Activate

a thesaurus of actions & tactics for dynamic genre fiction

by Damon Suede

Activate: a thesaurus of actions & tactics for dynamic genre fiction (Live Wire Writer Guides) by Damon Suede.

Published by Evil Mastermind, LLC
New York, NY
EvilMastermind.com
First Publication: 16 April 2019

Edited by Lynn West
Illustrations by Evil Mastermind, LLC
Book formatting by BB eBooks (1.1)

ISBN 978-1-945043-04-8 (Ebook)
ISBN 978-1-945043-05-5 (Print)

Website: DamonSuede.com/livewire

Contents

Foreword

This author-friendly thesaurus supplements ***Verbalize***, the first title in my Live Wire Writer Guides series, by offering thousands of active, dynamic verbs for use in fiction. Plenty of thesauri exist, but not one focused purely on writable actions and tactics for genre stories.

I came to fiction from showbiz, in which story and character cannot rely on traits, backstory, or other personal ad trivia because of the production process. My approach to genre fiction sprang from the idea that writers need tools that can deliver the goods on a deadline and that the "impersonal ad" approach to character is more of a time-suck than a credible method.

While most writing guides encourage the use of *characteristics* to portray people on the page, writers rarely use a tenth of the ancillary details demanded by popular methods, which is a waste of time and talent.

Working writers need tools that get results.

When most folks start writing fiction, adjectives and adverbs feel decorative and sexy...so many possibilities, so much ornamental specificity. Nouns seem reassuringly tangible and clear until you realize that no matter how solid or how beautiful all those other words are, **without verbs, nothing happens**. Verbs show, where all other words tell.

Action is all.

When I say a protagonist is “clever,” “freckled,” or “predatory,” I expect you to accept the provided descriptor at face value. If I describe that individual with a noun like “thief,” “gargoyle,” or “politician,” I must rely on your education and visualization to fill in the blanks with generic assumptions about those archetypal identities. On the other hand, the moment I make that character “volunteer,” “slash,” or “optimize” something, their actions paint a clear picture, their energy flows through the pages. Verbs give life to your fiction and power to your prose.

- **MODIFIERS tell**. Adjectives and adverbs only provide prechewed interpretation to explain other words, relying on preexisting opinion to decorate the story.
- **NOUNS suggest**. They populate a story's landscape with subjects and objects by evoking general assumptions, stereotypes, and simplifications.
- **VERBS show**. They express the energy of characters and direct their story because they relate actual forces shaping the narrative.

A smart writer learns to invest energy and time where it will pay dividends. That means getting to the marrow of the story, the fundamental actions and tactics that bring it to life.

Obviously, a book is more than a string of verbs. All the parts of speech help tell a tale, but a character simply has to take action to inspire opinions and feelings.

Stories are made of action like pigs are made of pork.

Readers look for meaning and significance to engage their feelings, and therefore every detail must work in service of your story. Rather than fumbling with trivia, interviews, archetypes, or psychological theory to create a "fully rounded" character, the author's task in characterization is to craft **action figures**, purpose-built narrative devices used to extract emotions from the audience. People read for emotional stimulation, and as a genre professional, you must structure that emotional ride with the precision and complexity of a roller coaster so they can expect a satisfying emotional ride, every time.

Great genre fiction evokes emotions by portraying dynamic characters and their transformations. Audiences show up to experience their actions and interactions as they battle the odds to achieve happiness. As the characters struggle toward their happy endings, they shape the story and impact everyone around them with ***verbs***.

When storytelling, modifiers can encumber and nouns can become obstacles, but by definition *verbs* have the power to do anything.

Because you want characters to change things and do things, you need verbs that have an impact, known grammatically as **transitive verbs**. A transitive verb is a verb that acts upon or interacts with an object, impacting someone or something external to the subject.

To verbalize a story effectively, authors need a steady supply of dynamic, transitive verbs appropriate to the task of spinning a yarn.

Most dictionaries and a few thesauri will let you know if verbs are transitive, but not all. For the past few years, my students have urged me to compile a list of verbs specifically appropriate for genre fictioneering to fill the gap in the available resources.

This thesaurus is a compendium of transitive verbs appropriate for use while verbalizing a story via character actions and tactics to facilitate the process of genre writing. I assembled this book as a supplement for working writers looking to verbalize their stories and deepen their knowledge of dynamic verbs in general. Inside these pages you'll find:

- a very brief **recap** of the techniques from ***Verbalize*** for anyone unfamiliar with my approach to structure and characterization.
- an **alphabetical** thesaurus of verbs useful as actions and tactics, along with antonyms suited to capturing chemistry on the page and characterizing powerful relationships.

- **genre** verbs especially useful for twelve categories of popular fiction and suggestive of that genre's prevalent tropes and subgenres.
- **directional** verbs sorting actions and tactics along two energetic axes to amplify shifts and complications between scenes.

I wanted to create the kind of resource I'd use daily in my own writing. I've used this resource at every stage of its creation, in fact. Obviously verbs will appear in more than one place, but I've tried to minimize repetition and maximize utility wherever possible.

Art is a hard dollar and everyone willing to do the job and support their genres deserves all the help they can get. Whether you use my verbalization technique or simply want a quick reference packed with juicy, active verbiage, I hope you'll find ***Activate*** a useful and inspiring resource.

Go write great books, because I want to read them.

"These are the things that matter—experiences that are almost impossible to render on the page. This is the grand project we are engaged in, why we worry about words, and why we must make them dance in our every sentence."

Constance Hale[1]

Verbalization

> "In short: **THERE ARE NO RULES.**
>
> And **HERE THEY ARE.**"
>
> Scott McCloud[2]

If you've read ***Verbalize*** or taken one of my workshops on characterization and story planning, feel free to skip past this section to the usage guide, but for everyone else, a word about verbalizing fiction.

As a reference, this book presupposes a passing familiarity with my method of characterization and story planning either from my teaching or writing. That said, I don't expect you to rush out and pick up another book to make this one useful, so I want to explain this guide's purpose even for first-time verbalizers. Again, if you know the drill, feel free to dive right into the verbs. If you do not, read on; I promise to make it swift.

In the spirit of "*Previously seen on...*" television recaps, I'll offer a quick summary of my book ***Verbalize*** and the techniques it covers:

Characters need to do stuff that matters, and for best results that means grappling with their intentions head-on via their choices and behavior in the story.

Characters are not faces, but *forces*...arcs of transformation revealed by high-stakes choices.

Given the scope and complexity of writing genre fiction, a savvy writer learns to align all of the components of a character so that each component supports and connects to every other to minimize effort and maximize effect.

Because human brains evolved to seek and solve patterns, stories work best when they attract attention and reward audiences with meaningful resolution. Readers discover interesting gaps in a story and fill them in, creating satisfying closure that connects the emotional dots between the characters and within themselves. The reader's imagination does most of the work, but only if the writer provides fascinating details...like grit for oysters primed to build a pearl.

Since art relies on attention and *disruption* is the primary generator of attention, significant contrast offers the single most powerful tool in the writer's toolkit. Opposing forces generate friction, which releases energy in a series of events that make up a story. That energy appears within the story as the actions of characters who must be not personalities, but *forces* of their own nature.

Stories make readers feel something at a distance via empathetic magic, by "sticking pins" in characters to create audiences' emotions. In grammatical structure of genre stories, the protagonist and problem of a story mirror the subject and predicate of sentences.

All characters wrestle with a personal, persistent **void** that drives all their actions and objectives...a persistent need/trauma/wound/error/lack/scar in their past that interferes with their happiness. Their *desire* for happiness changes them and drives them toward their ultimate story goal, and creates their Goal/Motivation/Conflict, but their essential energy characterizes them.

Consequently, ***action*** is the core of every character, the aligning principle of all characterization: **actions speak louder than words**. Those character actions are best expressed as active, dynamic verbs...expressive of the character's energy and impacting the world around them. The most powerful action always arises from the character's void because it reveals their idiosyncratic approach to life and hope for happiness. In essence, characters are sculptures that carve each other.

The unforgettable moments in any story spring from its *verbs*, which inevitably and explicitly dramatize energy and flow. Genre fiction is inherently grammatical, drawing power from the structure of language.

Aligning all of a characterization with a clear, dramatic action improves structure, drafting, and revision drastically. Since characters must do things that matter, their actions inevitably affect the world around them. For actions, the best verb options are transitive—taking an object—because they direct character efforts out in the world with meaningful impact.

Character actions will always be a **transitive** verb: a verb that acts upon or interacts with a person, object, entity, or idea *outside* the character. Transitive verbs keep your characters subjective by giving them an objective, and they create a subject by specifying an object. For example:

- She *writes* the novel. ("Writes" is the transitive verb.)
- He *revises* the chapter. ("Revises" is the transitive verb.)

Genre authors must draw on active, dramatic verbs to make anything happen in a story, but many common verbs make for feeble, forgettable character actions, some by their very nature.

Many verbs *cannot* impact the world around them, instead depicting the condition of a character without allowing them to *do* anything. These "simply existing" verbs that do not impact the outside world are **intransitive**. Intransitives cannot take a direct object because they describe a mood, state, or reflex.

- The assassin *sulked*. ("Sulked" is intransitive, conveying a mood.)
- Mimi *waltzed*. ("Waltzed" is intransitive, describing a state of being.)

- The goat *yawned*. ("Yawned" is intransitive, depicting a reflex.)

Intransitive verbs leave characters marooned inside their own head and heart. Result: passive beat, dead scene, inert character.

To complicate matters further, some flexible verbs can operate as either transitive or intransitive depending on whether a direct object receives the action. In "She drives away," *drive* is intransitive because it describes a state, but in "She drives *friends* away," *drive* is transitive because it affects an object.

Check out ***Verbalize*** for more in-depth information about this technique and its potential in characterization and dramatization.

Bottom line: **Strong verb, strong character**.

With those juicy transitives thrumming under the hood, characters need to direct their actions *at* something. Filmed entertainment often solves this action problem with a MacGuffin...a concrete target of pursuit and tension, visible onscreen, that gives characters something clear to struggle over. Because fiction is more innately subjective and internal, it benefits from giving characters subtle, complex story goals that are challenging, significant, relatable. This focuses a character upon an **objective**, like a mountain that needs climbing.

A character pursues that objective via their action with relentless focus. By choosing potent, positive actions for characters, an author keeps the story (and its writing) energized and clear. The character's action and objective persist for the length of the story, which creates coherence in their depiction.

Of course, a character cannot simply do one thing without variation for the course of the book, and so that action gives rise to strategically varied **tactics** specific to scenes. Though the character's action lasts the entire story, a new tactic—derived as *synonyms of* that action—appears in each scene like rungs on the action ladder.

Tactics are in effect *re*-actions, in which small shifts reveal internal complexity and narrative reversals, but since they are synonymous, the character coheres. Audiences experience a range of cohesive behavior, which allows them to extrapolate emotions and psychology.

Since tactics also use transitive verbs, they too require a target for their energy. **Objects** offer a character a distinct goal for each scene, like a problem that needs solving *now*.

Just as *objectives* are the character's story goal pursued via the action, the *objects* are a character's scene goals pursued by individual tactics in different contexts. In the same way, just as an action breaks down into tactics, the objective breaks down into specific, external, and dynamic objects that hold the energy of the scene like a battery.

Each new story beat requires a shift in tactic (and object) as the character *re*-acts to events and tries to pursue their overall story goal (objective). Taken together the tactics represent the character's overall action during the story.

Once you know your character's tactics, you can use them to craft a comprehensive character arc rising to the most dramatic tactic via significant moments, using character to shape plot and plot to explore character. Further, certain actions and tactics suggest genres, subgenres, and tropes because they convey categories of emotion.

Verbs shape vibe.

Character and plot are only two ways of understanding story, plot as external cause and effect; character as internal cause and effect. Transformation and escalation don't happen in straight lines, so shifting tactical directions will produce powerful results in any genre story. And each story will resolve conflict and tension as it escalates to an emotionally satisfying ending.

Verbalization is what most writers *do* unconsciously when they write a story. Exploring the process *consciously* simplifies the writing process and enhances the final product.

So… to break the process of verbalization down completely: Writers and readers in search of **meaning** pay **attention** via **alignment** to **characters** with **significance** that suggests **patterns** created by **contrast** that causes **friction** and **escalation** during **events** in order to generate **energy** expressed through a **void** that inspires **action** in pursuit of an **objective** through **relationships** that require **tactics** to handle **objects** in an **arc** varying **directions** to maximize **transformation** to reach the kind of **emotional experience** fans crave.

> "The changing wisdom of successive generations discards ideas, questions facts, demolishes theories. But the artist appeals to that part of our being which is not dependent on wisdom: to that in us which is a gift and not an acquisition—and, therefore, more permanently enduring."
>
> Joseph Conrad[3]

Usage

Before I unleash a torrent of sexy verbs, a few words about the organization of this book and why verbalization works so well. Everything that follows draws upon a few basic craft precepts:

- Every character has a core **action** in pursuit of their story goal (aka *objective*).
- Every action manifests as related **tactics** to achieve scene goals (aka *objects*).
- Because characters direct their actions and tactics at object(ive)s, those actions and tactics will always be transitive (active) verbs.
- Every character's action and tactics affect every other character's action and tactics via interactions.
- The stronger the relationship, the more oppositional (*antonymic*) the actions of the characters, the more powerful the effect on each other.

When verbalizing a story, the goal is to find the clearest, simplest expression of that character's energy so they can do what matters in a story. Every other component of that character's traits and identity will align with that essential action.

Verbs provide all the energy in writing. Actions are verbs. Tactics are verbs. Effective actions and tactics share transitivity, impact, and emotional legibility.

Focusing on the character's actions from the start ensures they're memorable and meaningful. The easiest way to identify that action is to identify the character's central void—the persistent injury/need/lack/scar of the past that impedes their present and future happiness. Invariably, a character's action springs from that void as a credible solution.

Every character wants to be happy, and their action reveals their innate approach. Compile a range of related verbs your character would consider a go-to solution in every situation and see which ones feel right. Each verb will subtly shift the portrayal, and each opens up a new set of dramatic possibilities.

Depending on how well you know your characters, you may start out with a solid grasp of what they do and why they do it at any moment. No one else knows this imaginary person as well as you do. As you bring them to life, their actions and tactics will portray them faithfully or falsely...and only you can judge how close you came. Give yourself permission to make bold choices boldly and also to nail your failures with unsentimental precision.

However well you know your cast, whatever your process for spinning a yarn, look for actions that are fun and physical, that direct energy outward so characters impact their community and environment.

Context changes the nuances of a verb, and when verbalizing a story, that goes *triple*. Be sure you know how the action or tactic operates and the specific object(ive) receiving the verb's action. If you cannot connect the dots, your audience won't.

The best actions and tactics operate internally and externally, with a tangible *physical* effect outside of the character as well as a *mental* resonance and an *emotional* impact that require no explanation to the reader. When verbalizing, keep an eye on all three levels:

- **PHYSICAL**: does the action/tactic direct energy outside of the character into clear, tangible goals that elicit emotional engagement? (e.g. a bully doesn't "gripe," but rather *torments* bystanders, a socialite doesn't "sparkle," but rather *dazzles* admirers.)
- **MENTAL**: does the action/tactic create clear, dynamic, dramatic images in the mind's eye through interesting sound and sense? (e.g. not "touch" but *massage*, not "harm" but *detonate*, not "admire" but *lionize*)
- **EMOTIONAL**: does the action/tactic offer variation and intensity evincing the full spectrum of your character's behavior and nature? (e.g. a "disguise" character can *impersonate* and *embellish* and *camouflage*, a

world you're writing, take a look at the directional grouping for sets of action/tactics that might lead you to a story idea. Let those verbs take you somewhere *fascinating*.

Exploring?

Activate sorts verbs alphabetically, generically, and directionally so you can approach your initial project planning from many angles so that it anchors the process in the power of *words*. If you're still trying to get a firm handle on the story and its characters, this book helps *anyone* splash around in the connotations and implications of the various possibilities of verbalization, whether you're a plotter or pantser, a newbie or an old hand.

When testing out a verb as an overarching character action, make sure you weigh the full array of meanings with an eye toward the possible tactics in individual scenes. Unpack the nuances, paradoxes, and contradictions in that verb's etymology. What is its origin, history, and evolution? Flag resonances, surprises, or significant details that feel germane to the character.

Shades of meaning play an outsized role in fiction. Associations, inference, and nuance play a large part in the emotional experience of the reader, so even a slight variation of verbalization can alter a character or a scene dramatically. Even without knowing the precise verbs in play, an audience will discern the pattern at work under the hood because that's how brains work: we extrapolate significance from the available info and discernible patterns. Because you're using words the audience knows, closure is instinctive, and the coherence inevitable. If you choose your words carefully, the character *feels* real.

Single out the most fascinating, specific *action* for that character, then round it out with an appealing range of secondary *tactics* to charge their scenes along the way. You already know some of them: most of your discarded actions will serve as perfect tactics. Think of tactics as rungs on the action ladder: as they accumulate, the character climbs toward their objective—one confrontation, one discovery, one object at a time.

Synonyms make a great starting point, especially with verbs that reveal a range of meanings and interpretations (e.g., Empress Livia's action *to poison* means "to murder" but also "to pollute," "to corrupt," and "to nullify."). To deepen characters, consider using synonyms of *those* synonyms to reveal more radical tactical possibilities. Tactics should offer further resonant variations to change the story's tune while honoring the melody. They'll help you as a writer, and the resultant scenes will appeal mightily to the reader.

Strong verbs will guarantee the writing and the reading stay emotional, evocative, and enjoyable.

Drafting?

Activate is chockablock with story spurs and character prompts. If you're hunkered down cranking out your pages and trying to keep the flow, you can use this book to lubricate the process.

Use these listings to nail down and upgrade the actions for the story and the tactics in the scenes. Especially in the early phases of committing words to paper, choosing potent, oppositional language will help activate a scene for all the participants, minimizing the need for exposition and qualification. Likewise, powerful verbs will keep that character in sharp focus so that they earn the attention they deserve.

When it comes to action and tactics, *any* choice is better than no choice. Get in the habit of replacing weaker options with stronger choices. Happily, the moment you write a beat, the scene will let you know if the tactics work and the story will let you know if the action does its job credibly.

When verbalizing your cast, keep those interdependent actions and tactics in mind: what seemed central may gradually reveal itself to be tactical as the character moves from identity to essence (as Michael Hague[4] puts it) over the story's course.

Whether for pantsers who prefer to discover character by improvising on the page or plotters who may structure events without a clear sense of intention, the initial knowledge of a character's capacities can give way to a deeper and more complex swath of possibilities. The action that seemed fundamental may turn out to be only a successful tactic to be supplanted by a more relevant, resonant option.

Write is a verb! By definition verbs *make* stuff, *take* stuff, *break* stuff, *fake* stuff. Learn to enjoy the depth and drama intrinsic to language. Let those actions and tactics drive your story as well as the process of putting it on the page for the first time.

Revising?

Activate offers a vast range of options that can enrich the language in your project during the editorial process. If the draft is done and your character feels passive, vague, or forgettable, look for an action or tactic upgrade that will amplify a pivotal beat in the story. If the plot suffers from logic leaps or inexplicable behavior, look to the tactics deployed in play during the problematic scenes to hone the emotional impact.

When facing a completed but imperfect manuscript, verbs can steer choices, solutions, and overhauls. Just eyeballing the language of a wonky chapter, scene, or section can diagnose the deficits. Refining, amplifying, and specifying character behavior has exponential impact on every element of storytelling. By starting at the root—the language of the story—you can pinpoint trouble spots with ruthless specificity. **Words work**.

Allow those actions and tactics to shift and reflect your knowledge of the story. If you notice initial "false" actions only express a certain mode or period of the character's behavior, dig deeper for the core action that connects all of the tactics.

Keep going back to pinpoint the precise action that expresses the character's energy as it flows through the story. Look for ways to escalate and transform their tactics (aka *re*-actions) in each scene for maximum emotional impact.

Remember: you're the writer, but outside perspectives can save your bacon. Listen to editors, betas, and trusted colleagues who call your bluff. Whether they're right or wrong, you'll only know if you pay attention to them and to the iffy writing that gives them pause. There's an old Yiddish proverb: if one person says you're drunk, have another, but when three people tell you you're drunk, go lie down.

If readers say a scene isn't working, you don't need to *obey* their suggestions blindly, but you should try to locate and solve the problem that gave them pause. When someone tells you there's a problem, nine times out of ten they're right. When they tell you how to solve it, nine times out of ten they're wrong. Besides, if they solve the problem, then *they're* writing the book. Learn to listen and also to clean up your own messes.

By clarifying and strengthening your language, you can transform your characters, their stories, and ultimately your career as a genre author.

Stretch yourself! Be wary of the impulse to stick with safe or expected options. Repeating the same actions and tactics is how lazy authors end up regurgitating the same book ad nauseam. Even the most fascinating, popular actions have traps built into them. And as an artist, you're either growing or you're dying.

As you verbalize your stories, you'll learn to explore the power and possibility buried in all these verbs, their motion and emotion, their scope and secrets. Mindbending treasure, infinite joy, and divine fire hide inside each one.

> "Using action verbs instead of adjectives is a way of approaching the emotional center of a scene in a way that is experiential and playable rather than descriptive and result-oriented. What we do affects our feelings and can create feeling."
>
> Judith Weston, director[5]

The following section makes up the bulk of ***Activate***, cross-referencing thousands of transitive verbs suited to use as actions and tactics in your fiction. This alphabetical listing includes more than 5,300 unique verbs distributed over 3,200 entries. I've included a healthy smattering of colorful jargon and slang but eliminated most archaisms and obsolete usages.

Each entry offers synonyms for the primary verb but also some synonyms of synonyms that vary in connotation and application. Many of the options are direct synonyms (=) but some are only *comparable* (≈) in meaning. In mathematical terms, many synonyms = their entries, but some ≈ their entries, to offer more variety and help you build more interesting sets of tactics for your characters. My goal wasn't to dissect their meanings, but to lay out an inspiring smorgasbord so you can follow your muse where she leads you.

In an attempt to curb redundancy in this alphabetical section, the less common synonyms only appear within listings for more common verbs.

Rather than trying to be exhaustive, I've tried to err on the side of dramatic potency and range. These are transitive verbs appropriate as actions or tactics, which can each take an object(ive). Please note that some of these verbs do have *in*transitive uses as well, so be careful to ask yourself who or what receives the force of the verb to keep your characters *interacting* with their world and doing stuff that matters.

Your characters don't act in a bubble. Relationships are shown by the effect characters have on each other (i.e., **no effect = no relationship**). For this reason, the greater the opposition between actions and tactics, the more powerful and significant the interactions between those characters. Antonyms will give you the greatest number of options for dramatic tension and transformation between the members of your cast.

In addition to omitting dedicated intransitives, I've also skipped phrasal verbs that can leech specificity from your writing. For example, your characters may *probe* the evidence, but they cannot *snoop* the evidence. "Snoop" is a phrasal verb that requires a preposition. You cannot snoop *something*; you can only snoop *through*, *in*, or *around* something. For that reason, "probe" appears in the pages that follow and "snoop" does not.

Remember: **keep things transitive**, interacting *with* and acting *upon* something outside of the character. When choosing an action or tactic, make certain you are using its full transitive power by identifying the object receiving the energy of the verb: Subject + Verb + Object.

Keep looking at your story and characters grammatically (**Verb + Target + Progress**) and you'll always know exactly *what* takes the energy of the verb.

- ACTION: Because the objective takes the entire story to achieve (or not), the character must continually adapt and re-strategize to get it. A character's ultimate path to happiness would be rendered as: **Action + Objective + Adjustment = Story.**
- TACTIC: Because the character must grapple with the object in a scene (or not), the character must process developments and *re*-actions to improve their next strategy for the next object. In each dramatic beat, a character's steps toward happiness would be rendered as: **Tactic + Object + Response = Scene.**

Although challenging, *any* action or tactic can work, but the more negative the action, the more ruthlessly specific the objective required to keep that action dramatic. If you have a character who *avoids*, they need to avoid one specific thing or person, not a concept, memory, or idea.

We want to see a character **win** a specific challenge, not **avoid** failure. Negatives derail and deaden character energy; a character cannot play a negative in a scene. Avoidance and deflection make your characters less specific and less intentional in their actions. For powerful scenes and characters, keep intentions positive so they stay significant, challenging, and relatable.

While I was compiling this thesaurus, a few negative transitive verbs cropped up repeatedly: **avoid**, **ignore**, **neglect**, **prevent**, etc. Their very *ubiquity* became comical because every time I couldn't find clear antonyms for a verb, those negatives turned up like sticky, fuzzy pennies perfectly poised to foil tactics and negate actions. In a sense they are *anti-*verbs.

Be wary of defaulting to these inherently inert, negative behaviors. They will generate hurdles and headaches because that's their *function*. Use them with conscious caution.

Yes, negatives serve a purpose, but when using them to verbalize a character, don't let them dilute or impede the story. All of them (and their synonyms) *can* make for fascinating tactics under the right circumstances, but as overarching character actions they steer a character towards generality, inertia, and passivity. Positive actions always yield better dramatic results than negative actions.

Rather than focusing on the negatives that motivate your character, see positive goals you can place before them to keep them moving in clear, specific directions. For this reason, I've marked some of the most inherently negative actions in the text with a minus sign (-) to denote their negativity. (i.e., -avoid, -ignore, -neglect, -prevent, etc.)

For best results, **accentuate positive intentions**.

Additionally, "stative" verbs lean towards moods, abstraction, and internal *states*. Statives only work as actions and tactics so long as that character pursues objectives and objects that are adamantly **specific**, **concrete**, and **challenging** in ways that require no explanation. Some statives are transitive and when used with care can serve as actions and tactics. The issue is the inherent *passivity* of stative verbs. Characters can "contemplate," "prefer," or "suspect" their way through a book, but dramatizing those behaviors will require concrete objects and serious ingenuity. To use abstract actions effectively, you'll want to balance their figurative, passive bent against some literal character conflict and pursuit.

To help you identify potential trouble and remind you that their abstraction may confuse readers, I've flagged these entries with a reversed question mark symbol and a warning: **(¿) ABSTRACTION ALERT. Concrete goals essential!**

All of this section's entries are listed alphabetically and include formatting and symbols to help you navigate swiftly.

- Each primary verb is given in ALL CAPS.
- The list of synonyms appear in *italicized lower case*.
- Each entry will be tagged with its primary "direction as indicated by the relevant symbol in parentheses.

  (→) PUSH verbs move away from the character.

(←) PULL verbs move toward the character.
(+) JOIN verbs connect something or someone external.
(/) SPLIT verbs divide something or someone external.

- At the end of each entry, you'll find a selection of relevant antonyms in parentheses flagged with a "not equal" sign, e.g., (≠ *antonym, antonym, antonym*)

Additionally, when a verb has more than one general meaning, each interpretation will be split into a new entry with its own set of synonyms and antonyms and the relevant directional tag.

Transitive verbs run the gamut as far as connotations and usages; some have multiple meanings which vary in direction. For example, "scour" has two major transitive meanings:

- SCOUR (→) means to *scrub*, as in "The janitor scoured the floor."...a **push** option that extends the energy from the character into the environment.
- SCOUR (←) means to *search*, as in "Alexis scoured the files."...a **pull** option that indicates investigation via a metaphor of scrutiny drawing information toward the character.

Likewise, some verbs offer multiple meanings that all operate along the same axis, such as "help," which has two **join** meanings, both interacting with an external entity:

- One HELP (+) means to *assist*, as in "Jerome helped rookies on the weekends."
- One HELP (+) means to *improve*, as in "The surgeon helped her patient."

Please don't take these direction groupings as absolute; context and connotations play havoc with meanings. But directions can prove useful when a scene needs a boost. For more information on these tactical modes, see Part III: Directions or the longer discussion in Chapter 12 of ***Verbalize***.

Just to help you navigate swiftly, here is a sample entry explaining the different areas and designations:

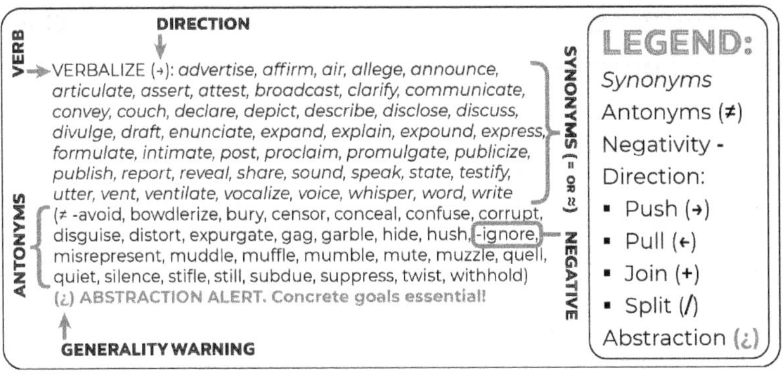

I always tell my students: when identifying your character's action and tactics, you'll feel the pull of the right option, in the way a dowser feels the tug towards water underground. Feel free to splash around in the verbs; some of my best characters and dramatic situations have arisen from instinctive reactions to groovy language.

The right word will reveal itself to you with a magnetic attraction that will not, cannot, and should not be denied. Just listen with your heart and your voice, and you will feel it: the inescapable *rightness* for this particular character (with actions) or this moment (for tactics) will ring in you consonant as a bell. Those *reverberations* connect the character to their world and to the lives of real people in your readers' lives.

You're a writer: **finding the right word is the whole gig**.

Allow the sound, sense, and symbolism of the verbs to inspire your work, to kick your butt, to push you out of the comfort zones that slowly, surely, steadily strangle your voice. Follow your gut and let the muse drag you into unexpected terrain. Give yourself permission to have fun!

-ABANDON (/): *abjure, chuck, deliver, depart, -desert, discard, -disown, -ditch, drop, dump, eject, -escape, evacuate, expel, -flee, fling, forfeit, -forsake, heave, isolate, jettison, jilt, junk, leave, maroon, offload, orphan, -quit, -reject, release, relinquish, -renounce, -repudiate, sacrifice, scrap, seclude, shed, shuck, -snub, strand, surrender, unload, vacate, withdraw, yield* (≠ acquire, adopt, cherish, colonize, defend, embrace, gather, guard, harbor, hold, indemnify, invade, keep, maintain, obtain, occupy, own, patrol, populate, possess, protect, pursue, reclaim, redeem, remainder, rescue, reserve, retain, retrofit, revisit, save, scavenge, steal, take, withhold)

-ABANDON (/): *-abort, abrogate, annul, call, -cancel, countermand, -discontinue, drop, end, -halt, interrupt, invalidate, -nullify, recall, recant, relinquish, repeal, -rescind, retract, reverse, revoke, scrap, scrub, stop, surrender, suspend, terminate, -void, withdraw* (≠ begin, brainstorm, commence, continue, engage, initiate, keep, pledge, promise, start, undertake)

-ABANDON (/): *abdicate, -abort, cease, cede, close, conclude, -discontinue, -ditch, drop, end, finish, forego, forswear, -halt, jettison, leave, pause, -quit, relinquish, -renounce, resign, sacrifice, scrap, surrender, terminate, waive, wrap, yield* (≠ begin, commence, continue, gentrify, keep, maintain, preserve, renew, reopen, restart, resume, start, stay, support, sustain, uphold)

ABASE (/): *bastardize, befoul, begrime, bestialize, blemish, canker, cheapen, contaminate, corrupt, damage, debase, debauch, deface, defile, demoralize, deprave, depreciate, destroy, deteriorate, dilute, dirty, disgrace, dishonor, downgrade, flaw, foul, harm, harshen, humble, humiliate, hurt, impair, lessen, mar, mutate, pervert, poison, pollute, profane, prostitute, ruin, shame, spoil, stain, suborn, subvert, sully, taint, tarnish, thin, vitiate, warp, weaken, wreck* (≠ ameliorate, amend, better, clarify, clean, cleanse, correct, elevate, enhance, enrich, improve, optimize, perfect, purify, rarefy, rectify, refine, reform, respect, restore, upgrade, uplift)

ABASE (/): *abash, affront, badmouth, belittle, blackguard, castigate, censure, chasten, cheapen, condemn, confound, confuse, criticize, damn, debase, decry, defame, defile, degrade, demean, demonize, denounce, depreciate, detract, diminish, discomfit, disconcert, -discount, discredit, disgrace, dishonor, disparage, downplay, embarrass, execrate, faze, fluster, foul, humble, humiliate, insult, libel, lower, malign, minimize, mortify, nonplus, pillory, rattle, ridicule, shame, sink, slander, smirch* (≠ advance, aggrandize, applaud, boast, boost, canonize, celebrate, commend, compliment, congratulate, dignify, ennoble, enshrine, enthrone, exalt, extol, glorify, heroicize, heroize, highlight, honor, hype, idealize, magnify, praise, promote, recognize, romanticize, salute, sentimentalize, spotlight, tout, uplift)

ABDUCT (←): *bind, bogart, bundle, capture, catch, disappear, enslave, entrap, grab, hijack, kidnap, lure, nab, pluck, ransom, remove, rustle, seize, shanghai, snatch, spirit, steal, take, trap, waylay* (≠ aid, defend, deliver, guard, house, protect, ransom, recover, redeem, release, rescue, restore, return, save, secure, shelter, shield, stash)

ABET (→): *activate, advance, brew, cultivate, detonate, encourage, energize, enliven, excite, ferment, fire, foment, forward, foster, further, galvanize, incite, inflame, inspire, instigate, invigorate, liven, motivate, nourish, nurture, pick, promote, provoke, quicken, raise, rouse, set, sow, stimulate, stir, trigger, vitalize* (≠ allay, bridle, calm, check, confound, confuse, counteract, curb, deactivate, discourage, hold, inhibit, quiet, regulate, rein, repress, restrain, settle, soothe, stagnate, stifle, still, strangle, subdue, tame, tranquilize)

ABET (+): *advance, advise, advocate, aid, assist, attend, back, benefit, bolster, boost, buttress, champion, comfort, condone, counsel, deliver, ease, embolden, encourage, endorse, energize, facilitate, favor, forward, foster, further, goad, guide, hearten, help, incite, inspire, instigate, kindle, launch, mentor, midwife, motivate, nurture, oblige, patronize, prod, profit, promote, prop, provoke, reinforce, rescue, sanction, save, second, serve, sponsor, spur, strengthen, succor, support, sustain, urge* (≠ baffle, -balk, bar, block, constrain, counter, damage, delay, -desert, -deter, disappoint, discourage, disfavor, dishearten, dissuade, fail, foil, -frustrate, hamper, handicap, harm, hinder, hold, hurt, impede, incommode, inconvenience, inhibit, injure, monkey-wrench, muzzle, obstruct, oppose, -prevent, repress, restrain, retard, sabotage, scotch, scupper, shelve, short-circuit, stifle, straiten, strangle, stunt, stymie, subvert, -thwart)

ABOLISH (/): *abnegate, abrogate, annihilate, annul, atomize, -blank, bulldoze, -cancel, decimate, deep-six, delete, demolish, -deny, desolate, destroy, devastate, disavow, disintegrate, dismantle, dismiss, dissolve, divorce, efface, eliminate, end, eradicate, erase, expunge, exterminate, extinguish, extirpate, flatten, invalidate, level, -negate, neutralize, -nullify, obliterate, overturn, pulverize, quash, raze, refute, -repudiate, retract, revoke, scotch, scrap, smash, snuff, stop, suppress, terminate, topple, undo, uproot, vaporize, -veto, vitiate, -void, wreck* (≠ authorize, begin, brainstorm, bring, build, catalyze, commence, create, enact, establish, fashion, forge, form, found, generate, greenlight, hatch, inaugurate, induce, initiate, institute, introduce, launch, legislate, make, notarize, ordain, retain, shape, spawn, survive, weather)

-ABORT (/): *-abandon, abrogate, annul, -cancel, check, conclude, countermand, -discontinue, drop, end, fail, finish, -frustrate, -halt, interrupt, invalidate, -negate, -nullify, recall, recant, relinquish, repeal, -rescind, retract, reverse, revoke, scrap, scratch, scrub, shorten, stop,* *surrender, suspend, terminate, -thwart, -void, withdraw* (≠ begin, commence, continue, engage, establish, initiate, instigate, institute, keep, launch, originate, pioneer, pledge, promise, prompt, start, undertake)

ABRADE (/): *bite, chafe, chew, coarsen, corrode, disintegrate, dissolve, eat, erase, erode, excoriate, file, fray, frazzle, fret, gall, gnaw, grate, graze, grind, hone, irritate, nibble, rasp, reduce, rub, sandblast, sandpaper, scour, scrape, scratch, scuff, sharpen, shave, wear, whet, wipe* (≠ aid, alleviate, assist, assuage, butter, calm, comfort, content, ease, fix, grease, heal, lube, lubricate, mend, oil, placate, polish, rectify, shine, smooth, soften, soothe, wax)

ABRIDGE (/): *abate, abbreviate, abstract, compress, concentrate, condense, constrict, contract, curtail, cut, decrease, de-escalate, deflate, digest, diminish, dock, downsize, elide, encapsulate, epitomize, focus, generalize, lessen, lower, miniaturize, minimize, moderate, modify, pare, prune, recapitulate, reduce, retrench, shorten, shrink, slash, subtract, summarize, syncopate, taper, trim, truncate* (≠ add, aggrandize, amplify, augment, balloon, boost, dilate, distend, elongate, enlarge, escalate, expand, expound, extend, heighten, increase, inflate, lengthen, maximize, prolong, protract, raise, stretch, supplement, swell)

ABROGATE (/): *abnegate, abolish, -abort, annul, -avoid, axe, ban, call, -cancel, challenge, chop, contradict, countermand, cripple, -deny, disable, disallow, disavow, dismiss, disqualify, dissolve, drop, dump, eliminate, end, enjoin, eradicate, erase, -forbid, hinder, impair, incapacitate, invalidate, -negate, neutralize, null, -nullify, outlaw, override, overrule, overturn, -prohibit, quash, rebut, recall, refute, -reject, remove, repeal, -repudiate, -rescind, retract, reverse, revoke, scotch, scrap, stop, strike, suspend, undercut, undermine, vacate, -veto, vitiate, -void, withdraw* (≠ allow, approve, authorize, command, confirm, decree, develop, enact, endorse, establish, formalize, foster, found, instigate, institute, introduce, legalize, legislate, legitimate, legitimize, mandate, order, pass, permit, prescribe, promulgate, ratify, reinstate, sanction, support, sustain, validate, warrant)

ABSOLVE (+): *acquit, bless, cleanse, clear, condone, defend, defray, discharge, dismiss, exculpate, excuse, exempt, exonerate, expiate, forgive, free, hallow, justify, liberate, loose, -overlook, pardon, purge, purify, rationalize, redeem, redress, release, relieve, remit, revenge, sanctify, sanitize, spare, spring, tolerate, unburden, vindicate, wash, whitewash* (≠ accuse, arraign, avenge, blame, castigate, charge, chasten, chastise, condemn, convict, defame, denounce, denunciate, doom, fault, finger, frame, implicate, imprison, incriminate, indict, penalize, punish, reprove, resent, revile, reward, satisfy, scapegoat, sentence)

ABSORB (←): *accept, access, acquire, admit, amalgamate, blend, combine, commingle, consume, coopt, devour, digest, drink, eat, embody, engorge, engulf, envelop, fuse, get, gobble, gulp, guzzle, imbibe, incorporate, ingest, inhale, inspire, integrate, intermingle, merge, mingle, pocket, process, quaff, receive, sip, slurp, sniff, sponge, suck, swallow,* *swig, swill, take* (≠ augment, blackball, build, conserve, disperse, dissipate, eject, emit, exhale, expel, exude, fortify, increase, peck, pick, preserve, protect, recoup, -refuse, reinforce, -reject, replace, restore, save, spew, splutter, -spurn, vent, vomit)

ABSORB (←): *allure, amuse, attract, beguile, bemuse, bewitch, busy, captivate, catch, charm, concern, consume, distract, divert, employ, enchant, engage, engross, entertain, enthrall, fascinate, fill, grip, hog, hold, hypnotize, immerse, interest, intrigue, involve, mesmerize, monopolize, obsess, occupy, possess, preoccupy, rivet, stimulate* (≠ annoy, bore, disgust, displease, distract, frustrate, irk, jade, offend, repel, revolt, tire, vex, weary) **(¿) ABSTRACTION ALERT. Concrete goals essential!**

ABSORB (+): *assimilate, catch, collect, compile, comprehend, coopt, digest, discover, follow, gain, gather, glean, grasp, grok, incorporate, integrate, internalize, learn, master, overhear, realize, receive, sense, study, suss, understand* (≠ -deny, forget, misapprehend, misconceive, misconstrue, misdiagnose, misinterpret, misperceive, misread, miss, mistake, misunderstand, -neglect, -reject, -spurn) **(¿) ABSTRACTION ALERT. Concrete goals essential!**

ABSORB (+): *acclimatize, accommodate, acculturate, accustom, adapt, adjust, adopt, amalgamate, assimilate, blend, combine, commingle, condition, coopt, embody, enculturate, fuse, habituate, include, incorporate, integrate, intermingle, merge, mingle, mix, naturalize, reunite, unite* (≠ alienate, banish, bar, contrast, diffuse, eliminate, -exclude, exile, expel, isolate, juxtapose, -omit, orphan, oust, -prevent, -prohibit, replace, -repudiate, resist, scatter, seclude, segregate)

ABUSE (←): *bamboozle, bleed, bully, cheat, coerce, commandeer, commercialize, commodify, compel, con, deceive, dragoon, embezzle, exploit, extort, fleece, gazump, gull, harass, impose, leverage, manipulate, milk, mistreat, overcharge, play, pressure, presume, skin, soak, stick, tap, use, work* (≠ aid, assist, benefit, guard, help, honor, -neglect, nurture, preserve, protect, respect, restore, save, support)

ABUSE (/): *bastardize, bestialize, cannibalize, consume, corrupt, debase, degrade, depredate, desecrate, dissipate, exhaust, exploit, fritter, misapply, mishandle, mismanage, misuse, overburden, overtax, overwork, pervert, profane, prostitute, ruin, spoil, squander, taint, twist, waste* (≠ apply, benefit, bless, defend, employ, esteem, guard, preserve, prize, respect, revere, support, use, utilize)

ABUSE (/): *anguish, assault, attack, batter, beat, brutalize, bully, burn, club, corrupt, crucify, damage, defile, degrade, deprave, desecrate, exploit, harass, harm, hit, hurt, ill-treat, impair, injure, maim, maltreat, manhandle, mar, menace, mishandle, mistreat, misuse, molest, oppress, outrage, persecute, pollute, rape, ruin, sandbag, soil, spoil, sully, taint, torment, torture, total, trample, use, victimize, violate, wound, wrong* (≠ adore, baby, cherish, coddle, defend, favor, foster, gratify, heal, help, honor, humor, indulge, mollycoddle, nurse, nurture, pamper, pity, preserve, protect, rescue, respect, revere, spoil, treasure)

ABUSE (/): *abase, affront, antagonize, assail, attack, backbite, badmouth, bait, bash, belabor, belittle, berate, besmirch, betray, blackguard, blaspheme, blast, blemish, browbeat, bully, bullyrag, calumniate, castigate, chastise, chide, criticize, curse, damn, debase, decry, defame, demean, demonize, denigrate, diminish, -discount, discredit, disfavor, disgrace, dishonor, disparage, excoriate, execrate, flannel, flatter, harangue, harass, harry, humble, humiliate, imprecate, impugn, insult, knock, lambaste, libel, malign, minimize, mortify, nag, offend, oppress, persecute, pillory, profane, rail, rebuke, reprimand, reproach, revile, ride, ridicule, savage, scathe, scold, shame, slam, slander, slap, slate, -slight, slur, smear, -snub, taunt, traduce, trash, upbraid, victimize, vilify, vituperate, whip, wrong, zing* (≠ acclaim, admire, adore, adulate, amuse, approve, boost, cajole, charm, cherish, commend, compliment, court, deify, delight, dignify, esteem, exalt, glorify, hail, hero-worship, idolize, laud, lionize, pity, praise, retort, revere, reverence, soap, support, sweet-talk, venerate, woo, worship)

ACCELERATE (→): *advance, aid, bundle, dispatch, drive, ease, encourage, expedite, facilitate, fast-forward, fast-track, forward, frogmarch, further, goad, gun, hasten, hurry, impel, march, midwife, precipitate, prod, promote, propel, push, quicken, race, railroad, rev, rush, spur, stimulate, stir, urge, whisk* (≠ -abort, brake, burden, choke, conclude, cripple, decelerate, delay, encumber, hamper, hamstring, hinder, hobble, impede, kill, obstruct, postpone, prolong, restrain, retard, shelve, short-circuit, slow, stall, stay, stifle, still, stop, tax, terminate, -thwart, weight)

ACCENTUATE (+): *accent, advertise, amplify, assert, belabor, bolster, boost, center, concentrate, deepen, display, elevate, emphasize, escalate, exaggerate, exhibit, favor, feature, flaunt, focus, foreground, heighten, highlight, hype, identify, illuminate, increase, intensify, magnify, mark, maximize, overemphasize, overplay, oversell, overstate, overstress, pinpoint, plug, present, press, prioritize, promote, publicize, punctuate, push, reinforce, sharpen, show, spotlight, strengthen, stress, underline, underscore, weight* (≠ abate, -avoid, belittle, bury, conceal, cover, curb, decrease, deemphasize, diminish, -discount, disparage, -disregard, downplay, -eschew, hide, -ignore, lessen, lighten, marginalize, mask, minimize, miss, mitigate, moderate, muffle, -neglect, obscure, obstruct, -omit, -overlook, quiet, reduce, sideline, silence, stifle, subdue, subordinate, temper, undercut, underemphasize, undermine, underrate, understate, weaken)

ACCEPT (←): *abide, absorb, access, acquire, admit, adopt, assimilate, authenticate, authorize, bear, brook, confirm, corroborate, countenance, devour, eat, embrace, endure, engorge, gain, gather, get, gobble, grasp, greenlight, gulp, import, incorporate, ingest, inhale, inspire, integrate, internalize, legalize, obtain, okay, permit, pocket, procure, ratify, receive, sanction, secure, shoulder, stand, stomach, support, sustain, swallow,* *sweat, take, tolerate, underwrite, warrant, welcome* (≠ accord, adjure, bestow, challenge, combat, comp, contest, counteract, countercheck, -decline, -deny, disallow, disapprove, discard, donate, eliminate, fight, give, oppose, protest, -refuse, -reject, repel, resist, scrap, -spurn, tender, tithe, -veto, withstand, yield)

ACCEPT (+): *acclaim, admire, adore, applaud, approve, back, bear, bless, commend, congratulate, countenance, endure, enjoy, favor, laud, love, okay, praise, recommend, respect, salute, stomach, support, sustain, tolerate, uphold* (≠ blacklist, boo, censure, condemn, criticize, damn, denounce, deprecate, depreciate, -detest, disfavor, disparage, fulminate, -hate, -loathe, malign, mind, mock, oppose, ridicule)

ACCEPT (+): *acknowledge, admit, affirm, allow, approve, assert, assume, assure, attest, believe, buy, certify, claim, conclude, contend, corroborate, credit, declare, deduce, endorse, express, gather, hold, infer, maintain, pledge, presume, proclaim, profess, promise, prove, ratify, sanction, state, stipulate, submit, support, suppose, sustain, swallow, take, testify, trust, understand, validate, verify, warrant, welcome* (≠ allege, challenge, consult, convince, cross-examine, debate, debunk, demonize, demonstrate, disbelieve, discredit, dispute, distrust, doubt, grill, impugn, interrogate, interview, mistrust, -negate, -nullify, pillory, question, -reject, -renounce, ridicule, scruple, suspect, wonder)

ACCEPT (+): *accede, adopt, advocate, assume, back, bear, champion, condone, embrace, endorse, espouse, integrate, obey, observe, shoulder, support, undertake, uphold* (≠ -abandon, abjure, -avoid, condemn, -decline, detour, disavow, disclaim, -disown, -forsake, -negate, offer, recant, -refuse, -reject, relinquish, -renounce, -repudiate, retract, spitball, -spurn, volunteer, withdraw)

ACCEPT (+): *abide, absorb, allow, bear, brave, brook, condone, countenance, endure, face, follow, hack, handle, meet, obey, permit, pocket, reconcile, respect, stand, stomach, suffer, support, sustain, swallow, sweat, take, tolerate, wear* (≠ -avoid, bandy, -bypass, -circumvent, combat, contest, counteract, -decline, dismiss, -dodge, -elude, -escape, -evade, fight, miss, oppose, -refuse, -reject, -repudiate, resist, -spurn)

ACCESS (→): *crack, crash, decode, discover, enter, gate-crash, infiltrate, infringe, invade, locate, open, penetrate, pierce, reach, read, retrieve, solve, trespass, uncover, unearth, unlock, use, utilize* (≠ -avoid, banish, block, botch, bury, cordon, depart, -exclude, hide, hinder, -ignore, leave, lose, miss, oust, shut)

ACCLAIM (+): *accredit, acknowledge, admire, adore, adulate, aggrandize, applaud, appreciate, approve, ballyhoo, beatify, blandish, boost, celebrate, cheer, commend, compliment, congratulate, deify, dignify, distinguish, elevate, emblazon, encourage, endorse, ennoble, eulogize, exalt, extol, favor, fête, flannel, flatter, glorify, gold-star, gratify, hail, heighten, high-five, honor, hype, idealize, idolize, laud, lift, lionize, magnify, plug, praise, promote, raise, recognize, recommend, respect,* *revere, reverence, reward, romanticize, salute, sanction, stroke, support, thank, toast, tout, trumpet, uplift, value, venerate, welcome* (≠ abuse, admonish, badmouth, belittle, berate, blame, blast, boo, castigate, censure, chastise, chide, condemn, criticize, damn, debase, decry, demean, demonize, denigrate, denounce, deride, -detest, diminish, discredit, disgrace, disparage, disrespect, excoriate, fault, finger, frame, fulminate, heckle, humiliate, insult, jeer, keelhaul, knock, lambaste, malign, minimize, mock, neg, pan, pillory, rebuke, reprimand, reproach, revile, ridicule, rue, savage, scold, -scorn, -shun, skewer, slag, slam, -snub, vilify, wrong)

ACCOMMODATE (+): *acclimate, acclimatize, accustom, acquaint, adapt, adjust, align, alter, arrange, array, attune, balance, bend, blend, calibrate, combine, compose, conciliate, condition, connect, convert, coordinate, correct, correlate, customize, defray, doctor, dovetail, edit, enable, equalize, equip, establish, even, facilitate, familiarize, fashion, fiddle, fine-tune, fit, fuse, gear, habituate, harden, harmonize, integrate, inure, join, key, match, merge, midwife, model, modify, naturalize, orchestrate, order, orient, orientate, pace, pair, pattern, phase, prepare, prime, proportion, readapt, readjust, ready, recast, reclaim, reconceive, reconceptualize, reconcile, recycle, redesign, redevelop, redo, reengineer, refashion, refit, refocus, register, regularize, regulate, rehearse, reintegrate, reinvent, rejigger, remake, remodel, reorient, restore, rethink, retool, reunite, revamp, revise, rework, rig, right, root, season, settle, shape, smooth, square, standardize, suit, synchronize, synthesize, tailor, time, toughen, transform, tune, unify, unite* (≠ alienate, botch, challenge, confuse, contradict, counteract, damage, disaffect, disarray, disorder, disorganize, disrupt, disturb, estrange, hamper, harm, impede, inconvenience, isolate, mar, misadjust, obstruct, occlude, -omit, oppose, sabotage, scupper, skew, tax, -thwart, trouble, undermine, upset)

ACCOMMODATE (+): *abet, aid, appease, assist, attend, boost, cheer, coddle, comfort, conciliate, delight, empower, encourage, equip, favor, gladden, grace, gratify, help, humor, indulge, mollify, mollycoddle, nurture, oblige, overindulge, pacify, pamper, placate, please, propitiate, provide, reassure, relieve, satisfy, soothe, succor, supply, support* (≠ bother, burden, constrain, -desert, disappoint, discommode, disfavor, disoblige, disturb, encumber, fail, -frustrate, hamper, hamstring, hinder, hobble, impede, incommode, inconvenience, obstruct, orphan, -ostracize, oust, restrain, sabotage, subvert, -thwart, trouble)

ACCOMMODATE (+): *barrack, bestow, billet, board, bunk, carry, chamber, contain, domicile, embattle, enclose, encompass, enfold, ensconce, fit, foster, garrison, harbor, help, hold, home, house, lodge, niche, place, quarter, roof, room, seat, secure, shed, shelter, stable, take, tent, welcome* (≠ alienate, ban, banish, bar, blackball, deport, eject, evict, exorcise, expel, isolate, -ostracize, oust, quarantine, -reject, remove, seclude, -shun)

ACCOMPANY (+): *accessorize, add, adorn, affix, attach, attend, bring, chaperone, chauffeur, conduct, convey, convoy, defend, escort, follow,* *garnish, guard, guide, lead, partner, pilot, protect, second, see, shadow, shepherd, squire, steer, supplement, tag, tail, usher, walk* (≠ -abandon, -desert, -ditch, drop, dump, -flee, follow, -forsake, jilt, leave, maroon, oppose, -quit, -reject, -shun, skip, -snub, strand, withdraw)

ACCOST (→): *address, ambush, annoy, approach, attack, bother, brace, buttonhole, challenge, confront, cross, dare, detain, entice, face, flag, greet, hail, -halt, high-five, importune, inveigle, molest, proposition, salute, solicit, stop, strike, waylay* (≠ accompany, aid, assure, befriend, defend, deflect, -dodge, -elude, encourage, -evade, guard, help, -ignore, insulate, invite, protect, rescue, retort, safeguard, save, -sidestep, support, welcome)

ACCUMULATE (←): *accrue, acquire, aggregate, amalgamate, amass, archive, arrange, assemble, ball, band, batch, bunch, cache, cluster, collate, collect, combine, compile, concentrate, congregate, connect, corral, double, download, expand, gain, garner, gather, glean, group, grow, heap, herd, hive, hoard, incorporate, increase, join, link, lump, mass, merge, multiply, muster, organize, pack, pile, pool, press, procure, profit, raise, rally, scavenge, stack, stockpile, store, swarm, systematize, throng, treble, triple, unite, wrangle* (≠ decrease, diffuse, diminish, disband, disintegrate, dismiss, dispel, disperse, dissipate, dissolve, divide, lessen, parcel, portion, scatter, send, separate, sever, spend, split, squander, waste)

ACCUSE (/): *allege, arraign, arrest, attack, attribute, betray, blame, book, brand, castigate, censure, challenge, charge, chastise, chide, cite, condemn, confront, criticize, damn, defame, denounce, disparage, expose, fault, finger, frame, impeach, implicate, impugn, incriminate, inculpate, indict, libel, litigate, name, out, prosecute, rebuke, report, reproach, reprove, resent, scapegoat, scold, slander, slur, sue, summon, tax* (≠ absolve, acquit, appeal, champion, clear, defend, exculpate, excuse, exonerate, forgive, justify, legalize, pardon, protect, release, remit, shrive, spare, support, vindicate)

ACCUSTOM (+): *accommodate, acquaint, adapt, adjust, advise, anchor, apprise, attune, balance, brief, calibrate, case-harden, center, coach, condition, discipline, educate, enlighten, expose, familiarize, ground, habituate, housebreak, housetrain, inform, initiate, instruct, introduce, inure, mentor, orient, orientate, present, reacquaint, school, season, subject, tame, tell, train, warn* (≠ addle, alarm, baffle, bother, brutalize, bug, confuse, deceive, discombobulate, distort, distress, fabricate, gaslight, hide, misinform, mislead, panic, perplex, puzzle, savage, terrorize, unnerve, upset, vex, withhold, worry)

ACE (→): *beat, best, clobber, conquer, dazzle, dominate, impress, master, outguess, outmaneuver, outperform, outsmart, outwit, overcome, overwhelm, rout, steamroller, stun, trounce, trump, vanquish* (≠ bobble, bomb, botch, bugger, bungle, choke, disappoint, fail, flub, flunk, fumble, lose, miss, muff, pass, skip, subvert)

ACHIEVE (→): *accomplish, acquire, actualize, answer, attain, claim, complete, conclude, consummate, crest, deliver, discharge, dispatch, earn, effect, effectuate, enact, end, execute, fill, finish, fulfill, gain, get, implement, keep, manage, manifest, meet, negotiate, obey, observe, obtain, perfect, perform, please, procure, produce, qualify, reach, realize, resolve, satisfy, score, seal, settle, sign, solve, suit, win* (≠ -abandon, -abort, -avoid, begin, breach, -cancel, commence, concede, destroy, displease, -disregard, dissatisfy, drop, fail, forfeit, forget, -halt, -ignore, leave, lose, miss, -neglect, -overlook, pass, question, scant, scrimp, skimp, start, stop, surrender, violate) **(¿) ABSTRACTION ALERT. Concrete goals essential!**

ACKNOWLEDGE (→): *accede, accept, address, admit, affirm, allow, announce, approve, avow, betray, blab, blurt, break, broadcast, bulletin, certify, communicate, concede, confess, confirm, declare, defend, disclose, divulge, endorse, expose, grant, greet, hail, high-five, impart, inform, leak, mark, notice, out, own, proclaim, profess, publish, rate, ratify, receive, recognize, reveal, spill, squeal, support, talk, telegraph, tell, thank, unburden, unload, unveil, warn, welcome* (≠ belittle, conceal, contradict, cover, debate, -deny, disallow, disavow, disclaim, -discount, dismiss, -disown, dispute, -disregard, distrust, doubt, forget, gainsay, hide, -ignore, impugn, -negate, obscure, -omit, -overlook, rebut, refute, -reject, -repudiate, scruple, -snub, -spurn, suspect, veil) **(¿) ABSTRACTION ALERT. Concrete goals essential!**

ACQUAINT (→): *accustom, advertise, advise, announce, appraise, apprise, befriend, brief, clue, coach, communicate, confess, disclose, divulge, educate, enlighten, familiarize, habituate, inform, instruct, notify, reveal, school, season, teach, tell, train, tutor* (≠ -avoid, baffle, befuddle, conceal, confuse, disguise, -disregard, forget, hide, -ignore, mask, misinform, mislead, obliterate, obscure, -overlook, pass, -reject, veil)

ACQUIRE (←): *access, accomplish, accumulate, achieve, amass, annex, appropriate, attain, bag, buy, capture, carry, catch, clear, collect, colonize, compile, cop, corral, debit, draw, earn, gain, garner, gather, get, glean, grab, gross, hustle, import, inherit, invade, land, make, net, notch, obtain, occupy, pick, procure, promote, pull, purchase, realize, reap, recapture, receive, regain, scavenge, score, secure, snag, source, stockpile, take, wangle, win* (≠ -abandon, accord, bandy, comp, contribute, -ditch, drop, dump, forfeit, forgo, -forsake, furnish, give, grant, hand, hard-sell, jettison, junk, leverage, lose, misplace, miss, offer, pay, peddle, pimp, prostitute, relinquish, sell, spare, stock, supply, surrender, tithe, toss, volunteer, yield)

ACQUIT (+): *absolve, affirm, champion, cleanse, clear, corroborate, defend, defray, deliver, discharge, dismiss, disprove, exculpate, excuse, exempt, exonerate, forgive, free, justify, liberate, mitigate, pardon, purge, purify, redeem, redress, refute, rehabilitate, release, relieve, remit, reprieve, shield, spare, support, vindicate, warrant, wash, whitewash* (≠ accuse, allege, blame, castigate, charge, condemn, convict, denounce, discipline, fault, frame, implicate, imprison, impugn, incriminate, indict, litigate, prosecute, punish, reprove, revile, ruin, scapegoat, sentence)

ACTIVATE (+): *accelerate, actuate, advance, animate, arouse, awaken, beget, begin, breed, bring, catalyze, charge, crank, create, cue, cultivate, deploy, develop, discharge, drive, electrify, enact, encourage, energize, engender, enliven, establish, excite, expedite, father, fire, forward, foster, found, fuel, further, galvanize, generate, ignite, impel, inaugurate, incite, induce, initiate, innovate, instigate, institute, introduce, invigorate, invoke, jump-start, kick-start, launch, make, mobilize, motivate, move, nourish, nurture, pioneer, power, prioritize, produce, promote, prompt, propel, prostrate, provoke, push, quicken, reactivate, reboot, recharge, release, render, revitalize, rouse, run, rush, set, spark, spawn, speed, spur, start, stimulate, stir, switch, trigger, trip, vitalize, wake* (≠ abolish, arrest, -avoid, block, brake, check, control, cripple, crush, curb, cut, dampen, deactivate, decelerate, delay, demolish, demotivate, destroy, -deter, disable, discourage, dissuade, end, extinguish, -halt, hamper, hamstring, hinder, hobble, impair, impede, inactivate, inhibit, jam, kill, limit, liquidate, -prevent, quash, quell, quench, repress, restrain, restrict, sabotage, shelve, short-circuit, slake, slow, smother, snuff, squash, squelch, stale, stall, stick, stifle, still, stop, stunt, stymie, subdue, suppress, terminate, -thwart, undermine)

ADAPT (+): *acclimate, acclimatize, accommodate, accustom, acquaint, adjust, align, alter, amend, approximate, attune, automate, bend, calibrate, case-harden, change, computerize, condition, convert, correct, customize, diversify, doctor, edit, embellish, embroider, emend, equalize, equip, establish, exchange, familiarize, fashion, fiddle, fine-tune, fit, game, gear, harden, harmonize, improve, inure, jerry-rig, match, mechanize, metamorphose, militarize, model, modernize, modify, mold, motorize, orient, overhaul, pace, pattern, phase, prepare, prime, qualify, radicalize, ready, realign, recalibrate, recast, reclaim, reconceive, reconceptualize, recycle, redesign, redevelop, redo, reengineer, refashion, refit, refocus, register, regulate, rehearse, reimagine, reinvent, rejigger, remake, remodel, reorient, reshape, restore, restructure, rethink, retool, retrofit, revamp, revise, revolutionize, rework, rig, right, root, sculpt, season, settle, shape, shift, shuffle, skew, square, substitute, suit, supplant, swap, switch, tailor, tone, toughen, transfigure, transform, transmute, transpose, tune, turn, tweak, update, vary, weaponize, wiggle, wriggle* (≠ abide, -abort, anesthetize, bolster, brace, complete, conclude, conserve, continue, deaden, debilitate, destroy, disable, disqualify, dull, endure, finalize, finish, fix, fortify, freeze, hamper, hamstring, harden, hinder, hold, immobilize, incapacitate, keep, leave, lock, maintain, misadjust, numb, paralyze, restrain, retain, set, settle, stabilize, steady, stop, strengthen, sustain, transfix, weather)

ADD (+): *accumulate, adjoin, affix, aggrandize, amplify, annex, append, attach, augment, beef, blend, boost, combine, complement, complete, compound, deepen, elongate, enforce, enhance, enlarge, escalate, expand, extend, fasten, fix, furnish, gather, graft, heighten, hike, hitch, improve, include, increase, infuse, inject, insert, intensify, interfuse, introduce, join, lengthen, magnify, maximize, mix, multiply, pad,* *piggyback, prolong, protract, raise, reinforce, spike, stockpile, strengthen, supplement, supply, sweeten, swell, tag, tie, unify, unite* (≠ abate, abbreviate, abridge, amputate, compress, condense, constrict, contract, curtail, cut, debit, decrease, deduct, detach, diminish, disconnect, disjoin, dissolve, excise, extract, lessen, lop, lower, miniaturize, minimize, reduce, release, remove, separate, sever, shorten, shrink, subtract, sunder, take, truncate, unfasten, withdraw)

ADD (+): *analyze, anatomize, appraise, assess, audit, calculate, check, cipher, compute, count, determine, divide, enumerate, evaluate, examine, figure, multiply, number, reckon, recompute, refigure, study, sum, synthesize, table, tabulate, tally, tell, total* (≠ abstract, deduct, -deny, disbelieve, -discount, -disregard, distrust, doubt, estimate, -exclude, guess, -ignore, mistrust, -negate, -neglect, -nullify, -omit, -overlook, question, subtract, suspect)

ADDLE (/): *abash, agitate, amaze, baffle, bamboozle, beat, befog, befuddle, bemuse, bewilder, bother, buffalo, chagrin, confound, confuse, deafen, deceive, discombobulate, discomfit, discomfort, discompose, disconcert, dismay, disorient, disquiet, distract, distress, disturb, dizzy, embarrass, faze, flummox, fluster, fox, gaslight, get, mismatch, mortify, muddle, muddy, mystify, nonplus, overset, perplex, perturb, puzzle, rattle, shake, stump, stun, throw, unhinge, unsettle, upset, vex* (≠ anchor, assure, calm, clarify, coach, edify, educate, encourage, enlighten, explain, guide, illuminate, illustrate, inform, instruct, reassure, rephrase, satisfy, school, simplify, solve, stabilize, steady, teach, tutor, unravel)

ADDRESS (→): *accost, acknowledge, approach, brave, buttonhole, challenge, command, communicate, compare, contact, control, convey, counter, cross, debate, direct, email, engineer, face, field, finesse, greet, guide, hack, hail, handle, harangue, impart, invite, invoke, jockey, lecture, manage, maneuver, manipulate, mediate, message, micromanage, name, negotiate, play, regulate, retort, run, send, steer, swing, take, text, treat* (≠ -avoid, botch, bungle, -bypass, -circumvent, -cut, -desert, -disregard, -elude, foozle, forget, fumble, goof, -ignore, mishandle, miss, muff, -omit, -overlook, pass, -shun, skip, -snub, -spurn) **(¿) ABSTRACTION ALERT. Concrete goals essential!**

ADJUDICATE (+): *adjudge, appraise, arbitrate, ascertain, assess, assist, broker, compromise, conciliate, conclude, consider, critique, decide, deliberate, determine, equalize, facilitate, find, hear, judge, mediate, moderate, mull, negotiate, pass, ponder, pronounce, prosecute, reconcile, referee, resolve, rule, sentence, settle, try, umpire, weigh* (≠ appeal, confound, confuse, debate, defer, disbelieve, -disregard, -ignore, leave, miss, muddy, -neglect, -overlook, overrule, postpone, praise, -reject, shelve, skirt) **(¿) ABSTRACTION ALERT. Concrete goals essential!**

ADJUST (+): *acclimate, acclimatize, accommodate, acquaint, adapt, align, alter, amend, approximate, arrange, attune, balance, bend, calibrate, case-harden, center, change, clarify, compose, computerize, condition, contemporize, convert, coordinate, correct, customize, dispose,* *doctor, edit, equalize, equip, establish, familiarize, fashion, fiddle, fine-tune, fit, fix, gear, habituate, harden, harmonize, improve, inure, jerry-rig, level, match, measure, mend, militarize, model, modernize, modify, modulate, naturalize, orient, pace, pattern, perfect, phase, polish, prepare, prime, readjust, ready, realign, recast, reclaim, recline, reconceive, reconceptualize, reconcile, rectify, recycle, redesign, redevelop, redo, reengineer, refashion, refit, refocus, register, regulate, rehearse, reimagine, reinvent, rejigger, remake, remodel, renovate, reorient, repair, rephrase, reshape, reshuffle, restore, restructure, rethink, retool, retrofit, reunite, revamp, revise, revolutionize, rework, rig, right, root, sculpt, season, set, settle, shape, shift, shine, shuffle, square, straighten, suit, tailor, temper, time, tone, toughen, transform, trouble-shoot, tune, tweak, update, weaponize, wiggle* (≠ abide, botch, break, cement, challenge, confuse, continue, corrode, damage, defy, derange, destroy, disarrange, disorder, disorganize, dissuade, disturb, endure, erode, freeze, fumble, hold, hurt, incite, increase, insist, keep, leave, maintain, misadjust, mismatch, paralyze, -rebuff, -refuse, repress, resist, retain, ruin, sabotage, scatter, spoil, stagnate, suppress, sustain, unsettle, upset)

ADMINISTER (→): *allocate, allot, allow, apply, apportion, appropriate, assign, authorize, bestow, bring, chunk, circulate, contribute, deal, deliver, disburse, discharge, dispense, disperse, disseminate, distribute, divide, divvy, dole, donate, drizzle, execute, extend, foist, force-feed, fuel, furnish, give, hand, impose, inflict, inject, issue, mainline, measure, mete, offer, overfeed, parcel, part, pledge, portion, proportion, prorate, provide, ration, reallocate, redistribute, scatter, serve, set, share, spare, split, spread, supply, tender, tithe, trickle, volunteer, vouchsafe* (≠ begrudge, -decline, -deny, deprive, disallow, grudge, hoard, hog, hold, keep, misallocate, monopolize, -neglect, pinch, -refuse, -reject, remove, scant, skimp, starve, stint, tap, withdraw, withhold, yank)

ADMINISTER (+): *boss, captain, chair, choreograph, command, conduct, control, designate, direct, disburse, dominate, execute, govern, guard, guide, handle, head, instruct, keep, lead, manage, micromanage, mind, negotiate, officiate, operate, orchestrate, organize, oversee, pace, pilot, police, protect, referee, regiment, regulate, rule, run, safeguard, spearhead, stage-manage, steer, steward, superintend, supervise, tend, watch* (≠ -abandon, abdicate, bobble, bomb, botch, bugger, bungle, collapse, debate, -deny, fake, flub, flunk, follow, forgo, -forsake, fudge, fumble, goof, half-ass, louse, mar, mess, mishandle, misjudge, mismanage, misrule, mistake, muff, -neglect, obey, overestimate, -overlook, -refuse, serve, -shirk, skip, squander, subvert, waste)

ADMIRE (+): *acclaim, accredit, adore, adulate, applaud, appreciate, approve, blandish, bless, boost, canonize, cherish, commend, compliment, congratulate, consider, credit, deify, dig, enjoy, esteem, extol, fancy, favor, flatter, glorify, hallow, honor, idolize, laud, love, praise, prize, regard, relish, respect, revere, reverence, savor, toast, treasure, trumpet, value, venerate, worship* (≠ abhor, abominate, -blank, boo, condemn, decry, deplore, -despise, -detest, disapprove, -discount, -disdain, disfavor, dismiss, -disregard, execrate, -hate, -loathe, -scorn, underestimate, vilify) **(¿) ABSTRACTION ALERT. Concrete goals essential!**

ADMIT (→): *accept, accord, acknowledge, adopt, affirm, allow, avow, bare, blab, blurt, communicate, concede, confess, confide, confirm, credit, declare, disclose, divulge, embrace, encompass, enumerate, expose, grant, initiate, involve, number, out, own, permit, proclaim, profess, receive, recognize, relate, reveal, spill, tolerate, uncover, unveil, yield* (≠ ban, banish, bar, conceal, confront, contradict, debate, -deny, discredit, disguise, -disown, dispute, distrust, doubt, eject, erase, -exclude, -forbid, gainsay, hide, hush, impugn, invalidate, obscure, -omit, oppose, -ostracize, oust, -prevent, -prohibit, protest, quiet, rebut, -refuse, -repudiate, -scorn, scruple, -spurn, suppress, -veto, withhold) **(¿) ABSTRACTION ALERT. Concrete goals essential!**

ADMONISH (/): *abuse, advise, assail, attack, badmouth, belittle, berate, blackguard, blame, blast, castigate, caution, censure, chastise, check, chide, condemn, correct, counsel, criticize, crucify, demonize, denounce, denunciate, deprecate, deride, ding, discipline, disparage, diss, excoriate, exhort, fault, finger, flay, fulminate, harangue, jaw, keelhaul, knock, lambaste, lash, lecture, minimize, mock, pan, pillory, punish, rate, ream, rebuke, reprimand, reproach, reprove, ridicule, scold, score, -scorn, slam, upbraid, warn, zap* (≠ applaud, approve, blandish, commend, compliment, congratulate, countersign, encourage, endorse, extol, flatter, gratify, hail, instigate, okay, permit, praise, salute, sanction, tout, unleash, urge)

ADOPT (←): *absorb, accept, adapt, affect, affirm, appoint, appropriate, approve, arrogate, assimilate, assume, borrow, cherish, choose, coopt, copy, cultivate, decide, determine, domesticate, elect, embrace, emulate, endorse, espouse, fancy, favor, feign, follow, heed, honor, imitate, incorporate, integrate, internalize, judge, maintain, mimic, naturalize, pick, prefer, pretend, prize, ratify, receive, seize, select, simulate, support, tap, treasure, use, usurp, utilize, welcome, wish* (≠ -abandon, abnegate, cease, discard, -discontinue, disfavor, -disown, -forsake, jettison, junk, -reject, relinquish, -renounce, -repudiate, repulse, -spurn, surrender, toss, withdraw)

ADOPT (+): *attend, choose, cradle, cultivate, discipline, educate, father, feed, foster, harbor, host, incubate, instruct, invite, mentor, mind, mother, naturalize, nourish, nurse, nurture, parent, pick, protect, raise, rear, receive, select, shelter, train, watch, welcome* (≠ -abandon, abuse, birth, -desert, discard, -disown, -ditch, dump, exile, expel, -forsake, hatch, -ignore, leave, maroon, mistreat, -neglect, offload, -reject, -shun, sire, wrong)

ADORE (+): *admire, adulate, applaud, appreciate, approve, canonize, cherish, deify, dig, endorse, enjoy, enshrine, esteem, exalt, extol, fancy, favor, hallow, hero-worship, honor, idealize, idolize, love, prefer, prize, regard, relish, respect, revere, reverence, savor, support, treasure, value, venerate, worship* (≠ abhor, abominate, antagonize, belittle, blackguard, boo, condemn, deprecate, -despise, -detest, -disdain, disfavor, disparage, displease, execrate, -hate, -loathe, ridicule, -scorn, -spurn) **(¿) ABSTRACTION ALERT. Concrete goals essential!**

ADORN (+): *accessorize, aggrandize, apparel, appliqué, array, attire, beautify, bedeck, bedizen, bejewel, bespangle, blazon, braid, brighten, caparison, clothe, costume, crown, dandify, deck, decorate, distinguish, drape, dress, elaborate, embellish, emblazon, emboss, embroider, enhance, enrich, fancify, feather, festoon, figure, filigree, flavor, flounce, freshen, frill, fringe, furbish, garland, garnish, gild, glitter, glitz, grace, hang, lace, lard, optimize, ornament, pad, paint, pigment, prettify, pretty, ribbon, smarten, spangle, spiff, spruce, stipple, stud, swag, tinsel, titivate, tool, trim, wreathe* (≠ bare, blemish, deface, deform, denude, disfigure, dismantle, display, divest, efface, expose, foul, harshen, mar, reveal, scar, simplify, spoil, streamline, strip, uglify, unbuckle, unbutton, uncover)

ADULTERATE (/): *alloy, amalgamate, attenuate, bastardize, befoul, blend, bowdlerize, canker, cheapen, commingle, contaminate, cook, corrupt, counterfeit, cut, debase, defile, degrade, depreciate, deteriorate, devalue, dilute, dirty, doctor, dose, envenom, extend, fake, falsify, foul, fudge, impair, infect, infiltrate, intermix, irrigate, lace, load, manipulate, mingle, misrepresent, mix, moderate, poison, pollute, qualify, soil, sophisticate, spike, spoil, sully, taint, temper, thin, transfuse, vitiate, water, weaken* (≠ augment, better, clarify, clean, cleanse, compact, concentrate, condense, decontaminate, delouse, distill, enhance, enrich, fertilize, filter, flush, focus, fortify, free, improve, lard, leach, optimize, pasteurize, purge, purify, rarefy, refine, reinforce, strengthen, supplement)

ADVANCE (→): *abet, advertise, advocate, aggrandize, aid, amplify, assist, back, ballyhoo, benefit, boost, champion, condone, cultivate, encourage, endorse, endow, energize, facilitate, favor, finance, float, forward, foster, fund, further, grow, heighten, help, hype, improve, increase, incubate, inspire, kindle, lift, limelight, magnify, motivate, nourish, nurse, nurture, patronize, plug, presell, present, prioritize, promote, provoke, publicize, push, sanction, second, spitball, spur, stake, strengthen, submit, subsidize, suggest, support, tout, underwrite, upgrade, uphold, uplift, urge* (≠ -abort, arrest, ban, bar, block, check, checkmate, cramp, curb, discourage, discredit, disfavor, disgrace, disinherit, -disown, encumber, enjoin, fetter, foil, -forbid, -frustrate, -halt, hamper, hamstring, harm, hinder, hobble, impede, inhibit, injure, -interdict, manacle, monkeywrench, obstruct, oppose, outlaw, pause, -prevent, -prohibit, proscribe, protest, repress, restrain, restrict, retard, shackle, slow, snuff, squash, squelch, stall, stifle, stop, stymie, subdue, suppress, -thwart)

ADVERTISE (→): *acclaim, announce, bait, ballyhoo, blare, blaze, blazon, blurb, broadcast, bulletin, champion, circulate, commodify, communicate, confess, confide, confirm, declare, disclose, display, disseminate, divulge, enunciate, feature, flash, herald, hustle, hype, impart, inform, intimate, introduce, laud, leverage, limelight, lure, mainstream, manifest, market, merchandize, notify, overestimate, overstate, peddle, pimp,* *pitch, placard, plug, popularize, post, praise, presell, proclaim, promo, promote, promulgate, publicize, publish, puff, push, recommend, release, report, reveal, sell, shill, show, sound, spotlight, spread, stimulate, telegraph, tout, trumpet* (≠ baffle, block, bury, chide, cloak, conceal, criticize, deceive, -deny, deride, -deter, -discount, discourage, disparage, ensconce, -halt, hide, hush, insult, lambaste, mock, niche, -prevent, protect, protest, recant, retract, revoke, ridicule, -scorn, screen, shield, -shun, silence, slam, suppress, withhold)

ADVISE (→): *acquaint, adjure, admonish, advocate, alert, appraise, apprise, arbitrate, beg, brief, caution, coach, commend, consult, convince, counsel, critique, cue, direct, dissuade, edify, educate, encourage, enjoin, enlighten, exhort, familiarize, forewarn, guide, impart, implore, induce, inform, instruct, lead, mediate, mentor, moderate, notify, persuade, pilot, prepare, prescribe, prompt, propose, ready, recommend, referee, report, school, shepherd, show, steer, suggest, teach, tout, tutor, update, urge, warn* (≠ -abandon, -avoid, betray, cheat, command, compromise, conceal, deceive, delude, demand, demotivate, -desert, discourage, endanger, fool, -forsake, imperil, mislead, -neglect, outwit, pretend, risk, trick, withhold)

ADVOCATE (→): *adopt, advance, advise, aid, approve, assist, back, bless, bolster, boost, buttonhole, champion, countenance, defend, encourage, endorse, espouse, favor, forward, further, help, justify, lobby, patronize, plug, preach, prescribe, press, promote, propose, propound, publicize, push, recommend, spitball, spur, strengthen, support, tout, upgrade, uphold, urge* (≠ assail, attack, baffle, block, chide, confound, counteract, criticize, decry, denounce, deride, -deter, discourage, dissuade, -frustrate, -halt, hinder, impede, impugn, obstruct, oppose, -prevent, protest, -refuse, -reject, -repudiate, sabotage, scold, -scorn, scotch, scupper, scuttle, shelve, -spurn, undermine)

AFFECT (→): *afflict, agitate, allure, alter, attack, attract, bewitch, bias, bother, captivate, change, charm, color, concern, contact, dazzle, discomfort, discompose, disquiet, distress, disturb, enchant, engage, enrapture, enthrall, entrance, fascinate, fluster, harass, harry, impact, impress, induce, influence, inspire, interest, involve, modify, move, overcome, penetrate, perturb, pester, pierce, plague, ravish, regard, relate, smite, stir, strain, stress, strike, sway, touch, transform, transport, trouble, try, upset, worry* (≠ -avert, -avoid, bore, -bypass, calm, -disregard, -dodge, -duck, -elude, -eschew, -evade, forego, -ignore, isolate, jade, -omit, -overlook, shelve, -sidestep, skip, stagnate, tire, underwhelm, weary) **(¿) ABSTRACTION ALERT. Concrete goals essential!**

AFFIX (+): *add, adhere, anchor, annex, append, attach, batten, bend, bind, bolt, button, cinch, clamp, clasp, clench, clinch, clip, connect, fasten, fix, fuse, glue, hang, harness, join, lace, lash, latch, link, nail, paste, pin, plaster, reaffix, reattach, refasten, resecure, rivet, screw, secure, shackle, solder, staple, stick, strap, stud, tack, tackle, tie, toggle, unite, weld, yoke* (≠ detach, disconnect, disjoin, disjoint, disunite, divide, divorce, loose, loosen, part, remove, separate, sever, slack, slacken, split, sunder, unbind, uncouple, undo, unfasten, unhook, unlash, unlink, untie, unyoke)

AFFLICT (/): *affect, aggravate, aggrieve, agitate, agonize, ail, anguish, annoy, assail, attack, badger, bedevil, besiege, bother, bug, burden, chafe, crucify, crush, curse, discomfort, discompose, disquiet, distress, disturb, dizzy, dog, exasperate, fluster, gall, get, grieve, hagride, harass, harm, harrow, harry, hound, hurt, irk, irritate, lacerate, martyr, menace, molest, nettle, oppress, overpower, overwhelm, pain, peeve, persecute, perturb, pester, pique, plague, prick, punish, pursue, rasp, ride, rile, smite, sorrow, stab, sting, strain, stress, strike, torment, torture, trouble, try, tyrannize, unhinge, upset, vex, victimize, worry, wound, wring, wrong* (≠ abet, aid, amuse, assist, comfort, console, content, deliver, doctor, ease, heal, help, nourish, nurse, nurture, pity, please, quiet, release, relieve, reprieve, solace, soothe, succor, support)

AFFRONT (/): *abase, abuse, accost, anger, annoy, bait, belittle, besmear, besmirch, blame, boo, confront, criticize, -cut, debase, defame, degrade, demean, demote, devalue, diminish, disgrace, dishonor, disparage, displease, disrespect, distress, disturb, humble, humiliate, hurt, injure, insult, jeer, libel, lower, malign, miff, mock, mortify, offend, oppress, outrage, pain, persecute, pillory, provoke, -rebuff, reduce, revile, ridicule, shame, slander, slap, -slight, slur, smear, -snub, soil, spoil, stain, sully, taint, taunt, torment, torture, trample, trouble, upset, vex, violate, wound, wrong, zing* (≠ acclaim, adulate, applaud, approve, assuage, blandish, commend, compliment, content, delight, eulogize, exalt, flannel, flatter, glorify, grace, gratify, hail, honor, please, praise, retort, satisfy, soothe, sweet-talk, thrill)

AGGRANDIZE (+): *acclaim, apotheosize, applaud, boost, canonize, commend, congratulate, deify, dignify, distend, distinguish, elevate, ennoble, enshrine, enthrone, exalt, extol, glorify, heighten, heroicize, heroize, honor, hype, idealize, inflate, intensify, laud, lift, magnify, praise, promote, raise, romanticize, sanitize, sentimentalize, shill, sugarcoat, swell, upgrade, uplift* (≠ abase, bastardize, belittle, bestialize, boo, condense, curtail, debase, decrease, decry, degrade, demean, diminish, disparage, erode, humble, humiliate, insult, lessen, minimize, reduce, shame, shrink, weaken)

AGGRAVATE (→): *accelerate, amplify, catalyze, complicate, compound, deepen, enhance, escalate, exacerbate, exaggerate, expand, extend, fuel, heighten, increase, inflame, intensify, lubricate, magnify, maximize, mount, overdramatize, rouse, worsen* (≠ allay, ameliorate, assuage, better, ease, help, improve, lessen, minimize, mitigate, relieve, shrink, slow)

AGGRAVATE (/): *affront, agitate, anger, annoy, antagonize, badger, bait, bother, bug, bullyrag, burn, chafe, chagrin, devil, discomfort, discompose, disquiet, distress, dog, earbash, eat, enrage, exacerbate, exaggerate, exasperate, exercise, freak, fret, frost, frustrate, gall, get, hagride, harass, harry, hassle, heckle, hector, hurt, impair, incense, inflame, infuriate, insult, irk, irritate, madden, magnify, maltreat, miff, mistreat, nag, needle,* *nettle, noodge, offend, outrage, peeve, persecute, perturb, pester, pique, plague, provoke, rankle, rasp, rile, roil, rouse, ruffle, spite, tease, torment, undo, unhinge, unsettle, upset, vex, wig, worry* (≠ allay, alleviate, amuse, appease, assuage, assure, calm, cheer, comfort, console, content, delight, gladden, gratify, lull, mitigate, mollify, oblige, pacify, placate, please, propitiate, quiet, reassure, satisfy, solace, soothe, sugarcoat, thrill)

AGITATE (→): *addle, alarm, arouse, beat, bug, burn, churn, concuss, confuse, convulse, craze, debate, dement, derange, discompose, disconcert, dishevel, disorient, dispute, disquiet, distract, distress, disturb, dizzy, excite, fan, faze, fluster, fret, froth, generate, harass, hassle, impel, incite, inflame, jumble, move, panic, perturb, press, psych, rattle, rock, rouse, ruffle, shake, shock, spook, startle, stimulate, stir, toss, trouble, unhinge, unnerve, unsettle, upset, vex, worry* (≠ allay, alleviate, appease, assuage, calm, compose, conciliate, hypnotize, lull, mellow, mesmerize, mollify, pacify, placate, propitiate, quiet, quieten, sedate, settle, smooth, soothe, stabilize, steady, still, tranquilize)

AID (+): *abet, accommodate, advance, advise, assist, attend, back, bail, befriend, benefit, bolster, boost, buttress, champion, comfort, condone, counsel, cultivate, deliver, ease, embolden, encourage, endorse, energize, facilitate, favor, forward, foster, further, guide, heal, hearten, help, improve, inspire, kindle, launch, mentor, midwife, motivate, nurse, nurture, oblige, patronize, profit, promote, prop, provoke, refresh, reinforce, reinvigorate, relieve, remedy, rescue, restimulate, restore, revive, sanction, save, school, second, serve, sponsor, spur, strengthen, subsidize, succor, support, sustain, teach, tutor* (≠ baffle, -balk, bar, block, boobytrap, checkmate, constrain, counteract, damage, daunt, demotivate, -desert, disappoint, discourage, discredit, disfavor, disgrace, dishearten, fail, foil, -frustrate, gaslight, hamper, handicap, harm, hinder, hold, hurt, impede, incommode, inconvenience, inhibit, injure, lynch, menace, monkey-wrench, muzzle, obstruct, oppose, pause, -prevent, protest, repress, restrain, retard, sabotage, scotch, scupper, scuttle, shelve, stall, stifle, straiten, strangle, stunt, stymie, subvert, -thwart)

ALARM (→): *abash, aggravate, agitate, ail, alert, amaze, anger, annoy, astonish, bedevil, blindside, bother, bug, caution, concern, confound, confuse, daunt, demoralize, demotivate, derail, discomfit, discomfort, discompose, disconcert, discountenance, discourage, dishearten, dismay, dispirit, disquiet, distemper, distract, distress, disturb, embarrass, exasperate, exercise, faze, fluster, frazzle, freak, fret, fuss, gall, get, harass, harry, haunt, irk, irritate, jar, jump, mortify, nettle, nonplus, peeve, perturb, pester, pique, plague, rattle, rile, shake, signal, surprise, threaten, undo, unhinge, unnerve, unsettle, upset, vex, warn, worry, wow* (≠ allay, alleviate, amuse, appease, assuage, calm, candy-coat, captivate, charm, compose, conciliate, content, delight, divert, entertain, flatter, gladden, gratify, help, humor, hush, indulge, lull, mollify, pacify, placate, please, propitiate, quiet, reassure, satisfy, sedate, settle, soothe, sugarcoat, suit, thrill, tranquilize)

ALARM (/): *affright, amaze, appall, astound, awe, brutalize, chill, daunt, demoralize, discomfort, discompose, disconcert, dismay, dispirit, disquiet, distract, distress, disturb, emasculate, floor, frighten, horrify, jolt, panic, perturb, petrify, rattle, rile, roil, savage, scare, shake, shock, spook, startle, terrify, terrorize, threaten, unman, unnerve, unsettle, unstring, upset, worry* (≠ anchor, assure, balance, bolster, brace, buoy, center, cheer, comfort, console, embolden, encourage, favor, fortify, hearten, inspire, mellow, mollify, pacify, placate, reassure, root, settle, solace, soothe, stabilize, steady, steel, strengthen, subdue, toughen)

ALERT (→): *admonish, adumbrate, advise, alarm, apprise, augur, awaken, bother, buzz, caution, clue, disconcert, dismay, enjoin, exhort, flag, forecast, foreshadow, foretell, forewarn, goad, harbinger, inform, nag, notify, predict, presage, prognosticate, prophesy, rattle, ring, signal, startle, surprise, threaten, tip, unsettle, wake, warn* (≠ anesthetize, bore, buffer, coddle, compromise, conceal, deaden, deafen, disguise, -disregard, drug, dull, endanger, forget, hide, hypnotize, imperil, miss, muffle, numb, -omit, -overlook, risk, sedate, stifle, tranquilize)

ALIENATE (/): *aggravate, anger, antagonize, arm, attack, disaffect, disenchant, disgruntle, disillusion, distance, disunite, divide, divorce, embitter, enrage, envenom, estrange, incense, inflame, infuriate, madden, outrage, poison, rankle, rile, roil, separate, sever, -shun, sour, split, sunder, uncouple, unlink, unyoke* (≠ appease, befriend, beguile, charm, connect, contact, disarm, endear, harbor, house, include, ingratiate, invite, marry, mollify, pacify, placate, propitiate, protect, reconcile, reunite, support, unite, welcome)

ALIGN (+): *adapt, adjust, ally, arrange, array, assimilate, associate, calibrate, chain, combine, compose, concatenate, contemporize, coordinate, enlist, equalize, even, fix, follow, harmonize, incorporate, integrate, internalize, join, level, link, order, pace, plumb, progress, queue, range, rank, rectify, refine, regiment, regulate, right, sequence, sort, straighten, string, succeed, thread, tune, unite, unskew* (≠ combat, confuse, contradict, crumple, derange, disarrange, discompose, dishevel, disjoint, dislocate, disorder, disorganize, disrupt, disturb, jar, jolt, jumble, oppose, ruffle, rumple, scramble, scrunch, separate, shift, shove, shuffle, shunt, skew, spoil, tousle, upset, wrinkle)

ALLAY (+): *abate, alleviate, ameliorate, amend, appease, assuage, better, blunt, calm, candy-coat, check, comfort, compose, correct, cure, decrease, defray, diminish, ease, emend, enhance, enrich, fix, heal, help, improve, lessen, lighten, lull, mend, mitigate, moderate, mollify, oil, pacify, palliate, perfect, placate, quell, quiet, rectify, reduce, refine, reform, relax, relieve, remedy, repair, right, settle, soften, soothe, square, still, sugarcoat, temper, tranquilize* (≠ aggravate, agitate, arouse, compound, exacerbate, excite, fan, harm, heighten, hurt, impair, increase, inflame, injure, intensify, kindle, provoke, rouse, sharpen, stir, worsen)

ALLEGE (→): *accuse, affirm, announce, argue, arraign, assert, attest, attribute, avow, blame, broadcast, charge, claim, condemn, confirm,* *contend, credit, criticize, declare, defend, denounce, fault, finger, frame, impeach, implicate, impugn, incriminate, insist, justify, maintain, plead, proclaim, profess, protest, purport, rationalize, reaffirm, reason, reassert, reproach, scold, support, telegraph, uphold, vindicate, warrant* (≠ -abandon, challenge, confute, consult, contradict, convince, counter, debate, demonstrate, -deny, disavow, disclaim, -disown, disprove, dispute, distrust, doubt, establish, gainsay, grill, interrogate, interview, invalidate, -negate, prove, question, rebut, refute, -reject, -repudiate, retort, scruple, substantiate, validate)

ALLEVIATE (+): *abate, aid, allay, anesthetize, appease, assuage, blunt, calm, candy-coat, check, comfort, compose, console, cool, cure, cushion, deaden, diminish, disencumber, dose, drug, dulcify, dull, ease, heal, help, lessen, lighten, lull, medicate, minimize, mitigate, moderate, mollify, narcotize, numb, pacify, palliate, quiet, reduce, relax, relieve, remedy, restore, restrain, sedate, soften, soft-pedal, soothe, still, subdue, sugarcoat, sweeten, syrup, temper, tranquilize* (≠ accentuate, aggravate, agitate, amp, amplify, deepen, derail, discomfort, disturb, encumber, exacerbate, heighten, increase, intensify, load, magnify, maximize, persecute, perturb, redouble, strengthen, torment, torture, unhinge, unsettle, worsen, wound)

ALLOCATE (→): *accord, administer, afford, allot, allow, apportion, assign, award, bequeath, bestow, budget, cede, chunk, comp, confer, contribute, convey, deal, deed, deliver, designate, dispense, distribute, divide, divvy, dole, dollop, donate, drizzle, earmark, endow, extend, furnish, give, grant, hand, impart, issue, measure, mete, meter, offer, parcel, part, place, portion, present, prioritize, proffer, prorate, provide, ration, reallocate, reapportion, reassign, redistribute, reserve, share, situate, slice, spare, split, supply, surrender, task, tender, time, tithe, transfer, transmit, trickle, volunteer, vouchsafe* (≠ abrogate, accept, acquire, appropriate, arrogate, begrudge, charge, commandeer, confiscate, debit, -decline, -deny, deprive, disinherit, dispossess, divest, gain, gather, glean, grab, hoard, hog, impound, inherit, invalidate, keep, monopolize, obtain, procure, -rebuff, -refuse, -reject, remove, repel, -repudiate, -rescind, retain, revoke, rob, seize, snatch, starve, stash, steal, stint, swipe, take, withhold)

ALLURE (←): *arrest, attract, bait, beckon, beguile, bewitch, cajole, candy-coat, captivate, charm, coax, decoy, delight, disarm, draw, enamor, enchant, engage, entice, entrance, entrap, fascinate, hook, induce, interest, inveigle, lure, magnetize, persuade, pull, seduce, tempt, win* (≠ block, bore, chill, dampen, demotivate, -deter, discourage, disgust, dissuade, nauseate, needle, -prevent, protest, -refuse, -reject, repel, repulse, -shun, view, warn) **(¿) ABSTRACTION ALERT. Concrete goals essential!**

ALTER (+): *adapt, adjust, affect, amend, amputate, automate, calibrate, change, commute, computerize, convert, customize, deform, diversify, doctor, edit, embellish, embroider, equalize, eviscerate, exchange, fine-tune, geld, improve, juggle, metamorphose, modernize, modify, mold,* *mutate, overhaul, qualify, radicalize, recalibrate, recast, reconceive, reconceptualize, redo, refashion, reform, regenerate, reimagine, reinvent, rejigger, remake, remodel, rephrase, reshape, restore, restructure, rethink, retool, retrofit, revamp, revise, revolutionize, rework, sculpt, sew, shape, shift, shuffle, stitch, substitute, supplant, swap, switch, tailor, transfigure, transform, transmogrify, transmute, transpose, tune, turn, tweak, update, vary, weaponize* (≠ abide, -abort, bolster, brace, complete, conclude, conserve, continue, destroy, endure, finalize, finish, fix, fortify, freeze, hamper, hamstring, harden, hinder, hold, immobilize, keep, leave, lock, maintain, paralyze, preserve, restrain, retain, set, settle, stabilize, steady, stop, strengthen, sustain, transfix, weather)

AMAZE (→): *affect, alarm, appall, astonish, astound, baffle, befuddle, bewilder, boggle, confound, confuse, daze, dazzle, discomfit, disconcert, dismay, dumbfound, electrify, exhilarate, flabbergast, flatten, floor, flummox, galvanize, gobsmack, gravel, horrify, impress, inspire, jar, jolt, move, muckrake, muddle, mystify, nonplus, perplex, puzzle, rock, scandalize, shake, shock, stagger, startle, stimulate, stir, strike, stun, stupefy, surprise, vex, wow* (≠ annoy, -balk, bore, bother, buffer, bug, -bypass, cushion, dampen, deaden, depress, disappoint, disenchant, dull, exhaust, explain, irk, irritate, muffle, nag, needle, nettle, normalize, numb, sedate, stifle, tire, underwhelm, vex, weary, worry)

AMBUSH (→): *accost, assail, assault, attack, blindside, bomb, boobytrap, bushwhack, capture, charge, compromise, corner, deceive, decoy, disguise, endanger, ensnare, entice, entrap, hide, hook, hunt, inveigle, jump, mug, net, sandbag, snare, stalk, storm, strike, surprise, surround, tackle, target, trap, trick, waylay* (≠ alert, announce, bluff, broadcast, bully, caution, confront, defend, discourage, dissuade, expose, forewarn, guard, intimidate, notify, protect, reveal, telegraph, threaten, trash-talk, warn)

AMEND (+): *adapt, adjust, alter, ameliorate, better, change, correct, enhance, fix, flavor, heal, improve, marinate, mend, modify, optimize, overhaul, patch, perfect, qualify, realign, reconceive, reconceptualize, rectify, redress, refine, reform, reinvent, remedy, repair, rephrase, restore, rethink, retool, revamp, revise, revolutionize, right, square, weaponize* (≠ aggravate, blemish, blight, break, canker, corrupt, damage, deface, degrade, destroy, diminish, disfigure, efface, exacerbate, harm, harshen, impair, injure, mar, ruin, spoil, tarnish, worsen)

AMPLIFY (→): *accelerate, accent, accentuate, accrue, accumulate, add, aggrandize, aggravate, amass, amp, assert, augment, beef, belabor, bolster, boost, breed, brighten, broaden, build, bump, buttress, catalyze, collect, color, complement, compound, concentrate, condense, consolidate, crank, darken, deepen, develop, dilate, distend, double, dramatize, elaborate, elevate, elongate, embellish, embroider, emphasize, enhance, enlarge, enliven, enrich, escalate, exacerbate, exaggerate, exalt, expand, extend, fan, fatten, feature, fill, fire, flavor, foreground, foster, fuel, further, glorify, grease, grow, hasten, heat, heighten, heroicize, heroize, highlight, hike, hype, hyperbolize, increase,* *inflame, inflate, intensify, lengthen, lighten, magnify, marinate, maximize, multiply, optimize, overdramatize, overemphasize, overhaul, overrate, overstate, pad, poeticize, prioritize, proliferate, prolong, propagate, protract, provoke, pump, punctuate, pyramid, quicken, raise, ratchet, redouble, reinforce, revolutionize, richen, rile, romanticize, satirize, scale, season, sentimentalize, sharpen, spice, spike, spotlight, spread, stoke, strengthen, stress, stretch, supersize, supplement, swell, treble, triple, trumpet, underline, underscore, unspool, up, upgrade, whet, widen, worsen* (≠ abate, abbreviate, abridge, alleviate, attenuate, blunt, buffer, bury, calm, cheapen, conceal, constrict, contract, curb, curtail, cushion, cut, dampen, deaden, decrease, deemphasize, de-escalate, depress, devalue, diminish, dismiss, downplay, downsize, dull, ease, elide, hide, lessen, lowball, lower, lull, mask, mellow, miniaturize, minify, minimize, mitigate, moderate, modulate, mollify, muffle, obscure, pacify, placate, postpone, rarefy, reduce, restrain, restrict, retrench, sedate, shorten, shrink, simplify, slow, smother, soothe, streamline, subdue, subtract, syncopate, taper, trim, truncate, underemphasize, understate, weaken)

AMPUTATE (/): *axe, behead, castrate, chop, cleave, cut, decapitate, dismember, dissect, eliminate, emasculate, excise, guillotine, hack, hew, lop, maim, mangle, maul, mutilate, razor, remove, separate, sever, slash, slice, split, sunder, truncate, vivisect* (≠ add, affix, attach, bond, connect, fix, fuse, graft, heal, implant, join, marry, merge, nurse, reconstruct, regenerate, regrow, splice, stitch, suture, transplant, unite)

AMUSE (+): *absorb, appease, beguile, bewitch, brighten, busy, captivate, chaff, charm, cheer, coddle, comfort, conciliate, console, content, convulse, delight, distract, divert, elate, enchant, encourage, engage, engross, enliven, entertain, enthrall, exhilarate, fascinate, gladden, grab, grace, gratify, grip, humor, hypnotize, immerse, indulge, interest, intrigue, involve, jolly, mesmerize, mollify, mollycoddle, oblige, occupy, overindulge, pacify, pamper, placate, please, pleasure, propitiate, razzle-dazzle, regale, solace, soothe, spoil, thrill, tickle, wow* (≠ aggravate, annoy, bore, bother, bug, chafe, depress, dismay, distress, disturb, drain, enervate, enrage, exasperate, exhaust, fatigue, fret, gall, harass, harry, infuriate, irk, irritate, jade, nettle, overset, peeve, perturb, pester, pique, sadden, sorrow, tire, upset, vex, wear, weary)

ANALYZE (←): *adjudge, anatomize, annotate, appraise, arrange, ascertain, assay, assess, assort, beta, calculate, catalog, categorize, check, classify, codify, compare, conclude, condense, connect, consider, contemplate, contrast, correlate, crack, criticize, critique, crosscheck, debate, decipher, decode, deconstruct, decrypt, deduce, delineate, determine, devise, diagnose, diagram, dissect, distill, distinguish, divide, elucidate, enumerate, estimate, evaluate, examine, explain, explore, extract, generalize, grade, index, infer, inspect, interpret, investigate, judge, mull, order, paraphrase, ponder, predict, probe, process, profile, prove, prowl, read, reduce, reference, render, rephrase, report, research, resolve, restate, review, sample, schematize, scrutinize, segment,* *separate, sift, simplify, solve, sort, study, subdivide, summarize, suss, tabulate, test, translate, try, verify, vivisect, weigh* (≠ accept, aggregate, amalgamate, assimilate, becloud, befog, believe, -blank, blur, -bypass, coalesce, concatenate, confound, confuse, conglomerate, consolidate, -discount, -disregard, distort, elide, forget, -ignore, integrate, jumble, miss, muddle, -neglect, obfuscate, -omit, -overlook, scramble, swallow, synthesize, tantalize, trust, unify) **(¿) ABSTRACTION ALERT. Concrete goals essential!**

ANCHOR (+): *affix, attach, balance, base, bed, brace, catch, check, clamp, clinch, compose, control, curb, deactivate, dock, embed, entrench, equalize, establish, fasten, fix, freeze, ground, -halt, hamstring, hitch, hobble, hold, immobilize, implant, inactivate, incapacitate, infuse, ingrain, instill, leash, lodge, moor, paralyze, pinion, place, plant, position, postpone, relax, restrain, root, secure, set, settle, soothe, stabilize, stay, steady, stick, still, stop, stuff, subdue, support, tie, transfix, wedge* (≠ accelerate, animate, boost, detach, discombobulate, disconnect, disengage, dislodge, displace, drive, eject, expel, extract, force, grease, hasten, launch, loose, loosen, mobilize, move, prize, propel, pry, pull, punt, quicken, release, remove, roil, rush, send, shake, shift, shoot, shunt, slack, slacken, speed, tear, thrust, unfasten, unleash, untie, uproot, weed, wiggle, wobble, wrench, wrest, yank)

ANESTHETIZE (←): *blunt, chloroform, daze, deactivate, deaden, desensitize, disable, dope, dose, drug, dull, enfeeble, etherize, gas, hamper, hamstring, hinder, hobble, impair, incapacitate, inject, medicate, narcotize, neutralize, numb, paralyze, petrify, poison, prostrate, relax, sap, scotch, sedate, spike, stun, stupefy, torpefy, treat, vitiate, weaken* (≠ activate, alarm, alert, amplify, animate, arouse, awaken, convulse, electrify, energize, excite, galvanize, hurt, ignite, incite, kindle, motivate, pain, prod, provoke, shake, shock, spur, stimulate, stir, trigger, wake)

ANGER (/): *affront, aggravate, annoy, antagonize, bother, bug, burn, cross, embitter, enrage, envenom, exasperate, gall, heckle, incense, inflame, infuriate, irk, irritate, madden, miff, needle, nettle, offend, outrage, peeve, pique, provoke, rankle, rile, roil, ruffle, steam, vex* (≠ allay, appease, assuage, beguile, bewitch, calm, charm, comfort, console, delight, disarm, gratify, lull, mollify, pacify, placate, please, quell, quiet, relax, relieve, sedate, settle, soothe, thrill, wow)

ANIMATE (→): *activate, actuate, agitate, arouse, awaken, bait, begin, boost, buoy, charge, coax, commandeer, compel, crank, drive, elate, electrify, elevate, empower, encourage, energize, engage, enliven, enthuse, excite, exhilarate, fire, flick, force, galvanize, gladden, goad, grease, hasten, hearten, incite, initiate, inspire, instigate, invigorate, kindle, lift, lubricate, mobilize, motivate, move, nerve, nudge, power, press, prompt, propel, provoke, quicken, raise, rally, recharge, reinvigorate, rejuvenate, reset, revive, rouse, shock, spark, spur, start, stimulate, stir, strengthen, thrill, throw, trigger, twiddle, uplift, urge, vitalize, vivify, wake, warm* (≠ anesthetize, bore, calm, check, curb, dampen, daunt, deaden, debilitate, demoralize, demotivate, depress, -deter, discourage, dissuade, drain, dull, enervate, enfeeble, exhaust, fatigue, freeze, -halt, inhibit, kill, paralyze, petrify, quell, quench, quiet, repress, restrain, sap, sedate, slow, stagnate, stale, stem, stop, stunt, suppress, tire, tucker, undermine, weaken, wear, weary, wither)

ANNEX (+): *acquire, add, adjoin, affix, aggrandize, amplify, append, appropriate, associate, attach, augment, boost, complement, compound, connect, conquer, double, elongate, enhance, enlarge, escalate, expand, extend, fasten, fix, graft, heighten, hitch, incorporate, increase, infuse, inject, insert, intensify, introduce, join, lengthen, magnify, maximize, multiply, occupy, procure, prolong, protract, raise, seize, strengthen, supplement, swell, tack, tag, tie, treble, triple, unite, usurp* (≠ abate, abbreviate, abridge, amputate, compress, condense, constrict, contract, curtail, cut, decrease, deduct, detach, diminish, disconnect, disjoin, divide, excise, lessen, lop, lower, minimize, recoup, reduce, remove, retrench, separate, sever, shorten, split, subtract, unfasten)

ANNIHILATE (/): *abolish, annul, atomize, bulldoze, -cancel, censor, checkmate, clobber, conquer, cream, crush, cut, decimate, deep-six, defeat, delete, demolish, depopulate, desolate, destroy, devastate, disintegrate, dismantle, drub, edit, eliminate, eradicate, erase, excise, execute, expunge, expurgate, exterminate, extinguish, extirpate, finish, flatten, immolate, level, liquidate, massacre, mortar, -negate, nuke, -nullify, obliterate, -omit, pulverize, quash, quell, ravage, raze, rout, ruin, scrub, slaughter, smash, strike, terminate, thrash, topple, trounce, vanquish, vaporize, vitiate, wallop, weed, wreck* (≠ armor, begin, bronze, constitute, defend, embalm, establish, eternalize, fabricate, found, guard, heal, help, inaugurate, initiate, innovate, introduce, machine, make, manufacture, mend, nurture, perpetuate, preserve, protect, reinvigorate, revive, save, secure, shield, survive, sustain, weather, withstand)

ANNOUNCE (→): *advertise, advise, air, apprise, bellow, bill, billboard, blare, blaze, blazon, blurb, broadcast, bulletin, choose, communicate, decide, declare, determine, disclose, disseminate, divulge, enunciate, expose, feature, flash, herald, hype, impart, inform, intimate, introduce, knell, limelight, manifest, notify, out, pick, pitch, placard, plug, post, proclaim, promote, promulgate, publicize, publish, release, report, reveal, ring, roar, select, shill, show, sound, spread, state, toll, trumpet* (≠ bury, censor, conceal, contain, cover, disguise, gag, hide, hush, interrupt, mask, muffle, mute, muzzle, -prevent, quash, quell, quiet, recall, recant, redact, retract, revoke, secrete, shush, silence, spin, stifle, suppress, swallow, withhold)

ANNOY (/): *abrade, aggravate, agitate, antagonize, badger, bait, bedevil, beleaguer, bore, bother, break, bug, chafe, chaff, chagrin, chivy, disconcert, displease, distress, disturb, earbash, exasperate, fret, gall, gnaw, goad, gravel, harass, harry, hassle, heckle, henpeck, hinder, incense, infuriate, irk, irritate, madden, miff, nag, needle, nettle, niggle, nitpick, nudge, peeve, perturb, pester, plague, provoke, rattle, ride, rile, ruffle, tease, trouble, vex, weary, worry* (≠ aid, appease, assist, butter, calm, candy-coat, charm, cheer, comfort, content, delight, gratify, grease, honor, inspire, lubricate, mitigate, oblige, please, quiet, reassure, soothe, sugarcoat, support, thrill)

ANNUL (/): *abate, abolish, -abort, abrogate, annihilate, -avoid, ban, call, -cancel, countermand, delete, disallow, dismiss, dissolve, drop, eliminate, enjoin, eradicate, erase, expunge, -forbid, invalidate, liquidate, -negate, -nix, null, -nullify, outlaw, override, overrule, overturn, -prohibit, quash, recall, -reject, remove, repeal, -rescind, retract, reverse, revoke, scrub, strike, suspend, vacate, -veto, -void, withdraw* (≠ allow, approve, authorize, clear, command, decree, enact, endorse, enforce, establish, formalize, found, institute, legalize, legislate, legitimate, legitimize, mandate, notarize, ordain, order, pass, permit, prescribe, ratify, restore, sanction, validate, warrant)

ANNUL (/): *-cancel, correct, counteract, counterbalance, counterpoise, expense, expiate, invalidate, -negate, neuter, neutralize, -nullify, offset, outbalance, outweigh, override, overrule, redeem, redress, relieve, remedy, right* (≠ advocate, aid, assist, compel, countenance, embolden, encourage, facilitate, help, incite, initiate, instigate, permit, promote, second, support, sustain, uphold, worsen)

ANOINT (+): *baptize, besmear, bless, coat, consecrate, daub, dedicate, grease, gum, hallow, lard, lubricate, oil, ordain, paint, plaster, rub, sanctify, slather, smear, smudge, syrup, tar* (≠ clean, cleanse, condemn, curse, defile, denigrate, dirty, disparage, dry, foul, impugn, malign, rinse, scour, scrape, scrub, shame, -shun, stain, sully, vilify, wash, wipe)

ANTAGONIZE (/): *afflict, aggravate, alarm, alienate, anger, anguish, annoy, badger, bait, bedevil, beleaguer, besiege, bother, browbeat, bug, bully, burden, chaff, chagrin, concern, contradict, counter, counteract, countercheck, curdle, demean, demonize, disaffect, disgruntle, dismay, distract, distress, disturb, dog, embitter, enrage, envenom, estrange, exasperate, faze, fluster, fret, fuss, goad, gravel, harass, harry, hassle, heckle, hector, hound, importune, incense, incommode, inconvenience, infuriate, insult, irk, irritate, isolate, jeer, kid, madden, militarize, mock, molest, nag, needle, niggle, nitpick, nudge, oppose, orphan, -ostracize, oust, outrage, perplex, perturb, pester, pillory, plague, poke, prod, provoke, rag, rally, razz, repel, rib, ride, ridicule, roast, slam, sorrow, sour, tantalize, taunt, tease, tickle, torment, trouble, unsettle, upset, vex, worry* (≠ amuse, appease, arm, armor, assist, assuage, defend, delight, demilitarize, disarm, dulcify, enchant, endear, entertain, grace, gratify, guard, heal, help, ingratiate, lull, mellow, mollify, nurture, pacify, placate, please, propitiate, protect, relax, rescue, restore, retort, reunite, save, shelter, shield, sugarcoat, support, sweeten, thrill, tranquilize, woo)

ANTICIPATE (→): *-abort, arrest, block, catch, check, deflect, delay, forestall, -frustrate, impede, intercept, interrupt, obstruct, preempt, -prevent, second-guess, seize, shelve, stop, stymie, -thwart, waylay* (≠ -abandon, accept, -avoid, -disregard, -dodge, forfeit, -ignore, -omit, -overlook, -shirk, -shun, withdraw)

ANTICIPATE (←): *alert, apprehend, assume, augur, await, caution, contemplate, descry, discern, divine, dread, envisage, envision, expect, eye, fear, forecast, foresee, foreshadow, foretell, forewarn, outguess, perceive, predetermine, predict, prefigure, presage, presume, presuppose, preview, prognosticate, prophesy, trust, view, visualize* (≠ bemoan, consult, dispute, distrust, doubt, forget, lament, question, recall, recollect, regret, -reject, remember, rue)

APE (←): *adopt, affect, caricature, clone, copy, counterfeit, ditto, dupe, duplicate, echo, emulate, feign, follow, ghostwrite, imitate, impersonate, mimic, mirror, mock, parody, parrot, playact, pretend, reflect, retrace, roleplay, simulate* (≠ alter, coin, contrast, create, customize, differentiate, distinguish, distort, hatch, individualize, initiate, invent, juxtapose, mint, originate, respect, separate, skew, spark, specify, tailor, twist)

APPALL (/): *affright, alarm, amaze, astonish, astound, awe, brutalize, chill, crush, daunt, deafen, demoralize, discomfort, discompose, disconcert, disgust, dismay, dispirit, displease, disquiet, distress, disturb, dumbfound, emasculate, flabbergast, floor, freak, frighten, horrify, intimidate, jolt, muckrake, nauseate, offend, outrage, overpower, overwhelm, panic, perturb, petrify, repel, revolt, savage, scandalize, scare, scarify, shake, shock, sicken, spook, startle, stun, stupefy, terrify, terrorize, throw, trash-talk, unman, unnerve, unsettle, unstring, upset* (≠ amuse, assure, blunt, buffer, charm, cheer, comfort, console, cushion, delight, entice, grace, gratify, please, reassure, rejoice, solace, soothe, tempt, thrill, tickle, woo) **(¿) ABSTRACTION ALERT. Concrete goals essential!**

APPEASE (+): *allay, alleviate, amuse, assuage, baby, blandish, cajole, calm, candy-coat, cater, coax, coddle, comfort, compose, console, content, delight, disarm, dulcify, ease, entertain, favor, gentle, gladden, gratify, humor, hush, indulge, infantilize, ingratiate, lull, mellow, mitigate, mollify, mollycoddle, oblige, overindulge, pacify, pamper, placate, please, propitiate, quell, quench, quiet, reconcile, relax, relieve, reunite, satisfy, serve, slake, soften, soothe, spoil, still, subdue, sugarcoat, sweeten, sweet-talk, syrup, tranquilize, wheedle, woo* (≠ affront, aggravate, agitate, anger, annoy, antagonize, appall, bother, bug, chafe, cross, discomfort, distress, disturb, enrage, exasperate, fret, gall, harass, harry, incense, inflame, infuriate, insult, irk, irritate, madden, nettle, offend, outrage, peeve, persecute, perturb, pester, pique, provoke, rankle, rile, roil, rouse, ruffle, sadden, -slight, tease, unhinge, unsettle, upset, vex, worry)

APPLAUD (+): *acclaim, accredit, acknowledge, admire, adore, adulate, aggrandize, appreciate, approve, ballyhoo, blandish, boost, celebrate, cheer, commend, compliment, congratulate, dignify, distinguish, elevate, emblazon, encourage, endorse, eulogize, exalt, extol, favor, fête, fetishize, flannel, flatter, glorify, gold-star, gratify, hail, high-five, honor, hype, idealize, idolize, laud, lionize, magnify, overpraise, plug, praise, promote, raise, recognize, recommend, respect, revere, reward, romanticize, salute, sanction, support, thank, toast, tout, trumpet, uplift, value, venerate, welcome* (≠ abuse, admonish, badmouth, belittle, blackguard, blast, blister, boo, castigate, chide, condemn, criticize, critique, damn, decry, demean, demonize, denigrate, denounce, deride, -detest, diminish, discredit, disgrace, disparage, disrespect, excoriate, execrate, fault, heckle, humiliate, insult, jeer, keelhaul, knock, lambaste, malign, minimize, mock, neg, pan, pillory, reproach, revile, ridicule, savage, scold, -scorn, skewer, slam, smear, vilify)

APPOINT (→): *accredit, allot, arrange, assign, authorize, charge, choose, command, commission, coopt, decide, decree, delegate, designate, detail, determine, direct, elect, employ, engage, enjoin, enlist, enroll, establish, finger, fix, hire, indicate, install, name, nominate, ordain, pick, recruit, select, set, settle, specify, tap, task* (≠ appropriate, blackball, -cancel, choose, confiscate, -deny, dismantle, dismiss, eject, expel, fire, -ignore, -neglect, oust, overthrow, predetermine, -refuse, -reject, remove, retain, sack, take, unsettle, wrack, wreck)

APPRAISE (←): *adjudge, advise, analyze, ascertain, assay, assess, audit, audition, beta, calculate, caliper, categorize, check, clock, compare, conclude, consider, contemplate, criticize, critique, decide, detect, determine, discover, educe, estimate, evaluate, examine, explore, eye, eyeball, fetishize, figure, gauge, guesstimate, infer, inspect, investigate, judge, learn, measure, misjudge, misprize, observe, ogle, overestimate, overvalue, peg, peruse, price, prioritize, prize, probe, prowl, rate, read, reappraise, reassess, reckon, reevaluate, regard, reinvestigate, review, sample, scan, scope, score, scrutinize, search, settle, sift, study, surmise, survey, suss, tally, test, time, underestimate, undervalue, valuate, value, vet, watch, weigh* (≠ assume, -blank, blind, blindfold, -bypass, conceal, confound, confuse, disguise, -disregard, forgive, guess, hide, -ignore, jumble, misgauge, miss, mistake, muddle, mystify, -neglect, -omit, -overlook, perplex, predetermine, puzzle, scramble, -shirk, -shun)

APPROACH (→): *accost, address, air, broach, buttonhole, cite, debate, express, greet, hail, high-five, introduce, meet, name, offer, propose, raise, reach, suggest, tackle, welcome* (≠ -avoid, -bypass, censor, -cut, detour, -elude, -evade, -ignore, -overlook, pass, quiet, redact, silence, -slight, suppress)

APPROPRIATE (←): *adopt, annex, arrogate, assume, attach, bogart, bootleg, borrow, burglarize, burgle, carjack, claim, collar, commandeer, confiscate, conquer, convert, defalcate, despoil, devour, dragoon, embezzle, filch, freeboot, grab, grasp, heist, hijack, hog, hook, hotwire, impound, infringe, invade, lift, loot, misapply, misappropriate, misuse, mooch, nab, nail, nip, nobble, occupy, own, pick, pilfer, pillage, pinch, pirate, plunder, poach, pocket, preempt, press, purloin, reap, reclaim, recoup, recover, recycle, redeem, repossess, requisition, rescue, retrieve, rifle, rob, rustle, sack, salvage, scavenge, seize, sequester, shoplift, snaffle, snag, snatch, snitch, sponge, steal, swipe, take, thieve, trespass, usurp, wrench, wrest* (≠ bestow, buy, comp, contribute, disseminate, dissipate, donate, fritter, furnish, give, hand, hoard, keep, offer, present, provide, purchase, -refuse, -reject, replace, replenish, restore, save, scatter, spare, squander, stock, tender, tithe, volunteer, yield)

APPROVE (+): *accept, acclaim, accord, accredit, acknowledge, adopt, advocate, affirm, allow, applaud, authorize, back, bless, boost, canonize, certify, champion, clear, commend, condone, confirm, countenance, empower, enable, encourage, endorse, favor, finalize, formalize, greenlight, initial, legalize, license, mandate, notarize, okay, pass, permit, ratify, reapprove, recommend, rubber-stamp, sanctify, sanction, second, sign, support, uphold, validate, warrant* (≠ ban, banish, bar, block, boo, -decline, -deny, disallow, disapprove, discredit, -disregard, enjoin, -exclude, -forbid, -ignore, -interdict, negative, -neglect, outlaw, -overlook, -prohibit, proscribe, -rebuff, rebut, -refuse, -reject, -spurn, turn down, -veto)

ARBITRATE (←): *adjudicate, ascertain, assess, broker, conclude, consider, control, decide, deliberate, determine, direct, equalize, hear, judge, manage, mediate, moderate, mull, negotiate, pacify, ponder, prosecute, reconcile, referee, resolve, reunite, rule, settle, skirt, solve, transact, try, umpire, weigh* (≠ accuse, aggravate, anguish, blame, cheat, claim, debate, disobey, -dodge, exacerbate, fault, frame, goad, manipulate, menace, predetermine, prompt, skew, skirt, subvert, torment, victimize, worsen) **(¿) ABSTRACTION ALERT. Concrete goals essential!**

ARM (→): *accoutre, appoint, array, bolster, brace, buttress, clout, defend, deliver, dispense, empower, equip, forearm, fortify, furnish, gird, grant, guard, harden, heel, interest, issue, load, offer, outfit, prepare, prime, protect, provide, ready, rearm, reinforce, rig, secure, steel, strengthen, supply, toughen* (≠ abrogate, botch, cripple, deactivate, demobilize, disable, disarm, disband, enfeeble, hamper, hamstring, handicap, hobble, immobilize, impair, incapacitate, neutralize, paralyze, prostrate, sabotage, scotch, scupper, subvert, undermine)

AROUSE (→): *abet, activate, aggravate, agitate, alert, anger, animate, annoy, bother, challenge, drive, encourage, energize, enrage, exasperate, excite, fan, ferment, fire, foment, gall, galvanize, goad, ignite, impassion, incite, incur, induce, inflame, infuriate, inspire, instigate, irritate, kindle, madden, motivate, move, pique, prod, prompt, provoke, quicken, raise, rev, sharpen, spark, spur, stimulate, stir, taunt, tease, trigger, upset, vex, warm, whet* (≠ anesthetize, appease, bore, calm, deactivate, -ignore, leave, mellow, mollify, -overlook, pacify, placate, sedate, settle, soothe, subdue, tranquilize)

AROUSE (←): *call, coax, conjure, educe, elicit, entice, evoke, excite, gain, galvanize, inspire, interest, intoxicate, intrigue, motivate, obtain, procure, provoke, raise, rouse, secure, summon, thrill, titillate* (≠ daunt, demotivate, discourage, disgust, dismay, hamper, hamstring, hinder, inhibit, -prevent, repel, repulse, retard, stymie, suppress, threaten)

AROUSE (+): *activate, agitate, animate, awaken, boost, charge, compel, disturb, dizzy, elate, electrify, energize, enliven, excite, exhilarate, force, galvanize, generate, goad, hasten, incite, incur, inspire, instigate,* *invigorate, kindle, lift, mobilize, motivate, move, nerve, provoke, raise, rally, reinvigorate, revive, rouse, roust, rout, shock, spark, spur, stimulate, stir, thrill, uplift, urge, vitalize, vivify, wake, warm* (≠ anesthetize, bore, calm, check, curb, dampen, daunt, deaden, demoralize, depress, discourage, dissuade, drain, dull, enervate, enfeeble, exhaust, fatigue, freeze, hamper, hypnotize, inhibit, lull, mellow, mesmerize, paralyze, petrify, quell, quench, quiet, repress, restrain, sap, sedate, slake, slow, stabilize, stem, still, stop, stunt, suppress, tantalize, tire, tranquilize, tucker, undermine, weaken, wear, weary, wither)

ARRANGE (+): *adapt, adjust, align, alter, array, assign, broker, calibrate, catalog, categorize, class, classify, codify, contrive, coordinate, design, determine, devise, dispose, distribute, equalize, file, fix, frame, grade, group, hierarchize, juxtapose, level, list, manipulate, marshal, negotiate, order, organize, pace, plan, position, prepare, project, ready, regiment, regulate, resolve, script, settle, sift, slot, sort, systematize, tailor, tidy, transact, tune* (≠ -abort, confuse, contest, counter, debate, derange, disarrange, dishevel, disorder, disorganize, dispute, disrupt, half-ass, improvise, jumble, mess, muddle, muss, oppose, protest, repeal, -rescind, resist, revoke, rumple, scramble, upset)

ARREST (←): *-abort, apprehend, bind, block, book, bridle, bust, capture, catch, check, collar, commit, confine, constrict, control, corner, delay, detain, disappear, dungeon, enmesh, ensnare, entangle, fetter, freeze, grab, -halt, handcuff, hinder, hogtie, hold, ice, immobilize, immure, impede, implicate, imprison, incarcerate, incriminate, inhibit, institutionalize, intern, interrupt, jail, keep, leash, nab, nail, nick, numb, obstruct, paralyze, pinch, restrain, retard, seize, shackle, shelve, slow, snaffle, snare, stall, stem, stop, stun, suppress, tether, trap, waylay, withhold* (≠ accelerate, acquit, activate, aid, alibi, -avoid, bail, budge, catalyze, convict, discharge, dismiss, -dodge, drive, -duck, eject, emancipate, empower, encourage, -escape, exonerate, expedite, expel, -flee, free, frogmarch, goad, help, liberate, loosen, lose, march, move, permit, propel, push, quicken, release, rescue, save, send, spring, spur, stir, unchain, unfasten, unfetter, unlock, unshackle, untie, vindicate)

ARREST (←): *absorb, amuse, assail, attract, captivate, capture, catch, charm, concern, consume, employ, enamor, enchant, engage, engross, entertain, fascinate, grip, hold, immerse, impress, interest, intrigue, involve, monopolize, obsess, occupy, possess, preoccupy, rivet, stimulate* (≠ anger, annoy, bore, bother, confuse, daunt, deflect, -deter, dissuade, distract, exasperate, frustrate, irk, irritate, repel, repulse, vex, weary) **(¿) ABSTRACTION ALERT. Concrete goals essential!**

ASSAIL (→): *abuse, accost, affront, ambush, arrest, assault, attack, badmouth, barrage, bash, batter, belabor, belittle, berate, besiege, blackguard, blaspheme, blast, blindside, bombard, bother, browbeat, brutalize, bully, burn, bushwhack, castigate, challenge, charge, chastise, chide, choke, combat, criticize, cross-examine, curse, -cut, defame, disparage, excoriate, execrate, fight, flay, grill, hammer, harangue,* *harass, harry, hit, hound, imprecate, impugn, insult, interrogate, inundate, invade, kick, lambaste, lash, libel, lunge, malign, menace, outmaneuver, pelt, pound, probe, profane, question, raid, ram, rebuke, reprimand, reprove, revile, savage, scarify, scathe, scold, scorch, slam, slander, slash, slur, sting, storm, strangle, strike, swamp, thrust, torment, traduce, trash, trounce, victimize, vilify, violate, vituperate, whip, wrong, zing* (≠ aid, armor, befriend, bulwark, commend, compliment, defend, deflect, exonerate, guard, heal, help, maintain, praise, preserve, protect, rescue, resist, retort, safeguard, save, secure, shelter, shield, support, sustain, uphold, withstand)

ASSASSINATE (/): *annihilate, behead, butcher, claim, croak, destroy, dispatch, eliminate, eradicate, execute, exterminate, fell, guillotine, kill, liquidate, massacre, murder, orphan, shoot, slaughter, slay, smite, snipe, terminate, whack, zap* (≠ animate, armor, defend, deflect, guard, protect, raise, reinvigorate, rescue, restore, resurrect, resuscitate, revive, save, secure, shelter, shield, survive, weather)

ASSAULT (/): *abuse, accost, advance, ambush, assail, attack, barrage, bash, batter, beleaguer, beset, besiege, bite, blast, blindside, blitz, bomb, bombard, bruise, brutalize, buffet, bully, bum-rush, burn, bushwhack, cannon, challenge, charge, choke, club, combat, cut, damage, deck, defile, disfigure, envelop, fight, flank, harm, harry, hit, impugn, invade, jump, kick, loot, menace, mob, molest, mug, nuke, overrun, pillage, plaster, plunder, press, punch, raid, rape, ravage, rob, ruin, rush, sack, sandbag, savage, slam, slice, storm, strangle, strike, surprise, swarm, trash, victimize, violate, waylay, wrong, zap* (≠ -avoid, bandage, cover, defend, deflect, -dodge, -elude, -escape, -evade, guard, heal, mend, nourish, nurse, nurture, pity, protect, repel, safeguard, secure, sentinel, shield, -sidestep, -thwart, withdraw)

ASSEMBLE (+): *begin, brew, build, carpenter, coin, collate, combine, compile, compose, conceive, concoct, connect, construct, contrive, cook, craft, create, design, devise, erect, establish, fabricate, fashion, fit, forge, form, found, frame, generate, hammer, handcraft, imagine, improvise, inaugurate, initiate, innovate, institute, invent, jerry-rig, join, machine, make, manufacture, model, mold, organize, originate, piece, prefabricate, produce, raise, rear, reassemble, rebuild, reconstruct, redevelop, regiment, retrofit, sculpt, shape, stitch, suture, unite, weld* (≠ atomize, break, crack, demolish, destroy, detach, devastate, disassemble, disconnect, disjoin, dismantle, dismember, disunite, divide, explode, flatten, fracture, level, pulverize, raze, ruin, separate, shatter, smash, split, strike, topple, wreck)

ASSERT (→): *accept, acknowledge, adjure, admit, affirm, approve, assure, attest, avow, belabor, certify, circulate, claim, confess, contend, corroborate, declare, demand, document, emphasize, endorse, entreat, evince, expect, express, hold, importune, maintain, order, overemphasize, pledge, postulate, press, proclaim, profess, promise, pronounce, ratify, reinforce, reiterate, repeat, request, require, state, stipulate, stress,* *submit, suggest, support, sustain, swear, testify, underline, urge, validate, verbalize, verify, vocalize, voice, vow, warrant* (≠ accord, allow, brook, challenge, conceal, counter, debate, debunk, -deny, discredit, -disown, disprove, dispute, distrust, doubt, endure, forget, gainsay, hide, -ignore, impugn, invalidate, minimize, -negate, prove, question, rebut, -reject, retort, retract, scruple, suspect, tolerate, underemphasize, understate) **(¿) ABSTRACTION ALERT. Concrete goals essential!**

ASSESS (←): *adjudge, analyze, appraise, apprise, ascertain, assay, audition, benchmark, beta, calculate, caliper, categorize, check, clock, compare, compute, conclude, connect, consider, contemplate, contrast, correlate, critique, decide, deduce, detect, determine, discover, distill, educe, estimate, evaluate, examine, explore, eye, eyeball, gauge, grade, guess, guesstimate, inspect, investigate, judge, learn, measure, monetize, observe, ogle, peg, peruse, price, prioritize, prize, probe, prowl, rank, rate, read, reckon, reevaluate, regard, sample, scan, scope, scrutinize, search, set, settle, sift, study, subdivide, survey, suss, test, time, triangulate, valuate, value, watch, weigh* (≠ accept, addle, assume, baffle, blind, blindfold, -bypass, confound, confuse, convince, deceive, disguise, -disregard, excuse, fake, forgive, fudge, -ignore, mask, miscalculate, misgauge, misjudge, mislead, misprize, miss, mistake, muddle, mystify, -neglect, overestimate, -overlook, pass, perplex, predetermine, pretend, puzzle, -shirk, trick, underestimate, undervalue)

ASSESS (←): *bleed, charge, coerce, compel, dock, exact, excise, extort, fine, fleece, force, gouge, impose, inflict, lay, levy, milk, mulct, penalize, skin, squeeze, tax, wreak, wrest, wring* (≠ abate, compensate, condone, diminish, -disregard, excuse, forgive, gloss, -ignore, indemnify, lessen, overpay, pardon, pay, release, remit, spare, stiff, tithe, underpay)

ASSIGN (→): *accord, administer, allocate, allot, allow, apportion, award, bestow, budget, chunk, contribute, deal, dispense, distribute, divide, dole, donate, earmark, give, grant, measure, mete, meter, parcel, part, portion, prorate, ration, reallocate, reassign, redistribute, reserve, share, sort, split, stock, supply, tender, tithe* (≠ appropriate, arrogate, begrudge, confiscate, -deny, deprive, grab, keep, remove, retain, skimp, snatch, starve, steal, stint, take, withhold)

ASSIGN (→): *bequeath, bestow, cede, commend, commit, confer, consign, contribute, convey, deed, deliver, donate, entrust, grant, hand, lease, leave, lend, loan, move, pass, present, release, relinquish, rent, surrender, transfer, transmit, trust, vest, will, yield* (≠ borrow, commandeer, confiscate, dragoon, filch, grab, harvest, mooch, poach, select, snaffle, snag, steal, swipe, take)

ASSIGN (+): *allocate, allot, anoint, appoint, attach, authorize, charge, choose, commission, commit, confer, consecrate, consign, create, crown, delegate, deputize, designate, detail, determine, draft, elect, empower, enthrone, entrust, fix, garrison, handpick, inaugurate, induct, install, instate, institute, invest, make, name, nominate, ordain, place, prioritize, rank, recommend, relegate, select, set, sideline, specify, station, stipulate,* *task, throne, trust* (≠ blackball, boot, -deny, depose, dethrone, discharge, dismiss, displace, eject, evict, expel, fire, hold, -ignore, keep, -neglect, oust, overthrow, -refuse, -reject, remove, retract, ruin, sack, unseat, wreck)

ASSIMILATE (←): *absorb, acclimatize, accommodate, acculturate, accustom, adapt, adjust, amalgamate, blend, calibrate, combine, commingle, condition, coopt, digest, embody, enculturate, equalize, fuse, grasp, habituate, hybridize, imbibe, incorporate, integrate, intermingle, internalize, learn, merge, mingle, mix, naturalize, reunite, synthesize, unite* (≠ contrast, denaturalize, detach, -deter, diffuse, -disregard, disseminate, dissolve, divide, divorce, -exclude, isolate, juxtapose, misconstrue, misinterpret, misread, misunderstand, -omit, orphan, oust, -reject, scatter, seclude, separate, sever, split, -spurn)

ASSIST (+): *abet, advocate, aid, allot, attend, award, back, bankroll, benefit, bequeath, bestow, bolster, boost, brace, buttress, comp, condone, deliver, donate, ease, encourage, endorse, endow, energize, expedite, facilitate, favor, foster, fund, furnish, further, give, grant, help, hype, inspire, kindle, lavish, lend, midwife, mother, motivate, nurse, offer, outlay, overpay, patronize, pay, pledge, plug, promote, provide, provoke, push, reinforce, relieve, rescue, sanction, save, second, serve, share, simplify, spur, strengthen, supply, support, sustain, tend, tender, tithe, underwrite, uphold, volunteer* (≠ -abort, -balk, bar, block, confound, constrain, counteract, cripple, damage, delay, demotivate, denounce, -desert, -deter, discourage, discredit, disfavor, disgrace, disinherit, -disown, dissuade, foil, -frustrate, -halt, hamper, hamstring, handicap, harm, hinder, hurt, impede, incommode, inconvenience, inhibit, injure, monkey-wrench, muzzle, obstruct, oppose, pause, -prevent, protest, resist, restrain, sabotage, scotch, scupper, scuttle, shelve, short-circuit, stem, stifle, stop, stump, stymie, subvert, -thwart, undermine, underpay)

ASSUAGE (+): *abate, allay, alleviate, ameliorate, amend, appease, better, calm, candy-coat, comfort, compose, console, cool, correct, cradle, cure, dulcify, ease, emend, enhance, enrich, fix, heal, help, improve, lessen, lighten, lower, lubricate, lull, mellow, mend, minimize, mitigate, moderate, mollify, pacify, palliate, perfect, placate, propitiate, quench, quiet, realign, rectify, reduce, refine, reform, relax, relieve, remedy, repair, right, sate, satisfy, slake, soften, soothe, still, sugarcoat, sweeten, syrup, temper, tranquilize* (≠ aggravate, bother, bug, daunt, deepen, disturb, exacerbate, harm, heighten, hurt, impair, increase, injure, intensify, irk, menace, sharpen, tantalize, threaten, traumatize, trouble, victimize, worsen)

ASSUME (←): *accept, acquire, add, adopt, amass, annex, appropriate, arrogate, bag, bear, buy, capture, catch, claim, collect, commandeer, corner, embrace, fetch, garner, get, harvest, heap, incur, land, lure, net, obtain, palm, pocket, preempt, procure, reap, receive, reclaim, recoup, recover, recycle, redeem, rescue, retrieve, salvage, scavenge, score, secure, seize, select, shoulder, take, undertake, usurp, win, wrangle* (≠ -abandon, abnegate, -avoid, blackball, -bypass, cede, -decline, deflect,

-deny, detour, disavow, disclaim, -disown, -disregard, expel, -forsake, jettison, -refuse, -reject, relinquish, -renounce, -repudiate, resign, shield, -shirk, -spurn, surrender)

ASSUME (←): *accept, adopt, affirm, allege, anticipate, apprehend, appropriate, arrogate, assert, avow, await, believe, claim, conceive, conclude, conjecture, contemplate, contend, credit, daydream, declare, deduce, desire, destine, dread, dream, embrace, envisage, envision, expect, fancy, figure, foresee, gather, generalize, guess, hold, hope, hypothesize, imagine, infer, insist, intend, judge, maintain, perceive, postulate, preempt, premise, presume, presuppose, profess, reckon, spitball, suppose, surmise, suspect, swallow, take, theorize, trust, understand, universalize, want, wish* (≠ ascertain, belie, cede, challenge, confute, consult, convince, cross-examine, debate, demonstrate, -deny, detect, determine, disavow, disbelieve, disclaim, -discount, discredit, -disown, disprove, dispute, -disregard, distrust, document, doubt, establish, exorcise, expel, grill, impugn, interrogate, interview, invalidate, jettison, learn, mistrust, -overlook, prove, question, rebut, -refuse, refute, -reject, -renounce, -repudiate, scruple, substantiate, validate, wonder) **(¿) ABSTRACTION ALERT. Concrete goals essential!**

ASSURE (+): *allay, alleviate, assuage, boost, buoy, calm, cheer, comfort, console, convince, elevate, embolden, encourage, hearten, lift, mellow, persuade, quiet, reassure, relax, relieve, sell, solace, soothe, tranquilize, uplift* (≠ aggravate, anguish, annoy, demoralize, demotivate, -deter, discourage, dishearten, distress, fret, harass, intensify, irk, irritate, pester, torment, torture, trouble, upset, worry, worsen)

ASSURE (+): *affirm, attest, certify, cinch, clinch, complete, confirm, crosscheck, ensure, guarantee, ice, indemnify, insure, lock, pledge, promise, prove, seal, secure, set, settle, stabilize, swear, verify, vow, warrant, witness* (≠ allege, cripple, daunt, debate, enfeeble, menace, panic, sabotage, scotch, scupper, subvert, threaten, undermine, weaken)

ASTONISH (→): *amaze, astound, baffle, befuddle, bewilder, boggle, confound, confuse, daze, dazzle, discomfit, disconcert, dismay, dumbfound, electrify, excite, flabbergast, floor, flummox, gobsmack, jar, jolt, muddle, mystify, nonplus, perplex, razzle-dazzle, rock, shake, shock, stagger, startle, stimulate, stir, strike, stun, stupefy, surprise, wow* (≠ abate, anesthetize, annoy, -balk, bore, bother, buffer, bug, calm, clarify, cushion, dampen, deaden, depress, disappoint, disenchant, dull, ease, elucidate, exhaust, explain, irk, irritate, lull, mellow, muffle, nag, needle, nettle, normalize, numb, pacify, sedate, solve, tire, tranquilize, underwhelm, vex, weary, worry)

ATTACH (+): *add, adhere, affix, annex, batten, bind, bolt, button, cinch, clamp, clasp, clench, clinch, clip, connect, couple, fasten, fix, glue, hang, harness, join, lace, lash, latch, link, nail, paste, pin, plaster, rivet, screw, secure, shackle, staple, stick, strap, tack, tackle, tie, toggle, unite, weld, yoke* (≠ break, cut, detach, disconnect, divide, eject, jettison, part, release, separate, sever, split, sunder)

ATTACK (→): *address, approach, begin, brave, commence, face, pursue, start, tackle, undertake* (≠ -avoid, -bypass, -circumvent, -elude, -evade, forget, misplace, -neglect, -overlook, pass, poke, -shirk, -shun, skirt)

ATTACK (→): *advance, ambush, assail, assault, barrage, bash, bat, batter, battle, bean, beat, beleaguer, beset, besiege, blast, blindside, blister, blitz, bomb, bombard, boot, box, brain, brutalize, buffet, bum-rush, burn, bushwhack, bust, charge, choke, chop, clip, clobber, clock, clout, club, combat, cut, damage, deck, disfigure, drub, envelop, fight, flank, harm, harry, hit, hurt, infest, infiltrate, injure, invade, jump, kick, lash, loot, maul, menace, mob, molest, mortar, mug, nuke, overrun, overwhelm, persecute, pillage, plunder, press, punch, raid, ram, ravage, rob, rush, sack, sandbag, savage, shank, shiv, slice, stab, steamroller, storm, strangle, strike, surprise, swarm, tackle, terrorize, thrash, threaten, thump, victimize, wallop, waylay, whack, whip, wrestle, wrong, zap* (≠ aid, armor, arrest, assist, -avoid, barricade, befriend, block, blockade, counterattack, cover, defend, deflect, -evade, guard, heal, help, maintain, pity, protect, rescue, resist, safeguard, secure, sentinel, shelter, shield, -shun, surrender, withstand)

ATTACK (/): *abuse, accost, affront, assail, badmouth, bash, belabor, belittle, berate, blackguard, blame, blaspheme, blast, blitz, boo, browbeat, bully, castigate, censure, challenge, charge, chastise, chide, criticize, curse, defame, demean, demonize, denounce, disparage, excoriate, execrate, fault, frame, fulminate, harangue, harass, harry, imprecate, impugn, indict, insult, knock, lambaste, lampoon, libel, malign, pillory, profane, rebuke, refute, reprimand, reprove, resent, revile, ridicule, roast, rubbish, savage, scapegoat, scathe, scold, -scorn, slam, slander, slate, slur, traduce, upbraid, vilify, vituperate, whip, wrong* (≠ acclaim, applaud, approve, commend, compliment, counter, defend, elevate, endorse, extol, hail, idolize, laud, praise, protect, respect, retort, revere, sanction, support, uphold, venerate, vindicate, withstand)

ATTAIN (←): *accomplish, accrue, accumulate, achieve, acquire, actualize, add, aggregate, annex, ascend, augment, complete, consummate, crest, dominate, earn, effect, find, fulfill, gain, get, grasp, hit, increase, net, obtain, overcome, procure, reach, realize, secure, stockpile, surmount, tally, touch, win* (≠ -abandon, bestow, comp, -desert, endow, fail, forfeit, forget, give, grant, -ignore, leave, lose, miss, -neglect, offer, relinquish, -renounce, sacrifice, spend, supply, surrender, yield)

ATTEND (→): *accompany, bring, chaperone, conduct, convoy, defend, escort, follow, guard, guide, lead, pilot, protect, see, serve, shadow, squire, steer, tag, tail, usher, walk* (≠ -abandon, betray, cheat, -desert, -ditch, dump, -forsake, kill, -scorn, wrong)

ATTEND (←): *analyze, appraise, assess, bear, categorize, check, clock, consider, contemplate, critique, deconstruct, dissect, esteem, examine, eye, follow, hear, heed, honor, inspect, mark, mind, note, notice, obey, observe, ogle, peruse, read, regard, scan, scope, scrutinize, study, surveil,* *survey, watch, weigh* (≠ -abandon, blind, blindfold, confuse, deceive, -desert, -discount, -disregard, -forsake, fudge, -ignore, maroon, misjudge, miss, mistake, -neglect, -overlook, perplex, -shirk, -sidestep, trick)

ATTEST (+): *accept, acknowledge, adduce, admit, affirm, allege, approve, assert, assure, authenticate, avow, certify, claim, concretize, confess, confirm, connote, contend, convince, corroborate, crosscheck, declare, demonstrate, depose, determine, display, document, endorse, ensure, establish, evince, exemplify, exhibit, express, forswear, guarantee, illustrate, maintain, manifest, observe, pledge, proclaim, profess, promise, pronounce, prove, ratify, show, state, submit, substantiate, support, sustain, swear, testify, validate, verbalize, verify, vocalize, vow, warrant, witness* (≠ belie, challenge, conceal, confound, consult, contest, contradict, cover, cross-examine, debate, debunk, deceive, -deny, disavow, disclaim, discredit, -disown, disprove, dispute, distrust, doubt, falsify, gainsay, grill, hide, impugn, interrogate, interview, invalidate, oppose, question, rebut, -refuse, refute, -reject, -repudiate, scruple, -veto)

ATTRACT (←): *bait, beckon, beguile, bewitch, bring, candy-coat, captivate, charm, court, delight, drag, draw, enamor, enchant, endear, engage, enthrall, entice, entrance, excite, fascinate, grab, hook, impress, incline, induce, interest, intrigue, inveigle, invite, kill, lasso, lure, pull, razzle-dazzle, rivet, rope, score, seduce, send, solicit, spellbind, steer, tempt, thrill, titillate, vamp, win, woo, wow* (≠ annoy, block, bore, caution, chill, damp, demotivate, -deter, discourage, disenchant, disgust, dissuade, nag, niggle, nitpick, offend, -prevent, -refuse, -reject, release, repel, repulse, revolt, -shun, warn, weary)

ATTUNE (+): *acclimate, accommodate, accustom, adapt, adjust, align, arrange, assimilate, balance, blend, calibrate, center, combine, connect, coordinate, correlate, counterbalance, dovetail, equalize, even, familiarize, fit, fix, fuse, habituate, harmonize, incorporate, integrate, internalize, join, key, match, merge, orchestrate, order, pace, pair, personalize, proportion, reconcile, regulate, square, standardize, suit, synchronize, synthesize, time, tune, unify, unite, unskew* (≠ alienate, confuse, disaffect, disarrange, disarray, discard, disorder, disorganize, disrupt, disturb, estrange, mismatch, muzzle, -omit, -refuse, -reject, skew, stifle, upset)

AUCTION (→): *barter, commodify, exchange, flog, hawk, leverage, market, monetize, offer, peddle, sell, stock, tout, trade, traffic* (≠ bid, buy, hoard, hold, import, keep, outbid, preserve, proposition, purchase, retain)

AUDIT (←): *analyze, ascertain, assess, assure, balance, benchmark, calculate, categorize, certify, check, classify, comb, compare, confirm, connect, contrast, correlate, deduce, demonstrate, determine, diagnose, dissect, distill, double-check, establish, estimate, evaluate, examine, explore, eyeball, grade, inspect, investigate, monitor, notice, observe, ogle, oversee, parse, peruse, plumb, probe, prove, rank, read, reference, reinvestigate, research, review, scan, scope, scrutinize, sift, study, subdivide, substantiate, survey, tally, test, verify, view, watch, weigh*

(≠ accept, addle, assume, baffle, -blank, blind, blindfold, cheat, confound, confuse, declare, -disregard, embezzle, estimate, falsify, forget, fudge, hocus-pocus, -ignore, mask, misconstrue, misdiagnose, misjudge, mislead, miss, mystify, -neglect, -overlook, overvalue, perplex, puzzle, scam, skim, swindle, undervalue)

AUDITION (←): *adjudge, analyze, appraise, ascertain, assess, benchmark, categorize, check, clock, compare, consider, critique, determine, evaluate, examine, eyeball, filter, gauge, heed, inspect, interview, investigate, judge, measure, peg, peruse, prioritize, prove, rank, rate, reevaluate, sample, screen, scrutinize, sift, sort, study, survey, test, verify, vet, watch, weigh* (≠ accept, contract, cull, discard, -discount, -disregard, eject, embrace, hire, -ignore, miss, overestimate, -overlook, pass, -refuse, -reject, skip, underestimate)

AUGMENT (+): *accelerate, accumulate, add, aggrandize, amass, amplify, beef, bolster, boost, broaden, build, bump, buttress, catalyze, collect, complement, compound, deepen, develop, dilate, distend, double, elaborate, elevate, elongate, encourage, enhance, enlarge, escalate, exacerbate, exaggerate, expand, extend, feed, fill, flavor, foster, fuel, grow, heighten, heroicize, heroize, hike, hype, increase, inflate, intensify, lengthen, magnify, marinate, maximize, modify, multiply, optimize, overdramatize, overhaul, pad, poeticize, prolong, protract, provoke, pump, pyramid, raise, ratchet, reinforce, rile, romanticize, season, sentimentalize, spice, spike, strengthen, stretch, supersize, supplement, sweeten, swell, treble, triple, up, widen* (≠ abate, abbreviate, abridge, compress, condense, constrict, contract, curtail, cut, decrease, de-escalate, diminish, downsize, lessen, lower, minimize, moderate, pare, prune, rarefy, reduce, remove, shave, shear, shorten, shrink, stunt, subtract, suppress, trim, truncate, weaken)

AUGUR (←): *alert, anticipate, await, caution, detect, determine, divine, forecast, foresee, foretell, forewarn, harbinger, herald, infer, outguess, portend, predetermine, predict, presage, proclaim, prognosticate, promise, prophesy, read, signify, soothsay, warn* (≠ calculate, establish, guess, investigate, lament, narrate, prove, recount, regret, relate, report, suspect, suss)

AUTHENTICATE (+): *accredit, affirm, argue, assert, attest, authorize, avow, buttress, certify, confirm, convince, corroborate, crosscheck, declare, demonstrate, document, endorse, ensure, establish, guarantee, justify, notarize, profess, prove, ratify, reinforce, substantiate, support, validate, verify, vindicate, warrant, witness* (≠ challenge, consult, contest, contradict, cross-examine, debate, -deny, disavow, disclaim, discredit, -disown, disprove, dispute, distrust, doubt, forge, gainsay, grill, interrogate, interview, invalidate, question, rebut, refute, scruple)

AUTHORIZE (+): *accept, accord, affirm, allow, appoint, approve, assign, authenticate, back, bless, certify, charge, commission, confirm, consign, corroborate, countenance, countersign, delegate, deputize, designate, empower, enable, endorse, enforce, enfranchise, entitle, entrust, favor,* *franchise, greenlight, legalize, legitimize, license, mandate, name, notarize, okay, ordain, permit, qualify, ratify, sanction, support, task, tolerate, underwrite, validate, warrant* (≠ -abort, ban, bar, block, constrain, criminalize, delegitimize, -deny, discourage, discredit, disfavor, disgrace, disqualify, -exclude, fight, -forbid, hinder, impede, invalidate, obstruct, -omit, oppose, oust, -preclude, -prevent, -prohibit, protest, -rebuff, rebut, -refuse, -reject, -spurn, stop, -veto)

AUTOMATE (+): *arm, assemble, centralize, computerize, depersonalize, design, develop, engineer, equip, expedite, improve, industrialize, invent, mechanize, modernize, motorize, power, program, remodel, reprogram, revolutionize, rig, streamline, systematize, update, upgrade* (≠ adapt, alter, break, customize, damage, -halt, hobble, humanize, hurt, modify, personalize, retain, ruin, stall, tailor, wreck)

AVENGE (/): *castigate, chasten, chastise, compensate, correct, crucify, defend, discipline, even, exact, exonerate, fix, get, incriminate, justify, lynch, match, penalize, persecute, punish, recompense, rectify, redress, repay, retort, return, revenge, right, scourge, square, torment, torture, vindicate, wreak* (≠ absolve, brook, comfort, condone, -disregard, encourage, excuse, forgive, pardon, permit, remit, spare, stomach, tolerate)

-AVERT (→): *-abort, anticipate, arrest, -avoid, baffle, -balk, bar, block, check, checkmate, -circumvent, counteract, counterbalance, deflect, -deter, divert, -dodge, -duck, -elude, -escape, -eschew, -evade, foil, -forbid, forestall, -frustrate, -halt, hamper, hinder, impede, inhibit, interrupt, -negate, neutralize, -nullify, obstruct, -obviate, occlude, offset, override, parry, pause, -preclude, -prevent, -prohibit, retard, save, shake, -shirk, short-circuit, -shun, shunt, stall, stem, stop, stymie, -thwart, turn, ward* (≠ abet, accelerate, advance, aid, allow, assist, await, brainstorm, catalyze, cultivate, ease, educe, enable, encourage, facilitate, forward, foster, further, instigate, leave, let, nurture, permit, promote, smooth, spark, spur, unclog)

-AVOID (→): *-avert, -balk, ban, bar, -blank, -boycott, -bypass, -circumvent, -decline, deflect, detour, -disregard, divert, -dodge, -duck, eliminate, -elude, -escape, -eschew, -evade, -exclude, finesse, -flee, foil, fox, -frustrate, miss, -neglect, -obviate, -omit, -ostracize, outfox, outsmart, outwit, overreach, override, parry, -preclude, -prevent, shake, -shirk, -shun, -sidestep, skirt, -thwart, ward* (≠ accept, arrest, buttonhole, catch, chase, claim, contact, contract, court, discover, embrace, engage, explore, find, grab, hold, hunt, include, incur, invite, prowl, pursue, seek, stalk, stop, waylay, welcome, woo)

AWARD (→): *accord, allocate, allot, allow, appoint, apportion, appropriate, assign, bequeath, bestow, comp, concede, confer, contribute, decorate, decree, designate, determine, dispense, distribute, dole, donate, dower, dub, endow, enrich, extend, fix, furnish, gift, give, grant, name, offer, outlay, overpay, present, proffer, provide, render, reward, set, show, spare, supply, tender, tithe, vest, volunteer, will, yield* (≠ -abort, abrogate, annul, call, claim, debit, drop, earn, grab, invalidate, merit, -nullify, quash, recall, recant, recover, repeal, -rescind, retract, revoke, snag, steal, swipe, take, tax, underpay, -veto, -void, withdraw, withhold)

AWARD (+): *acclaim, aggrandize, applaud, cite, commend, compensate, compliment, congratulate, decorate, elevate, hail, honor, lionize, magnify, pay, praise, promote, raise, recompense, refund, reimburse, remember, repay, reward, salute, tithe, tout* (≠ abash, boo, chastise, confound, discredit, disgrace, dishonor, embarrass, forget, humble, humiliate, -ignore, mortify, -neglect, -overlook, punish, rebuke, ridicule, shame, withhold)

AXE (→): *amputate, butcher, carve, chop, cleave, cut, dismember, divide, fell, gash, hack, halve, hew, incise, rend, rip, rive, saw, scissor, separate, sever, slam, slash, slice, slit, smite, split, sunder* (≠ affix, attach, bind, fasten, fuse, glue, grow, join, meld, mend, merge, patch, repair, seal, secure, sew, stitch, suture, unite, weld)

AXE (/): *abolish, boot, bounce, can, -cancel, cashier, chuck, discharge, dismiss, downsize, eliminate, expel, fire, furlough, pink-slip, release, remove, retire, sack, scrap, separate, terminate, trim, unseat, withdraw* (≠ brainstorm, contract, draft, employ, engage, enlist, hire, keep, place, promote, recruit, retain, save, select, sign, subcontract)

BABY (+): *accommodate, appease, assuage, buffer, calm, cherish, cocoon, coddle, content, cosset, cradle, cuddle, cultivate, cushion, dandle, delight, ease, encourage, featherbed, fondle, foster, gladden, gratify, guide, humor, indulge, infantilize, lull, mellow, mollify, mollycoddle, mother, nurse, nurture, nuzzle, oblige, overindulge, overprotect, pacify, pamper, parent, pet, pity, placate, please, propitiate, protect, safeguard, satisfy, serve, snuggle, soothe, spoil, spoon-feed, sugarcoat, wet-nurse* (≠ -abandon, abuse, annoy, attack, -avoid, bother, brutalize, bully, control, crucify, damage, -desert, discipline, dominate, harass, harm, hurt, ill-treat, injure, maltreat, manhandle, maul, menace, mishandle, mistreat, misuse, molest, -neglect, oppress, outrage, -overlook, pain, persecute, plague, punish, restrain, savage, -slight, threaten, torment, torture, victimize, violate, wound, wrong)

BACK (→): *abet, advance, advise, aid, assist, attend, authorize, bankroll, befriend, benefit, bolster, boost, buttress, capitalize, champion, comfort, condone, counsel, deliver, ease, embolden, encourage, endorse, facilitate, favor, finance, forward, foster, fund, furnish, further, greenlight, guide, hearten, help, launch, mentor, nurture, oblige, patronize, profit, promote, reinforce, rescue, save, serve, sponsor, subsidize, succor, supply, support, sustain, underwrite* (≠ -abandon, baffle, -balk, bar, beggar, betray, block, constrain, counter, damage, -desert, disappoint, discourage, discredit, disgrace, dishearten, disinherit, -disown, dissuade, drop, fail, foil, -frustrate, hamper, handicap, harm, hinder, hurt, impede, inconvenience, inhibit, injure, monkey-wrench, obstruct, oppose, restrain, retard, sabotage, scotch, scupper, scuttle, shelve, stifle, straiten, strangle, stunt, -thwart, undercut, undermine, wreck, wrong)

BACK (+): *adopt, advance, advocate, affirm, boost, champion, confirm, corroborate, countenance, countersign, cultivate, embrace, encourage, endorse, espouse, favor, forward, further, help, hype, legalize, patronize, plug, preach, promote, ratify, recommend, reinforce, sanction, second, spur, support, uphold, warrant* (≠ baffle, challenge, contradict, defeat, denounce, denunciate, -desert, disappoint, disfavor, fail, foil, -frustrate, fulminate, muzzle, oppose, reverse, sabotage, scotch, shelve, subvert, threaten, -thwart)

BADGER (→): *annoy, bait, besiege, browbeat, bug, bully, chaff, chivy, disturb, earbash, fret, goad, harass, harry, hassle, heckle, hector, hound, importune, irk, irritate, nag, needle, niggle, nitpick, noodge, nudge, persecute, pester, plague, press, pressure, rattle, ride, taunt, tease, torment, trouble, vex, worry* (≠ -abandon, aid, alleviate, amuse, assist, assuage, calm, comfort, delight, ease, help, -ignore, mellow, mollify, -neglect, pacify, placate, please, relax, settle, steady, support, woo)

BAFFLE (/): *abash, addle, agitate, amaze, astonish, bamboozle, beat, befog, befuddle, beguile, bemuse, bewilder, boggle, bother, buffalo, chagrin, cloud, confound, confuse, cozen, daze, deceive, delude, discombobulate, discomfit, discomfort, discompose, disconcert, dismay, disorient, disquiet, distress, disturb, dizzy, dumbfound, dupe, -elude, embarrass, faze, floor, flummox, fluster, foil, fool, fox, frustrate, get, gobsmack, gull, harass, hoax, hobble, hocus-pocus, hoodwink, humbug, jumble, misguide, mislead, mismatch, mortify, muddle, muddy, mystify, nonplus, obscure, obstruct, outguess, outwit, perplex, perturb, puzzle, rattle, snooker, snow, stick, stump, stun, tangle, throw, trick, trouble, unhinge, unsettle, upset, vex* (≠ assure, clarify, coach, decipher, deduce, edify, educate, enlighten, explain, guide, illuminate, inform, instruct, mentor, reassure, rephrase, satisfy, school, simplify, solve, steer, streamline, teach, train, tutor, untangle)

BAFFLE (/): *anticipate, arrest, -avert, -balk, bar, beat, block, bottleneck, brake, bung, burden, catch, check, checkmate, choke, clog, clutter, complicate, congest, conquer, constipate, constrain, counter, counteract, countercheck, cramp, crimp, cripple, curb, dam, defeat, delay, detain, -deter, discomfit, drag, encumber, entangle, entrap, fetter, foil, forestall, foul, -frustrate, -halt, hamper, hamstring, handicap, hinder, hobble, hold back, impair, impede, inhibit, interrupt, jam, manacle, mire, monkey-wrench, -negate, neutralize, -nullify, obstruct, -obviate, occlude, offset, oppose, overcome, paralyze, pause, plug, -preclude, -prevent, resist, restrain, restrict, shackle, shelve, short-circuit, snag, snarl, stall, stay, stem, stop, tangle, -thwart, trammel* (≠ abet, advance, aid, assist, await, content, cultivate, ease, educe, encourage, facilitate, forward, foster, further, hasten, nurture, promote, quicken, simplify, smooth, uncomplicate)

BAG (←): *acquire, apprehend, appropriate, arrest, capture, catch, commandeer, corner, download, gain, get, grab, hook, kill, land, nab, nail, net, obtain, procure, reserve, secure, shoot, snaffle, snag, source, take, trap* (≠ discharge, -disregard, emancipate, free, -ignore, liberate, loose, lose, miss, -overlook, release, restore, spring, unbind, unchain, waste)

BAIT (←): *allure, attract, bedevil, beguile, betray, bewitch, bribe, bullshit, cajole, candy-coat, captivate, catch, charm, cheat, coax, con, conjure, convince, decoy, defraud, draw, enchant, enmesh, ensnare, entice, entrap, fascinate, goad, hocus-pocus, hook, induce, inveigle, invite, lure, magnetize, mesh, mislead, outwit, persuade, provoke, pull, razzle-dazzle, rope, seduce, snare, snooker, snow, solicit, stoke, sucker, summon, sway, tangle, tantalize, taunt, tease, tempt, trap, trick, waylay* (≠ alarm, alert, annoy, -balk, block, bore, bother, bug, caution, cushion, dampen, deaden, demotivate, depress, disappoint, discourage, disenchant, dull, enrage, exhaust, forewarn, guard, hamper, impede, infuriate, irk, irritate, muffle, nag, needle, nettle, nobble, numb, offend, repel, repulse, scare, slake, spook, terrify, underwhelm, unnerve, vex, ward, warn, weary, withstand, worry)

BAIT (/): *aggravate, aggrieve, agitate, anger, annoy, badger, bedevil, beleaguer, bother, browbeat, bug, bully, burn, chafe, demean, demonize, deride, discomfort, disturb, dog, exasperate, fret, frost, gall, get, gibe, gnaw, goad, harass, harry, hassle, haze, heckle, hector, hound, irk, irritate, jeer, mock, nag, needle, nettle, nitpick, peeve, persecute, perturb, pester, pillory, pique, plague, provoke, rasp, ride, ridicule, rile, ruffle, spite, taunt, tease, terrorize, test, torment, torture, trouble, try, vex* (≠ allay, appease, -bypass, calm, compliment, defend, ease, forget, help, -ignore, mellow, -overlook, praise, protect, relax, respect, sedate, shield, -snub, -spurn, sugarcoat)

BALANCE (+): *accommodate, adjust, align, anchor, approximate, attune, calibrate, compensate, coordinate, counteract, counterbalance, counterpoise countervail, defray, equalize, equate, even, expense, fit, ground, harmonize, homogenize, indemnify, level, match, neutralize, normalize, offset, pace, parallel, personalize, poise, regularize, regulate, root, set, settle, square, stabilize, standardize, steady, tie, tune, weigh* (≠ bash, batter, bump, cant, capsize, cheat, convulse, customize, disturb, favor, jar, jolt, knock, mass, mismatch, overbalance, overset, overturn, rock, shake, shunt, tip, topple, unbalance, unhorse, violate, weight)

-BALK (→): *-abort, anticipate, arrest, -avert, baffle, bar, beat, block, check, checkmate, -circumvent, clog, conquer, counteract, cramp, dash, defeat, disappoint, discomfit, disconcert, encumber, fetter, foil, forestall, -frustrate, -halt, hamper, handicap, hinder, hobble, impede, inhibit, manacle, monkey-wrench, muzzle, -negate, neutralize, -nullify, obstruct, -obviate, occlude, offset, overcome, pause, -preclude, -prevent, protest, ruin, scruple, shackle, short-circuit, stall, stem, stop, stymie, -thwart, tie, trammel* (≠ abet, advance, aid, allow, assist, await, boost, brainstorm, catalyze, cultivate, ease, encourage, facilitate, forward, foster, further, grease, help, lubricate, nurture, permit, promote, smooth, spitball, spur, stimulate, support)

BALLYHOO (→): *acclaim, advance, advertise, announce, applaud, assert, bark, blare, blaze, blazon, boost, broadcast, bulletin, circulate, claim, commend, compliment, congratulate, declare, disseminate, endorse, eulogize, extol, glorify, hail, herald, hustle, hype, laud, limelight, magnify, merchandize, offer, peddle, pimp, pitch, plug, praise, presell, proclaim, promote, pronounce, publicize, publish, push, recommend, review, sell, shill, telegraph, tout, trumpet* (≠ blackguard, blame, boo, chide, conceal, demean, demonize, denigrate, deride, -disdain, dismiss, disparage, hide, hush, -ignore, insult, knock, mock, neg, pan, pillory, quiet, rib, ridicule, scold, -scorn, shame, -shun, silence, smother, stifle)

BAMBOOZLE (←): *beat, beguile, bemuse, bilk, bleed, bluff, bogart, buffalo, bullshit, burn, cadge, cajole, candy-coat, catch, cheat, chisel, con, convince, cozen, deceive, deflect, defraud, delude, diddle, dupe, euchre, exploit, fake, fiddle, finagle, fleece, flimflam, fool, fox, fudge, gouge, gull,* *hoax, hocus-pocus, hoodwink, humbug, hustle, impersonate, infiltrate, influence, juggle, kid, manipulate, misguide, misinform, mislead, outwit, pretend, roleplay, rook, scam, schmooze, screw, shaft, shortchange, skin, snooker, snow, spin, spoof, squeeze, stick, stiff, sting, sucker, swindle, tease, trick, underpay, upset, victimize, weasel, wrong* (≠ assume, assure, believe, blab, blurt, concede, confess, confide, confirm, confront, credit, debunk, disabuse, disclose, disenchant, disillusion, divulge, expose, help, honor, restore, reveal, show, support, tell, trust, uncloak, uncover, undeceive, unmask, unveil)

BAMBOOZLE (/): *abash, addle, agitate, amplify, baffle, beat, befog, befuddle, beguile, bemuse, bewilder, bother, buffalo, chagrin, confound, confuse, cozen, daze, deceive, delude, discombobulate, discomfit, discomfort, discompose, disconcert, dismay, disorient, disquiet, distress, disturb, dizzy, dumbfound, dupe, embarrass, faze, flummox, fluster, fool, fox, gaslight, get, gull, hoax, hocus-pocus, hoodwink, humbug, jumble, misguide, mislead, mortify, muddle, muddy, mystify, nonplus, perplex, perturb, puzzle, rattle, snooker, snow, spin, stick, stump, stun, tangle, throw, unhinge, unsettle, upset, vex* (≠ aid, assist, assure, calm, clarify, ease, elucidate, enlighten, explain, facilitate, floodlight, foster, further, hasten, illuminate, inform, nurture, promote, quicken, reassure, satisfy, simplify, smooth, solve, steady, streamline, unravel)

BAN (/): *amputate, banish, bar, blackball, blacklist, block, -boycott, censor, command, condemn, constrain, control, criminalize, curb, curse, curtail, damn, -deny, deport, disallow, disapprove, disbar, disqualify, doom, eject, eliminate, embargo, enjoin, eradicate, evict, excise, -exclude, -excommunicate, expatriate, expel, extradite, -forbid, -halt, -ignore, inhibit, -kibosh, -omit, oppress, -ostracize, oust, outlaw, picket, -preclude, -prevent, -prohibit, proscribe, protest, -refuse, -reject, relegate, remove, -renounce, -repudiate, restrict, sideline, stop, suppress, taboo, -veto* (≠ accord, admit, allow, approve, authorize, bear, brave, brook, countenance, cultivate, educe, embrace, enable, encourage, endorse, endure, entertain, face, facilitate, greenlight, include, legalize, nurture, permit, promote, sanction, suffer, support, tolerate, welcome)

BANDAGE (+): *address, attend, bind, cover, cure, doctor, dress, heal, medicate, mend, nurse, rehabilitate, remedy, repair, swaddle, swathe, treat, wrap* (≠ abuse, burn, cut, damage, expose, gash, harm, hurt, injure, lacerate, maim, mutilate, scar, slice, tear, unbandage, uncover, unwrap, wound)

BANISH (→): *axe, ban, bar, blackball, boot, bounce, -boycott, can, cashier, chase, defenestrate, denaturalize, deport, discard, discharge, dislodge, dismiss, dispel, displace, dispossess, eject, eliminate, eradicate, evict, -exclude, -excommunicate, exile, exorcise, expatriate, expel, extradite, extrude, fire, isolate, jettison, -omit, -ostracize, oust, outlaw, pink-slip, -prohibit, proscribe, quarantine, -reject, release, relegate, remove, -repudiate, retire, rout, sack, seclude, sequester, sideline, -spurn, terminate, transport* (≠ abduct, accept, admit, adopt, allow, entertain, harbor, house, keep, kidnap, lodge, naturalize, recall, receive, repatriate, reunite, shelter, take, welcome)

BANKRUPT (/): *beggar, blow, break, bust, cannibalize, compromise, consume, cripple, deplete, depredate, diminish, disinherit, -disown, drain, empty, exhaust, impoverish, leach, leech, misuse, pauperize, reduce, ruin, slather, spend, squander, straiten, waste, weaken, wreck* (≠ back, bankroll, bequeath, bestow, capitalize, dower, endow, enrich, finance, fund, restore, supplement, support, underwrite)

BAPTIZE (+): *admit, anoint, bless, call, christen, cleanse, consecrate, daub, dedicate, dip, douse, drench, dub, enroll, entitle, hallow, immerse, induct, initiate, introduce, name, purify, recruit, regenerate, rub, sanctify, sprinkle, style, term, title, wet* (≠ blemish, condemn, curse, damn, debauch, dirty, discharge, discredit, disparage, exile, exorcise, expel, -ignore, ruin, terminate, unmake)

BAR (/): *ban, barricade, blacklist, block, blockade, -boycott, check, condemn, deadbolt, -deny, disallow, discourage, disqualify, eliminate, enjoin, -exclude, exile, -forbid, -frustrate, hamper, hinder, impede, -interdict, limit, obstruct, occlude, -omit, -ostracize, oust, outlaw, override, picket, -preclude, -prevent, -prohibit, protest, -refuse, -reject, restrain, restrict, segregate, short-circuit, shut, -spurn, stem, stop, suspend, -veto* (≠ accord, admit, allow, approve, authorize, -bypass, -circumvent, cultivate, embrace, facilitate, force, include, legalize, loosen, nurture, open, outwit, permit, promote, sanction, -sidestep, suffer, support, tolerate, unlock, welcome)

BARRICADE (/): *bar, block, blockade, bolt, close, curtain, dam, defend, embattle, fence, fortify, garrison, gate, guard, hedge, hinder, lock, obstruct, occlude, protect, rampart, screen, secure, strengthen, stymie, -thwart, wall* (≠ abet, allow, breach, bulldoze, crack, invite, open, permit, railroad, ram, reopen, unbar, unblock, unbolt, welcome)

BARTER (+): *bandy, bootleg, broker, change, chop, commodify, commute, deal, debate, exchange, fence, leverage, negotiate, recoup, replace, sell, shift, substitute, swap, switch, trade, traffic, transact, transfer, truck* (≠ buy, cheat, -decline, donate, give, hide, hoard, import, keep, loan, loot, outbid, pilfer, purchase, sell, steal, swindle, swipe, tender, withhold)

BASH (→): *bat, batter, beat, belt, break, clip, clobber, clock, clout, club, concuss, crush, cudgel, cuff, flog, hammer, hit, knock, lash, lick, pelt, pound, pulverize, pummel, punch, slam, slap, slog, slug, smack, smash, smite, sock, spank, strike, swat, swipe, thump, wallop, whack* (≠ armor, -avert, block, caress, coddle, cuddle, defend, deflect, -dodge, -duck, -evade, guard, heal, nurture, parry, pet, protect, repel, rescue, shield, -sidestep, stroke)

BASTARDIZE (/): *abase, adulterate, animalize, attenuate, bestialize, blemish, blotch, bowdlerize, canker, cheapen, contaminate, corrupt, debase, debauch, degrade, demoralize, deprave, devalue, dilute, dirty,* *doctor, lessen, pervert, pollute, stain, suborn, subvert, sully, taint, tarnish, vitiate, warp, weaken* (≠ ameliorate, appreciate, augment, benefit, better, boost, clean, cleanse, dignify, embellish, enhance, enrich, heighten, honor, improve, legitimate, legitimize, moralize, optimize, overhaul, praise, purify, rarefy, refine, straighten, upgrade, value)

BATHE (+): *clean, cleanse, cover, dampen, decontaminate, deluge, dip, douse, drench, drizzle, -duck, dunk, engulf, flood, flush, hose, humidify, hydrate, immerse, impregnate, inundate, irrigate, lave, marinate, mist, moisten, moisturize, plunge, presoak, purify, rehydrate, rinse, sanitize, saturate, scour, scrub, shower, sink, slosh, sluice, soak, soap, splash, sponge, sprinkle, steep, sterilize, submerge, suffuse, swamp, syrup, trickle, wash, wet* (≠ blacken, contaminate, dehydrate, desiccate, dirty, dry, evaporate, harden, leach, muddy, parch, pollute, scorch, sear, soil, stain, sully, tarnish, towel, wring)

BATTER (→): *bash, beat, bombard, bruise, buffet, clip, clobber, clock, clout, concuss, conk, cuff, dash, drub, hammer, hit, knock, lash, lick, maul, pelt, pound, pulverize, pummel, punch, slap, slug, smack, smash, smite, sock, strike, swat, thrash, thump, thwack, wallop, whack* (≠ adorn, aid, beautify, block, build, compliment, construct, decorate, defend, deflect, -dodge, -duck, encourage, fix, help, mend, praise, preserve, protect, repair, repel, restore)

BATTER (/): *abuse, assail, assault, attack, blitz, bombard, break, bruise, club, combat, crack, cripple, crush, damage, demolish, destroy, disfigure, erode, fight, harry, hurt, ill-treat, injure, invade, maltreat, mangle, mar, maul, mortar, punish, ruin, savage, scarify, scathe, shatter, slash, storm, trash, trounce, violate, wreck, wrong* (≠ adore, cherish, cure, defend, guard, heal, honor, improve, indulge, mend, nurse, nurture, pamper, prize, protect, respect, revere, shield, treasure)

BATTLE (→): *antagonize, attack, block, challenge, checkmate, combat, confront, cross, debate, defy, distrust, emulate, engage, face, fight, -frustrate, gainsay, hassle, interrupt, jockey, jostle, maneuver, match, meet, neutralize, obstruct, oppose, oppress, override, overturn, parry, play, police, protest, race, refute, resist, restrain, rival, subvert, taunt, -thwart, train, withstand, work, wrestle* (≠ accept, accommodate, aid, allow, authorize, -avoid, befriend, -circumvent, concede, -dodge, -elude, encourage, endorse, -escape, -evade, favor, follow, foster, help, -ignore, join, nourish, nurture, obey, oblige, pass, permit, promote, protect, -quit, -shirk, -shun, -sidestep, support, surrender, tolerate, yield)

BATTLE (→): *assault, attack, bang, bash, bat, batter, beat, belt, bludgeon, bop, box, buffet, bump, clobber, club, combat, duel, fight, grapple, hammer, hit, knock, paste, pound, punch, slam, slap, slug, smack, smite, sock, strike, swat, swipe, tackle, thump, thwack, wallop, whack, whale, wrestle* (≠ absorb, align, -avoid, buffer, -bypass, -circumvent, defend, deflect, -duck, -elude, -escape, guard, nurture, protect, rescue, save, shelter, shield, -shun, -sidestep, treat, withstand)

BATTLE (/): *accost, address, agitate, argue, assail, baffle, bait, challenge, checkmate, combat, contest, counter, counteract, criticize, debate, defy, discredit, -disown, disprove, dispute, engage, face, fight, foil, -frustrate, impugn, invade, meet, monkey-wrench, oppose, oppugn, resist, short-circuit, straightjacket, tackle, -thwart, tug, withstand, wrestle* (≠ abide, advance, advocate, back, bear, champion, confess, cultivate, encourage, endorse, endure, forward, foster, further, nourish, nurture, promote, spitball, suffer, support, uphold)

BEAR (→): *beget, birth, breed, calve, create, deliver, develop, drop, engender, father, form, foster, generate, gestate, invent, kindle, litter, make, mother, multiply, produce, propagate, provide, reproduce, sire, spawn, whelp, yield* (≠ -abandon, -abort, bury, destroy, devour, digest, end, erase, kill, lose, malnourish, midwife, miscarry, murder, starve, terminate, throttle)

BEAR (←): *beam, bring, carry, cart, chauffeur, conduct, convey, deliver, ferry, fetch, forward, hand, harbor, haul, hump, lift, lug, move, pack, remove, schlep, send, shift, ship, take, tote, transfer, transmit, transport* (≠ -abandon, cant, discard, drop, dump, eliminate, forfeit, -forsake, give, leave, lose, mislay, misplace, miss, -neglect, -omit, -refuse, -reject, relinquish, send, steal, throw, trash)

BEAR (+): *abide, absorb, accept, admit, allow, brave, brook, buck, concede, condone, confront, countenance, endorse, endure, experience, face, hack, handle, harden, incur, indulge, know, meet, outlast, overcome, permit, pocket, receive, reconcile, respect, sanction, season, shoulder, stand, stomach, suffer, support, surmount, survive, sustain, swallow, sweat, take, tolerate, uphold, weather, withstand* (≠ -avoid, -balk, -bypass, challenge, -circumvent, combat, contest, counteract, -decline, defy, denounce, dismiss, -dodge, -elude, -escape, -evade, fight, -forbid, miss, oppose, -refuse, -reject, -repudiate, resist, -spurn, -thwart)

BEAT (→): *abuse, assail, assault, attack, bash, baste, bat, batter, belt, birch, bludgeon, box, break, bruise, buffet, bust, cane, castigate, chastise, clobber, clout, club, concuss, conk, cowhide, crack, cudgel, cuff, deck, drub, flagellate, flail, flay, flog, floor, hammer, hide, hit, horsewhip, knock, lace, lambaste, larrup, lash, lather, lick, maltreat, maul, paddle, paste, pelt, pistol-whip, pound, pulverize, pummel, punch, punish, ram, rap, rawhide, scourge, shake, slam, slap, slate, slug, smack, sock, spank, strap, strike, swat, swipe, switch, tan, thrash, thresh, thump, thwack, trample, trounce, wallop, whack, whale, whip, whomp, whup* (≠ aid, armor, assist, beautify, block, caress, cure, defend, deflect, doctor, fix, guard, heal, help, mend, nurse, parry, praise, protect, repair, restore, shield, stroke, strum, support)

BEAT (→): *accomplish, achieve, best, better, cap, capture, checkmate, clobber, conquer, crush, defeat, dispatch, drub, eclipse, exceed, foil, humble, lick, master, one-up, outclass, outcompete, outdistance, outdo, outfight, outguess, outgun, outlast, outmaneuver, outmatch, outpace, outperform, outplay, outrace, outrank, outreach, outrun, outscore,* *outsell, outshine, outsmart, outstrip, outweigh, outwit, overcome, overpower, overshadow, overtake, overthrow, overturn, overwhelm, quell, rival, score, shame, shellac, skunk, stop, subdue, subjugate, surmount, surpass, sweep, take, top, transcend, trounce, trump, unseat, upend, usurp, vanquish, wallop, whip, whup, win* (≠ -abandon, abdicate, aid, assist, boost, follow, forfeit, lose, mind, obey, relinquish, -renounce, resign, serve, surrender)

BEAT (/): *annihilate, assault, attack, bomb, break, bulldoze, bury, clobber, conquer, cow, cream, crush, decimate, defeat, demolish, devastate, discomfit, drub, enslave, finish, flatten, invade, obliterate, overthrow, overwhelm, quash, quell, reduce, rout, ruin, scotch, shellac, skin, slaughter, smash, smoke, steamroller, subdue, subjugate, tame, thrash, trounce, upset, vanquish, wallop, wax, whip, wrack, wreck* (≠ aid, build, construct, defend, found, free, guard, heal, help, liberate, preserve, promote, protect, raise, reinvigorate, rescue, restimulate, restore, revive, safeguard, save, shelter, shield, survive, treasure, weather)

BEAT (/): *-avert, -avoid, -bypass, -circumvent, deflect, disobey, -disregard, -ditch, divert, -dodge, -duck, -elude, -end-run, -escape, -eschew, -evade, flout, -ignore, -obviate, outflank, parry, -prevent, shake, -shirk, shortcut, -shun, -sidestep, skirt, subvert, ward* (≠ accept, acknowledge, authorize, catch, contact, contract, court, embrace, follow, honor, incur, institute, keep, obey, observe, pursue, respect, seek, serve, welcome)

BEAUTIFY (+): *accessorize, adorn, aggrandize, aid, appliqué, array, augment, barber, bedeck, bedizen, bejewel, benefit, better, blazon, bless, boost, braid, brighten, build, burnish, caparison, cleanse, clear, costume, deck, decorate, dignify, distinguish, drape, dress, elaborate, elevate, embellish, emblaze, emboss, embroider, enhance, ennoble, enrich, fancify, feather, festoon, figure, filigree, fillet, fix, flatter, flavor, flounce, freshen, frill, fringe, garland, garnish, gem, gild, glamorize, glitter, glitz, glorify, grace, groom, gussy, hang, help, illuminate, improve, jewel, lace, magnify, manicure, optimize, ornament, overhaul, paint, pearl, pigment, pomade, prettify, pretty, purify, rarefy, redecorate, redo, refine, revamp, revolutionize, ribbon, service, smarten, soften, spackle, spiff, spruce, stipple, stud, swag, tinsel, titivate, tool, transfigure, transform, trim, update, upgrade, wreathe* (≠ abase, bare, bedraggle, begrime, besmear, besmirch, blemish, blot, blur, botch, canker, cheapen, cloud, compromise, contaminate, corrupt, debase, decrease, deface, defile, deform, degrade, denude, destroy, deteriorate, dirty, discolor, disfigure, disgrace, dismantle, display, distort, divest, efface, embarrass, expose, foul, harm, harshen, humble, humiliate, hurt, infect, infest, injure, lessen, lower, mar, pollute, reduce, reveal, ruin, sabotage, scar, shame, simplify, smear, smirch, smudge, soil, spoil, streamline, strip, sully, taint, tar, tarnish, trash, uglify, uncover, undercut, undermine, violate, warp, weaken, wither, worsen, wound, wreck)

BECKON (+): *acknowledge, acquaint, advise, allure, ask, attract, bid, buzz, call, coax, command, conjure, demand, draw, entice, flag, flourish,* *induce, inform, invite, lure, persuade, pull, signal, summon, tempt, wave, welcome* (≠ -avoid, ban, bar, -deter, -disdain, -elude, -evade, -exclude, -neglect, -omit, -ostracize, oust, push, -reject, repel, repulse, -shun)

BED (+): *ball, bang, boff, boink, bone, bonk, debauch, deflower, devour, diddle, drill, enter, fuck, hump, impale, jump, nail, penetrate, pillage, pleasure, plow, plunder, poke, pork, pound, rail, ravish, ride, screw, seduce, shag, shtup, skewer, take, tap, tumble* (≠ -avoid, block, -deny, -desert, dismiss, -disregard, -ditch, drop, dump, -eschew, -ignore, jilt, -neglect, -rebuff, -refuse, -reject, -scorn, -shun, -snub, -spurn)

BEDEVIL (/): *afflict, aggravate, agitate, agonize, anguish, annoy, assail, assault, attack, badger, beset, besiege, bother, bug, chafe, confound, crush, curse, discomfort, discompose, disquiet, distress, disturb, dog, exasperate, excruciate, fluster, fret, frustrate, gall, get, gravel, grieve, hagride, harass, harm, harrow, harry, hound, hurt, impugn, injure, irk, irritate, lynch, martyr, menace, molest, nettle, oppress, overpower, overwhelm, pain, peeve, persecute, perturb, pester, pique, plague, prick, pursue, rack, rasp, ride, rile, smite, stab, sting, strain, stress, strike, tease, threaten, torment, torture, trouble, try, tyrannize, upset, vex, victimize, worry, wring, wrong* (≠ abet, aid, assist, assuage, calm, comfort, console, content, delight, deliver, encourage, gladden, heal, hearten, help, nurture, pacify, pity, please, protect, quiet, reassure, release, relieve, reprieve, shield, solace, soothe, succor)

BEFRIEND (←): *abet, acknowledge, acquaint, advise, aid, ally, assist, back, benefit, bolster, boost, cheer, comfort, commend, defend, encourage, favor, give, hearten, help, include, ingratiate, inspire, invite, offer, patronize, promote, protect, reassure, respect, satisfy, succor, support, sustain, uphold, welcome* (≠ abuse, assault, block, counteract, discourage, dissuade, harm, hinder, hurt, -ignore, injure, insult, -neglect, obstruct, oppose, -reject, resist, -shun, -snub, -spurn, -thwart, torment, vex, withstand, wrong)

BEFUDDLE (/): *abash, addle, agitate, amaze, baffle, bamboozle, beat, befog, bemuse, bewilder, bother, buffalo, bug, chagrin, cloud, confound, confuse, daze, deceive, delude, discombobulate, discomfit, discompose, disconcert, dismay, disorient, distract, distress, disturb, dizzy, dumbfound, dupe, embarrass, faze, floor, flummox, fluster, foil, fool, fox, gaslight, harass, hobble, hocus-pocus, inebriate, intoxicate, misguide, mislead, mismatch, mortify, muddle, muddy, mystify, nonplus, obscure, perplex, perturb, preoccupy, puzzle, rattle, shake, shock, snow, stick, stump, stun, stupefy, tangle, throw, trick, trouble, unhinge, unsettle, upset, vex* (≠ assure, clarify, contextualize, decipher, deduce, educate, enlighten, explain, floodlight, illuminate, inform, reassure, satisfy, school, simplify, teach, train, tutor)

BEG (←): *advocate, ask, beseech, besiege, canvass, claim, coerce, command, compel, conjure, covet, crave, demand, desire, entreat, force, implore, importune, insist, invoke, nag, petition, plead, pray, press,* *request, require, requisition, resent, solicit, sue, urge, woo, worry* (≠ appease, comfort, command, console, content, -deny, grace, gratify, hint, intimate, mollify, oblige, pacify, placate, please, provide, quiet, -refuse, satisfy)

BEG (←): *bilk, bite, borrow, bum, burn, buzz, cadge, chisel, ding, hustle, milk, mooch, nick, panhandle, scavenge, schnorr, score, scrounge, sponge, tap, touch* (≠ bequeath, bestow, comp, -disown, donate, endow, -forsake, furnish, give, junk, lend, -reject, relinquish, -renounce, -spurn, supply, tender, tithe, yield)

BEGRUDGE (/): *badmouth, blackguard, covet, crave, -deny, deprecate, deprive, desire, diminish, disallow, -discount, disparage, disrespect, drizzle, envy, fetishize, grudge, hoard, hog, hold, keep, mind, minimize, misallocate, mock, monopolize, -neglect, pinch, -refuse, -reject, remove, resent, ridicule, scant, skimp, starve, stint, trickle, want, wish, withdraw, withhold, yank* (≠ accord, administer, allocate, allow, apportion, bestow, celebrate, congratulate, contribute, deliver, dispense, disperse, donate, encourage, endow, extend, fuel, furnish, grant, invite, offer, pledge, praise, provide, share, spare, spitball, supply, tender, volunteer, welcome, wish)

BEGUILE (←): *allure, amuse, arrest, attract, beckon, bed, bewitch, blandish, cajole, candy-coat, captivate, charm, cheer, court, delight, disarm, distract, divert, draw, enamor, enchant, engage, engross, enliven, enrapture, entertain, enthrall, entrance, fascinate, flatter, fox, gratify, hypnotize, interest, intrigue, invite, kid, kill, lure, magnetize, mesmerize, occupy, please, pull, razzle-dazzle, seduce, solicit, spellbind, tempt, thrill, tickle, vamp, woo, wow* (≠ abuse, aggravate, anger, annoy, attack, bore, depress, disappoint, disgust, displease, disturb, drain, exhaust, fatigue, gall, harass, heckle, irk, menace, needle, nettle, nitpick, noodge, offend, pain, pester, repel, repulse, revolt, sorrow, tire, traumatize, upset, vex, victimize, weary, wound, wrong)

BEGUILE (←): *actuate, attract, bait, betray, bribe, capture, catch, coax, convince, decoy, draw, encourage, enmesh, ensnare, entice, entrap, induce, influence, inspire, inveigle, lasso, lead, lure, mesh, motivate, move, oblige, persuade, press, rope, seduce, seize, snare, snooker, snow, solicit, suborn, sway, tangle, target, tempt, trap, urge* (≠ alert, anguish, annoy, bother, browbeat, bug, bully, caution, coerce, compel, covet, crave, daunt, demand, demotivate, desire, -deter, discourage, dissuade, distract, fancy, favor, fetishize, force, forewarn, niggle, nobble, repulse, restrain, sandbag, threaten, -thwart, torment, ward, warn)

BEGUILE (←): *bamboozle, betray, bleed, bluff, buffalo, bullshit, burn, catch, cheat, chisel, con, convince, cozen, deceive, defraud, delude, diddle, double-cross, dupe, entice, euchre, exploit, fake, finesse, fleece, flimflam, fool, gull, gyp, hoax, hocus-pocus, hoodwink, hornswoggle, humbug, hustle, induce, inveigle, jockey, juggle, lure, manipulate, misguide, misinform, mislead, mulct, outthink, outwit, play, pretend, rook, scam, schmooze, seduce, shave, shortchange, skin, snooker, snow, spoof, squeeze, stick, sting, sucker, swindle, tease, trick, victimize* (≠ admit, assume, believe, blab, blurt, confess, confide, confront, debunk, detect, disabuse, disclose, disenchant, disillusion, divulge, expose, help, investigate, offer, protect, prove, respect, reveal, show, tell, trust, uncloak, uncover, undeceive, unmask, unveil, verify, wrong)

BEJEWEL (+): *accessorize, adorn, array, beautify, bedazzle, bedeck, bedizen, bestow, blazon, brighten, deck, decorate, elaborate, embellish, emblaze, enhance, enrich, fancify, festoon, flatter, garnish, gem, gild, glamorize, glitter, glitz, grace, gussy, hang, illuminate, impearl, improve, jewel, ornament, pearl, prettify, pretty, provide, redecorate, redo, revamp, set, stud, swag, tinsel, transfigure, transform, trim, upgrade* (≠ bare, befoul, blemish, blot, blotch, damage, darken, deface, denude, dirty, disfigure, disgrace, distort, divest, dull, efface, expose, harm, harshen, mar, muddy, obscure, roughen, scar, shame, simplify, smear, smudge, soil, spoil, stain, streamline, strip, sully, tarnish, uncover, vandalize)

BELABOR (→): *abuse, assail, assault, attack, bash, baste, bat, batter, beat, belt, beset, birch, blackjack, bludgeon, box, buffet, bust, cane, chop, clobber, clout, club, cowhide, crack, cudgel, cuff, curry, drub, flagellate, flay, flog, gore, hammer, hide, hit, horsewhip, jump, knock, lace, lacerate, lash, lather, lick, maim, mangle, maul, mutilate, paddle, paste, pelt, pistol-whip, pommel, pound, pummel, punch, raid, rawhide, rough, rush, sauce, scourge, slam, slap, slate, smack, smash, sock, spank, storm, strap, strike, swat, swipe, switch, tan, thrash, thresh, thump, thwack, wallop, whack, whale, wham, whip, whomp, whup, wound* (≠ assist, benefit, bless, buffer, cherish, conserve, consider, defend, favor, guard, heal, help, nurture, please, pleasure, preserve, protect, rescue, respect, safeguard, save, shield, sustain, tend)

BELABOR (→): *accent, accentuate, amplify, assert, deepen, emphasize, enforce, escalate, exaggerate, explain, flag, foreground, hammer, heighten, highlight, increase, insist, intensify, magnify, mark, outweigh, overemphasize, overestimate, overstate, punctuate, reiterate, sharpen, spotlight, stress, underline, underscore, weight* (≠ belittle, blur, bury, cloak, conceal, decrease, deemphasize, -deny, diminish, -discount, disguise, dismiss, disparage, -disregard, downplay, forget, hide, -ignore, lessen, marginalize, mask, minimize, -neglect, obscure, -omit, -overlook, pass, reduce, -slight, slur, subdue, trivialize, undercut, underemphasize, understate, weaken)

BELABOR (/): *abuse, affront, assail, attack, badmouth, bash, belittle, berate, blackguard, blaspheme, blast, boo, castigate, chastise, chide, criticize, curse, disparage, excoriate, execrate, fulminate, harangue, harass, harry, imprecate, insult, jump, lambaste, lash, libel, profane, rebuke, reprimand, reprove, resent, revile, savage, scathe, scold, slam, slander, slur, traduce, trash, vilify, vituperate, whip* (≠ acclaim, applaud, cheer, comfort, commend, compliment, congratulate, defend, delight, desire, encourage, esteem, flatter, gratify, hail, honor, idolize, inspire, laud, lionize, praise, prize, revere, treasure, uphold, venerate, vindicate)

BELIEVE (+): *accept, account, accredit, anticipate, assume, await, buy, conclude, conjecture, consider, consult, credit, decide, deduce, expect, fancy, gather, guess, imagine, infer, judge, predetermine, presume, reason, reckon, suppose, surmise, suspect, swallow, take, trust, understand* (≠ challenge, cross-examine, debate, debunk, disbelieve, discredit, dispute, distrust, double-deal, doubt, dread, fear, grill, imply, insinuate, interrogate, interview, mistrust, question, -reject, scruple, suspect) **(¿) ABSTRACTION ALERT. Concrete goals essential!**

BELITTLE (/): *abase, abuse, badmouth, bastardize, beguile, belittle, blister, boo, censure, cheapen, condemn, contaminate, corrupt, criticize, critique, debase, debauch, decry, deemphasize, defame, defile, degrade, demean, demote, denigrate, denounce, deprecate, deride, desecrate, devalue, diminish, -discount, discredit, disfavor, disgrace, dishonor, dismiss, disparage, disrespect, downgrade, downplay, humble, humiliate, insult, knock, lower, malign, minimize, mortify, neg, pan, patronize, pooh-pooh, reduce, rip, roast, scold, scorch, -scorn, shame, slam, slander, slur, smear, soil, squelch, stain, sully, taint, traduce, underestimate, underrate, undervalue, vilify, vilipend, violate, wrong* (≠ accentuate, acclaim, acknowledge, advance, affirm, aggrandize, apotheosize, applaud, approve, blandish, boost, brave, brook, canonize, celebrate, commend, compliment, congratulate, countenance, deify, dignify, elevate, encourage, endorse, ennoble, enshrine, eulogize, exalt, extol, face, favor, flannel, flatter, glorify, gratify, hail, heroicize, heroize, highlight, honor, idealize, idolize, ingratiate, laud, magnify, praise, prioritize, promote, raise, recognize, recommend, romanticize, salute, sanction, sentimentalize, spotlight, tout, uplift, venerate)

BEND (←): *affect, alter, bribe, compel, convince, direct, incline, induce, influence, maneuver, manipulate, modify, mold, persuade, predetermine, prejudice, shape, subdue, sway* (≠ allow, -deter, discourage, dissuade, enable, follow, hamper, hamstring, hinder, honor, impede, inhibit, mind, obey, permit, repel, restrain)

BEND (/): *adapt, adjust, angle, arch, bend, bow, break, buckle, circle, contort, crimp, crinkle, crook, crumple, curl, dangle, deflect, deform, distort, divert, double, flex, fold, hang, hook, incline, lean, loop, pervert, refract, ripple, roll, round, spiral, swerve, tilt, turn, twist, unsmooth, warp, wiggle, wilt, wind, wriggle, wrinkle, zigzag* (≠ align, correct, flatten, iron, level, realign, rectify, right, smooth, straighten, unbend, uncoil, uncrumple, uncurl, unfold, unroll, untwist)

BENEFIT (+): *advance, advantage, aid, ameliorate, assist, better, build, content, delight, enhance, enrich, favor, flavor, further, gain, gladden, grace, gratify, help, improve, optimize, outlay, overhaul, overpay, pay, please, profit, promote, rarefy, rectify, refine, relieve, satisfy, season, serve, spice, strengthen, succor* (≠ afflict, cheat, condemn, cripple, damage, deceive, destroy, discredit, disfavor, disgrace, distress, doom, hamper, handicap, harm, hinder, hurt, impair, impede, inhibit, injure, paralyze, ruin, short-circuit, underpay, upset, wound, wreck)

BEQUEATH (→): *allot, allow, assign, assist, attribute, award, bankroll, bestow, commit, consign, contribute, deed, deliver, devise, devote, disburse, dispense, dole, donate, dower, endow, entrust, expend, extend, fund, furnish, give, grant, help, impart, lavish, leave, legate, lend, mete, offer, outlay, overpay, pass, pay, pledge, present, provide, ration, render, send, serve, share, shower, submit, supply, tender, tithe, transfer, transmit, volunteer, will* (≠ accept, acquire, attain, bogart, cheat, claim, -deny, deprive, disinherit, -disown, earn, extract, find, gain, harvest, hoard, inherit, keep, make, obtain, pilfer, poach, procure, purloin, receive, remove, rob, secure, steal, swipe, take, win, withdraw, withhold)

BERATE (/): *abuse, admonish, advise, assail, attack, badmouth, belittle, blame, blast, browbeat, bully, castigate, caution, censure, chastise, chide, condemn, correct, counsel, criticize, crucify, demean, demonize, denigrate, denounce, discipline, disparage, diss, excoriate, exhort, fault, flay, fulminate, hammer, harangue, impugn, jeer, keelhaul, knock, lambaste, lash, lecture, mock, pan, persecute, pillory, punish, rag, rail, rate, ream, rebuke, reprimand, reproach, reprove, revile, ridicule, scold, score, -scorn, scourge, slam, slate, upbraid, vilify, vituperate, warn, wrong, zap* (≠ approve, blandish, cajole, coax, compliment, congratulate, endorse, extol, flannel, flatter, gratify, honor, idolize, ingratiate, lionize, pacify, placate, praise, revere, sanction, sweet-talk, venerate)

BESEECH (←): *accost, address, approach, ask, beg, besiege, bilk, buttonhole, cadge, claim, coerce, command, compel, covet, crave, demand, desire, entreat, exhort, extort, force, implore, importune, insist, invoke, mooch, panhandle, petition, plead, pray, request, require, scrounge, seek, solicit, sponge, sue, supplicate, target, urge* (≠ answer, appease, comfort, conciliate, console, content, -deny, fulfill, grace, gratify, hint, imply, intimate, mollify, oblige, pacify, placate, please, quiet, -refuse, satisfy, -scorn, -spurn, suggest)

BESIEGE (→): *assail, assault, attack, badger, barrage, barricade, beleaguer, beset, block, blockade, bombard, bother, bug, buttonhole, confine, congregate, crowd, encircle, encompass, envelop, harass, harry, hassle, hound, importune, insulate, invest, isolate, mortar, nag, oppress, outlast, overload, overwhelm, pester, plague, quarantine, sandbag, sap, surround, swamp, torment, trouble, worry* (≠ aid, armor, befriend, comfort, defend, deliver, emancipate, free, help, liberate, mollify, oblige, pacify, placate, protect, quiet, release, rescue, resist, shelter, shield, withstand)

BESMIRCH (/): *abase, abuse, bait, bastardize, belittle, besmear, besmirch, blackguard, boo, canker, contaminate, corrupt, debase, debauch, defame, defile, deflower, degrade, demean, demote, desecrate, devalue, diminish, disgrace, dishonor, embarrass, humble, humiliate, hurt, incriminate, injure, insult, libel, lower, malign, mortify, offend, outrage, pervert, -rebuff, reduce, ridicule, shame, -shun, slander, -slight, slur, -snub, soil, spoil, stain, suborn, sully, taint, taunt, trample, violate, wound, wrong* (≠ admire, applaud, benefit, bless, clean, cleanse, clear, commend, compliment, congratulate, dignify, elevate, enhance, enshrine, exalt, flannel, flatter, gratify, hallow, honor, improve, launder, lionize, moralize, praise, purify, revere, sanctify, treasure, worship)

BESMIRCH (/): *bedraggle, befoul, begrime, blacken, confuse, contaminate, daub, defile, dirty, disarrange, disarray, discolor, dishevel, disorder, draggle, foul, grime, jumble, mess, mire, muck, muddle, muddy, pollute, smirch, smudge, soil, stain, sully, taint, untidy* (≠ brighten, brush, clean, cleanse, decontaminate, delouse, deodorize, disinfect, dry-clean, dust, freshen, launder, mop, purge, purify, renew, rinse, sanitize, scour, scrub, spruce, straighten, sweep, tidy, wash, wipe)

BEST (→): *ace, annihilate, beat, better, blast, bomb, break, bulldoze, bury, cap, checkmate, clobber, conquer, cream, crush, deck, defeat, dispatch, drub, dwarf, eclipse, exceed, finish, flatten, floor, hammer, lambaste, lick, master, one-up, outclass, outdistance, outdo, outfight, outguess, outgun, outlast, outmaneuver, outpace, outperform, outplay, outrace, outrank, outreach, outrun, outsell, outshine, outslick, outsmart, outstrip, outthink, outweigh, outwit, overcome, overpower, overshadow, overtake, overthrow, overwhelm, pass, rout, ruin, score, shame, shellac, skin, skunk, slaughter, smoke, steamroller, stop, subdue, subjugate, surmount, surpass, sweep, take, thrash, top, topple, total, transcend, trash, trim, trounce, trump, unhorse, unseat, upend, upset, upstage, vanquish, wallop, waste, wax, whip, whomp, win, wipe, wrack, wreck, zap* (≠ aggrandize, aid, amplify, assist, augment, -avoid, back, bolster, bomb, boost, botch, brave, bungle, cede, coach, comfort, concede, defend, defer, develop, elevate, encourage, enhance, enlarge, exalt, expand, extend, extol, face, fail, flub, flunk, follow, forfeit, fumble, glorify, guard, heighten, help, highlight, hype, improve, increase, instruct, magnify, maximize, mind, nurture, obey, plug, promote, protect, publicize, -quit, raise, release, relinquish, -renounce, serve, showcase, stomach, submit, suffer, support, surrender, survive, train, uplift, weather, yield)

BESTOW (→): *accord, administer, aid, allot, apportion, assist, award, benefit, bequeath, commit, communicate, comp, confer, contribute, devote, dish, dispense, dispose, dole, donate, dower, endow, entrust, extend, feed, fuel, furnish, give, grant, hand, help, impart, issue, lavish, legate, mete, offer, overfeed, present, provide, regale, render, sacrifice, spare, tender, tithe, transmit, unspool, victual, volunteer, wreak* (≠ advance, -deny, deprive, disinherit, hoard, hold, inherit, keep, lend, leverage, loan, monetize, pocket, preserve, receive, retain, save, sell, take, withhold)

BET (→): *bid, chance, compromise, endanger, gamble, game, hazard, imperil, jeopardize, lay, offer, play, pledge, punt, risk, stake, trust, venture, wager* (≠ bank, conceal, defend, guard, hide, hoard, invest, lose, protect, restore, save, shield, win, withhold)

BETRAY (→): *advertise, air, announce, bare, bellow, blab, blaze, blurt, broadcast, circulate, communicate, concede, confess, confide, confirm, convince, declare, demonstrate, develop, disclose, discover, display, disseminate, divulge, evince, evolve, exhibit, expose, hype, impart, inform,* *leak, manifest, out, placard, plug, proclaim, project, publicize, publish, relate, represent, reveal, shout, show, showcase, signal, sound, spell, spill, squeal, suss, telegraph, tell, trumpet, uncloak, uncover, unfold, unlock, unmask, unveil* (≠ belie, bleep, camouflage, clothe, conceal, confront, costume, counterfeit, cover, disguise, distort, falsify, garble, gild, gloss, hide, hush, mask, misrepresent, obscure, quiet, rephrase, twist, varnish, veil, whitewash, withhold)

BETRAY (←): *-abandon, abdicate, abnegate, abuse, backstab, beguile, bilk, bluff, camouflage, cheat, con, counterfeit, cross, deceive, defraud, delude, -deny, -desert, disavow, discard, double-cross, double-deal, dupe, ensnare, entrap, falsify, finger, fool, forge, -forsake, gull, hocus-pocus, hoodwink, jilt, knife, misguide, mislead, outsmart, outwit, -reject, -renounce, retract, seduce, sucker, swindle, trick, two-time, underpay, victimize, wrong* (≠ aid, alert, assist, caution, defend, guard, help, honor, pity, protect, regret, repent, rue, safeguard, save, secure, shield, support, warn)

BETTER (+): *adapt, adjust, advance, alter, ameliorate, automate, benefit, calibrate, change, convert, correct, elevate, enhance, enrich, equalize, flavor, forward, further, help, improve, mend, modernize, optimize, overhaul, perfect, promote, raise, rarefy, realign, rectify, refine, reform, rephrase, restructure, revamp, revolutionize, right, season, shift, spice, transform, tune, tweak, update, upgrade* (≠ -abort, afflict, bastardize, bestialize, blemish, blight, damage, debase, freeze, harm, hurt, immobilize, impair, incapacitate, injure, paralyze, plague, stop, transfix, worsen)

BEWILDER (/): *amaze, astonish, astound, baffle, befuddle, bemuse, bother, cloud, confound, confuse, daze, disturb, dumbfound, embarrass, faze, floor, flummox, foil, forestall, gaslight, gobsmack, hobble, jumble, muddle, mystify, nonplus, obscure, outwit, perplex, puzzle, shock, stump, stun, stupefy, surprise, tangle, throw, -thwart, trouble* (≠ clarify, decipher, deduce, demonstrate, disentangle, edify, educate, explain, floodlight, illuminate, illustrate, instruct, profile, rephrase, reveal, school, simplify, solve, teach, train, tutor, untangle)

BEWITCH (→): *becharm, bespell, bind, brew, captivate, cast, charm, compel, conjure, constrain, curse, dazzle, dedicate, devise, devote, enchant, ensorcel, enthrall, entice, entrance, evoke, fascinate, force, glamour, hex, hoodoo, hypnotize, invoke, jinx, juggle, lure, maledict, mesmerize, possess, prophesy, seduce, spell, spellbind, strike, taint, tantalize, tempt, trigger, voodoo, weave, whammy, witch* (≠ aid, banish, bless, cleanse, consecrate, defend, disenchant, dislodge, dispel, dissipate, exorcise, expel, free, heal, liberate, protect, purge, purify, rectify, release, sanctify, shield, slake, unbind, ward)

BEWITCH (←): *allure, appropriate, arrest, attract, bait, beckon, beguile, candy-coat, captivate, capture, catch, charm, conquer, court, delight, disarm, draw, enamor, enchant, engage, engross, enrapture, ensnare, entangle, enthrall, entice, entrance, fascinate, grab, gratify, grip, hitch, hoodwink, hook, hypnotize, influence, interest, intrigue, invite, kill, lead,* *lure, magnetize, mesmerize, overtake, paralyze, please, pull, ravish, razzle-dazzle, seduce, seize, solicit, spellbind, strike, tangle, tantalize, tempt, thrill, transfix, transport, trap, win, woo, wow* (≠ aggravate, annoy, appall, badger, bore, bug, criticize, deplete, disenchant, disgust, dismay, displease, exasperate, exhaust, harass, hassle, horrify, insult, irk, irritate, lose, nag, nauseate, niggle, nitpick, offend, plague, -reject, repel, repulse, revolt, rile, sadden, sicken, tire, upset, vex, weary)

BID (→): *advance, bet, gamble, offer, play, present, propose, render, risk, spare, spitball, submit, tender, venture, volunteer, wager* (≠ accept, -deny, deprive, receive, -refuse, -reject, stiff, take, withhold)

BID (←): *ask, call, charge, command, conjure, demand, desire, direct, instruct, invite, order, request, require, solicit, summon, tell* (≠ allow, claim, command, defy, -deny, enforce, exact, extort, follow, mind, obey, permit, -refuse, serve, withstand)

BILK (←): *bamboozle, beat, beguile, betray, cheat, chisel, -circumvent, con, counterfeit, cozen, deceive, defraud, delude, diddle, disappoint, double-cross, dupe, entrap, euchre, falsify, fleece, flimflam, foil, fool, forge, frustrate, gull, hoax, hocus-pocus, manipulate, mislead, mulct, outwit, rook, ruin, scam, snooker, snow, sting, sucker, swindle, -thwart, trick, trim, victimize, wrong* (≠ accuse, aid, assist, assume, assure, believe, comp, compensate, confess, defend, donate, encourage, furnish, give, help, honor, indemnify, lose, offer, outbid, outlay, overpay, overspend, patronize, pay, protect, recoup, respect, supply, support)

BIND (→): *browbeat, bulldoze, bully, coerce, compel, daunt, dictate, dragoon, foment, force, frogmarch, galvanize, hijack, impel, incite, intimidate, march, motivate, muscle, muzzle, nag, oblige, order, prescribe, press, pressure, railroad, require, spark, steamroller, stimulate, stress, urge* (≠ allow, baffle, -balk, bar, block, check, convince, counteract, delay, foil, free, hamper, induce, let, obstruct, permit, persuade, -prevent, resist, stop, subvert, -thwart, unbind)

BIND (+): *affix, annex, attach, bale, betroth, bond, bracket, braid, buckle, capture, cement, chain, charm, clamp, clinch, commit, confine, connect, constrain, couple, cover, encumber, endear, engage, fasten, fix, fuse, glue, hinge, hitch, hold, join, juxtapose, knot, lace, lash, link, marry, merge, mortar, paste, plait, relate, rope, secure, splice, stay, stick, stitch, strap, string, suture, tether, tie, truss, unify, unite, weave, wed, weld, wrap, yoke, zip* (≠ break, cut, dissolve, divide, divorce, emancipate, free, liberate, loose, rend, rip, rupture, separate, sever, shred, slash, split, sunder, tatter, tear, unbind, unbrace, unbraid, unfasten, unlace, untie)

BIND (+): *attend, bandage, cover, cure, doctor, dress, heal, medicate, mend, nurse, rehabilitate, remedy, swaddle, swathe, treat, wrap* (≠ damage, expose, harm, hurt, injure, unbandage, uncover, unwrap)

BIND (/): *attach, band, belt, chain, cinch, clinch, coil, confine, constrain, constrict, cord, cuff, curb, enchain, encumber, enslave, entangle, fasten,* *fetter, gird, girdle, hamper, handcuff, hinder, hobble, hogtie, hold, impede, indenture, interlace, intertwine, interweave, iron, join, knot, lace, lash, leash, limit, link, manacle, pinion, restrain, restrict, rope, secure, shackle, snarl, straiten, strap, subjugate, tangle, tether, thread, tie, trammel, truss, twist, wind, wire* (≠ cut, detach, disengage, disentangle, emancipate, -escape, free, liberate, loose, open, razor, release, rescue, slice, unbind, uncoil, uncuff, undo, unfasten, unfetter, unhook, unlace, unlash, unleash, unlock, unravel, unshackle, unsnarl, unspool, unstrap, unstring, untangle, untether, unthread, untie, untwine, untwist, unwind)

BITE (/): *champ, chaw, chew, chomp, clamp, crunch, crush, cut, dispatch, eat, gnash, gnaw, grind, grip, gulp, gum, hold, masticate, munch, nibble, nip, nosh, peck, penetrate, pierce, pincer, pinch, rend, rip, ruminate, scrunch, seize, split, squeeze, tear, work, wound* (≠ defend, -disregard, guard, heal, -ignore, kiss, lick, protect, seal, shield, spit, stitch, stroke, swallow, unite)

BLACKBALL (/): *-abandon, ban, bar, blacklist, check, chop, cull, cut, debar, -decline, deep-six, -deny, disallow, disapprove, discard, discharge, disclaim, dismiss, disqualify, down, eject, eliminate, eradicate, excise, -exclude, exhaust, expel, fire, -forbid, -ignore, jettison, jilt, junk, kill, neg, -nix, -omit, oppugn, -ostracize, oust, -prohibit, proscribe, -refuse, -reject, relegate, -renounce, -repudiate, scrap, sideline, -snub, trash, -veto* (≠ admit, allow, appoint, approve, assign, boost, commission, confirm, designate, elect, embrace, encourage, greet, hail, high-five, host, include, invite, nominate, pass, praise, prioritize, ratify, receive, salute, sanction, support, task, welcome)

BLACKMAIL (←): *badger, bleed, bribe, bully, cheat, coerce, compel, cultivate, daunt, demand, exact, exploit, extort, fleece, force, frighten, gouge, induce, intimidate, leverage, manipulate, milk, muckrake, muscle, nobble, oblige, pressure, ransom, sandbag, scandalize, shake, shame, skin, squeeze, steamroller, suborn, swindle, terrorize, threaten, wrest, wring* (≠ broadcast, bury, buy, cloak, conceal, defy, exonerate, expose, give, hide, hush, out, pay, publicize, ransom, redeem, -refuse, rescue, reveal, save, vindicate)

BLAME (/): *accuse, admonish, allege, arraign, assail, attack, badmouth, belittle, berate, blast, boo, castigate, censure, charge, chasten, chastise, chide, clobber, condemn, criticize, crucify, decry, defame, defile, demean, demonize, denigrate, denounce, deprecate, deride, disapprove, discredit, disparage, drub, excoriate, fault, finger, flay, frame, gibbet, hammer, impeach, implicate, impugn, incriminate, inculpate, indict, keelhaul, knock, lambaste, lash, nag, pan, pillory, rebuke, -renounce, reprimand, reproach, reprove, resent, roast, saddle, scapegoat, scold, -scorn, skewer, skin, slam, slash, tax, tweak, upbraid, vilify* (≠ absolve, acclaim, acquit, alibi, applaud, approve, blandish, bless, cheer, clear, commend, credit, endorse, exalt, excuse, exonerate, extol, flatter, forgive, help, honor, ingratiate, justify, laud, pardon, praise, recommend, sanction, spare, thank, vindicate)

BLAST (→): *blaze, cast, catapult, discharge, fire, fling, heave, hurl, hurtle, launch, lob, loose, pelt, pepper, pitch, project, propel, shoot, sling, snipe, throw, toss, wing* (≠ catch, defend, deflect, drag, ease, hamper, heal, hold, holster, impede, nurse, receive, shield)

BLAST (→): *abuse, affront, assail, attack, badmouth, bash, beat, belabor, belittle, berate, blackguard, blaspheme, castigate, chastise, chide, clobber, criticize, critique, curse, defame, disparage, drub, excoriate, execrate, flay, fulminate, harangue, harass, harry, imprecate, impugn, insult, jump, lambaste, libel, lick, profane, rebuke, reprimand, reprove, revile, savage, scalp, scathe, scold, shellac, slam, slander, slate, slur, traduce, upbraid, vilify, vituperate, whip, zap* (≠ acclaim, approve, back, boost, commend, compliment, contradict, counter, defend, hail, honor, praise, promote, retort, uphold)

BLAST (/): *annihilate, assail, atomize, attack, blight, blow, bomb, break, burst, collapse, crack, damage, dash, decimate, demolish, destroy, detonate, discharge, doom, dynamite, explode, fracture, fragment, injure, kill, pop, pulverize, ruin, rupture, shatter, shrivel, smash, splinter, spoil, strike, stunt, torpedo, vaporize, wither, wreck* (≠ aid, armor, build, defend, erect, guard, implode, mend, raise, repair, rescue, restore, salvage, save, secure, shield, survive, sustain, weather, withstand)

BLEED (←): *blackmail, burgle, cannibalize, confiscate, consume, defalcate, deplete, depredate, drain, embezzle, empty, exhaust, extort, extract, fleece, gazump, impoverish, leach, leech, milk, overcharge, pauperize, reduce, rob, rook, sap, skin, squeeze, steal, stick, strong-arm, suck, tap* (≠ comfort, douse, earn, fill, infuse, inject, inundate, protect, reassure, recoup, recover, replenish, restore, staunch, swamp)

BLEMISH (/): *abase, adulterate, bastardize, bedraggle, begrime, besmear, besmirch, bestialize, blacken, blot, blur, botch, bungle, canker, chagrin, chasten, cheapen, cloud, compromise, contaminate, corrupt, crucify, curse, damn, darken, debase, debauch, debilitate, decay, defame, defile, deform, degrade, demean, demoralize, deprave, depress, desecrate, destroy, deteriorate, dirty, discolor, discredit, disgrace, dishonor, distort, embarrass, foul, -frustrate, hamper, hamstring, harshen, humble, humiliate, impair, incriminate, infect, infest, jinx, lessen, lower, malign, mar, mishandle, mock, monkey-wrench, mortify, -nullify, pervert, poison, pollute, prejudice, reduce, ruin, sabotage, shame, shrivel, sink, smear, smirch, smudge, soil, spoil, stain, stale, suborn, subvert, sully, taint, tar, tarnish, touch, trash, twist, undercut, undermine, violate, vitiate, warp, weaken, wither, wreck* (≠ adorn, advance, aggrandize, aid, alibi, apotheosize, assist, augment, benefit, better, bless, boost, build, buoy, burnish, cleanse, clear, decontaminate, defend, dignify, distinguish, elevate, encourage, enhance, ennoble, enrich, enshrine, exalt, exonerate, fancify, fix, glorify, guard, hallow, help, honor, improve, lionize, magnify, moralize, optimize, praise, promote, protect, purify, quarantine, raise, rarefy, rectify, refine, sanctify, serve, service, support, upgrade, uplift, vindicate)

BLEMISH (/): *abrade, afflict, annihilate, bang, bash, batter, blast, blight, blister, bloody, blot, blotch, blur, break, bruise, callous, check, chip, clobber, coarsen, crab, crack, crimp, cripple, crush, damage, dash, decimate, deface, deform, demolish, dent, desolate, destroy, deteriorate, devastate, ding, disable, discolor, disease, disfigure, distort, doom, dot, efface, enervate, enfeeble, erode, flaw, fleck, fracture, freckle, gash, gouge, hack, hamstring, harm, harshen, hurt, impair, inflict, injure, kink, lacerate, lame, maim, mangle, mar, mark, mutilate, nick, nock, notch, pockmark, pulverize, raze, ruin, rust, scalp, scar, scathe, score, scour, scourge, scrape, scratch, scuff, shatter, slit, smash, snag, speck, split, splotch, spoil, spot, stain, strike, taint, tarnish, tear, torment, torture, total, twist, undermine, vandalize, vitiate, waste, weaken, wear, welt, wound, wreck, wrinkle, zap* (≠ adorn, ameliorate, beautify, better, cure, decorate, doctor, edit, embellish, enhance, enrich, fix, glamorize, glitz, grace, heal, help, improve, mend, optimize, ornament, overhaul, patch, perfect, polish, rarefy, rebuild, recondition, reconstruct, rectify, refine, regret, rehabilitate, remedy, remodel, renovate, repair, revamp, revise, shine, tinsel, tool, weather, withstand)

BLEND (+): *add, alloy, amalgamate, beat, cement, churn, coalesce, collage, combine, commingle, composite, compound, concrete, conflate, conjoin, emulsify, fold, froth, fuse, homogenize, hybridize, incorporate, integrate, intermingle, intermix, intertwine, interweave, join, knit, link, meld, merge, mingle, mix, reintegrate, reunite, stir, synthesize, toss, unify, unite, weave, weld, whisk* (≠ break, cleave, detach, diffuse, disengage, disjoin, disperse, dissolve, disunite, divide, divorce, filter, isolate, orphan, part, purify, rupture, scatter, seclude, separate, sever, split, sunder, unmix)

BLESS (→): *accord, award, bequeath, bestow, boast, boost, clothe, confer, convey, cover, deliver, dispense, donate, empower, enable, endow, enhance, enrich, equip, favor, fund, furnish, gift, grant, heal, heighten, help, impart, improve, invest, leave, mend, offer, optimize, present, provide, restore, secure, spare, supply, support, tender, tithe, volunteer, will* (≠ bankrupt, beggar, blight, cannibalize, consume, -deny, deplete, depredate, deprive, diminish, discredit, disfavor, disgrace, disinherit, -disown, dispossess, divest, drain, exhaust, hoard, impoverish, keep, leach, leech, overextend, ruin, sap, scant, skimp, starve, stint, strip, tax, withdraw, withhold, wreck)

BLESS (+): *anoint, baptize, canonize, chasten, cleanse, commend, commit, consecrate, dedicate, devote, elevate, eulogize, exalt, exorcise, expurgate, extol, glorify, hallow, honor, laud, magnify, moralize, ordain, praise, purify, rarefy, reconsecrate, refine, sacrifice, sanctify, spiritualize, thank, worship* (≠ blaspheme, condemn, curse, cuss, damn, deconsecrate, defile, desacralize, desanctify, desecrate, dirty, doom, execrate, foul, pollute, profane, punish, soil, taint, violate)

BLIGHT (/): *afflict, annihilate, blast, blemish, blotch, botch, bruise, bungle, canker, contaminate, corrupt, crimp, cripple, crush, curse, damage, damn, dash, debilitate, decay, deface, defile, deform, deprave, desecrate,* *destroy, ding, disappoint, discolor, disease, disfigure, distort, doom, fracture, frost, -frustrate, hamper, hamstring, hurt, impair, infect, infest, inflict, injure, jinx, kill, mangle, mar, mishandle, monkey-wrench, mutilate, -nullify, pervert, poison, pollute, ruin, rust, sabotage, scar, scathe, shatter, shrivel, slash, slit, smash, snag, spoil, spot, stain, strike, taint, torment, trash, undercut, undermine, violate, vitiate, weaken, wither, wizen, wreck, wrinkle, zap* (≠ adorn, advance, aggrandize, aid, ameliorate, amend, assist, augment, benefit, better, bless, boost, build, burnish, cleanse, clear, decontaminate, defend, dignify, distinguish, elevate, encourage, enhance, ennoble, enrich, enshrine, exalt, exonerate, fancify, fix, flavor, glorify, guard, hallow, heal, help, honor, improve, lionize, magnify, mend, optimize, ornament, praise, promote, protect, purify, quarantine, raise, rarefy, rectify, refine, repair, sanctify, season, serve, service, spice, support, survive, sustain, upgrade, uplift, vindicate, weather, withstand)

BLIND (/): *baffle, bedazzle, blindfold, confuse, daze, dazzle, deceive, distract, gaslight, intimidate, mislead, overpower, overwhelm, stun, trap, trick, wow* (≠ bare, clarify, conceal, depict, edify, educate, explain, expose, floodlight, guide, illuminate, reveal, show, teach)

BLINDSIDE (→): *accost, ambush, assail, assault, attack, bushwhack, buttonhole, capture, catch, charge, corner, ensnare, entrap, fool, hit, hunt, impugn, intercept, invade, jump, mousetrap, mug, net, rush, sandbag, seize, snare, stalk, stampede, storm, strike, sucker-punch, surprise, tackle, trap, waylay* (≠ alert, announce, broadcast, caution, confess, confide, confirm, daunt, display, divulge, expose, forewarn, menace, notify, publicize, reveal, taunt, telegraph, threaten, warn)

BLOCK (/): *-abort, accost, anticipate, arrest, -balk, ban, bar, barricade, blockade, check, choke, clog, close, confound, confront, congest, cordon, cover, curb, dam, delay, -deter, forestall, -frustrate, gag, -halt, hamper, handicap, hinder, impede, inhibit, intercept, obscure, obstruct, occlude, pause, plug, preempt, -prohibit, proscribe, restrain, restrict, scotch, screen, seal, shackle, shelve, short-circuit, stall, stem, stonewall, stop, stopper, stump, stymie, tackle, -thwart, wrestle* (≠ await, benefit, boost, brainstorm, breach, break, catalyze, clear, crack, expose, free, frogmarch, goad, help, instigate, legalize, loosen, march, midwife, open, oxygenate, prioritize, release, spur, stimulate, unblock, ventilate)

BLOT (+): *absorb, anonymize, clean, cleanse, clear, dry, erase, mop, polish, purify, remove, scour, scrub, shine, sponge, swab, towel, wash, wipe* (≠ bathe, cover, dampen, dirty, douse, mark, moisten, overdo, rinse, soak, stain, wet)

BLOT (/): *bedraggle, befoul, bespatter, blacken, blemish, defile, dirty, discolor, disfigure, disgrace, draggle, foul, grime, harshen, mar, mark, mire, muck, muddy, smudge, smut, soil, spatter, spoil, spot, stain, stipple, streak, sully, taint, tar, tarnish* (≠ beautify, benefit, brighten, brush, clean, cleanse, clear, glamorize, glitz, grace, groom, launder, mop, prettify, purify, rinse, scour, scrub, spruce, wash, wipe)

BLUDGEON (→): *assail, assault, attack, bash, baste, bat, batter, beat, belabor, belt, beset, birch, blackjack, box, brain, bruise, buffet, bust, cane, chop, clobber, clout, club, concuss, conk, cowhide, crack, crush, cudgel, cuff, deck, defeat, drub, flog, hammer, hide, hit, injure, knock, lace, lambaste, lash, lather, lick, maim, mangle, maul, overcome, overemphasize, overpower, paddle, pelt, pistol-whip, pommel, pound, pulverize, pummel, punch, scourge, skull, slam, slate, smack, smash, strike, swat, swipe, switch, tan, thrash, thump, thwack, wallop, whack, whale, wham, whip, whomp, whup, wound* (≠ absorb, armor, -avoid, block, caress, counter, defend, deflect, -disregard, -escape, guard, -ignore, miss, parry, -prevent, protect, -rebuff, repel, rescue, resist, shield, stroke, strum, survive, tap, weather, withstand)

BLUFF (←): *bamboozle, beguile, betray, bleed, blind, buffalo, bullshit, burn, catch, cheat, chisel, con, convince, counterfeit, cozen, deceive, defraud, delude, diddle, double-cross, dupe, euchre, fake, fleece, fool, gull, hoax, hocus-pocus, hoodwink, humbug, hustle, jive, juggle, kid, lull, manipulate, misguide, misinform, mislead, mulct, pretend, rook, scam, schmooze, shortchange, skin, snooker, snow, spoof, squeeze, stick, sting, sucker, swindle, tease, trick* (≠ accuse, assume, authenticate, authorize, believe, certify, clarify, confess, confirm, debunk, disabuse, disclose, disenchant, disillusion, divulge, ensure, expose, guarantee, prove, rephrase, reveal, secure, show, substantiate, tell, trust, uncloak, uncover, undeceive, unmask, unveil, validate, verify)

BLUFF (←): *act, affect, assume, camouflage, clothe, conceal, convince, costume, counterfeit, disguise, dissimulate, fake, feign, forge, imitate, impersonate, make-believe, mask, play, playact, pose, pretend, profess, roleplay, simulate* (≠ authenticate, betray, communicate, confess, confront, convince, corroborate, demonstrate, disclose, discover, distinguish, divulge, endorse, evince, finger, flaunt, identify, nail, reveal, show, suss, uncloak, uncover, undress, unmask, unveil, validate, warrant)

BLUNT (/): *abate, allay, alleviate, anesthetize, attenuate, buffer, cauterize, cripple, damp, dampen, deaden, debilitate, decrease, desensitize, diminish, disable, dull, ease, enfeeble, lessen, lighten, lower, minimize, mitigate, moderate, muffle, mute, numb, reduce, round, sabotage, sap, soften, subdue, subvert, taper, underemphasize, undermine, weaken* (≠ accentuate, aim, amplify, animate, arouse, augment, boost, consolidate, deepen, develop, edge, emphasize, enhance, exaggerate, flavor, grind, heighten, hone, increase, intensify, magnify, marinate, maximize, needle, optimize, overdramatize, point, punctuate, rarefy, rectify, redouble, refine, season, sharpen, spice, stimulate, strengthen, whet)

BLUR (/): *becloud, befog, blear, blind, camouflage, cloak, clothe, cloud, complicate, conceal, confuse, cover, curtain, daze, dazzle, discompose, disguise, dishevel, disorder, dull, elaborate, entangle, fog, hide, implicate, jumble, mask, mist, muddle, muddy, obfuscate, obscure, perplex, scramble, snarl, soften, tangle, veil* (≠ analyze, clarify, clear, concentrate, decipher, decode, deduce, expose, focus, illuminate, reveal, sharpen, simplify, streamline, uncloud, uncover, unravel, unscramble, unveil)

BLUR (/): *bedim, besmirch, blacken, blemish, blot, blotch, cloud, darken, dim, dirty, discolor, eclipse, fog, haze, mist, obliterate, obscure, overshadow, screen, shade, shadow, shroud, smear, smudge, spot, stain, taint, tarnish* (≠ brighten, clarify, clean, cleanse, clear, illuminate, light, lighten, purify, rinse, shine)

BOLSTER (+): *aid, assist, augment, back, boost, brace, bulwark, buoy, buttress, carry, champion, condone, cushion, defend, egg, encourage, endorse, energize, enhance, favor, feed, force-feed, fortify, foster, fuel, guard, help, increase, inspire, kindle, maintain, motivate, nourish, nurse, nurture, patronize, pillow, prioritize, promote, prop, protect, ratify, reassure, reinforce, safeguard, sanction, second, secure, sponsor, stabilize, stay, strengthen, supplement, support, sustain, uphold* (≠ attack, betray, block, boobytrap, checkmate, corrode, counteract, decrease, -deny, destabilize, discredit, disfavor, dissolve, erode, foil, half-ass, hamstring, harm, hinder, -ignore, impede, injure, monkey-wrench, obstruct, -prevent, protest, sabotage, scupper, shelve, skim, stop, strip, stymie, -thwart, undercut, undermine, weaken)

BOLT (←): *consume, cram, devour, gobble, gorge, gulp, guzzle, inhale, scarf, seize, stuff, swallow, swill, wolf* (≠ belch, discard, disgorge, eject, empty, expel, nibble, peck, pick, -refuse, -reject, spew, spit, vomit)

BOLT (/): *bar, barricade, block, chain, close, cover, deadbolt, fasten, fortify, hinder, impede, latch, lock, obstruct, pin, protect, reinforce, rivet, screw, seal, secure, shut* (≠ admit, invite, loose, loosen, obtain, open, prize, pry, receive, release, unbolt, unfasten, unhook, unlock, welcome)

BOMBARD (→): *ambush, annoy, assail, assault, attack, barrage, batter, beset, besiege, blast, blindside, blitz, blitzkrieg, bomb, bother, bushwhack, catapult, catechize, club, cross-examine, debrief, deluge, demand, devastate, examine, flood, fusillade, grill, harass, hassle, hit, hound, interrogate, interview, inundate, launch, pelt, pester, pound, probe, pump, query, question, quiz, raid, rake, ravage, sandbag, shell, shower, stone, strafe, strike, swamp, torpedo, zap* (≠ armor, assist, conceal, cover, defend, deflect, disguise, harbor, hide, keep, nurture, parry, preserve, protect, repair, repel, save, screen, secure, shelter, shield, support)

BOOK (←): *arrange, bag, bespeak, calendar, charter, commit, contract, earmark, engage, hire, lease, order, organize, pencil, plan, prearrange, procure, program, promise, rent, reserve, retain, schedule* (≠ -abandon, -abort, abrogate, axe, -cancel, -decline, -deny, drop, dump, fire, forfeit, -halt, kill, -nix, pass, postpone, reconsider, -rescind, revoke, scrap, shelve, terminate, withdraw)

BOOST (→): *accent, accentuate, accrue, add, advance, advocate, affirm, aid, amplify, assert, assist, augment, back, bolster, brace, broaden, build, buttress, compliment, condone, double, egg, elevate, emphasize,* *encourage, endorse, energize, enhance, enlarge, enrich, exhilarate, expand, extend, fatten, favor, flavor, fortify, foster, further, grow, heighten, help, increase, inflate, inspire, intensify, invigorate, kindle, lengthen, lift, magnify, marinate, maximize, motivate, multiply, nourish, optimize, overhaul, patronize, promote, provoke, punctuate, raise, refine, reinforce, resuscitate, revolutionize, reward, richen, sanction, season, second, spice, spur, stimulate, strengthen, support, treble, triple, upgrade, uplift, urge, widen* (≠ -balk, block, checkmate, condemn, criticize, critique, curtail, dampen, delay, demotivate, depress, -deter, diminish, discourage, discredit, disfavor, disgrace, dissuade, downplay, downsize, encumber, foil, -frustrate, -halt, hamper, hamstring, harm, hinder, hurt, impede, incapacitate, inhibit, injure, lessen, lower, minimize, monkey-wrench, muzzle, obstruct, pause, -prevent, protest, rarefy, reduce, restrain, sabotage, scotch, scupper, scuttle, shelve, short-circuit, shrink, silence, sink, slow, stall, stem, subvert, suppress, -thwart, undercut, underemphasize, undermine, weaken)

BOOT (→): *axe, banish, can, cashier, defenestrate, deport, discharge, dismiss, displace, dispossess, eject, evict, exile, exorcise, expatriate, expel, fire, jettison, kick, -ostracize, oust, pink-slip, release, remove, retire, rout, sack, shed, shove, terminate* (≠ accept, admit, appoint, entertain, gather, glean, harbor, hire, house, keep, lodge, receive, retain, room, shelter, take, welcome)

BORE (/): *afflict, anesthetize, annoy, badger, bother, cloy, deaden, debilitate, demoralize, demotivate, disable, discomfort, discourage, dishearten, dispirit, drag, drain, dull, earbash, enervate, enfeeble, exhaust, fatigue, frustrate, irk, irritate, jade, nag, needle, niggle, nitpick, numb, pester, plague, sedate, stultify, tire, tranquilize, trouble, tucker, vex, wear, weary, worry* (≠ absorb, amuse, animate, attract, beguile, bewitch, captivate, charm, divert, enchant, energize, engage, engross, enliven, entertain, enthrall, entice, excite, fascinate, galvanize, grip, interest, intrigue, invigorate, involve, mesmerize, motivate, please, razzle-dazzle, stimulate, woo) **(¿) ABSTRACTION ALERT. Concrete goals essential!**

BORROW (←): *acquire, appropriate, beg, bite, bum, cadge, charter, chisel, coopt, debit, deduct, filch, hire, lease, lift, mooch, negotiate, obtain, pawn, pilfer, pledge, poach, procure, rent, scrounge, secure, siphon, soak, source, sponge, take, tap, touch* (≠ -abandon, bequeath, buy, discard, -disown, earn, forfeit, -forsake, give, jettison, lend, loan, lose, outbid, own, pay, provide, purchase, receive, recoup, -reject, relinquish, return, sell, steal, supply, tithe)

BORROW (←): *absorb, acquire, adopt, affect, appropriate, arrogate, assimilate, assume, cherish, copy, cultivate, derive, domesticate, draw, embrace, emulate, espouse, follow, foster, heed, honor, imitate, incorporate, integrate, internalize, mimic, naturalize, nurture, pirate, plagiarize, pretend, prize, quote, raise, rear, simulate, treasure, use, usurp, utilize* (≠ -abandon, abjure, abnegate, coin, conceive, concoct, create, devise, discard, -disown, -forsake, invent, jettison, junk, originate, -reject, relinquish, -renounce, -repudiate, spitball, -spurn, surrender)

BOTCH (/): *blemish, blight, blow, bobble, boggle, bollix, bugger, bungle, butcher, damage, destroy, -disregard, distort, doom, drop, fail, flaw, flub, fluff, foozle, forget, foul, fumble, half-ass, harm, harshen, hurt, impair, injure, jumble, lose, louse, mangle, mar, misapply, miscalculate, miscarry, misconstrue, misdiagnose, mishandle, misjudge, mislay, mismanage, miss, mistake, misunderstand, mix, muddle, muff, murder, mutilate, -neglect, -omit, -overlook, ruin, scramble, screw, spoil, vitiate, wreck* (≠ accomplish, achieve, actualize, ameliorate, bemoan, better, claim, crest, diagnose, doctor, enhance, fix, flavor, help, improve, lament, manage, mourn, nail, optimize, overhaul, patch, perfect, recondition, rectify, refine, reform, regret, remedy, renovate, repair, revamp, revolutionize, rue, season, steady)

BOTHER (/): *afflict, affront, aggravate, aggrieve, agitate, alarm, anger, annoy, antagonize, arouse, badger, bait, bedevil, beleaguer, besiege, browbeat, bug, bully, bullyrag, burden, burn, chafe, chaff, concern, devil, disappoint, discomfort, discommode, discompose, disgust, dismay, displease, disquiet, dissatisfy, distract, distress, disturb, dizzy, dog, earbash, eat, enrage, envenom, exacerbate, exasperate, exercise, faze, fluster, freak, fret, frost, fuss, gall, get, goad, grate, hagride, harass, harry, hassle, heckle, hector, importune, incense, incommode, inconvenience, inflame, infuriate, insult, irk, irritate, jar, jeer, kid, madden, miff, mock, molest, nag, nauseate, needle, nettle, niggle, nitpick, nudge, offend, outrage, overset, peeve, perplex, persecute, perturb, pester, pique, plague, poke, prod, provoke, rag, rally, rankle, rasp, razz, repel, rib, ride, ridicule, rile, roast, roil, rouse, ruffle, scandalize, shock, sicken, slam, spite, tantalize, taunt, tease, tickle, torment, trouble, undo, unhinge, unsettle, upset, vex, worry* (≠ accommodate, amuse, appease, assuage, assure, benefit, bless, calm, charm, cheer, comfort, console, content, delight, entertain, gladden, grace, gratify, hush, lull, mellow, mollify, oblige, pacify, placate, please, pleasure, propitiate, quiet, reassure, relax, satisfy, sedate, settle, smooth, soothe, steady, still, sugarcoat, thrill, tranquilize, woo, wow)

BOTTLE (←): *bury, check, collar, conceal, contain, corner, cramp, curb, curtail, disguise, enclose, hide, hold, hush, inhibit, keep, leash, limit, obstruct, occlude, -prevent, -prohibit, repress, restrain, restrict, silence, smother, stifle, straiten, strangle, suppress, throttle, trap* (≠ affirm, blab, blurt, circulate, confess, confide, confirm, disgorge, divuige, ejaculate, eject, expel, expose, out, reveal, share, spew, unleash, vent, vomit)

BOUNCE (→): *brush, bump, contact, dribble, drop, graze, hit, kiss, nudge, ping, rake, reflect, ricochet, shave, sideswipe, skim, skip, sweep, throw, toss, touch* (≠ catch, clench, deflate, grasp, grip, hold, keep, pin, puncture)

BOUNCE (→): *advance, advocate, arrange, articulate, calculate, chart, contrive, cover, detail, develop, dispense, draft, examine, express, file, formulate, forward, frame, introduce, lay, lodge, map, move, nominate,* *offer, place, plan, plot, pose, present, proffer, propose, recommend, shape, sketch, slate, specify, spitball, state, submit, suggest, table, tender, test, verbalize, vocalize, volunteer, vote* (≠ -abandon, adopt, choose, chuck, determine, discard, dismiss, -ditch, drop, dump, jettison, kill, pick, -reject, relinquish, remove, -repudiate, retain, scrap, select, shed, slam, trash)

BOUNCE (/): *axe, boot, can, cashier, chuck, discharge, dismiss, downsize, dump, eject, fire, furlough, kick, oust, pink-slip, release, remove, retire, sack, separate, terminate, trim, unseat* (≠ contract, employ, engage, hire, keep, recruit, reemploy, rehire, retain, sign, subcontract)

BOX (→): *attack, batter, battle, bludgeon, buffet, challenge, clobber, clout, combat, cuff, deck, fight, hammer, hit, maul, pummel, punch, rap, slap, slug, smack, sock, strike, thump, wallop, whack* (≠ block, counter, defend, deflect, guard, parry, protect, shield)

BOX (←): *cage, case, coffin, confine, contain, corner, crate, encase, encircle, enclose, hold, house, include, pack, package, parcel, pen, pigeonhole, pin, seal, surround, trap, wrap* (≠ dispense, expose, lose, -omit, open, release, reveal, spread, unbox)

-BOYCOTT (→): *-avoid, ban, bar, black, blackball, blacklist, -cold-shoulder, disallow, embargo, -eschew, -exclude, -ignore, -ostracize, outlaw, -prohibit, proscribe, -refuse, -reject, -snub, -spurn, strike* (≠ advocate, buy, champion, defend, encourage, import, patronize, promote, request, support)

BRACE (+): *bandage, bear, bind, bolster, bolt, bulwark, buttress, carry, clinch, fasten, fortify, gird, patch, prepare, prop, ready, reinforce, secure, shore, shove, splint, stabilize, stay, steady, steel, strap, strengthen, support, sustain, tie, tighten, truss, undergird, underpin, uphold* (≠ attack, boobytrap, burden, compromise, damage, endanger, harm, imperil, injure, loosen, lumber, mar, rattle, roil, sabotage, scotch, scupper, scuttle, shake, subvert, threaten, undercut, undermine, unfasten, wag, weaken, weaponize)

BRAID (+): *baste, bind, blend, coil, complicate, compose, concoct, connect, construct, contrive, couple, create, dress, enlace, entwine, fabricate, fashion, fasten, fuse, groom, improvise, incorporate, integrate, interlace, intermingle, intertwine, interweave, join, knit, knot, lace, lash, link, loop, make, manufacture, merge, mix, plait, pleat, ply, raddle, ravel, sew, snake, spin, splice, style, tangle, tether, twine, twist, unite, weave, wind, wreathe* (≠ brush, comb, cut, disentangle, divide, rip, separate, shred, slice, smooth, split, tatter, tear, unbraid, uncoil, unravel, unsew, unspool, untangle, untwine, unwind)

BRAINWASH (+): *adjust, alter, catechize, coax, condition, convert, convince, drill, educate, enchant, enthrall, equip, familiarize, gaslight, groom, ground, impress, inculcate, indoctrinate, influence, infuse, instill, instruct, modify, mold, persuade, prepare, prime, program, propagandize, proselytize, retrain, school, season, shape, sway, teach, temper,* *train, transform, tune, weaponize* (≠ awaken, -cancel, clean, contradict, debunk, deprogram, discredit, disprove, erase, expose, extract, forget, keep, -negate, -prevent, protest, reprogram, rescue, save, stop)

BRAND (→): *besmirch, burn, cauterize, censure, claim, denounce, discredit, disgrace, engrave, etch, fix, grade, impress, imprint, incriminate, ingrain, label, mark, monogram, scar, scorch, sear, set, singe, stain, stamp, stigmatize, taint, trademark, typecast* (≠ absolve, acquit, anonymize, -avoid, blot, clean, clear, erase, exonerate, expunge, honor, mislabel, mistake, normalize, obliterate, scour, scrub, wash)

BRANDISH (→): *display, exhibit, expose, flash, flaunt, flourish, parade, raise, shake, show, sport, swing, swish, twirl, unsheathe, vaunt, wag, wave, wield* (≠ -abandon, bury, cloak, conceal, cover, disguise, guard, hide, holster, mask, obscure, protect, save, sheathe, veil)

BRAVE (→): *abide, accost, affront, approach, battle, bear, beard, brazen, breast, challenge, combat, confront, contact, corner, court, dare, defy, endure, face, fight, front, meet, oppose, race, repel, resist, risk, stand, stomach, suffer, support, sweat, tolerate, venture, weather, withstand, woo* (≠ -abandon, -avoid, -circumvent, depart, -dodge, dread, -duck, -elude, -escape, -eschew, -evade, fear, -flee, forfeit, hide, -reject, resist, shake, -shirk, -shun, -sidestep, skip, spare)

BREACH (→): *break, burst, bust, cleave, contravene, cross, defy, dismiss, disobey, -disregard, flout, fracture, -ignore, -neglect, offend, open, outrage, pooh-pooh, rend, resist, rupture, -scorn, shatter, -slight, split, subvert, traduce, transgress, violate, withstand* (≠ attend, follow, fulfill, heed, mark, mind, note, notice, obey, observe, preserve, regard, satisfy, serve)

BREAK (→): *beat, better, eclipse, exceed, outdo, outperform, outreach, outshine, outstrip, surpass, top, transcend, trespass* (≠ -abandon, concede, forfeit, lose, relinquish, -renounce, sacrifice, surrender)

BREAK (+): *analyze, annotate, ascertain, calculate, condense, convert, crack, decipher, decode, decrypt, deduce, delineate, descramble, detect, determine, diagnose, discover, distinguish, elucidate, explain, explore, extract, guess, hack, indicate, interpret, learn, paraphrase, peg, penetrate, probe, profile, read, relate, render, rephrase, resolve, restate, scrutinize, settle, solve, study, summarize, suss, test, transcribe, translate, unravel, unscramble, untangle* (≠ assume, baffle, cipher, code, conceal, confuse, cypher, -disregard, encipher, encode, encrypt, fake, fudge, garble, hide, -ignore, jumble, miscalculate, misconstrue, misdiagnose, misinterpret, misjudge, misread, mistake, mix, mystify, obscure, -overlook, perplex, puzzle, scramble, stymie) **(¿) ABSTRACTION ALERT. Concrete goals essential!**

BREAK (/): *atomize, batter, beat, bend, burst, bust, club, concuss, corrode, crack, cripple, crumble, crush, damage, defeat, demolish, destroy, disable, disintegrate, dissolve, divide, erode, fissure, fracture, fragment,* *harm, impoverish, incapacitate, injure, mutate, pulverize, reduce, rend, rive, ruin, separate, sever, shatter, shiver, smash, snap, splinter, split, strike, tear, warp, wound* (≠ adapt, adjust, alter, amend, attach, calibrate, clout, concoct, correct, craft, create, fashion, fix, improve, mend, overhaul, patch, realign, rebuild, rectify, remedy, repair, restore, retool, revamp, revise, right, sculpt, seal, splint, tweak, weaponize)

BREAK (/): *bankrupt, beggar, bleed, break, bust, cannibalize, confound, consume, cow, cripple, crush, degrade, demoralize, demote, deplete, depredate, destroy, disprove, disqualify, doom, downgrade, drain, enervate, enfeeble, exhaust, humiliate, impair, impoverish, incapacitate, outlast, overcome, pauperize, rebut, reduce, refute, ruin, shatter, squander, subdue, tame, torpedo, undermine, waste, weaken* (≠ augment, bolster, boost, budget, conserve, develop, elevate, energize, enhance, enrich, foster, improve, inspire, maintain, optimize, squirrel, stow, strengthen, support, sustain, upgrade)

BREW (+): *abet, activate, advance, boil, concoct, contrive, cook, cultivate, detonate, devise, encourage, energize, enliven, excite, ferment, fire, foment, forward, foster, further, galvanize, hatch, improvise, incite, inflame, infuse, inspire, instigate, invigorate, machinate, make, manipulate, motivate, nourish, nurture, pick, plan, plot, prepare, project, promote, provoke, quicken, rabble-rouse, raise, ready, rouse, scheme, set, soak, sow, steep, stew, stimulate, stir, trigger, vitalize* (≠ abate, allay, bridle, calm, check, constrain, curb, discourage, hold, hush, inhibit, lull, mellow, mollify, quiet, regulate, restrain, settle, soothe, still, stymie, subdue, tame, tranquilize)

BRIBE (←): *allure, approach, bait, beguile, betray, bewitch, buy, candy-coat, captivate, catch, charm, coax, convince, corrupt, decoy, dulcify, enchant, enmesh, ensnare, entice, entrap, fascinate, fix, flatter, grease, hamper, honey, induce, influence, ingratiate, instigate, inveigle, lubricate, lure, magnetize, motivate, nobble, oil, outlay, overpay, patronize, pay, persuade, pervert, recompense, reward, rope, seduce, snare, snow, soap, solicit, spur, square, suborn, subvert, sugar, sugarcoat, sweeten, syrup, tangle, tantalize, tempt, tip, trap* (≠ alert, blackmail, bully, caution, coerce, demand, embezzle, expose, extort, extract, forewarn, milk, muscle, railroad, -refuse, repulse, sandbag, squeeze, ward, warn)

BRIDGE (+): *affix, associate, attach, bestride, bind, broker, clamp, combine, compare, connect, correlate, couple, cross, fasten, fill, ford, fuse, hybridize, interlink, join, link, marry, navigate, negotiate, reach, relate, reunite, secure, span, straddle, synthesize, tie, traverse, unite, yoke* (≠ alienate, breach, cleave, contrast, detach, disaffect, disconnect, disjoin, disunite, divide, -exclude, isolate, juxtapose, leave, maroon, -ostracize, oust, seclude, separate, sever, split, strand, sunder, unfasten, widen)

BRIDLE (←): *arrest, break, check, conquer, constrain, contain, control, corral, curb, domesticate, dominate, govern, -halt, harness, hold, inhibit, leash, master, moderate, muzzle, overpower, repress, restrain, rule, snaffle, staunch, stem, stop, subdue, suppress, train, withhold* (≠ air, arouse, -avoid, circulate, discharge, disseminate, emancipate, evince, express, free, -ignore, incite, liberate, loose, lose, -neglect, provoke, release, rouse, spur, unchain, unleash, verbalize, vocalize)

BRIEF (+): *abridge, admonish, advertise, advise, advocate, announce, apprise, assert, broadcast, caution, clue, communicate, confess, consult, contextualize, counsel, cue, declare, direct, disclose, disseminate, divulge, edify, enlighten, epitomize, exhibit, explain, express, guide, inform, initiate, instruct, notify, orient, prepare, prime, proclaim, recapitulate, recommend, reveal, suggest, summarize, testify, uncloak, update, warn* (≠ bury, conceal, confuse, deceive, disorient, edit, forget, grill, harbor, hide, interrogate, mislead, misrepresent, muddle, obscure, perplex, puzzle, question, redact, withhold)

BRIGHTEN (+): *animate, boost, buoy, burnish, cheer, clear, console, elate, elevate, encourage, enhance, enliven, excite, exhilarate, gladden, hearten, ignite, illuminate, illumine, improve, inspire, intensify, invigorate, kindle, light, lighten, optimize, overhaul, please, polish, raise, rectify, refine, refurbish, revitalize, rouse, shine, stimulate, uplift* (≠ blacken, bore, complicate, darken, deepen, demotivate, depress, dim, discourage, dishearten, dissuade, dull, enervate, fade, -frustrate, shadow, stymie, tarnish, upset, weary, worsen)

BRING (→): *accompany, attend, bear, bootleg, buck, carry, cart, chauffeur, conduct, convey, convoy, courier, deliver, dispatch, distribute, drive, drop, escort, ferry, fetch, give, guide, hand, hand-carry, haul, heel, help, lead, lug, move, pack, pass, piggyback, pilot, remit, ride, schlep, send, shepherd, shoulder, show, shuttle, smuggle, steer, supply, take, tote, tour, transport, trek, truck, usher, waft, whisk* (≠ -abandon, clutch, covet, demand, -desert, -ditch, drop, dump, forget, -forsake, grab, guard, hoard, hog, hold, -ignore, keep, leave, lose, maroon, meet, monopolize, -neglect, -refuse, request, retain, seize, -shirk, -shun, skip, stash, stay, stint, take, withhold)

BRING (+): *advance, beget, begin, breed, catalyze, create, cultivate, decide, determine, develop, draw, educe, effect, effectuate, elicit, enact, encourage, engender, establish, extract, father, force, forward, foster, found, further, generate, inaugurate, induce, initiate, innovate, inspire, institute, introduce, invoke, launch, make, nourish, nurture, obtain, pioneer, produce, promote, prompt, provoke, render, set, spawn, start, work, yield* (≠ abolish, arrest, check, control, crush, curb, dampen, demolish, -deny, destroy, doom, eradicate, erase, extinguish, hamper, hinder, impede, inhibit, kill, limit, liquidate, -prevent, -prohibit, quash, quell, quench, repress, restrain, restrict, retard, smother, snuff, squash, squelch, stifle, still, subdue, suppress, -thwart, weed)

BROACH (→): *advance, air, allege, approach, cite, debate, discuss, express, interject, interrupt, introduce, mention, name, offer, place, propose, raise, spitball, submit, suggest, vent, ventilate, verbalize, vocalize, volunteer*

loosen, lose, open, part, prize, pry, pull, relax, release, remove, rest, separate, sever, slack, slacken, slice, sunder, tear, unbuckle, unbutton, unchain, undress, unfasten, unhitch, unhook, unlace, unlink, unlock, unrestrict, unseal, untie, unwrap, unzip, uproot, wrest, yank)

BUCKLE (/): *bend, break, bulge, collapse, compress, compromise, contort, corrugate, crease, crumple, crush, distort, endanger, fold, jeopardize, mangle, mutate, ripple, slacken, smash, twist, undermine, unsmooth, warp, weaken, wiggle, wriggle, wrinkle, yield* (≠ align, bear, bolster, brace, endure, flatten, iron, level, plane, press, resist, roll, smooth, steady, straighten, uncrumple, unfold, weather, withstand)

BUDGET (←): *afford, allocate, allot, allow, apportion, assign, calculate, chunk, conserve, cut, deal, dispense, distribute, divide, drizzle, earmark, economize, estimate, give, measure, mete, moderate, parcel, partition, plan, portion, ration, save, scant, schedule, scrape, scrimp, segment, set, share, skimp, slice, split, stint, sustain, time, trickle, withhold* (≠ circulate, confuse, disburse, dissipate, exceed, expend, fritter, gamble, lavish, muddle, overcommit, risk, spend, squander, surpass, waste)

BUFF (→): *brighten, brush, burnish, dress, finish, furbish, glaze, gloss, grind, hone, polish, pumice, rub, sand, sandpaper, scour, scrub, shine, smooth* (≠ abrade, callous, chafe, coarsen, damage, harshen, roughen, score, scuff, sully, tarnish)

BUFFALO (←): *baffle, bamboozle, beguile, bemuse, betray, bilk, bleed, bluff, bullshit, burn, catch, cheat, chisel, con, confound, confuse, convince, cozen, daze, deceive, defraud, delude, diddle, disconcert, disorient, dupe, fake, faze, fleece, floor, flummox, fool, gammon, gaslight, gull, hoax, hocus-pocus, hoodwink, hornswoggle, humbug, hustle, josh, juggle, kid, manipulate, misguide, misinform, mislead, mix, muddle, mystify, nonplus, outwit, overawe, perplex, pretend, puzzle, rephrase, rook, schmooze, shortchange, skin, snooker, snow, spoof, squeeze, stump, stupefy, sucker, swindle, tease, trick, underpay, wrong* (≠ assure, believe, bolster, calm, clarify, confess, confide, confirm, confront, debunk, disabuse, disclose, disenchant, disillusion, divulge, educate, enlighten, explain, expose, face, help, illustrate, misunderstand, protect, reassure, relieve, reveal, settle, show, stabilize, steady, trust, uncloak, uncover, undeceive, unmask, unveil)

BUFFER (+): *absorb, allay, alleviate, armor, assuage, baby, baffle, blunt, cocoon, coddle, cordon, cushion, dampen, deaden, defend, diminish, dull, ease, fill, gentle, guard, insulate, isolate, lessen, lighten, line, lubricate, mitigate, moderate, modulate, overprotect, pack, pad, protect, reduce, relieve, seclude, shield, soften, soundproof, stuff, suppress, sustain, temper, upholster, wad, weaken, wrap* (≠ attack, compromise, endanger, exacerbate, expose, harass, heighten, imperil, intensify, jeopardize, risk, sharpen, strip, threaten)

BUG (→): *abrade, affront, aggravate, agitate, anger, annoy, antagonize, badger, bait, blister, bother, buttonhole, chafe, chaff, devil, discomfort,* *discompose, disquiet, distress, disturb, earbash, eat, enrage, exasperate, exercise, freak, fret, frost, gall, get, grate, hagride, harass, harry, hassle, heckle, incense, infuriate, insult, irk, irritate, madden, miff, nag, needle, nettle, niggle, nitpick, noodge, offend, outrage, overset, peeve, persecute, perturb, pester, pique, plague, provoke, rankle, rasp, rile, roil, rouse, ruffle, spite, tease, troll, undo, unhinge, unsettle, upset, vex, worry* (≠ alleviate, appease, assure, calm, candy-coat, cheer, comfort, conciliate, console, content, delight, disarm, -disregard, ease, encourage, engage, entertain, forget, gladden, gratify, hearten, hush, -ignore, leave, lull, mellow, mitigate, mollify, oblige, pacify, placate, please, propitiate, quiet, reassure, satisfy, -slight, solace, soothe, sugarcoat, thrill, tranquilize, welcome, wow)

BUG (←): *attend, case, cover, discover, espy, examine, eye, eyeball, glimpse, hear, heed, mind, monitor, note, notice, observe, overhear, recon, reconnoiter, regard, scout, scrutinize, sight, spy, surveil, tap, trace, view, watch, wire, wiretap, witness* (≠ -bypass, -disregard, expose, forget, -ignore, leave, miss, mistake, -neglect, -omit, skip, -slight)

BUILD (+): *assemble, automate, begin, carpenter, cast, coin, combine, compile, compose, conceive, concoct, configure, constitute, construct, contrive, cook, craft, create, design, devise, engineer, erect, establish, evolve, fabricate, fashion, father, forge, form, found, frame, generate, hammer, handcraft, imagine, inaugurate, initiate, innovate, institute, invent, jerry-build, jerry-rig, machine, make, manufacture, mechanize, model, mold, motorize, organize, originate, piece, prefabricate, produce, pyramid, raise, rear, reassemble, rebuild, reconstruct, redevelop, retrofit, rig, sculpt, shape, stitch, suture, synthesize, unite* (≠ atomize, bulldoze, deep-six, demolish, destroy, detach, detonate, devastate, disassemble, disconnect, disjoin, dismantle, dismember, dissolve, disunite, divide, doom, eradicate, explode, fell, flatten, fracture, level, obliterate, pulverize, raze, reshape, restructure, ruin, sabotage, scotch, scupper, scuttle, separate, shatter, shelve, smash, strike, tear, terminate, topple, undermine, wreck)

BULLDOZE (/): *abolish, annihilate, atomize, bore, clear, crash, crush, decimate, demolish, desolate, destroy, devastate, disintegrate, dismantle, drive, elbow, eradicate, exterminate, flatten, floor, force, jam, jostle, level, muscle, obliterate, press, pressure, propel, pulverize, push, ram, raze, scupper, shoulder, shove, smash, squash, squeeze, thrust, topple, vaporize, wreck* (≠ assemble, build, construct, craft, defy, -deny, ease, erect, erode, maintain, preserve, raise, repair, resist, restore, sabotage, secure, sideswipe, subvert, survive, sustain, undermine, withstand)

BULLDOZE (/): *admonish, badger, blackjack, bludgeon, bluff, bogart, browbeat, brutalize, bully, bullyrag, coerce, command, compel, constrain, control, cow, daunt, decree, demand, dictate, dragoon, drive, foment, force, forebode, frighten, harass, hector, hound, impel, intimidate, make, mandate, menace, muscle, nag, oblige, order, press, pressure, push, railroad, sandbag, savage, scare, steamroller, strong-arm, terrorize, threaten, torment, trample, trash-talk, unman, unnerve, victimize, warn,* *wrong* (≠ aid, allow, assist, beg, blandish, butter, cajole, cheer, coax, comfort, console, convince, embolden, encourage, grease, help, honor, induce, nurture, obey, permit, persuade, petition, protect, reassure, remedy, respect, soft-sell, soft-soap, solace, soothe, steel, subvert, support, sweet-talk, wheedle)

BULLY (/): *abuse, admonish, badger, beat, blackjack, blackmail, bluff, bogart, browbeat, brutalize, bulldoze, bullyrag, chide, coerce, compel, cow, daunt, dehumanize, dictate, domineer, dragoon, drive, earbash, forebode, frighten, goad, harangue, harass, haze, heckle, hector, henpeck, hijack, hint, hound, injure, insinuate, insult, intimidate, isolate, jeopardize, menace, mistreat, molest, motivate, muscle, nag, oblige, oppress, overwhelm, persecute, pester, press, pressure, punish, push, railroad, sandbag, scare, stalk, steamroller, stress, strong-arm, terrorize, threaten, torment, trash-talk, tyrannize, victimize, warn, wrong* (≠ alleviate, allow, blandish, cajole, champion, coax, commend, compliment, defend, endorse, favor, flatter, help, honor, laud, pity, praise, promote, protect, regret, rescue, respect, serve, soft-sell, soft-soap, support, sweet-talk, wheedle)

BUMP (→): *bang, bounce, box, buck, bunt, butt, clap, concuss, conk, crack, crash, elbow, hit, jab, jar, jerk, jolt, jostle, jounce, knock, nudge, pat, plop, plunk, pound, prod, punch, push, rap, rattle, shake, shunt, sideswipe, slam, slap, smack, strike, thump, thwack, whack* (≠ -avert, -avoid, block, brush, -bypass, catch, deflect, -disregard, -dodge, -duck, -elude, -evade, grasp, guard, miss, nudge, pass, protect, pull, repel, shave, -sidestep, skim, skip, yank)

BUMP (→): *budge, crowd, depose, disinherit, dislocate, dislodge, dismiss, displace, dispossess, disturb, eject, evict, exorcise, expel, extricate, fire, hustle, move, oust, overthrow, relegate, relocate, remove, replace, sack, shift, shove, shunt, sideline, supersede, supplant, topple, unhorse, uninstall, unseat, uproot* (≠ affix, attach, authorize, confirm, cram, embed, entrench, establish, greenlight, install, lodge, permit, promote, reinstate, renew, repair, restore, revive, stuff, support, wedge)

BUMP (→): *accent, accentuate, accrue, affirm, amplify, assert, augment, bolster, boost, cube, develop, double, emphasize, encourage, enhance, escalate, expand, flavor, foster, further, heighten, improve, increase, intensify, jack, magnify, marinate, maximize, multiply, prioritize, promote, punctuate, raise, refine, richen, season, spice, strengthen, treble, triple, upgrade* (≠ abate, contract, curtail, decrease, diminish, lessen, minimize, mitigate, rarefy, reduce, shorten, shrink, truncate, weaken)

BUNGLE (/): *blemish, blight, blow, bobble, boggle, botch, butcher, damage, destroy, dismiss, -disregard, doom, drop, fail, flaw, flub, fluff, foozle, forget, fumble, goof, half-ass, harm, hurt, -ignore, impair, jumble, lose, louse, mangle, mar, miscarry, mishandle, mislay, mismanage, misplace, miss, mistake, misunderstand, mix, muddle, muff, murder, -neglect, -omit, -overlook, overshoot, ruin, scramble, skip, spoil, undershoot, wreck* (≠ accomplish, achieve, actualize, ameliorate, bemoan, better, claim, crest, doctor, enhance, fix, help, improve, lament, manage, mourn, nail, optimize, overhaul, patch, perfect, recondition, rectify, refine, reform, regret, remedy, renovate, repair, revamp, revolutionize, rue, steady, succeed)

BURDEN (→): *baffle, block, bottleneck, charge, check, choke, clog, clutter, complicate, compromise, congest, constrain, cramp, cripple, crush, curb, delay, detain, -deter, drag, encumber, fetter, fill, foist, freight, -frustrate, hamper, hamstring, handicap, heap, hinder, impair, impede, inconvenience, inhibit, involve, jam, load, lumber, mound, obstruct, oppress, overburden, overextend, overload, overtax, overwhelm, pack, paralyze, pile, press, restrain, restrict, saddle, shelve, stack, strain, surcharge, task, tax, -thwart, tie, trammel, trouble, weigh, weight* (≠ aid, alleviate, assist, -avoid, boost, buoy, clear, discard, discharge, disencumber, dispatch, -ditch, divest, drop, -dump, ease, exempt, expedite, facilitate, further, hasten, hurry, lift, lighten, loosen, lose, mislay, misplace, open, organize, permit, promote, release, relieve, remove, separate, support, unblock, unburden, unclog, uncomplicate, unencumber, unload)

BURDEN (/): *afflict, agitate, agonize, ail, anguish, avenge, bother, bum, castigate, chain, chasten, concern, confine, constipate, curb, dash, daunt, delay, demoralize, demotivate, depress, derail, discomfort, discommode, discompose, discourage, dishearten, dismay, dispirit, disquiet, disrupt, distress, disturb, embarrass, enmesh, enslave, ensnare, entangle, execute, fetter, foil, freak, handcuff, handicap, hedge, hem, hinder, hobble, hogtie, hold, impede, imprison, incarcerate, inconvenience, incriminate, inhibit, lambaste, leash, manacle, mire, monkeywrench, oppress, persecute, perturb, pillory, -preclude, -prevent, rein, repress, reprise, retard, roadblock, sabotage, sadden, sentence, shackle, slow, smother, stifle, straightjacket, strain, strangle, stress, stump, stymie, subvert, suffocate, suppress, torment, torture, trouble, try, undo, unhinge, unnerve, unsettle, upset, weary, weigh, worry* (≠ animate, assure, benefit, boost, brighten, buoy, cheer, comfort, console, delight, elate, elevate, encourage, enliven, excite, exhilarate, free, gladden, gratify, hearten, help, inspire, invigorate, liberate, lift, lighten, please, prioritize, reassure, rejoice, rush, smooth, solace, soothe, speed, stimulate, thrill, uplift, wow)

BURGLE (←): *appropriate, bogart, boost, burglarize, cheat, comb, defraud, deprive, despoil, grab, gut, harry, hijack, hunt, invade, liberate, lift, loft, loot, maraud, nobble, pilfer, pillage, pluck, plunder, poach, raid, rake, ransack, ravage, ravish, relieve, requisition, rifle, rob, rummage, sack, salvage, snatch, steal, swindle, swipe, take, thieve, trespass* (≠ bestow, bury, conceal, defend, donate, furnish, give, guard, hide, hoard, hog, insure, keep, lock, lose, maintain, offer, police, preserve, protect, receive, refund, -refuse, reimburse, -reject, repay, rescue, restore, save, secure, shield, stash, supply, wall)

BURN (→): *bake, bank, barbecue, blacken, brand, broil, cauterize, char, consume, cook, cremate, crisp, damage, destroy, enkindle, fire, flame, frizzle, heat, ignite, immolate, incinerate, inflame, kindle, light, melt,* *parch, rekindle, roast, sauté, scald, scorch, sear, singe, smoke, stoke, toast, torch, wither* (≠ braise, chill, choke, cool, dim, douse, drench, embalm, extinguish, fortify, freeze, preserve, quench, rebuild, renew, repair, revive, smother, snuff, stifle, suffocate, wet)

BURN (←): *abuse, afflict, bamboozle, beat, beguile, betray, bilk, bluff, buffalo, catch, cheat, chisel, con, counterfeit, cozen, deceive, defraud, delude, double-cross, dupe, exploit, falsify, fiddle, fool, forge, gaslight, gull, harm, hoax, hoodwink, hornswoggle, humbug, juggle, maltreat, manipulate, misguide, misinform, mislead, misrepresent, mistreat, outwit, overreach, plague, ream, sandbag, scam, snooker, snow, stiff, sucker, swindle, trick, underpay, victimize, violate, wrong* (≠ aid, assume, assure, believe, clarify, comp, compensate, confess, confide, confirm, confront, counter, debunk, defend, disabuse, disclose, divulge, enlighten, explain, expose, foster, give, gratify, guard, help, inform, pity, placate, profit, protect, recoup, repay, replace, restore, reveal, reward, save, shield, support, treat, uncover, undeceive, unmask, unveil)

BURST (/): *annihilate, atomize, blast, blow, break, crack, dash, decimate, demolish, destroy, detonate, discharge, disintegrate, disrupt, doom, dynamite, erupt, explode, fracture, fragment, part, perforate, pierce, pop, prick, pulverize, puncture, rend, ruin, run, rupture, rush, shatter, shiver, smash, splinter, split, spout, spring, tear, vaporize, wreck* (≠ attach, bind, calm, close, collapse, combine, fasten, fix, fuse, implode, join, meld, mend, overhaul, rectify, renovate, repair, salvage, save, seal, secure, solder, unite, weld)

BURY (→): *cloak, coffin, conceal, cover, curtain, deposit, embalm, ensconce, enshrine, enshroud, entomb, hide, immure, inter, lay, mummify, obscure, plant, rebury, reinter, sepulcher, shade, shield, shroud* (≠ bare, burn, cremate, disclose, discover, disinter, display, exhibit, exhume, expose, resuscitate, reveal, revive, show, showcase, suss, uncoffin, uncover, unearth)

BURY (→): *cover, cram, embed, enclose, engulf, fix, graft, immerse, implant, insert, jam, lodge, place, plant, root, scatter, seed, set, sink, situate, sow, submerge, transplant, wedge* (≠ derive, distill, draw, elicit, exact, extract, free, gather, get, glean, obtain, pick, pluck, prize, pull, quarry, recover, remove, suck, tug, uproot, withdraw, worm, wrench, wrest, wring, yank)

BURY (←): *absorb, busy, concentrate, divert, employ, engage, engross, entertain, grip, hold, immerse, interest, involve, obsess, occupy, preoccupy, rivet* (≠ addle, anger, annoy, bore, bother, deflect, disorient, distract, divert, irk, irritate, nitpick, sidetrack, tire, vex, weary) **(¿) ABSTRACTION ALERT. Concrete goals essential!**

BURY (/): *archive, cache, camouflage, cloak, clothe, cloud, conceal, costume, cover, curtain, darken, disguise, eclipse, ensconce, enshroud, entomb, hide, hoard, holster, mask, obscure, obstruct, occult, -omit, plant, screen, secrete, shade, shadow, sheathe, shield, shroud, squirrel,* *stash, store, stow, suppress, tuck, veil, withhold* (≠ accost, bare, brandish, circulate, concede, confess, confide, confirm, confront, detect, disclose, discover, display, disseminate, divulge, exhibit, expose, externalize, flaunt, light, manifest, open, out, parade, present, reveal, show, showcase, strip, suss, uncover, unearth, unmask, unveil, unwrap, wag)

BURY (/): *ace, annihilate, beat, best, better, bomb, break, cap, clobber, conquer, cream, crush, deep-six, destroy, dispatch, drub, dust, eclipse, edge, exceed, finish, flatten, hurdle, lick, master, obliterate, outdistance, outdo, outfight, outlast, outrank, outsell, outshine, outstrip, outthink, overcome, overpower, overthrow, overwhelm, paste, rout, ruin, shellac, sink, skin, skunk, slaughter, snooker, snow, steamroller, subdue, subjugate, surmount, surpass, sweep, take, thrash, throw, top, topple, transcend, trim, trounce, upend, upset, vanquish, wallop, wax, whip, whomp, whup, wrack, wreck* (≠ aid, assist, augment, boost, cede, champion, defend, emancipate, empower, enfranchise, enhance, forfeit, free, guard, help, improve, liberate, preserve, prioritize, protect, release, safeguard, save, shield, surrender, survive, underwhelm, yield)

BUST (→): *abase, break, can, cashier, debase, degrade, demean, demote, dismiss, downgrade, downsize, fire, humble, humiliate, lower, reduce, relegate, sack, sideline* (≠ advance, elevate, foster, further, hire, promote, raise, recommend, upgrade)

BUST (←): *apprehend, arrest, bag, bind, capture, catch, collar, commit, confine, convict, cop, detain, enchain, fetter, get, grab, grapple, handcuff, hogtie, hold, hook, immure, imprison, incarcerate, jail, jug, land, manacle, nab, nail, pinch, police, raid, remand, restrain, search, seize, shackle, snaffle, snare, snatch, trammel, trap* (≠ absolve, acquit, alibi, clear, discharge, emancipate, exonerate, free, liberate, loose, loosen, redeem, release, spring, unbind, unchain, vindicate)

BUST (/): *bankrupt, beggar, bleed, break, cannibalize, consume, deplete, depredate, drain, exhaust, exploit, impoverish, pauperize, reduce, ruin, straiten, waste, weaken* (≠ bank, budget, compensate, conserve, earn, enrich, invest, pay, preserve, profit, protect, reward, stash, stow)

BUST (/): *atomize, blast, break, burst, chip, crack, crush, damage, destroy, detonate, dismember, disrupt, explode, fold, fracture, fragment, grind, harm, pestle, pop, powder, pulverize, reduce, rive, ruin, rupture, shatter, shiver, sliver, smash, splinter, split, vaporize, wreck* (≠ aid, doctor, fix, heal, mend, patch, rebuild, recondition, reconstruct, refurbish, renovate, repair, restore, save salvage, secure, stitch, suture, unify, unite)

BUTCHER (/): *annihilate, assassinate, behead, blitzkrieg, carve, castrate, clean, cleave, cure, cut, decapitate, decimate, depopulate, destroy, dispatch, dress, eradicate, execute, exterminate, fell, guillotine, joint, kill, liquidate, mangle, massacre, maul, murder, mutilate, portion, razor, slaughter, slay, slice, smite, snuff, stick, waste* (≠ aid, armor, assist, block, defend, doctor, grow, heal, mend, nurse, nurture, preserve, protect, repair, rescue, save, sew, shield, stitch, survive)

BUTCHER (/): *blemish, blight, blow, bobble, boggle, bollix, boot, botch, bungle, damage, destroy, disrupt, emasculate, flaw, flub, fluff, foozle, foul, fumble, half-ass, harm, harshen, hurt, impair, injure, lessen, louse, mangle, mar, mess, mishandle, mismanage, mistake, muddle, muff, murder, mutilate, poison, pollute, ruin, sabotage, scupper, spoil, stain, undercut, undermine, vitiate, weaken, worsen, wreck* (≠ accomplish, actualize, ameliorate, bandage, bemoan, better, broker, contrive, doctor, enhance, finagle, fix, handle, heal, help, improve, lament, machinate, manage, maneuver, mourn, negotiate, optimize, overhaul, patch, protect, recondition, rectify, refine, reform, regret, remedy, renegotiate, renovate, repair, repent, restore, revamp, revolutionize, rue, wangle)

BUTT (→): *batter, buck, buffet, bump, bunt, gore, hit, hook, horn, jab, knock, poke, prod, punch, push, ram, shove, smack, strike, thrust, toss* (≠ -bypass, calm, counter, defend, deflect, -disregard, guard, miss, parry, shield, skip, soften)

BUTTER (←): *adulate, anoint, applaud, blandish, blarney, bluff, brownnose, bullshit, cajole, candy-coat, charm, coat, coax, commend, compliment, con, congratulate, court, dulcify, endear, eulogize, felicitate, flannel, flatter, glad-hand, grease, hero-worship, honey, humor, hustle, idolize, ingratiate, inveigle, jolly, lard, leverage, lube, lubricate, massage, moisturize, oil, overpraise, pomade, praise, puff, romance, salve, schmooze, sell, slick, smear, smooth, snooker, snow, soften, soft-sell, soft-soap, stroke, sugarcoat, sweeten, sweet-talk, syrup, wheedle, woo, worship* (≠ abrade, badmouth, belittle, berate, boo, browbeat, bully, callous, case-harden, chafe, coarsen, compel, condemn, criticize, critique, decry, depreciate, disparage, force, harden, insult, intimidate, inure, mock, offend, railroad, repel, retort, ridicule, steamroller, toughen, trash-talk)

BUTTRESS (+): *anchor, anneal, back, base, bear, beef, bolster, brace, buffer, build, bulwark, carry, clinch, cover, cushion, defend, embattle, entrench, fence, fix, fortify, garrison, gird, ground, guard, harden, hinge, hold, patch, prepare, prop, protect, rampart, ready, reinforce, safeguard, secure, shore, stabilize, stand, stay, steady, steel, stiffen, strengthen, strut, support, sustain, temper, toughen, truss, undergird, underpin, uphold, wall* (≠ agitate, attack, boobytrap, breach, break, burden, canker, compromise, convulse, corrode, corrupt, crack, damage, destabilize, destroy, doom, drop, endanger, erode, fail, forget, harm, hurt, imperil, injure, lumber, mar, melt, monkey-wrench, -neglect, rattle, release, roil, sabotage, scotch, scupper, scuttle, shake, soften, subvert, threaten, undermine, weaken)

BUTTRESS (+): *affirm, assert, attest, authenticate, avow, back, bolster, certify, confirm, corroborate, demonstrate, document, ensure, establish, guarantee, notarize, prove, reinforce, substantiate, support, uphold, validate, verify, vindicate, warrant, witness* (≠ challenge, contest, contradict, -deny, disavow, disclaim, discredit, disprove, dispute, expose, gainsay, invalidate, -negate, question, rebut, refute, undercut, undermine, weaken)

BUY (+): *accept, account, accredit, affirm, assume, believe, comprehend, conclude, conjecture, credit, decide, declare, deduce, endorse, expect, gather, grok, hold, imagine, infer, judge, maintain, presume, profess, reason, reckon, recognize, suppose, surmise, swallow, take, trust, understand, wonder* (≠ challenge, consult, cross-examine, debate, -deny, determine, disbelieve, discredit, -disown, disprove, dispute, distrust, doubt, interrogate, invalidate, mistrust, -negate, oppugn, question, refute, -reject, scruple, suspect) **(¿) ABSTRACTION ALERT. Concrete goals essential!**

BUY (←): *acquire, attain, barter, bid, claim, earn, exchange, finance, find, gain, garner, get, horse-trade, land, negotiate, obtain, offer, outbid, overpay, pay, procure, purchase, renegotiate, secure, source, swap, take, trade, win* (≠ advertise, bootleg, broker, commodify, comp, deal, donate, give, lease, leverage, market, merchandize, monetize, offer, outlay, plug, promote, purloin, remainder, rent, retail, rob, sell, smuggle, steal, supply, swipe, tender, transact, vend)

BUY (/): *abase, allure, bait, beguile, bribe, corrupt, debase, debauch, defile, degrade, demean, deprave, dishonor, entice, fix, flatter, goad, induce, ingratiate, lure, motivate, nobble, persuade, pervert, poison, profane, prostitute, provoke, seduce, snare, spur, square, stimulate, suborn, subvert, taint, tempt, trap, warp* (≠ arrest, blackmail, bust, catch, collar, extort, indict, nab, nail, penalize, -refuse, -reject, resist, snaffle)

-BYPASS (→): *-avoid, -boycott, circumnavigate, -circumvent, detour, -discount, disobey, -disregard, divert, -dodge, -duck, -elude, -escape, -eschew, -evade, -flee, leapfrog, orbit, outflank, -overlook, pass, shake, shortcut, -shun, sidetrack, skirt, subvert, waive* (≠ accept, accost, catch, chase, confront, court, embrace, face, hunt, include, invite, keep, meet, pursue, seek, target, welcome, woo)

-BYPASS (→): *-blank, burke, -disdain, -disregard, -dodge, flout, forget, -ignore, miss, -neglect, -omit, -overlook, overtake, pass, pooh-pooh, -reject, scant, -scorn, shortcut, skimp, skip, -slight, slough, slur* (≠ appreciate, attend, bemoan, cherish, contact, cultivate, follow, foster, heed, indulge, invite, lament, mark, mind, mourn, note, notice, nurse, nurture, obey, observe, pamper, prize, pursue, regard, regret, remark, remember, rue, tend, treasure, value, watch)

-BYPASS (→): *-avert, -avoid, beat, -circumvent, deflect, disobey, -disregard, divert, -dodge, -duck, -elude, -end-run, -escape, -eschew, -evade, finesse, flout, -ignore, -obviate, outflank, override, parry, -prevent, shake, -shirk, -shun, shunt, -sidestep, skirt, ward* (≠ accede, accept, catch, clock, contract, court, embrace, follow, incur, keep, obey, observe, pursue, seek, treasure, welcome, woo)

C

CADGE (←): *abuse, appropriate, beg, bilk, blackmail, bleed, borrow, bum, cheat, coax, crib, drain, embezzle, employ, exploit, fleece, gouge, hunt, leech, lift, manipulate, milk, mooch, panhandle, pilfer, scam, schnorr, scrounge, seek, skim, solicit, sponge, swindle, tap, use, weasel, wheedle* (≠ bestow, comp, contribute, deserve, dispense, donate, dower, earn, endow, furnish, give, help, lend, merit, offer, pay, provide, recoup, replace, restore, serve, supply, support, volunteer)

CAGE (/): *armor, bound, box, bridle, circumscribe, closet, cocoon, collar, condemn, confine, contain, convict, coop, corner, corral, cover, embrace, encapsulate, encase, encircle, enclose, encompass, enfold, envelop, fence, fetter, handcuff, harness, hedge, hem, hold, house, immure, impound, imprison, incarcerate, include, institutionalize, intern, jail, limit, lock, manacle, mew, package, pen, restrain, restrict, ring, sentence, shackle, straightjacket, surround, tether, trap, wall* (≠ break, bust, deliver, discharge, emancipate, excuse, exonerate, forgive, free, liberate, parole, permit, release, rescue, save, unbind, uncage, unchain, unleash, vindicate)

CAJOLE (←): *adulate, beg, beguile, beseech, blandish, blarney, bootlick, bribe, brownnose, bullshit, butter, candy-coat, charm, coax, con, convince, court, cozen, crowd, deceive, decoy, delude, diddle, dupe, enlist, entice, entrap, finagle, flannel, flatter, glad-hand, gratify, honey, humbug, implore, importune, induce, influence, ingratiate, inveigle, jolly, juggle, lure, maneuver, massage, mislead, oil, overpraise, palaver, persuade, pressure, push, schmooze, seduce, snooker, snow, soap, soften, soft-sell, soft-soap, soothe, stroke, sugarcoat, sway, sweeten, sweet-talk, syrup, tantalize, tempt, trick, urge, wangle, wheedle, woo, work* (≠ berate, blackmail, browbeat, bug, bulldoze, bully, coerce, compel, constrain, cow, demand, force, harass, insult, intimidate, make, mock, muscle, nag, oblige, pester, railroad, repel, require, retort, sandbag, steamroller, supplicate, tease, trash-talk)

CALCULATE (+): *account, add, adjust, appraise, ascertain, assess, average, benchmark, calibrate, cast, cipher, compute, conjecture, count, debit, deduct, derive, determine, divide, enumerate, equalize, estimate, evaluate, factor, figure, forecast, foretell, gauge, itemize, measure, multiply, number, numerate, predetermine, prioritize, project, rate, read, recalculate, reckon, scale, solve, subtract, sum, tally, time, total, value, weigh* (≠ confuse, disbelieve, -disregard, distrust, doubt, forget, gather, guess, -ignore, miscalculate, misgauge, misread, mistake, mistrust, muddle, -neglect, -overlook, perplex, puzzle, question)

CALCULATE (+): *aim, arrange, blueprint, budget, build, chart, choreograph, consider, contemplate, contrive, design, devise, draft, figure, frame, graph, intend, judge, machinate, map, organize, outline, plan, plot, premeditate, prepare, project, reckon, shape, sketch, strategize, suppose, target, trust* (≠ ad-lib, assume, believe, botch, bungle, -discount, dismiss, -disregard, endanger, force, forget, fudge, fumble, gamble, guess, half-ass, -ignore, improvise, infer, mistake, misuse, presume, ravish, risk, wangle)

CALIBRATE (+): *accommodate, adapt, adjust, align, amend, attune, change, convert, correct, customize, diversify, doctor, edit, enhance, equalize, exchange, finalize, fine-tune, finish, fit, fix, flavor, fortify, harmonize, improve, level, match, mend, modernize, modify, mold, optimize, overhaul, pace, patch, perfect, rarefy, realign, reconceive, reconceptualize, rectify, redefine, refine, reform, regulate, reimagine, reinvent, rejigger, remodel, repair, reshuffle, restore, restructure, rethink, retool, retrofit, revamp, revise, revolutionize, right, sculpt, season, shape, shift, shuffle, spice, strengthen, substitute, suit, supplant, swap, switch, tailor, transform, transpose, tune, tweak, update, upgrade, weaponize* (≠ abide, -abort, bolster, brace, conserve, continue, defend, demolish, destroy, devastate, endure, freeze, hamper, hamstring, harden, hinder, hobble, hold, -ignore, immobilize, keep, leave, lock, mismatch, -neglect, paralyze, preserve, resist, restrain, retain, set, settle, stabilize, steady, stop, sustain, terminate, transfix, weather)

CALL (→): *address, baptize, brand, christen, denote, describe, designate, dub, entitle, label, mislabel, mistitle, name, nickname, nominate, package, rechristen, relabel, rename, specify, stigmatize, style, tag, term, title* (≠ anonymize, -deny, disavow, disclaim, -disown, erase, forget, -forsake, -reject, -repudiate, strip) **(¿) ABSTRACTION ALERT. Concrete goals essential!**

CALL (→): *allocate, appoint, ask, challenge, charge, claim, command, declare, decree, demand, dictate, direct, elect, entreat, exact, mandate, ordain, order, petition, postulate, proclaim, request, require, requisition, solicit, summon* (≠ annul, block, -cancel, countermand, end, -eschew, finish, -negate, -nullify, -prevent, -prohibit, -rescind, stop, terminate, withdraw)

CALL (←): *ask, assemble, beckon, beep, bid, buzz, cite, cold-call, command, contact, demand, dial, hail, invite, invoke, knell, order, page, phone, request, requisition, ring, subpoena, summon, telephone* (≠ banish, block, dismiss, -disregard, eject, fire, -ignore, -neglect, oust, -prevent, rout, -shun, -sidestep, skip, -slight, -thwart)

CALL (←): *amass, ask, assemble, bid, collect, conjure, contact, convene, convoke, gather, group, invite, knell, muster, order, rally, reassemble, reconvene, summon, unite* (≠ -cancel, diffuse, disband, dispel, disperse, dissipate, dissolve, divide, fragment, isolate, part, scatter, seclude, separate, split, stop)

CALL (+): *alert, announce, anticipate, augur, await, caution, consider, declare, detect, determine, divine, estimate, forecast, foresee, foretell, forewarn, guess, herald, judge, outguess, place, portend, predetermine, predict, presage, proclaim, prognosticate, project, promise, prophesy, read, reckon, regard, think, warn* (≠ challenge, debunk, describe, disprove, dispute, doubt, -ignore, narrate, oppose, recall, recount, refute, regret, relate, report)

CALLOUS (/): *abrade, adapt, adjust, blunt, brutalize, case-harden, chafe, chap, coarsen, deaden, debase, dehumanize, demoralize, deprave, desensitize, develop, dull, embitter, granulate, graze, habituate, harden, harshen, indurate, inure, numb, paralyze, rasp, roughen, scuff, season, steel, stiffen, strengthen, thicken, toughen, vitiate, vulgarize, warp* (≠ baby, buff, burnish, civilize, clean, cultivate, file, fix, groom, improve, indulge, manicure, neaten, oil, pamper, perfect, polish, protect, pumice, rectify, refine, sensitize, smarten, smooth, soften, spoil, tenderize, tidy, wax)

CALM (+): *abate, allay, alleviate, anesthetize, appease, assuage, collect, comfort, compose, contain, cool, defuse, drug, ease, focus, hush, hypnotize, lessen, lighten, lull, medicate, mesmerize, mitigate, moderate, mollify, narcotize, pacify, placate, quell, quiet, quieten, reconcile, relax, relieve, restrain, rock, salve, sedate, settle, silence, smooth, sober, soften, soothe, stabilize, steady, still, stroke, stupefy, subdue, sugarcoat, temper, torpefy, tranquilize* (≠ accelerate, aggravate, agitate, anger, appall, arouse, destabilize, disturb, energize, enrage, exacerbate, excite, foment, hasten, heighten, incite, infuriate, intensify, magnify, overset, rabble-rouse, rouse, ruffle, scramble, stir, unsettle, upset, vex, worry)

CAMOUFLAGE (/): *act, affect, assume, beard, blanket, bleep, bury, cloak, clothe, conceal, costume, counterfeit, cover, curtain, deceive, dim, disguise, dissimulate, dress, enshroud, fake, feign, gild, gloss, hide, holster, impersonate, mask, obfuscate, obscure, occult, -omit, play, playact, pose, pretend, roleplay, screen, sheathe, shroud, simulate, spackle, spin, varnish, veil, whitewash* (≠ accentuate, accost, bare, betray, brandish, confess, confide, confirm, confront, disclose, discover, display, divulge, exhibit, expose, feature, flaunt, flourish, highlight, parade, reveal, showcase, spotlight, suss, uncover, undrape, unmask, unveil, wag)

-CANCEL (/): *-abandon, abdicate, -abort, abrogate, annihilate, annul, axe, bury, call, censor, countermand, cut, delete, deselect, -desert, destroy, discard, disclaim, -discontinue, dismiss, -disown, dispel, dispose, doom, drop, edit, efface, eliminate, end, eradicate, erase, excise, expunge, expurgate, extirpate, forgo, -forsake, -halt, interrupt, invalidate, jettison, kill, leave, -negate, -nix, -nullify, obliterate, off, -omit, postpone, raze, recall, recant, -reject, release, relegate, relinquish, -renounce, repeal, -repudiate, -rescind, retract, reverse, revoke, rid, scrap, scrub, shed, sink, smash, squash, stop, strike, surrender, suspend, terminate, torpedo, total, trash, vacate, vent, -void, waive, wipe, withdraw, zap* (≠ begin, brainstorm, commence, continue, create, engage, form, found, initiate, institute, introduce, keep, launch, maintain, perpetuate, pledge, promise, restore, start, survive, undertake, uphold)

-CANCEL (/): *abate, abnegate, abolish, -abort, abrogate, annihilate, annul, -avoid, ban, call, countermand, counterpoise, deep-six, -deny, destroy, disallow, disavow, dismiss, dissolve, divorce, doom, drop, efface, eliminate, enjoin, eradicate, erase, extinguish, -forbid, invalidate, liquidate, -negate, neutralize, null, -nullify, obliterate, offset, outlaw, override, overrule, overturn, -prohibit, quash, recall, red-line, refute, -reject, remove, repeal, -repudiate, -rescind, retract, reverse, revoke, scotch, shelve, strike, suspend, undo, vacate, -veto, -void, withdraw* (≠ accord, allow, approve, authorize, clear, command, decree, enact, endorse, establish, formalize, found, greenlight, institute, legalize, legislate, legitimate, legitimize, mandate, order, pass, permit, prescribe, ratify, sanction, validate, warrant)

CAPTAIN (→): *administer, boss, bridle, chair, command, conduct, control, direct, discipline, dominate, drive, execute, fly, govern, guide, handle, harness, head, influence, lead, manage, maneuver, manipulate, monitor, navigate, negotiate, operate, order, oversee, pilot, quarterback, rule, run, sail, shepherd, skipper, spearhead, steer, superintend, supervise* (≠ -abandon, chase, crash, cripple, -deny, -desert, foil, follow, -frustrate, hamper, hamstring, heed, hinder, -ignore, maroon, mind, mishandle, mismanage, misrule, monkey-wrench, -neglect, obey, obstruct, pursue, -refuse, relinquish, ride, sabotage, serve, sideswipe, smash, submit, subvert, target)

CAPTIVATE (←): *allure, arrest, attract, beckon, bed, beguile, bewitch, bind, candy-coat, capture, catch, charm, coax, court, dazzle, delight, disarm, draw, enamor, enchant, endear, engage, engross, enrapture, enslave, ensnare, entertain, enthrall, entice, entrance, excite, fascinate, fixate, floor, glamour, gratify, grip, hold, hook, hypnotize, infatuate, interest, intrigue, invite, kill, lure, magnetize, mesmerize, please, pull, ravish, razzle-dazzle, rivet, seduce, seize, solicit, spellbind, stagger, stun, tantalize, tempt, thrill, titillate, vamp, win, woo, wow* (≠ annoy, appall, bore, burden, caution, chill, depress, -deter, disgust, disillusion, dismay, displease, dissuade, enrage, henpeck, irk, irritate, nag, nauseate, needle, nitpick, offend, repel, revolt, sicken, tire, warn, weary, worry)

CAPTURE (←): *accomplish, accumulate, achieve, acquire, amass, annex, attain, bag, bring, carry, catch, claim, clear, conquer, draw, earn, gain, garner, get, grab, gross, hunt, land, make, net, notch, obtain, occupy, pluck, procure, pull, reacquire, realize, reap, reattain, recapture, regain, remake, score, secure, seek, source, stockpile, take, win* (≠ accord, bequeath, forfeit, furnish, give, grant, hand, lose, offer, pay, relinquish, supply, surrender, tithe, yield)

CAPTURE (/): *abduct, apprehend, arrest, bag, block, bust, cage, catch, claim, clasp, clutch, collar, convict, cop, corner, corral, detain, disappear, enmesh, ensnare, entangle, entrap, get, glom, glove, grab, grapple, grasp, grip, halter, herd, hijack, hold, hook, imprison, incarcerate,* *institutionalize, intern, jail, kidnap, land, lasso, mesh, nab, nail, net, nick, overwhelm, rap, recapture, rend, rope, rush, rustle, secure, seize, snaffle, snag, snare, snatch, spirit, subjugate, take, trap, wrangle, wrest* (≠ -bypass, -decline, deliver, -desert, discharge, dismiss, -disown, drop, -escape, exonerate, forfeit, -forsake, free, guard, liberate, loosen, lose, miss, -prohibit, pursue, -rebuff, -refuse, -reject, release, rescue, save, unhand, vindicate)

CARESS (→): *brush, contact, cuddle, embrace, feel, finger, fondle, graze, grope, hug, kiss, lick, manipulate, massage, nuzzle, palm, palpate, pat, paw, pet, ply, rub, skim, stroke, strum, touch, twiddle* (≠ aggravate, annoy, disbelieve, displease, exasperate, insult, irritate, maltreat, manhandle, maul, mishandle, offend, provoke, release, tease, vex, wound)

CARRY (→): *advertise, air, announce, beam, bear, broadcast, circulate, communicate, conduct, convey, diffuse, display, disseminate, give, hype, offer, plug, presell, promulgate, publicize, publish, relay, release, report, scatter, send, show, spread, telegraph, televise, transfer, transmit, transport* (≠ bury, cloak, conceal, confuse, forget, garble, hide, mask, miscommunicate, misrepresent, obscure, scramble, screen, undermine, withhold)

CARRY (←): *beam, bear, bring, cart, channel, conduct, convey, convoy, deliver, displace, drive, ferry, fetch, freight, funnel, give, haul, heft, hoist, hump, import, lift, lug, move, pack, pipe, relay, release, relocate, remove, schlep, shift, shoulder, sustain, take, tote, transfer, transmit, transplant, transport, truck, waft* (≠ discard, drop, forfeit, keep, leave, lose, mislay, misplace, -reject, release, relinquish)

CART (←): *bear, bring, carry, chauffeur, convey, deliver, ferry, fetch, haul, hump, lug, move, pack, schlep, shift, ship, take, tote, transfer, transport* (≠ -abandon, -desert, -ditch, drop, leave, lose, misplace, skip)

CARVE (→): *chisel, crosshatch, deboss, decorate, embellish, emboss, engrave, etch, gouge, incise, indent, inscribe, mark, nick, nock, notch, ornament, tool, write* (≠ chip, deface, delete, dent, ding, efface, erase, expunge, fill, mangle, mar, obliterate, plaster, pulverize, remove, scour, scrub, shatter, spackle)

CARVE (+): *cast, chip, chisel, contour, cut, fashion, form, hew, model, mold, pattern, sculpt, sculpture, shape, whittle* (≠ break, crack, crush, deface, demolish, destroy, eradicate, fracture, pulverize, ruin, shatter, smash, wreck)

CARVE (/): *allocate, allot, apportion, butcher, chop, chunk, cut, dismember, dissect, distribute, divide, hack, hew, joint, portion, segment, slash, slice, sunder, trim, vivisect* (≠ accumulate, blend, collect, combine, fuse, gather, hoard, join, keep, meld, mix, pile, repair, restore, sew, stack, stitch, suture, unite, withhold)

CASE (←): *analyze, appraise, assess, canvas, check, clock, consider, contemplate, evaluate, examine, explore, eyeball, inspect, investigate, learn, measure, observe, peruse, prioritize, probe, prowl, read, scan, scope, scrutinize, search, sift, study, surveil, survey, watch* (≠ assume, -blank, blind, browse, -bypass, confound, confuse, deceive, -discount, disguise, -disregard, gloss, guess, -ignore, infer, misconstrue, misinterpret, misread, miss, mistake, -neglect, -overlook, pass, perplex, skim, skip, trick)

CAST (→): *belch, discharge, effuse, ejaculate, eject, eliminate, emit, erupt, evacuate, evolve, excrete, exhale, exorcise, expel, exude, give, gush, irradiate, issue, jet, ooze, pour, radiate, release, secrete, send, shoot, spew, spout, spray, spurt, squirt, throw, upchuck, vent, vomit* (≠ absorb, block, dim, impede, inhale, screen, shade, shadow, slurp, soak, sponge, suck, take, veil)

CAST (→): *bandy, bowl, buck, cant, catapult, chuck, dart, dash, diffuse, direct, drive, eject, fire, fling, flip, gun, heave, hook, hurl, hurtle, impel, launch, lob, loft, pass, peg, pelt, pitch, precipitate, project, propel, rifle, roll, scatter, shoot, shy, skitter, sling, spread, throw, thrust, toss, wing* (≠ accept, catch, clutch, gather, grab, grip, hold, keep, receive, seize, snag, take)

CAST (+): *adjust, allot, appoint, appraise, arrange, assess, assign, attach, audition, balance, categorize, choose, commission, compose, constitute, critique, delegate, designate, detail, draft, employ, engage, establish, form, handpick, integrate, judge, marshal, name, nominate, orchestrate, order, organize, pigeonhole, place, prepare, prioritize, ready, retain, screen, select, sort, stratify, task, test* (≠ blackball, blacklist, boot, cull, dismiss, expel, fire, oust, -refuse, -reject, remove, replace, terminate, winnow)

CASTRATE (/): *alter, caponize, change, cut, dampen, daunt, deaden, deball, demoralize, demotivate, desex, devitalize, discourage, dishearten, dispirit, drain, emasculate, enervate, enfeeble, exhaust, fatigue, fix, geld, knacker, lobotomize, mutilate, neuter, petrify, sap, snip, spay, sterilize, undermine, unman, unsex, weaken, wear* (≠ arouse, boost, brace, encourage, energize, enliven, excite, fortify, galvanize, inflame, invigorate, provoke, quicken, raise, refresh, revitalize, rouse, stimulate, stir, strengthen)

CATALOG (+): *alphabetize, categorize, chronicle, classify, compile, discern, discover, distinguish, docket, establish, file, identify, index, inscribe, label, list, note, organize, pinpoint, place, record, reference, register, research, schedule, slate, slot, specify, systematize, tabulate, tag, tally* (≠ abolish, anonymize, blot, confuse, consult, delete, efface, erase, expunge, jumble, misclassify, mislabel, missort, mistake, mix, muddle, obliterate, remove, scatter, scramble)

CATALYZE (→): *advance, beget, begin, breed, bring, create, cultivate, develop, effect, egg, enact, encourage, engender, establish, father, forward, foster, found, further, generate, hatch, inaugurate, induce,* *initiate, innovate, instigate, institute, introduce, invoke, launch, make, nourish, nurture, pioneer, produce, promote, prompt, render, set, sire, spawn, start, stimulate, yield* (≠ abolish, arrest, check, crush, curb, dampen, deaden, demolish, destroy, doom, extinguish, -forbid, hamper, hinder, impede, inhibit, kill, limit, muffle, mute, -nix, -nullify, -obviate, pause, -prevent, -prohibit, quash, quell, quench, repress, restrain, restrict, short-circuit, slake, smother, squash, squelch, stifle, subdue, suppress, throttle, -thwart)

CATCH (←): *apprehend, arrest, bag, blindside, bushwhack, bust, capture, clasp, claw, clench, clutch, collar, cop, corner, corral, ensnare, entangle, entrap, field, glom, grab, grasp, grip, hold, hook, hunt, lasso, nab, nail, net, nick, pick, pluck, recapture, rope, secure, seek, seize, snaffle, snag, snare, snatch, surprise, take, trap, wrangle* (≠ bequeath, dismiss, drop, -escape, forfeit, free, give, grant, launch, liberate, loosen, lose, misplace, miss, offer, pay, provide, receive, release, relinquish, skip, skitter, surrender, throw, tithe, toss, yield)

CATCH (←): *ascertain, clock, consult, descry, detect, discern, disclose, discover, distinguish, expose, grok, identify, note, notice, observe, perceive, recognize, reveal, sense, spot, spy, surprise, uncover, unearth, unmask* (≠ addle, baffle, blind, confound, confuse, disguise, distort, forget, garble, -ignore, mask, miscommunicate, misinterpret, misquote, misread, misrepresent, miss, mistake, mistranslate, misunderstand, -overlook, twist)

CATCH (←): *arrest, attract, bewitch, captivate, capture, charm, draw, enchant, engage, enmesh, ensnare, entangle, fascinate, grasp, hold, pull, seduce* (≠ alienate, bore, bug, caution, -deter, disappoint, dissuade, irk, lose, offend, -refuse, -reject, repel, tire, warn, weary)

CATEGORIZE (+): *align, alphabetize, arrange, array, assort, box, brand, cast, catalog, characterize, chart, class, classify, clump, cluster, codify, collate, compartment, compartmentalize, cull, designate, digest, distinguish, distribute, establish, file, frame, grade, group, hierarchize, identify, index, label, limit, list, marshal, methodize, orchestrate, order, organize, package, peg, pigeonhole, place, prepare, prioritize, program, range, rank, rate, recategorize, reclassify, recognize, regroup, regulate, relegate, schedule, schematize, score, screen, separate, shelve, sieve, sift, simplify, slot, sort, stamp, stereotype, structure, systematize, tab, tabulate, tag, typecast, unsnarl, winnow* (≠ addle, befuddle, blend, blur, boggle, churn, complicate, confuse, derange, disarrange, discombobulate, dishevel, disorganize, disorient, disrupt, disturb, -ignore, jumble, lump, misclassify, mislabel, mix, muddle, -neglect, pile, rummage, scatter, scramble, shuffle, toss, unsettle, untidy, upset)

CAUTION (→): *admonish, adumbrate, advise, alert, apprise, augur, counsel, -deter, exhort, flag, forecast, foreshadow, foretell, forewarn, harbinger, inform, notify, outguess, predict, presage, prognosticate, prophesy, signal, tip, urge, wake, warn, worry* (≠ attack, compromise, -disregard, embrace, endanger, expose, gamble, hasten, hazard, imperil, jeopardize, miss, -neglect, -overlook, regret, repent, risk, rue, -slight, target, threaten)

CELEBRATE (+): *acclaim, advocate, aid, amplify, bless, boost, broadcast, buoy, ceremonialize, cheer, chronicle, comfort, commemorate, commend, congratulate, consecrate, dedicate, distinguish, emblazon, embolden, encourage, enhance, enjoy, entertain, eulogize, exalt, expand, extol, feast, fête, foster, further, glorify, hallow, hold, honor, hype, incite, increase, inspire, intensify, keep, laud, limelight, lionize, magnify, mark, memorialize, observe, perform, praise, presell, prioritize, proclaim, promote, publicize, raise, record, remember, revere, ritualize, rouse, solemnize, sound, stir, strengthen, telegraph, toast, trumpet, urge* (≠ admonish, bemoan, blame, bury, chastise, chide, cloak, conceal, condemn, criticize, -disregard, fault, forget, frame, hide, -ignore, lambaste, lament, mourn, -neglect, obscure, -overlook, profane, rebuke, regret, repent, reprimand, rue, scold, -scorn, shame, -shun, veil, violate)

CEMENT (+): *affix, attach, bind, blend, bond, combine, connect, fasten, fix, fuse, glue, gum, hybridize, join, merge, mortar, paste, plaster, seal, solder, spackle, stick, unite, weld* (≠ break, chop, cleave, cut, detach, divide, extract, loosen, remove, rip, separate, sever, split, sunder, tear, unfasten, yank)

CENSOR (/): *abridge, adulterate, ban, blacklist, bleep, bowdlerize, conceal, control, criticize, cut, delete, edit, excise, -exclude, expurgate, gag, -omit, -prohibit, purge, restrain, restrict, sanitize, silence, squelch, sterilize, stifle, suppress, withhold* (≠ approve, authorize, bellow, blab, blurt, circulate, confess, disclose, disseminate, divulge, encourage, endorse, legalize, permit, promote, reveal, sanction, support, trumpet)

CENTER (+): *align, anchor, attune, balance, calibrate, collect, concentrate, consolidate, coordinate, direct, equalize, focus, gather, ground, harmonize, intensify, join, level, meet, poise, root, square, stabilize, steady, still, tune, unify* (≠ addle, baffle, befuddle, confuse, convulse, daze, diffuse, discombobulate, disconcert, disperse, dissipate, dizzy, -ignore, jangle, knock, muddle, rattle, rile, roil, scatter, shake, unnerve, upset)

CERTIFY (+): *accredit, affirm, allow, approve, ascertain, assure, attest, authenticate, authorize, avow, charter, clear, commission, confirm, corroborate, credential, crosscheck, declare, empower, enable, endorse, enfranchise, ensure, entitle, guarantee, inaugurate, induct, initiate, install, instate, invest, legalize, let, license, notarize, notify, okay, permit, privilege, profess, pronounce, prove, qualify, ratify, reassure, recognize, rubber-stamp, sanction, show, state, substantiate, swear, testify, validate, verify, vest, warrant, witness* (≠ abolish, ban, bar, block, constrain, contest, contradict, counteract, debate, decertify, -deny, disallow, disavow, disbar, discourage, discredit, disenfranchise, -disown, disprove, dispute, disqualify, distrust, doubt, enjoin, -exclude, -forbid, gainsay, hinder, impede, inhibit, invalidate, obstruct, outlaw, override, -prevent, -prohibit, proscribe, -reject, -renounce, -repudiate, scruple, stop, -veto)

CHAFE (→): *abrade, bind, bite, blister, burn, chew, corrode, decompose, disintegrate, dissolve, eat, erase, erode, excoriate, file, flay, fray, frazzle, fret, gall, gnaw, grate, graze, grind, hone, incense, inflame, irritate, nibble, peel, rasp, reduce, rub, sandblast, sandpaper, scour, scrape, scratch, scuff, sharpen, shave, skin, wear, whet, wipe* (≠ alleviate, anoint, bandage, butter, calm, caress, cool, grease, lube, lubricate, medicate, mend, moisturize, oil, relieve, salve, smooth, soothe, steady, still, wax)

CHAFE (/): *affront, aggravate, agitate, anger, annoy, antagonize, badger, bait, bother, bug, bullyrag, burn, chaff, devil, discomfort, discompose, disquiet, distress, eat, enrage, exasperate, exercise, freak, fret, frost, gall, get, gravel, hagride, harass, harry, hassle, heckle, henpeck, incense, inflame, infuriate, insult, irk, irritate, madden, miff, nag, nettle, offend, outrage, peeve, persecute, perturb, pester, pique, plague, provoke, rankle, rile, roil, rouse, ruffle, spite, tease, troll, undo, unhinge, unsettle, upset, vex, worry* (≠ allay, appease, assure, cheer, comfort, conciliate, console, content, delight, gladden, gratify, lull, mollify, oblige, pacify, placate, please, propitiate, quiet, reassure, satisfy, soothe, sugarcoat, thrill)

CHAIN (/): *attach, bind, cage, confine, constrain, constrict, cuff, curb, enchain, encumber, enslave, entangle, fasten, fetter, fix, hamper, handcuff, hinder, hitch, hobble, hogtie, hold, impede, imprison, indenture, join, lash, leash, limit, link, lock, manacle, pinion, restrain, restrict, rope, secure, shackle, straightjacket, straiten, subjugate, tether, tie, trammel, truss, yoke* (≠ break, cut, detach, emancipate, -escape, free, liberate, loose, open, release, rescue, unbind, unchain, uncuff, unfasten, unfetter, unleash, unlock, unshackle, untether)

CHAIR (→): *administer, boss, bridle, captain, command, conduct, control, convene, direct, discipline, dominate, execute, govern, handle, harness, lead, manage, master, moderate, order, oversee, pilot, rule, run, steer, superintend, supervise* (≠ begrudge, botch, bungle, collapse, -decline, -disregard, follow, fumble, -ignore, mishandle, misrule, -neglect, obey, -refuse, -reject, stint, subvert, yield)

CHALLENGE (→): *accost, attack, beard, block, brave, brazen, breast, champion, confront, dare, defy, face, intercept, invite, provoke, rival, stomach, stump, summon, tackle, weather, wrestle* (≠ ban, bar, blacklist, demotivate, -deter, discourage, dissuade, eliminate, -exclude, expel, -forbid, -ostracize, -prevent, -prohibit, protest, -refuse, -reject, stop, thwart)

CHALLENGE (→): *accuse, assault, attack, battle, combat, contest, counter, counteract, cross-examine, debate, defy, -deny, discredit, -disown, disprove, dispute, distrust, doubt, fight, grill, impeach, interrogate, invalidate, mistrust, oppose, oppugn, protest, query, question, race, resist, retort, scruple* (≠ abide, accept, advocate, approve, back, believe, champion, confirm, defend, embrace, endure, legalize, obey, promote, sanction, stomach, support, swallow, tolerate, trust)

CHALLENGE (/): *burden, drain, encumber, enervate, exact, exhaust, impose, load, lumber, overextend, overload, sap, strain, stretch, tax, test, threaten, tire, try, weaken, wear, weary, weigh* (≠ abate, alleviate, ameliorate, assuage, calm, diminish, facilitate, lessen, lighten, lull, mellow, mitigate, moderate, mollify, reduce, relax, relieve, soothe)

CHALLENGE (←): *ask, beg, claim, command, demand, enjoin, entail, exact, insist, involve, press, require, specify, stipulate, take, want, warrant* (≠ bequeath, bestow, confer, eliminate, grant, hold, -obviate, offer, own, possess, relinquish, surrender, yield)

CHAMPION (→): *abet, adopt, advance, advocate, affirm, aid, approve, assist, back, bolster, boost, buttress, commend, confirm, contend, defend, embrace, encourage, endorse, espouse, favor, forward, foster, further, guard, help, hold, legalize, maintain, patronize, plug, preach, prioritize, promote, protect, push, ratify, reinforce, represent, second, support, uphold, warrant* (≠ baffle, battle, betray, checkmate, counter, counteract, -deny, -desert, disappoint, discredit, disfavor, disgrace, fail, foil, -frustrate, hamper, hinder, hobble, minimize, monkey-wrench, muzzle, oppose, -reject, sabotage, scotch, scupper, scuttle, shelve, subvert, -thwart, undercut, undermine, wrong)

CHANCE (→): *attempt, beard, bet, brave, brazen, breast, challenge, compromise, confront, dare, defy, endanger, expose, face, gamble, hazard, imperil, jeopardize, menace, plunge, risk, spitball, stake, subject, tempt, try, venture, wager* (≠ appraise, arrange, calculate, defend, design, ensure, formulate, guarantee, machinate, mastermind, measure, organize, plan, plot, promise, protect, safeguard, scheme)

CHANGE (→): *accommodate, adapt, adjust, alter, alternate, amend, calibrate, commute, convert, customize, deform, develop, diminish, diversify, edit, equalize, evolve, exchange, gentrify, innovate, level, merge, metamorphose, moderate, modify, modulate, move, mutate, naturalize, recast, reconceive, reconceptualize, recondition, redefine, redo, reduce, refashion, reform, regenerate, reimagine, reinvent, rejigger, remake, remodel, renew, renovate, reorganize, rephrase, replace, reshape, reshuffle, resolve, restore, restructure, restyle, retool, revamp, revise, revolutionize, rework, sculpt, shape, shift, shunt, substitute, temper, transfer, transfigure, transform, translate, transmute, transpose, tune, turn, vary, warp, weaponize* (≠ affix, bear, brook, cage, cement, endure, fasten, fix, freeze, glue, guard, hold, immobilize, keep, maintain, paralyze, pin, pinion, preserve, -prevent, protect, restore, retain, safeguard, save, secure, set, stabilize, stay, steady, stomach, sustain, tolerate, weather)

CHANGE (→): *alternate, bandy, barter, cede, commute, convert, displace, exchange, interchange, invert, remove, replace, reverse, rotate, shift, substitute, supersede, supplant, surrender, swap, switch, trade, transmit, transpose, yield* (≠ clasp, -deny, grasp, grip, hold, keep, leave, pin, remove, reserve, retain, sustain, take, withhold)

CHANNEL (←): *beam, carry, choreograph, concentrate, conduct, consolidate, convey, direct, focus, force, funnel, guide, orchestrate, pipe, route, send, siphon, transmit, transport* (≠ block, derail, eject, -exclude, hamper, hinder, hobble, impair, impede, jettison, -omit, pause, -prevent, stop, -thwart)

CHAPERONE (+): *accompany, advise, assess, attend, audit, carry, check, conduct, control, convoy, counsel, detect, direct, escort, follow, gauge, govern, guard, guesstimate, guide, handle, herd, inspect, judge, manage, mind, monitor, nanny, note, observe, organize, oversee, patrol, plot, proctor, protect, record, referee, safeguard, scan, shepherd, supervise, survey, trace, track, umpire, watch* (≠ -abandon, abuse, bed, blindfold, challenge, compromise, debauch, deceive, deflower, -desert, -discount, dishonor, -ditch, dump, fake, forget, -forsake, -ignore, injure, mislead, miss, mistake, molest, -neglect, offload, -omit, -overlook, ravish, seduce, shame, trick)

CHARGE (→): *ambush, assail, assault, attack, barrage, batter, beleaguer, beset, besiege, blindside, blitz, bolt, bomb, bombard, buck, buffet, bum-rush, bushwhack, chase, dash, envelop, flank, harry, invade, jump, loot, lunge, mob, mug, overrun, pillage, plaster, plunder, press, raid, ram, ravage, rob, rush, sack, smash, stampede, storm, strike, surprise, swarm, tear, waylay* (≠ armor, -avoid, -bypass, -circumvent, cover, defend, detour, -disregard, -ditch, -dodge, -duck, -elude, guard, -ignore, parry, protect, secure, shield, -sidestep, skip, skirt)

CHARGE (→): *animate, arouse, awaken, bewitch, captivate, charm, delight, electrify, enchant, energize, enliven, enthrall, excite, exhilarate, fire, galvanize, hypnotize, incite, inspire, interest, intoxicate, intrigue, invigorate, jolt, mesmerize, move, power, prod, provoke, pump, quicken, razzle-dazzle, rivet, rouse, shock, spellbind, spur, startle, stimulate, stir, strengthen, tantalize, thrill, titillate, urge, vitalize, wow* (≠ bore, cannibalize, demoralize, demotivate, -deter, discourage, dishearten, dispirit, enervate, exhaust, fatigue, jade, sap, tire, undermine, weary)

CHARGE (→): *adjure, advise, appoint, ask, assign, authorize, beg, beseech, bid, boss, choreograph, coerce, command, commission, compel, conduct, constrain, control, counsel, direct, enjoin, entreat, force, instruct, lead, manage, muscle, oblige, orchestrate, order, oversee, petition, railroad, request, require, superintend, supervise, task, warn* (≠ accept, adopt, discharge, disobey, execute, follow, heed, honor, keep, mind, obey, observe, perform, -refuse, subvert, welcome)

CHARGE (→): *bloat, bulk, cram, crowd, crush, drench, energize, feed, fill, flood, fuel, glut, honeycomb, imbue, impregnate, infuse, instill, inundate, invigorate, load, mat, overcharge, overfill, overflow, overwhelm, pack, penetrate, permeate, pervade, press, railroad, ram, refill, refresh, regenerate, reinvigorate, rejuvenate, reload, renew, repack, replenish, restimulate, restore, resuscitate, revive, saturate, shove, squash, squeeze, steamroller, suffuse, surfeit, swamp, transfuse* (≠ bleed, cannibalize, clean, clear, consume, deplete, depredate, drain, draw, eliminate, empty, evacuate, exhaust, flush, leach, leech, lighten, purge, sap, scour, sweep, tap, unpack, vacate, void, weary)

CHARGE (←): *ask, assess, bill, blackmail, bleed, bring, coerce, command, commercialize, commodify, compel, debit, deduct, demand, dock, exact, excise, expense, extort, fetch, fine, fleece, force, gazump, gouge, impose, inflict, invoice, lay, levy, mark, milk, monetize, overcharge, overextend, penalize, price, require, sell, skin, squeeze, tax, toll, undercharge, value, wrest, wring* (≠ abate, borrow, comp, compensate, condone, diminish, -disregard, donate, earn, excuse, forgive, furnish, give, -ignore, lessen, loan, outbid, outlay, overpay, overspend, pardon, patronize, pay, release, remit, spare, steal, supply, tender, tithe, underpay)

CHARGE (/): *accuse, arraign, assail, blame, book, castigate, censure, chastise, chide, cite, condemn, criticize, damn, denounce, fault, finger, frame, impeach, implicate, impugn, incriminate, inculpate, indict, involve, name, peg, prosecute, rebuke, report, reproach, reprove, resent, scapegoat, scold, sue, summon, tax* (≠ absolve, acquit, alibi, clear, defend, exculpate, excuse, exonerate, forgive, free, justify, liberate, pardon, remit, shrive, spare, vindicate)

CHARM (→): *becharm, bespell, bewitch, bind, brew, captivate, cast, compel, conjure, constrain, curse, dazzle, dedicate, devise, devote, enchant, ensorcel, enthrall, entice, entrance, evoke, fascinate, force, glamour, hex, hoodoo, hypnotize, invoke, jinx, juggle, lure, maledict, mesmerize, possess, prophesy, seduce, spell, spellbind, strike, taint, tantalize, tempt, voodoo, weave, whammy, witch* (≠ aid, banish, bless, cleanse, consecrate, defend, disenchant, dislodge, dispel, dissipate, exorcise, expel, free, heal, liberate, protect, purge, purify, rectify, release, sanctify, shield, unbind, ward)

CHARM (←): *allure, amuse, arrest, attract, beckon, bed, beguile, bewitch, bind, blandish, cajole, captivate, caress, catch, cherish, coax, coddle, convince, court, cuddle, delight, disarm, distract, divert, drag, draw, enamor, enchant, endear, engage, engross, enlist, enrapture, entertain, enthrall, entice, entrance, fascinate, flannel, flatter, grab, gratify, hex, hug, hypnotize, implore, induce, ingratiate, interest, intrigue, inveigle, invite, kill, lure, magnetize, mesmerize, palaver, persuade, please, possess, pull, ravish, razzle-dazzle, refresh, relax, schmooze, seduce, serenade, snuggle, solicit, spellbind, stimulate, sway, take, tempt, thrill, tickle, titillate, transport, urge, vamp, win, woo, wow* (≠ afflict, affront, anguish, annoy, blackmail, bore, browbeat, bulldoze, bully, disgust, displease, enrage, heckle, infuriate, intimidate, irk, irritate, molest, nag, nauseate, needle, nettle, niggle, nitpick, offend, outrage, pester, plague, railroad, repel, repulse, revolt, sicken, tire, torment, trash-talk, vex, weary)

CHARTER (←): *allow, arrange, authorize, borrow, commission, contract, employ, engage, greenlight, hire, lease, let, license, order, permit, rent, reserve, sanction, sublease, sublet* (≠ ban, block, buy, -cancel, commodify, -forbid, leverage, obstruct, outlaw, own, -prohibit, sell, -veto)

CHASE (→): *bird-dog, capture, cull, dog, drag, drive, ferret, fish, follow, gun, harpoon, heel, hound, hunt, kill, net, poach, press, pursue, ride, run, scent, scratch, seek, shadow, shoot, snare, spoor, stalk, start, target, track, trail, trap* (≠ aid, conserve, defend, guard, husband, -ignore, nurture, preserve, protect, raise, ranch, rear, shield)

CHASE (←): *accompany, bird-dog, capture, cull, dog, drag, drive, escort, eye, ferret, follow, harpoon, hawk, hound, hunt, hurry, kill, net, observe, orbit, poach, pursue, retrace, run, rush, search, seek, shadow, shoot, sleuth, snare, spoor, stalk, tag, tail, trace, track, trail, trap, watch* (≠ baffle, blackball, blind, confound, confuse, corner, deceive, disguise, -dodge, -escape, -evade, expel, -flee, guide, head, lead, muddle, outrun, outwit, pilot, puzzle, trick)

CHASE (/): *axe, ban, banish, bar, boot, bounce, can, cashier, defenestrate, deport, discharge, dismiss, displace, dispossess, eject, evict, -exclude, exile, exorcise, expatriate, expel, extrude, fire, -ostracize, oust, out, pink-slip, proscribe, release, remove, retire, rout, sack, terminate* (≠ accept, admit, entertain, harbor, host, house, include, invite, lodge, receive, shelter, take, welcome)

CHASTEN (/): *abase, afflict, assess, berate, blister, castigate, charge, chastise, chide, condemn, convict, correct, cow, criticize, critique, curb, damn, daunt, denounce, discipline, dock, fine, housebreak, housetrain, humble, humiliate, impose, incriminate, keelhaul, levy, moderate, penalize, punish, rebuke, repress, reprimand, reproach, reprove, restrain, scold, sentence, soften, subdue, tame, upbraid, wreak* (≠ absolve, acquit, assist, boost, commend, commute, encourage, exculpate, excuse, exonerate, forfeit, help, honor, inspire, pardon, ransom, release, reprieve, spare, uplift, vindicate)

CHASTISE (/): *abate, admonish, afflict, avenge, beat, berate, blame, boo, burden, cane, castigate, censure, chasten, chide, condemn, confine, correct, criticize, crucify, deduct, defame, defile, demean, demonize, denigrate, denounce, deprecate, deride, discipline, discredit, disparage, distress, encumber, execute, fault, fine, fix, flog, forfeit, fulminate, handicap, imprison, incarcerate, judge, lambaste, lash, penalize, persecute, pillory, pummel, punish, ream, rectify, reform, remedy, -renounce, reprimand, reproach, reprove, scold, -scorn, scourge, sentence, smack, spank, strap, thrash, torture, upbraid, vilify, whip* (≠ absolve, acquit, applaud, approve, cheer, comfort, commend, compliment, congratulate, cuddle, encourage, endorse, exculpate, excuse, exonerate, extol, forgive, guard, pardon, praise, promote, release, reward, sanction, spare, support, vindicate)

CHEAPEN (/): *abase, adulterate, bastardize, bedraggle, befoul, begrime, belittle, bestialize, betray, blemish, contaminate, corrupt, damage, debase, debauch, -decline, decry, deface, defile, degrade, demean, demoralize, demote, denigrate, deprave, depreciate, destroy, deteriorate, devalue, dilute, dirty, discredit, disgrace, dishonor, disparage, down-*

grade, flaw, harm, harshen, humble, humiliate, hurt, impair, lessen, lowball, lower, mar, minimize, misapply, misuse, pervert, poison, pollute, profane, prostitute, reduce, relegate, ruin, sacrifice, shame, spoil, stain, subvert, taint, tarnish, thin, underbid, undervalue, vitiate, warp, water, weaken, whore, wreck (≠ accent, accentuate, accrue, advance, ameliorate, amend, amplify, better, clarify, clean, cleanse, dignify, elevate, enhance, ennoble, enrich, exalt, honor, improve, moralize, optimize, overhaul, perfect, promote, purify, raise, rarefy, rectify, refine, restore, revolutionize, upgrade, uplift)

CHEAPEN (/): *abase, abash, affront, badmouth, belittle, boo, castigate, censure, chasten, condemn, confound, confuse, criticize, damn, debase, decry, defame, defile, degrade, demean, denounce, depreciate, detract, diminish, discomfit, disconcert, -discount, discredit, disgrace, dishonor, disparage, embarrass, execrate, faze, fluster, foul, humble, humiliate, insult, libel, lower, malign, minimize, mortify, nonplus, pillory, rattle, ridicule, shame, sink, slander, smirch* (≠ acclaim, advance, aggrandize, apotheosize, applaud, boost, canonize, celebrate, deify, dignify, elevate, ennoble, enshrine, eulogize, exalt, extol, glorify, hail, heroicize, heroize, highlight, honor, idealize, magnify, praise, prioritize, promote, raise, romanticize, spotlight, tout, upgrade, uplift)

CHEAT (+): *bait, bamboozle, beard, beat, beguile, betray, bilk, bleed, bluff, bootleg, bottom-deal, buffalo, bullshit, bunk, burgle, burn, cajole, catch, chisel, clip, con, convince, cook, cozen, crib, deacon, deceive, defraud, delude, diddle, disinform, doctor, double-cross, double-deal, double-talk, dupe, embezzle, enmesh, ensnare, entangle, entice, euchre, exploit, fake, fiddle, finagle, fleece, flimflam, fool, fox, frame, fudge, game, gas, goldbrick, gouge, gull, gyp, hoax, hocus-pocus, hoodwink, hook, hornswoggle, hose, humbug, hustle, hype, ice, inveigle, juggle, lure, manipulate, milk, misdirect, misguide, misinform, mislead, misrepresent, mousetrap, nobble, outfox, outslick, outwit, overreach, palaver, pervert, plant, pluck, pretend, rob, rook, rope, salt, sandbag, scam, screw, seduce, shaft, short, shortchange, shuck, skin, snooker, snow, soak, spoof, squeeze, steal, stick, stiff, sting, stonewall, sucker, swindle, take, tantalize, tempt, thimblerig, trick, two-time, underpay, vamp, victimize, whitewash, wrong* (≠ accuse, afford, assume, audit, authenticate, believe, comp, confess, confide, confirm, corroborate, credit, crosscheck, debunk, deflate, disabuse, disclose, discredit, disgrace, disprove, dispute, distrust, divulge, document, doubt, evince, expose, fund, give, honor, humiliate, malign, mock, offer, -ostracize, pillory, pity, protect, prove, provide, regret, -repudiate, respect, restore, reveal, scruple, shame, stigmatize, substantiate, supply, support, trust, validate, verify, vilify)

CHECK (+): *affirm, analyze, ascertain, assert, assess, audit, authenticate, avow, benchmark, beta, buttress, calculate, caliper, categorize, certify, compare, conclude, confirm, connect, consult, contrast, correlate, corroborate, crosscheck, cross-examine, debunk, declare, deduce, demonstrate, determine, discover, distill, document, ensure, establish, estimate, evaluate, examine, explore, eyeball, frisk, gauge, grill,* *guarantee, inspect, interrogate, interview, investigate, learn, measure, monitor, notarize, police, prioritize, probe, proctor, profess, prove, prowl, rank, read, reference, reinforce, research, sample, scan, scope, screen, scrutinize, search, study, subdivide, substantiate, support, survey, test, time, validate, verify, vet, vindicate, warrant, weigh, witness* (≠ accept, assume, -bypass, challenge, contest, contradict, debate, -deny, disavow, disclaim, -discount, discredit, disprove, dispute, -disregard, distrust, doubt, excuse, fake, gainsay, -ignore, invalidate, misgauge, misjudge, mislead, miss, mistake, -neglect, overestimate, -overlook, pass, pretend, question, rebut, refute, scruple, suspect, underestimate, undershoot)

CHECK (←): *-abort, arrest, bar, block, bottle, bridle, choke, constrain, contain, control, curb, damp, delay, gag, govern, -halt, hamper, handcuff, hinder, hold, housebreak, housetrain, impede, inhibit, interrupt, keep, limit, measure, mince, muffle, muzzle, obstruct, pace, pause, pocket, -prevent, -prohibit, protest, regulate, rein, repress, restrain, retard, rule, shelve, short-circuit, silence, sink, slow, smother, squelch, staunch, stem, stifle, stop, straightjacket, strangle, stymie, suppress, swallow, tame, -thwart* (≠ air, encourage, evince, express, frogmarch, incite, instigate, liberate, loose, loosen, lose, march, punctuate, slack, slacken, spur, unleash, vent)

CHERISH (←): *bear, bronze, carry, conserve, cultivate, embrace, entertain, foster, harbor, hold, honor, house, hug, keep, maintain, nourish, nurse, nurture, pet, preserve, protect, remember, respect, retain, shelter, support, sustain, treasure, value* (≠ -abandon, abjure, -decline, -deny, -desert, discard, -disdain, -disregard, drop, erase, expunge, forget, -forsake, -ignore, -neglect, -overlook, -quit, -refuse, -reject, -renounce, repel, -repudiate, -scorn, torment)

CHERISH (+): *admire, adore, adulate, appreciate, canonize, caress, deify, dig, encourage, enjoy, enshrine, esteem, exalt, extol, fancy, glamorize, glorify, hero-worship, idealize, idolize, immortalize, lionize, love, memorialize, praise, prize, regard, relish, respect, revere, reverence, romanticize, savor, treasure, value, venerate, worship* (≠ -abandon, abhor, abominate, antagonize, -avoid, badmouth, belittle, decry, demean, demonize, deride, -despise, -detest, -disdain, disfavor, disparage, -disregard, execrate, forget, -forsake, -hate, high-hat, -ignore, -loathe, minimize, -neglect, pillory, -renounce, ridicule, -scorn, -slight, -snub, -spurn, undervalue) **(¿) ABSTRACTION ALERT. Concrete goals essential!**

CHEW (/): *bite, bolt, champ, chaw, chomp, consume, crunch, devour, dispatch, eat, gnash, gnaw, gobble, gorge, grind, gulp, gum, ingest, masticate, munch, nibble, nip, nosh, peck, rend, ruminate, scarf, wolf* (≠ cut, dismiss, drink, forget, -ignore, mash, -neglect, spit, swallow)

CHIDE (/): *admonish, berate, blame, boo, browbeat, bully, castigate, censure, chasten, chastise, check, condemn, criticize, critique, curse, defame, defile, denigrate, denounce, deprecate, deride, disapprove, discredit, disparage, disrespect, fault, flay, fulminate, harass, hector, henpeck, intimidate, lecture, lesson, nag, rate, -rebuff, rebuke, -renounce,* *reprimand, reproach, reprove, scold, -scorn, trash-talk, upbraid, vilify* (≠ applaud, approve, blandish, brave, brook, celebrate, compliment, congratulate, countenance, encourage, endorse, flatter, ingratiate, instigate, laud, praise, salute, sanction, tolerate, tout, vindicate)

CHILL (←): *air-condition, congeal, cool, depress, discourage, freeze, frost, ice, numb, refrigerate, supercool, ventilate* (≠ bake, barbecue, boil, broil, cook, crisp, heat, roast, sauté, steam, thaw, toast, warm)

CHILL (/): *afflict, blackmail, bother, browbeat, bully, cloud, cow, damp, dampen, dash, daunt, deaden, debilitate, demoralize, demotivate, depress, discourage, dishearten, dismay, disparage, dispirit, distress, enfeeble, frighten, frustrate, horrify, intimidate, irk, petrify, sadden, scare, terrify, trouble, undermine, unman, unnerve, vex, weaken, weigh, worry* (≠ amuse, assure, bolster, buoy, charm, cheer, delight, embolden, encourage, energize, excite, fortify, galvanize, gladden, hearten, incite, inspire, invigorate, nerve, provoke, rally, relieve, safeguard, spur, steady, steel)

CHIP (/): *break, chisel, chop, clip, crack, crumble, damage, dent, flake, fragment, gash, hack, hew, incise, nick, nock, notch, shape, shear, slash, slice, sliver, snick, snip, splinter, split, whack, whittle* (≠ combine, fix, increase, join, mend, patch, plaster, polish, rectify, repair, restore, sand, shine, smooth, spackle)

CHISEL (→): *carve, chip, contour, crosshatch, cut, engrave, etch, fashion, form, hew, incise, indent, mold, notch, roughcast, sculpt, sculpture, shape, whittle, write* (≠ blur, cloud, erase, fill, muddle, muddy, obliterate, pad, plaster, polish, sand, smooth, smudge, spackle, stuff)

CHISEL (←): *bamboozle, beat, bilk, blackmail, bleed, bluff, cheat, clip, con, cozen, deceive, defraud, diddle, dupe, embezzle, euchre, exploit, extort, fast-talk, fiddle, fleece, flimflam, fool, gazump, gouge, gull, hocus-pocus, hustle, milk, nick, outwit, overcharge, pluck, ream, rob, rook, scam, screw, short, shortchange, skin, skunk, soak, squeeze, steal, stick, stiff, sting, sucker, swindle, trick, underpay, victimize, wrench, wrest, wring* (≠ appropriate, assist, assume, assure, bankroll, believe, bequeath, bestow, compensate, confess, contribute, donate, exonerate, expose, fund, give, help, indemnify, offer, pay, receive, refund, reimburse, repay, respect, restore, return, support, trust, underwrite, volunteer)

CHOKE (/): *asphyxiate, bar, block, clog, close, congest, constrict, drown, extinguish, gag, garrote, kill, lynch, muffle, obstruct, occlude, overpower, overwhelm, plug, repress, restrain, shush, smother, squeeze, squelch, stagnate, stifle, stop, straiten, strangle, stunt, subdue, suffocate, suppress, throttle, wring* (≠ aerate, clear, free, loose, loosen, open, oxygenate, release, restimulate, restore, resuscitate, revitalize, revive, save, slacken, unblock, unclog, ventilate)

CHOOSE (←): *accept, accumulate, acquire, adopt, amass, appoint, approve, assemble, bag, cache, capture, cherry-pick, claim, collect,* *compile, covet, cull, decide, designate, desire, download, elect, embrace, espouse, fancy, favor, fix, gain, garner, gather, glean, grasp, handpick, harvest, hoard, hunt, invite, locate, mark, name, nominate, obtain, peg, pick, pile, pluck, predetermine, prefer, preselect, prioritize, procure, pull, reap, salvage, scavenge, secure, seize, select, set, slot, snag, snare, source, stockpile, store, stow, strip, tab, tag, take, tap, winnow* (≠ -abandon, -avoid, bandy, -decline, deep-six, deselect, discard, discredit, disfavor, dismiss, dissipate, -ditch, donate, drop, dump, eliminate, -eschew, -exclude, -forsake, furnish, give, -ignore, jettison, junk, lavish, lose, -neglect, -nix, offer, -omit, predetermine, -refuse, -reject, remove, -repudiate, retain, scatter, -scorn, scrap, skip, -spurn, squander, supply, toss, trash, -veto, waste)

CHOP (/): *amputate, axe, butcher, carve, circumcise, cleave, cut, dice, dismember, dissect, divide, fell, hack, halve, hash, hew, joint, kibble, mash, mince, purée, rend, saw, separate, sever, slam, slash, slice, smite, split, subtract, sunder* (≠ add, affix, assemble, attach, bind, build, combine, embed, fuse, graft, grow, implant, join, meld, merge, regenerate, repair, restore, sew, sprout, stitch, strengthen, suture, transplant, unify, unite, weld)

CHOREOGRAPH (+): *administer, aim, allocate, arrange, blueprint, budget, calculate, chart, coerce, compel, concert, conduct, constrain, contemplate, contrive, control, correct, design, devise, dictate, direct, draft, drill, engineer, figure, force, frame, govern, handle, instruct, intend, intrigue, lead, machinate, manage, map, mastermind, meditate, oblige, orchestrate, order, organize, outline, oversee, pace, plan, plot, point, premeditate, prepare, project, ready, regulate, require, run, script, shape, sketch, space, steer, strategize, superintend, supervise, teach, time, train, tutor* (≠ blow, bobble, botch, bugger, bungle, butcher, discharge, disorganize, execute, flub, follow, fulfill, fumble, half-ass, heed, -ignore, improvise, keep, mangle, mind, mishandle, muddle, muff, obey, observe, perform, ruin, wreck)

CHURN (→): *agitate, animate, beat, blend, boil, convulse, disturb, ferment, froth, joggle, jolt, mingle, mix, paddle, puddle, pump, reel, rock, roil, shake, splash, stir, swirl, toss, upset, wash, wheel, whip, whirl, whisk* (≠ align, balance, brace, calibrate, calm, center, classify, equalize, fix, hush, level, lull, mellow, mollify, order, organize, regiment, regulate, secure, stabilize, steady, still, tranquilize)

CIRCLE (+): *belt, circuit, circulate, circumnavigate, circumscribe, coil, compass, curve, embrace, encircle, enclose, encompass, envelop, gird, girdle, hedge, hem, loop, orbit, pivot, revolve, ring, roll, rotate, -sidestep, skirt, spiral, surround, tour, whirl, wind, wrap* (≠ accept, -avoid, -bypass, confront, court, -dodge, -escape, face, free, liberate, meet, -neglect, open, pursue, release, seek, welcome)

-CIRCUMVENT (→): *-avert, -avoid, beat, beguile, bilk, -blank, -bypass, circle, circumnavigate, cramp, crimp, deceive, deflect, detour, disappoint,* *disobey, -disregard, divert, -dodge, -duck, dupe, -elude, -end-run, ensnare, entrap, -escape, -eschew, -evade, -flee, flout, foil, fool, frustrate, hoodwink, -ignore, leapfrog, mislead, -obviate, outflank, outwit, overreach, parry, -prevent, queer, ruin, shake, -shirk, -shun, -sidestep, skirt, stump, stymie, subvert, -thwart, trick, ward* (≠ accept, accost, aid, approve, assist, authorize, brave, catch, confront, contact, court, embrace, face, follow, guide, help, meet, mind, obey, observe, permit, pursue, seek, support, welcome, woo)

CIVILIZE (+): *acculturate, acquaint, advance, better, coach, cultivate, develop, discipline, domesticate, drill, edify, educate, elevate, enlighten, ennoble, enrich, foster, housebreak, housetrain, humanize, idealize, implant, improve, indoctrinate, influence, inform, inspire, institute, instruct, mentor, mitigate, moderate, mold, motivate, nurture, pacify, perfect, polish, predispose, prepare, promote, reclaim, refine, school, shape, shine, socialize, sophisticate, spiritualize, sway, tame, teach, train, uplift* (≠ abase, abuse, barbarize, bestialize, brutalize, callous, coarsen, condemn, debase, degrade, dehumanize, enrage, hurt, -ignore, infuriate, menace, mislead, -neglect, outrage, savage, subjugate, threaten, torment, unleash, victimize, worsen, wrong)

CLAIM (→): *accept, acknowledge, adjure, admit, advance, affirm, allege, announce, approve, argue, assert, assume, assure, attest, avow, believe, broadcast, certify, confess, confirm, contend, convince, corroborate, declare, defend, endorse, express, feign, hold, insist, justify, maintain, plead, pledge, postulate, pretend, proclaim, profess, promise, pronounce, protest, purport, ratify, rationalize, reason, state, submit, support, sustain, testify, uphold, urge, validate, verbalize, verify, vindicate, voice, warrant* (≠ -abandon, admit, challenge, confess, confute, consult, contradict, counter, cross-examine, debate, debunk, -deny, disavow, disclaim, discredit, -disown, disprove, dispute, distrust, doubt, gainsay, grill, interrogate, interview, invalidate, -negate, prove, question, rebut, refute, -reject, -repudiate, retort, scruple, suspect) **(¿) ABSTRACTION ALERT. Concrete goals essential!**

CLAIM (←): *accumulate, acquire, add, amass, annex, appropriate, ask, assume, badger, bag, buy, capture, catch, challenge, collect, colonize, command, commandeer, compile, confiscate, conquer, corner, covet, crave, demand, deserve, download, dun, embezzle, enjoin, exact, fetch, garner, gather, get, glean, grab, grasp, harass, harvest, heap, hoard, hotwire, hound, import, impose, impound, incur, insist, invade, land, lure, net, nobble, obtain, occupy, outbid, overrun, own, palm, pilfer, plead, pluck, poach, pocket, press, procure, purchase, purloin, reap, receive, recover, request, require, requisition, retrieve, scavenge, score, secure, seize, select, snaffle, snag, snatch, source, steal, stipulate, stockpile, swipe, take, target, trademark, usurp, vanquish, want, warrant, win, wrangle* (≠ -abandon, anonymize, bandy, bequeath, challenge, commodify, comp, concede, -desert, diffuse, discard, disclaim, -disown, disperse, dispute, -ditch, drop, dump, forfeit, forgo, -forsake, give, grant, hand, jettison, junk, lose, miss, monetize, offload, pass, pay, -reject, release, relinquish, -renounce, sacrifice, scatter, scrap, sell, shed, shuck, slough, spend, squander, surrender, throw, tithe, undershoot, unload, waive, yield)

CLAIM (←): *ask, bear, beg, challenge, command, covet, demand, enjoin, entail, exact, insist, involve, press, require, stipulate, take, want, warrant* (≠ boast, enjoy, hold, keep, maintain, own, possess, retain) **(¿) ABSTRACTION ALERT. Concrete goals essential!**

CLAIM (←): *act, affect, allege, bamboozle, bilk, bluff, bullshit, cheat, con, counterfeit, cover, deceive, defraud, diddle, disguise, dupe, fabricate, fake, falsify, feign, fiddle, fleece, forge, imitate, impersonate, manipulate, outwit, pose, pretend, profess, purport, roleplay, rook, rope, show, simulate, snooker, snow, stage, sucker, swindle, trick, underpay, victimize* (≠ accuse, assume, authenticate, believe, confess, confide, confirm, corroborate, debunk, disabuse, discredit, disgrace, dispute, divulge, doubt, expose, humiliate, malign, mock, notarize, -ostracize, pillory, -repudiate, reveal, shame, stigmatize, substantiate, trust, verify)

CLAIM (/): *annihilate, assassinate, butcher, croak, decimate, deep-six, demolish, destroy, dispatch, doom, eliminate, end, eradicate, erase, execute, fell, finish, get, kill, martyr, massacre, molochize, mow, murder, obliterate, orphan, slaughter, slay, smite, snuff, terminate, topple, waste* (≠ animate, bear, birth, gestate, heal, mend, nourish, nurture, raise, reinvigorate, restore, resurrect, resuscitate, revive, survive, sustain, weather, withstand)

CLARIFY (+): *accent, accentuate, affirm, amplify, analyze, annotate, assert, clear, construe, contextualize, contrast, convey, convince, decipher, decode, deduce, define, delineate, demonstrate, demystify, disentangle, distinguish, elucidate, emphasize, expand, explain, explicate, explore, expound, extract, factor, formulate, generalize, gloss, illuminate, illumine, illustrate, interpret, paraphrase, pinpoint, profile, punctuate, rephrase, resolve, settle, sharpen, simplify, solve, specify, straighten, strip, summarize, teach, translate, uncomplicate, undo, unpack, unravel, unriddle, unscramble, untangle* (≠ baffle, befog, churn, cloud, complicate, confound, confuse, elaborate, embellish, exaggerate, froth, gaslight, jumble, mess, minimize, mix, muddle, muddy, obfuscate, obscure, perplex, puzzle, scramble)

CLARIFY (+): *clean, cleanse, clear, decontaminate, disinfect, distill, extract, filter, leach, perfect, process, purge, purify, rarefy, rectify, reduce, refine, sanitize, screen, sieve, sift, wash* (≠ bedraggle, begrime, besmirch, camouflage, cloud, contaminate, defile, dirty, dull, foul, muddle, muddy, pollute, soil, sully, taint)

CLASP (←): *bear-hug, catch, clamp, clinch, clutch, cradle, crush, cuddle, embrace, encircle, enclasp, enfold, entwine, envelop, fasten, fold, fondle, gather, grab, grasp, grip, hold, hook, hug, lock, nab, nestle, nuzzle, pet, press, seize, snatch, snuggle, squeeze, squoosh, take, twine, wrap* (≠ deliver, drop, entrust, free, give, hand, loose, loosen, pass, release, relinquish, send, slack, slacken, transfer, transmit, unchain, unclasp, unclench, unfasten, unleash)

CLASSIFY (+): *align, allocate, allot, alphabetize, analyze, arrange, array, assign, assort, brand, calculate, catalog, categorize, choose, class, clump, cluster, codify, comb, compartment, compartmentalize, concatenate, conclude, connect, contrast, coordinate, correlate, cue, cull, deduce, designate, digest, display, dispose, distill, distinguish, distribute, divide, docket, document, embody, file, grade, groom, group, hierarchize, identify, incorporate, index, label, line, link, list, map, mark, marshal, match, name, number, order, organize, package, peg, pigeonhole, place, prioritize, queue, range, rank, rate, recategorize, reclassify, recognize, record, refer, regiment, register, regroup, relegate, riddle, screen, segregate, separate, sequence, set, shelve, sieve, sift, size, slot, sort, specify, spruce, stamp, stereotype, straighten, string, subcategorize, subdivide, systematize, tab, tabulate, tag, thread, ticket, tidy, type, typecast, unscramble, winnow* (≠ anonymize, baffle, clutter, collect, confuse, derange, disarrange, disarray, disorder, disorganize, gather, heap, jumble, lump, mess, misclassify, mislabel, missort, mix, muddle, muss, nonplus, perplex, pile, puzzle, rumple, scatter, scramble, shuffle, tangle, upset)

CLASSIFY (/): *bleep, block, bury, camouflage, cloak, conceal, couch, cover, -deny, disguise, distort, encrypt, enshroud, fabricate, guard, hide, hush, kill, maintain, mask, mislead, muddy, obfuscate, obscure, obstruct, occlude, -omit, redact, repress, reserve, screen, seclude, secrete, secure, shroud, smother, stash, stifle, subdue, suppress, withhold* (≠ admit, advertise, air, announce, bare, betray, broadcast, clarify, concede, confess, confide, confirm, debrief, declassify, disclose, discover, display, divulge, expose, flaunt, herald, hint, identify, leak, out, proclaim, publish, reveal, showcase, spread, telegraph, uncover, unmask, volunteer)

CLAW (/): *break, butcher, cleave, crab, cut, dig, dismember, dissect, gash, graze, hack, hurt, incise, injure, itch, lacerate, mangle, maul, open, rend, rip, rive, rupture, scrape, scratch, shred, slash, split, tatter, tear* (≠ aid, armor, bandage, bind, block, close, heal, mend, nurse, remedy, repair, restore, retract, salve, seal, smooth, soothe, stitch, suture)

CLEAN (+): *bathe, brighten, brush, cauterize, clarify, cleanse, clear, comb, dab, decontaminate, delete, delouse, deodorize, disinfect, distill, dredge, dry, dry-clean, dust, erase, filter, flush, freshen, launder, mop, muck, neaten, -nullify, order, organize, polish, purge, purify, rake, refine, remove, rinse, rub, sanitize, scour, scrape, scrub, shampoo, shine, shower, smear, soak, soap, sponge, spruce, sterilize, straighten, swab, sweep, sweeten, tidy, unclutter, vacuum, wash, wipe* (≠ bedraggle, befoul, begrime, blacken, contaminate, corrupt, defile, dirty, discolor, foul, infect, mar, muddy, pollute, replace, smear, smudge, soil, spill, spoil, spot, stain, sully, taint, tarnish, untidy)

CLEANSE (+): *absolve, acquit, alibi, amend, baptize, clarify, clean, clear, decontaminate, delouse, disinfect, elevate, ennoble, exonerate, expunge,* *expurgate, heal, improve, launder, moralize, purge, purify, refine, regenerate, restore, rinse, sanitize, scour, scrub, sterilize, uplift, vindicate* (≠ besmirch, canker, corrode, corrupt, debase, debauch, defile, degrade, demean, deprave, incriminate, pervert, poison, profane, prostitute, stain, sully, tarnish, warp)

CLEAR (→): *aerate, anonymize, -blank, clean, cleanse, delouse, disengage, disentangle, empty, erase, evacuate, filter, fine, free, lighten, move, oxygenate, refine, relieve, remove, shift, shunt, solve, tidy, unblock, unburden, uncomplicate, unload, unpack, vacate, vent, ventilate, void, wipe* (≠ affix, block, burden, clog, complicate, cram, elaborate, embalm, fasten, fix, glue, insert, jam, load, lumber, maintain, overstuff, pack, pin, preserve, restore, sustain, -thwart)

CLEAR (+): *absolve, acquit, alibi, avenge, condone, defend, defray, discharge, disengage, disentangle, dismiss, dispel, except, exculpate, excuse, exempt, exonerate, forget, forgive, free, justify, liberate, license, mitigate, -overlook, pardon, permit, privilege, refute, release, relieve, remit, reprieve, spare, stay, tolerate, vindicate* (≠ accuse, arraign, blame, charge, condemn, contradict, convict, -deny, -desert, destroy, discredit, -disown, disprove, dispute, distrust, doom, doubt, fault, forget, frame, gainsay, grill, -ignore, impeach, implicate, imprison, incriminate, indict, interrogate, oppose, prove, punish, question, rebut, refute, reproach, ruin, sentence)

CLEAVE (/): *amputate, axe, carve, chop, crack, cut, detach, disconnect, dismember, dissect, divide, divorce, hack, halve, hew, incise, joint, open, part, pierce, razor, rend, rip, rive, separate, sever, slash, slice, slit, smite, split, stab, sunder, tear, vivisect, whack* (≠ annex, attach, combine, connect, fuse, join, marry, meld, mend, merge, part, repair, restore, secure, sew, solder, stitch, suture, tie, unite, weld)

CLENCH (←): *bag, bear, capture, carry, catch, clasp, clutch, collar, corral, cradle, embrace, enfold, envelop, fasten, feel, finger, grab, grapple, grasp, grip, handle, hold, hook, hug, land, nab, nail, paw, press, seize, snare, snatch, squeeze, squoosh, take, trap, wrap* (≠ bequeath, cede, deliver, drop, free, give, hand, liberate, loose, loosen, release, relinquish, render, slacken, unchain, unclasp, unclench, unfasten, unhand, unleash, yield)

CLIMB (→): *ascend, crest, escalate, lift, mount, scale, span, straddle, surmount, thrust, top* (≠ descend, dip, dismount, drop, lower, plunge, sink, slide)

CLINCH (+): *affirm, assure, clarify, conclude, confirm, consult, convince, decide, define, demonstrate, determine, end, ensure, establish, finish, illuminate, insure, nail, prove, rubber-stamp, seal, secure, settle, show, specify, state, stipulate, verify* (≠ addle, baffle, confuse, debate, discredit, disprove, dispute, doubt, invalidate, muddle, muddy, mystify, perplex, puzzle, question, scruple, unnerve, unsettle, wrangle)

CLIP (→): *bang, bash, bat, batter, bean, beat, belt, bludgeon, bob, bonk, bop, box, brain, buffet, bump, bung, bunt, bust, butt, cane, chop, clap, clobber, clock, clout, club, concuss, conk, crack, cream, cudgel, cuff, deck, drub, fell, flail, flick, flog, floor, graze, hammer, hit, jab, jostle, kick, knee, knock, lace, lambaste, lash, level, lick, mangle, maul, nail, paste, pelt, pepper, poke, pommel, pound, prod, pummel, punch, push, rabbit-punch, rap, rough, sap, scuff, shove, skull, slam, slap, slash, sledge, sledgehammer, slog, slug, smack, smite, sock, spear, stab, stamp, strike, sucker-punch, swat, swipe, switch, tap, thrash, thump, thwack, wallop, whack, whale, whip, zap* (≠ armor, -avoid, block, caress, cuddle, deflect, -dodge, -duck, guard, hold, miss, parry, pet, protect, repel, secure, shelter, shield, stroke, undershoot)

CLIP (/): *abbreviate, bob, crop, curtail, cut, dock, lop, manicure, mow, nip, pare, pinch, poll, pollard, prune, shave, shear, shorten, skive, snip, stump, trim, truncate, whittle* (≠ augment, cultivate, develop, elongate, expand, extend, foster, grow, increase, lengthen, pad, protect, protract, spin, stretch, sustain, unspool)

CLOAK (/): *act, affect, assume, blanket, bleep, camouflage, clothe, conceal, costume, counterfeit, cover, curtain, disguise, dissimulate, dress, enshroud, fake, feign, gild, hide, impersonate, mask, obscure, occult, palliate, play, playact, pose, pretend, roleplay, screen, sheathe, shield, shroud, simulate, spackle, varnish, veil, whitewash* (≠ bare, betray, brandish, circulate, confess, confide, confirm, denude, disclose, discover, display, disrobe, divulge, exhibit, expose, flaunt, parade, reveal, show, showcase, strip, uncloak, unclothe, uncover, undrape, unmask, unveil, wag)

CLOAK (/): *becloud, bedim, befog, belie, blanket, block, bury, camouflage, clothe, cloud, conceal, cover, curtain, darken, disguise, eclipse, ensconce, enshroud, envelop, gild, gloss, hide, mask, obscure, obstruct, occlude, occult, overshadow, rephrase, screen, shade, shadow, shield, shroud, smother, spin, suppress, varnish, veil, whitewash, wrap* (≠ advertise, air, bare, broadcast, clarify, confess, confide, confirm, confront, detect, disclose, display, disseminate, divulge, expose, floodlight, hype, illuminate, light, peel, present, proclaim, publicize, publish, reveal, show, spread, telegraph, uncloak, uncover, unmask, unveil)

CLOBBER (→): *bang, bash, bat, batter, bean, beat, belt, bludgeon, bob, bonk, bop, box, brain, buffet, bump, bung, bunt, burst, bust, butt, cane, chop, clap, clip, clock, clout, club, concuss, conk, crack, cream, cudgel, cuff, deck, ding, drub, fell, flail, flick, flog, floor, hammer, hit, jab, jostle, kick, knee, knock, lace, lambaste, lash, level, lick, mangle, maul, nail, paste, pelt, pepper, poke, pommel, pound, prod, pulverize, pummel, punch, push, rap, rough, sap, scuff, shove, skull, slam, slap, slash, sledge, sledgehammer, slog, slug, smack, smash, smite, sock, spank, spear, stab, stamp, strike, stroke, sucker-punch, swat, swipe, switch, tap, thrash, thump, thwack, wallop, whack, whale, whip, zap* (≠ armor, defend, deflect, -dodge, -duck, guard, harbor, heal, help, nurse, parry, preserve, protect, repel, safeguard, save, sentinel, shelter, shield, -sidestep, uphold)

CLOBBER (/): *annihilate, beat, best, better, bomb, break, bulldoze, bury, cap, checkmate, conquer, cream, crush, defeat, destroy, devastate, dispatch, doom, drub, dust, eclipse, exceed, finish, flatten, hurdle, knock, lick, master, one-up, outdistance, outdo, outfight, outgun, outmatch, outperform, outreach, outsell, outshine, outstrip, outthink, overcome, overpower, overthrow, overwhelm, paste, quell, rout, ruin, shellac, sink, skin, skunk, slaughter, steamroller, subdue, subjugate, surmount, surpass, sweep, take, thrash, throw, top, transcend, trim, trounce, upend, upset, vanquish, wallop, wax, whip, whomp, whup, wrack, wreck* (≠ back, barricade, blockade, bolster, buttress, champion, contest, cover, defend, defy, -deter, guard, hold, maintain, oppose, preserve, protect, rescue, resist, safeguard, save, screen, secure, shelter, shield, support, survive, sustain, uphold, vindicate, weather, withstand)

CLOCK (→): *bang, bash, bat, batter, bean, belt, bludgeon, bonk, bop, brain, buffet, bump, clip, clobber, clout, club, concuss, conk, crack, cream, cudgel, cuff, deck, drub, fell, floor, hammer, hit, jab, knock, level, nail, paste, pepper, pound, prod, pummel, punch, rabbit-punch, rap, sap, skull, sledgehammer, slug, smack, smite, sock, strike, sucker-punch, swat, swipe, thrash, thump, thwack, wallop, whack, whale, zap* (≠ armor, assist, bandage, block, buffer, counter, cushion, defend, deflect, -dodge, -duck, endure, guard, heal, help, -ignore, mend, miss, pad, parry, pet, protect, repel, shelter, shield, stroke, support, weather)

CLOCK (←): *analyze, assay, case, check, consider, contemplate, cross-check, examine, eyeball, inspect, learn, notice, observe, ogle, patrol, peg, peruse, read, regard, review, scan, scope, scout, scrutinize, search, sift, spot, spy, study, survey, verify, watch, winnow* (≠ -blank, blind, block, bury, -bypass, -circumvent, cloak, conceal, confound, confuse, deceive, -discount, -disregard, excuse, face, forget, guard, hide, -ignore, misjudge, mislead, miss, mistake, -neglect, -overlook, pass, perplex, protect, puzzle, screen, shield, -sidestep, skirt, trick, withhold)

CLOG (/): *baffle, bar, block, bottleneck, brake, bung, burden, catch, check, choke, close, complicate, congest, constipate, constrain, counter, cramp, crimp, cripple, curb, dam, delay, detain, -deter, drag, encumber, entangle, entrap, fetter, fill, foul, -frustrate, hamper, hamstring, handicap, hinder, impair, impede, inhibit, interrupt, jam, lumber, mire, obstruct, occlude, oppose, oppress, overload, paralyze, plug, resist, restrain, restrict, retard, seal, snag, snarl, stem, stop, stopper, stuff, stymie, tangle, -thwart, wedge* (≠ accelerate, advantage, aerate, breach, catalyze, clear, compel, decongest, edge, expedite, facilitate, fast-track, hasten, hurry, jump, midwife, open, oxygenate, penetrate, pierce, pull, quicken, rupture, scour, speed, unblock, unclog, unplug, unstop, untangle, ventilate)

CLONE (←): *adopt, ape, bootleg, copy, counterfeit, double, duplicate, echo, emulate, freeboot, ghostwrite, imitate, impersonate, mirror, multiply,* *photocopy, pirate, playact, repeat, replicate, reproduce, roleplay, simulate* (≠ challenge, coin, contradict, counter, create, -deny, destroy, develop, discredit, dispute, doubt, eliminate, eradicate, expose, exterminate, gainsay, initiate, introduce, invent, oppose, originate, refute, reveal, reverse, spark)

CLOSE (+): *acquire, adjudicate, arbitrate, arrange, broker, clinch, complete, conclude, confirm, contract, decide, determine, establish, execute, land, mediate, negotiate, organize, procure, renegotiate, resolve, seal, secure, settle, transact, verify* (≠ botch, bungle, debate, -deny, dispute, half-ass, lose, offer, predetermine, propose, -refuse, ruin, seek, solicit, spitball, spoil, squander, suggest)

CLOSE (/): *bar, barricade, batten, block, blockade, bolt, chain, clog, cork, deadbolt, fasten, fill, fix, latch, lock, obstruct, occlude, padlock, plug, pucker, seal, secure, shut, slam, stopper, tighten* (≠ broach, crack, expose, open, unbar, unbolt, unchain, unfasten, unlatch, unlock, unseal)

CLOSE (/): *adjourn, cease, complete, conclude, -discontinue, end, finish, -halt, recess, stop, suspend, terminate, wrap* (≠ begin, build, commence, expand, found, inaugurate, initiate, instigate, kick-start, open, prolong, spur, start)

CLOTHE (+): *adjust, adorn, arrange, array, attire, buckle, button, caparison, clean, comb, costume, cover, deck, decorate, don, drape, dress, fit, garb, garnish, groom, gussy, outfit, prepare, primp, rig, robe, straighten, style, tidy, trim, uniform, wear, zip* (≠ bare, denude, disorder, display, disrobe, divest, exhibit, expose, flash, peel, remove, reveal, shed, strip, unbuckle, unbutton, unclothe, uncover, undrape, undress, unveil, unzip)

CLOUD (/): *adumbrate, becloud, befog, blacken, blur, camouflage, churn, cloak, clothe, complicate, conceal, confuse, cover, curtain, darken, dim, disarrange, disarray, discompose, disguise, dishevel, disorder, disorient, disrupt, disturb, dull, eclipse, elaborate, embellish, entangle, extinguish, fog, froth, hide, implicate, jumble, mantle, mask, mix, muddle, muddy, obfuscate, obliterate, obscure, overshadow, perplex, scramble, screen, shade, shadow, shroud, shuffle, snarl, sophisticate, tangle, tousle, upset, veil* (≠ analyze, brighten, clarify, cleanse, clear, decipher, decode, disentangle, explain, expose, floodlight, illuminate, light, reveal, simplify, straighten, streamline, uncloud, uncomplicate, uncover, undo, unravel, unscramble, untangle, unveil)

CLUB (→): *abuse, assail, assault, attack, bang, bash, baste, bat, batter, bean, beat, belt, beset, birch, blackjack, bludgeon, bonk, bop, box, brain, buffet, bust, cane, chop, clip, clobber, clock, clout, concuss, conk, cowhide, crack, cream, crush, cudgel, cuff, deck, drub, fell, flagellate, flatten, flog, floor, fracture, hammer, hide, hit, knock, lace, lambaste, lash, lather, level, lick, mangle, mar, maul, nail, paddle, paste, pelt, pistol-whip, pommel, pound, pulverize, pummel, punch, rap, rough, sap, scourge, skull, slam, slap, slate, sledge, sledgehammer, slug, smack, smash, smite, sock,* *spank, strap, strike, swat, swipe, switch, tan, tap, thrash, thresh, thump, thwack, trounce, wallop, whack, whale, whip, whomp, whup* (≠ aid, armor, assist, bandage, block, buffer, caress, coddle, cure, cushion, defend, deflect, -dodge, -duck, endure, fix, guard, heal, help, hold, -ignore, mend, miss, pad, parry, pet, protect, repair, rescue, shelter, shield, stroke, support, weather)

CLUTCH (←): *bag, bear, capture, carry, catch, cherish, clasp, clench, clinch, collar, corral, cradle, embrace, fasten, feel, finger, grab, grapple, grasp, grip, handle, harbor, hold, hook, hug, keep, land, nab, nail, paw, seize, snag, snare, snatch, take, trap* (≠ -abandon, bequeath, bestow, cede, deliver, donate, drop, give, hand, impart, lose, miss, provide, release, relinquish, render, restore, unclasp, unfasten, unhand, yield)

COACH (+): *accompany, advise, assist, attend, brainwash, brief, chaperone, choreograph, civilize, condition, consult, convince, convoy, counsel, cram, cultivate, demonstrate, develop, direct, discipline, drill, edify, educate, engineer, enhance, enlighten, escort, expand, extend, familiarize, foster, godfather, groom, guide, help, hone, improve, inculcate, indoctrinate, influence, inform, instruct, lead, mentor, monitor, nurture, optimize, orchestrate, oversee, pilot, prepare, prime, question, ready, retrain, school, shepherd, show, steer, stretch, superintend, supervise, sway, teach, test, train, tutor, upgrade* (≠ -abandon, abuse, accept, cheat, decondition, decrease, deflect, destroy, doom, follow, forfeit, forget, hocus-pocus, -ignore, interview, learn, mislead, -neglect, obey, play, practice, sabotage, scupper, shelve, -shun, sidetrack, undermine, wrong)

COARSEN (/): *abase, abrade, adulterate, bastardize, blunt, callous, chafe, cheapen, contaminate, corrupt, damage, deaden, debase, defile, degrade, demean, desensitize, devalue, dirty, disgrace, dishonor, dull, harden, harshen, indurate, lessen, lower, pollute, roughen, score, scuff, sully, taint, tarnish, thicken, toughen, vulgarize* (≠ brush, buff, burnish, civilize, clarify, cultivate, edify, educate, elevate, enhance, enlighten, glitz, heighten, hone, humanize, improve, indulge, instruct, perfect, polish, purify, rarefy, rectify, refine, sand, scrub, sensitize, shine, smooth, socialize, soften, sophisticate, spoil, tame, thin, upgrade, weaken)

COAT (→): *apply, blanket, bury, cake, carpet, circle, cloak, clothe, cover, curtain, daub, encircle, enclose, encompass, encrust, enshroud, envelop, lard, layer, mantle, overlay, paint, pave, pigment, plaster, shawl, shroud, slather, smear, spread, swathe, syrup, veil, wrap* (≠ bare, betray, clean, clear, disclose, display, divulge, erase, excoriate, expose, peel, remove, reveal, skin, stipple, strip, uncover, unearth)

COAX (←): *adulate, allure, barter, beckon, beg, beguile, beseech, blandish, blarney, bribe, bullshit, butter, cajole, candy-coat, charm, con, convince, cozen, decoy, draw, enlist, entice, facilitate, finagle, flannel, flatter, glad-hand, gratify, grease, hook, hustle, importune, indoctrinate, induce, influence, ingratiate, inveigle, juggle, lubricate, lure, massage, oil,* *overpraise, palaver, persuade, pester, press, schmooze, seduce, sell, snooker, soft-sell, soft-soap, soothe, sway, sweet-talk, tantalize, tease, tempt, urge, wangle, wheedle, woo, worm* (≠ allow, blackmail, bluff, browbeat, bug, bulldoze, bully, chill, claim, coerce, command, commandeer, compel, constrain, cow, dampen, demand, -deter, dictate, discourage, disenchant, disgust, dissuade, dragoon, drive, exact, force, harass, intimidate, make, muscle, nag, oblige, order, pester, railroad, repel, repulse, require, sandbag, solicit, stall, steamroller, stem, stipulate, tease, trash-talk, warn)

COBBLE (+): *assemble, build, clout, compound, concoct, craft, create, design, engineer, fabricate, fashion, forge, formulate, frame, fudge, half-ass, handcraft, improvise, jerry-build, jerry-rig, patch, sculpt, shape, weave* (≠ annihilate, batter, break, damage, demolish, destroy, discard, dismantle, mangle, raze, ruin, shred, smash, wreck)

COCOON (←): *bind, blanket, camouflage, circle, cloak, cloister, clothe, costume, cover, curtain, cushion, defend, disguise, drape, embed, embrace, encase, encircle, enclose, encompass, enfold, enlace, enshroud, envelop, insulate, involve, isolate, lap, mantle, mask, muffle, overprotect, pad, preserve, protect, seclude, sheathe, shroud, swaddle, swathe, truss, veil, wrap* (≠ bare, compromise, denude, display, endanger, excoriate, expose, harm, imperil, injure, jeopardize, menace, open, peel, present, reunite, reveal, show, strip, target, threaten, uncover, unite, unveil)

CODDLE (←): *accommodate, baby, caress, cherish, cosset, cotton, cradle, cuddle, favor, featherbed, fondle, gratify, humor, indulge, infantilize, mollycoddle, nurse, nurture, overindulge, overprotect, pamper, pet, pity, protect, smother, spoil, spoon-feed, sugarcoat, treat* (≠ abuse, assault, control, crucify, discipline, disfavor, harass, harm, hurt, -ignore, injure, mangle, menace, mistreat, molest, -neglect, -overlook, persecute, restrain, straightjacket, threaten, torment, torture, victimize, violate, wound, wrong)

CODIFY (+): *align, alphabetize, arrange, array, assort, catalog, categorize, class, classify, clump, cluster, compartment, compartmentalize, cull, digest, distinguish, distribute, docket, file, grade, group, hierarchize, identify, index, list, map, marshal, order, organize, peg, pigeonhole, place, prioritize, queue, range, rank, recategorize, reclassify, regiment, regroup, relegate, screen, separate, set, shelve, sieve, sift, slot, sort, stereotype, straighten, systematize, type, unscramble, winnow* (≠ churn, confuse, derange, disarrange, disorganize, jumble, lump, misclassify, missort, mistype, mix, muddle, rumple, scramble, upset)

COERCE (→): *badger, blackjack, blackmail, bludgeon, bluff, browbeat, bulldoze, bully, compel, constrain, cow, daunt, dominate, drag, dragoon, drive, egg, force, frighten, harass, hector, hound, impel, impress, intimidate, make, menace, muscle, nobble, obligate, oblige, press, press-gang, pressure, push, railroad, repress, restrict, sandbag, scare, shame, squeeze, steamroller, strong-arm, suppress, terrorize, threaten, urge* (≠ allow, argue, bait, bribe, cajole, coax, convince, entice, hinder, -ignore, induce, influence, invite, let, lure, move, permit, persuade, satisfy, schmooze, seduce, subvert, sway, tantalize, tease, tempt, welcome)

COIL (←): *arch, belt, bend, circle, corkscrew, crook, curl, curve, encircle, enlace, entwine, fake, girdle, hook, interlace, intertwine, lace, loop, orbit, rotate, snake, spiral, sweep, swerve, swirl, tie, turn, twine, twirl, twist, weave, wheel, whirl, wind, wreathe, zigzag* (≠ align, flatten, neaten, order, right, straighten, tidy, tug, unbend, uncoil, uncurl, unspool)

COLLAPSE (/): *abbreviate, abridge, capsule, capsulize, compact, compress, concentrate, condense, consolidate, constrict, contract, cram, crowd, curtail, decrease, diminish, downsize, jam, jam-pack, lessen, narrow, pack, shorten, shrink, simplify, squeeze, streamline, telescope, wedge* (≠ augment, bulge, decompress, diffuse, dilate, disperse, dissipate, distend, expand, increase, inflate, open, outstretch, scatter, swell)

COLLAR (←): *abduct, apprehend, arrest, bag, capture, catch, clasp, clutch, cop, corner, corral, detain, enmesh, ensnare, entangle, entrap, get, glom, grab, grapple, grasp, grip, halter, hold, hook, kidnap, land, lasso, nab, nail, net, rap, rend, rope, secure, seize, snaffle, snag, snatch, wrangle, wrest* (≠ discharge, drop, free, liberate, loosen, miss, release, slacken, unhand)

COLLAR (←): *apprehend, arrest, bind, bust, capture, catch, commit, confine, convict, detain, enchain, fetter, get, grab, handcuff, haul, hogtie, hold, immure, imprison, incarcerate, intern, jail, jug, manacle, nab, nail, nick, pinch, restrain, seize, shackle, snare, snatch, stop, straightjacket, trammel, trap* (≠ coddle, discharge, emancipate, free, liberate, loose, loosen, pamper, release, spring, unbind, unchain)

COLLECT (←): *accrue, accumulate, aggregate, amass, arrange, assemble, ball, band, batch, bind, brigade, bunch, cluster, collate, combine, compile, concentrate, congregate, connect, consolidate, corral, garner, gather, glean, group, heap, herd, hive, hoard, join, lasso, link, lump, merge, muster, organize, pack, pile, pool, press, raise, rally, rope, round, save, source, stack, stash, stockpile, swarm, systematize, throng, tuck, unite, wrangle* (≠ banish, cant, chuck, diffuse, disband, discard, disintegrate, dismiss, dispel, disperse, dissipate, dissolve, eject, jettison, scatter, send, separate, sever, split)

COLLECT (←): *acquire, beg, beseech, court, covet, crave, cultivate, demand, entreat, fetishize, gain, implore, importune, inherit, invite, lobby, obtain, petition, procure, prompt, pursue, request, seek, solicit, target, win, woo, wow* (≠ afford, bankroll, bequeath, bestow, comp, contribute, deliver, donate, endow, equip, fund, furnish, gift, give, hand, offer, pay, provide, secure, spare, supply, tender, tithe, volunteer, yield)

COLLECT (+): *assemble, assure, calm, compile, compose, contain, content, control, enlighten, form, gather, hush, inform, lull, mellow, mollify, order, organize, pace, pacify, placate, prepare, propitiate, quiet, rally, ready, reassure, recollect, recover, regulate, restore, restrain, satisfy, settle,* *silence, soothe, steady, still, tranquilize* (≠ alarm, baffle, bewilder, blindside, confuse, discombobulate, discomfit, disconcert, dismay, disturb, dizzy, embarrass, faze, fluster, gaslight, nonplus, perplex, perturb, rattle, ruffle, shake, startle, surprise, throw, unnerve, unsettle, upset)

COLLECT (+): *accumulate, acquire, aggregate, amass, anthologize, assemble, collate, commission, compile, download, edit, garner, gather, glean, group, recompile, redact, redraft, reedit, revamp, revise, rework* (≠ censor, destroy, diffuse, disarrange, disassemble, disorder, disorganize, disperse, distribute, divide, -reject, scatter, separate, spread)

COLONIZE (+): *annex, appropriate, base, begin, build, create, discover, form, found, inaugurate, inhabit, install, institute, introduce, invade, lodge, occupy, organize, people, pioneer, plant, populate, secure, settle, shelter, start, tenant* (≠ -abandon, annihilate, circumnavigate, clear, decimate, depopulate, evacuate, -forsake, leave, level, maroon, massacre, relinquish, relocate, remove, -renounce, ruin, slaughter, uproot, vacate)

COMB (→): *ascertain, assess, audit, browse, check, descry, detect, determine, dig, discover, dredge, examine, explore, ferret, find, frisk, get, grub, hit, hunt, inspect, investigate, learn, locate, peruse, plumb, poke, probe, prowl, rake, ransack, read, reinvestigate, review, riffle, rifle, rummage, scan, scope, scour, screen, scrutinize, search, sift, sort, study, survey, sweep, track* (≠ -abandon, block, bury, -bypass, conceal, ensconce, hide, -ignore, jumble, lose, miss, mistake, -neglect, -overlook, scramble, screen, shield, veil)

COMB (+): *adjust, arrange, brush, clean, curry, disentangle, dress, fix, groom, gussy, manicure, neaten, order, prepare, prime, primp, sleek, slick, smarten, smooth, spiff, spruce, tidy, titivate, untangle* (≠ dirty, dishevel, disorder, entangle, jumble, kink, knot, mess, muss, snarl, tangle, untidy)

COMBAT (→): *agitate, argue, assault, bash, batter, battle, beat, belt, bludgeon, box, buffet, bump, clobber, confront, contest, debate, dispute, duel, engage, fight, hammer, hit, knock, paste, pound, punch, slam, slap, slug, smack, smite, sock, strike, swat, swipe, thump, thwack, wallop, whack, whale, wrestle* (≠ alleviate, allow, -bypass, calm, defend, defuse, endorse, forfeit, -ignore, join, lose, miss, mitigate, mollify, pacify, permit, placate, quell, second, skirt, subdue, support)

COMBAT (/): *accost, attack, baffle, -balk, bar, battle, challenge, check, checkmate, confound, confront, contest, contradict, counter, counteract, countercheck, curb, defeat, defy, face, fight, foil, -frustrate, hamper, hinder, impede, meet, minimize, monkey-wrench, muzzle, obstruct, oppose, oppugn, -prevent, protest, race, resist, stymie, -thwart, withstand* (≠ abide, accord, advance, advocate, back, bear, champion, cultivate, encourage, endorse, endure, forward, foster, further, nourish, nurture, promote, rubber-stamp, suffer, support, uphold)

COMBINE (+): *add, amalgamate, annex, associate, attach, beat, bind, blend, bond, cement, churn, coalesce, collage, commingle, composite, compound, concrete, conflate, conjoin, connect, couple, emulsify, entwine, fasten, fold, fuse, glue, homogenize, hybridize, incorporate, integrate, intermingle, intermix, intertwine, interweave, join, knit, link, marry, match, meld, mend, merge, mingle, mix, mortar, reintegrate, splice, stir, synthesize, tie, toss, unify, unite, weave, weld, yoke* (≠ atomize, bisect, break, chop, chunk, cleave, crack, detach, diffuse, disengage, disjoin, disperse, dissolve, disunite, divide, divorce, fracture, fragment, halve, kibble, part, partition, pulverize, razor, rip, rupture, scatter, separate, sever, shatter, slice, split, sunder, tear, unmix)

COMFORT (+): *abate, aid, allay, alleviate, ameliorate, appease, assist, assuage, assure, bolster, boost, brace, buoy, calm, cheer, coddle, confirm, console, convince, cuddle, delight, divert, ease, elevate, embolden, encourage, enliven, free, gladden, heal, hearten, help, hush, inspire, inspirit, invigorate, lift, lubricate, lull, mellow, midwife, mitigate, mollify, nourish, nurture, pacify, placate, please, quiet, reanimate, reassure, refresh, reinvigorate, relax, relieve, remedy, restimulate, revitalize, revive, rock, salve, sedate, soften, solace, soothe, steady, stimulate, strengthen, stroke, subdue, succor, sugarcoat, support, sustain, tranquilize, treat, uplift* (≠ afflict, aggravate, agonize, annoy, antagonize, arouse, avenge, badger, bait, bedevil, bother, burden, castigate, chafe, chasten, chastise, correct, crucify, daunt, demean, demonize, discipline, distress, disturb, enrage, exacerbate, exasperate, fine, grate, harry, hassle, horrify, inflame, infuriate, irk, irritate, judge, lumber, mar, menace, nag, needle, nettle, niggle, nitpick, overset, pain, peeve, penalize, persecute, perturb, pester, pillory, punish, rankle, rile, roil, sadden, sorrow, sting, tease, threaten, torment, torture, upset, vex, victimize, wound, wrong)

COMMAND (→): *adjure, advise, appoint, ask, assign, authorize, beg, beseech, bid, boss, call, charge, coerce, commission, compel, conduct, constrain, control, counsel, curb, decree, demand, determine, dictate, direct, enjoin, entreat, exact, force, guide, hinder, influence, instruct, lead, manage, mandate, muscle, oblige, operate, ordain, order, oversee, petition, prescribe, push, railroad, request, require, restrain, stop, superintend, supervise, sway, task, tell, warn* (≠ allow, -cancel, contradict, countermand, -deny, follow, gainsay, keep, mind, -negate, obey, observe, refute, -rescind)

COMMAND (→): *administer, boss, captain, choreograph, coach, conduct, conquer, control, dictate, direct, dominate, domineer, govern, head, lead, manage, master, micromanage, officiate, oppress, orchestrate, override, oversee, pace, regulate, rule, run, skipper, spearhead, subdue, subjugate, superintend, supervise, tyrannize* (≠ challenge, counteract, defy, follow, mind, misrule, obey, oppose, plead, pursue, -refuse, resist, serve, subvert)

COMMAND (←): *bear, boast, carry, claim, enjoy, exhibit, hold, keep, own, possess, reserve, retain, show, showcase, sport, stock, sustain, withhold*

(≠ cede, discard, dump, relinquish, require, -spurn, squander, surrender, want, yield)

COMMAND (←): *anticipate, ask, assess, await, bill, bring, charge, demand, discount, exact, expect, fetch, invoice, obtain, overcharge, price, secure, undercharge, value* (≠ acquire, afford, beg, bestow, bid, buy, compensate, fund, furnish, meet, obtain, offer, outbid, pay, purchase, recompense, refund, reimburse, repay, reward, stiff, treat)

COMMAND (←): *ask, badger, beg, claim, coerce, demand, dun, enjoin, exact, expect, foist, harass, hound, impose, plead, request, require, requisition, stipulate, take, want, warrant* (≠ bequeath, bestow, comp, donate, give, hand, hint, imply, insinuate, offer, pledge, relinquish, spare, suggest, surrender, volunteer, yield)

COMMANDEER (←): *annex, appropriate, arrogate, assume, attach, bogart, bootleg, claim, collar, colonize, confiscate, conscript, convert, despoil, draft, embezzle, enslave, gate-crash, grab, grasp, hijack, hotwire, impound, infringe, invade, liberate, loot, misapply, misappropriate, misuse, occupy, pillage, pirate, poach, preempt, press, reap, recoup, recover, repossess, requisition, retrieve, scavenge, seize, sequester, snag, snatch, steal, swipe, take, trespass, usurp, wrench, wrest* (≠ -abandon, deliver, disengage, forfeit, give, keep, offer, pass, pledge, provide, receive, -refuse, -reject, resign, retreat, return, sacrifice, secede, spare, stop, supply, surrender, vacate, volunteer, withdraw, yield)

COMMEMORATE (+): *bless, bronze, celebrate, ceremonialize, congratulate, consecrate, fête, honor, immortalize, keep, lament, laud, lionize, mark, memorialize, mourn, observe, praise, recognize, regret, remember, ritualize, salute, sanctify, solemnize* (≠ break, cheat, discredit, disgrace, dishonor, dismiss, -disregard, -exclude, forget, -ignore, -neglect, -omit, -overlook, regret, repent, reproach, rue, skip, transgress, violate)

COMMEND (→): *advance, advocate, approve, assign, bid, commit, confer, confide, consign, deliver, entrust, extend, give, hand, offer, present, proffer, propose, relegate, render, resign, rubber-stamp, spare, submit, suggest, tender, trust, volunteer, yield* (≠ accept, begrudge, blackball, debit, -deny, deprive, detain, dismiss, hold, keep, oust, -prevent, receive, -refuse, -reject, remove, resent, reserve, retain, take, withdraw, withhold)

COMMEND (+): *acclaim, accredit, advocate, applaud, approve, back, befriend, boost, build, champion, compliment, congratulate, countenance, endorse, eulogize, extol, hail, honor, idolize, laud, lionize, praise, prioritize, promote, recommend, sanction, stroke, support* (≠ admonish, attack, blame, blast, boo, censure, chastise, condemn, criticize, critique, denigrate, denounce, denunciate, disparage, diss, fault, frame, fulminate, knock, lambaste, neg, pan, rebuke, reprimand, -scorn, slam, zap)

COMMISSION (+): *accredit, affirm, appoint, approve, arrange, assign, authorize, bid, certify, charge, command, commit, confirm, consign, contract, countersign, crown, delegate, deputize, designate, dispatch,* *employ, empower, enable, enfranchise, engage, enlist, enroll, entitle, entrust, greenlight, hire, inaugurate, induct, instruct, invest, license, mandate, name, nominate, notarize, ordain, order, permit, request, sanction, select, send, task, validate, warrant* (≠ ban, bar, blackball, blacklist, block, debar, -deny, disallow, disapprove, -exclude, expel, -forbid, -nix, -ostracize, oust, -prevent, -prohibit, protest, -reject, -repudiate, retract, -snub, -veto, wait-list, withhold)

COMMIT (→): *accomplish, ace, achieve, actualize, attain, claim, compass, complete, crest, effect, effectuate, enact, end, execute, finish, fulfill, implement, make, nail, negotiate, perform, perpetrate, practice, prosecute, realize, reenact, repeat* (≠ baffle, blow, defeat, -ditch, fail, -frustrate, mar, miscarry, ruin, scant, -shirk, -shun, skimp, -slight, slur, spoil)

COMMIT (→): *advance, assign, bequeath, commend, confer, confide, consign, contribute, deal, delegate, deliver, deposit, dispense, disperse, distribute, divide, entrust, furnish, give, grant, hand, leave, lend, loan, pass, recommend, release, relinquish, submit, supply, surrender, transfer, transmit, trust, vest, will, yield* (≠ accept, detain, hold, keep, occupy, own, possess, receive, reserve, retain, take, withhold)

COMMIT (+): *affiance, betroth, bind, contract, covenant, decide, dedicate, engage, enlist, enroll, mortgage, obligate, overcommit, pledge, predetermine, promise, swear, vow* (≠ betray, cheat, contradict, debate, -deny, discredit, disprove, dispute, distrust, doubt, gainsay, invalidate, mistrust, oppose, refute, -repudiate, retract, stiff, wait-list, waive)

COMMIT (/): *admit, apprehend, arrest, assign, bar, bind, bust, capture, catch, confine, constrain, convict, detain, enchain, fetter, gate, handcuff, hold, immure, impound, impress, imprison, incarcerate, institutionalize, intern, jail, jug, keep, limit, manacle, nab, pinch, restrain, restrict, seize, send, shackle, shanghai, shut, straightjacket, trammel* (≠ discharge, emancipate, enfranchise, free, liberate, manumit, release, unbind, uncage, unchain, unfetter)

COMPEL (→): *badger, bind, blackjack, blackmail, bludgeon, bluff, browbeat, bulldoze, bully, coerce, command, constrain, cow, daunt, dictate, drag, dragoon, drive, enforce, entrance, exact, extort, fascinate, foment, force, frogmarch, galvanize, harass, hector, hijack, hound, hustle, impel, importune, impress, incite, insist, instruct, intimidate, make, mandate, march, menace, mesmerize, motivate, muscle, nag, nobble, obligate, oblige, overcommit, pester, press, press-gang, pressure, railroad, require, restrain, sandbag, shame, sic, spark, squeeze, steamroller, stimulate, stipulate, straightjacket, stress, strong-arm, terrorize, threaten, trammel, trash-talk, urge* (≠ absolve, accord, acquit, allow, argue, ask, blandish, block, bribe, cajole, clear, coax, convince, curb, delay, discharge, exculpate, exempt, exonerate, forgive, free, -frustrate, hinder, impede, induce, liberate, move, obstruct, pardon, permit, persuade, release, satisfy, schmooze, shelve, shield, soft-sell, soft-soap, solicit, spare, sweet-talk, -thwart, wheedle, win)

COMPENSATE (→): *balance, bankroll, bribe, -cancel, correct, counteract, counterbalance, countervail, defray, disburse, discharge, dole, expense, indemnify, neutralize, nobble, -nullify, offset, outlay, overpay, patronize, pay, -quit, realign, rebate, recompense, recoup, redress, refund, reimburse, remedy, remit, remunerate, repair, repay, reward, satisfy, set, settle, square, tune* (≠ beggar, burgle, cheat, deprive, disinherit, -disown, divest, fine, forfeit, lose, relinquish, remove, rob, sacrifice, shortchange, steal, stiff, underpay, withhold)

COMPENSATE (+): *abrogate, accommodate, adjust, allow, annul, appease, balance, better, calibrate, -cancel, compromise, concede, counteract, counterbalance, equalize, fix, improve, invalidate, mediate, -negate, neutralize, -nullify, offset, outweigh, reconcile, recoup, redeem, redress, repair, replace, restitute, restore* (≠ burden, capsize, damage, deprive, encumber, exacerbate, hamstring, impair, injure, overbalance, overburden, overwhelm, penalize, tilt, topple, upset, wrong)

COMPILE (+): *accumulate, amass, anthologize, arrange, assemble, collate, collect, compose, craft, cull, edit, garner, gather, glean, group, marshal, organize, recompile, redact, redraft, reedit, retool, revamp, revise, rework, scavenge* (≠ delete, destroy, diffuse, disarrange, disassemble, discard, disorder, disorganize, disperse, distribute, divide, extract, forget, -ignore, miss, ransack, rummage, scatter, separate, spread)

COMPLEMENT (+): *accompany, accomplish, achieve, approximate, benefit, cap, clinch, complete, conclude, consummate, contrast, crown, finalize, finish, fulfill, improve, integrate, juxtapose, match, perfect, satisfy, top* (≠ degrade, deplete, diminish, downsize, fail, impair, lessen, mismatch, -neglect, reduce, subtract, vulgarize, worsen)

COMPLETE (+): *accomplish, achieve, actualize, cap, claim, clinch, close, conclude, consummate, crest, crown, discharge, discover, end, execute, finalize, finish, fulfill, make, perfect, perform, plumb, realize, settle, terminate, win* (≠ begin, commence, continue, delay, establish, extend, inaugurate, institute, introduce, open, prolong, resurrect, revive, shelve, stall, start, sustain)

COMPLICATE (/): *churn, compound, confound, confuse, develop, elaborate, embarrass, embroider, entangle, expand, implicate, intensify, jumble, magnify, mix, muddle, perplex, scramble, snarl, sophisticate, tangle* (≠ abbreviate, align, cut, disentangle, ease, facilitate, lubricate, midwife, organize, oversimplify, shorten, simplify, straighten, streamline, transact, unravel, untangle)

COMPLICATE (/): *aggravate, amplify, compound, deepen, exacerbate, exaggerate, heighten, increase, inflame, intensify, magnify, overdramatize, worsen* (≠ allay, alleviate, ameliorate, assuage, better, ease, help, improve, lubricate, midwife, mitigate, relieve, simplify)

COMPLIMENT (+): *acclaim, admire, adulate, applaud, blandish, boost, butter, cajole, celebrate, charm, cheer, commemorate, commend,* *congratulate, endorse, eulogize, exalt, extol, felicitate, flannel, flatter, glorify, greet, hail, high-five, honor, hype, idolize, ingratiate, laud, lionize, magnify, panegyrize, please, plug, praise, presell, recommend, salute, sanction, schmooze, soothe, toast, worship* (≠ abuse, badmouth, belittle, blame, blast, boo, castigate, chasten, chide, condemn, criticize, critique, debase, decry, defame, demean, demonize, denounce, dishonor, disparage, disrespect, diss, fault, frame, fulminate, humiliate, insult, lambaste, libel, mock, pillory, ridicule, scold, -scorn, shame, slander, tease, vilify, wrong)

COMPOSE (+): *arrange, assemble, author, brew, build, cast, choreograph, coin, conceive, concoct, construct, contour, contrive, cook, craft, create, design, devise, discover, draw, fabricate, fashion, forge, form, formulate, frame, fudge, ghostwrite, imagine, invent, make, orchestrate, originate, pen, plan, produce, score, script, sculpt, write* (≠ annihilate, break, bulldoze, demolish, destroy, dismantle, disperse, forget, half-ass, improvise, inspire, instigate, motivate, obliterate, raze, ruin, sabotage, scotch, scupper, scuttle, shelve, spur, topple, undermine, wreck) **(¿) ABSTRACTION ALERT. Concrete goals essential!**

COMPOSE (+): *adjust, align, allay, appease, arrange, assuage, attune, balance, calibrate, calm, center, collect, comfort, compile, console, consolidate, contain, control, cool, coordinate, direct, ease, equalize, focus, gather, ground, harmonize, lull, mellow, mitigate, moderate, modulate, mollify, pace, pacify, placate, poise, quell, quiet, reconcile, regiment, regulate, relax, repress, resolve, restrain, sculpt, sedate, settle, sober, soften, soothe, square, stabilize, steady, still, suppress, temper, tranquilize, tune, unify* (≠ aggravate, agitate, alarm, anger, annoy, arouse, confuse, convulse, daze, disarrange, discombobulate, disconcert, disorganize, disquiet, distress, disturb, dizzy, excite, fan, foment, heckle, heighten, hurt, incense, incite, increase, intensify, irritate, kindle, mismatch, nag, needle, nitpick, provoke, rattle, rouse, scatter, shake, stir, troll, trouble, unsettle, upset, vex, worry, worsen)

COMPOUND (+): *alloy, ally, amalgamate, blend, cement, chain, churn, coalesce, combine, concatenate, conjugate, connect, couple, dovetail, fuse, hitch, hook, hybridize, incorporate, integrate, interconnect, interlink, intermingle, intermix, join, link, merge, mingle, mix, reintegrate, string, synthesize, unify, unite, weld, wire, yoke* (≠ cleave, detach, disconnect, disengage, disjoin, disjoint, distill, disunite, divide, part, rupture, separate, sever, split, sunder, unchain, uncouple, unhitch, unlink, unyoke)

COMPOUND (+): *accelerate, accent, accentuate, accrue, accumulate, add, affirm, aggrandize, amass, amplify, animate, assert, augment, boost, build, bulge, bump, buttress, collect, complement, complicate, corroborate, cube, deepen, develop, dilate, distend, double, elaborate, elongate, embellish, emphasize, enhance, enlarge, escalate, expand, extend, flavor, foster, heighten, hype, increase, inflate, inspire, intensify, lengthen, magnify, marinate, maximize, multiply, prioritize, prolong, protract, punctuate, raise, ratchet, reinforce, restore, season, spice, spike,* *strengthen, stretch, supersize, supplement, swell, treble, triple, unspool, up* (≠ abate, abbreviate, abridge, balance, -cancel, compress, condense, constrict, contract, counteract, curtail, cut, decrease, de-escalate, diminish, downsize, edit, erase, lessen, lower, minimize, rarefy, reduce, shorten, subtract, truncate, underemphasize, undo)

COMPOUND (/): *aggravate, complicate, embitter, enrage, exacerbate, exaggerate, expand, extend, heighten, impair, increase, inflame, inflate, infuriate, intensify, irritate, overdramatize, provoke, vex, worsen* (≠ alleviate, assuage, better, calm, correct, ease, help, improve, lull, mellow, minimize, mitigate, mollify, offset, outweigh, overcome, placate, rectify, redress, relieve, remedy, sedate, soothe, subdue)

COMPRESS (/): *abbreviate, abridge, capsule, capsulize, collapse, compact, concentrate, condense, consolidate, constrict, contract, cram, crowd, crush, curtail, decrease, diminish, downsize, flatten, focus, generalize, impact, jam, jam-pack, lace, lessen, miniaturize, minimize, narrow, pack, pincer, pinch, press, pressurize, pump, reduce, sardine, screw, shoehorn, shorten, shrink, simplify, squash, squeeze, squoosh, strain, straiten, strangle, streamline, stuff, summarize, synopsize, tamp, telescope, wedge, wrinkle* (≠ accrue, amplify, augment, balloon, broaden, bulge, decompress, diffuse, dilate, disperse, dissipate, distend, elaborate, expand, fatten, increase, inflate, magnify, maximize, open, scatter, spread, swell, unfold, unfurl)

COMPROMISE (/): *blackjack, blackmail, blight, bludgeon, chance, cripple, endanger, explode, expose, gamble, harm, harshen, hazard, hobble, hurt, impair, impede, imperil, implicate, infect, inhibit, intimidate, jeopardize, mar, menace, poison, pollute, predetermine, prejudice, risk, ruin, sabotage, scotch, scupper, scuttle, spike, spoil, subject, target, threaten, undermine, venture, wager, weaken* (≠ aid, armor, block, comfort, cure, defend, disinfect, guard, heal, help, immunize, imperil, inoculate, preserve, protect, quarantine, rescue, resume, safeguard, save, secure, shelter, shield, treat, vaccinate)

COMPROMISE (/): *besmirch, blacken, blemish, coarsen, contaminate, damage, degrade, demean, diminish, discredit, disgrace, dishonor, embarrass, humiliate, implicate, incriminate, involve, malign, prejudice, shame, stain, sully, taint, tarnish, vulgarize* (≠ aid, assist, beautify, benefit, brighten, clean, defend, dignify, elevate, enhance, freshen, glorify, honor, moralize, optimize, overhaul, polish, praise, purify, rarefy, rectify, refine, restore, sanitize, shine, spruce, straighten, tidy, upgrade, wash)

COMPUTE (+): *add, appraise, ascertain, assess, benchmark, calculate, categorize, chart, cipher, conclude, consider, count, deduce, determine, discern, divide, enumerate, evaluate, examine, figure, gauge, grade, graph, hack, infer, jack, judge, measure, multiply, number, numerate, plan, plot, prove, quantify, rank, rate, rationalize, read, reckon, scan, study, subtract, sum, tally, test, time, total, triangulate, value, weigh* (≠ approximate, assume, believe, challenge, cheat, claim, conjecture, contradict, deceive, distrust, doubt, estimate, fake, falsify, fancy, fudge, gainsay, guess, guesstimate, mistrust, question, refute, surmise, trick, wonder)

CON (+): *bamboozle, beguile, bilk, bluff, bullshit, cajole, cheat, coax, deceive, defraud, delude, diddle, double-cross, dupe, entrap, exploit, fleece, flimflam, fool, fox, gammon, goldbrick, gull, hoax, hocus-pocus, hoodwink, hornswoggle, humbug, inveigle, lure, manipulate, mislead, outslick, outwit, palaver, rook, scam, shortchange, snooker, snow, spin, stiff, sweet-talk, swindle, trick, underpay, victimize, wheedle, wrong* (≠ absolve, acquit, assume, assure, believe, blab, blurt, clear, confess, confide, confront, crosscheck, debunk, divulge, exonerate, expose, honor, pardon, protect, regret, remedy, shame, trust, validate, verify, vindicate)

CONCEAL (/): *blanket, bury, cache, coffer, cover, -ditch, ensconce, entomb, harbor, hide, hoard, holster, inter, niche, palm, plant, secrete, sheathe, shelter, sneak, squirrel, stash, store, stow, submerge, tuck, wrap* (≠ bare, brandish, disinter, display, exhibit, exhume, expose, exteriorize, externalize, flaunt, manifest, open, present, reveal, show, showcase, strip, uncover, unearth, unmask, unveil, unwrap)

CONCEAL (/): *beard, -blank, blanket, bleep, block, blur, bury, camouflage, candy-coat, classify, cloak, clothe, cloud, costume, couch, cover, curtain, darken, -deny, disguise, -duck, eclipse, enshroud, gild, gloss, guard, hide, holster, hood, hush, kill, maintain, manage, mask, muddy, obfuscate, obscure, obstruct, occlude, occult, -omit, overshadow, plant, repress, screen, seclude, shade, sheathe, shroud, smother, spackle, spin, stifle, subdue, sugarcoat, suppress, varnish, veil, whitewash* (≠ accost, admit, advertise, air, bare, betray, brandish, broadcast, bulletin, clarify, concede, confess, confide, confirm, confront, disclose, discover, divulge, expose, flaunt, floodlight, herald, identify, illuminate, light, limelight, out, parade, plug, present, proclaim, publicize, reveal, showcase, sport, spread, telegraph, uncloud, uncover, unmask, volunteer, wag)

CONCEDE (+): *accept, acknowledge, admit, affirm, allow, announce, avow, betray, blab, blurt, break, broadcast, caution, circulate, communicate, confess, confide, confirm, declare, disclose, disseminate, divulge, expose, give, grant, impart, inform, leak, own, proclaim, profess, publish, recognize, reveal, spill, telegraph, tell, unburden, unload, unveil, warn, yield* (≠ conceal, confront, contradict, debate, -deny, disallow, disavow, disclaim, discredit, -disown, disprove, dispute, distrust, doubt, gainsay, hide, -negate, obscure, rebut, refute, -reject, -repudiate, scruple, veil) **(¿) ABSTRACTION ALERT. Concrete goals essential!**

CONCEDE (/): *-abandon, abnegate, bequeath, cede, commit, consign, deliver, -desert, discard, entrust, forfeit, -forsake, release, relinquish, render, -renounce, resign, sacrifice, shed, surrender, survive, transfer, waive, yield* (≠ claim, colonize, conquer, defend, defy, -deny, deprive, hold, invade, keep, maintain, obtain, oppose, protect, retain, stint, vanquish, withhold)

CONCENTRATE (+): *accumulate, aggregate, amass, assemble, bunch, center, centralize, cluster, collect, combine, compact, compile, compress, condense, congregate, consider, consolidate, crowd, direct, distill, evaporate, focus, gather, hoard, integrate, intensify, localize, mass, mind, muster, narrow, overcrowd, pile, reduce, rivet, stockpile, store, strengthen, swarm, thicken, unify* (≠ adulterate, diffuse, dilute, disband, disintegrate, disperse, dissipate, dissolve, divide, enlarge, expand, extend, loosen, part, rarefy, release, scatter, segregate, separate, sever, spend, split, spread, squander, stretch, thin, waste, water, weaken)

CONCERN (+): *abash, aggravate, agitate, ail, alarm, anger, annoy, appall, bedevil, bother, bug, chafe, chivy, confound, confuse, daunt, demoralize, demotivate, derail, discomfit, discomfort, discompose, disconcert, discountenance, discourage, dishearten, dismay, dispirit, disquiet, distemper, distract, distress, disturb, embarrass, exasperate, exercise, faze, fluster, frazzle, freak, fret, fuss, gall, get, harass, harry, haunt, interest, involve, irk, irritate, jar, mortify, nettle, niggle, nitpick, nonplus, peeve, perturb, pester, pique, plague, rattle, rile, sadden, shake, touch, trouble, undo, unhinge, unnerve, unsettle, upset, vex, worry* (≠ allay, alleviate, appease, assuage, calm, comfort, compose, conciliate, console, delight, entertain, forget, hush, lull, mellow, mollify, pacify, placate, propitiate, quiet, sedate, settle, soothe, sugarcoat, thrill, tranquilize) **(¿) ABSTRACTION ALERT. Concrete goals essential!**

CONCLUDE (+): *accept, adjudge, affirm, ascertain, assume, believe, conjecture, construe, contemplate, credit, decide, declare, deduce, derive, detect, determine, draw, educe, extrapolate, figure, gather, guess, hold, infer, interpret, judge, maintain, presume, profess, profile, rationalize, read, reason, reckon, suppose, surmise, suss, think, trust, understand, wonder* (≠ addle, baffle, conceal, confuse, disprove, -disregard, doubt, forget, hide, -ignore, invalidate, lose, mask, misplace, miss, mystify, -overlook, perplex, predetermine, puzzle, scruple, shroud, stun, trouble, unlearn, veil) **(¿) ABSTRACTION ALERT. Concrete goals essential!**

CONCLUDE (+): *accomplish, achieve, adjudge, adjudicate, arbitrate, arrange, ascertain, broker, chew, choose, claim, clinch, close, consider, consult, contemplate, crest, cull, decide, decree, deliberate, determine, effect, elect, entertain, establish, execute, figure, fill, finalize, find, fix, fulfill, handpick, integrate, judge, learn, meditate, mull, name, negotiate, pick, ponder, prefer, question, referee, resolve, rule, select, settle, study, umpire, weigh* (≠ confuse, debate, -decline, delay, discourage, dissuade, -halt, hinder, mismanage, misplace, miss, muddle, muddy, -overlook, perplex, predetermine, -prevent, prolong, puzzle, -refuse, -reject, renegotiate, shelve, skirt, stall, stop, suppress, undershoot, unsettle) **(¿) ABSTRACTION ALERT. Concrete goals essential!**

CONCLUDE (/): *-abort, cap, cease, close, complete, consummate, crown, -discontinue, end, finish, -halt, perfect, stop, suspend, terminate, wrap*

(≠ begin, brainstorm, commence, concoct, continue, create, extend, follow, inaugurate, initiate, inspire, instigate, launch, open, originate, spur, start)

CONCOCT (+): *ad-lib, blend, brainstorm, brew, churn, coin, conceive, construct, contrive, cook, daydream, design, develop, devise, dream, envisage, envision, extemporize, fabricate, fantasize, fix, formulate, foster, half-ass, hallucinate, hatch, imagine, improvise, invent, machine, make, manufacture, mix, picture, plan, plot, prepare, produce, ready, script, visualize* (≠ adopt, clone, copy, copycat, criticize, demolish, destroy, devastate, duplicate, emulate, ghostwrite, imitate, mangle, mimic, reduplicate, replicate, reproduce, ruin, terminate, wreck)

CONDEMN (/): *abhor, abominate, admonish, assail, attack, badmouth, ban, bar, belittle, berate, blacklist, blame, blast, boo, castigate, censure, chastise, chide, coerce, compel, criticize, critique, crucify, curse, cuss, damn, decry, demean, demolish, demonize, denounce, denunciate, deplore, deprecate, deride, destroy, -detest, disparage, disrespect, diss, doom, drub, -excommunicate, excoriate, execrate, fault, flay, force, frame, fulminate, gibbet, hammer, -hate, imprecate, impugn, keelhaul, knock, lambaste, lash, lecture, -loathe, neg, ordain, -ostracize, pan, pillory, proscribe, rag, rake, rate, -rebuff, rebuke, reprimand, reproach, reprove, resent, revile, scalp, scapegoat, scold, skewer, skin, slam, slate, tweak, upbraid, vituperate* (≠ acclaim, applaud, approve, bless, commend, congratulate, consecrate, endorse, eulogize, exalt, expiate, extol, glorify, hail, hallow, honor, laud, legalize, praise, recommend, revere, rubber-stamp, salute, sanctify, sanction, tout, venerate)

CONDEMN (/): *accuse, admonish, arraign, blister, castigate, censure, charge, chasten, chastise, conclude, consign, convict, correct, damn, decide, decree, denounce, determine, discipline, doom, find, impeach, incriminate, indict, judge, outlaw, penalize, predetermine, punish, rebuke, reprimand, reproach, reprove, resolve, rule, sentence* (≠ absolve, acquit, alibi, approve, bless, cite, clear, commend, endorse, exculpate, exonerate, expiate, honor, pardon, reprieve, right, sanction, spare, tout, vindicate)

CONDENSE (→): *abbreviate, abridge, capsule, capsulize, collapse, compact, compress, concentrate, consolidate, constrict, contract, cram, crowd, curtail, decrease, digest, diminish, downsize, jam, jam-pack, lessen, miniaturize, narrow, pack, prune, reduce, shorten, shrink, simplify, squeeze, streamline, telescope, truncate* (≠ bulge, decompress, diffuse, dilate, disperse, dissipate, distend, enlarge, expand, expound, increase, inflate, open, scatter, stretch, swell)

CONDENSE (+): *boil, clarify, clean, cleanse, coagulate, concentrate, deepen, distill, enhance, enrich, evaporate, extract, flush, fortify, harden, heighten, intensify, leach, precipitate, purge, purify, reduce, refine, remove, solidify, strengthen, thicken* (≠ adulterate, cut, dilute, disperse, dissolve, divide, flux, liquefy, melt, open, rarefy, separate, soften, thin, unclot, water, weaken)

CONDITION (+): *accustom, adapt, adjust, arm, brainwash, calibrate, case-harden, convince, drill, educate, equip, familiarize, groom, habituate, improve, indoctrinate, influence, inure, modify, mold, nourish, practice, prepare, prime, program, ready, reinvigorate, restimulate, restore, retrain, revive, school, season, shape, sharpen, teach, temper, tone, train, transform, treat, tune* (≠ brutalize, cannibalize, consume, cripple, debilitate, decondition, deplete, deprogram, disqualify, enervate, exhaust, gaslight, hamstring, incapacitate, sap, soften, weaken, wither, worsen)

CONDONE (+): *abet, absolve, accept, accord, acquit, allow, approve, authorize, back, bless, brook, buy, clear, concede, -discount, dismiss, -disregard, endorse, enfranchise, exculpate, excuse, exonerate, explain, forget, forgive, gloss, -ignore, justify, legalize, let, license, okay, -overlook, pardon, permit, ratify, rationalize, release, remit, reprieve, rubber-stamp, sanction, spare, support, tolerate, vindicate, waive, whitewash* (≠ accuse, arraign, assess, avenge, blame, censure, charge, condemn, criticize, critique, fault, -forbid, frame, heed, impose, incriminate, indict, mark, mind, -nix, note, -prevent, prosecute, protest, punish, reprimand, -repudiate, resent, scapegoat)

CONDUCT (→): *administer, chair, channel, choreograph, concentrate, consolidate, control, direct, engineer, focus, funnel, govern, guard, guide, handle, head, keep, lead, manage, maneuver, micromanage, mind, operate, orchestrate, order, organize, oversee, pace, pilot, pipe, protect, regulate, rule, run, safeguard, siphon, stage-manage, steer, steward, superintend, supervise, tend, time, watch* (≠ botch, bungle, -desert, -disregard, follow, -forsake, half-ass, leave, lose, maroon, mishandle, mismanage, misrule, -neglect, obey)

CONDUCT (←): *accompany, attend, beam, bear, bring, carry, chaperone, chauffeur, control, convey, convoy, direct, escort, guide, lead, manage, marshal, pilot, route, schlep, shepherd, show, steer, take, transmit, usher* (≠ -abandon, compromise, damage, dog, drop, endanger, follow, forget, harm, hound, -neglect, shadow, tail, tailgate, trail)

CONFESS (→): *accept, acknowledge, admit, affirm, allow, announce, assert, attest, avow, bare, betray, blab, blaze, blurt, break, breathe, broadcast, communicate, concede, confide, confirm, convey, corroborate, declare, disclose, dish, divulge, expose, grant, hint, impart, inform, leak, out, own, proclaim, profess, promulgate, publish, recall, recognize, regret, relay, repent, report, reveal, scandalize, shock, shrive, spill, spread, unbosom, unburden, unload, unveil, verbalize, verify, vocalize, voice, warn, whisper, yield* (≠ betray, bluff, bullshit, bury, cheat, conceal, contradict, cover, deceive, defraud, defuse, -deny, disallow, disavow, disclaim, disguise, -disown, dispute, gainsay, hide, hush, mask, mislead, -negate, negative, obscure, rebut, recant, refute, -reject, -repudiate, retract, revoke, scam, silence, suppress, swindle, trick, veil, withhold)

CONFINE (/): *abduct, apprehend, arrest, bar, bind, bound, bust, cage, capture, catch, chain, commit, constrain, constrict, control, convict,* *cramp, delimit, detain, enchain, encircle, enclose, encumber, enslave, fetter, fix, gate, hamper, handcuff, hogtie, hold, immure, impound, imprison, incarcerate, inhibit, institutionalize, intern, jail, jug, keep, limit, lock, manacle, nab, pen, pinch, pinion, regulate, repress, restrain, restrict, seize, shackle, shanghai, shut, straightjacket, tie, trammel, trap, waylay, wrap* (≠ aid, allow, aquit, discharge, emancipate, encourage, enfranchise, expand, expose, extricate, free, grant, liberate, loose, manumit, release, rescue, unbind, unbury, uncage, unchain, unfetter)

CONFIRM (+): *accept, adduce, affirm, approve, ascertain, assert, assure, attest, authenticate, authorize, back, certify, champion, check, clinch, clock, concretize, connote, contextualize, corroborate, crosscheck, declare, demonstrate, depose, determine, document, endorse, ensure, establish, evidence, evince, exemplify, exhibit, favor, greenlight, guarantee, illustrate, instance, manifest, notarize, observe, permit, pledge, promise, prove, ratify, recommend, rubber-stamp, sanction, settle, showcase, state, substantiate, support, testify, underwrite, validate, verify, warrant, witness* (≠ addle, annul, assume, baffle, blind, blindfold, -cancel, challenge, confound, confuse, consult, contest, contradict, debate, debunk, deceive, -deny, discredit, disgrace, disguise, -disown, disprove, dispute, distrust, doubt, fake, -forbid, fudge, gainsay, invalidate, mislead, -negate, oppose, overthrow, pretend, -prohibit, proscribe, puzzle, quash, question, -rebuff, -refuse, refute, -reject, -repudiate, revoke, scotch, scruple, suspect, trick, -veto, void)

CONFISCATE (←): *abduct, acquire, amass, annex, appropriate, arrogate, assume, attach, bag, capture, catch, collect, commandeer, demand, deprive, garnish, gather, get, glean, grab, harvest, hijack, impound, levy, liberate, monopolize, nab, occupy, pinch, preempt, procure, reap, remove, request, requisition, scavenge, seize, select, sequester, snag, steal, swipe, take, usurp* (≠ abdicate, abnegate, allocate, allot, allow, appoint, apportion, assign, award, bequeath, bestow, cede, comp, deliver, distribute, divide, donate, forfeit, free, give, grant, hand, mete, offer, portion, ration, release, relinquish, render, -renounce, resign, restore, return, select, spare, surrender, tender, tithe, volunteer, win, yield)

CONFOUND (/): *amaze, astonish, astound, baffle, bamboozle, beat, bedevil, befuddle, bemuse, bewilder, blindside, block, boggle, bother, chagrin, checkmate, cloud, confuse, confute, curb, curse, daze, deafen, defeat, dement, derange, disturb, dumbfound, -elude, embarrass, embroil, ensnare, faze, flabbergast, floor, flummox, foil, frustrate, gaslight, gobsmack, harass, hobble, jumble, mislabel, monkey-wrench, muddle, muzzle, mystify, nonplus, obscure, obstruct, outguess, outwit, overthrow, overwhelm, perplex, puzzle, stump, stun, stupefy, surprise, tangle, throw, -thwart, trouble, upset, wrack* (≠ advise, assure, authenticate, believe, buoy, clarify, comfort, confirm, corroborate, counsel, decipher, decode, deduce, demonstrate, direct, distinguish, document, educate, elucidate, encourage, enlighten, establish, explain, facilitate, guide, help, illuminate, inform, instruct, lead, manifest, navigate, orient, prove, rally, reassure, right, satisfy, simplify, solve, soothe, steer, straighten, substantiate, support, teach, tidy, train, tutor, uphold, validate, verify)

CONFRONT (→): *accost, address, affront, antagonize, approach, assail, assault, attack, battle, beard, block, brave, brazen, breast, buttonhole, challenge, combat, contrast, corner, dare, debate, defend, defy, dispute, disturb, embattle, face, fight, flout, front, -frustrate, -halt, hassle, impugn, intercept, juxtapose, meet, obstruct, oppose, picket, present, protest, race, reach, repel, resist, -scorn, show, stand, tackle, withstand, wrangle, wrestle* (≠ -abandon, -avoid, -boycott, -bypass, circumnavigate, -circumvent, concede, detour, -dodge, -duck, -elude, -escape, -eschew, -evade, forfeit, shake, -shirk, shortcut, -shun, -sidestep, skip)

CONFUSE (/): *abash, addle, amaze, astonish, baffle, bamboozle, bedevil, befuddle, bemuse, bewilder, blindside, boggle, bother, buffalo, chagrin, cloud, clutter, complicate, confound, darken, daze, defeat, demoralize, discomfit, discompose, disconcert, disorient, distract, disturb, dizzy, dumbfound, -elude, embarrass, embroil, ensnare, faze, flabbergast, floor, flummox, fluster, fog, foil, frustrate, gaslight, gobsmack, hocus-pocus, intoxicate, involve, jumble, misinform, mislabel, mislead, monkey-wrench, mortify, muddle, mystify, nonplus, obfuscate, obscure, obstruct, outwit, overwhelm, perplex, perturb, psych, puzzle, rattle, shame, stump, stun, stupefy, surprise, tangle, throw, -thwart, trouble, unhinge, unsettle, upset, worry* (≠ advise, analyze, assuage, assure, buoy, clarify, clear, coach, comfort, confirm, corroborate, counsel, crystallize, decipher, decode, deduce, demonstrate, direct, distinguish, educate, elucidate, encourage, enlighten, explain, facilitate, floodlight, guide, help, illuminate, inform, instruct, lead, light, navigate, orient, profile, rally, reassure, right, satisfy, school, settle, simplify, solve, soothe, steer, straighten, support, systematize, teach, tidy, train, tutor)

CONFUSE (/): *addle, agitate, befuddle, blend, blur, bollix, churn, clutter, complicate, compound, confound, convulse, derange, diffuse, disarrange, disarray, discombobulate, discompose, dishevel, disjoint, dislocate, disorder, disorganize, displace, disrupt, disturb, elaborate, embroil, encumber, entangle, faze, garble, hash, implicate, intermingle, jumble, mess, mingle, mislabel, mislay, mismatch, misplace, mix, muddle, muss, overset, perplex, perturb, ripple, roil, roughen, ruffle, rummage, rumple, scatter, scramble, shuffle, snarl, stir, swirl, tangle, toss, tousle, trouble, tumble, unsettle, untidy, upset, whip, whisk* (≠ abbreviate, adjust, align, ameliorate, arrange, array, calibrate, classify, clean, codify, coordinate, cut, disconnect, disentangle, distinguish, divide, ease, -exclude, extricate, fix, free, groom, gussy, hierarchize, line, manicure, marshal, methodize, mitigate, neaten, order, organize, pace, queue, regiment, regulate, remove, right, separate, shorten, sift, simplify, sort, straighten, streamline, systematize, tidy, tune, uncloud, uncomplicate, unravel, unscramble, unsnarl, untangle)

CONGRATULATE (+): *acknowledge, admire, adulate, affirm, applaud, blandish, bless, boost, cheer, commend, compliment, eulogize, exalt,* *extol, flatter, glorify, gold-star, hail, high-five, honor, hug, laud, lionize, magnify, praise, salute, stroke, toast* (≠ abuse, accuse, badmouth, belittle, berate, blast, boo, chastise, chide, criticize, critique, decry, demean, demonize, deprecate, diminish, -discount, disparage, minimize, mock, pillory, rebuke, ridicule, scold, -scorn, taunt, tease)

CONJURE (←): *awaken, beg, beseech, bewitch, brew, charm, compel, conceive, concoct, create, daydream, dream, educe, elicit, enchant, entrance, entreat, envisage, envision, evoke, excite, exorcise, fabricate, fancy, fantasize, fascinate, glamour, hallucinate, imagine, importune, insinuate, invent, invoke, levitate, manufacture, materialize, picture, plan, produce, project, raise, recall, recollect, rouse, see, solicit, suggest, summon, urge, visualize, witch* (≠ -avert, banish, bless, block, counter, destroy, disenchant, eject, eliminate, eradicate, exorcise, expel, -forbid, -halt, oust, -prevent, -prohibit, remove, repel, shield, -thwart, ward)

CONNECT (+): *adhere, affix, articulate, attach, cement, chain, clamp, coalesce, combine, compound, concatenate, conflate, conjugate, constellate, cord, couple, dovetail, fasten, hitch, hook, integrate, interconnect, interlink, join, link, mortar, network, secure, span, string, tack, tag, tie, unite, weld, wire, yoke* (≠ cleave, detach, disconnect, disengage, disjoin, disjoint, disunite, divide, part, rupture, separate, sever, split, sunder, unchain, uncouple, unhitch, unlink, unyoke)

CONNECT (+): *ally, assemble, bestride, bond, bridge, chain, cluster, coalesce, combine, compile, compound, concatenate, congregate, conjoin, conjugate, convene, couple, fuse, gather, hybridize, join, marry, mate, meet, meld, melt, recombine, reconnect, reintegrate, rejoin, reunify, reunite, span, splice, straddle, synthesize, unify, unite, wed* (≠ alienate, diffuse, disband, disconnect, disjoin, disjoint, disperse, disunite, divide, divorce, isolate, orphan, part, resolve, scatter, seclude, section, separate, sever, split, sunder)

CONNECT (+): *ally, associate, bracket, compare, conjoin, correlate, couple, emulate, equate, group, identify, join, liken, link, match, mimic, network, parallel, relate* (≠ categorize, characterize, classify, contrast, differentiate, disconnect, distinguish, divorce, juxtapose, seclude, separate, sever, sort)

CONQUER (→): *annex, annihilate, appropriate, beat, besiege, best, better, capture, checkmate, clobber, command, commandeer, control, crush, defeat, demolish, dethrone, dominate, dragoon, exterminate, floor, foil, hammer, humble, install, lick, master, obtain, occupy, oppress, outdo, outlast, outmaneuver, outperform, outplay, outsmart, outwit, overcome, overpower, overrun, oversee, overthrow, overturn, overwhelm, possess, prostrate, quell, remove, repress, rout, ruin, rule, seize, slaughter, subdue, subject, subjugate, subordinate, succeed, suppress, surmount, take, thrash, top, trounce, trump, usurp, vanquish, whip, win, wrack, wreck* (≠ aid, assist, deliver, emancipate, enfranchise, follow, forfeit, heal, help, liberate, loosen, lose, manumit, obey, relinquish, serve, submit, subvert, support, surrender, survive, sustain, unbind, uncage, unchain, weather)

CONSECRATE (+): *adore, anoint, apotheosize, beatify, bless, dedicate, deify, devote, enshrine, exalt, glorify, hallow, honor, idolize, ordain, revere, sanctify, venerate, vow, worship* (≠ blame, blaspheme, canker, condemn, corrupt, desacralize, desanctify, desecrate, despoil, disparage, fault, insult, mock, revile, -scorn, -shun, sully, taint, violate)

CONSERVE (←): *accumulate, amass, archive, brine, coffer, deprive, guard, hoard, hog, husband, keep, pickle, pile, preserve, protect, reserve, retain, safeguard, save, scant, scrimp, skimp, squirrel, starve, stash, steward, stockpile, store, stow, stuff, support, suppress, sustain, treasure, tuck, withhold* (≠ blow, cannibalize, circulate, consume, deplete, depredate, destroy, diffuse, disperse, disseminate, dissipate, doom, exhaust, expend, fritter, impoverish, lavish, overfeed, scatter, spend, squander, waste)

CONSERVE (+): *cure, defend, fix, guard, heal, husband, maintain, manage, mend, nurse, patch, preserve, protect, rebuild, reconstruct, rehabilitate, rejuvenate, remedy, rescue, restore, safeguard, salvage, save, screen, secure, service, shield, support, sustain* (≠ annihilate, break, damage, destroy, -disregard, doom, end, harm, hurt, -ignore, impair, injure, -neglect, -nix, obliterate, pulverize, ruin, terminate, torch, wreck)

CONSIDER (←): *acknowledge, adjudge, analyze, appraise, ascertain, assess, believe, bemoan, benchmark, calculate, categorize, compare, concede, consult, contemplate, count, credit, critique, envisage, estimate, evaluate, examine, eye, favor, gauge, grade, grant, inspect, judge, lament, learn, liken, measure, mourn, mull, number, numerate, observe, ogle, peg, peruse, ponder, prioritize, rank, rate, read, reappraise, reassess, reckon, recognize, reflect, regard, regret, remember, respect, scan, scope, scrutinize, sense, study, suppose, weigh, wonder* (≠ -abandon, addle, baffle, blind, blindfold, -bypass, cheat, clothe, confound, confuse, costume, deceive, determine, disbelieve, discard, -discount, discredit, disfavor, disgrace, disguise, dismiss, -disregard, doubt, -exclude, fake, forget, -forsake, fudge, -ignore, leave, mask, misgauge, misjudge, mislead, miss, muddle, -neglect, -omit, -overlook, perplex, pooh-pooh, question, -reject, scam, -scorn, scruple, suspect, trick, vilify) **(¿) ABSTRACTION ALERT. Concrete goals essential!**

CONSOLE (+): *aid, allay, alleviate, appease, assuage, brighten, calm, cheer, comfort, compose, cool, cure, ease, embolden, encourage, enliven, gladden, hearten, help, hush, inspire, lift, lighten, lull, mellow, mollify, nurture, pacify, placate, please, quell, quiet, reassure, relieve, remedy, sedate, soothe, still, subdue, support, tranquilize, upraise* (≠ aggravate, agitate, anguish, annoy, antagonize, crucify, demoralize, depress, discourage, dishearten, dissuade, distress, disturb, exacerbate, grieve, harass, hassle, hurt, injure, irk, irritate, nettle, niggle, nitpick, overset, sadden, torment, torture, trouble, upset, worry, worsen, wound)

CONSOLIDATE (+): *align, amalgamate, assemble, blend, center, centralize, coalesce, collate, collect, combine, compact, compile, concentrate, conjoin, coordinate, focus, fuse, gather, harmonize, hybridize, incorporate, integrate, join, link, merge, orchestrate, polarize,* *reduce, reintegrate, reunify, reunite, synthesize, unify, unite* (≠ atomize, chunk, decentralize, deconcentrate, diffuse, disperse, divide, fracture, fragment, partition, portion, pulverize, scatter, segregate, separate, shatter, sift, split, spread, winnow)

CONSOLIDATE (+): *accelerate, accent, accentuate, accrue, aggravate, amp, amplify, augment, beef, boost, broaden, catalyze, cement, deepen, emphasize, enforce, enhance, enlarge, enliven, exacerbate, expand, extend, fortify, hasten, heighten, increase, intensify, lengthen, magnify, maximize, quicken, redouble, reinforce, secure, sharpen, stabilize, strengthen, stress, supplement* (≠ abate, adulterate, alleviate, decrease, diminish, ease, lessen, lighten, minimize, moderate, reduce, subdue, weaken)

CONSTRAIN (→): *bully, coerce, command, compel, demand, dragoon, drive, force, impel, muscle, obligate, oblige, overcommit, press, pressure, railroad, sandbag, strong-arm, urge* (≠ allege, block, daunt, -frustrate, -halt, impede, insinuate, obstruct, occlude, -prevent, -prohibit, stymie, suggest, -thwart)

CONSTRAIN (←): *arrest, ban, bar, bind, bottle, bound, box, bridle, cage, chain, check, confine, constrict, control, convict, cork, cramp, curb, -deny, deprive, disallow, encumber, fetter, fix, hamper, hinder, hogtie, immure, imprison, incarcerate, inhibit, institutionalize, intern, jail, limit, obligate, pace, package, pause, pigeonhole, press, pressure, regulate, restrain, restrict, stereotype, stifle, stop, straightjacket, straiten, tie, withhold* (≠ authorize, circulate, disseminate, emancipate, encourage, endorse, facilitate, free, legalize, liberate, lubricate, motivate, permit, sanction, spur, unleash, unlock, urge)

CONSTRICT (←): *bind, chain, check, choke, circumscribe, clench, close, compress, concentrate, condense, confine, constrain, contract, cramp, curb, encumber, fetter, hamper, hinder, impede, inhibit, limit, narrow, obstruct, occlude, pinch, pucker, restrain, restrict, shrink, squeeze, straightjacket, strangle, tauten, tense, tighten, tuck* (≠ aerate, decompress, diffuse, dilate, disperse, dissipate, enlarge, expand, extend, free, grow, increase, inflate, lengthen, liberate, loose, loosen, open, oxygenate, release, scatter, slack, slacken, stretch, swell, unspool, ventilate)

CONSTRUCT (+): *assemble, automate, begin, build, carpenter, coin, combine, compose, concoct, constitute, contour, contrive, cook, craft, create, elevate, engineer, erect, establish, fabricate, fashion, father, forge, form, found, frame, generate, hammer, handcraft, jerry-build, jerry-rig, machine, make, manufacture, mechanize, model, mold, motorize, organize, patch, piece, prefabricate, produce, raise, rear, reassemble, rebuild, reconstruct, redevelop, repair, retrofit, rig, sculpt, sew, shape, stitch, structure, suture, unify, unite, weave, weld* (≠ atomize, bulldoze, bust, clone, demolish, destroy, detach, devastate, disassemble, disconnect, disengage, disjoin, dismantle, dismember, disunite, divide, doom, explode, flatten, fracture, fragment, level, pulverize, raze, reproduce, reshape, restructure, ruin, separate, shatter, smash, strike, topple, wreck)

CONSTRUCT (+): *ad-lib, brainstorm, brew, coin, conceive, concoct, contrive, design, devise, dream, envisage, envision, extemporize, fabricate, fantasize, formulate, hatch, imagine, improve, improvise, inaugurate, initiate, innovate, institute, invent, originate, picture, produce, visualize* (≠ adopt, ape, clone, copy, copycat, demoralize, duplicate, emulate, forget, -ignore, imitate, mimic, mock, reduplicate, replicate, reproduce, sabotage, scotch, scupper, scuttle, shelve, undermine)

CONSUME (←): *absorb, accept, access, acquire, admit, appreciate, appropriate, assimilate, banquet, bolt, chew, corrode, cram, demolish, devour, digest, dispatch, dissolve, down, drink, eat, engorge, engulf, enjoy, envelop, feast, finish, get, glut, gnaw, gobble, gorge, gulp, gum, guzzle, hoover, imbibe, incorporate, ingest, inhale, inspire, integrate, internalize, lap, lick, manage, metabolize, mouth, munch, nibble, nosh, nurse, overwhelm, pick, pocket, procure, quaff, raven, receive, regale, relish, ruminate, savor, scarf, sip, slop, slurp, snarf, sniff, stuff, suck, surfeit, swallow, swig, swill, take, taste, try, vacuum, welcome, wolf* (≠ -avoid, barf, belch, brew, -bypass, concoct, content, cook, covet, crave, create, -decline, desire, disgorge, disperse, -ditch, drop, dump, eject, excrete, expel, exude, famish, fancy, favor, feed, fetishize, force-feed, forgo, fuel, furnish, grace, gratify, heave, hunt, jettison, make, malnourish, miss, nourish, offer, order, overfeed, pass, please, prepare, puke, quench, -refuse, regurgitate, -reject, request, satisfy, serve, skimp, skip, slake, spew, spit, splutter, starve, stint, supply, toss, trash, underfeed, victual, vomit, withhold)

CONSUME (←): *abate, absorb, access, bankrupt, beggar, blow, burn, cannibalize, clean, cripple, debilitate, decrease, de-escalate, deplete, devour, diminish, disable, dissipate, downsize, drain, draw, eat, empty, enfeeble, exhaust, expend, fritter, guzzle, impoverish, lavish, leech, lessen, lower, misspend, reduce, sap, spend, squander, undermine, use, waste, weaken, wither* (≠ augment, bolster, boost, budget, buttress, charge, conserve, dent, deprive, drizzle, enforce, enlarge, fill, fortify, fuel, increase, pickle, preserve, rebuild, recoup, refill, reinforce, reinvigorate, reload, renew, repair, replace, replenish, restimulate, restore, revive, save, scant, skimp, stimulate, stint, stock, strengthen, trickle, withhold)

CONSUME (←): *absorb, allure, arrest, beckon, beguile, bewitch, captivate, charm, court, delight, disarm, draw, enchant, engage, engross, enrapture, enthrall, entice, entrance, fascinate, floor, gratify, grip, hold, interest, intrigue, invite, involve, kill, lure, magnetize, monopolize, obsess, occupy, please, preoccupy, pull, rivet, seduce, solicit, tempt, thrill, woo, wow* (≠ annoy, -balk, bore, bother, bug, burden, dampen, deaden, depress, disappoint, disenchant, disgust, displease, dull, frustrate, irk, irritate, nag, needle, nettle, nitpick, numb, offend, repel, replace, revolt, satisfy, sedate, slake, stifle, tire, weary) **(¿) ABSTRACTION ALERT. Concrete goals essential!**

CONSUME (+): *annihilate, burn, corrode, damage, decimate, demolish, deplete, depredate, desolate, destroy, devastate, devour, disintegrate,* *dissipate, dominate, doom, drain, eat, employ, eradicate, erase, erode, exhaust, expend, exterminate, extinguish, extirpate, finish, fritter, gut, leach, obliterate, pulverize, ravage, raze, remove, ruin, shatter, slather, smash, spend, squander, topple, utilize, waste, wear, wreck* (≠ assemble, build, conserve, construct, erect, fortify, lard, manufacture, pickle, preserve, protect, raise, renew, repair, restore, revive, save, stimulate, strengthen, survive, sustain, weather)

CONTAIN (+): *accept, accommodate, carry, confine, corral, embody, embrace, encircle, enclose, encompass, envelop, hold, include, incorporate, integrate, involve, orbit, possess, seat, subsume, surround, take, wrap* (≠ alienate, banish, bar, block, -deny, eject, eliminate, estrange, evict, -exclude, hinder, inconvenience, obstruct, -omit, oppose, -ostracize, oust, -refuse, -reject, relocate, -shun) **(¿) ABSTRACTION ALERT. Concrete goals essential!**

CONTAIN (+): *attach, bandage, bind, bottle, chain, check, clamp, close, collect, control, cool, cork, cover, curb, dress, fasten, fetter, hamper, harness, hinder, hogtie, hold, impede, inhibit, leash, limit, lock, rein, repress, restrain, restrict, secure, shackle, smother, stifle, stop, straight-jacket, strap, suppress, tether, tie, truss, wrap* (≠ allow, detach, disconnect, emancipate, excuse, free, liberate, loose, loosen, lose, open, permit, release, remove, rescue, separate, unbind, uncover, unlace, unleash, unshackle, untangle)

CONTAMINATE (/): *abase, adulterate, alloy, bastardize, bedraggle, befoul, begrime, besmear, besmirch, blacken, blight, canker, corrupt, damage, debase, debauch, decay, defile, degrade, demean, demote, deprave, desecrate, devalue, dilute, diminish, dirty, disgrace, dishonor, doctor, foul, harm, humble, humiliate, impair, incriminate, infect, injure, lower, mortify, muddy, overdose, pervert, poison, pollute, profane, reduce, rot, shame, smear, smudge, soil, spike, spoil, stain, suborn, sully, taint, tarnish, violate, vulgarize* (≠ clarify, clean, cleanse, cure, decontaminate, delouse, disinfect, distill, filter, fumigate, immunize, inoculate, moralize, purge, purify, quarantine, refine, sanctify, sanitize, sterilize, vaccinate, wash)

CONTEMPLATE (+): *anticipate, await, clock, compare, consider, deliberate, design, envisage, evaluate, examine, expect, eye, eyeball, foresee, gauge, inspect, measure, mull, note, observe, plan, ponder, propose, regard, scan, scope, scrutinize, spitball, study, survey, time, view, weigh, witness* (≠ -avoid, baffle, blind, confound, disbelieve, discard, -discount, dismiss, -disregard, -eschew, forget, -ignore, -neglect, -overlook, pooh-pooh, -reject, -scorn, -slight, -spurn, trick) **(¿) ABSTRACTION ALERT. Concrete goals essential!**

CONTENT (+): *amuse, appease, assuage, bewitch, calm, captivate, charm, coddle, comfort, credit, delight, divert, enrapture, entertain, excite, feast, fulfill, galvanize, gladden, gratify, humor, hush, indulge, lull, mellow, mollify, mollycoddle, pacify, pamper, placate, please, quench, reconcile, rejoice, relieve, sate, satiate, satisfy, slake, soothe, spoil,* *sugarcoat, suit, thrill, tickle, titillate, treat, warm, welcome* (≠ aggravate, agitate, anger, annoy, bother, bug, chaff, challenge, cross, displease, distress, disturb, enrage, exasperate, harass, heckle, incense, infuriate, irk, irritate, nag, needle, nettle, niggle, nitpick, outrage, peeve, pester, provoke, rankle, rile, ruffle, sadden, tantalize, tease, tempt, troll, upset, vex, weary, worry)

CONTEST (→): *abnegate, abrogate, antagonize, argue, blast, challenge, combat, confront, confute, consult, contend, contradict, contrast, counter, counteract, debate, debunk, -deny, disavow, discredit, -disown, disprove, dispute, doubt, face, fight, hassle, impeach, impugn, invalidate, litigate, mistrust, -negate, oppose, oppugn, protest, push, query, question, rebut, refute, -repudiate, resist, scruple, suspect, tangle, withstand, wrestle* (≠ abide, accept, accord, advocate, allow, approve, authorize, back, believe, certify, champion, concede, consult, corroborate, defend, embrace, endure, further, indulge, permit, persuade, promote, sanction, shoulder, stomach, support, swallow, sway, tolerate, uphold, validate, weather)

CONTORT (/): *bend, corrugate, crimp, crumple, crush, curve, deform, disfigure, distort, gnarl, knot, mangle, misshape, mutate, ripple, rotate, torture, twist, warp, wiggle, wind, wrench, wriggle, yank* (≠ align, beautify, flatten, iron, mend, press, rectify, repair, right, smooth, soothe, straighten, unbend, uncrumple, uncurl)

CONTRACT (+): *appoint, arrange, covenant, employ, engage, enlist, hire, negotiate, promise, retain, settle, sign, stipulate, subscribe, underwrite* (≠ argue, -cancel, contest, debate, dismiss, dispute, dissolve, fire, release, remove, revoke, terminate)

CONTRACT (/): *abbreviate, abridge, concentrate, consolidate, cram, crowd, curtail, decrease, diminish, distill, downsize, jam, jam-pack, lessen, pack, shorten, shrink, simplify, streamline* (≠ bulge, decompress, diffuse, dilate, disperse, dissipate, distend, expand, increase, inflate, open, outstretch, scatter, spread, swell)

CONTRADICT (/): *abnegate, abrogate, annul, antagonize, belie, buck, -cancel, challenge, check, confront, confute, contrast, contravene, controvert, counter, counteract, counterattack, counterbalance, cross, dare, debate, debunk, defend, defy, -deny, differentiate, disallow, disavow, disclaim, discredit, -disown, disprove, dispute, distrust, doubt, efface, fight, gainsay, hinder, impede, impugn, inhibit, intercept, invalidate, invert, juxtapose, -negate, neutralize, -nullify, obstruct, offset, oppose, oppress, override, overturn, parry, protest, question, -rebuff, rebut, refute, -reject, rejoin, -renounce, repeal, repel, repress, -repudiate, repulse, resist, retort, reverse, scruple, subvert, suspect, void* (≠ accept, acknowledge, admit, adopt, affirm, allow, announce, assert, authenticate, avow, back, champion, claim, concede, confess, confirm, consult, convince, corroborate, crosscheck, declare, defend, detect, determine, embrace, espouse, maintain, notarize, own, profess, prove, second, submit, substantiate, validate, verify)

CONTRIVE (+): *ad-lib, arrange, brainstorm, coin, conceive, concoct, construct, cook, create, daydream, design, devise, dream, envisage, envision, extemporize, fabricate, fantasize, half-ass, hallucinate, hatch, imagine, improvise, invent, machine, manage, manufacture, picture, produce, visualize* (≠ adopt, clone, copy, copycat, duplicate, emulate, ghostwrite, imitate, mimic, reduplicate, replicate, reproduce)

CONTRIVE (+): *arrange, brew, broker, captain, chart, choreograph, command, compass, concert, conclude, concoct, conduct, construct, cook, create, design, devise, direct, engineer, fabricate, finagle, finesse, frame, gerrymander, handle, hatch, invent, jerry-build, jerry-rig, jockey, machinate, manage, maneuver, manipulate, map, mastermind, negotiate, orchestrate, plan, plot, quarterback, renegotiate, run, scheme, script, shape, stage-manage, time, wangle* (≠ blow, bobble, botch, bungle, butcher, flub, fumble, mangle, mishandle, muddle, muff, ruin, screw, wreck)

CONTROL (→): *administer, advise, angle, arrange, blackmail, bluff, boss, brew, browbeat, bully, call, captain, chair, command, compass, concert, conclude, concoct, conduct, conquer, contrive, dictate, direct, discipline, dominate, domineer, engineer, finagle, finesse, frame, govern, hammer, handle, head, instruct, intimidate, intrigue, lead, lobby, machinate, manage, maneuver, manipulate, master, mastermind, micromanage, muscle, negotiate, oppress, order, oversee, pace, plan, plot, police, quarterback, railroad, regiment, regulate, rule, run, scheme, shepherd, steamroll, subdue, subject, subjugate, superintend, supervise, tend, time, tyrannize, wangle* (≠ abdicate, botch, bugger, bungle, butcher, -disregard, flub, follow, forfeit, -forsake, fumble, -ignore, loose, loosen, lose, mangle, mind, mishandle, misrule, muff, -neglect, obey, relinquish, -renounce, resign, -shirk, -sidestep, slacken, subvert)

CONTROL (→): *check, choreograph, command, conduct, direct, drive, employ, engineer, exert, fly, guide, handle, juxtapose, maneuver, manipulate, moderate, monitor, operate, orchestrate, order, organize, pace, pilot, ply, position, program, regiment, regulate, run, script, steer, steward, tend, turn, use, wield, work* (≠ -abandon, baffle, bewilder, confuse, crash, deprogram, deregulate, discombobulate, lose, -neglect, ruin, sideswipe, smash, unleash, vent, wreck)

CONTROL (←): *-abort, adjust, arrest, awe, block, bottle, bridle, calibrate, calm, check, choke, collect, compose, constrain, contain, cool, corner, cow, curb, daunt, gag, govern, hamper, handcuff, hinder, hold, housebreak, housetrain, hush, impede, inhibit, intercept, interrupt, keep, leash, limit, lull, measure, mellow, mince, moderate, mollify, monopolize, muffle, muzzle, obstruct, occlude, pace, pause, pocket, possess, punctuate, quell, quiet, rally, recover, regiment, regulate, rein, repress, restrain, rule, settle, silence, sink, smother, soothe, squelch, stabilize, steady, stifle, still, stop, straightjacket, strangle, subdue, suppress, swallow, tame, time, tranquilize, tune* (≠ air, chance, churn, encourage, evince, exacerbate, express, flip, initiate, instigate, liberate, loose, loosen, lose, prompt, release, rile, risk, rush, slack, slacken, spur, unleash, unsettle, upset, urge, vent)

CONVENE (+): *amass, assemble, call, collect, congregate, convoke, corral, gather, group, herd, meet, muster, open, rally, summon, unite, wrangle* (≠ adjourn, ban, bar, -cancel, disband, disperse, dissolve, expel, prorogue, recess, repel, scatter, separate, split)

CONVERT (→): *adapt, adjust, alter, apply, appropriate, automate, calibrate, change, commute, customize, deform, disfigure, displace, distort, download, exchange, interchange, make, mechanize, metamorphose, modify, motorize, mutate, rebuild, recast, reconceive, reconceptualize, reconstruct, redefine, redesign, redo, reengineer, refashion, refine, reform, regenerate, reimagine, reinvent, remake, remodel, reorganize, replace, reshape, reshuffle, restore, restructure, restyle, rethink, retool, revamp, revise, rework, sculpt, substitute, supersede, supplant, swap, switch, transfer, transfigure, transform, translate, transmogrify, transmute, transpose, tune, turn, vary, weaponize* (≠ block, conserve, embalm, endure, freeze, hold, keep, maintain, paralyze, preserve, protect, resist, retain, stand, sustain, uphold, withstand)

CONVERT (←): *actuate, adopt, allure, alter, assimilate, baptize, beguile, bend, bias, blandish, blarney, brainwash, bribe, bring, budge, cajole, coax, convince, drill, entreat, evangelize, exhort, fast-talk, gain, get, ground, impel, impress, incline, incorporate, inculcate, indoctrinate, induce, influence, instill, instruct, integrate, lead, lure, move, persuade, predetermine, prejudice, prompt, propagandize, propagate, proselytize, redeem, reform, regenerate, retrain, satisfy, save, school, seduce, sell, snow, sway, teach, tempt, train, turn, urge, wheedle* (≠ believe, challenge, debunk, demotivate, -deter, discourage, disprove, dissuade, doubt, hold, interrogate, invalidate, mistrust, mock, nobble, question, scruple, unsell)

CONVEY (←): *beam, bear, bring, carry, cart, channel, chauffeur, conduct, courier, deliver, dispatch, distribute, drive, ferry, fetch, forward, funnel, give, guide, hand, hand-carry, haul, lug, move, pack, pass, pipe, remove, schlep, send, shift, ship, smuggle, supply, take, tote, transfer, transmit, transport, truck, waft* (≠ -abandon, -bypass, catch, detour, drop, forget, hoard, hold, keep, lose, misplace, retain, stash, stint, withhold)

CONVICT (/): *accuse, admonish, arraign, arrest, castigate, censure, charge, chastise, condemn, damn, denounce, discipline, impeach, imprison, incarcerate, incriminate, indict, intern, jail, judge, penalize, punish, rebuke, reprimand, reproach, reprove, sentence* (≠ absolve, acquit, alibi, approve, bless, cite, clear, commend, dismiss, endorse, exculpate, excuse, exonerate, forgive, pardon, permit, sanction, spare, vindicate)

CONVINCE (→): *allure, argue, assure, beguile, blandish, blarney, brainwash, bribe, bring, cadge, cajole, coax, convert, egg, entreat, exhort, fast-talk, gain, gaslight, get, incline, induce, influence, lead, lobby, lure, move, palaver, persuade, prepossess, promise, prompt, prove, retrain, satisfy,* *schmooze, scrounge, seduce, sell, snooker, snow, sway, swear, tempt, urge, vow, wheedle, win, woo* (≠ baffle, befuddle, believe, bewilder, block, check, confuse, daunt, demoralize, demotivate, -deter, discourage, disincline, dissuade, doubt, fluster, -forbid, frustrate, hinder, mystify, obscure, overwhelm, -prohibit, repel, restrain, spook, unsell, wonder)

COOK (+): *bake, barbecue, blanch, boil, braise, brew, broil, brown, burn, churn, crisp, curry, deep-fry, devil, doctor, fix, flavor, fricassee, frizzle, froth, fry, griddle, grill, heat, imbue, marinate, melt, microwave, mix, nuke, panfry, parboil, parch, percolate, poach, prep, prepare, ready, reduce, roast, ruin, sauté, scald, scorch, sear, simmer, singe, sizzle, spoil, steam, steep, stew, toast, warm* (≠ -abandon, botch, bungle, clean, consume, cool, devour, eat, feast, feed, force-feed, freeze, gobble, grow, -ignore, ingest, -neglect, snarf, swallow, victual, wet)

COOK (/): *belie, bend, bowdlerize, camouflage, censor, color, complicate, confound, confuse, disguise, distort, falsify, fudge, garble, gloss, mask, misdescribe, misinterpret, misrepresent, misstate, mistake, mistranslate, obscure, pervert, rephrase, slant, spin, twist, veil, warp, whitewash* (≠ clarify, clear, confess, decipher, deduce, explain, expose, illuminate, illustrate, interpret, reveal, straighten, tidy)

COOL (←): *aerate, air-condition, chill, fan, freeze, frost, ice, refresh, refrigerate, supercool, ventilate* (≠ bake, boil, broil, crisp, heat, sauté, scorch, sear, steam, toast, warm)

COOL (+): *abate, allay, assuage, block, blunt, calm, check, compose, curb, curtail, dampen, decrease, defuse, diminish, ease, hush, lessen, lull, mellow, minimize, moderate, mollify, pacify, -prevent, quell, quiet, reduce, relieve, sober, soothe, temper, tranquilize* (≠ accent, accentuate, amplify, augment, emphasize, exacerbate, excite, fuel, increase, instigate, intensify, maximize, stimulate, strengthen)

COORDINATE (+): *align, arrange, assort, balance, blend, bond, conjoin, correlate, defray, dovetail, fuse, groove, harmonize, hybridize, integrate, match, meet, merge, mesh, order, organize, pace, parallel, pool, quarterback, regiment, regulate, square, synchronize, systematize, tabulate, tally* (≠ alienate, bar, -cancel, confuse, contradict, contrast, counter, counteract, disband, dismiss, disorder, -exclude, jar, jumble, juxtapose, mismatch, muddle, -negate, offset, override, scramble, tangle)

COORDINATE (+): *accommodate, adapt, adjust, align, approximate, arrange, array, attune, balance, blend, calibrate, center, combine, complement, connect, contemporize, correlate, dovetail, equalize, even, fit, fuse, harmonize, hybridize, integrate, join, key, match, merge, network, orchestrate, order, pair, personalize, proportion, reconcile, regularize, reintegrate, relate, reunite, square, standardize, suit, synchronize, synthesize, time, tune, unify, unite, unskew* (≠ alienate, confuse, customize, disaffect, disarray, disintegrate, disorder, disorganize, disrupt, disturb, estrange, -ignore, interrupt, jar, mismatch, -omit, -ostracize, -reject, rock, shake, skew, unsettle, upset)

COP (←): *appropriate, filch, grab, hook, lift, misappropriate, nab, nobble, pinch, pluck, plunder, poach, pocket, remove, seize, shanghai, shoplift, snaffle, snag, snatch, sneak, steal, swindle, swipe, take* (≠ buy, comp, defend, donate, earn, give, offer, protect, recover, rescue, restore, return, secure, shield)

COPY (←): *bootleg, cartoon, clone, counterfeit, crib, delineate, depict, ditto, draw, dupe, duplicate, engrave, engross, fake, forge, freeboot, imitate, limn, mirror, mold, paint, paraphrase, photocopy, picture, pirate, plagiarize, portray, print, reduplicate, reflect, repeat, replicate, represent, reproduce, retrace, rewrite, scan, sculpt, trace, transcribe* (≠ authenticate, coin, compose, concoct, create, devise, discover, fabricate, formulate, invent, notarize, originate, verify)

COPY (+): *adopt, affect, ape, borrow, burlesque, caricature, echo, embody, emulate, epitomize, express, exteriorize, externalize, fake, follow, illustrate, imitate, impersonate, incorporate, mimic, mirror, mock, model, parody, parrot, personify, phony, playact, prefigure, pretend, repeat, replicate, roleplay, simulate, steal, travesty, typify* (≠ confess, contradict, counter, direct, divulge, expose, -halt, oppose, originate, -prevent, prove, reveal, reverse, stop)

CORK (→): *block, bung, cap, choke, close, congest, contain, cover, fill, jam, pack, plug, ram, seal, stem, stopper, stopple, stuff* (≠ broach, burst, clear, crack, decant, drizzle, effuse, open, pour, syrup, trickle, uncover, unseal)

CORNER (→): *absorb, bogart, burden, clog, command, consume, control, copyright, corner, dictate, direct, dominate, employ, engross, -exclude, exploit, flood, govern, hog, hold, inundate, keep, manage, monopolize, overload, overwhelm, own, patent, possess, restrain, rule, saturate, syndicate, use, utilize* (≠ allocate, allot, bestow, dispense, -disregard, distribute, divide, forfeit, furnish, lose, offer, provide, -reject, release, scatter, share)

CORNER (←): *block, bottle, box, cage, capture, catch, collar, confine, constrain, curb, fool, force, hamper, hinder, hunt, impede, limit, mousetrap, nab, pinion, restrict, seize, snare, trap, trick, trouble, waylay* (≠ -abandon, allow, chase, emancipate, free, liberate, loose, miss, permit, release, unleash)

CORRAL (←): *abduct, apprehend, arrest, bag, capture, catch, clasp, clutch, collar, cop, corner, detain, ensnare, entangle, entrap, get, glom, grab, grapple, grasp, grip, halter, hold, hook, kidnap, land, lasso, nab, nail, net, rap, rope, secure, seize, snaffle, snag, snare, snatch, trap, wrangle* (≠ -abandon, -bypass, discharge, -disregard, drop, free, liberate, loosen, lose, miss, release, unhand)

CORRAL (+): *accumulate, amass, archive, armor, arrange, assemble, attract, band, bound, box, brand, brigade, bring, bunch, cage, circum-*

scribe, closet, cluster, cocoon, collate, collect, combine, compile, concentrate, confine, congregate, conjure, connect, constellate, contain, convene, coop, cover, crate, draw, embrace, encapsulate, encase, encircle, enclose, encompass, enfold, envelop, fence, fold, frame, garner, gather, glean, graze, group, guide, heap, hedge, hem, herd, hive, hold, house, immure, impound, imprison, include, join, limit, link, lump, manage, marshal, merge, milk, muster, organize, pack, pen, pile, pool, press, pull, raise, rally, regiment, regroup, restrict, reunite, ring, scavenge, stable, stack, stockpile, summon, surround, swarm, systematize, throng, unite, wall, wrangle (≠ -abandon, alienate, diffuse, disaffect, disband, discard, disgorge, disintegrate, dismiss, dispel, disperse, dissipate, dissolve, divide, eject, expel, forfeit, isolate, jettison, loose, -omit, -reject, remove, scatter, seclude, segregate, send, separate, sever, share, split, unbridle, unleash)

CORRECT (→): *adapt, adjust, align, annul, balance, calibrate, -cancel, check, compensate, counteract, counterbalance, counterpoise, defeat, defray, equalize, expense, foil, -frustrate, harmonize, hinder, indemnify, invalidate, level, minimize, -negate, neuter, neutralize, -nullify, offset, oppose, outbalance, outweigh, override, overrule, -prevent, redeem, redress, relieve, remedy, resist, set, square, -thwart, tune, undo* (≠ accent, accentuate, accrue, aggravate, amplify, assert, assist, augment, boost, deepen, emphasize, exacerbate, fuel, heighten, increase, inflame, irritate, maximize, provoke, sharpen, support, vex, worsen)

CORRECT (+): *adjust, advance, alter, ameliorate, amend, better, blue-pencil, calibrate, change, clean, critique, cure, cut, debug, disabuse, doctor, edit, elaborate, embellish, emend, enhance, finesse, fix, flavor, further, garnish, grace, help, improve, launder, mend, modify, modulate, optimize, overhaul, pace, patch, perfect, polish, proofread, punctuate, reclaim, reconceive, reconceptualize, reconstruct, rectify, red-pen, red-pencil, redraft, redraw, redress, refine, reform, regulate, reimagine, reinvent, rejigger, remedy, remodel, renovate, reorganize, repair, rephrase, reshape, reshuffle, restyle, rethink, retool, retouch, revamp, review, revise, revolutionize, rework, rewrite, right, scrub, shine, shorten, shuffle, sort, straighten, sugarcoat, tweak, upgrade* (≠ aggravate, bastardize, blemish, botch, break, callous, canker, coarsen, corrupt, cripple, damage, debase, deface, depress, destroy, disable, disfigure, disorder, doom, efface, half-ass, -halt, harm, harshen, hurt, impair, injure, kill, maim, maintain, mangle, mar, mutilate, -neglect, ruin, scotch, spoil, suborn, tarnish, upset, wear, worsen, wreck, wrong)

CORRECT (/): *afflict, agonize, anguish, assess, avenge, burden, castigate, charge, chasten, chastise, condemn, confine, convict, criticize, crucify, damn, deduct, demonize, denounce, discipline, distress, dock, encumber, fine, foist, handicap, impose, judge, keelhaul, lambaste, levy, mulct, penalize, persecute, pillory, punish, rebuke, reprimand, reprove, sentence, torture, wreak* (≠ absolve, acquit, commute, exculpate, excuse, exonerate, forfeit, forgive, -ignore, pardon, ransom, release, reprieve, spare, vindicate)

CORROBORATE (+): *accept, acknowledge, adduce, adjure, admit, affirm, approve, argue, assert, assure, attest, authenticate, avow, back, bolster, buttress, certify, check, claim, concretize, confess, confirm, connote, consult, contend, contextualize, convince, crosscheck, cross-examine, declare, demonstrate, depose, determine, document, double-check, endorse, ensure, establish, evidence, evince, exemplify, exhibit, express, externalize, grill, guarantee, illustrate, instance, interrogate, interview, justify, maintain, manifest, notarize, observe, okay, pledge, proclaim, profess, promise, pronounce, prove, ratify, reinforce, rubber-stamp, showcase, strengthen, substantiate, support, sustain, testify, underpin, uphold, validate, verbalize, verify, vindicate, voice, warrant, witness* (≠ baffle, blind, challenge, confound, confuse, contest, contradict, debate, debunk, -deny, disavow, disclaim, discredit, -disown, disprove, dispute, distrust, doubt, fake, fudge, gainsay, invalidate, mislead, mistake, mystify, -overlook, puzzle, question, rebut, refute, -reject, -repudiate, scruple, suspect, trick, undercut, undermine, weaken)

CORRODE (/): *abrade, bite, blemish, burn, canker, consume, corrupt, crumble, damage, decimate, destroy, deteriorate, devastate, disintegrate, dissolve, eat, erode, fret, gnaw, harshen, impair, mar, nibble, rot, roughen, ruin, rust, scour, spot, sully, tarnish, waste, wreck* (≠ aid, bronze, build, construct, embalm, enhance, fortify, freshen, help, preserve, protect, refresh, regenerate, rejuvenate, renew, restore, revitalize, revive, seal, strengthen)

CORRUPT (←): *allure, bait, bed, beguile, bribe, bully, butter, buy, coerce, convince, debase, debauch, deceive, defile, degrade, demean, deprave, dishonor, doctor, entice, falsify, finagle, fix, flatter, fudge, goad, grease, hustle, induce, influence, lure, massage, misinform, mislead, misrepresent, motivate, nobble, oil, overpay, patronize, pay, persuade, pervert, poison, profane, prostitute, provoke, schmooze, seduce, snare, spur, square, stimulate, suborn, subvert, sway, sweet-talk, taint, tempt, trap, urge, warp* (≠ absolve, acquit, defend, discipline, excuse, expose, free, guard, honor, maintain, moralize, pardon, preserve, protect, punish, purify, redeem, -refuse, -reject, rescue, save, sustain, uphold)

CORRUPT (/): *abase, abuse, adulterate, animalize, bastardize, befoul, begrime, belittle, bend, besmear, besmirch, bestialize, blemish, blight, boot, bowdlerize, brutalize, canker, cheapen, contaminate, contort, corrode, crook, damage, debase, debauch, decay, decompose, deface, defile, deflower, deform, degrade, dehumanize, demean, demoralize, demote, deprave, depreciate, desecrate, despoil, destroy, deteriorate, devalue, dilute, diminish, dirty, disfigure, disgrace, dishonor, distort, doctor, doom, downgrade, efface, fix, flaw, harm, harshen, humble, humiliate, hurt, impair, incriminate, infect, injure, lessen, lower, lure, maltreat, mangle, mar, mistreat, misuse, mortify, mutate, outrage, pervert, poison, pollute, profane, prostitute, ravage, reduce, rot, ruin, sabotage, savage, seduce, shame, soil, spoil, stain, suborn, subvert, sully, taint, tarnish, twist, undercut, undermine, victimize, violate, vitiate, vulgarize, warp, waste, weaken, wreck, wrong* (≠ better, bless, chasten, cherish, clarify, clean, cleanse, decontaminate, dignify, elevate, enhance, ennoble, enrich, enshrine, exalt, hallow, honor, improve, moralize, optimize, overhaul, perfect, pity, praise, protect, purge, purify, quarantine, rarefy, rectify, refine, regret, respect, restore, revere, revolutionize, sanctify, shrive, treasure, upgrade, uplift, worship)

COUNSEL (→): *admonish, advise, advocate, alert, apprise, brief, caution, charge, confer, consult, convince, cue, direct, edify, educate, encourage, enjoin, enlighten, exhort, forewarn, guide, inform, instruct, notify, order, prescribe, prompt, recommend, school, shepherd, steer, suggest, teach, tout, tutor, urge, warn* (≠ answer, betray, brake, check, conceal, constrain, curb, deceive, demotivate, -deter, discourage, dissuade, feign, fool, -forbid, mask, outwit, pretend, restrain, trick, withhold)

COUNTER (→): *affront, answer, antagonize, baffle, battle, beat, bilk, buck, challenge, check, checkmate, -circumvent, combat, confront, contradict, contravene, counteract, countermand, cross, dare, dash, debate, defy, disappoint, discredit, -disown, disprove, dispute, distrust, doubt, face, fight, foil, -frustrate, gaslight, hamper, hinder, impede, inhibit, intercept, invalidate, match, meet, monkey-wrench, muzzle, obstruct, offset, oppose, override, parry, pit, protest, race, -rebuff, resist, retort, return, ruin, scruple, -thwart, withstand* (≠ abide, accept, advance, allow, back, brave, champion, cultivate, encourage, endorse, endure, foster, nourish, permit, promote, rubber-stamp, stomach, suffer, support, uphold, weather)

COUNTERACT (/): *annul, buck, -cancel, challenge, check, checkmate, confound, confront, contravene, correct, counter, counterbalance, countermand, countervail, cross, defeat, defy, disobey, expiate, fix, foil, -frustrate, -halt, hinder, invalidate, monkey-wrench, muzzle, -negate, neuter, neutralize, -nullify, offset, oppose, outbalance, outweigh, override, overrule, -prevent, protest, realign, rectify, redeem, redress, relieve, remedy, resist, retort, right, subvert, -thwart, undo* (≠ advance, aid, approve, assist, augment, boost, elevate, encourage, enhance, escalate, foster, further, hasten, help, maintain, prioritize, promote, quicken, support, sustain)

COUNTERFEIT (←): *adulterate, cheat, concoct, cook, copy, crib, doctor, duplicate, fabricate, fake, forge, fudge, hocus-pocus, imitate, invent, juggle, manipulate, phony, plagiarize, reduplicate, replicate, reproduce, simulate* (≠ attest, authenticate, certify, confirm, convince, corroborate, crosscheck, debunk, endorse, expose, notarize, police, ratify, substantiate, validate, verify)

COUNTERFEIT (→): *act, adopt, affect, assume, bluff, camouflage, clone, conceal, costume, disguise, dissimulate, dupe, emulate, fake, feign, forge, imitate, impersonate, mask, mimic, play, playact, pose, pretend, profess, roleplay, simulate* (≠ bare, betray, confess, confirm, confront, convince, disclose, discover, divulge, expose, flaunt, reveal, show, uncloak, unmask)

COUPLE (+): *ally, assemble, associate, attach, bind, bracket, buckle, chain, clasp, cluster, coalesce, combine, compound, congregate, conjoin, conjugate, connect, constellate, convene, fasten, fuse, gather, harness, hitch, hook, hybridize, integrate, join, link, marry, match, mate, network, pair, recombine, reconnect, rejoin, reunify, reunite, splice, synthesize, unify, unite, wed, yoke* (≠ break, detach, diffuse, disband, disconnect, disperse, divide, divorce, isolate, mismatch, orphan, part, scatter, seclude, section, separate, sever, split, sunder, uncouple, unlink)

COURT (←): *allure, attend, beckon, beguile, beseech, bewitch, blandish, captivate, charm, chase, coddle, date, desire, enchant, encourage, engage, engross, enthrall, entice, escort, fancy, fascinate, flatter, hypnotize, interest, invite, lure, magnetize, mesmerize, propose, pursue, razzle-dazzle, rivet, romance, seduce, see, serenade, spark, spoon, sway, sweet-talk, target, tease, tempt, urge, win, woo, wow* (≠ abuse, affront, aggravate, alienate, annoy, assault, attack, -avoid, bore, chill, -cut, -deter, disgust, -disregard, dissuade, -elude, foil, -ignore, irk, irritate, nauseate, -neglect, offend, -ostracize, -rebuff, -refuse, -reject, repel, repulse, revolt, -shun, sicken, -snub, -spurn, terrorize, torment, weary, worry)

COURT (←): *attract, blandish, bootlick, congratulate, cultivate, entreat, facilitate, flatter, follow, hunt, importune, incite, ingratiate, invite, please, praise, prompt, provoke, pursue, risk, search, seek, solicit, spark, tantalize, tease, tempt, woo* (≠ complicate, delay, demotivate, discourage, -disregard, hamper, hinder, -ignore, impede, obstruct, -prevent, protest, shelve, -spurn, stall, stymie, -thwart, troll)

COVER (→): *accoutre, attire, blanket, bronze, buckle, button, cake, canopy, cap, carpet, circle, cloak, clothe, coat, costume, crown, curtain, daub, deck, drape, dress, encase, encircle, enclose, encompass, enfold, enshroud, envelop, gild, layer, mantle, overlap, overlay, panel, paper, pave, plaster, plate, roughcast, shawl, sheathe, shroud, spackle, spread, surface, swaddle, swathe, tent, thatch, tile, veil, wallpaper, wrap* (≠ bare, denude, disrobe, excoriate, expose, find, peel, remove, reveal, scour, scrub, shuck, strip, unbuckle, unbutton, uncover, unearth, unwrap)

COVER (←): *comprehend, concern, consider, contain, describe, detail, embody, embrace, encompass, entail, examine, include, incorporate, instance, investigate, involve, meet, mention, name, note, notice, orbit, present, quote, reach, report, review, specify, survey, treat* (≠ -disregard, eliminate, -exclude, forget, -ignore, miss, -neglect, -omit, oust, -overlook, -reject, skip, -slight) **(¿) ABSTRACTION ALERT. Concrete goals essential!**

COVER (+): *armor, bulwark, buttress, canopy, cap, cloak, clothe, costume, crown, defend, disguise, drape, guard, harbor, hood, house, mask, obscure, pall, patrol, protect, reinforce, safeguard, screen, secure, shade, shelter, shield, stash, tuck, veil, watch* (≠ -abandon, attack, bare, denude, -disregard, expose, forget, harm, -ignore, reveal, sabotage, scotch, scupper, strip, uncover, undermine)

COVER (/): *becloud, bedim, befog, belie, blanket, bleep, block, blot, bury, cache, camouflage, cloak, cloud, conceal, curtain, darken, disguise, eclipse, encase, enclose, ensconce, enshroud, gild, gloss, hide, holster, hood, mask, niche, obscure, obstruct, occlude, occult, -omit, overlap, overshadow, screen, secrete, shade, sheathe, shroud, smother, spackle, spin, suppress, varnish, veil, whitewash, wrap, wreathe* (≠ accost, advertise, air, bare, betray, brandish, broadcast, circulate, clarify, confess, confide, confirm, confront, disclose, discover, display, disseminate, divulge, expose, flaunt, floodlight, hype, illuminate, parade, presell, present, proclaim, publicize, publish, reveal, show, showcase, spread, telegraph, uncloak, uncover, unmask, unveil, wag)

COVET (←): *admire, adore, anticipate, appreciate, await, begrudge, cherish, choose, crave, demand, desire, dig, enjoy, envy, expect, fancy, favor, fetishize, grasp, grudge, hope, hunt, love, prefer, prize, pursue, relish, resent, seek, stalk, target, treasure, value, want, welcome, wish* (≠ abhor, abjure, abominate, -avoid, -decline, -despise, -detest, disfavor, forfeit, -forsake, give, -hate, -loathe, nauseate, -refuse, -reject, -renounce, -scorn, -shun, -spurn)

CRACK (→): *break, debug, decipher, decode, decrypt, deduce, descramble, detect, explore, fathom, hack, infiltrate, jack, profile, render, resolve, solve, translate, unravel, unriddle, unscramble, work* (≠ baffle, cipher, code, defend, encipher, encode, encrypt, garble, jumble, miscommunicate, misunderstand, muddle, perplex, puzzle, scramble, stymie)

CRACK (/): *atomize, break, burst, chip, chop, cleave, crash, damage, detonate, explode, fissure, fracture, fragment, hurt, impair, injure, pop, pulverize, rend, ring, rive, sever, shatter, shiver, snap, splinter, split* (≠ cobble, correct, fix, heal, meld, mend, patch, plaster, realign, rectify, remedy, renew, renovate, repair, restore, seal, solder)

CRADLE (←): *assuage, baby, bear, carry, clasp, clutch, cuddle, cushion, embrace, fondle, grasp, hold, hug, lull, mollify, nestle, nourish, nurse, nurture, pacify, pillow, pity, placate, protect, rock, shelter, support, tend, watch* (≠ -abandon, abuse, attack, discard, -disregard, drop, expel, harm, -ignore, injure, menace, -neglect, repel, -shun, threaten, torment, victimize, wound, wrong)

CRAFT (+): *assemble, author, brew, build, cast, coin, compose, compound, conceive, concoct, construct, contrive, cook, create, design, devise, draft, draw, erect, establish, fabricate, fashion, forge, form, formulate, frame, ghostwrite, handcraft, imagine, improvise, institute, invent, machine, make, manufacture, mint, mold, organize, originate, patch, pen, prepare, produce, raise, ready, rear, redraft, reformulate, reframe, sculpt, sculpture, shape, structure, verbalize, weave, word, write* (≠ atomize, break, crush, damage, demolish, destroy, dismantle, fracture, fragment, harm, mangle, obliterate, pulverize, reshape, ruin, sabotage, scotch, scupper, scuttle, shatter, shelve, smash, wreck)

CRAM (→): *charge, chock, choke, compact, compress, crowd, crush, devour, drive, fill, force, glut, gobble, gorge, guzzle, heap, jam, jam-pack, load, overcrowd, overeat, overfill, pack, press, ram, sandwich, sardine, satiate, shoehorn, shove, slop, slosh, squash, squeeze, stuff, surfeit, tamp, thrust, wedge, wolf* (≠ calibrate, clean, clear, drain, draw, empty, evacuate, extract, leach, leech, loosen, measure, open, regulate, release, unpack, vacate, void, withdraw)

CRAMP (/): *arrest, bang, bash, batter, break, bridle, bump, check, circumscribe, clamp, clasp, clog, collapse, confine, constrain, damage, dash, disintegrate, encumber, fasten, fracture, fragment, -frustrate, grip, hamper, hamstring, handicap, hinder, hit, impede, inhibit, kill, knock, limit, obstruct, oppress, plunge, pound, rein, restrain, restrict, shackle, shatter, shiver, short-circuit, shunt, smash, splinter, stymie, -thwart, tie, topple* (≠ aid, allow, assist, comfort, ease, encourage, free, help, loosen, open, permit, promote, release, support, unfasten, unlock)

CRASH (/): *bang, bash, batter, break, bump, collapse, crack, damage, dash, disintegrate, fracture, fragment, hit, kill, knock, plunge, pound, pulverize, shatter, shiver, shunt, smash, splinter, topple, whack* (≠ -bypass, defend, drive, guard, leave, miss, operate, preserve, rescue, save, sustain)

CRAVE (←): *admire, adore, anticipate, appreciate, await, cherish, covet, demand, desire, dig, enjoy, expect, fancy, favor, grasp, hog, imagine, love, monopolize, prefer, prize, relish, require, resent, treasure, value, want, welcome, wish* (≠ abhor, abominate, -avoid, -decline, -despise, -detest, discredit, disfavor, dread, execrate, fear, forget, -hate, -loathe, -refuse, -reject, skip, -spurn) **(¿) ABSTRACTION ALERT. Concrete goals essential!**

CREATE (+): *actualize, ad-lib, appoint, author, brainstorm, breed, brew, build, carve, code, coin, compose, conceive, concoct, conjure, construct, contrive, cook, craft, design, develop, devise, draft, effect, engender, erect, establish, evolve, expedite, fabricate, fashion, forge, form, formulate, foster, found, frame, generate, guarantee, hasten, hatch, improvise, inaugurate, initiate, install, instigate, institute, introduce, invent, invest, launch, make, manufacture, mint, model, mold, occasion, ordain, organize, originate, paint, parent, perform, plan, produce, program, prompt, propagate, propel, provide, rear, script, sculpt, shape, sire, spawn, spearhead, spur, start, sustain, trigger, warrant, weave, whelp, write* (≠ adopt, arrest, -avoid, borrow, break, can, -cancel, check, conclude, copy, crush, curb, deep-six, demolish, -deny, destroy, dismantle, doom, duplicate, emulate, end, eradicate, finish, ghostwrite, -halt, -ignore, impede, inhibit, lose, mimic, mutate, obliterate, obstruct, poach, -prevent, quash, quell, raze, repress, restrain, restrict, ruin, smother, snuff, squelch, steal, stifle, stop, subdue, suppress, -thwart, wreck)

CREDIT (+): *accept, assign, attribute, believe, blame, buy, charge, connect, entrust, honor, link, swallow, thank, trust* (≠ adjudge, criticize, critique, disbelieve, discredit, fault, -ignore, judge, nag, -overlook, scold, shame)

CRIPPLE (/): *bash, batter, beat, belt, bench, bludgeon, boobytrap, break, bruise, buffet, castrate, club, crack, crucify, damage, debilitate, defeat, demoralize, deprive, destroy, disable, disfigure, dismember, disqualify, drub, enervate, enfeeble, flog, fracture, fragment, freeze, -frustrate, gore, hammer, hamper, hamstring, handicap, harm, hobble, hurt, immobilize, impair, impede, incapacitate, injure, kill, kneecap, lacerate, lambaste, lame, lash, maim, mangle, maul, murder, mutilate, palsy, paralyze, paste, pelt, pound, prostrate, pummel, ruin, sabotage, scar, scotch, scupper, scuttle, shatter, short-circuit, shrivel, sideline, smash, spoil, stifle, thrash, thump, torment, torture, undercut, undermine, wallop, weaken, whip, wing, wither, wizen, wound* (≠ aid, assist, bandage, bolster, boost, brace, brave, cure, defend, doctor, dress, enable, face, fix, guard, heal, help, hospitalize, improve, medicate, mend, midwife, militarize, nurse, oblige, outlast, overcome, patch, prioritize, promote, quicken, rehabilitate, reintegrate, rejuvenate, relieve, remedy, renew, repair, restore, rush, speed, splint, steady, strengthen, support, suture, tolerate, train, treat, unify, unite, weaponize, weather, weld, withstand)

CRIPPLE (/): *abrogate, abuse, anesthetize, anguish, annihilate, arrest, baffle, -balk, bash, batter, bind, blemish, blight, block, blockade, bloody, bog, boobytrap, botch, break, castrate, chain, check, checkmate, choke, clobber, clog, club, compromise, confine, constrain, crab, cramp, crimp, cross, crush, curb, damage, dash, deaden, deafen, debilitate, decimate, deface, delay, demolish, dent, derail, desolate, destroy, deteriorate, devastate, ding, disable, disarm, disfigure, disqualify, disrupt, doom, dull, emasculate, embarrass, encumber, enervate, enfeeble, erode, fetter, flaw, foil, -frustrate, halter, hamper, hamstring, handicap, harm, hem, hinder, hobble, hogtie, hold, hurt, immobilize, impair, impede, incapacitate, inhibit, injure, invalidate, kneecap, lame, leash, maim, manacle, mar, mire, monkey-wrench, mutilate, neutralize, obstruct, occlude, paralyze, prostrate, pulverize, raze, rein, restrain, restrict, retard, roadblock, ruin, sabotage, sap, scotch, scourge, scupper, scuttle, shackle, shatter, shelve, short-circuit, shrivel, smash, smother, spoil, stagger, stifle, straightjacket, strangle, stump, stun, stupefy, stymie, subvert, suffocate, suppress, tarnish, -thwart, tie, topple, torment, total, trammel, undercut, undermine, unman, vitiate, waste, weaken, wear, wither, wizen, worsen, wound, wreck* (≠ accelerate, advance, aid, ameliorate, assist, bemoan, better, boost, buoy, catalyze, clear, compel, cure, disencumber, doctor, ease, edit, empower, encourage, energize, enhance, enrich, expedite, facilitate, fast-track, fix, fortify, free, freshen, fuel, further, galvanize, gentrify, grease, hasten, heal, help, improve, invigorate, lament, liberate, loosen, lubricate, mend, midwife, mourn, oblige, open, optimize, overhaul, patch, perfect, prioritize, promote, quicken, rebuild, recondition, reconstruct, rectify, refine, refresh, regenerate, regret, rehabilitate, reimagine, reinvent, reinvigorate, rejuvenate, release, remedy, remodel, renew, renovate, repair, restimulate, restore, retool, revamp, revise, revitalize, revive, revolutionize, rush, smooth, speed, steady, stimulate, strengthen, survive, transcend, unclog, unleash, unstop, untangle, untie, urge, vitalize, weather)

CRITICIZE (/): *abuse, admonish, analyze, appraise, assail, assess, attack, badmouth, belittle, berate, blame, blast, blister, boo, browbeat, canvass, castigate, censure, chastise, chide, clobber, condemn, correct, critique, crucify, decry, defame, demean, demonize, denigrate, denounce, denunciate, deprecate, deride, devalue, diminish, -discount, dismiss, disparage, downplay, drub, excoriate, fault, flay, fulminate, gibbet, hammer, harass, hector, henpeck, humble, humiliate, impugn, insult, judge, keelhaul, knock, lambaste, lash, malign, minimize, mortify, nag, neg, nitpick, pan, patronize, pillory, read, -rebuff, rebuke, reprimand, reproach, reprove, resent, review, rip, roast, rubbish, scalp, scapegoat, scold, scorch, second-guess, shame, skewer, slam, slander, slate, smear, traduce, trash, trash-talk, tweak, underestimate, underrate, undervalue, upbraid, vilify, vituperate, zap, zing* (≠ acclaim, acknowledge, adore, advance, affirm, aggrandize, apotheosize, applaud, approve, blandish, boost, brave, brook, canonize, celebrate, cherish, commend, compliment, congratulate, countenance, deify, dignify, elevate, encourage, endorse, enshrine, esteem, eulogize, exalt, extol, face, favor, flannel, flatter, glorify, gold-star, gratify, hail, heroicize, high-five, honor, idealize, idolize, ingratiate, laud, lionize, magnify, praise, prize, promote, raise, recognize, recommend, regard, relish, revere, romanticize, rubber-stamp, salute, sanction, sentimentalize, tout, treasure, uplift, value, venerate, worship)

CROSS (→): *cover, crisscross, explore, follow, ford, frequent, hike, intersect, navigate, negotiate, pace, pass, patrol, perambulate, ride, roam, run, track, transit, travel, traverse, tread, visit, walk, wander* (≠ -avoid, -bypass, circle, circumnavigate, -ditch, -dodge, -duck, -elude, -escape, -evade, miss, orbit, pass, -sidestep, skip, skirt)

CROSS (+): *alloy, assemble, blend, breed, combine, compose, compound, concoct, couple, crossbreed, cross-fertilize, cross-pollinate, fuse, hybridize, incorporate, infuse, inseminate, interbreed, intermix, marry, merge, mingle, mix, mongrelize, stir, synthesize* (≠ disconnect, disunite, divide, divorce, filter, keep, preserve, purify, separate, sever, strain, sunder, uncouple, unmix)

CROSS (/): *antagonize, block, buck, check, checkmate, combat, constrain, contradict, counteract, counterattack, cramp, debate, defy, delay, -deny, -deter, discredit, -disown, disprove, dispute, distrust, doubt, fight, flummox, foil, -frustrate, hamper, hamstring, hinder, impede, inhibit, intercept, monkey-wrench, obstruct, oppose, oppress, protest, -rebuff, repel, repress, repulse, resist, scruple, stall, stonewall, stop, stump, stymie, suppress, suspect, -thwart* (≠ abet, aid, assist, boost, charm, defuse, disarm, encourage, facilitate, help, instigate, mollify, neutralize, nurture, placate, prioritize, promote, support, urge)

CROSS (/): *-abandon, abdicate, abnegate, backstab, betray, deceive, denounce, -deny, -desert, disavow, double-cross, incriminate, -renounce, retract, sell, two-time* (≠ advance, aid, assist, defend, endorse, follow, guard, help, honor, mind, obey, promote, protect, reassure, rescue, safeguard, save, shield, support)

CROSS-EXAMINE (→): *annoy, challenge, check, consult, cross-question, debrief, examine, grill, harass, hound, interrogate, interview, investigate, nettle, niggle, nitpick, pester, probe, pump, query, question, quiz, sweat* (≠ accept, address, answer, -avoid, baffle, confuse, -dodge, -duck, evince, gaslight, hamper, impede, judge, prove, puzzle, skirt, stall, stymie, swear, trust)

CROWD (→): *bump, bundle, cluster, compress, congest, cram, crush, elbow, fill, frogmarch, gather, heap, henpeck, hustle, jam, jam-pack, jostle, load, march, muster, nudge, overstuff, pack, pile, press, push, ram, sandwich, sardine, shoehorn, shove, squash, squeeze, squish, stuff, swarm, throng, thrust, wedge* (≠ -abandon, accommodate, -bypass, decompress, diffuse, dilate, disband, disperse, dissipate, expand, leave, loosen, open, organize, scatter, -sidestep, split)

CROWN (+): *adorn, anoint, authorize, bedeck, bedizen, cap, complete, conclude, dandify, decorate, delegate, dignify, dower, emblazon, enable, endow, ennoble, enrich, enthrone, exalt, fancify, festoon, finalize, finish, fulfill, garnish, gild, heighten, honor, inaugurate, induct, install, invest, ornament, perfect, prettify, raise, reward, strengthen, terminate, trim, wrap* (≠ banish, begin, blemish, defame, deform, denounce, destroy, dethrone, disfigure, dishonor, -disregard, drop, fine, harm, hurt, -ignore, initiate, injure, insult, mar, -neglect, overthrow, -prevent, punish, raze, ruin, topple, unhorse, unsettle, usurp, weaken)

CRUCIFY (/): *afflict, agonize, anguish, assault, attack, avenge, bedevil, blister, bother, burden, castigate, censure, chasten, chastise, confine, correct, criticize, critique, demean, demonize, denigrate, discipline, distress, dun, excoriate, excruciate, execute, fine, frustrate, hang, harangue, harrow, ill-treat, imprison, incarcerate, judge, keelhaul, kill, lambaste, lampoon, lynch, martyr, massacre, menace, mistreat, mock, murder, mutilate, pain, pan, penalize, persecute, pillory, punish, rack, rag, reprise, ridicule, rubbish, savage, scalp, sentence, slam, slate, slaughter, smite, stigmatize, strangle, terrorize, threaten, torment, torture, tyrannize, victimize, wound, wrack, wrong* (≠ aid, celebrate, commend, compliment, congratulate, defend, endorse, exalt, extol, glorify, gold-star, guard, harbor, help, honor, laud, nurture, pity, please, praise, protect, regret, rescue, save, secure, shelter, shield, soothe, tout, welcome)

CRUSH (→): *atomize, batter, beat, break, bruise, champ, club, compress, confute, crease, crowd, crumble, crumple, crunch, fracture, fragment, gnash, grind, hammer, mangle, mash, mill, pestle, pincer, pinch, pound, powder, press, pulp, pulverize, quash, repress, rumple, scrunch, shatter, smash, squash, squeeze, squelch, squish, subdue, suppress, trample, wallop, wrinkle* (≠ caress, defend, guard, heal, help, lift, loosen, mend, nurse, preserve, protect, release, remove, restore, uncrumple, unwrinkle)

CRUSH (/): *abash, annihilate, asphyxiate, beat, blitzkrieg, capture, checkmate, conquer, decimate, defeat, dehumanize, demolish, demoralize, desolate, destroy, dethrone, devastate, dispirit, dominate, doom, douse, end, exterminate, extinguish, foil, humble, humiliate,* *master, mortify, nuke, obliterate, oppress, outdo, outlast, outmaneuver, outperform, outplay, overcome, overpower, overthrow, overturn, overwhelm, prostrate, quash, quell, quench, repress, rout, ruin, scotch, shame, shatter, shellac, silence, slaughter, smash, smear, smother, snuff, squash, squelch, steamroller, stifle, strangle, subdue, subject, subjugate, suffocate, suppress, surmount, terminate, throttle, topple, trounce, trump, tyrannize, upset, vanquish, waste, whip, win, wrack, wreck* (≠ abet, advance, aid, arm, assist, back, bless, bolster, brace, buoy, buttress, calm, cheer, cover, cultivate, defend, embattle, encourage, endure, energize, entrench, establish, feed, foment, fortify, forward, foster, fuel, further, garrison, gird, guard, harden, hatch, hearten, help, hone, honor, incite, inspire, instigate, inure, invigorate, nerve, nourish, nurture, optimize, prepare, prime, promote, prop, protect, provoke, rabble-rouse, ready, reassure, reinforce, rescue, respect, revive, save, secure, sharpen, steel, stir, stomach, support, survive, sustain, toughen, wall, weaponize, weather)

CUDDLE (←): *baby, bundle, caress, clasp, coddle, cosset, dandle, embrace, encircle, enfold, fondle, hold, hug, indulge, kiss, love, nestle, nurse, nuzzle, overprotect, pamper, pet, protect, smooch, snog, snuggle, squeeze, squoosh, touch* (≠ -abandon, abuse, anguish, assault, attack, -avoid, beat, harm, hit, injure, maim, menace, mutilate, -reject, scalp, smack, terrorize, threaten, thump, torment, torture, victimize, wound, wrong)

CUE (→): *activate, actuate, buzz, catalyze, charge, dig, drive, electrify, energize, fire, fuel, generate, goad, ignite, incite, initiate, instigate, jog, jump-start, kick-start, launch, move, nudge, poke, power, prod, prompt, provoke, push, reactivate, rouse, run, signal, spark, spur, start, stimulate, switch, trigger, trip* (≠ -abort, arrest, baffle, block, brake, check, confuse, deactivate, forget, -halt, inactivate, jam, kill, miss, muddle, obstruct, repress, skip, stall, stick, stop, stunt, stymie, suppress)

CULL (←): *accept, accumulate, adopt, amass, appoint, assemble, bag, cherry-pick, choose, collect, compile, designate, elect, espouse, extract, fix, garner, gather, glean, handpick, hoard, hunt, mark, name, nominate, pick, pluck, poach, prefer, preselect, pull, reap, rob, scavenge, seize, select, set, settle, sift, steal, stockpile, tab, tag, take, tap* (≠ -abandon, -decline, disapprove, discard, disperse, dissipate, distribute, -ignore, jettison, -neglect, -refuse, -reject, -repudiate, -scorn, skip, spend, -spurn, squander, supply, waste)

CULL (/): *annihilate, attenuate, blitzkrieg, butcher, -cancel, clean, clear, cut, decimate, decrease, delete, depose, destroy, diminish, discard, dismiss, -ditch, doom, efface, eject, eradicate, erase, excise, expel, expunge, exterminate, extirpate, finish, hunt, jettison, kill, lessen, narrow, obliterate, oust, pulverize, purge, raze, reduce, -reject, remove, scrap, shatter, slaughter, smash, snuff, terminate, thin, trash, trim, waste, weed, zap* (≠ build, conserve, construct, create, develop, diffuse, disclaim, dismiss, disperse, dissipate, double, expand, extend, fashion, forge, form, foster, increase, insert, leave, mend, multiply, patch, preserve, protect, -reject, renovate, restore, retain, save, scatter, sustain, treble, triple)

CULTIVATE (→): *collect, cut, develop, dig, domesticate, dress, fallow, farm, fertilize, garden, germinate, gestate, grow, harrow, hoe, husband, inseminate, manage, manure, mature, mow, nourish, nurture, originate, plant, plow, pot, prepare, produce, proliferate, promote, propagate, pull, raise, ready, rear, replant, reseed, ripen, rototill, seed, sow, sprout, tend, till, transplant, work* (≠ -abandon, afflict, blight, consume, contaminate, cull, damage, destroy, devour, diminish, eat, exterminate, gather, glean, harvest, -ignore, impair, indispose, jettison, junk, kill, mow, -neglect, pick, pickle, pluck, poison, pollute, pull, raze, reap, recycle, ruin, scavenge, scorch, select, shrivel, sicken, squander, stunt, uproot, waste, weed, wither, yield)

CULTIVATE (+): *advance, aid, ameliorate, assist, back, better, bolster, brownnose, butter, check, cherish, civilize, coach, court, develop, discipline, drill, edify, educate, elevate, encourage, enhance, enlighten, enrich, forward, foster, further, help, improve, inform, instruct, legalize, mentor, nourish, nurse, nurture, optimize, patronize, perfect, polish, prepare, promote, pursue, raise, rarefy, rear, refine, school, shine, support, teach, train, tutor, win, woo, wow* (≠ arrest, ban, bar, barbarize, battle, block, callous, coarsen, combat, condemn, counter, damage, demolish, -desert, destroy, diminish, discourage, -ditch, doom, dump, encumber, fight, -forsake, -halt, hinder, hobble, hurt, -ignore, impede, inhibit, injure, -neglect, obstruct, oppose, poison, -reject, scrap, shackle, slough, snuff, stifle, worsen)

CURB (←): *-abort, baffle, bar, block, bottleneck, brake, bridle, bung, burden, catch, check, choke, clog, complicate, confound, congest, constipate, constrain, constrict, contain, control, counter, cramp, crimp, cripple, dam, dampen, daunt, delay, demotivate, -deny, depress, detain, -deter, discourage, dishearten, disincline, dissuade, drag, encumber, entangle, entrap, fetter, foul, -frustrate, gag, -halt, hamper, hamstring, handicap, hinder, hobble, hogtie, hold, housebreak, housetrain, ice, impair, impede, inhibit, interrupt, jam, leash, lumber, manacle, minimize, mire, moderate, muzzle, obstruct, occlude, oppose, oppress, paralyze, pause, plug, quiet, reduce, rein, repress, resist, restrain, restrict, retard, shackle, shelve, short-circuit, silence, snag, snarl, stall, stay, stem, stifle, still, stop, straightjacket, stymie, subdue, suppress, tame, tangle, throttle, -thwart, tie* (≠ abet, accelerate, accent, accentuate, accrue, actuate, affirm, aid, allow, amp, amplify, assert, assist, brainstorm, brew, bring, catalyze, effectuate, emphasize, encourage, energize, engender, exhort, foment, foster, frogmarch, generate, help, incite, incur, induce, instigate, invigorate, invoke, liven, loosen, make, march, maximize, midwife, nudge, permit, prod, promote, propel, provoke, punt, quicken, stampede, stimulate, tolerate, uncomplicate, uncork, unleash, unlock, vent, vitalize)

CURE (+): *allay, alleviate, ameliorate, assuage, bandage, better, brace, correct, depress, diagnose, doctor, dose, dress, drug, ease, fix, fortify, heal, help, hospitalize, improve, lighten, medicate, mend, moderate, nurse, palliate, physic, quarantine, realign, rectify, redress, regenerate, rehabilitate, reinvigorate, rejuvenate, relieve, remedy, renew, repair,* *restimulate, restore, resuscitate, revitalize, revive, right, salve, soothe, temper, treat* (≠ afflict, aggravate, ail, cripple, damage, debilitate, depress, disable, enervate, enfeeble, harm, hurt, impair, indispose, infect, injure, lacerate, lame, maim, mangle, misdiagnose, mutilate, overdose, palsy, poison, sap, shrivel, sicken, spike, undermine, waste, weaken, wither, wizen, worsen, wound)

CURSE (/): *abuse, admonish, afflict, anathematize, anguish, bedevil, beset, bespell, bewitch, blame, blast, blight, censure, chastise, chide, condemn, confound, criticize, cuss, damn, dash, denounce, doom, drat ensorcel, execrate, fault, fulminate, harm, haunt, hex, imprecate, insult, jinx, judge, maledict, plague, profane, rebuke, reprimand, reproach, reprove, revile, ruin, scapegoat, scourge, smite, threaten, torment, voodoo, whammy, witch, zap* (≠ applaud, bless, commend, compliment, congratulate, consecrate, enshrine, expiate, extol, glorify, gold-star, hail, hallow, high-five laud, magnify, praise, salute, sanctify, worship)

CURTAIL (/): *abate, abbreviate, abridge, abstract, chop, clip, compress, constrict, contract, cramp, cut, decrease, de-escalate, deflate, digest, diminish, dock, downsize, elide, encapsulate, epitomize, guillotine, lessen, limit, lop, lower, minimize, moderate, modify, pare, prune, recapitulate, reduce, restrict, retrench, shorten, shrink, slash, slim, subtract, summarize, syncopate, taper, trim, truncate* (≠ accent, accentuate, accrue, add, affirm, aggrandize, allow, amplify, assert, augment, balloon, boost, dilate, distend, elongate, emphasize, enlarge, escalate, exacerbate, expand, extend, heighten, increase, inflate, lengthen, maximize, prioritize, prolong, protract, raise, stretch, supplement, swell)

CUSHION (+): *absorb, allay, alleviate, armor, assuage, baffle, blunt, bolster, buffer, buttress, cradle, dampen, deaden, defend, diminish, dull, ease, gentle, insulate, lessen, lighten, lubricate, midwife, minimize, mitigate, moderate, modulate, muffle, pad, pillow, prop, protect, quiet, reduce, relieve, seclude, shield, soften, soundproof, stifle, sugarcoat, support, suppress, temper* (≠ accent, accentuate, amplify, boost, chafe, discomfit, emphasize, harm, heighten, intensify, irritate, jab, maximize, penetrate, pierce, poke, puncture, sharpen, transmit)

CUSTOMIZE (+): *accommodate, adapt, adjust, alter, attune, balance, calibrate, change, contrive, convert, custom-make, design, equalize, fashion, fine-tune, improvise, modify, personalize, reconceive, reconceptualize, reconstruct, refine, reimagine, reinvent, rejigger, remodel, rephrase, reshuffle, restyle, rethink, retool, revamp, reverse, revise, sculpt, shuffle, suit, tailor, tailor-make, transform, tune, tweak, vary, weaponize* (≠ adopt, copy, depersonalize, duplicate, emulate, formalize, homogenize, leave, mimic, normalize, pace, preserve, regularize, regulate, restore, retain, standardize)

CUT (→): *amputate, anatomize, bite, butcher, carve, chip, chisel, chop, circumcise, cleave, clip, crop, crosscut, dice, dismember, dissect, divide, dock, excise, gash, gouge, hack, hacksaw, hew, hurt, incise, knife, lacerate, lance, lop, mangle, mince, nick, nock, notch, perforate, pierce,* *prick, prune, raze, razor, rend, rip, rive, saw, scissor, score, scratch, scythe, section, segment, separate, sever, shank, shear, shiv, shred, slash, slice, slit, snip, split, stab, sting, strike, sunder, tear, vivisect, wound* (≠ armor, bandage, block, defend, doctor, fuse, grow, guard, heal, integrate, join, meld, mend, nurse, protect, reintegrate, seal, sew, shield, stitch, suture, unify, unite, weld)

-CUT (/): *-avoid, -blank, -boycott, -cold-shoulder, deflect, -disdain, -disregard, forget, high-hat, humiliate, -ignore, insult, isolate, -neglect, -ostracize, -overlook, -rebuff, -reject, repel, repulse, -scorn, seclude, -shun, -slight, -snub, -spurn* (≠ acknowledge, approve, attend, compliment, contact, embrace, favor, flatter, glad-hand, greet, heed, high-five, host, include, invite, note, praise, respect, reunite, welcome)

CUT (/): *abbreviate, abridge, alienate, alleviate, axe, bob, clip, concentrate, condense, crop, curb, curtail, decrease, delete, detach, diminish, disburden, discharge, divide, dock, dump, ease, edit, estrange, excise, expurgate, halve, lessen, lighten, lop, lower, nip, -omit, pare, part, poll, précis, prune, reduce, relieve, remove, shave, shear, shorten, skive, slash, snip, split, subdivide, summarize, trim, whittle* (≠ amplify, augment, boost, elongate, enlarge, expand, extend, heighten, increase, inflate, lengthen, maximize, permit, raise, strengthen, stretch, supplement, unspool, unwind)

DAMAGE (/): *annihilate, bash, batter, blemish, blight, boobytrap, botch, break, clobber, compromise, crab, cripple, crucify, crush, dash, decimate, deface, demolish, dent, desolate, destroy, deteriorate, devastate, ding, disable, disfigure, emasculate, enervate, enfeeble, erode, flaw, fracture, fragment, hamstring, harm, harshen, hurt, impair, infect, injure, lacerate, lame, maim, mangle, mar, mutilate, nock, poison, pulverize, queer, raze, ruin, sabotage, scalp, scotch, scour, scourge, scupper, shatter, smash, spike, spoil, subvert, tarnish, torment, torture, total, trounce, undercut, undermine, vitiate, waste, weaken, wear, welt, wound, wreck* (≠ alleviate, ameliorate, bemoan, better, defend, edit, endure, enhance, enrich, fix, improve, lament, mend, mourn, optimize, overhaul, patch, perfect, protect, quarantine, rarefy, rebuild, recondition, reconstruct, rectify, refine, regret, rehabilitate, remedy, remodel, renovate, repair, restore, rethink, retool, revamp, revise, survive, weather)

DAMAGE (/): *abuse, afflict, aggrieve, assault, batter, bedraggle, blemish, blight, bloody, blow, break, bruise, burn, callous, canker, castrate, club, coarsen, contaminate, contuse, corrode, corrupt, crack, crease, cripple, cut, deface, defame, defile, desecrate, destroy, dirty, disable, discolor, disfigure, disintegrate, dismantle, disqualify, efface, fade, fissure, gash, gnaw, gore, graze, hamstring, harm, hit, hurt, impair, incapacitate, indispose, infect, injure, lacerate, lame, maim, maltreat, mangle, mar, mistreat, monkey-wrench, mutilate, nick, pollute, ravage, razor, rend, rot, ruin, rust, sabotage, savage, scald, scar, scathe, scorch, scrape, scratch, sear, shank, shiv, sicken, singe, slash, slice, smash, split, spoil, stab, stain, sting, strain, subvert, taint, tarnish, tear, torment, torture, undercut, undermine, vandalize, vitiate, weaken, wound, wreck, wrinkle, wrong, zap* (≠ advantage, armor, bandage, benefit, bless, comfort, correct, cure, decontaminate, doctor, enhance, fix, flavor, guard, heal, help, improve, inoculate, mend, nourish, nurse, nurture, optimize, overhaul, patrol, polish, realign, remedy, repair, revolutionize, right, season, shelter, shield, shine, spice)

DAMN (/): *abuse, admonish, anathematize, attack, ban, banish, berate, blackball, blacken, blame, blast, boo, censure, chide, convict, criticize, curse, cuss, decry, denigrate, denounce, denunciate, discredit, drat, -excommunicate, excoriate, execrate, expel, flame, imprecate, jinx, knock, pan, penalize, proscribe, punish, rebuke, reprimand, reproach, reprove, revile, sentence, slam, slate, wrong* (≠ applaud, approve, commend, compliment, defend, endorse, exalt, exonerate, exorcise, favor, glorify, idolize, laud, lionize, magnify, praise, protect, reward, salute)

DAMN (/): *abhor, abominate, admonish, attack, belittle, berate, blacklist, blame, blaspheme, blast, castigate, censure, chastise, chide, condemn, criticize, curse, decry, denounce, deprecate, -detest, disfavor, disgrace, disparage, disrespect, diss, -excommunicate, execrate, fault, -hate, imprecate, knock, lambaste, -loathe, maledict, -ostracize, pan, rake, rebuke, reprimand, reproach, reprove, revile, scapegoat, scold, slam, upbraid, vituperate, zap* (≠ acclaim, anoint, applaud, bless, cherish, commend, congratulate, consecrate, eulogize, exalt, expiate, extol, glorify, hail, hallow, high-five, honor, idolize, laud, praise, redeem, respect, revere, salute, sanctify, sanction, tout, treasure, value, venerate, worship)

DAMN (/): *adjudge, castigate, censure, chasten, chastise, conclude, condemn, correct, decide, decree, determine, discipline, doom, find, judge, penalize, punish, resolve, rule, sentence* (≠ absolve, acquit, clear, excuse, exonerate, forgive, free, pardon, reprieve, spare, vindicate)

DAMPEN (/): *abate, allay, alleviate, blunt, buffer, castrate, cauterize, check, chill, cloud, cool, curb, damp, dash, daunt, deactivate, deaden, debilitate, decrease, dehydrate, demoralize, demotivate, depress, desiccate, -deter, devitalize, diminish, discourage, dishearten, dismay, dispirit, drain, dull, ease, enervate, enfeeble, exhaust, fatigue, humble, inactivate, inhibit, lessen, lighten, lobotomize, lower, minimize, moderate, muffle, mute, numb, petrify, reduce, restrain, sap, smother, stem, stifle, subdue, taper, tucker, underemphasize, undermine, weaken, wear, wither* (≠ accent, accentuate, accrue, affirm, amplify, arouse, assert, augment, boost, brace, buoy, charge, cheer, deepen, electrify, emphasize, encourage, energize, enhance, enliven, excite, exhilarate, fire, flavor, foment, fortify, galvanize, heighten, incite, increase, inflame, inspire, instigate, intensify, invigorate, kindle, lift, magnify, marinate, maximize, perfect, prioritize, promote, provoke, redouble, refine, rouse, season, sharpen, spark, spice, stimulate, stir, strengthen, trigger, uplift, vitalize, whet)

DANGLE (→): *balance, drape, festoon, flap, flutter, garland, hang, hook, mount, pin, poise, sling, string, suspend, sway, swing, tack, trail, wave* (≠ affix, anchor, coil, conceal, hide, loop, pin, pinion, reel, retract, withdraw)

DANGLE (←): *bait, brandish, bribe, convince, encourage, entice, flaunt, flourish, lure, motivate, offer, parade, persuade, prod, seduce, showcase, spur, sway, tantalize, tease, tempt, unsheathe, urge, wag* (≠ alarm, alert, caution, chill, -deter, disenchant, disgust, dissuade, holster, pin, repel, repulse, sheathe, warn)

DARE (→): *bet, brave, chance, compromise, defy, endanger, gamble, hazard, imperil, jeopardize, lay, play, risk, stake, target, venture, wager* (≠ block, defend, guard, keep, preserve, protect, rescue, resume, save, shelter, shield)

DARE (→): *accost, affront, approach, battle, beard, brave, brazen, breast, challenge, combat, confront, corner, counteract, defy, face, fight, flout, front, goad, invite, meet, oppose, provoke, race, repel, resist, stand,* *stump, taunt, troll, withstand* (≠ accept, -avoid, -deny, -dodge, -duck, -elude, -escape, -eschew, -evade, follow, frighten, funk, hide, -ignore, preserve, scare, shake, -shirk, -shun, -sidestep)

DARKEN (/): *adumbrate, becloud, bedim, befog, blacken, blear, blot, blur, camouflage, cloak, cloud, conceal, cover, curtain, dim, disguise, eclipse, fade, fog, fuzz, haze, hide, mask, mist, obliterate, obscure, overcloud, overshadow, screen, shade, shadow, shroud, veil* (≠ brighten, clean, expose, floodlight, illuminate, illumine, light, lighten, polish, reveal, shine, uncloud, uncover, unveil, wash)

DARKEN (/): *afflict, agitate, ail, bother, bum, burden, concern, dash, daunt, demoralize, demotivate, depress, discomfort, discompose, discourage, dishearten, dismay, dispirit, disquiet, distress, disturb, freak, oppress, perturb, sadden, sorrow, torment, torture, trouble, undo, unhinge, unnerve, unsettle, upset, weigh, worry* (≠ animate, assure, boost, brighten, buoy, cheer, comfort, console, delight, elate, elevate, encourage, enliven, excite, exhilarate, gladden, grace, gratify, hearten, inspire, invigorate, lift, lighten, please, reassure, rejoice, solace, soothe, stimulate, thrill, uplift)

DASH (→): *batter, beat, bowl, buck, cant, cast, catapult, chuck, crash, eject, fire, fling, heave, hurl, hurtle, impel, lash, launch, lob, loft, peg, pelt, pitch, pound, precipitate, project, propel, rifle, roll, shoot, skitter, slam, sling, strike, throw, thrust, toss, wing* (≠ armor, block, catch, defend, deflect, endure, face, guard, help, nurture, parry, protect, receive, shield, sustain, weather)

DASH (/): *afflict, agitate, ail, appall, blight, bother, break, burden, concern, confound, crush, dampen, daunt, demoralize, demotivate, depress, destroy, devastate, disappoint, discomfort, discompose, discourage, dishearten, dismay, dispirit, disquiet, distress, disturb, fracture, fragment, freak, frustrate, oppress, perturb, pulverize, ruin, sadden, shatter, smash, spoil, -thwart, torment, torture, trouble, undo, unhinge, unnerve, unsettle, upset, worry, wreck* (≠ animate, assure, boost, brighten, buoy, cheer, comfort, console, delight, elate, elevate, encourage, enliven, excite, exhilarate, gladden, gratify, hearten, inspire, invigorate, lift, lighten, please, prioritize, reassure, rejoice, soothe, stimulate, thrill, uplift)

DAUNT (/): *abash, afflict, alarm, appall, bluff, bother, browbeat, bug, bully, chill, cow, damp, dampen, deaden, debilitate, demoralize, demotivate, depress, -deter, discomfit, disconcert, discourage, dishearten, disillusion, dismay, dispirit, distress, emasculate, enfeeble, faze, flummox, frighten, frustrate, funk, horrify, intimidate, irk, muscle, overawe, psych, railroad, rattle, ruffle, sadden, scare, shake, spook, steamroller, trash-talk, trouble, try, undermine, unman, unnerve, vex, weaken, weigh, worry* (≠ animate, assure, bolster, boost, buoy, buttress, cheer, embolden, encourage, energize, enforce, enliven, excite, fortify, galvanize, gladden, hearten, inspire, invigorate, lift, nerve, prioritize, provoke, quicken, rally, reassure, reinforce, spark, steel, stimulate, stir, strengthen, troll)

DAZE (/): *amaze, anesthetize, astonish, astound, baffle, bemuse, bewilder, blind, boggle, confuse, dazzle, deaden, deafen, desensitize, distract, drug, dull, dumbfound, faze, flabbergast, floor, flummox, gobsmack, impress, narcotize, numb, overwhelm, paralyze, perplex, puzzle, shock, stagger, startle, steamroller, stun, stupefy, subdue, surprise, torpefy, wow* (≠ alarm, alert, anchor, arouse, balance, center, concentrate, energize, focus, ground, reinvigorate, revive, rouse, stabilize, steady, stimulate, stir, wake)

DAZZLE (→): *amaze, astonish, astound, awe, bedazzle, bewitch, blind, blur, captivate, confound, confuse, daze, dumbfound, energize, excite, fascinate, flabbergast, flummox, gobsmack, hypnotize, impress, overawe, overpower, overwhelm, razzle-dazzle, shock, stagger, startle, strike, stun, stupefy, surprise, wow* (≠ anger, annoy, bore, bother, buffer, bug, calm, deaden, depress, dim, distress, dull, enrage, exhaust, irk, irritate, lull, mellow, mitigate, moderate, sadden, sedate, tire, upset, vex, weary, worry)

DEACTIVATE (/): *abolish, -abort, anesthetize, arrest, brake, cut, disable, disarm, disband, dismantle, disqualify, dissolve, eighty-six, end, erase, extinguish, -halt, immobilize, incapacitate, jam, kill, mothball, paralyze, prostrate, retire, snuff, stall, stick, stop, terminate* (≠ activate, charge, crank, drive, electrify, energize, fuel, launch, move, power, propel, reactivate, reboot, spark, start, trigger)

DEADEN (/): *castrate, damp, dampen, daunt, daze, deactivate, deafen, debilitate, dehydrate, demoralize, demotivate, depress, desiccate, destroy, devitalize, discourage, dishearten, dispirit, disqualify, drain, enervate, enfeeble, exhaust, fatigue, freeze, frustrate, impair, inactivate, incapacitate, injure, leech, lobotomize, paralyze, petrify, sap, smother, stagnate, stale, stun, stupefy, tire, torpefy, tucker, undermine, unnerve, weaken, wear* (≠ arouse, boost, brace, buoy, charge, cheer, electrify, energize, enliven, excite, foment, fortify, galvanize, ignite, incite, inflame, inspire, instigate, invigorate, kindle, prioritize, provoke, quicken, raise, rouse, spark, stimulate, stir, trigger, vitalize, vivify)

DEADEN (/): *abate, allay, alleviate, anesthetize, assuage, blunt, buffer, cauterize, check, chloroform, consume, cushion, damp, dampen, daze, debilitate, decrease, deprive, desensitize, dim, diminish, dope, drown, dull, ease, enfeeble, etherize, exhaust, gas, harden, hush, lessen, lighten, lower, minimize, mitigate, moderate, muffle, mute, numb, quell, quiet, reduce, repress, retard, sedate, slow, smother, soften, soothe, stifle, stultify, subdue, suppress, taper, torpefy, tranquilize, weaken, wither* (≠ accent, accentuate, accrue, affirm, aggravate, amplify, animate, arouse, augment, beef, boost, consolidate, deepen, emphasize, enhance, exacerbate, flavor, heighten, increase, intensify, magnify, marinate, maximize, prioritize, redouble, rouse, season, sensitize, sharpen, spice, stimulate, strengthen, whet)

DEAL (→): *accord, allot, apportion, assign, bestow, bid, circulate, confer, deliver, diffuse, discharge, dispense, disperse, disseminate, distribute,* *divide, dole, dollop, drizzle, give, grant, hand, issue, mete, outbid, pass, pour, scatter, share, spread, supply, tender, transmit, trickle* (≠ begrudge, collect, -decline, -deny, deprive, -disregard, -ignore, -neglect, pinch, -refuse, -reject, scant, scavenge, skimp, steal, stint, take, withhold)

DEAL (→): *administer, apply, burden, deliver, direct, dispense, enforce, exact, foist, force-feed, impose, inflict, lay, levy, mete, overfeed, perpetrate, wreak* (≠ baffle, checkmate, defeat, -deny, deprive, disallow, -frustrate, mar, miss, ruin, spoil, take, withhold)

DEAL (→): *auction, bandy, barter, bootleg, broker, buy, cold-call, commercialize, commodify, corner, distribute, exchange, export, fence, flog, handle, hard-sell, horse-trade, import, invest, leverage, market, merchandize, monetize, monopolize, negotiate, operate, peddle, prescribe, purchase, push, remainder, renegotiate, retail, sell, smuggle, stock, supply, swap, take, trade, traffic, transact, treat, undersell, vend, wholesale* (≠ -avoid, ban, bar, blackball, blacklist, -boycott, -cold-shoulder, curb, disallow, embargo, -eschew, -exclude, -forbid, -ignore, -omit, -ostracize, outlaw, picket, -prohibit, proscribe, protest, -refuse, -reject, -snub, -spurn, suppress)

DEBASE (/): *abase, animalize, barbarize, befoul, begrime, bestialize, betray, blemish, canker, cheapen, contaminate, corrupt, damage, debauch, debilitate, deface, defile, degrade, demean, demoralize, deprave, depreciate, destroy, deteriorate, devalue, dilute, dirty, disable, downgrade, flaw, harm, harshen, hurt, impair, lessen, lower, mar, misapply, misuse, mutate, nobble, pervert, pimp, poison, pollute, profane, prostitute, reduce, ruin, sacrifice, sink, sophisticate, spike, spoil, stain, suborn, subvert, taint, tarnish, undermine, vitiate, vulgarize, warp, whore, wreck, wrong* (≠ ameliorate, amend, better, bless, clarify, clean, cleanse, decontaminate, dignify, elevate, enhance, ennoble, enrich, exalt, glorify, hallow, honor, improve, magnify, moralize, optimize, overhaul, perfect, praise, purify, rarefy, rectify, refine, respect, restore, revolutionize, upgrade, uplift)

DEBASE (/): *abase, adulterate, alloy, attenuate, bastardize, bedraggle, befoul, cheapen, contaminate, corrupt, counterfeit, cut, damage, defile, degrade, dilute, dirty, doctor, dope, dose, envenom, extend, fake, falsify, foul, fudge, impair, infect, jade, lace, load, manipulate, misrepresent, moderate, poison, pollute, qualify, sap, soil, sophisticate, spike, spoil, sully, taint, temper, thin, vitiate, water, weaken, weight, worsen* (≠ augment, better, bolster, clarify, clean, cleanse, clear, compact, concentrate, condense, decontaminate, delouse, distill, enhance, enrich, fertilize, filter, flush, fortify, improve, lard, leach, pasteurize, purge, purify, refine, reinforce, strengthen, supplement, upgrade)

DEBASE (/): *abash, affront, badmouth, belittle, blackguard, blame, boo, castigate, censure, chasten, cheapen, condemn, confound, confuse, criticize, damn, decry, defame, defile, degrade, demean, demonize, denounce, depreciate, detract, diminish, discomfit, disconcert, -discount,* *discredit, disgrace, dishonor, disparage, embarrass, execrate, faze, fluster, foul, humble, humiliate, insult, libel, lower, malign, minimize, mortify, nonplus, pillory, rattle, ridicule, shame, sink, slander, smirch, vulgarize, weaken* (≠ acknowledge, advance, affirm, aggrandize, apotheosize, applaud, boast, boost, canonize, celebrate, commend, compliment, congratulate, deify, dignify, elevate, ennoble, enshrine, exalt, extol, glorify, hail, heroicize, heroize, highlight, honor, idealize, magnify, praise, prioritize, promote, raise, recognize, romanticize, salute, sentimentalize, spotlight, tout, uplift)

DEBAUCH (/): *abase, abuse, adulterate, animalize, assault, befoul, begrime, belittle, besmear, besmirch, bestialize, blemish, brutalize, cheapen, contaminate, corrupt, damage, debase, deface, defile, deflower, deform, degrade, demean, demoralize, demote, deprave, depreciate, desecrate, despoil, destroy, deteriorate, devalue, dilute, diminish, dirty, disgrace, dishonor, distort, downgrade, flaw, harm, humble, humiliate, hurt, ill-treat, impair, lessen, lower, maltreat, mar, misuse, molest, mortify, pervert, poison, pollute, profane, prostitute, ravish, reduce, ruin, savage, seduce, shame, soil, spoil, stain, subvert, sully, taint, tarnish, twist, victimize, violate, vitiate, warp, wreck, wrong* (≠ better, clean, cleanse, decontaminate, dignify, elevate, enhance, ennoble, enrich, exalt, expiate, honor, improve, moralize, perfect, pity, protect, purge, purify, rarefy, reclaim, rectify, redeem, refine, reform, regenerate, regret, rehabilitate, respect, restore, sanctify, uplift, worship)

DEBILITATE (/): *afflict, attenuate, bleed, blunt, cannibalize, castrate, consume, cripple, damage, deplete, depredate, depress, deprive, devitalize, diminish, disable, drain, emasculate, enervate, enfeeble, eviscerate, exhaust, fatigue, hamstring, harm, hurt, impair, impoverish, incapacitate, injure, invalid, invalidate, leech, maim, mar, palsy, paralyze, prostrate, reduce, relax, restrict, sabotage, sap, scotch, scupper, shelve, soften, spoil, subvert, tire, undercut, undermine, unhinge, unman, unnerve, waste, weaken, weary* (≠ aid, beef, bolster, boost, brace, cure, defend, enable, energize, feed, fortify, fuel, galvanize, harden, heal, invigorate, nourish, nurture, protect, recruit, rejuvenate, restore, revitalize, season, shield, strengthen, tone, toughen, vitalize)

DEBRIEF (+): *consult, cross-examine, cross-question, examine, grill, inform, interrogate, interview, investigate, probe, question, quiz, scrutinize, study, test* (≠ answer, conceal, dismiss, -disregard, falsify, hide, -ignore, mislead, muffle, -overlook, silence)

DEBUG (+): *adjust, amend, calibrate, cure, decontaminate, emend, fix, improve, patch, perfect, quarantine, rectify, red-pen, red-pencil, redress, reform, regulate, remedy, repair, restore, rethink, retool, revamp, revise, right, tweak* (≠ afflict, attack, contaminate, corrupt, damage, hack, infect, infiltrate, invade, plague, puzzle, short-circuit, taint)

DEBUNK (+): *belie, challenge, confound, confront, confute, consult, contest, crosscheck, cross-examine, debate, deflate, demean, demolish, -deny, disbelieve, discard, disclose, -discount, discredit, discuss, disprove,* *dispute, distrust, divulge, doubt, explode, expose, falsify, grill, interrogate, invalidate, lampoon, mistrust, mock, nail, overthrow, overturn, pillory, puncture, quash, query, question, rebuke, rebut, refute, -reject, reveal, ridicule, scathe, -scorn, scruple, show, suspect, tell, trust, uncloak, uncover, undress, unmask, unveil* (≠ adduce, attest, authenticate, back, believe, buttress, camouflage, certify, chronicle, cloak, clothe, cloud, conceal, concede, confirm, consult, convince, corroborate, credit, demonstrate, disguise, display, document, endorse, establish, evidence, evince, hide, identify, illustrate, interview, manifest, mask, notarize, prove, record, rubber-stamp, secrete, show, substantiate, support, trust, validate, veil, verify, witness)

DECANT (→): *draw, drizzle, fill, ladle, offer, pour, serve, siphon, sprinkle, syrup, tap, transfer, trickle* (≠ drain, infuse, leach, leech, refill, replace, replenish, restock, restore, spout, stock)

DECEIVE (←): *abuse, affect, bait, bamboozle, beat, beguile, betray, bilk, bleed, blind, bluff, buffalo, bullshit, bunk, burn, cajole, camouflage, catch, cheat, chisel, claim, cloak, clothe, cloud, con, conceal, convince, costume, counterfeit, cover, cozen, crib, deacon, defraud, delude, diddle, disguise, double-cross, double-deal, double-talk, dupe, embezzle, enmesh, ensnare, entangle, entice, entrap, euchre, exploit, fake, falsify, feign, fiddle, finagle, flannel, flatter, fleece, flimflam, fool, forge, fox, fudge, goldbrick, gouge, gull, hoax, hocus-pocus, hoodwink, hornswoggle, hose, humbug, hustle, imitate, impersonate, inveigle, juggle, lure, manipulate, mask, milk, misdirect, misguide, misinform, mislead, misrepresent, misuse, mulct, outmaneuver, outslick, outsmart, outwit, overreach, palaver, pervert, playact, pose, pretend, rob, roleplay, rook, rope, sandbag, scam, screw, seduce, shaft, short, shortchange, show, skin, snooker, snow, spin, spoof, squeeze, stage, stick, stiff, sting, sucker, swindle, tempt, trap, trick, two-time, underpay, victimize, wrong* (≠ accuse, assume, audit, authenticate, believe, blab, blaze, blurt, confess, confide, confirm, confront, corroborate, crosscheck, debunk, deflate, disabuse, disclose, discredit, disenchant, disgrace, disillusion, -disown, dispute, distrust, divulge, document, doubt, evince, expose, honor, humiliate, malign, mock, -ostracize, pillory, pity, protect, regret, -repudiate, respect, restore, reveal, scruple, shame, stigmatize, substantiate, support, suspect, tell, trust, uncloak, uncover, undeceive, unmask, unveil, validate, verify, vilify)

DECIMATE (/): *annihilate, atomize, beat, best, blast, blitzkrieg, blot, break, bulldoze, butcher, clobber, conquer, cream, cripple, crush, damage, deep-six, deface, defeat, demolish, depopulate, desolate, despoil, destroy, deteriorate, devastate, dilapidate, disassemble, disfigure, disintegrate, dismantle, dissolve, doctor, doom, drub, dynamite, efface, eliminate, eradicate, erode, execute, explode, expunge, exterminate, extinguish, extirpate, fix, flatten, fracture, fragment, gut, harm, impair, injure, lick, liquidate, loot, mangle, mar, massacre, master, mend, mortar, mutilate, nuke, obliterate, outlast, overcome, patch, pillage, plunder, pulverize, ravage, raze, recondition, remove, repair, revamp, rout, ruin, sack, scotch,* *scour, shatter, skunk, slaughter, smash, snuff, spoil, subdue, surmount, thrash, topple, total, trample, trash, trounce, unbuild, undo, unmake, vandalize, vaporize, vitiate, wallop, waste, whip, wrack, wreck* (≠ assemble, build, conserve, constitute, construct, create, erect, establish, fabricate, fashion, father, forge, form, found, frame, heal, institute, invent, make, manufacture, mold, organize, preserve, produce, protect, raise, rear, rebuild, reconstruct, remodel, renovate, restore, resuscitate, save, shape, sire, survive, weather)

DECIPHER (+): *analyze, ascertain, break, cipher, compare, convert, crack, decode, decrypt, deduce, delineate, descramble, determine, discover, disentangle, elucidate, evaluate, examine, explain, explore, expound, extract, infer, inspect, interpret, investigate, learn, probe, profile, read, render, reveal, scan, scrutinize, search, settle, solve, spell, study, survey, test, translate, understand, unfold, unravel, unriddle, unscramble* (≠ baffle, cipher, cloak, cloud, code, conceal, confuse, disguise, encipher, encode, encrypt, garble, hide, jumble, mask, miscommunicate, misinterpret, misread, mistake, misunderstand, mystify, puzzle, scramble, trick)

DECIPHER (+): *absorb, appreciate, apprehend, assimilate, catch, compass, comprehend, conceive, decode, dig, digest, discern, fathom, get, grasp, grok, intuit, know, make, penetrate, perceive, pierce, plumb, realize, recognize, register, savvy, see, seize, sense, simplify, suss, understand* (≠ conflate, confuse, misapprehend, misconceive, misconstrue, misdiagnose, misinterpret, misperceive, misread, miss, mistake, misunderstand)

DECK (→): *assail, assault, attack, batter, beat, bulldoze, capsize, club, crush, defeat, demolish, fell, flatten, floor, hit, knock, level, overturn, overwhelm, prostrate, pulverize, punch, raze, smash, steamroller, subdue, tackle, topple, unhorse, upset, wreck, wrestle* (≠ block, boost, counterpunch, defend, -dodge, elevate, guard, lift, miss, parry, preserve, protect, raise, rear, restore, shield, -sidestep, support)

DECK (+): *accessorize, accoutre, adorn, appliqué, appoint, array, attire, beautify, bedeck, bedizen, bejewel, blazon, braid, brighten, buckle, button, caparison, clothe, costume, dandify, decorate, drape, dress, elaborate, embellish, emboss, embroider, enrich, fancify, feather, festoon, figure, filigree, fillet, flounce, freshen, frill, fringe, garland, garnish, gild, glitter, glitz, grace, hang, lace, ornament, paint, pigment, prettify, pretty, primp, ribbon, smarten, spruce, stipple, stud, swag, tinsel, titivate, tool, trim, wreathe* (≠ bare, blemish, deface, denude, disfigure, dismantle, display, disrobe, divest, efface, expose, harshen, humble, mar, reveal, scar, simplify, spoil, streamline, strip, uglify, unbuckle, unbutton, uncover, undress)

-DECLINE (/): *abjure, -avoid, -bypass, contradict, controvert, debate, -deny, detour, ding, disallow, disapprove, disavow, disclaim, discredit, -disdain, dismiss, -disown, dispute, flush, -forbid, forgo, forswear, gainsay, -ignore, -negate, -nix, overrule, pass, -prohibit, proscribe, -rebuff, rebut, recall, recant, -refuse, refute, -reject, -renounce, -repudiate, retract,* *revoke, -scorn, scout, -spurn, stick, -veto, withdraw* (≠ accede, accept, acquire, adopt, approve, brook, choose, condone, countenance, embrace, espouse, face, grasp, handpick, invite, obtain, procure, receive, seize, select, source, support, swallow, take, tolerate, welcome)

-DECLINE (/): *ban, check, constrain, curb, -deny, disallow, disapprove, enjoin, -forbid, hinder, hold, impede, keep, negative, -nix, obstruct, override, -prohibit, proscribe, -rebuff, -refuse, -reject, repel, repress, restrain, restrict, -spurn, stall, stymie, -veto, withhold* (≠ accord, afford, allow, authorize, commission, concede, dispense, furnish, give, grant, let, license, okay, permit, provide, sanction, supply, vouchsafe, warrant)

DECODE (+): *break, crack, decipher, decrypt, deduce, descramble, detect, interpret, read, render, solve, translate, understand, unravel, unriddle, unscramble, untangle, work* (≠ baffle, cipher, code, encipher, encode, encrypt, garble, jumble, mix, muddle, puzzle, scramble)

DECONSTRUCT (/): *analyze, anatomize, arrange, assay, assess, bare, catalog, categorize, classify, codify, compare, contrast, correlate, crack, cut, decipher, decode, deduce, detect, diagnose, diagram, dismantle, dissect, distill, divide, enumerate, evaluate, examine, explore, index, inspect, investigate, learn, order, probe, profile, read, reduce, schematize, scrutinize, segment, separate, sort, study, subdivide, tabulate, vivisect* (≠ agglomerate, aggregate, amalgamate, assemble, assimilate, baffle, build, coalesce, code, combine, compile, confuse, conglomerate, consolidate, construct, craft, encrypt, incorporate, integrate, internalize, misdiagnose, reshape, restructure, signify, synthesize, unify)

DECONTAMINATE (+): *bleach, bless, clean, cleanse, clear, delouse, deodorize, disinfect, distill, filter, fumigate, hallow, perfect, purge, purify, quarantine, rectify, redeem, refine, rinse, sanctify, sanitize, soak, soap, sterilize, wash* (≠ adulterate, canker, contaminate, corrode, corrupt, foul, harm, infect, infest, poison, pollute, soil, spoil, stain, sully, taint, tarnish)

DECORATE (+): *accessorize, adorn, appliqué, arrange, array, beautify, bedeck, beribbon, blazon, braid, brighten, buckle, burnish, button, caparison, color, contour, costume, crown, deck, diamond, dignify, drape, dress, edge, elaborate, embellish, emblazon, emboss, embroider, enhance, enrich, fancify, feather, festoon, figure, filigree, fillet, finish, fix, flounce, freshen, frill, fringe, garland, garnish, gem, gild, glamorize, glitter, glitz, grace, groom, gussy, hang, illuminate, impearl, jewel, lace, neaten, optimize, order, ornament, overhaul, paint, pearl, perfect, pigment, prettify, pretty, provide, redecorate, redo, renovate, ribbon, sculpt, smarten, spangle, spruce, stipple, stud, swag, tidy, tinsel, tool, trim, wallpaper, wreathe* (≠ bare, blemish, darken, decrease, deface, deform, denude, disfigure, dismantle, display, divest, dull, efface, expose, harshen, hurt, mar, reduce, reveal, ruin, scar, simplify, spoil, streamline, strip, uglify, unbuckle, unbutton, uncover)

DECOY (←): *allure, attract, bait, beguile, betray, bewitch, blind, captivate, capture, catch, charm, con, deceive, delude, draw, enchant, enmesh, ensnare, entice, entrap, fascinate, inveigle, lead, lure, magnetize, mesh, mislead, persuade, rope, seduce, shill, snare, snooker, snow, solicit, steer, tangle, tantalize, tease, tempt, tout, trap, trick* (≠ alert, belie, betray, bore, caution, chill, dampen, daunt, -deter, dissuade, expose, forewarn, -prevent, repel, repulse, reveal, signal, telegraph, ward, warn)

DECREASE (/): *abate, abbreviate, abridge, absorb, appreciate, apprehend, assimilate, attenuate, broaden, catch, choke, clip, compass, comprehend, compress, conceive, concentrate, condense, constrict, contract, crop, curtail, cut, decode, de-escalate, deflate, dent, deplete, dig, digest, diminish, discern, dock, downscale, downsize, drop, ease, fathom, get, grasp, grok, impede, intuit, kill, lessen, limit, lower, make, minimize, moderate, modify, modulate, nick, pare, penetrate, perceive, pierce, -prohibit, prune, qualify, realize, recognize, reduce, register, retrench, savvy, see, seize, sense, shorten, shrink, sink, slacken, slash, taper, trim, truncate, whittle* (≠ accent, accentuate, accrue, add, aggrandize, amplify, augment, boost, bulge, complement, develop, dilate, distend, elongate, emphasize, enhance, enlarge, escalate, expand, extend, foster, heighten, incorporate, increase, inflate, integrate, intensify, lengthen, maximize, prioritize, prolong, protract, raise, redouble, refine, supplement, swell, unspool)

DECRY (/): *abhor, abominate, abuse, admonish, attack, badmouth, belittle, berate, blacklist, blame, blast, blister, boo, castigate, censure, chastise, chide, condemn, criticize, curse, damn, defame, denigrate, denounce, denunciate, deprecate, depreciate, -detest, devalue, diminish, -discount, discredit, disfavor, disgrace, dismiss, disparage, disrespect, diss, downgrade, -excommunicate, excoriate, execrate, fault, fulminate, -hate, imprecate, knock, lambaste, -loathe, lower, malign, minimize, -ostracize, pan, rake, rebuke, reprimand, reproach, reprove, resent, revile, rip, scapegoat, scold, -scorn, slam, slander, slate, slur, traduce, underestimate, underrate, undervalue, upbraid, vilify, vilipend, vituperate, wrong, zap* (≠ accentuate, acclaim, affirm, amplify, applaud, approve, assert, bless, brook, commend, compliment, congratulate, consecrate, countenance, endorse, eulogize, exalt, extol, face, favor, glorify, gold-star, hail, hallow, honor, laud, magnify, praise, protect, recommend, respect, revere, salute, sanctify, sanction, support, tolerate, tout, treasure, venerate)

DEDICATE (+): *address, allocate, apply, assign, bestow, bind, bless, budget, commit, confide, consecrate, consign, devote, earmark, employ, entrust, give, hallow, inscribe, name, offer, pledge, present, reserve, sacrifice, sanctify, save, surrender, task, use, volunteer* (≠ conceal, deduct, -ignore, misapply, misuse, -neglect, profane, -refuse, stint, take, withhold)

DEDUCE (←): *analyze, appraise, ascertain, assess, benchmark, calculate, categorize, chart, collect, compare, comprehend, conceive, conclude, conjecture, consider, construe, contemplate, count, critique, decide, derive, detect, determine, draw, educe, enumerate, estimate, evaluate,* *extrapolate, fancy, figure, gather, gauge, glean, infer, interpret, judge, learn, make, number, numerate, plan, plot, postulate, presume, presuppose, prioritize, rank, rationalize, read, reason, reckon, regard, scheme, study, suppose, surmise, suss, systematize, tally, think, triangulate, understand, weigh* (≠ addle, assume, baffle, believe, bewilder, bury, conceal, confound, confuse, deceive, defraud, disbelieve, disguise, disperse, -disregard, distribute, divide, forget, guess, hide, -ignore, imply, instruct, leave, mask, misgauge, misjudge, misread, misunderstand, muddle, mystify, obscure, perplex, predetermine, puzzle, -reject, scatter, teach, trick, trust, wonder) **(¿) ABSTRACTION ALERT. Concrete goals essential!**

DEDUCT (/): *abate, abbreviate, abridge, abstract, borrow, clip, compact, compress, concentrate, contract, crop, curtail, cut, debit, decrease, deflate, deplete, diminish, discount, -ditch, dock, downsize, drain, dump, erode, leach, leech, lessen, lose, lower, minimize, offload, pare, prune, rebate, reduce, remove, retrench, shorten, shrink, slash, subtract, trim, truncate, whittle, withdraw* (≠ accentuate, accrue, add, affix, aggrandize, allege, amplify, annex, append, augment, boost, complement, compound, double, emphasize, enhance, enlarge, expand, increase, inject, insert, insinuate, intensify, interpolate, interpose, intersperse, introduce, magnify, mainline, maximize, multiply, pad, prioritize, raise, supplement, tack, treble, triple)

DEFACE (/): *annihilate, blemish, boobytrap, break, damage, deform, demolish, dent, depredate, desecrate, despoil, destroy, devastate, dilapidate, disfigure, efface, fracture, fragment, graffiti, harm, harshen, hurt, impair, injure, loot, mar, maraud, mutilate, nock, obliterate, pillage, plunder, pulverize, ransack, ravage, raven, raze, ruin, sabotage, sack, scalp, scorch, scourge, scratch, shatter, smash, spoil, stain, sully, tag, tarnish, tear, total, trash, vandalize, violate, waste, wrack, wreck* (≠ aid, assist, build, clean, clear, conserve, guard, heal, mend, patch, preserve, protect, rebuild, recycle, refresh, refurbish, repaint, repair, salvage, save, scour, scrub, survive, wash)

DEFAME (/): *abase, abrade, abuse, accuse, admonish, antagonize, badmouth, besmear, besmirch, blacken, blame, blemish, blister, calumniate, castigate, censure, chasten, chastise, chide, cloud, condemn, criticize, damage, decry, deface, defile, degrade, demean, demonize, denigrate, denounce, deprecate, deride, diminish, disapprove, -discount, discredit, disfavor, disgrace, dishonor, disparage, disrespect, embarrass, fault, frame, incriminate, knock, lessen, libel, malign, mock, muckrake, pan, pillory, reduce, -renounce, reproach, roast, scandalize, scorch, -scorn, shame, slam, slander, smear, stigmatize, sully, tarnish, traduce, traumatize, upbraid, vilify, villainize, vituperate, vulgarize, wrong, zing* (≠ admire, adore, alibi, approve, benefit, champion, clear, commend, compliment, congratulate, defend, deify, esteem, eulogize, exalt, excuse, exonerate, favor, glorify, gold-star, magnify, pardon, praise, respect, revere, shield, spare, venerate, vindicate)

DEFANG (←): *attenuate, blunt, buffer, castrate, dampen, deaden, debilitate, decrease, demilitarize, devitalize, dilute, diminish, disable, disarm, disqualify, dull, emasculate, enervate, enfeeble, exhaust, hamper, hamstring, handicap, hinder, hobble, impair, incapacitate, lessen, moderate, neuter, neutralize, paralyze, prostrate, reduce, relieve, sabotage, sap, scotch, soften, starve, stun, stupefy, subdue, subvert, temper, undermine, vitiate, weaken* (≠ arm, edge, enrage, equip, exacerbate, fortify, gird, hone, intensify, militarize, nerve, prepare, prime, ready, reinforce, sharpen, steel, weaponize, whet)

DEFEAT (/): *bar, beat, best, better, block, break, cap, capture, checkmate, confound, conquer, crush, dethrone, dominate, drub, eclipse, exceed, finish, floor, foil, hinder, humble, impede, master, monkey-wrench, muzzle, -nullify, obstruct, outclass, outdo, outlast, outmaneuver, outmatch, outperform, outplay, outrank, outrun, outscore, outsell, outshine, outsmart, outstrip, outwit, overcome, overpower, overshadow, overtake, overthrow, overturn, overwhelm, pulverize, quash, quell, railroad, -rebuff, repel, rival, rout, ruin, shellac, smash, steamroller, subdue, surmount, surpass, thrash, -thwart, top, transcend, trounce, trump, usurp, vanquish, whip, whup, win, wrack, wreck* (≠ abdicate, boost, build, confirm, congratulate, crown, defend, elect, encourage, establish, guard, inspire, install, lose, maintain, motivate, praise, preserve, prioritize, protect, reinstate, reinvigorate, release, relinquish, renew, repair, restore, revive, settle, stimulate, subvert, support, uphold)

DEFEND (+): *absolve, acquit, aid, argue, arm, armor, assist, -avert, bar, barricade, battle, blockade, blunt, bolster, buffer, bulwark, buttress, champion, cherish, conserve, contend, contest, counter, counterattack, counterpunch, cover, cushion, -deter, embattle, escort, exonerate, fence, fight, forfend, fortify, foster, garrison, guard, hold, house, insulate, insure, keep, maintain, mine, nourish, oppose, patrol, patronize, police, preserve, -prevent, protect, ransom, reclaim, recover, redeem, repel, rescue, resist, retain, retrieve, safeguard, salvage, save, screen, secure, sentinel, shelter, shield, support, sustain, uphold, ward, watch, withstand* (≠ -abandon, abuse, assail, assault, attack, beset, besiege, blitz, bombard, -desert, forget, -forsake, impugn, jeopardize, mortar, outlast, overrun, protest, relinquish, sic, storm, submit, violate, withdraw, wrong, yield)

DEFEND (+): *accentuate, advocate, affirm, argue, assert, avow, champion, claim, confirm, contend, crosscheck, debate, discuss, emphasize, espouse, insist, justify, maintain, plead, proclaim, profess, protest, state, stress, support, underline, underscore, uphold, vindicate, warrant* (≠ -abandon, abjure, assert, contradict, controvert, disprove, -forsake, invalidate, -negate, overturn, parry, rebut, recant, refute, resent, retract, reverse, subvert, switch, withdraw)

DEFILE (/): *abase, abuse, adulterate, affront, assault, bed, befoul, begrime, besmirch, bestialize, blacken, blaspheme, canker, contaminate, corrupt, curse, damage, debase, debauch, deconsecrate, defame, deflower, degrade, denigrate, desanctify, desecrate, despoil, dilute, dirty,* *disgrace, dishonor, doctor, foul, grime, infect, insult, mire, molest, muddy, offend, outrage, pervert, poison, pollute, profane, rot, shame, smear, smirch, smudge, soil, spoil, stain, sully, taint, tarnish, violate, wrong* (≠ anoint, apotheosize, benefit, bless, cherish, clarify, clean, cleanse, clear, consecrate, decontaminate, dedicate, deify, delouse, disinfect, distill, expiate, filter, hallow, honor, praise, protect, purge, purify, quarantine, redeem, respect, sanctify, sanitize, sterilize, vindicate)

DEFLATE (/): *appall, bulldoze, cannibalize, chagrin, chasten, collapse, consume, contract, crush, curb, dampen, dash, debunk, decrease, demoralize, demotivate, deplete, depreciate, depress, devalue, diminish, disabuse, disappoint, disconcert, discourage, disenchant, dishearten, disillusion, dismay, dispirit, empty, enlighten, exhaust, flatten, humble, humiliate, inhibit, lessen, lower, minimize, mortify, prick, puncture, reduce, shake, shrink, squash, squeeze, subdue, unpack, void* (≠ accrue, aerate, aggrandize, aid, amplify, assist, augment, bloat, boost, build, bulge, develop, dilate, distend, elongate, encourage, enlarge, escalate, expand, extend, fill, help, increase, inflate, magnify, prioritize, raise, stretch, swell)

DEFLECT (/): *-abort, anticipate, -avert, -avoid, bar, bend, block, -bypass, check, chill, -circumvent, contort, counter, counterpunch, curve, dampen, daunt, derail, -deter, discourage, dissuade, divert, -dodge, -duck, -elude, -evade, fence, field, focus, foil, forestall, hook, inhibit, intercept, misdirect, move, obstruct, parry, -preclude, -prevent, realign, -rebuff, rebuke, rechannel, redirect, refract, reorient, repel, repulse, reroute, resist, retort, reverse, shift, -shirk, -shun, shunt, -sidestep, sidetrack, stop, sway, swing, switch, swivel, -thwart, transfer, turn, twist, warp, withdraw* (≠ accept, accost, attack, await, brave, buttonhole, confront, contact, face, fight, invite, meet, oppose, receive, seek, stay, straighten, suffer, tackle, taunt, waylay, welcome, wrestle)

DEFLOWER (/): *abase, assault, attack, bed, beguile, belittle, besmirch, boink, compromise, corrupt, debase, debauch, defile, degrade, demean, demote, desecrate, despoil, devalue, devour, disgrace, dishonor, force, fuck, harm, hump, mar, molest, outrage, penetrate, possess, rape, ravage, ravish, ruin, screw, seduce, shame, soil, spoil, stain, sully, taint, violate* (≠ aid, assist, defend, dignify, elevate, enshrine, guard, help, honor, preserve, protect, revere, save, shield, worship)

DEFORM (/): *abuse, blemish, buckle, coil, contort, cripple, crucify, crumple, crush, curl, damage, deface, disfigure, distort, efface, flaw, gnarl, harm, harshen, hurt, impair, injure, kink, knot, loop, maim, mangle, mar, misshape, mutate, mutilate, pervert, rotate, ruin, screw, skew, spiral, spoil, squinch, torture, twine, twist, warp, wind, wreathe, wreck, wrench, wrest, wring, wrong* (≠ align, beautify, correct, glamorize, glitz, improve, maintain, mend, patch, preserve, realign, rectify, remedy, right, smooth, straighten, unbend, uncrumple, uncurl)

DEFRAUD (←): *bamboozle, beard, beat, beguile, bilk, bleed, bluff, bootleg, bottom-deal, burn, cajole, cheat, chisel, clip, con, convince, cook, cozen,* *crib, deceive, defalcate, diddle, disinform, doctor, double-cross, double-talk, dupe, embezzle, euchre, exploit, fiddle, finagle, fleece, flimflam, fool, fox, frame, fudge, gas, goldbrick, gouge, gull, gyp, hoax, hocus-pocus, hoodwink, hook, hornswoggle, hose, humbug, hype, ice, manipulate, milk, mislead, mousetrap, outfox, outwit, plant, pluck, rob, rook, salt, sandbag, scam, screw, shaft, short, shortchange, shuck, skin, snooker, snow, soak, stick, stiff, sting, stonewall, sucker, swindle, take, trick, two-time, underpay, vamp, victimize, whitewash, wrong* (≠ accuse, afford, assume, audit, authenticate, bankroll, believe, capitalize, comp, confess, confide, confirm, confront, crosscheck, debunk, defray, disclose, discredit, disperse, divulge, donate, evince, exonerate, expose, fund, give, honor, indemnify, offer, -ostracize, permit, protect, prove, provide, refund, regret, reimburse, repay, respect, restore, reveal, scatter, shame, square, substantiate, supply, support, tender, trust)

DEFUSE (+): *allay, alleviate, ameliorate, amend, arrest, assuage, better, brake, bridle, calm, check, console, constrain, contain, control, cool, curb, deactivate, defang, demilitarize, diminish, disable, disarm, dismantle, dull, ease, -halt, help, hush, immobilize, improve, inactivate, inhibit, jam, lubricate, lull, mellow, midwife, mitigate, mollify, pace, pacify, placate, quell, quieten, reassure, reconcile, regulate, rein, relax, relieve, restrain, reunite, sedate, settle, soothe, stabilize, stall, steady, still, tranquilize* (≠ aggravate, agitate, charge, crank, detonate, electrify, exacerbate, fuel, incite, induce, inflame, instigate, intensify, kindle, militarize, propel, provoke, push, spark, stir, trigger, troll, vex)

DEFY (/): *accost, baffle, beard, brave, breach, break, buck, challenge, combat, confront, contest, contradict, counter, counteract, counter-check, dare, debate, defeat, -despise, -deter, discredit, dismiss, disobey, disoblige, -disown, disprove, dispute, -disregard, disrespect, distrust, doubt, -elude, -evade, face, fight, flout, foil, -frustrate, gibe, -ignore, infringe, insult, invalidate, jeer, mock, monkey-wrench, oppose, pooh-pooh, provoke, -reject, repel, repulse, resist, retort, ridicule, -scorn, -shun, -slight, -spurn, stick, subvert, -thwart, transgress, venture, violate, withstand* (≠ admire, allow, assist, -avoid, blandish, boost, command, concede, demand, -dodge, dominate, -duck, -elude, encourage, -escape, -eschew, flatter, follow, heed, help, hide, ingratiate, keep, mind, obey, oblige, observe, permit, prioritize, regard, respect, serve, -sidestep, support, urge)

DEGRADE (/): *abase, abuse, affront, bed, belittle, besmear, besmirch, bestialize, brutalize, canker, cheapen, contaminate, corrupt, debase, debauch, declass, defile, dehumanize, demean, demoralize, demote, desecrate, devalue, diminish, discredit, disgrace, dishonor, downgrade, fuck, humble, humiliate, hump, incriminate, insult, mortify, patronize, prostitute, reduce, savage, screw, seduce, shame, sideline, soil, spoil, stain, suborn, subvert, sully, taint, victimize, violate, wrong* (≠ acclaim, applaud, bless, boost, cherish, decontaminate, dignify, elevate, exalt, extol, glorify, hallow, honor, magnify, pity, praise, profane, protect, regret, revere, upgrade, venerate, worship)

DEHUMANIZE (/): *abase, abuse, animalize, assault, attack, barbarize, bestialize, brutalize, bulldoze, bully, callous, case-harden, contaminate, corrupt, crucify, deaden, debauch, degrade, demean, depersonalize, deprave, desensitize, disgrace, gaslight, harden, humble, humiliate, intimidate, inure, menace, mistreat, mutate, objectify, pervert, poison, pollute, pressure, profane, prostitute, sabotage, savage, subvert, taint, terrorize, threaten, torment, torture, undermine, victimize, warp, whore, wound, wrong* (≠ amend, better, civilize, cleanse, cultivate, dignify, edify, educate, elevate, enlighten, ennoble, exalt, heal, help, honor, humanize, improve, inspire, nurture, pity, polish, protect, purify, refine, respect, restore, uplift)

DEIFY (+): *admire, adore, apotheosize, beatify, bless, canonize, commemorate, consecrate, delight, dignify, eternalize, exalt, extol, follow, glorify, gratify, hallow, honor, immortalize, laud, lionize, love, magnify, memorialize, mind, obey, panegyrize, please, praise, regard, respect, revere, reverence, ritualize, sanctify, satisfy, serve, solemnize, venerate, worship* (≠ abase, abominate, affront, anathematize, attaint, bestialize, blaspheme, challenge, curse, damn, debase, defame, demonize, desecrate, disgrace, dishonor, disobey, disparage, displease, disrespect, execrate, fault, -ignore, insult, libel, malign, offend, outrage, pique, profane, repent, ridicule, -scorn, slander, slur, smear, violate)

DEIFY (+): *acclaim, adore, adulate, appreciate, approve, blandish, canonize, celebrate, cheer, cherish, commend, compliment, congratulate, endorse, esteem, eulogize, fancy, favor, fête, flannel, flatter, gold-star, gratify, hail, hallow, hero-worship, high-five, honor, idealize, idolize, limelight, lionize, prefer, prize, regard, respect, revere, romanticize, salute, sentimentalize, stroke, support, treasure, value, venerate, worship* (≠ abhor, abominate, accuse, admonish, affront, belittle, berate, betray, blackguard, blame, chide, condemn, degrade, demean, denounce, deprecate, -despise, -detest, -disdain, dishonor, -disown, disparage, disrespect, -hate, humble, humiliate, -ignore, -loathe, malign, misprize, offend, outrage, -overlook, pillory, reproach, rue, scathe, scold, -scorn, shame, -shun, -slight, slur, vilify, violate)

DEIFY (+): *accentuate, acclaim, accrue, add, affirm, aggrandize, amplify, applaud, appreciate, assert, augment, boost, canonize, compound, dignify, elevate, enhance, enlarge, ennoble, enshrine, enthrone, escalate, exaggerate, exalt, expand, extend, extol, fetishize, glorify, heighten, heroicize, heroize, highlight, honor, hype, idealize, increase, inflate, intensify, laud, lift, magnify, maximize, multiply, optimize, overestimate, overprice, overrate, overvalue, panegyrize, plug, praise, presell, prioritize, promote, push, raise, recommend, romanticize, salute, sanction, sanitize, sentimentalize, spotlight, sugarcoat, trumpet, upgrade, uplift, value, whitewash* (≠ abase, abhor, abominate, badmouth, belittle, blast, blemish, boo, castigate, chastise, condemn, criticize, critique, decry, degrade, demean, denigrate, depreciate, detract, disparage, -disregard, disrespect, fault, flaw, frame, humble, humiliate, incriminate, insult, libel, lower, malign, minimize, rebuke, reprimand, ridicule, -scorn, -shun, slander, -slight, smear, trash, vilify)

DELAY (←): *adjourn, arrest, bar, battle, block, check, choke, clog, confine, cripple, curb, defer, demotivate, detain, -deter, discourage, drag, encumber, fetter, fight, filibuster, -halt, hamper, hamstring, hinder, hold, impede, inhibit, keep, obstruct, oppose, pause, postpone, -prevent, prolong, protest, restrain, restrict, retard, shelve, short-circuit, slow, stall, stay, stem, stonewall, stop, stymie, suspend, table, -thwart, withhold* (≠ accelerate, advance, brainstorm, catalyze, ease, encourage, expedite, facilitate, fast-forward, fast-track, forward, further, hasten, help, hurry, midwife, precipitate, press, prompt, push, quicken, race, rush, speed, support, unblock, urge, whisk)

DELEGATE (→): *accredit, allot, appoint, assign, authorize, cast, charge, choose, commend, commission, commit, consign, constitute, deliver, demote, deputize, designate, elect, empower, entitle, entrust, give, leave, license, mandate, name, nominate, ordain, relinquish, replace, select, substitute, task, warrant* (≠ abdicate, abrogate, accept, bar, blackball, command, control, demand, -deny, detain, discharge, eject, fire, hog, hold, -ignore, keep, micromanage, monopolize, occupy, oust, own, -refuse, -reject, remove, reserve, retain, withdraw)

DELETE (/): *abbreviate, anonymize, bleep, blot, blue-pencil, bowdlerize, -cancel, censor, clip, crop, cut, deep-six, destroy, doom, edit, efface, elide, eliminate, eradicate, erase, excise, expunge, expurgate, kill, launder, obliterate, -omit, redact, red-pen, red-pencil, remove, repress, root, scratch, shorten, silence, strike, suppress, take* (≠ add, augment, begin, build, conceive, construct, copy, create, embed, inject, insert, introduce, place, print, replace, rescue, restore, save, write)

DELIGHT (+): *amuse, animate, appease, assuage, attract, bewitch, boost, brighten, calm, captivate, charm, cheer, coddle, comfort, console, content, divert, elate, elevate, embolden, enchant, encourage, engage, enliven, enrapture, entertain, enthrall, entrance, excite, exhilarate, fascinate, fire, fortify, galvanize, gladden, grace, gratify, humor, indulge, inspire, invigorate, jolly, lighten, lull, mellow, mollify, mollycoddle, pacify, pamper, placate, please, pleasure, quench, rally, razzle-dazzle, reassure, refresh, reinvigorate, revive, rouse, sate, satiate, satisfy, seduce, slake, soothe, spellbind, spoil, stimulate, stir, strengthen, suit, sustain, thrill, tickle, titillate, treat, uplift, vitalize, warm, woo, wow* (≠ abuse, affront, aggravate, agitate, anger, annoy, appall, applaud, bore, bother, brutalize, bug, chafe, cross, degrade, depress, dismay, displease, distress, disturb, enrage, exasperate, gall, gaslight, grate, harass, harm, harry, heckle, hurt, incense, inflame, infuriate, injure, insult, irk, irritate, madden, menace, nag, needle, nettle, niggle, nitpick, offend, outrage, peeve, perturb, pester, pique, plague, provoke, rankle, rile, roil, rouse, ruffle, sadden, savage, terrorize, threaten, unnerve, upset, vex, victimize, wound, wrong)

DELIVER (→): *bear, bootleg, bring, carry, cart, chauffeur, convey, courier, dispatch, distribute, drop, give, hand, hand-carry, pass, remit, schlep,* *send, smuggle, supply, take, transport, truck, waft* (≠ -abandon, acquire, collect, discard, -ditch, dump, guard, hoard, hog, hold, keep, lose, remove, retain, squirrel, stash, stint, trash, tuck, withhold)

DELIVER (→): *-abandon, abnegate, administer, advance, allocate, apportion, assign, beam, bequeath, cede, commend, commit, confer, confide, consign, deal, deed, delegate, -desert, discard, dispense, disperse, distribute, divide, dollop, entrust, force-feed, forfeit, -forsake, furnish, give, grant, hand, leave, lend, loan, mete, overfeed, parcel, pass, portion, prorate, recommend, release, relinquish, render, -renounce, resign, shed, submit, supply, surrender, transfer, transmit, trust, vest, waive, will, yield* (≠ accept, budget, capture, conserve, detain, hold, inherit, keep, limit, occupy, own, possess, preserve, receive, reserve, restrain, restrict, retain, take, withhold)

DELIVER (→): *administer, aim, beam, contribute, deal, direct, dispatch, drizzle, fling, fulfill, give, hurl, implement, inflict, launch, pitch, pour, provide, provision, reprovision, send, strike, supply, target, throw, transmit, trickle, wing* (≠ -abort, block, -cancel, -disregard, foil, -halt, hamper, impede, monkey-wrench, -neglect, oppose, -prevent, -prohibit, stop, stymie, -thwart, weaken)

DELIVER (+): *acquit, discharge, disentangle, emancipate, extricate, free, liberate, loose, ransom, recover, redeem, release, rescue, salvage, save, unchain, unshackle* (≠ compromise, confine, detain, endanger, hazard, imperil, imprison, jeopardize, restrain, restrict, risk, straightjacket)

DEMAND (←): *abuse, arrogate, ask, assail, badger, batter, beg, beseech, besiege, bid, bombard, challenge, charge, cite, claim, coerce, command, compel, constrain, covet, crave, dictate, direct, dun, enforce, enjoin, entreat, exact, expect, fetishize, flay, foist, force, hammer, harass, harry, hit, hound, implore, importune, impose, insist, interrogate, invade, invite, involve, knock, lash, lunge, muscle, nag, oblige, order, outlast, pester, petition, plead, postulate, pound, press, pressure, question, reclaim, recoup, recover, request, require, requisition, rescue, retrieve, sandbag, savage, scarify, scathe, scavenge, scorch, seek, solicit, stipulate, sue, summon, tackle, take, target, tax, urge, want, warrant* (≠ bequeath, bestow, blandish, cajole, coax, contribute, dispense, eliminate, give, grant, locate, mind, obey, -obviate, offer, palaver, produce, relinquish, rid, schmooze, soft-sell, soft-soap, spare, supply, surrender, sweet-talk, volunteer, wheedle, yield)

DEMAND (←): *accommodate, ask, bear, beg, challenge, claim, command, constrain, enjoin, entail, exact, favor, indulge, insist, involve, oblige, press, railroad, require, stipulate, take, want, warrant* (≠ -decline, -deny, deprive, eliminate, hoard, hog, hold, keep, lend, loan, -obviate, own, possess, starve, stint, withhold)

DEMAND (←): *anticipate, ask, assess, await, bill, bring, charge, command, discount, expense, fetch, gazump, invoice, mark, overcharge, price,* *undercharge, value* (≠ bankroll, buy, comp, compensate, donate, fund, import, indemnify, inherit, meet, offer, pay, scant, skimp, spare, starve, stint, tender, underwrite, volunteer, yield)

DEMEAN (/): *abase, abash, abuse, affront, badmouth, bedraggle, befoul, begrime, belittle, besmear, besmirch, bestialize, blemish, boo, brutalize, castigate, castrate, censure, chasten, cheapen, condemn, confound, confuse, contaminate, corrupt, criticize, damage, damn, debase, debauch, decry, deface, defame, defile, degrade, dehumanize, demonize, demoralize, demote, denounce, deprave, depreciate, desecrate, destroy, deteriorate, detract, devalue, dilute, diminish, dirty, discomfit, disconcert, -discount, discredit, disgrace, dishonor, disparage, downgrade, emasculate, embarrass, execrate, faze, flaw, fluster, foul, harm, humble, humiliate, hurt, impair, incriminate, insult, lessen, libel, lower, malign, mar, minimize, mortify, nonplus, pervert, pillory, poison, pollute, profane, prostitute, rattle, ravish, reduce, ridicule, ruin, savage, seduce, shame, sideline, sink, slander, smirch, soil, spoil, stain, subvert, sully, taint, tarnish, violate, vitiate, vulgarize, warp, weaken, wreck, wrong* (≠ admire, advance, affirm, aggrandize, amplify, applaud, approve, better, boost, canonize, celebrate, cleanse, commend, compliment, congratulate, decorate, deify, dignify, elevate, enhance, ennoble, enrich, enshrine, enthrone, exalt, glorify, gold-star, heroicize, heroize, high-five, honor, idealize, improve, magnify, moralize, optimize, perfect, praise, prioritize, promote, purify, raise, rarefy, reclaim, rectify, redeem, refine, reform, rehabilitate, respect, restore, revere, romanticize, salute, sanctify, sentimentalize, tout, upgrade, uplift, value, worship)

DEMOLISH (/): *abolish, annihilate, assault, atomize, attack, batter, beat, blast, bomb, break, bulldoze, burst, bury, cannibalize, checkmate, clobber, collapse, conquer, cow, cream, crush, decimate, deep-six, defeat, desolate, destroy, detonate, devastate, devour, discomfit, disintegrate, dismantle, dispatch, doom, drub, dust, dynamite, eclipse, end, engulf, enslave, eradicate, explode, exterminate, extirpate, fell, finish, flatten, floor, fracture, fragment, gulp, knock, level, lick, master, obliterate, overthrow, overturn, overwhelm, plunder, prostrate, pulverize, quash, quell, ravage, raven, raze, reduce, rout, ruin, shatter, shellac, sink, skin, skunk, slaughter, smash, smoke, smother, steamroller, subdue, subjugate, suppress, surpass, tame, thrash, topple, torpedo, trample, trounce, trump, vanquish, vaporize, wallop, wax, whip, whomp, whup, wrack, wreck* (≠ assemble, augment, begin, boost, brainstorm, bring, build, catalyze, commence, conceive, construct, craft, create, design, develop, elevate, engender, enhance, erect, establish, fabricate, fashion, foster, found, generate, gentrify, improve, machine, maintain, manufacture, mend, organize, perpetuate, preserve, produce, prop, protect, raise, rear, rebuild, rectify, renovate, repair, rescue, restore, salvage, save, sculpt, secure, shape, strengthen, support, survive, sustain, upgrade, weather, withstand)

DEMORALIZE (/): *abash, afflict, appall, blackmail, boobytrap, bother, break, browbeat, brutalize, bug, bully, chagrin, cheapen, chill, cow, craze,* *cripple, crush, dampen, daunt, deaden, debilitate, decry, defame, deflate, demotivate, deplete, depress, deprive, derange, -deter, devitalize, diminish, disable, disappoint, discompose, disconcert, discourage, dishearten, dismay, disorganize, disparage, dispirit, disquiet, distress, disturb, douse, drain, emasculate, embarrass, enervate, enfeeble, exhaust, fatigue, faze, frighten, frustrate, horrify, impair, incapacitate, indispose, intimidate, irk, jade, jumble, madden, muddle, neuter, nonplus, oppress, overset, paralyze, perturb, prostrate, psych, rattle, sabotage, sadden, sap, scare, shake, shelve, snarl, soften, stymie, subvert, terrify, terrorize, tire, trash-talk, trouble, unbalance, undercut, undermine, undo, unhinge, unman, unnerve, unsettle, unstring, upset, vex, waste, weaken, weigh, worry* (≠ animate, bolster, boost, brace, buoy, buttress, comfort, dignify, elate, encourage, energize, exalt, excite, fortify, galvanize, inspire, intoxicate, invigorate, nerve, quicken, rally, reassure, reinforce, restore, steady, steel, stimulate, stir, strengthen, uplift)

DEMORALIZE (/): *abase, befoul, begrime, blemish, cheapen, contaminate, corrupt, damage, debase, debauch, deface, defile, degrade, demean, deprave, depreciate, destroy, deteriorate, dilute, dirty, disgrace, dishonor, doom, downgrade, flaw, harm, humble, humiliate, hurt, impair, lessen, mar, pervert, poison, pollute, profane, prostitute, ruin, shame, spoil, stain, suborn, subvert, taint, tarnish, thin, vitiate, warp, water, weaken, wreck* (≠ ameliorate, amend, better, clarify, clean, cleanse, dignify, elevate, enhance, ennoble, enrich, exalt, honor, improve, moralize, perfect, purify, refine, respect, restore, uplift)

DEMOTE (/): *abase, belittle, bench, boot, break, bump, bust, can, cashier, debase, declass, degrade, demean, denigrate, depose, deprecate, depreciate, detract, devalue, discipline, -discount, discredit, disfavor, disgrace, dismiss, disparage, downgrade, fire, flunk, humble, humiliate, lower, punish, reduce, relegate, sack, shame, sideline* (≠ advance, aggrandize, boost, catapult, certify, commend, elevate, encourage, exalt, favor, further, hire, honor, impress, improve, nominate, optimize, overhaul, prefer, prioritize, promote, propel, raise, revolutionize, upgrade)

DENIGRATE (/): *abuse, admonish, assail, badmouth, belittle, besmear, besmirch, betray, blacken, blackguard, blame, blister, boo, burlesque, calumniate, caricature, castigate, censure, chasten, chastise, cheapen, chide, condemn, criticize, decry, defame, defile, demean, demonize, denounce, deprecate, deride, detract, diminish, disapprove, -discount, discredit, disfavor, disgrace, dishonor, dismiss, disparage, disrespect, diss, fault, frame, fulminate, humiliate, impugn, incriminate, insult, jeer, kid, knock, libel, malign, mimic, minimize, mock, neg, pillory, rag, razz, -renounce, reproach, revile, ride, ridicule, rip, roast, scandalize, scape-goat, scold, -scorn, shame, slander, slur, smear, stigmatize, sully, tarnish, taunt, traduce, upbraid, vilify, wrong* (≠ acclaim, affirm, applaud, approve, boost, brave, brook, cherish, commend, compliment, congratulate, countenance, dignify, endorse, eulogize, exaggerate, exalt, extol, face, favor, fetishize, glamorize, glorify, gold-star, heroicize, heroize, high-five, idealize, lionize, magnify, overvalue, poeticize, praise, prioritize, recommend, romanticize, sensationalize, sentimentalize, stomach, tolerate)

DENOUNCE (/): *accuse, allege, anathematize, arraign, attack, badmouth, berate, besmear, besmirch, betray, blacken, blacklist, blame, boo, -boycott, brand, calumniate, castigate, censure, charge, chastise, cite, condemn, contemn, contradict, criticize, damn, declaim, decry, defame, demean, demonize, denunciate, -deny, deplore, detract, disavow, discredit, disfavor, dishonor, disparage, excoriate, execrate, expose, fault, finger, frame, impeach, implicate, impugn, incriminate, inculpate, indict, knock, libel, malign, muckrake, -ostracize, picket, pillory, proscribe, prosecute, protest, rebuke, refute, reprimand, reproach, reprove, -repudiate, resent, revile, rubbish, scandalize, scapegoat, scold, shame, skin, slander, slate, smear, stigmatize, sully, tarnish, threaten, traduce, trash, upbraid, vilify, vituperate* (≠ absolve, accept, advocate, aid, alibi, applaud, assist, brave, brook, clear, commend, congratulate, countenance, elevate, embolden, encourage, exculpate, exonerate, face, glorify, honor, incite, instigate, legalize, pardon, praise, promote, prove, recognize, salute, spare, stomach, support, tolerate, tout, uphold, venerate)

-DENY (/): *abjure, abnegate, begrudge, challenge, confute, contradict, counteract, debate, deplete, deprive, disallow, disavow, disbelieve, disclaim, discredit, -disown, disprove, dispute, distrust, doubt, forswear, gainsay, impoverish, invalidate, malnourish, -negate, negative, -nullify, oppose, rebut, recant, refute, -reject, repossess, -repudiate, revoke, scant, scruple, seize, skimp, starve, stint, suspect, traverse, withhold* (≠ accede, accept, acknowledge, admit, adopt, affirm, allow, announce, approve, assert, authenticate, avow, bestow, blab, blaze, blurt, circulate, claim, concede, confess, confirm, convince, corroborate, crosscheck, declare, disseminate, embrace, espouse, grant, maintain, offer, own, pour, profess, submit, substantiate, validate, verify, volunteer) **(¿) ABSTRACTION ALERT. Concrete goals essential!**

-DENY (/): *amputate, -balk, ban, banish, bar, block, -boycott, check, constrain, control, curb, -decline, deport, disallow, disapprove, discard, dismiss, -disown, disqualify, enjoin, -eschew, evict, -exclude, -excommunicate, exile, expatriate, expel, extradite, -forbid, forgo, -forsake, hinder, hold, -ignore, impede, inhibit, keep, -nix, obstruct, -omit, oppress, -ostracize, oust, outlaw, -preclude, -prevent, -prohibit, proscribe, -rebuff, -refuse, -reject, relegate, remove, repel, repress, restrain, restrict, sacrifice, -spurn, straightjacket, suppress, -veto, withhold* (≠ accede, accord, afford, allow, authorize, commission, concede, contribute, disburse, dispense, encourage, furnish, give, grant, greenlight, legalize, let, license, obtain, okay, permit, provide, ratify, recover, request, restore, sanction, seek, source, supply, validate, vindicate, vouchsafe, warrant)

DEPICT (→): *caricature, delineate, describe, diagram, document, draw, illustrate, image, outline, paint, picture, portray, render, represent, show, silhouette, sketch, trace* (≠ blot, cloak, conceal, delete, eclipse, efface, erase, expunge, mask, obliterate, remove, smear, smudge, veil, wipe)

DEPICT (←): *characterize, chronicle, conjure, define, delineate, demonstrate, describe, detail, display, draft, draw, exhibit, hint, illustrate, image, label, limn, narrate, outline, paint, picture, portray, précis, profile, qualify, recite, record, recount, rehearse, relate, render, report, represent, reproduce, show, showcase, silhouette, sketch, spiel, suggest, summarize, tell, trace, vignette* (≠ color, distort, falsify, garble, miscommunicate, misdescribe, mislabel, misrepresent, misstate, pervert, twist, warp) **(¿) ABSTRACTION ALERT. Concrete goals essential!**

DEPLETE (←): *abate, abbreviate, abridge, attenuate, bankrupt, beggar, bleed, bob, cannibalize, clip, compact, compress, concentrate, condense, consume, contract, crop, cull, curtail, debilitate, decrease, deduct, deflate, depredate, deprive, devitalize, devour, diminish, disable, dispel, disperse, dissipate, downgrade, drain, draw, dry, eat, empty, enervate, enfeeble, erode, exhaust, expend, fatigue, finish, impair, impoverish, incapacitate, jade, leach, leech, lessen, lighten, lower, milk, minimize, nip, overextend, overtax, overwork, pare, prune, reduce, sap, shave, shear, shorten, shrink, slather, spend, squander, strain, straiten, taper, tax, tire, trim, truncate, undermine, unhinge, -void, waste, weaken, weary, weed, whittle, wither* (≠ accent, accentuate, accrue, amplify, augment, bolster, boost, budget, bulge, buttress, complement, conserve, create, develop, dilate, distend, elongate, emphasize, energize, enhance, enlarge, escalate, expand, extend, fill, fortify, heighten, hoard, increase, inflate, intensify, invigorate, lard, lengthen, maximize, pickle, preserve, prolong, raise, rebuild, recoup, refresh, reinforce, reinvigorate, rejuvenate, renew, repair, replace, replenish, restimulate, restore, revive, save, strengthen, supplement)

DEPLOY (→): *activate, allocate, apply, arrange, brandish, cannibalize, circulate, diffuse, direct, display, disseminate, distribute, embattle, employ, exercise, expand, exploit, extend, garrison, handle, harness, manipulate, operate, position, recycle, redistribute, reuse, run, scatter, station, unfold, use, utilize, wield, work* (≠ conceal, conclude, -decline, defer, delay, -deny, disallow, displace, disturb, end, finish, hide, -ignore, keep, misapply, misuse, -neglect, -nix, postpone, -refuse, -reject, withhold)

DEPORT (/): *banish, denaturalize, dismiss, displace, eject, eliminate, evict, -exclude, exile, expatriate, expel, extradite, -ostracize, oust, -reject, relegate, repatriate, transport* (≠ accept, admit, adopt, entertain, harbor, house, invite, naturalize, permit, receive, shelter, welcome)

DEPOSE (/): *banish, boot, bounce, can, cashier, chase, chuck, defrock, degrade, demote, deprive, dethrone, discharge, dismiss, displace, downgrade, eject, expel, extrude, fire, impeach, oust, overpower, overthrow, remove, retire, rout, ruin, sack, sideline, subvert, supplant, topple, uncrown, unfrock, unmake, unseat, unthrone, upset, usurp, wrack, wreck* (≠ anoint, appoint, baptize, crown, designate, elect, elevate, enhance, enthrone, honor, inaugurate, induct, initiate, install, instate, invest, reward, support, throne, uplift)

DEPOSIT (→): *affix, anchor, array, assemble, berth, bung, carry, clap, collect, deliver, depose, dispose, -ditch, drop, dump, ensconce, establish, fix, install, juxtapose, land, lay, locate, lock, lodge, move, niche, orient, park, place, plank, plant, plonk, plop, plump, plunk, position, precipitate, queue, rank, rearrange, reorder, rest, set, settle, shift, situate, slap, stash, stick, stow, tuck, wedge* (≠ banish, dislodge, disperse, displace, dissipate, divide, draw, expend, move, pay, relegate, relocate, remove, replace, scavenge, supersede, supplant, take, use, waste)

DEPOSIT (←): *accumulate, amass, archive, bank, cache, capitalize, coffer, commit, consign, entrust, file, fund, garner, hoard, invest, keep, lodge, reserve, save, squirrel, stash, stockpile, store, stow, transfer, treasure, tuck* (≠ cash, charge, claim, diffuse, disburse, disperse, expend, give, lose, pay, remove, scatter, spend, squander, stiff, take, tender, waste, withdraw, yield)

DEPRAVE (/): *abase, adulterate, animalize, bastardize, bed, befoul, begrime, bestialize, blemish, brutalize, canker, cheapen, contaminate, corrupt, damage, debase, debauch, deface, defile, deform, degrade, dehumanize, demean, demoralize, depreciate, desecrate, destroy, deteriorate, dilute, dirty, disgrace, dishonor, distort, downgrade, flaw, harm, humble, humiliate, hurt, impair, infect, lessen, mar, pervert, poison, pollute, profane, prostitute, ravish, ruin, seduce, shame, soil, spoil, stain, subvert, sully, taint, tarnish, twist, victimize, vitiate, warp, wreck, wrong* (≠ benefit, better, clean, cleanse, correct, dignify, elevate, enhance, ennoble, enrich, exalt, honor, improve, moralize, perfect, protect, purify, rarefy, rectify, refine, reform, respect, restore, uplift)

DEPRESS (/): *abase, afflict, agitate, ail, appall, beat, bother, bug, bum, burden, chill, concern, cow, darken, dash, daunt, debase, degrade, demoralize, demotivate, desolate, discomfort, discompose, discourage, dishearten, dismay, dispirit, disquiet, distress, disturb, freak, lower, mock, mortify, oppress, overburden, perturb, sadden, -scorn, sorrow, torment, torture, trouble, undo, unhinge, unnerve, unsettle, upset, weigh, worry* (≠ animate, assure, boost, brighten, buoy, cheer, comfort, console, delight, elate, elevate, encourage, enliven, excite, exhilarate, gladden, grace, gratify, heal, hearten, help, inspire, invigorate, lift, lighten, please, reassure, rejoice, soothe, stimulate, thrill, uplift, wow)

DEPRESS (/): *consume, cripple, damage, dampen, debilitate, deplete, devitalize, disable, drag, drain, dull, enervate, enfeeble, exhaust, faze, grind, hamstring, harm, hurt, impair, impoverish, incapacitate, injure, lessen, level, lower, paralyze, press, prostrate, reduce, sap, slow, soften, tire, undermine, unman, waste, weaken, weary, weight* (≠ boost, energize, excite, fortify, harden, invigorate, recruit, rejuvenate, season, stimulate, strengthen, tone, toughen, vitalize)

DEPRESS (/): *abridge, attenuate, break, cheapen, compress, contract, cut, debase, de-escalate, deflate, demonetize, depreciate, devaluate, devalue, diminish, downgrade, downsize, impair, lessen, lowball, lower, moderate, reduce, shrink, sink, slash, underestimate, underprice,* *underrate, undervalue* (≠ appreciate, bloat, boost, bump, enhance, fetishize, heighten, improve, increase, inflate, jack, monetize, overestimate, overprice, overrate, overvalue, raise, upgrade)

DEPRIVE (←): *abate, bankrupt, bare, beggar, bereave, bogart, burgle, cheat, confiscate, cripple, damage, debilitate, defraud, denude, -deny, deplete, despoil, disinherit, dismantle, dispossess, disrobe, divest, dock, enfeeble, famish, fatigue, hold, impair, impoverish, incapacitate, keep, leach, lessen, lose, malnourish, -omit, oust, recall, recant, reduce, -refuse, reserve, retain, retract, revoke, rob, sap, scant, seize, shortchange, skim, skimp, starve, steal, stiff, stint, straiten, strip, suppress, swindle, underfeed, weaken, withdraw, withhold, wrest* (≠ accord, accoutre, administer, allocate, allot, allow, apportion, arm, assign, bestow, contribute, dispense, distribute, dole, dollop, dower, endow, enrich, equip, feed, force-feed, fuel, furnish, grant, hand, indulge, infuse, invest, mete, obtain, offer, overfeed, present, prioritize, provide, provision, source, stock, suffuse, supply, task, victual, volunteer)

DERAIL (/): *abash, aggravate, agitate, ail, alarm, alter, anger, annoy, -avert, bedevil, bother, bug, cant, capsize, chafe, change, chivy, concern, confound, confuse, convulse, daunt, deflect, demoralize, demotivate, destabilize, discomfit, discomfort, discompose, disconcert, discourage, dishearten, dismay, dispirit, displace, disquiet, disrupt, distemper, distract, distress, disturb, divert, dizzy, embarrass, exasperate, exercise, faze, fluster, frazzle, freak, fret, funnel, fuss, gall, get, hamper, harass, harry, haunt, heckle, impede, indispose, irk, irritate, jar, misguide, mislead, mortify, needle, nettle, niggle, nitpick, nonplus, obstruct, overset, overthrow, overturn, peeve, perturb, pester, pique, plague, -prevent, protest, rankle, rattle, redirect, refocus, reorient, rile, roil, ruin, shake, short-circuit, sideline, sidetrack, spill, startle, swerve, switch, tip, topple, undo, unhinge, unhorse, unnerve, unsettle, unsteady, upset, vex, worry, wreck* (≠ advance, aid, aim, allay, alleviate, appease, assist, assuage, balance, boost, brace, calibrate, calm, center, chair, compose, concentrate, conciliate, continue, dedicate, direct, enable, encourage, equalize, expedite, facilitate, focus, forward, further, guide, help, hush, keep, lull, maintain, mellow, mollify, pacify, placate, prioritize, propitiate, quiet, settle, smooth, soothe, stabilize, steady, steer, sugarcoat, support, sustain, target, tranquilize, tune, tweak)

DERANGE (/): *confound, confuse, craze, dement, destabilize, disarrange, disarray, discommode, discompose, disconcert, dislocate, disorder, disorganize, displace, distract, disturb, dizzy, frenzy, jumble, madden, mess, misplace, muss, perplex, puzzle, ruffle, rummage, shuffle, trouble, unbalance, unhinge, unnerve, unsettle, untidy, upset* (≠ align, arrange, balance, calm, center, clarify, comfort, compose, fix, groom, hush, lull, mellow, mollify, order, organize, pace, pacify, place, please, queue, quiet, regiment, regulate, relax, right, settle, sober, soothe, sort, spruce, stabilize, straighten, systematize, tidy, tranquilize, unscramble)

DERIDE (/): *ape, badmouth, bait, belittle, boo, bug, burlesque, caricature, catcall, condemn, decry, demean, detract, -disdain, disparage, disrespect, diss, flout, gibe, harass, harry, hassle, heckle, imitate, insult, jeer, kid, knock, lampoon, mimic, mock, needle, neg, pan, parody, parrot, pester, pillory, pooh-pooh, quiz, rag, razz, rib, ride, ridicule, roast, satirize, -scorn, skewer, slam, target, taunt, tease, torment, travesty, tweak* (≠ applaud, approve, blandish, boost, commend, congratulate, elevate, endorse, exalt, extol, flannel, flatter, glorify, gold-star, gratify, ingratiate, praise, prioritize, promote, revere, salute, sanction, support)

DESECRATE (/): *abase, abuse, adulterate, bastardize, besmirch, bestialize, canker, contaminate, corrupt, curse, damn, debase, debauch, defile, deform, degrade, demean, demonize, demoralize, deprave, desacralize, desanctify, despoil, devalue, diminish, dirty, disgrace, dishonor, distort, foul, humiliate, ill-treat, insult, maledict, maltreat, misuse, mortify, pervert, pollute, seduce, shame, soil, spoil, stain, sully, taint, twist, violate, vitiate, warp, wrong* (≠ benefit, bless, boost, build, cherish, clean, cleanse, consecrate, construct, decontaminate, dedicate, dignify, elevate, esteem, exalt, expiate, extol, glorify, hallow, help, honor, improve, magnify, praise, prize, profane, protect, purge, purify, rebuild, redeem, repair, respect, revere, sanctify, save, value, venerate, worship)

-DESERT (/): *-abandon, abdicate, beach, betray, -boycott, chuck, discard, -discontinue, disfavor, -disown, -ditch, drop, -duck, dump, -escape, -eschew, evacuate, fail, -flee, fly, forfeit, -forsake, jettison, jilt, leave, maroon, offload, -quit, -refuse, -reject, relinquish, -renounce, -repudiate, resign, sacrifice, -shun, -snub, split, strand, surrender, vacate, waive, withdraw* (≠ adopt, aid, assist, chauffeur, cherish, claim, colonize, court, cultivate, defend, embalm, face, favor, forgive, foster, guard, harbor, haunt, help, hold, invade, keep, maintain, occupy, pardon, patrol, possess, preserve, protect, provide, pursue, reclaim, redeem, rescue, retain, save, seek, serve, support, tend, undertake, uphold, vindicate, woo)

DESIGN (→): *cast, chart, concoct, construct, contrive, create, delineate, describe, devise, diagram, draft, draw, effect, execute, fashion, form, frame, fulfill, graph, invent, map, outline, perform, plan, plot, produce, project, script, sculpt, sketch, trace* (≠ -abort, baffle, blur, cloud, confuse, delete, disorder, disorganize, erase, muddle, oppose, perplex, puzzle, rumple, upset)

DESIGN (+): *accomplish, achieve, arrange, blueprint, budget, calculate, chart, choreograph, coin, compose, conceive, construct, contrive, create, develop, devise, fabricate, fashion, form, frame, hatch, invent, make, model, orchestrate, originate, produce, sculpture, style* (≠ abolish, break, crush, demolish, -deny, destroy, doom, -ignore, impede, quash, -refuse, ruin, snuff, suppress, wreck)

DESIGN (+): *aim, arrange, chart, contemplate, contrive, destine, devise, figure, gear, graph, intend, make, map, mind, organize, plan, plot, premeditate, prepare, project, propose, ready, scheme, script, shape,* *spitball, strategize, tailor* (≠ -abandon, dismiss, -disregard, forget, -ignore, mismanage, miss, -neglect, -overlook, pooh-pooh, -reject, -shirk, skip, -slight) **(¿) ABSTRACTION ALERT. Concrete goals essential!**

DESIGNATE (→): *baptize, call, christen, class, classify, describe, dub, entitle, label, name, nickname, nominate, style, term, title* (≠ anonymize, cloak, cloud, conceal, confuse, costume, disguise, forget, hide, mask, mislabel, miss, muddle, -overlook, -scorn, -shun, skip, strike)

DESIGNATE (→): *allocate, allot, appoint, apportion, appropriate, assign, authorize, budget, characterize, charge, choose, commission, connote, constitute, define, delegate, denote, deputize, describe, dictate, earmark, elect, evidence, favor, finger, individualize, make, mark, mete, name, nominate, package, peg, pick, pinpoint, prefer, reserve, select, set, show, slot, specify, stipulate, tab, tag, tap, task* (≠ appropriate, begrudge, commandeer, confiscate, deprive, disfavor, envy, impound, -neglect, -refuse, reserve, scant, seize, sequester, skimp, stint, withhold)

DESIRE (←): *admire, adore, appreciate, cherish, choose, covet, crave, demand, dig, enjoy, envy, fancy, favor, fetishize, love, prefer, prize, relish, target, treasure, value, want* (≠ abhor, abominate, -decline, -despise, -detest, disfavor, -hate, -loathe, -refuse, -reject, -spurn) **(¿) ABSTRACTION ALERT. Concrete goals essential!**

-DESPISE (/): *abhor, abominate, condemn, contemn, deplore, deprecate, deride, -detest, discredit, -disdain, disfavor, -disregard, disrespect, -eschew, execrate, flout, -hate, -loathe, mock, -neglect, -reject, -renounce, -repudiate, resent, revile, -scorn, -shun, -slight, -snub, -spurn, undervalue* (≠ admire, adore, appreciate, approve, cherish, covet, crave, desire, enjoy, esteem, fancy, favor, fetishize, hallow, idolize, love, praise, prefer, prize, relish, respect, revere, treasure, venerate, worship) **(¿) ABSTRACTION ALERT. Concrete goals essential!**

DESTABILIZE (/): *addle, agitate, antagonize, baffle, befuddle, blacklist, bother, -boycott, cant, capsize, challenge, chase, churn, confuse, convulse, corrupt, counter, counteract, debase, debauch, demoralize, deprave, depress, derail, derange, discompose, dislocate, dislodge, disrupt, disturb, dizzy, extinguish, fluster, foment, gaslight, invalidate, knock, menace, mix, mystify, overset, overthrow, overturn, perplex, pervert, raze, reverse, ruffle, ruin, sabotage, scotch, scupper, shake, sink, spill, subvert, supersede, supplant, suppress, terrorize, threaten, tip, topple, trouble, tumble, unbalance, undercut, undermine, unhinge, unhorse, unseat, unsettle, unsteady, upset, victimize, vitiate, weaken, wrack, wreck* (≠ add, anchor, balance, bolster, boost, brace, build, buttress, calibrate, center, compose, enlarge, equalize, erect, establish, extend, fix, govern, increase, plant, prop, regulate, reinforce, root, settle, stabilize, steady, strengthen, support, toughen, tune, tweak)

DESTROY (/): *abolish, annihilate, assault, atomize, attack, batter, beat, best, blast, blow, bludgeon, break, bulldoze, burst, -cancel, checkmate, clobber, collapse, conquer, cow, cripple, crush, damage, decimate, deep-*

six, deface, defeat, demolish, despoil, deteriorate, detonate, devastate, dilapidate, disassemble, discomfit, disfigure, disintegrate, dismantle, dissolve, drub, dynamite, efface, eliminate, enslave, eradicate, erode, excise, execute, explode, expunge, exterminate, extirpate, finish, flatten, floor, fracture, fragment, gut, harm, impair, incinerate, injure, kill, knock, level, lick, liquidate, loot, mangle, mar, master, mortar, murder, mutilate, nuke, -nullify, obliterate, orphan, outlast, outmaneuver, overcome, overthrow, overturn, pillage, plunder, pulverize, quash, quell, ravage, raze, reduce, remove, rout, ruin, sack, scotch, scour, scupper, shatter, skunk, slaughter, smash, snuff, spoil, subdue, subjugate, suppress, surmount, tame, thrash, torpedo, trample, trash, trounce, vandalize, vanquish, vitiate, wallop, whip, wrack, wreck, zap (≠ assemble, bronze, build, concoct, conserve, construct, craft, create, defend, embalm, establish, fabricate, fashion, fix, forge, form, found, guard, heal, make, mend, nurture, organize, patch, patrol, pickle, preserve, produce, promote, protect, raise, rear, rebuild, regret, reinvigorate, repair, rescue, restore, restructure, resurrect, revamp, revive, save, sculpt, secure, stimulate, support, survive, sustain, weather, withstand)

DETACH (/): *break, chunk, cleave, cut, decouple, disassemble, disconnect, disengage, disentangle, dismantle, dismount, divide, excise, fragment, free, halve, insulate, isolate, loosen, -omit, orphan, part, partition, remove, rend, rip, rupture, segregate, separate, sever, split, sunder, tear, uncouple, unfasten, unhitch, withdraw, wrench* (≠ add, affix, associate, attach, combine, complete, conjoin, connect, desegregate, fasten, fix, fuse, glue, hold, increase, integrate, join, link, meld, melt, merge, strengthen, weld)

DETACH (/): *alienate, antagonize, disaffect, disassociate, disengage, distance, disunite, divorce, estrange, -exclude, free, isolate, loose, loosen, maroon, oppose, orphan, -ostracize, oust, quarantine, seclude, segregate, separate, sequester, sever, -snub, split, -spurn, strand* (≠ assimilate, blend, bridge, churn, combine, connect, couple, incorporate, integrate, involve, join, link, marry, merge, mix, network, reconcile, reintegrate, restore, reunite, span, stay, straddle, unify, unite, wed)

DETAIN (←): *accost, ambush, attack, baffle, bar, block, bottleneck, brake, bung, burden, buttonhole, catch, check, choke, clog, complicate, congest, constipate, constrain, counter, cramp, crimp, cripple, curb, curtail, dam, deactivate, deaden, debilitate, decelerate, delay, -deter, disable, distract, divert, drag, encumber, entangle, entrap, fetter, foul, freeze, -frustrate, hamper, hamstring, handicap, hinder, hold, immobilize, impair, impede, implicate, incapacitate, inconvenience, inhibit, intercept, interrupt, jam, keep, lame, limit, mire, numb, obstruct, oppose, oppress, overload, paralyze, pause, pin, plug, resist, restrain, restrict, retard, saddle, seize, shelve, sidetrack, slow, snag, snarl, stay, stem, stop, straightjacket, surprise, tangle, -thwart, waylay* (≠ accelerate, activate, advance, aid, allow, assist, boost, budge, catalyze, compel, discharge, dismiss, ease, encourage, expedite, extricate, facilitate, fast-forward, fast-track, force, forward, free, frogmarch, fuel, give, grease, hasten, help, hurry, legalize, lubricate, march, midwife, oblige, offer, open, permit, prioritize, prod, propel, punt, push, quicken, release, rush, send, simplify, slacken, smooth, speed, spur, stimulate, stir, stoke, support, unclog, uncomplicate, unleash, untangle, urge)

DETAIN (/): *apprehend, arrest, bind, block, book, bridle, bust, capture, catch, collar, commit, confine, constrict, control, convict, corner, delay, dungeon, enmesh, ensnare, entangle, fetter, freeze, grab, -halt, handcuff, hinder, hogtie, hold, ice, immobilize, immure, impede, imprison, incarcerate, inhibit, institutionalize, intern, interrupt, jail, keep, leash, nab, nail, nick, obstruct, paralyze, pause, pinch, restrain, seize, shackle, slow, snaffle, snag, snare, stall, stop, stun, suppress, tether, trap, withhold* (≠ acquit, aid, alibi, bail, discharge, emancipate, empower, excuse, exonerate, free, liberate, permit, release, rescue, save, spring, unfetter, unlock, unshackle, untie, vindicate)

DETECT (←): *ascertain, catch, clock, consult, cross-examine, decipher, decode, decrypt, deduce, descry, determine, discern, disclose, discover, disinter, distinguish, dredge, elicit, espy, excavate, expose, fathom, ferret, find, get, grill, hit, hunt, identify, inspect, interrogate, interview, learn, locate, meet, note, notice, observe, perceive, police, profile, question, realize, recognize, reveal, root, rout, rummage, scent, scout, search, seek, sense, sight, sleuth, solve, spoor, spot, spy, strip, suss, track, uncover, unearth, unlock, unmask, unravel, untangle, unveil* (≠ -avoid, baffle, bewilder, blind, bullshit, bury, -bypass, conceal, confound, confuse, couch, deceive, defraud, disbelieve, disguise, -disregard, ensconce, fake, forget, fudge, gaslight, guess, hide, hoard, -ignore, imply, lose, mask, misgauge, mislay, mislead, misplace, misread, miss, mistake, misunderstand, mystify, niche, obscure, -overlook, pass, perplex, predetermine, puzzle, screen, shield, -sidestep, spackle, stash, stow, trick, trust, tuck, wonder) **(¿) ABSTRACTION ALERT. Concrete goals essential!**

-DETER (→): *admonish, anticipate, -avert, baffle, -balk, ban, bar, blackmail, block, bottleneck, brake, burden, catch, caution, check, checkmate, chill, clog, complicate, constipate, constrain, cool, counter, countercheck, cramp, cripple, curb, dam, damp, dampen, daunt, deflect, delay, demotivate, depress, derail, detain, discourage, dishearten, disincline, dissuade, divert, encumber, entrap, fetter, foil, forestall, frighten, -frustrate, hamper, hamstring, handicap, hinder, hogtie, impair, impede, inhibit, interrupt, intimidate, jam, -kibosh, lumber, mire, monkey-wrench, muzzle, -nix, nobble, obstruct, oppose, paralyze, pause, -preclude, -prevent, -prohibit, protest, resist, restrain, restrict, scare, scotch, shelve, snag, stay, stop, stultify, stump, stymie, tangle, -thwart, warn* (≠ absorb, accelerate, advance, aid, allow, assist, await, brainstorm, bribe, calm, catalyze, comfort, convince, egg, encourage, facilitate, forward, goad, hearten, heat, help, impel, incite, inspirit, instigate, legalize, lull, mellow, mollify, permit, persuade, promote, prompt, push, stimulate, support, sway, urge, warm)

DETERMINE (→): *affect, affirm, assure, choreograph, clarify, clear, clinch, conclude, condition, control, decide, define, demonstrate, dictate, direct, end, ensure, establish, finish, govern, guide, illuminate, impel, influence, insure, nail, orchestrate, ordain, order, organize, pace, prompt, prove, regiment, regulate, rule, secure, settle, show, specify, state, steer, stipulate* (≠ churn, confuse, delay, derail, disrupt, disturb, jumble, misrule, mix, muddle, muddy, obscure, overturn, predetermine, -refuse, -reject, scramble, shelve, unsettle, upset)

DETERMINE (→): *adjudge, adjudicate, arbitrate, broker, choose, cinch, clinch, conclude, consider, consult, contemplate, cull, decide, decree deliberate, elect, entertain, establish, figure, find, finish, handpick, hear, judge, learn, meditate, moderate, mull, name, negotiate, pick, ponder, prefer, prosecute, question, referee, renegotiate, resolve, rule, select, set, settle, size, study, umpire, weigh* (≠ -avoid, challenge, debate, -decline, delay, -halt, hinder, prolong, -refuse, -reject, skirt, stall, wonder) **(¿) ABSTRACTION ALERT. Concrete goals essential!**

DETERMINE (←): *analyze, ascertain, assess, audit, benchmark, categorize, check, consult, cross-examine, descry, detect, disclose, discover, double-check, dredge, educe, elicit, espy, establish, expose, fathom, ferret, find, gauge, get, grill, hit, hunt, identify, inspect, interrogate, interview, learn, locate, prioritize, question, rank, read, realize, recognize, reveal, root, rout, rummage, scout, seek, sight, slot, solve, spot, suss, track, unearth, unmask, unravel, verify* (≠ accept, assume, baffle, believe, bewilder, bury, conceal, confound, confuse, conjecture, deceive, defraud, disbelieve, -discount, disguise, -disregard, fake, gaslight, guess, hide, -ignore, imply, lose, mask, misgauge, misjudge, mislay, mislead, misplace, misprize, misread, miss, mistake, misunderstand, muddle, mystify, obscure, overestimate, -overlook, perplex, pretend, puzzle, -reject, skip, trick, trust, underestimate, wonder)

DETHRONE (/): *banish, boot, bounce, can, cashier, chase, checkmate, conquer, defeat, defrock, degrade, depose, deprive, discharge, dismiss, displace, eject, expel, extrude, fire, oust, overcome, overthrow, remove, retire, rout, ruin, sack, subdue, subjugate, subvert, succeed, supersede, supplant, topple, uncrown, unmake, unseat, unthrone, usurp, vanquish, wrack* (≠ anoint, appoint, assign, baptize, crown, designate, elect, elevate, enthrone, inaugurate, induct, initiate, install, instate, invest, nominate, promote, raise, support, throne)

DETONATE (/): *atomize, bang, blast, blow, burst, discharge, explode, fire, fracture, fragment, fulminate, ignite, kindle, knock, pop, pulverize, shatter, shoot, short-circuit, smash, spark, splinter, trigger, vaporize, zap* (≠ block, choke, collapse, dampen, defuse, dismantle, douse, hamper, implode, snuff, stifle, -thwart)

DEVALUE (/): *attenuate, bastardize, belittle, break, cheapen, contract, cut, debase, decrease, decry, de-escalate, deflate, degrade, demean, depreciate, depress, devaluate, diminish, -discount, dismiss, disparage, downgrade, downsize, knock, lessen, lowball, lower, minimize, moderate, pare, reduce, shave, shrink, sink, slam, slash, slate, trim, underbid, underestimate, underprice, underrate, undervalue, vulgarize* (≠ accentuate, accrue, add, affirm, aggrandize, amplify, appreciate, assert, augment, balloon, bloat, boost, compound, dilate, enhance, enlarge, escalate, exaggerate, expand, extend, fetishize, heighten, heroicize, heroize, increase, inflate, magnify, maximize, multiply, optimize, overestimate, overhaul, overprice, overrate, overvalue, praise, prioritize, raise, refine, revolutionize, romanticize, sentimentalize, swell, upgrade)

DEVASTATE (/): *annihilate, assassinate, atomize, beat, best, blast, blitzkrieg, break, butcher, cannibalize, clobber, conquer, consume, cream, cripple, crush, damage, decimate, deface, defeat, demolish, depopulate, depredate, desecrate, desolate, despoil, destroy, deteriorate, devour, dilapidate, disassemble, disfigure, disintegrate, dismantle, dispatch, dissolve, doom, drub, dynamite, efface, eradicate, erase, erode, execute, expunge, exterminate, extinguish, extirpate, fell, flatten, fracture, fragment, gut, harm, harry, impair, injure, kill, level, lick, liquidate, loot, mangle, mar, maraud, massacre, master, murder, mutilate, -negate, nuke, obliterate, orphan, overpower, overrun, overthrow, overwhelm, pillage, plunder, pulverize, raid, ransack, ravage, raze, remove, rout, ruin, sabotage, sack, scotch, scour, scourge, scupper, shatter, skunk, slaughter, slay, smash, snuff, splinter, spoil, steamroller, strip, subdue, surmount, thrash, topple, total, trample, trash, trounce, vandalize, vaporize, victimize, vitiate, waste, whip, wrack, wreck, wrong, zap* (≠ assemble, build, conserve, construct, create, defend, doctor, enhance, erect, establish, fabricate, fashion, father, fix, forge, form, found, frame, guard, heal, help, improve, institute, invent, make, manufacture, mend, mold, organize, patch, patrol, pity, preserve, produce, protect, raise, rear, rebuild, recondition, reconstruct, recover, redeem, rehabilitate, remodel, renovate, repair, restore, revamp, save, sculpt, shape, shield, sire, survive, sustain, weather, withstand)

DEVASTATE (/): *appall, astound, break, confound, confute, crush, daze, defeat, deluge, demoralize, depress, discomfit, discompose, disconcert, dismay, distress, disturb, drown, floor, grieve, horrify, hurt, indispose, nonplus, numb, offend, oppress, outrage, overcome, overpower, overwhelm, paralyze, perturb, prostrate, pulverize, refute, rock, shatter, shock, sink, stagger, startle, stun, stupefy, swamp, throw, torpefy, traumatize, unman, unnerve, upset* (≠ amuse, appease, assist, assuage, cherish, comfort, console, encourage, energize, entertain, heal, inspire, invigorate, motivate, nourish, nurture, please, protect, rectify, redeem, rescue, rouse, save, stimulate, sugarcoat)

DEVELOP (→): *accent, accentuate, actualize, add, advance, amplify, augment, beautify, beef, broaden, complement, cultivate, deepen, dilate, elaborate, emphasize, enlarge, enrich, evolve, expand, exploit, extend, finish, flesh, heighten, improve, increase, intensify, lengthen, magnify, materialize, maximize, perfect, polish, promote, punctuate, realize, refine, shine, spread, strengthen, stretch, supplement, unfold, weaponize, widen* (≠ abbreviate, abridge, adumbrate, callous, coarsen, compress, concentrate, condense, confine, contract, decrease, lessen, limit, minimize, narrow, outline, shorten, summarize, underemphasize)

DEVELOP (←): *absorb, accrue, achieve, acquire, adopt, attain, begin, break, breed, commence, conceive, contract, create, cultivate, effect,* *embrace, establish, follow, form, foster, found, gain, generate, get, initiate, institute, invent, invest, nourish, nurture, obtain, originate, pioneer, produce, promote, reach, start* (≠ -abandon, -abort, cease, -desert, discard, -discontinue, -ditch, dump, end, -forsake, -halt, jettison, junk, lose, -reject, scrap, shed, shuck, slough, stop, terminate, -thwart, toss, unload)

DEVELOP (+): *abet, accommodate, accomplish, achieve, actualize, advance, affirm, aid, assert, assist, automate, boost, brainstorm, brew, carve, change, civilize, coach, cobble, coin, compose, conceive, concoct, construct, contrive, cook, craft, create, cultivate, customize, decontaminate, devise, discipline, drill, edify, educate, effect, encourage, engineer, enlarge, enlighten, evolve, expand, fabricate, fashion, favor, feed, force-feed, forge, form, fortify, foster, frame, fuel, generate, grow, hatch, help, improve, improvise, increase, instruct, invent, manufacture, mature, mechanize, mentor, mint, model, motorize, nourish, nurse, nurture, originate, prioritize, progress, raise, rear, refine, school, sculpt, shape, spread, support, sustain, tailor, teach, train, tutor, weaponize, weave* (≠ abuse, attack, barbarize, brutalize, callous, coarsen, collapse, contaminate, decrease, dehumanize, demolish, derail, destroy, dismantle, doom, -forbid, forget, hamper, hinder, impair, incapacitate, injure, mutate, pervert, -prevent, -prohibit, protest, raze, reshape, restructure, ruin, stagnate, stale, stunt, topple, undo, unmake, wreck, wrong)

DEVISE (+): *ad-lib, arrange, brainstorm, brew, cast, chart, coin, compose, conceive, concoct, construct, contrive, cook, craft, create, design, discover, envisage, envision, extemporize, fabricate, fantasize, forge, form, formulate, frame, hatch, imagine, improvise, invent, machinate, machine, manufacture, mastermind, originate, picture, plan, plot, prepare, produce, project, ready, scheme, script, shape, spark, visualize, weave* (≠ adopt, ape, borrow, clone, copy, copycat, destroy, doom, duplicate, emulate, ghostwrite, imitate, mimic, obstruct, poach, reduplicate, replicate, reproduce, ruin, steal, -thwart, wreck)

DEVOTE (→): *accord, allocate, allot, apply, appropriate, assign, bestow, bless, budget, commit, confer, confide, consecrate, consign, dedicate, earmark, employ, endow, enshrine, entrust, give, grant, hallow, offer, pledge, reserve, sacrifice, sanctify, save, surrender, tender, use, volunteer* (≠ check, conceal, deduct, degrade, desecrate, disrespect, exploit, hold, -ignore, keep, misapply, misappropriate, misuse, -neglect, profane, recoup, -refuse, steal, take, waste, withhold)

DEVOUR (←): *absorb, accept, access, acquire, admit, appreciate, appropriate, assimilate, bolt, chew, consume, corrode, cram, digest, dispatch, dissolve, down, drink, eat, engorge, engulf, enjoy, envelop, finish, get, glut, gnaw, gobble, gorge, gulp, gum, guzzle, hoover, imbibe, incorporate, ingest, inhale, inspire, integrate, lap, lick, manage, metabolize, mouth, munch, nibble, nosh, nurse, overwhelm, pocket, procure, quaff, raven, receive, relish, ruminate, savor, scarf, sip, slop, slurp, snarf, sniff, stuff, suck, surfeit, swallow, swill, take, taste, try, vacuum, welcome, wolf* (≠ -avoid, barf, belch, brew, -bypass, concoct, cook, create,

-decline, disgorge, -ditch, drop, dump, eject, excrete, expel, feed, force-feed, forgo, fuel, heave, hunt, jettison, make, miss, nourish, offer, order, overfeed, pass, prepare, puke, -refuse, regurgitate, -reject, request, skip, spew, spit, splutter, starve, supply, toss, trash, victual, vomit)

DEVOUR (/): *absorb, annihilate, cannibalize, consume, deplete, depredate, desolate, destroy, devastate, dispatch, doom, empty, engulf, envelop, exhaust, pillage, ravage, raze, ruin, sack, spend, spoil, waste* (≠ assemble, build, construct, establish, fashion, furnish, mend, produce, renew, restore, save, supply, survive, sustain, weather, withstand)

DIAGNOSE (←): *analyze, ascertain, check, confirm, contextualize, crosscheck, deduce, detect, determine, distinguish, establish, explain, explore, eyeball, identify, inspect, interpret, investigate, isolate, learn, locate, pinpoint, place, profile, pronounce, quarantine, recognize, scan, scrutinize, settle, spot, study, test, verify* (≠ afflict, baffle, bewilder, bullshit, bury, cloak, cloud, conceal, confuse, damage, deceive, defraud, disguise, fake, harm, hide, hurt, infect, injure, mask, misdiagnose, mislead, miss, mistake, misunderstand, mystify, -neglect, -overlook, perplex, pretend, scam, trick)

DICTATE (→): *bid, bulldoze, call, chair, charge, choreograph, coerce, command, control, decree, demand, direct, enjoin, foist, govern, guide, impose, insist, instruct, lead, manage, mandate, muscle, orchestrate, ordain, order, prescribe, promulgate, pronounce, railroad, regiment, require, rule, set* (≠ ask, beseech, -cancel, countermand, entreat, implore, plead, propose, recommend, request, -rescind, spitball, suggest, urge)

DIFFUSE (/): *broadcast, circulate, detach, disburse, disconnect, disintegrate, dislocate, disorder, dispense, disperse, disseminate, dissipate, dissolve, distribute, dole, evaporate, expand, extend, penetrate, permeate, promulgate, propagate, radiate, refract, scatter, separate, spread* (≠ abridge, compile, compress, concentrate, condense, confine, contain, fuse, gather, hoard, hold, hybridize, join, keep, limit, link, meld, reserve, restrict, shorten, synthesize, tighten)

DIG (→): *bore, chuck, drill, drive, goad, gouge, jab, jog, knock, nag, nudge, perforate, pierce, plunge, poke, prick, prod, propel, punch, puncture, ram, shank, shiv, spur, stab, stick* (≠ brake, caress, check, constrain, curb, -deter, discourage, dissuade, grasp, grip, hold, inhibit, pull, restrain, stroke, tug, yank)

DIG (←): *access, bore, bulldoze, channel, claw, cultivate, deepen, depress, disinter, -ditch, dredge, drill, drive, enter, entrench, excavate, exhume, fork, gouge, grub, harrow, harvest, hoe, hollow, mine, penetrate, pierce, pit, plow, quarry, root, rout, sap, scoop, scratch, shovel, sift, spade, spit, spud, till, trench, uncover, undermine, unearth, work* (≠ block, bury, congest, cover, cram, fill, jam, load, lose, obscure, obstruct, occlude, pack, pile, plug, ram, replenish, restore, seal, smooth, stash, stow, stuff, tuck, wedge, withdraw)

DIG (←): *analyze, anatomize, assay, audit, check, debunk, decipher, decode, deduce, detect, determine, dissect, elucidate, examine, explore, expose, extricate, ferret, find, gather, inspect, interpret, investigate, peruse, plumb, poke, probe, produce, prospect, ransack, reference, reinvestigate, research, retrieve, review, root, rummage, scan, scout, scrutinize, search, seek, sift, study, surf, survey, uncover, unearth, verify, winnow* (≠ -avoid, bury, camouflage, cloak, clothe, cloud, conceal, disguise, -disregard, ensconce, hide, mask, misconstrue, misdiagnose, misinterpret, misperceive, misread, miss, mistake, misunderstand, -neglect, obscure, repress, screen, secrete, shield, stash, submerge, suppress, whitewash)

DIGEST (←): *absorb, accept, access, acquire, admit, assimilate, consume, devour, dissolve, eat, engorge, get, incorporate, ingest, integrate, macerate, metabolize, process, receive, swallow, take* (≠ assemble, belch, concoct, cook, create, -decline, disgorge, eject, excrete, expel, hunt, make, offer, -omit, prepare, -refuse, -reject, spit, vomit)

DIGEST (←): *absorb, analyze, assimilate, comprehend, consider, contemplate, deliberate, discover, glean, grasp, incorporate, integrate, internalize, learn, master, mull, ponder, read, realize, study, suss, understand* (≠ aggregate, amalgamate, -avoid, consolidate, -ignore, integrate, miss, mistake, misunderstand, synthesize, unify) **(¿) ABSTRACTION ALERT. Concrete goals essential!**

DIGNIFY (+): *acclaim, admire, advance, affirm, aggrandize, apotheosize, applaud, approve, blandish, boost, canonize, commend, compliment, congratulate, deify, distinguish, elevate, endorse, enhance, ennoble, enshrine, enthrone, eulogize, exalt, extol, flatter, glorify, grace, heighten, heroicize, heroize, honor, idealize, idolize, inflate, intensify, laud, lift, lionize, magnify, optimize, overhaul, praise, prefer, prioritize, promote, raise, rarefy, recommend, refine, romanticize, sanction, sanitize, sentimentalize, sugarcoat, upgrade, uplift* (≠ abase, belittle, blame, blast, boo, condemn, corrupt, decry, degrade, demean, denounce, depreciate, detract, disgrace, disparage, humble, humiliate, -ignore, insult, lower, minimize, -overlook, pervert, reduce, ruin, -scorn, shame, -shun, slander, vulgarize, worsen, wreck)

DILUTE (/): *adulterate, alter, attenuate, cook, cut, decrease, deprive, diffuse, diminish, doctor, lace, lessen, mitigate, mix, moderate, modify, plant, qualify, rarefy, reduce, rephrase, sap, shave, spike, temper, thin, underemphasize, water, weaken* (≠ accentuate, accrue, concentrate, condense, consolidate, distill, emphasize, enrich, evaporate, increase, intensify, pasteurize, punctuate, purify, strengthen, sully, thicken)

DIM (/): *blacken, blear, blur, cloud, darken, dull, eclipse, efface, fade, fog, fuzz, haze, lower, mist, muddy, obfuscate, obscure, overshadow, shade, shadow, shroud, smudge, tarnish* (≠ blanch, brighten, clarify, disclose, expose, floodlight, ignite, illuminate, kindle, light, lighten, reveal, uncloud, uncover, unveil, whiten, whitewash)

DIMINISH (/): *abate, abbreviate, abridge, attenuate, bastardize, bob, cannibalize, castrate, clip, compact, compress, compromise, concentrate, condense, consume, contract, crop, cull, curtail, cut, deactivate, deaden, debilitate, debit, decrease, deduct, deflate, deplete, depredate, depress, -discontinue, downgrade, drain, drop, emasculate, enfeeble, erode, exhaust, fatigue, fragment, impair, impoverish, leach, lessen, lighten, lowball, lower, mince, miniaturize, minimize, moderate, nip, pare, prune, reduce, retrench, sap, shave, shear, shorten, shrink, shrivel, sink, straiten, taper, temper, trim, truncate, undercut, underemphasize, undermine, weaken, weed, whittle, wither* (≠ accent, accentuate, accrue, acquire, add, aggravate, amplify, append, assert, boost, broaden, build, bulge, complement, develop, dilate, distend, double, elongate, emphasize, enhance, enlarge, exaggerate, expand, extend, foment, foster, grow, improve, increase, inflate, lengthen, maximize, mount, multiply, obtain, optimize, overdramatize, overhaul, prioritize, prolong, punctuate, raise, rarefy, recoup, refine, reinvigorate, revive, revolutionize, stoke, stretch, supplement, swell, treble, triple, unspool, upgrade, wax)

DIMINISH (/): *abuse, badmouth, belittle, berate, chastise, cheapen, debase, decry, defame, degrade, demean, denigrate, deprecate, depreciate, deride, detract, devaluate, devalue, -discount, discredit, disfavor, disgrace, disparage, disrespect, downgrade, humble, insult, knock, malign, minimize, neg, pan, persecute, rebuke, scold, -scorn, shame, shred, slash, -slight, tatter, underbid, undersell, vilify, vulgarize, wrong* (≠ acclaim, affirm, aggrandize, approve, blandish, boost, brook, commend, compliment, countenance, defend, dramatize, endorse, exalt, extol, favor, flatter, glorify, heroicize, heroize, idealize, ingratiate, poeticize, praise, prioritize, recommend, romanticize, sanction, sensationalize, sentimentalize, strengthen, tolerate, treasure)

DIRECT (→): *beam, carry, channel, concentrate, conduct, consolidate, convey, deliver, dispense, distribute, focus, force, funnel, guide, pipe, send, siphon, steer, transmit, transport* (≠ barricade, block, blockade, choke, clog, constipate, dam, delay, foil, hamper, impede, interrupt, monkeywrench, obstruct, pause, -prevent, shelve, stall, stem, stop, stymie, -thwart, waylay)

DIRECT (→): *accompany, administer, admonish, advise, advocate, appoint, ask, assign, attend, authorize, beg, beseech, bid, boss, bridle, brief, call, caution, chaperone, charge, choreograph, coerce, command, commission, compel, conduct, confer, constrain, consult, control, counsel, cue, decree, deliver, demand, dictate, discipline, dominate, encourage, enjoin, entreat, escort, execute, force, govern, guard, guide, handle, harness, head, influence, inform, instruct, keep, lead, manage, mandate, maneuver, marshal, mastermind, micromanage, mind, motivate, notify, oblige, operate, orchestrate, ordain, order, organize, oversee, pace, petition, pilot, prompt, protect, recommend, regiment, regulate, request, require, route, rule, run, safeguard, see, shepherd, spearhead, stage-manage, steer, steward, suggest, superintend, supervise, task, tell, tend, usher, warn, watch* (≠ -cancel, challenge, contradict, counter, countermand, defer, defy, disobey, disrespect, dog, follow, hound, keep, mind, mismanage, misrule, muzzle, -neglect, obey, observe, -refuse, -rescind, shadow, subvert, tail, topple, trail)

DIRECT (+): *advise, aim, apply, bear, bend, cast, concentrate, conduct, designate, devote, escort, face, fix, focus, give, guide, head, hold, incline, inform, inscribe, instruct, label, lead, lecture, level, mail, mark, navigate, orient, pilot, pinpoint, point, present, route, school, send, set, settle, shepherd, show, sight, slant, steer, target, teach, throw, train, try, turn, tutor, usher, warn* (≠ -avert, confuse, curve, deflect, detour, divert, follow, heed, misdirect, misguide, mislabel, mislead, rechannel, refract, shunt, sidetrack)

DIRTY (/): *adulterate, befoul, begrime, besmirch, bestialize, blacken, blotch, blur, canker, coat, contaminate, corrode, corrupt, debase, decay, defile, discolor, encrust, foul, grime, imbrue, mess, muddy, poison, pollute, rot, smear, smirch, smoke, smudge, smut, soil, spatter, splash, spoil, spot, stain, suborn, sully, sweat, taint, tar, tarnish* (≠ bleach, brush, clean, cleanse, decontaminate, disinfect, distill, filter, launder, mop, purify, rinse, scour, scrub, sponge, sterilize, sweep, uncloud, wash, wipe)

DISABLE (/): *attenuate, batter, blunt, boobytrap, break, cannibalize, castrate, club, consume, crack, cripple, damage, deactivate, debilitate, defuse, deplete, depredate, devitalize, disarm, disqualify, emasculate, enervate, enfeeble, exhaust, fracture, fragment, hamstring, handicap, harm, hinder, hogtie, hurt, immobilize, impair, inactivate, incapacitate, invalidate, -kibosh, lame, maim, mangle, mar, mutilate, muzzle, paralyze, pinion, prostrate, pulverize, reduce, restrict, ruin, sabotage, sap, scotch, scupper, scuttle, shatter, shrivel, spoil, stop, stymie, subvert, total, undercut, undermine, unhinge, unplug, weaken, wing, wither, wizen, wound, wreck* (≠ activate, advantage, aid, assist, benefit, build, connect, cure, doctor, empower, enable, energize, fix, fortify, galvanize, heal, help, improve, include, increase, invigorate, mend, mobilize, patch, permit, refresh, regenerate, rehabilitate, reinvigorate, rejuvenate, remedy, renew, repair, restimulate, restore, revitalize, revive, stimulate, strengthen, weaponize)

DISABUSE (/): *adduce, advise, apprise, attest, belie, chagrin, confess, confide, confirm, confound, confront, crush, dampen, debate, debunk, deflate, demoralize, disappoint, disclose, disconcert, discourage, discredit, disenchant, dishearten, disillusion, dispirit, disprove, dispute, dissatisfy, divulge, document, enlighten, expose, gainsay, invalidate, jade, pooh-pooh, rebut, recant, refute, -repudiate, retract, shake, sophisticate, spill, tell, testify, uncloak, uncover, undeceive, unmask, unveil* (≠ bamboozle, bluff, bullshit, cheat, con, convince, deceive, delude, dupe, fool, gull, hoax, hocus-pocus, hoodwink, kid, manipulate, misguide, misinform, mislead, misrepresent, snooker, snow, stiff, sucker, trick)

DISAPPOINT (/): *-abort, aggrieve, anger, annoy, baffle, -balk, betray, bother, bugger, bungle, chagrin, -circumvent, crush, dampen, dash, deceive, deflate, delude, demoralize, demotivate, disabuse, disconcert,* *discourage, disenchant, disgruntle, disgust, dishearten, disillusion, dismay, dispirit, displease, dissatisfy, disturb, dumbfound, embitter, enlighten, fail, foil, -frustrate, grate, hamper, hinder, irritate, jade, jar, louse, miscarry, mislead, monkey-wrench, offend, provoke, repel, rile, sabotage, sadden, scandalize, scupper, shake, shelve, shock, subvert, tease, -thwart, torment, undercut, undermine, vex, wrong* (≠ accommodate, advantage, allow, assist, benefit, cheer, content, delight, encourage, endorse, excite, explain, fill, forward, fulfill, gladden, glut, grace, gratify, help, inspire, oblige, patronize, permit, please, rubber-stamp, sate, satiate, satisfy, surfeit, thrill, wow)

DISARM (←): *allure, amaze, amuse, attract, beguile, bewitch, cajole, captivate, charm, coax, convince, delight, distract, divert, enchant, engross, entertain, enthrall, entice, fascinate, implore, induce, invite, lighten, magnetize, palaver, persuade, please, refresh, relax, schmooze, seduce, stimulate, sway, thrill, unarm, urge, win* (≠ affront, aggravate, antagonize, appall, bother, bug, chafe, cross, disgust, enrage, exasperate, gall, grate, harass, infuriate, irk, irritate, jar, nauseate, nettle, offend, provoke, rankle, repel, repulse, rile, roil, rouse, sicken, tire, troll, upset, vex, worry)

DISARM (/): *abrogate, anesthetize, botch, cramp, cripple, deactivate, deaden, debilitate, de-escalate, defang, demilitarize, demobilize, disable, disband, disqualify, dull, enfeeble, hamper, hamstring, handicap, hinder, hobble, immobilize, impair, inactivate, incapacitate, invalidate, lame, neutralize, occupy, pacify, paralyze, prostrate, remove, sap, scotch, skin, strip, stun, stupefy, subdue, subjugate, unarm, undermine, vitiate, weaken* (≠ alarm, alert, arm, defend, enable, equip, furnish, militarize, mobilize, outfit, prepare, provide, ready, reequip, rouse, steel, strengthen, supply, unnerve, weaponize)

DISBAND (/): *alienate, ban, banish, bar, demob, demobilize, diffuse, dismiss, dispel, disperse, disseminate, dissipate, dissolve, estrange, expel, isolate, part, prorogue, scatter, segregate, separate, split, spread* (≠ accompany, assemble, cluster, collect, compile, congregate, consolidate, convene, gather, incorporate, join, muster, reintegrate, reunite, unify, unite, weaponize)

DISBELIEVE (/): *contradict, counter, cross-examine, -discount, discredit, dismiss, -disregard, distrust, -eschew, grill, -ignore, interrogate, mistrust, -overlook, question, -reject, -repudiate, -scorn, scout, suspect* (≠ accept, acknowledge, affirm, analyze, believe, consider, consult, follow, judge, recognize, regard, support, sway, trust, weigh) **(¿) ABSTRACTION ALERT. Concrete goals essential!**

DISCARD (→): *-abandon, abdicate, abjure, betray, can, -cancel, chuck, deep-six, -desert, discharge, disclaim, dislodge, dismiss, -disown, dispatch, -ditch, divorce, drop, dump, eject, eliminate, evacuate, expel, forfeit, -forsake, jettison, junk, leave, offload, oust, plonk, -reject, release, relinquish, remove, -renounce, repeal, -repudiate, sack, sacrifice, scrap, shed, -spurn, surrender, waive, withdraw, wrong, yield* (≠ accumulate, acquire, amass, brine, claim, collect, defend, embrace, foster, guard, harvest, hoard, hog, hold, keep, maintain, monopolize, obtain, pickle, possess, preserve, protect, pursue, ration, remainder, rescue, retain, save, shield, stash, stockpile, store, stow, support, sustain, tend)

DISCERN (←): *analyze, ascertain, attend, catch, categorize, check, clock, consider, deduce, descry, detect, determine, diagnose, differentiate, discover, distinguish, espy, examine, explore, eye, eyeball, get, heed, identify, inspect, judge, learn, mark, mind, note, notice, observe, perceive, pinpoint, profile, recognize, regard, remark, sample, scan, scope, scrutinize, see, sight, specify, spot, spy, study, survey, test, view, watch, witness* (≠ addle, baffle, -blank, blind, -bypass, churn, confound, confuse, deceive, disguise, -disregard, doubt, forget, -ignore, lose, lump, mask, mingle, misconstrue, misdiagnose, mishear, misinterpret, misread, miss, mistake, misunderstand, mix, muddle, mystify, -neglect, -overlook, puzzle, scruple, suspect, trick) **(¿) ABSTRACTION ALERT. Concrete goals essential!**

DISCHARGE (→): *blast, blaze, cast, catapult, detonate, explode, fire, fling, heave, hurl, hurtle, launch, lob, loose, pelt, pepper, pitch, project, shoot, skitter, sling, snipe, throw, toss, wing, zap* (≠ catch, clasp, clutch, deflect, field, grab, grasp, grip, guard, hold, holster, load, protect, receive, repel, seize, shield, snag, snatch)

DISCHARGE (→): *clear, disencumber, empty, evacuate, free, lighten, offload, relieve, remove, send, unburden, unload, unpack, vacate, void* (≠ archive, burden, charge, cram, fill, heap, jam, jam-pack, load, overstuff, pack, stash, store, stow, stuff, tuck, wedge)

DISCHARGE (→): *bandy, belch, cast, disgorge, dispense, drizzle, effuse, ejaculate, eject, eliminate, emit, empty, erupt, evacuate, evolve, excrete, exhale, expel, exude, gush, irradiate, issue, jet, leak, ooze, pour, radiate, release, secrete, send, shoot, spew, splutter, spout, spray, spurt, squirt, throw, trickle, upchuck, vent, void, vomit* (≠ absorb, bleed, block, check, dam, decant, drain, draw, drink, impede, inhale, leach, leech, milk, plug, pull, quaff, sip, siphon, sniff, soak, sponge, staunch, stem, suck)

DISCHARGE (→): *axe, banish, boot, bounce, bump, bust, can, cashier, chuck, discard, dislodge, dismiss, displace, dispossess, downsize, drum, eject, excuse, exempt, exorcise, expel, fire, furlough, -nix, oust, pink-slip, release, relieve, remove, replace, retire, rout, sack, separate, spare, supersede, supplant, suspend, terminate, toss, trim, turf, unload, unseat* (≠ appoint, assign, contract, delegate, employ, engage, hire, invite, keep, promote, protect, recruit, reemploy, rehire, retain, sign, subcontract, task)

DISCHARGE (→): *ante, balance, clear, compensate, defray, equalize, expense, foot, honor, indemnify, liquidate, meet, offset, outlay, overpay, pay, -quit, rebate, recompense, rectify, redress, refund, reimburse, relieve, remedy, remit, remunerate, repay, satisfy, settle, square, stand, swing* (≠ -abandon, abrogate, annul, -cancel, challenge, cheat, contest, disinherit, dispute, -dodge, lend, loan, oppose, owe, poach, protest, refute, -repudiate, scant, skimp, skirt, steal, stiff, stint, underpay, void)

DISCHARGE (+): *accomplish, achieve, actualize, answer, claim, complete, conclude, consummate, dispense, effect, execute, fill, finish, fulfill, implement, keep, meet, obey, observe, perfect, perform, qualify, realize, satisfy* (≠ -abandon, abnegate, abrogate, breach, -disregard, fail, forfeit, forget, -forsake, lose, miss, -neglect, -overlook, quash, skimp, -slight, slur, stint, vacate, violate)

DISCHARGE (+): *absolve, acquit, alibi, bail, clear, deliver, disencumber, disengage, disentangle, dismiss, emancipate, enfranchise, enlarge, exculpate, exonerate, extricate, free, liberate, loose, loosen, manumit, pardon, parole, ransom, redeem, release, relieve, rescue, save, spare, spring, unbind, unburden, uncage, unchain, unfetter, unshackle, untie* (≠ arrest, bind, commit, confine, conquer, convict, detain, enchain, enslave, fetter, handcuff, hogtie, hold, immure, imprison, incarcerate, institutionalize, intern, jail, keep, lock, manacle, restrain, seal, shackle, straightjacket, subdue, subjugate, trammel, trap)

DISCIPLINE (→): *assess, beat, break, cane, castigate, charge, chasten, chastise, check, civilize, coach, condemn, control, convict, correct, criticize, critique, cultivate, curb, damn, denounce, develop, dock, drill, edify, educate, enlighten, exercise, fine, flagellate, flog, foster, govern, ground, hide, housebreak, housetrain, hurt, impose, inculcate, indoctrinate, inform, instruct, inure, keelhaul, lash, lather, levy, lick, limit, mold, mulct, paddle, pain, penalize, punish, realign, rebuke, regulate, reprimand, reprove, restrain, restrict, school, sentence, slap, slipper, slug, smack, spank, straightjacket, strap, strike, subjugate, tame, tan, teach, thrash, thwack, torment, train, tutor, wallop, whack, whip, wreak* (≠ absolve, acquit, alibi, baby, barbarize, commute, exculpate, excuse, exonerate, forfeit, indulge, infantilize, -neglect, pamper, pardon, permit, praise, ransom, release, reprieve, reward, spare, spoil, vindicate)

DISCLAIM (/): *-abandon, abdicate, abjure, challenge, confute, contradict, criticize, debate, debunk, -decline, -deny, disallow, disavow, discard, discredit, -disown, disprove, dispute, gainsay, invalidate, -negate, question, rebuke, rebut, recant, -refuse, refute, -reject, -renounce, -repudiate, retract, -spurn* (≠ accept, acknowledge, admit, adopt, affirm, announce, assert, authenticate, avow, claim, concede, confess, confirm, consult, convince, corroborate, declare, embrace, espouse, grant, maintain, notarize, own, profess, recognize, submit, substantiate, validate, verify)

DISCLOSE (→): *acknowledge, admit, advertise, announce, avow, bare, betray, blab, blast, blurt, broadcast, bulletin, circulate, communicate, confess, confide, confirm, confront, convince, declare, develop, discover, disinter, display, disseminate, divulge, exhibit, expose, hype, impart, leak, light, open, placard, post, presell, proclaim, promulgate, publicize, publish, relate, reveal, share, show, showcase, sound, spill, spotlight,* *telegraph, tell, uncloak, uncover, unearth, unfold, unfurl, unlock, unmask, unveil, utter, vouchsafe* (≠ bleep, camouflage, candy-coat, cloak, clothe, cloud, conceal, costume, cover, darken, disguise, eclipse, enshroud, gild, gloss, hide, mask, obscure, secrete, shroud, spackle, spin, varnish, veil, whitewash, withhold)

DISCOMBOBULATE (/): *abash, addle, agitate, alarm, amaze, baffle, bamboozle, beat, befog, befuddle, beguile, bemuse, bewilder, blindside, bother, buffalo, bug, chagrin, confound, confuse, cozen, craze, daze, deafen, deceive, delude, discomfit, discomfort, discompose, disconcert, dismay, disorient, disquiet, distress, disturb, dizzy, double-talk, dupe, embarrass, faze, flummox, fluster, fool, fox, gaslight, gull, hoax, hocus-pocus, hoodwink, humbug, indispose, intoxicate, jangle, manipulate, misguide, mislead, mortify, muddle, muddy, mystify, nonplus, perplex, perturb, puzzle, rattle, ruffle, shake, snooker, snow, startle, stick, stump, stun, surprise, throw, trick, trouble, unbalance, unhinge, unnerve, unsettle, upset, vex* (≠ aid, assist, assure, bolster, brace, buoy, calm, cheer, clarify, comfort, encourage, enlighten, explain, floodlight, hallucinate, hearten, help, hush, illuminate, inform, lull, mellow, mollify, nerve, order, organize, rally, reassure, regiment, regulate, satisfy, soothe, steady, support)

DISCOMFIT (←): *arrest, -avert, baffle, -balk, bar, beat, block, check, checkmate, clog, confound, conquer, counteract, defeat, encumber, faze, fetter, foil, forestall, frustrate, gravel, -halt, hamper, handicap, hinder, hobble, hold, impede, inhibit, manacle, -negate, neutralize, -nullify, obstruct, -obviate, offset, outlast, outwit, overcome, -preclude, -prevent, shackle, short-circuit, stall, stop, -thwart, trammel, trump* (≠ abet, advance, aid, assist, buoy, cede, cultivate, ease, enable, encourage, expedite, explain, facilitate, forfeit, forward, foster, further, help, inspire, lose, nurture, organize, promote, rush, smooth, stimulate, support)

DISCOMFIT (/): *abash, agitate, annoy, bother, chagrin, confound, confuse, debase, debunk, degrade, demean, demoralize, discomfort, discompose, disconcert, discountenance, disgrace, dishonor, dismay, displease, disquiet, distress, disturb, embarrass, expose, faze, fluster, gaslight, heckle, humble, humiliate, irk, malign, mock, mortify, nag, needle, nettle, nitpick, nonplus, -ostracize, perplex, perturb, pillory, queer, rattle, ridicule, ruffle, scandalize, shame, stigmatize, unhinge, unsettle, upset, vex, vilify, worry* (≠ appease, assure, buoy, calm, cheer, comfort, compose, console, delight, embolden, encourage, enlighten, hearten, help, hush, lull, mellow, mollify, order, pacify, placate, please, reassure, relax, relieve, settle, soothe, stabilize, sugarcoat, thrill)

DISCONCERT (/): *abash, agitate, alarm, baffle, -balk, bewilder, blindside, bug, chagrin, confound, confuse, deflate, dement, demoralize, derange, disappoint, discombobulate, discomfit, discompose, dismay, distract, distress, disturb, embarrass, faze, floor, fluster, frighten, frustrate, gaslight, hinder, humiliate, mismatch, muddle, nonplus, perplex, perturb, puzzle, rattle, rile, ruffle, shake, shame, startle, surprise, throw, trouble,* *unbalance, unnerve, unsettle, upset, worry* (≠ approve, assist, assure, buoy, calm, cheer, clarify, comfort, console, encourage, enlighten, explain, hearten, help, hush, inspirit, lull, mellow, mollify, order, pacify, permit, placate, please, quiet, rally, reassure, relax, relieve, soothe, support)

DISCONNECT (/): *bisect, break, chunk, cleave, cut, decompose, de-energize, detach, disassemble, disassociate, disengage, disentangle, disintegrate, disjoin, disjoint, dissect, dissolve, disunite, divide, divorce, estrange, fracture, halve, insulate, isolate, orphan, part, partition, pull, quarter, rend, resolve, rip, rive, rupture, seclude, segment, segregate, separate, sequester, sever, split, subdivide, sunder, tear, uncouple, undo, unhitch, unhook, unlink, unplug, unravel, untie, unyoke* (≠ accumulate, assemble, associate, attach, bind, blend, cement, close, combine, connect, couple, fasten, fuse, integrate, join, knit, link, mingle, mix, mortar, network, reintegrate, reunite, stick, unify, unite, weld)

DISCOUNT (/): *abate, cheapen, curtail, cut, decrease, deduct, depreciate, diminish, lessen, lowball, lower, minimize, modify, rebate, redeem, reduce, remove, slash, subtract, underbid, underemphasize, undersell* (≠ accent, accentuate, accrue, amplify, augment, boost, bump, elevate, emphasize, escalate, heighten, hike, increase, inflate, intensify, jack, list, maximize, pad, prioritize, raise, up)

-**DISCOUNT (/):** *absolve, acquit, belittle, -bypass, clear, condone, depreciate, disbelieve, discredit, dismiss, -disregard, doubt, exculpate, excuse, exonerate, explain, fail, forget, forgive, gloss, -ignore, interrogate, justify, minimize, misprize, miss, mistake, mistrust, -neglect, -omit, -overlook, pardon, pooh-pooh, question, rationalize, -reject, remit, scruple, -slight, spare, suspect, underestimate, undervalue, vindicate, waive, whitewash* (≠ accept, acknowledge, adjudge, affirm, analyze, appraise, assert, assume, attend, believe, check, compare, consider, consult, contemplate, critique, evaluate, examine, eyeball, heed, honor, inspect, investigate, judge, learn, mark, mind, note, prize, prowl, recognize, regard, respect, scrutinize, study, test, value, weigh)

DISCOUNT (/): *abuse, badmouth, belittle, blame, blast, boo, censure, condemn, cow, criticize, critique, cross-examine, decry, defame, denigrate, denounce, deprecate, depreciate, diminish, discredit, disfavor, disgrace, dismiss, disparage, diss, incriminate, malign, minimize, rip, scold, slander, slur, traduce, trash, trash-talk, vilify, vilipend, wrong* (≠ acclaim, applaud, approve, brave, brook, commend, compliment, congratulate, countenance, endorse, eulogize, exalt, extol, face, favor, glorify, gold-star, gratify, laud, magnify, praise, recommend, sanction, stomach, support, tolerate)

DISCOURAGE (←): *-abort, baffle, bar, block, bottleneck, brake, bung, burden, -cancel, catch, caution, check, chill, choke, clog, complicate, congest, constipate, constrain, control, crimp, curb, dam, dampen, daunt, defeat, delay, demolish, demotivate, deprecate, depress, detain, -deter, dishearten, disincline, dissuade, divert, drag, encumber, entangle, entrap, fetter, foul, freeze, frighten, -frustrate, hamper, hinder, impede,* *indispose, inhibit, interrupt, jam, mire, obstruct, paralyze, pause, plug, -preclude, preempt, -prevent, quiet, repress, restrain, restrict, scare, shake, shelve, short-circuit, snag, snarl, stay, stem, stifle, stop, stymie, tangle, throttle, -thwart, warn, weaken, withhold* (≠ advance, assist, bolster, boost, brace, buoy, buttress, calm, egg, encourage, facilitate, fortify, galvanize, goad, help, impel, induce, inspire, invigorate, invite, lull, mellow, midwife, nerve, permit, prioritize, prod, prompt, provoke, rally, reassure, reinforce, spur, steady, steel, stimulate, stir, strengthen, support, uncomplicate, urge, welcome)

DISCOURAGE (/): *abash, admonish, afflict, agitate, alarm, appall, -avert, awe, ban, bar, blackmail, bother, browbeat, bug, bulldoze, bully, caution, check, chill, confuse, cow, damp, dampen, dash, daunt, deflect, demoralize, demotivate, deprecate, depress, derail, -deter, disappoint, disconcert, dishearten, disillusion, disincline, dismay, disparage, dispirit, dissuade, distress, disturb, divert, forebode, frighten, harass, harrow, haunt, hint, horrify, inhibit, intimidate, irk, nobble, panic, petrify, -preclude, -prevent, prostrate, protest, rattle, repress, restrain, scare, terrify, threaten, -thwart, torment, trash-talk, trouble, unnerve, vex, warn, weigh* (≠ animate, assure, cheer, comfort, commend, compliment, congratulate, encourage, energize, enliven, excite, facilitate, galvanize, gladden, gold-star, hasten, hearten, high-five, inspire, legalize, motivate, please, praise, soothe, spark, uplift)

DISCOVER (←): *ascertain, bare, catch, debunk, descry, detect, determine, dig, disclose, disinter, dredge, educe, elicit, espy, explore, expose, fathom, ferret, find, get, hit, hunt, identify, investigate, learn, locate, plumb, probe, prowl, recognize, reveal, root, rout, rummage, scout, search, seek, sight, solve, spot, track, uncover, unearth, unmask, unravel, unriddle, unsheathe, unveil, unwrap* (≠ bury, cloak, clothe, cloud, conceal, costume, deceive, disguise, double-talk, ensconce, hide, lose, mislay, misplace, miss, niche, obscure, -overlook, pass, spackle, varnish, veil, whitewash)

DISCOVER (←): *analyze, ascertain, calculate, clock, consult, deduce, descry, detect, determine, discern, distinguish, divine, espy, establish, fathom, find, hear, identify, lay, learn, locate, mind, note, notice, observe, perceive, pinpoint, place, position, post, realize, recognize, retrace, see, sense, set, situate, spot, spy, station, suss, trace, unmask* (≠ blanket, blind, blindfold, blot, cloak, conceal, confound, confuse, cover, curtain, deceive, disguise, -disregard, enshroud, fake, forget, fudge, hide, -ignore, lose, mask, mislead, miss, mistake, muddle, mystify, -neglect, occult, -overlook, perplex, puzzle, screen, shroud, trick, unlearn, veil)

DISCOVER (+): *anticipate, begin, brainstorm, colonize, compose, conceive, contrive, create, design, develop, devise, establish, explore, foreshadow, found, initiate, instigate, institute, introduce, invent, launch, lead, map, open, originate, pioneer, prepare, spearhead, start, trail-blaze* (≠ abolish, adopt, annihilate, annul, ape, close, conceal, copy, damage, destroy, duplicate, emulate, end, exterminate, finish, -halt, hide, mimic, -nullify, ruin, shut, stop, terminate, wrap, wreck)

DISCREDIT (/): *abase, abash, affront, anathematize, badmouth, belittle, bestialize, blackguard, blame, blast, boo, castigate, censure, chasten, cheapen, condemn, confound, confuse, criticize, damage, damn, debase, decry, defame, defile, degrade, demean, demonize, denounce, depreciate, destroy, detract, diminish, discomfit, disconcert, -discount, disgrace, dishonor, disparage, disprove, doom, embarrass, execrate, explode, expose, faze, fluster, foul, fulminate, humble, humiliate, incriminate, insult, invalidate, libel, lower, malign, minimize, mock, mortify, nonplus, pillory, pooh-pooh, puncture, rattle, reproach, ridicule, rubbish, ruin, shame, shoot, sink, slam, slander, slate, slur, smear, smirch, tarnish, topple, trash, vilify, vulgarize* (≠ accentuate, acclaim, acknowledge, advance, affirm, aggrandize, applaud, assert, boast, boost, canonize, celebrate, cheer, cite, commend, compliment, congratulate, decorate, deify, dignify, elevate, ennoble, enshrine, enthrone, eulogize, exalt, extol, glorify, hail, heroicize, highlight, honor, idealize, laud, lift, lionize, magnify, praise, promote, raise, recognize, respect, romanticize, salute, sentimentalize, spotlight, tout, upgrade, uplift)

DISCREDIT (/): *belie, challenge, confound, confront, confute, consult, contest, crosscheck, cross-examine, debate, debunk, deflate, demean, demolish, -deny, disbelieve, discard, -discount, discuss, disprove, dispute, distrust, divulge, doubt, explode, expose, falsify, grill, interrogate, invalidate, lampoon, mistrust, mock, nail, overthrow, overturn, pillory, puncture, quash, query, question, rebuke, rebut, refute, -reject, reveal, ridicule, scathe, -scorn, scruple, show, suspect, tell, trust, uncloak, uncover, undress, unmask, unveil* (≠ adduce, attest, authenticate, back, believe, buttress, camouflage, certify, chronicle, cloak, clothe, cloud, conceal, concede, confirm, consult, convince, corroborate, credit, demonstrate, disguise, display, document, endorse, establish, evidence, evince, hide, identify, illustrate, interview, manifest, mask, notarize, prove, record, rubber-stamp, secrete, show, substantiate, support, trust, validate, veil, verify, witness)

-DISDAIN (/): *abhor, abominate, belittle, -cold-shoulder, condemn, demean, deplore, deprecate, deride, -despise, -detest, disavow, discredit, disfavor, disgrace, disparage, -disregard, disrespect, execrate, -hate, high-hat, -ignore, jeer, -loathe, mock, pillory, pooh-pooh, -rebuff, -reject, ridicule, -scorn, scout, -slight, -snub, -spurn, undervalue* (≠ accept, admire, appreciate, brave, brook, cherish, countenance, esteem, face, favor, hallow, honor, lionize, okay, prize, respect, revere, tolerate, treasure, value, venerate, worship)

DISEMBOWEL (/): *bone, clean, cut, dissect, draw, dress, empty, eviscerate, excise, extract, gore, gut, harvest, mangle, maul, remove, transplant, unpack, vivisect, withdraw, yank* (≠ clog, cram, fill, jam, load, pack, reinstate, replace, restore, seal, stuff, wedge)

DISENCHANT (/): *advise, apprise, chagrin, confess, confide, confront, crush, curb, dampen, debunk, deflate, demoralize, demotivate, disabuse, disappoint, disclose, disconcert, discourage, dishearten, disillusion,* *dispirit, dissatisfy, divulge, enlighten, expose, frustrate, inhibit, jade, refute, shake, sophisticate, sour, spill, tell, trust, uncloak, uncover, undeceive, unmask, unveil, upset* (≠ beguile, bewitch, bluff, captivate, cheat, cozen, delude, dupe, enchant, enrapture, enthrall, fascinate, fool, gull, hoax, hoodwink, josh, kid, mesmorize, misguide, misinform, mislead, misrepresent, snow, stiff, trick)

DISENGAGE (/): *alienate, amputate, axe, bisect, break, clear, cleave, cut, decouple, deliver, detach, disaffect, disarticulate, disassemble, disassociate, disconnect, disentangle, disintegrate, disjoin, dismantle, dismiss, dissect, disunite, divide, divorce, drop, ease, emancipate, estrange, excise, extricate, fragment, free, halve, incise, insulate, isolate, liberate, loose, loosen, -omit, -ostracize, oust, pare, part, partition, release, remove, rend, reprieve, rip, rupture, scissor, segregate, separate, sever, slice, split, sunder, unbind, uncouple, undo, unfasten, unglue, unhinge, unhitch, unhook, untie, withdraw* (≠ attach, bind, burden, chain, clasp, clip, collect, combine, connect, embroil, encumber, engage, entangle, fasten, gather, hamper, hinder, hold, impede, implicate, join, keep, link, load, maintain, network, obstruct, reunite, secure, span, straddle, tie, unite)

DISFIGURE (/): *blemish, blight, bloody, botch, break, compromise, crab, cripple, damage, deface, defile, deform, dent, ding, disable, distort, efface, erode, flaw, hamstring, harm, harshen, hurt, impair, injure, lacerate, lame, maim, mangle, mar, mutilate, palsy, razor, ruin, scalp, scar, scour, scourge, smash, spoil, tarnish, torment, torture, vitiate, welt, wound, wreck* (≠ ameliorate, beautify, better, cure, doctor, enhance, fix, glamorize, glitz, heal, help, improve, mend, optimize, overhaul, patch, rebuild, reconstruct, rectify, refine, regret, rehabilitate, remedy, remodel, renovate, repair, revamp)

DISGRACE (/): *abase, abuse, bed, belittle, besmirch, bestialize, blackguard, blame, blast, blot, boo, canker, contaminate, corrupt, debase, debauch, debunk, defame, defile, deflower, degrade, demean, demonize, demote, depress, deride, desecrate, devalue, diminish, discomfit, discredit, dishonor, disparage, disrespect, embarrass, expose, humble, humiliate, insult, libel, lower, malign, mock, mortify, muckrake, -ostracize, out, pillory, ravish, reduce, reproach, ridicule, scandalize, seduce, shame, sideline, slander, slur, -snub, soil, spoil, stain, stigmatize, sully, taint, tarnish, vilify, violate, vulgarize, wrong* (≠ aggrandize, applaud, blandish, boost, canonize, celebrate, commend, congratulate, decorate, dignify, elevate, ennoble, enthrone, esteem, exalt, flatter, glorify, heroicize, heroize, highlight, honor, idealize, ingratiate, praise, promote, purify, raise, recognize, regard, respect, reverence, reward, romanticize, salute, sentimentalize, spotlight, tout, upgrade, uplift)

DISGUISE (+): *act, adopt, affect, ape, assume, beard, blanket, bleep, blot, camouflage, cloak, conceal, copy, costume, counterfeit, cover, curtain, deceive, double-talk, dress, dupe, emulate, enshroud, fake, feign, gild, gloss, hide, impersonate, mantle, mask, mimic, obscure, occult, -omit, paint, play, playact, pose, pretend, roleplay, screen, sheathe, shroud,* *simulate, spackle, spin, varnish, veil, whitewash* (≠ bare, betray, brandish, circulate, confess, confide, confirm, confront, convince, disclose, discover, display, divulge, exhibit, expose, flaunt, parade, reveal, show, showcase, uncloak, unclothe, uncover, undrape, unmask, unveil, wag)

DISGUISE (/): *act, affect, alter, beard, becloud, bedim, befog, belie, blanket, bleep, block, blot, blur, bury, camouflage, candy-coat, change, cloak, clothe, cloud, color, conceal, costume, couch, counterfeit, cover, curtain, darken, -deny, dissimulate, dress, -duck, eclipse, ensconce, enshroud, fake, falsify, feign, fudge, gild, gloss, guard, hide, holster, hood, hush, impersonate, kill, mask, misrepresent, muddy, muffle, obfuscate, obscure, obstruct, occlude, occult, -omit, overshadow, paint, play, playact, pretend, rephrase, repress, roleplay, screen, shade, sheathe, shield, shrink, shroud, simulate, smother, spackle, sugarcoat, suppress, varnish, veil, whitewash* (≠ accost, admit, advertise, air, amplify, augment, bare, betray, boost, brandish, broadcast, circulate, clarify, concede, confess, confide, confirm, confront, disclose, discover, display, disseminate, divulge, elevate, enhance, enlarge, exhibit, expand, expose, extend, flaunt, floodlight, glorify, heighten, herald, highlight, hype, identify, illuminate, limelight, magnify, maximize, out, parade, present, proclaim, publicize, publish, reveal, show, showcase, sport, spotlight, spread, telegraph, trumpet, uncloak, uncover, unmask, unveil, volunteer)

DISGUST (/): *abuse, affront, aggrieve, anger, annoy, appall, bother, depress, disappoint, dismay, displease, disquiet, distress, disturb, grate, horrify, incense, insult, irk, irritate, jar, muckrake, nauseate, offend, outrage, provoke, repel, repulse, revolt, rile, scandalize, shock, sicken, -slight, -snub, trigger, troll, upset, vex* (≠ allure, attract, beguile, bewitch, captivate, charm, comfort, delight, enchant, enrapture, enthrall, entice, entrance, fascinate, gratify, lure, magnetize, please, razzle-dazzle, rejoice, restore, seduce, tantalize, tease, tempt, thrill, tickle, woo)

DISH (→): *administer, allocate, apportion, assign, chunk, contribute, deliver, dispense, distribute, dole, dollop, feed, force-feed, fuel, furnish, give, hand, ladle, offer, portion, present, prorate, provide, scoop, serve, spoon, supply, transfer* (≠ budget, conserve, -deny, deprive, hold, keep, maintain, preserve, remove, reserve, retain, save, seize, starve, withdraw, withhold)

DISH (→): *admit, analyze, anatomize, broadcast, chide, circulate, communicate, confess, consider, criticize, critique, debate, declare, disclose, discuss, dissect, disseminate, divulge, estimate, evaluate, examine, interpret, investigate, judge, knock, muckrake, neg, process, promulgate, provoke, review, rumor, scandalize, scold, -scorn, scrutinize, share, slam, spill, spite, spread, study, test, transmit, weigh* (≠ applaud, bury, camouflage, censor, conceal, contradict, defend, -deny, disguise, dispute, flatter, gainsay, hide, honor, hush, muzzle, obscure, praise, promote, protect, quiet, redact, refute, shield, silence, suppress, withhold)

DISHEARTEN (/): *afflict, appall, bother, browbeat, bully, chagrin, chill, cow, crush, curb, damp, dampen, daunt, deaden, debilitate, deflate,* *demoralize, demotivate, depress, -deter, disabuse, disappoint, disconcert, discountenance, discourage, disenchant, disillusion, dismay, dispirit, distress, enervate, enfeeble, enlighten, frighten, frustrate, horrify, intimidate, irk, oppress, sadden, scare, shake, sicken, -thwart, trouble, try, undermine, unman, unnerve, vex, weaken, weigh, worry, wrong* (≠ animate, assure, boost, buoy, cheer, comfort, congratulate, console, embolden, encourage, energize, enforce, enliven, excite, fortify, galvanize, gladden, gold-star, hearten, high-five, inspire, invigorate, lift, nerve, provoke, quicken, rally, reassure, reinforce, revitalize, steel, stimulate, stir, strengthen)

DISHONOR (/): *abase, attaint, bed, belittle, besmear, besmirch, blacken, blot, contaminate, corrupt, debase, debauch, declass, defame, defile, deflower, degrade, demean, demote, desecrate, devalue, diminish, discredit, disgrace, disoblige, disparage, humble, humiliate, insult, libel, lower, mortify, reduce, seduce, shame, sideline, slander, soil, spoil, stain, sully, taint, violate, wrong* (≠ acclaim, aggrandize, cleanse, compliment, credit, dignify, elevate, enhance, esteem, exalt, glorify, honor, praise, purify, raise, respect, revere, reverence, reward, treasure, upgrade)

DISILLUSION (/): *advise, alienate, appall, apprise, caution, chill, confess, confide, confirm, confront, crush, curb, dampen, debunk, deflate, demoralize, demotivate, depress, disabuse, disaffect, disappoint, disclose, disconcert, discourage, disenchant, dishearten, dismay, dispirit, dissatisfy, divulge, embitter, enlighten, expose, frustrate, jade, quash, refute, sadden, shake, sophisticate, sour, spill, tell, uncloak, uncover, undeceive, unmask, unveil, warn* (≠ beguile, bluff, bullshit, cozen, delight, delude, dupe, enchant, fascinate, fool, gull, hoax, hoodwink, kid, mesmerize, misguide, misinform, mislead, misrepresent, ravish, snooker, snow, trick)

DISINTEGRATE (/): *abolish, anatomize, annihilate, atomize, break, collapse, corrode, crumble, decay, decimate, decompose, demolish, desolate, destroy, devastate, diffuse, digest, disburse, dislocate, dismantle, disorder, disperse, dissolve, distribute, doom, eradicate, erode, exterminate, extirpate, flatten, fracture, fragment, fuse, level, liquefy, melt, mortify, pulverize, radiate, refract, rot, rupture, scatter, separate, shatter, shred, smash, soften, splinter, split, spoil, tatter, thaw, turn, vaporize, weaken, wreck* (≠ accumulate, amass, assemble, attach, brace, build, collect, combine, compose, concentrate, connect, constellate, couple, craft, crystallize, develop, fix, freeze, garner, gather, harden, incorporate, integrate, join, link, meld, mend, petrify, renew, reshape, restore, set, solidify, steel, strengthen, survive, sustain, temper, toughen, unite, weather, withstand)

DISLODGE (→): *budge, bulldoze, bump, butt, catapult, convulse, crash, discard, disentangle, dislocate, dismiss, displace, dispossess, disturb, drive, eject, elbow, evacuate, evict, exorcise, expel, extricate, fire, force, goad, hustle, impel, jab, jettison, jog, joggle, jolt, jostle, knock, move, muscle, nudge, oust, poke, press, prod, push, ram, relegate, relocate,* *remove, sack, shake, shift, shove, shunt, slam, strike, supersede, supplant, thrust, uproot* (≠ affix, attach, block, bolster, cram, ensconce, fasten, fill, fortify, glue, jam, link, lodge, obstruct, occlude, order, overstuff, paste, pin, pinion, plant, plug, sow, stash, stick, stow, strengthen, stuff, tack, tuck, wedge)

DISMANTLE (/): *annihilate, bankrupt, beggar, decimate, deconstruct, demolish, deprive, destroy, detach, disarticulate, disassemble, disconnect, disjoin, disjoint, dismember, dismount, disunite, divest, divide, fell, level, raze, ruin, separate, strike, strip, subvert, topple, unsew, wrack, wreck* (≠ assemble, build, combine, construct, craft, erect, fashion, machine, make, manufacture, pitch, raise, sculpt, sew, stitch, survive, sustain, suture, unite, weather, weld, withstand)

DISMAY (/): *alarm, appall, bewilder, bother, bug, chagrin, concern, daunt, demoralize, demotivate, depress, disappoint, disconcert, discourage, dishearten, disillusion, dispirit, distress, disturb, dread, enervate, flummox, frighten, horrify, irk, irritate, paralyze, puzzle, rattle, rile, sadden, scare, shake, shock, sorrow, trouble, unnerve, unsettle, upset, worry* (≠ amuse, appease, assure, calm, comfort, congratulate, content, delight, ease, elate, embolden, encourage, entertain, grace, gratify, hallucinate, help, intoxicate, lull, mellow, mollify, mollycoddle, pacify, placate, please, quiet, reassure, restore, satisfy, settle, soothe, sugarcoat, thrill, uplift, wow)

DISMEMBER (/): *amputate, axe, behead, butcher, chop, cleave, crack, cripple, crush, cut, damage, decapitate, deface, deform, disable, disarticulate, disfigure, disjoint, dislocate, dissect, distort, divide, excise, guillotine, hack, hew, hurt, impair, injure, joint, lacerate, lame, lop, maim, mangle, mar, mutilate, ravage, razor, remove, rend, ruin, scratch, separate, sever, slash, slice, split, spoil, sunder, truncate, vivisect, weaken* (≠ aid, assemble, build, combine, connect, construct, cure, doctor, erect, fix, heal, help, join, mend, patch, pitch, rebuild, recondition, reconstruct, rehabilitate, remedy, renovate, repair, restore, unite)

DISMISS (→): *axe, banish, boot, bounce, can, cashier, chase, chuck, deport, discard, discharge, dislodge, displace, dispossess, eject, evict, exile, exorcise, expatriate, expel, fire, furlough, -ostracize, oust, pink-slip, release, remove, retire, rout, sack, spare, supersede, terminate, unseat* (≠ accept, admit, appoint, assign, contract, delegate, employ, engage, entertain, harbor, hire, house, invite, keep, lodge, promote, protect, receive, recruit, reemploy, rehire, retain, shelter, sign, subcontract, take, task, welcome)

DISMISS (/): *abuse, badmouth, belittle, blame, blast, boo, censure, condemn, criticize, critique, decry, defame, denigrate, denounce, deprecate, depreciate, diminish, disbelieve, -discount, discredit, disfavor, disgrace, disparage, -disregard, -ignore, incriminate, malign, minimize, -overlook, rip, scold, slander, slur, traduce, trash, vilify, wrong* (≠ accent, accentuate, accept, acclaim, acknowledge, affirm, amplify, analyze, applaud, approve, assert, assess, believe, brook, commend, compare, compliment, consider, countenance, endure, evaluate, face, favor, honor, judge, mark, mull, note, ponder, punctuate, read, recognize, recommend, regard, sanction, spitball, stomach, tolerate, value, weigh)

DISOBEY (/): *breach, break, buck, challenge, combat, contest, contradict, contravene, counter, counteract, debate, defy, dismiss, disoblige, dispute, -disregard, disrespect, exceed, fight, flout, gate-crash, -ignore, infringe, mock, offend, oppose, -overlook, overstep, pooh-pooh, -reject, resist, -scorn, transgress, trespass, violate, withstand* (≠ abide, accept, attend, command, demand, dominate, follow, hear, heed, insist, keep, mandate, mark, mind, note, notice, obey, oblige, observe, regard, require, serve, watch)

DISORGANIZE (/): *agitate, blur, botch, capsize, churn, clutter, complicate, confound, confuse, convulse, derange, destroy, disarrange, disarray, disband, discompose, dishevel, dislocate, disorder, disperse, displace, disrupt, disturb, embroil, half-ass, hash, infuse, jumble, litter, mislay, misplace, mix, muddle, muss, perturb, roil, roughen, ruffle, rummage, rumple, scatter, scramble, shuffle, swirl, toss, tousle, trouble, tumble, unsettle, unstring, untidy, upset, whip, whisk* (≠ adapt, adjust, align, arrange, calibrate, catalog, clarify, classify, codify, collect, compile, compose, coordinate, enlighten, explain, fix, gather, groom, gussy, hierarchize, line, methodize, neaten, order, organize, pace, plan, regiment, regulate, right, script, shelve, soothe, spruce, straighten, systematize, systemize, tidy, tweak, uncomplicate, unscramble)

DISORIENT (/): *abash, addle, agitate, baffle, bamboozle, beat, befog, befuddle, beguile, bemuse, bewilder, blind, bother, buffalo, chagrin, cloud, confound, confuse, cozen, daze, deafen, deceive, delude, discombobulate, discomfit, discomfort, discompose, disconcert, dismay, disquiet, distress, disturb, dizzy, double-talk, dupe, embarrass, faze, flummox, fluster, fool, fox, gaslight, gull, hoax, hocus-pocus, hoodwink, humbug, lose, manipulate, misguide, mislead, mortify, muddle, muddy, mystify, nonplus, perplex, perturb, puzzle, rattle, shunt, snooker, snow, stump, stun, stupefy, trick, unbalance, unhinge, unsettle, upset, vex* (≠ anchor, assure, balance, calibrate, center, compose, enlighten, explain, floodlight, illuminate, inform, orient, pinpoint, reassure, satisfy, settle, solve, stabilize, steady, tune)

-DISOWN (/): *-abandon, abdicate, abjure, abnegate, blackball, -cancel, contradict, -deny, -desert, disallow, disavow, discard, disclaim, disinherit, dismiss, dispel, dispose, drop, exile, expel, -forsake, gainsay, jettison, leave, -negate, recall, recant, -refuse, refute, -reject, release, relegate, -renounce, -repudiate, revoke, shed, -shun, vacate, withdraw* (≠ accept, acknowledge, admit, allow, avow, bequeath, cherish, claim, colonize, declare, defend, honor, include, invite, involve, maintain, nurture, own, permit, preserve, protect, recognize, redeem, retain, support, welcome, will)

DISPARAGE (/): *abrade, abuse, accuse, admonish, anathematize, attaint, belittle, blackguard, blame, blast, blister, boo, castigate, censure, charge,* *chasten, chastise, cheapen, chide, condemn, criticize, critique, decry, defame, defile, degrade, demean, demonize, demoralize, denigrate, denounce, denunciate, deprecate, depreciate, deride, detract, diminish, disapprove, -discount, discourage, discredit, -disdain, dishonor, dismiss, disrespect, diss, fault, frame, fulminate, impeach, incriminate, jeer, knock, lessen, malign, minimize, mock, neg, pan, pillory, rebuke, reduce, -renounce, reproach, resent, ridicule, roast, scalp, scapegoat, scold, scorch, -scorn, slam, slander, slate, slur, smear, trash, underestimate, underrate, undervalue, upbraid, vilify, wrong* (≠ admire, advantage, affirm, applaud, benefit, blandish, brave, brook, commend, compliment, congratulate, countenance, encourage, endorse, endure, esteem, eulogize, exalt, face, flannel, flatter, glorify, gold-star, hearten, high-five, honor, ingratiate, inspire, overestimate, overrate, panegyrize, praise, protect, raise, recommend, regard, respect, sanction, shield, sustain, tend, tolerate, uphold, vindicate)

DISPATCH (→): *accelerate, address, advance, beam, bestow, consign, contribute, convey, courier, deliver, donate, drop, expedite, export, express, forward, give, hand, import, launch, mail, pack, pass, post, present, remit, render, resend, return, send, ship, shoot, transfer, transmit, transport* (≠ accept, acquire, beg, download, draw, earn, gain, garner, get, obtain, plead, procure, receive, request, secure, solicit, source)

DISPATCH (/): *accomplish, actualize, arrange, cease, clinch, close, complete, conclude, decide, determine, discharge, -discontinue, end, establish, finish, negotiate, perform, resolve, settle* (≠ activate, begin, birth, commence, establish, found, inaugurate, initiate, instigate, launch, originate, spur, start, trigger)

DISPATCH (/): *ace, annihilate, beat, best, better, break, bury, cap, checkmate, clobber, conquer, cream, crush, defeat, drub, eclipse, exceed, finish, flatten, lick, master, outdistance, outdo, outfight, outlast, outmaneuver, outperform, outrank, outsell, outshine, outstrip, overcome, overpower, overthrow, overwhelm, rout, ruin, score, shellac, skin, skunk, slaughter, smoke, subdue, subjugate, succeed, surmount, surpass, sweep, take, thrash, top, transcend, trim, trounce, unseat, upend, upset, upstage, vanquish, wallop, wax, whip, wrack, wreck* (≠ cede, concede, defend, forfeit, fortify, guard, maintain, preserve, protect, redeem, rescue, salvage, save, stabilize, strengthen, sustain, weather)

DISPATCH (/): *annihilate, assassinate, behead, butcher, claim, croak, decimate, depopulate, destroy, doom, eliminate, eradicate, euthanize, execute, exterminate, fell, finish, get, guillotine, kill, liquidate, martyr, massacre, mow, murder, orphan, shoot, slaughter, slay, smite, snipe, snuff, take, terminate, waste, zap* (≠ aid, animate, armor, assist, defend, guard, heal, mend, nurse, nurture, raise, repair, restore, resurrect, resuscitate, revive, save, secure, shelter, shield, survive, withstand)

DISPEL (/): *allay, banish, chase, clear, diffuse, disband, dismiss, disperse, disseminate, dissipate, drive, eliminate, exorcise, expel, isolate, part, rid, rout, scatter, segregate, separate, shed, split, spread, squander* (≠ affix, agglomerate, assemble, cluster, collect, concentrate, conglomerate, congregate, gather, glean, integrate, muster, pile, reintegrate, unify, unite)

DISPENSE (→): *administer, allocate, allot, allow, apportion, appropriate, assign, bestow, chunk, circulate, comp, contribute, deal, decant, diffuse, disburse, dish, disperse, disseminate, distribute, divide, divvy, dole, dollop, donate, dose, drizzle, force-feed, furnish, give, hand, inflict, inject, issue, mainline, measure, mete, overfeed, parcel, part, pass, pledge, portion, pour, proportion, prorate, provide, ration, reallocate, reapportion, redistribute, scatter, set, share, split, spread, supply, tender, tithe, trickle, yield* (≠ amass, begrudge, collect, debit, -decline, -deny, deprive, disallow, gather, guard, hoard, hold, keep, misallocate, pinch, -refuse, -reject, remove, reserve, scant, skimp, starve, stint, withdraw, withhold)

DISPENSE (→): *accomplish, administer, apply, assess, complete, deliver, discharge, effect, effectuate, enforce, execute, finagle, foist, fulfill, implement, impose, issue, levy, operate, perform, realize* (≠ abolish, arrest, can, check, control, crush, curb, demolish, extinguish, impede, inhibit, limit, quash, quell, quench, rein, repress, restrain, restrict, smother, snuff, squash, squelch, stifle, subdue, suppress)

DISPERSE (/): *break, broadcast, cast, circulate, deal, diffuse, disband, disburse, dismiss, dispel, dispense, disseminate, dissipate, dissolve, distribute, dole, isolate, melt, part, propagate, radiate, release, scatter, segregate, separate, split, spread, sprinkle, squander, strew, thin, toss* (≠ accumulate, affix, agglomerate, assemble, attach, call, cluster, collect, combine, compile, concentrate, conglomerate, congregate, conjure, garner, gather, glean, herd, hoard, integrate, keep, maintain, marry, reintegrate, reunite, scavenge, summon, unify, unite)

DISPIRIT (/): *afflict, appall, bother, browbeat, bully, chagrin, chill, cow, crush, damp, dampen, dash, daunt, deaden, debilitate, deflate, demoralize, demotivate, depress, -deter, disabuse, disappoint, disconcert, discourage, disenchant, dishearten, disillusion, dismay, dissatisfy, dissuade, distress, enfeeble, enlighten, frighten, frustrate, horrify, intimidate, irk, jade, sadden, scare, shake, suppress, trash-talk, trouble, try, undermine, unman, unnerve, vex, weaken, weigh, worry* (≠ animate, assure, boost, buoy, cheer, congratulate, embolden, encourage, energize, enliven, excite, fortify, galvanize, gladden, hearten, inspire, invigorate, lift, nerve, please, provoke, quicken, rally, reassure, reinforce, satisfy, steel, stimulate, stir, strengthen)

DISPLACE (←): *alter, bear, budge, carry, cart, convey, dislocate, dislodge, disturb, drive, flush, haul, lug, misplace, modify, move, relegate, relocate, remodel, remove, replace, reposition, revamp, shift, shuttle, supersede, supplant, tote, transfer, transmit, transplant, transport, transpose* (≠ anchor, embed, entrench, fix, freeze, implant, ingrain, lodge, moor, place, root, secure, set, situate, stabilize)

DISPLACE (/): *banish, -cold-shoulder, deport, dismiss, dispossess, eject, eliminate, evict, -exclude, -excommunicate, exile, expatriate, expel, flush,*

-ostracize, oust, -reject, relegate, -repudiate, -shun, -snub, -spurn, transport (≠ accept, admit, adopt, entertain, harbor, host, house, naturalize, rear, receive, repatriate, room, shelter, welcome)

DISPLACE (/): *banish, boot, bounce, can, cashier, chase, defrock, depose, deprive, dethrone, discharge, dislodge, dismiss, eject, evict, exorcise, expel, extrude, fire, force, oust, override, overthrow, -rebuff, remove, replace, retire, rout, sack, subvert, succeed, supersede, supplant, topple, unhorse, unmake, unseat, uproot, usurp* (≠ appoint, baptize, crown, designate, elect, enthrone, hire, inaugurate, induct, initiate, install, instate, invest, name, nominate, ordain, propose, throne)

DISPLAY (→): *blazon, boast, brandish, broadcast, concede, confirm, convince, divulge, exhibit, expose, flash, flaunt, flourish, parade, post, present, produce, promote, publicize, reveal, show, showcase, sport, telegraph, televise, trumpet, uncloak, uncover, unmask, unsheathe, unveil, wag, wave* (≠ camouflage, cloak, clothe, cloud, conceal, costume, cover, curtain, disguise, enshroud, hide, holster, hood, mask, obscure, occlude, occult, -omit, screen, sheathe, shield, shroud, spackle, veil)

DISPLAY (→): *advertise, air, announce, bare, bellow, betray, blaze, broadcast, circulate, communicate, declare, demonstrate, disclose, disseminate, evince, expose, exteriorize, externalize, manifest, placard, proclaim, project, publicize, reveal, show, showcase, sound, telegraph, trumpet, uncloak, uncover* (≠ belie, camouflage, cloak, cloud, conceal, costume, counterfeit, cover, disguise, distort, falsify, garble, gild, gloss, hide, mask, miscommunicate, misrepresent, obscure, occlude, rotate, twist, varnish, veil, whitewash)

DISPLEASE (/): *affront, aggravate, aggrieve, agitate, alienate, anger, annoy, antagonize, bother, bug, chagrin, curdle, depress, disaffect, disappoint, discompose, discontent, disgruntle, disgust, disoblige, disquiet, dissatisfy, disturb, enrage, estrange, exasperate, fret, frustrate, gall, harass, heckle, hurt, incense, infuriate, irk, irritate, nag, nauseate, needle, nettle, niggle, nitpick, nonplus, offend, peeve, perplex, perturb, pique, provoke, repel, revolt, rile, roil, sadden, sicken, troll, upset, vex, worry, zing* (≠ amuse, appease, baby, calm, coddle, compose, content, delight, entertain, flatter, gladden, grace, gratify, humor, hush, indulge, inspire, lull, mellow, mollify, oblige, pacify, placate, please, praise, romance, satisfy, settle, soothe, sugarcoat, thrill, tickle, tranquilize, woo, wow)

DISPROVE (/): *abnegate, abrogate, belie, break, bury, challenge, confound, confute, contest, contradict, contravene, controvert, crush, debate, debunk, defend, deflate, -deny, disabuse, disavow, discredit, discuss, dispute, double-check, doubt, explode, expose, falsify, gainsay, impugn, invalidate, mistrust, -negate, negative, oppose, overthrow, overturn, parry, pooh-pooh, puncture, query, question, rebut, recant, refute, rejoin, repeal, -repudiate, retract, scruple, shoot, subvert, weaken, withdraw* (≠ adduce, affirm, approve, attest, authenticate, back, buttress, certify, chronicle, claim, concede, confirm, convince, corroborate, credit, crosscheck, demonstrate, display, document, endorse, establish, evidence, evince, hide, identify, illustrate, manifest, notarize, praise, prove, record, rubber-stamp, show, strengthen, substantiate, support, suspect, testify, uphold, validate, verify, witness)

DISPUTE (/): *abnegate, abrogate, antagonize, argue, blast, challenge, combat, confront, confute, contend, contest, contradict, contrast, counter, counteract, debate, debunk, -deny, disavow, discredit, discuss, -disown, disprove, doubt, face, fight, hassle, impeach, impugn, invalidate, litigate, mistrust, -negate, oppose, oppugn, protest, query, question, rebut, refute, rejoin, -repudiate, resist, scruple, suspect, withstand, wrestle* (≠ abide, accept, accord, advocate, allow, approve, aúthorize, back, believe, certify, champion, consult, corroborate, defend, embrace, endorse, endure, further, indulge, permit, persuade, promote, recommend, sanction, shoulder, stomach, support, swallow, sway, tolerate, uphold, validate, verify, weather)

DISQUALIFY (/): *ban, banish, bar, blackball, blacklist, block, -boycott, constrain, control, curb, curtail, debilitate, -deny, disable, disallow, disapprove, disbar, eighty-six, eject, eliminate, eradicate, evict, except, excise, -exclude, -excommunicate, exile, expel, -forbid, handicap, -ignore, immobilize, impair, incapacitate, inhibit, invalidate, -nix, -omit, oppress, -ostracize, oust, outlaw, paralyze, -preclude, -prevent, -prohibit, proscribe, -refuse, -reject, relegate, remove, -renounce, -repudiate, restrain, restrict, suppress, suspend* (≠ accredit, add, aid, allow, approve, assist, authorize, certify, charter, empower, enable, encourage, entitle, fit, help, include, invest, legalize, mobilize, permit, prepare, qualify, ready, vest, weaponize, welcome)

DISREGARD (+): *absolve, acquit, clear, condone, disbelieve, -discount, exculpate, excuse, exonerate, explain, forgive, gloss, -ignore, justify, -overlook, pardon, rationalize, remit, spare, spin, vindicate, waive, whitewash* (≠ accuse, allege, ascertain, blame, charge, fault, finger, frame, heed, implicate, indict, mark, mind, note, prove, remember, verify)

-DISREGARD (/): *belittle, -blank, condemn, -cut, deprecate, deride, -despise, -disdain, dismiss, disparage, disrespect, drop, eliminate, -exclude, forget, -neglect, oust, -overlook, pass, -rebuff, -scorn, -slight, -snub, -spurn* (≠ accept, acknowledge, admire, approve, blandish, butter, compliment, credit, employ, esteem, flannel, flatter, gratify, greet, high-five, honor, ingratiate, love, praise, regard, respect, use)

-DISREGARD (/): *-abandon, -avoid, -bypass, challenge, contradict, contravene, counteract, defy, -disdain, disobey, fail, flout, forget, -forsake, gainsay, -ignore, miss, -neglect, -omit, oppose, -overlook, pooh-pooh, -refuse, -reject, -repudiate, scant, -scorn, skimp, -slight, slough, -spurn, subvert, trespass, violate* (≠ appreciate, attend, bemoan, cherish, clock, cultivate, detect, examine, eye, follow, foster, heed, lament, mark, mind, mourn, note, notice, nurse, nurture, obey, observe, pamper, prize, recognize, regard, regret, remark, remember, respect, scan, scope, scrutinize, serve, study, tend, treasure, value, watch)

DISRUPT (→): *-abort, -avert, block, breach, break, broach, check, end, foil, fracture, -frustrate, -halt, hamper, hinder, inhibit, intercept, interrupt, jog, jolt, jostle, monkey-wrench, obstruct, open, postpone, -preclude, -prevent, rupture, short-circuit, shunt, stop, stymie, suspend, -thwart* (≠ accelerate, aid, assist, brainstorm, catalyze, enable, encourage, expedite, facilitate, frogmarch, grease, hasten, help, lubricate, march, midwife, oil, quicken, rush, smooth, speed, spur)

DISRUPT (/):*agitate, alarm, bobble, botch, bungle, capsize, churn, clutter, confuse, derange, disarrange, disarray, discombobulate, discompose, disconcert, dishevel, disjoint, dislocate, disorder, disorganize, disturb, embroil, entangle, faze, flub, fluff, fumble, hamper, hash, impede, interrupt, jumble, louse, mess, mismatch, mix, muddle, muss, oppose, overthrow, perturb, protest, rattle, rile, roil, rumple, sabotage, scramble, shake, shelve, shuffle, snarl, spoil, stir, subvert, tangle, throw, topple, tousle, tumble, undercut, undermine, unnerve, unsettle, untidy, upset* (≠ adjust, align, arrange, array, brace, calibrate, calm, classify, codify, control, coordinate, dispose, equalize, fix, groom, humor, line, lull, marshal, mellow, methodize, mollify, order, organize, pace, pacify, placate, queue, range, ready, regiment, regulate, right, sort, spruce, stabilize, steady, straighten, systematize, systemize, tidy, tune, tweak, unscramble)

DISRUPT (/): *atomize, blast, break, burst, bust, chip, crack, crush, destroy, detonate, disintegrate, dismember, doom, explode, fracture, fragment, grind, implode, pop, powder, pulverize, reduce, rive, ruin, shatter, shiver, slice, smash, splinter, split, wreck, zap* (≠ doctor, fix, fuse, glue, heal, join, meld, melt, mend, patch, rebuild, recondition, reconstruct, reintegrate, renovate, repair, restore, unify, unite)

DISS (/): *abase, abuse, aggravate, anger, annoy, antagonize, arouse, badger, bait, bedevil, belittle, bother, burn, chafe, defame, demean, denigrate, discompose, disconcert, disgrace, disturb, enrage, envenom, exacerbate, exasperate, fret, frustrate, grate, harass, harry, hassle, humiliate, hurt, inflame, infuriate, injure, irk, irritate, jar, jeer, libel, malign, mock, nag, needle, nettle, offend, outrage, peeve, perturb, pester, pillory, plague, provoke, rankle, rattle, ridicule, rile, shame, slander, -slight, -snub, stain, sully, taint, taunt, tease, torment, trample, troll, trouble, upset, vex, violate, wound, wrong* (≠ admire, adore, appease, assuage, blandish, boost, cherish, commend, compliment, conciliate, congratulate, defend, dignify, disarm, flannel, flatter, gold-star, gratify, guard, high-five, ingratiate, mollify, pacify, placate, praise, prioritize, propitiate, protect, respect, support, treasure)

DISSATISFY (/): *affront, aggravate, aggrieve, agitate, alienate, anger, annoy, antagonize, bother, bug, chagrin, cheat, deceive, delude, depress, disaffect, disappoint, discompose, discontent, disenchant, disgruntle, disgust, disillusion, displease, disquiet, distress, disturb, enrage, estrange, exasperate, fail, fret, frustrate, gall, hurt, incense, irk, irritate, mock, nag,* *needle, nettle, nitpick, offend, peeve, perplex, perturb, provoke, repel, revolt, rile, roil, sadden, stiff, upset, vex, worry, zing* (≠ amuse, appease, baby, calm, coddle, compose, content, delight, divert, entertain, fulfill, gladden, grace, gratify, humor, hush, indulge, inspire, lull, mellow, mollify, nourish, nurture, pacify, pamper, placate, please, satisfy, soothe, thrill, tickle, tranquilize, treat)

DISSECT (/): *analyze, anatomize, assess, audit, benchmark, carve, categorize, check, cleave, cut, deconstruct, dichotomize, disarticulate, dismember, divide, examine, explore, inspect, investigate, joint, learn, prioritize, probe, quarter, rank, razor, read, saw, scan, scope, scrutinize, section, separate, sever, slash, slice, split, study, subdivide, sunder, survey, vet, vivisect* (≠ combine, connect, -discount, dismiss, -disregard, fix, fuse, generate, grow, heal, -ignore, meld, mend, misread, mistake, -overlook, rebuild, regenerate, repair, restore, sew, stitch, suture, unify, unite, weld)

DISSEMINATE (→): *advertise, announce, bellow, blaze, blazon, broadcast, bulletin, circulate, declare, diffuse, dish, disperse, dissipate, distribute, hype, plug, presell, proclaim, promulgate, propagate, publicize, publish, radiate, scatter, sow, spread, strew, telegraph, televise, trumpet* (≠ bury, cloak, cloud, collect, conceal, disguise, ensconce, gather, glean, hide, hoard, hush, keep, mask, mislead, muffle, obscure, -omit, silence, smother, stifle, store, veil, withhold)

DISSIPATE (/): *blow, cannibalize, consume, deplete, depredate, diffuse, disburse, drain, dump, exhaust, expend, fritter, impoverish, indulge, lard, lavish, leach, leech, lose, misspend, misuse, overfeed, overindulge, overspend, scatter, shoot, slather, spend, squander, waste* (≠ accumulate, bank, budget, collect, conserve, economize, gather, hoard, hog, invest, keep, monopolize, pickle, preserve, protect, retain, save, scant, scavenge, scrimp, skimp, stockpile, withhold)

DISSOLVE (+): *defrost, diffuse, flux, fuse, heat, liquefy, melt, pour, render, run, soften, stream, thaw, thin, warm, weaken* (≠ coagulate, concentrate, congeal, crystallize, freeze, harden, petrify, set, solidify, thicken)

DISSOLVE (/): *abrogate, adjourn, anatomize, annihilate, annul, atomize, -cancel, collapse, corrode, crumble, decimate, demolish, destroy, digest, disarm, discharge, -discontinue, disintegrate, dismiss, disorganize, disunite, divorce, doom, end, eradicate, erode, fracture, fragment, invalidate, loose, metabolize, mortify, -nullify, overthrow, postpone, pulverize, quash, repeal, revoke, ruin, rupture, scotch, separate, sever, shatter, shoot, spoil, suspend, terminate, unmake, vacate, -void, wrack, wreck* (≠ arm, beef, bolster, brace, brainstorm, buttress, concoct, continue, create, empower, enliven, fortify, harden, institute, invigorate, marry, prop, reinforce, resolve, stabilize, steady, steel, strengthen, support, sustain, temper, toughen, validate, weather, withstand)

DISSUADE (/): *advise, caution, contradict, counsel, counter, counteract, countercheck, curb, dampen, demotivate, derail, -deter, discourage,* *disincline, divert, exhort, faze, -frustrate, goad, hamper, hinder, impede, impel, induce, inhibit, malign, nobble, oppose, paralyze, -preclude, -prevent, prick, prompt, protest, repel, restrain, stifle, stop, stymie, throttle, -thwart, unsell, warn* (≠ accelerate, bribe, catalyze, convince, encourage, entice, excite, foment, grease, hasten, incite, incur, induce, instigate, lure, persuade, prod, rabble-rouse, spur, tantalize, tease, tempt, trigger, urge)

DISTANCE (/): *alienate, detach, disaffect, disassemble, disassociate, disconnect, disengage, disentangle, disintegrate, disjoin, disjoint, dissolve, disunite, divide, divorce, estrange, insulate, isolate, orphan, outdo, outpace, outrun, outstrip, part, pass, remove, resolve, seclude, segregate, separate, sequester, sever, split, sunder, uncouple, unlink, unyoke, withdraw* (≠ accumulate, assemble, associate, attach, bind, blend, cement, close, combine, connect, corral, couple, fasten, fuse, gather, herd, hybridize, integrate, invite, join, knit, link, mingle, mix, muster, network, rally, reunite, stick, synthesize, unify, unite, welcome, weld, wrangle)

DISTILL (←): *brew, clarify, clean, cleanse, clear, concentrate, condense, cook, cut, decontaminate, derive, disinfect, evaporate, express, extract, ferment, filter, fine, infuse, leach, perfect, precipitate, press, process, purge, purify, rarefy, rectify, refine, sanitize, screen, sieve, sift, sublimate, trim, vaporize, wash* (≠ adulterate, begrime, besmirch, blend, churn, cloud, contaminate, defile, dirty, dull, foul, froth, infect, mix, muddle, muddy, poison, pollute, soil, sully, taint)

DISTINGUISH (←): *analyze, catch, clock, consult, define, descry, detect, differentiate, dig, discern, discover, eye, eyeball, flash, focus, identify, individualize, know, mark, note, notice, observe, perceive, read, recognize, remark, scan, scope, scrutinize, separate, signify, specialize, spot, spy* (≠ baffle, bewilder, -blank, blind, -bypass, conceal, confound, confuse, connect, deceive, disguise, -disregard, equate, forget, fudge, hide, identify, lose, mask, mislead, misplace, miss, mistake, misunderstand, muddle, mystify, -neglect, -overlook, perplex, puzzle, relate, trick, wholesale)

DISTINGUISH (+): *acclaim, acknowledge, admire, adore, apotheosize, applaud, approve, blandish, celebrate, cherish, commend, compliment, deify, devote, dignify, earn, endorse, ennoble, eulogize, exalt, extol, flatter, glorify, honor, idolize, immortalize, praise, pray, recommend, respect, revere, sanction, venerate, win, worship* (≠ abase, abuse, belittle, blast, boo, cheapen, -cut, defame, defile, deflate, degrade, despoil, devaluate, devalue, diminish, -discount, disgrace, dishonor, disrespect, embarrass, -ignore, ill-treat, lower, malign, maltreat, misuse, mock, pare, reduce, -scorn, shame, shave, -spurn, trash, trim, violate, vulgarize)

DISTINGUISH (+): *ascertain, categorize, characterize, classify, collate, decide, deduce, demarcate, determine, diagnose, differentiate, divide, estimate, extricate, finger, grade, identify, individualize, judge, know, label, mark, monogram, name, notice, package, part, particularize, pinpoint, place, prioritize, profile, qualify, recognize, select, separate, sift,* *slot, sort, specify, spot, stamp, tag* (≠ anonymize, blend, churn, compare, conflate, confound, confuse, consolidate, misdiagnose, mislabel, mistake, mix, muddle, predetermine, puzzle, shuffle, synthesize, unify)

DISTORT (/): *alter, bend, buckle, callous, change, coarsen, coil, compress, contort, crimp, crumple, crush, curl, curve, deface, deform, disfigure, dishevel, gnarl, hamper, jumble, kink, knot, loop, mangle, mar, melt, misshape, rack, ripple, rotate, screw, spiral, squash, squinch, squish, stretch, torment, torture, twine, twist, wad, warp, wiggle, wind, wreathe, wrench, wrest, wriggle, wring* (≠ align, beautify, build, burnish, clear, equalize, even, flatten, improve, keep, level, plane, polish, preserve, rectify, refine, right, sand, shine, smooth, straighten, unbend, uncrumple, uncurl, untwist)

DISTORT (/): *belie, bend, bias, bleep, bowdlerize, camouflage, censor, churn, cloak, clothe, cloud, color, complicate, con, conceal, confound, confuse, cook, corrupt, costume, deceive, disguise, doctor, double-talk, elaborate, embellish, fake, falsify, fudge, garble, gloss, harshen, mangle, mask, miscommunicate, misconstrue, misdiagnose, mishear, misinterpret, mislead, misread, misrepresent, misstate, mistake, mistranslate, mix, muddle, mutate, mystify, obscure, pervert, predetermine, prejudge, prejudice, pretend, redact, rephrase, scam, scramble, skew, slant, spin, twist, veil, warp, whitewash* (≠ authorize, clarify, decipher, deduce, detect, diagnose, elucidate, explain, expose, illuminate, illustrate, interpret, profile, prove, realize, reveal, simplify, suss, unskew, vindicate)

DISTRACT (+): *absorb, amuse, beguile, charm, cheer, delight, detract, -disregard, divert, engage, engross, entertain, enthrall, gladden, interest, occupy, please, regale, relax, sidetrack, stall, thrill, tickle, wow* (≠ bore, concentrate, consider, displease, focus, harass, irk, irritate, regard, repel, sadden, sicken, tire, vex, weary, worry)

DISTRACT (/): *aggravate, agitate, ail, alarm, anger, annoy, bedevil, bother, bug, chafe, chivy, concern, confound, daunt, deflect, demoralize, discomfort, discourage, dishearten, dismay, dispirit, disquiet, distress, disturb, embarrass, exasperate, exercise, fret, fuss, gall, harass, harry, haunt, irk, irritate, madden, mortify, nag, nettle, nitpick, nonplus, peeve, perturb, pester, pique, plague, rile, torment, undo, unhinge, unnerve, unsettle, upset, vex* (≠ allay, alleviate, appease, assuage, calm, comfort, compose, favor, help, humor, hush, lull, mellow, mollify, pacify, placate, propitiate, quiet, relax, settle, soothe, tranquilize)

DISTRACT (/): *abash, addle, befuddle, bewilder, blind, confound, confuse, daze, derail, derange, discomfit, discompose, disconcert, disorient, disturb, embarrass, faze, fluster, frazzle, freak, jar, mislead, muddle, perplex, puzzle, rattle, shake, throw, trouble, unbalance, unhinge, upset, worry* (≠ clarify, compose, concentrate, decipher, detect, floodlight, focus, illuminate, instruct, settle, simplify, steady, untangle)

DISTRESS (/): *abash, afflict, aggravate, agitate, agonize, ail, alarm, anger, anguish, annoy, appall, badger, bedevil, bother, bug, chafe, concern,* *confound, confuse, daunt, demoralize, demotivate, depress, derail, discomfit, discomfort, discompose, disconcert, discountenance, discourage, dishearten, dismay, dispirit, disquiet, distemper, distract, disturb, dizzy, dog, embarrass, exasperate, exercise, faze, fluster, frazzle, freak, fret, fuss, gall, gravel, grieve, harass, harrow, harry, hassle, haunt, heckle, hector, hurt, irk, irritate, jar, mortify, nag, needle, nettle, nitpick, nonplus, pain, peeve, persecute, perturb, pester, plague, rankle, rattle, rile, rock, sadden, shake, sweat, tease, torment, traumatize, trouble, undo, unhinge, unnerve, unsettle, upset, vex, worry* (≠ allay, alleviate, amuse, appease, assuage, balance, brace, calm, center, comfort, compose, conciliate, entertain, humor, hush, lull, mellow, mollify, pacify, placate, propitiate, quiet, reassure, relax, settle, soothe, stabilize, steady, tranquilize)

DISTRIBUTE (→): *accord, administer, allocate, allot, allow, apportion, appropriate, assign, award, bestow, budget, chunk, circulate, comp, contribute, deal, diffuse, disburse, dispense, disperse, disseminate, divide, divvy, dole, dollop, donate, drizzle, earmark, force-feed, furnish, give, grant, hand, issue, measure, mete, meter, overfeed, parcel, part, pledge, portion, pour, proportion, prorate, provide, provision, ration, reallocate, reapportion, reassign, redistribute, reprovision, reserve, scatter, set, share, split, spread, supply, tender, trickle, yield* (≠ appropriate, arrogate, begrudge, confiscate, -decline, -deny, deprive, disallow, keep, misallocate, pinch, -refuse, -reject, retain, scant, skimp, stint, withhold)

DISTRIBUTE (+): *alphabetize, array, assort, catalog, categorize, class, classify, clump, cluster, codify, compartment, compartmentalize, cull, digest, dispose, distinguish, file, grade, group, hierarchize, identify, index, list, marshal, order, organize, peg, pigeonhole, place, prioritize, range, rank, recategorize, reclassify, recognize, refer, regroup, relegate, screen, separate, set, shelve, sieve, sift, slot, sort, subcategorize, systematize, type, winnow* (≠ churn, confuse, disarrange, dishevel, jumble, lump, misclassify, missort, mistype, mix, scramble, stir)

DISTRUST (/): *attend, beware, cross-examine, disbelieve, discern, -discount, discredit, doubt, dread, fear, grill, heed, interrogate, mark, mind, mistrust, -negate, note, notice, observe, perceive, question, scruple, suspect, watch, wonder* (≠ accept, anticipate, assume, assure, await, believe, consult, count, detect, determine, -discount, -disregard, expect, expose, hope, -ignore, imagine, miss, -overlook, presume, suppose, trust) **(¿) ABSTRACTION ALERT. Concrete goals essential!**

DISTURB (→): *alter, bear, budge, cant, capsize, carry, cart, collapse, confuse, convey, derange, dethrone, disarrange, disarray, discompose, dishevel, dislocate, disorder, disorganize, displace, distort, drive, haul, jumble, lug, modify, move, muddle, oust, poke, prod, redo, refashion, relegate, relocate, remake, remodel, remove, replace, reposition, revamp, revise, rework, rock, scramble, shift, shock, shunt, startle, stir, supersede, supplant, tire, topple, tote, touch, transfer, transmit, transplant, transport, transpose, trouble, unhorse, unseat, unsettle, upset, vary*

(≠ affix, anchor, arrange, attach, blunt, bolster, brace, buffer, calm, comfort, embed, entrench, fix, freeze, glue, humor, hush, implant, ingrain, lodge, lull, mellow, mollify, moor, organize, pacify, placate, reassure, root, secure, set, settle, sort, stabilize, steady)

DISTURB (→): *accost, annoy, antagonize, beleaguer, beset, besiege, bother, bug, burden, chaff, chivy, confront, defy, dement, derail, discommode, discompose, disconcert, disrupt, distract, embarrass, enrage, fluster, gate-crash, humiliate, incense, incommode, inconvenience, inflame, infuriate, interrupt, invade, irk, madden, molest, mortify, outlast, pester, provoke, rile, shame, sidetrack, threaten, trespass, trouble, violate, waylay, wrong* (≠ -avoid, -bypass, comfort, console, content, delight, disarm, -disregard, forget, gladden, gratify, -ignore, leave, miss, mollify, oblige, -overlook, placate, please, satisfy, -shun, -sidestep, -slight, -snub, thrill)

DISTURB (/): *agitate, blend, blur, capsize, churn, clutter, confound, confuse, convulse, derange, diffuse, disarrange, disarray, discompose, dishevel, disjoint, dislocate, disorder, disorganize, displace, disrupt, embroil, entangle, harshen, hash, jumble, mess, mislay, misplace, mix, muddle, muss, perturb, pillage, ransack, rifle, ripple, roil, roughen, ruffle, rummage, rumple, scatter, scramble, shuffle, snarl, stir, swirl, tangle, toss, tousle, trouble, tumble, unsettle, untidy, upset, whip, whisk* (≠ adjust, align, arrange, array, calibrate, catalog, categorize, classify, codify, coordinate, dispose, equalize, fix, groom, gussy, marshal, methodize, order, organize, pace, prioritize, queue, range, regiment, regulate, shelve, slot, spruce, straighten, systematize, tidy, tune, tweak, unscramble)

DISTURB (/): *abash, addle, afflict, affront, aggravate, agitate, ail, alarm, amaze, anger, annoy, appall, arouse, astound, badger, bedevil, bother, bug, chafe, complicate, concern, confound, confuse, daunt, demoralize, demotivate, depress, derail, derange, devil, discombobulate, discomfit, discomfort, discompose, disconcert, discountenance, discourage, dishearten, dismay, disorient, dispirit, displease, disquiet, distemper, distract, distress, dizzy, dog, dun, earbash, embarrass, exasperate, excite, exercise, faze, fluster, frazzle, freak, fret, frighten, fuss, gall, get, gnaw, grate, grieve, harass, harry, hassle, haunt, heckle, hector, henpeck, infest, irk, irritate, jar, jolt, molest, mortify, muddle, nag, needle, nettle, nitpick, nonplus, outrage, pain, peeve, perplex, persecute, perturb, pester, pique, plague, provoke, puzzle, rankle, rasp, rattle, rile, rock, roil, rouse, ruffle, sadden, shake, sorrow, startle, stir, tease, tire, torment, touch, trouble, undo, unhinge, unnerve, unsettle, upset, vex, worry* (≠ allay, alleviate, appease, assuage, calm, charm, coddle, comfort, compose, conciliate, delight, ease, entertain, favor, gratify, humor, hush, indulge, lull, mellow, mollify, oblige, pacify, placate, please, pleasure, propitiate, quiet, reassure, relax, satisfy, settle, soothe, stabilize, steady, sugarcoat, thrill, tranquilize, wow)

-DITCH (/): *-abandon, abdicate, abolish, annihilate, cant, chuck, -cold-shoulder, -cut, -desert, discard, dismiss, drop, dump, eighty-six, eject, eliminate, empty, eradicate, exorcise, expunge, exterminate, extinguish, extirpate, -forsake, high-hat, jettison, jilt, junk, leave, liquidate, lose, maroon, offload, pitch, plonk, -quit, -reject, remove, scrap, shed, shuck,*

-slight, -snub, -spurn, toss, unload (≠ adopt, archive, befriend, carry, chauffeur, conserve, embalm, embrace, employ, hoard, hold, keep, latch, pile, preserve, remainder, retain, save, stack, stock, store, take, utilize, welcome)

DIVERT (→): *alter, -avert, bend, change, curve, deflect, distract, funnel, intercept, modify, move, obstruct, rechannel, redirect, refocus, refract, reorient, reroute, reverse, rotate, shift, shunt, sidetrack, stall, sway, swerve, swing, switch, swivel, transfer, turn, twist, wheel, whip, whirl, zigzag* (≠ aim, chair, concentrate, direct, focus, insist, maintain, preserve, pursue, seek, stay, sustain, target)

DIVERT (←): *absorb, amuse, appease, beguile, bewitch, busy, captivate, charm, cheer, coddle, comfort, conciliate, console, content, delight, distract, enchant, engage, engross, entertain, enthrall, fascinate, gladden, gratify, grip, humor, hypnotize, immerse, indulge, infantilize, interest, intrigue, involve, mesmerize, mollify, mollycoddle, oblige, occupy, overindulge, pacify, pamper, placate, please, pleasure, propitiate, razzle-dazzle, regale, relax, slay, solace, soothe, spoil, thrill, tickle, wow* (≠ aggravate, anger, annoy, -balk, bore, bother, bug, chafe, chaff, dampen, deaden, depress, disappoint, disenchant, disturb, drain, dull, enervate, exasperate, exhaust, fatigue, fret, gall, harass, harry, heckle, irk, irritate, jade, nag, needle, nettle, nitpick, numb, peeve, perturb, pester, pique, rankle, sadden, sedate, stifle, tire, underwhelm, upset, vex, wear, weary, worry)

DIVIDE (→): *administer, allocate, allot, allow, apportion, appropriate, assign, bestow, budget, chunk, circulate, comminute, contribute, deal, diffuse, disburse, dispense, disperse, disseminate, distribute, divvy, dole, donate, furnish, hand, issue, measure, mete, parcel, part, pledge, portion, proportion, provide, ration, redistribute, scatter, share, split, spread, supply, tender, tithe* (≠ accumulate, acquire, begrudge, collect, conserve, -decline, -deny, deprive, disallow, hoard, hog, hold, keep, misallocate, monopolize, obtain, pinch, -refuse, -reject, retain, scant, scavenge, skimp, starve, stash, stint, stockpile, stow, withhold)

DIVIDE (+): *alphabetize, arrange, array, assort, catalog, categorize, class, classify, codify, compartment, compartmentalize, cull, digest, dispose, distinguish, distribute, file, grade, group, hierarchize, identify, index, list, marshal, order, organize, peg, pigeonhole, place, polarize, prioritize, range, rank, recategorize, reclassify, recognize, refer, regiment, regroup, relegate, screen, segregate, separate, set, shelve, sieve, sift, slot, sort, subcategorize, systematize, type, winnow* (≠ blend, churn, confuse, disarrange, jumble, lump, meld, misclassify, mistype, mix, muddle, scramble)

DIVIDE (/): *alienate, bisect, break, chunk, cleave, cut, detach, disaffect, disassemble, disassociate, disconnect, disengage, disentangle, disintegrate, disjoin, disjoint, dissect, dissolve, disunite, divorce, estrange, fracture, halve, insulate, isolate, orphan, part, partition, polarize, pull,* *quarter, rend, rip, rive, rupture, seclude, segment, segregate, separate, sequester, sever, split, subdivide, sunder, tear, uncouple, unlink, unravel, untie, unyoke* (≠ accumulate, add, assemble, associate, attach, augment, bind, blend, cement, close, combine, connect, couple, double, fasten, fuse, hybridize, integrate, join, knit, link, mingle, mix, mortar, multiply, network, reintegrate, reunite, stick, synthesize, treble, triple, unify, unite, weld)

DIVINE (+): *alert, anticipate, apprehend, augur, caution, conjecture, consult, deduce, discern, envision, forebode, forecast, foresee, foreshadow, foretell, forewarn, guess, harbinger, herald, infer, intuit, outguess, perceive, portend, predict, profile, prognosticate, prophesy, reveal, soothsay, suppose, surmise, suspect, understand, warn* (≠ ascertain, assure, bemoan, calculate, deduce, demonstrate, detect, determine, ensure, establish, guarantee, insure, investigate, lament, narrate, prove, recount, regret, relate, report, settle, verify, warrant)

DIVORCE (/): *-abandon, annul, -cancel, detach, disconnect, disjoin, dissolve, disunite, divide, estrange, -forsake, isolate, jilt, -nullify, part, -reject, -repudiate, separate, sever, split, sunder, unmarry* (≠ betroth, bind, cement, combine, connect, couple, court, fuse, join, link, marry, meld, reunite, unite, wed, weld, win, woo)

DIVULGE (→): *admit, advertise, amplify, announce, bare, bellow, betray, blab, blazon, blurt, brandish, broadcast, bulletin, circulate, clue, communicate, concede, confess, confide, debunk, declare, disclose, discover, dish, disinter, disseminate, email, exhibit, expose, flaunt, highlight, hype, impart, inform, leak, magnify, message, placard, post, proclaim, promote, promulgate, prove, publicize, publish, relate, reveal, share, shout, showcase, sound, spill, spotlight, squeal, talk, telegraph, tell, text, trumpet, uncloak, unclothe, uncover, undrape, unearth, unmask, unveil, verify, vouchsafe* (≠ befog, belie, bleep, bluff, bullshit, camouflage, cheat, cloak, clothe, cloud, con, conceal, costume, cover, darken, deceive, defraud, disguise, eclipse, enshroud, gild, gloss, hide, keep, mask, obscure, overshadow, scam, secrete, shade, shroud, spackle, stash, trick, varnish, veil, whitewash)

DIZZY (/): *addle, agitate, befuddle, bemuse, bewilder, bother, confound, confuse, daze, derange, discompose, disconcert, disorient, disquiet, disturb, embarrass, faze, flap, flummox, fluster, inebriate, intoxicate, muddle, perplex, puzzle, rattle, razzle-dazzle, ruffle, stir, thrill, unbalance, unnerve, unsettle, upset* (≠ alleviate, balance, bolster, brace, calm, center, compose, hallucinate, help, humor, lull, mellow, mitigate, moderate, mollify, pacify, placate, settle, sober, soothe, stabilize, steady)

DOCTOR (+): *administer, aid, alleviate, attend, bandage, cure, diagnose, dose, drug, fix, heal, hospitalize, medicate, mend, nurse, overhaul, patch, physic, prescribe, quarantine, rebuild, recondition, reconstruct, rectify, rehabilitate, remedy, repair, revamp, stitch, strengthen, supply, support, treat* (≠ abuse, afflict, damage, deform, disfigure, harm, harshen, hurt, indispose, infect, injure, maim, mangle, misdiagnose, mutilate, ruin, sicken, weaken, welt, wound, wreck)

DOCTOR (+): *acclimate, acclimatize, accommodate, accustom, adapt, adjust, aid, align, alter, ameliorate, attune, automate, bend, better, calibrate, case-harden, condition, convert, correct, cure, customize, decorate, edit, enhance, enrich, equip, establish, familiarize, fashion, fiddle, fine-tune, fit, fix, flavor, freshen, furbish, gear, habituate, harden, harmonize, heal, help, improve, inure, maintain, marinate, match, mechanize, mend, model, modify, motorize, naturalize, optimize, orient, overhaul, pace, patch, pattern, perfect, phase, prepare, preserve, prime, punctuate, readapt, readjust, ready, realign, rebuild, recast, reclaim, reconceive, reconceptualize, recondition, reconstruct, recover, rectify, recycle, redesign, redevelop, redo, reengineer, refashion, refine, refit, refocus, refresh, refurbish, regenerate, register, regulate, rehearse, reinvent, reinvigorate, rejigger, rejuvenate, remake, remodel, renew, renovate, reorient, repair, rephrase, restimulate, restore, resuscitate, revamp, revise, revitalize, revive, rework, richen, rig, right, root, sculpt, season, service, settle, shape, spice, square, stimulate, suit, sustain, tailor, toughen, transform, tune, weaponize* (≠ blemish, break, cripple, damage, deface, disable, disfigure, efface, flaw, harm, harshen, hurt, impair, injure, maim, mangle, mar, misadjust, monkey-wrench, mutilate, ruin, sabotage, scotch, scupper, spoil, subvert, undermine, vandalize, wreck)

DOCTOR (/): *adulterate, alter, calibrate, change, cloud, contort, cook, deacon, debase, dilute, disguise, distort, exaggerate, falsify, fiddle, fudge, game, garble, gloss, manipulate, massage, minimize, misconstrue, misinterpret, misquote, misread, misreport, misrepresent, misstate, pervert, rephrase, slant, twist, weight* (≠ accentuate, amplify, analyze, assess, audit, balance, benchmark, categorize, check, confirm, examine, inspect, investigate, prove, read, reinvestigate, review, scrutinize, test, verify)

DOCTOR (/): *administer, contaminate, corrupt, cut, defile, dilute, dope, dose, drug, foul, harm, infect, lace, load, pollute, soil, spike, spoil, sully, taint, vitiate, water, weaken* (≠ clean, cleanse, concentrate, decontaminate, filter, fix, purge, purify, remedy, sift)

DOCUMENT (+): *chart, chronicle, cite, detail, enter, graph, inscribe, jot, journalize, keep, list, log, mark, minute, notate, notch, note, record, register, report, research, score, track, transcribe* (≠ anonymize, bury, censor, conceal, delete, eradicate, erase, expunge, forget, hide, -ignore, -neglect, obliterate, redact, remove)

DOCUMENT (+): *adduce, attest, authenticate, back, buttress, certify, clinch, confirm, corroborate, crosscheck, demonstrate, detect, determine, establish, evidence, evince, identify, nail, notarize, prove, record, reference, settle, substantiate, support, sustain, uphold, validate, verify, witness* (≠ allege, assume, challenge, conjecture, debate, debunk, discredit, -disown, disprove, dispute, distrust, doubt, guess, hint, invalidate, presume, rebut, refute, scruple, surmise, suspect, wonder)

-DODGE (/): *-avert, -avoid, beat, -blank, -bypass, -circumvent, deflect, detour, disobey, -disregard, divert, -duck, -elude, -end-run, -escape,*

-eschew, -evade, -flee, flout, -ignore, -obviate, outflank, outrun, parry, -prevent, shake, shift, -shirk, shortcut, -shun, -sidestep, skirt, subvert, ward (≠ accept, buttonhole, catch, chase, contact, contract, court, embrace, follow, incur, keep, obey, observe, pursue, seek, waylay, welcome, win, woo, wow)

DOG (→): *accompany, bird-dog, chaperone, chase, escort, eye, follow, harry, haunt, hound, hunt, observe, plague, pursue, retrace, run, seek, shadow, spoor, stalk, tag, tail, trace, track, trail, trouble, watch, worry* (≠ -abandon, -bypass, dismiss, -disregard, -ditch, -forsake, guide, head, lead, lose, miss, mistake, pilot, -scorn, -shun, skirt, spearhead, steer)

DOMESTICATE (+): *acclimatize, accustom, arrest, assimilate, barber, block, bottle, break, breed, bridle, bust, cage, calm, check, choke, collar, conquer, constrain, contain, control, corral, correct, curb, discipline, dominate, enslave, familiarize, farm, gag, gentle, govern, groom, habituate, hamper, handcuff, harness, herd, hinder, hitch, hold, housebreak, housetrain, humble, impede, incorporate, inhibit, integrate, interrupt, keep, lasso, leash, master, measure, mellow, mince, mitigate, moderate, muffle, mute, muzzle, naturalize, obstruct, overcome, pacify, program, quell, raise, ranch, reclaim, rectify, regulate, rein, repress, restrain, rule, school, silence, sink, smother, soften, squelch, stifle, stop, strangle, subdue, subjugate, suppress, tame, teach, temper, train, vanquish, whip, whup, wrangle, yoke* (≠ -abandon, abuse, agitate, air, brutalize, craze, dehumanize, deprogram, enrage, express, inflame, infuriate, liberate, loose, loosen, lose, maltreat, menace, -neglect, release, savage, scare, terrorize, threaten, unhinge, unleash, upset, vent, victimize)

DOMINATE (→): *annihilate, antagonize, bar, beat, best, better, blackmail, block, bluff, boss, break, browbeat, bully, checkmate, choreograph, clobber, coerce, command, conquer, control, coordinate, crush, defeat, demand, dictate, direct, discipline, domineer, drub, eclipse, enslave, execute, govern, grasp, grip, handle, harness, head, hinder, hold, impede, influence, inform, instruct, intimidate, lead, lick, manage, manipulate, master, menace, monopolize, muscle, nobble, obstruct, oppress, orchestrate, order, outlast, outmaneuver, outperform, outrank, outshine, outthink, overcome, overpower, override, overrule, oversee, overshadow, pacify, pilot, provoke, quash, quell, railroad, repress, rout, rule, run, sandbag, scotch, shrink, silence, skunk, smash, smother, snuff, squash, squelch, steamroller, steer, subdue, subject, subjugate, subordinate, supervise, suppress, sway, thrash, threaten, train, trash-talk, trounce, trump, tyrannize, vanquish* (≠ abide, accept, aggrandize, amplify, augment, baby, back, bear, bolster, boost, calm, challenge, coach, coddle, concede, contest, contradict, cosset, counteract, defend, defer, defy, develop, discharge, elevate, emancipate, enfranchise, enhance, enlarge, exalt, expand, extend, extol, follow, forfeit, free, glorify, heighten, highlight, humor, hype, illuminate, improve, increase, indulge, liberate, lull, magnify, manumit, maximize, mellow, mind, mollify, nurture, obey, oppose, pacify, pamper, placate, plug, promote, protect, publicize, release, relinquish, short-circuit, showcase, soften, spoil, spotlight, spring, support, surrender, survive, unbind, uncage, unchain, unfetter, uplift, weaken, yield)

DOMINATE (→): *abut, best, bestride, climb, command, dwarf, eclipse, face, front, menace, mount, overhang, overlook, overshadow, straddle, survey, threaten* (≠ aid, augment, back, bolster, boost, elevate, support, sustain, underpin)

DONATE (→): *accord, administer, aid, allot, allow, assign, assist, attribute, award, bankroll, benefit, bequeath, bestow, board, cater, clothe, confer, consign, contribute, deliver, deploy, devote, disburse, dispense, dole, endow, expend, extend, feed, fork, fuel, fund, furnish, gift, give, grant, hand, help, impart, issue, lavish, lend, mete, offer, outlay, overpay, patronize, pay, pledge, present, provide, ration, regale, reinforce, reload, render, replenish, sacrifice, send, serve, share, shower, submit, subscribe, supply, tender, underwrite, volunteer* (≠ accept, advance, bogart, cheat, clutch, commercialize, commodify, debit, -deny, deprive, disinherit, -disown, embezzle, filch, grab, grasp, grip, hoard, hog, hold, keep, lend, leverage, loan, misappropriate, monetize, monopolize, pilfer, pocket, preserve, purchase, purloin, remove, request, retain, rob, save, scant, secure, sell, skim, skimp, stash, steal, stiff, stint, stockpile, swindle, swipe, thieve, underpay, withdraw, withhold)

DOSE (→): *administer, allocate, anesthetize, bestow, chloroform, disburse, dispense, distribute, doctor, drug, etherize, force-feed, furnish, immunize, inject, inoculate, issue, lace, mainline, medicate, narcotize, overdose, physic, pour, prescribe, provide, sedate, share, sniff, spike, stick, stupefy, supply, tranquilize, treat, vaccinate* (≠ afflict, begrudge, cleanse, -decline, -deny, deprive, disallow, expel, extract, infect, injure, palm, pinch, purge, -refuse, -reject, remove, scant, skimp, skip, stint, vomit, withdraw, withhold, wound)

DOUBLE-CROSS (/): *-abandon, abuse, backstab, beguile, betray, bluff, cheat, con, cozen, cross, deceive, defraud, delude, -desert, double-deal, double-talk, dupe, embezzle, exploit, fiddle, fleece, fool, -forsake, hoodwink, humbug, juggle, mislead, mistreat, outwit, rook, scam, screw, sell, shaft, skin, snooker, snow, split, stiff, sting, sucker, swindle, torment, trick, two-time, victimize, wrong* (≠ aid, confess, defend, expose, guarantee, guard, help, honor, maintain, pledge, preserve, promise, protect, rescue, respect, reveal, safeguard, salvage, save, secure, shield, swear)

DOUBT (/): *assume, challenge, cross-examine, debunk, -deny, disbelieve, -discount, discredit, disprove, distrust, dread, fancy, fear, feel, gather, grill, guess, imagine, impugn, infer, interrogate, invalidate, mistrust, -negate, presume, question, reckon, scruple, suppose, surmise, suspect, wonder* (≠ accept, await, believe, buy, consult, defend, detect, determine, discover, ensure, guarantee, insure, know, maintain, pledge, promise, prove, respect, swear, trust, validate, verify, vindicate, warrant) **(¿) ABSTRACTION ALERT. Concrete goals essential!**

DOUSE (→): *bathe, bedew, bedraggle, damp, dampen, deluge, dip, drench, drown, -duck, dunk, engulf, flood, flush, hose, humidify, hydrate, imbrue, imbue, immerse, impregnate, infuse, inundate, irrigate, lave, mist, moisten, moisturize, overflow, plunge, puddle, quench, rehydrate, rinse, saturate, shower, slop, slosh, sluice, soak, sop, souse, spatter, splash, splatter, sprinkle, squench, steep, submerge, swamp, syrup, thrust, wash, water, waterlog, wet* (≠ barbecue, broil, dehumidify, dehydrate, desiccate, drip-dry, drizzle, dry, evaporate, parch, scorch, sear, staunch, towel, trickle, wipe, wring)

DOUSE (/): *blanket, choke, extinguish, quench, smother, snuff, stamp, stub, suffocate* (≠ barbecue, burn, fire, ignite, inflame, kindle, light, scorch, singe, torch)

DOWN (←): *bolt, chew, consume, devour, dispatch, drink, eat, engulf, finish, gnaw, gobble, gorge, gulp, guzzle, imbibe, ingest, lap, lick, mouth, munch, nibble, nosh, scarf, sip, snarf, swallow, wolf* (≠ assemble, belch, choke, concoct, cook, create, -decline, disgorge, excrete, expel, make, offer, prepare, -refuse, -reject, spew, splutter, vomit)

DOWN (/): *bang, bash, beat, belt, bludgeon, clobber, concuss, conk, crash, defeat, drop, fell, flatten, floor, hammer, hit, jab, knock, level, mow, overthrow, overwhelm, paste, poke, pound, prostrate, punch, slam, slap, slug, smack, smite, sock, steamroller, swat, swipe, thump, thwack, topple, unhorse, unseat, wallop, whack, whale* (≠ assemble, bolster, brace, build, buttress, construct, elevate, erect, fabricate, fling, guard, launch, lift, maintain, pitch, preserve, protect, raise, shield, steady, throw, toss)

DOWNGRADE (/): *abase, abridge, attenuate, bastardize, belittle, bench, bestialize, break, cheapen, clip, compress, condense, contract, curtail, cut, debase, declass, decrease, decry, de-escalate, defile, deflate, degrade, demarcate, demonetize, demote, denigrate, deplete, depose, depreciate, depress, deprive, devaluate, devalue, diminish, -discount, disparage, downsize, drain, erode, humble, lessen, lighten, lowball, lower, minimize, moderate, pare, reduce, relegate, shave, shorten, shrink, sideline, sink, slash, squeeze, strip, trim, truncate, underbid, underestimate, underprice, underrate, undervalue, vulgarize, wither* (≠ accentuate, accrue, amplify, appreciate, augment, bloat, boost, commend, dignify, elevate, emphasize, enhance, fetishize, honor, increase, inflate, magnify, monetize, optimize, overestimate, overhaul, overprice, overrate, overvalue, prioritize, promote, rarefy, rectify, refine, revolutionize, upgrade)

DOWNGRADE (/): *abase, break, bust, can, cashier, chasten, chastise, debase, degrade, demean, demote, denounce, dismiss, downsize, fire, humble, humiliate, lower, reduce, relegate, sack, strip, terminate, topple* (≠ advance, advocate, aid, assist, back, boost, catapult, champion, elevate, encourage, endorse, exalt, foster, further, help, hire, honor, nurture, prioritize, promote, raise, recommend, sponsor, support, upgrade)

DOWNPLAY (/): *abridge, belittle, bury, compress, conceal, contract, cover, decrease, demean, deprecate, depreciate, diminish, -discount, -disdain,* *disguise, dismiss, disparage, -disregard, downgrade, -exclude, forget, hide, -ignore, lessen, lower, marginalize, minimize, -overlook, reduce, relegate, shrink, sideline, -slight, soft-pedal, spin, trivialize, underemphasize, underestimate, underplay, underrate, understate, undervalue* (≠ amplify, belabor, color, dramatize, embellish, embroider, emphasize, enlarge, exaggerate, magnify, overdo, overdramatize, overemphasize, oversell, overstate, romanticize, stress, stretch)

DRAG (←): *attract, carry, convey, draw, ferry, haul, heave, jerk, lug, magnetize, move, pull, schlep, shuttle, tow, trail, transport, trek, truck, tug, yank* (≠ drive, drop, eject, lose, nudge, propel, punt, push, ram, shove, shunt, thrust)

DRAGOON (←): *badger, blackjack, blackmail, bogart, browbeat, bulldoze, bully, coerce, commandeer, compel, constrain, cow, daunt, dictate, domineer, drag, drive, extort, foment, force, galvanize, goad, harass, hector, hijack, hound, impel, impress, incite, intimidate, make, mandate, menace, motivate, muscle, nag, nobble, obligate, oblige, press, pressure, propel, push, railroad, sandbag, shame, spark, stimulate, stress, strong-arm, terrorize, threaten, urge* (≠ allow, argue, baffle, bar, block, check, convince, counteract, delay, discuss, embarrass, foil, -frustrate, hamper, impede, induce, let, move, obstruct, oppose, permit, persuade, -prevent, resist, satisfy, stop, sway, -thwart, win)

DRAIN (←): *bleed, blot, catheterize, clean, clear, decant, decrease, deduct, deflate, dehumidify, dehydrate, deplete, diminish, draft, draw, effuse, embezzle, empty, evacuate, evaporate, exhaust, extort, flush, juice, knacker, lessen, lower, milk, pump, purge, reduce, sap, shrink, siphon, slurp, staunch, suck, tap, vacate, vacuum, -void, wither* (≠ augment, bathe, conserve, deluge, douse, drench, drown, endow, engulf, fill, flood, impregnate, increase, inundate, invest, macerate, marinate, overwhelm, pack, presoak, puddle, recoup, replace, restore, soak, souse, spike, staunch, submerge, swamp, wash, water, wet)

DRAIN (/): *abate, absorb, bankrupt, beggar, blackmail, blow, burn, cannibalize, consume, cripple, debilitate, deplete, depredate, devitalize, devour, disable, dissipate, downsize, eat, empty, enervate, enfeeble, exhaust, expend, extract, fatigue, fritter, guzzle, impoverish, incapacitate, lessen, lower, reduce, sap, spend, squander, tap, tire, undermine, use, waste, weaken, weary, wither* (≠ amp, amuse, bank, bless, bolster, budget, conserve, divert, energize, enforce, enlarge, enliven, entertain, fortify, invigorate, jump-start, liven, preserve, quicken, rebuild, reinforce, reinvigorate, renew, repair, restimulate, revive, save, stabilize, stimulate, strengthen, vitalize, vivify)

DRAMATIZE (→): *accent, accentuate, act, adapt, aggrandize, amplify, assert, augment, burlesque, color, elaborate, embellish, emphasize, enact, enhance, exacerbate, exaggerate, execute, hoke, maximize, overdo, overdramatize, overplay, oversell, overstate, perform, playact, poeticize, produce, punctuate, refine, script, show, splash, stage, stretch* (≠ belittle, bore, calm, conceal, deemphasize, dismiss, downplay, hide, hush, mellow, minimize, sedate, simplify, soft-pedal, subdue, tranquilize, underemphasize, understate)

DRAW (←): *acquire, bring, carry, choose, conclude, convey, convince, cull, debit, deduct, draft, drag, drain, elicit, evoke, extract, fascinate, fetch, gather, get, haul, hook, incline, induce, infer, influence, jerk, leach, leech, lug, milk, obtain, persuade, pick, pluck, procure, prompt, pull, pump, rake, receive, remove, select, siphon, slurp, source, subtract, suck, take, tap, tow, trail, trawl, tug, vacuum, withdraw, wrench, yank* (≠ cast, clamp, drive, fasten, fling, force, heave, holster, impel, lob, pitch, propel, punt, push, ram, repel, shoot, shove, skitter, sling, throw, thrust, toss)

DRAW (←): *allure, attract, beckon, beguile, bewitch, captivate, charm, coddle, court, deduce, enchant, engage, engross, enthrall, entice, evoke, fascinate, hypnotize, interest, invite, lure, magnetize, mesmerize, razzle-dazzle, rivet, romance, seduce, sway, tantalize, tease, tempt, trigger, win, woo, wow* (≠ alienate, annoy, banish, bore, caution, chill, daunt, -deter, disaffect, disappoint, disgust, disillusion, displease, dissuade, disturb, irk, lose, nauseate, offend, -omit, -ostracize, pain, -refuse, -reject, repel, repulse, revolt, sicken, -thwart, torment, warn, weary)

DRAW (+): *caricature, chart, compose, delineate, depict, design, doodle, draft, engrave, etch, express, frame, graph, illuminate, limn, map, mark, model, outline, paint, pencil, pictorialize, picture, portray, profile, represent, scribble, sketch, trace, visualize* (≠ blot, conceal, destroy, efface, eradicate, erase, expunge, -ignore, obliterate, rub, ruin, smudge, wipe, wreck)

DREDGE (←): *ascertain, audit, browse, check, comb, descry, detect, determine, dig, discover, drag, examine, explore, ferret, find, frisk, hunt, inspect, investigate, learn, locate, peruse, plumb, probe, prowl, raise, rake, ransack, reinvestigate, review, rifle, rummage, scan, scoop, scour, scrutinize, search, seek, study, survey, uncover, unearth* (≠ -abandon, block, bury, -discount, -disregard, forgo, -forsake, glance, hide, -ignore, lose, -neglect, -omit, -overlook, -renounce, skim, waive)

DRENCH (→): *bathe, bedraggle, dampen, deluge, dip, douse, drown, -duck, dunk, engulf, flood, flush, hose, hydrate, imbue, immerse, impregnate, infuse, inundate, irrigate, lave, marinate, mist, moisten, permeate, presoak, puddle, rehydrate, rinse, saturate, shower, slosh, sluice, soak, sop, souse, splash, sprinkle, steep, submerge, swamp, syrup, wash, water, waterlog, wet* (≠ barbecue, burn, dehumidify, dehydrate, deplete, desiccate, drain, drip-dry, drizzle, dry, empty, evaporate, ignite, mummify, parch, scorch, sear, shrivel, staunch, torch, trickle, void, wither, wring)

DRESS (+): *accoutre, adjust, adorn, arm, arrange, array, attire, barber, bind, buckle, button, caparison, clean, clothe, comb, compose, costume, cover, curry, deck, decorate, develop, don, drape, equip, fit, furnish, garb, garnish, groom, gussy, jacket, manicure, outfit, pomade, prepare, prime, primp, ready, rig, robe, straighten, style, suit, tidy, tinsel, titivate, tog, trim,* *uniform, wear, wrap, zip* (≠ bare, bedraggle, cut, denude, dirty, dishevel, dismantle, disorder, disrobe, divest, doff, draggle, expose, muss, peel, reveal, ruffle, rumple, shed, strip, unbuckle, unbutton, unclothe, uncover, undress, unzip)

DRILL (→): *bore, core, dig, excavate, exhume, gaff, gouge, groove, hollow, impale, penetrate, perforate, pierce, plumb, poke, prick, punch, puncture, riddle, sink* (≠ block, clog, cover, fill, mend, patch, plaster, plug, repair, resist, seal)

DRILL (+): *break, coach, condition, cultivate, develop, discipline, edify, educate, enlighten, exercise, groom, habituate, hone, indoctrinate, inform, instruct, learn, mentor, perfect, practice, prepare, ready, refine, rehearse, repeat, review, school, study, teach, train, tutor* (≠ cease, confound, confuse, decondition, forget, -ignore, impede, indulge, learn, misunderstand, muddle, -neglect, withhold)

DRINK (←): *absorb, belt, consume, down, drain, gulp, guzzle, hoist, imbibe, indulge, irrigate, kill, lap, lick, mouth, pound, quaff, sip, slug, slurp, suck, swallow, swig, swill, toast* (≠ belch, decant, disgorge, eject, emit, expel, parch, pour, -refuse, regurgitate, spew, spill, spit, spout, vomit)

DRIVE (→): *animate, compel, compress, depress, egg, encourage, exhort, force, goad, guide, herd, hound, impel, jam, motivate, move, muscle, operate, press, pressure, prick, prod, prompt, propel, provoke, punch, punt, push, railroad, ram, rouse, run, rush, send, shepherd, shove, spur, squash, squeeze, steamroll, steer, stimulate, thrust, urge, weigh, whip, wrangle* (≠ -abort, -balk, bar, block, check, curb, delay, -deter, encumber, foil, -frustrate, hamper, hinder, impede, monkey-wrench, obstruct, oppose, pause, -preclude, -prevent, pull, resist, restrain, shelve, short-circuit, stall, stem, stop, stymie, -thwart, yank)

DRIVE (→): *abet, activate, actuate, arouse, excite, ferment, fire, foment, galvanize, impel, incite, inflame, inspire, instigate, motivate, move, propel, provoke, raise, rouse, start, stimulate, stir, trigger, trip, work* (≠ bridle, cage, cannibalize, check, constrain, consume, contain, control, curb, deactivate, deplete, drain, exhaust, inhibit, kill, leash, pace, regulate, rein, restrain, stop, straightjacket)

DRIVE (/): *badger, blackjack, blackmail, bluff, browbeat, bulldoze, bully, coerce, compel, constrain, cow, dog, drag, dragoon, flog, force, harass, hector, hound, impel, impress, intimidate, make, menace, muscle, nag, nobble, obligate, oblige, overcommit, press, pressure, railroad, sandbag, scourge, shame, steamroller, terrorize, threaten, trash-talk, whip* (≠ allow, argue, bribe, cajole, coax, convince, encourage, glad-hand, induce, let, move, permit, persuade, satisfy, schmooze, soft-sell, soft-soap, urge, wheedle, win)

DROP (→): *-abandon, blackball, bobble, bungle, chuck, depress, -desert, discard, -disown, -disregard, -ditch, divorce, dump, eject, eliminate, -exclude, expel, finish, flatten, floor, foozle, forfeit, -forsake, fumble,* *immerse, jilt, leave, level, lower, offload, -omit, oppose, -ostracize, oust, plop, -reject, relinquish, -renounce, -repudiate, separate, sink, -spurn, submerge, throw, topple* (≠ acquire, add, bequeath, claim, collect, cultivate, gain, gather, hoard, hog, keep, lift, maintain, manage, marry, monopolize, obtain, protect, pursue, raise, refine, renew, retain, save, secure, seek, store, woo)

DROWN (→): *asphyxiate, bury, deluge, dip, douse, drench, engulf, envelop, flood, immerse, infuse, inundate, marinate, overcome, overflow, overpower, overwhelm, plunge, saturate, sink, soak, sop, stifle, submerge, suffocate, swamp, syrup* (≠ barbecue, buoy, burn, dehydrate, desiccate, drain, dry, elevate, empty, float, hoist, leach, leech, lift, parch, rescue, save, scorch, sear, staunch)

DRUG (←): *allay, alleviate, anesthetize, assuage, balance, benumb, blunt, calm, compose, daze, deaden, defuse, desensitize, dope, dose, dull, ease, etherize, hush, hypnotize, intoxicate, lighten, lull, medicate, mellow, mesmerize, mitigate, moderate, mollify, narcotize, numb, pacify, placate, quell, quiet, quieten, relax, relieve, restrain, sedate, settle, shanghai, silence, smooth, soften, soothe, stabilize, steady, still, stupefy, subdue, torpefy, tranquilize, treat, unruffle* (≠ aggravate, agitate, anger, arouse, bait, bother, chafe, charge, convulse, discompose, disturb, dizzy, energize, enliven, enrage, excite, fluster, foment, goad, incite, inflame, infuriate, irk, irritate, jolt, madden, needle, nettle, perturb, provoke, rankle, rattle, rile, roil, rouse, shake, spur, stimulate, stir, terrorize, trouble, unnerve, upset, vex, wake, worry)

DULL (/): *allay, alleviate, anesthetize, assuage, blunt, blur, buffer, cloud, cushion, dampen, darken, daze, deaden, decrease, depress, desensitize, dim, diminish, disable, disarm, discourage, dishearten, drug, enfeeble, hamper, hamstring, handicap, hinder, hobble, impair, lessen, lower, lubricate, minimize, mitigate, moderate, muffle, neutralize, numb, obscure, paralyze, quiet, reduce, relieve, sadden, sap, soften, soundproof, stupefy, subdue, temper, torpefy, tranquilize, undermine, weaken* (≠ accent, accentuate, aggravate, amplify, assert, boost, concentrate, edge, emphasize, enhance, exaggerate, file, flavor, grind, heighten, hone, increase, intensify, magnify, marinate, maximize, optimize, overdramatize, overhaul, poeticize, prioritize, refine, reveal, richen, rile, romanticize, season, serrate, sharpen, spice, strengthen, strop, uncloud, whet)

DUMP (/): *abdicate, abolish, annihilate, blackball, boot, cant, cashier, cast, chuck, deep-six, deposit, -desert, discard, discharge, dismiss, dispatch, -ditch, drain, drop, eject, eliminate, empty, eradicate, evacuate, exorcise, expel, expunge, exterminate, extinguish, extirpate, exude, fence, fling, flush, -forsake, jettison, junk, leach, leave, liquidate, lose, offload, pitch, plonk, purge, -reject, remove, replace, scrap, sell, shed, shuck, slough, stamp, tip, toss, trash, unload, unpack, waste* (≠ adopt, archive, cherish, cradle, embrace, employ, hold, keep, load, maintain, prize, recoup, remainder, retain, save, survive, take, use, utilize, weather)

DUMP (/): *-abandon, banish, -cold-shoulder, -cut, -desert, -ditch, divorce, -forsake, high-hat, jilt, leave, maroon, -quit, -renounce, -slight, -snub, -spurn, unmarry* (≠ adopt, befriend, chauffeur, court, invite, marry, pursue, romance, take, welcome, win, woo)

DUPE (←): *abuse, baffle, bamboozle, beguile, betray, bleed, bluff, buffalo, bullshit, burn, cajole, catch, cheat, chisel, -circumvent, con, convince, cozen, deceive, defraud, delude, diddle, double-cross, double-talk, euchre, exploit, fake, fiddle, fleece, flimflam, fool, fox, fudge, gaslight, goldbrick, gull, hoax, hocus-pocus, hoodwink, hornswoggle, humbug, hustle, josh, juggle, kid, manipulate, misguide, misinform, mislead, mulct, nobble, outwit, overreach, palaver, pretend, rob, rook, scam, schmooze, shaft, shortchange, skin, snooker, snow, spoof, squeeze, stick, stiff, sting, sucker, swindle, tease, trick, victimize, wrong* (≠ admit, assume, assure, believe, blab, blaze, blurt, clue, concede, confess, confide, confirm, confront, crosscheck, debunk, disabuse, disclose, disenchant, disillusion, divulge, expose, face, help, prosecute, respect, restore, reveal, support, tell, trust, uncloak, uncover, undeceive, unmask, unveil)

E

EARMARK (→): *allocate, apply, apportion, assign, bestow, bless, commit, confide, consecrate, consign, dedicate, designate, devote, employ, entrust, hallow, label, mete, package, reserve, sanctify, save, tag, use* (≠ anonymize, block, -deny, deprive, hamper, -ignore, impede, misapply, mislabel, misuse, -neglect, -refuse, -reject, scant, skimp, squander, stall, stint, waste, withhold)

EARN (←): *accomplish, accumulate, achieve, acquire, amass, annex, attain, bag, capture, carry, catch, claim, clear, collect, cop, crest, derive, draw, effect, gain, garner, gather, get, gross, hustle, land, make, net, notch, obtain, occupy, perform, pocket, procure, profit, pull, rate, reacquire, realize, reap, reattain, recapture, receive, regain, remake, scavenge, score, secure, snag, sock, take, turn, win, wrangle* (≠ accord, bequeath, cost, forfeit, give, grant, lose, outlay, overpay, patronize, pay, relinquish, spend, stiff, surrender, underpay, yield)

EARN (←): *achieve, acquire, attain, bag, claim, conquer, deserve, entitle, gain, harvest, make, master, merit, net, obtain, qualify, rate, reap, score, secure, warrant, win* (≠ -abandon, damage, fail, forfeit, grant, lose, miss, -omit, relinquish, shame, surrender, undershoot, yield)

EASE (+): *abate, advance, aid, allay, alleviate, ameliorate, anesthetize, appease, assist, assuage, calm, cheer, comfort, compose, conciliate, console, content, cool, cure, defuse, disencumber, disentangle, doctor, emancipate, encourage, expedite, facilitate, favor, free, further, humor, hush, improve, indulge, lessen, liberate, lighten, lubricate, lull, mellow, midwife, mitigate, moderate, mollify, nurse, pacify, palliate, placate, promote, quell, quiet, quieten, reassure, reconcile, reduce, relax, release, relieve, reprieve, salve, sedate, settle, simplify, smooth, soften, solace, soothe, speed, stabilize, still, subdue, sugarcoat, tranquilize, unbind, unchain, unfetter, unleash, unload, untie* (≠ agitate, agonize, anguish, annoy, constrain, crucify, discipline, discomfort, disquiet, embarrass, exacerbate, harass, impair, inhibit, injure, irritate, nag, needle, nettle, nitpick, pain, perplex, pressure, rankle, repress, reserve, restrain, rile, sting, strain, stress, suffer, suppress, torment, torture, trouble, vex, worry)

EAT (←): *absorb, accept, access, acquire, admit, appreciate, appropriate, assimilate, banquet, bolt, chew, chop, consume, corrode, cram, demolish, devour, digest, dispatch, dissolve, down, drink, engorge, engulf, enjoy, envelop, feast, finish, get, glut, gnaw, gobble, gorge, gulp, gum, guzzle, hoover, imbibe, incorporate, ingest, inhale, inspire, integrate, internalize, lap, lick, manage, metabolize, mouth, munch, nibble, nosh, nurse, overwhelm, pick, pocket, procure, quaff, raven, receive, regale, relish,* *ruminate, savor, scarf, sip, slop, slurp, snarf, sniff, stuff, suck, surfeit, swallow, swig, swill, take, taste, try, vacuum, welcome, wolf* (≠ -avoid, barf, belch, brew, -bypass, concoct, content, cook, covet, crave, create, -decline, desire, disgorge, disperse, -ditch, drop, dump, eject, excrete, expel, exude, famish, fancy, favor, feed, fetishize, force-feed, forgo, fuel, furnish, grace, gratify, heave, hunt, jettison, make, malnourish, miss, nourish, offer, order, overfeed, pass, please, prepare, puke, quench, -refuse, regurgitate, -reject, request, satisfy, serve, skimp, skip, slake, spew, spit, splutter, -spurn, starve, stint, supply, toss, trash, underfeed, victual, vomit, withhold)

EAT (←): *bite, cannibalize, condense, consume, corrode, crumble, decay, decimate, decompose, deplete, depredate, destroy, devastate, disintegrate, dissipate, dissolve, drain, erode, exhaust, fret, gnaw, leech, liquefy, melt, nibble, rot, ruin, rust, squander, undermine, waste, wear, wreck* (≠ aid, build, conserve, construct, create, fortify, freshen, help, improve, pickle, preserve, recreate, refresh, regenerate, reinvigorate, rejuvenate, renew, repair, restore, revitalize, revive, shield, stimulate, sustain)

ECHO (←): *adopt, ape, belabor, copy, counterfeit, ditto, duplicate, emulate, feign, flatter, ghostwrite, imitate, impersonate, mime, mimic, mirror, mock, overemphasize, parallel, parrot, playact, portray, pretend, quote, recall, redouble, reflect, reiterate, repeat, replicate, reproduce, retort, roleplay, rubber-stamp, simulate* (≠ cue, dampen, deaden, end, muffle, mute, muzzle, oppose, originate, prompt, question, silence, smother, stifle, suppress, terminate, throttle, translate, voice)

ECLIPSE (→): *ace, annihilate, beat, best, better, bury, cap, checkmate, clobber, conquer, cream, crush, defeat, dispatch, drub, dwarf, exceed, finish, flatten, floor, lambaste, lick, master, one-up, outbalance, outclass, outdistance, outdo, outfight, outguess, outgun, outmaneuver, outpace, outperform, outplay, outrace, outrank, outreach, outrun, outsell, outshine, outslick, outsmart, outstrip, outthink, outweigh, outwit, overcome, overpower, overshadow, overtake, overthrow, overwhelm, pass, rout, ruin, shame, shellac, skunk, slaughter, smoke, steamroller, stop, subdue, subjugate, surmount, surpass, sweep, take, thrash, top, topple, total, transcend, trash, trounce, trump, unhorse, unseat, upend, upset, upstage, vanquish, wallop, waste, wax, whip, whomp, wipe, wrack, wreck, zap* (≠ aggrandize, aid, amplify, assist, augment, -avoid, back, bolster, bomb, boost, botch, brave, bungle, cede, coach, comfort, concede, defend, defer, develop, elevate, encourage, enhance, exalt, extol, face, fail, flub, flunk, follow, forfeit, fumble, glorify, guard, help, improve, instruct, lose, mind, nurture, obey, promote, protect, publicize, raise, relinquish, -renounce, serve, showcase, spotlight, stomach, suffer, support, surrender, survive, train, uplift, weather, yield)

ECLIPSE (/): *adumbrate, becloud, bedim, befog, blacken, blear, block, blot, blur, camouflage, cloak, cloud, conceal, cover, curtain, darken, dim, disguise, drape, extinguish, fog, haze, hide, mask, mist, muddy, mystify, obfuscate, obliterate, obscure, occlude, occult, overcloud, overshadow,* *screen, shade, shadow, shroud, veil* (≠ brandish, brighten, clear, elevate, enlarge, expand, explain, expose, extend, flaunt, floodlight, focus, heighten, highlight, hype, illuminate, illumine, increase, light, lighten, magnify, maximize, parade, plug, reveal, show, showcase, uncloud, uncover, unveil)

EDIFY (+): *better, civilize, coach, counsel, cultivate, develop, discipline, drill, educate, elevate, enlighten, ennoble, enrich, ensoul, exalt, foster, glorify, guide, illuminate, illumine, improve, inform, inspire, instruct, lift, mentor, nurture, regenerate, renew, school, teach, train, transfigure, transform, tutor, uplift* (≠ addle, baffle, barbarize, becloud, bestialize, bewilder, blur, cloud, confound, confuse, darken, lower, muddle, muddy, mystify, nonplus, obscure, perplex, puzzle, stump)

EDIT (+): *acclimate, acclimatize, accommodate, adapt, adjust, align, alter, attune, bend, calibrate, condition, convert, correct, customize, doctor, equip, fashion, fine-tune, fit, fix, gear, harden, harmonize, inure, match, mend, model, modify, overhaul, pattern, perfect, phase, prepare, prime, punctuate, ready, realign, recast, reclaim, reconceive, reconceptualize, rectify, recycle, redesign, redevelop, redo, reengineer, refashion, refit, refocus, rehearse, reimagine, reinvent, rejigger, remake, remodel, renovate, reorient, repair, rephrase, reshuffle, restore, rethink, retool, revamp, revise, rework, rig, right, sculpt, season, shape, shuffle, square, suit, tailor, toughen, transform, tune, tweak, weaponize* (≠ -abandon, botch, bungle, draft, fake, flub, force, freeze, fudge, half-ass, hamper, hinder, improvise, maintain, mar, misadjust, preserve, propose, retain, ruin, sketch, spoil, wing, wreck)

EDUCATE (+): *advise, apprise, brainwash, brief, civilize, clarify, coach, contextualize, convince, correct, counsel, cultivate, describe, develop, direct, discipline, drill, edify, elevate, enlighten, enrich, exercise, explain, familiarize, foster, grade, groom, guide, illuminate, impart, implant, improve, inculcate, indoctrinate, inform, initiate, instill, instruct, introduce, lead, lecture, mentor, mold, nourish, nurture, prepare, prime, qualify, ready, realign, rear, refine, retrain, school, shape, show, teach, train, tutor* (≠ addle, baffle, bamboozle, barbarize, becloud, bewilder, blind, cloud, confuse, corrupt, darken, degrade, dim, forget, gaslight, hamper, hamstring, hinder, -ignore, learn, manipulate, mystify, obscure, perplex, pervert, puzzle, resist, study, stump, stymie, vulgarize, worsen)

EJECT (-): *axe, banish, belch, boot, bounce, bump, can, cashier, chase, deport, disbar, discard, discharge, disgorge, dislodge, dismiss, displace, dispossess, -ditch, drop, dump, eighty-six, ejaculate, eliminate, eradicate, evacuate, evict, -exclude, excrete, exile, exorcise, expectorate, expel, extrude, fire, offload, -omit, oppose, -ostracize, oust, pink-slip, propel, -reject, release, remove, retire, rout, sack, scrap, spew, spit, splutter, spout, -spurn, terminate, upchuck, vomit* (≠ absorb, accept, accompany, admit, approve, consume, contain, devour, embrace, entertain, greet, harbor, house, ingest, invite, lodge, pull, receive, room, shelter, take, unite, welcome)

ELABORATE (+): *accent, accentuate, accrue, adorn, advance, affirm, amplify, assert, complexify, complicate, confound, decorate, develop, devise, embellish, embroider, emphasize, enhance, enlarge, enrich, evolve, exaggerate, expand, explain, fancify, festoon, flavor, forge, foster, garnish, glitter, glitz, grow, heroicize, heroize, idealize, idolize, improve, involve, materialize, mature, maximize, ornament, overdramatize, overdraw, oversell, poeticize, polish, punctuate, refine, ripen, romanticize, sentimentalize, sophisticate, tangle, tool, unfold* (≠ abridge, compact, concentrate, condense, consolidate, contract, devalue, downplay, elide, focus, integrate, minimize, reduce, simplify, soft-pedal, streamline, uncomplicate, underemphasize, unify)

ELATE (→): *animate, boost, brighten, charge, cheer, console, content, delight, dizzy, elevate, energize, enrapture, enthuse, excite, exhilarate, gladden, gratify, hearten, inspire, intoxicate, please, raise, rejoice, rouse, satisfy, spark, stimulate, thrill, transport, uplift, warm, wow* (≠ appall, bore, burden, demoralize, demotivate, depress, discourage, dismay, dispirit, distress, enervate, frighten, grieve, harass, lumber, oppress, perplex, sadden, scare, sorrow, terrify, weary, weight)

ELBOW (→): *bulldoze, bump, crash, crowd, hook, hustle, jam, jostle, knock, muscle, nudge, press, push, ram, shoulder, shove, squeeze, steamroll, thrust* (≠ -avoid, -bypass, dissuade, draw, -halt, haul, hinder, jerk, pull, tow, tug, wrench, yank)

ELECT (→): *accept, adopt, appoint, cherry-pick, choose, conclude, coopt, cull, decide, designate, determine, embrace, endorse, espouse, fancy, favor, fix, handpick, judge, mark, name, nominate, pick, prefer, preselect, resolve, return, rubber-stamp, select, set, settle, tab, take, tap, wish* (≠ blackball, block, -decline, defame, depose, deprive, dethrone, disapprove, discard, disclaim, discredit, disfavor, disgrace, dismiss, displace, jettison, leave, -nix, oust, predetermine, -refuse, -reject, -repudiate, -spurn, unseat, -veto)

ELECTRIFY (→): *activate, agitate, amaze, animate, arouse, astonish, astound, bewitch, captivate, charge, charm, delight, disquiet, disturb, dizzy, enchant, energize, enliven, enthrall, enthuse, excite, exhilarate, fire, frenzy, galvanize, gobsmack, hypnotize, impassion, incite, inflame, inspire, interest, intoxicate, intrigue, invigorate, jar, jolt, mesmerize, motivate, power, provoke, quicken, razzle-dazzle, rivet, rouse, shock, spellbind, stagger, startle, stimulate, stir, strike, stun, tantalize, thrill, titillate, vitalize, wire, wow* (≠ baffle, blunt, bore, bother, bug, confound, confuse, dampen, deaden, demoralize, demotivate, depress, discourage, dishearten, drain, dull, exhaust, fatigue, flatten, jade, leech, nag, perplex, puzzle, repulse, sadden, sap, sicken, tire, weary, worry)

ELEVATE (→): *ascend, boost, crane, exalt, heave, heft, heighten, hike, hoist, intensify, jack, lift, magnify, mount, raise, ramp, rear, soar, up, upend, uphold, uplift, upraise* (≠ bear, depress, descend, dip, drop, lessen, lower, pitch, plonk, plunge, press, push, sink, slip, submerge, topple)

ELEVATE (+): *acclaim, advance, affirm, aggrandize, apotheosize, applaud, augment, blackball, boost, canonize, celebrate, cite, commend, commission, compliment, congratulate, cultivate, decorate, deify, dignify, distinguish, edify, educate, empower, enhance, enlighten, ennoble, enshrine, ensoul, enthrone, eulogize, exalt, extol, forward, further, glorify, gold-star, hail, heighten, heroicize, heroize, honor, idealize, idolize, improve, inform, instruct, intensify, knight, laud, lift, magnify, nurture, optimize, overhaul, praise, prefer, prioritize, promote, pump, raise, rarefy, refine, revolutionize, romanticize, salute, sanitize, school, sentimentalize, strengthen, sugarcoat, swell, teach, upgrade, uplift* (≠ abase, anathematize, attaint, belittle, bench, blast, blister, boo, censure, condemn, declass, decry, degrade, demean, demote, denounce, depose, depreciate, dethrone, detract, disgrace, dishonor, dismiss, disparage, downgrade, expel, fulminate, humble, humiliate, impeach, incriminate, lower, minimize, mortify, oust, overthrow, reduce, remove, ruin, shame, sideline, -spurn, unmake, unseat, vulgarize, wrack, wreck)

ELEVATE (+): *affirm, boost, brighten, buoy, cheer, content, delight, elate, enrapture, excite, exhilarate, gladden, grace, gratify, inspire, intoxicate, please, rejoice, rouse, satisfy, stimulate, thrill, transport, uplift, warm, wow* (≠ bother, bug, crush, demoralize, depress, discourage, dishearten, dispirit, distress, irk, oppress, pain, sadden, vex, weary, worry)

ELICIT (←): *bare, bring, coax, derive, detect, determine, disclose, discover, disinter, divulge, drag, draw, dredge, educe, effect, engender, evince, evoke, exact, expose, extort, extract, fathom, fetch, find, gain, generate, get, identify, induce, inspire, make, motivate, obtain, procure, produce, provoke, pull, raise, realize, recognize, reveal, secure, solve, source, uncloak, uncover, unearth, unmask, unravel, unveil, wangle, wrest, wring* (≠ bury, comp, conceal, contribute, cover, -deny, -disregard, donate, ensconce, exterminate, forget, furnish, give, hide, -ignore, keep, miss, -neglect, -overlook, quash, -refuse, repress, reserve, soothe, subdue, supply, suppress, tender, tithe, withhold, yield)

ELIMINATE (/): *abolish, annihilate, ban, banish, bar, beat, behead, blackball, blacklist, block, -cancel, cease, checkmate, conquer, debar, deep-six, defeat, delete, deport, destroy, -deter, -discontinue, -disregard, doom, drop, eject, eradicate, erase, euthanize, except, excise, -exclude, -excommunicate, exile, exorcise, expel, expunge, exterminate, extinguish, extirpate, -halt, hinder, impede, kill, lick, murder, obliterate, obstruct, -obviate, -omit, oppose, orphan, -ostracize, oust, overwhelm, -preclude, -prevent, -prohibit, raze, -reject, remove, slay, suppress, suspend, terminate, thrash, uproot, ward, weed, whack* (≠ accept, adapt, admit, adopt, begin, brainstorm, celebrate, create, defend, embrace, entertain, foster, found, include, initiate, invite, keep, legalize, preserve, promote, receive, retain, shield, sustain, take, weather, welcome)

-ELUDE (→): *anticipate, -avert, -avoid, baffle, ban, bar, bilk, block, burke, -bypass, -circumvent, confound, -decline, deflect, detour, divert, -dodge, -duck, eliminate, -escape, -eschew, -evade, except, -exclude, finesse, -flee,* *foil, forestall, fox, -frustrate, lose, miss, -obviate, -ostracize, outfox, outmaneuver, outrun, outsmart, outwit, overreach, parry, -preclude, -prevent, puzzle, shake, -shirk, shortcut, shrink, shuffle, -shun, -sidestep, skip, skirt, stall, stonewall, stump, -thwart, underpay, ward, weasel* (≠ accept, accost, attract, catch, confront, contact, contract, court, embrace, entice, face, incur, invite, meet, pursue, seek, solicit, target, victimize, waylay, welcome, win, woo)

EMANCIPATE (+): *acquit, alibi, alleviate, deliver, discharge, disengage, disentangle, enfranchise, exonerate, extricate, free, liberate, loose, loosen, manumit, parole, ransom, redeem, release, relieve, rescue, save, spring, unbind, unburden, uncage, unchain, uncuff, unfetter, unleash, unlock, unshackle, untie* (≠ bind, commit, confine, conquer, convict, cuff, enchain, enslave, fetter, handcuff, hogtie, immure, imprison, incarcerate, institutionalize, intern, jail, lock, manacle, restrain, shackle, straightjacket, subdue, subjugate, trammel)

EMASCULATE (/): *alter, brutalize, castrate, cripple, daunt, deball, debilitate, demoralize, demotivate, desex, devitalize, discourage, dishearten, dismay, dispirit, enervate, enfeeble, fix, frighten, geld, impoverish, intimidate, neuter, paralyze, prostrate, sap, savage, scare, soften, spay, terrify, terrorize, tire, unman, unnerve, unsex, unstring, vitiate, waste, weaken, wither* (≠ aid, arouse, assist, boost, embolden, encourage, fortify, galvanize, harden, heal, hearten, help, invigorate, mend, nerve, nurture, renew, restore, rouse, stimulate, strengthen, toughen, vitalize)

EMBALM (/): *anoint, archive, bank, bottle, brine, bury, can, cherish, consecrate, conserve, cremate, enshrine, entomb, fossilize, freeze, immortalize, inter, keep, marinate, mummify, perpetuate, petrify, pickle, plant, prepare, preserve, process, ready, refrigerate, save, store, treasure, wrap* (≠ activate, corrupt, disintegrate, energize, exhume, heal, invigorate, -neglect, rejuvenate, renew, restore, resuscitate, revive, ruin, spoil, squander, waste, wither)

EMBARRASS (/): *abash, agitate, annoy, appall, bewilder, bother, bug, chagrin, confound, confuse, crush, debase, degrade, demean, discombobulate, discomfit, discomfort, discompose, disconcert, discountenance, discourage, dismay, disquiet, distract, distress, disturb, dumbfound, faze, fluster, humble, humiliate, injure, irk, jeer, mock, mortify, nag, nitpick, nonplus, perplex, perturb, pillory, plague, puzzle, rattle, ridicule, shame, -slight, -snub, stun, tease, throw, unhinge, unsettle, upset, wound* (≠ assist, assure, boost, buoy, calm, cheer, comfort, compliment, conceal, congratulate, console, cover, dignify, embolden, encourage, gladden, gold-star, gratify, hearten, help, hide, high-five, honor, humor, lull, mellow, mollify, pacify, placate, please, prioritize, reassure, relieve, soothe, support)

EMBATTLE (+): *arm, array, barricade, blockade, bolster, brace, buttress, cover, defend, entrench, equip, fence, fortify, furnish, garrison, guard, mobilize, patrol, prepare, protect, ready, reinforce, secure, steady, strengthen, supply, support* (≠ boobytrap, damage, discourage, dissuade,

-dodge, -elude, -evade, exhaust, expose, hurt, impair, -neglect, sabotage, scotch, scupper, subvert, undercut, undermine, weaken, withhold)

EMBED (→): *bed, bury, connect, cram, deposit, disgorge, drive, enclose, ensconce, entrench, establish, fasten, fix, graft, hammer, imbue, impact, implant, infiltrate, infuse, ingrain, initiate, inject, inlay, insert, inset, insinuate, install, instate, instill, interpose, introduce, juxtapose, locate, lodge, niche, penetrate, pierce, place, plant, plunge, position, press, root, set, settle, sink, stick, stuff, wedge* (≠ budge, delouse, detach, dislocate, dislodge, disturb, eject, eliminate, eradicate, excise, exorcise, expel, extract, purge, relegate, relocate, remove, reposition, uninstall, uproot, weed, withdraw)

EMBELLISH (→): *accessorize, adorn, amplify, appliqué, array, beautify, bedeck, bedizen, bespangle, blazon, braid, brighten, caparison, color, costume, dandify, deck, decorate, drape, dress, drizzle, elaborate, emblaze, emblazon, emboss, embroider, enhance, enrich, exaggerate, fancify, feather, festoon, figure, filigree, fillet, flavor, flounce, freshen, frill, fringe, fudge, garland, garnish, gild, glamorize, glitter, glitz, grace, hang, lace, magnify, marinate, optimize, ornament, overhaul, overstate, paint, perfume, pigment, raddle, refine, ribbon, season, smarten, spangle, spice, spiff, spruce, stipple, stud, swag, tinsel, tool, trim, wreathe* (≠ bare, besmirch, blemish, damage, deface, defile, deform, denude, disfigure, dismantle, display, divest, dull, efface, expose, harm, harshen, injure, mangle, mar, maul, mutilate, reveal, scar, simplify, smear, spoil, stain, streamline, strip, sully, taint, tarnish, uglify, uncover)

EMBELLISH (←): *accent, accentuate, aggrandize, amplify, assert, belabor, bounce, caricature, color, distend, dramatize, dress, elaborate, embroider, emphasize, enhance, enlarge, exaggerate, expand, fudge, glitz, grace, heighten, heroicize, heroize, honor, hyperbolize, idealize, idolize, increase, magnify, maximize, overdo, overdramatize, overdraw, overemphasize, overplay, oversell, overstate, pad, poeticize, puff, punctuate, romanticize, satirize, sensationalize, sentimentalize, sharpen, sophisticate, stress, stretch* (≠ abolish, abridge, belittle, dampen, deaden, decrease, decry, deemphasize, deprecate, -discount, dismiss, disparage, downplay, eliminate, eradicate, erode, lessen, minimize, muffle, obliterate, reduce, soften, soft-pedal, trivialize, underemphasize, underrate, understate)

EMBEZZLE (←): *acquire, annex, appropriate, arrogate, assume, attach, burglarize, claim, collar, commandeer, convert, defalcate, filch, grab, grasp, harvest, heist, hijack, hook, lift, loot, misapply, misappropriate, misuse, mooch, nab, nail, nick, nip, nobble, peculate, pick, pilfer, pillage, pinch, pirate, plunder, poach, pocket, preempt, press, procure, purloin, reap, rifle, rob, rustle, sack, seize, snaffle, snatch, snooker, sponge, steal, swindle, swipe, take, thieve, usurp, wrench, wrest* (≠ avenge, bankroll, bestow, capitalize, contribute, defend, donate, earn, finance, fund, furnish, generate, give, grant, indemnify, invest, present, provide, reclaim, recoup, recover, repay, replace, restore, retrieve, salvage, subsidize, supply, tender)

EMBOLDEN (→): *animate, assure, boost, buoy, cheer, convince, encourage, energize, enliven, excite, fire, fortify, galvanize, hearten, inflame, inspire, inspirit, invigorate, nerve, prioritize, provoke, quicken, rally, reassure, reinforce, rouse, steel, stimulate, stir, strengthen, vitalize* (≠ blackmail, chide, daunt, debilitate, demoralize, demotivate, depress, discourage, dishearten, dispirit, enfeeble, hamstring, hinder, intimidate, sadden, sap, scold, sicken, tire, undermine, unnerve, weaken)

EMBRACE (→): *accost, acknowledge, address, adopt, approach, buttonhole, call, detain, enjoy, flag, glad-hand, greet, hail, high-five, hold, hug, kiss, meet, name, notice, prefer, receive, recognize, salute, select, signal, stop, wave, waylay, welcome* (≠ affront, -avoid, -bypass, cashier, circumnavigate, -circumvent, -cold-shoulder, counter, -cut, daunt, -decline, -elude, -evade, -exclude, manhandle, oppose, -ostracize, oust, -rebuff, -refuse, -reject, repel, repulse, -snub, -spurn, threaten)

EMBRACE (→): *blanket, bower, bracket, camouflage, circle, cloak, clothe, cocoon, curtain, disguise, drape, embed, encase, encircle, enclose, encompass, enfold, enlace, enshroud, envelop, invest, involve, lap, mantle, mask, muffle, orbit, overlay, shroud, subsume, swaddle, swathe, veil, wrap* (≠ bare, denude, display, divest, expel, expose, jettison, lose, open, remove, reveal, shed, shuck, strip, uncover)

EMBRACE (←): *bear-hug, caress, clamp, clasp, clinch, clutch, confine, contain, cradle, crush, cuddle, encircle, enclasp, enclose, encompass, enfold, entwine, envelop, fold, fondle, grab, grapple, grasp, grip, hold, hug, lock, nestle, nuzzle, pat, pet, press, seize, snog, snuggle, squeeze, squoosh, strain, stroke, surround, swathe, trap, twine, wrap* (≠ alienate, -avoid, disaffect, -ditch, drop, -duck, -evade, lose, miss, -neglect, orphan, -overlook, release, -sidestep, toss, unclasp)

EMBRACE (+): *absorb, accept, accommodate, admit, adopt, affect, appropriate, arrogate, assimilate, assume, borrow, cherish, cherry-pick, choose, cull, comprehend, contain, copy, cover, cultivate, domesticate, elect, embody, enclose, encompass, enjoin, espouse, follow, foster, grab, handpick, heed, hold, honor, imitate, include, incorporate, integrate, internalize, involve, keep, mind, naturalize, nurture, obey, pick, pretend, prize, quote, raise, rear, receive, retain, reunite, seize, simulate, subsume, take, treasure, use, usurp, utilize, welcome* (≠ -abandon, -boycott, contradict, discard, distrust, -eschew, -exclude, -forsake, give, isolate, jettison, junk, -negate, -nix, -omit, oppugn, -ostracize, oust, picket, protest, -reject, relinquish, -renounce, -repudiate, seclude, -shun, -spurn, threaten) **(¿) ABSTRACTION ALERT. Concrete goals essential!**

EMBROIDER (+): *accent, accentuate, accrue, adorn, advance, amplify, beautify, bedeck, better, braid, color, correct, deck, decorate, dignify, dress, elaborate, elevate, embellish, emblazon, emphasize, enhance, enrich, exaggerate, fancify, further, garnish, gild, glitz, grace, heighten, heroicize, heroize, honor, idealize, idolize, illuminate, improve, increase, intensify, magnify, ornament, overdramatize, oversell, personalize, poeticize, prettify, progress, punctuate, refine, renovate, revamp, revolutionize, romanticize, sentimentalize, sew, sophisticate, stitch,* *stretch, tinsel, tool, transform, trim, upgrade* (≠ abridge, bare, belittle, besmirch, blemish, condense, contract, decrease, deface, denude, diminish, disfigure, divest, dull, efface, expose, harm, harshen, lessen, mar, minimize, mutilate, reduce, reveal, scar, shorten, shrink, simplify, smear, spoil, stain, streamline, strip, sully, taint, tarnish, uglify, uncover, underemphasize, understate, unsew)

EMBROIL (←): *bog, broil, complicate, compromise, confound, confuse, derange, disorder, disturb, disunite, encumber, enmesh, ensnare, ensnarl, entangle, entrap, implicate, incriminate, involve, jumble, mingle, mire, muddle, perplex, snare, snarl, tangle, trap, trouble* (≠ banish, blackball, -bypass, disentangle, disgorge, eject, emancipate, -evade, -exclude, expel, free, isolate, jettison, liberate, -omit, oust, release, remove, separate, -shun, -sidestep, simplify, spew, streamline, uncomplicate)

EMPHASIZE (→): *accent, accentuate, advertise, amplify, assert, augment, beef, belabor, bellow, bolster, boost, build, bump, caricature, color, deepen, double, dramatize, elaborate, embellish, embroider, enhance, enlarge, enrich, exaggerate, expand, feature, focus, foreground, glorify, heighten, highlight, hike, hyperbolize, identify, illuminate, inflate, intensify, magnify, maximize, misrepresent, overdramatize, overemphasize, overestimate, overplay, overrate, oversell, overstate, pad, pinpoint, plug, press, promote, publicize, puff, punctuate, refine, reinforce, romanticize, satirize, sentimentalize, spotlight, strengthen, stress, stretch, supplement, swell, treble, triple, trumpet, underline, underscore, up* (≠ abate, abbreviate, abridge, belittle, bury, compress, conceal, curb, curtail, cut, decrease, deemphasize, demean, diminish, -discount, dismiss, disparage, downplay, hide, lessen, mask, minimize, mitigate, moderate, modulate, muffle, obscure, reduce, -scorn, shorten, shrink, smother, stifle, subdue, subtract, underemphasize, understate, weaken)

EMPLOY (→): *apply, bestow, cannibalize, choreograph, deploy, direct, engage, exercise, exert, exploit, fill, handle, harness, manipulate, occupy, operate, orchestrate, ply, recycle, reuse, run, spend, unsheathe, use, utilize, weaponize, wield, work* (≠ block, -ditch, drop, dump, forget, -ignore, invalid, lose, misapply, misplace, misuse, -neglect, -omit, -overlook, shed, -shun, toss, unload)

EMPLOY (←): *advance, appoint, apprentice, assume, commission, contract, engage, enlist, fill, headhunt, hire, ink, keep, obtain, occupy, partner, pay, place, procure, promote, recruit, reemploy, reengage, rehire, retain, scout, secure, sign, subcontract, upgrade* (≠ axe, bench, boot, can, cashier, demote, discharge, dismiss, eighty-six, fire, furlough, retire, sack, sideline, terminate)

EMPOWER (+): *activate, advantage, aid, assist, benefit, bless, bolster, brace, buttress, charge, confirm, consolidate, drive, enable, encourage, energize, enforce, enliven, ensoul, entrench, fire, force, forearm, fortify, harden, help, invigorate, power, prop, recharge, reinforce, reinvigorate, revitalize, revive, rouse, spark, steady, steel, stimulate, support, temper,* *tone, toughen, vivify* (≠ arrest, block, cripple, debilitate, deplete, depredate, diminish, disqualify, encumber, enervate, enfeeble, enslave, exhaust, fatigue, hamper, hinder, incapacitate, lessen, oppress, sap, stymie, suppress, -thwart, weaken, wither)

EMPOWER (+): *accredit, affirm, allow, approve, arm, authorize, certify, charge, clear, commission, confirm, credential, delegate, endorse, enforce, enfranchise, entitle, entrust, equip, facilitate, grant, greenlight, inaugurate, induct, initiate, install, instate, invest, legitimize, let, license, okay, permit, privilege, qualify, rubber-stamp, sanction, strengthen, validate, vest, warrant* (≠ abolish, ban, bar, block, -cancel, castrate, constrain, demotivate, -deny, disallow, disbar, discourage, disenfranchise, disqualify, enjoin, -exclude, -forbid, hinder, impair, impede, incapacitate, inhibit, -interdict, legalize, -nullify, obstruct, outlaw, -preclude, -prevent, -prohibit, proscribe, -refuse, -reject, -rescind, reverse, revoke, stop, -thwart, -veto, weaken, withdraw)

EMPTY (/): *belch, bleed, cannibalize, clean, clear, consume, decant, deplete, depredate, discharge, disgorge, drain, draw, drink, drizzle, dump, eject, eliminate, -escape, evacuate, exhaust, exorcise, expel, flush, gut, guzzle, issue, leach, leak, leave, leech, milk, offload, pour, pump, purge, release, scour, siphon, sweep, tap, trickle, unburden, unload, unpack, upchuck, use, vacate, void, vomit* (≠ accumulate, acquire, add, assemble, augment, collect, cram, fill, flood, gather, hoard, keep, load, obtain, overstuff, pack, pile, replenish, restore, retain, stack, stash, stock, stow, stuff, supplement, supply, tuck, wedge)

EMULATE (←): *ape, approximate, burlesque, caricature, challenge, copy, copycat, counterfeit, ditto, duplicate, echo, feign, flatter, follow, imitate, impersonate, lampoon, match, mime, mimic, mirror, mock, model, pantomime, parallel, parody, parrot, pattern, perform, play, playact, portray, pretend, reflect, repeat, replicate, reproduce, rival, roleplay, simulate, travesty* (≠ begin, challenge, coach, conceive, contradict, counter, counteract, create, gainsay, generate, inaugurate, institute, invent, mentor, mismatch, oppose, originate, pioneer, refute, seed, -spurn, -thwart)

ENABLE (→): *abet, accelerate, advance, advantage, aid, allow, assist, augment, bankroll, benefit, boost, brainstorm, catalyze, condition, dower, ease, encourage, endow, enhance, equip, expedite, facilitate, fast-track, foster, fund, furnish, further, grease, hasten, help, hurry, improve, initiate, instigate, invest, lube, lubricate, midwife, mother, motivate, nourish, nurture, permit, prioritize, promote, quicken, relieve, serve, simplify, smooth, spark, spur, stimulate, support, sustain, tend, underwrite, weaponize* (≠ challenge, checkmate, counter, cripple, disable, disinherit, -disown, disqualify, foil, freeze, -frustrate, hamstring, handicap, hinder, hobble, immobilize, impair, impede, inactivate, incapacitate, inhibit, monkey-wrench, muzzle, obstruct, occlude, paralyze, -preclude, -prevent, -prohibit, restrict, spike, stifle, stop, stymie, suffocate, -thwart)

ENABLE (+): *accredit, affirm, allow, approve, arm, authenticate, authorize, bless, certify, commission, confirm, corroborate, countersign, delegate, deputize, designate, empower, endorse, endow, enfranchise, entitle, equip, fit, grant, greenlight, implement, legalize, license, notarize, ordain, permit, prepare, qualify, ready, sanction, task, validate, warrant* (≠ -abort, abrogate, annul, ban, bar, bench, blackball, blacklist, block, -boycott, -cancel, castrate, counter, demote, emasculate, -exclude, -halt, -negate, neutralize, oppose, -ostracize, outlaw, -overlook, picket, -prohibit, protest, quash, -rescind, revoke, -shun, sideline, -snub, stop, -veto, vex, weaken, withdraw)

ENAMOR (←): *allure, amaze, attract, awe, beguile, bewitch, charm, dazzle, delight, dumbfound, enchant, enrapture, enthrall, fascinate, get, hypnotize, infatuate, lure, mesmerize, seduce, thrill, win, woo, wow* (≠ affront, bore, disgust, displease, irk, nauseate, offend, repel, repulse, sicken, vex, worry) **(¿) ABSTRACTION ALERT. Concrete goals essential!**

ENCASE (/): *armor, bale, bound, box, cage, circumscribe, closet, cocoon, coffin, conceal, confine, contain, corral, cover, curb, encapsulate, encircle, enclose, encompass, enfold, enlace, entomb, envelop, fence, frame, hedge, hem, hide, house, immure, include, limit, orbit, package, pen, restrict, ring, sheathe, spackle, surround, wall, wrap* (≠ bare, divulge, eject, -exclude, excoriate, exhume, expose, jettison, -omit, open, peel, reveal, shuck, strip, unbind, uncover, unlash, unmask, unshackle, untie, unwind, wrap)

ENCHANT (→): *becharm, bespell, bewitch, bind, brew, captivate, cast, charm, compel, conjure, constrain, curse, dazzle, dedicate, devise, devote, ensorcel, enthrall, entice, entrance, evoke, fascinate, force, glamour, hex, hoodoo, hypnotize, invoke, jinx, juggle, lure, mesmerize, possess, prophesy, seduce, spell, spellbind, strike, taint, tantalize, tempt, trigger, voodoo, weave, whammy, witch* (≠ aid, banish, bless, cleanse, consecrate, defend, disenchant, dislodge, dispel, dissipate, exorcise, expel, free, guard, heal, liberate, protect, purge, purify, rectify, sanctify, shield, unbind, ward)

ENCHANT (←): *absorb, allure, arrest, astonish, attract, beckon, bedazzle, beguile, bewitch, captivate, catch, charm, court, dazzle, delight, disarm, dizzy, draw, enamor, endear, engage, engross, enrapture, enthrall, entice, entrance, fascinate, grab, gratify, grip, hold, hypnotize, interest, intoxicate, intrigue, invite, involve, kill, lure, magnetize, mesmerize, mystify, please, pull, ravish, razzle-dazzle, seduce, solicit, spellbind, tantalize, tease, tempt, thrill, transfix, win, woo, wow* (≠ annoy, bore, disenchant, disgust, disillusion, disperse, displease, dissipate, distract, eject, hallucinate, heckle, irk, jade, nag, needle, nettle, nitpick, offend, repel, revolt, tire, weary, worry)

ENCIRCLE (+): *bale, band, circle, circuit, circumscribe, compass, cover, crowd, enclose, encompass, enfold, envelop, gird, girdle, halo, hem, orbit, ring, surround, wrap, wreathe* (≠ bar, eject, -exclude, expel, expose, free, -ignore, loose, -neglect, -omit, open, oust, -rebuff, release, unwrap)

ENCLOSE (←): *barricade, blockade, bound, box, cage, circle, circumscribe, cocoon, coffin, confine, coop, corral, cover, delimit, embrace, encase, encircle, encompass, enfold, enshroud, envelop, fence, frame, hedge, hem, hold, imbue, immure, implant, impound, imprison, include, induct, insert, institutionalize, jail, limit, package, pen, restrict, ring, sheathe, surround, tent, veil, wrap* (≠ bare, besiege, brandish, conceal, denude, display, emancipate, -exclude, expose, face, flaunt, free, hide, liberate, loose, meet, -omit, open, -reject, release, reveal, show, showcase, uncover, unloose)

ENCODE (/): *bury, cipher, cloak, cloud, code, conceal, costume, disguise, encipher, encrypt, garble, hide, obscure, perplex, puzzle, ravel, scramble* (≠ clarify, crack, decipher, decode, decrypt, deduce, detect, interpret, solve, translate, unravel, untangle)

ENCOURAGE (→): *abet, activate, anger, animate, annoy, arouse, bother, drive, energize, enrage, exasperate, excite, fan, ferment, fire, foment, gall, galvanize, ignite, impassion, incite, incur, induce, inflame, inspire, instigate, irritate, kindle, madden, motivate, move, pique, provoke, quicken, rabble-rouse, raise, rev, spark, stimulate, stir, taunt, tease, trigger, upset, vex, vitalize* (≠ appease, calm, dampen, deactivate, heckle, humor, hush, lull, mellow, mollify, nag, needle, nettle, niggle, nitpick, numb, pacify, placate, sedate, soothe, subdue, sugarcoat, tranquilize)

ENCOURAGE (→): *adjure, beseech, blandish, bully, cajole, coax, coerce, drive, egg, exhort, fast-track, foment, frogmarch, goad, greenlight, hurry, hustle, implore, importune, incite, instigate, kindle, lobby, march, muscle, nag, needle, nudge, press, pressure, prod, prompt, propel, provoke, push, railroad, rush, shove, soft-soap, spark, spur, steamroller, stimulate, stir, urge, wheedle* (≠ battle, brake, check, constrain, curb, -deter, discourage, dissuade, fight, hamper, hamstring, hold, inhibit, oppose, -prevent, protest, restrain, short-circuit, slow, soft-sell, stall, stem, stop)

ENCOURAGE (+): *advance, animate, assure, boost, buoy, cheer, convince, ease, embolden, energize, enforce, enliven, excite, expedite, fortify, fuel, galvanize, hearten, inspire, inspirit, invigorate, prioritize, promote, provoke, quicken, rally, reassure, reinforce, simplify, steel, stimulate, stir, stoke, streamline, strengthen* (≠ blackmail, daunt, debilitate, demoralize, demotivate, depress, discourage, dishearten, dispirit, enfeeble, hamstring, intimidate, sadden, threaten, undermine, weaken)

ENCOURAGE (+): *abet, advance, advantage, advertise, advise, advocate, agitate, aid, arouse, assist, assure, attend, augment, back, befriend, benefit, bolster, boost, bribe, champion, coach, comfort, condone, console, convince, cultivate, drive, endorse, endow, enthuse, facilitate, favor, feed, finance, force-feed, forward, foster, fuel, fund, further, goad, greenlight, help, incite, incubate, inflame, influence, legalize, lift, lobby, mentor, midwife, mother, motivate, nerve, nourish, nurse, nurture, patronize, persuade, plug, prioritize, prod, promote, publicize, reinvigorate, relieve, revitalize, revive, rouse, second, serve, spark, spitball, spur, stake, stimulate, subsidize, support, sustain, teach, tend, tout, under-*

write, uphold, urge (≠ arrest, ban, bar, block, check, checkmate, demotivate, discourage, discredit, disfavor, disgrace, encumber, enjoin, fetter, foil, -forbid, -frustrate, -halt, harm, hinder, hobble, impede, inhibit, -interdict, manacle, monkey-wrench, muzzle, nobble, obstruct, outlaw, paralyze, -preclude, -prevent, -prohibit, proscribe, protest, repress, retard, shackle, smother, snuff, squash, squelch, stifle, strangle, subdue, suffocate, suppress, throttle, -thwart)

ENCRYPT (/): *baffle, bury, cipher, cloak, cloud, code, conceal, confuse, disguise, encipher, encode, garble, hide, mystify, obscure, perplex, puzzle, ravel, scramble* (≠ clarify, crack, decipher, decode, decrypt, deduce, delineate, detect, explore, extract, interpret, solve, translate, unravel, untangle)

ENCUMBER (→): *afflict, burden, clog, clutter, fill, foist, freight, hamper, handicap, heap, load, lumber, mound, oppress, overburden, overextend, overload, overtax, pack, pile, press, restrict, saddle, stack, strain, surcharge, tax, weigh, weight* (≠ alleviate, assist, discard, discharge, disencumber, drop, -dump, ease, lighten, lose, mislay, misplace, relieve, unburden, unload)

ENCUMBER (←): *arrest, baffle, -balk, barricade, bind, block, blockade, brake, burden, chain, check, choke, clog, compromise, confine, congest, constipate, constrain, constrict, contain, cramp, curb, delay, derail, discommode, disrupt, embarrass, enmesh, enslave, ensnare, entangle, fetter, foil, -frustrate, halter, hamper, handcuff, handicap, hedge, hem, hinder, hobble, hogtie, hold, impede, implicate, inconvenience, inhibit, involve, leash, load, manacle, mire, monkey-wrench, muzzle, obstruct, oppress, overload, -preclude, -prevent, rein, repress, restrain, retain, retard, roadblock, sabotage, saddle, shackle, slow, smother, stifle, straightjacket, strain, strangle, stress, stump, stymie, subvert, suffocate, suppress, tether, -thwart, tie, trammel, weigh* (≠ aid, alleviate, assist, benefit, boost, buoy, clear, discharge, dispatch, ease, encourage, expedite, facilitate, free, further, gladden, hasten, help, hurry, liberate, lift, lighten, loosen, open, organize, permit, promote, release, relieve, remove, rush, separate, smooth, speed, support, unblock, unburden, unclog, uncomplicate, unencumber, unload, unplug, unstop, untie)

ENDANGER (/): *boobytrap, bully, chance, compromise, corrupt, cripple, damage, enfeeble, expose, gamble, hamstring, hazard, imperil, implicate, intimidate, jeopardize, menace, out, risk, sabotage, scupper, subject, subvert, taint, target, threaten, undercut, undermine, venture, wager, weaken* (≠ aid, analyze, armor, assist, bolster, brace, comfort, defend, embalm, guard, harbor, help, maintain, nurture, patrol, preserve, protect, rescue, resume, retain, save, secure, shelter, shield, store, support, sustain, weigh)

ENDEAR (←): *absorb, allure, amuse, attach, attract, bait, bedazzle, beguile, bewitch, bind, blandish, butter, captivate, caress, charm, cherish, coddle, compel, contact, court, cuddle, dazzle, delight, disarm, draw,* *enamor, enchant, engage, engross, enrapture, entertain, enthrall, entice, fascinate, flannel, flatter, grab, gratify, grip, hold, hook, hug, hypnotize, include, influence, interest, intrigue, inveigle, invite, involve, lure, magnetize, mesmerize, monopolize, nuzzle, occupy, ogle, please, preoccupy, prize, pull, razzle-dazzle, rivet, romance, seduce, serenade, snuggle, solicit, spellbind, spoon, take, tantalize, tempt, thrill, tickle, treasure, value, win, woo, wow* (≠ affront, alienate, annoy, antagonize, attack, bore, bother, bug, burden, chagrin, disaffect, disconnect, disenchant, disgruntle, disgust, displease, distance, embitter, enrage, envenom, estrange, frustrate, harass, -hate, heckle, infuriate, insult, irk, irritate, isolate, menace, nag, nauseate, needle, nettle, niggle, nitpick, offend, -omit, oppress, -ostracize, oust, release, repel, repulse, revolt, shame, -shun, sicken, threaten, tire, torment, vex, victimize, weary, wound, wrong) **(¿) ABSTRACTION ALERT. Concrete goals essential!**

ENDORSE (+): *abet, adopt, advance, advocate, affirm, aid, approve, assist, authorize, back, bolster, boost, buttress, champion, confirm, countersign, crosscheck, elect, embrace, empower, entitle, espouse, favor, forward, further, help, patronize, permit, plug, preach, prioritize, prop, ratify, recommend, reinforce, sanction, second, sign, support, sustain, uphold, vindicate, warrant* (≠ baffle, block, conceal, -deny, -desert, disappoint, disavow, discredit, disfavor, disgrace, -disown, fail, foil, -frustrate, oppose, -repudiate, sabotage, scupper, shelve, subvert, -thwart, undercut, undermine)

ENDOW (→): *advocate, aid, award, back, bequeath, bestow, boost, champion, clear, confer, discharge, establish, favor, found, furnish, give, grant, grubstake, invest, leave, legate, liquidate, maintain, nourish, organize, patronize, present, promote, provide, settle, stand, subscribe, supply, support, will* (≠ borrow, cannibalize, chisel, consume, demand, -deny, deplete, deprive, drain, draw, exhaust, leach, leech, lend, loan, poach, receive, remove, scant, skimp, steal, stint, swipe, withdraw, withhold)

ENDOW (→): *accord, arm, award, bankroll, bequeath, bestow, bless, capitalize, clothe, cofinance, comp, confer, contribute, cover, defray, disburse, dispense, donate, dower, empower, enable, enhance, enrich, equip, favor, finance, foot, fund, gift, grant, heighten, invest, patronize, pay, provide, recompense, refinance, reimburse, sponsor, stake, subsidize, supply, tender, tithe, underwrite, will* (≠ beggar, cheat, defund, deplete, disinherit, -disown, dispossess, divest, drain, embezzle, exhaust, purloin, refund, repay, rob, scam, skimp, steal, stiff, stint, strip, swindle)

ENDURE (+): *abide, absorb, accept, allow, assimilate, bear, brave, brook, buck, concede, condone, confront, countenance, digest, experience, face, feel, hack, handle, harden, incur, indulge, know, meet, outlast, overcome, pass, permit, pocket, process, receive, sanction, season, see, shoulder, stand, stomach, suffer, support, surmount, survive, sustain, swallow, sweat, take, taste, tolerate, weather, withstand, witness* (≠ -abandon, -abort, alter, -avoid, -bypass, cease, change, -circumvent, combat, contest, convert, -decline, -deny, dismiss, -dodge, -elude, embrace, enjoy, -escape, -evade, fight, -forbid, -halt, lose, maintain, miss, modify, oppose, outlaw, -prevent, -prohibit, protest, -refuse, -reject, -repudiate, resist, -shun, -spurn, stop, substitute, terminate, transform, -veto)

ENERGIZE (→): *abet, accelerate, activate, actuate, amp, amplify, animate, arouse, awaken, boost, brace, brainstorm, buoy, catalyze, charge, cheer, drive, electrify, embolden, empower, engage, enkindle, enliven, excite, ferment, fire, foment, fortify, galvanize, generate, ginger, goad, goose, hearten, impel, incite, inflame, infuse, inspire, instigate, invigorate, jazz, juice, jump-start, kindle, lift, liven, maximize, motivate, move, prime, prioritize, propel, prostrate, provoke, quicken, raise, rally, reactivate, reanimate, reawaken, recharge, recreate, reenergize, refresh, regenerate, reinforce, reinvigorate, rejuvenate, rekindle, renew, restimulate, restore, resurrect, resuscitate, revitalize, revive, rouse, spark, spike, spur, steel, stimulate, stir, strengthen, sustain, tantalize, tempt, trigger, vitalize, vivify, wake, zap* (≠ check, consume, curb, damp, dampen, daunt, deactivate, deaden, debilitate, demoralize, demotivate, deplete, discourage, dishearten, dispirit, drain, dull, enervate, enfeeble, exhaust, fatigue, harass, inactivate, inhibit, jade, kill, leech, minimize, overextend, overload, quell, quench, repress, restrain, sap, sedate, slow, stagnate, stale, still, stunt, suppress, tax, tire, undermine, weaken, wear, weary, wither)

ENERVATE (/): *attenuate, break, cannibalize, castrate, consume, cripple, damp, dampen, daunt, deaden, debilitate, dehydrate, demoralize, demotivate, deplete, depredate, deprive, desiccate, devitalize, diminish, disable, discourage, dishearten, dismay, dispirit, dissipate, drain, emasculate, empty, enfeeble, exhaust, fatigue, impair, impoverish, incapacitate, jade, lobotomize, numb, paralyze, petrify, reduce, restrict, sap, spend, squander, stagnate, stale, stultify, tap, tire, tucker, undercut, undermine, unhinge, unman, unnerve, waste, weaken, wear, wither* (≠ arouse, boost, brace, buoy, catalyze, charge, electrify, energize, enliven, excite, fire, fortify, galvanize, hearten, incite, inspire, invigorate, kindle, lift, nourish, provoke, quicken, reanimate, reawaken, recharge, regenerate, rejuvenate, rekindle, restore, resurrect, resuscitate, revitalize, rouse, spark, stimulate, stir, strengthen, toughen)

ENFOLD (←): *blanket, bower, camouflage, circle, clasp, clinch, cloak, clothe, clutch, cocoon, costume, cuddle, curtain, disguise, drape, embed, embrace, encase, encircle, enclose, encompass, engulf, enlace, enshroud, envelop, fold, hold, hug, invest, involve, lap, mantle, mask, muffle, orbit, overlay, press, shroud, squeeze, squoosh, surround, swaddle, swathe, veil, wrap, wreathe* (≠ -abandon, bare, denude, display, disrobe, drop, -exclude, exhibit, expose, free, loose, peel, release, reveal, shuck, strip, unclothe, uncover, unveil, unwrap)

ENFORCE (→): *administer, adopt, apply, authorize, bulldoze, cite, coerce, command, compel, constrain, discharge, dispense, effect, effectuate, empower, enact, energize, exact, execute, foist, force, fulfill, honor, implement, impose, invigorate, invoke, legislate, mount, muscle,* *obligate, oblige, observe, pressure, promulgate, prosecute, railroad, realize, reinforce, render, require, rouse, steamroll, strengthen, uphold, urge* (≠ allow, beg, -cancel, demoralize, discourage, -disregard, erase, exempt, expunge, free, -frustrate, -ignore, -neglect, -overlook, permit, quash, relieve, -rescind, scotch)

ENGAGE (→): *accost, affront, ambush, assail, assault, attack, batter, battle, blindside, bombard, brave, bushwhack, buttonhole, challenge, combat, confront, contest, counter, counteract, cross, dare, defy, drive, emulate, face, fight, flay, hammer, harry, impugn, invade, jump, lash, launch, meet, oppose, pillage, pound, race, resist, retort, rival, savage, scathe, scorch, scramble, slash, strike, tackle, trounce, violate, waylay, withstand, wrestle* (≠ -avoid, -bypass, -circumvent, detour, -ditch, -dodge, -duck, -elude, -escape, -evade, miss, -scorn, -shun, skip, -slight, -snub, -spurn)

ENGAGE (←): *advance, appoint, apprentice, assume, bind, book, charter, commission, commit, contract, employ, enlist, enroll, headhunt, hire, ink, keep, lease, obligate, occupy, overcommit, partner, pay, place, promote, recruit, rehire, rent, reserve, retain, scout, secure, sign, subcontract, time, upgrade, utilize* (≠ axe, can, -cancel, discharge, dismiss, eject, fire, furlough, oust, sack, terminate)

ENGAGE (←): *absorb, allure, arrest, attract, beguile, bemuse, betroth, bewitch, busy, captivate, capture, catch, charm, delight, distract, divert, draw, employ, enamor, enchant, endear, energize, engross, enrapture, enthrall, entrance, fascinate, fill, gain, grip, hog, hold, hook, hypnotize, immerse, include, interest, intrigue, involve, join, mesmerize, monopolize, obsess, occupy, preoccupy, soak, tackle, thrill, transport, win, wow, wrestle* (≠ alienate, -avoid, banish, bore, -decline, disaffect, distance, distract, estrange, -exclude, isolate, jade, -omit, orphan, -ostracize, pall, rebuke, -refuse, -reject, seclude, separate, -shun, -snub, -spurn, tire, weary) **(¿) ABSTRACTION ALERT. Concrete goals essential!**

ENGENDER (→): *arouse, beget, breed, create, develop, encourage, excite, foment, foster, generate, hatch, incite, incur, induce, inspire, instigate, kindle, make, muster, nurture, precipitate, produce, proliferate, propagate, provoke, quicken, rouse, spawn, stimulate, stir, whelp* (≠ abolish, conclude, demolish, destroy, doom, end, erase, exterminate, extinguish, -halt, mutate, obliterate, quash, scotch, snuff, squelch, suppress, terminate)

ENGINEER (+): *adjust, align, angle, arrange, assemble, balance, brew, broker, build, calibrate, captain, chair, chart, choreograph, command, compass, compose, conceive, conclude, concoct, conduct, contrive, control, cook, coordinate, create, design, devise, direct, doctor, establish, finagle, finesse, form, frame, game, gerrymander, handle, hatch, integrate, intrigue, machinate, manage, maneuver, manipulate, mastermind, negotiate, operate, orchestrate, organize, originate, outsell, outthink, pace, place, plan, plant, plot, prep, prepare, program, quarterback, ready, regiment, regulate, renegotiate, rig, run, scam,* *schedule, scheme, script, settle, shape, solve, spearhead, stage-manage, steer, strategize, structure, superintend, supervise, swing, synchronize, synthesize, systematize, time, transact, tune, tweak, unify, upstage, wangle, weave, work* (≠ addle, abolish, ad-lib, blow, bobble, bomb, botch, break, bugger, bungle, butcher, capsize, clutter, confound, confuse, damage, demolish, destroy, devastate, discover, dismantle, disorganize, disrupt, disturb, doom, duplicate, eradicate, flatten, flub, forget, fracture, fragment, fudge, fumble, half-ass, harm, -ignore, impede, improvise, jumble, maintain, mangle, mar, mess, mishandle, muddle, muff, obey, pulverize, raze, restore, ruin, scotch, scramble, shatter, smash, spoil, squelch, steal, terminate, wreck)

ENGROSS (←): *absorb, arrest, attract, bewitch, captivate, consume, corner, engage, engulf, enrapture, enthrall, entrance, envelop, fascinate, fixate, grip, hog, hold, immerse, interest, intrigue, involve, monopolize, obsess, occupy, preoccupy, razzle-dazzle, rivet, spellbind* (≠ addle, annoy, befuddle, bore, disgust, distract, forget, -ignore, irk, irritate, nag, needle, nettle, offend, rankle, -reject, release, repel, repulse, tire, weary) **(¿) ABSTRACTION ALERT. Concrete goals essential!**

ENGULF (←): *absorb, arrest, avalanche, bury, consume, cover, deluge, devour, douse, drench, drown, encompass, enfold, engross, envelop, flood, hold, immerse, inundate, marinate, overcome, overrun, overtake, overwhelm, plunge, preoccupy, smother, soak, steamroller, submerge, swamp, wet* (≠ bare, beat, dehydrate, drain, dry, -escape, expose, leach, leech, -neglect, parch, peel, reveal, shed, shuck, staunch, strip, surpass, uncover, underwhelm, unwrap)

ENHANCE (+): *accelerate, accent, accentuate, adorn, aggrandize, aggravate, ameliorate, amend, amp, amplify, assert, augment, automate, beautify, beef, better, bolster, boost, broaden, burnish, buttress, candy, complement, computerize, consolidate, correct, decorate, deepen, dulcify, edit, elaborate, elevate, embellish, embroider, emend, emphasize, enforce, enlarge, enliven, enrich, exacerbate, exaggerate, exalt, expand, extend, fancify, fine-tune, flavor, fortify, glamorize, glitter, glitz, grace, hasten, heighten, help, hone, honey, improve, increase, intensify, jazz, lengthen, lift, magnify, marinate, maximize, modernize, moralize, pad, perfect, perfume, polish, prioritize, punctuate, pyramid, quicken, raise, realign, reconceive, reconceptualize, rectify, redefine, redouble, redraft, refine, reform, refurbish, rehab, rehabilitate, reimagine, reinforce, reinvent, remedy, repair, rephrase, restore, restructure, rethink, retool, retouch, revamp, revise, revolutionize, rework, richen, right, sensationalize, sharpen, shine, sophisticate, spiff, spruce, stabilize, strengthen, stress, supplement, sweeten, swell, syrup, titivate, update, upgrade* (≠ abate, alleviate, barbarize, blemish, blight, callous, coarsen, compromise, damage, decrease, deface, demolish, diminish, disfigure, disrupt, ease, efface, eradicate, flaw, harm, harshen, hurt, impair, injure, lessen, lighten, lower, mar, minimize, moderate, pulverize, reduce, ruin, sabotage, scotch, scupper, scuttle, shatter, shelve, spoil, subdue, subvert, tarnish, undermine, vitiate, weaken, worsen, wreck)

ENJOY (→): *bear, boast, carry, claim, command, exert, experience, hold, keep, maintain, occupy, own, possess, preserve, process, reserve, retain, sport, sustain, use, wield, withhold* (≠ -abandon, beg, cede, -decline, discard, disclaim, -disown, dump, -forsake, lose, miss, -omit, -reject, relinquish, -renounce, -repudiate, require, -spurn, surrender, want, yield) **(¿) ABSTRACTION ALERT. Concrete goals essential!**

ENJOY (←): *acclaim, admire, adore, appreciate, celebrate, cheer, cherish, commemorate, covet, crave, devour, dig, drink, eat, esteem, fancy, favor, fête, fetishize, glorify, hail, hallow, honor, idolize, indulge, laud, love, memorialize, observe, praise, prefer, prize, relish, revere, salute, savor, taste, treasure, trumpet, value, venerate, worship* (≠ abhor, abominate, bemoan, condemn, deplore, deprecate, -despise, -detest, disfavor, endure, execrate, -hate, -loathe, mind, regret, repent, rue, -scorn, -shun, -spurn, stomach, suffer) **(¿) ABSTRACTION ALERT. Concrete goals essential!**

ENLARGE (+): *accelerate, accent, accentuate, accrue, accumulate, add, advance, aggrandize, amass, amplify, assert, augment, beef, bolster, boost, breed, broaden, build, bulge, bump, buttress, collect, complement, compound, deepen, develop, dilate, distend, double, elevate, elongate, emphasize, enhance, escalate, expand, extend, fatten, foster, further, grow, heighten, hype, increase, inflate, intensify, lengthen, magnify, maximize, multiply, optimize, overemphasize, overhaul, prioritize, proliferate, prolong, propagate, protract, pump, punctuate, raise, ratchet, reinforce, revolutionize, scale, spread, stoke, strengthen, stretch, supersize, supplement, swell, treble, triple, unspool, up, upgrade, widen* (≠ abate, abbreviate, abridge, cheapen, compress, concentrate, condense, constrict, contract, curtail, cut, decrease, de-escalate, depress, devaluate, devalue, diminish, downsize, elide, lessen, lowball, lower, miniaturize, minify, minimize, mitigate, moderate reduce, restrain, restrict, retrench, shorten, shrink, subtract, syncopate, trim, truncate, underemphasize)

ENLIGHTEN (→): *acquaint, advise, apprise, better, brief, circulate, civilize, coach, concede, confess, confide, confirm, confront, convert, convince, counsel, cultivate, deflate, develop, direct, disabuse, disappoint, discipline, disclose, disenchant, disillusion, divulge, drill, edify, educate, elevate, elucidate, ennoble, enrich, ensoul, exalt, foster, guide, illuminate, illumine, imbue, improve, inculcate, indoctrinate, inform, inspire, instill, instruct, lift, light, mentor, notify, nurture, persuade, renew, reveal, save, school, shake, teach, tell, train, transfigure, transform, tutor, uncloud, undeceive, update, uplift* (≠ baffle, barbarize, bewilder, bluff, blur, cloud, conceal, confound, confuse, darken, deceive, delude, dement, derange, double-talk, foil, fool, gaslight, harm, hide, hurt, learn, misinform, mislead, -neglect, obfuscate, obscure, -omit, perplex, puzzle, stonewall, stultify, suppress, unhinge, unnerve, upset, worry)

ENLIST (←): *admit, appoint, assign, conscript, draft, employ, engage, enroll, gather, hire, induct, initiate, join, muster, place, recruit, register, task, volunteer* (≠ ban, bar, blacklist, discharge, fire, -quit, release, remove, terminate, wait-list, withdraw)

ENLIST (←): *allure, attract, cajole, charm, coax, commandeer, convince, encourage, engage, enter, entice, gather, get, implore, incorporate, indoctrinate, induce, influence, interest, levy, mobilize, muster, oblige, obtain, palaver, persuade, procure, record, reserve, schmooze, secure, seduce, sell, sway, tempt, urge, win* (≠ ban, bar, blackball, blacklist, -bypass, caution, check, daunt, -deter, discourage, disincline, dissuade, drop, forget, frighten, hamper, hinder, inhibit, intimidate, lose, miss, -overlook, -prevent, -prohibit, restrain, scare, -shun, stop, warn)

ENLIVEN (→): *abet, activate, actuate, amp, animate, arouse, awaken, boost, brace, brighten, buoy, catalyze, charge, cheer, drive, electrify, embolden, energize, excite, exhilarate, ferment, fire, foment, fortify, galvanize, ginger, gladden, hearten, impel, incite, inflame, infuse, inspire, instigate, invigorate, jazz, jump-start, kindle, lift, liven, motivate, move, propel, provoke, quicken, raise, rally, reactivate, reanimate, recharge, refresh, reinvigorate, rejuvenate, renew, resurrect, resuscitate, revitalize, revive, rouse, spark, spike, steel, stimulate, stir, strengthen, tantalize, trigger, vitalize, vivify, wake* (≠ cannibalize, castrate, check, curb, damp, dampen, daunt, deactivate, deaden, debilitate, demoralize, demotivate, deplete, discourage, dishearten, dispirit, drain, dull, enervate, enfeeble, exhaust, fatigue, harass, inactivate, inhibit, jade, kill, leech, quell, quench, repress, restrain, sap, slow, stagnate, stale, still, straightjacket, stunt, subdue, suppress, undermine, weaken, wear, weary, wither)

ENNOBLE (+): *acclaim, adorn, advance, aggrandize, apotheosize, augment, boost, canonize, commend, correct, crown, deify, develop, dignify, distinguish, elevate, enhance, enrich, enshrine, enthrone, entitle, exalt, extol, glorify, heighten, heroicize, heroize, honor, idealize, idolize, immortalize, increase, intensify, laud, lift, lionize, magnify, moralize, optimize, overhaul, perfect, praise, prioritize, promote, raise, rarefy, rectify, refine, revere, romanticize, sanitize, sentimentalize, sugarcoat, upgrade, uplift, venerate* (≠ abase, animalize, bastardize, belittle, canker, chasten, cheapen, darken, debase, debauch, decry, degrade, dehumanize, demean, depreciate, detract, disparage, humble, humiliate, lessen, minimize, mortify, subvert, tarnish, vitiate, vulgarize, worsen)

ENRAGE (/): *affront, aggravate, agitate, anger, annoy, antagonize, bug, cross, embitter, envenom, exasperate, harass, heckle, hector, incense, incite, inflame, infuriate, irk, irritate, madden, miff, nag, needle, nettle, niggle, nitpick, offend, outrage, peeve, pique, provoke, rankle, rile, roil, ruffle, troll, vex* (≠ allay, amuse, appease, assuage, beguile, bewitch, calm, captivate, charm, comfort, console, delight, disarm, enchant, gratify, humor, lull, mellow, mitigate, mollify, pacify, placate, please, quiet, relieve, settle, soothe, sugarcoat, thrill)

ENRAPTURE (←): *absorb, amaze, astonish, attract, beguile, bewitch, captivate, charm, delight, elate, electrify, enamor, enchant, endear, engage, engross, entangle, entertain, enthrall, entrance, fascinate, gladden, gobsmack, grace, gratify, hypnotize, inspire, mesmerize, occupy, pierce, please, ravish, razzle-dazzle, rivet, seduce, spellbind,* *surprise, thrill, transfix, transport, wow* (≠ annoy, bore, demoralize, depress, disappoint, discourage, disenchant, disgust, dishearten, dispirit, displease, distress, disturb, harry, heckle, irk, irritate, nag, nauseate, needle, nitpick, offend, oppress, pain, rankle, repel, repulse, rile, sadden, upset, worry) **(¿) ABSTRACTION ALERT. Concrete goals essential!**

ENRICH (→): *accrue, advantage, augment, award, back, bankroll, benefit, bestow, boost, capitalize, compensate, donate, dower, endow, expand, finance, fund, grant, heighten, increase, inflate, magnify, outlay, overpay, pad, patronize, pay, present, profit, promote, raise, recompense, refund, reimburse, remunerate, repay, reward, sponsor, subsidize, support, swell, tender, underwrite* (≠ beggar, blemish, blight, bluff, cheat, decrease, defraud, defund, deplete, deprive, disgrace, disinherit, -disown, divest, harm, impair, impoverish, reduce, scar, spoil, squander, starve, steal, stiff, stint, swindle, swipe, take, withhold, worsen)

ENRICH (+): *aggrandize, ameliorate, amend, augment, better, boost, civilize, correct, cultivate, develop, educate, emend, endow, enhance, fine-tune, fortify, foster, grace, help, hone, improve, intensify, lavish, optimize, overhaul, perfect, polish, prioritize, pyramid, rectify, refine, reform, refurbish, rehabilitate, reinforce, retouch, revamp, revise, revolutionize, sophisticate, strengthen, supplement, sweeten, upgrade* (≠ barbarize, blemish, blight, callous, coarsen, damage, deface, deprive, diminish, disfigure, flaw, harm, harshen, hurt, impair, impoverish, injure, lessen, mar, spoil, straiten, tarnish, worsen)

ENROLL (←): *accept, admit, appoint, book, catalog, classify, compile, conscript, docket, draft, employ, engage, enlist, enter, file, index, induct, inscribe, join, list, muster, note, obtain, overcommit, record, recruit, register, reschedule, schedule, serve, sign, slate, tabulate, tally, wait-list* (≠ blackball, blacklist, -cancel, delete, discard, discharge, dismiss, -dodge, eject, erase, -exclude, expel, expunge, -ignore, jettison, -omit, oust, -overlook, pass, -refuse, -reject, -shun, -snub, withdraw)

ENSCONCE (→): *allocate, allot, anchor, appoint, arrange, assign, commission, consign, convey, delegate, deliver, deploy, designate, detail, dispose, distribute, embattle, entrench, establish, fit, fix, garrison, graft, harbor, house, implant, insert, install, instate, locate, lodge, nestle, nominate, park, place, plant, position, protect, relegate, room, root, seat, send, set, settle, shelter, situate, specify, station, stipulate, task, transfer, transmit* (≠ ban, bar, block, boot, confound, confuse, disarrange, disorder, disorganize, displace, dump, extract, extricate, fire, forget, free, impede, invalidate, leave, liberate, loose, lose, move, remove, -thwart, unleash, unsettle, upset)

ENSCONCE (/): *archive, bury, cache, coffer, conceal, cover, -ditch, embed, entomb, entrench, establish, exhume, hide, hoard, holster, inter, -omit, pack, protect, screen, secrete, shade, sheathe, shield, squirrel, stash, store, stow, stuff, tuck, wedge* (≠ bare, brandish, circulate, concede, confide, disclose, disinter, display, disseminate, divulge, exhibit, exhume, expose, flaunt, open, parade, reveal, show, showcase, uncover, unearth, unmask, unveil, unwrap)

ENSHRINE (+): *adore, affirm, bless, bronze, celebrate, ceremonialize, cherish, consecrate, conserve, dedicate, deify, devote, embalm, esteem, eternalize, exalt, fête, guard, hallow, honor, idolize, immortalize, lionize, memorialize, preserve, prize, protect, purify, respect, revere, ritualize, sanctify, shield, treasure, value, venerate, worship* (≠ -abandon, bastardize, belittle, bestialize, condemn, contaminate, debase, decry, defile, demean, desecrate, disparage, disrespect, humble, insult, minimize, pollute, profane, regret, rue, tarnish, vandalize)

ENSLAVE (/): *bind, cage, capture, chain, coerce, compel, confine, conquer, constrain, deprive, disenfranchise, dominate, enchain, enclose, enthrall, fetter, hobble, hogtie, hold, immure, imprison, incarcerate, indenture, jail, keep, lock, manacle, oppress, reduce, restrain, restrict, secure, shackle, subdue, subjugate, suppress, tether, tie, trammel, trap, yoke* (≠ allow, deliver, emancipate, embolden, enfranchise, extricate, free, honor, liberate, loose, loosen, manumit, permit, ransom, redeem, release, rescue, save, spring, subvert, unbind, uncage, unchain, unfetter, unshackle)

ENSNARE (←): *ambush, bed, capture, catch, cheat, confound, confuse, corner, deceive, decoy, double-talk, embroil, encumber, enmesh, entangle, entice, entrap, hijack, hook, impersonate, implicate, induce, inveigle, involve, lasso, lure, mislead, nab, net, rope, seduce, seize, snag, snare, tangle, trap, trick* (≠ -bypass, clear, detach, disenchant, disentangle, disgust, dissuade, -ditch, -dodge, dump, -exclude, free, liberate, lose, miss, release, repulse, restore, -shun, -sidestep, skip, untangle)

ENSURE (+): *arrange, assure, attest, certify, cinch, clinch, confirm, convince, crosscheck, establish, guarantee, guard, indemnify, insure, okay, pledge, promise, protect, prove, provide, safeguard, secure, swear, warrant, witness* (≠ boobytrap, damage, dent, disrupt, doubt, enfeeble, erode, injure, sabotage, scotch, scruple, scupper, shelve, subvert, suspect, undercut, undermine, weaken)

ENTANGLE (←): *baffle, bar, bewilder, block, bottleneck, brake, burden, catch, check, choke, clog, complicate, compromise, confound, confuse, congest, constipate, constrain, corner, counter, cramp, crimp, cripple, curb, dam, delay, detain, -deter, drag, embarrass, embroil, encumber, enmesh, ensnare, entrap, fetter, foul, -frustrate, hamper, hamstring, handicap, hinder, hook, impair, impede, implicate, incriminate, inhibit, interrupt, intertwine, involve, jam, jumble, knot, mire, muddle, obstruct, paralyze, perplex, plug, puzzle, ravel, resist, restrain, restrict, shelve, snag, snare, snarl, stall, stay, stop, swamp, swindle, tangle, -thwart, trammel, trap, twist, unsettle* (≠ abbreviate, assist, clarify, clear, cut, detach, disconnect, disengage, disentangle, distinguish, ease, enlighten, -exclude, explain, extricate, facilitate, free, help, liberate, loose, order, organize, oust, release, remove, resolve, separate, sever, shorten, simplify, straighten, streamline, support, unbind, uncomplicate, unfasten, unfold, unknot, unravel, unscramble, unsnarl, untangle, untie, untwist)

ENTERTAIN (←): *absorb, amuse, beguile, busy, captivate, charm, cheer, comfort, content, convulse, delight, distract, divert, elate, enchant, engage, engross, enliven, enrapture, enthrall, exhilarate, fascinate, gladden, grab, gratify, host, humor, hypnotize, immerse, indulge, inspire, interest, intrigue, involve, mesmerize, occupy, pacify, please, pleasure, razzle-dazzle, regale, relax, satisfy, slay, solace, spoil, stimulate, thrill, tickle, wow* (≠ aggravate, annoy, bore, deplete, drain, earbash, enervate, exasperate, exhaust, fatigue, fret, gall, grieve, heckle, irk, irritate, nag, needle, nettle, niggle, nitpick, rankle, rile, sadden, sorrow, tire, upset, vex, weary)

ENTERTAIN (+): *accommodate, admit, bear, board, cherish, compère, cultivate, emcee, feast, feed, foster, fuel, give, harbor, hold, host, house, include, introduce, invite, keep, lodge, maintain, nourish, nurse, nurture, present, provide, quarter, receive, regale, support, sustain, treat, welcome* (≠ -abandon, abjure, banish, -deny, -desert, -disdain, -disregard, -forsake, -neglect, -refuse, -reject, -renounce, repel, -repudiate, -scorn, -spurn, withhold)

ENTHRALL (←): *absorb, amuse, beguile, bewitch, bind, captivate, charm, constrain, delight, distract, divert, enamor, enchant, endear, engage, engross, enrapture, enslave, entertain, entrance, fascinate, glamour, grab, grip, hold, hook, hypnotize, intrigue, lighten, mesmerize, obsess, please, preoccupy, razzle-dazzle, refresh, relax, rivet, spellbind, stimulate, subdue, subject, subjugate, subordinate, thrill, transfix, wow* (≠ annoy, bore, bug, daunt, disenchant, disillusion, dull, earbash, heckle, irk, jade, nag, nauseate, needle, nettle, nitpick, rankle, repel, repulse, rile, sadden, sicken, tire, vex, weary, worry) **(¿) ABSTRACTION ALERT. Concrete goals essential!**

ENTHRONE (+): *acclaim, adorn, aggrandize, anoint, boost, canonize, crown, decorate, deify, dignify, elevate, ennoble, enshrine, exalt, extol, festoon, glorify, heighten, heroicize, heroize, honor, idealize, idolize, induct, install, intensify, invest, laud, lift, magnify, praise, promote, raise, reward, romanticize, sanitize, sugarcoat, upgrade, uplift* (≠ abase, belittle, conquer, decry, degrade, demean, depose, depreciate, dethrone, detract, disparage, humble, humiliate, minimize, overthrow, topple, unseat, usurp, vanquish)

ENTICE (←): *allure, arouse, arrest, attract, award, bait, bamboozle, beckon, bedevil, beguile, bewitch, bribe, cajole, candy-coat, captivate, capture, catch, charm, coax, conquer, convince, court, dare, dazzle, decoy, delight, disarm, draw, dulcify, educe, enamor, enchant, engage, engross, enlist, enrapture, ensnare, entangle, enthrall, entrance, entrap, fascinate, grab, grant, gratify, grip, honey, hoodwink, hook, hypnotize, incite, indoctrinate, induce, influence, instigate, interest, intrigue, inveigle, invite, lead, lure, magnetize, manipulate, mesmerize, motivate, move, oil, outbid, overpay, palaver, paralyze, persuade, please, provoke, pull, ravish, razzle-dazzle,* *reward, rouse, schmooze, seduce, seize, sell, snooker, solicit, spellbind, stimulate, strike, suborn, sugarcoat, suggest, sway, sweeten, tangle, tantalize, taunt, tease, tempt, test, thrill, titillate, train, transfix, transport, trap, treat, trigger, urge, vamp, welcome, wheedle, whet, win, woo, wow* (≠ affront, alarm, annoy, appall, assuage, badger, baffle, -balk, beleaguer, bore, browbeat, bug, bully, burden, caution, cloy, command, content, covet, crave, daunt, demand, demotivate, -deter, disappoint, discourage, disgust, dismay, displease, dissuade, exhaust, fill, force, frustrate, fulfill, glut, gratify, hassle, horrify, hunt, irk, irritate, lose, menace, nag, nauseate, needle, niggle, nitpick, offend, pester, plague, pursue, quench, -reject, repel, repulse, revolt, sadden, sate, satiate, satisfy, scare, seek, shake, shock, sicken, slake, surfeit, terrify, threaten, -thwart, tire, torment, upset, vex, warn, weary, worry, wound)

ENTITLE (+): *accredit, affirm, allow, approve, authenticate, authorize, bless, certificate, certify, charter, commission, confirm, countersign, delegate, deputize, designate, empower, enable, endorse, enfranchise, ennoble, legalize, legitimize, license, notarize, ordain, permit, privilege, qualify, rate, ratify, reapprove, recertify, revalidate, sanction, validate, warrant* (≠ ban, blackball, -cancel, decertify, delegitimize, disable, disallow, disenfranchise, disqualify, -forbid, incapacitate, invalidate, -nullify, proscribe, stop, -thwart, topple)

ENTOMB (/): *bury, cloak, conceal, cover, curtain, embalm, ensconce, enshrine, enshroud, hide, inter, obscure, plant, sepulcher, shade, shield, shroud* (≠ bare, cremate, disclose, discover, disinter, display, excavate, exhume, expose, resurrect, reveal, show, unbury, unearth)

ENTRANCE (+): *amaze, anesthetize, astonish, attract, beguile, bewilder, bewitch, captivate, charm, compel, daze, delight, dizzy, dumbfound, enamor, enchant, endear, engross, enrapture, enthrall, fascinate, gladden, gobsmack, hold, hypnotize, intoxicate, involve, mesmerize, numb, overpower, overwhelm, please, ravish, razzle-dazzle, rejoice, spellbind, stagger, stun, stupefy, thrill, torpefy, transport, wow* (≠ annoy, -balk, bore, bother, bug, dampen, deaden, depress, disappoint, disenchant, disgust, displease, dull, earbash, exhaust, hallucinate, heckle, irk, irritate, nag, needle, nettle, numb, offend, -reject, repel, repulse, revolt, stifle, tire, underwhelm, vex, weary, worry) **(¿) ABSTRACTION ALERT. Concrete goals essential!**

ENTRAP (+): *abduct, ambush, await, bag, bait, bamboozle, bed, beguile, blindside, cage, capture, catch, con, convince, corner, deceive, decoy, defraud, delude, double-talk, embroil, enmesh, ensnare, entangle, entice, frame, gull, hoax, hook, implicate, induce, inveigle, lasso, lure, manipulate, net, rope, seduce, snare, snooker, snow, sucker, swindle, tantalize, tease, tempt, trap, trick, waylay* (≠ assume, assure, believe, credit, discard, discourage, disentangle, disgust, dissuade, -exclude, extricate, free, liberate, loose, lose, miss, release, restore, spring, trust, untangle)

ENTREAT (+): *beg, beseech, blandish, coax, conjure, covet, crave, enjoin, exhort, implore, importune, invoke, panhandle, pester, petition, plague,* *plead, press, request, solicit, supplicate, urge, wheedle* (≠ answer, claim, command, demand, -deny, enforce, exact, extort, give, insist, mollify, oblige, offer, please, provide, -refuse, -reject, supply, volunteer)

ENTRUST (→): *advance, assign, bank, bequeath, commend, commit, confer, confide, consign, credit, delegate, deliver, dispense, disperse, distribute, divide, endow, furnish, give, grant, hand, leave, lend, loan, lumber, pass, recommend, release, relinquish, submit, supply, surrender, transfer, transmit, trust, vest, will, yield* (≠ accept, confiscate, detain, hold, keep, occupy, own, possess, receive, reserve, retain, seize, take, withhold)

ENTRUST (→): *allocate, allot, appoint, assign, authorize, charge, commission, commit, confer, confide, consign, delegate, deputize, designate, empower, foist, impose, invest, name, recommend, relegate, shift, task, trust* (≠ appropriate, bench, betray, blackball, bungle, -decline, demote, discharge, dismiss, fire, flub, incriminate, oust, overthrow, -refuse, sideline, wrong)

ENTWINE (←): *braid, coil, embroil, entangle, interlace, intertwine, join, knit, knot, link, plait, raddle, ravel, rotate, tie, twine, twist, weave, wind, wreathe* (≠ cut, extricate, free, loose, release, separate, unbraid, unravel, untangle, untwist)

ENVELOP (←): *absorb, blanket, circle, clasp, cloak, conceal, consume, contain, corral, cover, deluge, drown, embrace, encase, encircle, enclose, encompass, enfold, engross, engulf, enshroud, guard, hide, hold, hug, obscure, orbit, overwhelm, pen, protect, roll, sheathe, shield, shroud, surround, swaddle, swamp, swathe, veil, wrap* (≠ bare, denude, display, excoriate, expose, extract, open, peel, remove, scour, scrape, shed, show, shuck, strip, uncover, undress, unwrap)

EQUAL (→): *approach, approximate, balance, beat, better, complement, connote, counterbalance, denote, echo, eclipse, emulate, equalize, express, image, import, level, make, match, meet, mirror, outdistance, outdo, outperform, outshine, outstrip, parallel, reach, repeat, rival, signify, suggest, supplement, surpass, tally, tie, top, total, touch, transcend* (≠ bias, cant, contradict, exceed, forfeit, lose, mismatch, miss, oppose, outrank, outreach, outshine, predetermine, prejudge, prejudice, rephrase, skew, slant, tilt, unbalance) **(¿) ABSTRACTION ALERT. Concrete goals essential!**

EQUIP (→): *accommodate, accoutre, adorn, allocate, allot, apparel, appoint, apportion, arm, array, assign, attire, bestow, clothe, contribute, costume, deal, deck, decorate, dispense, distribute, dole, donate, dress, embattle, endow, fortify, furnish, gear, gird, give, hand, heel, implement, issue, man, outfit, portion, prep, prepare, present, prorate, provide, provision, ready, rig, stake, stock, store, supply, tender, uniform, yield* (≠ bare, commandeer, coopt, -deny, deprive, dispossess, divest, expose, -forsake, -neglect, ransack, -refuse, remove, request, require, stint, strip, weaken, withdraw, withhold)

ERADICATE (/): *abnegate, abolish, annihilate, annul, anonymize, atomize, banish, bulldoze, -cancel, censor, -cut, decimate, deep-six, delete, delouse, demolish, -deny, desolate, destroy, devastate, disavow, disclaim, disintegrate, dismantle, dismiss, dissolve, divorce, doom, draw, edit, efface, eliminate, erase, excavate, excise, expunge, expurgate, exterminate, extinguish, extirpate, extract, extricate, flatten, invalidate, kill, level, liquidate, -negate, neutralize, -nullify, obliterate, off, -omit, pulverize, purge, raze, redact, refute, -reject, remove, -repudiate, retract, revoke, scratch, scrub, smash, squash, strike, suppress, torpedo, total, trash, undo, uproot, vaporize, -veto, waste, weed, withdraw, wreck* (≠ aid, assist, authorize, bear, bronze, build, cherish, confirm, conserve, construct, continue, create, embalm, embed, enact, enshrine, entrench, establish, fabricate, fashion, fix, forge, form, help, implant, institute, introduce, keep, legalize, make, manufacture, mend, nurture, patch, perpetuate, plant, preserve, promote, protect, ratify, rebuild, reconstruct, reinstate, reinvigorate, renovate, repair, restore, revive, root, save, schedule, sculpt, seed, shape, shelter, sow, stimulate, support, survive, sustain, weather, withstand)

ERASE (/): *abolish, annihilate, annul, atomize, blackball, -blank, blast, blot, bury, -cancel, censor, clean, consume, -cut, dash, decimate, delete, demolish, destroy, devastate, devour, discard, dismantle, dispatch, dissolve, -ditch, doom, dynamite, eclipse, efface, eject, eliminate, eradicate, excise, exorcise, expel, expunge, exterminate, extirpate, finish, flatten, forget, fragment, hide, jettison, kill, liquidate, -negate, -nullify, obliterate, obscure, oust, powder, prune, pulverize, ravage, raze, remove, rub, ruin, scratch, shatter, smash, snuff, splinter, strike, sweep, terminate, total, trim, waste, wipe, withdraw, wreck, zap* (≠ accept, add, aggrandize, amplify, brainstorm, bronze, build, chronicle, conserve, construct, create, defend, develop, document, embalm, enhance, enlarge, exalt, expand, extend, fabricate, fashion, fix, forge, form, frame, highlight, hype, illuminate, include, insert, magnify, make, manufacture, maximize, mend, nurture, patch, plug, preserve, promote, protect, prove, publicize, rebuild, recondition, reconstruct, renew, renovate, repair, restore, retain, revamp, save, sculpt, shape, showcase, spotlight, support, survive, sustain, weather, withstand)

ERECT (+): *assemble, boost, brace, build, buttress, compose, configure, construct, craft, crane, create, elevate, escalate, establish, exalt, fabricate, fashion, forge, form, found, heave, heft, heighten, hike, hoist, initiate, institute, jack, join, lift, machine, make, manufacture, mount, organize, pitch, plant, produce, prop, raise, rear, rebuild, sculpt, shape, steady, support, upend, uplift, upraise* (≠ annihilate, atomize, bend, bulldoze, capsize, consume, decimate, demolish, destroy, devastate, devour, disassemble, dismantle, flatten, fracture, fragment, level, mortar, nuke, overturn, prostrate, pulverize, raze, restructure, shatter, topple, vaporize, wrack)

ERODE (/): *abrade, bite, consume, corrode, crumble, decimate, deplete, destroy, devastate, disintegrate, dissolve, doom, eat, excoriate, fragment, gnaw, melt, nibble, ruin, scour, spoil, undermine, waste, wreck* (≠ build, construct, erect, fix, freshen, gentrify, preserve, rebuild, refresh, renew, repair, restore, revitalize, revive)

ESCALATE (→): *accelerate, accent, accentuate, accrue, accumulate, add, aggrandize, amass, amplify, ascend, assert, augment, beef, belabor, boost, broaden, build, catalyze, climb, collect, complement, compound, deepen, develop, disturb, elaborate, elongate, emphasize, enhance, enlarge, exaggerate, expand, extend, gather, grow, heighten, hike, hype, increase, inflame, inflate, intensify, lengthen, magnify, maximize, mount, multiply, outgrow, overdramatize, overemphasize, oversell, plug, prioritize, prolong, pump, punctuate, raise, rally, reinforce, scale, sharpen, spread, stoke, strengthen, stress, stretch, supersize, supplement, swell, treble, underline, up, wax, widen* (≠ abbreviate, abridge, compress, condense, constrict, curtail, decrease, de-escalate, diminish, downsize, -halt, lessen, limit, lower, minimize, reduce, restrain, shorten, shrink, slow, stop, subtract, underemphasize, weaken)

-ESCAPE (→): *-avoid, -bypass, -circumvent, depart, -desert, detour, disentangle, emancipate, enfranchise, evacuate, extricate, -flee, fly, foil, free, leave, liberate, loose, loosen, lose, manumit, outrun, -quit, redeem, release, rescue, shake, -sidestep, skip, slip, spring, unbind, uncage, unchain, unfetter* (≠ abide, brave, capture, chase, endure, face, follow, hunt, retain, seek, stomach, target, track, weather)

-ESCAPE (→): *-avert, -avoid, ban, bar, -bypass, -circumvent, debar, deflect, -ditch, divert, -dodge, -duck, eliminate, -elude, -eschew, -evade, except, -exclude, finagle, finesse, foil, fox, -frustrate, miss, -obviate, outfox, outmaneuver, outsmart, outwit, parry, -preclude, -prevent, shake, -shirk, -shun, skirt, -thwart, ward* (≠ accept, catch, contract, court, embrace, incur, invite, pursue, seek, solicit, welcome, woo)

-ESCHEW (/): *-abandon, abjure, -avert, -avoid, ban, bar, -boycott, burke, -bypass, -circumvent, debar, deflect, -deny, discard, -disown, divert, -dodge, -duck, eliminate, -elude, -escape, -evade, except, -exclude, finesse, foil, -forsake, fox, -frustrate, jettison, miss, -obviate, -omit, oppose, -ostracize, oust, outfox, outsmart, outwit, overreach, parry, picket, -preclude, -prevent, -prohibit, protest, -refuse, -reject, relinquish, -renounce, -repudiate, shake, -shirk, -shun, skirt, -spurn, -thwart, waive, ward* (≠ accept, accost, adopt, advocate, catch, colonize, confront, contact, contract, court, deliver, demand, embrace, encourage, espouse, face, incur, indulge, invite, keep, legalize, love, permit, pursue, seek, support, welcome, woo)

ESCORT (+): *accompany, attend, bring, chaperone, chauffeur, conduct, convey, convoy, court, defend, deliver, direct, follow, guard, guide, herald, lead, marshal, navigate, partner, pilot, protect, provide, safeguard, schlep, second, see, serve, shadow, shepherd, show, squire, steer, tag, tail, take, transfer, usher, walk* (≠ -abandon, accost, assault, attack, -avoid, block, -bypass, chuck, cripple, -desert, -ditch, dump, -forsake, hamstring, harm, hinder, hurt, impair, incapacitate, injure, jilt, maroon, molest, offload, -shun, -sidestep, -spurn, stall, stop, strand)

ESPOUSE (→): *absorb, accept, adopt, advocate, affect, appropriate, approve, arrogate, assimilate, assume, back, champion, cherish, choose, coopt, copy, cultivate, decide, defend, determine, embrace, fancy, favor, follow, foster, heed, honor, imitate, incorporate, integrate, internalize, maintain, nurture, patronize, pick, prefer, pretend, prize, quote, second, select, simulate, support, treasure, uphold, use, usurp, utilize, wish* (≠ -abandon, abjure, abnegate, attack, contradict, debate, debunk, discard, discredit, disfavor, -disown, dispute, distrust, -ditch, doubt, dump, -forsake, jettison, junk, oppose, -refuse, refute, -reject, relinquish, -renounce, -repudiate, scruple, -spurn, surrender, suspect)

ESTABLISH (+): *adjust, align, arrange, array, balance, base, begin, brainstorm, build, calendar, calibrate, cast, categorize, chart, classify, coin, collate, compose, connect, constitute, control, create, decree, design, devise, embed, enact, endow, ensconce, entrench, erect, fix, form, found, frame, grade, graft, ground, group, harmonize, implant, inaugurate, inculcate, initiate, insert, install, institute, integrate, introduce, juxtapose, lodge, maintain, marshal, mediate, methodize, moor, open, orchestrate, order, organize, originate, pace, pigeonhole, place, plan, plant, plot, position, prepare, prioritize, provide, rank, rate, rationalize, ready, regiment, regulate, root, schedule, schematize, secure, separate, set, settle, shape, sift, slot, sort, stabilize, start, station, structure, synchronize, systematize, time, unify* (≠ abolish, -abort, adapt, adjourn, annihilate, annul, can, cease, close, conclude, destroy, discharge, dismiss, doom, end, finish, fire, -frustrate, -halt, invalidate, -nullify, obstruct, retract, round, ruin, shut, stop, terminate, uninstall)

ESTABLISH (+): *adduce, affirm, ascertain, assure, attest, audit, authenticate, authorize, base, certify, check, clock, concretize, confirm, connote, contextualize, convince, corroborate, crosscheck, declare, deduce, demonstrate, depose, determine, diagnose, discover, document, double-check, evince, exemplify, exhibit, externalize, find, formulate, illustrate, instance, learn, legalize, legislate, legitimize, manifest, observe, prescribe, profile, prove, ratify, rest, show, showcase, state, substantiate, support, testify, validate, verify, witness* (≠ baffle, conceal, confuse, contradict, cover, debunk, delegitimize, disprove, -disregard, enshroud, expose, forget, gaslight, hide, -ignore, invalidate, lose, mask, misconstrue, misdiagnose, mislay, misplace, miss, misunderstand, -neglect, -overlook, refute, screen, shroud, unlearn, unsettle, veil) **(¿) ABSTRACTION ALERT. Concrete goals essential!**

ESTEEM (+): *adjudge, admire, adore, applaud, appreciate, approve, believe, celebrate, cherish, commend, consider, count, encourage, enjoy, extol, fancy, favor, heed, hold, honor, idolize, judge, laud, lionize, love, mark, mind, notice, observe, praise, prefer, prize, rate, recommend, regard, relish, respect, revere, reverence, think, treasure, value, venerate,* *view, welcome, worship* (≠ -abandon, abhor, abuse, belittle, blackguard, blame, blast, boo, condemn, contemn, criticize, decry, defame, demean, demonize, denounce, denunciate, deplore, deride, -detest, discredit, -disdain, disfavor, disgrace, dishonor, disparage, -disregard, disrespect, execrate, -ignore, incriminate, insult, jeer, -loathe, mistrust, mock, -neglect, pillory, regret, -reject, -renounce, repent, ridicule, rue, -scorn, slander, suspect, wrong) **(¿) ABSTRACTION ALERT. Concrete goals essential!**

ESTIMATE (←): *account, acquaint, adjudge, adumbrate, advise, analyze, appraise, ascertain, assay, assess, audition, believe, benchmark, budget, call, cipher, class, classify, compare, conclude, conjecture, consider, contemplate, criticize, critique, decide, deduce, determine, discover, enumerate, evaluate, examine, extrapolate, figure, fudge, gather, gauge, guess, guesstimate, infer, judge, learn, make, misjudge, misprize, outline, overestimate, place, plan, predict, price, prize, profile, rank, rate, read, reappraise, reason, reassess, reckon, reevaluate, revalue, sample, scan, scope, scrutinize, set, settle, suppose, surmise, survey, suspect, test, underestimate, understand, undervalue, valuate, value, vet* (≠ assume, -blank, calculate, calibrate, compute, cost, count, disbelieve, -discount, -disregard, fake, forget, identify, -ignore, invoice, know, measure, miscalculate, misgauge, misjudge, mislead, mistake, -neglect, number, numerate, pinpoint, predetermine, prove, scale, skip, time)

EVACUATE (→): *barf, belch, bleed, blow, clean, clear, cull, deep-six, deplete, discard, discharge, disclaim, disgorge, dislodge, dispossess, -ditch, drain, draw, drop, dump, ease, eject, eliminate, emit, empty, excise, -exclude, excrete, exhaust, exile, exorcise, expel, exude, flush, jettison, junk, oust, purge, -reject, relieve, remove, scour, scrap, shed, snip, spew, sweep, trash, unpack, vent, void, vomit, waste* (≠ cram, feed, fill, fuel, furnish, insert, invite, jam, load, overstuff, pack, replenish, stash, stow, stuff, supply, tuck, wedge, welcome)

EVACUATE (/): *-abandon, abdicate, abstract, clear, depart, -desert, -discontinue, drop, empty, -escape, -flee, -forsake, leave, -omit, -quit, relinquish, remove, resign, surrender, vacate, -void, withdraw* (≠ access, annex, colonize, conquer, defend, enter, haunt, inhabit, invade, occupy, people, populate, possess, settle, tenant, vanquish)

-EVADE (→): *-avert, -avoid, baffle, -balk, block, -bypass, check, -circumvent, -decline, defeat, deflect, defy, detour, disobey, -ditch, -dodge, -duck, -elude, -escape, fence, -flee, foil, -frustrate, fudge, obstruct, outrun, parry, -prevent, -refuse, shift, -shirk, shortcut, shuffle, -shun, -sidestep, skip, snooker, -spurn, stall, stymie, subvert, -thwart, waive* (≠ abide, absorb, accept, accost, attack, beard, bide, brave, confront, contact, court, dare, defy, divulge, embrace, endure, engage, face, habituate, incur, meet, oppose, pursue, seek, stomach, sustain, tolerate, waylay, weather, welcome, woo)

EVALUATE (←): *adjudge, advise, allot, analyze, appraise, apprise, ascertain, assay, assess, assign, audit, audition, benchmark, beta, budget, calculate, calibrate, categorize, check, class, classify, codify,* *compare, compute, conclude, connect, consider, contemplate, contrast, correlate, count, criticize, critique, deduce, detect, determine, diagnose, distill, enumerate, estimate, examine, explore, eye, eyeball, gauge, grade, group, guesstimate, hierarchize, identify, inspect, interpret, investigate, invoice, judge, learn, liken, mark, measure, number, numerate, observe, ogle, outline, part, peg, peruse, pigeonhole, price, prioritize, probe, profile, prove, quantify, quantize, rank, rate, read, reckon, regard, reinvestigate, review, sample, scan, scope, score, scrutinize, search, second-guess, sift, size, slot, stereotype, study, subdivide, survey, systematize, tally, test, time, total, triangulate, try, underestimate, valuate, value, vet, watch, weigh* (≠ accept, addle, assume, await, baffle, believe, bewilder, blind, blindfold, bury, -bypass, cheat, conceal, confound, confuse, deceive, defraud, -discount, disguise, -disregard, dupe, erase, excuse, fake, fancy, fool, forgive, fudge, -ignore, mask, miscalculate, misconstrue, misdiagnose, misgauge, mishear, misinterpret, misjudge, mislead, misprize, misread, miss, mistake, misunderstand, muddle, mystify, -neglect, obscure, -omit, outwit, overestimate, -overlook, overstate, pass, perplex, predetermine, pretend, puzzle, scam, -shirk, skew, skip, trick, underestimate, undervalue)

EVICT (→): *alienate, ban, banish, bar, blackball, blacklist, boot, bounce, -boycott, cloister, confine, cordon, -deny, deport, detach, disallow, disbar, dislodge, dismiss, disqualify, eject, eliminate, eradicate, excise, -exclude, -excommunicate, exile, exorcise, expatriate, expel, extirpate, extradite, -forbid, -ignore, insulate, isolate, -ostracize, oust, -prohibit, proscribe, -reject, relegate, remove, -renounce, -repudiate, screen, seclude, segregate, separate, sequester* (≠ accept, admit, board, forgive, harbor, hold, house, include, install, invite, keep, lease, lodge, maintain, receive, renew, rent, room, shelter, support, take, welcome)

EVISCERATE (/): *amputate, bone, butcher, castrate, claw, clean, cleave, core, cut, deball, disembowel, disfigure, dismember, dissect, draw, dress, empty, excise, extract, geld, gouge, gut, hack, harvest, hollow, impale, injure, lacerate, mangle, maul, mutilate, razor, remove, scoop, sever, slice, slit, sunder, torture, vivisect, withdraw, yank* (≠ armor, bandage, close, doctor, fill, guard, heal, help, nurse, nurture, protect, remedy, repair, restore, resuscitate, revive, seal, shield, stitch, stuff, suture, transplant)

EVOKE (←): *arouse, awaken, bare, beckon, call, coax, conjure, disclose, discover, divulge, drag, dredge, educe, elicit, evince, excite, expose, extort, extract, gain, get, induce, inspire, invoke, kindle, milk, obtain, procure, provoke, pull, raise, rally, recall, reveal, rouse, secure, stimulate, stir, summon, uncloak, uncover, unmask, unveil, wake, wangle, wrest, wring* (≠ -disregard, erase, forget, -halt, -ignore, miss, -neglect, -overlook, quell, repress, squench, stifle, suppress, -thwart)

EXACERBATE (→): *accent, accentuate, aggravate, amplify, anguish, annoy, antagonize, arouse, assert, badger, bait, bother, chafe, complicate, compound, deepen, disturb, emphasize, enrage, envenom, escalate, exaggerate, exasperate, excite, fret, harass, harry, hassle, heckle, heighten, increase, inflame, infuriate, intensify, irk, irritate,* *madden, magnify, maximize, nag, needle, nettle, niggle, nitpick, overdramatize, peeve, perturb, pester, provoke, rankle, sharpen, tease, torment, trigger, troll, trouble, unsettle, upset, vex, worsen* (≠ allay, alleviate, ameliorate, assuage, better, calm, ease, expiate, help, humor, hush, improve, lighten, lubricate, lull, mellow, minimize, mitigate, moderate, mollify, pacify, placate, relieve, salve, soothe, uncomplicate)

EXACT (←): *ask, assess, badger, blackmail, bleed, challenge, charge, cheat, claim, coerce, command, commandeer, compel, constrain, demand, dock, dragoon, dun, enjoin, excise, extort, extract, fine, fleece, force, gouge, gyp, harass, hound, impose, inflict, insist, lay, levy, milk, mulct, oblige, obtain, penalize, pinch, reap, reclaim, recoup, recover, request, require, requisition, rescue, retrieve, scavenge, skin, solicit, source, squeeze, stipulate, swindle, take, tax, warrant, wreak, wrench, wrest, wring* (≠ abate, bequeath, bestow, comp, condone, contribute, diminish, dispense, -disregard, donate, excuse, foist, forfeit, forgive, furnish, give, grant, -ignore, lessen, pardon, patronize, pay, provide, push, -refuse, release, relinquish, remit, spare, steal, stiff, stint, supply, surrender, tender, yield)

EXAGGERATE (→): *accent, accentuate, aggrandize, amplify, assert, belabor, boast, bolster, boost, caricature, color, cook, corrupt, deceive, deepen, distend, distort, double-talk, dramatize, elaborate, embellish, embroider, emphasize, enhance, enlarge, enrich, exalt, expand, fabricate, fake, falsify, forge, fudge, glorify, goliathize, grace, heighten, heroicize, heroize, hike, honor, hyperbolize, idealize, idolize, inflate, intensify, magnify, maximize, mislead, misreport, misrepresent, overdo, overdramatize, overdraw, overemphasize, overestimate, overplay, overrate, oversell, overstate, pad, paint, pigment, poeticize, puff, punctuate, pyramid, romanticize, satirize, scam, sentimentalize, stress, stretch, up* (≠ belittle, bury, conceal, curb, curtail, cut, deemphasize, diminish, dismiss, downplay, hide, lessen, mask, minimize, moderate, modulate, muffle, obscure, reduce, restrain, screen, shrink, smother, spackle, spin, stifle, underemphasize, understate, varnish, whitewash)

EXALT (+): *acclaim, acknowledge, admire, adore, aggrandize, anoint, apotheosize, applaud, appreciate, approve, ballyhoo, beatify, blandish, bless, boost, celebrate, cheer, cherish, commend, compliment, congratulate, consecrate, dedicate, deify, devote, dignify, elevate, endorse, ennoble, enthrone, erect, eulogize, extol, flatter, glorify, gold-star, gratify, hail, hallow, heighten, hoist, honor, idolize, laud, lift, lionize, magnify, ordain, praise, pray, prioritize, promote, raise, recognize, recommend, respect, revere, reverence, reward, salute, sanctify, sanction, strengthen, swell, thank, toast, tout, trumpet, uplift, venerate, worship* (≠ abase, badmouth, bastardize, belittle, bestialize, blacken, blackguard, blame, blast, boo, brutalize, chasten, cheapen, chide, condemn, criticize, critique, debase, debauch, decry, defame, degrade, dehumanize, demean, demonize, demoralize, demote, denigrate, denounce, deprave, desacralize, desanctify, desecrate, diminish, discredit, disgrace, dishonor, dismiss, disparage, execrate, fulminate, humble, humiliate, incriminate, lower, minimize, offend, pillory, profane, reduce, reproach, revile, ridicule, savage, smear, subvert, threaten, traduce, trash-talk, victimize, vilify, vulgarize, wound, wrong)

EXAMINE (←): *analyze, appraise, assess, audit, benchmark, browse, calculate, caliper, case, categorize, check, clock, collate, comb, compute, con, consider, contemplate, criticize, critique, cruise, diagnose, dissect, estimate, explore, eye, eyeball, finger, frisk, inspect, investigate, learn, mull, notice, number, numerate, observe, oversee, parse, peruse, plumb, police, ponder, prioritize, probe, process, prove, prowl, rank, read, reconnoiter, reference, reinvestigate, research, review, revise, riffle, rifle, sample, scan, scope, screen, scrutinize, search, sift, study, surf, survey, sweep, test, vet, watch, weigh, winnow, x-ray* (≠ accept, anonymize, assume, baffle, believe, blind, blindfold, -bypass, cheat, confound, confuse, deceive, -discount, disguise, -disregard, dupe, erase, estimate, fake, fancy, fool, forget, fudge, -ignore, mask, miscalculate, misconstrue, misdiagnose, mishear, misinterpret, mislead, misread, miss, mistake, misunderstand, muddle, mystify, -neglect, -omit, -overlook, overstate, perplex, puzzle, scam, skew, skim, skip, skirt, stiff, trick)

EXAMINE (←): *annoy, canvass, certify, consult, cross-examine, cross-question, debrief, gauge, grill, harass, hound, interrogate, interview, judge, measure, nag, niggle, nitpick, pester, pump, query, question, quiz, test, time, weigh* (≠ answer, -avoid, believe, conceal, -duck, feign, hide, misgauge, mislead, observe, -refuse, rejoin, remark, retort, study, trust)

EXASPERATE (→): *affront, aggravate, agitate, anger, annoy, antagonize, arouse, badger, bait, bedevil, bother, bug, chafe, chaff, chagrin, devil, discomfort, discompose, disquiet, distress, disturb, earbash, eat, enrage, envenom, exacerbate, exaggerate, exercise, fret, frost, frustrate, gall, get, goad, grate, gravel, hagride, harass, harry, hassle, heckle, hector, hurt, impair, incense, inflame, infuriate, insult, irk, irritate, itch, madden, magnify, maltreat, miff, mistreat, nag, needle, nettle, nitpick, offend, outrage, overdramatize, peeve, persecute, perturb, pester, pique, plague, provoke, rankle, rasp, rile, roil, rouse, ruffle, spite, tease, torment, troll, trouble, undo, unhinge, unsettle, upset, vex, weary, worry* (≠ aid, alleviate, ameliorate, amend, appease, assist, assuage, better, calm, cheer, comfort, compose, console, content, delight, ease, favor, gladden, gratify, help, honor, humor, improve, indulge, lull, mellow, mollify, oblige, pacify, placate, please, quiet, reassure, satisfy, soothe, sugarcoat, thrill, tranquilize, woo)

EXCAVATE (←): *claw, core, cut, dig, discover, disinter, dredge, empty, exhume, explore, gouge, grub, hollow, investigate, mine, plumb, probe, quarry, reveal, scoop, scrape, shovel, spade, spud, trench, uncover, unearth, unpack* (≠ bury, conceal, cover, ensconce, entomb, fill, hide, -ignore, inter, shield, smooth, spackle)

EXCEED (→): *beat, best, better, cap, clobber, conquer, crush, defeat, drub, eclipse, expand, extend, flaunt, lick, magnify, master, maximize, one-up, outbalance, outclass, outdistance, outdo, outgrow, outgun, outlast,* *outpace, outperform, outrace, outrank, outreach, outrun, outsell, outshine, outstrip, outweigh, overcome, overshadow, overstep, overtake, pass, rout, shame, skunk, subdue, surmount, surpass, thrash, top, transcend, trim, trounce, trump, vanquish, wallop, whip* (≠ -abandon, ape, approximate, clone, concede, copy, defer, diminish, -dodge, emulate, follow, forfeit, -forsake, lose, match, mimic, minimize, miss, relinquish, -renounce, resign, shrink, shrivel, wither)

EXCHANGE (+): *alternate, assign, bandy, barter, cede, change, commercialize, commodify, commute, consign, convert, displace, grant, hand, imitate, interchange, invert, leverage, market, monetize, network, rearrange, rejigger, replace, represent, reverse, rotate, second, sell, shift, shuffle, substitute, supersede, supplant, surrender, swap, switch, trade, traffic, transfer, transpose, yield* (≠ abide, bide, continue, -decline, -deny, endure, grasp, grip, hoard, hold, -ignore, keep, maintain, preserve, reserve, retain, stash, stay, steal, sustain, take, tolerate)

EXCISE (/): *amputate, axe, bisect, break, butcher, circumcise, cleave, cut, delete, destroy, disassemble, disconnect, disengage, disjoin, dismantle, dissect, disunite, divide, doom, draw, edit, elide, eliminate, eradicate, erase, estrange, excavate, expunge, expurgate, exterminate, extract, extricate, fragment, gut, halve, pare, razor, remove, rend, -rescind, rip, sacrifice, scissor, scratch, sever, slash, slice, split, strike, sunder, trim, uncouple, vivisect, withdraw* (≠ add, affix, allow, amplify, augment, bear, bury, defend, develop, embed, endure, engender, enlarge, generate, gestate, graft, grow, implant, include, insert, intensify, keep, lose, maintain, plant, preserve, protect, replace, restore, sustain)

EXCITE (→): *abet, activate, agitate, amaze, anger, animate, annoy, arouse, astonish, astound, awaken, bother, chafe, charge, congratulate, delight, discompose, disturb, dizzy, drive, elate, electrify, encourage, energize, engender, enliven, enrage, enthuse, evoke, exasperate, exhilarate, fan, ferment, fire, flush, fluster, foment, gall, galvanize, gobsmack, high-five, ignite, impassion, impress, incite, incur, induce, inflame, infuriate, inspire, instigate, intoxicate, invigorate, irritate, jar, jeer, jolt, kindle, madden, mock, motivate, move, offend, pique, provoke, quicken, raise, rev, rouse, shock, spark, startle, stimulate, stir, taunt, tease, thrill, tickle, touch, trigger, uplift, upset, vex, vitalize, wake, warm, whet, worry, wow* (≠ appease, bar, bore, bother, bug, burden, calm, deaden, demoralize, depress, dishearten, dispirit, encumber, hush, inhibit, lull, lumber, mellow, mitigate, moderate, mollify, nag, nauseate, needle, pacify, placate, quiet, repress, sadden, sedate, sicken, soothe, stagnate, subdue, suppress, tire, tranquilize, weary, worry)

EXCITE (→): *accelerate, boost, catalyze, electrify, elicit, encourage, engender, evoke, facilitate, fan, foment, galvanize, generate, goad, hasten, ignite, impel, incite, incur, induce, instigate, intensify, lubricate, midwife, motivate, precipitate, prioritize, provoke, quicken, rally, spark, spur, start, stimulate, stoke, sway, trigger, urge* (≠ -abort, block, burden, dampen, deactivate, deaden, dull, encumber, exterminate, foil, -frustrate,

-halt, hamper, hamstring, hinder, impede, inactivate, lower, lumber, obstruct, -prevent, restrain, slow, stall, stop, stymie, -thwart, weaken)

EXCITE (←): *amuse, arouse, awaken, bewitch, captivate, charm, delight, enchant, entertain, enthrall, entice, grab, hook, hypnotize, inflame, interest, intrigue, jazz, mesmerize, provoke, rivet, rouse, spellbind, stimulate, tantalize, tease, tempt, thrill, tickle, titillate, wow* (≠ appease, bore, bug, chagrin, dampen, deaden, demotivate, discourage, dull, fatigue, inhibit, nonplus, repel, repress, repulse, sadden, sicken, still, subdue, tire, weary, worry)

-**EXCLUDE (/):** *ban, banish, bar, blackball, blacklist, -blank, block, bounce, -boycott, cordon, delegitimize, delete, disallow, disbar, disqualify, -disregard, drop, eject, eliminate, embargo, evict, except, exempt, expel, -forbid, -ignore, -interdict, leave, obstruct, -obviate, occlude, -omit, -ostracize, oust, outlaw, picket, -preclude, -prevent, -prohibit, proscribe, protest, -refuse, -reject, remove, -repudiate, sideline, skip, -spurn, suspend, -veto* (≠ accept, add, admit, allow, approve, choose, consider, count, embrace, entertain, help, include, incorporate, invite, involve, keep, legalize, legitimize, open, permit, ratify, receive, sanction, support, take, welcome)

EXCUSE (+): *absolve, acquit, alibi, alleviate, appease, clear, confess, contextualize, discharge, ease, exculpate, exonerate, expiate, explain, forgive, free, -ignore, indulge, justify, legalize, lessen, liberate, lighten, mitigate, moderate, -overlook, palliate, pardon, rationalize, release, remit, reprieve, shrive, soften, soft-pedal, spare, spin, sugarcoat, temper, tolerate, varnish, vindicate* (≠ arrest, castigate, chastise, crucify, discipline, fine, imprison, indict, penalize, punish, rebuke, reprimand, sentence, shame, warn)

EXCUSE (+): *clear, condone, cover, defend, -discount, -disregard, exempt, explain, forgive, gloss, -ignore, justify, minimize, mitigate, -omit, -overlook, pardon, rationalize, remit, spare, tolerate, vindicate, waive, whitewash* (≠ adjudge, assert, blame, censure, chasten, condemn, damn, denounce, denunciate, deplore, fault, finger, frame, fulminate, heed, incriminate, judge, mark, mind, note, reproach, resent, resist, scapegoat, slam)

EXECUTE (→): *accomplish, ace, achieve, act, actualize, administer, apply, attain, automate, broker, cite, claim, commit, compass, complete, consummate, crest, deliver, discharge, dispatch, effect, effectuate, enact, end, enforce, engage, engineer, expedite, finish, fulfill, govern, hack, honor, implement, invoke, legislate, make, manage, mechanize, nail, negotiate, observe, perform, perpetrate, practice, promulgate, prosecute, realize, reduplicate, reenact, render, repeat, score, serve, stage, transact, uphold, validate, work* (≠ -abandon, -desert, -disregard, forget, -ignore, mismanage, miss, -neglect, scamp, -shirk, skimp, -slight, slur, undershoot)

EXECUTE (/): *annihilate, assassinate, behead, blot, bump, butcher, claim, croak, crucify, decapitate, destroy, dispatch, doom, drown, electrocute,* *eliminate, eradicate, exterminate, fell, finish, gas, guillotine, hang, ice, impale, kill, liquidate, lynch, massacre, murder, neutralize, off, orphan, purge, shoot, slaughter, slay, smite, snipe, snuff, terminate, whack, zap* (≠ acquit, alibi, animate, bear, exonerate, gestate, guard, heal, protect, raise, reinvigorate, release, rescue, restore, resurrect, resuscitate, revive, save, survive, withstand)

EXEMPT (/): *absolve, acquit, alibi, clear, discharge, dismiss, dispense, except, -exclude, excuse, exonerate, forgive, free, liberate, -omit, -overlook, pardon, release, relieve, remit, spare, waive* (≠ accuse, blame, condemn, convict, disrespect, enforce, fault, finger, frame, obligate, oblige, overcommit, punish, scapegoat, -scorn, -shun)

EXERCISE (→): *abuse, apply, bestow, direct, discharge, employ, enjoy, exert, exploit, handle, harness, implement, maneuver, manipulate, operate, ply, practice, recycle, reuse, run, try, use, utilize, weaponize, wield, work* (≠ break, damage, discard, drop, -ignore, jettison, misapply, misuse, -neglect, -reject, scrap)

EXERCISE (+): *break, condition, cultivate, develop, discipline, drill, edify, foster, groom, habituate, hone, improve, inure, learn, limber, perfect, practice, prepare, ready, refine, rehearse, repeat, review, school, sharpen, strain, study, teach, train, tune* (≠ -abandon, -disregard, forget, hamper, hamstring, hinder, impede, -neglect, -omit, -overlook, stall, stiffen, stymie, weaken, worsen)

EXERCISE (/): *abash, aggravate, agitate, ail, alarm, anger, annoy, appall, bedevil, bother, bug, chafe, concern, confound, confuse, daunt, demoralize, derail, discomfit, discomfort, discompose, disconcert, discourage, dishearten, dismay, dispirit, disquiet, distemper, distract, distress, disturb, dizzy, embarrass, exasperate, faze, fluster, frazzle, fret, fuss, gall, harass, harry, haunt, irk, irritate, jar, mortify, nettle, nonplus, peeve, perturb, pester, pique, plague, rattle, rile, shake, undo, unhinge, unnerve, unsettle, upset, vex, worry* (≠ allay, alleviate, appease, assuage, calm, comfort, compose, conciliate, console, help, humor, mellow, mitigate, moderate, mollify, pacify, placate, propitiate, quiet, settle, soothe, stabilize, steady, tranquilize)

EXHAUST (/): *bankrupt, beggar, bleed, castrate, consume, debilitate, decondition, deplete, devour, diminish, disable, dispel, disperse, dissipate, drain, draw, dry, eat, empty, enervate, enfeeble, erode, expend, fatigue, finish, impoverish, incapacitate, jade, knacker, leach, leech, milk, overextend, overtax, overwork, reduce, sap, slather, spend, squander, strain, straiten, stultify, tax, tire, unhinge, -void, waste, weaken, weary, wither* (≠ augment, bank, boost, budget, condition, conserve, deposit, embattle, energize, fortify, invigorate, lard, refresh, reinvigorate, rejuvenate, renew, replenish, restimulate, restore, revive, stimulate, strengthen)

EXHIBIT (→): *adduce, advertise, air, amplify, announce, array, assert, attest, bare, bear, bellow, blaze, brandish, brief, broadcast, carry, certify, circulate, communicate, concede, confess, confide, confirm, confront,* *corroborate, declare, demonstrate, disclose, discover, display, disseminate, divulge, document, elevate, embody, establish, evidence, evince, exemplify, expose, express, exteriorize, externalize, extol, feature, flash, flaunt, flourish, glorify, herald, highlight, hype, illuminate, illustrate, indicate, magnify, manifest, mark, materialize, offer, parade, placard, plug, possess, post, presell, present, proclaim, produce, promote, prove, publicize, reveal, show, showcase, sound, sport, spotlight, state, substantiate, support, telegraph, testify, trumpet, uncloak, uncloud, uncover, unmask, unsheathe, unveil, validate, volunteer, wag, wave, wear* (≠ baffle, belie, blacken, blind, block, blur, bury, camouflage, censor, cloak, clothe, cloud, conceal, confuse, costume, cover, curtain, darken, dim, disguise, eclipse, ensconce, enshroud, fog, forget, hide, holster, hush, mask, misconstrue, miss, mistake, muddle, muddy, niche, obfuscate, obscure, occlude, occult, -omit, -overlook, overshadow, perplex, remove, screen, shade, shadow, sheathe, shroud, skip, spackle, veil, withhold)

EXHILARATE (+): *activate, amuse, animate, arouse, awaken, boost, brighten, buoy, charge, cheer, delight, elate, electrify, elevate, energize, enliven, excite, freshen, generate, gladden, ignite, inflame, inspire, intoxicate, invigorate, jolt, juice, lift, light, motivate, quicken, raise, razzle-dazzle, refresh, rejoice, restimulate, restore, revitalize, revive, rouse, spark, stimulate, thrill, uplift, vitalize, wake, wow* (≠ agitate, bore, bother, bug, burden, deaden, demoralize, demotivate, depress, discourage, dishearten, dispirit, dissuade, distress, dull, encumber, enervate, frustrate, harass, hassle, hurt, insult, jade, offend, oppress, punish, receive, repress, sadden, sicken, suppress, tire, tranquilize, upset, weaken, weary, worry)

EXHORT (→): *admonish, advise, beseech, bid, caution, coerce, convince, counsel, encourage, enjoin, entreat, force, goad, implore, incite, inflame, insist, inspire, instigate, persuade, plead, preach, press, pressure, prick, prod, prompt, propel, rally, sandbag, spur, stimulate, urge, warn* (≠ answer, block, brake, check, constrain, curb, daunt, demotivate, -deter, discourage, dissuade, -forbid, hamper, hinder, impede, inhibit, -preclude, -prevent, -prohibit, protest, restrain, stall, stem, -thwart)

EXHUME (←): *dig, disclose, disinter, excavate, expose, resurrect, reveal, revive, unbury, unearth, unveil* (≠ bury, conceal, ensconce, entomb, hide, inter, obscure, plant, shroud, stash, store)

EXILE (→): *ban, banish, bar, denaturalize, deport, displace, dispossess, eject, evacuate, -excommunicate, expatriate, expel, extradite, -ostracize, oust, outlaw, proscribe, relegate, repatriate, separate, transport, uproot* (≠ accept, admit, allow, collect, conjure, embrace, greet, harbor, hold, host, invite, keep, permit, receive, repatriate, solicit, summon, welcome)

EXONERATE (+): *absolve, acquit, affirm, alibi, avenge, champion, cleanse, clear, condone, consult, corroborate, defend, defray, deliver, discharge, dismiss, disprove, endorse, exculpate, excuse, exempt, expiate, forget, forgive, free, justify, liberate, mitigate, -omit, -overlook, pardon, purge, purify, redeem, redress, refute, rehabilitate, release, relieve, remit, reprieve, second, shield, spare, substantiate, support, tolerate, unburden,* *uphold, vindicate, warrant, wash* (≠ accuse, allege, anathematize, attaint, bind, blame, burden, charge, compel, condemn, contradict, convict, damn, denounce, discipline, doom, doubt, fault, finger, frame, gainsay, implicate, imprison, impugn, incarcerate, incriminate, indict, institutionalize, intern, jail, litigate, obligate, oblige, prosecute, punish, question, restrain, revile, ruin, scapegoat, sentence, subvert)

EXORCISE (/): *-abandon, abdicate, abolish, adjure, annihilate, ban, bar, cashier, chuck, deep-six, -desert, discard, discharge, dismiss, -ditch, dump, eighty-six, eject, eliminate, eradicate, evacuate, evict, exile, expel, expunge, exterminate, extinguish, extirpate, -forsake, free, jettison, junk, liquidate, lose, oust, pitch, purify, -reject, remove, scrap, shed, shuck, sideline, slough, toss, unload, uproot* (≠ accept, adopt, colonize, conjure, dominate, embrace, employ, encourage, guard, harbor, hold, inhabit, invite, keep, possess, retain, shelter, shield, summon, use, utilize, welcome)

EXPAND (→): *diffuse, diversify, extend, fan, flare, open, outstretch, spread, stretch, unfold, unfurl, unravel, unroll, unspool, wax* (≠ close, compact, compress, concentrate, condense, contract, crush, fold, press, reduce, wrinkle)

EXPAND (+): *accelerate, accent, accentuate, accrue, accumulate, affirm, aggrandize, amass, amplify, assert, augment, beef, belabor, bloat, bolster, boost, broaden, build, bulge, buttress, caricature, collect, color, complement, compound, deepen, develop, dilate, distend, double, dramatize, elaborate, elongate, emphasize, enhance, enlarge, escalate, extend, fatten, flesh, foster, fudge, glitz, grow, heighten, heroicize, heroize, hike, hype, hyperbolize, idealize, idolize, increase, inflate, intensify, lengthen, magnify, maximize, mount, multiply, optimize, overdo, overdramatize, overdraw, overemphasize, overhaul, overplay, oversell, overstate, pad, parlay, piggyback, poeticize, prioritize, prolong, protract, puff, punctuate, pyramid, raise, ratchet, reinforce, romanticize, satirize, sensationalize, sentimentalize, sharpen, sophisticate, spread, stockpile, stoke, strengthen, stress, stretch, supersize, supplement, swell, thicken, treble, triple, up, widen* (≠ abate, abbreviate, abridge, belittle, compress, condense, constrict, contract, curtail, decrease, decry, deemphasize, de-escalate, deflate, deprecate, diminish, -discount, dismiss, disparage, downplay, downsize, lessen, lower, miniaturize, minify, minimize, reduce, retrench, shorten, shrink, soften, soft-pedal, subtract, trivialize, underemphasize, underrate, understate)

EXPAND (+): *add, amplify, broaden, complement, deepen, detail, develop, dilate, elaborate, embellish, embroider, enlarge, exaggerate, flesh, supplement, widen* (≠ abbreviate, abridge, adumbrate, compress, concentrate, condense, contract, curtail, edit, generalize, outline, précis, reduce, shorten, summarize, truncate)

EXPEDITE (+): *accelerate, advance, assist, brainstorm, catalyze, discharge, dispatch, facilitate, fast-forward, fast-track, forward, frogmarch, further, grease, hasten, hurry, hustle, lube, lubricate, march,* *midwife, precipitate, press, promote, push, quicken, railroad, rush, speed, spur, urge* (≠ -abort, block, -cancel, cripple, curb, decelerate, delay, -halt, hamper, hamstring, hinder, hobble, pause, shelve, slacken, slow, stall, stop, stymie, -thwart)

EXPEL (→): *barf, belch, blow, breathe, cast, discharge, disgorge, ejaculate, eject, emit, erupt, evacuate, exhale, expectorate, fire, fling, gush, heave, hurl, hurtle, issue, jet, jettison, launch, pitch, pour, puke, regurgitate, release, shoot, spew, spit, splutter, spout, spring, spurt, squirt, stream, toss, upchuck, vent, void, vomit* (≠ absorb, bottle, consume, contain, devour, eat, engulf, gobble, ingest, inhale, inspire, receive, restrain, smell, sniff, swallow)

EXPEL (→): *alienate, amputate, antagonize, axe, ban, banish, bar, blackball, blacklist, boot, bounce, -boycott, bust, can, cashier, cast, chase, cloister, closet, confine, cordon, defenestrate, -deny, deport, detach, disallow, disbar, discard, discharge, dislodge, dismiss, displace, dispossess, disqualify, divorce, drop, eject, eliminate, eradicate, estrange, evacuate, evict, excise, -exclude, -excommunicate, exile, expatriate, extirpate, extradite, extrude, fire, -forbid, -ignore, impel, insulate, isolate, offload, -omit, -ostracize, oust, out, outlaw, pink-slip, -prohibit, propel, proscribe, protest, -reject, release, relegate, remove, -renounce, -repudiate, retire, rout, sack, screen, seclude, segregate, separate, sequester, sever, sideline, -spurn, suspend, target, terminate, turf* (≠ accept, admit, entertain, greet, harbor, house, include, invite, lodge, permit, receive, reunite, room, shelter, take, welcome)

EXPEL (→): *cast, discharge, ejaculate, eject, eliminate, emit, erupt, evacuate, evolve, excrete, exhale, exude, give, gush, irradiate, issue, jet, ooze, pour, radiate, release, secrete, send, shoot, spew, spout, spray, spurt, squirt, throw, vent* (≠ absorb, draw, drink, infuse, inhale, lap, marinate, slurp, smell, sniff, soak, sponge, steep, suck, take, taste, vacuum)

EXPEND (→): *afford, blow, buy, disburse, dissipate, drop, fritter, give, lard, lavish, misspend, outbid, outlay, overfeed, overpay, overspend, pay, procure, purchase, rain, slather, spend, squander, waste* (≠ acquire, cache, earn, gain, garner, hoard, make, procure, realize, save, secure, starve, stiff, stint, win)

EXPEND (←): *absorb, bankrupt, beggar, burn, cannibalize, consume, cripple, debilitate, deplete, devour, diminish, disable, dissipate, drain, draw, eat, employ, empty, enfeeble, exhaust, guzzle, impoverish, leech, overextend, sap, spend, undermine, use, utilize, weaken, wither* (≠ augment, bank, bolster, budget, conserve, enforce, enlarge, fortify, increase, preserve, rebuild, recoup, reinforce, reinvigorate, renew, repair, replace, restore, revive, save, stabilize, steal, stimulate, strengthen, withhold)

EXPLAIN (+): *analyze, annotate, circulate, cite, clarify, classify, clear, construe, contrast, decipher, decode, define, delineate, demonstrate, demystify, describe, disclose, disentangle, distinguish, elaborate,* *elucidate, explicate, explore, expound, extract, floodlight, generalize, gloss, illuminate, illustrate, interpret, paraphrase, predict, profile, resolve, school, simplify, solve, specify, summarize, teach, translate, uncomplicate, undo, unfold, unravel, unriddle, unscramble, untangle* (≠ addle, baffle, befog, cloud, complicate, confound, confuse, flummox, muddy, mystify, nonplus, obfuscate, obscure, perplex, puzzle, scramble, stump, tangle, trouble, vex) **(¿) ABSTRACTION ALERT. Concrete goals essential!**

EXPLAIN (+): *absolve, acquit, alibi, attribute, condone, defend, exculpate, excuse, exonerate, forgive, justify, rationalize, vindicate* (≠ -abandon, abjure, accuse, blame, condemn, fault, -forsake, indict, refute, -scorn)

EXPLOIT (→): *apply, choreograph, direct, employ, exercise, exert, handle, harness, mine, operate, orchestrate, recycle, reuse, run, tap, use, utilize, weaponize, wield, work* (≠ -bypass, -ignore, leave, misapply, misuse, -neglect, -reject, -shun)

EXPLOIT (/): *abuse, bastardize, beguile, bestialize, betray, bleed, bluff, cheapen, cheat, chisel, commercialize, commodify, con, cozen, debase, deceive, defraud, degrade, delude, demean, devalue, devise, dupe, engineer, euchre, finagle, finesse, fleece, fool, gazump, gull, handle, hoax, hoodwink, hustle, ill-treat, leverage, maneuver, manipulate, mastermind, milk, misapply, mistreat, misuse, oppress, outsmart, outthink, outwit, overcharge, pervert, profane, prostitute, remainder, sacrifice, shanghai, skin, snooker, snow, soak, stiff, sucker, swindle, trick, use, whore, work, wrong* (≠ afford, bankroll, bestow, confess, confront, contribute, defend, dower, endow, fund, furnish, give, guard, honor, maintain, offer, preserve, protect, provide, repair, rescue, restore, save, supply, support, sustain, underwrite, volunteer)

EXPLORE (←): *analyze, anatomize, appraise, ascertain, ask, assay, audit, browse, canvass, case, catch, catechize, challenge, check, chew, clock, consider, consult, contemplate, criticize, critique, cross-examine, cruise, debate, debunk, detect, determine, diagnose, discern, disclose, dispute, dissect, distinguish, elicit, espy, examine, excavate, eyeball, frisk, glimpse, grill, hear, hunt, identify, inspect, interpolate, interrogate, interview, investigate, learn, locate, monitor, mull, notice, observe, parse, perceive, peruse, pick, pioneer, poll, ponder, probe, prove, query, question, quiz, read, realize, recognize, reconnoiter, reference, reinvestigate, research, resolve, reveal, review, riffle, rifle, sample, scan, scope, screen, scrutinize, search, see, seek, sense, sift, size, skim, spitball, spot, study, surf, survey, suss, sweep, test, vet, view, weigh* (≠ addle, assimilate, baffle, bewilder, -blank, blind, blindfold, bury, cloud, conceal, confound, confuse, consolidate, deceive, defraud, digest, disguise, -disregard, fake, forget, fudge, gaslight, grok, -ignore, integrate, leave, mask, misconstrue, misdiagnose, misgauge, mislead, misread, miss, misunderstand, muddle, mystify, -neglect, obscure, -omit, -overlook, perplex, puzzle, skim, skip, synthesize, -thwart, trick, trust, unify)

EXPLORE (←): *analyze, beat, comb, consult, dig, disclose, discover, dredge, examine, excavate, expose, fathom, ferret, gouge, grub, hunt, inspect,* *investigate, observe, pace, patrol, perambulate, pilfer, plumb, plunder, probe, prospect, prowl, question, raid, rake, ransack, ravage, reconnoiter, research, reveal, rummage, scoop, scour, scout, scrounge, scrutinize, search, seek, shovel, sift, sound, spade, survey, test, tour, transit, travel, traverse, tread, trowel, unearth, visit, wander* (≠ -abandon, -avoid, bestow, blind, bury, buy, -bypass, circumnavigate, -circumvent, clean, conceal, confound, contribute, cover, defend, donate, -evade, fill, free, give, guard, hide, -ignore, keep, lose, mislead, miss, mistake, neaten, -neglect, offer, -omit, orbit, order, organize, -overlook, present, protect, purchase, receive, -refuse, -reject, return, shield, skip, skirt, -slight, -snub, stash, stow, supply, tidy, volunteer, yield)

EXPOSE (→): *accost, accuse, admit, attaint, betray, circulate, clarify, concede, confess, confide, confront, confute, crack, debunk, denounce, detect, disclose, display, disseminate, divulge, exhibit, exteriorize, externalize, floodlight, illuminate, leak, manifest, open, out, present, prove, reveal, show, showcase, spill, uncover, unearth, unmask, unveil* (≠ bleep, bullshit, bury, camouflage, candy-coat, censor, cloud, conceal, confuse, cover, -deny, gloss, hide, mask, obscure, overshadow, protect, puzzle, redact, refute, shroud, snooker, snow, spackle, suppress, trick, varnish, veil, whitewash, withhold)

EXPOSE (→): *advertise, air, amplify, announce, bare, bellow, betray, blab, blaze, blurt, boost, brandish, broadcast, bulletin, circulate, communicate, confide, confirm, debunk, declare, demonstrate, disclose, discover, disinter, display, disseminate, divulge, elevate, evince, exhibit, feature, flaunt, flourish, heighten, herald, highlight, hype, illuminate, impart, inform, leak, light, magnify, manifest, out, parade, placard, post, proclaim, produce, project, promote, promulgate, publicize, publish, rake, relate, report, reveal, share, show, showcase, sound, spill, sport, spotlight, telegraph, tell, trumpet, uncloak, unclothe, uncover, undrape, unearth, unmask, unsheathe, unshroud, unveil, wave* (≠ bleep, camouflage, censor, cloak, clothe, cloud, conceal, costume, couch, counterfeit, cover, curtain, darken, disguise, distort, eclipse, enshroud, falsify, garble, gild, gloss, hide, holster, hood, mask, miscommunicate, misrepresent, obscure, occlude, occult, -omit, overshadow, redact, shade, sheathe, shroud, twist, varnish, veil, whitewash)

EXPOSE (+): *bare, bark, clear, defoliate, deforest, denude, discard, disentangle, disrobe, divest, excoriate, flash, flay, free, loose, loosen, open, peel, release, relinquish, remove, shed, shuck, skin, slough, streak, strip, unbuckle, unbutton, unclothe, uncover, undrape, undress, unfasten, unfold, unmask, untie, unveil, unwrap, unzip* (≠ accoutre, adorn, apparel, arm, array, attire, buckle, button, caparison, cloak, clothe, costume, cover, deck, decorate, drape, dress, equip, furnish, garb, ornament, outfit, robe, spackle, swaddle, swathe, veil, zip)

EXPOSE (+): *accost, belittle, blacken, chasten, chastise, concede, confess, confirm, confront, debase, debunk, deflate, degrade, demean, demolish, denounce, denunciate, -deny, diminish, disclose, discomfit, discredit,* *disgrace, dismay, disprove, divulge, embarrass, hound, humble, humiliate, hurt, incriminate, invalidate, malign, mortify, nail, oppose, out, pillory, prove, rattle, ridicule, sabotage, shame, shrivel, taunt, trust, uncloak, uncover, undermine, undress, unmask, unveil, validate, wither* (≠ bluff, bolster, brace, bullshit, buoy, bury, buttress, camouflage, cloak, clothe, comfort, conceal, costume, deceive, -deny, disguise, double-talk, ensconce, flannel, flatter, gratify, hide, mask, mislead, mollify, placate, praise, -rebuff, secrete, settle, veil)

EXPOSE (/): *chance, compromise, endanger, gamble, hazard, imperil, intimidate, jeopardize, menace, risk, stake, subject, threaten, venture, wager* (≠ block, bluff, conceal, guard, hide, preserve, protect, rescue, save, secure, shelter, shield)

EXPUNGE (/): *abolish, annihilate, annul, anonymize, atomize, blackout, blast, blot, -cancel, consume, -cut, dash, decimate, deep-six, delete, demolish, destroy, devastate, devour, discard, dismantle, dissolve, -ditch, doom, drop, dump, dynamite, efface, eject, eradicate, erase, excise, -exclude, exorcise, expel, exterminate, extinguish, extirpate, finish, flatten, fragment, gut, jettison, kill, launder, liquidate, -negate, neutralize, obliterate, offload, -omit, oppose, -ostracize, oust, powder, pulverize, ravage, raze, remove, ruin, scrub, shatter, smash, snuff, splinter, strike, terminate, toss, total, trim, waste, weed, wipe, wreck, zap* (≠ add, approve, arrange, build, chronicle, confirm, conserve, construct, create, encourage, fabricate, fashion, fix, forge, form, frame, help, include, incorporate, insert, institute, introduce, keep, legalize, maintain, make, manufacture, mend, notate, note, patch, permit, perpetuate, plant, preserve, promote, protect, ratify, rebuild, recondition, reconstruct, record, remainder, renew, renovate, repair, restore, retain, revamp, save, sculpt, shape, start, survive, sustain, weather, welcome, withstand)

EXTEND (→): *accord, advance, allocate, allot, allow, approach, assign, assist, attempt, attribute, award, bankroll, bequeath, bestow, bid, cite, comp, confer, consign, contribute, deal, deed, deliver, devote, disburse, dispense, dole, dollop, donate, endow, expend, fund, furnish, give, grant, help, impart, invite, issue, lavish, lend, offer, patronize, pay, pledge, pose, present, proffer, propose, provide, quote, ration, render, send, serve, share, shower, spare, spitball, submit, supply, tender, underwrite, volunteer, yield* (≠ accept, check, coerce, conceal, control, curb, debit, -decline, deduct, defund, demand, -deny, deprive, disallow, disinherit, -disown, -disregard, hide, hold, -ignore, keep, maintain, -neglect, -overlook, pinch, poach, -rebuff, rebut, receive, -refuse, -reject, repress, request, reserve, restrain, retain, retract, -spurn, starve, steal, stiff, stint, suppress, take, -veto, withdraw, withhold)

EXTEND (+): *accentuate, accrue, add, advance, aggrandize, amplify, assert, attenuate, augment, boost, broaden, crane, deepen, develop, dilate, distend, double, draw, elevate, elongate, emphasize, engorge, enhance, enlarge, expand, fatten, foster, grow, heighten, increase, inflate, intensify, lengthen, magnify, mantle, maximize, multiply, open,* *optimize, outstretch, overhaul, pad, prioritize, prolong, protract, raise, reinforce, revolutionize, spin, spread, stall, stretch, supplement, swell, take, thicken, treble, triple, unfold, unfurl, unroll, unwind, upgrade, widen* (≠ abbreviate, -abort, abridge, concentrate, conclude, condense, contract, curtail, cut, decrease, deplete, diminish, downsize, elide, encapsulate, end, finish, lessen, lower, miniaturize, minimize, pare, prune, reduce, shorten, shrink, stop, synopsize, terminate, truncate, underemphasize)

EXTERMINATE (/): *abolish, annihilate, asphyxiate, assassinate, atomize, blitzkrieg, bulldoze, butcher, crush, decimate, delouse, demolish, depopulate, desolate, destroy, devastate, disintegrate, dismantle, dispatch, doom, drown, eliminate, eradicate, erase, execute, extinguish, extirpate, finish, flatten, hang, hunt, ice, kill, level, liquidate, massacre, obliterate, overdose, poison, pulverize, purge, ravage, raze, remove, sacrifice, savage, shred, slaughter, slay, smash, smite, smother, snuff, strangle, suffocate, vanquish, vaporize, weed, wreck, zap* (≠ augment, authorize, bear, beget, breed, build, cherish, colonize, confirm, conserve, construct, create, develop, establish, fashion, foster, frame, gestate, help, increase, institute, introduce, legalize, mend, plant, populate, preserve, proliferate, promote, propagate, protect, rebuild, reinstate, reinvigorate, renew, repair, replenish, rescue, restore, revamp, revive, save, stimulate, support, survive, sustain, weather)

EXTINGUISH (/): *abolish, annihilate, assassinate, beat, best, blanket, butcher, choke, clobber, conquer, cream, cripple, crush, decimate, deep-six, defeat, demolish, desolate, destroy, devastate, disintegrate, dismantle, dispatch, doom, douse, drench, drub, end, eradicate, erase, execute, expunge, exterminate, extirpate, fell, flatten, gut, hush, kill, massacre, murder, mute, nuke, -nullify, obliterate, orphan, overcome, pulverize, quell, quench, quiet, ravage, raze, rout, ruin, scotch, scour, settle, shatter, shush, silence, skunk, slake, slaughter, slay, smash, smother, snuff, squash, squelch, squench, stifle, strangle, subdue, suffocate, suppress, throttle, total, trample, trash, trounce, vaporize, waste, whip, wrack, wreck, zap* (≠ activate, agitate, build, burn, construct, defend, erect, fire, fuel, ignite, inflame, initiate, kindle, light, oxygenate, preserve, raise, rear, spark, start, still, stimulate, stir, survive, sustain, torch, ventilate, weather, withstand)

EXTOL (+): *acclaim, admire, adore, adulate, aggrandize, apotheosize, applaud, approve, blandish, bless, boost, cajole, celebrate, cheer, cherish, commemorate, commend, compliment, congratulate, consecrate, deify, dignify, endorse, enjoy, eulogize, exalt, fête, flannel, flatter, glorify, gold-star, gratify, hail, hallow, hero-worship, high-five, honor, hype, idealize, idolize, immortalize, laud, limelight, lionize, magnify, memorialize, observe, panegyrize, plug, praise, prioritize, promote, publicize, push, recommend, revere, romanticize, salute, sanction, sentimentalize, solemnize, stroke, treasure, trumpet, venerate, worship* (≠ abominate, accuse, admonish, anathematize, attaint, badmouth, belittle, berate, blame, blast, boo, castigate, chastise, chide, condemn, criticize, critique, debase, defame, denigrate, denounce, -detest, disgrace, dishonor, disparage, disrespect, execrate, fault, frame, fulminate, humiliate, incriminate, lambaste, profane, rebuke, regret, repent, reprimand, reproach, ridicule, rue, scathe, scold, -scorn, shame, slander, trash, vilify)

EXTORT (←): *acquire, badger, blackmail, bleed, bluff, bully, cheat, clip, coerce, compel, defraud, demand, educe, evince, exact, extract, fleece, force, gain, gouge, ice, milk, nobble, obtain, pilfer, pinch, procure, ransom, screw, secure, shake, skin, soak, squeeze, stick, stiff, sting, strong-arm, swindle, threaten, victimize, wrench, wrest, wring, wrong* (≠ bankroll, beg, bequeath, beseech, bestow, comp, contribute, donate, entreat, finance, fund, furnish, grant, implore, offer, outbid, outlay, overpay, overspend, patronize, pay, petition, pity, protect, provide, regret, request, solicit, spare, steal, stiff, stint, supply, tender, underpay, volunteer, yield)

EXTRACT (←): *acquire, blackmail, cull, debit, derive, detach, distill, draw, elicit, eradicate, evoke, exact, excise, express, extort, extricate, garner, gather, get, glean, gut, mine, obtain, pick, pluck, prize, pry, pull, quarry, reap, recover, remove, root, secure, select, separate, siphon, source, squeeze, suck, take, tear, uninstall, uproot, vacuum, weed, withdraw, worm, wrench, wrest, wring, yank* (≠ add, blend, compile, cram, entangle, fill, implant, inject, insert, install, instill, introduce, jam, mainline, overstuff, pack, penetrate, plant, ram, saturate, stuff, wedge)

EXTRACT (←): *blackmail, coerce, cull, derive, distill, draw, elicit, garner, gather, get, glean, secure, select, siphon, worm* (≠ disperse, dissipate, plant, -refuse, -reject, spend, spread)

EXTRICATE (←): *clear, deliver, detach, disencumber, disengage, disentangle, extract, free, liberate, loose, loosen, redeem, release, relieve, remove, rescue, save, unburden, unravel, unsnarl, untangle, untie, withdraw* (≠ block, burden, embroil, encumber, entangle, hamper, hinder, impede, involve, load, lumber, obstruct, occlude, stall, stop, weigh)

EYEBALL (←): *absorb, analyze, appraise, assess, assimilate, benchmark, calculate, catch, categorize, check, clock, compare, conclude, connect, consider, consult, contemplate, contrast, correlate, critique, deduce, diagnose, digest, discern, distinguish, estimate, evaluate, examine, explore, eye, gauge, heed, identify, inspect, investigate, learn, mark, measure, mind, note, notice, number, numerate, observe, ogle, peruse, prioritize, probe, prowl, rank, read, regard, reinvestigate, review, scan, scope, scrutinize, search, sift, spot, study, survey, time, watch, weigh, witness* (≠ -avoid, -blank, blind, confuse, -discount, disguise, dismiss, -disregard, fake, fudge, -ignore, mask, misconstrue, misdiagnose, misgauge, misinterpret, mislead, misread, miss, mistake, muddle, mystify, -neglect, -overlook, perplex, pooh-pooh, puzzle, skim, skip)

F

FABRICATE (←): *ad-lib, brainstorm, coin, con, concoct, contrive, counterfeit, deceive, devise, double-talk, extemporize, fake, falsify, feign, forge, form, fudge, half-ass, hatch, imitate, improvise, invent, jive, misrepresent, pretend, scam, spin* (≠ authenticate, confirm, corroborate, crosscheck, document, endorse, notarize, prove, sanction, substantiate, support, validate, verify)

FABRICATE (+): *assemble, begin, brainstorm, brew, build, carpenter, coin, combine, compose, conceive, concoct, configure, constitute, construct, contour, contrive, cook, craft, create, design, devise, erect, establish, fashion, father, forge, form, formulate, found, frame, generate, ghostwrite, hammer, handcraft, imagine, improvise, inaugurate, initiate, innovate, institute, invent, jerry-build, join, machine, make, manufacture, mix, mold, organize, originate, piece, produce, raise, rear, reassemble, rebuild, reconstruct, redevelop, retrofit, rig, sculpt, shape, structure, unite, weave* (≠ atomize, break, crack, crush, demolish, destroy, devastate, disassemble, dismantle, flatten, fracture, fragment, level, pulverize, raze, rend, rip, ruin, shatter, shred, smash, splinter, strike, tatter, tear, wreck)

FACE (→): *abide, accept, accost, affront, allow, approach, battle, bear, beard, brace, brave, brazen, breast, brook, buttonhole, challenge, combat, confront, consult, contact, corner, countenance, court, cross, dare, defy, embrace, endure, experience, eyeball, fight, front, intercept, meet, oppose, race, repel, resist, risk, seek, stand, stomach, submit, suffer, sustain, swallow, tackle, take, tolerate, venture, weather, withstand, woo, wrestle* (≠ -avoid, block, -bypass, -circumvent, detour, -dodge, -duck, -elude, -escape, -eschew, -evade, -forsake, funk, hide, outwit, -overlook, run, shake, -shirk, -shun, -sidestep, skip, skirt, -thwart, withdraw)

FACE (→): *abut, adjoin, annex, append, block, border, bound, command, confront, dominate, edge, embrace, encircle, enclose, fence, flank, fringe, front, juxtapose, line, margin, meet, orbit, overlook, rim, skirt, surround, touch, watch* (≠ alienate, -avoid, back, conceal, detach, -discount, -disregard, hide, -ignore, isolate, oust, screen, seclude, separate)

FACE (→): *apparel, array, blanket, bronze, clothe, coat, costume, cover, decorate, dress, encase, enclose, enshroud, envelop, finish, front, garb, invest, lap, level, line, mantle, overlay, pave, plaster, polish, redecorate, refinish, remodel, robe, roughcast, sheathe, shine, shingle, shroud, smooth, spackle, surface, surround, swathe, veil, veneer, wrap* (≠ bare, denude, discard, excoriate, expose, peel, remove, scour, scrape, scrub, shed, shuck, skin, strip, uncover, unswathe)

FACILITATE (+): *abet, accelerate, advance, aid, assist, brainstorm, butter, catalyze, decongest, disentangle, ease, enable, encourage, enhance, expedite, fast-track, forward, further, grease, hasten, help, hurry, improve, loosen, lubricate, midwife, oil, promote, quicken, rush, simplify, smooth, speed, streamline, unclog, uncomplicate, untangle, upgrade* (≠ aggravate, block, complicate, confound, constipate, cripple, freeze, -halt, hamper, hamstring, harm, hinder, hobble, impair, impede, inhibit, muddy, obstruct, occlude, paralyze, perplex, -prevent, -prohibit, retard, sabotage, scotch, scupper, scuttle, shelve, sophisticate, stall, stifle, stymie, subvert, -thwart, transact, undermine, worsen)

FAIL (/): *-abandon, annoy, betray, chagrin, cheat, deceive, delude, disappoint, discontent, disenchant, disgruntle, disillusion, displease, dissatisfy, distress, -ditch, -forsake, frustrate, lose, mock, -neglect, nonplus, -quit, sadden, stiff, -thwart, upset* (≠ accomplish, ace, achieve, claim, complete, consummate, content, crest, execute, finalize, finish, fulfill, gladden, gratify, realize, satisfy, undertake, win)

FAKE (←): *adulterate, ape, bootleg, camouflage, cloak, clothe, concoct, copy, counterfeit, crib, disguise, doctor, duplicate, fabricate, falsify, fashion, forge, fudge, imitate, impersonate, invent, juggle, manipulate, phony, pirate, plagiarize, playact, pretend, reduplicate, replicate, reproduce, roleplay, sculpt, simulate* (≠ coin, develop, discover, form, invent, launch, originate, pioneer, plant, produce, start)

FAKE (/): *act, adopt, affect, assume, bluff, bullshit, camouflage, cloud, con, conceal, copy, costume, counterfeit, deceive, defraud, disguise, dissimulate, dupe, emulate, fabricate, feign, forge, fudge, ghostwrite, imitate, impersonate, improvise, mask, mimic, pirate, playact, pretend, profess, roleplay, simulate, spackle, spoof, trick, varnish, whitewash, wing* (≠ bare, confess, confirm, confront, corroborate, debunk, discredit, divulge, expose, face, out, reveal, sample, shame, test, validate, verify)

FALSIFY (/): *adulterate, alter, belie, bend, bowdlerize, camouflage, censor, change, cloak, clothe, cloud, color, complicate, con, confound, confuse, contort, contradict, contravene, cook, costume, counterfeit, crib, deceive, -deny, disguise, distort, doctor, double-talk, dress, embellish, embroider, exaggerate, fabricate, fake, fiddle, forge, frame, fudge, garble, gloss, heighten, heroicize, idealize, invent, juggle, manipulate, mask, massage, miscommunicate, misdescribe, mishear, misinterpret, misquote, misread, misrepresent, misstate, mistake, mistranslate, mystify, obscure, overdramatize, oversell, pervert, poeticize, pretend, promote, rig, romanticize, salt, sentimentalize, slant, spin, twist, warp, whitewash* (≠ attest, authenticate, betray, certify, clarify, clear, confirm, correct, corroborate, crosscheck, decipher, deduce, demonstrate, detect, document, explain, expose, illuminate, illustrate, interpret, notarize, prove, rectify, reveal, right, spell, substantiate, validate, witness)

FAMILIARIZE (+): *acclimatize, accustom, acquaint, adapt, adjust, advise, apprise, brief, calibrate, case, coach, condition, discipline, domesticate, enlighten, habituate, housebreak, housetrain, indoctrinate, inform,* *initiate, instruct, introduce, inure, mentor, mix, naturalize, orient, personalize, popularize, post, present, prime, reacquaint, school, season, standardize, tame, teach, tell, train* (≠ addle, alienate, baffle, confuse, customize, disaffect, disarrange, disorder, disorient, -exclude, forget, gaslight, learn, misinform, mislead, mystify, -neglect, -ostracize, perplex, puzzle, stymie, upset)

FAN (→): *accent, accentuate, affirm, agitate, amplify, animate, arouse, assert, begin, breathe, bring, congratulate, deepen, emphasize, encourage, energize, enliven, excite, expand, extend, fire, foment, fuel, galvanize, generate, goad, ignite, impassion, impress, incite, increase, induce, inflame, influence, initiate, inject, inspire, instigate, intensify, kindle, lubricate, midwife, motivate, move, press, prod, produce, prompt, provoke, punctuate, quicken, rabble-rouse, raise, rouse, ruffle, spark, spread, spur, start, stimulate, stir, trigger, urge, whip, winnow* (≠ appease, balance, blunt, bolster, brace, bridle, buffer, calm, center, confound, constrain, counteract, curb, deactivate, demotivate, -deter, diminish, discourage, dissuade, equalize, finish, fix, -frustrate, -halt, hinder, hold, impede, inactivate, inhibit, lessen, mellow, minimize, mitigate, moderate, mollify, obstruct, pacify, placate, -preclude, -prevent, quiet, satisfy, settle, soothe, stabilize, steady, still, stop, subdue, suppress, tame, underemphasize)

FANCY (←): *acclaim, accredit, admire, adore, anticipate, applaud, appreciate, approve, begrudge, cherish, consider, covet, crave, demand, desire, devour, dig, endorse, enjoy, envy, esteem, expect, extol, favor, fetishize, idealize, idolize, indulge, love, praise, prefer, prize, regard, relish, respect, revere, romanticize, sanction, savor, sentimentalize, target, toast, treasure, trumpet, value, venerate, want, worship* (≠ abhor, abominate, assuage, -avoid, censure, check, condemn, control, curb, decry, -despise, -detest, discard, discredit, -disdain, disfavor, -disregard, dread, fear, -flee, -hate, -ignore, judge, -loathe, moderate, -neglect, oppose, pacify, -refuse, regulate, -reject, repress, resent, restrain, -scorn, -shun, -spurn, subdue, tame, underestimate, vilify) **(¿) ABSTRACTION ALERT. Concrete goals essential!**

FANCY (+): *await, believe, conceive, concoct, conjecture, conjure, contemplate, daydream, dream, envisage, envision, fabricate, fantasize, feature, guess, hallucinate, imagine, infer, invent, manufacture, mull, picture, plan, ponder, project, realize, reckon, reflect, relive, spark, spitball, suppose, surmise, suspect, suss, think, visualize, wonder* (≠ analyze, ascertain, calculate, conclude, detect, determine, disbelieve, discover, doubt, ensure, evaluate, gauge, guarantee, know, measure, promise, prove, question, sample, scruple, swear, test, verify) **(¿) ABSTRACTION ALERT. Concrete goals essential!**

FARM (+): *collect, crop, cull, cultivate, culture, develop, dig, domesticate, fallow, fertilize, garden, gather, germinate, gestate, glean, grow, harrow, harvest, hay, hoe, husband, implant, manage, manure, mature, mow, nourish, nurture, originate, pick, plant, plow, pluck, pot, prepare, produce,* *promote, propagate, pull, raise, reap, rear, replant, reseed, ripen, rototill, scatter, seed, select, sharecrop, sow, sprout, start, stock, tend, till, transplant, work, yield* (≠ -abandon, afflict, blight, consume, contaminate, damage, defoliate, destroy, devour, diminish, eat, exterminate, -ignore, infest, kill, mow, -neglect, poison, pollute, raze, recycle, ruin, scavenge, scorch, shrivel, sicken, squander, stunt, uproot, waste, wither)

FASCINATE (←): *absorb, allure, arouse, arrest, attract, bait, beckon, bedazzle, beguile, bemuse, bewitch, busy, captivate, charm, compel, court, dazzle, delight, disarm, distract, draw, enamor, enchant, engage, engross, enrapture, entertain, enthrall, entice, entrance, generate, grab, gratify, grip, hog, hold, hook, hypnotize, immerse, influence, interest, intrigue, invite, involve, lure, magnetize, mesmerize, monopolize, mystify, obsess, occupy, perplex, pique, please, preoccupy, pull, puzzle, razzle-dazzle, rivet, seduce, solicit, spellbind, tantalize, tease, tempt, thrill, titillate, transfix, win, woo, wow* (≠ annoy, answer, bore, bother, bug, burden, chagrin, disgust, displease, earbash, encumber, explain, frustrate, harass, heckle, irk, irritate, jade, nag, needle, nettle, niggle, nitpick, offend, oppress, repel, revolt, satisfy, solve, subdue, tire, weary) **(¿) ABSTRACTION ALERT. Concrete goals essential!**

FASHION (+): *acclimate, acclimatize, accommodate, accustom, acquaint, adapt, adjust, alter, attune, automate, bend, calibrate, case-harden, condition, convert, correct, customize, doctor, edit, equip, establish, fake, familiarize, fine-tune, fit, gear, habituate, harden, harmonize, improvise, inure, match, mechanize, model, modify, mold, motorize, naturalize, orient, orientate, pattern, phase, prepare, prime, readapt, readjust, ready, recast, reclaim, reconceive, recycle, redesign, redevelop, redo, reengineer, refashion, refit, refocus, register, regulate, rehearse, reinvent, rejigger, remake, remodel, rephrase, restore, retool, revamp, revise, rework, rig, right, root, salvage, season, settle, shape, square, suit, tailor, toughen, transform, tune, tweak, weaponize, wing* (≠ adopt, borrow, break, confuse, copy, damage, destroy, disorder, disperse, disturb, dull, duplicate, hurt, misadjust, mismatch, ruin, scatter, scramble, spoil, unsettle, upset, worsen)

FASHION (+): *ad-lib, assemble, brainstorm, brew, build, coin, conceive, concoct, configure, construct, contrive, cook, craft, create, design, devise, envision, erect, establish, execute, fabricate, father, forge, form, frame, handcraft, hatch, hew, imagine, improvise, innovate, institute, invent, machine, make, manufacture, mint, mold, organize, originate, patch, picture, plan, prefabricate, produce, raise, rear, refashion, remake, rethink, script, shape, stitch, structure, visualize, weave, weld, wing* (≠ abolish, annihilate, atomize, botch, break, bungle, demolish, destroy, devastate, disassemble, dismantle, dismember, eradicate, explode, exterminate, extinguish, find, flatten, fracture, fragment, half-ass, mangle, mar, pulverize, raze, repair, restore, ruin, shatter, shred, smash, steal, tear, wreck)

FASTEN (+): *adhere, affix, anchor, attach, batten, belt, bind, bolt, bond, brace, buckle, button, catch, cement, chain, clamp, cleave, clinch, clip, close, concentrate, connect, corset, couple, deadbolt, direct, embed, establish, fix, focus, glue, grip, hitch, hogtie, hold, hook, implant, jam, join, knot, lace, latch, leash, link, lock, lodge, moor, mortar, mortise, nail, pin, rivet, rope, screw, seal, secure, set, settle, shut, solder, stick, strengthen, string, tack, tag, tether, tie, tighten, truss, unite, wedge, weld, zip* (≠ crack, discharge, disconnect, disengage, displace, divide, extract, free, leave, liberate, loose, loosen, lose, open, part, prize, pry, pull, release, remove, separate, sever, slacken, tear, unbuckle, unchain, unfasten, unhitch, unhook, unlace, unlink, unlock, unseal, untie, uproot, wrest, yank)

FATHER (→): *baby, bequeath, bestow, carry, cherish, coddle, cradle, cultivate, discipline, educate, engender, fertilize, foster, guard, host, impregnate, indulge, inseminate, nanny, nourish, nurse, nurture, overindulge, overprotect, pamper, parent, produce, protect, raise, rear, respect, reward, school, scold, shelter, sire, spoil, teach, tend, train, welcome* (≠ -abandon, abuse, betray, -deny, -desert, disclaim, -disown, exterminate, -forsake, murder, orphan, -reject, -renounce, -repudiate)

FATHOM (←): *ascertain, catch, comprehend, detect, determine, diagnose, dig, discover, disinter, divine, educe, elicit, examine, expose, find, follow, gauge, grasp, grok, identify, interpret, know, measure, penetrate, perceive, pinpoint, plumb, probe, realize, recognize, reveal, savvy, search, see, solve, sound, suss, understand, unearth, unmask, unravel* (≠ calculate, confuse, -disregard, estimate, forget, guess, -ignore, misconstrue, misdiagnose, misgauge, mishear, misinterpret, misread, miss, mistake, misunderstand, -neglect)

FATIGUE (/): *break, cannibalize, consume, cripple, debilitate, deplete, depredate, deprive, devitalize, diminish, drain, enervate, enfeeble, exhaust, frazzle, harass, incapacitate, kill, leech, overextend, overtire, overwork, prostrate, sap, stultify, tax, tire, tucker, unhinge, weaken, wear, weary, wither* (≠ activate, animate, energize, enthuse, heal, ignite, inspire, invigorate, kindle, muster, reinvigorate, rejuvenate, relax, rest, restimulate, restore, revive, spark, stimulate, stir, strengthen, vitalize)

FAULT (/): *admonish, anathematize, assail, attack, badmouth, belittle, berate, blame, blast, castigate, censure, chastise, chide, clobber, condemn, criticize, critique, crucify, decry, demean, demonize, denounce, deride, disparage, drub, excoriate, finger, flay, frame, gibbet, hammer, impeach, impugn, incriminate, judge, keelhaul, knock, lambaste, lash, nag, neg, nibble, nitpick, pan, pillory, rebuke, reprimand, reproach, reprove, resent, scapegoat, scold, shame, shred, skewer, slam, slash, slate, trash, tweak, upbraid* (≠ approve, commend, correct, credit, defend, endorse, enhance, excuse, explain, extol, glamorize, idealize, idolize, justify, laud, lionize, moralize, optimize, overhaul, perfect, praise, rationalize, realign, recommend, rectify, revolutionize, reward, right, romanticize, sanction, substantiate, validate, vindicate, warrant)

FAVOR (→): *accommodate, advance, advantage, aid, assist, benefit, boost, charm, cheer, confirm, congratulate, cosset, delight, encourage, endorse, endow, enrich, forward, foster, fulfill, gladden, gold-star, grace, gratify, help, honor, humor, include, indulge, oblige, overindulge, pamper, patronize, placate, please, prioritize, promote, protect, reward, satisfy, spoil, succor, support, sustain, thrill, welcome, woo* (≠ baffle, bench, blacklist, boobytrap, -boycott, checkmate, declass, demote, denounce, -desert, disappoint, fail, foil, -frustrate, monkey-wrench, oppose, picket, protest, sabotage, scotch, scupper, scuttle, shelve, sideline, -snub, subvert, -thwart, undercut)

FAVOR (→): *accord, arm, award, bankroll, bequeath, bestow, bless, clothe, comp, confer, contribute, cover, dispense, donate, dower, empower, enable, endow, enhance, enrich, entrust, equip, fund, furnish, gift, give, grant, heighten, impart, invest, lavish, offer, present, provide, spare, supply, tender, transmit, underwrite, volunteer, will, yield* (≠ bilk, burgle, cadge, cannibalize, cheat, commandeer, consume, debilitate, defund, demand, deplete, disinherit, dispossess, divest, drain, exhaust, leach, mooch, poach, rob, scant, scrounge, skimp, steal, stiff, stint, strip, usurp, weasel, withhold)

FAVOR (+): *accept, acclaim, admire, adore, advocate, applaud, approve, authorize, back, bear, befriend, champion, choose, commend, congratulate, countenance, covet, crave, cull, desire, dig, endorse, endure, enjoy, face, fancy, fetishize, handpick, laud, name, okay, pick, praise, prefer, recommend, relish, salute, sanction, select, support, sustain, target, tolerate, uphold, want* (≠ abhor, abuse, belittle, blackguard, blacklist, blame, blast, boo, condemn, criticize, critique, damn, denounce, deprecate, -detest, discard, -disown, disparage, -hate, jettison, -loathe, malign, mind, oppose, -refuse, -reject, ridicule, -shun, -spurn, wrong)

FAVOR (+): *abet, accommodate, aid, appease, assist, attend, coddle, comfort, conciliate, delight, gladden, gratify, harbor, help, humor, indulge, infantilize, mollify, mollycoddle, nourish, nurture, oblige, pacify, pamper, placate, please, relieve, satisfy, succor, support* (≠ bother, burden, -desert, disappoint, disturb, encumber, faze, -forsake, -frustrate, hamper, hamstring, hobble, impede, incommode, inconvenience, obstruct, oppose, sabotage, saddle, scotch, shelve, subvert, -thwart, trouble)

FAZE (/): *abash, addle, agitate, amaze, annoy, appall, baffle, bewilder, blindside, bother, chagrin, confound, confuse, daunt, daze, dazzle, deafen, debase, degrade, demean, discomfit, discomfort, discompose, disconcert, discountenance, discourage, dismay, disquiet, distress, disturb, dizzy, dumbfound, embarrass, flummox, fluster, freak, gaslight, harass, harry, haunt, heckle, horrify, humble, humiliate, incommode, irritate, jumble, mortify, muddle, mystify, needle, nettle, nitpick, nonplus, perplex, perturb, puzzle, rankle, rattle, roil, shake, shame, shock, startle, stun, surprise, unhinge, unnerve, unsettle, upset, vex, worry* (≠ anchor, assure, buoy, calm, cheer, comfort, console, convince, embolden, encourage, explain, favor, ground, hearten, help, humor, mellow, mitigate, moderate, mollify, pacify, placate, reassure, relieve, root, save, settle, soothe, stabilize, steady)

FEATURE (→): *accent, accentuate, advertise, assert, belabor, bolster, boost, concentrate, deepen, display, elevate, emphasize, escalate, exaggerate, exhibit, favor, flaunt, focus, foreground, heighten, highlight, hype, identify, illuminate, increase, intensify, magnify, mark, maximize, overemphasize, overplay, oversell, overstate, overstress, pinpoint, plug, present, press, prioritize, promote, publicize, punctuate, push, reinforce, sharpen, show, spotlight, stress, underline, underscore, upgrade, weight* (≠ -avoid, belittle, bury, conceal, cover, curb, decrease, deemphasize, delegate, diminish, -discount, disparage, -disregard, downgrade, downplay, -eschew, hide, -ignore, lessen, lighten, marginalize, mask, minimize, miss, -neglect, obscure, obstruct, -omit, -overlook, quiet, reduce, sideline, silence, stifle, subdue, temper, tune, underemphasize, undermine, underrate, understate, weaken)

FEED (→): *banquet, batten, board, bottle-feed, cater, fatten, feast, fill, force-feed, foster, fuel, hand-feed, nourish, nurture, overfeed, provision, regale, reprovision, serve, spoon-feed, stuff, suckle, surfeit, sustain, victual* (≠ -deny, deplete, deprive, drain, famish, hurt, -ignore, injure, leech, malnourish, -neglect, -refuse, starve, stint, underfeed, withhold)

FEED (→): *administer, allocate, apportion, assign, augment, beef, bolster, buttress, cede, contribute, deal, deed, deliver, deploy, dispense, distribute, dole, dollop, donate, encourage, endow, fill, fortify, foster, fuel, furnish, grant, gratify, hand, mete, nurse, nurture, parcel, portion, promote, prorate, provide, reinforce, reload, replenish, satisfy, stock, strengthen, supply, support, transfer* (≠ conserve, -deny, deplete, deprive, drain, extract, harm, hoard, hold, hurt, -ignore, injure, keep, malnourish, -neglect, preserve, -refuse, remove, reserve, retain, sabotage, save, scupper, subvert, undermine, withhold)

FEIGN (←): *act, affect, assume, bluff, camouflage, cloak, clothe, cloud, conceal, costume, counterfeit, devise, disguise, dissimulate, embellish, embroider, fabricate, fake, falsify, forge, ghostwrite, imagine, imitate, impersonate, invent, mask, play, playact, pretend, profess, roleplay, simulate, stonewall* (≠ assess, attest, authenticate, benchmark, check, confess, confirm, confront, corroborate, crosscheck, debunk, discredit, divulge, document, expose, out, prove, reveal, shame, substantiate, test, unmask, validate, verify)

FELL (/): *annihilate, assassinate, bulldoze, butcher, claim, cleave, croak, -cut, dash, decimate, demolish, destroy, dispatch, doom, down, drop, euthanize, execute, finish, flatten, floor, gash, ground, hack, hew, ice, kill, level, mangle, martyr, massacre, mow, murder, neutralize, off, overthrow, raze, rive, ruin, sever, shoot, skittle, slash, slaughter, slay, smite, snuff, split, sunder, take, terminate, topple, tumble, unhorse, unseat, waste, whack, wrack, wreck* (≠ animate, armor, assemble, bolster, brace, build, buttress, construct, craft, elevate, erect, grow, guard, maintain, nurture, preserve, protect, raise, rescue, restore, resurrect, resuscitate, revive, save, secure, shield, stabilize, steady, steel, sustain)

FENCE (/): *bound, cage, circumscribe, confine, coop, corral, delimit, encircle, enclose, girdle, hedge, hem, immure, pen, rail, restrict, separate, surround, wall, wrap* (≠ break, broach, emancipate, expose, free, liberate, open, release, unchain, uncoop, unfasten, unleash)

FENCE (/): *armor, -avert, battle, bulwark, circumscribe, conserve, cover, defend, -dodge, fight, forfend, fortify, guard, keep, oppose, parry, preserve, -prevent, protect, repel, resist, safeguard, save, screen, secure, shield, ward, withstand* (≠ -abandon, assail, assault, attack, beset, besiege, bombard, compromise, endanger, -forsake, harm, imperil, jeopardize, overrun, risk, storm)

FERRET (←): *ascertain, chase, descry, detect, determine, discover, dredge, espy, exhume, extract, find, forage, get, hit, hunt, learn, locate, penetrate, pierce, probe, pry, pursue, retrace, rifle, root, rout, rummage, scour, scout, search, seek, sight, sleuth, spot, trace, track, trail, unearth, uproot* (≠ bury, conceal, cover, disguise, dismiss, -disregard, ensconce, forget, hide, lose, mislay, misplace, miss, obscure, -overlook, safeguard, shroud, squirrel, stash, stow)

FERRY (←): *beam, bear, bring, buck, carry, cart, chauffeur, convey, deliver, drive, fetch, forward, haul, lug, move, pack, ply, remove, run, schlep, send, shift, ship, shuttle, smuggle, take, taxi, tote, transfer, transmit, transport* (≠ abandon, -deny, -desert, discard, -ditch, drop, -dump, hoard, hold, jettison, keep, leave, lose, maintain, paralyze, reconsider, -refuse, unload)

FESTOON (+): *accessorize, adorn, appliqué, array, beautify, bedeck, bedizen, blazon, braid, brighten, caparison, chase, costume, dandify, deck, decorate, drape, dress, drizzle, elaborate, embellish, emblaze, emboss, embroider, encircle, enfold, enrich, fancify, feather, figure, filigree, fillet, flounce, freshen, frill, fringe, garland, garnish, gild, glitter, glitz, grace, gussy, hang, impearl, jewel, lace, ornament, paint, pearl, pretty, redecorate, redo, ribbon, smarten, spruce, stud, swag, swathe, tinsel, tool, trim, wreathe* (≠ bare, blemish, deface, denude, disfigure, dismantle, display, divest, efface, expose, harshen, mar, reveal, scar, simplify, spoil, streamline, strip, uglify, uncover)

FETCH (←): *accumulate, acquire, amass, assume, bag, bear, bring, buck, buy, capture, carry, catch, chauffeur, claim, collect, conduct, convey, deliver, download, earn, elicit, escort, garner, harvest, import, land, lead, lug, monetize, net, obtain, pack, piggyback, procure, produce, purchase, realize, reap, reclaim, recoup, recover, recycle, rescue, retrieve, ride, salvage, scavenge, schlep, secure, sell, shoulder, shuttle, source, stockpile, take, target, tote, transport, truck, wangle* (≠ covet, crave, demand, -deny, deprive, -ditch, drop, dump, fancy, fetishize, furnish, give, hand, hoard, -ignore, lose, misplace, offer, offload, plonk, -reject, request, seek, shed, spare, stash, stockpile, supply, tuck, volunteer, welcome, withdraw, withhold)

FETCH (←): *ask, bill, bring, charge, command, cost, debit, demand, earn, exact, expense, gross, levy, merit, net, pocket, rate, receive, run, total, yield* (≠ accept, buy, consign, -decline, -deny, disburse, pay, purchase, -refuse, scant, skimp, spend, starve, steal, stiff, stint)

FETISHIZE (+): *adore, appreciate, bless, bronze, celebrate, ceremonialize, cherish, commemorate, covet, crave, depersonalize, desire, elevate, enshrine, esteem, eternalize, eulogize, exaggerate, exalt, extol, fancy, hail, honor, idolize, immortalize, laud, lionize, love, magnify, memorialize, objectify, overestimate, overpraise, overvalue, panegyrize, praise, require, revere, ritualize, romanticize, seek, sentimentalize, treasure, value, venerate, want, wish, worship* (≠ belittle, criticize, denigrate, denounce, deride, -despise, devalue, diminish, discredit, -disdain, dishonor, dismiss, -disregard, knock, malign, minimize, mock, -neglect, -omit, -overlook, regret, ridicule, roast, rue, -scorn, -shun, slam, slate, underestimate, underrate, undervalue, vilify)

FIDDLE (←): *bamboozle, betray, bilk, bleed, cheat, chisel, clip, con, cook, cozen, deceive, defraud, diddle, double-cross, double-talk, dupe, embellish, embroider, exploit, extort, fake, falsify, fast-talk, finagle, fix, fleece, flimflam, fool, game, gazump, gouge, graft, gull, hoodwink, hornswoggle, hose, hustle, juggle, maneuver, manipulate, milk, mulct, nick, overcharge, pluck, ream, rook, rope, scam, screw, short, shortchange, skin, skunk, soak, squeeze, stick, stiff, sting, sucker, swindle, thimblerig, trick, underpay, victimize, wrench, wrest, wring* (≠ accuse, aid, appraise, assist, assume, audit, believe, confess, contribute, examine, expose, fail, give, help, honor, inspect, inventory, investigate, lose, maintain, offer, preserve, receive, recoup, rectify, refund, -refuse, repay, respect, restore, review, straighten, support, trust)

FIGHT (→): *accost, affront, ambush, assail, assault, attack, batter, battle, besiege, blindside, blitz, bombard, box, brave, bushwhack, challenge, champion, combat, confront, contest, contradict, counter, defy, dispute, disrespect, duel, face, flay, flout, hammer, harry, hit, humiliate, impugn, incite, insult, invade, lash, lunge, offend, oppose, outrage, pound, punish, race, refute, repel, repulse, resist, savage, scarify, scathe, scorch, slash, trounce, violate, withstand, wrestle* (≠ allow, appease, armor, block, -bypass, calm, defend, endorse, forfeit, guard, heal, -ignore, lose, mellow, miss, mollify, nurture, outmaneuver, -overlook, pacify, permit, placate, quiet, rubber-stamp, second, settle, shield, skirt, soothe, support)

FIGHT (←): *antagonize, baffle, -balk, battle, block, buck, challenge, check, checkmate, combat, confront, contain, contest, contradict, control, counter, counteract, countercheck, cross, curb, debate, defy, discredit, dispute, face, foil, -frustrate, hamper, hamstring, hinder, impede, inhibit, intercept, meet, monkey-wrench, muzzle, obstruct, oppose, oppress, oppugn, outlast, override, repel, repress, repulse, resist, restrain, short-circuit, smother, stem, stifle, straightjacket, stymie, suppress, -thwart, withstand* (≠ abide, accelerate, accord, advance, advocate, assist, back, bear, boost, brainstorm, catalyze, champion, cultivate, diffuse, enable, encourage, endorse, endure, expedite, facilitate, forward, foster, further, grease, hasten, nourish, nurture, permit, prioritize, promote, quicken, stomach, suffer, support, uphold)

FILCH (←): *bag, bilk, burglarize, burgle, cadge, cop, crib, defalcate, defraud, embezzle, extort, fleece, freeboot, grab, haul, heist, hijack, hustle, lift, loot, misappropriate, mug, nick, nip, nobble, palm, pilfer, pinch, pirate, plagiarize, plunder, poach, pocket, purloin, rob, rustle, scrounge, shanghai, shoplift, snaffle, snag, sneak, snipe, steal, swindle, swipe, take, thieve, weasel* (≠ bequeath, bestow, buy, comp, compensate, contribute, donate, fund, give, guard, inherit, keep, offer, pay, present, protect, purchase, receive, refund, reimburse, repay, return, secure, stash, stint, supply, tuck, volunteer)

FILE (+): *archive, book, catalog, categorize, classify, compile, enter, index, list, note, organize, pigeonhole, prioritize, process, record, register, reschedule, slate, slot, sort, store, tabulate, tally* (≠ access, -cancel, delete, drop, erase, find, forget, lose, misfile, mislay, misplace, miss)

FILE (/): *abrade, buff, burnish, chafe, dress, edge, gloss, grate, grind, hone, plane, polish, pumice, rasp, rub, sand, sandblast, scour, scrape, shape, sharpen, shave, shine, smooth, strop, whet* (≠ blunt, callous, coarsen, dull, harshen, indurate, roughen, scuff, soften)

FILL (→): *bloat, brim, bulge, charge, contribute, crowd, crush, distend, drench, flood, furnish, glut, gorge, heap, imbue, impregnate, inflate, interpenetrate, inundate, jam, jam-pack, load, marinate, occupy, overcrowd, overfill, overflow, penetrate, permeate, pervade, provide, refill, refresh, reload, repack, replenish, riddle, sardine, sate, satiate, satisfy, saturate, soak, stock, store, stretch, stuff, suffuse, supply, surfeit, swamp, swell, top* (≠ bleed, cannibalize, consume, cripple, debilitate, deplete, depredate, drain, empty, evacuate, exhaust, extract, honeycomb, leach, leech, milk, overextend, pump, remove, siphon, spend, take, unpack, use, vacate, void)

FILL (→): *block, bulk, bung, caulk, chink, choke, clog, close, clot, congest, cork, cram, dam, jam, mat, obstruct, occlude, overstuff, pack, plug, press, ram, repack, restuff, seal, shove, squash, squeeze, stem, stop, stopper, stopple, stuff* (≠ clear, core, dent, dig, excavate, furrow, gouge, groove, hollow, scoop, shovel, unearth)

FILL (→): *accomplish, achieve, answer, assign, carry, claim, commit, compass, complete, conclude, consummate, crest, discharge, dispatch, distribute, effect, elect, engage, execute, finalize, finish, fix, fulfill, hold, keep, make, meet, name, occupy, perfect, perform, redeem, satisfy* (≠ abdicate, botch, breach, break, -disregard, forfeit, forget, fumble, half-ass, -ignore, -neglect, -overlook, -quit, resign, -slight, transgress, violate)

FILM (←): *bare, broadcast, chronicle, depict, detail, disclose, divulge, document, enumerate, expose, express, itemize, memorialize, photograph, record, recount, relate, render, report, reveal, roll, shoot, take,* *televise, video, videotape, visualize* (≠ bury, -cancel, cloak, clothe, cloud, conceal, costume, delete, disguise, -disregard, erase, forget, hide, hush, mask, obscure, -overlook, screen, sequester, silence, suppress)

FILTER (←): *clarify, clean, cleanse, clear, decontaminate, disinfect, distill, drain, extract, fine, launder, leach, leak, neaten, order, penetrate, percolate, perfect, permeate, process, purge, purify, rectify, refine, sanitize, screen, scrub, sieve, sift, sterilize, strain, tidy, wash, winnow, wipe* (≠ accumulate, begrime, besmirch, churn, cloud, collect, combine, compile, contaminate, defile, dirty, dull, foul, froth, garble, gather, jumble, mingle, mix, muddy, pollute, pour, scramble, soil, sully, taint)

FINAGLE (→): *arrange, brew, broker, captain, choreograph, command, compass, concert, conclude, concoct, conduct, contrive, cook, direct, engineer, finesse, frame, gerrymander, handle, hatch, improvise, intrigue, jockey, lobby, machinate, manage, maneuver, manipulate, mastermind, negotiate, orchestrate, outsmart, outthink, plot, quarterback, renegotiate, run, scheme, wangle, wing* (≠ blow, bobble, botch, bugger, bungle, butcher, flub, fumble, half-ass, louse, mangle, mess, mishandle, mismanage, muff, ruin, spoil, tank, wreck)

FINAGLE (←): *bamboozle, bluff, bullshit, cheat, clinch, con, cook, deceive, double-talk, euchre, falsify, fiddle, finesse, fudge, game, half-ass, hornswoggle, jerry-build, jerry-rig, manage, maneuver, manipulate, outwit, plot, rig, scheme, secure, snooker, snow, stiff, sucker, swindle, trick* (≠ admit, block, confess, confront, -deny, disabuse, disclose, disillusion, divulge, expose, hamper, hinder, impede, -prevent, reveal, stymie, -thwart, uncover, undeceive, unmask)

FINANCE (→): *advantage, aid, assist, award, back, bankroll, benefit, bequeath, bestow, capitalize, clear, cofinance, compensate, contribute, defray, discharge, dispense, donate, dower, endorse, endow, enrich, ensure, establish, extend, facilitate, feed, float, foot, force-feed, foster, found, fuel, fund, furnish, grant, grubstake, guarantee, help, house, invest, keep, lend, liquidate, loan, maintain, nourish, nurture, offer, organize, overfeed, patronize, pay, proffer, profit, promote, provide, -quit, recompense, refinance, refund, reward, serve, settle, sponsor, stake, stand, subscribe, subsidize, suckle, supplement, supply, support, sustain, tend, underwrite* (≠ -abandon, accept, acquire, bankrupt, beggar, bilk, borrow, break, bust, cadge, consume, cripple, defund, demand, deplete, deprive, -desert, diminish, disappoint, disinherit, -disown, drain, draw, exhaust, expect, expend, exploit, famish, fleece, foil, -frustrate, hamper, hamstring, hinder, impoverish, leech, -neglect, obtain, overextend, pauperize, receive, reduce, request, ruin, sabotage, sap, scant, scotch, scrounge, scupper, skimp, spend, squander, starve, stiff, stint, straiten, subvert, take, tap, tax, -thwart, waste, weaken, withhold)

FINESSE (→): *arrange, brew, broker, captain, choreograph, command, compass, concert, conclude, concoct, conduct, contrive, direct, engineer, finagle, frame, game, gerrymander, handle, hatch, improvise, intrigue, machinate, manage, maneuver, manipulate, mastermind, negotiate,* *orchestrate, outsmart, outthink, plot, quarterback, renegotiate, run, scheme, transact, trick, wangle, wing* (≠ blow, bobble, botch, bugger, bungle, butcher, flub, fumble, half-ass, mangle, mess, mishandle, muff, ruin, tank, wreck)

FINESSE (/): *-avert, -avoid, ban, bar, -bypass, -circumvent, debar, deflect, divert, -dodge, -duck, eliminate, -elude, -escape, -evade, except, -exclude, foil, fox, -frustrate, miss, -obviate, oppose, -ostracize, outfox, outmaneuver, outsmart, outwit, overreach, parry, -preclude, -prevent, shake, -shirk, shuffle, -shun, skirt, steer, -thwart, ward* (≠ accept, catch, contract, court, embrace, incur, pursue, seek, welcome, win, woo)

FINE-TUNE (+): *accommodate, adapt, adjust, align, alter, arm, attune, balance, bend, calibrate, case-harden, convert, correct, customize, doctor, edit, equalize, equip, fashion, fit, harden, harmonize, inure, match, modify, personalize, prepare, prime, punctuate, ready, realign, reconceive, reconceptualize, redefine, refine, reimagine, reinvent, rejigger, remodel, repair, rephrase, restore, rethink, retool, revamp, revise, rig, right, sculpt, season, shape, square, suit, tailor, tone, toughen, transform, tune, tweak, weaponize* (≠ blemish, break, cripple, damage, deface, deform, destroy, disable, disfigure, disqualify, disrupt, doom, efface, -halt, hamper, hamstring, harm, harshen, hinder, hobble, impair, incapacitate, mar, misadjust, mismatch, monkey-wrench, ruin, sabotage, scar, scupper, shelve, spoil, stymie, -thwart, undermine, vandalize, weaken, wreck)

FINGER (→): *allege, ascertain, betray, check, clock, determine, diagnose, disclose, discover, distinguish, examine, find, hit, identify, inspect, investigate, isolate, locate, name, notice, observe, pick, pin, pinpoint, place, recall, recognize, remember, reveal, scrutinize, spot* (≠ camouflage, cloak, cloud, conceal, costume, counterfeit, disguise, feign, hide, lose, misdiagnose, misplace, simulate)

FINISH (←): *cannibalize, consume, deplete, depredate, devour, dispatch, down, drain, drink, eat, empty, exhaust, expend, guzzle, leech, overextend, spend, use* (≠ concoct, cook, feed, fill, fuel, keep, maintain, prepare, ready, replenish, restore, save, stock, store, victual)

FINISH (/): *-abort, absolve, accomplish, achieve, attain, cap, cease, claim, clinch, close, complete, conclude, consummate, crest, crown, determine, discharge, -discontinue, effect, end, execute, finalize, fold, fulfill, -halt, perfect, realize, scratch, scrub, settle, shutter, stop, terminate, wrap* (≠ begin, block, brainstorm, commence, hamper, hinder, inaugurate, initiate, inspire, -preclude, -prevent, scamp, spark, stall, start, trigger)

FINISH (/): *annihilate, assassinate, atomize, best, checkmate, conquer, crush, defeat, destroy, dispatch, doom, down, euthanize, execute, exterminate, kill, leach, liquidate, outlast, overcome, overpower, overthrow, overwhelm, rout, ruin, slaughter, slay, steamroller, terminate, topple, unhorse, unseat, vaporize, whup, wrack, wreck* (≠ armor, bear, build, construct, create, defend, embalm, establish, found, gestate, preserve, protect, rescue, revive, save, secure, shield, support, survive, sustain, weather)

FIRE (→): *axe, ban, banish, boot, bounce, bump, bust, can, cashier, chuck, depose, discard, discharge, dislodge, dismiss, displace, dispossess, downsize, drop, drum, eject, excuse, exempt, expel, furlough, -nix, -ostracize, oust, pink-slip, release, relieve, remove, replace, retire, rout, sack, separate, spare, supersede, supplant, suspend, terminate, toss, trim, turf, unload, unseat* (≠ appoint, assign, boost, contract, delegate, employ, engage, hire, invite, keep, nominate, promote, propose, protect, pursue, recruit, reemploy, rehire, retain, sign, subcontract, task, welcome)

FIT (←): *accommodate, carry, contain, enclose, encompass, enfold, harbor, hold, house, include, incorporate, involve, room, seat, shelter, shield, take* (≠ banish, blackball, dismiss, eject, endanger, expel, harm, hurt, imperil, oust, -refuse, -reject, relegate) **(¿) ABSTRACTION ALERT. Concrete goals essential!**

FIT (+): *acclimate, accommodate, accustom, adapt, adjust, align, alter, approximate, arm, attune, automate, balance, bend, calibrate, condition, convert, correct, customize, doctor, edit, equalize, equip, fashion, fine-tune, gear, habituate, harden, harmonize, inure, match, mechanize, model, modify, motorize, naturalize, orient, pattern, phase, prepare, prime, punctuate, ready, realign, recast, reclaim, recycle, redesign, redevelop, reengineer, refashion, refocus, register, regulate, rehearse, reinvent, rejigger, remake, remodel, reorient, repair, rephrase, rethink, retool, revamp, revise, rework, rig, right, sculpt, season, shape, square, suit, tailor, toughen, transform, tune, tweak* (≠ -boycott, damage, -eschew, freeze, harm, hinder, hold, homogenize, keep, misadjust, mismatch, picket, -prohibit, protest, standardize)

FIT (+): *accept, accommodate, align, balance, blend, combine, connect, dovetail, equal, follow, graft, harmonize, join, link, match, meet, square, suit, tally, unify, unite* (≠ alienate, battle, challenge, contradict, counter, defy, disrupt, estrange, gainsay, integrate, jar, -negate, -nullify, rattle, reintegrate, resist, rile, roil, shake, skew, unsettle) **(¿) ABSTRACTION ALERT. Concrete goals essential!**

FIX (→): *affix, anchor, attach, bind, bond, catch, cement, chain, clamp, clinch, congeal, connect, consolidate, couple, embed, entrench, establish, fasten, glue, graft, harden, hitch, implant, inculcate, ingrain, install, instill, join, juxtapose, link, locate, lodge, moor, mortar, nail, peg, pin, place, plant, position, rigidify, rivet, root, screw, secure, set, settle, situate, solidify, stabilize, station, steady, stick, stiffen, stud, stuff, thicken, tie, wedge* (≠ alter, change, crack, destroy, detach, disorganize, extract, loose, loosen, prize, pry, pull, remove, sever, tear, unfasten, unsettle, uproot, wrest, yank)

FIX (←): *arrange, bribe, buy, coerce, cook, corrupt, distort, doctor, embellish, embroider, fake, falsify, fiddle, finagle, finesse, forge, game,* *grease, hamper, influence, lubricate, maneuver, manipulate, massage, misrepresent, nobble, pervert, pretend, reach, rig, square, suborn, subvert, twist* (≠ accuse, bobble, botch, bugger, bungle, confess, confirm, corroborate, debunk, expose, flub, fumble, honor, indict, investigate, mishandle, obey, recoup, resist, restore, save, validate, verify)

FIX (+): *absorb, aim, attract, channel, concentrate, direct, draw, fasten, focus, hold, level, point, rivet, target, turn* (≠ addle, blur, bore, confuse, -disregard, distract, -ignore, muddle, -omit, -overlook, -sidestep)

FIX (+): *adjust, aid, align, alter, ameliorate, amend, automate, balance, better, calibrate, center, clout, compose, computerize, condition, connect, coordinate, correct, cure, debug, doctor, edit, emend, enhance, enrich, equalize, face-lift, fine-tune, fit, focus, freshen, furbish, gentrify, grind, heal, help, improve, maintain, mend, modernize, optimize, overhaul, pace, patch, perfect, polish, prepare, punctuate, readjust, ready, realign, reassemble, rebuild, reconceive, reconceptualize, recondition, reconstruct, rectify, refine, refresh, refurbish, regenerate, regulate, rehabilitate, reimagine, reinvent, reinvigorate, rejuvenate, remedy, renew, renovate, repair, rephrase, reshuffle, restore, restructure, retool, retread, revamp, revise, revitalize, revive, revolutionize, right, service, set, sharpen, shine, shuffle, sort, square, stimulate, tighten, troubleshoot, update, upgrade* (≠ -abandon, blemish, break, callous, coarsen, cripple, damage, deface, destroy, disable, disfigure, doom, efface, flaw, -frustrate, half-ass, harm, harshen, hurt, impair, injure, maim, mangle, mar, monkey-wrench, mutilate, -neglect, ruin, scotch, short-circuit, spoil, vandalize, wound, wreck)

FIX (+): *adjust, align, arm, arrange, array, balance, barber, batten, brace, brush, cast, categorize, chart, class, classify, collate, comb, compose, control, design, devise, draft, dress, equip, establish, fit, forearm, form, fortify, frame, furnish, gird, grade, groom, group, gussy, harmonize, integrate, lay, machinate, maintain, manicure, marshal, mediate, methodize, mount, neaten, normalize, orchestrate, order, organize, outfit, pace, pigeonhole, place, plan, plot, prep, prepare, prime, primp, prioritize, program, provide, rank, rate, rationalize, ready, regulate, reintegrate, right, schedule, schematize, scheme, school, score, screen, separate, set, settle, shape, sift, sleek, smarten, smooth, sort, spread, stabilize, steady, steel, straighten, stratify, structure, subordinate, supply, support, synchronize, systematize, tidy, time, titivate, train, type, unify, unsnarl* (≠ bedraggle, break, churn, confuse, destroy, dirty, disarrange, disarray, disconnect, dishevel, disorder, disorganize, disperse, disrupt, disturb, jumble, knot, mess, mix, move, muddle, muss, ruin, rumple, scatter, scramble, snarl, soil, strew, tangle, untidy, upset)

FIX (+): *assemble, barbecue, blend, brew, brown, combine, compose, compound, concoct, cook, craft, fit, flavor, fricassee, frizzle, froth, fry, fuse, griddle, grill, heat, incorporate, infuse, make, marinate, mash, meld, merge, microwave, mingle, mix, prepare, produce, ready, richen, roast, sauté, sear, season, serve, singe, sizzle, spice, stew, toast, warm*

(≠ consume, crave, demand, devour, eat, fancy, guzzle, ingest, order, relish, request, ruin, savor, spoil, wolf)

FIXATE (←): *absorb, bewitch, captivate, compel, concern, direct, enchant, engage, engross, excite, fascinate, grip, haunt, hypnotize, infatuate, interest, intrigue, involve, mesmerize, obsess, occupy, preoccupy, prepossess, razzle-dazzle, rivet, settle, steady* (≠ annoy, bore, bug, chagrin, confound, deflect, -disregard, distract, exhaust, fluster, frustrate, offend, -overlook, repulse, sidetrack, tire, weary) **(¿) ABSTRACTION ALERT. Concrete goals essential!**

FLABBERGAST (→): *abash, amaze, appall, astonish, astound, befuddle, bewilder, bewitch, blindside, boggle, confound, confuse, daze, discomfit, disconcert, dismay, dumbfound, energize, excite, floor, flummox, gobsmack, grab, interest, jar, move, needle, nettle, nitpick, nonplus, outlast, overcome, overwhelm, perplex, razzle-dazzle, rock, rouse, shake, shock, stagger, startle, stun, stupefy, surprise, sway, throw, wow* (≠ anesthetize, annoy, anticipate, bore, bother, calm, exhaust, expect, help, irk, mellow, mitigate, moderate, mollify, pacify, placate, soothe, tranquilize, vex, weary)

FLAG (→): *acquaint, advise, alert, beckon, buzz, cue, flourish, guide, hail, inform, mime, motion, notify, nudge, pantomime, prompt, relate, salute, sign, signal, tell, wave* (≠ block, cloak, clothe, cloud, conceal, discourage, disguise, hide, -ignore, mask, -neglect, obscure, -rebuff, repel, withhold)

FLAG (→): *brand, budget, caption, caution, denote, designate, earmark, hallmark, identify, label, mark, monogram, name, note, stamp, stigmatize, tab, tag, ticket, warn* (≠ allow, anonymize, -blank, -bypass, -disregard, forget, -ignore, mislabel, -neglect, -omit, -overlook, permit, skip, -slight)

FLATTEN (→): *abrade, compress, crush, depress, flush, grade, ground, iron, level, plane, plaster, press, roll, sleek, smooth, squash, straighten, uncrumple, unfold, unwrinkle* (≠ break, buckle, crease, crimp, crumple, dent, fold, nock, pit, round, ruck, rumple, wrinkle)

FLATTEN (/): *annihilate, atomize, bastardize, beat, best, better, blast, bomb, break, bulldoze, bury, cap, checkmate, clobber, collapse, conquer, cow, cream, crush, debase, decimate, deep-six, defeat, deflate, demolish, desolate, destroy, devastate, dismantle, dispatch, doom, drub, dust, dynamite, eclipse, end, eradicate, exceed, explode, exterminate, fell, finish, floor, fragment, hurdle, level, lick, master, obliterate, outdistance, outdo, outfight, outshine, outstrip, overcome, overpower, overthrow, overturn, overwhelm, plunder, prostrate, pulverize, quash, quell, ravage, raven, raze, rout, ruin, shatter, shellac, sink, skin, skunk, slaughter, smash, smoke, smother, squelch, steamroller, subdue, subjugate, succeed, suppress, surmount, surpass, sweep, take, tame, thrash, throw, top, topple, torpedo, trample, transcend, trim, tromp, trounce, trump, unhorse, unseat, upend, upset, vanquish, vaporize, wallop, wax, whip, whomp, whup, wreck* (≠ assemble, augment, boost, build, catalyze, commence, conceive, construct, craft, create, design, develop, elevate, engender, enhance, erect, establish, fabricate, fashion, foster, found, generate, gentrify, improve, maintain, manufacture, mend, organize, perpetuate, preserve, produce, prop, protect, raise, rear, rebuild, rectify, renovate, repair, restore, salvage, save, sculpt, secure, shape, stand, strengthen, support, survive, sustain, upgrade, weather, withstand)

FLATTER (←): *adulate, applaud, blandish, blarney, bootlick, brownnose, butter, cajole, charm, coax, commend, compliment, con, congratulate, court, deceive, double-talk, endear, eulogize, extol, felicitate, flannel, gammon, glad-hand, glorify, grease, hero-worship, honey, humbug, humor, idolize, ingratiate, inveigle, jolly, laud, magnify, massage, mislead, oil, overpraise, oversell, palaver, persuade, pet, praise, promote, puff, pursue, respect, revere, romance, rub, salve, schmooze, seduce, sell, serenade, snow, soap, soften, soft-soap, solicit, soothe, stroke, sucker, sugarcoat, sway, sweeten, sweet-talk, swindle, syrup, tempt, treasure, venerate, wheedle, win, woo, worship* (≠ abuse, anathematize, badmouth, belittle, blackguard, blame, blast, blister, boo, castigate, chide, condemn, criticize, critique, decry, demean, demonize, denounce, denunciate, deride, disparage, disrespect, flay, fulminate, humble, humiliate, insult, mock, offend, pillory, ridicule, scalp, scold, -scorn, -shun, -slight, -snub, -spurn, tease)

FLATTER (+): *adorn, advance, amplify, augment, balance, beautify, bejewel, benefit, better, boost, complement, deck, decorate, dignify, elevate, embellish, enhance, enlarge, ennoble, enrich, exaggerate, fancify, finish, fit, glamorize, glitter, glitz, glorify, grace, harmonize, heighten, heroicize, heroize, honor, idealize, idolize, improve, inflate, magnify, match, ornament, perfect, poeticize, polish, prioritize, rectify, romanticize, sensationalize, sentimentalize, suit, supplement* (≠ blacken, blemish, chide, clash, compromise, damage, deface, disfigure, distort, efface, flaw, harshen, humble, humiliate, impair, jar, mangle, mar, mismatch, ruin, -scorn, shame, -shun, spoil, -spurn, stain, sully, taint, tarnish)

FLAUNT (→): *accent, accentuate, advertise, air, announce, assert, bare, belabor, bellow, boast, bolster, boost, brandish, broadcast, circulate, confess, confirm, confront, dangle, declare, disclose, discover, display, disseminate, divulge, elevate, emphasize, escalate, exaggerate, exhibit, expose, favor, feature, flash, flourish, flutter, focus, foreground, heighten, herald, highlight, hype, illuminate, insist, intensify, limelight, magnify, mark, out, overemphasize, overplay, oversell, overstate, overstress, parade, plug, post, present, prioritize, proclaim, produce, promote, pronounce, publicize, push, reinforce, reveal, shill, shout, show, showcase, sound, sport, spotlight, state, stress, telegraph, trumpet, uncloak, uncover, underline, underscore, unmask, unsheathe, unveil, wag, wave, wield* (≠ -avoid, belittle, bury, camouflage, censor, cloak, clothe, cloud, conceal, costume, cover, curb, curtain, deemphasize, diminish, -discount, disguise, disparage, -disregard, downplay, enshroud, -eschew, hide, holster, -ignore, lessen, marginalize, mask, minimize, miss, -neglect, obscure, obstruct, occlude, occult, -omit, -overlook, quiet, reduce, screen, sheathe, shroud, sideline, silence, spackle, stow, subdue, temper, underemphasize, undermine, underrate, understate, veil, withhold)

FLAVOR (+): *animate, appetize, brighten, dress, drizzle, dulcify, energize, enhance, enliven, enrich, entice, garnish, ginger, honey, imbue, impart, improve, infuse, invigorate, lace, leaven, liven, marinate, mix, optimize, overhaul, pepper, perfume, prepare, revolutionize, richen, rouse, salt, saturate, sauce, savor, season, sour, spice, spike, stimulate, stir, sugar, sweeten, syrup, vitalize, zest, zing* (≠ blunt, bore, dampen, deaden, disenchant, dull, homogenize, muddle, poison, simplify, sully, taint)

FLAY (/): *abuse, admonish, anathematize, assail, attack, badmouth, baste, belittle, berate, blame, blast, blister, castigate, censure, chastise, chide, condemn, criticize, crucify, demean, demonize, denounce, deride, discipline, disparage, disrespect, diss, excoriate, execrate, fault, hammer, harangue, impugn, incriminate, keelhaul, knock, lambaste, lash, lecture, mock, pan, pillory, punish, rag, rate, ream, rebuke, reprimand, reproach, reprove, revile, ridicule, scalp, scold, -scorn, scourge, slam, slate, upbraid, vituperate, wrong* (≠ absolve, approve, bless, commend, defend, endorse, excuse, extol, laud, pardon, praise, sanction, spare, support, vindicate)

FLAY (/): *bare, bark, denude, excoriate, expose, flog, hull, husk, pare, peel, scale, scourge, shell, shuck, skin, strip, uncover, whip* (≠ alleviate, armor, block, cloak, cover, envelop, guard, heal, nurse, protect, remedy, shield, veil, wrap)

-FLEE (→): *-avert, -avoid, ban, bar, blow, bolt, break, -bypass, -circumvent, debar, deflect, depart, -desert, -ditch, divert, -dodge, -duck, eliminate, -elude, -escape, -eschew, evacuate, -evade, -exclude, finesse, fly, foil, fox, -frustrate, leave, lose, miss, -obviate, outfox, outrun, outsmart, outwit, overreach, parry, -preclude, -prevent, -quit, rush, shake, -shirk, -shun, skip, skirt, split, -thwart, withdraw* (≠ accept, accost, beard, brave, brook, catch, chase, confront, contact, contract, court, covet, crave, dare, defy, embrace, endure, face, hunt, incur, meet, pursue, seek, stand, stay, stomach, target, weather, welcome)

FLEECE (←): *bamboozle, beat, betray, bilk, blackmail, bleed, buffalo, bullshit, burn, cadge, cheat, chisel, clip, con, convince, cozen, deceive, defalcate, defraud, despoil, diddle, double-cross, dupe, embezzle, euchre, exploit, extort, fast-talk, fiddle, flimflam, fool, gouge, gull, gyp, hocus-pocus, hose, hustle, manipulate, milk, mislead, outwit, overcharge, pluck, plunder, poach, ream, rifle, rob, rook, screw, shaft, short, shortchange, skin, skunk, snooker, snow, soak, squeeze, steal, stick, stiff, sting, strip, sucker, swindle, thimblerig, trick, underpay, victimize, wheedle, wrench, wring, wrong* (≠ accuse, afford, allege, assume, assure, audit, authenticate, believe, bestow, blame, comp, confess, credit, defend, disabuse, disclose, discredit, disgrace, dispute, distrust, donate, doubt, evince, expose, fault, frame, fund, give, guard, offer, pillory, pity, protect, prove, provide, regret,

-repudiate, respect, restore, reveal, scruple, shame, stigmatize, supply, support, trust, undercharge, validate, verify, vilify)

FLIMFLAM (←): *bamboozle, beat, betray, bilk, bleed, bluff, bullshit, burn, cadge, cheat, chisel, clip, con, convince, cozen, deceive, defraud, diddle, double-cross, double-talk, dupe, exploit, extort, fake, fast-talk, feign, fiddle, fleece, fool, gazump, gouge, gull, hoodwink, hornswoggle, hose, hustle, impersonate, manipulate, milk, mislead, mooch, mulct, nick, outwit, overcharge, play, playact, pluck, poach, pretend, ream, roleplay, rook, rope, sandbag, scam, schnorr, screw, shaft, short, shortchange, skin, snooker, snow, soak, squeeze, steal, stick, stiff, sting, sucker, swindle, trick, victimize, wrench, wrest, wring, wrong* (≠ accuse, assume, assure, believe, confess, confirm, confront, crosscheck, defend, deserve, divulge, earn, expose, merit, refund, reimburse, repay, respect, restore, reveal, support, trust)

FLING (→): *bowl, buck, cant, cast, catapult, chuck, dart, dash, dump, eject, fire, flip, gun, heave, hook, hurl, hurtle, impel, jerk, launch, lob, loft, pass, peg, pelt, pitch, precipitate, project, propel, rifle, roll, send, shoot, shy, skitter, sling, throw, thrust, toss, wing* (≠ bring, carry, catch, clutch, convey, give, grab, grasp, grip, hand, hold, keep, pull, receive, retain, schlep, seize, snag, snatch, tug, yank)

FLIP (→): *cant, careen, cast, change, chuck, click, exchange, flap, flick, fling, hurl, interchange, invert, jerk, overset, overturn, pitch, reverse, riffle, rotate, shift, skittle, snap, spin, substitute, supersede, supplant, swap, switch, throw, topple, toss, transpose, turn, twirl, twist, unhorse, unseat, upset, yank* (≠ affix, balance, bolster, brace, buttress, calm, cement, center, embed, fix, freeze, glue, harden, hold, keep, level, maintain, nail, paralyze, pin, plant, preserve, secure, stabilize, steady, sustain)

FLOG (→): *bash, bat, batter, beat, belabor, belt, birch, bludgeon, buffet, cane, castigate, chastise, clout, discipline, drub, flagellate, flay, hammer, hide, hit, lambaste, lash, lather, maul, paddle, penalize, pound, pummel, punish, scourge, slap, slug, smack, smite, spank, strap, strike, stripe, switch, tan, thrash, wallop, whack, whip* (≠ aid, block, caress, coddle, defend, guard, heal, nurture, protect, shield)

FLOG (→): *advertise, circulate, cold-call, commercialize, commodify, deal, deliver, handle, hawk, hustle, hype, leverage, limelight, market, monetize, offer, peddle, pimp, plug, presell, publicize, push, sell, shill, solicit, tout, trade, traffic, vend* (≠ bury, buy, cloud, conceal, cover, discard, disguise, give, hide, hold, import, keep, limit, obscure, purchase, restrict, steal, suppress, withhold)

FLOOD (→): *avalanche, deluge, douse, drench, drown, engulf, fill, immerse, inundate, marinate, overcome, overflow, overrun, overwhelm, rinse, saturate, smother, soak, spatter, splatter, submerge, swamp, swell, syrup, transgress, wash, wet* (≠ check, curb, dehydrate, drain, dry, hold, leach, leech, parch, reserve, restrain, staunch, withhold)

FLOOR (→): *affright, alarm, amaze, appall, astonish, astound, awe, baffle, beat, bewilder, chill, confound, conquer, daunt, defeat, demoralize, discomfit, discomfort, discompose, disconcert, disgust, dismay, dispirit, displease, disquiet, distress, disturb, dumbfound, emasculate, flabbergast, flummox, freak, frighten, frustrate, gobsmack, horrify, indispose, level, nauseate, nonplus, offend, outrage, overawe, overpower, overwhelm, panic, perplex, perturb, prostrate, puzzle, repel, revolt, scandalize, scare, scarify, shake, sicken, spook, startle, stump, stun, stupefy, terrify, throw, undo, unman, unnerve, unsettle, upset* (≠ assure, buffer, calm, charm, cheer, comfort, console, cushion, delight, enlighten, entice, explain, gratify, help, humor, mellow, mitigate, moderate, mollify, pacify, placate, please, reassure, rejoice, satisfy, settle, solace, soothe, steady, tempt, thrill, tickle)

FLOOR (→): *bang, bash, beat, belt, bludgeon, clobber, concuss, conk, deck, defeat, down, drop, fell, flatten, ground, hammer, hit, jab, knock, level, overthrow, paste, poke, pound, prostrate, punch, raze, slam, slap, slug, smack, smite, sock, swat, swipe, thump, thwack, topple, wallop, whack, whale, wrack* (≠ aid, assist, bolster, brace, build, construct, erect, guard, help, lift, nurture, preserve, protect, raise, shelter, shield, steady, strengthen, support, sustain, toughen)

FLOOR (/): *annihilate, boggle, break, crush, daze, deaden, defeat, deluge, demoralize, devastate, distress, disturb, drown, numb, oppress, overcome, overpower, overwhelm, paralyze, prostrate, pulverize, refute, rock, shatter, sink, stagger, stupefy, swamp, throw, unhorse, unman, unnerve, unseat, upset* (≠ anchor, bore, buoy, calm, clarify, comfort, encourage, enlighten, enliven, explain, inspire, mellow, mollycoddle, organize, reassure, root, sedate, settle, stabilize, steady, survive, tire, underwhelm, withstand)

FLOURISH (→): *brandish, convince, dangle, demonstrate, display, evince, exhibit, expose, flaunt, illustrate, indicate, manifest, mark, parade, present, reveal, shake, show, swing, swish, thrash, twirl, uncover, unmask, unveil, vaunt, wag, wave, wield* (≠ bury, conceal, cover, disguise, drop, forget, hide, lose, mask, -omit, reserve, -scorn, sheathe, shroud, -spurn, withdraw, withhold)

FLOUT (/): *affront, belittle, break, defy, demean, deprecate, deride, -despise, -disdain, dismiss, disobey, disparage, -disregard, disrespect, forget, gate-crash, gibe, gird, insult, jeer, mock, -neglect, offend, outrage, -overlook, pillory, -reject, -repudiate, ridicule, -scorn, -slight, -spurn, subvert, taunt, upset, violate* (≠ accept, advocate, approve, back, compliment, defend, endorse, follow, honor, maintain, mind, obey, observe, praise, promote, regard, respect, restore, save, sustain, uphold)

FLUB (/): *blemish, blight, blow, bobble, boggle, boot, botch, bugger, bungle, butcher, damage, destroy, doom, flaw, fluff, foozle, foul, fumble, goof, half-ass, harm, hurt, impair, injure, louse, mangle, mar, mess, mishandle, mismanage, miss, muddle, muff, murder, mutilate, ruin, spoil, waste, wreck* (≠ ace, ameliorate, bemoan, better, correct, doctor, enhance, fix, help, improve, lament, manage, nail, perfect, realign, rectify, refine, reform, regret, remedy, repair, revamp, right, sophisticate)

FLUMMOX (/): *addle, amaze, astonish, baffle, bamboozle, beat, befog, befuddle, bemuse, bewilder, buffalo, confound, confuse, daze, defeat, discombobulate, disconcert, disorient, dumbfound, faze, floor, fox, gaslight, gobsmack, hocus-pocus, manipulate, mismatch, muddle, muddy, mystify, nonplus, perplex, pose, puzzle, stump, stymie, throw, vex* (≠ assure, clarify, coach, edify, educate, enlighten, explain, floodlight, guide, help, illuminate, inform, reassure, satisfy, school, settle, simplify, solve, steady, teach, tutor, uncomplicate, untangle)

FLUNK (→): *assess, benchmark, compare, evaluate, fail, gauge, grade, judge, mark, pigeonhole, rank, rate, scold, value* (≠ accept, allow, approve, coach, commend, educate, esteem, pass, praise, school, teach, tutor, validate, verify)

FLUNK (/): *blow, bobble, bomb, botch, bungle, chagrin, cheat, close, collapse, crash, deceive, delude, disappoint, discontent, disenchant, disgruntle, disillusion, displease, dissatisfy, distress, fail, flub, fold, fumble, half-ass, implode, miss, mock, muff, sink, tank, upset* (≠ content, deliver, fulfill, gladden, gratify, handle, learn, manage, master, pass, prove, satisfy, study, test, validate, verify, win)

FLUSH (→): *cleanse, clear, deluge, douse, drench, eject, empty, engulf, evacuate, exorcise, expel, flood, gush, hose, inundate, irrigate, rinse, rush, saturate, scour, slosh, sluice, soak, splash, stream, swab, swamp, void, wash* (≠ bake, burn, dehydrate, desiccate, dirty, dry, fill, foul, pack, parch, soil, staunch, stuff, taint)

FLUSTER (/): *agitate, baffle, bewilder, bother, bug, chagrin, churn, cloud, confound, confuse, craze, discombobulate, discomfit, discompose, disconcert, discountenance, disquiet, distract, distress, disturb, dizzy, embarrass, excite, faze, flap, flip, frustrate, gaslight, harass, hassle, heckle, hurry, jar, jolt, misconstrue, mistake, muddle, mystify, nonplus, obscure, overset, palpitate, panic, perplex, perturb, psych, puzzle, quiver, rattle, rile, ruffle, shake, spook, stir, trouble, unhinge, unnerve, unsettle, upset, vex* (≠ appease, assure, calm, comfort, compose, console, embolden, encourage, enlighten, explain, help, humor, lull, mellow, mitigate, moderate, mollify, order, organize, pacify, placate, quiet, reassure, regiment, relieve, sedate, settle, soothe, stabilize, steady)

FOCUS (+): *adapt, adjust, aim, attend, attract, calibrate, center, centralize, chair, concentrate, convene, direct, equalize, fasten, fix, ground, heed, join, level, meet, mind, nail, orient, pinpoint, point, refocus, reorient, rivet, set, sharpen, spotlight, sweat, target, train, tune, turn, tweak, uncloud* (≠ blur, cloud, confuse, dim, discombobulate, -ignore, miss, -neglect, obfuscate, obscure, obstruct, puzzle, secrete, smudge, veil)

FOIL (←): *-abort, anticipate, arrest, -avert, baffle, -balk, bar, beat, bilk, block, bollix, buffalo, check, checkmate, -circumvent, clog, complicate,* *conquer, constipate, counter, counteract, countervail, crab, cramp, crimp, curb, dash, daunt, defeat, deflect, disappoint, discomfit, disconcert, -ditch, -dodge, -duck, -elude, encumber, faze, fetter, forestall, foul, -frustrate, -halt, hamper, handicap, hassle, heckle, hinder, hobble, hocus-pocus, impede, indispose, inhibit, manacle, monkey-wrench, -negate, neutralize, -nullify, obstruct, -obviate, occlude, offset, outlast, outmaneuver, outslick, outsmart, outwit, overcome, override, parry, -preclude, -prevent, protest, rattle, restrain, retort, scupper, scuttle, shackle, shake, short-circuit, skip, stall, stop, straightjacket, stump, stymie, -thwart, tie, trammel* (≠ abet, accelerate, advance, aid, assist, boost, brainstorm, catalyze, cultivate, ease, encourage, facilitate, forward, foster, further, grease, hasten, help, midwife, nurture, prioritize, promote, quicken, smooth, support, uncomplicate)

FOIST (→): *burden, camouflage, compel, con, counterfeit, disguise, distort, doctor, embellish, encumber, entail, extort, fake, falsify, fleece, force, forge, fudge, gouge, impose, inflict, introduce, juggle, manipulate, mask, misrepresent, obscure, oversell, palm, ram, saddle, scam, slant, snooker, snow, squeeze, sucker, thrust, unload, whitewash, wreak* (≠ allow, attest, authenticate, block, confess, confirm, convince, corroborate, crosscheck, debunk, detect, diminish, divulge, excuse, expose, forgive, impede, pardon, permit, -refuse, -reject, -shun, -spurn, substantiate, suggest, -thwart, validate, verify)

FOLLOW (→): *accompany, attend, bird-dog, chaperone, chase, convoy, dog, escort, eye, harry, haunt, hound, hunt, monitor, observe, orbit, persecute, pursue, retrace, scent, search, seek, shadow, shag, spook, spoor, stalk, tag, tail, tailgate, target, trace, track, trail, undertake, watch* (≠ -abandon, -avoid, -desert, direct, -disregard, -elude, -escape, -forsake, guide, head, -ignore, lead, leave, lose, miss, -neglect, -overlook, pass, pilot, -shun, skip, spearhead, steer)

FOLLOW (←): *accept, adopt, align, ape, attend, clock, consider, contemplate, coopt, copy, cultivate, emulate, harmonize, hear, heed, imitate, keep, mark, match, mimic, mind, mirror, mull, note, notice, notify, obey, observe, ponder, practice, reflect, regard, repeat, replace, respect, retrace, serve, succeed, supersede, supplant, support, take, watch, weigh* (≠ breach, break, buck, chair, challenge, choreograph, combat, command, contest, dare, defy, -deny, deride, direct, -discount, discredit, dismiss, disobey, dispute, -disregard, doubt, fight, flout, -ignore, infringe, institute, lead, mismatch, mock, -neglect, oppose, orchestrate, order, originate, -overlook, pooh-pooh, -refuse, -reject, -renounce, -repudiate, resist, -scorn, scruple, steer, subvert, suggest, transgress, violate) **(¿) ABSTRACTION ALERT. Concrete goals essential!**

FOLLOW (+): *accept, appreciate, apprehend, catch, comprehend, dig, fathom, gather, get, grasp, grok, know, master, perceive, realize, savvy, see, suss, twig, understand, visualize* (≠ confuse, -disregard, forget, misconstrue, mishear, misinterpret, misread, miss, mistake, misunderstand, -overlook, perplex, study) **(¿) ABSTRACTION ALERT. Concrete goals essential!**

FOMENT (→): *abet, activate, advance, agitate, arouse, brew, cultivate, detonate, encourage, energize, enliven, excite, ferment, fire, forward, foster, further, galvanize, goad, incite, inflame, inspire, instigate, invigorate, kindle, motivate, nourish, nurse, nurture, pick, promote, prompt, provoke, quicken, raise, rouse, set, sow, spur, start, stimulate, stir, trigger, vitalize* (≠ -abort, allay, block, bridle, calm, cease, check, constrain, curb, deactivate, demotivate, discourage, dissuade, hamper, hold, inactivate, inhibit, leash, lull, mellow, mitigate, moderate, mollify, pace, pacify, placate, quash, quell, quiet, regulate, restrain, settle, soothe, squench, still, stop, straightjacket, subdue, suppress, tame, tranquilize)

FONDLE (←): *baby, caress, clutch, coddle, cosset, cradle, cuddle, dandle, embrace, enfold, feel, gentle, grab, grope, hug, indulge, infantilize, knead, love, massage, mollycoddle, nestle, nose, nuzzle, pamper, pat, paw, pet, smuggle, snuggle, spoil, spoon, squeeze, stroke, strum, touch* (≠ abuse, attack, -avoid, -disregard, drop, harm, injure, maltreat, manhandle, maul, -neglect, plonk, release, repel, repulse, rolf, smack, strike, torture)

FOOL (←): *bamboozle, beguile, bluff, buffalo, bullshit, burn, cheat, con, convince, cozen, deceive, defraud, delude, diddle, double-talk, dupe, feign, fleece, flimflam, fox, gull, hoax, hocus-pocus, hoodwink, humbug, hustle, jive, josh, kid, manipulate, misguide, misinform, mislead, outfox, outmaneuver, outslick, outsmart, outwit, pretend, rook, scam, shortchange, skin, snooker, snow, spoof, squeeze, stick, stiff, sting, sucker, swindle, tease, trick, victimize, wrong* (≠ assume, assure, believe, confess, confide, confirm, confront, debunk, disabuse, disclose, divulge, expose, face, honor, pity, protect, restore, reveal, trust, uncloak, uncover, undeceive, unmask)

-FORBID (/): *ban, banish, bar, blacklist, block, -cancel, censor, check, condemn, cordon, criminalize, damn, -deny, deprive, disallow, embargo, enjoin, -exclude, -excommunicate, freeze, -halt, hinder, impede, inhibit, -interdict, -kibosh, -nix, obstruct, -omit, oppose, outlaw, -preclude, -prevent, -prohibit, proscribe, -refuse, restrain, restrict, spike, stop, straightjacket, stymie, taboo, -veto, withhold* (≠ approve, brook, circulate, cultivate, disseminate, endorse, endure, invite, legalize, motivate, nourish, order, require, rubber-stamp, stomach, support, tolerate, welcome)

FORCE (→): *apply, bind, blackmail, bluff, browbeat, bulldoze, bully, bump, burden, catapult, charge, choke, coerce, command, compel, conscript, constrain, contract, defeat, demand, draft, drag, dragoon, drive, enforce, enjoin, entrance, exact, exhort, extort, fascinate, fix, fling, foment, frogmarch, goad, grease, hasten, heave, hurl, hustle, impel, impose, impress, inflict, instigate, instruct, intimidate, jerk, jog, jolt, jostle, knock, launch, limit, lob, make, march, mesmerize, motivate, move, muscle, nobble, nudge, obligate, oblige, overcome, overcommit, pitch, poke, press, pressure, prod, prompt, propel, punt, push, railroad, ram, require, restrain, restrict, sandbag, shove, sling, squeeze, steamroller, stimulate,* *strike, strong-arm, throw, thrust, trigger, urge, wrench, wrest, wring* (≠ assist, beguile, blandish, block, bribe, cajole, coax, comfort, consider, console, convince, curb, deactivate, delay, encourage, entice, flatter, follow, -frustrate, glad-hand, heed, help, hinder, impede, inactivate, inveigle, lure, maneuver, mark, mind, nobble, obey, obstruct, occlude, palaver, persuade, praise, reassure, respect, schmooze, seduce, serve, shelve, short-circuit, soothe, steel, sweet-talk, tantalize, tease, tempt, -thwart, wheedle)

FORCE (/): *assault, blast, blow, break, burst, bust, crack, defile, dislodge, exact, explode, extort, extract, fracture, fragment, free, heave, hoist, jimmy, lever, lift, move, open, pinch, pop, prize, propel, pry, pulverize, push, raise, ram, rape, ravish, rend, rive, rotate, ruin, rupture, shatter, shift, smash, snap, splinter, split, spoil, squeeze, thrust, twist, unfasten, unlock, violate, wrench, wrest, wring* (≠ attach, benefit, block, blunt, buffer, close, connect, defend, fasten, fix, guard, help, join, mend, protect, -rebuff, repair, seal, secure, shield, solder, sustain, tend, unite, weld)

FORECAST (→): *alert, announce, anticipate, augur, calculate, call, caution, conclude, conjecture, declare, demonstrate, determine, discern, divine, envisage, envision, espy, estimate, expect, extrapolate, forebode, foresee, foreshadow, foretell, forewarn, gather, gauge, guess, harbinger, herald, infer, outguess, perceive, plan, portend, predetermine, predict, presage, proclaim, prognosticate, project, promise, prophesy, read, reason, reveal, scent, second-guess, smell, soothsay, surmise, telegraph, understand, visualize, warn* (≠ bemoan, describe, distrust, doubt, dread, fear, forget, -ignore, lament, mourn, narrate, recall, recite, recollect, recount, regret, relate, remember, report, scruple, suspect, tell)

FORESTALL (←): *-abort, anticipate, -avert, -avoid, -balk, deflect, -deter, divert, foil, -frustrate, -halt, hamper, hinder, impede, intercept, monkey-wrench, obstruct, -obviate, occlude, parry, -preclude, preempt, -prevent, second-guess, shunt, stem, stop, -thwart, turn, ward* (≠ accelerate, advance, aid, allow, assist, catalyze, cultivate, ease, encourage, facilitate, foster, further, grease, hasten, help, nurture, permit, promote, quicken, require, smooth, support, unclog)

FORETELL (→): *announce, anticipate, apprehend, augur, call, caution, declare, disclose, divine, divulge, dope, figure, forebode, forecast, foresee, foreshadow, forewarn, harbinger, portend, predict, prefigure, presage, proclaim, prognosticate, prophesy, read, reveal, signify, soothsay, warn* (≠ ascertain, bemoan, calculate, deduce, demonstrate, determine, insure, lament, mourn, prove, recount, regret, relate, report, settle, warrant)

FORFEIT (→): *-abandon, bomb, cede, -desert, discard, -disdain, dismiss, -disown, -ditch, drop, dump, flunk, forgo, -forsake, jettison, jilt, lose, muff, offload, -quit, -reject, release, relinquish, -renounce, -repudiate, sacrifice, scratch, -spurn, surrender, waive, yield* (≠ accomplish, achieve, acquire, actualize, attain, award, claim, colonize, conquer, demand, embrace, gain, keep, obtain, procure, profit, reclaim, recoup, recover, retain, retrieve, reward, source, take, win)

FORGE (→): *beat, boast, carve, chase, chisel, clout, coin, contour, cut, draw, fabricate, fashion, form, hammer, hew, knap, knead, mint, model, mold, pat, pound, sculpt, sculpture, shape, stamp, work* (≠ break, demolish, destroy, dissolve, fracture, fragment, obliterate, pulverize, raze, ruin, sabotage, scotch, scupper, scuttle, shatter, shelve, splinter, wreck)

FORGE (←): *adulterate, bootleg, clone, coin, concoct, cook, copy, counterfeit, crib, design, doctor, dupe, duplicate, embellish, embroider, fabricate, fake, falsify, fashion, feign, frame, fudge, half-ass, imitate, invent, jerry-build, jerry-rig, juggle, manipulate, phony, pirate, plagiarize, produce, replicate, reproduce, scratch, simulate, trace, transcribe* (≠ authenticate, confirm, corroborate, crosscheck, debunk, document, explain, expose, illuminate, notarize, prove, substantiate, validate, verify)

FORGE (+): *accomplish, achieve, actualize, assemble, brainstorm, build, carve, cast, coin, compose, conceive, concoct, construct, contrive, cook, craft, create, customize, develop, devise, effect, engineer, fabricate, fashion, form, found, frame, generate, hatch, invent, machine, make, manufacture, mint, model, originate, sculpt, shape, tailor, weave* (≠ -abandon, -abort, break, -cancel, copy, crack, demolish, destroy, dismantle, doom, duplicate, end, eradicate, jumble, muddle, pulverize, raze, ruin, shatter, stall, stop, terminate, topple, undo, unmake, wreck)

FORGIVE (+): *absolve, accept, acquit, allow, clear, commute, condone, defray, discharge, -discount, dismiss, dispel, -disregard, efface, except, exculpate, excuse, exempt, exonerate, explain, forget, free, gloss, -ignore, justify, legalize, liberate, mitigate, -omit, -overlook, palliate, pardon, permit, pocket, purge, rationalize, redeem, release, relieve, remit, reprieve, rescue, shrive, spare, spring, tolerate, unburden, undercharge, vindicate, waive, whitewash* (≠ abhor, abominate, accuse, allege, assess, avenge, blame, castigate, charge, chastise, condemn, convict, defame, -despise, -detest, discipline, execrate, fault, finger, frame, -hate, heed, impeach, implicate, impugn, incriminate, indict, -loathe, maintain, mark, mind, note, offend, penalize, prosecute, punish, rebuke, redress, refund, remunerate, repay, resent, revenge, reward, satisfy, scapegoat, -scorn, sentence, summon, transgress)

FORM (+): *arrange, assemble, brainstorm, brew, build, cast, chart, complete, compose, conceive, concoct, configure, construct, contrive, cook, craft, create, cultivate, cut, design, develop, devise, envisage, erect, establish, fabricate, fashion, father, finish, fix, forge, formulate, foster, found, frame, handcraft, hew, imagine, improvise, institute, invent, machine, make, manufacture, mint, model, mold, order, organize, originate, outline, pattern, perfect, plan, plot, produce, project, raise, rear, refashion, remake, script, sculpt, shape, sire, structure, weave* (≠ annihilate, atomize, break, canker, corrode, crack, crush, demolish, destroy, devastate, disassemble, dismantle, disperse, dissect, dissolve, disturb, doom, end, eradicate, explode, exterminate, extinguish, flatten, fracture, fragment, -halt, hurt, melt, powder, -prevent, pulverize, raze, ruin, scatter, shatter, shiver, shred, smash, splinter, tatter, tear, vivisect, wreck)

FORMULATE (+): *ad-lib, articulate, brainstorm, brew, cast, chart, clothe, codify, coin, communicate, compose, conceive, concoct, contrive, cook, couch, craft, create, define, describe, design, detail, develop, devise, disclose, draft, evince, evolve, express, forge, form, found, frame, graph, hatch, improvise, invent, itemize, map, originate, particularize, plan, prepare, propose, render, script, specify, spitball, state, systematize, vocalize, weave* (≠ addle, baffle, bewilder, cloud, confuse, delete, destroy, disorganize, erase, -frustrate, -halt, hamper, hinder, impair, impede, inhibit, jumble, muddle, mystify, -negate, perplex, puzzle, raze, ruin, scramble, stall, stop, stymie, tangle, wreck)

-FORSAKE (/): *-abandon, abdicate, abjure, betray, -boycott, -deny, -desert, discard, disclaim, -disown, -ditch, divorce, double-cross, double-deal, drop, dump, -escape, -eschew, fling, forgo, forswear, jettison, jilt, junk, leave, maroon, offload, -prohibit, protest, -quit, -refuse, -reject, relinquish, -renounce, -repudiate, resign, scrap, shed, shuck, -shun, -spurn, strand, surrender, unmarry, vacate, waive, wrong, yield* (≠ accept, advocate, annex, colonize, embrace, espouse, harbor, hold, invade, keep, own, permit, possess, reclaim, redeem, rediscover, rescue, reserve, retain, save, support, withhold)

FORTIFY (→): *arm, arouse, bolster, boost, brace, buoy, buttress, cheer, comfort, confirm, embolden, encourage, energize, enforce, enliven, forearm, harden, hearten, inspire, inure, invigorate, nerve, poise, prioritize, prop, prostrate, rally, ready, reassure, refresh, reinforce, reinvigorate, renew, restore, revive, rouse, season, steady, steel, stiffen, stimulate, stir, strengthen, support, sustain, toughen* (≠ chill, convulse, dampen, daunt, debilitate, demoralize, demotivate, discourage, dishearten, dispirit, dissuade, drain, enervate, enfeeble, leech, prostrate, sap, shake, soften, tax, tire, undercut, undermine, unnerve, weaken, wither)

FORTIFY (+): *acclimate, accustom, adapt, adjust, anneal, armor, barricade, blockade, bolster, boost, brace, buffer, bulwark, buttress, case-harden, condition, consolidate, cover, defend, embattle, enforce, entrench, fence, garrison, gird, guard, habituate, harden, immunize, indurate, inure, limber, mound, patrol, prepare, prop, prostrate, protect, rampart, ready, reinforce, season, secure, shield, steady, steel, strengthen, support, temper, tone, toughen, train, vaccinate, wall* (≠ attack, battle, boobytrap, canker, cannibalize, capsize, consume, corrode, cripple, debilitate, decrease, deplete, depredate, diminish, drain, emasculate, enervate, enfeeble, erode, exhaust, hamstring, hurt, incapacitate, injure, knacker, leach, level, mar, overextend, sabotage, sap, scotch, scupper, scuttle, sensitize, soften, subvert, topple, unhorse, unman, unseat, weaken)

FOSTER (+): *abet, advance, advantage, advertise, advocate, aid, assist, back, bankroll, bolster, boost, capitalize, champion, cultivate, develop, encourage, endorse, endow, entertain, expand, facilitate, favor, feed, finance, foment, forward, fuel, fund, furnish, further, grant, grubstake, guarantee, help, hold, hype, incubate, nourish, nurse, nurture, offer,* *patronize, plug, prioritize, proffer, promote, publicize, reward, serve, sponsor, stake, stimulate, stoke, subsidize, suckle, supplement, supply, support, sustain, tend, tout, underwrite, uphold, volunteer* (≠ attack, ban, bankrupt, bar, battle, beggar, challenge, check, combat, counter, cripple, damage, defund, demotivate, deprive, discourage, encumber, enjoin, exhaust, exploit, famish, fight, fleece, foil, -forbid, -frustrate, -halt, hamstring, hinder, hobble, impair, impede, impoverish, inhibit, obstruct, oppose, outlaw, -prevent, -prohibit, proscribe, repress, retard, ruin, sabotage, scotch, scupper, scuttle, shackle, shelve, snuff, squander, squash, squelch, stifle, strangle, subdue, subvert, suppress, undermine, waste, weaken, withhold)

FOSTER (+): *accommodate, adopt, advance, attend, breed, cherish, coach, cradle, cultivate, defend, direct, discipline, edify, educate, enlighten, father, feed, forward, furnish, further, guide, harbor, hatch, help, house, incubate, indoctrinate, instruct, keep, lead, maintain, mentor, mind, mother, nourish, nurse, nurture, prepare, preserve, promote, protect, provide, raise, rear, rescue, respect, save, school, shelter, shepherd, shield, show, supply, teach, train, treasure, tutor, watch* (≠ -abandon, abuse, anguish, assault, -avoid, brutalize, bully, defile, degrade, exploit, harass, harm, hurt, -ignore, ill-treat, ill-use, injure, maltreat, menace, mishandle, mistreat, -neglect, oppress, persecute, savage, terrify, torment, torture, traumatize, victimize, violate, wound, wrong)

FOUL (/): *bedraggle, befoul, begrime, besmirch, blacken, contaminate, corrupt, daub, defile, desecrate, dirty, discolor, draggle, infect, mire, muck, muddy, poison, pollute, profane, rot, smear, smirch, smudge, soil, spike, spoil, spot, stain, sully, taint, tarnish* (≠ clean, cleanse, decontaminate, delouse, disinfect, distill, exalt, filter, freshen, launder, purge, purify, quarantine, rinse, sanitize, scour, scrub, sterilize, wash)

FOUL (/): *block, catch, choke, clog, confuse, derange, disarrange, disarray, discompose, dishevel, dislocate, disorder, disorganize, disturb, draggle, ensnare, entangle, fill, jam, jumble, knot, mess, muddle, obstruct, occlude, ruffle, scramble, shuffle, snarl, tangle, twist, unsettle, untidy* (≠ adjust, align, arrange, array, clear, consolidate, distribute, empty, loosen, marshal, methodize, open, order, organize, regulate, solve, sort, straighten, systematize, tidy, unpack, untangle, void)

FOUND (+): *arrange, assemble, author, bankroll, begin, commence, conceive, concoct, constitute, construct, contrive, create, develop, devise, endow, enlarge, erect, establish, expand, fabricate, fashion, father, finance, fix, form, foster, fund, generate, hatch, inaugurate, initiate, innovate, institute, introduce, invent, launch, make, manufacture, organize, originate, pioneer, plant, produce, raise, settle, start, subsidize, systematize, underwrite* (≠ abolish, -abort, adjourn, annihilate, annul, -cancel, close, conclude, defund, destroy, dismantle, doom, end, finish, -forbid, -forsake, -halt, -nullify, -prevent, -prohibit, ruin, shut, stop, suppress, terminate)

FOUND (+): *anchor, base, build, construct, embed, erect, establish, fix, ground, install, locate, plant, position, predicate, raise, rear, rest, root, set, settle, stabilize, stay, steady, support, sustain* (≠ cripple, damage, destroy, disable, disrupt, doom, erode, impair, incapacitate, rock, ruin, sabotage, scotch, scupper, scuttle, shelve, spoil, subvert, topple, undermine, weaken, wreck)

FRACTURE (/): *atomize, blast, break, burst, bust, chip, crack, crush, damage, deface, destroy, detonate, disfigure, disintegrate, dismember, disrupt, divide, efface, explode, fissure, flaw, fragment, grind, harshen, hurt, implode, kink, mar, pop, powder, pulverize, reduce, rive, ruin, rupture, scar, score, scrape, scratch, shatter, shiver, sliver, smash, snap, splinter, split, spoil, wreck, zap* (≠ assemble, brace, buffer, buttress, clamp, doctor, fix, heal, join, mend, nurse, patch, plaster, rebuild, recondition, reconstruct, rehabilitate, remedy, renovate, repair, restore, save, shield, splint, unite, withstand)

FRAGMENT (/): *anatomize, atomize, axe, blast, break, burst, bust, chip, cleave, crack, crumb, crumble, crush, cut, decay, decompose, destroy, detach, detonate, diffuse, disconnect, disengage, disintegrate, dismantle, dismember, disrupt, dissect, dissolve, disunite, divide, divorce, estrange, excise, explode, fracture, grind, implode, mortify, part, pop, powder, pulverize, reduce, remove, rend, rip, rive, rot, ruin, rupture, scatter, scissor, segregate, separate, sever, shatter, shiver, slice, sliver, smash, splinter, split, sunder, vivisect, wreck* (≠ affix, assemble, attach, bind, blend, bridge, cement, chain, clasp, clip, combine, complete, connect, corral, doctor, fashion, fasten, fix, forge, fuse, glue, heal, hybridize, join, meld, mend, patch, rebuild, recondition, reconstruct, renovate, repair, restore, sculpt, secure, synthesize, tie, unify, unite, weld)

FRAME (+): *arrange, assemble, brew, build, captain, cast, command, compass, conceive, concert, conclude, concoct, conduct, construct, contrive, cook, craft, create, design, devise, direct, engineer, envisage, erect, establish, fashion, father, finagle, finesse, forge, hammer, handcraft, handle, hatch, hew, imagine, institute, invent, machinate, make, manage, maneuver, manipulate, mastermind, mint, mold, negotiate, organize, originate, picture, plan, plot, prefabricate, quarterback, raise, rear, refashion, remake, run, scheme, script, sculpt, shape, structure, visualize, wangle* (≠ abolish, annihilate, blow, bobble, botch, break, bungle, butcher, -cancel, demolish, destroy, devastate, disassemble, dismantle, dismember, eradicate, erase, explode, exterminate, extinguish, flatten, flub, fracture, fragment, fumble, half-ass, louse, mangle, mess, mishandle, muff, obliterate, pulverize, raze, ruin, shatter, smash, wreck)

FRAME (/): *accuse, allege, anathematize, arraign, attaint, blame, book, censure, charge, chide, cite, condemn, criticize, damn, denounce, fault, finger, impeach, implicate, impugn, incriminate, indict, involve, plant, prosecute, rebuke, report, reproach, reprove, scapegoat, sue, summon, trap* (≠ absolve, acquit, advocate, aid, alibi, applaud, champion, clear, commend, defend, exculpate, excuse, exonerate, forgive, glorify, honor, justify, legalize, pardon, praise, prove, remit, salute, shrive, support, uphold, vindicate)

FREE (+): *absolve, acquit, alibi, bail, clear, deliver, discharge, disencumber, disengage, disentangle, emancipate, enfranchise, enlarge, except, excuse, exempt, exonerate, extricate, liberate, loose, loosen, manumit, pardon, parole, ransom, redeem, release, relieve, rescue, rid, save, spare, spring, unbind, unburden, uncage, unchain, uncuff, undo, unfetter, unhook, unleash, unlock, unshackle, untie* (≠ bind, cage, chain, commit, confine, conquer, constrain, convict, cuff, enchain, enslave, fetter, handcuff, hogtie, immure, imprison, incarcerate, incriminate, institutionalize, intern, jail, keep, lock, manacle, -prevent, restrain, shackle, subdue, subjugate, trammel)

FREE (+): *clear, deliver, discharge, disembody, disencumber, disengage, disentangle, divest, emancipate, enfranchise, extricate, liberate, loose, loosen, manumit, redeem, release, relieve, rescue, rid, save, slack, slacken, spring, unbind, unburden, uncage, unchain, uncuff, unfetter, unravel, unsnarl, untangle, untie, untwine* (≠ block, bog, burden, cuff, embroil, encumber, entangle, fetter, hamper, hinder, impede, load, lumber, obstruct, restrain, saddle, shackle, straightjacket, subject, weigh, weight)

FREE (+): *aerate, clean, clear, decongest, ease, facilitate, loosen, open, oxygenate release, smooth, strip, unblock, unclog, unclutter, unplug, unstop, ventilate* (≠ barricade, block, blockade, clog, close, clutter, constrict, dam, encumber, hamper, hinder, impede, obstruct, occlude, plug, stem, stop, trammel)

FREEZE (/): *calcify, chill, clot, coagulate, concrete, congeal, cool, crystallize, deep-freeze, embalm, firm, glaciate, harden, ice, indurate, ossify, petrify, preserve, refrigerate, rigidify, set, solidify, stiffen, thicken* (≠ de-ice, dissolve, flux, fuse, liquefy, loosen, melt, smelt, soften, steam, thaw, unfreeze)

FREEZE (/): *-abort, arrest, cripple, deactivate, disable, fix, -halt, hold, immobilize, inactivate, numb, paralyze, peg, stop, stun, suspend* (≠ accelerate, catalyze, free, grease, hasten, loose, midwife, mobilize, move, quicken, speed, stir, unleash, weaponize)

FRESHEN (+): *activate, aerate, air, assist, brace, cheer, clean, cleanse, cool, disburse, dispense, energize, enliven, exhilarate, fortify, galvanize, gentrify, heal, invigorate, liven, modernize, neaten, overhaul, prod, prompt, purify, quarantine, quicken, recharge, reclaim, recondition, reconstitute, recreate, redesign, redevelop, redo, reengineer, refill, refresh, refurbish, regenerate, rehab, rehabilitate, reinvigorate, rejuvenate, remake, remodel, renew, renovate, repair, replenish, reshuffle, restimulate, restore, restructure, resupply, resuscitate, revitalize, revive, revolutionize, rouse, shuffle, stimulate, sweeten, tidy, update, upgrade, ventilate* (≠ age, bleed, blemish, blight, cannibalize, consume, cripple, damage, debilitate, deplete, depredate, destroy, doom, drain, enervate, exhaust, hamstring, harm, impair, infect, injure, leech, mangle, mar, overextend, paralyze, ruin, shrivel, trouble, weaken, wither, wizen, wreck)

FRIGHTEN (/): *affright, agitate, alarm, amaze, appall, astound, awe, blackjack, blackmail, bludgeon, boggle, browbeat, brutalize, bulldoze, bully, chill, cow, daunt, deafen, demoralize, demotivate, -deter, discomfort, discompose, disconcert, discourage, dishearten, dismay, dispirit, disquiet, distract, distress, disturb, emasculate, faze, floor, freeze, funk, haunt, horrify, intimidate, jolt, menace, numb, panic, paralyze, perturb, petrify, railroad, rattle, repel, sandbag, savage, scare, shake, shock, spook, startle, strong-arm, stun, stupefy, terrify, terrorize, threaten, trash-talk, traumatize, unhinge, unman, unnerve, unsettle, unstring, upset, victimize, warn, worry* (≠ allay, amuse, assuage, assure, baby, boost, buoy, calm, charm, cheer, coddle, comfort, compose, console, delight, embolden, enchant, encourage, entertain, exhilarate, fortify, gladden, guard, hearten, help, humor, inspire, invigorate, lull, mellow, mitigate, moderate, mollify, nurture, pacify, placate, please, protect, quiet, reassure, release, relieve, save, secure, seduce, soothe, stabilize, steady, steel, stimulate, strengthen, thrill, uplift, vamp, woo, wow)

FRISK (←): *browse, check, despoil, examine, explore, fan, ferret, grope, inspect, investigate, learn, peruse, probe, ransack, rifle, scan, scope, scrutinize, search, study, survey, toss* (≠ -abandon, conceal, hide, -ignore, miss, mistake, -neglect, -overlook, pocket, stash, stow, tuck, wedge)

-FRUSTRATE (/): *anticipate, arrest, -avert, baffle, -balk, bar, battle, beat, block, check, checkmate, clog, conquer, counteract, defeat, discomfit, encumber, fetter, fight, foil, forestall, -halt, hamper, handicap, hinder, hobble, impede, inhibit, manacle, monkey-wrench, -negate, neutralize, nobble, -nullify, obstruct, -obviate, occlude, offset, oppose, outlast, overcome, override, -preclude, -prevent, protest, shackle, short-circuit, stall, stop, stultify, stymie, -thwart* (≠ abet, advance, aid, assist, cultivate, ease, encourage, facilitate, forward, foster, further, midwife, nurture, promote, smooth)

FRUSTRATE (/): *afflict, alarm, bother, browbeat, bully, chill, cow, dampen, daunt, deaden, debilitate, demoralize, demotivate, depress, discourage, dishearten, dismay, dispirit, distress, enfeeble, frighten, horrify, intimidate, irk, sadden, scare, sicken, trouble, undermine, unman, unnerve, vex, weaken, weigh, wither, worry* (≠ animate, boost, buoy, cheer, encourage, energize, enliven, excite, fortify, galvanize, inspire, invigorate, prioritize, reassure, reinforce, steel, stir, strengthen)

FRY (+): *barbecue, brown, cook, fricassee, frizzle, griddle, grill, roast, sauté, sear, singe, sizzle, toast* (≠ bake, baste, butter, chill, cool, douse, drench, freeze, grease, ice, oil, refrigerate, soak, wet)

FUEL (→): *augment, beef, bolster, boost, buttress, charge, contribute, dispense, encourage, energize, fan, feed, fill, fire, force-feed, gas, incite, inflame, nourish, nurture, overfeed, power, prioritize, service, stimulate,* *stoke, strengthen, supply, sustain, victual* (≠ bleed, cannibalize, consume, cripple, debilitate, demotivate, deplete, depredate, discourage, drain, empty, exhaust, finish, knacker, leach, leech, overextend, sap, spend, squander, tap, tax, withhold)

FULFILL (+): *accomplish, achieve, acquire, actualize, answer, attain, claim, complete, conclude, consummate, crest, deliver, discharge, dispatch, earn, effect, effectuate, enact, end, execute, fill, finish, gain, get, implement, keep, manage, manifest, meet, negotiate, obey, observe, obtain, perfect, perform, please, procure, produce, qualify, reach, realize, resolve, satisfy, score, seal, settle, sign, solve, suit, win* (≠ -abandon, -abort, -avoid, begin, breach, -cancel, commence, concede, create, destroy, displease, -disregard, dissatisfy, drop, fail, forfeit, forget, -halt, -ignore, introduce, leave, lose, miss, -neglect, -overlook, pass, question, scant, scrimp, skimp, -slight, start, stop, violate) **(¿) ABSTRACTION ALERT. Concrete goals essential!**

FUMBLE (/): *blemish, blight, blow, bobble, boggle, boot, botch, bugger, bungle, butcher, damage, destroy, dismiss, -disregard, doom, drop, fail, flaw, flub, fluff, foozle, forget, goof, half-ass, harm, hurt, -ignore, impair, injure, jumble, lose, louse, mangle, mar, mess, miscarry, mishandle, mislay, mismanage, misplace, miss, mistake, misunderstand, mix, muddle, muff, murder, -neglect, -omit, -overlook, overshoot, ruin, scramble, skip, spoil, undershoot, vitiate, wreck* (≠ accomplish, achieve, actualize, ameliorate, bemoan, better, claim, crest, doctor, enhance, fix, handle, help, improve, lament, manage, mourn, nail, optimize, outsell, outshine, overhaul, pass, patch, perfect, recondition, rectify, refine, reform, regret, remedy, renovate, repair, revamp, revolutionize, steady, surpass, transfer)

FUMIGATE (/): *circulate, cleanse, decontaminate, delouse, deodorize, disinfect, fan, freshen, oxygenate, purify, quarantine, sanitize, smoke, sterilize, vaporize* (≠ afflict, choke, cloud, contaminate, foul, infect, infest, plague, pollute, sully, taint)

FUND (→): *advantage, advocate, aid, assist, award, back, bankroll, benefit, bequeath, bestow, capitalize, champion, clear, cofinance, compensate, contribute, defray, discharge, dispense, dower, endorse, endow, enrich, ensure, extend, facilitate, feed, finance, float, foot, force-feed, foster, fuel, furnish, grant, grubstake, guarantee, help, house, keep, lend, liquidate, loan, maintain, nourish, nurture, offer, overfeed, patronize, pay, pony, proffer, profit, promote, provide, -quit, recompense, refinance, refund, reward, serve, settle, sponsor, stake, stand, subsidize, suckle, supplement, supply, support, sustain, tend, underwrite, volunteer* (≠ -abandon, accept, acquire, bankrupt, beggar, bilk, borrow, break, bust, cadge, consume, cripple, defund, demand, deplete, deprive, -desert, diminish, disappoint, disinherit, -disown, drain, earn, exhaust, expect, expend, exploit, famish, fleece, foil, -frustrate, hinder, impoverish, inherit, leech, -neglect, obtain, overextend, pauperize, reduce, request, ruin, sabotage, sap, scant, scotch, skimp, spend, squander, starve, stiff, stint, straiten, subvert, take, tap, tax, -thwart, waste, weaken, withhold)

FURNISH (→): *accoutre, afford, allocate, allot, apparel, appoint, apportion, arm, array, assign, award, bequeath, bestow, clothe, comp, contribute, decorate, deliver, dispense, distribute, dole, dollop, donate, dower, endow, enrich, equip, feather, feed, fill, force-feed, fortify, fuel, gird, give, grant, hand, lend, loan, offer, outfit, overfeed, prepare, present, provide, provision, refill, rig, spare, stock, store, supply, tender, transfer, victual, volunteer, yield* (≠ bank, borrow, budget, cadge, claim, commandeer, confiscate, conserve, debit, deduct, demand, -deny, deprive, dispossess, divest, grab, impound, keep, maintain, pickle, preserve, -refuse, reserve, retain, rob, save, scant, scrounge, seize, skimp, starve, steal, stint, strip, swipe, take, weasel, withdraw, withhold)

FURTHER (→): *abet, advance, advertise, advocate, aid, amplify, assist, back, ballyhoo, benefit, boost, champion, condone, cultivate, encourage, endorse, endow, energize, facilitate, favor, finance, float, forward, foster, fund, grow, heighten, help, hype, improve, increase, incubate, inspire, kindle, lift, limelight, magnify, motivate, nourish, nurse, nurture, patronize, plug, presell, present, prioritize, promote, provoke, publicize, push, sanction, second, spitball, spur, stake, strengthen, submit, subsidize, suggest, support, tout, underwrite, upgrade, uphold, uplift, urge* (≠ -abort, arrest, ban, bar, block, check, checkmate, cramp, curb, discourage, discredit, disfavor, disgrace, disinherit, -disown, encumber, enjoin, fetter, foil, -forbid, -frustrate, -halt, hamper, hamstring, harm, hinder, hobble, impede, inhibit, injure, -interdict, manacle, monkey-wrench, obstruct, oppose, outlaw, pause, -prevent, -prohibit, proscribe, protest, repress, restrain, restrict, retard, shackle, slow, snuff, squash, squelch, stall, stifle, stop, stymie, subdue, suppress, -thwart)

FUSE (+): *add, amalgamate, annex, attach, bind, blend, bond, cement, coalesce, combine, commingle, composite, compound, concrete, conflate, conjoin, connect, couple, emulsify, entwine, fasten, flux, fold, glue, homogenize, incorporate, integrate, intermingle, intermix, intertwine, interweave, join, knit, link, marry, match, meld, melt, mend, merge, mingle, mix, mortar, network, reintegrate, run, smelt, solder, splice, stir, synthesize, tie, toss, unify, unite, weave, weld, yoke* (≠ atomize, break, cleave, detach, diffuse, disengage, disjoin, disperse, dissolve, disunite, divide, divorce, estrange, fracture, fragment, kibble, part, pulverize, rend, rupture, scatter, separate, sever, shatter, split, sunder, tear, unmix, vaporize)

GAG (/): *asphyxiate, bar, bind, block, censor, check, choke, clog, close, constrict, curb, hinder, muffle, mute, muzzle, obstruct, overpower, overwhelm, plug, -prevent, -prohibit, quiet, repress, restrain, shush, silence, smother, squeeze, squelch, stifle, still, stop, straightjacket, strangle, subdue, suffocate, suppress, throttle* (≠ aid, air, allow, amplify, assist, augment, boost, broadcast, clear, disseminate, encourage, expose, extend, free, help, loose, magnify, oxygenate, publicize, release, restore, reveal, share, soothe, spread, unclog, vent, ventilate, voice)

GAIN (←): *accept, accrue, achieve, acquire, apprehend, attain, bag, bilk, bogart, borrow, buy, cadge, capture, catch, claim, cop, crest, download, earn, enlist, exact, extract, find, get, grab, gross, harvest, import, increase, inherit, lease, milk, mine, mooch, nab, net, obtain, occupy, pilfer, poach, possess, procure, pull, purchase, reclaim, recoup, rent, scoop, scrounge, secure, seize, select, snag, snare, snatch, source, steal, swipe, take, tap, weasel, win, wrest* (≠ -abandon, bequeath, bestow, cost, debit, decrease, deduct, deplete, disburse, disinherit, expend, forfeit, give, grant, lessen, lose, lower, miss, reduce, relinquish, scrounge, shrink, subtract, thin, undershoot, yield)

GALVANIZE (→): *activate, amaze, animate, arouse, astonish, awaken, bewitch, captivate, catalyze, charge, charm, delight, egg, electrify, empower, enchant, encourage, energize, enliven, enthrall, excite, exhilarate, fire, foment, freshen, frighten, fuel, hypnotize, incite, inspire, interest, intoxicate, intrigue, invigorate, jolt, mesmerize, motivate, move, pique, power, prime, prod, provoke, quicken, razzle-dazzle, rivet, rouse, shock, spellbind, spur, startle, stimulate, stir, stun, tantalize, thrill, titillate, urge, vitalize, wake, wow, zap* (≠ bore, calm, comfort, cripple, dampen, deaden, demoralize, demotivate, depress, -deter, discourage, dishearten, dispirit, dissuade, dull, hamper, hamstring, hinder, hobble, impair, incapacitate, inhibit, jade, lull, mellow, mesmerize, numb, pacify, quiet, retard, sadden, sedate, sicken, tire, weaken, weary)

GAMBLE (→): *ante, back, bet, bid, brave, challenge, chance, compromise, dare, defy, endanger, face, game, hazard, imperil, invest, jeopardize, lay, offer, parlay, play, risk, spare, spitball, stake, venture, volunteer, wager* (≠ assure, clinch, crosscheck, defend, design, ensure, guarantee, indemnify, insure, plan, promise, protect, prove, script, secure, verify, vouchsafe, warrant)

GARBLE (/): *alter, belie, bend, bleep, bowdlerize, buckle, camouflage, censor, churn, cloud, color, complicate, confound, confuse, contort, cook, corrupt, deceive, deform, disguise, distort, doctor, double-talk, embellish,* *embroider, fake, falsify, fudge, gloss, half-ass, heave, interpolate, jumble, manipulate, mask, misdescribe, mishear, misinterpret, mislead, misquote, misread, misrepresent, misstate, mistake, mistranslate, misunderstand, mix, muddle, mutilate, mystify, obscure, pervert, redact, scramble, slant, spin, tinge, twist, veil, warp, whitewash* (≠ align, clarify, clear, correct, crack, decipher, decode, decrypt, deduce, detect, distill, edit, elaborate, elucidate, explain, filter, grok, illuminate, illustrate, interpret, order, punctuate, purify, realign, rectify, rephrase, represent, right, simplify, solve, strain, streamline, translate, uncomplicate, unravel, unscramble, untangle)

GARNER (+): *accumulate, amass, archive, arrange, assemble, ball, band, batch, brigade, bunch, cluster, collate, collect, combine, compile, concentrate, congregate, connect, corral, cull, deposit, gather, glean, group, heap, herd, hive, hoard, husband, join, link, lump, merge, muster, organize, pack, pile, pool, press, raise, rally, reserve, save, scavenge, scrape, stack, stockpile, store, stow, swarm, systematize, throng, treasure, unite* (≠ break, diffuse, disband, disintegrate, dismiss, dispel, disperse, disseminate, dissipate, dissolve, offload, part, scatter, send, separate, sever, split, squander, waste)

GARNER (←): *accomplish, accumulate, achieve, acquire, actualize, amass, annex, attain, bag, bring, capture, carry, catch, claim, clear, clinch, crest, download, draw, earn, gain, get, gross, land, make, net, notch, obtain, occupy, procure, pull, reacquire, realize, reap, recapture, regain, score, secure, source, win* (≠ accord, bequeath, bestow, confer, forfeit, give, grant, hand, impart, lose, offer, pay, relinquish, spare, starve, surrender, undershoot, volunteer, yield)

GARNISH (←): *cull, cut, debit, decrease, deduct, diminish, dock, downsize, excise, extract, lessen, mitigate, pull, reduce, remove, reserve, subtract, take, tax, withhold* (≠ accord, augment, boost, donate, earn, furnish, give, increase, make, offer, pay, recoup, spare, stiff, stint, supply, tender, volunteer, yield)

GARNISH (+): *accessorize, adorn, amplify, appliqué, array, beautify, bedeck, bedizen, bespangle, better, blazon, braid, brighten, caparison, color, costume, crown, dandify, deck, decorate, drape, dress, drizzle, elaborate, embellish, emblaze, emblazon, emboss, embroider, enhance, enrich, exaggerate, fancify, feather, festoon, filigree, fillet, fix, flavor, flounce, freshen, frill, fringe, further, garland, gild, glamorize, glitter, glitz, grace, hang, improve, increase, lace, magnify, marinate, optimize, ornament, overhaul, paint, perfume, pigment, prettify, refine, renovate, ribbon, season, sensationalize, smarten, sophisticate, spangle, spice, spiff, spruce, stipple, stud, swag, tinsel, titivate, tool, trim, upgrade, wreathe* (≠ bare, besmirch, blemish, damage, decrease, deface, defile, deform, denude, disfigure, dismantle, display, divest, dull, efface, expose, harm, harshen, hurt, injure, mangle, mar, mutilate, remove, reveal, scalp, scar, simplify, smear, spoil, stain, streamline, strip, sully, taint, tarnish, uglify, uncover)

GASH (/): *bite, carve, claw, cleave, cut, damage, flay, furrow, gore, gouge, hack, harm, hurt, incise, injure, lacerate, lance, mark, maul, mutilate, nick, nip, notch, perforate, pierce, puncture, razor, rend, rip, scalp, scar, score, scrape, scratch, slash, slice, slit, split, tear, wound* (≠ aid, armor, block, close, cure, defend, deflect, fix, guard, heal, help, join, mend, parry, protect, repair, seal, sew, shield, stitch, suture)

GATHER (→): *accrue, accumulate, add, advance, amass, amplify, augment, boost, broaden, build, deepen, develop, double, elevate, enhance, enlarge, enrich, excite, expand, extend, gain, grow, heighten, improve, increase, intensify, jack, maximize, mingle, mount, progress, raise, ramp, stimulate, swell, thicken, triple* (≠ abate, cut, decrease, diffuse, diminish, dismiss, dissipate, divide, lessen, lose, scatter, spend, squander, taper)

GATHER (←): *accept, adjudge, affirm, anticipate, apprehend, ascertain, assume, await, believe, conceive, conclude, conjecture, construe, contemplate, credit, decide, declare, deduce, derive, detect, determine, diagnose, dread, educe, envision, expect, extrapolate, fancy, fear, feel, follow, foresee, grant, guess, hear, hold, imagine, infer, interpret, judge, learn, maintain, premise, presume, presuppose, profess, profile, rationalize, read, reason, reckon, suppose, surmise, suspect, think, trust, understand* (≠ bury, conceal, -disregard, ensconce, forget, hide, -ignore, lose, mask, misapprehend, misconceive, misconstrue, misdiagnose, mishear, misinterpret, misperceive, misread, miss, mistake, misunderstand, -overlook, predetermine) **(¿) ABSTRACTION ALERT. Concrete goals essential!**

GATHER (←): *bend, corrugate, crease, crimp, crinkle, crumple, curl, double, fold, furrow, pleat, pucker, ridge, ripple, ruck, rumple, tuck, twist, wrinkle* (≠ compress, crush, even, expand, extend, flatten, iron, level, press, roll, smooth, spread, squash, stretch, uncrumple, unfold)

GATHER (←): *accrue, accumulate, acquire, aggregate, bag, capture, choose, claim, collect, commandeer, confiscate, conjure, crop, cull, -cut, download, draw, extract, fish, forage, garner, get, glean, grab, grow, harvest, hay, heap, hoard, hunt, impound, levy, mass, monopolize, mow, nab, net, pick, pile, pluck, procure, raise, reap, reclaim, recover, recycle, rescue, retrieve, salvage, scavenge, scoop, seek, select, snag, snare, stack, stockpile, summon, take, trap* (≠ -abandon, bury, cultivate, diffuse, distribute, dump, find, grow, implant, lose, miss, nurture, plant, scatter, seed, seek, skip, sow, transplant, waste)

GATHER (+): *accumulate, amass, annex, arrange, assemble, attract, ball, band, batch, brigade, build, bunch, cluster, collate, collect, combine, compile, concentrate, congregate, connect, convene, corral, crowd, draw, garner, group, heap, herd, hive, integrate, join, link, lump, marshal, mass, meet, merge, muster, network, organize, overcrowd, pack, pile, pool, press, pull, raise, rake, rally, reintegrate, reunite, stack, summon, swarm, systematize, throng, unify, unite, wrangle* (≠ allot, bestow, break, deal, diffuse, disband, disintegrate, dismiss, dispel, disperse, disseminate, dissipate, dissolve, distribute, divide, furnish, offload, prorogue, scatter, send, separate, sever, split, spread, supply)

GAUGE (←): *analyze, appraise, apprise, ascertain, assay, assess, audit, audition, benchmark, beta, calculate, calibrate, caliper, categorize, check, clock, compare, compute, conclude, connect, consider, consult, contemplate, contrast, correlate, count, critique, deduce, detect, determine, estimate, evaluate, examine, explore, eye, eyeball, figure, grade, guess, guesstimate, inspect, investigate, judge, learn, measure, meter, monitor, number, numerate, observe, ogle, peg, peruse, prioritize, probe, prowl, quantify, rank, rate, read, reckon, regard, sample, scan, score, scrutinize, search, set, sift, size, study, survey, suss, tally, test, time, total, valuate, value, watch, weigh* (≠ accept, addle, assume, baffle, bewilder, blind, bury, cloud, conceal, confound, confuse, deceive, defraud, disguise, -disregard, fake, forget, fudge, half-ass, hide, -ignore, mask, miscalculate, misjudge, mislead, misread, miss, mistake, misunderstand, muddle, muddy, mystify, -neglect, -nullify, obfuscate, obscure, -omit, overestimate, -overlook, perplex, predetermine, puzzle, skim, skip, trick, trust, underestimate)

GENERALIZE (+): *abbreviate, abridge, abstract, adumbrate, assume, compress, conclude, condense, contract, deduce, depersonalize, digest, distill, distort, educe, encapsulate, epitomize, infer, minute, outline, oversimplify, précis, profile, shorten, standardize, summarize, synopsize, theorize, universalize* (≠ ascertain, complicate, customize, denote, detail, except, -ignore, miss, narrow, -neglect, -overlook, particularize, personalize, pinpoint, specialize, specify, unsettle) **(¿) ABSTRACTION ALERT. Concrete goals essential!**

GENERATE (+): *activate, advance, agitate, arouse, awaken, beget, brainstorm, breed, bring, build, catalyze, concoct, create, cultivate, develop, effect, effectuate, enact, encourage, energize, engender, establish, fashion, father, form, foster, found, further, galvanize, hatch, inaugurate, incite, incur, induce, initiate, innovate, inspire, institute, intrigue, introduce, invigorate, invoke, kindle, launch, make, move, nourish, nurture, originate, pioneer, produce, proliferate, promote, prompt, propagate, provoke, quicken, raise, reinvigorate, render, revive, rouse, sculpt, sire, spark, spawn, spur, start, stimulate, stir, trigger, vitalize, wake, whelp, yield* (≠ abolish, arrest, check, control, crush, curb, damage, dampen, deactivate, demolish, destroy, doom, eradicate, exterminate, extinguish, impede, inactivate, inhibit, limit, liquidate, -prevent, quash, quell, quench, repress, restrain, restrict, retard, satisfy, scotch, slake, smother, squash, squelch, squench, stall, stifle, subdue, suppress)

GIVE (→): *administer, afford, aid, allocate, apportion, assign, assist, award, benefit, bestow, cede, comp, confer, contribute, deal, deed, deliver, dish, dispense, distribute, dole, donate, endow, extend, feed, furnish, hand, help, impart, issue, lavish, mete, offer, parcel, pay, portion, present, proffer, prorate, provide, regale, render, sacrifice, supply, tender, transfer, volunteer* (≠ advance, conserve, -deny, hold, keep, lend, loan, maintain,

-neglect, -omit, pocket, preserve, reserve, retain, save, sell, -spurn, take, withhold)

GIVE (→): *advance, assign, bequeath, commend, commit, confer, confide, consign, deal, deed, delegate, deliver, deposit, dispense, disperse, distribute, divide, endow, entrust, fund, furnish, grant, hand, leave, lend, loan, pass, recommend, release, relinquish, submit, supply, surrender, transfer, transmit, trust, vest, will, yield* (≠ accept, detain, hold, keep, occupy, own, possess, receive, reserve, retain, take, withhold)

GIVE (→): *advertise, air, allege, announce, articulate, broadcast, circulate, communicate, convey, declare, denounce, describe, disseminate, enunciate, expound, express, hype, offer, present, proclaim, promote, publicize, publish, raise, sound, state, submit, vent, ventilate, verbalize, voice, write* (≠ -avoid, bowdlerize, censor, expurgate, gag, muffle, -omit, -overlook, purge, restrain, restrict, -scorn, stifle, suppress) **(¿) ABSTRACTION ALERT. Concrete goals essential!**

GIVE (→): *allocate, allot, blow, disburse, dispense, dissipate, drop, expend, fritter, lavish, outlay, pay, rain, scatter, spend, squander, throw, waste* (≠ acquire, cache, earn, gain, garner, gross, hoard, make, net, obtain, procure, realize, save, secure, source, win)

GIVE (→): *broadcast, communicate, conduct, contaminate, convey, deliver, diffuse, disseminate, impart, infect, pass, poison, propagate, spread, surrender, transfer, transfuse, transmit* (≠ accept, catch, claim, contract, decontaminate, disallow, gather, isolate, oppose, purge, purify, quarantine, receive, -refuse, sequester, suppress, withdraw)

GIVE (→): *act, carry, depict, display, dramatize, enact, exhibit, expose, extend, impersonate, mount, offer, parade, perform, play, portray, present, preview, produce, proffer, render, represent, show, stage, tender, unveil* (≠ bury, censor, conceal, curtain, gag, hide, mask, obscure, -prevent, -prohibit, shroud, stifle, stop, suppress, -thwart) **(¿) ABSTRACTION ALERT. Concrete goals essential!**

GIVE (→): *acclaim, admonish, advise, advocate, applaud, back, brief, caution, commend, compliment, confer, consult, counsel, cue, direct, encourage, endorse, eulogize, exalt, exhort, extend, extol, glorify, guide, inform, instruct, notify, offer, plan, pose, praise, proffer, prompt, propose, proposition, recommend, sanction, spare, submit, suggest, tender, uphold, urge, volunteer, warn* (≠ accept, accredit, approbate, approve, authorize, clear, confirm, -decline, -deny, disallow, -disregard, finalize, formalize, -ignore, -neglect, okay, -overlook, ratify, -rebuff, rebut, receive, -refuse, -reject, retract, sanction, -spurn, take, -veto, warrant, withdraw) **(¿) ABSTRACTION ALERT. Concrete goals essential!**

GLADDEN (+): *amuse, appease, assuage, boost, brighten, buoy, calm, captivate, charm, cheer, comfort, content, delight, divert, elate, encourage, enliven, entertain, excite, exhilarate, feast, galvanize, grace, gratify, help, humor, indulge, invigorate, jolly, lift, lull, mellow, oblige,* *pacify, pamper, placate, please, sate, satiate, satisfy, soothe, spoil, suit, thrill, tickle, titillate, treat, warm, wow* (≠ aggravate, anger, appall, bore, bother, bug, burden, chafe, cross, depress, dismay, displease, distress, enrage, exasperate, gall, harass, infuriate, irk, nag, nauseate, nettle, outrage, pester, rankle, rile, sadden, sicken, terrorize, troll, upset, vex, victimize, weary, worry, wound)

GLAD-HAND (↔): *accept, acclaim, befriend, beguile, blandish, butter, cajole, charm, coax, compliment, convince, court, embrace, flannel, flatter, grease, greet, hail, high-five, honey, hustle, include, influence, ingratiate, inveigle, invite, lure, massage, meet, palaver, persuade, receive, salute, schmooze, soft-soap, stroke, sway, welcome, wheedle, win, woo* (≠ abuse, affront, anger, -avoid, bother, bug, disconnect, disgust, disjoin, divide, enrage, insult, offend, outrage, -reject, repel, repulse, -scorn, separate, -snub, -spurn, terrorize, tyrannize, upset)

GLAMORIZE (+): *adorn, adulate, advance, aggrandize, amplify, array, canonize, cherish, commend, deck, decorate, defend, deify, dignify, distinguish, elevate, embellish, endorse, enhance, enlarge, ennoble, enrich, enshrine, enthrone, euphemize, exaggerate, exalt, extol, garnish, gild, glitz, glorify, grace, heroicize, heroize, hype, idealize, idolize, improve, inflate, justify, laud, lionize, magnify, optimize, ornament, overhaul, perfect, poeticize, praise, promote, rationalize, recommend, respect, revere, revolutionize, reward, romanticize, sanction, sentimentalize, smarten, soften, sweeten, treasure, upgrade, validate, venerate, vindicate, warrant, worship* (≠ admonish, assail, badmouth, belittle, blast, blemish, blight, blotch, caricature, castigate, chastise, chide, condemn, criticize, crucify, debase, decry, deglamorize, demean, demonize, denigrate, denounce, deride, disparage, excoriate, fault, flay, hammer, impugn, judge, keelhaul, knock, lambaste, lash, malign, minimize, mock, neg, nitpick, pan, pillory, rebuke, reprimand, reproach, resent, ridicule, scapegoat, scold, -scorn, shame, shred, -shun, skewer, slam, slash, slate, spoil, stain, trash, upbraid)

GLEAN (↔): *accumulate, acquire, amass, ascertain, choose, collect, compile, conclude, cull, deduce, develop, earn, extract, find, gain, garner, gather, harvest, learn, obtain, pick, pluck, procure, profile, reap, recover, rescue, retrieve, salvage, scavenge, secure, select, sift, source, stockpile, win, winnow* (≠ assign, bestow, bury, circulate, conceal, confuse, diffuse, disseminate, dissipate, encode, ensconce, garble, hide, mystify, perplex, puzzle, -reject, scatter, screen, shield, spread, withhold)

GLORIFY (+): *acclaim, acknowledge, admire, adore, affirm, aggrandize, anoint, apotheosize, applaud, appreciate, approve, ballyhoo, beatify, blandish, bless, boost, canonize, celebrate, cheer, cherish, commend, compliment, congratulate, consecrate, dedicate, deify, devote, dignify, distinguish, elevate, emblazon, endorse, ennoble, enshrine, enthrone, erect, eulogize, exalt, extol, fête, fetishize, flatter, glorify, gold-star, gratify, hail, hallow, heighten, heroicize, heroize, high-five, hoist, honor, idealize, idolize, intensify, laud, lift, lionize, magnify, ordain, praise, pray, prioritize,* *proclaim, promote, raise, recognize, recommend, respect, revere, reverence, reward, romanticize, salute, sanctify, sanction, sanitize, sentimentalize, strengthen, sugarcoat, swell, thank, toast, tout, trumpet, upgrade, uplift, venerate, worship* (≠ abase, admonish, badmouth, bastardize, belittle, bestialize, blackguard, blame, blast, blister, boo, brutalize, cheapen, chide, condemn, criticize, critique, damn, debase, debauch, decry, defame, defile, degrade, dehumanize, demean, demonize, demote, denigrate, denounce, deprave, desanctify, desecrate, detract, diminish, discredit, disgrace, dishonor, dismiss, disparage, -disregard, disrespect, execrate, fault, forget, frame, fulminate, humble, humiliate, -ignore, incriminate, insult, lower, malign, minimize, mock, -neglect, offend, pillory, profane, rebuke, reduce, regret, repent, reprimand, reproach, revile, ridicule, savage, scold, -scorn, shame, -shun, slander, smear, subvert, threaten, trash-talk, victimize, vilify, violate, vulgarize, wound, wrong)

GLUE (+): *adhere, affix, attach, bolt, bond, cement, cinch, clamp, clasp, clench, clinch, clip, connect, fasten, fix, gum, hang, join, link, mortar, paste, pin, plaster, reaffix, reattach, refasten, resecure, seal, staple, stick, stud, tack, tie, unite* (≠ break, cut, detach, disconnect, disjoin, divide, divorce, loose, loosen, part, separate, sever, split, sunder, tear, unbind, uncouple, undo, unfasten, unlash, untie)

GNAW (/): *bite, canker, champ, chaw, chew, chomp, consume, corrode, crunch, decimate, destroy, devastate, devour, disintegrate, dissolve, eat, erode, fret, gum, masticate, munch, nibble, ruin, ruminate, waste, wear, wreck* (≠ armor, conserve, defend, freshen, preserve, protect, recreate, refresh, regenerate, rejuvenate, renew, restore, revitalize, revive, shield, sustain)

GNAW (/): *aggravate, anguish, annoy, bedevil, beleaguer, bug, displease, distress, exasperate, fret, gall, harass, harry, hassle, haunt, irritate, madden, nag, needle, nettle, niggle, nitpick, pester, plague, rankle, rile, ruffle, tease, torment, trouble, vex, worry* (≠ allay, alleviate, appease, assuage, calm, comfort, compose, help, humor, lull, mellow, mitigate, moderate, mollify, pacify, placate, please, propitiate, quiet, settle, soothe, tranquilize)

GOAD (→): *abet, accelerate, adjure, animate, annoy, arouse, badger, beseech, blandish, browbeat, bully, cajole, catalyze, coax, coerce, convince, drive, earbash, encourage, energize, excite, exhort, fast-forward, fast-track, foment, force, frogmarch, goose, gravel, grease, harass, hasten, hound, hurry, hustle, impel, implore, importune, incite, incur, induce, influence, inspire, instigate, irritate, jolt, lubricate, march, midwife, motivate, muscle, nag, needle, nudge, palaver, persuade, poke, press, pressure, prick, prod, prompt, propel, provoke, push, quicken, rabble-rouse, railroad, rankle, rile, rush, sandbag, schmooze, soft-soap, spark, spur, stimulate, sting, stir, taunt, tease, trash-talk, trigger, urge, vex, wheedle, worry* (≠ brake, check, constrain, cripple, curb, deactivate, demotivate, -deter, discourage, dissuade, freeze, hinder, inactivate, inhibit, paralyze, -prevent, protest, restrain, soft-sell, stall, stem, stop, straightjacket, stymie)

GOBBLE (←): *absorb, accept, acquire, assimilate, bolt, consume, cram, devour, eat, engorge, engulf, get, gorge, gulp, guzzle, hog, incorporate, ingest, inhale, integrate, overeat, ram, raven, receive, scarf, snarf, stuff, swallow, swill, take, wolf* (≠ -bypass, -decline, lick, nibble, -omit, peck, pick, -refuse, regurgitate, -reject, relish, savor, skip, spill, spit, splutter, taste, vomit)

GOUGE (←): *bleed, cheat, clip, con, deceive, defraud, embezzle, euchre, exaggerate, fleece, fool, gazump, hornswoggle, hustle, hyperbolize, inflate, magnify, milk, nobble, overcharge, overstate, pluck, rob, rook, scalp, scam, shortchange, skin, snooker, soak, steal, stick, stiff, sting, sucker, surcharge, swindle, trick, undercut* (≠ bankroll, bestow, capitalize, comp, compensate, disburse, donate, endow, fund, indemnify, pay, recompense, recoup, refund, reimburse, remit, remunerate, repay, return, reward, settle, square, undercharge)

GOUGE (/): *chisel, claw, cleave, coarsen, core, cut, dent, dig, ding, dredge, excavate, extract, furrow, gash, groove, hack, hollow, incise, knife, lacerate, maul, nick, notch, penetrate, perforate, pick, pierce, poke, rut, scoop, score, scrape, scratch, shovel, slash, slit, split, tear, wound* (≠ augment, block, buff, even, fill, flatten, heal, mend, plaster, plug, polish, restore, seal, shine, smooth, stroke, wax)

GOVERN (→): *administer, boss, captain, chair, choreograph, command, conduct, conquer, control, dictate, direct, discipline, dominate, domineer, execute, guard, guide, handle, head, influence, keep, lead, manage, master, micromanage, mind, occupy, operate, oppress, orchestrate, order, override, overrule, oversee, pace, pilot, protect, regulate, render, rule, run, safeguard, shepherd, spearhead, stage-manage, steer, steward, subdue, subjugate, superintend, supervise, sway, tend, time, tyrannize, watch* (≠ battle, buck, challenge, contradict, counter, defy, disobey, follow, mind, obey, oppose, -refuse, resist, subvert, topple)

GOVERN (+): *arrest, block, bottle, bridle, check, choke, conduct, constrain, contain, control, curb, decide, determine, direct, dispose, gag, guide, hamper, handcuff, handle, hinder, hold, impede, incline, inhibit, interrupt, keep, measure, mince, muffle, muzzle, obstruct, order, pace, pocket, predispose, quell, regulate, rein, repress, restrain, rule, silence, sink, smother, squelch, stabilize, steady, steer, stifle, stop, straightjacket, strangle, subdue, suppress, swallow, sway, tame* (≠ air, deregulate, destabilize, exacerbate, express, liberate, loose, loosen, lose, panic, release, unleash, vent)

GRAB (←): *abduct, annex, apprehend, appropriate, arrest, bag, capture, catch, clasp, clutch, collar, commandeer, cop, corner, corral, detain, disappear, embrace, enmesh, ensnare, entangle, entrap, get, glom, glove, grapple, grasp, grip, halter, hold, hook, kidnap, land, lasso, mesh,* *nab, nail, net, pluck, pull, rap, rend, rope, rustle, secure, seize, snaffle, snag, snap, snare, snatch, swipe, take, trap, tug, usurp, wrench, wrest* (≠ discharge, drop, free, liberate, loosen, lose, miss, plonk, release, seek, surrender, unhand, yield)

GRAB (←): *absorb, arouse, arrest, attract, bait, beckon, beguile, bewitch, captivate, charm, court, dazzle, delight, disarm, draw, enchant, engage, engross, enrapture, entertain, enthrall, entice, entrance, fascinate, gratify, hook, hypnotize, interest, intrigue, invite, lure, magnetize, mystify, please, pull, puzzle, razzle-dazzle, rivet, seduce, solicit, tantalize, tease, tempt, thrill, transfix, win, woo, wow* (≠ affront, anger, annoy, bore, bug, burden, disgust, dismay, displease, enrage, frustrate, horrify, irk, irritate, nag, needle, nettle, nitpick, offend, rankle, repel, repulse, revolt, rile, satisfy, sour, tire, weary, worry)

GRACE (→): *accessorize, adorn, appliqué, array, beautify, bedeck, bedizen, blazon, boss, braid, brighten, caparison, chase, costume, crown, dandify, deck, decorate, dignify, distinguish, drape, dress, drizzle, elevate, embellish, emblaze, emboss, embroider, enhance, enrich, fancify, favor, feather, festoon, figure, filigree, fillet, flavor, flounce, freshen, frill, fringe, garland, garnish, gild, glitter, glitz, glorify, hang, honor, lace, optimize, ornament, overhaul, paint, pigment, ribbon, season, smarten, spice, spiff, spruce, stipple, stud, swag, tinsel, titivate, tool, trim, wreathe* (≠ bare, blemish, botch, damage, deface, denude, disfigure, disgrace, dismantle, display, divest, efface, expose, harm, harshen, injure, mar, repulse, reveal, scar, simplify, spoil, streamline, strip, tarnish, uglify, uncover)

GRADE (+): *alphabetize, arrange, array, assess, assort, benchmark, brand, catalog, categorize, class, classify, clump, cluster, codify, compare, compartment, compartmentalize, cull, digest, dispose, distinguish, distribute, evaluate, file, group, hierarchize, identify, index, label, list, mark, marshal, order, organize, peg, pigeonhole, place, prioritize, range, rank, rate, recategorize, reclassify, recognize, refer, regroup, relegate, screen, separate, set, shelve, sieve, sift, size, slot, sort, systematize, type, value, winnow* (≠ assume, confuse, disarrange, -disregard, estimate, guess, guestimate, half-ass, -ignore, jumble, lump, miscalculate, misclassify, miss, missort, mistake, mistype, mix, -neglect, overestimate, -overlook, scramble, skip, underestimate)

GRAFT (+): *affix, attach, bud, clip, connect, embed, ensconce, establish, fasten, fix, implant, initiate, inoculate, insert, install, Instate, introduce, join, locate, pin, place, plant, position, propagate, root, secure, situate, splice, tie, transplant, unite* (≠ cut, detach, divide, draw, eliminate, excise, extract, pick, pluck, prize, remove, separate, split, withdraw, wrench, wrest)

GRANT (→): *accord, afford, allocate, allot, appoint, apportion, assign, award, bequeath, bestow, cede, comp, confer, contribute, convey, deed, deliver, designate, dispense, dole, donate, drop, dub, endow, extend, fix, furnish, gift, give, hand, impart, invest, name, offer, present, proffer, provide, relinquish, set, show, spare, stake, supply, surrender, tender,* *transfer, transmit, vest, volunteer, yield* (≠ -abort, abrogate, accept, acquire, appropriate, commandeer, confiscate, debit, -decline, -deny, derive, disinherit, dispossess, divest, drop, gain, gather, glean, impound, inherit, invalidate, -nullify, obtain, procure, -rebuff, -refuse, -reject, remove, repel, -repudiate, -rescind, retract, revoke, rob, seize, source, -spurn, swipe, take, -void, withdraw, withhold)

GRANT (→): *accede, accept, accord, acknowledge, admit, affirm, allow, announce, assume, avow, betray, blab, bless, blurt, break, broadcast, circulate, communicate, concede, confess, confide, confirm, declare, disclose, disseminate, divulge, expose, give, impart, inform, leak, let, permit, proclaim, profess, publish, recognize, reveal, spill, suppose, telegraph, tell, unburden, unload, unveil, vouchsafe, warn, yield* (≠ conceal, condemn, contradict, cover, debate, debunk, -deny, disallow, disavow, disclaim, discredit, -disown, disprove, dispute, distrust, doubt, gainsay, hide, neg, -negate, obscure, rebut, refute, -reject, -repudiate, scruple, suspect, veil, -veto) **(¿) ABSTRACTION ALERT. Concrete goals essential!**

GRAPPLE (←): *accost, battle, clasp, clinch, clutch, combat, confront, engage, face, fight, grab, grasp, grip, hold, seize, snatch, tackle, wrestle* (≠ -avoid, -dodge, drop, -duck, dump, -elude, -escape, -evade, -overlook, shake, -sidestep, skip, skirt)

GRASP (←): *bag, catch, clasp, clench, clinch, clutch, collar, corral, crush, embrace, encircle, enclose, grab, grapple, grip, hold, hook, hug, land, nab, seize, snag, snatch, squeeze, squoosh, take, wrap* (≠ -avoid, bequeath, bestow, deliver, drop, forfeit, give, hand, lose, misplace, offer, plonk, receive, -refuse, release, relinquish, spare, surrender, transfer, transmit, volunteer, yield)

GRASP (+): *appreciate, assimilate, comprehend, conceive, diagnose, discern, fathom, follow, grok, incorporate, integrate, internalize, know, master, penetrate, perceive, realize, sense, suspect, suss, understand, visualize* (≠ confuse, forget, misconstrue, misdiagnose, mishear, misinterpret, misread, miss, mistake, misunderstand, -neglect, -overlook) **(¿) ABSTRACTION ALERT. Concrete goals essential!**

GRATIFY (+): *appease, assuage, baby, cocoon, coddle, conciliate, content, cosset, favor, fulfill, humor, indulge, infantilize, mollify, mollycoddle, oblige, overindulge, overprotect, pacify, pamper, placate, quench, recompense, reconcile, resolve, sate, satiate, satisfy, slake, soothe, spoil, square* (≠ abuse, appall, betray, bridle, check, constrain, cripple, curb, deceive, disappoint, disfavor, disgrace, dismay, frustrate, harm, hobble, hurt, impair, incapacitate, inhibit, injure, restrain, stifle, upset, wrong)

GRATIFY (+): *amuse, attract, beguile, bewitch, brighten, cajole, calm, captivate, charm, cheer, comfort, content, delight, distract, divert, draw, elate, electrify, enamor, enchant, encourage, engage, engross, enliven, enrapture, entertain, excite, exhilarate, fascinate, favor, galvanize, gladden, gratify, hearten, help, humor, indulge, interest, intrigue, lull,* *mellow, mesmerize, mitigate, moderate, mollify, occupy, pacify, placate, please, pleasure, rejoice, rouse, sate, satisfy, schmooze, stimulate, suit, thrill, tickle, titillate, treat, warm, win, woo* (≠ affront, aggravate, agitate, anger, annoy, bore, bother, bug, burden, chafe, depress, disgust, displease, distress, disturb, earbash, enrage, exasperate, fret, gall, grate, harass, harry, incense, infuriate, insult, irk, irritate, madden, nag, needle, nettle, nitpick, offend, outrage, pain, peeve, perturb, pester, pique, provoke, rankle, rile, roil, rouse, ruffle, sadden, scare, sicken, upset, vex, weary, worry)

GREASE (+): *anoint, bathe, butter, cream, douse, drench, lard, lube, lubricate, marinate, moisten, moisturize, oil, pomade, schmooze, slick, smear, soak, soften, souse, wash, water, wax, wet* (≠ abrade, callous, chafe, coarsen, dehydrate, desiccate, dry, harden, harshen, parch, rough, roughen, scratch, scuff, sear, stiffen)

GREASE (+): *abet, accelerate, advance, aid, alleviate, ameliorate, assist, assuage, boost, brainstorm, bribe, buy, catalyze, cherish, comfort, corrupt, disentangle, ease, enable, encourage, entertain, entice, expedite, facilitate, fast-forward, fast-track, fix, forward, foster, further, glad-hand, hasten, heal, help, hurry, hustle, improve, influence, instigate, keep, kick-start, loosen, lubricate, midwife, mitigate, nobble, nourish, nurse, nurture, outbid, outlay, overpay, overspend, palaver, pay, press, promote, prompt, protect, quicken, relieve, remedy, rush, simplify, smooth, solve, soothe, speed, spur, straighten, streamline, suborn, support, sustain, trigger, unclog, uncomplicate, untangle* (≠ aggravate, -avert, bear, block, checkmate, clog, complicate, confound, constipate, delay, -deter, expose, filibuster, foil, -frustrate, -halt, hamper, hamstring, harm, hinder, hobble, impair, impede, inhibit, monkey-wrench, muddle, obstruct, occlude, oppose, postpone, -prevent, -prohibit, protest, retard, ruin, scotch, shelve, short-circuit, slow, spoil, stall, starve, steal, stem, stiff, stint, stop, stump, stymie, -thwart, -veto, withhold, worsen)

GREET (+): *accost, acknowledge, address, approach, attend, buttonhole, call, compliment, detain, embrace, flag, glad-hand, hail, high-five, hug, meet, notice, receive, recognize, salaam, salute, signal, stop, waylay, welcome* (≠ affront, -bypass, -cold-shoulder, daunt, detour, -disdain, dismiss, -disregard, -dodge, -duck, -ignore, miss, -omit, -sidestep, -slight, -snub, -spurn, threaten)

GRIEVE (/): *afflict, agitate, ail, anguish, appall, bother, bum, burden, concern, crucify, crush, dash, daunt, demoralize, depress, discomfort, discompose, discourage, dishearten, dismay, dispirit, disquiet, distress, disturb, freak, horrify, hurt, offend, oppress, pain, perturb, sadden, shock, sicken, torment, torture, trouble, undo, unhinge, unnerve, unsettle, upset, weigh, worry, wound* (≠ animate, boost, brighten, buoy, cheer, comfort, console, delight, elate, encourage, excite, exhilarate, gladden, gratify, heal, hearten, inspire, invigorate, lift, please, prioritize, reassure, soothe, stimulate, thrill, transcend, uplift)

GRILL (←): *annoy, ask, besiege, bombard, canvass, catechize, chaff, challenge, check, consult, cross-examine, cross-question, debate, debrief,* *disbelieve, discredit, disprove, dispute, doubt, earbash, examine, hammer, harass, hector, hound, interrogate, interview, investigate, irk, irritate, nag, needle, nettle, niggle, nitpick, pester, poll, probe, pump, query, question, quiz, research, roast, scruple, survey, suspect, test* (≠ answer, -avoid, conceal, confide, -deny, -dodge, -duck, -evade, feign, hide, -ignore, mislead, -neglect, observe, rejoin, remark, retort, silence, stonewall, suppress, withhold)

GRIND (→): *bob, bone, brighten, buff, burnish, clean, dress, edge, face, file, finish, furbish, glaze, gloss, hone, lap, plane, polish, pumice, rasp, rub, sand, sandblast, sandpaper, scour, scrape, scrub, serrate, sharpen, shine, sleek, slick, smooth, strop, veneer, wax, whet* (≠ abrade, blunt, callous, chafe, coarsen, dull, granulate, graze, harshen, rasp, roughen, ruffle, scuff, soften)

GRIND (→): *abrade, callous, chafe, clash, coarsen, crunch, gnash, grate, grit, harden, harshen, hinder, jangle, jar, rasp, roughen, rub, scrape, scratch, scrunch* (≠ anoint, assist, butter, drench, ease, grease, lard, lube, lubricate, marinate, moisturize, oil, polish, shine, slick, smear, smooth, wax, wet)

GRIND (/): *atomize, beat, break, bust, chew, comminute, crumble, crunch, crush, dash, disintegrate, fracture, fragment, grate, kibble, mill, pestle, pound, powder, pulverize, ruminate, shatter, smash, splinter* (≠ assemble, build, create, doctor, fabricate, fashion, fix, forge, form, meld, melt, mend, mold, patch, preserve, produce, protect, renovate, repair, restore, sculpt, shape)

GRIP (←): *bag, bear, capture, carry, catch, clasp, clench, clutch, collar, corral, cradle, embrace, feel, finger, grab, grapple, grasp, handle, hold, hook, hug, land, nab, nail, paw, seize, snag, snare, snatch, take, trap* (≠ -abandon, bequeath, bestow, cant, cede, chuck, deliver, drop, forfeit, give, hand, plonk, -reject, release, relinquish, render, unclasp, unhand, yield)

GRIP (←): *absorb, amuse, arrest, bedazzle, beguile, bewitch, catch, charm, compel, delight, distract, divert, enchant, engage, engross, enrapture, entertain, enthrall, entrance, fascinate, hypnotize, involve, lighten, mesmerize, please, refresh, relax, rivet, spellbind, stimulate, thrill, wow* (≠ annoy, bore, bug, burden, disgust, displease, exhaust, irk, irritate, jade, nag, needle, nitpick, offend, repel, revolt, sadden, sicken, tire, vex, weary, worry)

GROOM (+): *adjust, adorn, arrange, array, beautify, brush, clean, comb, costume, curry, dandify, decorate, delouse, dress, embellish, enhance, festoon, fix, garnish, gild, glamorize, glitter, glitz, grace, improve, manicure, moisturize, neaten, oil, optimize, ornament, overhaul, paint, perfume, polish, pomade, preen, prep, prepare, prettify, pretty, primp, ready, refine, renovate, scent, shave, shine, sleek, slick, smarten, smooth, spackle, spiff, spruce, tidy, titivate, trim, wash* (≠ bedraggle, callous, coarsen, dirty, disfigure, dishevel, draggle, harm, harshen, impair, injure, maim, mangle, mar, muss, scalp, scar, soil, spoil, tangle, untidy, wound)

GROOM (+): *adapt, adjust, alter, arm, clean, coach, convince, drill, educate, equip, inculcate, influence, instruct, mentor, modify, mold, nurture, persuade, polish, prep, prepare, prime, program, ready, refine, refresh, school, season, shape, sharpen, sophisticate, teach, temper, toughen, train, transform, tutor* (≠ barbarize, callous, coarsen, compromise, deprogram, extract, forget, freeze, -negate, -omit, -overlook, paralyze, purge, rescue, study)

GROPE (→): *abuse, brush, caress, clasp, clutch, contact, cuddle, feel, finger, fondle, fumble, goose, grasp, graze, grip, handle, knead, manhandle, manipulate, massage, maul, molest, nuzzle, palm, palpate, pat, paw, pet, pluck, ply, poke, press, probe, rub, search, seize, skim, smack, squeeze, stimulate, stroke, strum, touch, twiddle* (≠ -avoid, bar, block, defend, deflect, discourage, -dodge, -elude, -escape, -evade, foil, guard, -ignore, inhibit, injure, intercept, -neglect, obstruct, parry, protect, -refuse, resist, shield, -sidestep, support, -thwart)

GROSS (←): *accumulate, aggregate, amass, clear, collect, draw, earn, gain, get, increase, make, obtain, pocket, produce, pull, realize, reap, receive, take, total, yield* (≠ borrow, forfeit, give, grant, loan, lose, net, pay, relinquish, spend, squander, steal, stiff, stint, surrender, waste, yield)

GROUND (+): *acquaint, adjust, align, anchor, assume, attune, balance, base, calibrate, center, coach, compose, concentrate, counteract, counterbalance, discipline, drill, educate, equalize, establish, even, familiarize, fit, fix, focus, found, hang, harmonize, indoctrinate, inform, initiate, instruct, introduce, level, match, mentor, neutralize, offset, pace, parallel, plant, poise, postulate, predicate, premise, prepare, presume, presuppose, prime, qualify, ready, regulate, rest, root, school, secure, set, settle, square, stabilize, stay, steady, suppose, teach, tie, train, tune, tutor* (≠ challenge, confuse, convulse, cross-examine, discombobulate, disconcert, discredit, disprove, dizzy, doubt, eliminate, heckle, interrogate, jolt, mismatch, mistrust, -negate, -obviate, question, rattle, rebut, refute, -reject, -repudiate, roil, scruple, shake, suspect, unbalance, upset)

GROUND (/): *anchor, bar, beach, berth, bind, block, chasten, confine, curtail, detain, dock, down, fell, fix, floor, hinder, impede, land, level, limit, maroon, -preclude, -prevent, -prohibit, restrain, restrict, stop, strand, suppress, -thwart* (≠ aid, emancipate, encourage, free, incite, liberate, loose, permit, release, spring, transcend, urge)

GROUP (+): *accumulate, amass, arrange, assemble, associate, ball, band, batch, bracket, brigade, bulk, bunch, bundle, clump, cluster, collate, collect, combine, compile, concentrate, congregate, connect, corral, garner, gather, harmonize, heap, herd, hive, join, lasso, link, lump, mass, merge, muster, network, organize, pack, pile, pool, press, raise, rally, stack, stockpile, swarm, systematize, throng, unite, wrangle* (≠ alienate, break, diffuse, disband, disintegrate, dismiss, dispel, disperse, dissipate, dissolve, -ditch, dump, eject, estrange, -exclude, expel, jettison, -omit, -ostracize, oust, scatter, send, separate, sever, split, spread, toss)

GROUP (+): *align, alphabetize, arrange, array, assemble, associate, assort, band, bracket, catalog, categorize, class, classify, clump, cluster, codify, compartment, compartmentalize, coordinate, cull, digest, dispose, distinguish, distribute, draw, file, gather, glean, grade, hierarchize, identify, index, link, list, marshal, order, organize, peg, pigeonhole, place, prioritize, range, rank, recognize, regiment, relegate, screen, separate, set, shelve, sieve, sift, slot, sort, stereotype, systematize, tidy, type, typecast, winnow* (≠ churn, confuse, disarrange, dislocate, disorder, disorganize, disturb, jumble, lump, mess, misclassify, missort, mistype, mix, muddle, scramble, shuffle, tangle, unsettle, untidy)

GROW (+): *breed, create, crop, cultivate, culture, deliver, develop, double, dress, embed, engender, evoke, farm, fertilize freshen, gather, generate, germinate, glean, ground, harvest, help, implant, improve, invent, make, nourish, nurture, originate, outgrow, plant, pot, prepare, produce, promote, propagate, provoke, quicken, raise, rear, replant, reseed, revive, ripen, root, seed, sow, sprout, stimulate, tend, transplant, yield* (≠ afflict, blight, consume, crop, cull, cut, defoliate, deforest, demolish, destroy, devour, dig, diminish, doom, drain, eat, extirpate, gather, glean, -halt, harvest, hay, -ignore, kill, lose, mow, -neglect, pick, pluck, poison, pull, raze, reap, reduce, ruin, scavenge, scorch, shrivel, sicken, squander, stop, stunt, uproot, waste, weaken, wither, worsen, yield)

GUARANTEE (→): *accent, accentuate, advance, advertise, advocate, affirm, amplify, announce, assert, assure, avow, blaze, boost, call, champion, convince, declare, defend, emphasize, espouse, explain, justify, persuade, plug, prioritize, proclaim, profess, promote, pronounce, publicize, rationalize, reaffirm, reassert, stress, support, underline, underscore, uphold* (≠ challenge, contradict, counter, debate, -deny, disavow, disclaim, discredit, disprove, dispute, doubt, gainsay, -ignore, minimize, -negate, -neglect, -overlook, question, rebut, refute, -reject, -repudiate, scruple, understate)

GUARANTEE (+): *affirm, assert, assure, attest, avow, back, bond, certify, cinch, clinch, confirm, corroborate, countersign, cover, crosscheck, declare, demonstrate, depose, endorse, ensure, establish, guard, ice, indemnify, insure, maintain, pledge, promise, protect, prove, reassure, recoup, register, safeguard, secure, shield, show, sponsor, state, stipulate, substantiate, support, swear, underwrite, verify, vouchsafe, vow, warrant, witness* (≠ attack, break, compromise, damage, deceive, -deny, -disown, disprove, distrust, double-talk, doubt, endanger, enfeeble, imperil, injure, invalidate, predict, refute, -reject, -repudiate, risk, scruple, suspect, undermine, weaken, worry)

GUARANTEE (+): *adhere, assert, assure, attest, authenticate, avow, bond, certify, confirm, contract, corroborate, covenant, declare, demonstrate, insist, insure, notarize, pledge, promise, second, stipulate, substantiate, support, swear, testify, undertake, uphold, validate, verify, vow, warrant,* *witness* (≠ challenge, cheat, consult, contest, contradict, debate, debunk, deceive, -deny, disavow, disclaim, discredit, disgrace, disprove, dispute, distrust, double-talk, doubt, gainsay, grill, interrogate, invalidate, question, rebut, refute, stiff)

GUARD (+): *armor, assure, attend, -avert, babysit, barricade, battle, beware, block, blockade, budget, bulwark, chaperone, chauffeur, conduct, conserve, convoy, cover, defend, embattle, escort, fence, fight, fortify, house, inoculate, insulate, insure, keep, mind, observe, oppose, oversee, patrol, police, preserve, -prevent, protect, resist, safeguard, sanction, save, screen, secure, sentinel, shelter, shepherd, shield, stonewall, superintend, supervise, support, tend, ward, watch, withstand* (≠ -abandon, assail, assault, attack, beset, besiege, betray, blind, blindfold, blitz, bombard, compromise, confound, deceive, -desert, -disregard, endanger, forget, -forsake, harm, hurt, -ignore, imperil, injure, jeopardize, leave, lose, -neglect, open, outlast, overrun, risk, storm, submit, target, trick, unbar, unblock, unbolt, uncover)

GUIDE (→): *administer, chair, choreograph, command, conduct, control, direct, engineer, govern, guard, handle, keep, lead, manage, micromanage, mind, operate, orchestrate, oversee, pace, pilot, protect, regulate, rule, run, safeguard, spearhead, stage-manage, steer, steward, superintend, supervise, tend, watch* (≠ bobble, botch, bugger, bungle, doom, flub, follow, fumble, half-ass, mar, mind, mishandle, mismanage, obey, ruin, serve, spoil, wreck)

GUIDE (+): *accompany, aim, attend, beacon, chaperone, conduct, control, convey, convoy, direct, dispatch, escort, forward, influence, lead, manage, maneuver, marshal, navigate, oversee, pilot, point, route, see, send, shepherd, show, steer, target, usher* (≠ -abandon, abuse, baffle, block, confuse, dog, follow, forget, hamper, harm, hinder, hobble, hound, leave, mystify, perplex, puzzle, shadow, stall, stop, stymie, tail, tailgate, terrorize, -thwart, trail)

GUIDE (+): *accompany, advise, attend, brainwash, brief, chair, chaperone, coach, convince, convoy, counsel, cultivate, direct, drill, edify, educate, engineer, enlighten, escort, foster, godfather, govern, help, improve, inculcate, indoctrinate, influence, inform, instruct, lead, manage, maneuver, marshal, mentor, nurture, operate, oversee, pastor, pilot, retrain, rule, school, see, shepherd, show, spearhead, squire, steer, superintend, supervise, sway, teach, train, tutor* (≠ -abandon, abuse, addle, baffle, bury, compromise, conceal, confound, confuse, -desert, endanger, forget, -forsake, gaslight, hide, -ignore, imperil, misinform, mislead, mystify, -neglect, perplex, puzzle, risk, target, unhinge, unsettle)

GUT (/): *burgle, cannibalize, clean, clear, consume, cripple, debilitate, decimate, deplete, depredate, despoil, destroy, devastate, dilapidate, discharge, disembowel, doom, drain, draw, dress, empty, evacuate, eviscerate, exhaust, gore, issue, loot, pillage, plunder, ransack, ravage, rifle, rob, sack, strip, unload, unpack, vacate, void* (≠ build, cram, devour, dispense, fill, furnish, gorge, ingest, load, nurse, nurture, pack, preserve, protect, replace, replenish, restore, stock, stuff, supply, sustain, swallow)

GUZZLE (←): *absorb, belt, bolt, consume, cram, demolish, devour, dispatch, down, drink, eat, engorge, engulf, finish, glut, gobble, gorge, gulp, hog, hoist, hoover, imbibe, ingest, inhale, kill, lap, lick, overeat, pound, quaff, raven, scarf, siphon, slurp, snarf, stuff, suck, swallow, swig, swill, vacuum, wolf* (≠ -avoid, barf, belch, -bypass, covet, crave, -decline, disgorge, eject, expel, force-feed, forgo, furnish, gratify, heave, jettison, nibble, offer, pass, peck, pick, puke, quench, -refuse, regurgitate, -reject, sip, skimp, skip, slake, spew, spill, spit, starve, stint, taste, vomit, withhold)

HABITUATE (+): *accustom, acquaint, adapt, adjust, coach, condition, counsel, discipline, domesticate, drill, edify, educate, familiarize, housebreak, housetrain, inform, instruct, inure, mentor, pacify, placate, school, season, tame, teach, tone, toughen, train, tutor* (≠ agitate, baffle, bother, bug, confuse, destabilize, discompose, disconcert, disturb, dizzy, fluster, perplex, rattle, rile, ruffle, shake, trouble, unbalance, unhinge, unnerve, unsettle, upset)

HACK (→): *access, attack, automate, bootleg, breach, break, code, control, crack, debug, decode, decrypt, formulate, freeboot, infect, infiltrate, invade, jack, manage, mechanize, operate, penetrate, pierce, pirate, program, punch, rend, reprogram, rip, rupture, -sidestep, sneak, solve, wipe, wire* (≠ ban, bar, block, defend, expel, guard, maintain, protect, purge, quarantine, remove, screen, shield, sustain)

HACK (+): *address, command, control, direct, engineer, field, finesse, grapple, guide, handle, jockey, manage, maneuver, manipulate, micromanage, negotiate, play, pull, regulate, run, steer, swing, take, treat* (≠ bobble, botch, bugger, bungle, foozle, fumble, half-ass, mishandle, mismanage, muff, ruin, spoil, wreck)

HACK (+): *abide, accept, admit, allow, bear, brave, brook, countenance, endure, face, outlast, overcome, permit, resist, respect, sanction, stand, stomach, suffer, surmount, survive, swallow, tolerate, warrant, weather, withstand* (≠ -avoid, -bypass, -circumvent, combat, contest, -decline, dismiss, -dodge, -elude, -escape, -evade, fight, oppose, -refuse, -reject, resist, -shirk, -sidestep, skirt, -spurn)

HACK (/): *axe, behead, butcher, chop, clear, clip, cut, damage, decapitate, disfigure, dismember, fell, gash, gore, guillotine, harm, hew, hurt, knife, lacerate, maim, mangle, mutilate, notch, penetrate, pierce, puncture, razor, rend, saw, scar, sever, slash, slice, split, stab, sunder, unsew, whack, wound* (≠ armor, attach, block, defend, doctor, heal, mend, parry, patch, preserve, protect, repair, rescue, restore, save, sew, shield, stitch, suture)

HAIL (→): *accost, acknowledge, address, approach, buttonhole, confront, detain, embrace, face, flag, greet, high-five, hug, kiss, notice, receive, salaam, salute, shoulder, shout, signal, stop, wave, waylay, welcome* (≠ -avoid, -cut, -elude, -evade, -ignore, -overlook, pass, repel, -shun, -sidestep, skirt, whisper)

HAIL (←): *ask, assemble, beckon, bid, buzz, call, cite, command, convene, convoke, demand, include, invite, invoke, knell, muster, order, page, request, requisition, ring, subpoena, welcome* (≠ banish, blackball, boot, dismiss, eject, exorcise, expel, -ostracize, oust, out, push, -rebuff, rout, send, skip)

HAIL (+): *acclaim, accredit, acknowledge, adulate, applaud, approve, ballyhoo, blandish, celebrate, cheer, commemorate, commend, compliment, congratulate, deify, emblazon, endorse, enjoy, eulogize, exalt, extol, favor, fête, flatter, glorify, gold-star, gratify, greet, hallow, high-five, honor, idolize, inaugurate, laud, magnify, memorialize, observe, overpraise, praise, proclaim, recognize, recommend, rejoice, salute, solemnize, support, tout, trumpet, venerate* (≠ accuse, admonish, belittle, berate, blame, boo, castigate, censure, chastise, chide, criticize, critique, denigrate, discredit, -disdain, disfavor, disparage, excoriate, keelhaul, knock, lambaste, neg, pan, rebuke, regret, repent, reprimand, reproach, reprove, rue, scold, -scorn, skewer, slam, -slight, -snub, -spurn, vilify)

HALLOW (+): *anoint, baptize, bless, canonize, chasten, cleanse, commit, consecrate, dedicate, devote, elevate, enshrine, exalt, exorcise, expurgate, extol, ordain, purify, respect, revere, sanctify, spiritualize, treasure, venerate, worship* (≠ abuse, blaspheme, condemn, curse, cuss, damn, deconsecrate, defile, desacralize, desanctify, desecrate, dirty, execrate, foul, maledict, pollute, profane, punish, soil, taint, violate, wrong)

-HALT (←): *abolish, -abort, accost, adjourn, annul, arrest, baffle, -balk, bar, block, blockade, bottleneck, brake, call, -cancel, catch, cease, check, clog, close, complete, conclude, confront, cripple, crush, curb, -cut, dam, deactivate, delay, demolish, destroy, detain, -deter, -discontinue, dissolve, end, finish, foil, freeze, -frustrate, hamper, hinder, hobble, hold, immobilize, impede, inactivate, interrupt, -kibosh, kill, -nix, obstruct, occlude, paralyze, pause, -prevent, punctuate, -quit, rein, repress, rest, restrain, ruin, scuttle, shelve, short-circuit, snag, snuff, squash, squelch, stall, staunch, stay, stem, still, stop, straightjacket, stunt, stymie, suppress, suspend, terminate, -thwart* (≠ activate, actuate, advance, authorize, begin, brainstorm, budge, commence, continue, create, drive, employ, enact, encourage, establish, extend, forward, goad, greenlight, impel, initiate, instigate, introduce, keep, move, permit, prolong, propel, punt, push, reboot, restart, resuscitate, spur, start, stir, sustain)

HALVE (/): *allocate, allot, assign, bisect, break, cleave, cut, divide, earmark, give, lessen, part, partition, portion, ration, reduce, sever, share, split, sunder, tear* (≠ blend, combine, connect, double, fuse, hybridize, join, marry, meld, mend, mix, pair, patch, repair, synthesize, unify, unite)

HAMMER (→): *attack, bang, bash, bat, batter, bean, beat, belt, bludgeon, bob, bonk, bop, box, brain, buffet, bump, bung, bunt, bust, butt, cane, chop, clap, clip, clobber, clock, clout, club, concuss, conk, crack, cream, crush, cudgel, cuff, deck, defeat, drive, drub, fell, flail, flatten, flick, flog, floor, fracture, fragment, hit, jab, jostle, kick, knee, knock, lace, lambaste, lash, level, lick, mangle, maul, nail, paste, pelt, pepper, poke, pommel, pound, prod, pulverize, pummel, punch, push, rabbit-punch, rap, rough, sap, scuff, shove, skull, slam, slap, slash, sledge, sledgehammer, slog, slug, smack, smite, sock, spear, stab, stamp, strike, sucker-punch, swat,* *swipe, switch, tap, thrash, thump, thwack, trounce, wallop, whack, whale, whip, zap* (≠ aid, armor, block, caress, defend, deflect, -dodge, -duck, guard, help, hold, miss, parry, riffle, shelter, shield, stroke, support)

HAMMER (→): *annoy, canvass, catechize, cross-examine, cross-question, debate, debrief, discredit, dispute, distrust, earbash, examine, grill, harass, hound, interrogate, interview, nag, needle, niggle, nitpick, pester, poll, pump, query, question, quiz, rankle, rile, roast, sweat, test* (≠ answer, contradict, counter, -deny, -dodge, doubt, -evade, explain, mislead, parry, rebut, refute, -reject, -repudiate, retort, retract, scruple)

HAMMER (+): *abate, beat, boast, build, carve, chase, chisel, coin, craft, cut, draw, fabricate, fashion, forge, form, hew, knap, knead, make, mint, model, mold, pat, pound, sculpt, sculpture, shape, stamp, work* (≠ break, contort, crumple, deform, destroy, disfigure, distort, mar, ruin, shatter, shiver, spoil, warp, wreck)

HAMMER (/): *abuse, admonish, assail, attack, badmouth, belittle, berate, blame, blast, boo, castigate, censure, chastise, chide, condemn, criticize, critique, crucify, decry, demean, demonize, denigrate, denounce, disparage, disrespect, diss, earbash, excoriate, fault, finger, flay, fulminate, harangue, heckle, impugn, incriminate, jaw, keelhaul, knock, lambaste, lash, lecture, mock, nag, needle, neg, pan, pillory, pulverize, rag, rail, rate, ream, rebuke, reprimand, reproach, reprove, revile, ridicule, scold, score, -scorn, scourge, -shun, slam, slate, tongue-lash, upbraid, vilify, vituperate* (≠ acclaim, applaud, approve, congratulate, endorse, exalt, extol, gold-star, gratify, high-five, idolize, ingratiate, laud, lionize, outmaneuver, praise, sanction, trumpet, worship)

HAMPER (←): *anticipate, baffle, -balk, bar, block, bottleneck, brake, bung, burden, catch, chain, check, checkmate, choke, clog, complicate, congest, constipate, constrain, counter, cramp, crimp, cripple, curb, dam, dampen, daunt, delay, demotivate, depress, detain, -deter, disadvantage, discommode, discourage, dishearten, disincline, disrupt, dissuade, drag, encumber, entangle, entrap, fetter, foil, forestall, foul, freeze, -frustrate, hamstring, handicap, hinder, hogtie, impair, impede, inconvenience, inhibit, interrupt, jam, kneecap, knot, limit, lumber, mire, monkey-wrench, obstruct, occlude, oppose, overload, paralyze, pause, plug, preempt, -prevent, -prohibit, resist, restrain, restrict, retard, scotch, shackle, shelve, short-circuit, slow, snag, snarl, stagnate, stall, stay, stem, stifle, stop, straightjacket, stultify, stunt, stymie, tangle, throttle, -thwart, trammel, wing* (≠ accelerate, accommodate, advance, aid, assist, boost, brainstorm, catalyze, clear, compel, disencumber, disentangle, ease, encourage, expedite, extricate, facilitate, fast-forward, fast-track, free, frogmarch, fuel, further, grease, hasten, heal, help, hurry, improve, liberate, loosen, lubricate, march, mend, midwife, oblige, open, prioritize, promote, prompt, propel, quicken, release, relieve, remedy, rush, smooth, spark, speed, spur, steady, stimulate, stir, stoke, strengthen, transcend, unclog, uncomplicate, unleash, unlock, untangle, untie, urge)

HANDLE (→): *apply, command, control, direct, drive, exercise, exert, exploit, grapple, guide, maneuver, manipulate, operate, pilot, ply, run, steer, unsheathe, use, utilize, weaponize, wield, work* (≠ bobble, botch, bugger, bungle, -disregard, foozle, fumble, mishandle, misuse, muff, -neglect, wreck)

HANDLE (→): *address, administer, advise, bestow, boss, broker, captain, chair, choreograph, command, conduct, control, debate, direct, discuss, dispense, dole, dominate, employ, engineer, finesse, govern, guard, guide, hack, head, jockey, keep, lead, manage, manipulate, micromanage, mind, monitor, negotiate, orchestrate, order, oversee, pace, pilot, play, protect, pull, regulate, renegotiate, rule, run, safeguard, serve, shepherd, show, skipper, spearhead, stage-manage, steward, superintend, supervise, swing, tackle, take, tend, transact, treat, watch, wrestle* (≠ bobble, botch, bungle, -disregard, foozle, forget, fumble, goof, half-ass, mess, mismanage, misuse, muddle, muff, -neglect, scamp, subvert)

HANDLE (→): *abide, absorb, accept, allow, bear, brave, brook, countenance, endure, face, field, hack, meet, permit, pocket, respect, stand, stomach, suffer, support, sustain, swallow, sweat, take, tolerate, weather* (≠ -avoid, -bypass, -circumvent, combat, contest, -decline, dismiss, -dodge, -elude, -escape, -evade, fight, miss, oppose, -refuse, -reject, -repudiate, resist, skip, skirt, -spurn)

HANDLE (→): *auction, bandy, barter, bootleg, carry, commercialize, commodify, deal, dispense, dispose, distribute, dole, exchange, export, flog, import, keep, market, merchandize, monetize, offer, peddle, provide, retail, sell, smuggle, stock, supply, swap, trade, traffic, vend, wholesale* (≠ borrow, buy, hoard, hold, import, keep, lease, lend, loan, possess, preserve, -prohibit, purchase, -refuse, rent, retain)

HANDLE (→): *accept, bounce, caress, catch, clasp, cradle, dandle, dribble, embrace, enfold, feel, finger, fondle, grasp, grip, hold, hug, knead, manhandle, massage, pat, paw, pet, pick, riffle, stroke, strum, touch* (≠ -avoid, -circumvent, -disregard, drop, -ignore, mishandle, miss, -ostracize, -refuse, release, -shun)

HANG (→): *bait, balance, bend, brandish, dangle, drape, drop, extend, flap, flaunt, flourish, flutter, lean, lure, poise, project, showcase, sling, suspend, sway, swing, tantalize, tempt, trail, unspool, wave* (≠ block, bury, cloak, conceal, draw, drop, hide, hold, holster, pull, retract, screen, sheathe, shield, stash, tuck, veil, wedge, withdraw)

HANG (+): *affix, append, attach, cement, drape, fasten, festoon, fix, garland, glue, hook, mount, paste, pin, stick, string, tack* (≠ cut, detach, down, drop, lift, lose, prop, pull, release, remove, tear, yank)

HANG (/): *asphyxiate, choke, execute, gibbet, kill, lynch, pillory, punish, smother, stifle, strangle, throttle* (≠ bear, create, drop, exonerate, free, release, resuscitate, revive)

HARANGUE (→): *accost, address, annoy, buttonhole, declaim, earbash, exhort, expound, filibuster, harass, harry, hassle, lambaste, lecture, mouth, nag, needle, niggle, nitpick, preach, press, push, recite, spiel, spout* (≠ assuage, calm, censor, choke, commend, console, -deny, gag, gratify, hush, -ignore, please, praise, quiet, repress, satisfy, silence, smother, stifle, suppress, withhold) **(¿) ABSTRACTION ALERT. Concrete goals essential!**

HARASS (/): *afflict, aggravate, agitate, annoy, antagonize, attack, badger, bait, bedevil, beleaguer, besiege, blackmail, bombard, bother, break, browbeat, bug, bully, burn, bust, chaff, chide, criticize, debilitate, distract, distress, disturb, drain, earbash, eat, enervate, enfeeble, exasperate, exhaust, fatigue, frazzle, fret, frustrate, gnaw, goad, harry, hassle, heckle, hector, henpeck, hound, intimidate, irk, irritate, kill, nag, needle, nettle, niggle, nitpick, noodge, oppress, pain, perplex, persecute, pester, plague, provoke, pursue, raid, rankle, ride, rile, sap, scold, strain, stress, taunt, tease, tire, torment, trash-talk, troll, trouble, try, tucker, upset, vex, waste, weaken, wear, weary, worry* (≠ activate, alleviate, appease, assuage, calm, champion, ease, endorse, energize, favor, help, honor, humor, invigorate, laud, lull, mellow, mitigate, moderate, mollify, pacify, placate, praise, rejuvenate, relax, rest, settle, soothe, strengthen, support, unwind, vitalize)

HARBOR (+): *accommodate, barrack, bestow, billet, board, bunk, chamber, conceal, cover, defend, domicile, ensconce, guard, hide, hold, home, house, lodge, maintain, niche, place, protect, quarter, roof, room, safeguard, screen, secure, shade, shadow, shed, shelter, shield, stable, take, tent, ward, welcome* (≠ banish, compromise, -disown, eject, endanger, evict, exile, expose, imperil, inhabit, jeopardize, occupy, -refuse, -reject, -renounce, -repudiate, -shun, target, tenant, threaten)

HARDEN (→): *acclimate, acclimatize, accustom, adapt, adjust, anneal, blunt, bolster, boost, brace, brutalize, buttress, callous, case-harden, coarsen, condition, deaden, dehumanize, desensitize, develop, discipline, dull, embitter, enforce, familiarize, forearm, fortify, habituate, harshen, immunize, indurate, inure, invigorate, naturalize, numb, paralyze, prop, reinforce, roughen, school, season, steel, stiffen, strengthen, stun, stupefy, substantiate, support, teach, temper, toughen, train, victimize, vitalize* (≠ ameliorate, blunt, buffer, change, cripple, cushion, dampen, debilitate, discourage, dissuade, ease, emasculate, enervate, enfeeble, exhaust, flex, hamstring, harm, hurt, impair, incapacitate, indulge, injure, moderate, overextend, paralyze, sap, sensitize, soften, spoil, stretch, tenderize, undercut, undermine, unman, unsettle, upset, weaken)

HARDEN (+): *amalgamate, anneal, bake, brace, buttress, cake, calcify, callous, cement, close, clot, coagulate, compact, compress, concentrate, congeal, consolidate, contract, crystallize, curdle, dry, encrust, firm, fix, fortify, fossilize, freeze, gird, indurate, nerve, ossify, petrify, precipitate, press, reinforce, rigidify, set, settle, solidify, starch, steady, steel, stiffen, strengthen, temper, thicken, toughen* (≠ bend, dilute, disperse, dissolve, liquefy, loosen, marinate, melt, presoak, rarefy, relax, separate, slacken, smelt, soak, soften, steep, tenderize, thaw, thin, water, weaken, wet)

HARD-SELL (→): *auction, ballyhoo, cold-call, commercialize, commodify, hawk, hype, leverage, market, monetize, peddle, pimp, pitch, plug, presell, pressure, promote, prostitute, push, sell, shill, tout, whore* (≠ borrow, buy, cajole, furnish, give, hoard, import, keep, lease, loan, offer, -refuse, -reject, rent, schmooze, stash, supply)

HARM (/): *abuse, afflict, aggrieve, assault, batter, blemish, bloody, break, bruise, canker, castrate, contort, contuse, crease, cripple, crucify, cut, damage, deform, disfigure, distress, fracture, gash, gore, graze, hamstring, harshen, hurt, impair, infect, injure, insult, lacerate, lame, maim, maltreat, mangle, mar, molest, mutilate, nick, offend, pain, poison, prejudice, ravage, razor, rend, savage, scald, scalp, scar, scathe, scrape, shank, shiv, slice, spoil, stab, sting, strain, stymie, tear, torment, torture, traumatize, trouble, undermine, upset, weaken, welt, wound, wrinkle, wrong* (≠ advantage, aid, assist, bandage, benefit, cure, doctor, fix, heal, help, mend, nurse, nurture, perfect, quarantine, rectify, rehabilitate, remedy, treat)

HARM (/): *annihilate, bash, batter, blemish, blight, bloody, boobytrap, botch, break, canker, castrate, clobber, club, compromise, corrode, crab, cripple, crush, damage, dash, decimate, deface, demolish, dent, desolate, destroy, devastate, ding, disable, disadvantage, disfigure, efface, emasculate, enervate, enfeeble, erode, flaw, fracture, fragment, half-ass, hamper, hamstring, hurt, ill-treat, impair, injure, mangle, mar, mistreat, mutilate, overdose, perforate, pulverize, queer, raze, rend, rip, ruin, sabotage, scotch, scour, scourge, scupper, shatter, shred, smash, splinter, spoil, subvert, sully, tarnish, tatter, tear, torment, torture, total, undercut, undermine, unman, vitiate, waste, weaken, wreck* (≠ ameliorate, benefit, better, bless, doctor, edit, elevate, enhance, enrich, fix, help, improve, mend, optimize, overhaul, patch, perfect, rarefy, rebuild, recondition, reconstruct, rectify, refine, rehabilitate, remedy, remodel, renovate, repair, rephrase, restore, retool, revamp, revise, revolutionize, survive, sustain, weather, withstand)

HARMONIZE (+): *accommodate, accord, adapt, adjust, align, approximate, arrange, attune, balance, blend, calibrate, center, combine, compose, contemporize, coordinate, correlate, equalize, fit, heal, integrate, match, mix, orchestrate, proportion, reconcile, reintegrate, relate, reunite, set, settle, soothe, suit, synthesize, time, tune, tweak, unify, unite, unskew* (≠ addle, alarm, alienate, battle, break, challenge, churn, confound, confuse, contradict, convulse, counteract, disaffect, disorganize, disrupt, interrupt, isolate, jar, jostle, jumble, mismatch, muddle, -omit, oppose, oust, race, rattle, rile, rock, roil, scramble, shake, skew, unsettle, upset)

HARNESS (+): *access, apply, bind, bridle, cannibalize, channel, check, choreograph, cinch, clinch, collar, constrain, control, couple, curb, direct, domesticate, employ, equip, exercise, exert, exploit, fasten, fetter, fit,* *focus, funnel, furnish, gear, govern, handle, hitch, hold, leash, limit, manipulate, mobilize, muzzle, operate, orchestrate, outfit, recycle, reuse, rig, rope, run, saddle, secure, strap, tackle, tame, tap, tie, use, utilize, weaponize, wield, work, yoke* (≠ allow, detach, discard, disconnect, emancipate, free, -ignore, liberate, loose, loosen, lose, misapply, misuse, -neglect, permit, release, slack, slacken, spur, unchain, unfasten, unharness, unlock, unshackle, untie, waste)

HARVEST (←): *accumulate, acquire, amass, assemble, bag, cache, capture, clutch, collect, compile, crop, cull, cut, discover, download, excavate, fish, forage, gain, garner, gather, glean, grasp, grow, harrow, hay, hoard, hunt, locate, mine, mow, net, obtain, pick, pile, plow, pluck, procure, pull, raise, reap, recycle, salvage, scavenge, secure, seize, snare, source, stash, stockpile, store, stow, strip, take, trap, uncover* (≠ -abandon, blow, deprive, diffuse, discard, dissipate, donate, drop, -eschew, fallow, -forsake, furnish, give, grow, junk, lavish, lose, misuse, offer, pickle, plant, -reject, scatter, scrap, seed, skimp, skip, sow, squander, starve, stint, supply, trash, waste, withhold)

HASSLE (/): *aggravate, aggrieve, agitate, annoy, antagonize, attack, badger, bait, bedevil, beleaguer, besiege, bother, browbeat, bug, bully, burn, chafe, chaff, challenge, chide, chivy, contest, criticize, critique, demean, denigrate, deride, despoil, discomfort, disparage, disturb, dog, earbash, exasperate, fluster, fret, frost, gall, get, goad, harass, harry, haze, heckle, hector, henpeck, hound, importune, intimidate, irk, irritate, jeer, mock, nag, needle, nettle, niggle, noodge, oppose, oppress, peeve, persecute, perturb, pester, pillory, pique, plague, provoke, pursue, railroad, ride, ridicule, rile, ruffle, scold, spite, taunt, tease, terrorize, test, threaten, torment, torture, trash-talk, troll, trouble, try, vex, worry* (≠ amuse, appease, assist, assuage, baby, calm, coddle, delight, endear, entertain, fascinate, gratify, help, humor, hush, indulge, lull, mellow, mitigate, moderate, mollify, pacify, placate, please, relax, satisfy, sedate, smooth, stabilize, steady, thrill, woo)

HASTEN (→): *accelerate, advance, aid, assist, boost, catalyze, dispatch, encourage, expedite, fast-forward, fast-track, -flee, fly, forward, frogmarch, fuel, further, goad, help, hurry, hustle, march, precipitate, press, prioritize, push, quicken, race, rush, speed, spur, tear, urge* (≠ -abort, block, counteract, delay, end, finish, hamper, impede, interfere, interrupt, oppose, override, postpone, -prevent, short-circuit, stall, stop, stymie, terminate, -thwart)

HATCH (+): *birth, brainstorm, breed, brood, conceive, concoct, contrive, create, cultivate, culture, design, develop, devise, engender, enlarge, evolve, expand, feed, form, formulate, foster, fuel, generate, gestate, grow, improvise, incubate, initiate, invent, lay, machinate, nourish, nurture, originate, plan, plot, produce, project, propagate, scheme, spawn, whelp* (≠ -abandon, alter, botch, bungle, crush, damage, depopulate, destroy, doom, eradicate, exterminate, half-ass, hamper, impair, impede, inhibit, injure, kill, massacre, mutate, oppose, smash, snuff, starve, stifle, suppress, -thwart)

HAUL (←): *attract, bear, bring, buck, carry, cart, chauffeur, convey, convoy, deliver, drag, draw, ferry, fetch, forward, heave, hoist, hump, jerk, lift, lug, move, pack, piggyback, pull, push, raise, remove, ride, schlep, send, shift, ship, shoulder, shuttle, smuggle, take, tote, tow, trail, transfer, transmit, transport, trawl, truck, tug, yank* (≠ chuck, -desert, discard, -disown, -ditch, drive, drop, dump, eject, -forsake, jettison, keep, leave, lose, lower, offload, -omit, plonk, propel, punt, push, ram, -rebuff, -reject, repel, scrap, shove, -spurn, thrust)

HAUNT (→): *assail, attend, claim, frequent, habituate, hound, infest, inhabit, invade, occupy, overrun, patronize, permeate, pervade, possess, stalk, stay, stop, swarm, travel, traverse, visit* (≠ -abandon, -avoid, -desert, -disown, -disregard, -ditch, -dodge, -duck, -elude, -escape, -eschew, -evade, -flee, forget, leave, lose, -neglect, shake, -shun)

HAUNT (/): *affect, agitate, agonize, alarm, anguish, annoy, appall, bedevil, besiege, burden, depress, devastate, dismay, disquiet, distress, disturb, frighten, harass, harrow, harry, horrify, hound, infest, intimidate, madden, manifest, materialize, molest, nag, nettle, obsess, oppress, outlast, overrun, panic, persecute, pester, petrify, plague, possess, rattle, return, scare, spook, tease, terrify, terrorize, threaten, torment, trouble, unnerve, upset, vex, worry, wrack* (≠ -abandon, aid, assist, bolster, bore, brace, buoy, calm, cheer, comfort, console, delight, encourage, -forsake, hearten, help, humor, inspire, lull, mellow, mitigate, moderate, mollify, pacify, placate, please, reassure, relax, settle, soothe, stabilize, steady, steel, thrill, uplift)

HAWK (→): *auction, bootleg, cold-call, commercialize, commodify, deal, distribute, hard-sell, hustle, hype, leverage, market, merchandize, monetize, peddle, pimp, plug, presell, pressure, promote, prostitute, retail, sell, trade, vend, wholesale, whore* (≠ borrow, buy, cadge, denigrate, discard, disparage, hoard, -ignore, import, keep, lease, -overlook, purchase, -refuse, -reject, rent, retain, -scorn, squirrel, stash, store)

HAZARD (→): *ante, beard, bet, brave, brazen, breast, challenge, chance, compromise, confront, dare, defy, endanger, expose, face, gamble, imperil, jeopardize, menace, offer, risk, spare, spitball, stake, subject, submit, suggest, tempt, threaten, venture, volunteer, wage, wager* (≠ assure, certify, crosscheck, defend, ensure, guarantee, guard, indemnify, insure, maintain, nurture, pledge, preserve, promise, protect, prove, rescue, save, secure, shelter, shield, sustain, warrant)

HEAD (→): *address, administer, boss, captain, chair, choreograph, command, control, direct, dominate, govern, guide, handle, lead, manage, maneuver, monitor, orchestrate, order, oversee, pioneer, quarterback, rule, run, shepherd, show, skipper, spearhead, steer, superintend, supervise* (≠ accept, challenge, defy, deride, -disregard, disrespect, follow, heed, -ignore, mind, misrule, obey, -refuse, respect, -scorn, subvert, trail)

HEAD (→): *accompany, aim, announce, attend, bear, bend, cast, concentrate, conduct, direct, escort, face, focus, guide, herald, hold, incline, lead, level, navigate, orient, pilot, pinpoint, set, show, sight, steer, train, usher* (≠ -avert, conclude, curve, deflect, detour, divert, dog, end, finish, follow, rechannel, shunt, sidetrack, stop, tail, tailgate, terminate, trail)

HEAL (+): *aid, align, allay, alleviate, ameliorate, assuage, attend, bandage, better, comfort, compose, cure, diagnose, doctor, dose, dress, drug, ease, fix, fortify, harmonize, help, hospitalize, improve, inoculate, lighten, medicate, mend, moderate, nurse, palliate, patch, physic, quarantine, reanimate, rebuild, reconcile, regenerate, rehabilitate, reinvigorate, rejuvenate, relieve, remedy, renew, renovate, repair, restimulate, restore, resuscitate, reunite, revitalize, revive, salve, set, settle, soothe, splint, temper, treat, vaccinate* (≠ abuse, afflict, aggravate, ail, castrate, cripple, damage, debilitate, disable, enervate, enfeeble, harm, hurt, impair, indispose, infect, injure, lacerate, lame, maim, mangle, misdiagnose, mutilate, overextend, sap, scar, shrivel, sicken, waste, weaken, welt, wither, wizen, worsen, wound, wrong)

HEAP (←): *accumulate, add, amass, archive, arrange, assemble, augment, bank, bestow, build, bunch, burden, clump, collect, compile, concentrate, confer, congest, deposit, dump, fill, garner, gather, group, hoard, increase, jam-pack, lavish, layer, load, lumber, lump, mass, mound, mow, pack, pile, pour, pyramid, ruck, shower, stack, stockpile, store, stuff, swell* (≠ confiscate, -deny, deprive, disperse, distribute, ditch, divest, downsize, economize, empty, fling, keep, -refuse, reserve, retain, scant, scatter, scrimp, skimp, squander, stint, strip, withhold)

HEAT (→): *animate, annoy, arouse, bake, barbecue, boil, burn, char, cook, crisp, de-ice, enrage, excite, fire, flush, griddle, grill, inflame, microwave, overheat, parch, reheat, rewarm, roast, rouse, sauté, scald, scorch, sear, singe, steam, stimulate, stir, superheat, thaw, toast, warm* (≠ chill, congeal, cool, douse, extinguish, freeze, frost, glaciate, harden, ice, refrigerate, solidify, supercool, temper)

HEAVE (→): *bowl, buck, cant, cast, catapult, chuck, dart, dash, disgorge, eject, fire, fling, flip, gun, hook, hurl, hurtle, impel, launch, lob, loft, pass, peg, pelt, pitch, precipitate, project, propel, puke, punt, ram, rifle, roll, shoot, skitter, sling, spew, spit, throw, thrust, toss, upchuck, vomit* (≠ capture, clutch, contract, engulf, extract, field, grab, grasp, grip, hold, hook, inhale, keep, net, receive, seize, snag, snare, snatch, stop, swallow, take, trap, withhold, yank)

HEAVE (←): *boost, crane, elevate, force, heft, heighten, hike, hoist, jack, levitate, lift, pull, pulley, raise, rear, up, upend, uphold, uplift, upraise, winch* (≠ bear, compress, decrease, depress, descend, dip, drop, hide, lower, pitch, plonk, plunge, press, push, shrink, sink, slip, submerge, topple)

HECKLE (/): *abuse, aggravate, aggrieve, agitate, annoy, antagonize, badger, bait, barrack, bedevil, beleaguer, belittle, blame, blast, blister, boo, bother, browbeat, bug, bully, catcall, chafe, chaff, chivy, demean, deride, discomfit, discomfort, disconcert, disrupt, diss, disturb, dog, embarrass, exasperate, faze, fret, frost, gall, get, gnaw, goad, harass, harry, hassle, haze, hector, hound, insult, interrupt, irk, irritate, jeer, mock, needle, nettle, niggle, nitpick, peeve, persecute, perturb, pester, pillory, pique, plague, rattle, ride, ridicule, rile, ruffle, spite, taunt, tease, terrorize, test, torment, torture, trash-talk, vex, worry* (≠ -abandon, aid, appease, applaud, assist, assuage, buoy, calm, celebrate, cheer, cherish, commend, congratulate, delight, encourage, facilitate, gratify, heed, help, high-five, humor, indulge, lull, mellow, mitigate, moderate, mollify, pacify, placate, please, praise, promote, respect, support, treasure)

HEDGE (←): *-avoid, border, -bypass, circle, circumnavigate, -circumvent, detour, -dodge, -duck, -elude, -eschew, -evade, flank, fudge, miss, -omit, orbit, shake, -shirk, shuffle, -sidestep, skirt, stall, stonewall, straddle* (≠ accost, brave, challenge, claim, confront, contradict, debunk, defy, expound, face, fight, insist, meet, oppose, promote, provoke, -renounce, support)

HEDGE (+): *abut, belt, block, border, cage, confine, coop, corral, cover, edge, encircle, enclose, fence, fortify, girdle, guard, hinder, immure, indemnify, insure, limit, obstruct, pen, protect, restrict, ring, safeguard, shield, surround, wrap* (≠ allow, bare, broaden, discharge, encourage, exceed, expand, expose, free, -ignore, imperil, liberate, loose, open, outreach, permit, release, reveal)

HEED (←): *abide, accept, answer, attend, catch, clock, consider, contemplate, discharge, embrace, execute, follow, fulfill, hear, keep, mark, mind, mull, note, notice, obey, observe, perform, ponder, regard, respect, scan, scope, scrutinize, see, serve, spot, watch, weigh* (≠ -blank, defy, -discount, dismiss, disobey, -disregard, flout, gloss, -ignore, mind, -neglect, -overlook, pass, pooh-pooh, resist, -scorn, -slight, -snub, subvert, violate) **(¿) ABSTRACTION ALERT. Concrete goals essential!**

HEIGHTEN (→): *accelerate, accent, accentuate, accrue, add, advance, affirm, aggravate, amp, amplify, assert, augment, beef, boost, broaden, build, consolidate, deepen, develop, elaborate, elevate, emphasize, enforce, enhance, enlarge, enliven, escalate, exacerbate, exaggerate, exalt, expand, extend, fatten, flavor, foster, hasten, heroicize, heroize, idealize, idolize, improve, increase, inflate, intensify, jazz, lengthen, lift, magnify, marinate, maximize, multiply, optimize, overdramatize, overhaul, oversell, poeticize, prioritize, punctuate, quicken, raise, redouble, reinforce, revolutionize, richen, romanticize, season, sentimentalize, sharpen, spice, strengthen, stress, stretch, supplement, swell, underline, upgrade, widen* (≠ abate, abridge, alleviate, compress, concentrate, condense, curtail, decrease, deepen, depress, diminish, discourage, drop, ease, lessen, lighten, lower, minimize, moderate, reduce, shorten, shrink, subdue, submerge, underemphasize, weaken, worsen)

HELM (→): *administer, captain, chair, choreograph, command, commandeer, conduct, control, direct, drive, govern, guide, head, hijack, lead, manage, navigate, orchestrate, oversee, pilot, rein, skipper, spearhead, steer, usher* (≠ -abandon, block, checkmate, crash, defy, disobey, follow, misrule, -neglect, obey, overthrow, resist, serve, shadow, tail, trail, undermine, wreck)

HELP (+): *abet, accommodate, advance, advantage, advise, advocate, affirm, aid, alleviate, assist, attend, augment, back, ballyhoo, befriend, benefit, bless, bolster, boost, buttress, champion, comfort, condone, console, content, counsel, decongest, delight, deliver, develop, drive, ease, embolden, encourage, endorse, endow, energize, facilitate, favor, feed, finance, forward, foster, fuel, fund, further, gladden, grant, gratify, greenlight, guide, heal, hearten, hype, incite, incubate, inspire, kindle, launch, legalize, lift, maintain, mentor, midwife, mother, motivate, nerve, nourish, nurse, nurture, oblige, patronize, please, plug, prioritize, profit, promote, prop, provoke, publicize, push, reinforce, reinvigorate, relieve, remedy, rescue, restore, revitalize, revive, rubber-stamp, sanction, satisfy, save, second, serve, spark, sponsor, spur, stimulate, strengthen, subsidize, support, sustain, tout, tutor, unclog, underwrite, uphold, urge* (≠ afflict, antagonize, baffle, -balk, ban, bar, block, checkmate, constrain, contradict, counter, counteract, countercheck, cramp, curb, damage, delay, demotivate, depress, -desert, -deter, disappoint, discourage, discredit, disfavor, disgrace, dissuade, distress, encumber, fail, fight, foil, -frustrate, -halt, hamper, handicap, harm, hide, hinder, hobble, hurt, impede, incommode, inconvenience, inhibit, injure, monkey-wrench, muzzle, -neglect, neutralize, obstruct, occlude, oppose, outlaw, paralyze, -prevent, -prohibit, protest, repress, restrain, restrict, retard, sabotage, sadden, scotch, scupper, scuttle, shelve, short-circuit, slow, squash, stagnate, stale, stall, stifle, stop, straightjacket, strangle, stunt, subdue, subvert, suppress, terrorize, throttle, -thwart, traumatize, undermine, upset)

HELP (+): *advance, alleviate, ameliorate, amend, attend, augment, automate, beef, better, boost, coach, correct, cultivate, cure, decontaminate, develop, doctor, ease, edit, emend, enhance, enrich, facilitate, fine-tune, fortify, foster, grow, heal, hone, improve, increase, intensify, mend, mentor, mitigate, modernize, nourish, optimize, overhaul, palliate, perfect, polish, realign, reconceive, reconceptualize, recover, rectify, redraft, refine, reform, refurbish, rehabilitate, reimagine, reinforce, reinvent, reinvigorate, relieve, remediate, remedy, repair, restore, restructure, rethink, retool, retouch, revamp, revise, revive, rework, right, shine, splint, stimulate, streamline, strengthen, teach, tend, treat, update, upgrade* (≠ afflict, attack, blemish, blight, callous, coarsen, contaminate, cripple, damage, decrease, deface, destroy, diminish, disease, disfigure, distort, doom, efface, eradicate, exacerbate, flaw, hamper, hamstring, handicap, harm, harshen, hinder, hobble, hurt, impair, impede, infect, infest, injure, lessen, lower, malign, mar, poison, pollute, reduce, ruin, spoil, stunt, sully, tarnish, vitiate, worsen, wound, wreck, wrong)

HENPECK (/): *abuse, accuse, admonish, berate, blame, blast, browbeat, castigate, caution, censure, chasten, chastise, chide, condemn, criticize, critique, denigrate, denounce, disparage, earbash, exasperate, fault, fulminate, harass, hector, lambaste, lecture, mock, nag, punish, ream, rebuke, reprimand, reproach, ridicule, scold, taunt, upbraid, villainize* (≠ appease, approve, blandish, brook, commend, compliment, countenance, delight, endorse, endure, eulogize, flannel, flatter, gratify, help, ingratiate, mollify, please, praise, recommend, sanction, soften, soothe, support, thank, thrill, tolerate, tout)

HEX (+): *becharm, bespell, bewitch, bind, brew, captivate, cast, charm, compel, conjure, constrain, curse, dazzle, dedicate, devise, devote, enchant, ensorcel, enthrall, entice, entrance, evoke, fascinate, force, glamour, hoodoo, hypnotize, invoke, jinx, juggle, lure, maledict, mesmerize, possess, prophesy, seduce, spell, spellbind, strike, taint, tantalize, tempt, trigger, voodoo, weave, whammy, witch* (≠ aid, banish, bless, cleanse, consecrate, defend, disenchant, dislodge, dispel, dissipate, exorcise, expel, free, heal, liberate, protect, purge, purify, rectify, release, sanctify, shield, unbind, ward)

HIDE (+): *archive, bank, box, bury, cache, conceal, cover, cram, deposit, -ditch, dump, embed, enclose, engulf, ensconce, enshroud, entomb, harbor, hoard, holster, immerse, implant, insert, inter, jam, niche, package, pickle, plant, reserve, secrete, secure, sheathe, shelter, sink, smuggle, squirrel, stash, stockpile, store, stow, stuff, submerge, thrust, tuck, veil, wedge, wrap* (≠ ascertain, bare, brandish, comb, detect, discover, disinter, display, dredge, exhibit, exhume, explore, expose, find, flaunt, hunt, parade, probe, prowl, pursue, ransack, reveal, rifle, scan, scour, scrutinize, search, seek, share, show, showcase, track, uncover, unearth, unmask, unveil, unwrap)

HIDE (/): *beard, becloud, bedim, befog, belie, blanket, blind, block, blot, bury, cache, camouflage, censor, cloak, clothe, cloud, conceal, costume, couch, cover, curtain, darken, deceive, disguise, double-talk, eclipse, enshroud, gild, gloss, harbor, hood, hush, mask, obscure, obstruct, occlude, occult, -omit, overshadow, pocket, redact, screen, shade, shadow, shroud, smother, sneak, spackle, spin, stifle, submerge, sugarcoat, suppress, varnish, veil, whitewash, withhold, wrap* (≠ accost, advertise, air, bare, betray, broadcast, bulletin, candy-coat, circulate, clarify, concede, confess, confide, confirm, confront, disclose, display, disseminate, divulge, expose, exteriorize, externalize, flaunt, floodlight, herald, hype, identify, illuminate, light, limelight, manifest, out, parade, presell, present, proclaim, publicize, publish, reveal, shill, show, showcase, spread, telegraph, uncloak, uncover, unmask, unveil)

HIGHLIGHT (+): *accent, accentuate, advertise, assert, belabor, bolster, boost, concentrate, deepen, display, elevate, emphasize, escalate,* *exaggerate, exhibit, favor, feature, flaunt, focus, foreground, heighten, hype, identify, illuminate, increase, intensify, magnify, mark, overemphasize, overplay, oversell, overstate, overstress, pinpoint, plug, present, press, prioritize, promote, publicize, punctuate, push, reinforce, sharpen, show, spotlight, stress, underline, underscore, weight* (≠ -avoid, belittle, bury, censor, conceal, cover, curb, decrease, deemphasize, delegate, diminish, -discount, disparage, -disregard, downplay, -eschew, hide, -ignore, lessen, marginalize, minimize, miss, -neglect, obscure, obstruct, -omit, -overlook, quiet, reduce, sideline, silence, subdue, temper, tune, underemphasize, undermine, underrate, understate)

HIJACK (←): *appropriate, bogart, capture, carjack, commandeer, confiscate, disappear, ensnare, hotwire, kidnap, pluck, poach, seize, shanghai, skyjack, snaffle, snatch, steal, terrorize, threaten, waylay* (≠ -abandon, -bypass, cede, chauffeur, defend, deliver, forfeit, guard, leave, protect, release, relinquish, render, rescue, restore, return, supply, surrender)

HINDER (←): *anticipate, baffle, -balk, bar, block, bottleneck, brake, bung, burden, catch, check, choke, clog, complicate, congest, constipate, constrain, counter, cramp, crimp, cripple, curb, dam, dampen, daunt, delay, demotivate, depress, detain, -deter, disadvantage, discourage, dishearten, disincline, dissuade, drag, encumber, entangle, entrap, fetter, foil, forestall, foul, -frustrate, hamper, hamstring, handicap, hogtie, impair, impede, inhibit, interrupt, jam, kneecap, lumber, mire, monkey-wrench, obstruct, oppose, paralyze, pause, plug, preempt, -prevent, -prohibit, resist, restrain, restrict, retard, shelve, short-circuit, snag, snarl, stagnate, stay, stem, stifle, stop, straightjacket, stunt, stymie, tangle, throttle, -thwart, trammel, wing* (≠ accelerate, accommodate, advance, aid, assist, boost, brainstorm, catalyze, clear, compel, disencumber, disentangle, ease, encourage, expedite, extricate, facilitate, fast-forward, fast-track, free, frogmarch, fuel, further, grease, hasten, heal, help, hurry, improve, inspire, legalize, liberate, loosen, lubricate, march, mend, midwife, oblige, open, prioritize, prod, promote, prompt, propel, quicken, release, relieve, remedy, rush, slacken, smooth, speed, steady, stimulate, stir, stoke, strengthen, support, transcend, unclog, uncomplicate, unleash, unlock, untangle, untie, urge)

HIRE (←): *book, charter, commission, contract, engage, lease, let, obtain, occupy, order, rent, reserve, sublease, sublet, utilize* (≠ bogart, -cancel, -decline, drop, -eschew, forget, postpone, -reject, scrap)

HIRE (←): *advance, appoint, apprentice, assume, audition, authorize, contract, delegate, draft, employ, empower, engage, enlist, exploit, headhunt, interview, partner, pay, pick, place, pledge, procure, promise, promote, recruit, retain, scout, secure, select, sign, subcontract, upgrade* (≠ axe, ban, blackball, blacklist, boot, can, discharge, dismiss, fire, furlough, jettison, pink-slip, -refuse, -reject, sack, stiff, terminate, -veto)

HIT (→): *backhand, bang, bash, bat, batter, bean, beat, belt, biff, blast, blitz, bludgeon, bob, bonk, bop, box, brain, buffet, bump, bung, bunt,* *bust, butt, cane, chop, clap, clip, clobber, clock, clout, club, concuss, conk, crack, cream, cudgel, cuff, dab, deck, ding, drub, fell, flail, flick, flog, floor, hammer, hook, jab, jostle, kick, knee, knock, lace, lambaste, lash, level, lick, mangle, maul, nail, paste, pelt, pepper, poke, pommel, pop, pound, prod, pummel, punch, push, rabbit-punch, rap, rough, sap, scuff, shove, skull, slam, slap, slash, sledge, sledgehammer, slug, smack, smite, sock, spear, stab, stamp, stone, strike, stroke, sucker-punch, swat, swipe, switch, tap, thrash, thump, thwack, trash, uppercut, wallop, whack, whale, whip, zap* (≠ armor, block, build, defend, deflect, -disregard, dissuade, -dodge, -duck, forget, guard, help, leave, lose, miss, -neglect, offer, protect, repel, secure, shelter, shield, skirt, tap, unite)

HIT (→): *bang, buffet, bump, butt, clip, crash, damage, harm, jostle, knock, meet, rap, scrape, sideswipe, smash, tap, thump* (≠ -avoid, -bypass, -circumvent, -dodge, -duck, -elude, -evade, miss, -sidestep, skip, skirt)

HIT (→): *accomplish, achieve, actualize, affect, attain, claim, complete, consummate, crest, execute, finalize, finish, gain, hack, influence, manage, overwhelm, reach, score, secure, strike, touch* (≠ -abandon, botch, bugger, bungle, forfeit, -forsake, fumble, half-ass, leave, lose, miss, -neglect, -nullify, relinquish, -renounce, sacrifice, skimp, start, stop, undershoot)

HITCH (+): *affix, anchor, articulate, attach, bind, cement, chain, cinch, clamp, coalesce, combine, compound, concatenate, conjugate, connect, cord, couple, dovetail, fasten, fix, fuse, harness, hogtie, hook, hybridize, integrate, interconnect, interlink, interlock, join, lash, link, lodge, moor, secure, strap, string, tether, tie, unite, weld, wire, yoke* (≠ break, cleave, cut, detach, disconnect, disengage, divide, extract, free, loose, part, pry, pull, release, rupture, separate, sever, split, sunder, unchain, uncouple, unfasten, unhitch, unlink, unlock, unyoke, wrest, yank)

HOARD (←): *accumulate, acquire, amass, archive, assemble, bank, budget, bury, buy, cache, coffer, collect, compile, conceal, concentrate, conserve, deposit, embalm, ensconce, garner, gather, glean, heap, hide, hold, husband, import, keep, pickle, pile, preserve, procure, recycle, reserve, retain, salt, salvage, save, scavenge, scrimp, secrete, squirrel, stack, stash, stock, stockpile, store, stow, treasure, tuck, warehouse, withhold* (≠ bequeath, blow, cannibalize, consume, deplete, diffuse, discard, dispel, disperse, dissipate, -ditch, dump, exhaust, fritter, impoverish, jettison, lavish, lose, misspend, offload, relinquish, scatter, share, spend, squander, surrender, unload, use, waste)

HOAX (←): *bamboozle, bluff, buffalo, bullshit, cheat, con, convince, deceive, defraud, delude, diddle, double-cross, double-talk, dupe, embellish, embroider, entrap, fake, falsify, fiddle, fleece, flimflam, fool, forge, frame, goldbrick, gull, hocus-pocus, hoodwink, hornswoggle, josh, kid, manipulate, mislead, outwit, persuade, play, pretend, rook, scam, snooker, snow, stiff, sting, sucker, sway, swindle, trap, trick, victimize* (≠ accuse, admit, aid, assist, assume, assure, believe, confess, confirm, confront, contribute, debunk, divulge, esteem, expose, fail, fund, give, help, honor, lose, offer, punish, refund, -refuse, repay, replace, reveal, support, trust, uncover)

HOBBLE (←): *abuse, arrest, baffle, -balk, barricade, bind, block, blockade, bog, boobytrap, brake, castrate, chain, check, checkmate, choke, clog, confine, constrain, cramp, crimp, cripple, curb, damage, debilitate, delay, derail, destroy, disable, disqualify, disrupt, doom, emasculate, embarrass, encumber, fasten, fetter, foil, -frustrate, halter, hamper, hamstring, handcuff, handicap, hem, hinder, hogtie, hold, immobilize, impair, impede, incapacitate, inhibit, injure, kneecap, lame, leash, maim, manacle, mire, monkey-wrench, mutilate, muzzle, obstruct, occlude, paralyze, rein, repress, restrain, restrict, retain, retard, roadblock, ruin, sabotage, scotch, scupper, scuttle, shackle, shelve, short-circuit, shrivel, smother, spoil, stifle, straightjacket, strangle, stump, stymie, subvert, suffocate, suppress, tether, -thwart, tie, trammel, undercut, undermine, unman, weaken, wither, wizen, worsen, wound* (≠ accelerate, advance, aid, assist, boost, catalyze, clear, compel, disencumber, ease, encourage, expedite, facilitate, fast-track, free, fuel, further, grease, hasten, heal, help, improve, liberate, loosen, lubricate, mend, midwife, oblige, open, prioritize, promote, quicken, release, remedy, rush, smooth, speed, steady, stimulate, strengthen, transcend, unclog, unleash, unstop, untangle, untie, urge)

HOCK (→): *bond, borrow, deposit, flog, guarantee, hazard, monetize, mortgage, offload, pawn, peddle, pledge, sell, stake, trade* (≠ buy, collect, lend, loan, ransom, reclaim, recoup, recover, redeem, refund, reimburse, repay, repurchase)

HOG (←): *absorb, accumulate, amass, appropriate, bogart, command, consume, control, copyright, corner, dominate, employ, engross, -exclude, hoard, hold, keep, manage, monopolize, own, patent, pile, possess, restrain, stash, stock, stockpile, store, stow, syndicate, use, utilize, withhold* (≠ allocate, allot, bestow, circulate, comp, discard, dispense, disseminate, distribute, divide, donate, dump, give, lose, offer, share, spare, split, squander, supply, tender, tithe, volunteer, waste)

HOIST (←): *ascend, boost, crane, elevate, erect, escalate, exalt, heave, heft, heighten, hike, jack, levitate, lift, mount, raise, rear, up, uphold, uplift, upraise, winch* (≠ -abandon, depress, descend, dip, drop, lower, offload, pitch, plonk, plunge, press, push, sink, submerge)

HOLD (←): *bag, bear, bind, bottle, capture, carry, catch, check, cherish, clasp, clench, clinch, clutch, collar, command, confine, conserve, control, corner, corral, cradle, cuddle, cup, detain, direct, embrace, enjoy, exert, feel, finger, fondle, freeze, grab, grapple, grasp, grip, guard, handle, hang, hook, hug, keep, land, lock, maintain, manage, nab, nail, nourish, occupy, own, palm, paw, pickle, possess, preserve, press, protect, reserve, restrain, retain, rule, save, secure, seize, shoulder, smuggle, snag, snare, snatch, squeeze, squoosh, stick, subsume, support, take, trap, treasure, unsheathe, wield, withhold, wring* (≠ -abandon, beam, bequeath, cede, comp, contribute, -decline, deliver, discard, discharge, donate, drop, dump, eject, entrust, give, hand, loose, lose, offload, plonk, -reject, release, relinquish, render, -repudiate, -spurn, surrender, tender, tithe, transfer, transmit, unclasp, unhand, yield)

HOLD (←): *arrest, block, bottle, bridle, cage, check, checkmate, choke, collar, constrain, contain, control, curb, gag, govern, hamper, handcuff, hinder, housebreak, housetrain, impede, inhibit, interrupt, keep, leash, measure, mince, muffle, muzzle, obstruct, pace, pocket, regulate, rein, repress, restrain, rule, silence, sink, smother, snaffle, squelch, stifle, stop, straightjacket, strangle, suppress, swallow, tame, throttle* (≠ air, announce, articulate, embody, exhibit, express, liberate, loose, loosen, lose, manifest, slacken, testify, unleash, vent, verbalize, vocalize, voice)

HOLD (←): *accommodate, bear, boast, carry, case, contain, encase, enclose, encompass, enfold, engulf, envelop, fit, harbor, holster, house, imprison, lodge, seat, sheathe, shelter, sport, take, warehouse, wrap* (≠ ban, banish, bar, chuck, disgorge, dislodge, eject, eradicate, estrange, evict, exorcise, expel, extricate, -forbid, jettison, relegate, remove, require, spew)

HOLD (←): *absorb, arrest, captivate, catch, charm, clutch, cradle, cup, dazzle, delight, draw, enamor, enchant, endear, engage, engross, enthrall, entrance, fascinate, fill, hypnotize, intoxicate, maintain, mesmerize, monopolize, mystify, obsess, occupy, preoccupy, rivet, spellbind, thrill, transfix, wow* (≠ affront, annoy, bore, bug, disgust, enrage, harass, heckle, irritate, needle, nettle, nitpick, offend, release, repel, revolt, vex, worry) **(¿) ABSTRACTION ALERT. Concrete goals essential!**

HOLD (+): *aid, assist, augment, bear, bolster, brace, budget, buoy, buttress, carry, conserve, cushion, defend, fortify, foster, guard, help, lock, maintain, nourish, nurture, prop, protect, reinforce, safeguard, secure, shore, shoulder, stabilize, stay, steady, strengthen, supplement, support, sustain, take, truss, undergird, underpin, uphold* (≠ attack, boobytrap, compromise, convulse, corrode, crumble, damage, destabilize, disrupt, dissolve, endanger, erode, half-ass, hamstring, harm, impede, injure, monkey-wrench, rock, sabotage, scotch, scupper, shake, shiver, subvert, threaten, topple, undermine, unhorse, unseat, upset, weaken)

HOLD (+): *accept, account, adjudge, assume, await, believe, call, conceive, conclude, consider, consult, count, deduce, detect, determine, esteem, fancy, feel, figure, guess, imagine, infer, judge, perceive, premise, presume, presuppose, rate, reckon, regard, sense, suppose, surmise, think, trust, view* (≠ counter, cross-examine, debunk, disbelieve, discredit, distrust, doubt, grill, interrogate, interview, mistrust, question, -reject, scruple, suspect, undermine, wonder) **(¿) ABSTRACTION ALERT. Concrete goals essential!**

HOLD (+): *amass, assemble, call, celebrate, collect, compile, conduct, continue, convene, convoke, corral, gather, glean, group, herd, host, muster, officiate, organize, rally, run, schedule, solemnize, summon,* *supervise, synchronize, time* (≠ attend, -cancel, diffuse, disband, disperse, dissolve, miss, -overlook, scatter, skip, terminate)

HOLD (/): *arrest, bind, book, cage, capture, chain, check, closet, commit, confine, contain, convict, curb, detain, dungeon, enclose, enslave, fetter, -halt, hamper, handcuff, harbor, hinder, hogtie, ice, immure, impede, impound, imprison, incarcerate, institutionalize, intern, jail, keep, lock, manacle, nab, obstruct, pen, pinion, possess, remand, restrain, restrict, retain, sentence, shackle, snaffle, stockade, stop, straightjacket, tie, trap, wrap* (≠ accuse, acquit, alibi, bail, convict, exonerate, free, judge, liberate, ransom, release, sentence, spring, uncage, vindicate)

HOLLOW (/): *channel, chase, corrugate, dent, dig, disembowel, dish, -ditch, empty, eviscerate, excavate, furrow, gorge, gouge, groove, indent, notch, pit, remove, rut, scoop, shovel, trench* (≠ add, augment, bury, cram, ensconce, fill, jam, overstuff, pack, raise, replenish, stash, store, stuff, tuck, wedge)

HONEY (←): *adulate, alleviate, appease, applaud, assuage, blandish, blarney, butter, cajole, candy, candy-coat, coax, commend, compliment, congratulate, court, cushion, dulcify, ease, endear, eulogize, extol, felicitate, flannel, flatter, glad-hand, gold-star, gratify, harmonize, hero-worship, idolize, ingratiate, laud, massage, mellow, mitigate, mollify, overpraise, pacify, palaver, placate, praise, propitiate, puff, relieve, romance, schmooze, soften, soft-soap, soothe, stroke, sugar, sugarcoat, sweeten, sweet-talk, syrup, temper, wheedle, win, woo, worship* (≠ annoy, badmouth, belittle, blast, blister, boo, decry, depreciate, disparage, displease, disrupt, embitter, enrage, harden, heckle, infuriate, insult, nag, needle, nettle, niggle, nitpick, outrage, salt, sour, trouble, vex, worry)

HONOR (+): *acclaim, acknowledge, admire, adore, aggrandize, applaud, appreciate, award, celebrate, cheer, cite, commemorate, commend, compliment, congratulate, credit, decorate, dignify, discharge, distinguish, elevate, enshrine, erect, esteem, exalt, execute, extol, fête, fulfill, glorify, gold-star, gratify, hail, hallow, high-five, keep, laud, lionize, magnify, memorialize, mourn, observe, ordain, perform, praise, prize, recognize, remember, respect, revere, reward, ritualize, salute, sanctify, thank, toast, tout, treasure, value, venerate, worship* (≠ attaint, badmouth, belittle, betray, blackguard, blame, blast, boo, censure, cheat, condemn, damn, deceive, deface, defame, demean, demonize, denounce, discredit, disgrace, dishonor, disrespect, double-talk, humble, humiliate, incriminate, injure, insult, libel, malign, mock, neg, pillory, regret, repent, reproach, ridicule, rue, shame, slander, -slight, stiff)

HOOK (←): *bag, beguile, capture, catch, cinch, clasp, clinch, crook, curve, engage, enmesh, ensnare, entangle, entrap, fasten, fix, glom, grab, lasso, net, pin, rope, secure, snag, snare, strike, trap, trick* (≠ boot, cleave, dismiss, divide, drop, -escape, estrange, free, liberate, loose, loosen, lose, miss, -overlook, release, repel, separate, sever, split, sunder, unfasten, unhitch, unhook, unlock)

HORRIFY (/): *affright, alarm, amaze, appall, astound, awe, blackmail, brutalize, chill, consternate, daunt, demoralize, discomfort, discompose, disconcert, disgust, dismay, dispirit, disquiet, distract, distress, disturb, emasculate, floor, frighten, indispose, intimidate, jolt, nauseate, offend, outrage, panic, perturb, petrify, repel, revolt, savage, scandalize, scare, shake, shock, sicken, spook, startle, terrify, terrorize, undo, unman, unnerve, unsettle, unstring, upset, worry* (≠ amuse, assure, baby, buffer, calm, charm, cheer, coddle, comfort, console, defend, delight, embolden, encourage, entertain, flatter, gladden, heal, hearten, help, humor, indulge, inspire, lull, mellow, mitigate, moderate, mollify, nurture, pacify, placate, please, protect, reassure, soothe, steel, thrill, toughen)

HOST (+): *accommodate, admit, attend, befriend, board, cherish, compère, emcee, entertain, feast, feed, foster, gather, give, harbor, house, include, introduce, invite, join, lodge, meet, nourish, nurture, present, provide, quarter, receive, regale, room, treat, welcome* (≠ ban, banish, bar, -cold-shoulder, cordon, disinvite, -exclude, frequent, jettison, -ostracize, oust, -rebuff, -refuse, -reject, repel, -shun, -snub, -spurn, visit, withhold)

HOUND (→): *accompany, bird-dog, chaperone, chase, dog, escort, eye, eyeball, follow, hunt, observe, pursue, retrace, run, scout, search, seek, shadow, spoor, tag, tail, target, trace, track, trail, watch* (≠ -abandon, direct, dismiss, -disregard, -dodge, -evade, guide, head, hide, -ignore, lead, lose, -neglect, -overlook, pilot, spearhead, steer)

HOUND (/): *annoy, badger, bait, beg, besiege, blandish, blitz, bombard, bother, bug, bully, cajole, chivy, coax, contact, disturb, dog, drive, earbash, egg, exasperate, exhort, force, goad, harass, harry, hassle, haunt, heckle, hector, henpeck, impel, importune, incite, insist, irk, nag, needle, nitpick, noodge, outlast, persecute, pester, plague, plead, press, pressure, prod, prompt, provoke, push, ride, scratch, spur, stalk, tail, track, trail, urge, vex, wheedle* (≠ acclaim, applaud, boost, commend, compliment, defend, endorse, eulogize, extol, glorify, guard, hype, laud, plug, praise, promote, protect, publicize, recommend, secure, tout)

HOUSE (+): *accommodate, barrack, bestow, billet, board, bunk, chamber, domicile, ensconce, harbor, home, host, lodge, niche, quarter, reunite, roof, room, secure, shed, shelter, stable, tent, warehouse, welcome* (≠ alienate, attack, ban, banish, bar, deport, -desert, dismiss, displace, eject, evict, exile, incommode, inconvenience, inhabit, isolate, oppose, orphan, -ostracize, oust, relegate, repel, tenant, torment, turf, withhold)

HOUSE (+): *archive, armor, bound, box, cage, carry, circumscribe, closet, cocoon, confine, contain, coop, corral, cover, encapsulate, encase, encircle, enclose, encompass, enfold, enlace, envelop, fence, frame, guard, hem, hold, holster, immure, include, incorporate, keep, limit, mew, package, pen, place, preserve, protect, receive, restrict, ring, secure, sheathe, shelter, shield, store, stow, surround, wall, wrap* (≠ block, disgorge, displace, disseminate, eject, -exclude, exorcise, expel, extract, extricate, launch, loosen, -omit, -ostracize, oust, remove, spew, uninstall, vent)

HUMBLE (/): *abase, abash, affront, badmouth, bastardize, belittle, bench, besmear, besmirch, bestialize, blast, blister, boo, castigate, censure, chagrin, chasten, cheapen, condemn, confound, confuse, criticize, critique, crush, damn, debase, decry, defame, defile, deflate, degrade, demean, demote, denounce, -deny, depreciate, detract, devalue, diminish, discomfit, disconcert, -discount, discredit, disgrace, dishonor, disparage, downgrade, efface, embarrass, execrate, faze, fluster, foul, fulminate, hide, humiliate, insult, libel, lower, malign, minimize, mortify, neg, nonplus, outlast, overcome, pillory, rattle, reduce, ridicule, shame, sideline, silence, sink, slander, smirch, -snub, soil, spoil, squash, squelch, stain, subdue, sully, taint, upset, violate, vulgarize* (≠ acknowledge, advance, affirm, aggrandize, apotheosize, applaud, assert, boast, boost, canonize, celebrate, cheer, cherish, cite, commend, compliment, congratulate, crown, decorate, deify, dignify, elevate, ennoble, enshrine, enthrone, eulogize, exalt, extol, fetishize, glorify, gold-star, gratify, hail, heighten, heroicize, heroize, high-five, highlight, honor, idealize, idolize, laud, lift, magnify, praise, prioritize, promote, raise, recognize, revere, romanticize, salute, spotlight, tout, upgrade, uplift, venerate, worship)

HUMILIATE (/): *abase, abash, attaint, beat, belittle, bench, besmear, besmirch, bestialize, blame, blast, blister, boo, break, chagrin, chasten, chastise, checkmate, confound, confuse, conquer, crush, -cut, debase, debauch, defame, defeat, defile, deflate, degrade, demean, demote, denigrate, depress, devalue, diminish, discomfit, disgrace, dishonor, disparage, downplay, embarrass, expose, flog, humble, insult, lower, mock, mortify, pan, pillory, reduce, ridicule, rip, -scorn, shame, -shun, sideline, slam, slander, -slight, smear, -snub, soil, spoil, squash, stain, subdue, sully, taint, tease, trounce, vilify, violate, whup, wither* (≠ acclaim, applaud, blandish, boost, canonize, celebrate, cherish, commend, compliment, congratulate, decorate, deify, dignify, elevate, ennoble, enshrine, enthrone, eulogize, exalt, extol, fête, flatter, glorify, gold-star, gratify, high-five, highlight, honor, idealize, ingratiate, praise, prioritize, promote, raise, recognize, respect, revere, romanticize, salute, sentimentalize, spotlight, tout, upgrade, worship)

HUMOR (+): *abide, accommodate, appease, blandish, brook, coax, coddle, condone, cosset, countenance, delight, endure, face, favor, flannel, flatter, gratify, indulge, infantilize, jolly, mollify, mollycoddle, overindulge, pamper, permit, please, pleasure, prioritize, sate, satiate, satisfy, spoil, stomach, suffer, swallow, tolerate* (≠ attack, bridle, challenge, check, confront, constrain, contradict, counter, curb, defy, -deny, discipline, discomfit, disfavor, disrespect, fight, inhibit, oppose, oppress, -prohibit, punish, resist, restrain, -scorn, shame, stifle, straightjacket, torment)

HUMP (→): *ball, bang, bed, boff, boink, bone, bonk, debauch, deflower, devour, diddle, drill, enter, fuck, impale, jump, nail, penetrate, pillage, pleasure, plow, plunder, poke, pork, pound, probe, prong, rail, ram, ravish, ream, ride, screw, seduce, shag, shtup, skewer, tap, tumble* (≠ -avoid, -deny, -neglect, -refuse, -reject, -spurn)

HUMP (←): *bear, carry, cart, chauffeur, convey, convoy, deliver, dispatch, drag, draw, express, haul, heave, hoist, jerk, lift, lug, move, pull, remove, schlep, send, shift, ship, shoulder, shuttle, smuggle, tote, tow, trail, transfer, transmit, transport, tug, yank* (≠ -abandon, -desert, discard, drop, leave, lose, offload, plonk, push, -rebuff, -refuse, -reject, repel, repulse, scrap, shove, stash, thrust)

HUNT (→): *backtrack, bag, bird-dog, capture, chase, cull, decoy, dog, drag, drive, ferret, fish, follow, forage, harpoon, harry, hound, kill, net, persecute, poach, pursue, root, scent, scrounge, search, seek, shadow, shoot, sift, snare, spoor, stalk, tail, target, track, trail, trap, winnow* (≠ acquire, capture, catch, corner, -evade, find, free, hide, -ignore, lead, liberate, lose, miss, -neglect, obtain, procure, secure, -sidestep, skip, source)

HUNT (→): *case, check, disclose, discover, examine, explore, fathom, grill, interrogate, investigate, plumb, probe, prospect, prowl, question, ransack, reconnoiter, retrace, reveal, root, rummage, scour, scout, search, sound, trace, track, trail, unearth* (≠ -boycott, -bypass, conceal, detect, discern, discover, -disregard, -eschew, expose, forget, hide, -ignore, learn, lose, -neglect, -omit, -overlook, -prohibit, protest, realize, reveal, spot)

HURL (→): *bowl, buck, bung, cant, cast, catapult, chuck, dart, dash, eject, fire, fling, flip, gun, heave, hook, hurtle, impel, launch, lob, loft, pass, peg, pelt, pitch, precipitate, project, propel, rifle, roll, send, shoot, skitter, sling, throw, thrust, toss, wing* (≠ accept, acquire, bring, carry, catch, clasp, clutch, convey, drag, give, grab, grasp, grip, hand, hold, keep, obtain, procure, pull, receive, retain, schlep, secure, snag, tow, tug, yank)

HURRY (→): *accelerate, advance, agitate, aid, assist, bundle, catalyze, dispatch, dizzy, drive, ease, encourage, expedite, facilitate, fast-track, fluster, frogmarch, goad, grease, hasten, hustle, incite, lubricate, march, midwife, nudge, oil, prod, prompt, propel, punt, push, quicken, race, rush, speed, spur, stimulate, stir, urge, whisk* (≠ -abort, arrest, brake, check, decelerate, delay, encumber, fetter, freeze, hamper, hinder, hobble, hold, impede, leash, manacle, obstruct, pause, plant, restrain, retard, root, shackle, shelve, short-circuit, slow, stall, stay, still, stop, straightjacket, stymie, -thwart, trammel)

HURT (/): *annihilate, bash, batter, blemish, blight, bloody, botch, break, callous, canker, castrate, clobber, club, coarsen, compromise, contaminate, corrode, corrupt, crab, crack, cripple, cross, crucify, crush, damage, dash, debilitate, decimate, deface, defile, demolish, dent, desecrate, desolate, destroy, deteriorate, devastate, ding, dirty, disable, discolor, disfigure, disintegrate, dismantle, doom, efface, emasculate, enervate, enfeeble, erode, fade, flaw, fracture, gnaw, half-ass, hamper, hamstring, harm, harshen, hinder, impair, incapacitate, injure, kneecap, lacerate, lame, maim, mangle, mar, mutilate, pollute, pulverize, queer, ravage, raze, rot, ruin, rust, sabotage, scotch, scour, scourge, scupper, shatter, smash, spoil, stain, taint, tarnish, tear, torment, torture, total, undercut, undermine, unman, vandalize, vitiate, waste, weaken, wear, welt, whip,* *wound, wreck* (≠ advantage, ameliorate, benefit, better, boost, cure, decontaminate, doctor, edit, enhance, enrich, fix, guard, heal, help, improve, mend, patch, perfect, polish, protect, rebuild, recondition, reconstruct, rectify, refine, rehabilitate, remedy, remodel, renovate, repair, restore, revamp, revise, save, secure, sophisticate, splint, survive, sustain, withstand)

HURT (/): *abuse, afflict, aggrieve, assault, attack, batter, beat, blemish, blight, bloody, break, bruise, brutalize, burn, burst, castrate, club, contuse, crease, cripple, cut, damage, disfigure, fracture, gash, gore, graze, hamstring, harm, hit, impair, infect, injure, lacerate, lame, maim, maltreat, mangle, mar, mutilate, nick, punish, razor, rend, rupture, savage, scald, scalp, scar, scathe, scorch, scrape, scratch, shank, shiv, sicken, slash, slice, smash, split, spoil, stab, sting, strain, tear, torment, torture, traumatize, wound* (≠ aid, alleviate, armor, assist, bandage, bind, cure, defend, doctor, dose, dress, drug, ease, fix, heal, hospitalize, maintain, medicate, mend, nurse, preserve, -prevent, protect, quarantine, remedy, renew, repair, restore, resuscitate, revive, sew, shelter, shield, splint, stitch, support, treat)

HURT (/): *afflict, aggrieve, agonize, anguish, bleed, crucify, defame, discipline, grieve, harass, harm, indispose, injure, insult, malnourish, menace, mistreat, -neglect, oppress, outrage, persecute, plague, rack, sadden, sicken, sorrow, threaten, torment, torture, traumatize, upset, vex, victimize, violate, wound, wrong* (≠ accommodate, amuse, appease, assure, baby, cheer, cherish, comfort, console, cuddle, defend, delight, ease, endure, entertain, favor, featherbed, foster, gratify, guard, humor, indulge, mollify, nourish, nurture, oblige, pacify, placate, please, reassure, satiate, satisfy, shield, solace, soothe, spoon-feed, support, thrill, tolerate, weather)

HUSH (/): *anesthetize, appease, calm, compose, devoice, help, humor, lull, mellow, mitigate, moderate, mollify, muffle, mute, muzzle, pacify, placate, quell, quiet, sedate, settle, shush, silence, soothe, squelch, squench, stifle, still, subdue, suppress, tranquilize* (≠ aggravate, agitate, alarm, communicate, deafen, disrupt, disturb, exacerbate, express, intensify, kindle, mobilize, rally, rattle, rile, roil, rouse, say, shake, stir, verbalize, worsen)

HUSTLE (→): *accelerate, bulldoze, bump, bundle, bustle, crowd, dash, drive, elbow, fast-forward, fast-track, fly, force, grease, hasten, hurry, impel, jog, jostle, manhandle, move, nudge, outpace, outrun, outstrip, overtake, press, prod, push, quicken, race, rush, shove, speed, spur, stir, thrust* (≠ decelerate, defer, delay, drag, hamper, hinder, impede, pacify, pause, postpone, shelve, short-circuit, -sidestep, slow, stall, stymie, -thwart)

HUSTLE (←): *bamboozle, beat, betray, bilk, blackmail, bleed, bluff, butter, charm, cheat, chisel, clip, cold-call, commodify, con, convince, cozen, dazzle, deceive, defraud, double-cross, double-talk, dupe, elbow, encourage, euchre, exploit, extort, fast-talk, fiddle, finagle, finesse, fleece,* *flimflam, fool, force, gazump, glad-hand, gouge, grease, gull, gyp, hoodwink, hornswoggle, leverage, lobby, manipulate, milk, monetize, nick, nudge, oil, overcharge, pressure, ream, rook, schmooze, screw, sell, short, shortchange, skin, soak, squeeze, stick, stiff, sting, sucker, swindle, trick, underpay, victimize, wrench, wrest, wring, wrong* (≠ accept, assume, assure, believe, confess, defend, doubt, expose, face, guard, help, honor, indemnify, preserve, protect, refund, regret, reimburse, repay, rescue, respect, safeguard, save, shield, support, suspect, trust, verify)

HYBRIDIZE (+): *adulterate, allow, alloy, amalgamate, bastardize, blend, braid, commingle, compound, conjoin, cross, crossbreed, cross-fertilize, cross-pollinate, fuse, graft, incorporate, infiltrate, infuse, inseminate, instill, interbreed, intermingle, knit, lump, merge, mingle, mix, stir, suffuse, synthesize, tangle, transfuse, unite, weave* (≠ amputate, cleanse, detach, disconnect, disengage, divide, excise, -exclude, expunge, insulate, isolate, part, purge, purify, quarantine, remove, segregate, separate, sequester, sever, simplify, split, uncomplicate, unmix)

HYPE (→): *acclaim, advertise, aggrandize, aid, announce, back, bait, ballyhoo, boost, broadcast, bulletin, champion, circulate, commend, commercialize, commodify, disseminate, elevate, encourage, endorse, favor, feature, further, handle, hawk, highlight, hustle, inspire, laud, leverage, limelight, lobby, lure, mainstream, market, mention, merchandize, monetize, motivate, notify, offer, overestimate, overstate, peddle, pimp, pitch, plug, popularize, praise, presell, prioritize, promo, promote, promulgate, propagandize, publicize, publish, puff, push, recommend, sanction, sell, shill, spark, spotlight, spur, stimulate, support, telegraph, tout* (≠ attack, ban, battle, -boycott, bury, buy, camouflage, conceal, condemn, criticize, critique, demean, demonize, denigrate, denounce, deride, discourage, discredit, disguise, dismiss, disparage, distrust, -eschew, foil, hide, insult, knock, mock, monkey-wrench, muffle, muzzle, neg, pan, picket, pillory, -prohibit, protest, prove, purchase, recall, recant, -reject, ridicule, -scorn, -shun, slam, -snub, -spurn, suppress, undersell, understate)

HYPE (+): *accelerate, accent, accentuate, accumulate, add, affirm, aggrandize, amass, amp, amplify, assert, augment, boost, build, bump, collect, complement, compound, deepen, develop, dilate, distend, emphasize, enhance, enlarge, escalate, expand, extend, foster, heighten, increase, inflate, intensify, lengthen, magnify, maximize, multiply, prioritize, prolong, pump, raise, ratchet, reinforce, spike, strengthen, stretch, supersize, supplement, swell, up* (≠ abate, abbreviate, abridge, compress, condense, constrict, contract, crush, curtail, cut, decrease, de-escalate, deflate, diminish, downplay, downsize, kill, lessen, lower, mellow, minimize, mitigate, moderate, modulate, reduce, retrench, shorten, subdue, subtract, underemphasize)

HYPNOTIZE (←): *absorb, amaze, anesthetize, appease, arrest, assuage, bedazzle, beguile, bewitch, calm, captivate, charm, command, compel, control, dazzle, deaden, distract, dizzy, drug, ease, enchant, engage,* *engross, enrapture, enslave, ensnare, entertain, enthrall, entrance, fascinate, fixate, galvanize, grab, gratify, grip, hold, hush, immerse, immobilize, involve, lull, magnetize, mellow, mesmerize, mitigate, mollify, monopolize, motivate, narcotize, numb, pacify, paralyze, quell, quiet, razzle-dazzle, relax, relieve, rivet, settle, silence, soothe, spellbind, still, stun, stupefy, subdue, subjugate, suggest, thrill, torpefy, tranquilize, transfix, vamp, win, wow* (≠ aggravate, agitate, alarm, annoy, bore, bother, bug, convulse, crucify, disenchant, disgust, disillusion, displease, disturb, drain, dull, enliven, enrage, excite, exhilarate, harass, hector, horrify, incite, infuriate, inspire, irk, irritate, jar, jolt, knacker, menace, numb, offend, poke, prod, rankle, rattle, repel, repulse, rile, roil, rouse, shake, shock, sicken, spur, startle, stimulate, stir, terrify, terrorize, threaten, tire, torment, trouble, unnerve, upset, victimize, violate, wake, weary, worry, wound, wrong)

I

IDEALIZE (+): *admire, adore, adulate, aggrandize, amplify, apotheosize, canonize, celebrate, cherish, commemorate, defend, deify, dignify, dramatize, elevate, embellish, ennoble, enshrine, enthrone, eulogize, euphemize, exaggerate, exalt, extol, fantasize, fetishize, flatter, glamorize, glorify, hail, heighten, heroicize, heroize, hype, idolize, immortalize, inflate, intensify, lionize, magnify, overdramatize, overemphasize, oversell, overstate, panegyrize, poeticize, praise, respect, reverence, romanticize, sensationalize, sentimentalize, shield, treasure, varnish, venerate, worship* (≠ bare, belittle, chide, condemn, criticize, decry, deemphasize, defile, deglamorize, demean, denigrate, deprecate, deride, diminish, disparage, downplay, humble, humiliate, insult, judge, knock, libel, marginalize, minimize, mock, pan, regret, ridicule, rue, scold, -scorn, -shun, slam, slander, slate, -spurn, trash, trivialize, vilify)

IDENTIFY (←): *ascertain, betray, catalog, check, classify, clock, deduce, define, detect, determine, diagnose, discern, disclose, discover, distinguish, establish, examine, find, finger, hierarchize, inspect, investigate, know, label, locate, monogram, name, notice, observe, package, perceive, pick, pinpoint, place, profile, recognize, reveal, scrutinize, specify, spot, suss, tag* (≠ anonymize, baffle, bleep, blind, bury, camouflage, cloak, clothe, cloud, conceal, contrast, costume, counterfeit, deceive, disguise, feign, hide, -ignore, juxtapose, mask, misdiagnose, mislabel, miss, obscure, -overlook, screen, simulate, spackle, trick, varnish, whitewash) **(¿) ABSTRACTION ALERT. Concrete goals essential!**

IDOLIZE (+): *admire, adore, adorn, apotheosize, appreciate, approve, beatify, canonize, cherish, deify, endorse, enshrine, esteem, exalt, fancy, favor, fetishize, glorify, hallow, hero-worship, laud, limelight, lionize, praise, prefer, prize, regard, respect, revere, sanctify, support, treasure, value, venerate, worship* (≠ abhor, abominate, belittle, defile, demean, demonize, denounce, deprecate, -despise, -detest, discredit, -disdain, disfavor, disgrace, disparage, fulminate, -hate, -ignore, -loathe, malign, pillory, ridicule, slam, vilify)

IGNITE (+): *animate, arouse, awaken, bake, bank, barbecue, blast, brighten, broil, burn, burst, char, cook, cremate, electrify, embolden, encourage, enkindle, enliven, excite, exhilarate, explode, fire, frizzle, fuel, galvanize, generate, illuminate, immolate, incinerate, inflame, inspire, invigorate, irradiate, jolt, kindle, launch, light, motivate, provoke, quicken, reignite, rekindle, relight, rouse, scald, scathe, scorch, sear, shock, spark, stimulate, stoke, strengthen, thrill, torch, trigger, vitalize, waken, zap* (≠ blacken, bury, chill, choke, dampen, darken, deactivate, deaden, dim, douse, drown, dull, extinguish, freeze, inactivate, obscure, paralyze, quench, smother, snuff, soak, suffocate, trample, wet)

-IGNORE (/): *belittle, blackball, -blank, -boycott, -bypass, condone, -cut, defy, deprecate, -despise, detour, disbelieve, -discount, -disdain, dismiss, disobey, -disown, disparage, -disregard, disrespect, -ditch, drop, -dump, -exclude, fail, flout, forget, lose, miss, mistake, -neglect, -omit, -ostracize, -overlook, pass, pooh-pooh, -refuse, -reject, -repudiate, scant, -scorn, skimp, skip, -slight, slough, slur, -snub, -spurn, starve* (≠ accept, acknowledge, appreciate, attend, await, believe, bemoan, buttonhole, cherish, clock, consider, cultivate, follow, foster, greet, heed, indulge, infantilize, lament, mark, mind, mourn, note, notice, nurse, nurture, observe, overindulge, pamper, prize, recognize, regard, regret, remark, remember, scan, scrutinize, tend, treasure, value, watch, waylay, weigh)

-IGNORE (/): *absolve, acquit, clear, condone, -discount, -disregard, exculpate, excuse, exonerate, explain, forgive, gloss, justify, -overlook, pardon, rationalize, remit, spare, spin, underemphasize, vindicate, waive, whitewash, wipe* (≠ accent, accentuate, amplify, assert, belabor, blame, emphasize, heed, highlight, incriminate, mark, mind, note, punctuate, regret, -scorn, spotlight, stress, underline)

ILLUMINATE (→): *accent, accentuate, advertise, assert, belabor, bolster, boost, concentrate, deepen, emphasize, exaggerate, feature, focus, foreground, heighten, highlight, hype, identify, magnify, overemphasize, overplay, oversell, pinpoint, plug, press, prioritize, promote, publicize, punctuate, push, reinforce, sharpen, spotlight, stress, underline, underscore* (≠ belittle, bury, conceal, cover, decrease, deemphasize, diminish, -discount, disparage, -disregard, downplay, hide, -ignore, lessen, marginalize, minimize, miss, obscure, obstruct, -omit, -overlook, quiet, reduce, silence, subdue, tune, underemphasize, understate)

ILLUMINATE (+): *bathe, beacon, beam, bedazzle, blind, brighten, burn, daze, dazzle, flame, flash, floodlight, halo, highlight, ignite, illumine, incinerate, irradiate, kindle, light, lighten, limelight, radiate, spotlight* (≠ blacken, block, bury, cloud, cover, curtain, darken, dim, douse, dull, ensconce, entomb, extinguish, obfuscate, obscure, quench, shade, shadow, shroud, snuff, veil)

ILLUMINATE (+): *analyze, annotate, clarify, clear, construe, contextualize, decipher, decode, define, demonstrate, demystify, depict, disentangle, edify, elucidate, enlighten, explain, explicate, expose, expound, gloss, illustrate, inform, instruct, interpret, pictorialize, resolve, reveal, school, show, simplify, solve, specify, teach, train, translate, uncloud, uncomplicate, unravel, unriddle, unscramble, untangle* (≠ befog, blur, cloud, complicate, conceal, confound, confuse, cypher, distract, encode, encrypt, garble, hide, jumble, misconstrue, mishear, misinterpret, misread, mistake, misunderstand, mix, muddle, mystify, obfuscate, obscure, perplex, puzzle, scramble, suppress)

ILLUMINATE (+): *better, boost, buoy, canonize, dignify, distinguish, edify, educate, elevate, enlighten, ennoble, enrich, enshrine, ensoul, exalt, glorify, illume, illumine, improve, inspire, lift, magnify, nurture, promote, purify, raise, regenerate, renew, sanctify, transfigure, transform, uplift* (≠ abase, becloud, cloud, condemn, confuse, contaminate, corrupt, damn, darken, degrade, demean, discourage, humiliate, lessen, lower, mar, mystify, obscure, perplex, pervert, pollute, puzzle, reduce, weaken)

ILLUSTRATE (→): *adduce, analyze, annotate, ape, attest, authenticate, cast, certify, chart, cite, clarify, clear, confirm, connote, construe, convince, copy, corroborate, decipher, declare, decode, define, demonstrate, demystify, depict, depose, describe, detail, determine, disentangle, display, document, doodle, draw, duplicate, edify, elaborate, elucidate, embellish, embroider, enlighten, enumerate, establish, etch, evince, exemplify, exhibit, explain, explicate, expose, expound, externalize, flaunt, flourish, gloss, graph, illuminate, image, imitate, instance, interpret, list, manifest, map, mention, model, name, observe, outline, paint, parade, photograph, pictorialize, picture, portray, present, profile, prove, quote, render, replicate, represent, resolve, show, showcase, silhouette, simplify, simulate, sketch, solve, specify, spell, state, substantiate, support, testify, trace, uncover, unmask, unravel, unriddle, unscramble, untangle, unveil, validate, visualize, witness* (≠ baffle, becloud, befog, belie, blur, cloak, clothe, cloud, complicate, conceal, confound, confuse, confute, contort, costume, darken, debunk, disguise, disprove, distort, erase, expunge, expurgate, falsify, fog, garble, hide, mask, misinterpret, misread, misrepresent, misstate, muddle, muddy, obfuscate, obliterate, obscure, perplex, puzzle, rebut, refute, scramble, screen, veil)

IMAGINE (+): *anticipate, assume, await, believe, conceive, conclude, conjecture, deduce, dread, dream, expect, fancy, fear, feel, gather, guess, hypothesize, infer, judge, presume, reckon, suppose, surmise, suspect, theorize, think, wonder* (≠ adjudge, ascertain, conclude, corroborate, deduce, demonstrate, detect, determine, discern, discover, document, establish, know, learn, prove, substantiate, validate, verify) **(¿) ABSTRACTION ALERT. Concrete goals essential!**

IMBUE (+): *animate, bathe, blend, brine, charge, deluge, diffuse, drown, enliven, ensoul, fill, flavor, flood, implant, impregnate, inculcate, infuse, ingrain, inject, inoculate, inspire, instill, interpenetrate, inundate, invest, invigorate, leaven, marinate, overwhelm, permeate, pervade, plant, presoak, saturate, steep, submerge, suffuse, tinge, tint* (≠ bleed, clear, deplete, deprive, distill, divest, drain, draw, eliminate, empty, expel, extract, filter, flush, jettison, leach, leech, offload, pour, purge, purify, remove, screen, separate, siphon, spew, strain, strip, take, tap, unload, unpack, withdraw, withhold)

IMITATE (←): *adopt, ape, approximate, burlesque, caricature, clone, copy, copycat, counterfeit, ditto, duplicate, echo, emulate, fake, falsify, feign, forge, ghostwrite, impersonate, lampoon, match, mime, mimic, mirror, mock, pantomime, parallel, parody, parrot, perform, play, playact,* *pretend, reconstruct, recreate, reflect, regurgitate, render, repeat, replicate, reproduce, roleplay, simulate, spoof, travesty* (≠ battle, coin, combat, conceal, concoct, construct, contradict, contrive, counter, create, design, develop, devise, -disdain, disguise, -disregard, -eschew, fabricate, flip, initiate, introduce, invent, mismatch, -negate, oppose, originate, patent, reverse, -shun, -spurn)

IMMOBILIZE (/): *anchor, arrest, attenuate, cripple, crush, damage, deactivate, debilitate, disable, disqualify, enervate, fix, freeze, -halt, hamstring, hobble, impair, inactivate, incapacitate, kneecap, lame, maim, mangle, mutilate, numb, palsy, paralyze, petrify, pin, pinion, prostrate, rivet, root, sabotage, sap, scotch, shelve, splint, stop, stun, torpefy, transfix, undercut, undermine, weaken, wither, wound* (≠ accelerate, animate, boost, catalyze, empower, energize, fortify, galvanize, grease, hasten, heal, invigorate, mobilize, quicken, rally, recline, refresh, regenerate, reinvigorate, rejuvenate, restore, revitalize, revive, sedate, shift, speed, stimulate, strengthen, tranquilize, vitalize, weaponize)

IMMORTALIZE (+): *apotheosize, beatify, bronze, canonize, celebrate, cherish, commemorate, consecrate, conserve, defend, deify, ennoble, enshrine, eternalize, eulogize, exalt, fetishize, glorify, guard, honor, idealize, idolize, laud, maintain, memorialize, perpetuate, preserve, protect, revere, romanticize, safeguard, support, sustain, treasure, venerate, worship* (≠ abuse, annihilate, betray, crush, decimate, decry, defile, demean, demolish, demonize, denounce, desecrate, destroy, devastate, disparage, eradicate, erase, expunge, extinguish, extirpate, forget, -ignore, malign, -neglect, obliterate, regret, repent, rue, -scorn, shame, snuff, -spurn, vilify, wrong)

IMPAIR (/): *abuse, aggrieve, bash, batter, blemish, blight, bloody, blunt, botch, break, castrate, cloud, club, compromise, contaminate, corrupt, crab, cripple, crush, damage, dash, debase, debilitate, decrease, deface, defile, deform, dement, demoralize, dent, deplete, deprive, derange, deteriorate, diminish, ding, disable, disfigure, emasculate, enervate, enfeeble, erode, flaw, half-ass, hamper, hamstring, handicap, harm, harshen, hinder, hurt, injure, kneecap, lacerate, lame, lessen, maim, mangle, mar, maul, modify, mutilate, overextend, palsy, reduce, retard, ruin, sap, scotch, short-circuit, shrivel, sorrow, spoil, taint, tarnish, undermine, unman, vitiate, warp, weaken, wing, wither, worsen, wound* (≠ aid, align, allay, alleviate, ameliorate, assist, assuage, better, conserve, correct, cure, debug, decontaminate, develop, doctor, embattle, enhance, enrich, fix, fortify, foster, heal, help, improve, increase, invigorate, maintain, mend, mitigate, mollify, optimize, overhaul, patch, perfect, preserve, purify, raise, realign, rebuild, recondition, reconstruct, rectify, refine, reform, rehabilitate, relieve, remedy, renovate, repair, revamp, revolutionize, strengthen, sugarcoat, tone, toughen, upgrade)

IMPALE (→): *bayonet, bore, broach, burst, core, crack, cut, disembowel, drill, drive, enter, fill, gaff, gash, gimlet, gore, gouge, groove, gut, harpoon, hollow, honeycomb, insert, invade, jab, kebab, knife, lance, peck,* *penetrate, perforate, pick, pierce, pike, pin, pink, poke, poniard, prick, probe, prong, punch, puncture, ream, rend, riddle, rupture, screw, shank, shiv, skewer, spear, spike, spindle, spit, split, stab, stake, stick, tap, tear, thrust, transfix* (≠ armor, bandage, block, buffer, close, cover, defend, deflect, draw, eject, extract, fill, guard, heal, mend, parry, patch, plaster, plug, protect, pull, remove, repair, seal, secure, shield, withdraw)

IMPEDE (←): *-abort, arrest, baffle, -balk, ban, bar, barricade, bind, block, blockade, boobytrap, brake, burden, chain, check, checkmate, choke, clog, confine, constipate, constrain, constrict, cramp, curb, delay, demotivate, derail, -deter, discourage, disrupt, embarrass, encumber, faze, fetter, foil, freeze, -frustrate, -halt, halter, hamper, hamstring, handcuff, handicap, hem, hinder, hobble, hogtie, hold, impair, inconvenience, inhibit, intercept, -interdict, interrupt, leash, lumber, manacle, mire, monkey-wrench, muzzle, obstruct, occlude, oppress, overload, paralyze, pause, postpone, -prevent, protest, rein, repress, restrain, restrict, retain, retard, roadblock, sabotage, saddle, scotch, shackle, shelve, short-circuit, slow, smother, stall, stem, stifle, stop, strangle, stultify, stump, stymie, subvert, suffocate, suppress, tether, -thwart, tie, trammel, undercut, undermine* (≠ accelerate, accommodate, advance, aerate, aid, assist, boost, brainstorm, catalyze, clear, compel, disencumber, disentangle, ease, encourage, expedite, extricate, facilitate, fast-forward, fast-track, free, frogmarch, fuel, further, grease, hasten, heal, help, hurry, improve, inspire, legalize, liberate, loosen, lubricate, march, mend, midwife, oblige, open, oxygenate, prioritize, prod, promote, prompt, propel, quicken, release, relieve, remedy, rush, slacken, smooth, speed, spur, steady, stimulate, stir, stoke, strengthen, support, transcend, unclog, uncomplicate, unleash, unlock, untangle, untie, urge, ventilate)

IMPERIL (/): *boobytrap, bully, chance, compromise, corrupt, cripple, damage, endanger, enfeeble, expose, gamble, hamstring, hazard, implicate, intimidate, jeopardize, menace, out, risk, sabotage, scupper, subject, subvert, taint, target, threaten, undercut, undermine, venture, wager, weaken* (≠ aid, analyze, armor, assist, bolster, brace, comfort, defend, embalm, guard, harbor, help, maintain, nurture, patrol, preserve, protect, rescue, resume, retain, save, secure, shelter, shield, store, support, sustain, weigh)

IMPERSONATE (←): *act, adopt, ape, caricature, copy, costume, depict, disguise, ditto, dramatize, duplicate, emulate, enact, fake, ghostwrite, hoke, imitate, interpret, mask, mime, mimic, mirror, mock, pantomime, parody, perform, play, playact, portray, pretend, render, replicate, represent, roleplay, travesty* (≠ buck, challenge, confess, confront, contradict, counter, direct, -disregard, divulge, expose, gainsay, -halt, -ignore, oppose, originate, -prevent, reverse, stop)

IMPLANT (→): *bed, bury, connect, embed, ensconce, entrench, establish, fix, graft, imbue, impact, inculcate, infiltrate, infuse, ingrain, initiate, inject, insert, inset, insinuate, install, instate, instill, interpose, introduce, invest, juxtapose, locate, lodge, modify, penetrate, pierce, place, plant,* *position, root, settle, sow, steep, stick, suffuse, transplant* (≠ blackball, budge, detach, disconnect, disengage, dislocate, dislodge, displace, disturb, eject, eliminate, eradicate, expel, leach, relegate, relocate, remove, reposition, transfer, transpose, uninstall, uproot, weed, withdraw, wrest, wring)

IMPLICATE (→): *accuse, affect, allege, arraign, associate, attaint, blackmail, blame, book, castigate, censure, charge, chide, cite, compromise, concern, condemn, connect, criticize, damn, denounce, embarrass, embroil, endanger, enmesh, entangle, fault, finger, frame, impeach, impugn, include, incriminate, inculpate, indict, inform, insinuate, involve, link, mire, name, prosecute, rebuke, report, reproach, reprove, scapegoat, stigmatize, sue, suggest, summon, tangle, target, tax, threaten* (≠ absolve, acquit, advocate, alibi, champion, clear, defend, disconnect, disentangle, distinguish, exculpate, excuse, exonerate, extricate, forgive, justify, pardon, protect, remit, remove, separate, shrive, spare, support, untangle, vindicate)

IMPLORE (←): *accost, address, ask, beg, beseech, besiege, buttonhole, cadge, claim, coerce, command, compel, conjure, covet, crave, demand, desire, entreat, exhort, force, importune, insist, invoke, mooch, panhandle, petition, plead, pray, press, request, require, resent, scrounge, seek, solicit, sponge, supplicate, target, urge* (≠ answer, appease, comfort, command, conciliate, console, content, -deny, extort, fulfill, grace, gratify, hint, imply, intimate, mollify, oblige, pacify, placate, please, -refuse, satisfy, -scorn, -spurn, suggest)

IMPLY (→): *allege, allude, clue, confide, convey, couch, denote, entail, hint, impart, indicate, infer, insinuate, intimate, involve, mention, propose, require, rumor, scandalize, signal, signify, suggest, whisper, withhold* (≠ announce, assert, broadcast, clarify, confirm, declare, define, delineate, describe, elucidate, explain, express, proclaim, profile, reveal, spill, state, telegraph, voice) **(¿) ABSTRACTION ALERT. Concrete goals essential!**

IMPOSE (→): *apply, assess, blackmail, bleed, burden, charge, coerce, compel, decree, dock, encumber, enforce, establish, exact, excise, extort, fine, fix, fleece, foist, force, gouge, inflict, institute, introduce, lay, levy, milk, penalize, saddle, set, skin, squeeze, tax, thrust, wreak, wrest, wring* (≠ abate, carry, condone, diminish, discourage, -disregard, excuse, forgive, gloss, haul, -ignore, lessen, overlook, pardon, release, relieve, remit, spare, tackle, undertake, volunteer)

IMPOUND (←): *abduct, acquire, amass, annex, appropriate, arrogate, attach, bag, capture, catch, collect, commandeer, confiscate, deprive, dragoon, gather, get, grab, harvest, levy, monopolize, nab, pound, procure, reap, remove, repossess, requisition, rob, salvage, seize, select, sequester, take, usurp* (≠ afford, assign, bestow, contribute, dispense, donate, extend, give, grant, lavish, lend, offer, present, provide, replace, restore, return, secure, share, spare, supply, tender, volunteer, yield)

IMPOUND (/): *bridle, cage, capture, catch, collar, condemn, confine, contain, convict, coop, corral, cover, detain, embrace, encircle, enclose, encompass, entrap, envelop, fence, fetter, gain, grab, handcuff, harness, hold, immure, imprison, incarcerate, institutionalize, intern, jail, keep, land, manacle, pen, pluck, secure, seize, sentence, shackle, snag, snatch, straightjacket, surround, take, tether, trap, wrest* (≠ -abandon, bail, bestow, deliver, discharge, drop, emancipate, free, furnish, give, liberate, loose, manumit, mislay, misplace, miss, offer, pardon, ransom, redeem, release, rescue, supply, tender, unhand, volunteer)

IMPOVERISH (/): *bankrupt, beggar, blight, break, bust, cannibalize, consume, cripple, debilitate, deplete, depredate, deprive, diminish, drain, enervate, exhaust, famish, fleece, harm, injure, leech, malnourish, overextend, pauperize, reduce, ruin, sap, starve, straiten, tap, tax, underfeed, weaken* (≠ advantage, award, benefit, bequeath, bestow, capitalize, compensate, enrich, finance, force-feed, fuel, fund, furnish, grant, offer, overfeed, pay, profit, reward, subsidize, supplement, supply, sustain, volunteer)

IMPREGNATE (→): *bathe, brine, charge, color, conceive, dampen, dip, douse, drench, drown, fertilize, fill, flood, humidify, hydrate, imbue, immerse, implant, infiltrate, infuse, inoculate, inseminate, interpenetrate, inundate, macerate, marinate, moisten, penetrate, perfume, permeate, pervade, presoak, saturate, scent, soak, sop, souse, spread, steep, submerge, suffuse, swamp, swill, transfuse, wash, water* (≠ -abort, blight, clear, close, dehumidify, dehydrate, deplete, deprive, desiccate, divest, drain, dry, eliminate, empty, extract, leach, parch, remove, sear, strip, void, withdraw, wring)

IMPRESS (→): *affect, afflict, agitate, allure, amaze, arouse, astonish, astound, attract, awe, bewilder, bewitch, bias, bother, buffalo, bulldoze, captivate, carry, charm, color, concern, daze, dazzle, discomfort, discompose, disquiet, distress, disturb, drive, dumbfound, electrify, enchant, enforce, engage, enrapture, enthrall, enthuse, entrance, excite, fascinate, faze, fluster, galvanize, gobsmack, grab, harass, harry, hocus-pocus, impact, influence, inspire, interest, involve, kill, move, overawe, overwhelm, penetrate, perturb, pester, pierce, pique, plague, possess, predetermine, prejudge, prejudice, prepossess, provoke, ravish, razzle-dazzle, reach, rouse, score, slay, smite, stimulate, stir, strain, stress, strike, stun, stupefy, surprise, sway, thrill, touch, transport, trouble, try, upset, worry, wow, wring* (≠ affront, annoy, appall, baffle, -balk, bobble, bomb, bore, bungle, confound, depress, disappoint, disenchant, disgust, dismay, displease, earbash, embarrass, flunk, fumble, heckle, irk, jade, lower, muff, nag, nauseate, needle, nettle, niggle, nitpick, offend, repel, revolt, shame, tire, underwhelm, weary) **(¿) ABSTRACTION ALERT. Concrete goals essential!**

IMPRESS (→): *brand, carve, copy, deboss, dent, draw, drill, emboss, engrave, etch, fix, imbue, implant, imprint, inculcate, indent, infuse, ingrain, inscribe, instill, mark, nock, outline, pound, print, reproduce, set,* *stamp, strike, tool* (≠ anonymize, blot, -cancel, delete, erase, expunge, fill, flatten, iron, obliterate, plaster, polish, pumice, remove, sand, scour, shine, smooth, spackle)

IMPRISON (/): *apprehend, arrest, bar, bind, book, bust, cage, can, capture, catch, chain, closet, commit, confine, constrain, contain, convict, detain, dungeon, enchain, enclose, enslave, fetter, -halt, hamper, handcuff, harbor, hinder, hogtie, hold, ice, immure, impound, impress, incarcerate, institutionalize, intern, jail, keep, limit, lock, manacle, nab, pen, pinch, pinion, remand, restrain, restrict, secure, seize, sentence, shackle, shanghai, shut, snaffle, stockade, straightjacket, tie, trammel, trap* (≠ accuse, acquit, allow, bail, clear, deliver, discharge, emancipate, enfranchise, excuse, exonerate, free, liberate, manumit, pardon, parole, release, unbind, uncage, unchain, unfetter)

IMPROVE (+): *adapt, adjust, advance, aid, alter, ameliorate, amend, assist, augment, automate, barber, beautify, better, boost, brighten, burnish, calibrate, calm, change, chasten, civilize, clean, clear, coach, computerize, convert, correct, cultivate, cure, develop, dulcify, ease, edify, edit, educate, elevate, enhance, enlighten, enrich, exercise, fine-tune, flavor, fortify, glamorize, glitter, glitz, groom, grow, guide, gussy, help, hone, humanize, increase, manicure, mellow, mend, modernize, modify, moralize, normalize, nurture, optimize, overhaul, pace, perfect, polish, prioritize, promote, punctuate, purify, raise, rally, realign, rebuild, reclaim, reconceive, reconceptualize, recover, rectify, redefine, redress, reeducate, refine, reform, refurbish, regenerate, regulate, rehabilitate, reimagine, reinforce, reinvent, remedy, remodel, repair, rephrase, restore, restructure, resuscitate, rethink, retool, retouch, retrofit, revamp, revise, revitalize, revolutionize, richen, right, school, season, shape, sharpen, shift, shine, smarten, sophisticate, spice, streamline, strengthen, sweeten, teach, titivate, train, transform, tune, tutor, tweak, update, upgrade, weaponize* (≠ aggravate, barbarize, bastardize, bestialize, blemish, blight, callous, castrate, coarsen, compromise, damage, debase, debilitate, deface, deteriorate, diminish, disfigure, dismantle, drain, efface, emasculate, encumber, enervate, flaw, harm, harshen, hurt, immobilize, impair, injure, lessen, lower, maim, mar, pervert, pollute, reduce, ruin, scotch, spoil, tarnish, unman, vitiate, weaken, worsen)

IMPROVISE (+): *ad-lib, arrange, brainstorm, brew, coin, concoct, contrive, cook, extemporize, fabricate, fake, fiddle, fix, hatch, improv, invent, jerry-build, jerry-rig, manage, maneuver, manipulate, manufacture, pretend, rig, scheme, vamp, wangle, wing* (≠ arrange, calculate, chart, design, devise, engineer, graph, orchestrate, organize, plan, plot, practice, premeditate, prepare, ready, regiment, rehearse, script, strategize, structure)

IMPUGN (/): *abuse, admonish, assail, attack, berate, betray, blame, blast, break, censure, challenge, chastise, chide, contradict, contravene, counter, criticize, critique, cross, cross-examine, debate, debunk, defame, denigrate, denounce, -deny, discredit, -disown, disprove, dispute, distrust,* *doubt, fault, finger, frame, gainsay, grill, impeach, insult, interrogate, invalidate, knock, neg, -negate, oppose, question, rebuke, reprimand, resent, resist, revile, ridicule, rip, scapegoat, scold, shame, shred, -shun, slam, slander, smear, -spurn, suspect, tar, traduce, trash, upbraid, vilify, vituperate, wrong, zap, zing* (≠ aid, allow, approve, assist, blandish, boost, compliment, concede, confirm, corroborate, defend, elevate, flannel, flatter, help, honor, ingratiate, join, praise, prioritize, promote, protect, prove, support, uphold, validate, vindicate)

INACTIVATE (/): *arrest, cripple, damage, deactivate, deaden, defuse, disable, disqualify, freeze, -halt, hamstring, hobble, immobilize, impair, impede, incapacitate, inhibit, mothball, paralyze, prostrate, restrain, sabotage, scotch, scupper, scuttle, shelve, stabilize, stagnate, stale, stop, stymie, subdue, subvert, -thwart, undermine, weaken* (≠ activate, agitate, animate, correct, cure, fix, ignite, initiate, mend, mobilize, remedy, repair, right, rile, roil, spark, spur, start, stimulate, stir, trigger, wake, weaponize)

INAUGURATE (+): *arrange, author, begin, brainstorm, commence, commission, conceive, concoct, constitute, construct, contrive, create, dedicate, develop, devise, endow, enlarge, establish, expand, fabricate, father, finance, found, fund, induct, initiate, innovate, install, instate, instigate, institute, introduce, invent, invest, launch, manufacture, open, ordain, organize, originate, pioneer, plant, produce, refound, reinitiate, reinstitute, relaunch, start, subsidize, systematize, systemize* (≠ abolish, -abort, adjourn, annihilate, annul, axe, can, -cancel, cease, close, conclude, discharge, end, expel, finish, fire, -halt, impeach, -nullify, oust, recess, remove, retract, shut, stop, terminate, uninstall)

INCAPACITATE (/): *anesthetize, attenuate, bang, bash, batter, beat, belt, bludgeon, boobytrap, box, break, bruise, buffet, castrate, chloroform, club, concuss, conk, cripple, crucify, damage, debilitate, demilitarize, deprive, devitalize, disable, disarm, disfigure, dismember, disqualify, drain, drub, emasculate, enervate, enfeeble, exhaust, fatigue, flog, gore, hammer, hamstring, harm, hinder, hit, hobble, hogtie, hurt, immobilize, impair, injure, kill, knacker, kneecap, lace, lacerate, lambaste, lame, lash, leech, lick, maim, mangle, maul, murder, mutilate, overextend, palsy, paralyze, paste, pelt, pommel, pound, prostrate, pummel, punch, restrict, sabotage, sap, scar, scotch, scupper, scuttle, sedate, shelve, shrivel, slap, smack, smash, sock, spank, swat, swipe, thrash, thump, thwack, tire, torment, torpefy, torture, trank, tranquilize, undercut, undermine, unman, unnerve, vanquish, wallop, weaken, whack, whip, wing, wither, wizen, wound* (≠ advantage, benefit, cure, doctor, embattle, empower, encourage, energize, enhance, facilitate, fix, fortify, freshen, galvanize, heal, invigorate, mend, militarize, optimize, overhaul, patch, permit, refresh, regenerate, rehabilitate, reinvigorate, rejuvenate, remedy, renew, repair, restore, revitalize, revive, revolutionize, stimulate, strengthen, supercharge, support, teach, train, vitalize, weaponize)

INCARCERATE (/): *apprehend, arrest, bar, bind, book, bust, cage, can, capture, catch, closet, commit, confine, constrain, detain, dungeon,* *enchain, fetter, gate, handcuff, hogtie, hold, ice, immure, impound, impress, imprison, institutionalize, jail, jug, keep, limit, lock, manacle, nab, pen, pinch, remand, restrain, restrict, seize, sentence, shackle, shanghai, shut, snaffle, stockade, straightjacket, trammel, trap* (≠ accuse, acquit, alibi, bail, clear, deliver, discharge, emancipate, enfranchise, excuse, exonerate, free, liberate, manumit, pardon, parole, redeem, release, spare, unbind, uncage, unchain, unfetter, vindicate)

INCENSE (→): *affront, aggravate, agitate, anger, annoy, antagonize, bug, burn, cross, embitter, enrage, envenom, exasperate, gravel, hassle, heckle, incite, inflame, infuriate, irk, irritate, madden, miff, nag, needle, nettle, niggle, nitpick, offend, outrage, peeve, pique, provoke, rankle, rile, roil, ruffle, troll, vex* (≠ allay, appease, assuage, beguile, bewitch, calm, captivate, charm, comfort, conciliate, console, delight, disarm, enchant, entertain, gratify, help, humor, hush, lull, mellow, mitigate, moderate, mollify, pacify, placate, please, quiet, relax, relieve, sedate, settle, soothe, thrill, woo, wow)

INCINERATE (/): *annihilate, barbecue, blacken, blaze, brand, broil, burn, cauterize, char, consume, cook, cremate, damage, destroy, flame, ignite, immolate, kindle, light, melt, obliterate, parch, rekindle, roast, scald, scorch, sear, singe, torch* (≠ chill, cool, douse, drench, drown, extinguish, freeze, smother, stifle, suffocate, survive, weather, wet)

INCITE (→): *abet, activate, advance, agitate, animate, arouse, awaken, beget, boost, brew, call, convince, cultivate, detonate, drive, egg, embolden, encourage, energize, enliven, enrage, excite, exhort, facilitate, fan, fast-forward, fast-track, ferment, fire, foment, forward, foster, fuel, further, galvanize, generate, goad, hurry, ignite, impassion, impel, induce, inflame, influence, infuriate, inspire, instigate, invigorate, jazz, juice, kindle, liven, lubricate, midwife, motivate, move, nourish, nurture, persuade, pick, pique, prick, prod, promote, prompt, propel, provoke, psych, quicken, rabble-rouse, raise, rally, rev, rouse, set, sow, spark, spur, stimulate, stir, supercharge, taunt, trigger, urge, vitalize* (≠ allay, appease, bridle, calm, check, confound, constrain, counteract, cripple, curb, deactivate, demotivate, -deter, discourage, dissuade, freeze, help, hold, humor, inactivate, inhibit, lull, mellow, mitigate, moderate, mollify, obstruct, occlude, override, pace, pacify, paralyze, placate, quiet, regulate, rein, restrain, settle, soothe, stall, stem, still, straightjacket, stymie, subdue, suppress, tame, tranquilize)

INCLUDE (←): *accommodate, add, admit, allow, append, bear, build, carry, combine, constitute, contain, count, cover, embody, embrace, encircle, enclose, encompass, enjoin, entail, enter, greet, hold, implicate, incorporate, inject, insert, integrate, interject, interpolate, introduce, invite, involve, number, orbit, permit, receive, reckon, span, subsume, take, welcome* (≠ -abandon, ban, bar, cordon, -cut, -deny, discard, divide, drop, eject, eliminate, erase, -exclude, forget, jettison, leave, misplace, -neglect, offload, -omit, oppose, -ostracize, oust, -prevent, -prohibit, -refuse, -reject, release, remove, separate, -shun, subtract, withdraw)

INCONVENIENCE (←): *aggravate, agitate, anger, annoy, bother, bug, burden, chafe, discombobulate, discommode, discompose, disfavor, disoblige, disrupt, disturb, encumber, exacerbate, exasperate, fetter, fuss, gall, get, grate, -halt, hamper, hamstring, handicap, harass, hassle, hinder, hobble, impede, incommode, inhibit, irk, lumber, manacle, mismatch, nag, needle, nettle, niggle, nitpick, obstruct, overload, peeve, perturb, pique, provoke, retard, rile, saddle, shackle, trammel, trouble, try, upset, vex, weigh, worry* (≠ abet, accommodate, advantage, aid, alleviate, appease, assist, benefit, comfort, conciliate, console, content, delight, disarm, ease, enhance, facilitate, favor, gladden, gratify, grease, help, lubricate, mollify, oblige, oil, pacify, placate, please, profit, satisfy, smooth, support)

INCORPORATE (←): *absorb, acculturate, accustom, assimilate, blend, combine, commingle, condition, coopt, digest, embody, embrace, encompass, enculturate, fuse, habituate, ingest, integrate, intermingle, internalize, merge, metabolize, mingle, naturalize, reunite, subsume* (≠ alienate, chuck, disaffect, discard, disgorge, -ditch, divide, eject, estrange, -exclude, exorcise, expel, isolate, jettison, -omit, oppose, -ostracize, oust, resist, seclude, spew, vomit)

INCORPORATE (+): *add, amalgamate, associate, blend, coalesce, collage, combine, commingle, composite, compound, concrete, conflate, conjoin, consolidate, contain, cover, emulsify, fold, form, fuse, homogenize, hybridize, include, integrate, intermingle, intermix, intertwine, interweave, join, knit, link, meld, merge, mingle, mix, organize, pool, reintegrate, stir, synthesize, toss, unify, unite, weave* (≠ cleave, detach, diffuse, disengage, disjoin, disperse, dissolve, disunite, divide, divorce, isolate, part, rupture, scatter, seclude, separate, sever, split, sunder, unmix)

INCREASE (+): *accent, accentuate, accrue, accumulate, add, advance, aggrandize, aggravate, amplify, annex, assert, augment, boost, broaden, build, deepen, develop, dilate, distend, double, emphasize, enhance, enlarge, escalate, exaggerate, expand, extend, flavor, foster, further, gain, gather, grow, heighten, improve, inflate, intensify, lengthen, magnify, marinate, maximize, multiply, optimize, overhaul, pad, prioritize, progress, prolong, protract, punctuate, raise, recoup, redouble, reinforce, revolutionize, richen, rouse, season, sharpen, spice, spread, strengthen, supplement, swarm, swell, thicken, treble, triple, unspool, wax, widen* (≠ abate, abbreviate, abridge, compact, compress, concentrate, contract, curb, curtail, debit, decrease, deduct, deflate, deplete, diminish, drain, erode, leach, leech, lessen, lose, lower, minimize, moderate, reduce, shorten, shrink, subtract, truncate, underemphasize)

INCRIMINATE (/): *accuse, allege, arraign, attack, attaint, attribute, blame, book, brand, castigate, censure, charge, chide, cite, condemn, criticize, damn, denounce, fault, finger, frame, impeach, implicate, impugn, inculpate, indict, inform, insinuate, involve, name, prosecute, rebuke, report, reproach, reprove, sue, summon, try* (≠ absolve, acquit, alibi, champion, clear, confess, defend, exculpate, excuse, exonerate, forgive, free, ingratiate, justify, pardon, release, shrive, spare, vindicate)

INCUBATE (+): *birth, brainstorm, breed, brew, brood, conceive, concoct, contrive, create, cultivate, design, develop, devise, engender, enlarge, evolve, expand, feed, form, formulate, foster, fuel, generate, gestate, grow, hatch, improvise, initiate, invent, lay, machinate, nourish, nurture, originate, plan, plot, produce, project, propagate, scheme, spawn* (≠ -abandon, annihilate, battle, combat, counter, damage, exterminate, fight, foil, hamper, hinder, impede, injure, kill, murder, mutate, obliterate, oppose, -prevent, -prohibit, snuff, squelch, starve, stifle, suppress, terminate)

INCUBATE (+): *abet, advance, advertise, advocate, agitate, aid, assist, back, boost, champion, cultivate, encourage, endorse, endow, finance, forward, foster, fund, further, nourish, nurse, nurture, patronize, plug, promote, publicize, stake, subsidize, support, tout, underwrite, uphold* (≠ arrest, ban, bar, check, discourage, encumber, enjoin, fetter, -forbid, -frustrate, -halt, hobble, impede, inhibit, obstruct, outlaw, -prevent, -prohibit, proscribe, repress, retard, shackle, snuff, squash, squelch, stifle, subdue, suppress)

INCUR (←): *achieve, arouse, awaken, bait, brave, brook, contract, earn, elicit, endure, engender, entice, evoke, excite, experience, face, gain, generate, goad, incite, induce, inflame, inspire, instigate, kindle, motivate, move, prod, produce, promote, prompt, provoke, risk, rouse, run, shoulder, spark, spur, stimulate, stir, suffer, sustain, tolerate, urge, weather* (≠ -avert, -avoid, -bypass, deduct, discourage, -ditch, -dodge, forfeit, lessen, lose, miss, misunderstand, pass, -prevent, push, reduce, -sidestep, stop, subtract, withhold)

INDEX (+): *access, account, adjust, align, alphabetize, archive, arrange, array, audit, book, budget, calibrate, card, catalog, categorize, check, chronicle, classify, clock, codify, collect, compile, coordinate, count, detail, docket, document, enroll, enter, enumerate, file, generalize, grade, hierarchize, inscribe, inventory, invoice, itemize, label, list, log, methodize, minute, notate, note, order, organize, prioritize, queue, record, reference, register, regulate, reschedule, scan, schedule, score, scrutinize, slate, slot, sort, store, straighten, summarize, systematize, table, tabulate, tag, tally, tidy, total, unscramble, wait-list* (≠ addle, anonymize, baffle, churn, clutter, confound, confuse, delete, disarrange, dishevel, disorder, disorganize, displace, disrupt, disturb, entangle, erase, faze, garble, hash, intermix, jumble, mess, mingle, mislabel, mislay, misplace, mix, muddle, muddy, muss, mystify, perplex, randomize, roil, ruffle, rummage, rumple, scatter, scramble, shuffle, snarl, stir, swirl, tangle, toss, tousle, untidy)

INDICT (/): *accuse, allege, arraign, attaint, attribute, blame, book, castigate, censure, charge, chide, cite, condemn, criticize, damn, decry, denounce, denunciate, deride, fault, finger, frame, impeach, implicate, impugn, incriminate, litigate, name, prosecute, rebuke, report, reproach,* *reprove, subpoena, sue, summon, tax, try* (≠ absolve, acquit, advocate, alibi, appeal, champion, defend, excuse, exonerate, forgive, free, justify, liberate, pardon, release, remit, shrive, spare, vindicate)

INDOCTRINATE (+): *brainwash, brief, catechize, coach, colonize, condition, consult, convert, convince, direct, discipline, drill, edify, educate, enlighten, familiarize, fix, gaslight, ground, guide, hypnotize, imbue, implant, impress, imprint, inculcate, influence, inform, infuse, ingrain, initiate, instill, instruct, introduce, lead, lecture, mentor, plant, prepare, prime, program, propagandize, qualify, rear, retrain, school, show, teach, train, tutor* (≠ -abandon, accept, assail, believe, buck, challenge, champion, contest, criticize, cross-examine, debunk, defend, defy, deprogram, disbelieve, discredit, disprove, dispute, distrust, doubt, embrace, fight, forget, grill, impugn, interrogate, interview, learn, liberate, mistrust, -neglect, oppose, promote, protest, question, resist, support, swallow, trust, vilify)

INDUCE (←): *abet, activate, actuate, breed, bribe, bulldoze, cajole, coax, convince, draw, encourage, engender, entreat, force, generate, glad-hand, goose, impel, incite, influence, inspire, instigate, lubricate, lure, midwife, motivate, move, originate, palaver, persuade, press, procure, produce, promote, prompt, provoke, schmooze, seduce, soft-soap, spark, spur, squeeze, steamroll, suborn, sway, sweet-talk, tantalize, tease, tempt, trigger, urge, wheedle* (≠ arrest, cripple, curb, dampen, deactivate, demotivate, -deter, discourage, dissuade, freeze, hamper, hobble, impede, inactivate, inhibit, limit, nobble, paralyze, -prevent, -prohibit, protest, quash, quell, restrain, restrict, scotch, smother, snuff, squash, squelch, squench, stall, stem, straightjacket, stymie, suppress, -thwart)

INDULGE (←): *abate, allay, alleviate, appease, appreciate, approve, assuage, cater, celebrate, cloy, consume, content, demolish, devour, eat, enjoy, experience, extinguish, fancy, feast, fill, fulfill, glut, gorge, gratify, gulp, guzzle, humor, ingest, inhale, lighten, mitigate, moderate, moisten, oblige, overfill, prize, quench, reduce, relieve, relish, sample, sate, satiate, satisfy, saturate, savor, slake, smell, snarf, sniff, surfeit, swallow, swig, swill, taste, touch, treasure, whiff, wolf* (≠ abuse, amplify, annoy, arouse, betray, covet, crave, demand, -deny, depress, deprive, desire, disappoint, dissatisfy, distress, entice, envy, -eschew, exacerbate, excite, expect, famish, fancy, forfeit, forgo, frustrate, inhibit, intensify, lure, provoke, -refuse, regret, -reject, -renounce, repent, restrain, rue, scant, scrimp, seek, -shun, skimp, starve, stifle, stimulate, stint, tantalize, target, taunt, tease, tempt, trigger, underfeed, want, withhold, wrong)

INDULGE (+): *accommodate, amuse, appease, baby, caress, cherish, coddle, conciliate, cosset, cotton, cradle, cuddle, delight, entertain, favor, featherbed, fondle, foster, gratify, humor, infantilize, lavish, mitigate, moderate, mollycoddle, nourish, nurse, nurture, oblige, overindulge, pacify, pamper, pet, placate, please, pleasure, regale, reward, satiate, satisfy, smother, soothe, spoil, spoon-feed, tickle, tolerate, treat* (≠ anguish, bridle, check, constrain, control, crucify, curb, discipline, disfavor, -frustrate, harass, harm, hurt, injure, malnourish, menace, -neglect, oppress, outrage, persecute, restrain, sadden, sicken, threaten, torment, torture, traumatize, underfeed, upset, victimize, violate, wound, wrong)

INFATUATE (←): *absorb, allure, arouse, attract, bait, bedazzle, beguile, bewitch, captivate, charm, compel, court, dazzle, delight, disarm, draw, enamor, enchant, engross, enrapture, enthrall, entice, entrance, fascinate, glamour, grab, gratify, grip, hog, hold, hook, hypnotize, influence, interest, intrigue, invite, involve, lure, magnetize, mesmerize, monopolize, obsess, occupy, please, possess, pull, razzle-dazzle, rivet, seduce, solicit, spellbind, tantalize, tempt, thrill, titillate, transfix, win, woo, wow* (≠ anger, annoy, appall, -balk, bore, bother, bug, dampen, deaden, depress, disappoint, disenchant, disgust, dull, enrage, exhaust, frustrate, infuriate, irk, irritate, nag, nauseate, needle, nettle, niggle, nitpick, numb, offend, outrage, repulse, revolt, sicken, stifle, tire, underwhelm, vex, weary) **(¿) ABSTRACTION ALERT. Concrete goals essential!**

INFECT (→): *activate, affect, agitate, animate, arouse, charge, churn, drive, empower, encourage, energize, enliven, enthuse, excite, fan, fire, force, freshen, fuel, generate, incite, influence, inspire, instigate, invigorate, kindle, motivate, move, overwhelm, power, prompt, provoke, quicken, recharge, reinvigorate, restore, revive, rouse, spark, spread, spur, stimulate, stoke, strengthen, swamp, tempt, touch, trigger* (≠ alienate, barricade, block, confuse, dampen, daunt, deaden, discourage, dull, enervate, hamper, hinder, isolate, menace, -prevent, quiet, sedate, sequester, stall, stop, stymie, -thwart)

INFECT (/): *afflict, blight, carry, contaminate, corrupt, curse, damage, defile, dirty, disease, give, harm, injure, mar, overcome, pass, pervert, plague, poison, pollute, sicken, spoil, spread, sully, taint, transmit, ulcerate, vitiate, weaken* (≠ cure, decontaminate, disinfect, doctor, dose, heal, help, immunize, inoculate, isolate, medicate, nurse, -prevent, protect, quarantine, sanitize, seclude, treat, vaccinate)

INFEST (→): *annoy, assail, beset, besiege, colonize, contaminate, crowd, defile, fill, flood, harass, harry, honeycomb, infect, infiltrate, infuse, inject, instill, invade, overload, overrun, overwhelm, pack, penetrate, permeate, pervade, pester, plague, pollute, press, ravage, spread, swamp, swarm, throng, worry* (≠ cleanse, clear, defend, delouse, destroy, eject, eliminate, eradicate, expel, expurgate, exterminate, guard, maintain, oust, protect, purge, purify, quarantine, remove, rescue, save, scour, ward, wash)

INFILTRATE (→): *access, colonize, crack, embed, enter, filter, foist, hack, impregnate, infect, infest, infuse, insert, insinuate, instill, interpenetrate, interpolate, interpose, introduce, invade, marinate, penetrate, percolate, permeate, pervade, pierce, presoak, puncture, saturate, slip, sneak, soak, tinge, wiggle, wind, worm, wriggle* (≠ blackball, block, clarify, clean, clear, cordon, delouse, disgorge, -exclude, exorcise, expel, extract, filter, jettison, purge, quarantine, remove, separate, sift, strip, tug, withdraw, yank)

INFLAME (→): *afflict, affront, aggravate, agitate, agonize, anger, anguish, animate, annoy, antagonize, arouse, awaken, badger, bait, bedevil, bother, burn, chafe, compound, cramp, cross, discompose, disquiet, distress, disturb, electrify, embitter, embolden, encourage, energize, enrage, envenom, escalate, exacerbate, exasperate, excite, exhilarate, fan, fire, fret, fuel, gall, galvanize, generate, grate, harass, harry, hassle, heat, hurt, ignite, Impassion, impel, incense, incite, increase, infuriate, inspire, intensify, intoxicate, invigorate, irk, irritate, kindle, light, madden, miff, militarize, motivate, nag, needle, nerve, nettle, niggle, nitpick, offend, outrage, pain, peeve, perturb, pester, pique, prod, propel, provoke, rankle, rile, roil, rouse, ruffle, steam, stimulate, sting, stir, stitch, stoke, strengthen, tantalize, tease, tempt, torment, torture, trigger, troll, trouble, upset, vex, vitalize, worsen, wrack, wrench* (≠ allay, appease, assuage, beguile, bewitch, calm, captivate, castrate, charm, comfort, conciliate, console, cool, dampen, deactivate, deaden, delight, demilitarize, devitalize, disarm, douse, emasculate, enchant, enervate, extinguish, freeze, gratify, help, humor, hush, lull, mellow, mitigate, moderate, mollify, pacify, paralyze, petrify, placate, please, propitiate, quench, quiet, relieve, satisfy, settle, slake, smother, soothe)

INFLATE (→): *accent, accentuate, accrue, aerate, affirm, aggrandize, amplify, assert, augment, boost, bulge, deepen, dilate, distend, elevate, emphasize, enlarge, escalate, exaggerate, exalt, expand, extend, fill, heighten, heroicize, heroize, honor, idealize, idolize, increase, intensify, lift, magnify, maximize, overdramatize, overestimate, overrate, oversell, overstate, poeticize, punctuate, raise, romanticize, sentimentalize, strengthen, swell* (≠ abridge, collapse, compress, concentrate, condense, constrict, contract, curtail, decrease, deflate, diminish, flatten, lessen, lower, minimize, précis, puncture, reduce, shrink, shrivel, summarize, tighten, underemphasize)

INFLICT (/): *administer, apply, blackmail, burden, command, deal, deliver, dispense, dole, enforce, exact, execute, expose, express, extort, foist, force, force-feed, give, impose, invite, levy, loose, mete, perpetrate, precipitate, require, saddle, spark, strike, subject, unleash, vent, visit, wreak* (≠ -avert, check, curb, foil, hide, hold, inhibit, keep, -preclude, -prevent, stop, stymie, suppress, take, -thwart, withhold)

INFLUENCE (←): *affect, afflict, agitate, allure, alter, arouse, attract, bewitch, bias, bother, bribe, buttonhole, captivate, carry, change, charm, choreograph, color, compel, concern, condition, control, convince, dazzle, determine, direct, discomfort, discompose, dispose, disquiet, distress, disturb, dizzy, dominate, enchant, encourage, engage, enrapture, enthrall, entrance, fascinate, fluster, goad, guide, harass, harry, impact, impel, impress, incite, incline, induce, infect, inspire, instigate, interest, involve, manage, maneuver, manipulate, modify, mold, motivate, move, operate, orchestrate, outsmart, outthink, outwit, penetrate, permeate, persuade, perturb, pester, pierce, plague, predetermine, prejudge, prejudice, prepossess, prompt, ravish, reach, rouse, shape, smite, steer, stir, strain, stress, strike, sway, tantalize, tease, tempt, touch, train,* *transform, transmute, transport, trigger, trouble, try, upset, urge, win, woo, work, worry, wring* (≠ allow, -avoid, bore, -bypass, -deter, discourage, dissuade, hinder, -ignore, impede, inhibit, miss, -neglect, nobble, -omit, permit, -prevent, quarantine, restrain, -shun, -sidestep, subvert, tire, underwhelm, weary)

INFORM (→): *acquaint, advise, announce, apprise, betray, blab, blaze, blurt, brief, caution, certify, clue, coach, communicate, cultivate, debrief, discipline, drill, edify, educate, email, endow, enlighten, familiarize, forewarn, illuminate, impart, influence, inspire, instruct, invest, leak, level, mentor, message, notify, nurture, possess, post, relate, school, snitch, squeal, teach, tell, text, tip, tout, train, tutor, update, warn* (≠ conceal, contradict, debate, -deny, discredit, disprove, dispute, distrust, doubt, gainsay, hide, misinform, mislead, refute, -reject, retract, scruple, suspect, withhold)

INFRINGE (→): *breach, break, contravene, crash, defy, dismiss, disobey, -disregard, disrespect, flout, fracture, -ignore, invade, -neglect, offend, -overlook, pooh-pooh, resist, -scorn, subvert, traduce, transgress, violate, withstand* (≠ attend, -bypass, -circumvent, -dodge, follow, hear, heed, mark, mind, note, notice, obey, observe, regard, serve, shunt, skirt, watch)

INFRINGE (←): *bootleg, borrow, breach, break, contravene, defy, dismiss, disobey, -disregard, flout, fracture, freeboot, -ignore, impose, lift, -neglect, offend, -overlook, overstep, pirate, poach, pooh-pooh, presume, resist, -scorn, steal, traduce, transgress, violate, withstand* (≠ attend, follow, hear, heed, honor, mark, mind, note, notice, obey, observe, regard, respect, serve, watch)

INFURIATE (/): *affront, aggravate, agitate, anger, annoy, antagonize, arouse, badger, bait, bedevil, bother, bug, burn, chafe, challenge, confront, contradict, counter, cross, defy, discompose, disconcert, displease, disturb, earbash, embitter, enrage, envenom, exacerbate, exasperate, fret, frustrate, gall, get, goad, grate, harass, harry, hassle, heckle, hector, hound, incense, incite, inflame, irk, irritate, madden, miff, nag, needle, nettle, niggle, nitpick, offend, outrage, peeve, persecute, perturb, pester, pique, provoke, rankle, rattle, rile, roil, rouse, ruffle, tease, torment, troll, trouble, upset, vex* (≠ allay, appease, assuage, beguile, bewitch, calm, captivate, charm, comfort, conciliate, console, content, delight, disarm, enchant, expiate, gladden, gratify, help, humor, lull, mellow, mitigate, moderate, mollify, pacify, placate, please, propitiate, quiet, rejoice, relieve, satisfy, sedate, settle, soothe, sugarcoat, thrill, tranquilize)

INFUSE (+): *animate, brew, brine, charge, deluge, dose, draw, drizzle, drown, endow, enliven, fill, flavor, flood, glut, imbue, impart, implant, impregnate, inculcate, indoctrinate, infiltrate, ingrain, inject, inoculate, insinuate, inspire, instill, interpenetrate, intersperse, introduce, inundate, invest, invigorate, lace, leaven, lend, mainline, marinate, meld, mingle, overwhelm, penetrate, permeate, pervade, plant, presoak, saturate, soak, steep, submerge, suffuse, surfeit, tinge, tint* (≠ bleed, cleanse, clear, debit, deplete, deprive, distill, divest, drain, draw, eliminate, empty, expel, extract, filter, flush, jettison, leach, leech, offload, pour, purge, purify, remove, screen, separate, siphon, spew, strain, strip, take, tap, unload, unpack, withdraw, withhold)

INGEST (←): *absorb, accept, access, acquire, admit, appreciate, appropriate, assimilate, banquet, bolt, chew, consume, corrode, cram, demolish, devour, digest, dispatch, dissolve, down, drink, eat, engorge, engulf, enjoy, envelop, feast, finish, get, glut, gnaw, gobble, gorge, gulp, gum, guzzle, hoover, imbibe, incorporate, inhale, inspire, integrate, internalize, lap, lick, manage, metabolize, mouth, munch, nibble, nosh, nurse, overwhelm, pick, pocket, procure, quaff, raven, receive, regale, relish, ruminate, savor, scarf, sip, slop, slurp, snarf, sniff, stuff, suck, surfeit, swallow, swig, swill, take, taste, try, vacuum, welcome, wolf* (≠ -avoid, barf, belch, brew, -bypass, concoct, content, cook, covet, crave, create, -decline, desire, disgorge, disperse, -ditch, drop, dump, eject, excrete, expel, exude, famish, fancy, favor, feed, fetishize, force-feed, forgo, fuel, furnish, grace, gratify, heave, hunt, jettison, make, malnourish, miss, nourish, offer, order, overfeed, pass, please, prepare, puke, quench, -refuse, regurgitate, -reject, request, satisfy, serve, skimp, skip, slake, spew, spit, splutter, starve, stint, supply, toss, trash, underfeed, victual, vomit, withhold)

INHABIT (+): *abide, annex, claim, colonize, crash, locate, lodge, occupy, park, people, populate, possess, settle, stay, tenant* (≠ -abandon, -avoid, depart, -desert, evacuate, -flee, forfeit, -forsake, leave, lose, miss, move, -reject, -shun, vacate)

INHERIT (←): *accede, accept, acquire, assume, claim, collect, derive, gain, harvest, obtain, procure, reap, receive, recover, salvage, scavenge, secure, succeed, take* (≠ bequeath, bestow, compensate, concede, deed, -deny, deprive, dower, endow, entrust, forfeit, grant, leave, lose, offer, surrender, will, withhold, yield)

INHIBIT (←): *admonish, antagonize, -avert, baffle, -balk, ban, bar, bind, block, bottleneck, brake, bridle, burden, catch, challenge, check, checkmate, chill, choke, clog, collar, complicate, confront, congest, constipate, constrain, constrict, contradict, counter, counteract, counterattack, cramp, crimp, cripple, cross, curb, dam, dampen, daunt, deflect, defy, delay, demotivate, depress, derail, detain, -deter, discourage, dishearten, disincline, dispute, dissuade, divert, drag, encumber, entangle, entrap, fetter, fight, -forbid, foul, -frustrate, hamper, hamstring, handicap, hinder, impair, impede, intercept, interrupt, intimidate, jam, leash, lumber, mire, obstruct, occlude, oppose, oppress, override, paralyze, pause, plug, postpone, -prevent, -prohibit, protest, -rebuff, repel, repress, repulse, resist, restrain, restrict, shackle, shelve, short-circuit, snag, snarl, stall, staunch, stay, stem, stop, straightjacket, straiten, stymie, suppress, tangle, tether, -thwart* (≠ accelerate, accommodate, advance, aid, assist, augment, boost, brainstorm, catalyze, clear, compel, disencumber, disentangle, ease, encourage, expedite, extricate, facilitate, fast-forward, fast-track, feed, free, frogmarch, fuel, further, grease, hasten, heal, help, hurry, improve, inspire, legalize, liberate, lift, loosen, lubricate, march, mend, midwife, motivate, oblige, open, oxygenate, prioritize, prod, promote, prompt, propel, quicken, release, relieve, remedy, rush, slacken, smooth, speed, spur, steady, stimulate, stir, stoke, strengthen, support, transcend, unclog, uncomplicate, unleash, unlock, untangle, untie, urge, ventilate)

INITIATE (→): *activate, arrange, author, bankroll, begin, brainstorm, brew, conceive, concoct, constitute, construct, contrive, create, develop, devise, endow, establish, engineer, fabricate, father, finance, foster, found, fund, galvanize, generate, hatch, ignite, inaugurate, induce, innovate, instigate, institute, introduce, invent, kick-start, launch, manufacture, open, organize, originate, patent, pioneer, plant, produce, prompt, seed, sire, sow, spark, spur, start, stimulate, subsidize, systematize, trigger, underwrite* (≠ abolish, -abort, adjourn, annihilate, annul, axe, -cancel, close, conclude, crush, defund, deep-six, dismiss, dissolve, drop, eliminate, end, extinguish, finish, -halt, impede, kill, -nullify, perfect, quash, sabotage, scratch, scrub, shelve, slow, stop, suspend, terminate, wrap, wreck)

INITIATE (+): *accept, accustom, acquaint, admit, advise, apprise, brainwash, brief, crash, drill, educate, enlighten, enroll, enter, expose, familiarize, greet, ground, habituate, inculcate, induct, inform, install, instill, instruct, introduce, invest, ordain, orient, present, reacquaint, receive, retrain, school, subject, teach, train, tutor, wait-list, warn, welcome* (≠ banish, blackball, clear, confound, confuse, -cut, deprive, divest, eliminate, empty, -exclude, exile, expel, learn, mystify, -neglect, -ostracize, oust, -refuse, -reject, remove, -spurn, strip, terminate)

INJECT (→): *add, administer, append, attach, cram, cure, dose, drug, ease, force-feed, imbue, immunize, implant, impregnate, include, infuse, inlay, inoculate, inseminate, insert, inset, insinuate, install, instill, interject, interpolate, interpose, intersperse, introduce, lard, mainline, medicate, ram, sandwich, shoot, shove, thrust, treat, vaccinate, weave, wedge* (≠ bleed, deduct, detach, disgorge, drain, draw, eject, eliminate, -exclude, expel, extract, jettison, leach, leech, milk, -omit, oust, pull, -reject, remove, subtract, suck, withdraw)

INJURE (/): *abuse, afflict, aggrieve, anguish, attack, bark, bash, batter, beat, blemish, blight, blind, bloody, bludgeon, break, bruise, brutalize, burn, castrate, choke, concuss, conk, contort, contuse, crease, cripple, crucify, cut, damage, deaden, debilitate, deface, deform, disable, disadvantage, disfigure, dislocate, distress, fracture, gash, gore, graze, hamstring, harm, hit, hurt, ill-treat, impair, incapacitate, infect, insult, kneecap, lacerate, lame, maim, maltreat, mangle, mar, misdiagnose, mistreat, mutilate, nick, offend, overdose, pain, paralyze, pinch, poison, prejudice, razor, rend, ruin, sadden, savage, scald, scalp, scar, scathe, scorch, scrape, sear, shank, shatter, shiv, shoot, shrivel, sicken, slice, smash, sorrow, spoil, sprain, stab, sting, strain, target, tarnish, tear, torment, torture, traumatize, undermine, upset, victimize, vitiate, weaken, welt, wing, wither, wound, wrench, wrong* (≠ aid, armor, assuage, bandage, brace, cure, diagnose, doctor, drug, fix, heal, help, hospitalize, medicate, mend, nurse, nurture, pacify, pamper, patch, pity, protect, regret, shield, soothe, splint, spoil, spoon-feed, stabilize, steady, strengthen, treat)

INJURE (/): *abrade, adulterate, affect, annihilate, attack, backhand, bang, bash, batter, betray, blemish, blight, blister, botch, break, canker, clobber, club, compromise, corrode, corrupt, crab, crack, crash, cripple, cross, crush, damage, dash, decimate, deface, demolish, dent, desecrate, desolate, despoil, destroy, deteriorate, devastate, ding, disable, disfigure, disqualify, distress, doom, efface, emasculate, enervate, enfeeble, erode, flaw, fracture, gash, graze, grieve, hamstring, harm, hurt, impair, impoverish, incapacitate, jam, lacerate, lame, maim, mangle, mar, mark, mutilate, offend, overload, pollute, prejudice, pulverize, raze, ruin, rust, sabotage, scorch, scour, scourge, scrape, scuff, shatter, sideline, sideswipe, smash, snag, snarl, spoil, squash, stain, straiten, sully, tarnish, tear, torment, torture, total, trample, undercut, undermine, unman, vandalize, vitiate, warp, waste, weaken, wear, wreck, wrench* (≠ align, ameliorate, augment, better, boost, doctor, edit, enhance, enrich, fix, help, improve, mend, patch, perfect, rebuild, recondition, reconstruct, rectify, refine, rehabilitate, remedy, remodel, renovate, repair, restore, revamp, revise, survive, weather, withstand)

INOCULATE (+): *animate, charge, defend, deluge, dose, drown, enliven, fill, flood, imbue, immunize, implant, impregnate, inculcate, infuse, ingrain, inject, instill, insulate, inundate, invest, invigorate, leaven, mainline, medicate, overwhelm, permeate, pervade, plant, -prevent, protect, quarantine, remedy, safeguard, saturate, shield, steep, submerge, suffuse, treat, vaccinate* (≠ afflict, clear, damage, deprive, divest, eliminate, empty, endanger, extract, harm, -ignore, infect, injure, jeopardize, remove, -shirk, sicken, strip, take)

INSINUATE (→): *allude, connote, couch, embed, foist, hint, implant, imply, infect, infer, infiltrate, inject, insert, instill, interpolate, interpose, intimate, introduce, lodge, mention, penetrate, pierce, propose, purport, signal, signify, sneak, suggest, whisper, worm* (≠ announce, ascertain, broadcast, conceal, debunk, declare, delineate, describe, discern, elucidate, explain, hide, isolate, plug, proclaim, profile, quarantine, segregate, sequester, telegraph, withhold) **(¿) ABSTRACTION ALERT. Concrete goals essential!**

INSINUATE (+): *add, append, attach, braid, cram, embed, implant, inject, inlay, insert, inset, install, interject, interpenetrate, interpolate, interpose, intersperse, introduce, jam, lard, penetrate, permeate, pervade, plait, possess, ram, sandwich, saturate, shove, slide, suffuse, thrust, weave, wedge* (≠ blackball, deduct, detach, disgorge, eject, eliminate, excise, -exclude, exorcise, expel, extract, leach, leech, -omit, oppose, oust, -reject, remove, repel, subtract, withdraw)

INSPECT (←): *analyze, anatomize, appraise, assess, attend, audit, benchmark, browse, calculate, case, categorize, chart, check, clock, comb, con, conclude, connect, consider, consult, contemplate, contextu-*

alize, contrast, correlate, criticize, critique, crosscheck, deconstruct, deduce, differentiate, discern, dissect, distill, examine, explore, eye, eyeball, frequent, frisk, heed, inspect, investigate, learn, monitor, notice, number, numerate, observe, oversee, parse, perceive, peruse, plumb, police, prioritize, probe, prove, prowl, rank, read, reconnoiter, reference, regard, reinvestigate, research, review, riffle, rifle, scan, scope, scout, scrutinize, search, study, subdivide, superintend, supervise, survey, suss, travel, verify, vet, view, visit, vivisect, watch, witness, x-ray (≠ -blank, blind, blindfold, confound, confuse, deceive, -discount, disguise, -disregard, fake, forget, fudge, half-ass, hide, -ignore, lose, mask, mislead, miss, mistake, muddle, mystify, -neglect, -omit, -overlook, perplex, puzzle, skim, skip, trick)

INSPIRE (+): *animate, arouse, awaken, carry, elate, encourage, energize, enliven, ensoul, enthrall, enthuse, exalt, excite, exhilarate, galvanize, goad, hearten, ignite, imbue, impel, impress, incite, infect, inflame, influence, inform, infuse, inject, instigate, instill, invigorate, kindle, light, motivate, produce, prompt, propel, provoke, quicken, rally, razzle-dazzle, reassure, rouse, spark, spur, stimulate, stir, strike, sway, thrill, touch, trigger, urge, vitalize* (≠ blackjack, blackmail, bore, chill, confuse, daunt, deaden, debilitate, demotivate, depress, -deter, discourage, dissuade, dull, enervate, enfeeble, extinguish, -halt, hamstring, hinder, inhibit, intimidate, paralyze, perplex, puzzle, quiet, repress, restrain, stop, suppress, undermine, wither)

INSTALL (+): *affix, clinch, embed, establish, fit, fix, furnish, graft, implant, insert, introduce, juxtapose, lay, line, locate, lodge, place, plant, plumb, position, settle, site, situate, station, transplant* (≠ cut, detach, disconnect, eject, erase, excise, extract, pluck, pull, purge, remove, unfasten, wrench, yank)

INSTALL (+): *consecrate, ensconce, entrench, establish, inaugurate, induct, instate, institute, introduce, invest, locate, lodge, nestle, niche, ordain, place, settle, situate* (≠ banish, discharge, dislodge, dismiss, dump, eradicate, fire, remove, terminate)

INSTIGATE (→): *abet, activate, advance, animate, arouse, begin, brew, convince, cultivate, detonate, drive, encourage, energize, enliven, excite, fan, ferment, fire, foment, forward, foster, fuel, further, galvanize, generate, goad, heckle, ignite, impassion, impel, incite, incur, induce, inflame, influence, initiate, insinuate, inspire, invigorate, kindle, lubricate, midwife, motivate, move, needle, nourish, nurture, persuade, pick, pique, plan, plot, press, prod, promote, prompt, provoke, quicken, rabble-rouse, raise, rouse, scheme, sow, spark, spur, start, stimulate, stir, trigger, urge, vitalize* (≠ allay, appease, bridle, calm, check, complicate, constrain, curb, deactivate, demotivate, discourage, end, freeze, -halt, hamper, hold, humor, inhibit, lull, mellow, mitigate, moderate, mollify, muddle, oppose, pace, pacify, paralyze, placate, -prevent, quiet, regulate, rein, restrain, settle, soothe, stall, still, stop, straightjacket, stymie, subdue, tame, -thwart, tranquilize)

INSTITUTE (+): *appoint, arrange, author, begin, build, commence, conceive, concoct, constitute, contrive, create, develop, devise, enact, endow, enlarge, establish, expand, fabricate, father, finance, fix, found, fund, inaugurate, induct, initiate, innovate, install, introduce, invent, invest, launch, manufacture, open, ordain, organize, originate, pioneer, plant, produce, rev, settle, start, subsidize, systematize, trigger* (≠ abolish, -abort, annihilate, annul, banish, cease, close, conclude, -deny, dismiss, end, eradicate, finish, -forbid, -halt, -nix, -nullify, -prevent, protest, -reject, -rescind, shut, stop, terminate, wrap)

INSTRUCT (→): *acquaint, advise, aid, apprentice, apprise, assist, brainwash, brief, catechize, civilize, coach, command, compel, condition, convince, counsel, cram, cultivate, demonstrate, develop, direct, discipline, domesticate, drill, edify, educate, elevate, enlighten, expand, extend, familiarize, fit, foster, groom, ground, guide, help, housebreak, housetrain, impart, implant, improve, inculcate, indoctrinate, inform, initiate, inspire, instill, introduce, lead, lecture, mentor, monitor, moralize, notify, nurture, order, parrot, perfect, preach, prepare, prime, proctor, qualify, question, quiz, read, ready, rear, rehearse, retrain, reveal, school, scold, season, shape, sharpen, show, steer, strain, stretch, supervise, take, tame, tax, teach, test, train, tutor, update* (≠ abuse, addle, attend, baffle, barbarize, bewilder, bury, censor, cheat, conceal, confound, confuse, consult, debase, deceive, defraud, delude, demean, discombobulate, disguise, fabricate, fluster, follow, gaslight, hamper, heed, hide, hinder, -ignore, impede, keep, learn, lower, mind, misinform, mislead, muddle, mystify, -neglect, nonplus, obey, obscure, observe, perplex, pester, puzzle, ruffle, study, stump, suppress, surprise, withhold)

INSTRUCT (→): *adjure, advise, appoint, ask, assign, authorize, beg, beseech, bid, boss, captain, charge, choreograph, coerce, command, commission, compel, conduct, constrain, control, counsel, direct, enjoin, entreat, force, lead, manage, oblige, orchestrate, order, oversee, petition, request, require, superintend, supervise, tell, warn* (≠ allow, brook, countenance, endorse, follow, keep, mind, obey, observe, permit, sanction, support)

INSULATE (+): *abstract, armor, barricade, blockade, blunt, buffer, coat, cocoon, confine, cover, cushion, defend, detach, detain, disengage, encase, envelop, -exclude, guard, hold, holster, immure, incarcerate, inlay, inoculate, institutionalize, isolate, jail, keep, line, -omit, oppose, pad, protect, quarantine, remove, restrain, restrict, safeguard, seclude, segregate, separate, sequester, sheathe, shelter, shield, soundproof, tape, treat, wrap* (≠ assimilate, associate, attack, burn, chill, combine, connect, damage, desegregate, discharge, expose, free, incorporate, infiltrate, insinuate, integrate, internalize, join, liberate, link, loose, -neglect, penetrate, pierce, reintegrate, release, reunite, unite)

INSULT (/): *abase, abuse, affront, antagonize, bait, belittle, bench, besmear, besmirch, bestialize, blacken, blackguard, blame, blast, blister, boo, bruise, chide, criticize, curse, cuss, -cut, debase, defame, degrade,* *demean, demote, denigrate, devalue, diminish, disgrace, dishonor, disparage, displease, disrespect, distress, disturb, humble, humiliate, hurt, injure, jeer, libel, lower, malign, miff, mock, mortify, offend, oppress, outrage, pain, persecute, -rebuff, reduce, revile, ridicule, shame, sideline, slander, slap, -slight, slur, smear, -snub, soil, spoil, stain, sully, taint, taunt, torment, torture, trample, trouble, upset, villainize, violate, vulgarize, wound, wrong* (≠ acclaim, admire, applaud, approve, blandish, bless, boost, cherish, commend, compliment, congratulate, defend, delight, dignify, eulogize, exalt, flannel, flatter, glad-hand, glorify, gratify, guard, hail, high-five, honor, ingratiate, please, praise, prioritize, promote, protect, retort, revere, satisfy, sweet-talk, thank, welcome, worship)

INSURE (+): *assure, attest, certify, cinch, clinch, compensate, cover, crosscheck, ensure, guarantee, guard, ice, indemnify, maintain, patrol, pledge, preserve, promise, protect, reassure, register, reimburse, safeguard, secure, shield, support, sustain, swear, underwrite, warrant, witness* (≠ attack, bemoan, break, burden, compromise, cost, damage, disrupt, doubt, endanger, enfeeble, imperil, injure, mourn, predict, regret, risk, sabotage, scotch, scruple, scupper, shelve, suspect, target, threaten, undermine, weaken, worry)

INTEGRATE (+): *accommodate, align, amalgamate, arrange, articulate, assimilate, associate, attune, blend, coalesce, combine, compact, concatenate, concentrate, conflate, conjoin, consolidate, contemporize, coordinate, desegregate, embody, equalize, fuse, harmonize, homogenize, hybridize, incorporate, intermix, internalize, join, knit, link, mainstream, meld, merge, mesh, mingle, mix, orchestrate, organize, proportion, reconcile, reintegrate, reunite, synthesize, systematize, time, tune, unify, unite, wed* (≠ alienate, chunk, cleave, detach, differentiate, diffuse, disaffect, disengage, disintegrate, disjoin, disperse, dissolve, disunite, divide, divorce, estrange, isolate, mismatch, -omit, orphan, -ostracize, oust, part, partition, rupture, scatter, seclude, segregate, separate, sever, split, sunder)

INTENSIFY (+): *accelerate, accent, accentuate, accrue, accumulate, add, aggrandize, aggravate, amp, amplify, assert, augment, beef, belabor, bolster, boost, breed, brighten, broaden, build, bump, buttress, catalyze, collect, color, complement, compound, concentrate, condense, consolidate, crank, darken, deepen, develop, dilate, distend, double, dramatize, elaborate, elevate, elongate, embellish, embroider, emphasize, enforce, enhance, enlarge, enliven, enrich, escalate, exacerbate, exaggerate, exalt, expand, extend, fan, fatten, feature, fire, flavor, foreground, foster, fuel, further, grease, grow, hasten, heat, heighten, highlight, hike, hype, hyperbolize, increase, inflate, lengthen, lighten, magnify, marinate, maximize, multiply, optimize, overemphasize, overhaul, overstate, pad, point, prioritize, proliferate, prolong, propagate, protract, pump, punctuate, quicken, raise, ratchet, redouble, reinforce, revolutionize, richen, romanticize, rouse, satirize, scale, season, sentimentalize, sharpen, spice, spike, spotlight, spread, stoke, strengthen,* *stress, stretch, supersize, supplement, swell, treble, triple, trumpet, underline, underscore, unspool, up, upgrade, whet, widen, worsen* (≠ abate, abbreviate, abridge, alleviate, attenuate, blunt, buffer, bury, calm, cheapen, compress, conceal, constrict, contract, curb, curtail, cushion, cut, deaden, decrease, deemphasize, de-escalate, depress, devalue, diminish, dismiss, downplay, downsize, dull, ease, elide, hide, lessen, lighten, lowball, lower, lull, mask, mellow, miniaturize, minify, minimize, mitigate, moderate, modulate, mollify, muffle, obscure, pacify, placate, postpone, reduce, restrain, restrict, retrench, sedate, shorten, shrink, slow, smother, soothe, subdue, subtract, syncopate, taper, trim, truncate, underemphasize, understate, weaken)

INTERCEPT (←): *ambush, appropriate, arrest, blindside, block, brave, bushwhack, buttonhole, capture, catch, check, checkmate, collar, commandeer, corner, corral, counter, curb, deflect, delay, divert, face, -frustrate, grab, hijack, hinder, impede, interpose, interrupt, obstruct, oppose, pause, postpone, -prevent, refract, seize, shelve, short-circuit, snag, snare, snatch, stall, stop, take, -thwart, trap, waylay, wrangle* (≠ abet, allow, assist, -avoid, -bypass, -disregard, -dodge, -duck, -elude, -escape, -evade, -flee, forget, forward, fumble, further, help, leave, miss, observe, originate, overshoot, -sidestep, skip, skirt)

INTEREST (←): *absorb, affect, amuse, arm, arouse, attract, captivate, concern, dazzle, divert, engage, engross, excite, fascinate, generate, grip, impress, inspire, intrigue, involve, move, occupy, rivet, thrill, tickle, touch* (≠ alienate, annoy, bore, deaden, depress, disaffect, discourage, dissuade, earbash, fatigue, irk, nag, niggle, nitpick, tire, trouble, vex, weary) **(¿) ABSTRACTION ALERT. Concrete goals essential!**

INTERPRET (←): *adapt, annotate, clarify, compare, construe, contextualize, contrast, decipher, decode, deduce, define, delineate, depict, describe, diagnose, distinguish, elucidate, explain, explicate, explore, expound, extract, gather, generalize, gloss, illuminate, illustrate, infer, limn, mimic, paraphrase, perform, picture, play, portray, predict, profile, rationalize, read, reenact, render, represent, scan, solve, summarize, take, translate, understand, untangle, view* (≠ bury, cloud, con, confound, confuse, corrupt, deceive, falsify, garble, -ignore, mangle, misconstrue, misdiagnose, mishear, misinterpret, mislead, misread, misrepresent, mistake, misunderstand, muddle, obfuscate, obscure, -overlook, scramble, twist)

INTERROGATE (←): *annoy, ask, besiege, bombard, canvass, catechize, challenge, check, consult, cross-examine, cross-question, debrief, depose, disbelieve, discredit, disprove, dispute, distrust, doubt, examine, grill, hammer, harass, hound, interview, investigate, nag, needle, nitpick, pester, poll, probe, pump, query, question, quiz, roast, survey, suspect, test* (≠ answer, -avoid, conceal, confide, -discount, -disregard, -duck, -evade, feign, hide, -ignore, mislead, -neglect, obstruct, -overlook, -rebuff, retort, -sidestep, silence, stall, stonewall)

INTERRUPT (→): *-abort, arrest, battle, block, bother, break, -cancel, check, crash, cut, defer, delay, disconnect, -discontinue, disrupt, disturb, disunite, divide, end, -halt, hinder, impede, infringe, insinuate, intercept, obstruct, oppose, pause, postpone, -prevent, protest, punctuate, separate, sever, shelve, short-circuit, stall, stay, stop, suspend* (≠ advance, aid, assist, begin, connect, continue, defend, expedite, facilitate, free, frogmarch, grease, hasten, help, march, permit, promote, quicken, support)

INTERRUPT (/): *add, barrack, blackjack, bother, bully, contribute, disrupt, disturb, harass, heckle, impede, inject, interject, interpolate, interpose, intimidate, postpone, punctuate, relieve* (≠ allow, assist, attend, combine, compel, encourage, expedite, facilitate, further, heed, leave, support)

INTERSECT (→): *bisect, cleave, connect, contact, crisscross, cross, crosscut, cut, divide, entwine, interconnect, interweave, meet, overlap, part, pass, separate, sever, split, tangle, touch, traverse* (≠ abut, -avoid, -bypass, -circumvent, combine, detour, disjoin, hedge, hem, miss, nudge, observe, overlook, -sidestep, skip, skirt, unite, watch)

INTERVIEW (←): *ask, canvass, challenge, check, consult, cross-examine, cross-question, debrief, examine, grill, hammer, inspect, interrogate, investigate, parry, poll, probe, pump, query, question, quiz, research, solicit, survey, test* (≠ answer, assure, attest, blab, blaze, blurt, confess, confirm, counterpunch, deflect, -dodge, hint, parry, report, retort, stonewall)

INTIMATE (→): *allege, allude, camouflage, communicate, couch, embed, evoke, hint, impart, implant, imply, infer, infiltrate, inject, insert, insinuate, instill, introduce, lodge, mention, signal, suggest, veil* (≠ announce, bellow, blab, blurt, conceal, conclude, confess, confirm, deduce, derive, expose, extrapolate, gather, hide, prove, publicize, scan, scrutinize, surmise, trumpet) **(¿) ABSTRACTION ALERT. Concrete goals essential!**

INTIMIDATE (/): *affright, alarm, appall, awe, badger, bait, blackjack, blackmail, bludgeon, browbeat, brutalize, buffalo, bulldoze, bully, bullyrag, caution, chide, chill, coerce, compel, constrain, cow, daunt, demoralize, -deter, discompose, disconcert, dishearten, dismay, disquiet, distress, disturb, domineer, dragoon, enforce, extort, force, frighten, harass, hector, henpeck, horrify, hound, menace, muscle, oblige, overawe, perturb, press, pressure, psych, railroad, repress, ride, ruffle, savage, scare, shock, spook, startle, steamroller, strong-arm, subdue, terrify, terrorize, threaten, torment, trash-talk, unman, unnerve, upset, vex, victimize, warn, wrong* (≠ amuse, assist, assure, blandish, bolster, buoy, buttress, cajole, calm, charm, cheer, coax, comfort, console, convince, delight, embolden, encourage, flatter, glad-hand, hearten, help, humor, inspire, lull, mellow, mitigate, moderate, mollify, pacify, palaver, persuade, pity, placate, please, protect, reassure, release, schmooze, soft-soap, solace, soothe, steady, steel, sweet-talk, toughen, wheedle, woo)

INTOXICATE (→): *animate, arouse, bewitch, captivate, charge, charm, compel, delight, distract, electrify, enchant, engross, enliven, enrapture, enslave, ensnare, enthrall, entice, entrance, excite, exhilarate, fascinate, fixate, fuel, galvanize, grab, grip, hold, hook, hypnotize, immerse, incite, inspire, interest, intrigue, inveigle, invigorate, lure, mellow, mesmerize, mitigate, mollify, occupy, overpower, overwhelm, please, possess, preoccupy, provoke, razzle-dazzle, relax, relieve, rivet, spellbind, stimulate, stun, tantalize, thrill, tickle, titillate, tranquilize, transfix* (≠ aggravate, agitate, alarm, annoy, bore, bother, bug, convulse, demoralize, demotivate, discourage, dishearten, disillusion, dispirit, enrage, hallucinate, harass, hector, horrify, incite, infuriate, jade, jar, jolt, knacker, menace, poke, prod, rankle, rattle, repel, repulse, rile, roil, rouse, shake, shock, sicken, spur, startle, stir, terrify, tire, torment, tranquilize, unnerve, upset, wake, weary, worry, wound)

INTOXICATE (←): *activate, amuse, awaken, boost, brighten, buoy, charge, cheer, content, dazzle, delight, elate, electrify, elevate, energize, enliven, enrapture, enthuse, excite, exhilarate, gladden, gratify, ignite, inflame, inspire, invigorate, jolt, juice, lift, light, motivate, please, quicken, razzle-dazzle, refresh, rejoice, restimulate, restore, revitalize, revive, rouse, satisfy, spark, stimulate, thrill, transport, uplift, vitalize, wake, warm, wow* (≠ bore, bother, bug, burden, deaden, demoralize, demotivate, depress, discourage, dishearten, dispirit, dissuade, distress, dull, encumber, enervate, frustrate, harass, hassle, hurt, oppress, punish, repress, sadden, sicken, suppress, tire, upset, weaken, weary, worry)

INTOXICATE (/): *anesthetize, appease, assuage, befuddle, bewilder, calm, confound, confuse, daze, deaden, discomfit, disconcert, dismay, dizzy, dope, dose, drug, dull, hush, immobilize, inebriate, inflame, jar, lull, medicate, muddle, narcotize, nonplus, numb, pacify, paralyze, perplex, puzzle, quell, quench, quiet, relax, sedate, settle, shake, silence, soothe, still, stupefy, subdue, torpefy, unbalance* (≠ alarm, alert, awaken, center, clear, concentrate, focus, hallucinate, jolt, poke, rouse, shake, sober, startle, steady, stir, wake)

INTRIGUE (←): *absorb, amuse, animate, arouse, arrest, attract, bait, beguile, bemuse, bewitch, busy, captivate, charm, consume, dazzle, delight, distract, draw, electrify, enchant, energize, engage, engross, entertain, enthrall, enthuse, excite, exhilarate, fascinate, generate, grab, grip, hog, hook, hypnotize, immerse, impress, inspire, interest, involve, kindle, mesmerize, monopolize, motivate, mystify, obsess, occupy, perplex, pique, please, preoccupy, pull, puzzle, rivet, stimulate, stir, tantalize, thrill, tickle, titillate, wow* (≠ answer, bore, bother, bug, burden, clarify, discourage, disturb, explain, frustrate, henpeck, irk, irritate, jade, nag, nauseate, needle, nettle, pigeonhole, repel, repulse, sadden, satisfy, sicken, solve, sour, tire, unnerve, upset, weary, worry) **(¿) ABSTRACTION ALERT. Concrete goals essential!**

INTUIT (←): *appreciate, apprehend, assume, clock, comprehend, conclude, conjecture, deduce, derive, detect, diagnose, discern, divine,* *experience, extrapolate, feel, foretell, gather, grasp, grok, guess, infer, notice, observe, perceive, presume, prognosticate, realize, reason, recognize, sense, suppose, surmise, suspect, suss, understand, wonder* (≠ adjudge, authenticate, corroborate, detect, determine, discover, misapprehend, misconstrue, misdiagnose, misinterpret, misread, miss, misunderstand, prove, substantiate, verify) **(¿) ABSTRACTION ALERT. Concrete goals essential!**

INURE (+): *acclimate, acclimatize, accustom, adapt, adjust, anneal, balance, bolster, boost, brace, buttress, calibrate, case-harden, center, compose, condition, desensitize, embattle, enforce, familiarize, forearm, fortify, habituate, harden, immunize, indurate, invigorate, limber, naturalize, prop, quarantine, reinforce, root, season, steady, steel, strengthen, support, temper, tone, toughen, train, vitalize* (≠ castrate, cripple, debilitate, emasculate, enervate, enfeeble, exhaust, frighten, hamstring, harm, incapacitate, infect, sap, sensitize, shrivel, soften, unman, unnerve, weaken, wither, wizen, worry)

INVADE (→): *assail, assault, attack, battle, beleaguer, beset, besiege, blockade, breach, burst, charge, colonize, combat, conquer, cross, crush, despoil, dominate, fight, garrison, gate-crash, harass, infect, infest, infiltrate, infringe, interrupt, loot, maraud, occupy, overcome, overpower, overrun, overthrow, overwhelm, penetrate, permeate, pervade, pillage, plunder, possess, raid, ransack, ravage, rush, sack, seize, steamroller, storm, strike, strip, subdue, subject, subjugate, swarm, trespass, vanquish, violate* (≠ aid, ban, bar, barricade, befriend, block, cede, cover, defend, defy, evacuate, exorcise, expel, guard, oppose, patrol, protect, quarantine, repel, resist, safeguard, shelter, shield, submit, support, surrender, survive, sustain, uphold, ward, withdraw, withstand, yield)

INVALIDATE (/): *abnegate, abolish, abrogate, annul, -cancel, challenge, confute, contradict, counteract, counterbalance, debate, debilitate, deep-six, delegitimize, delete, -deny, destroy, disable, disavow, disclaim, discredit, dismiss, -disown, disprove, dispute, disqualify, dissolve, divorce, doubt, efface, eliminate, eradicate, extinguish, impair, -negate, neutralize, -nullify, obliterate, override, overrule, overthrow, quash, rebut, refute, -reject, -repudiate, -rescind, retract, revoke, scotch, scruple, suspect, terminate, undercut, undermine, undo, -veto, vitiate, -void, weaken, withdraw* (≠ affirm, authorize, certify, confer, confirm, constitute, corroborate, demonstrate, enact, endorse, entitle, establish, formalize, legalize, legislate, legitimize, notarize, ordain, prove, qualify, ratify, rubber-stamp, sanction, substantiate, validate)

INVEIGLE (←): *allure, bait, bamboozle, beguile, blandish, blarney, bluff, bribe, bullshit, butter, cajole, charm, cheat, coax, con, convince, court, decoy, dupe, ensnare, entice, entrap, flannel, flatter, fool, fox, fudge, glad-hand, gull, honey, hook, influence, ingratiate, leverage, lure, maneuver, manipulate, massage, milk, oil, palaver, persuade, schmooze, seduce, sell, snooker, snow, soap, stroke, sucker, sweet-talk, tantalize, tease, tempt, trick, trigger, urge, wheedle, win, woo, wow* (≠ assume, assure, believe, browbeat, bully, chill, coerce, demand, demotivate, -deter, discourage, disenchant, disgust, dissuade, force, free, insist, liberate, muscle, nobble, order, -prevent, railroad, release, repel, repulse, sandbag, steamroll, trash-talk, trust, warn)

INVENT (+): *ad-lib, author, brainstorm, brew, coin, compose, conceive, concoct, construct, contrive, create, design, devise, discover, envisage, envision, execute, extemporize, fabricate, fake, fashion, find, forge, form, formulate, frame, ghostwrite, hallucinate, hatch, imagine, improve, improvise, inaugurate, initiate, innovate, machine, make, manufacture, mint, originate, picture, pioneer, plan, produce, script, sculpt, visualize, weave, wing* (≠ adopt, approximate, borrow, clone, coopt, copy, copycat, duplicate, emulate, eradicate, follow, ghostwrite, imitate, match, mimic, repeat, replicate, reproduce, steal)

INVENTORY (+): *account, add, appraise, assess, audit, calculate, catalog, categorize, check, classify, clock, collect, compute, conclude, deduce, determine, distribute, divide, document, enumerate, evaluate, figure, file, gauge, group, inspect, itemize, journalize, learn, list, log, measure, note, number, numerate, order, organize, profile, quantify, quantize, rank, reckon, record, register, scan, scope, scrutinize, slot, sort, stock, study, summarize, supply, systematize, tabulate, tally, total, weigh* (≠ confuse, delete, diffuse, disorder, disorganize, dispense, dole, estimate, guess, jumble, lose, mislay, misplace, miss, mistake, presume, scatter, scramble, surmise)

INVEST (→): *advance, back, bankroll, bestow, capitalize, contribute, dedicate, devote, endow, entrust, fund, furnish, give, grant, infuse, lend, loan, offer, place, plunge, provide, sink, spend, sponsor, stake, subsidize, supply, support, underwrite* (≠ bankrupt, beggar, borrow, cadge, cheat, defund, deprive, divest, draw, embezzle, extract, mooch, pilfer, remove, rob, ruin, squander, steal, stiff, stint, waste, withdraw, withhold)

INVEST (→): *accord, authorize, award, bequeath, bestow, bless, charge, confer, consecrate, cover, create, dignify, dower, empower, enable, endow, enhance, enrich, enthrone, establish, favor, gift, grant, heighten, honor, inaugurate, induct, initiate, install, instate, license, mandate, ordain, provide, sanction, supply, vest, will* (≠ banish, bum, cannibalize, consume, cripple, debilitate, deplete, dethrone, disbar, disinherit, -disown, dispossess, divest, drain, exhaust, expel, leech, overthrow, ruin, skimp, stint, strip, topple)

INVEST (+): *accoutre, apparel, arm, array, attire, bedeck, caparison, cloak, clothe, costume, deck, drape, dress, equip, frock, furnish, garb, gown, jacket, mantle, outfit, robe, suit, swaddle, swathe, tailor, tog, uniform, vest, wrap* (≠ denude, disarray, disrobe, divest, strip, unbuckle, unbutton, unclothe, uncover, undrape, undress, unveil)

INVEST (+): *accredit, affirm, allow, approve, authorize, certify, clear, commission, confirm, credential, empower, enable, endorse, enfranchise, entitle, greenlight, inaugurate, induct, initiate, install, instate, let, license, okay, permit, privilege, qualify, sanction, validate, vest, warrant* (≠ ban, bar, block, constrain, -deny, disallow, disbar, discourage, disenfranchise, disqualify, enjoin, -exclude, foil, -forbid, hinder, impede, inhibit, -interdict, monkey-wrench, obstruct, -omit, outlaw, -prevent, -prohibit, proscribe, stop, -veto)

INVESTIGATE (←): *analyze, browse, bug, calculate, case, categorize, comb, conclude, connect, consider, consult, contrast, correlate, cross-examine, cruise, deduce, differentiate, distill, examine, explore, expose, extrapolate, eye, eyeball, frisk, grill, hunt, inspect, interrogate, interview, learn, muckrake, out, peruse, poke, police, probe, prowl, question, rake, ransack, read, reconnoiter, reference, reinvestigate, research, review, rifle, scan, scour, scout, scrutinize, search, seek, sift, skim, sleuth, sort, spy, study, subdivide, surf, suss, tap, trawl, uncover, unearth, wiretap* (≠ answer, assume, blind, block, bury, camouflage, censor, cloak, cloud, conceal, -discount, disguise, -disregard, ensconce, forget, garble, hide, hush, -ignore, muddy, mystify, -neglect, niche, obfuscate, obscure, -overlook, presume, redact, scramble, screen, secure, shield, stash, stifle, tuck, veil, witness)

INVIGORATE (+): *abet, activate, actuate, amp, animate, arouse, assure, awaken, boost, brace, brighten, buoy, charge, cheer, comfort, console, drive, elate, electrify, elevate, embolden, encourage, energize, enkindle, enliven, exalt, excite, exhilarate, ferment, fire, foment, fortify, freshen, galvanize, generate, gentrify, ginger, gladden, harden, hearten, impel, incite, inflame, infuse, inspire, instigate, intoxicate, jazz, jolly, jolt, juice, jump-start, kindle, lift, lighten, liven, motivate, move, nerve, prioritize, promote, propel, provoke, quicken, raise, rally, reactivate, reanimate, reassure, reawaken, recharge, recreate, reenergize, refresh, regenerate, reinvigorate, rejuvenate, rekindle, renew, restimulate, restore, resurrect, resuscitate, revitalize, revive, rouse, shock, spark, spike, steel, stiffen, stimulate, stir, strengthen, supercharge, sustain, tantalize, tease, tempt, trigger, uplift, vitalize, vivify, wake* (≠ bore, cannibalize, castrate, check, concern, consume, cripple, curb, dampen, daunt, deactivate, deaden, debilitate, demoralize, demotivate, deplete, depress, -deter, discourage, dishearten, dispirit, drain, dull, emasculate, enervate, enfeeble, exhaust, fatigue, freeze, frustrate, harass, inactivate, inhibit, jade, kill, knacker, leech, overextend, paralyze, quell, quench, repress, restrain, sap, sedate, shrivel, slow, stagnate, stale, stall, still, stunt, suppress, tire, tucker, undermine, unman, weaken, wear, weary, wither, wizen, worry, wound)

INVITE (←): *allow, ask, beg, bid, call, command, conjure, countenance, demand, encourage, entertain, entreat, face, insist, invoke, lead, legalize, permit, persuade, petition, ply, press, propose, provoke, request, seek, solicit, suggest, summon, urge, welcome, will* (≠ -avoid, baffle, ban, bar, battle, block, combat, condemn, confound, daunt, -desert, -deter, discourage, dissuade, fight, -halt, hamper, hinder, hobble, -ignore, obstruct, oppose, -prevent, protest, -refuse, -reject, stall, stop, stymie, -thwart, undermine)

INVITE (←): *allure, attract, beguile, coax, court, draw, entice, hail, hunt, inveigle, lead, lure, provoke, search, seek, solicit, tantalize, tease, tempt, vamp, welcome, woo* (≠ ban, bar, barricade, block, discourage, disenchant, disgust, -ignore, -refuse, -reject, repel, repulse, -shun, -spurn)

INVOKE (→): *advance, apply, beget, begin, breed, bring, catalyze, cite, create, cultivate, decide, deploy, determine, develop, effect, effectuate, enact, encourage, enforce, engender, establish, execute, father, forward, foster, found, further, generate, implement, inaugurate, induce, initiate, innovate, institute, introduce, launch, make, midwife, nourish, nurture, pioneer, produce, promote, prompt, render, set, spawn, start, use, yield* (≠ abolish, crush, curb, dampen, demolish, destroy, doom, extinguish, impede, limit, quash, quell, repress, restrict, smother, squash, stifle, subdue, suppress)

INVOKE (←): *accost, address, adjure, approach, beg, beseech, bring, charge, conjure, covet, crave, entice, entreat, foster, further, greet, implore, importune, imprecate, induce, invite, muster, nourish, nurture, petition, plead, prompt, rally, request, seek, solicit, spawn, summon, woo* (≠ banish, block, dispel, eject, -exclude, -forbid, impede, inhibit, limit, -ostracize, oust, quell, restrain, restrict)

INVOLVE (←): *absorb, admit, allege, allure, attract, beguile, bemuse, bewitch, busy, buttonhole, captivate, charm, commit, concern, distract, embroil, enchant, encompass, encumber, engage, engross, engulf, enmesh, ensnare, entangle, enthrall, entrance, fascinate, grip, hog, hold, hypnotize, immerse, implicate, include, incorporate, incriminate, interest, intrigue, mesmerize, monopolize, obsess, occupy, preoccupy, rivet* (≠ bore, -bypass, -circumvent, detour, -elude, -evade, extricate, jade, miss, -omit, release, remove, separate, -shirk, -shun, tire, weary) **(¿) ABSTRACTION ALERT. Concrete goals essential!**

INVOLVE (+): *access, add, admit, align, amalgamate, assimilate, blend, bracket, carry, combine, compose, comprehend, consolidate, constitute, contain, cover, embody, embrace, enclose, encompass, entail, enter, form, harmonize, hold, homogenize, include, incorporate, insert, integrate, introduce, join, make, merge, mingle, mix, number, overlap, own, possess, receive, reckon, span, subsume, take, unite* (≠ alienate, ban, bar, debar, -deny, disaffect, eliminate, except, -exclude, isolate, leave, lose, mislay, misplace, -omit, oppose, orphan, -ostracize, oust, -preclude, -prevent, -prohibit, -refuse, -reject, seclude, -shun)

INVOLVE (/): *accuse, associate, attaint, blame, charge, compromise, concern, connect, embarrass, embroil, ensnare, entangle, fault, finger, frame, impeach, implicate, include, incriminate, indict, mortify, shame* (≠ absolve, acquit, alibi, clear, exculpate, excuse, exonerate, forgive, free, pardon, release, spare, vindicate)

IRK (/): *abrade, affront, aggravate, agitate, anger, annoy, antagonize, badger, bait, bedevil, bother, bug, bullyrag, burn, chafe, chagrin, devil, discomfort, discommode, discompose, disconcert, disgust, displease, disquiet, distress, disturb, eat, enrage, exasperate, exercise, freak, fret, frost, gall, get, hagride, harass, harry, hassle, heckle, hector, hound, incense, incommode, inconvenience, inflame, infuriate, insult, irritate, madden, miff, nag, needle, nettle, niggle, nitpick, noodge, offend, outrage, overset, peeve, persecute, perturb, pester, pique, plague, provoke, rankle, rasp, rattle, rile, roil, rouse, ruffle, spite, tease, trouble, undo, unhinge, unsettle, upset, vex, weary, worry* (≠ amuse, appease, assuage, assure, baby, buffer, calm, cheer, coddle, comfort, console, content, delight, gladden, gratify, humor, lull, mellow, mitigate, moderate, mollify, oblige, pacify, pamper, placate, please, propitiate, quiet, reassure, satisfy, settle, soothe, stabilize, steady, thrill, woo, wow)

IRRITATE (/): *affront, aggravate, agitate, anger, annoy, antagonize, badger, bait, bedevil, bother, bug, bullyrag, burn, chafe, chaff, chagrin, confuse, devil, discomfort, discompose, disconcert, displease, disquiet, distemper, distress, disturb, earbash, eat, enrage, exasperate, exercise, fret, frost, gall, get, goad, hagride, harass, harry, hassle, heckle, hound, hurt, incense, inflame, infuriate, insult, irk, jar, madden, miff, nag, needle, nettle, niggle, nitpick, offend, outrage, pain, peeve, persecute, perturb, pester, pique, plague, provoke, rankle, rasp, rattle, rile, roil, rouse, ruffle, sour, spite, tease, torment, try, undo, unhinge, unsettle, upset, vex, victimize, wear, worry, wrong* (≠ accommodate, aid, amuse, appease, assuage, assure, buffer, calm, cheer, comfort, console, content, cushion, delight, entertain, favor, featherbed, gladden, gratify, help, humor, lull, mellow, mitigate, moderate, mollify, nurture, oblige, pacify, pamper, placate, please, propitiate, protect, quiet, reassure, relax, reward, satiate, satisfy, solace, soothe, spoil, spoon-feed)

IRRITATE (/): *abrade, afflict, aggravate, burn, chafe, excoriate, flay, fret, gall, graze, hurt, inflame, intensify, itch, pain, peel, rub, scrape, scratch, sensitize, sharpen, skin, sting, swell* (≠ advantage, alleviate, assist, benefit, butter, calm, cool, ease, grease, heal, lubricate, moisturize, nurse, oil, salve, smooth, soothe, treat)

ISOLATE (/): *alienate, ban, banish, bar, blackball, blacklist, -boycott, cloister, closet, compartmentalize, confine, cordon, decouple, deport, -desert, detach, disaffect, disbar, disconnect, disengage, divide, divorce, eject, eliminate, evict, -exclude, -excommunicate, exile, expatriate, expel, extirpate, extradite, insulate, marginalize, maroon, -omit, -ostracize, oust, part, picket, -prohibit, protest, quarantine, -reject, remove, screen, seclude, segregate, separate, sequester, sever, sunder, uncouple, unhitch* (≠ abut, assimilate, associate, attach, bind, blend, border, combine, confuse, conjoin, connect, couple, desegregate, discharge, embrace, fuse, gather, hybridize, include, incorporate, integrate, join, liberate, link, loose, marry, meld, mingle, network, reintegrate, release, reunite, synthesize, unify, unite, wed)

ITEMIZE (+): *calculate, catalog, chart, check, cite, compute, count, delineate, detail, diagram, document, enumerate, estimate, figure, graph, instance, inventory, list, mark, mention, name, number, numerate, outline, particularize, pinpoint, reckon, record, rehearse, specify, stipulate, tabulate, tally* (≠ addle, baffle, bury, conceal, confound, confuse, disguise, disorganize, -disregard, estimate, generalize, guess, hide, -ignore, jumble, lose, mask, miss, muddle, mystify, -omit, -overlook, perplex, puzzle, scramble, shuffle)

J

JAB (→): *bayonet, blow, box, breach, break, buck, bump, bunt, contact, cut, damage, dig, elbow, flick, gaff, gimlet, gore, harpoon, hit, impale, jog, knife, knock, lance, lunge, nudge, peck, perforate, pick, pierce, pike, pink, poke, poniard, prick, prod, prong, punch, puncture, push, ram, riddle, shank, shiv, skewer, slice, spear, spike, spindle, spit, stab, stick, tap, thrust, touch, transfix* (≠ armor, -avoid, block, close, counterpunch, defend, deflect, dissuade, -dodge, drag, draw, -duck, fill, guard, heal, help, hold, miss, parry, patch, plug, protect, pull, repel, seal, sew, shield, -shun, withdraw, yank)

JACK (←): *bilk, bogart, boost, cadge, defraud, elevate, filch, grab, hijack, hike, hoist, hotwire, increase, inflate, lift, nobble, poach, program, pull, purloin, raise, schnorr, scrounge, seize, shanghai, snaffle, snag, snatch, steal, swipe, take, weasel, wheedle* (≠ block, calm, defend, guard, maintain, place, position, preserve, protect, restore, return, safeguard, secure, shield)

JADE (/): *annoy, bore, bother, bug, dampen, deaden, debilitate, demoralize, demotivate, desensitize, devitalize, diminish, disable, disappoint, discourage, disenchant, dishearten, dispirit, drain, dull, enervate, enfeeble, exhaust, fatigue, frustrate, irk, irritate, knacker, nauseate, needle, nettle, numb, paralyze, sap, stagnate, stale, stifle, tire, trouble, underwhelm, vex, weaken, wear, weary, worry* (≠ absorb, amuse, attract, busy, captivate, charm, enchant, energize, engage, engross, entertain, enthrall, excite, fascinate, galvanize, grip, hypnotize, immerse, inspire, interest, intrigue, involve, mesmerize, monopolize, obsess, occupy, preoccupy, rally, rouse, seduce, stimulate, stir) **(¿) ABSTRACTION ALERT. Concrete goals essential!**

JAIL (/): *apprehend, arrest, bar, bind, book, bust, cage, can, capture, catch, closet, commit, condemn, confine, constrain, convict, detain, dungeon, enchain, fetter, gate, handcuff, hold, ice, immure, impound, impress, imprison, incarcerate, institutionalize, intern, jug, keep, limit, lock, manacle, nab, pen, pinch, remand, restrain, restrict, seize, sentence, shackle, shanghai, shut, snaffle, stockade, straightjacket, trammel, trap* (≠ accuse, acquit, alibi, bail, discharge, emancipate, enfranchise, exculpate, exonerate, free, incriminate, liberate, loose, manumit, pardon, redeem, release, spare, unbind, uncage, unchain, unfetter, vindicate)

JAM (→): *bloat, block, brim, bulk, bung, charge, chock, choke, clog, close, clot, confine, congest, constipate, cork, cram, crowd, crush, dam, drench, elbow, fill, flood, force, glut, gum, -halt, heap, honeycomb, insert, inundate, jam-pack, jostle, load, lock, mat, obstruct, occlude, overcharge,* *overcrowd, overfill, overflow, overstuff, overwhelm, pack, penetrate, plug, press, push, ram, refill, refresh, reload, repack, replenish, sandwich, sardine, saturate, shoehorn, shove, silt, squash, squeeze, squish, stall, stem, stick, stop, stopper, stopple, stuff, stymie, surfeit, swamp, thrust, -thwart, wedge* (≠ aerate, bleed, clean, clear, consume, core, deplete, dislodge, drain, draw, eliminate, empty, evacuate, excavate, exhaust, extract, flush, free, hollow, leach, lighten, open, oxygenate, purge, remove, scoop, scour, sweep, unblock, unclog, unpack, unstop, vacate, ventilate, void)

JAR (→): *agitate, annoy, bandy, chafe, challenge, clash, consider, contest, dare, debate, defy, disconcert, discuss, dispute, disturb, fight, gall, grate, grind, hassle, irk, irritate, jangle, jerk, jog, jolt, jostle, kick, mismatch, nag, needle, nitpick, offend, overset, protest, rasp, rattle, shake, trouble, upset, wrangle* (≠ accept, accord, align, balance, blend, -bypass, calm, center, compose, drag, drop, equalize, fit, harmonize, lull, match, mitigate, pacify, pull, push, root, set, settle, smooth, soothe, steady, still)

JEOPARDIZE (/): *bet, bias, blackjack, bluff, bobble, botch, brutalize, bugger, bungle, chance, compromise, endanger, expose, fumble, gamble, half-ass, hazard, imperil, intimidate, menace, predetermine, prejudice, risk, stake, subject, target, terrorize, threaten, undermine, venture, wager, weaken* (≠ defend, guard, maintain, patrol, preserve, protect, rescue, resume, safeguard, save, shelter, shield)

JERK (←): *bounce, buck, bump, dislodge, drag, draw, force, grab, haul, heave, hitch, jig, jiggle, jog, joggle, jolt, jounce, lug, move, pitch, pluck, pull, rip, shake, snag, snatch, stagger, strain, tear, throw, tug, tweak, twitch, wrench, wrest, wring, yank* (≠ bash, elbow, grasp, grip, hold, jog, jostle, nudge, pin, press, push, ram, release, shove, shunt, stroke, thrust)

JETTISON (→): *-abandon, abdicate, abolish, annihilate, bandy, belch, cant, cashier, cast, chuck, -desert, discard, disgorge, dismiss, -ditch, drop, dump, eject, eliminate, eradicate, exorcise, expel, expunge, exterminate, extinguish, extirpate, fling, -forsake, heave, junk, liquidate, lose, offload, pitch, plonk, -reject, relinquish, remove, -repudiate, root, scrap, shed, shuck, skitter, sling, slough, throw, toss, trash, unload, upchuck, vomit* (≠ accept, accumulate, acquire, adopt, allow, approve, burden, choose, collect, compile, embrace, employ, gather, glean, hold, hound, keep, load, lumber, maintain, pick, poach, procure, ratify, recycle, remainder, retain, retrofit, return, salvage, sanction, save, scavenge, secure, steal, stockpile, sustain, take, use, utilize)

JEWEL (+): *adorn, array, beautify, bedazzle, bedeck, bedizen, bejewel, bestow, brighten, deck, decorate, diamond, embellish, enrich, fancify, garnish, gem, gild, glamorize, glitter, glitz, grace, impearl, ornament, pearl, provide, set, spangle, spruce, stud, tinsel, tool, trim* (≠ bare, besmirch, blemish, blot, deface, disgrace, dismantle, divest, dull, efface, expose, harshen, mar, roughen, scar, shame, simplify, smudge, spoil, stain, strip, sully, tarnish)

JILT (/): *-abandon, bar, belch, betray, blackball, blacklist, check, chop, chuck, clip, crop, cull, curtail, -cut, deceive, deep-six, -deny, -desert, disallow, disappoint, disapprove, discard, discharge, disclaim, disgorge, dismiss, -ditch, drop, dump, eject, eliminate, evacuate, excise, -exclude, -forsake, jettison, junk, leave, lop, offload, oppugn, -ostracize, oust, -reject, relinquish, scrap, shear, shed, snip, spew, -spurn, trash, vent, vomit, wrong* (≠ befriend, charm, chase, court, entice, hold, keep, latch, maintain, oblige, pursue, regard, romance, shadow, stalk, take, tantalize, target, tease, tempt, track, win, woo)

JIMMY (→): *access, blow, breach, break, bust, crack, crowbar, detach, disengage, disjoin, divide, elevate, expose, force, hack, hoist, invade, jack, jam, lever, lift, open, part, penetrate, pick, pierce, prize, pry, pull, reveal, separate, split, unbolt, unfasten, unlock, unseal* (≠ bar, barricade, bolt, brace, clinch, close, connect, defend, defy, fasten, guard, join, keep, lock, maintain, padlock, preserve, protect, repair, resist, seal, secure, shield, shut)

JINX (/): *afflict, anguish, annoy, bedevil, beset, besiege, bespell, bewitch, blight, charm, checkmate, condemn, confound, cripple, crush, curse, damn, discourage, distress, doom, enchant, ensorcel, fret, frustrate, harass, harm, hex, impair, irk, irritate, maledict, mar, pester, plague, poison, pollute, ruin, scourge, spike, stain, tease, torment, torture, trouble, vex, whammy, witch, worry* (≠ advantage, aid, assist, benefit, bless, boost, cure, defend, enhance, further, nurture, optimize, overhaul, profit, promote, protect, rectify, remedy, rescue, secure, shield, ward)

JOG (→): *activate, arouse, elicit, encourage, energize, goad, hasten, impel, incite, incur, induce, inspire, instigate, joggle, jostle, make, motivate, move, nudge, prod, produce, prompt, propel, provoke, remind, spur, stimulate, stir, trigger, urge* (≠ block, deactivate, demotivate, discourage, dissuade, freeze, -halt, hamper, hinder, impede, jam, knock, pinion, postpone, -prevent, pull, repress, stall, stop, stunt, stymie, suppress)

JOIN (+): *add, adhere, amalgamate, annex, articulate, assemble, associate, attach, bind, blend, bond, braid, button, cement, chain, cluster, coalesce, combine, compile, compound, concatenate, congregate, conjoin, conjugate, connect, convene, cord, couple, dovetail, entwine, fasten, fuse, gather, glue, hitch, hook, hybridize, incorporate, integrate, interconnect, interlink, intertwine, knit, link, marry, match, mate, meet, mend, merge, mortar, network, raddle, recombine, reconnect, reintegrate, rejoin, reunify, reunite, sew, splice, string, synthesize, tie, unify, unite, weave, weld, wire, yoke, zip* (≠ break, cleave, detach, diffuse, disband, disconnect, disengage, disjoin, disjoint, disperse, disunite, divide, divorce, estrange, isolate, mismatch, orphan, part, rupture, scatter, seclude, section, separate, sever, split, sunder, tear, unbraid, unchain, uncouple, unhitch, unlink, unmarry, unsew, unyoke)

JOIN (+): *accompany, ally, associate, attend, buttonhole, chaperone, combine, conduct, direct, enlist, enroll, escort, follow, guide, incorporate, integrate, lead, partner, pilot, reintegrate, shepherd, show, squire, steer,* *team, unify, unite, usher, waylay* (≠ -abandon, alienate, -avoid, -bypass, -circumvent, -desert, detour, disband, -ditch, divorce, dump, -exclude, exile, fire, follow, -forsake, isolate, -omit, -ostracize, oust, quarantine, -reject, seclude, separate, split)

JOLT (→): *buck, bump, churn, convulse, crank, drag, elbow, grab, hitch, jar, jerk, jig, jiggle, jog, joggle, jostle, jounce, knock, lug, nudge, pitch, pluck, pull, rip, rock, shake, shove, shunt, snatch, stagger, sway, tear, tug, tweak, twitch, wrench, wrest, wring, yank* (≠ calm, -circumvent, comfort, -dodge, freeze, hold, lull, mellow, order, pacify, paralyze, placate, -sidestep, skip, soothe, stabilize, steady)

JOLT (→): *affright, alarm, amaze, appall, astonish, astound, awe, blindside, chill, crush, daunt, demoralize, discomfort, discompose, disconcert, disgust, dismay, dispirit, displease, disquiet, distress, disturb, dumbfound, electrify, emasculate, excite, fire, flabbergast, floor, freak, frighten, galvanize, gobsmack, horrify, invigorate, jar, nauseate, offend, outrage, overpower, overwhelm, panic, perturb, razzle-dazzle, repel, revolt, rouse, scandalize, scare, scarify, shake, shock, sicken, spook, stagger, startle, stimulate, stir, stun, stupefy, surprise, terrify, terrorize, thrill, undo, unman, unnerve, unsettle, unstring, upset, wow* (≠ anesthetize, assure, blunt, bore, buffer, calm, charm, cheer, comfort, console, cushion, dampen, deaden, delight, dull, entice, gratify, help, humor, knacker, lull, mellow, mitigate, moderate, mollify, numb, pacify, pad, placate, please, reassure, rejoice, sap, sedate, soothe, stagnate, stale, stall, tempt, tickle, torpefy, tranquilize, weaken)

JOSTLE (→): *bang, bulldoze, bump, butt, catapult, crash, crowd, drive, elbow, frogmarch, goad, hustle, impel, jab, jam, jog, joggle, jolt, knock, march, move, muscle, nudge, poke, press, prod, push, ram, scramble, shake, shoulder, shove, slam, squeeze, strike, throng, thrust, trigger, urge* (≠ balance, bind, -bypass, center, chain, compose, -evade, fasten, grasp, grip, hobble, hold, immobilize, manacle, pin, pinion, shackle, -sidestep, skirt, stabilize, steady, still)

JUDGE (←): *account, add, analyze, appraise, ascertain, assess, benchmark, calculate, call, compare, compute, conclude, conjecture, consider, count, critique, deduce, detect, determine, discern, distinguish, divide, educe, enumerate, estimate, evaluate, examine, extrapolate, figure, gather, gauge, guess, infer, measure, number, numerate, place, quantify, rank, rate, rationalize, read, reason, reckon, review, sample, schedule, scheme, score, second-guess, study, sum, suppose, systematize, tally, total, triangulate, try, understand, value, weigh* (≠ addle, assume, baffle, befuddle, bewilder, bury, calibrate, conceal, confound, confuse, deceive, defraud, disguise, -disregard, gaslight, hide, -ignore, imagine, mask, miscalculate, misgauge, misinterpret, misjudge, misread, miss, mistake, misunderstand, muddle, mystify, -neglect, obscure, overestimate, perplex, puzzle, trick, trust, underestimate, wonder)

JUDGE (←): *accept, affirm, ascertain, assume, await, believe, conclude, conjecture, construe, contemplate, decide, deduce, derive, determine, discern, extrapolate, find, gather, guess, hold, imagine, infer, interpret, maintain, presume, profess, rationalize, read, reason, suppose, surmise, think, trust, understand* (≠ challenge, contest, counter, debunk, -deny, discover, discredit, expose, oppose, perceive, predetermine, prove, verify)

JUDGE (+): *adjudge, adjudicate, arbitrate, conclude, condemn, consider, decide, decree, deliberate, determine, discipline, find, hear, mediate, moderate, mull, negotiate, penalize, ponder, pronounce, prosecute, punish, referee, resolve, rule, sentence, settle, try, umpire, weigh* (≠ absolve, acquit, alibi, -avoid, -bypass, commute, compliment, debate, -duck, exculpate, excuse, exonerate, favor, forgive, help, incriminate, legalize, pardon, ransom, release, reprieve, reward, skirt, spare, vindicate) **(¿) ABSTRACTION ALERT. Concrete goals essential!**

JUGGLE (←): *adjust, alter, balance, bamboozle, beguile, betray, bluff, buffalo, burn, catch, change, cheat, con, conjure, cook, cozen, dazzle, deceive, delude, disguise, doctor, double-cross, dupe, equalize, fake, falsify, fiddle, finagle, finesse, fix, fool, game, gull, handle, hoax, hocus-pocus, hoodwink, humbug, hustle, kid, maneuver, manipulate, massage, misguide, misinform, mislead, misrepresent, modify, prestidigitate, rearrange, rejigger, rig, rook, scam, shortchange, shuffle, skin, snow, spoof, squeeze, stick, sting, sucker, swindle, tease, trick, wow* (≠ confess, confront, debunk, disabuse, disclose, disenchant, disillusion, divulge, drop, expose, -neglect, reveal, stabilize, steady, tell, trust, uncloak, uncover, undeceive, unmask, unveil)

JUICE (→): *abet, activate, actuate, amp, animate, arouse, awaken, boost, brace, buoy, charge, cheer, drive, electrify, embolden, energize, enkindle, enliven, enthuse, excite, exhilarate, ferment, fire, foment, fortify, galvanize, ginger, hearten, impel, incite, inflame, infuse, inspire, instigate, invigorate, jazz, jump-start, kindle, lift, liven, motivate, move, prioritize, propel, provoke, psych, quicken, raise, rally, reactivate, reanimate, reawaken, recharge, recreate, reenergize, refresh, regenerate, reinvigorate, rejuvenate, rekindle, renew, restimulate, resurrect, resuscitate, revitalize, revive, rouse, shock, spark, spike, steel, stimulate, stir, strengthen, supercharge, trigger, vitalize, vivify, wake* (≠ bore, castrate, check, cripple, curb, dampen, daunt, deactivate, deaden, debilitate, demoralize, demotivate, -deter, discourage, dishearten, dispirit, drain, dull, emasculate, enervate, enfeeble, exhaust, fatigue, foil, freeze, frustrate, harass, hinder, hobble, impair, impede, inactivate, inhibit, irk, jade, kill, knacker, leech, overextend, paralyze, quell, quench, repress, restrain, sap, sedate, slow, still, stunt, suppress, tire, tucker, undermine, weaken, wear, weary)

JUICE (←): *acquire, cull, decant, deplete, derive, distill, draft, drain, draw, elicit, empty, evacuate, exhaust, exploit, express, extract, flush, garner, gather, glean, harvest, leech, milk, obtain, press, prize, procure, pry, pull, pump, purge, remove, select, siphon, squeeze, suck, take, tap, use,* *vacate, vacuum, -void, withdraw, wrest, wring* (≠ bathe, cram, deluge, douse, drench, drown, fill, flood, infuse, insert, install, instill, inundate, jam, marinate, ram, replace, restore, soak, souse, staunch, submerge, swamp, swell, wash, water, wet)

JUMBLE (/): *addle, agitate, befuddle, blend, blur, churn, clutter, confound, confuse, convulse, derange, diffuse, disarrange, disarray, discompose, dishevel, disjoint, dislocate, disorder, disorganize, displace, disrupt, disturb, embroil, entangle, faze, garble, hash, mess, mingle, mislabel, mislay, misplace, mix, muddle, muss, overset, perplex, perturb, ripple, roil, roughen, ruffle, rummage, rumple, scatter, scramble, shuffle, snarl, stir, swirl, tangle, toss, tousle, trouble, tumble, unsettle, untidy, upset, whip, whisk* (≠ adjust, align, arrange, array, calibrate, classify, clean, codify, coordinate, fix, groom, gussy, hierarchize, line, manicure, methodize, order, organize, pace, queue, regiment, regulate, right, sort, straighten, systematize, tidy, tune, uncloud, unscramble)

JUMP (→): *accost, ambush, antagonize, assail, assault, attack, bash, batter, blindside, block, bushwhack, buttonhole, capture, catch, challenge, charge, check, checkmate, clip, clutch, combat, confront, corner, counter, crush, down, flip, -frustrate, grab, grapple, grasp, -halt, harass, hassle, hunt, intercept, manhandle, menace, mug, nail, obstruct, ram, rush, sack, sandbag, seize, shove, slam, smash, smear, smite, stalk, stop, storm, strike, surprise, tackle, take, threaten, throw, topple, trap, unhorse, unseat, upend, upset, victimize, waylay, wrestle* (≠ armor, assist, -avoid, block, brave, -bypass, -circumvent, defend, deflect, -dodge, -duck, -elude, embrace, endure, -evade, face, free, guard, help, -ignore, invite, liberate, loose, observe, protect, receive, release, rescue, save, shelter, shield, -shirk, -sidestep, skip, skirt, weather, welcome, withstand)

JUMP (/): *-avoid, -bypass, clear, cover, -cut, -disregard, -dodge, -elude, -escape, -evade, -exclude, hop, hurdle, -ignore, leap, leapfrog, leave, miss, negotiate, -nullify, -omit, -overlook, overshoot, pass, postpone, shelve, -shun, skip, spring, surmount, vault* (≠ access, accost, address, approach, attack, brave, choose, confront, engage, face, grasp, handle, intercept, mark, meet, oppose, pinpoint, seek, seize, select, tackle, target, threaten)

JUNK (/): *-abandon, abdicate, bar, blackball, blacklist, cashier, chop, chuck, clip, crop, cull, -cut, deep-six, demolish, -desert, disallow, disassemble, discard, disclaim, disgorge, dismantle, dismiss, -ditch, drop, dump, eject, eliminate, eradicate, excise, -exclude, expunge, -forsake, jettison, jilt, liquidate, lose, offload, -omit, oppugn, oust, pitch, -reject, relinquish, remove, -repudiate, scrap, separate, shed, shuck, slough, snip, strip, toss, trash, unload, vomit* (≠ acquire, adopt, assemble, borrow, cherish, claim, craft, cultivate, defend, develop, embrace, employ, foster, hold, keep, maintain, pickle, preserve, procure, protect, recover, recycle, remainder, repair, rescue, retain, retrieve, retrofit, salvage, save, scavenge, secure, utilize)

JUSTIFY (+): *absolve, accent, accentuate, acquit, advocate, affirm, argue, assert, authorize, avow, belabor, champion, claim, clear, condone,* *confirm, contend, contextualize, debate, defend, deserve, discuss, -disregard, emphasize, espouse, establish, excuse, exonerate, explain, forgive, gloss, -ignore, insist, maintain, overemphasize, pardon, plead, proclaim, profess, protest, prove, rationalize, remit, spin, state, stress, substantiate, support, sustain, underline, underscore, uphold, validate, verify, vindicate, warrant, whitewash* (≠ -abandon, abjure, accuse, attack, blame, charge, condemn, contradict, controvert, convict, damn, debate, -deny, -desert, discredit, disprove, dispute, distrust, doubt, fault, -forsake, frame, implicate, impugn, incriminate, invalidate, -neglect, oppose, rebut, recant, refute, resent, retract, reverse, scapegoat, scruple, suspect, switch, underemphasize, -veto, withdraw)

KEEP (→): *abet, advantage, aid, assist, back, bankroll, benefit, capitalize, compensate, contribute, dispense, dower, endow, ensure, facilitate, feed, finance, foster, fuel, fund, guarantee, harbor, help, house, maintain, nourish, nurture, patronize, pay, promote, provide, room, serve, sponsor, stake, subsidize, suckle, supply, support, sustain, tend, underwrite, victual* (≠ -abandon, accept, acquire, antagonize, anticipate, beggar, bilk, cadge, condemn, defund, demand, -desert, disappoint, discourage, disinherit, -disown, expect, exploit, fail, foil, -frustrate, hinder, hurt, -ignore, maroon, -neglect, oppose, sabotage, scant, scotch, scupper, scuttle, shelve, skimp, stiff, stint, subvert, take, -thwart, withhold)

KEEP (←): *accumulate, acquire, amass, archive, bear, boast, bronze, budget, cache, carry, cellar, cherish, coffer, collect, command, conduct, conserve, control, deal, deposit, detain, direct, embalm, enjoy, file, furnish, garage, garner, grasp, grip, guard, hangar, harbor, heap, hoard, hold, house, maintain, manage, own, pack, pickle, pile, place, possess, preserve, protect, recycle, reserve, retain, rule, salvage, save, scavenge, season, shelve, skimp, stack, stint, stock, stockpile, store, stow, sustain, treasure, warehouse, withhold* (≠ -abandon, bequeath, bestow, cede, circulate, commodify, comp, consume, contribute, -decline, diffuse, discard, dispense, disperse, disseminate, distribute, dole, dollop, donate, drop, dump, eat, give, hand, leverage, lose, monetize, offer, offload, plonk, -reject, release, relinquish, remainder, -repudiate, scatter, sell, spare, -spurn, squander, surrender, tender, tithe, transfer, volunteer, waste, yield)

KEEP (+): *administer, attend, board, chair, choreograph, command, conduct, continue, control, defend, direct, endure, feed, foster, govern, guard, guide, handle, lead, maintain, manage, micromanage, mind, nourish, nurture, operate, orchestrate, ordain, order, oversee, pace, parent, patrol, pilot, preserve, protect, provision, raise, rear, regulate, run, safeguard, serve, shelter, shield, stage-manage, steer, steward, subsidize, superintend, supervise, support, sustain, tend, watch* (≠ -abandon, botch, bungle, damage, -disregard, flub, forget, -forsake, fumble, half-ass, harm, -ignore, injure, misrule, -neglect, ruin, -shirk, stagnate, stunt, wreck)

KEEP (+): *acknowledge, believe, bless, celebrate, ceremonialize, commemorate, consecrate, fête, fulfill, hold, honor, laud, maintain, mark, memorialize, mind, mourn, obey, observe, perform, perpetuate, praise, recognize, regard, regret, remember, respect, revere, ritualize, sanctify, solemnize, venerate* (≠ break, dishonor, -disregard, disrespect, forget, -forsake, -ignore, mock, -neglect, -overlook, ridicule, -scorn, transgress, violate) **(¿) ABSTRACTION ALERT. Concrete goals essential!**

KEEP (+): *accomplish, achieve, answer, commit, compass, complete, conclude, consummate, discharge, effect, execute, fill, finalize, finish, fulfill, meet, perfect, perform, redeem, satisfy* (≠ -abandon, breach, break, -disregard, fail, forget, -ignore, lose, -neglect, -nullify, -overlook, -slight, transgress, violate)

KEEP (+): *-avert, battle, bulwark, conserve, cover, defend, fence, fight, forfend, guard, oppose, outlast, patrol, preserve, -prevent, protect, resist, safeguard, save, screen, secure, shield, ward, withstand* (≠ ambush, assail, assault, attack, barrage, beset, besiege, blindside, bombard, bushwhack, -desert, forfeit, -forsake, overrun, pillage, ravage, ruin, sack, storm, wreck)

KEEP (/): *arrest, -avert, block, bottle, bridle, cage, chain, check, checkmate, choke, confine, constrain, contain, control, counter, curb, delay, detain, -deter, foil, frustrate, gag, govern, hamper, hamstring, handcuff, hinder, hold, housebreak, housetrain, impede, imprison, inhibit, institutionalize, interrupt, jail, leash, limit, measure, mince, muffle, muzzle, obstruct, pace, pause, pocket, -prevent, regulate, rein, repress, restrain, retard, rule, shackle, shelve, short-circuit, silence, sink, smother, squelch, stall, stifle, stop, straightjacket, strangle, stymie, suppress, swallow, tame, tie, withhold* (≠ accelerate, adapt, aid, air, boost, circulate, disseminate, encourage, express, liberate, loose, loosen, lose, permit, prioritize, release, unleash, urge, vent)

KICK (→): *ban, bar, blackball, blacklist, boot, bounce, chop, cull, -cut, deep-six, -deny, discharge, dislodge, dismiss, disqualify, drop, dump, eighty-six, eject, eliminate, evict, -exclude, exorcise, expel, -forbid, jettison, jilt, -omit, oppugn, oust, -prohibit, propel, -reject, relegate, scrap, shed, -spurn, trash* (≠ accept, admit, allow, cooperate, embrace, employ, engage, enlist, grant, greet, high-five, hold, include, invite, involve, join, keep, partake, participate, permit, receive, settle, steady, summon, welcome)

KICK-START (→): *abet, activate, advance, arrange, author, bankroll, begin, brainstorm, brew, conceive, concoct, constitute, construct, contrive, create, cultivate, detonate, develop, devise, encourage, endow, energize, enlarge, enliven, establish, excite, expand, fabricate, father, ferment, finance, fire, foment, forward, foster, found, fund, further, galvanize, generate, hatch, ignite, improvise, inaugurate, incite, inflame, initiate, innovate, inspire, instigate, institute, introduce, invent, invigorate, launch, manufacture, mobilize, motivate, move, nourish, nurture, organize, originate, pick, pioneer, plant, produce, promote, prompt, propel, provoke, quicken, rabble-rouse, raise, rouse, set, sire, sow, spark, spur, start, stimulate, stir, subsidize, systematize, trigger, trip, underwrite, vitalize* (≠ abolish, allay, annihilate, annul, bridle, calm, check, constrain, cripple, curb, deactivate, defund, demotivate, discourage, end, finish, freeze, -halt, hamper, hobble, hold, impede, inactivate, inhibit, lull, mitigate, -nullify, pace, paralyze, -prohibit, quiet, regulate, rein, restrain, settle, short-circuit, slow, soothe, stall, still, stop, straightjacket, stymie, subdue, tame, terminate, -thwart, tranquilize, wrap)

KIDNAP (←): *abduct, bundle, capture, catch, disappear, entrap, extort, grab, hijack, lure, nab, pluck, poach, ransom, remove, seize, shanghai, skyjack, snatch, spirit, steal, take, waylay* (≠ chauffeur, defend, deliver, guard, protect, ransom, recover, redeem, rescue, restore, return, save, secure, shield)

KILL (←): *allure, arrest, beckon, beguile, bewitch, captivate, charm, court, delight, disarm, draw, enchant, engross, enrapture, entertain, enthrall, entice, entrance, fascinate, galvanize, gratify, grip, hypnotize, inspire, interest, intrigue, invite, lure, magnetize, mesmerize, monopolize, please, pull, seduce, solicit, tempt, thrill, woo* (≠ annoy, appall, bore, bother, bug, deaden, depress, disappoint, disgust, displease, frustrate, irk, irritate, knacker, nauseate, needle, nettle, numb, offend, repel, repulse, revolt, tire, trouble, underwhelm, weary)

KILL (/): *annihilate, asphyxiate, assassinate, behead, bump, butcher, claim, croak, crucify, decapitate, decimate, depopulate, destroy, dispatch, doom, electrocute, eliminate, euthanize, execute, exterminate, fell, finish, garrote, guillotine, hang, liquidate, lynch, martyr, massacre, mow, murder, mutilate, neutralize, off, orphan, sacrifice, shank, shiv, shoot, slaughter, slay, smite, smother, snuff, stab, strangle, suffocate, take, terminate, throttle, waste, zap* (≠ animate, bear, birth, doctor, gestate, grow, heal, nurse, nurture, raise, reanimate, reinvigorate, rescue, restore, resurrect, resuscitate, revive, save, stimulate, survive, withstand)

KILL (/): *abolish, axe, blackball, blacklist, -cancel, -decline, deep-six, delete, destroy, devastate, disallow, disapprove, dismiss, dispatch, doom, down, eliminate, end, eradicate, erase, monkey-wrench, -negate, -nix, obliterate, -refuse, retire, ruin, scupper, terminate, -veto, weed, wreck* (≠ admit, allow, approve, begin, brainstorm, champion, confirm, create, cultivate, elect, establish, generate, initiate, legalize, nurture, pass, promote, protect, ratify, renew, sanction, start, support, sustain, weather)

KILL (/): *arrest, brake, choke, cripple, crush, curb, dampen, deactivate, deaden, dismantle, dull, freeze, -halt, hobble, inactivate, jam, mothball, muffle, paralyze, quash, quell, scotch, smother, squench, stall, stifle, stop, suppress, terminate* (≠ accelerate, activate, actuate, amp, charge, crank, discharge, drive, electrify, energize, fire, fuel, generate, intensify, launch, power, propel, reboot, recharge, release, run, spark, start, trigger, trip)

KILL (/): *break, bust, castrate, debilitate, drain, emasculate, enervate, enfeeble, exhaust, fatigue, frazzle, harass, leach, overextend, sap, shrivel, strain, tire, unman, waste, weaken, wear, weary, wither, worsen* (≠ activate, energize, enliven, invigorate, leech, rejuvenate, relax, rest, stimulate, strengthen, survive, unwind, vitalize, withstand)

KINDLE (+): *agitate, animate, arouse, awaken, bake, bank, barbecue, blast, brighten, broil, burn, burst, challenge, char, cook, cremate, electrify, embolden, encourage, enkindle, enliven, exasperate, excite, exhilarate, fan, fire, foment, frizzle, fuel, galvanize, generate, ignite, illuminate, immolate, incinerate, incite, incur, induce, inflame, inspire, invigorate,* *irradiate, jolt, launch, light, motivate, provoke, quicken, rabble-rouse, rally, reignite, rekindle, relight, rouse, scald, scathe, scorch, sear, sharpen, shock, singe, spark, spur, stimulate, stir, stoke, strengthen, tantalize, tease, tempt, thrill, torch, trigger, vitalize, wake, whet* (≠ blacken, check, chill, choke, cripple, crush, curb, darken, deactivate, delay, dim, douse, dull, extinguish, freeze, hamper, hinder, impair, impede, inhibit, obscure, obstruct, paralyze, quench, slake, smother, snuff, still, stop, strangle, suffocate, throttle)

KNEAD (→): *alter, blend, contour, form, grip, knuckle, manipulate, massage, mix, mold, pinch, ply, pound, press, pummel, push, rolf, rub, shape, squeeze, stroke, strum, twist, work* (≠ caress, discard, drop, forget, freeze, hold, -ignore, -neglect, paralyze, pierce, poke, toss)

KNIFE (→): *bayonet, carve, chop, clip, cut, gouge, hurt, impale, kill, lacerate, lance, pierce, razor, rip, scar, shank, shiv, skewer, slash, slice, slit, spit, stab, stick, thrust, wound* (≠ armor, block, blunt, close, cover, defend, deflect, dull, guard, miss, parry, protect, seal, sew, sheathe, shield, stitch)

KNIGHT (+): *advance, aggrandize, commend, compliment, decorate, dignify, distinguish, elevate, ennoble, exalt, glorify, honor, immortalize, magnify, praise, promote, raise, recognize, reward, salute, upgrade, uplift* (≠ bastardize, cheapen, degrade, dehumanize, demoralize, demote, diminish, downgrade, humble, humiliate, lessen, reduce, sideline, strip, tarnish)

KNIT (+): *ally, baste, bind, bracket, braid, buckle, buttonhole, cement, chain, clinch, connect, corrugate, couple, crease, crochet, cross-stitch, draw, embroider, fasten, furrow, fuse, gather, glue, hitch, hybridize, interlace, intertwine, knot, lace, lash, link, mend, mortar, paste, plait, pucker, raddle, seam, secure, sew, splice, stay, stitch, strap, string, suture, synthesize, tack, tether, tie, tighten, unite, unsmooth, weave, weld, wrinkle, zip* (≠ cut, detach, disconnect, disentangle, disjoin, divide, fray, harm, hurt, injure, loose, loosen, lose, release, separate, shred, slice, smooth, tear, unbind, unbraid, unfasten, unknit, unravel, unsew, untie, wear)

KNOCK (→): *assault, backhand, bang, bash, bat, batter, bean, beat, belt, biff, blow, bludgeon, bob, bonk, bop, box, brain, buffet, bump, bung, bunt, bust, butt, cane, chop, clap, clip, clobber, clock, clout, club, concuss, conk, crack, cream, cudgel, cuff, deck, drub, elbow, fell, flick, flog, floor, hammer, hit, jab, jostle, kick, knee, lace, lambaste, lash, level, lick, mangle, maul, nail, nudge, paste, pelt, pepper, poke, pommel, pound, prod, pummel, punch, push, rap, sap, scuff, shove, skull, slam, slap, sledge, slug, smack, smite, sock, stamp, strike, swat, swipe, tag, tap, thrash, thump, thwack, topple, unhorse, wallop, whack, whale, whip* (≠ armor, block, caress, defend, deflect, -dodge, -duck, -elude, -escape, -evade, guard, protect, repel, safeguard, secure, shield, sustain)

KNOCK (/): *abuse, admonish, assail, attack, badmouth, belittle, berate, blame, blast, castigate, censure, chastise, chide, clobber, condemn,* *criticize, critique, crucify, decry, defame, demean, demonize, denigrate, denounce, denunciate, deride, ding, disparage, diss, drub, excoriate, fault, finger, flay, fulminate, gibbet, hammer, impugn, keelhaul, lambaste, lash, neg, pan, pillory, -rebuff, rebuke, reprimand, reproach, scold, -scorn, skewer, slag, slam, slander, slash, tweak, upbraid, wrong* (≠ adore, approve, commend, compliment, defend, endorse, exalt, extol, idolize, ingratiate, laud, lionize, praise, protect, recommend, revere, sanction, support, treasure, venerate, worship)

KNOT (+): *bind, braid, complicate, cord, enlace, entangle, entwine, interlace, intertwine, interweave, jumble, knit, lash, leash, loop, plait, ravel, scramble, secure, snarl, tangle, tether, tie, twine, weave, wind, wreathe* (≠ cut, disentangle, loosen, unbraid, uncomplicate, unknot, unravel, unscramble, unsnarl, untangle, untie, untwine, untwist)

L

LABEL (→): *baptize, brand, call, caption, christen, denote, designate, dub, earmark, entitle, hallmark, identify, mark, mistitle, monogram, name, nickname, nominate, specify, stamp, sticker, stigmatize, style, tab, tag, term, title, trademark, typecast* (≠ camouflage, cloak, clothe, cloud, conceal, costume, counterfeit, cover, disguise, feign, hide, mask, veil)

LABEL (+): *arrange, assort, bracket, brand, call, cast, catalog, categorize, characterize, class, classify, contrast, define, describe, designate, differentiate, dub, group, identify, judge, juxtapose, mark, name, order, package, pigeonhole, prioritize, pronounce, slot, sort, specify, stamp, stereotype, tally, term, type, typecast* (≠ baffle, blur, confuse, disorder, disorganize, jumble, lump, mislabel, misrepresent, mix, muddle, perplex, puzzle, scramble)

LACE (+): *attach, bind, blend, braid, cinch, clinch, close, enlace, entwine, fasten, fortify, fuse, interlace, intertwine, join, knot, link, mix, plait, ply, secure, strap, string, thread, tie, twine, twist, weave, wreathe* (≠ cut, disentangle, sever, slice, uncoil, unfasten, unlace, unspool, untangle, untie, untwine, unwind)

LACE (+): *add, alternate, amalgamate, assimilate, blend, combine, commingle, embody, enhance, enrich, flavor, fuse, incorporate, insert, integrate, interlace, intermingle, intersperse, interweave, juxtapose, magnify, marinate, maximize, merge, mingle, mix, pepper, perfume, richen, salt, sauce, savor, season, spice, thread, weave, wreathe* (≠ deduct, delete, edit, eject, eliminate, excise, -exclude, -omit, oust, purge, remove, simplify, streamline, subtract, withhold)

LACE (/): *add, adulterate, attenuate, bastardize, befoul, blend, cheapen, contaminate, corrupt, counterfeit, cut, debase, defile, degrade, dilute, dirty, doctor, envenom, extend, fake, falsify, flavor, fortify, foul, fudge, infect, load, manipulate, misrepresent, mix, moderate, overdose, poison, pollute, qualify, soil, sophisticate, spike, spoil, strengthen, sully, taint, temper, thin, weaken* (≠ augment, better, clarify, clean, cleanse, clear, compact, concentrate, condense, decontaminate, distill, enhance, enrich, filter, flush, fortify, improve, lard, leach, pasteurize, purge, purify, refine, reinforce, remove, separate, strain, strengthen, supplement)

LACERATE (/): *afflict, claw, cleave, cut, distress, gash, gore, gouge, hack, harm, harrow, hurt, injure, lance, maim, mangle, mutilate, puncture, razor, rend, rip, score, serrate, shank, shiv, slash, slit, stab, tear, torment, torture, wound* (≠ block, blunt, close, cure, defend, doctor, fix, guard, heal, join, mend, nurse, nurture, protect, remedy, repair, restore, seal, secure, sew, smooth, solder, stitch, unite, weld)

LAMBASTE (/): *admonish, afflict, agonize, anguish, assail, assault, attack, avenge, badmouth, baste, batter, beat, belabor, belittle, berate, blame, blast, blister, bludgeon, boo, buffet, burden, castigate, censure, chasten, chastise, clobber, confine, correct, criticize, crucify, cudgel, demean, demonize, denigrate, denounce, denunciate, discipline, disparage, distress, drub, excoriate, execute, fine, flay, flog, fulminate, hammer, hit, hurt, imprison, impugn, incarcerate, judge, keelhaul, lash, pan, pelt, penalize, persecute, pillory, pound, pummel, punish, rap, rebuke, reprimand, reprise, reproach, reprove, roast, rubbish, scalp, scathe, scold, scorch, scourge, sentence, shellac, slam, slap, slash, smear, smother, strike, thrash, torture, trim, try, upbraid, wallop, whip* (≠ absolve, accredit, adulate, applaud, bless, boost, celebrate, coddle, commend, compliment, congratulate, defend, emblazon, embrace, encourage, exalt, excuse, exonerate, extol, flatter, glorify, ingratiate, laud, magnify, pardon, placate, praise, protect, spare, support, tout, uphold)

LAME (/): *batter, break, bruise, cripple, damage, debilitate, destroy, disable, disfigure, dismember, fracture, gore, hamper, hamstring, handicap, harm, hobble, hurt, immobilize, impair, impede, incapacitate, injure, kneecap, lacerate, maim, mangle, maul, mutilate, paralyze, pulverize, ruin, sabotage, scar, scotch, scupper, shatter, shrivel, spoil, torment, torture, undercut, undermine, weaken, wing, wither, wound* (≠ assist, brace, cure, defend, doctor, empower, enable, enhance, facilitate, fix, fortify, heal, help, improve, invigorate, mend, mobilize, nurse, patch, perfect, promote, rebuild, reconstruct, rectify, refine, regenerate, rehabilitate, rejuvenate, remedy, renew, repair, restore, splint, strengthen, support)

LAMPOON (/): *blackguard, blast, blister, burlesque, caricature, counterfeit, demean, distort, exaggerate, fake, misrepresent, mock, overdramatize, parody, pasquinade, pillory, pretend, rail, ridicule, roast, satirize, spoof, travesty* (≠ applaud, approve, celebrate, congratulate, defend, elevate, enshrine, guard, high-five, honor, praise, respect, support, venerate, worship)

LANCE (→): *bore, broach, burst, core, cut, dart, deflate, drill, gaff, gash, gimlet, gore, gouge, harpoon, impale, incise, invade, jab, kebab, knife, notch, penetrate, perforate, pierce, pin, pink, pit, poke, prick, probe, prong, punch, puncture, rend, rupture, shank, shiv, skewer, slash, slice, slit, spear, spike, spit, split, stab, stake, stick, tap, tear, thrust, transfix* (≠ absorb, armor, block, close, defend, deflect, eject, extract, fill, fuse, guard, heal, inflate, mend, obstruct, occlude, parry, patch, plaster, plug, praise, protect, prove, rectify, repair, repel, seal, sew, shield, smooth, stitch, withdraw, yank)

LASH (→): *attack, bang, bash, batter, beat, belt, birch, blackjack, bludgeon, buffet, bullwhip, bust, cane, chastise, clap, clip, clobber, clout, club, cowhide, crack, cudgel, cuff, cut, discipline, drub, drum, flagellate,* *flail, flay, flog, hammer, harm, hide, hit, horsewhip, injure, knock, lace, lacerate, lather, lick, mangle, martyr, maul, mortify, paddle, paste, pelt, pistol-whip, pound, pummel, punch, punish, rawhide, scourge, slap, slash, slog, slug, smack, smite, sock, spank, sting, strap, strike, swat, swipe, switch, tan, thrash, thump, thwack, wallop, welt, whack, whip, whup* (≠ aid, alleviate, assist, assuage, block, buffer, comfort, console, content, cushion, defend, delight, ease, gratify, guard, heal, help, nurture, pity, protect, save, shield, soothe, succor, suffer, support, weather)

LASH (+): *affix, attach, bind, chain, cinch, clamp, clinch, clip, confine, connect, constrain, curb, entangle, fasten, fetter, fix, hamper, hang, harness, hinder, hobble, hogtie, impede, join, knot, lace, latch, leash, limit, link, pin, pinion, reaffix, reattach, refasten, resecure, restrict, rope, secure, seize, shackle, stick, strap, tack, tangle, tether, tie, toggle, trammel, truss, unite, yoke* (≠ cut, detach, disconnect, disengage, divide, drop, emancipate, free, liberate, loose, loosen, lose, open, part, release, rescue, separate, sever, slice, split, sunder, tear, unbind, uncouple, unfasten, unhook, unlace, unlash, unlink, untangle, untie, unyoke)

LASH (/): *abuse, attack, belabor, belittle, berate, blame, blister, castigate, censure, chasten, chastise, chide, criticize, dehumanize, demonize, denigrate, deride, disparage, fault, flay, fulminate, hammer, harangue, humiliate, insult, lambaste, lampoon, malign, menace, mistreat, mock, neg, pan, persecute, pillory, plague, razz, rebuke, reprimand, reprove, ridicule, satirize, scold, -scorn, slate, tongue-lash, tyrannize, upbraid, victimize* (≠ approve, blandish, boost, cherish, commend, compliment, congratulate, defend, endorse, flannel, flatter, glorify, gratify, help, idealize, idolize, lionize, praise, protect, respect, reward, sanction, support, treasure, uplift, venerate)

LASSO (←): *apprehend, arrest, bridle, capture, catch, collar, corner, corral, ensnare, entrap, harness, herd, hook, nab, net, nick, recapture, rope, secure, seize, snaffle, snag, snare, tie, trap, wrangle* (≠ drop, emancipate, expel, free, loose, lose, miss, -reject, release, skip, unbind, unchain, unleash)

LATHER (+): *bathe, foam, froth, launder, lave, massage, rub, scrub, shampoo, slather, soap, wash* (≠ bedraggle, clean, cleanse, dirty, flatten, lose, marinate, presoak, rinse, soak, surrender)

LAUNCH (→): *barrage, bombard, bowl, buck, bung, cast, catapult, chuck, dart, dash, discharge, dispatch, drive, eject, fire, fling, flip, float, gun, heave, hook, hurl, hurtle, impel, lob, loft, mortar, pass, peg, pelt, pitch, precipitate, project, propel, punt, rifle, roll, send, shoot, skitter, sling, throw, thrust, toss, trigger, wing* (≠ barricade, blockade, bulwark, defend, deflect, encumber, grasp, grip, guard, hoard, hold, keep, load, pin, protect, repel, reset, retain, shield)

LAUNCH (+): *arrange, author, bankroll, begin, brainstorm, brew, commence, conceive, concoct, constitute, construct, contrive, cook, create, develop, devise, endow, enlarge, establish, expand, fabricate, father, finance, foster, found, fund, galvanize, generate, hatch, inaugu-*

rate, initiate, innovate, instigate, institute, introduce, invent, kick-start, manufacture, open, organize, originate, patent, pioneer, plant, produce, sire, spark, spur, start, subsidize, systematize, underwrite (≠ abolish, -abort, adjourn, annihilate, annul, -cancel, cease, close, deep-six, defund, dismantle, -disown, dissolve, drop, eliminate, end, extinguish, finish, -halt, impede, kill, -nullify, perfect, ruin, sabotage, scotch, scupper, scuttle, shelve, shut, stop, suspend, terminate, wrap, wreck)

LAUNDER (+): *abbreviate, anonymize, bleep, blue-pencil, bowdlerize, censor, censure, clean, cleanse, condemn, delete, delouse, denounce, edit, examine, excise, expunge, expurgate, gut, presoak, purge, purify, redact, red-pen, red-pencil, repress, review, screen, scrub, scrutinize, shorten, silence, spin, suppress, wash* (≠ allege, approve, authorize, bedraggle, besmirch, contaminate, dirty, draggle, endorse, implicate, incriminate, rubber-stamp, sanction, smear, smudge, sully, taint)

LAVISH (→): *bestow, blow, bombard, consume, deluge, deplete, disburse, dissipate, exhaust, expend, flood, fritter, give, heap, impoverish, indulge, inundate, lard, lose, misspend, overindulge, overspend, overwhelm, pamper, pour, rain, scatter, shoot, shower, slather, spend, squander, swamp, syrup, waste* (≠ bank, budget, conserve, debit, -deny, deprive, divest, drizzle, economize, famish, hoard, keep, limit, malnourish, pinch, preserve, protect, reserve, retain, save, scant, scrimp, skimp, starve, stint, underfeed, withdraw, withhold)

LEACH (←): *bleed, cannibalize, consume, cripple, debilitate, deplete, depredate, drain, drink, empty, exhaust, extract, filter, filtrate, knacker, leech, quaff, remove, sap, sluice, slurp, strain, suck, swallow, vacuum, void, withdraw* (≠ cram, fill, furnish, hoard, imbue, keep, lavish, maintain, preserve, provide, refresh, reload, replace, replenish, restore, retain, saturate, stock, stuff, supply)

LEAD (→): *boss, bring, captain, chair, choreograph, command, contribute, control, convert, convince, direct, dominate, draw, govern, handle, head, helm, incline, induce, introduce, manage, motivate, move, orchestrate, oversee, pace, persuade, produce, prompt, quarterback, regulate, rule, run, serve, shepherd, spearhead, spur, superintend, supervise, tend, trail-blaze* (≠ deregulate, follow, liberate, loose, loosen, lose, mind, mislead, mismanage, misrule, obey, serve, subvert, unleash)

LEAD (→): *accompany, attend, chaperone, coerce, compel, conduct, control, convey, convoy, direct, drive, escort, force, get, guard, guide, impel, induce, manage, marshal, muscle, persuade, pilot, protect, quarterback, route, safeguard, see, shepherd, show, span, squire, steer, traverse, usher, watch* (≠ -abandon, -desert, -ditch, dog, follow, -forsake, haunt, hound, maroon, mind, obey, shadow, tail, tailgate, track, trail)

LEAD (→): *beat, best, better, clobber, conquer, crush, defeat, drub, eclipse, exceed, lick, master, outbalance, outclass, outdistance, outdo, outpace, outperform, outrank, outreach, outrun, outsell, outshine, outstrip, outweigh, overcome, overshadow, overtake, rout, shame, skunk, subdue,* *surmount, surpass, thrash, top, transcend, trounce, trump, wallop, whip* (≠ aggrandize, back, bolster, boost, cede, concede, defend, defer, develop, elevate, enhance, forfeit, -forsake, highlight, hype, improve, magnify, maximize, plug, promote, protect, publicize, relinquish, sacrifice, serve, showcase, spotlight, support, survive)

LEAD (+): *accompany, affect, alter, attend, brief, change, coach, counsel, cultivate, direct, dispose, drill, encourage, engineer, enlighten, foster, godfather, guide, impact, incline, inculcate, indoctrinate, induce, influence, inform, instruct, mentor, modify, motivate, move, nurture, oversee, persuade, pilot, prompt, school, shepherd, show, steer, supervise, sway, teach, train, transform, tutor* (≠ arrest, ban, bar, block, checkmate, cripple, demotivate, -deter, discourage, dissuade, -frustrate, -halt, hamstring, harm, hinder, impede, inhibit, obstruct, -prevent, restrain, stall, undercut, weaken)

LEAK (→): *blab, blaze, blurt, break, circulate, clue, concede, confess, confide, confirm, disclose, divulge, impart, out, publicize, relate, reveal, spill, spread, squeal, tell* (≠ block, bury, censor, cloak, cloud, conceal, control, costume, disguise, expurgate, gag, hide, hush, mask, mute, muzzle, redact, secrete, stifle, suppress)

LEARN (←): *absorb, acquire, apprehend, assimilate, comprehend, cram, digest, discern, gain, gather, get, glean, grasp, imbibe, incorporate, integrate, internalize, know, master, memorize, procure, read, receive, study, train, understand* (≠ -blank, -disregard, forget, -ignore, miss, misunderstand, -neglect, -overlook, unlearn)

LEARN (←): *ascertain, calculate, catch, clock, descry, detect, determine, discern, discover, divine, espy, find, gather, get, glean, hear, locate, mind, note, observe, perceive, realize, scan, scout, scrutinize, search, see, seek, sight, spot, suss, track, understand, unearth* (≠ bewilder, blanket, bury, cloak, conceal, cover, curtain, -disregard, enshroud, forget, hide, -ignore, lose, mask, mislay, misplace, miss, occult, -overlook, screen, shroud, unlearn, veil)

LEARN (←): *absorb, accept, apprehend, comprehend, con, digest, grasp, know, memorize, mourn, recall, recollect, regret, relive, remember, retain, study, understand* (≠ addle, baffle, bury, confuse, -disregard, forget, -ignore, misremember, mystify, -neglect, -overlook, unlearn) **(¿) ABSTRACTION ALERT. Concrete goals essential!**

LEASE (←): *arrange, bespeak, book, charter, contract, engage, hire, let, license, loan, order, possess, register, rent, reserve, sublet* (≠ banish, buy, commodify, dismiss, eject, -exclude, expel, fire, hold, keep, monetize, oust, purchase, release, sell, take)

LEASH (/): *bind, break, bridle, calm, check, conquer, control, curb, discipline, domesticate, dominate, guide, harness, hogtie, hold, housebreak, housetrain, humble, lead, lull, master, mellow, mitigate, moderate, mollify, overcome, pacify, placate, quell, rein, repress, restrain,* *soften, straightjacket, subdue, subjugate, suppress, tame, temper, tether, tie, train* (≠ -abandon, agitate, -desert, dismiss, free, liberate, loose, manumit, outrage, provoke, rankle, release, rouse, spring, stir, subvert, unbind, uncage, unchain, unfetter, unhinge, unhook, unleash, untie)

LEAVE (→): *-abandon, cease, cede, chuck, -desert, -ditch, drop, dump, forgo, -forsake, hand, jettison, jilt, maroon, offload, plonk, -quit, relinquish, -renounce, resign, stop, surrender, terminate, waive, yield* (≠ chauffeur, defend, guard, hold, keep, maintain, preserve, protect, remember, retain)

LEAVE (→): *allocate, allot, apportion, assign, bequeath, bestow, cede, commit, confer, consign, deliver, donate, dower, endow, entrust, hand, legate, refer, tender, transfer, transmit, will* (≠ block, clutch, -deny, dispute, grasp, grip, hoard, hold, keep, -refuse, squander, withhold)

LECTURE (+): *address, admonish, brief, catechize, coach, consult, deliver, direct, drill, edify, educate, enlighten, expound, familiarize, filibuster, guide, harangue, impart, implant, inculcate, indoctrinate, inform, initiate, instill, instruct, introduce, mentor, mouth, preach, prepare, prime, qualify, read, recite, school, sermonize, show, spiel, spout, talk, teach, tutor, update* (≠ abbreviate, abridge, censor, confound, confuse, cross-examine, disrespect, doubt, forget, grill, -ignore, interrogate, interview, learn, mystify, -neglect, obscure, question, -repudiate, restrain, -scorn, scruple, stifle, stonewall, study, suspect, withhold) **(¿) ABSTRACTION ALERT. Concrete goals essential!**

LECTURE (/): *abuse, admonish, assail, attack, badmouth, belittle, berate, blame, blast, blister, castigate, censure, chastise, chide, condemn, criticize, critique, crucify, denounce, disparage, disrespect, diss, excoriate, fault, flay, hammer, harangue, impugn, keelhaul, knock, lambaste, lash, mock, pan, rag, rate, ream, rebuke, reprimand, reproach, reprove, revile, ridicule, scold, -scorn, scourge, slam, tongue-lash, upbraid, vituperate* (≠ absolve, acclaim, adopt, applaud, approve, blandish, celebrate, cheer, commend, compliment, congratulate, emulate, endorse, exalt, exonerate, extol, flatter, forgive, gratify, help, honor, idealize, laud, pardon, praise, revere, romanticize, sanction, spare, venerate)

LEECH (←): *beg, bilk, bleed, bum, cadge, cannibalize, coerce, consume, cripple, debilitate, exhaust, extract, leach, milk, mooch, overextend, schnorr, scrounge, sluice, sponge, tap, tax, weasel* (≠ clasp, clutch, compensate, confess, expose, grasp, hoard, keep, replace, replenish, restore, retain, withhold)

LEGISLATE (+): *administer, allow, approve, authorize, codify, confirm, constitute, control, decree, dictate, effect, enact, establish, execute, formulate, govern, legalize, make, manage, ordain, order, pass, permit, prescribe, proclaim, ratify, regulate, rule, sanction, set* (≠ abolish, abrogate, annul, -blank, -cancel, invalidate, kill, misrule, -nullify, overturn, repeal, -rescind, reverse, revoke, void)

LEGITIMIZE (+): *accredit, allow, approve, authorize, back, certificate, certify, charter, commission, confirm, decriminalize, empower, enable, endorse, entitle, guarantee, legalize, legitimate, license, mandate, notarize, permit, ratify, reward, rubber-stamp, sanction, support, sustain, underwrite, validate, warrant* (≠ abolish, abrogate, annul, -cancel, chastise, criminalize, -exclude, -forbid, invalidate, marginalize, -negate, -nix, -nullify, outlaw, proscribe, punish, rectify, -rescind)

LEND (→): *add, advance, afford, allot, allow, assign, assist, attribute, award, bankroll, bequeath, bestow, confer, consign, contribute, credit, deliver, devote, disburse, dispense, dole, endow, entrust, expend, extend, fund, furnish, give, grant, help, impart, lavish, lease, lend-lease, let, loan, mortgage, oblige, offer, pawn, pay, permit, pledge, present, provide, ration, render, send, serve, share, shower, stake, sublet, submit, supply, tender, trust, underwrite, volunteer* (≠ acquire, appropriate, bestow, bilk, borrow, cadge, cheat, chisel, claim, contribute, defraud, defund, derive, disinherit, -disown, donate, draw, earn, give, obtain, procure, scrounge, secure, seize, source, sponge, steal, stiff, tithe, use)

LESSEN (/): *abate, abbreviate, abridge, accent, allay, alleviate, amplify, amputate, assuage, attenuate, bob, calm, clip, compact, compress, concentrate, condense, contract, crop, cull, curtail, cut, deaden, debit, decrease, deduct, deflate, deplete, deprive, diffuse, dilute, diminish, -discount, downgrade, downsize, drain, dull, ease, erode, impair, leach, leech, lighten, lower, lull, mellow, minimize, mitigate, moderate, narrow, nip, palliate, pare, prune, rarefy, reduce, relieve, shave, shear, shorten, shrink, slow, soft-pedal, soothe, subordinate, taper, trim, truncate, unload, weaken, weed* (≠ accelerate, accent, accentuate, accrue, accumulate, add, adjoin, affirm, affix, aggrandize, ameliorate, amend, amp, amplify, annex, append, assert, assess, attach, augment, balloon, belabor, boost, brew, broaden, compile, consolidate, deepen, double, emphasize, enhance, enlarge, enrich, escalate, expand, extend, flavor, foist, gather, glitz, heighten, impose, improve, increase, intensify, lengthen, magnify, marinate, maximize, multiply, optimize, overhaul, prioritize, proliferate, prolong, punctuate, recoup, redouble, refine, revolutionize, season, sophisticate, spice, stoke, strengthen, supplement, treble, triple, underscore)

LEVEL (+): *adjust, align, approximate, balance, burnish, calibrate, center, compose, counteract, counterbalance, defray, equalize, equate, even, flatten, flush, glaze, gloss, grade, grind, homogenize, iron, juggle, lay, match, mow, neutralize, offset, override, pave, plane, polish, press, right, roll, sand, set, shine, slick, smooth, spackle, square, stabilize, steady, straighten, surface, tune, tweak, unbend, uncrumple, uncurl, unfold, unwrinkle* (≠ bend, coarsen, crease, deform, dent, disfigure, fold, harshen, jar, mismatch, nock, pit, pock, roughen, ruffle, rumple, serrate, sharpen, unbalance, unsettle, warp, wrinkle)

LEVEL (/): *abolish, annihilate, atomize, bulldoze, compress, crop, decimate, deflate, demolish, desolate, destroy, devastate, disintegrate,* *dismantle, doom, down, drop, eradicate, erase, exterminate, extirpate, fell, flatten, floor, ground, mow, obliterate, pulverize, raze, remove, ruin, scythe, shear, smash, squish, topple, vaporize, waste, wipe, wreck* (≠ assemble, build, concoct, configure, construct, craft, create, devise, engineer, erect, fabricate, fashion, found, make, manufacture, plan, raise, survive, weather, withstand)

LEVERAGE (→): *abuse, adapt, adopt, apply, bleed, cannibalize, channel, cheat, commercialize, commodify, control, develop, direct, embrace, employ, exercise, exploit, fleece, handle, harness, lobby, manipulate, milk, misappropriate, mistreat, misuse, mobilize, muster, operate, organize, overcharge, pimp, process, rally, recycle, reuse, run, salvage, skin, soak, stick, use, utilize, wield, work* (≠ -abandon, -avoid, -boycott, -bypass, -circumvent, -discount, -eschew, -exclude, -forbid, forfeit, -forsake, -ignore, lose, misapply, -neglect, -nix, -omit, -prohibit, -reject, relinquish, -renounce, sacrifice, -scorn, -spurn, surrender, -veto, weaken, wound)

LIBERATE (+): *absolve, acquit, alibi, deliver, discharge, disembody, disencumber, disengage, disentangle, emancipate, enfranchise, enlarge, exonerate, extricate, free, loose, loosen, manumit, pardon, parole, ransom, redeem, release, rescue, save, slack, slacken, spare, spring, unbind, unburden, uncage, unchain, unfetter, unravel, unshackle, unsnarl, untie, untwine* (≠ bind, cage, chain, commit, confine, conquer, convict, enchain, enslave, fetter, handcuff, hogtie, immure, imprison, incarcerate, incriminate, institutionalize, intern, jail, keep, limit, lock, manacle, -prevent, restrain, shackle, straightjacket, subdue, subjugate, tie, trammel, truss, unchain, unfetter, unhook, unleash, unshackle, untie)

LICENSE (+): *accredit, affirm, allow, approve, authenticate, authorize, bless, certify, commission, confirm, countersign, deputize, designate, empower, enable, enfranchise, entitle, franchise, legalize, legitimize, notarize, ordain, permit, privilege, qualify, sanction, suffer, task, validate, warrant* (≠ ban, bar, blacklist, delegitimize, -deny, disallow, -exclude, -forbid, outlaw, -prohibit, -refuse, restrict, sabotage, undermine, -veto, withhold)

LICK (→): *brush, calm, caress, clean, contact, fondle, gloss, graze, lap, moisten, osculate, soothe, stroke, sweep, taste, tongue, touch, wash, wet* (≠ bite, chew, dry, gnaw, harm, injure, spit, wound)

LICK (/): *assail, assault, attack, backhand, bash, baste, bat, batter, beat, belabor, belt, beset, birch, blackjack, bludgeon, box, buffet, bust, cane, chop, clobber, clout, club, cowhide, crack, cudgel, cuff, curry, drub, flagellate, flog, hammer, hide, hit, horsewhip, knock, lace, lambaste, lash, lather, maim, mangle, maul, paddle, paste, pelt, pistol-whip, pommel, pound, pummel, punch, raid, rush, scourge, slam, slap, slate, smack, smash, sock, spank, storm, strap, strike, swat, swipe, switch, tan, thrash, thresh, thump, thwack, wallop, whack, whale, wham, whip, whomp, wound* (≠ -avoid, block, build, -bypass, caress, -circumvent, defend, deflect, -disregard, dissuade, -dodge, -duck, -elude, -evade, forget, guard, help,

-ignore, miss, -neglect, pet, protect, repel, secure, shelter, shield, -sidestep, skip, skirt, tap)

LICK (/): *annihilate, beat, best, better, bomb, break, bury, cap, checkmate, clobber, conquer, cream, crush, defeat, demolish, dispatch, down, drub, eclipse, exceed, finish, flatten, master, outdistance, outdo, outfight, outlast, outmaneuver, outperform, outreach, outshine, outstrip, outthink, overcome, overpower, overtake, overthrow, overwhelm, rout, ruin, score, shellac, skin, skunk, slaughter, smoke, stop, subdue, subjugate, surmount, surpass, sweep, take, thrash, throw, top, transcend, trounce, unseat, upend, upset, vanquish, wallop, whip, whup, wrack, wreck* (≠ aid, arm, assist, bobble, bomb, defend, empower, enable, equip, flunk, forfeit, fumble, guard, lose, maintain, muff, preserve, protect, release, rescue, restore, save, secure, steady, survive, sustain, unchain, weather, withstand)

LIFT (→): *ascend, bear, boost, crane, elevate, erect, escalate, heave, heft, heighten, hike, hoist, jack, levitate, mount, raise, rear, soar, up, upend, uphold, uplift, upraise* (≠ anchor, bear, bury, depress, descend, dip, discard, drop, lower, offload, pitch, plonk, plunge, press, push, restrain, root, sink, submerge)

LIFT (→): *activate, actuate, advance, ameliorate, animate, arouse, beef, bolster, boost, bring, buoy, cheer, comfort, console, dignify, draw, elevate, embolden, encourage, enhance, enthuse, exalt, excite, goad, goose, hearten, hike, impel, incite, induce, initiate, inspire, kick-start, kindle, lubricate, motivate, move, persuade, please, prompt, propel, provoke, push, raise, rally, reassure, rouse, spur, stimulate, stir, support, trigger, upgrade, uplift, urge* (≠ appall, bench, blackjack, blackmail, bore, browbeat, bully, confuse, daunt, demoralize, demote, demotivate, depress, disconcert, discourage, dishearten, dismay, dull, intimidate, menace, prioritize, sadden, sideline, sink, stall, stifle, threaten, upset, weaken, worry)

LIFT (→): *adduce, airlift, bear, bring, carry, cart, conduct, convey, deliver, dispatch, draw, express, fetch, fly, forward, haul, impart, induce, move, provide, remove, run, schlep, send, shift, ship, shuttle, take, transfer, transmit, transport, truck* (≠ -abandon, capture, chuck, conceal, -deny, discard, -ditch, dump, eject, endanger, expel, forget, -forsake, hide, imperil, jeopardize, jettison, leave, lose, miss, offload, plonk, receive, -refuse, -reject, reserve, retain, withhold)

LIFT (←): *abduct, appropriate, bilk, bogart, boost, bootleg, borrow, burglarize, burgle, cadge, carjack, collar, cop, copy, crib, filch, freeboot, grab, grasp, heist, hijack, hook, kidnap, loot, misappropriate, mooch, nail, nick, nip, pick, pickpocket, pilfer, pillage, pinch, pirate, plagiarize, plunder, poach, pocket, purloin, rifle, rob, rustle, sack, scrounge, seize, shanghai, shoplift, snaffle, snag, snatch, snitch, spirit, sponge, steal, swipe, take, thieve* (≠ bestow, buy, comp, contribute, deliver, donate, drop, give, hand, hoard, keep, lose, offer, present, purchase, receive, replace, replenish, restore, return, save, stock, supply, volunteer)

LIFT (/): *abolish, -abort, abrogate, annihilate, annul, -avoid, ban, -cancel, countermand, delegitimize, disallow, dismantle, dismiss, dissolve, drop, eliminate, end, enjoin, eradicate, erase, -forbid, invalidate, liquidate, -negate, -nullify, outlaw, override, overrule, overturn, -prohibit, quash, recall, -reject, relax, remove, repeal, -rescind, retract, reverse, revoke, scrap, stop, strike, suspend, terminate, vacate, -veto, -void, withdraw* (≠ allow, approve, authorize, clear, command, create, decree, dictate, enact, endorse, establish, foist, formalize, found, impose, institute, legalize, legislate, legitimate, legitimize, mandate, order, pass, permit, prescribe, ratify, retain, sanction, validate, warrant)

LIGHT (→): *bake, bank, barbecue, beacon, brighten, broil, burn, char, cook, cremate, enkindle, fire, floodlight, frizzle, ignite, illuminate, illumine, immolate, incinerate, inflame, irradiate, kindle, lighten, radiate, reignite, rekindle, relight, scald, scathe, scorch, sear, spark, spur, stoke, torch, trigger* (≠ blacken, choke, dampen, darken, dim, douse, dull, eclipse, extinguish, mute, obscure, overshadow, quench, shade, smother, snuff, stifle, suffocate)

LIGHTEN (+): *amuse, beguile, bolster, brighten, buoy, captivate, charm, cheer, console, delight, distract, divert, elate, enchant, encourage, energize, engage, enliven, entertain, enthrall, excite, gladden, hearten, inspire, lift, liven, mesmerize, please, rally, refresh, reinvigorate, relax, restore, revive, rouse, stimulate, thrill, uplift* (≠ anger, annoy, bore, bother, bug, darken, debilitate, demoralize, depress, discourage, drain, encumber, exhaust, fatigue, irk, irritate, knacker, nag, needle, nettle, niggle, nitpick, numb, pain, paralyze, sadden, stifle, tire, trouble, vex, weary, worry)

LIGHTEN (+): *abbreviate, abridge, allay, alleviate, ameliorate, assuage, attenuate, buoy, calm, change, comfort, cull, curtail, decrease, deflate, deplete, dilute, diminish, disencumber, drain, ease, empty, eradicate, erode, facilitate, free, help, jettison, leach, lessen, levitate, lift, lull, mellow, minimize, mitigate, moderate, mollify, pacify, palliate, pare, placate, prune, rarefy, reduce, relieve, remedy, remove, shave, shear, shift, shorten, shrink, soothe, take, taper, thin, trim, truncate, unburden, unload, unpack, weed* (≠ accent, accentuate, accrue, aggravate, amplify, assert, ballast, burden, deepen, emphasize, exacerbate, harm, heighten, hurt, impair, increase, injure, intensify, load, lumber, saddle, sharpen, weight, worsen)

LIMIT (/): *arrest, assign, ban, bar, bind, block, bottle, bound, box, bridle, cage, cap, categorize, chain, check, circumscribe, classify, confine, constrain, constrict, contain, contract, control, cork, cramp, curb, define, delimit, delineate, demarcate, -deny, deprive, describe, determine, dictate, disallow, encumber, fetter, fix, govern, hamper, hamstring, hem, hinder, hogtie, ice, immure, impede, imprison, incarcerate, inhibit, institutionalize, intern, jail, label, lessen, modify, narrow, number, obligate, obstruct, overcommit, pace, package, pigeonhole, pinch, prescribe, press, pressure, pucker, qualify, quell, ration, reduce, regulate, rein, repress, restrain, restrict, set, slot, specify, squeeze, stereotype, stifle,* *stop, stopple, straightjacket, suppress, terminate, tie, tighten, withhold* (≠ aid, allow, assist, broaden, circulate, develop, disclose, disseminate, emancipate, encourage, enlarge, exceed, expand, extend, foster, free, help, increase, legalize, lengthen, liberate, loose, loosen, open, outreach, overextend, overreach, permit, promote, raise, release, slack, slacken, stretch, unbind, unfasten, unleash, untie, widen)

LINK (+): *ally, amalgamate, associate, attach, baste, befriend, bestride, bind, bracket, bridge, combine, concatenate, conjoin, conjugate, connect, constellate, contact, couple, fasten, group, hitch, hook, identify, include, incorporate, integrate, interlink, involve, join, knit, lash, merge, network, plait, reintegrate, relate, sew, span, straddle, tether, tie, unify, unite, weave, yoke, zip* (≠ alienate, break, cede, cut, deactivate, detach, disaffect, disconnect, disengage, divide, divorce, eject, estrange, evict, -exclude, expel, forfeit, forget, loose, loosen, lose, -omit, -ostracize, oust, release, relinquish, remove, retain, separate, sever, slacken, split, unfasten, unmarry, unplug)

LIONIZE (+): *acclaim, admire, adore, adulate, aggrandize, apotheosize, applaud, approve, blandish, bless, boost, cajole, celebrate, cheer, cherish, commemorate, commend, compliment, congratulate, consecrate, deify, dignify, endorse, enjoy, eulogize, exalt, extol, fête, flannel, flatter, glorify, gold-star, gratify, hail, hallow, hero-worship, high-five, honor, hype, idealize, idolize, immortalize, laud, limelight, magnify, memorialize, observe, panegyrize, plug, praise, presell, prioritize, promote, publicize, push, recommend, revere, romanticize, salute, sanction, sentimentalize, solemnize, stroke, treasure, trumpet, venerate, worship* (≠ abominate, accuse, admonish, anathematize, attaint, badmouth, belittle, berate, bestialize, blame, blast, boo, castigate, censure, chastise, chide, condemn, criticize, critique, debase, defame, denigrate, denounce, -detest, disgrace, dishonor, disparage, disrespect, execrate, fault, frame, fulminate, humiliate, incriminate, lambaste, profane, rebuke, regret, repent, reprimand, reproach, ridicule, rue, scathe, scold, -scorn, shame, slander, trash, vilify)

LIQUEFY (/): *dilute, dissolve, flux, fuse, heat, liquidize, melt, rarefy, render, run, smelt, soften, thaw, thin* (≠ clot, coagulate, congeal, freeze, harden, reduce, set, solidify, steel, thicken, toughen)

LIQUIDATE (→): *balance, cash, clear, commodify, convert, defray, disband, discharge, dissolve, exchange, foot, honor, meet, monetize, pay, -quit, realize, recompense, reimburse, remainder, repay, satisfy, sell, service, settle, shutter, square, stand, substitute, swap, switch* (≠ aggravate, dispute, exacerbate, -ignore, invest, keep, owe, -repudiate, retain, stiff, sustain, withhold)

LIQUIDATE (/): *abolish, annihilate, annul, assassinate, atomize, blast, -cancel, consume, cut, dash, decimate, demolish, destroy, devastate, devour, discard, dismantle, dispatch, dissolve, -ditch, doom, dynamite, efface, eject, eliminate, eradicate, erase, excise, expel, expunge, exterminate, extirpate, finish, flatten, fragment, jettison, kill, massacre,* *murder, obliterate, oust, powder, pulverize, purge, ravage, raze, remove, ruin, scour, shatter, silence, smash, snuff, splinter, terminate, total, vaporize, waste, wreck, zap* (≠ budget, build, conserve, construct, create, embalm, erect, fabricate, fashion, fix, forge, form, frame, maintain, make, manufacture, mend, patch, preserve, protect, rebuild, recondition, reconstruct, renew, renovate, repair, restore, revamp, save, shape, survive, sustain)

LITIGATE (/): *accuse, appeal, argue, arraign, charge, contest, debate, dispute, indict, press, prosecute, sue, summon, try* (≠ accuse, acquit, alibi, clear, exonerate, free, judge, justify, pardon, prove, spare, vindicate)

LOAD (→): *afflict, block, burden, clog, clutter, compromise, congest, constipate, constrain, cramp, curb, delay, disrupt, encumber, enmesh, ensnare, entangle, fetter, fill, foil, freight, -frustrate, hamper, handicap, heap, hinder, hobble, impede, inconvenience, inhibit, involve, lumber, mire, monkey-wrench, mound, obstruct, oppress, overburden, overextend, overload, overtax, overwhelm, pack, pile, -preclude, press, -prevent, rein, repress, restrain, retard, roadblock, sabotage, saddle, slow, smother, stack, stifle, straightjacket, strain, stress, stuff, stump, stymie, subvert, suffocate, suppress, surcharge, tax, tether, -thwart, tie, trammel, trouble, weigh, weight* (≠ aid, alleviate, assist, benefit, boost, buoy, clear, discharge, disencumber, dispatch, ease, encourage, expedite, facilitate, free, further, gladden, grease, hasten, help, hurry, liberate, lift, lighten, loosen, open, organize, permit, promote, propel, release, relieve, remove, rush, separate, smooth, speed, spur, stir, stroke, support, unblock, unburden, unclog, uncomplicate, unencumber, unload, unstop, untie)

LOAD (→): *bloat, brim, bulk, charge, cram, crowd, crush, drench, equip, fill, flood, glut, heap, honeycomb, insert, inundate, jam, jam-pack, lard, mat, overcharge, overfill, overflow, overstuff, pack, penetrate, press, prime, ram, refill, refresh, reload, repack, replenish, sardine, saturate, shove, squash, squeeze, stuff, surfeit, swamp* (≠ bleed, cannibalize, clean, clear, consume, deplete, drain, draw, eliminate, empty, evacuate, exhaust, flush, leach, leech, lighten, purge, scour, sweep, unload, unpack, vacate, void)

LOAN (→): *accommodate, advance, allow, bankroll, contribute, credit, fund, furnish, give, grant, invest, lease, lend, provide, rent, score, scratch, stake, touch, underwrite* (≠ beg, borrow, charge, cheat, earn, mortgage, pawn, pay, receive, refund, reimburse, repay, restore, seize, steal, take)

LOBBY (→): *advance, affect, alter, bill, billboard, boost, bribe, change, convince, demand, drum, flannel, flatter, further, glad-hand, hard-sell, hype, induce, influence, inveigle, leverage, lubricate, midwife, mitigate, moderate, modify, persuade, pitch, plug, presell, press, pressure, prioritize, procure, promote, push, request, sell, soft-sell, soft-soap, solicit, splash, spot, sway, sweet-talk, thump, urge* (≠ block, continue, demotivate, -deter, discourage, dishearten, disincline, dissuade, -forbid, -halt, hinder, insult, -negate, nobble, -prevent, protest, pull, repress, stop, stymie, subvert, suppress, -thwart, undermine, warn)

LOCATE (→): *access, ascertain, clock, deduce, descry, detect, determine, discover, dredge, espy, establish, ferret, find, flag, get, hit, hook, hunt, identify, lay, learn, mark, note, notice, orient, pinpoint, place, position, read, rout, rummage, scan, scout, scrutinize, search, seek, sight, sleuth, spot, station, strike, track, uncover, unearth* (≠ -abandon, -bypass, detour, discard, -discount, -disregard, -ditch, dump, forget, -forsake, -ignore, lose, mislay, misplace, miss, -neglect, -overlook, -sidestep, skip, skirt)

LOCATE (+): *allocate, build, connect, contextualize, dispose, embed, ensconce, establish, fix, graft, implant, inhabit, initiate, insert, install, juxtapose, lay, niche, park, place, plant, position, post, root, seat, set, settle, site, situate, stand, station* (≠ banish, depart, dislodge, dismantle, displace, -escape, extricate, -flee, leave, move, relocate, remove, replace, shift, shunt, supersede, supplant, take)

LOCK (←): *adhere, clasp, clench, clutch, embrace, encircle, enclose, grapple, grasp, grip, hold, hug, keep, press, retain, seize* (≠ -avoid, drop, -evade, loose, loosen, offer, release, repel, -shun, slacken, unclasp)

LOCK (+): *bind, embody, encompass, engage, enmesh, entangle, entwine, envelop, include, incorporate, integrate, jam, join, link, marry, mesh, stick, unite, wed* (≠ break, cut, dissolve, divide, scatter, sever, split, sunder, untangle)

LOCK (+): *bar, barricade, block, bolt, button, clinch, close, deadbolt, fasten, foil, jam, join, latch, padlock, -prevent, seal, secure, shut, stop, stymie, -thwart, zip* (≠ expose, free, invite, loose, open, unlock, unseal, untie, welcome)

LOOSE (→): *blast, cast, catapult, discharge, fire, fling, heave, hurl, hurtle, launch, lob, pelt, pitch, project, shoot, skitter, sling, throw, toss, wing, zap* (≠ accept, block, catch, deflect, hit, hold, holster, keep, obtain, penetrate, receive, smash, strike)

LOOSE (→): *aerate, air, announce, articulate, assert, communicate, concede, confess, confide, confirm, convey, declare, demonstrate, denote, depict, discharge, disclose, divulge, embody, emit, evince, exhibit, express, formulate, manifest, oxygenate, release, report, reveal, share, show, showcase, spill, state, testify, unleash, vent, ventilate, verbalize, vocalize, voice, vouchsafe* (≠ bottle, bridle, check, choke, constrain, contain, control, curb, inhibit, muffle, quell, quiet, rein, repress, restrain, smother, soothe, stifle, still, straightjacket, strangle, suppress, swallow, tame)

LOOSE (+): *air, deliver, detach, discharge, disconnect, disencumber, disengage, disentangle, emancipate, enfranchise, enlarge, express, extricate, free, liberate, loosen, manumit, parole, ransom, redeem, release, rescue, save, separate, spring, unbind, unbolt, unbuckle, unbutton, uncage, unchain, unclasp, uncork, uncouple, undo, unfasten, unfetter, unhitch, unhook, unlace, unlash, unlatch, unleash, unlock, unmoor, unpin, unshackle, unstrap, untie, vent* (≠ bale, bind, box, bridle, cage, chain, check, clinch, commit, confine, conquer, constrain, contain, control, convict, curb, enchain, enslave, fasten, fetter, fix, govern, halter, hamper, handcuff, hold, immure, imprison, incarcerate, inhibit, intern, jail, leash, limit, lock, manacle, pace, package, pen, regulate, rein, restrain, restrict, secure, shackle, smother, subdue, subjugate, tame, trammel)

LOOSEN (+): *allay, alleviate, break, detach, diminish, disarticulate, disconnect, disjoin, disperse, ease, free, lessen, mitigate, moderate, open, reduce, relax, release, slack, slacken, unbind, unclamp, undo, unfasten, unscrew, untie, weaken* (≠ affix, attach, bridle, clamp, clinch, close, constrict, cramp, crush, encumber, hamper, heighten, increase, obstruct, occlude, pucker, regulate, restrain, seize, squeeze, stiffen, strain, stymie, tighten)

LOOT (←): *appropriate, bogart, boost, burglarize, burgle, cheat, comb, defraud, despoil, grab, gut, harry, hijack, hunt, liberate, lift, loft, maraud, nobble, pilfer, pillage, pluck, plunder, poach, raid, rake, ransack, ravage, ravish, relieve, requisition, rifle, rob, rummage, sack, salvage, snatch, steal, swipe, take, thieve* (≠ bestow, bury, conceal, defend, donate, furnish, give, guard, hide, hoard, hog, insure, keep, lock, lose, maintain, offer, police, preserve, protect, receive, refund, -refuse, reimburse, -reject, repay, rescue, restore, save, secure, shield, stash, supply, wall)

LOSE (→): *-abandon, abdicate, bereave, cede, -desert, discard, displace, dispossess, drop, fail, forfeit, forget, -forsake, mislay, misplace, miss, oust, -overlook, relinquish, resign, sacrifice, suffer, surrender, waste, yield* (≠ acquire, adopt, detect, download, enjoy, find, gain, guard, hold, keep, lament, locate, mourn, own, patrol, possess, procure, protect, regret, remember, retain, safeguard, save, secure, survive, track, win)

LOSE (/): *-abandon, abdicate, abolish, annihilate, -avoid, cant, cashier, chuck, clear, -desert, discard, dismiss, -ditch, -dodge, -duck, dump, eliminate, -elude, eradicate, -escape, -evade, exorcise, expunge, exterminate, extinguish, extirpate, fling, -forsake, jettison, junk, leave, liquidate, offload, outrun, pitch, -reject, remove, rid, root, scrap, shake, shed, shuck, slough, toss, unburden, unload* (≠ adopt, ascertain, attach, confront, connect, embrace, employ, face, hold, keep, locate, meet, nail, pinpoint, procure, retain, secure, use, utilize)

LOSE (/): *bleed, blow, burgle, consume, deplete, disburse, disinherit, -disregard, dissipate, divest, drain, exhaust, expend, fritter, impoverish, indulge, lavish, leach, miss, misspend, -neglect, overindulge, overspend, rob, shoot, spend, squander, waste* (≠ bank, budget, conserve, defend, economize, embalm, guard, hoard, invest, maintain, pickle, preserve, procure, protect, regain, retain, save, scant, scrimp, secure, skimp, take)

LOWBALL (←): *assess, bait, belittle, con, defraud, depreciate, devalue, dismiss, disparage, entice, gauge, guess, infer, inveigle, leverage, lure, minimize, miscalculate, misjudge, rank, underbid, undercharge, underemphasize, underestimate, undermine, underprice, underrate,* *undersell, undervalue* (≠ accentuate, accrue, amplify, assert, augment, boost, emphasize, fetishize, hike, hype, inflate, measure, overvalue, presell, prioritize, read, weigh)

LOWER (→): *bobble, bungle, couch, deepen, depress, down, drop, flatten, floor, foozle, fumble, ground, immerse, knock, land, level, plonk, plop, plunge, plunk, sink, submerge, throw, topple* (≠ boost, buoy, crane, draw, elevate, expand, extend, float, fly, heave, hoist, launch, lift, pull, raise)

LOWER (/): *abate, abbreviate, abridge, attenuate, bob, clip, compact, compress, concentrate, condense, constrict, contract, crop, curtail, cut, decrease, decry, deduct, deepen, de-escalate, deflate, delete, demote, dent, deplete, depreciate, detract, devalue, dilute, diminish, discount, dock, downscale, downsize, drain, drop, ease, erode, halve, leach, leech, lessen, lowball, minimize, moderate, modify, modulate, pare, prune, qualify, reduce, retrench, shave, shear, shorten, shrink, slash, soften, subtract, trim, truncate, underbid, underemphasize, undervalue, whittle* (≠ accent, accentuate, accrue, aggrandize, amplify, augment, boost, broaden, complement, dilate, distend, elongate, emphasize, enhance, enlarge, escalate, expand, extend, heighten, increase, inflate, intensify, lengthen, magnify, maximize, optimize, overhaul, prolong, protract, punctuate, raise, redouble, revolutionize, stretch, supplement, swell)

LOWER (/): *abase, abash, affront, badmouth, bastardize, belittle, bench, bestialize, blacken, blackguard, blame, blast, boo, castigate, censure, chasten, cheapen, collapse, condemn, confound, confuse, contaminate, cow, criticize, crush, damn, debase, decay, decry, deemphasize, defame, defile, degrade, demean, denounce, depreciate, depress, detract, devalue, diminish, discomfit, disconcert, -discount, discredit, disfigure, disgrace, dishonor, dismiss, disparage, downgrade, downplay, embarrass, execrate, faze, flatten, fluster, foul, harm, harshen, humble, humiliate, incriminate, injure, insult, libel, malign, mar, marginalize, minimize, mortify, nonplus, pollute, rattle, ridicule, shame, sideline, sink, slam, slander, slash, slate, smirch, subordinate, trivialize, underrate, vulgarize, weaken, worsen* (≠ acclaim, acknowledge, advance, affirm, aggrandize, aid, apotheosize, applaud, assert, blandish, boast, boost, canonize, celebrate, cheer, cite, commend, compliment, congratulate, decontaminate, decorate, deify, dignify, elevate, ennoble, enshrine, enthrone, eulogize, exalt, extol, fête, flatter, glorify, gold-star, gratify, hail, heighten, help, heroicize, heroize, highlight, honor, hype, idealize, idolize, laud, lift, limelight, magnify, plug, praise, presell, prioritize, promote, push, raise, recognize, revere, romanticize, salute, sentimentalize, spotlight, strengthen, tout, upgrade, uplift)

LUBRICATE (+): *accelerate, advance, anoint, assist, bathe, butter, cream, douse, drench, ease, encourage, expedite, facilitate, forward, further, grease, help, lard, lube, make, marinate, moisturize, oil, promote, quicken, slick, smear, smooth, soak, souse, speed, wash, water, wax, wet* (≠ abrade, callous, chafe, coarsen, dehydrate, desiccate, dry, exfoliate, harden, harshen, hinder, parch, roughen, rub, scratch)

LUG (←): *bear, bring, buck, carry, cart, chauffeur, convey, deliver, drag, draw, ferry, fetch, forward, haul, heave, hump, jerk, lift, move, pack, pull, rake, remove, schlep, send, shift, ship, shuttle, smuggle, take, tote, tow, transfer, transmit, transport, trawl, tug, yank* (≠ -abandon, drive, drop, -forsake, hold, hurl, jettison, keep, lose, offload, plonk, propel, punt, push, ram, -refuse, repel, shove, thrust, wing)

LULL (←): *abate, allay, alleviate, ameliorate, appease, assuage, butter, calm, comfort, compose, conciliate, cool, cradle, crush, defuse, demilitarize, dulcify, ease, help, humor, hush, lay, mellow, mitigate, moderate, mollify, narcotize, pacify, placate, propitiate, quell, quiet, quieten, reconcile, relax, relieve, salve, satisfy, sedate, settle, silence, smooth, soften, soft-pedal, solace, soothe, still, stupefy, subdue, sweeten, tame, temper, tranquilize* (≠ aggravate, agitate, annoy, arouse, bother, discompose, disquiet, disturb, earbash, enrage, excite, foment, heckle, incite, infuriate, instigate, irritate, militarize, nag, needle, nettle, niggle, nitpick, perturb, rabble-rouse, rouse, stir, terrify, unnerve, upset, vex)

LUMBER (→): *afflict, burden, charge, clog, clutter, constipate, encumber, fill, foist, freight, hamper, handicap, heap, impede, impose, land, load, mound, oppress, overburden, overextend, overload, overtax, pack, pile, press, saddle, stack, strain, surcharge, tax, weigh, weight* (≠ allay, alleviate, assuage, comfort, discharge, disencumber, disperse, ease, lessen, lift, lighten, mitigate, relieve, unburden, unload)

LURE (←): *allure, attract, bag, bait, beckon, bed, beguile, betray, bewitch, bribe, cajole, call, captivate, capture, catch, charm, convince, decoy, drag, draw, enchant, enmesh, ensnare, entice, fascinate, grab, haul, hook, induce, inveigle, invite, magnetize, persuade, pull, rope, schmooze, seduce, snare, solicit, steer, tangle, tantalize, tease, tempt, train, trap, trigger, urge* (≠ alert, antagonize, ban, banish, block, caution, demotivate, -deter, discourage, disenchant, disgust, dissuade, divert, -evade, hamper, hinder, nobble, repel, repulse, -shun, stymie, -thwart, ward, warn)

LYNCH (/): *asphyxiate, assassinate, assault, attack, butcher, crucify, demonize, dispatch, eliminate, execute, exterminate, hang, hunt, ice, kill, martyr, massacre, murder, orphan, persecute, pillory, punish, purge, remove, sacrifice, slaughter, slay, smite, smother, snuff, stifle, stigmatize, strangle, suffocate, throttle, torment, torture, tyrannize, victimize* (≠ acquit, aerate, aid, alibi, assist, bear, create, defend, excuse, exonerate, guard, harbor, heal, liberate, nourish, nurture, oxygenate, pardon, protect, rescue, save, shelter, shield, spare, ventilate, vindicate)

MAGNIFY (→): *accelerate, accent, accentuate, accrue, add, aggravate, amp, amplify, assert, augment, belabor, boost, broaden, build, consolidate, deepen, develop, elaborate, emphasize, enforce, enhance, enlarge, enliven, exacerbate, exaggerate, expand, extend, fill, flavor, hasten, heighten, heroicize, heroize, honor, idealize, idolize, increase, inflame, inflate, intensify, lengthen, maximize, optimize, overdramatize, overemphasize, overhaul, oversell, pad, poeticize, prioritize, provoke, punctuate, pyramid, quicken, raise, redouble, reinforce, revolutionize, richen, rile, romanticize, season, sentimentalize, sharpen, spice, strengthen, stress, stretch, supplement, swell, unspool, up, widen* (≠ abate, abridge, alleviate, blunt, buffer, compress, concentrate, condense, curtail, decrease, diminish, ease, lessen, lighten, miniaturize, minimize, mitigate, moderate, précis, reduce, shorten, shrink, subdue, summarize, taper, underemphasize, weaken)

MAIM (/): *bang, bash, batter, beat, belt, bloody, bludgeon, box, break, bruise, buffet, castrate, club, cripple, crucify, crush, damage, deball, deform, disable, disfigure, dismember, drub, emasculate, flog, gore, hack, hammer, hamstring, harm, hit, hobble, hogtie, hurt, impair, incapacitate, injure, kill, kneecap, lace, lacerate, lambaste, lame, lash, lick, mangle, mar, maul, murder, mutilate, paralyze, paste, pelt, pommel, pound, pummel, punch, razor, scar, slap, slash, slice, smack, smash, sock, spank, spoil, swat, swipe, thrash, thump, thwack, torment, torture, wallop, whack, whip, wing, wound* (≠ aid, alleviate, armor, bandage, bind, block, brace, cure, defend, doctor, dress, fix, guard, heal, help, maintain, mend, nurse, patch, preserve, protect, recondition, rehabilitate, rejuvenate, remedy, renovate, repair, rescue, restore, save, secure, sew, shield, splint, stitch, support, sustain, suture, tend, treat)

MAINTAIN (→): *advocate, affirm, allege, announce, argue, assert, attest, avow, await, believe, broadcast, champion, claim, colonize, confirm, contend, debate, declare, defend, espouse, hold, insist, justify, perpetuate, plead, proclaim, profess, promise, protest, purport, rationalize, reaffirm, reason, state, support, swear, telegraph, testify, uphold, vindicate, warrant* (≠ -abandon, challenge, consult, contradict, counter, cross-examine, debate, -deny, disavow, disclaim, discredit, -disown, disprove, dispute, distrust, doubt, -forsake, gainsay, grill, interrogate, -negate, question, rebut, recant, refute, -reject, -renounce, -repudiate, retract, scruple, suspect, withdraw) **(¿) ABSTRACTION ALERT. Concrete goals essential!**

MAINTAIN (+): *armor, bronze, budget, conserve, cure, defend, embalm, fix, guard, heal, husband, keep, manage, mend, patch, patrol, pickle,* *preserve, protect, rebuild, reconstruct, recover, recycle, rehabilitate, rejuvenate, remedy, repair, rescue, restore, safeguard, salvage, save, screen, service, shield, support, sustain* (≠ boobytrap, break, conclude, damage, destroy, -disregard, doom, eradicate, erase, harm, hurt, -ignore, impair, injure, monkey-wrench, -neglect, ruin, sabotage, scotch, scupper, scuttle, shelve, subvert, terminate, undermine, vandalize, weed, wreck)

MAINTAIN (+): *aid, assist, bankroll, contribute, feed, finance, fuel, fund, harbor, house, keep, nourish, nurture, patronize, provide, room, shelter, sponsor, stake, supply, support, sustain, underwrite, victual* (≠ banish, bleed, cheat, defund, -deny, -disown, famish, malnourish, -neglect, -rebuff, -reject, -repudiate, reserve, starve, suppress, underfeed, withhold)

MAKE (→): *badger, blackjack, blackmail, bluff, browbeat, bulldoze, bully, coerce, compel, constrain, cow, drag, dragoon, drive, force, harass, hector, hound, impel, impress, intimidate, menace, muscle, obligate, oblige, overcommit, press, pressure, railroad, require, sandbag, shame, steamroller, strong-arm, terrorize, threaten, urge* (≠ allow, argue, bribe, cajole, coax, convince, entice, follow, induce, let, lubricate, midwife, move, obey, pay, permit, persuade, satisfy, schmooze, serve)

MAKE (→): *advance, begin, brainstorm, breed, bring, catalyze, create, cultivate, decide, determine, develop, effect, effectuate, enact, encourage, engender, establish, father, forward, foster, found, further, generate, hatch, inaugurate, induce, initiate, innovate, institute, introduce, invoke, launch, midwife, nourish, nurture, pioneer, produce, promote, prompt, render, set, sire, spawn, start, whelp, work, yield* (≠ abolish, check, control, crush, curb, dampen, demolish, destroy, erase, exterminate, extinguish, impede, inhibit, liquidate, quash, quell, quench, restrain, restrict, retard, smother, squash, squelch, squench, stifle, subdue, suppress, terminate)

MAKE (←): *accomplish, accumulate, achieve, acquire, actualize, amass, annex, attain, bag, bring, capture, carry, catch, claim, clear, crest, draw, earn, gain, garner, get, gross, land, net, notch, obtain, occupy, procure, pull, realize, reap, score, secure, win* (≠ accord, bequeath, bestow, forfeit, give, grant, lose, pay, relinquish, spend, squander, stiff, surrender, undershoot, waste, withhold, yield)

MAKE (+): *arrange, assemble, brainstorm, brew, build, compose, conceive, concoct, configure, construct, contrive, cook, craft, create, design, devise, envisage, erect, establish, fabricate, fashion, father, fix, forge, form, formulate, frame, generate, handcraft, hatch, hew, imagine, improv, improvise, institute, invent, machine, manufacture, mass-produce, mint, model, mold, organize, originate, patent, picture, prepare, produce, raise, ready, rear, refashion, sculpt, serve, sew, shape, sire, stitch, structure, visualize, weave, write* (≠ atomize, break, canker, corrode, corrupt, crack, crumple, demolish, destroy, disassemble, dismantle, dissolve, doom, explode, flatten, fracture, fragment, pulverize, raze, repair, restore, ruin, shatter, shred, smash, splinter, tatter, tear, topple, wreck)

MALIGN (/): *abase, abuse, accuse, antagonize, attack, attaint, badmouth, bait, belittle, besmirch, bestialize, blacken, blame, blast, calumniate, curse, debase, decry, defame, defile, degrade, denigrate, deride, dirty, discredit, -disdain, disfavor, disgrace, dishonor, disparage, disrespect, envenom, harm, humble, humiliate, impugn, injure, insult, libel, misrepresent, muckrake, pollute, revile, roast, scandalize, -scorn, shame, slam, slander, slate, slur, smear, soil, spatter, stain, sully, taint, tarnish, traduce, trash, vilify, villainize, vituperate, wrong* (≠ admire, adore, advantage, applaud, benefit, cherish, commend, congratulate, esteem, eulogize, exalt, extol, favor, glorify, gold-star, gratify, high-five, honor, ingratiate, praise, protect, respect, revere, romanticize, salute, sentimentalize, shield, venerate, vindicate, worship)

MANAGE (→): *administer, advocate, boss, captain, chair, chaperone, command, conduct, control, counsel, designate, direct, disburse, dominate, govern, guard, guide, handle, head, inspect, instruct, keep, lead, maintain, micromanage, mind, monitor, navigate, negotiate, observe, operate, organize, oversee, pace, pilot, police, protect, referee, regiment, regulate, rule, run, safeguard, spearhead, stage-manage, steer, steward, superintend, supervise, survey, tend, train, watch* (≠ abdicate, bobble, bomb, botch, bugger, bungle, collapse, debate, -deny, fake, flub, flunk, follow, fudge, fumble, goof, half-ass, louse, mess, mishandle, misjudge, mismanage, misrule, mistake, muff, -neglect, obey, overestimate, -overlook, -refuse, -shirk, skip, subvert, underestimate)

MANAGE (→): *choreograph, conduct, control, direct, employ, exert, guide, handle, influence, keep, maneuver, manipulate, master, operate, orchestrate, order, organize, pace, play, regulate, request, steer, time, use, wield, work* (≠ addle, baffle, botch, bungle, confuse, crash, destroy, discard, disorder, doom, flub, flunk, fumble, permit, release, ruin, scramble, wreck)

MANAGE (+): *accomplish, achieve, address, arbitrate, arrange, automate, broker, command, control, doctor, engineer, execute, field, finagle, finesse, fix, game, grapple, guide, hack, handle, jockey, maneuver, manipulate, mechanize, micromanage, negotiate, pace, plant, play, pull, regulate, renegotiate, rig, run, scam, steer, swing, take, transact, treat, upstage, wangle, work* (≠ -abandon, bobble, bomb, botch, bugger, bungle, doom, fake, flub, flunk, foozle, forfeit, -forsake, fudge, fumble, half-ass, lose, louse, mess, mishandle, miss, muff, -neglect, -overlook, -refuse, scamp, -shirk, skimp, skip, subvert)

MANEUVER (→): *aid, assist, benefit, berth, broker, chart, conduct, contrive, control, devise, direct, dock, drive, ease, engineer, exercise, finagle, govern, guide, handle, help, jockey, juxtapose, lobby, machinate, man, manage, manipulate, move, navigate, negotiate, outsmart, outthink, outwit, pilot, plan, plot, position, rescue, restore, rule, salvage, save, scheme, script, steer, transact, turn, wangle* (≠ blow, bobble, botch, bungle, crash, damage, -discount, drop, fail, flub, foozle, fumble, half-ass, harm, miscalculate, mishandle, misjudge, mismanage, miss, muff, -neglect, quit, seek, smash, stop)

MANGLE (/): *batter, behead, break, bruise, brutalize, butcher, carve, club, contort, cripple, crush, cut, damage, decapitate, deface, deform, destroy, disembowel, disfigure, distort, efface, eviscerate, flay, gash, gnarl, gore, gut, hack, harm, hash, impair, injure, joint, knife, lacerate, lop, maim, mar, maul, mutilate, razor, rend, rip, ruin, savage, scalp, separate, sever, shear, slash, slay, slice, slit, split, spoil, sunder, tear, truncate, twist, wound, wreck* (≠ aid, alleviate, armor, assist, beautify, benefit, build, construct, cure, doctor, embalm, enhance, fix, guard, heal, help, improve, join, mend, patch, preserve, protect, rectify, refine, remedy, repair, restore, reunite, revive, secure, sew, shield, solder, splint, stitch, sustain, unite, weld)

MANGLE (/): *bend, blemish, blight, blow, bobble, boggle, boot, botch, bugger, bungle, butcher, contort, corrupt, crook, damage, deform, destroy, disfigure, distort, doom, flaw, flub, fluff, flunk, foozle, foul, fumble, harm, hurt, impair, injure, louse, mar, mishandle, mismanage, muddle, muff, murder, mutilate, pervert, ruin, spoil, vitiate, wreck* (≠ aid, alleviate, ameliorate, assist, better, correct, doctor, enhance, fix, help, improve, maintain, patch, preserve, protect, recondition, rectify, refine, reform, remedy, renovate, repair, rescue, revamp, save, sustain, tune)

MANHANDLE (→): *abuse, ambush, assail, attack, backhand, bash, batter, beat, brutalize, buffet, bulldoze, clobber, clout, club, drub, fight, harm, hit, hurt, ill-treat, injure, jostle, jump, knock, lambaste, lick, maltreat, mangle, maul, menace, mishandle, mistreat, misuse, molest, muscle, oppress, persecute, pommel, pound, pummel, push, railroad, savage, shove, slap, steamroller, thrash, threaten, torment, torture, victimize, wound, wrestle, wrong* (≠ appease, baby, caress, coddle, cotton, cuddle, delight, entertain, fondle, foster, guard, humor, indulge, maintain, mollycoddle, nurse, nurture, oblige, overprotect, pacify, pamper, pet, placate, please, protect, riffle, satisfy, soothe, spoil, spoon-feed, stroke, strum, tickle, touch)

MANHANDLE (←): *carry, convey, drag, draw, drive, ferry, haul, heave, hump, jerk, lug, move, propel, pull, push, ram, schlep, shove, thrust, tow, transport, tug, yank* (≠ -abandon, cherish, defend, drop, -forsake, guard, lose, miss, plonk, protect, save, secure, treasure)

MANIFEST (→): *advertise, air, announce, attest, bare, bellow, betray, blaze, broadcast, communicate, confess, confirm, declare, demonstrate, disclose, display, establish, evince, exhibit, expose, express, flash, illustrate, mark, out, parade, placard, present, proclaim, project, prove, publicize, reveal, show, showcase, sport, telegraph, trumpet, uncloak, uncover, verbalize, vocalize, voice* (≠ belie, bleep, camouflage, cloak, clothe, cloud, conceal, costume, counterfeit, cover, disguise, distort, embellish, embroider, falsify, garble, gild, gloss, hide, mask, misrepresent, obscure, occlude, spackle, twist, varnish, veil, whitewash)

MANIFEST (→): *actualize, concretize, conjure, embody, epitomize, exemplify, express, exteriorize, externalize, illustrate, image, incarnate, incorporate, instance, materialize, objectify, personalize, personify, realize, reify, signify, substantiate, typify* (≠ annihilate, bury, cloak, conceal, deep-six, -deny, destroy, disembody, dissolve, ensconce, erase, hide, -negate, -nullify, obliterate, veil, withhold) **(¿) ABSTRACTION ALERT. Concrete goals essential!**

MANIPULATE (→): *arrange, brew, broker, captain, coerce, command, compass, concert, conclude, concoct, conduct, contrive, control, direct, drive, engineer, finagle, finesse, frame, gerrymander, guide, handle, hatch, influence, intrigue, lobby, machinate, manage, maneuver, mastermind, milk, mold, move, navigate, negotiate, operate, plot, position, quarterback, renegotiate, run, scheme, sculpt, shape, situate, steer, supervise, turn, wangle* (≠ -abandon, blow, bobble, botch, bungle, butcher, confuse, flub, follow, fumble, half-ass, louse, mangle, mishandle, mismanage, muff, muscle, obey, perplex, puzzle)

MANIPULATE (→): *caress, contact, contour, employ, exert, feel, finger, fondle, form, knead, knuckle, massage, maul, mold, operate, ply, pound, press, pummel, riffle, rolf, rub, shape, squeeze, swing, thumb, touch, unsheathe, use, wield, work* (≠ -avoid, cripple, drop, harm, hit, -ignore, injure, -neglect, punch, -shun, withhold)

MANIPULATE (←): *arrange, beguile, bluff, buffalo, bullshit, cheat, chisel, con, contrive, convince, cook, cozen, deceive, defraud, delude, devise, doctor, double-talk, dupe, embellish, embroider, engineer, euchre, exploit, falsify, fiddle, finagle, finesse, fleece, fool, game, gerrymander, gull, gyp, hoax, hocus-pocus, hoodwink, hustle, influence, intrigue, jockey, josh, juggle, kid, machinate, maneuver, massage, mastermind, misrepresent, outwit, persuade, play, plot, rig, rook, scheme, shanghai, shuffle, skin, snooker, snow, sucker, sway, swindle, take, thimblerig, trick, upstage, use* (≠ accuse, badmouth, bulldoze, bungle, challenge, compensate, confess, confide, confirm, confront, defend, defy, -deny, divulge, expose, fumble, help, oppose, protect, railroad, -refuse, resist, respect, restore, steamroll, support)

MANUFACTURE (←): *alter, bootleg, camouflage, copy, counterfeit, disguise, distort, doctor, embellish, embroider, fabricate, fake, falsify, feign, fiddle, forge, generate, imitate, impersonate, manipulate, massage, misrepresent, misstate, pervert, pirate, playact, pretend, reproduce, rig, roleplay, simulate* (≠ authenticate, betray, certify, conceal, confess, confirm, corroborate, denounce, detect, divulge, expose, hide, -overlook, prove, reveal, uncover, unmask, validate, verify)

MANUFACTURE (+): *accomplish, assemble, build, carve, cast, cobble, complete, compose, concoct, configure, construct, contrive, cook, craft, create, erect, execute, fabricate, fashion, forge, form, frame, fudge, handcraft, hew, machine, make, mass-produce, mill, model, mold, prefab, prefabricate, process, produce, raise, rear, refashion, remake, sculpt, shape, structure, synthesize, tool, weave* (≠ break, corrode, crumble, damage, destroy, disassemble, dismantle, dissolve, explode, flatten, fracture, fragment, pulverize, raze, ruin, shatter, shiver, shred, smash, splinter, tatter, tear, wreck)

MANUFACTURE (+): *arrange, brew, coin, compose, conceive, concoct, construct, contrive, create, daydream, design, devise, dream, envisage, establish, fabricate, father, formulate, frame, generate, hatch, imagine, institute, invent, mint, organize, originate, picture, plan, plot, produce, script, visualize, weave* (≠ adopt, clone, copy, copycat, derive, duplicate, emulate, imitate, mimic, reduplicate, replicate, reproduce)

MAP (+): *arrange, blueprint, bound, calculate, chart, choreograph, compass, define, delineate, design, diagram, draft, draw, frame, fringe, graph, heed, margin, mark, mind, note, notice, observe, organize, outline, plan, plot, prepare, profile, project, regard, retrace, scheme, script, shape, silhouette, sketch, strategize, survey, trace, triangulate* (≠ addle, adumbrate, baffle, bewilder, confound, confuse, disorganize, -disregard, erase, gloss, -ignore, jumble, lose, mislead, muddle, mystify, -omit, -overlook, perplex, puzzle, skip)

MAR (/): *abrade, abuse, afflict, batter, bend, blemish, blight, blister, blot, blotch, botch, break, bruise, bugger, bungle, chafe, cheapen, check, chip, contaminate, contort, corrupt, cripple, crosshatch, cut, damage, deface, defile, deform, deprave, desecrate, despoil, detract, ding, disable, discolor, disfigure, distort, dot, efface, flaw, fleck, fluff, fracture, freckle, fumble, gash, hack, harm, harshen, hinder, hurt, ill-treat, impair, infect, injure, kink, maim, maltreat, mangle, mark, miscalculate, misconstrue, mishandle, misjudge, mutate, mutilate, nick, notch, pervert, pillage, pockmark, pollute, prejudice, ransack, ravage, rend, ruin, sabotage, scalp, scar, score, scotch, scrape, scratch, scuff, slit, smash, speck, splotch, spoil, spot, stain, sully, taint, tarnish, torment, torture, traumatize, twist, vandalize, violate, vitiate, warp, welt, wither, wound, wreck* (≠ accomplish, achieve, adorn, aid, align, ameliorate, appreciate, assist, barbarize, beautify, better, bless, build, cherish, clean, cleanse, create, cure, decontaminate, decorate, defend, dignify, doctor, edit, elevate, embellish, enhance, ennoble, enrich, enshrine, fancify, fix, flatter, glitz, glorify, grace, grow, guard, hallow, heal, help, improve, increase, manage, mend, optimize, ornament, overhaul, patch, perfect, preserve, protect, purify, raise, rarefy, rebuild, recondition, reconstruct, rectify, refine, rehabilitate, remedy, remodel, renovate, repair, respect, restore, rethink, retool, revamp, revise, revolutionize, right, save, sophisticate, straighten, strengthen, tinsel, tool, trim, upgrade)

MARAUD (←): *attack, burgle, capture, despoil, devastate, filch, fleece, forage, grab, hijack, lift, loot, misappropriate, nab, pilfer, pillage, pinch, pluck, plunder, poach, pocket, purloin, raid, ransack, ravage, raze, remove, rifle, rob, sack, seize, shanghai, snatch, sneak, spoil, steal, strip, swindle, take, vandalize* (≠ aid, assist, bestow, contribute, defend, entrust, furnish, guard, offer, patrol, police, preserve, protect, rebuild, recover, rescue, restore, retain, return, safeguard, save, secure, shelter, shield, withstand)

MARGINALIZE (/): *abjure, abstract, alienate, -avoid, ban, banish, bar, bench, blackball, blacklist, bump, -cold-shoulder, consign, degrade, delegate, demote, deport, detach, diminish, disaffect, disconnect, dispatch, divorce, downgrade, eject, -eschew, -exclude, exile, expel, humble, isolate, lower, maroon, minimize, -omit, orphan, -ostracize, oust, reduce, -refuse, -reject, relegate, remove, seclude, segregate, separate, sequester, -shirk, -shun, sideline, -snub, -spurn, strand, transfer, underemphasize* (≠ absorb, accentuate, acclaim, accommodate, adopt, advance, aggrandize, assimilate, celebrate, commend, compliment, elevate, embrace, emphasize, ennoble, exalt, feature, foreground, highlight, include, incorporate, integrate, internalize, join, lift, praise, present, promote, refine, spotlight, support, upgrade, value, welcome)

MARK (→): *brand, budget, call, caption, chalk, characterize, designate, distinguish, dub, earmark, entitle, flag, hallmark, identify, inscribe, invoice, label, monogram, name, package, stamp, stigmatize, style, tab, tag, term, ticket, title* (≠ anonymize, baffle, conceal, confuse, hide, -ignore, mask, mislabel, muddle, mystify, obfuscate, obscure, perplex, stump)

MARK (←): *analyze, appraise, ascertain, assay, assess, benchmark, categorize, clock, compare, correct, critique, decide, determine, discover, estimate, evaluate, grade, guesstimate, judge, learn, misjudge, misprize, price, prioritize, prize, rank, rate, read, reappraise, reassess, reevaluate, revalue, scan, scrutinize, set, settle, survey, test, underestimate, undervalue, valuate, value* (≠ -blank, -bypass, -disregard, -ignore, miss, -neglect, -omit, -overlook, predetermine, -sidestep, skip)

MARK (+): *acknowledge, bless, celebrate, ceremonialize, commemorate, consecrate, enshrine, exalt, fête, fetishize, glorify, honor, keep, laud, memorialize, mourn, observe, praise, recognize, regret, remember, ritualize, sanctify, solemnize* (≠ break, contemn, -despise, disgrace, dishonor, -disregard, forget, -ignore, -neglect, -overlook, profane, transgress, violate)

MARK (/): *blemish, blot, blotch, brand, bruise, chip, crosshatch, cut, damage, dapple, daub, dent, discolor, dot, fleck, freckle, gash, gouge, groove, indent, marble, mottle, nick, nock, notch, pepper, scar, score, scratch, serrate, smudge, snick, soil, speck, speckle, splash, splatter, splotch, spot, spray, sprinkle, stain, stipple, streak, stripe, stud, taint, tally, vandyke* (≠ anonymize, blanch, bleach, blot, -cancel, clean, cleanse, delete, efface, eradicate, erase, even, excise, expunge, fade, fix, heal, launder, level, miss, obliterate, polish, rectify, remove, repair, rinse, shine, smooth, wash, wipe)

MARKET (→): *advertise, aggrandize, aid, announce, assist, auction, back, ballyhoo, barter, boost, broadcast, carry, champion, circulate, commend, commercialize, commodify, condone, declare, display, disseminate, distribute, elevate, encourage, endorse, exchange, export, favor, further,* *handle, hawk, hype, import, inform, inspire, keep, kindle, leverage, license, limelight, mainstream, merchandize, monetize, motivate, notify, peddle, pimp, plug, popularize, praise, presell, proclaim, promo, promote, promulgate, provide, publicize, publish, push, retail, sanction, sell, shill, spark, spur, stimulate, stock, supply, support, swap, telegraph, tout, trade, traffic, upgrade, wholesale* (≠ ban, -boycott, buy, camouflage, conceal, criticize, critique, deride, disguise, disparage, -eschew, foil, hide, insult, knock, mock, neg, pan, picket, pillory, -prohibit, protest, purchase, recall, recant, -refuse, -reject, reserve, ridicule, -scorn, -shun, slam, -spurn, suppress, -thwart, withhold)

MAROON (/): *-abandon, abjure, banish, beach, deliver, -desert, discard, -disown, -ditch, dump, -escape, -exclude, exile, fling, -forsake, isolate, jettison, junk, leave, marginalize, offload, -ostracize, oust, -quit, -reject, relinquish, -renounce, -repudiate, scrap, seclude, segregate, shed, shuck, strand, surrender, vacate, yield* (≠ befriend, chase, chauffeur, harbor, hold, invite, join, keep, maintain, own, possess, reclaim, redeem, rescue, reserve, retain, reunite, save, seek, welcome, withhold)

MARRY (+): *ally, amalgamate, assemble, associate, bind, chain, cluster, coalesce, combine, compound, congregate, conjoin, conjugate, connect, convene, couple, fuse, gather, hitch, hook, hybridize, integrate, join, knit, link, match, mate, meet, merge, pair, recombine, reconnect, reintegrate, rejoin, reunify, reunite, splice, synthesize, unify, unite, weld, yoke* (≠ cleave, detach, disband, disconnect, disjoin, disjoint, disperse, disunite, divide, divorce, estrange, isolate, mismatch, -ostracize, oust, part, resolve, scatter, section, separate, sever, split, sunder, uncouple, unmarry, unyoke)

MARSHAL (→): *accompany, attend, chair, chaperone, conduct, control, convoy, direct, escort, guide, lead, manage, pilot, route, see, shepherd, show, spearhead, steer, take, usher* (≠ concede, dog, follow, hound, obey, shadow, tail, tailgate, trail)

MARSHAL (+): *activate, arrange, assemble, call, collect, congregate, conjure, convene, gather, group, include, integrate, invoke, mobilize, muster, order, organize, rally, reassemble, reform, regroup, reorganize, summon, unify, unite* (≠ alienate, deactivate, demobilize, detach, diffuse, disarrange, disband, dismiss, disorder, disorganize, disperse, disrupt, dissolve, disturb, divide, estrange, -ostracize, oust, part, scatter, split)

MARSHAL (+): *align, alphabetize, arrange, array, assemble, classify, codify, collect, compile, coordinate, cue, deploy, display, dispose, file, gather, glean, groom, group, line, map, muster, order, organize, place, prioritize, queue, range, rank, regiment, sequence, set, spruce, straighten, systematize, tidy, unscramble* (≠ derange, disarrange, disarray, dishevel, disorder, jumble, mess, muss, rumple, scramble, tangle, untidy, upset)

MASH (/): *beat, crush, extract, extrude, grind, mangle, mince, pestle, pound, powder, press, pulp, pulverize, pummel, purée, ream, smash, squash, squeeze* (≠ assemble, build, construct, forge, form, mend, mold, preserve, produce, protect, raise, reconstitute, repair, restore, save, shape)

MASK (/): *act, affect, assume, becloud, bedim, befog, belie, blanket, bleep, block, blot, bury, camouflage, cloak, clothe, cloud, conceal, costume, counterfeit, cover, curtain, darken, disguise, dissimulate, dress, eclipse, ensconce, enshroud, fake, feign, gild, gloss, hide, holster, hood, impersonate, obscure, obstruct, occlude, occult, -omit, overlap, overshadow, paper, play, playact, pose, pretend, roleplay, screen, shade, sheathe, shield, shroud, simulate, smother, spackle, suppress, varnish, veil, whitewash* (≠ accost, advertise, air, augment, bare, bellow, betray, boost, brandish, broadcast, circulate, clarify, concede, confess, confide, confirm, confront, disclose, discover, display, disseminate, divulge, elevate, enhance, enlarge, exhibit, expose, flaunt, floodlight, illuminate, limelight, magnify, maximize, parade, present, proclaim, publicize, publish, reveal, shout, show, showcase, spread, telegraph, trumpet, uncloak, unclothe, uncover, undrape, unmask, unveil)

MASS (+): *accumulate, agglomerate, amass, assemble, bank, build, clump, cluster, collect, compile, concentrate, conglomerate, congregate, crowd, gather, glean, heap, lump, muster, overcrowd, pile, rally, salvage, scavenge, stack, stockpile, swarm, throng* (≠ deplete, diffuse, disperse, dissipate, donate, empty, estrange, exhaust, gut, -omit, scatter, separate, spend, spill, split, squander, use, waste)

MASSACRE (/): *annihilate, assassinate, axe, blitzkrieg, butcher, croak, decimate, defeat, destroy, devastate, dispatch, doom, eradicate, erase, execute, exterminate, fell, kill, liquidate, murder, obliterate, orphan, rout, slaughter, slay, smite, snuff, terminate, thrash, vanquish, waste, weed, wreck* (≠ armor, bear, birth, build, create, defend, embalm, entomb, gestate, harbor, heal, help, maintain, nourish, nurture, preserve, protect, repair, rescue, save, shelter, shield, survive, sustain, withstand)

MASSAGE (→): *caress, curb, knead, manipulate, mold, pat, press, pummel, push, relax, rolf, rub, shampoo, stimulate, stretch, stroke, strum, touch* (≠ aggravate, damage, distress, -ignore, injure, irritate, -neglect, pain)

MASSAGE (→): *adulterate, alter, bend, cook, counterfeit, diddle, distort, doctor, elaborate, embellish, embroider, fake, falsify, fiddle, fix, forge, fudge, game, half-ass, maneuver, manipulate, misrepresent, misstate, outsmart, outwit, pervert, pretend, rig, twist* (≠ authenticate, certify, clarify, confirm, correct, corroborate, decipher, detect, document, establish, evidence, expose, illuminate, illustrate, protect, prove, realign, rectify, right, show, substantiate, support, validate, verify, witness)

MASTER (→): *ace, administer, annihilate, beat, best, better, block, bomb, boss, break, bridle, bury, cap, capture, charge, check, checkmate, clobber, command, conduct, conquer, control, coordinate, cream, crush, curb, defeat, direct, discipline, dispatch, dominate, drub, eclipse, exceed, finish, flatten, foil, get, govern, grip, handle, head, hold, housebreak, housetrain, humble, lead, lick, manage, one-up, outdistance, outdo, outfight, outgrow, outgun, outlast, outmaneuver, outperform, outplay, outrank, outreach, outshine, outstrip, outthink, overcome, overpower, oversee, overtake, overthrow, overturn, overwhelm, prejudice, pressure,* *quell, rout, rule, shellac, skin, skunk, slaughter, smoke, spearhead, subdue, subject, subjugate, superintend, supervise, suppress, surmount, surpass, sway, sweep, take, tame, thrash, top, transcend, trim, trounce, trump, unseat, upend, upset, vanquish, wallop, wax, whip, win* (≠ -abandon, adulate, aid, assist, bobble, bomb, botch, bungle, copy, defy, deregulate, fail, flunk, fold, follow, forfeit, -forsake, fumble, half-ass, help, liberate, lose, mind, mismanage, misrule, muff, -neglect, obey, permit, release, resign, respect, retire, serve, submit, subvert, surrender, survive, trail, unleash, withstand, worship, yield)

MASTER (+): *absorb, acquire, analyze, apprehend, assimilate, comprehend, consider, contemplate, cram, diagnose, digest, discover, examine, get, glean, grasp, grok, imbibe, incorporate, integrate, internalize, investigate, know, learn, manage, meditate, memorize, mull, ponder, procure, read, realize, reference, research, revise, scan, scrutinize, secure, study, survey, suss, train, understand, work* (≠ botch, confuse, dismiss, -disregard, flunk, forget, garble, half-ass, -ignore, misconstrue, misdiagnose, mishear, misinterpret, misread, misremember, miss, misunderstand, -neglect, -omit, -overlook, unlearn, wipe) **(¿) ABSTRACTION ALERT. Concrete goals essential!**

MASTERMIND (→): *adjust, arrange, assemble, automate, brew, broker, calibrate, captain, chair, chart, choreograph, command, compass, compose, conceive, concert, conclude, concoct, conduct, contrive, control, cook, coordinate, design, devise, direct, engineer, facilitate, finagle, finalize, finesse, forge, frame, gerrymander, graph, handle, hatch, improvise, inspire, lead, machinate, manage, maneuver, manipulate, marshal, mechanize, mediate, negotiate, orchestrate, order, organize, originate, outsmart, outthink, outwit, plan, plot, prep, prepare, program, quarterback, ready, regulate, renegotiate, run, schedule, scheme, script, settle, shape, solve, spearhead, stage, stage-manage, steer, strategize, structure, supervise, synthesize, transact, wangle, weave* (≠ addle, baffle, bewilder, blow, bobble, bomb, botch, bungle, butcher, capsize, clutter, confound, confuse, damage, destroy, disorder, disorganize, disrupt, disturb, doom, drop, flub, fluff, flunk, forget, fudge, fumble, half-ass, -ignore, jumble, mangle, mar, mishandle, mismanage, miss, muddle, muff, muss, -neglect, perplex, puzzle, ruffle, ruin, scotch, scramble, -shirk, spoil, upset, wreck)

MATCH (→): *approach, beat, better, compare, eclipse, equal, meet, oppose, outclass, outdistance, outdo, outpace, outperform, outrank, outshine, outstrip, overtake, parallel, rival, suggest, surpass, tie, top, touch, transcend, trump, vanquish* (≠ abide, advance, aggrandize, back, bear, bolster, boost, cede, coach, concede, endure, fail, flunk, foster, further, half-ass, improve, nurture, promote, suffer, support, survive, train, uplift)

MATCH (+): *accompany, accord, adapt, align, balance, blend, complement, connect, coordinate, counterbalance, counterpoise, echo, equalize, fit, harmonize, image, mirror, pattern, relate, repeat, square,* *suit, supplement, tally* (≠ -abandon, challenge, contradict, counter, defy, -deny, disavow, disclaim, -disown, disprove, dispute, gainsay, invalidate, mismatch, -negate, question, rebut, refute, -reject, -repudiate)

MATCH (+): *affiance, ally, betroth, combine, commit, couple, engage, espouse, hitch, join, link, marry, mate, pair, pledge, promise, team, unite, wed, yoke* (≠ break, dissolve, divide, divorce, estrange, isolate, mismatch, -ostracize, oust, part, separate, split, sunder, unmarry)

MATERIALIZE (←): *actualize, attest, compel, concretize, conjure, create, demonstrate, display, engender, establish, evince, evoke, exhibit, expose, express, exteriorize, externalize, form, generate, illustrate, initiate, invoke, make, manifest, originate, present, produce, propagate, prove, raise, reify, reveal, rouse, show, showcase, summon* (≠ abolish, annihilate, conceal, deep-six, delete, destroy, dissolve, eliminate, end, eradicate, erase, expunge, exterminate, hide, kill, nullify, obliterate, terminate)

MATURE (+): *advance, age, brew, concoct, correct, develop, edify, educate, evolve, gray, grow, harden, mellow, open, perfect, prepare, realign, rectify, ripen, school, season, soften, sophisticate, teach, temper, toughen, train, unfold, weather* (≠ baby, cocoon, coddle, -decline, fade, infantilize, pamper, refresh, rejuvenate, shrivel, spoil, weaken, wilt, wither, worsen)

MAUL (/): *abuse, assault, attack, backhand, bang, bash, batter, beat, belt, bite, bludgeon, buffet, claw, clout, club, concuss, conk, drub, flagellate, flail, hamstring, hit, hobble, hurt, ill-treat, lacerate, lash, maim, maltreat, mangle, manhandle, molest, mug, muscle, mutilate, paste, paw, pelt, pound, pummel, rend, savage, skin, tear, thrash, trample, wallop, wax, whip* (≠ aid, armor, assist, bandage, block, coddle, comfort, doctor, fix, fondle, guard, heal, help, lose, maintain, mend, nurse, nurture, preserve, protect, repair, replace, rescue, restore, sew, shelter, shield, stitch, support, surrender)

MAXIMIZE (→): *accelerate, accent, accentuate, accrue, accumulate, add, advance, aggrandize, amass, amplify, assert, augment, beef, bolster, boost, breed, broaden, build, bump, buttress, collect, complement, compound, deepen, develop, dilate, distend, double, elevate, elongate, emphasize, enhance, enlarge, escalate, expand, extend, fatten, flavor, foster, further, grow, heighten, hype, increase, inflate, intensify, lengthen, magnify, multiply, optimize, overemphasize, overhaul, prioritize, proliferate, prolong, propagate, protract, pump, punctuate, raise, ratchet, reinforce, revolutionize, richen, scale, season, spice, spread, stoke, strengthen, stretch, supersize, supplement, swell, treble, triple, unspool, up, upgrade, widen* (≠ abate, abbreviate, abridge, attenuate, cheapen, compress, concentrate, condense, constrict, contract, curtail, cut, decrease, de-escalate, depreciate, depress, devaluate, devalue, diminish, downsize, elide, lessen, lowball, lower, miniaturize, minify, minimize, mitigate, moderate, reduce, restrain, restrict, retrench, shorten, shrink, subtract, syncopate, trim, truncate, underemphasize)

MEASURE (→): *allocate, allot, allow, apportion, assign, balance, budget, cut, deal, dispense, distribute, earmark, give, level, mete, parcel, partition, portion, ration, regulate, restore, segment, set, share, slice, split, square* (≠ check, conceal, control, curb, deduct, deprive, hide, hold, keep, -refuse, repress, reserve, restrain, retain, suppress, withhold)

MEASURE (←): *appraise, ascertain, assess, benchmark, calculate, calibrate, caliper, categorize, check, cipher, compare, compute, conjecture, consider, contemplate, critique, demarcate, detect, determine, discover, estimate, evaluate, eyeball, fathom, figure, gauge, grade, guesstimate, judge, mark, meter, number, numerate, plumb, portion, prioritize, quantify, rank, rate, read, reckon, record, scale, size, sound, span, sum, suppose, survey, tally, time, total, triangulate, valuate, value, weigh* (≠ assume, bewilder, conceal, confound, confuse, deceive, defraud, disguise, disorder, disorganize, -disregard, fancy, guess, hide, hypothesize, -ignore, lose, mask, misgauge, mismeasure, misread, miss, mistake, misunderstand, muddle, mystify, -neglect, obscure, -overlook, perplex, predict, puzzle, surmise, trick, wonder) **(¿) ABSTRACTION ALERT. Concrete goals essential!**

MECHANIZE (+): *arm, assemble, automate, centralize, computerize, decentralize, depersonalize, design, develop, engineer, equip, expedite, improve, industrialize, invent, modernize, motorize, patent, power, program, remodel, revolutionize, rig, streamline, systematize, update, upgrade, weaponize* (≠ antiquate, break, corrode, customize, damage, disassemble, dismantle, fragment, hobble, humanize, hurt, personalize, preserve, retain, ruin, stagnate, wreck)

MEDIATE (+): *adjudicate, arbitrate, bother, broker, chair, control, decide, determine, direct, equalize, interpose, invade, judge, manage, moderate, negotiate, pacify, propitiate, reconcile, referee, renegotiate, resolve, restore, reunite, settle, solve, transact, umpire, weigh* (≠ -avoid, battle, challenge, cheat, confront, debate, defy, demand, -disregard, -eschew, -ignore, inflame, instigate, manipulate, -overlook, provoke, race, -shun)

MEDICATE (→): *anesthetize, apply, bandage, chloroform, cure, deaden, diagnose, doctor, dose, drug, heal, immunize, inject, inoculate, lace, mainline, narcotize, numb, nurse, physic, prescribe, quarantine, remedy, sedate, spike, stupefy, tranquilize, treat, vaccinate* (≠ afflict, contaminate, damage, harm, hurt, -ignore, incapacitate, infect, infest, injure, maim, misdiagnose, -neglect, overdose, plague, poison, pollute, sicken, weaken, worsen)

MEET (→): *accost, bear, bump, catch, confront, contact, crisscross, cross, discover, endure, experience, face, greet, handle, hit, manage, pass, salute, stomach, strike, suffer, tackle, tolerate, weather, wrestle* (≠ -avoid, -disregard, -ditch, -dodge, -duck, -elude, -escape, -evade, -flee, -ignore, -neglect, -omit, -overlook, shake, -shirk, -shun)

MEET (+): *accomplish, achieve, answer, claim, commit, compass, complete, conclude, consummate, crest, discharge, effect, equal,* *execute, fill, finalize, finish, fulfill, keep, make, match, perfect, perform, qualify, redeem, satisfy* (≠ breach, break, -disregard, forget, -ignore, mismatch, -neglect, -overlook, -slight, transgress, violate)

MEET (+): *assemble, associate, cluster, collect, concentrate, conglomerate, congregate, conjoin, connect, consolidate, convene, couple, cross, gather, intersect, join, link, merge, muster, rally, reassemble, reconvene, touch, unite* (≠ -abandon, -avoid, break, depart, disband, disjoin, disperse, disunite, -elude, -escape, -eschew, -evade, -flee, leave, scatter, split)

MELD (+): *add, alloy, amalgamate, beat, blend, coalesce, collage, combine, commingle, composite, compound, concrete, conflate, conjoin, emulsify, fold, fuse, homogenize, hybridize, incorporate, integrate, intermingle, intermix, intertwine, interweave, join, knit, link, merge, mingle, mix, stir, synthesize, toss, unite, weave, whisk* (≠ break, cleave, detach, diffuse, disengage, disjoin, disperse, dissolve, disunite, divide, divorce, join, part, rupture, scatter, separate, sever, split, sunder, unmix)

MELD (+): *accommodate, adapt, align, arrange, attune, balance, blend, complement, compose, equalize, fit, harmonize, match, mix, suit* (≠ confuse, disarrange, dislocate, disorganize, disrupt, disturb, hamper, impede, interrupt, mismatch, sabotage, unsettle, upset)

MELLOW (+): *age, develop, dulcify, grow, improve, mature, mollify, pacify, perfect, placate, relax, ripen, season, settle, soften, subdue, sweeten, temper* (≠ agitate, callous, constrain, energize, excite, hurry, hustle, rush, sharpen, strain, stress, tire, toughen)

MELT (/): *canker, collapse, corrode, crumble, defrost, digest, dilute, disintegrate, dissolve, erode, flux, fuse, liquefy, rarefy, separate, smelt, soften, thaw, thin, weaken* (≠ brace, clot, coagulate, concentrate, condense, congeal, cool, freeze, harden, petrify, separate, set, solidify, steel, temper, thicken, toughen)

MENACE (/): *alarm, appall, blackjack, blackmail, bluff, browbeat, brutalize, bully, chance, chill, coerce, compromise, daunt, dismay, endanger, expose, frighten, funk, gamble, hazard, imperil, intimidate, jeopardize, lower, muscle, overhang, press, pressure, railroad, risk, scare, spook, subject, target, terrify, terrorize, threaten, torment, trash-talk, venture, wager* (≠ calm, defend, guard, harbor, help, house, humor, lull, mellow, mitigate, moderate, mollify, nurture, pacify, patrol, placate, preserve, protect, reassure, rescue, resume, safeguard, save, shelter, shield)

MEND (+): *aid, ameliorate, amend, bandage, better, cobble, cure, darn, doctor, fix, heal, knit, overhaul, patch, reassemble, rebuild, recondition, reconstruct, recover, rectify, redress, refit, refurbish, regenerate, rejuvenate, remedy, renew, renovate, repair, restore, retool, retouch, revamp, revise, right, service, sew, solder, splint, treat* (≠ afflict, blemish, break, bust, damage, deface, disable, disfigure, efface, eradicate, flaw, harm, harshen, impair, inflict, maim, mangle, mar, monkey-wrench, mutilate, ruin, sabotage, scotch, scupper, scuttle, shred, splinter, spoil, tatter, tear, undercut, undermine, unsew, vandalize, wreck)

MENTOR (+): *accompany, attend, brief, chaperone, coach, convoy, counsel, cultivate, direct, drill, engineer, enlighten, escort, foster, godfather, guide, inculcate, indoctrinate, inform, instruct, lead, nurture, oversee, pilot, school, shepherd, show, squire, steer, superintend, supervise, sway, teach, train, tutor* (≠ abuse, crucify, damage, decondition, exploit, hinder, hurt, -ignore, impede, inhibit, injure, maltreat, mislead, molest, obstruct, oppress, -thwart, torture, wrong)

MERGE (+): *add, amalgamate, assimilate, beat, blend, coalesce, collage, combine, commingle, composite, compound, concrete, conflate, conjoin, consolidate, emulsify, fold, fuse, homogenize, hybridize, incorporate, integrate, intermingle, intermix, internalize, intertwine, interweave, join, knit, link, meet, meld, melt, mingle, mix, stir, synthesize, toss, unite, weave* (≠ break, cleave, detach, diffuse, disengage, disjoin, disperse, dissolve, disunite, divide, divorce, estrange, -ostracize, oust, part, rupture, scatter, separate, sever, split, sunder, unmix)

MESMERIZE (←): *absorb, allure, amaze, anesthetize, appease, arouse, arrest, assuage, attract, bedazzle, beguile, bewitch, cajole, calm, captivate, charm, command, compel, control, dazzle, deaden, delight, distract, dizzy, draw, drug, dull, ease, enchant, engage, engross, enrapture, enslave, ensnare, entertain, enthrall, enthuse, entice, entrance, fascinate, fixate, galvanize, grab, gratify, grip, hold, hook, hush, hypnotize, immerse, immobilize, infatuate, interest, intoxicate, intrigue, inveigle, involve, lull, lure, magnetize, mellow, mitigate, mollify, monopolize, motivate, narcotize, numb, obsess, occupy, overpower, overwhelm, pacify, paralyze, please, possess, preoccupy, provoke, quell, quiet, ravish, razzle-dazzle, relax, relieve, rivet, seduce, settle, silence, soothe, spellbind, still, stimulate, stir, stun, stupefy, subdue, subjugate, suggest, tantalize, tempt, thrill, tickle, titillate, torpefy, tranquilize, transfix, transport, vamp, win, wow* (≠ aggravate, agitate, alarm, annoy, bore, bother, bug, convulse, crucify, disenchant, disgust, disillusion, displease, disturb, drain, dull, enliven, enrage, excite, exhilarate, harass, hector, horrify, incite, infuriate, inspire, irk, irritate, jar, jolt, knacker, menace, numb, offend, poke, prod, rankle, rattle, repel, repulse, rile, roil, rouse, shake, shock, sicken, spur, startle, stimulate, stir, terrify, terrorize, threaten, tire, torment, trouble, unnerve, upset, victimize, violate, wake, weary, worry, wound, wrong) **(¿) ABSTRACTION ALERT. Concrete goals essential!**

MIDWIFE (←): *accelerate, advance, aid, alleviate, ameliorate, assist, assuage, boost, brainstorm, catalyze, cherish, comfort, cure, ease, enable, encourage, entertain, expedite, facilitate, forward, foster, further, grease, harbor, hasten, heal, help, improve, instigate, keep, lubricate, mitigate, nourish, nurse, nurture, promote, prompt, protect, quicken, relieve, remedy, smooth, soothe, speed, support, sustain, trigger* (≠ -avert, bear, block, checkmate, delay, -deter, foil, -frustrate, gestate, -halt, hamper, hamstring, harm, hinder, impede, inhibit, monkey-wrench, obstruct, occlude, oppose, postpone, -prevent, protest, ruin, scotch, shelve, short-circuit, spoil, stall, stem, stump, stymie, -thwart)

MILK (+): *access, acquire, deflate, derive, drain, draw, elicit, exact, exhaust, express, extract, gather, glean, lap, leech, obtain, press, procure, pull, pump, render, siphon, squeeze, suck, tap, use, vacuum, withdraw, wrench, wrest, wring* (≠ augment, boost, cache, fill, guard, hoard, keep, recoup, replace, reserve, restore, save, stash, stockpile)

MILK (/): *abuse, beggar, bleed, cheat, commercialize, commodify, diddle, exploit, fleece, gazump, hard-sell, hawk, hype, leverage, manipulate, mistreat, oppress, overcharge, pimp, plug, promote, push, rook, skin, soak, stick, stiff, sting, tout, use, work, wrong* (≠ bankroll, benefit, capitalize, create, donate, endow, favor, finance, foster, fund, furnish, increase, protect, replenish, restore, supply, support, undercharge, underwrite)

MIMIC (+): *act, adopt, ape, burlesque, caricature, copy, copycat, ditto, duplicate, echo, emulate, enact, fake, feign, ghostwrite, hoke, imitate, impersonate, improv, mime, mirror, mock, pantomime, parody, parrot, perform, play, playact, pretend, replicate, ridicule, roleplay, simulate* (≠ cloak, clothe, coin, conceal, concoct, construct, contradict, contrive, create, design, develop, devise, -disdain, disguise, -disregard, -eschew, fabricate, introduce, invent, -negate, originate, patent, -prevent, reverse, -shun, -spurn, vamp)

MINCE (/): *butcher, carve, chip, chop, crumble, cut, dice, dissect, divide, grate, grind, hack, hash, kibble, mash, pulverize, purée, shred, slice* (≠ accumulate, build, collect, combine, expand, extend, fuse, grow, increase, join, meld, melt, restore, solidify, unify, unite)

MIND (+): *accept, allow, analyze, attend, consider, contemplate, entertain, evaluate, examine, follow, fulfill, hear, heed, investigate, keep, learn, mark, mull, note, notice, obey, observe, peruse, ponder, recognize, regard, research, respect, scan, scrutinize, see, study, survey, take, watch, weigh, wonder* (≠ buck, challenge, contest, defy, -desert, -discount, dismiss, disobey, disoblige, dispute, -disregard, fight, flout, forget, -ignore, miss, mock, -neglect, oppose, -overlook, -refuse, resist, -scorn, -snub, subvert, transgress, violate, withstand) **(¿) ABSTRACTION ALERT. Concrete goals essential!**

MIND (+): *attend, begrudge, bemoan, beware, consider, contemplate, discern, ensure, follow, guard, heed, keep, lament, learn, mark, mourn, mull, note, notice, obey, observe, perceive, ponder, regard, regret, remember, respect, scrutinize, see, study, trouble, watch, weigh* (≠ -blank, defy, -discount, dismiss, -disregard, disrespect, flout, -ignore, miss, -neglect, -overlook, pooh-pooh, -scorn, -slight, -snub) **(¿) ABSTRACTION ALERT. Concrete goals essential!**

MIND (+): *baby, babysit, chaperone, conduct, control, direct, govern, guard, guide, handle, manage, mother, nanny, nurse, nurture, operate, oversee, pace, parent, patrol, protect, regulate, run, safeguard, sentinel, shepherd, shield, sort, steward, superintend, supervise, tend, watch* (≠ -abandon, abuse, -desert, -disown, -disregard, forget, -forsake, -ignore, lose, maroon, -neglect, -quit, -reject, -renounce, -repudiate, -shun, -snub, wrong)

MINE (←): *claw, dig, dredge, drill, excavate, extract, grub, hew, pan, pluck, plumb, prize, quarry, recover, remove, scoop, search, shovel, spade, unearth, withdraw, work, wrench* (≠ archive, bury, conceal, cover, embed, engulf, ensconce, fill, hide, plant, replace, sink, smooth, store, submerge)

MINE (/): *ambush, arm, attack, blindside, bomb, boobytrap, bushwhack, decoy, detonate, dupe, entrap, explode, militarize, rig, sandbag, snare, trap, trick* (≠ build, defuse, demilitarize, disable, disarm, guard, protect, recover, repair, rescue, restore, save, shield)

MINGLE (+): *add, alloy, amalgamate, blend, churn, coalesce, collage, combine, commingle, composite, compound, concrete, conflate, conjoin, emulsify, fold, fuse, homogenize, hybridize, incorporate, integrate, intermingle, intermix, intertwine, interweave, join, knit, link, marry, meld, merge, mix, stir, synthesize, toss, unite, weave, wed* (≠ break, cleave, detach, diffuse, disengage, disjoin, disperse, dissolve, disunite, divide, divorce, part, rupture, scatter, separate, sever, split, sunder, unmix)

MINIMIZE (/): *abbreviate, abridge, attenuate, bob, clip, compact, compress, concentrate, condense, contract, crop, cull, curtail, cut, decrease, deflate, deplete, depreciate, diminish, downgrade, drain, dwarf, erode, leach, lessen, lighten, lowball, miniaturize, minify, nip, pare, prune, reduce, shave, shear, shrink, slash, taper, trim, truncate, weed, whittle* (≠ amplify, augment, broaden, build, develop, elevate, enlarge, expand, extend, grow, heighten, hyperbolize, increase, inflate, lengthen, maximize, overestimate, prolong, raise, strengthen, stretch, swell)

MINIMIZE (/): *abrade, badmouth, belittle, besmear, besmirch, blacken, calumniate, cheapen, decry, deemphasize, defame, demean, denigrate, denounce, deprecate, depreciate, deride, detract, diminish, -discount, discredit, dishonor, disparage, disrespect, downplay, dwarf, eclipse, knock, lessen, libel, lower, malign, marginalize, mock, needle, neg, outperform, outrank, overshadow, pan, pillory, pooh-pooh, reduce, ridicule, scandalize, -scorn, shame, slam, slander, smear, soft-pedal, spin, stigmatize, sully, tarnish, traduce, trash, trivialize, underbid, underestimate, underplay, underrate, upstage, vilify, weaken* (≠ aggrandize, apotheosize, canonize, commend, deify, dignify, dramatize, elevate, ennoble, enshrine, enthrone, exalt, feature, fetishize, glorify, highlight, hype, idealize, idolize, lionize, magnify, overestimate, overrate, praise, promote, romanticize, sensationalize, sentimentalize, spotlight)

MIRROR (←): *adopt, ape, clone, copy, depict, ditto, double, duplicate, echo, embody, emulate, epitomize, exemplify, fake, follow, ghostwrite,* *illustrate, image, imitate, mimic, parrot, personify, pretend, reduplicate, reflect, repeat, replicate, represent, reproduce, show, simulate, typify* (≠ absorb, conceal, concoct, cover, create, discard, dismiss, -disregard, establish, forget, generate, hide, -ignore, invent, -neglect, originate, patent, produce, take, withhold) **(¿) ABSTRACTION ALERT. Concrete goals essential!**

MISCALCULATE (/): *blow, botch, bungle, confuse, cook, corrupt, distort, doctor, fetishize, foozle, garble, half-ass, jumble, misapprehend, misconceive, misconstrue, miscount, misdiagnose, misgauge, misinterpret, misjudge, mismeasure, misread, misrepresent, mistake, misunderstand, muddle, mutilate, overestimate, overrate, overvalue, scramble, screw, slant, spoil, twist, underestimate, underrate, undervalue, wreck* (≠ ascertain, attend, calculate, compute, correct, deduce, detect, determine, diagnose, discern, evaluate, figure, get, grok, notice, number, numerate, perceive, rectify, regard, respect, right, scan, scrutinize, spot, total, understand)

MISDIRECT (+): *-avert, befuddle, blindfold, cheat, coerce, confuse, convince, deceive, deflect, delude, divert, double-talk, fool, hoodwink, misapply, misappropriate, misguide, misinform, mislead, misrepresent, misuse, refract, trick, waste* (≠ advise, benefit, counsel, direct, disenchant, fix, guard, guide, handle, help, inform, lead, manage, protect, respect, straighten, support)

MISHANDLE (/): *abuse, appropriate, blow, bobble, botch, bugger, bungle, cheat, damage, defalcate, doctor, drop, embezzle, fiddle, flub, fluff, fumble, half-ass, harm, hurt, ill-treat, lose, maltreat, mess, misappropriate, misjudge, mismanage, misrule, mistreat, misuse, muff, pilfer, plonk, skim, steal, stiff, violate* (≠ ace, aid, assist, benefit, boost, enhance, govern, handle, help, husband, improve, manage, nurture, pilot, preserve, protect, redeem, regulate, rescue, restore, rule, salvage, save, score, steer, win)

MISJUDGE (/): *accept, assume, believe, confuse, corrupt, distort, doctor, expect, fancy, fetishize, foozle, fumble, garble, guess, imagine, infer, jumble, misapprehend, miscalculate, misconceive, misconstrue, miscount, misdiagnose, misgauge, mishear, misinterpret, mismeasure, misread, misrepresent, mistake, misunderstand, muddle, mutilate, overestimate, overrate, overvalue, postulate, prejudge, presume, presuppose, scramble, slant, spoil, suppose, twist, underestimate, underrate, undervalue, wreck* (≠ adjudge, ascertain, attend, calculate, compute, correct, deduce, detect, determine, diagnose, discern, educe, evaluate, figure, get, grok, judge, notice, perceive, profile, rectify, regard, respect, right, scan, scrutinize, spot, understand)

MISLABEL (/): *bewilder, clutter, complicate, conceal, confound, confuse, disarrange, disorganize, disturb, garble, hide, -ignore, implicate, involve, jumble, mingle, misdirect, mislead, mistake, mistitle, mix, muddle, -overlook, perplex, pigeonhole, puzzle, scramble, shuffle, snarl, stereotype, tangle, tumble, upset* (≠ brand, call, caption, catalog, categorize, classify, denote, designate, docket, earmark, hallmark, identify, index, label, mark, monogram, name, prioritize, slot, specify, stamp, stigmatize, tab, tag, ticket, title)

MISLAY (/): *clutter, confound, confuse, disarrange, discompose, dishevel, disorder, disorganize, displace, dissipate, disturb, drop, forfeit, forget, jumble, lose, misapply, misassign, misfile, misplace, miss, mix, muddle, muss, -overlook, remove, scatter, scramble, strew, toss, unsettle, untidy, upset* (≠ adjust, array, assort, classify, collect, compose, detect, dispose, enjoy, find, gather, group, hold, keep, leave, locate, maintain, neaten, occupy, order, organize, own, place, possess, retain, scout, sort, systematize, tidy, track)

MISLEAD (←): *baffle, bait, bamboozle, beard, beat, befuddle, beguile, betray, bilk, bleed, blind, blindfold, bluff, bottom-deal, buffalo, bullshit, bunk, burn, candy-coat, catch, cheat, chisel, clip, cloud, con, confuse, convince, cook, cozen, deacon, deceive, defraud, delude, diddle, disinform, doctor, double-cross, double-talk, dupe, enmesh, ensnare, entangle, entice, euchre, fake, fleece, flimflam, fool, fox, frame, fudge, gas, gaslight, gouge, gull, gyp, hoax, hocus-pocus, hoodwink, hook, hornswoggle, hose, humbug, hustle, hype, ice, inveigle, juggle, lure, manipulate, misdirect, misguide, misinform, misrepresent, mousetrap, mystify, outfox, outwit, overreach, perplex, pervert, plant, pluck, presell, pretend, puzzle, rephrase, rook, rope, salt, sandbag, scam, screw, seduce, shaft, shortchange, skin, snooker, snow, soak, spin, spoof, squeeze, stick, stiff, sting, stonewall, sucker, swindle, take, tempt, trick, two-time, underpay, vamp, victimize, whitewash, wrong* (≠ acknowledge, advise, assume, assure, believe, concede, confess, confide, confirm, confront, counsel, debunk, defend, -deny, disabuse, disclose, disenchant, disillusion, divulge, expose, guard, lead, out, protect, respect, reveal, show, trust, uncloak, uncover, undeceive, unmask, unveil, verify)

MISMANAGE (/): *abuse, betray, blackjack, blackmail, bobble, bomb, botch, browbeat, bugger, bully, bungle, cheat, damage, deceive, dissipate, exploit, fake, flub, flunk, fritter, fudge, fumble, half-ass, harm, hurt, ill-treat, intimidate, jumble, lavish, maltreat, mar, mishandle, misjudge, misrule, misspend, mistreat, misuse, muff, muscle, -neglect, overestimate, -overlook, pretend, railroad, -shirk, skip, squander, trash-talk, trick, underestimate, violate, waste* (≠ aid, coach, follow, govern, handle, help, husband, lead, manage, mentor, mind, navigate, nurture, obey, pilot, preserve, protect, rescue, rule, save, secure, serve, shield, steer, win)

MISPLACE (/): *clutter, confound, confuse, disarrange, discompose, dishevel, disorder, disorganize, displace, dissipate, disturb, drop, forfeit, forget, jumble, lose, misapply, misassign, misfile, mislay, miss, mix, muddle, muss, -overlook, remove, scatter, scramble, strew, toss, unsettle, untidy, upset* (≠ adjust, array, assort, classify, collect, compose, detect, dispose, enjoy, find, gather, group, hold, keep, leave, locate, maintain, neaten, occupy, order, organize, own, place, possess, retain, scout, sort, systematize, tidy, track)

MISREPRESENT (←): *ballyhoo, beard, belie, bend, blarney, bluff, bowdlerize, bullshit, camouflage, censor, cloak, clothe, cloud, color, complicate, con, confound, confuse, contort, cook, costume, disguise, distort, doctor, embellish, embroider, exaggerate, falsify, fudge, garble, gloss, heighten, heroicize, heroize, idealize, idolize, jolly, manipulate, mask, minimize, miscommunicate, misconstrue, misdescribe, mishear, misinterpret, misquote, misread, misreport, misstate, mistake, mistranslate, mystify, obscure, -omit, overdramatize, oversell, paint, pervert, poeticize, promote, puff, rephrase, romanticize, scam, sentimentalize, slant, snooker, snow, spin, sucker, twist, veil, warp, whitewash* (≠ affirm, bare, betray, clarify, clear, contextualize, decipher, deduce, demonstrate, detect, disclose, discover, elaborate, evince, exhibit, explain, expose, flaunt, illuminate, illustrate, interpret, out, parade, represent, reveal, showcase)

MISS (←): *bemoan, covet, crave, demand, desire, fetishize, grieve, lament, lose, mourn, recall, recollect, regret, remember, target, want, wish* (≠ -avoid, -detest, -discount, -disregard, forget, -hate, misremember, -scorn, -shun, skirt, -spurn)

MISS (/): *blow, bobble, botch, bungle, -bypass, -cut, detour, disbelieve, -discount, dismiss, -disregard, drop, fail, flub, fluff, forget, fumble, -ignore, juggle, lose, louse, miscarry, mislay, misplace, mistake, misunderstand, muff, -neglect, -omit, -overlook, overshoot, pass, skip, -slight, trip, undershoot* (≠ achieve, aim, attain, attend, balance, claim, conquer, crest, find, get, hit, locate, manage, outguess, realize, recollect, regret, remember, score, steady, suss, target, waylay)

MISTAKE (/): *addle, botch, bungle, confound, confuse, flub, fluff, flunk, goof, jumble, louse, misapprehend, miscalculate, misconceive, misconstrue, miscount, misdiagnose, mishear, misinterpret, misjudge, mislabel, misprize, misread, miss, misunderstand, muddle, muff, -omit, overestimate, -overlook, snarl, tangle, underestimate* (≠ appreciate, apprehend, catch, compare, comprehend, diagnose, evaluate, fathom, get, grasp, grok, interpret, learn, outguess, perceive, regret, savvy, seize, survey, suss, understand)

MISTREAT (/): *-abandon, abuse, alienate, attack, backbite, bash, batter, betray, blackjack, blackmail, browbeat, brutalize, bully, burn, crucify, damage, dehumanize, depersonalize, devalue, disaffect, discredit, disfavor, disgrace, dump, exploit, gaslight, hamstring, harass, harm, humiliate, hurt, ill-treat, injure, intimidate, isolate, maltreat, manhandle, maul, mishandle, misuse, molest, muscle, -neglect, objectify, oppress, -ostracize, outrage, penalize, persecute, railroad, -reject, rip, sandbag, savage, shaft, shake, shortchange, sicken, taunt, torment, torture, trample, trash, trash-talk, tyrannize, upstage, vex, victimize, violate, wound, wrong* (≠ accommodate, advantage, aid, amuse, appease, assist, baby, benefit, cherish, coddle, cosset, cotton, cure, delight, entertain, favor, featherbed, foster, gratify, guard, heal, help, humor, indulge, infantilize, mollycoddle, nourish, nurture, oblige, overindulge, overprotect, pacify, pamper, pet, pity, placate, please, protect, reward, satiate, satisfy, soothe, spoil, spoon-feed, thrill, treat, woo)

MITIGATE (+): *abate, allay, alleviate, ameliorate, amend, appease, assuage, better, blunt, buffer, calm, candy-coat, check, control, cool, correct, curb, cure, cushion, decrease, diminish, dulcify, dull, ease, emend, enhance, enrich, fix, heal, help, humor, improve, lessen, lighten, lull, mellow, mend, moderate, modify, mollify, pace, pacify, palliate, perfect, placate, qualify, quiet, realign, rectify, reduce, refine, reform, regulate, relieve, remedy, remit, repair, right, sedate, slake, soften, soothe, spin, still, subdue, sugarcoat, sweeten, temper, tranquilize, weaken* (≠ aggravate, agitate, alarm, amplify, deepen, exacerbate, exaggerate, exasperate, harden, harm, heighten, hurt, impair, increase, inflame, injure, intensify, irritate, overdramatize, oversell, sharpen, troll, worry, worsen)

MIX (+): *add, adulterate, alloy, amalgamate, associate, blend, braid, churn, coalesce, combine, commingle, composite, compound, concrete, conflate, cross, crossbreed, cross-fertilize, cross-pollinate, fold, froth, fuse, homogenize, hybridize, incorporate, infiltrate, infuse, instill, integrate, interbreed, intermingle, intermix, intertwine, interweave, introduce, join, jumble, knead, knit, link, lump, mash, meld, merge, mingle, mongrelize, raddle, saturate, scramble, stir, suffuse, synthesize, tangle, toss, transfuse, unite, weave, whisk* (≠ cleave, detach, diffuse, disconnect, disengage, disjoin, disperse, dissolve, disunite, divide, divorce, part, remove, rupture, scatter, separate, sever, split, sunder, unmix)

MIX (+): *associate, circulate, gather, include, integrate, invite, join, meet, mingle, reintegrate, socialize, unify, unite, welcome* (≠ -avoid, divide, -eschew, -exclude, -omit, oust, segregate, separate, -shun, -slight, -snub, split) **(¿) ABSTRACTION ALERT. Concrete goals essential!**

MOBILIZE (→): *activate, actuate, animate, arrange, assemble, brainstorm, call, catalyze, circulate, collect, conscript, convene, corral, drive, encourage, energize, enlist, galvanize, gather, group, herd, impel, incite, influence, inspire, instigate, marshal, midwife, motivate, muster, order, organize, prepare, prompt, propel, provoke, punt, rally, ready, rouse, spark, spur, stimulate, summon, weaponize* (≠ check, curb, deactivate, demobilize, demotivate, detain, -deter, disband, discourage, dismiss, disorganize, disperse, disrupt, dissolve, dissuade, disturb, divide, end, -halt, hamper, hinder, hold, inactivate, repress, retard, scatter, separate, short-circuit, slow, split, stall, stop, stymie, -thwart)

MOCK (←): *act, adopt, amplify, ape, burlesque, caricature, copycat, counterfeit, deride, duplicate, embellish, embroider, emulate, enhance, exaggerate, expand, fake, feign, imitate, impersonate, lampoon, magnify, mime, mimic, overdramatize, overdraw, overstate, pad, pantomime, parody, parrot, perform, play, pretend, replicate, reproduce, ridicule, satirize, simulate, spoof, stretch, travesty* (≠ counter, create, follow, heed, invent, mark, mind, note, notice, obey, observe, oppose, originate, oversell, poeticize, -prevent, reverse, romanticize, sentimentalize, serve)

MOCK (/): *ape, badmouth, bait, belittle, blackguard, blast, blister, bug, burlesque, caricature, cartoon, catcall, chaff, crucify, decry, deflate, demean, deride, disparage, disrespect, diss, expose, flout, harass, harry, hassle, haze, heckle, hound, humiliate, imitate, insult, josh, kid, knock, lampoon, mimic, needle, neg, pan, parody, parrot, patronize, pester, pillory, poke, pooh-pooh, quiz, rag, razz, rib, ride, ridicule, roast, satirize, -scorn, scout, shame, skewer, -slight, target, taunt, tease, torment, travesty, tweak, twit, unmask* (≠ admire, applaud, approve, blandish, commend, compliment, encourage, endorse, esteem, exalt, flannel, flatter, glad-hand, heroicize, honor, idealize, idolize, -ignore, praise, recommend, respect, revere, sanction, support, sweet-talk, venerate)

MOCK (/): *battle, breach, break, buck, challenge, combat, contest, defy, discredit, dismiss, disobey, disoblige, dispute, -disregard, fight, flout, -ignore, infringe, oppose, -overlook, pooh-pooh, protest, question, -reject, resist, revolt, -scorn, subvert, tax, test, transgress, violate, withstand* (≠ attend, follow, hear, heed, honor, keep, mark, mind, note, notice, obey, oblige, observe, regard, respect, serve, watch)

MODERATE (+): *abate, allay, alleviate, appease, assuage, attenuate, calm, chasten, check, compress, condense, constrain, constrict, contract, control, cool, curb, decrease, de-escalate, deflate, diminish, domesticate, drain, dull, ease, help, humor, leash, lessen, limit, lower, lull, mellow, mitigate, modify, modulate, mollify, pace, pacify, palliate, pen, placate, qualify, quiet, reduce, regulate, relax, relieve, repress, restrain, shrink, slacken, slow, soften, soft-pedal, subdue, tame, taper, temper* (≠ aggravate, amplify, brighten, build, darken, deepen, embellish, embroider, enlarge, escalate, exacerbate, exaggerate, exasperate, expand, flub, harden, incite, increase, inflate, intensify, irritate, lengthen, provoke, sharpen, swell, toughen, unleash, vex)

MODERNIZE (+): *amend, automate, computerize, correct, enhance, gentrify, improve, mechanize, modify, motorize, network, optimize, overhaul, realign, rebuild, recast, reconceive, reconceptualize, reconstruct, redefine, redesign, redevelop, redo, reengineer, refashion, refine, reform, refresh, refurbish, regenerate, reimagine, reinvent, reinvigorate, rejuvenate, remake, remodel, renew, renovate, restimulate, restore, restructure, rethink, retool, revamp, revise, revive, revolutionize, rework, streamline, transform, update, upgrade, wire* (≠ -abandon, antique, conserve, corrode, damage, date, destroy, doom, dump, -forsake, hurt, kill, maintain, outmode, preserve, resist, ruin, sabotage, scotch, scupper, scuttle, shelve, toss, trash, undermine, wear, wreck)

MODIFY (+): *abate, accrue, adapt, adjust, affect, align, alter, amend, amplify, calibrate, case-harden, change, contort, contour, convert, correct, customize, degrade, diversify, doctor, downgrade, edit, enhance, flavor, gnarl, harden, impair, improve, increase, invert, jack, magnify, marinate, maximize, minimize, mitigate, moderate, mutate, optimize,* *overhaul, override, overrule, pervert, punctuate, realign, recast, redesign, reduce, refashion, reform, reimagine, rejigger, remodel, remold, reorganize, repair, rephrase, reshape, reshuffle, restore, retool, retrofit, revamp, revise, revolutionize, rework, right, rotate, sculpt, season, shift, shuffle, soften, spice, strengthen, switch, temper, touch, transfigure, transform, transmogrify, transmute, tune, turn, tweak, twist, upgrade, vary, warp, weaken, weaponize* (≠ abide, conserve, continue, defend, endure, freeze, grow, -halt, hold, incite, increase, intensify, keep, leave, maintain, paralyze, pickle, preserve, retain, set, spoil, stabilize, stagnate, stale, stop, sustain)

MODULATE (+): *adjust, align, alter, attune, balance, calibrate, center, change, commute, compose, convert, exchange, fine-tune, harmonize, lower, minimize, moderate, modify, pace, recast, redo, refashion, regenerate, regulate, rejigger, remake, remodel, restrain, retool, revamp, reverse, revise, revolutionize, rework, soften, supplant, swap, switch, temper, tone, transfigure, transform, transmogrify, transmute, tune, tweak, vary* (≠ abuse, accentuate, aggravate, amplify, attack, boost, compound, emphasize, exacerbate, exaggerate, fight, fix, force, freeze, heighten, heroicize, idealize, inflate, intensify, maximize, -neglect, overdramatize, paralyze, poeticize, punctuate, push, resist, romanticize, sentimentalize, set, stabilize, steady, unleash, weaponize)

MOISTEN (→): *bathe, braise, damp, dampen, dip, douse, drench, drizzle, drown, flood, hose, humidify, imbue, irrigate, lick, marinate, moisturize, permeate, presoak, rinse, saturate, slake, sluice, soak, soften, sop, spatter, splash, splatter, spray, sprinkle, steep, swamp, wash, water, wet* (≠ abrade, bake, barbecue, broil, chafe, congeal, dehydrate, desiccate, dry, harden, mop, parch, scorch, sear, staunch, toughen, towel)

MOLD (→): *assemble, bend, bronze, build, carve, cast, coin, compose, concoct, configure, construct, contour, craft, crease, create, design, devise, erect, fashion, forge, form, frame, integrate, knead, make, model, pat, plan, plant, plot, pour, round, scheme, script, sculpt, shape, stamp, structure, whittle, work* (≠ -abandon, annihilate, atomize, break, crack, demolish, destroy, dismantle, dissolve, eradicate, erase, forget, fracture, fragment, melt, -neglect, nuke, pulverize, raze, ruin, shatter, split, strip, vaporize, wreck)

MOLD (+): *affect, alter, better, bias, brainwash, cleanse, coach, condition, control, convince, corrupt, direct, dominate, educate, form, guide, impart, improve, induce, influence, infuse, inject, instruct, manipulate, mentor, nobble, persuade, predetermine, prejudice, purify, refresh, renew, restore, retrain, school, shape, suborn, sway, teach, transform* (≠ attack, -bypass, -circumvent, dissuade, gaslight, -ignore, impede, inhibit, -neglect, -prevent, sabotage, -sidestep, subvert, undermine)

MOLEST (→): *abuse, accost, adulterate, assail, assault, attack, befoul, besmirch, contaminate, debase, debauch, deflower, degrade, dirty, disgrace, dishonor, displace, disturb, fondle, harm, hinder, hurt, ill-treat, injure, maltreat, manhandle, mistreat, misuse, profane, rape, ravish,* *seduce, shame, smear, soil, stain, sully, tar, tarnish, trash, vitiate, wrong* (≠ cherish, defend, guard, heal, help, honor, preserve, protect, purify, respect, shelter, shield, support)

MOLEST (/): *abuse, afflict, aggravate, agitate, alarm, annoy, appall, assault, badger, bait, bash, bedevil, berate, blast, blister, bore, bother, browbeat, bug, bust, charge, chivy, concern, confuse, criticize, cross, discommode, discompose, disconcert, disgust, dismay, displease, disquiet, distress, disturb, eat, embarrass, exacerbate, exasperate, fluster, frighten, gate-crash, goad, grieve, harass, harry, hassle, heckle, hector, hound, impede, impugn, inconvenience, insult, interrupt, invade, irk, irritate, lambaste, malign, maltreat, mistreat, nag, needle, nudge, pain, perplex, persecute, perturb, pester, plague, provoke, pursue, revile, ride, scare, spite, tantalize, taunt, tease, terrify, torment, trash-talk, troll, trouble, upset, vex, worry, wrong* (≠ alleviate, appease, assist, assuage, baby, calm, cheer, coddle, comfort, defend, guard, help, humor, indulge, lull, mellow, mitigate, mollify, mollycoddle, pacify, pamper, placate, please, protect, quiet, reassure, relax, rescue, save, shield, soothe)

MOLLIFY (+): *abate, aid, allay, alleviate, anesthetize, appease, assuage, blunt, calm, comfort, compose, conciliate, console, content, cool, cushion, defuse, demilitarize, dulcify, ease, help, humor, hush, indulge, lessen, lighten, lull, mellow, mitigate, moderate, modify, overindulge, pacify, placate, propitiate, quell, quiet, quieten, reconcile, relax, relieve, rock, sedate, settle, silence, smooth, sober, soften, soothe, stabilize, steady, still, stroke, subdue, sugarcoat, sweeten, syrup, temper, tranquilize* (≠ affront, aggravate, agitate, alienate, anger, annoy, antagonize, appall, disaffect, distress, disturb, earbash, enrage, exacerbate, exasperate, excite, gravel, harden, hurt, incense, infuriate, insult, irritate, lynch, maim, militarize, nag, needle, nettle, niggle, nitpick, noodge, offend, -ostracize, outrage, persecute, pester, provoke, rankle, rile, roil, rouse, ruffle, shock, troll, unhinge, upset, vex, worry)

MONETIZE (→): *alter, amass, apply, appropriate, cannibalize, cash, change, claim, collect, earn, employ, exploit, garner, garnish, harness, manipulate, mint, pocket, raise, reclaim, recoup, recover, recycle, skim, tap, transfigure, transform, transmute, utilize* (≠ bequeath, break, comp, contribute, demolish, destroy, dismantle, donate, -ignore, lose, misapply, misuse, -neglect, raze, ruin, take)

MONITOR (←): *advise, analyze, anatomize, assess, audit, backtrack, benchmark, calculate, categorize, chaperone, chart, check, chronicle, clock, conclude, consult, contextualize, control, correlate, counsel, cover, crosscheck, deconstruct, deduce, detect, dissect, double-check, eye, eyeball, follow, gauge, glimpse, graph, guesstimate, inspect, judge, mind, nanny, note, notice, observe, organize, oversee, patrol, perceive, plot, police, proctor, quarterback, rank, read, record, referee, regard, retrace, review, safeguard, sample, scan, scope, scrutinize, shepherd, spy, superintend, supervise, surveil, survey, trace, track, umpire, usher, verify, watch, witness* (≠ -abandon, baffle, -blank, blind, blindfold, confound, confuse, deceive, disguise, -disregard, erase, fake, forget, fudge, -ignore, lose, mask, miss, mistake, muddle, mystify, -neglect, obliterate, -omit, -overlook, perplex, puzzle, skim, skip, trick) **(¿) ABSTRACTION ALERT. Concrete goals essential!**

MONOPOLIZE (←): *absorb, appropriate, buttonhole, command, consume, control, corner, demand, dictate, direct, dominate, engross, govern, handle, hog, hold, manage, obsess, occupy, own, possess, preoccupy, rule, syndicate, waylay* (≠ allocate, apportion, -avoid, -bypass, chunk, denounce, diffuse, -discount, distribute, divide, drop, dump, forget, give, grant, -ignore, lose, offer, -omit, portion, -reject, release, -repudiate, scatter, share, -shun, -sidestep, subvert, volunteer)

MOOCH (←): *abuse, appropriate, beg, bilk, blackmail, bleed, bluff, borrow, buffalo, bum, cadge, cheat, crib, drain, embezzle, employ, exploit, fleece, gouge, hunt, leech, lift, manipulate, milk, panhandle, pilfer, scam, schnorr, scrounge, seek, sponge, stiff, sucker, swindle, tap, use, weasel, wheedle* (≠ bestow, comp, contribute, deserve, dispense, donate, earn, endow, furnish, give, help, lend, merit, offer, patronize, pay, provide, recoup, replace, restore, serve, supply, support, volunteer)

MORTIFY (/): *abase, abash, affront, agitate, annoy, appall, belittle, blacken, blackguard, blister, bother, chagrin, chasten, chastise, confound, confuse, control, crush, debase, deflate, degrade, demean, -deny, diminish, disappoint, discipline, discomfit, discomfort, discompose, disconcert, discountenance, discredit, disgrace, dishonor, dismay, displease, disquiet, distress, disturb, embarrass, expose, faze, fluster, harass, heckle, horrify, hound, humble, humiliate, hurt, insult, malign, mock, nag, needle, nettle, niggle, nitpick, nonplus, offend, out, outrage, perturb, pillory, rattle, ridicule, shame, shrivel, -slight, -snub, subdue, taunt, unhinge, unsettle, upset, vex, wither, worry, wound* (≠ assure, blandish, bolster, brace, buoy, buttress, calm, cheer, comfort, compliment, console, encourage, flannel, flatter, gratify, help, humor, inspire, lull, mellow, mitigate, moderate, mollify, nurture, pacify, placate, please, praise, reassure, relieve, settle, soothe, steady, support)

MORTIFY (/): *abuse, afflict, agonize, anguish, avenge, bench, burden, castigate, chasten, chastise, confine, conquer, control, correct, crucify, deduct, demote, -deny, discipline, -discount, distress, encumber, fine, forfeit, handicap, imprison, incarcerate, judge, lambaste, penalize, persecute, pillory, punish, reduce, reprise, restrain, sentence, sideline, subdue, subjugate, suppress, torture, wrong* (≠ animate, assist, boost, coddle, comfort, ease, forgive, fortify, gratify, heal, indulge, mend, pamper, prioritize, promote, rally, release, reward, stimulate, stroke, supply)

MOTHER (←): *accommodate, adopt, aid, appease, assist, attend, baby, bear, benefit, bequeath, bestow, bottle-feed, carry, cherish, coddle, cosset, cotton, cradle, create, cuddle, cultivate, develop, discipline, educate, embrace, encourage, endow, facilitate, favor, feed, form, foster, fuel, generate, gestate, gratify, guard, help, host, humor, indulge, infantilize, mollycoddle, motivate, nag, nanny, nourish, nurse, nurture,* *originate, overindulge, overprotect, pacify, pamper, parent, produce, protect, raise, rear, relieve, respect, reward, satisfy, school, scold, serve, shelter, sire, soothe, spoil, spoon-feed, support, sustain, teach, tend, tolerate, train, treat, welcome* (≠ -abandon, abuse, anguish, antagonize, betray, bother, brutalize, cripple, crucify, damage, -desert, destroy, -disown, -disregard, end, -forsake, harm, hurt, impair, infect, injure, irritate, kill, malnourish, molest, murder, -neglect, orphan, persecute, poison, -reject, sacrifice, savage, sicken, smother, stifle, strangle, stunt, terrorize, threaten, -thwart, torment, torture, traumatize, underfeed, upset, victimize, wound, wrong)

MOTIVATE (→): *activate, actuate, animate, arouse, assist, bribe, bring, compel, convince, direct, draw, drive, electrify, encourage, energize, enliven, excite, facilitate, fire, galvanize, goad, goose, impel, incite, incur, induce, influence, initiate, inspire, inspirit, instigate, invigorate, kick-start, kindle, lead, lubricate, move, persuade, prod, prompt, propel, provoke, push, quicken, rouse, spark, spearhead, spur, stimulate, stir, suggest, supercharge, sway, trigger, urge, vitalize, whet* (≠ blackjack, blackmail, confuse, cripple, daunt, deactivate, demoralize, demotivate, depress, discourage, dissuade, hamper, hobble, impede, intimidate, nobble, paralyze, perplex, sadden, sicken, torpefy, undermine, weaken)

MOUNT (→): *ascend, boost, cant, climb, crest, elevate, escalate, incline, lean, lift, raise, ride, scale, slant, slope, surmount, thrust, tilt, tip, top, uplift, vault* (≠ -decline, descend, dismount, drop, lower, plunge, settle, sink, slide)

MOUNT (→): *affix, arrange, carry, clinch, depict, display, dramatize, enact, exhibit, expose, extend, fit, frame, give, install, juxtapose, launch, offer, organize, parade, perform, place, play, portray, position, prepare, present, preview, produce, proffer, render, represent, show, showcase, stage, tender, unveil* (≠ bury, -cancel, close, conceal, conclude, disband, dismantle, end, -forbid, hide, stymie, terminate, -thwart, withdraw)

MOVE (→): *alter, beam, bear, bring, budge, bustle, carry, cart, chauffeur, convey, deliver, dislocate, dispatch, displace, distribute, disturb, drive, express, fetch, haul, juxtapose, lug, modify, operate, pass, position, pull, push, recline, redo, refashion, relegate, relocate, remake, remodel, remove, replace, reposition, revamp, revise, rework, roll, run, schlep, send, shift, ship, shove, shunt, shuttle, smuggle, stir, supersede, supplant, swing, switch, take, tote, transfer, transmit, transplant, transport, transpose, vary, waft* (≠ anchor, block, cage, drop, dump, embed, fix, freeze, hamper, hoard, hog, implant, leave, lodge, lose, monopolize, moor, paralyze, pause, pin, pinion, root, secure, set, stabilize, stash, stop, stow, -thwart, withhold)

MOVE (→): *activate, actuate, advance, advocate, affect, agitate, animate, arouse, bribe, bring, catalyze, convert, convince, drive, excite, facilitate, fast-forward, fast-track, fire, foment, frogmarch, galvanize, generate, hurry, hustle, ignite, impel, impress, incite, incline, induce, influence, inspire, instigate, introduce, lead, lubricate, march, motivate, persuade, prompt, propel, propose, provoke, pull, punt, push, quicken, rabble-rouse,* *raise, recommend, rouse, shift, shove, spearhead, start, stimulate, stir, strike, suggest, sway, touch, trigger, trip, tug, turn, urge, wag, wave, wiggle, work* (≠ bridle, check, constrain, contain, control, cripple, curb, deactivate, demotivate, discourage, dissuade, freeze, -halt, hamper, hinder, hobble, impair, impede, inhibit, jam, pace, regulate, rein, restrain, stall, stop, straightjacket, suppress, terrify, -thwart)

MOVE (←): *affect, afflict, agitate, allure, amuse, anger, arouse, astound, attract, awe, bewitch, bias, bother, captivate, charm, cheer, color, concern, dazzle, depress, discomfort, discompose, disgust, disquiet, distress, disturb, enchant, energize, engage, engross, enrage, enrapture, entertain, enthrall, entice, entrance, excite, fascinate, fluster, galvanize, gladden, grip, harass, harry, hypnotize, impact, impress, influence, infuriate, inspire, interest, intrigue, involve, irritate, mesmerize, monopolize, obsess, overawe, overpower, overwhelm, penetrate, perturb, pester, pierce, plague, predetermine, prejudice, preoccupy, rally, rattle, ravish, razzle-dazzle, reach, rouse, sadden, scare, shake, shock, smite, stimulate, stir, strain, stress, strike, sway, tantalize, tease, tempt, terrify, tickle, touch, transport, trigger, trouble, try, upset, worry, wow, wring* (≠ anesthetize, annoy, bore, bother, bug, deaden, debilitate, demoralize, desensitize, discourage, dispirit, drain, enervate, exhaust, fatigue, frustrate, irk, irritate, jade, knacker, numb, pall, paralyze, sedate, stagnate, tire, trouble, underwhelm, vex, wear, weary) **(¿) ABSTRACTION ALERT. Concrete goals essential!**

MUDDY (/): *bedaub, bedraggle, befoul, begrime, besmirch, bespatter, blacken, cloud, confuse, contaminate, daub, defile, dirty, disarrange, disarray, discolor, dishevel, disorder, draggle, foul, grime, jumble, mess, mire, muck, muddle, pollute, puddle, smear, smirch, smudge, soil, stain, sully, taint, untidy* (≠ brighten, brush, clean, cleanse, decontaminate, deodorize, disinfect, dry-clean, dust, freshen, launder, mop, purge, purify, quarantine, rarefy, renew, rinse, sanitize, scour, scrub, straighten, sweep, tidy, wash, wipe)

MUDDY (/): *abash, addle, agitate, baffle, bamboozle, beat, becloud, befog, befuddle, beguile, bemuse, bewilder, blur, bother, buffalo, chagrin, churn, cloud, complicate, confound, confuse, cozen, deceive, delude, disarrange, disarray, discombobulate, discomfit, discomfort, discompose, disconcert, dishevel, dismay, disorder, disorganize, disorient, disquiet, disrupt, distress, disturb, double-talk, dupe, embarrass, entangle, faze, flummox, fluster, fog, fool, fox, gaslight, gull, hoax, hocus-pocus, hoodwink, humbug, jumble, manipulate, misguide, mislead, mix, mortify, muddle, mystify, nonplus, obfuscate, perplex, perturb, puzzle, rattle, scramble, shuffle, snarl, snow, sophisticate, stump, stun, tangle, tousle, trick, trouble, unhinge, unsettle, upset, vex* (≠ analyze, assure, clarify, clear, decipher, decode, deduce, detect, disentangle, enlighten, floodlight, illuminate, inform, order, organize, profile, reassure, regiment, satisfy, simplify, straighten, streamline, uncloud, uncomplicate, undo, unravel, unscramble, untangle)

MUFFLE (←): *bandage, blanket, bower, bundle, camouflage, circle, cloak, cocoon, cover, curtain, disguise, drape, embed, embosom, embower, embrace, encase, encircle, enclose, encompass, enfold, enlace, enshroud, enswathe, envelop, invest, lap, mantle, mask, overlay, pack, shroud, surround, swaddle, swathe, veil, wrap, wreathe* (≠ bare, denude, expose, open, peel, reveal, shuck, strip, tear, uncover, unwrap)

MUFFLE (/): *baffle, bleep, censor, cloak, conceal, cover, cushion, dampen, deaden, decrease, devoice, drown, dull, envelop, gag, hide, hush, insulate, mellow, minimize, mute, muzzle, pad, quiet, quieten, repress, silence, smother, soften, soft-pedal, soundproof, squelch, stifle, strangle, subdue, suppress, swaddle, swathe, throttle, underemphasize, wrap* (≠ accent, accentuate, accost, amplify, assert, bare, blab, blaze, blurt, boost, confess, confront, deafen, deepen, disclose, divulge, emphasize, encourage, enhance, expose, free, heighten, increase, intensify, magnify, maximize, open, punctuate, release, reveal, sharpen, strengthen, uncover)

MUG (→): *assail, assault, attack, bash, batter, boost, grab, haul, hijack, hold, jump, lift, pocket, rob, rustle, seize, shanghai, snatch, steal, swipe, waylay* (≠ defend, -evade, guard, police, repel, replace, rescue, restore, save, secure, skirt)

MULTIPLY (+): *accelerate, accentuate, accrue, accumulate, add, aggrandize, aggregate, amass, amplify, augment, boost, breed, build, collect, complement, compound, cube, deepen, develop, double, elongate, emphasize, enhance, enlarge, escalate, expand, extend, foster, generate, grow, heighten, hype, increase, inflate, intensify, lengthen, magnify, maximize, mount, populate, prioritize, produce, proliferate, prolong, propagate, protract, raise, reinforce, repeat, reproduce, spread, square, stretch, supersize, supplement, swell, triple* (≠ abate, abbreviate, abridge, compress, concentrate, condense, constrict, contract, curtail, decrease, de-escalate, diminish, divide, downsize, lessen, lower, minimize, reduce, shorten, shrink, subtract)

MURDER (/): *abolish, annihilate, asphyxiate, assassinate, axe, behead, bludgeon, butcher, club, crush, decapitate, defeat, depopulate, destroy, dispatch, doom, drown, dust, electrocute, eliminate, eradicate, erase, execute, exterminate, extinguish, finish, garrote, guillotine, hang, hit, ice, kill, knife, liquidate, lynch, mangle, massacre, neutralize, purge, remove, ruin, sacrifice, savage, shank, shiv, shoot, slaughter, slay, smite, smother, snuff, spoil, stab, strangle, suffocate, terminate, thrash, throttle, waste, whack* (≠ aid, bear, begin, build, continue, create, defend, develop, encourage, establish, feed, foster, guard, heal, help, initiate, institute, keep, maintain, nourish, nurture, preserve, protect, raise, rescue, resuscitate, revive, save, shelter, shield, spare, spark, start, survive, withstand)

MUSCLE (→): *abuse, affright, alarm, appall, assault, awe, badger, blackjack, blackmail, bleed, bludgeon, bluff, bogart, browbeat, brutalize, bulldoze, bully, bullyrag, coerce, compel, constrain, cow, daunt, demoralize, discompose, disconcert, dismay, disquiet, distress, disturb, drag, dragoon, drive, entreat, force, frighten, harass, hector, hijack,* *horrify, hound, impel, implore, importune, impose, impress, intimidate, make, manhandle, mau-mau, menace, molest, nobble, obligate, oblige, oppress, perturb, petrify, press, pressure, push, railroad, sandbag, scare, shame, shock, shove, spook, startle, steamroller, strong-arm, terrify, terrorize, threaten, trash-talk, unman, unnerve, upset, victimize, violate, wound, wrong* (≠ accommodate, allow, amuse, assuage, baby, bamboozle, bribe, cajole, calm, cheer, coax, coddle, comfort, con, console, convince, court, delight, embolden, encourage, gratify, hearten, help, hint, humor, induce, influence, lubricate, lull, manipulate, mellow, midwife, mitigate, moderate, mollify, nurture, outmaneuver, outslick, outsmart, outwit, pacify, palaver, pamper, permit, persuade, placate, please, reassure, reward, satiate, satisfy, schmooze, solace, soothe, spoil, steel, suggest, sway, tantalize, tease, tempt, trick, trigger, wheedle, woo)

MUSTER (←): *accumulate, activate, arrange, assemble, call, cluster, collect, compile, concentrate, congregate, conjure, convene, enlist, enroll, gather, group, herd, include, invite, marshal, mass, meet, mobilize, order, organize, raise, rally, reconvene, scavenge, scrounge, summon, throng, welcome* (≠ adjourn, -avoid, banish, block, -cancel, deactivate, demobilize, destroy, diffuse, disband, discharge, dismiss, disorganize, disperse, dissolve, divide, -dodge, -exclude, -forbid, -ignore, -neglect, prorogue, remove, scatter, separate, split, stop)

MUTATE (/): *adapt, adjust, alter, change, convert, deform, evolve, metamorphose, modify, modulate, remake, remodel, reshape, transfigure, transform, translate, transmogrify, transmute, transpose, transubstantiate, vary* (≠ balance, clone, copy, distill, duplicate, establish, fix, freeze, maintain, purify, refine, secure, settle, stabilize, steady, sustain)

MUTILATE (/): *amputate, axe, bash, batter, behead, bludgeon, break, bruise, brutalize, butcher, castrate, chop, circumcise, cleave, contort, cripple, crush, cut, damage, deball, decapitate, deface, deform, disable, disfigure, dismember, distort, drub, efface, emasculate, eviscerate, excise, gash, gore, hack, hammer, hamstring, harm, hew, hobble, hurt, impair, incapacitate, injure, kill, kneecap, lacerate, lame, lash, lop, maim, mangle, mar, maul, murder, paralyze, pummel, ravage, razor, remove, ruin, savage, scalp, scar, scratch, separate, sever, slash, slice, smash, split, spoil, sunder, thump, torment, torture, truncate, unman, whip, wing, wound* (≠ adorn, aid, armor, assist, bandage, beautify, build, craft, create, cultivate, cure, decorate, defend, doctor, embellish, enable, fancify, fashion, fix, garnish, guard, heal, help, manufacture, mend, nurse, nurture, ornament, pamper, patch, preserve, protect, rectify, refurbish, rehabilitate, rejuvenate, remedy, renew, repair, rescue, restore, save, sculpt, secure, shield, splint, stitch, strengthen, support, suture, toughen)

MUZZLE (/): *block, censor, check, choke, clog, close, constrict, cover, curb, dampen, devoice, fetter, gag, hinder, hush, inhibit, minimize, muffle, mute, obstruct, quiet, redact, restrain, shush, silence, stifle, stop, straightjacket, subdue, suppress, underemphasize* (≠ accent, accentuate, affirm, amplify, assert, bellow, blab, blurt, boost, broadcast, confess, confirm, declare, dish, emphasize, expose, free, intensify, loose, magnify, maximize, prioritize, release, restore, share, shout, show, telegraph, trumpet)

MYSTIFY (/): *abash, addle, agitate, amaze, astonish, astound, baffle, bamboozle, beat, befog, befuddle, beguile, bemuse, bewilder, blur, bother, buffalo, bullshit, chagrin, cloud, clutter, confound, confuse, cozen, daze, deceive, delude, discombobulate, discomfit, discomfort, discompose, disconcert, dismay, disorient, disquiet, distress, disturb, dizzy, double-talk, dumbfound, dupe, -elude, embarrass, -escape, faze, floor, flummox, fluster, fog, foil, fool, forestall, fox, gaslight, gobsmack, gull, hoax, hobble, hocus-pocus, hoodwink, humbug, jumble, manipulate, misguide, mislead, mismatch, mortify, muddle, muddy, nonplus, obfuscate, obscure, outwit, perplex, perturb, puzzle, rattle, shock, snooker, snow, stick, stump, stun, stupefy, surprise, tangle, throw, -thwart, trick, trouble, unhinge, unsettle, upset, vex* (≠ aid, assist, assure, catalog, clarify, classify, comfort, decipher, deduce, demystify, detect, determine, educate, encourage, enlighten, explain, expose, floodlight, guide, help, illuminate, index, inform, instruct, lead, order, organize, orient, reassure, satisfy, school, settle, simplify, solve, soothe, stabilize, steer, streamline, support, teach, uncloud, uncomplicate, uncover, untangle)

N

NAB (←): *abduct, acquire, amass, annex, apprehend, appropriate, arrest, bag, bust, capture, catch, clutch, collar, collect, commandeer, confiscate, cop, deprive, detain, download, ensnare, gather, get, glean, grab, harvest, impound, levy, monopolize, nail, net, nick, nobble, obtain, pinch, pluck, procure, reap, salvage, scavenge, secure, seize, select, snaffle, snag, snatch, source, take, usurp* (≠ accuse, acquit, alibi, deliver, dismiss, drop, emancipate, enhance, exonerate, forgive, free, give, liberate, lose, miss, misunderstand, pardon, receive, reinstate, release, restore, return, spring, unfasten, unlock, vindicate)

NAG (→): *aggravate, alarm, annoy, antagonize, arouse, badger, bait, bedevil, berate, besiege, blame, bother, browbeat, bug, bully, burden, chafe, chastise, chide, concern, criticize, critique, crowd, denigrate, deride, discompose, distress, disturb, dog, earbash, enrage, exasperate, fault, force, fret, frighten, gall, hack, harass, harry, hassle, heckle, hector, henpeck, hound, inflame, infuriate, intimidate, irk, irritate, needle, nettle, niggle, nitpick, noodge, peeve, perturb, pester, pique, plague, provoke, rankle, rebuke, reprimand, reproach, ruffle, scold, tease, threaten, torment, trouble, unsettle, upbraid, upset, vex, worry* (≠ aid, answer, appease, approve, assist, assuage, blandish, cajole, coax, commend, compliment, delight, discourage, dissuade, ease, flatter, gladden, glad-hand, glorify, gratify, help, lionize, mollify, please, praise, schmooze, soften, soft-soap, soothe, support, sweet-talk, thrill, titillate, wheedle, woo)

NAIL (→): *apprehend, arrest, attach, capture, catch, clinch, corner, fasten, fix, grab, hammer, join, pin, secure, seize, snaffle, snatch, tack, trap* (≠ acquit, camouflage, conceal, confuse, -disregard, drop, free, liberate, lose, miss, release, vindicate)

NAME (→): *address, baptize, brand, call, characterize, christen, classify, define, denote, designate, distinguish, dub, entitle, identify, label, mistitle, nickname, nominate, package, specify, stigmatize, style, tag, term, ticket, title* (≠ anonymize, camouflage, cloak, clothe, cloud, conceal, confuse, costume, counterfeit, delete, disguise, -disregard, erase, hide, -ignore, mislabel, miss, muddle, -neglect, skip)

NAME (←): *accept, adopt, appoint, cherry-pick, choose, consign, cull, designate, elect, embrace, espouse, fix, handpick, mark, nominate, pick, prefer, preselect, select, set, tab, tag, take, tap* (≠ -abandon, -decline, discard, dismiss, erase, jettison, -negate, -refuse, -reject, -repudiate, shed, -spurn, toss)

NAME (←): *announce, anoint, appoint, assign, authorize, charge, choose, cite, classify, commission, connote, consecrate, create, crown, declare, delegate, denote, deputize, designate, draft, elect, enthrone, entrust, finger, handpick, identify, inaugurate, index, induct, install, instance, instate, institute, invest, list, make, mark, mention, nominate, ordain, peg, pick, recognize, refer, remark, select, signify, slot, specify, suggest, tab, tag, tap, task, throne* (≠ accuse, banish, bench, blackball, blame, demote, depose, dethrone, discharge, dismiss, displace, eject, evict, expel, fault, fire, frame, oust, -overlook, overthrow, remove, ruin, shame, sideline, topple, uncrown, unmake, unseat)

NAUSEATE (/): *afflict, affront, agitate, appall, discomfit, discompose, disgust, dismay, displease, disquiet, distress, horrify, indispose, infect, inflict, insult, offend, outrage, pain, rattle, repel, repulse, revolt, sadden, scandalize, shake, shock, sicken, terrorize, traumatize, trigger, unhinge, unnerve, unsettle, upset, weary, wound* (≠ allure, attract, bed, beguile, bewitch, captivate, charm, comfort, console, delight, disarm, draw, entertain, entice, entrance, fascinate, gratify, heal, intrigue, lure, please, pull, restore, seduce, settle, steady, tantalize, tease, tempt, thrill, tickle, woo, wow) **(¿) ABSTRACTION ALERT. Concrete goals essential!**

NAVIGATE (→): *captain, chart, command, conduct, control, cover, crisscross, cross, direct, drive, escort, execute, follow, ford, govern, guide, handle, harness, head, helm, hike, influence, lead, manage, maneuver, manipulate, monitor, negotiate, operate, order, oversee, pace, pass, perambulate, pilot, plan, plot, quarterback, ride, roam, run, sail, shepherd, skipper, spearhead, steer, superintend, supervise, track, transit, travel, traverse, tread, usher, wander* (≠ -abandon, -avoid, crash, cripple, -desert, -disregard, -eschew, -evade, fail, flub, foil, follow, forget, -frustrate, hamper, hamstring, heed, hinder, -ignore, maroon, mind, miscalculate, mishandle, misjudge, mismanage, misrule, miss, mistake, monkey-wrench, muddle, -neglect, obey, obstruct, -omit, -overlook, pursue, puzzle, quit, -refuse, relinquish, ride, sabotage, serve, sideswipe, skip, smash, subvert, target, wreck)

NEATEN (+): *arrange, barber, brush, clean, clear, clip, dandify, declutter, edge, groom, gussy, iron, launder, maintain, manicure, order, organize, police, pomade, preen, primp, rectify, right, sleek, slick, smarten, sort, spiff, spruce, square, straighten, tauten, tidy, titivate, trim, uncrumple, wash* (≠ bedraggle, clutter, crumple, diffuse, dirty, dishevel, disorder, disorganize, draggle, jumble, muss, scatter, scramble, shuffle, smudge, soil, trash, untidy, wreck, wrinkle)

NEEDLE (→): *aggravate, annoy, antagonize, arouse, badger, bait, bedevil, bother, bug, chafe, chaff, discompose, disturb, earbash, enrage, envenom, exacerbate, examine, exasperate, fret, gnaw, goad, grill, harass, harry, hassle, heckle, hector, henpeck, inflame, infuriate, interrogate, irk, irritate, jeer, mock, nag, nettle, niggle, nitpick, nudge, peeve, perturb, pester, plague, poke, prick, prod, provoke, question, quiz, rankle, retort, ride, ridicule, rile, roast, ruffle, spur, sting, taunt, tease,* *torment, troll, trouble, tweak, upset, vex, worry, wound* (≠ aid, appease, assist, assuage, calm, charm, comfort, defend, delight, discourage, dissuade, guard, help, humor, lull, mellow, mitigate, moderate, mollify, pacify, placate, please, praise, rescue, respect, sedate, shield, soothe, woo)

-NEGATE (/): *abnegate, abolish, abrogate, annihilate, annul, -cancel, check, confute, contradict, counterbalance, countermand, countervail, deep-six, delete, -deny, destroy, disavow, disclaim, discredit, dismiss, disprove, dissolve, divorce, doom, efface, eliminate, eradicate, erase, expense, extinguish, gainsay, invalidate, invert, neutralize, -nullify, obliterate, offset, oppose, oppugn, -prohibit, quash, refute, -reject, -renounce, repeal, -repudiate, -rescind, retract, reverse, revoke, scotch, stultify, undo, -veto, -void, withdraw* (≠ adopt, advance, affirm, approve, assert, avow, back, confirm, corroborate, enact, insist, institute, maintain, mandate, order, pledge, profess, promote, sanction, substantiate, support, survive, sustain, warrant, weather)

-NEGLECT (→): *-abandon, -avoid, -blank, -bypass, confound, confuse, deceive, -desert, -discount, -disdain, disguise, dismiss, disobey, -disregard, disrespect, erase, excuse, fail, fake, forget, -forsake, fudge, half-ass, -ignore, infringe, leave, miss, mistake, -omit, overestimate, -overlook, pass, pooh-pooh, -rebuff, -reject, scant, -scorn, -shirk, skip, -slight, slur, -snub, -spurn, subvert, underestimate* (≠ admire, appreciate, attend, bemoan, cherish, clock, concern, cultivate, follow, foster, guard, heed, indulge, infantilize, keep, lament, mark, mind, mourn, note, notice, nurse, nurture, observe, overindulge, pamper, patrol, prize, protect, regard, remark, remember, respect, tend, treasure, value, watch, worship)

-NEGLECT (/): *-bypass, defer, detour, discard, dismiss, -disregard, elide, -evade, fail, famish, forget, leapfrog, malnourish, miss, -omit, -overlook, postpone, scant, -shirk, skimp, skip, starve, stint, suspend, underfeed, withhold* (≠ accomplish, achieve, brave, complete, confront, discharge, execute, face, feed, finish, force-feed, fuel, fulfill, furnish, maintain, meet, mind, overfeed, perform, practice, regret, remember, satisfy, stomach, supply, tend, victual)

NEGOTIATE (→): *bestride, bridge, clear, crisscross, cross, ford, guide, hurdle, leapfrog, maneuver, navigate, pace, pass, perambulate, plan, plot, range, roam, span, straddle, surmount, transit, travel, traverse, tread, vault, wander* (≠ -avoid, -bypass, circumnavigate, -circumvent, destroy, -dodge, -duck, -eschew, -evade, -ignore, miss, -shun, -sidestep, skip, skirt)

NEGOTIATE (→): *accommodate, accost, address, adjust, brave, buttonhole, challenge, charm, command, concede, concert, confront, consider, consult, contract, control, deal, debate, direct, discuss, engineer, face, field, finesse, gauge, grapple, guide, hack, handle, jockey, judge, manage, maneuver, manipulate, mediate, micromanage, moderate, pacify, play, pull, referee, regulate, request, resolve, review, run, steer, stipulate, swing, take, treat* (≠ bobble, botch, bungle, foozle, fumble, louse, mishandle, mismanage, muff, ruin, scotch, wreck)

NEGOTIATE (→): *arrange, brew, captain, chart, command, compose, conclude, concoct, conduct, contrive, direct, engineer, finagle, finesse, frame, gerrymander, handle, hatch, lobby, machinate, manage, maneuver, manipulate, mastermind, outsmart, outthink, outwit, plot, quarterback, run, wangle* (≠ blow, bobble, botch, bungle, butcher, crash, disorganize, flub, fumble, gum, mangle, mishandle, muff, screw, wreck)

NEGOTIATE (→): *accomplish, ace, achieve, actualize, attain, claim, commit, compass, complete, conclude, effect, effectuate, end, execute, finish, fulfill, implement, make, nail, perform, perpetrate, practice, prosecute, realize, reenact, repeat, succeed* (≠ attempt, bobble, botch, bungle, drop, fail, flunk, fumble, lose, miss, skimp, -slight, slur, try, undershoot, venture)

NEGOTIATE (←): *adjudicate, appraise, arbitrate, argue, arrange, assess, bandy, barter, broker, buy, challenge, charm, commodify, compare, concert, conclude, confront, connect, contract, covenant, deal, debate, discuss, estimate, evaluate, exchange, fight, gauge, handle, hassle, hawk, horse-trade, import, judge, leverage, lower, manipulate, mediate, moderate, offer, peddle, presell, price, purchase, raise, renegotiate, request, resolve, risk, sell, settle, stipulate, substitute, swap, switch, talk, trade, traffic, transact, truck, umpire, valuate, weigh, wrangle* (≠ -abandon, -avoid, bill, charge, demand, exact, foist, force, impose, insult, invoice, levy, mishandle, mock, -prevent, -refuse, -shun, withhold)

NET (←): *accumulate, acquire, add, amass, annex, assume, bag, buy, capture, catch, claim, collar, collect, corner, enmesh, ensnare, entangle, entrap, fetch, garner, get, harvest, heap, hook, incur, land, lasso, lure, nab, obtain, palm, pocket, procure, purchase, reap, receive, recoup, recover, redeem, rescue, retrieve, rope, salvage, score, secure, snare, source, take, trap, win, wrangle* (≠ detach, discharge, disengage, disentangle, drop, emancipate, -exclude, extricate, free, give, hunt, liberate, loosen, lose, miss, -omit, receive, release, seek, slacken, spring, unfasten, unhand, untangle)

NET (←): *accumulate, aggregate, clear, collect, draw, earn, gain, get, make, obtain, pocket, produce, pull, realize, reap, receive, scavenge, source, take, total* (≠ bequeath, bestow, borrow, charge, disburse, expense, forfeit, give, grant, gross, loan, lose, outlay, pay, relinquish, spend, squander, stiff, surrender, waste, yield)

NETTLE (/): *affront, aggravate, agitate, anger, annoy, antagonize, badger, bait, bother, bug, bullyrag, burn, chafe, chagrin, craze, devil, discomfort, discompose, disgust, disquiet, distress, disturb, earbash, eat, enrage, exasperate, exercise, freak, fret, frost, frustrate, gall, goad, grate, hagride, harass, harry, hassle, heckle, incense, inflame, infuriate, insult, irk, irritate, itch peeve, madden, miff, nag, needle, niggle, nitpick, offend, outrage, peeve, persecute, perturb, pester, pique, plague, provoke, rankle, rasp, rile, roil, rouse, ruffle, spite, stew, sting, tease, torment, undo, unhinge, unsettle, upset, vex, worry* (≠ allay, amuse, appease, assure, baby, calm, cheer, coddle, comfort, conciliate, console, content, delight, entertain, gladden, gratify, help, humor, lull, mellow, mitigate, moderate, mollify, oblige, pacify, placate, please, propitiate, quiet, reassure, satisfy, settle, solace, soothe, steady, thrill)

NEUTER (/): *alter, caponize, castrate, deball, desex, doctor, dress, emasculate, excise, extract, fix, geld, mutilate, remove, spay, sterilize, unman, unsex* (≠ arouse, boost, buoy, charge, fertilize, heal, invigorate, keep, renew, replace, restore, retain, stimulate)

NEUTRALIZE (/): *abrogate, annul, balance, -cancel, center, checkmate, compose, conquer, correct, counteract, counterbalance, counterpoise, countervail, defeat, disqualify, erase, expense, -frustrate, ground, incapacitate, invalidate, minimize, -negate, negative, neuter, normalize, -nullify, offset, outbalance, outweigh, overcome, override, overrule, realign, redeem, redress, relieve, remedy, right, stultify, subdue, undo* (≠ accent, accentuate, aggravate, amplify, animate, assert, corroborate, deepen, emphasize, exacerbate, exaggerate, increase, inspire, intensify, maximize, overdramatize, punctuate, raise, reinvigorate, restore, resurrect, resuscitate, revive, stimulate, strengthen)

NICK (←): *apprehend, arrest, bag, bind, bust, capture, catch, collar, commit, confine, convict, detain, enchain, fetter, get, grab, grapple, handcuff, hold, hook, immure, imprison, incarcerate, intern, jail, jug, land, manacle, nab, nail, pinch, remand, restrain, seize, shackle, snaffle, snare, snatch, stop, trammel, trap* (≠ acquit, bail, discharge, eject, emancipate, -escape, expel, free, liberate, loose, loosen, release, spring, unbind, unchain, uncuff)

NICK (←): *abduct, acquire, appropriate, bogart, boost, burglarize, burgle, collar, filch, grab, grasp, heist, hook, kidnap, lift, loot, misappropriate, mooch, nail, nip, nobble, obtain, pick, pilfer, pillage, pinch, pluck, plunder, poach, pocket, procure, purloin, remove, rifle, rob, rustle, sack, seize, shanghai, shoplift, snaffle, snag, snatch, sneak, snitch, spirit, sponge, steal, swipe, take, thieve* (≠ bestow, buy, comp, contribute, donate, -forsake, give, guard, hand, leave, present, protect, purchase, recover, restore, return, safeguard, secure)

NICK (/): *abrade, blemish, blot, chip, crosshatch, cut, damage, deface, deform, dent, disfigure, distort, dot, efface, flaw, fleck, fracture, gash, hack, hurt, indent, kink, knock, mar, mark, nock, notch, pockmark, scar, score, scrape, scratch, scuff, slit, snick, splotch, spoil, spot, taint, tarnish, wound* (≠ beautify, block, burnish, cover, fix, fortify, heal, mend, patch, perfect, polish, rectify, reinforce, remedy, repair, shield, shine, smooth)

NIP (/): *bite, catch, clasp, clip, clutch, compress, crimp, dock, grasp, grip, hold, lop, munch, nibble, pinch, snag, snap, snip, squeeze, take, tweak* (≠ drop, eject, expel, free, loose, loosen, maim, mutilate, numb, release, savage, sedate, spit, spring, swallow)

NIP (/): *bob, clip, crop, curtail, cut, dock, lop, manicure, mow, pare, pinch, poll, prune, shave, shear, shorten, skive, snip, stump, trim, whittle*

(≠ augment, cultivate, elongate, expand, extend, grow, lengthen, nurture, preserve, stretch, unspool)

NOMINATE (→): *anoint, appoint, assign, attach, authorize, broker, cherry-pick, choose, commission, consign, constitute, crown, delegate, deputize, designate, detail, draft, elect, elevate, enthrone, finger, handpick, inaugurate, induct, install, instate, institute, invest, license, name, ordain, pick, place, postulate, present, propose, propound, recommend, select, spitball, submit, suggest, task* (≠ accuse, bar, blackball, blacklist, blame, -boycott, condemn, depose, dethrone, discharge, dismiss, displace, eject, evict, -exclude, expel, fire, oppose, -ostracize, oust, -overlook, overthrow, picket, -prohibit, protest, -reject, remove, -repudiate, shame, -shun, -spurn, -thwart uncrown, unmake, unseat)

NORMALIZE (+): *accredit, adapt, adjust, align, average, calibrate, certify, clear, codify, compose, control, coordinate, depersonalize, equalize, even, formalize, govern, harmonize, homogenize, institute, integrate, manage, marshal, mend, methodize, neutralize, order, organize, pace, rebuild, reconcile, recondition, reconstitute, reconstruct, redeem, reform, regiment, regularize, regulate, rehab, rehabilitate, reinstate, reintegrate, renew, restore, rule, save, square, stabilize, standardize, straighten, structure, synthesize, systematize, systemize, tune* (≠ adapt, alter, change, contrast, criticize, customize, differentiate, disparage, disprove, distinguish, individualize, juxtapose, malign, mismatch, -negate, personalize, rattle, rebut, roil, separate, tailor, vilify)

NOTCH (/): *abrade, blemish, blot, chip, chisel, cleave, crimp, crosshatch, cut, damage, deface, deform, dent, disfigure, distort, efface, flaw, fleck, fracture, gash, gouge, groove, hack, hurt, incise, indent, kink, knock, mar, mark, mill, nick, nock, pockmark, scallop, scar, score, scrape, scratch, scuff, serrate, slit, snick, spoil, tally, wound* (≠ augment, beautify, block, burnish, cover, erase, even, fill, fix, flatten, fortify, heal, mend, patch, perfect, plaster, plug, polish, rectify, reinforce, remedy, repair, shield, shine, smooth)

NOTIFY (→): *acquaint, admonish, advise, advocate, air, alert, announce, apprise, assert, beckon, blazon, brief, broadcast, bulletin, cable, caution, circulate, clue, communicate, concede, confer, confess, confide, confirm, consult, convey, counsel, cue, debrief, declare, disclose, disseminate, divulge, email, enlighten, evince, express, flag, guide, herald, hint, hype, illuminate, impart, inform, instruct, mention, message, motion, note, nudge, plug, post, presell, proclaim, prompt, promulgate, publicize, publish, radio, recommend, report, reveal, school, signal, spread, state, suggest, talk, teach, telegraph, telephone, tell, text, verbalize, vocalize, warn, wire, write* (≠ addle, baffle, blind, bury, cloak, cloud, collect, conceal, confuse, cover, deceive, disguise, double-talk, encrypt, ensconce, gather, glean, hide, hush, keep, mislead, obscure, perplex, puzzle, screen, secrete, suppress, veil, withhold) **(¿) ABSTRACTION ALERT. Concrete goals essential!**

NOURISH (+): *abet, advance, advertise, advocate, aid, assist, back, boost, champion, cherish, comfort, cultivate, encourage, endorse, endow, finance, force-feed, forward, foster, fund, further, help, incubate, maintain, nurse, nurture, overfeed, patronize, plug, prioritize, promote, publicize, rear, stake, stimulate, stoke, strengthen, subsidize, support, tend, tout, underwrite, uphold* (≠ arrest, ban, bar, check, defund, -desert, discourage, encumber, -forbid, -forsake, -frustrate, -halt, hinder, hobble, impede, inhibit, -neglect, obstruct, outlaw, -prevent, -prohibit, proscribe, repress, retard, snuff, squash, squelch, starve, stifle, subdue, suppress, -thwart, withhold)

NOURISH (+): *accord, attend, board, cater, cloy, contribute, disburse, dispense, entertain, feed, fill, fortify, fuel, furnish, nurse, nurture, provide, provision, replenish, sate, satiate, satisfy, strengthen, suckle, supply, surfeit, sustain, victual, wean* (≠ -abandon, curb, -deny, deprive, famish, -forsake, hoard, malnourish, scant, sicken, skimp, skip, starve, stint, underfeed, withdraw, withhold)

NUDGE (→): *alert, beckon, bump, buzz, contact, crowd, cue, dig, egg, elbow, encourage, entice, exhort, flag, force, frogmarch, goad, guide, hasten, hustle, impel, incite, induce, inspire, instigate, jab, jog, jostle, knock, march, motivate, move, notify, poke, prod, prompt, propel, provoke, push, remind, shoulder, shove, shunt, signal, stimulate, tap, touch, trigger, urge* (≠ backhand, ban, bang, bash, beat, cripple, deflect, delay, demotivate, -deter, discourage, dishearten, dissuade, -forbid, -ignore, inhibit, miss, pause, postpone, -prohibit, punch, ram, restrain, restrict, shelve, short-circuit, smack, smash, stall, stem, stop, thwack, -thwart, wallop, warn)

-NULLIFY (/): *abate, abolish, -abort, abrogate, annihilate, annul, -avoid, ban, -blank, call, -cancel, checkmate, counteract, countermand, counterpoise countervail, deactivate, defeat, delegitimize, destroy, disallow, -discontinue, dismiss, dissolve, doom, drop, efface, eliminate, enjoin, eradicate, erase, expense, foil, -forbid, inactivate, invalidate, liquidate, monkey-wrench, -negate, null, offset, outlaw, override, overrule, overturn, -prohibit, quash, recall, -reject, remove, -renounce, repeal, -rescind, retract, reverse, revoke, suspend, vacate, -veto, -void, withdraw* (≠ allow, approve, authorize, boost, cherish, clear, command, craft, create, decree, enact, endorse, establish, formalize, found, institute, legalize, legislate, legitimate, legitimize, mandate, order, pass, permit, prescribe, promote, propose, ratify, recommend, restore, rubber-stamp, sanction, survive, sustain, validate, warrant, withstand)

NUMB (/): *abate, alleviate, anesthetize, arrest, blunt, buffer, cauterize, chill, chloroform, cushion, damp, dampen, daze, deactivate, deaden, debilitate, decrease, desensitize, diminish, dose, drug, dull, ease, enfeeble, freeze, hypnotize, immobilize, inactivate, lessen, lighten, lower, medicate, mesmerize, minimize, moderate, muffle, mute, narcotize, paralyze, reduce, sedate, stultify, stun, stupefy, subdue, torpefy, tranquilize, weaken* (≠ accentuate, activate, agitate, amplify, animate, arouse, augment, boost, consolidate, deepen, energize, enhance, enliven, heighten, increase, intensify, invigorate, magnify, maximize, prod, redouble, rouse, sensitize, sharpen, stimulate, stir, strengthen, wake, whet)

NURSE (+): *abet, aid, assist, attend, baby, babysit, bolster, boost, bottle-feed, cherish, clean, cleanse, coddle, conserve, cradle, cultivate, cure, decontaminate, doctor, dose, drug, encourage, feed, foster, further, harbor, heal, help, hospitalize, humor, immunize, indulge, infantilize, inoculate, medicate, mollycoddle, mother, nourish, nurture, overprotect, pamper, preserve, prioritize, promote, provide, relieve, remedy, serve, splint, spoil, sterilize, strengthen, succor, support, sustain, tend, treat, vaccinate, wash* (≠ abuse, afflict, aggravate, anguish, assault, attack, -avoid, contaminate, forget, gore, harm, hurt, -ignore, infect, injure, lacerate, malnourish, menace, nauseate, -neglect, overdose, -overlook, persecute, plague, poison, pollute, shock, -shun, sicken, -slight, terrorize, threaten, torment, torture, traumatize, trouble, victimize, violate, wound, wrong)

NURTURE (+): *abet, accommodate, advance, advertise, advocate, aid, assist, back, bankroll, bolster, boost, buttress, champion, cherish, coach, cultivate, culture, develop, discipline, edify, educate, elevate, encourage, endorse, endow, enhance, enlighten, entertain, father, favor, feed, finance, foment, force-feed, forward, foster, fuel, fund, further, groom, guide, harbor, hatch, help, hold, improve, incubate, inform, mentor, mother, nourish, nurse, optimize, overfeed, pastor, patronize, plug, preserve, prioritize, promote, protect, publicize, raise, rear, school, serve, sire, stake, stimulate, stoke, strengthen, subsidize, support, sustain, teach, tend, touch, tout, train, underwrite, uphold, uplift, victual* (≠ abuse, arrest, ban, bar, battle, betray, brutalize, check, checkmate, counter, defund, degrade, dehumanize, demotivate, discourage, discredit, disfavor, disgrace, disinherit, -disown, encumber, enjoin, fetter, -forbid, -frustrate, -halt, harm, hinder, hobble, hurt, impede, inhibit, injure, -interdict, manacle, -neglect, obstruct, oppose, outlaw, -prevent, -prohibit, proscribe, repress, retard, sabotage, scotch, scupper, scuttle, shackle, shelve, snuff, squash, squelch, stifle, stymie, subdue, suppress, -thwart, undermine, -veto, wrong)

OBEY (+): *abide, accept, admit, aid, allow, answer, assist, attend, cede, discharge, embrace, enthrone, execute, favor, follow, fulfill, hear, heed, help, hold, honor, imitate, keep, maintain, mark, mind, note, notice, oblige, observe, perform, preserve, protect, recognize, regard, respect, retain, serve, submit, support, surrender, survive, sustain, take, watch, welcome, worship, yield* (≠ break, buck, bulldoze, bully, challenge, command, contest, dare, debate, decree, defy, demand, depose, dictate, dismiss, disobey, dispute, -disregard, disrespect, enslave, fight, flout, mock, muscle, oppose, oppress, -overlook, overstep, pooh-pooh, railroad, -refuse, -renounce, -repudiate, resist, -scorn, steamroll, subjugate, subvert, test, topple, transgress, violate)

OBLIGATE (→): *bind, bludgeon, browbeat, bulldoze, bully, charge, coerce, commit, compel, constrain, enforce, engage, excise, force, impel, make, mandate, muscle, oblige, overcommit, press, pressure, railroad, require, restrain, restrict, sandbag, stipulate* (≠ absolve, acquit, advise, allow, bribe, clear, convince, discharge, exculpate, excuse, exempt, exonerate, forgive, free, imply, liberate, pardon, permit, persuade, release, spare)

OBLIGE (→): *badger, blackjack, blackmail, browbeat, bulldoze, bully, coerce, command, compel, constrain, cow, demand, drag, dragoon, drive, force, harass, hector, hound, impel, impress, intimidate, make, menace, muscle, nobble, obligate, overcommit, press, pressure, railroad, require, sandbag, shame, terrorize, threaten, tie* (≠ allow, argue, bribe, coax, convince, ease, encourage, facilitate, hint, induce, let, lubricate, midwife, move, permit, persuade, request, satisfy, suggest)

OBLIGE (+): *abet, accommodate, advantage, aid, appease, assist, attend, benefit, coddle, comfort, contribute, delight, favor, gladden, gratify, help, humor, indulge, infantilize, mind, mollify, mollycoddle, obey, offer, pacify, pamper, placate, please, pledge, profit, relieve, satisfy, serve, succor, support, volunteer* (≠ alienate, bother, burden, constrain, -desert, disaffect, disappoint, discommode, disfavor, disoblige, disturb, encumber, fail, -frustrate, hamper, hamstring, hinder, hobble, impede, incommode, inconvenience, obstruct, oppose, -ostracize, restrain, sabotage, saddle, scotch, subvert, -thwart, trouble, weigh)

OBSCURE (/): *adumbrate, becloud, bedim, befog, belie, blacken, blanket, blear, blind, blindfold, block, blur, bury, camouflage, censor, cloak, clothe, cloud, complicate, conceal, confound, confuse, costume, cover, curtain, darken, dim, disguise, eclipse, ensconce, enshroud, extinguish, falsify, fog, fuzz, gild, gloss, haze, hide, holster, hood, hush, mask, misrepresent, mist, muddle, muddy, niche, obfuscate, obliterate, obstruct, occlude, occult,* *outperform, overcast, overcloud, overlap, overshadow, redact, screen, shade, shadow, sheathe, shroud, smother, stonewall, suppress, varnish, veil, whitewash, wrap* (≠ advertise, air, bare, blab, blaze, blazon, blurt, boost, brandish, brighten, broadcast, clarify, clock, confess, disclose, discover, display, divulge, edify, exalt, expose, extol, flaunt, floodlight, flutter, glorify, heighten, highlight, hype, illuminate, illumine, light, lighten, observe, parade, plug, present, proclaim, promote, publicize, publish, reveal, scan, scope, scrutinize, show, showcase, spotlight, spread, uncloak, uncloud, uncomplicate, uncover, unmask, unveil)

OBSERVE (←): *attend, bird-dog, catch, clock, consider, consult, descry, detect, discern, discover, distinguish, espy, examine, eye, eyeball, follow, glimpse, guard, heed, identify, inspect, learn, mark, mind, monitor, note, notice, patrol, perceive, police, proctor, read, recognize, regard, remark, scan, scope, scrutinize, see, sight, spot, spy, study, survey, view, ward, watch, witness* (≠ -blank, bury, cloak, conceal, -discount, dismiss, disprove, dispute, -disregard, doubt, ensconce, forget, gloss, handle, hide, -ignore, miss, -neglect, niche, obscure, obstruct, occlude, -overlook, -repudiate, -scorn, scruple, skim, skip, tackle, touch, wrestle) **(¿) ABSTRACTION ALERT. Concrete goals essential!**

OBSERVE (+): *bemoan, bless, celebrate, ceremonialize, commemorate, consecrate, fête, honor, keep, lament, laud, memorialize, mourn, praise, regret, remember, ritualize, sanctify, solemnize, venerate* (≠ break, -disregard, forget, -ignore, -neglect, -overlook, regret, rue, transgress, violate)

OBSERVE (+): *accept, acknowledge, attend, concede, disoblige, follow, fulfill, hear, heed, honor, mark, mind, note, notice, obey, regard, remember, respect, satisfy, take, watch* (≠ breach, break, buck, challenge, combat, contest, debate, defy, deride, discredit, dismiss, disobey, dispute, -disregard, doubt, fight, flout, gainsay, mock, oppose, refute, -repudiate, resist, -scorn, subvert, violate)

OBSTRUCT (/): *anticipate, arrest, baffle, -balk, bar, barricade, block, blockade, bottleneck, brake, burden, cage, catch, check, checkmate, choke, -circumvent, clog, complicate, confront, confuse, congest, constipate, constrain, cordon, counter, crab, cramp, crimp, cripple, cross, curb, dam, dampen, daunt, defeat, deflect, defy, delay, demotivate, detain, -deter, disappoint, discourage, dissuade, divert, double-cross, -duck, -elude, encumber, entangle, entrap, -exclude, fetter, flummox, foil, forestall, foul, -frustrate, -halt, hamper, hamstring, handicap, hinder, hogtie, impair, impede, inhibit, intercept, interrupt, jam, -kibosh, kneecap, limit, lumber, mire, monkey-wrench, muzzle, obscure, oppose, oust, outwit, paralyze, parry, pause, plug, postpone, preempt, -prevent, -prohibit, protest, resist, restrain, restrict, retard, ruin, sandbag, scotch, shelve, short-circuit, skin, slow, snag, snarl, snooker, spite, stagnate, stall, stem, stifle, stop, straightjacket, stultify, stump, stunt, stymie, taboo, tangle, throttle, -thwart, trammel, waylay* (≠ accelerate, accommodate, advance, aerate, aid, assist, boost, brainstorm, catalyze, clear, compel, decongest, ease, encourage, enhance, excavate, expedite, facilitate, fast-forward, fast-track, forward, free, fuel, further, grease, hasten, help, hollow, hurry, inspire, liberate, lighten, loosen, lubricate, midwife, oblige, observe, open, optimize, oxygenate, prioritize, prod, promote, prompt, propel, quicken, release, relieve, remedy, revolutionize, rush, scoop, slacken, smooth, speed, spur, stimulate, stir, stoke, strengthen, support, transcend, unblock, unclog, uncomplicate, unleash, unlock, untie, urge, ventilate, watch)

OBTAIN (+): *abduct, accomplish, accumulate, achieve, acquire, add, amass, annex, apprehend, appropriate, arrest, assume, attain, bag, bilk, bogart, borrow, buy, cadge, capture, carry, catch, claim, clear, clinch, collar, collect, corner, download, draw, earn, enlist, fetch, gain, garner, get, grab, gross, harvest, heap, import, incur, inherit, land, lease, lure, make, net, nobble, notch, occupy, palm, pilfer, poach, pocket, possess, preempt, procure, purchase, rack, reacquire, realize, reap, reattain, recapture, receive, reclaim, recoup, recover, recycle, redeem, regain, remake, rent, rescue, retrieve, rustle, salvage, scavenge, score, scrounge, secure, seize, select, snaffle, snag, snare, snatch, steal, stockpile, swipe, take, weasel, wheedle, win, wrangle* (≠ -abandon, accord, bankroll, bequeath, bestow, commend, comp, confer, contribute, deliver, disburse, dispense, donate, dower, drop, endow, equip, fail, forfeit, fumble, fund, furnish, give, grant, lose, miss, offer, pay, present, -quit, relinquish, send, spare, starve, stiff, stint, supply, surrender, tender, tithe, transfer, underwrite, volunteer, yield)

OCCUPY (+): *absorb, allure, amuse, attend, attract, beguile, bemuse, bewitch, busy, captivate, charm, distract, divert, employ, enchant, energize, engage, engross, entertain, enthrall, excite, fascinate, fill, galvanize, grip, hog, hold, hypnotize, immerse, interest, intrigue, involve, mesmerize, monopolize, obsess, possess, preoccupy, retain, soak, stimulate, wow* (≠ annoy, appall, bore, bother, bug, dampen, deaden, desensitize, distract, drain, dull, exasperate, exhaust, fatigue, frustrate, irk, jade, knacker, nag, nauseate, needle, nettle, niggle, nitpick, numb, paralyze, pester, sicken, tire, trouble, underwhelm, vex, weary) **(¿) ABSTRACTION ALERT. Concrete goals essential!**

OCCUPY (+): *abide, billet, colonize, cover, embattle, embed, ensconce, establish, fill, fortify, hold, house, impregnate, infiltrate, inhabit, keep, lodge, maintain, own, penetrate, permeate, pervade, populate, possess, quarter, saturate, settle, stay, tenant* (≠ -abandon, -desert, dislodge, displace, evict, exile, forfeit, -forsake, leave, maroon, -omit, -ostracize, oust, relegate, relocate, strand)

OFFEND (/): *abase, abuse, affront, aggrieve, anger, annoy, antagonize, bait, belittle, besmear, besmirch, bestialize, bother, confound, debase, defame, deflate, degrade, demean, demote, devalue, diminish, disappoint, disgrace, disgust, dishonor, displease, disturb, exasperate, gravel, harass, hassle, heckle, humble, humiliate, hurt, incense, injure, insult, irritate, jar, jeer, libel, lower, malign, miff, mock, mortify, muckrake,* *nag, nauseate, needle, nettle, niggle, nitpick, outrage, provoke, -rebuff, reduce, repel, repulse, revolt, ridicule, rile, ruffle, scandalize, shame, shock, sicken, sideline, slander, -slight, slur, -snub, soil, spoil, stain, sully, taint, taunt, trample, troll, upset, violate, wound, wrong* (≠ admire, amuse, appease, assuage, beguile, boost, buoy, butter, captivate, charm, comfort, compliment, content, court, delight, disarm, enchant, entertain, expiate, fascinate, flannel, flatter, forgive, glad-hand, gratify, honor, inveigle, mollify, pacify, placate, please, prioritize, propitiate, repent, revere, rue, satisfy, settle, steady, sweet-talk, thrill, woo)

OFFER (→): *advance, commercialize, commodify, contribute, extend, forward, give, introduce, leverage, market, monetize, present, proffer, recommend, remainder, sell, submit, suggest, supply, tender, volunteer* (≠ accept, -decline, -deny, -rebuff, receive, -refuse, -reject, retract, -spurn, take, -veto, withdraw)

OFFER (→): *advance, arrange, bid, bounce, calculate, chart, contrive, cover, frame, lodge, map, nominate, plan, plot, pose, posit, present, proffer, propose, recommend, shape, spare, spitball, submit, suggest, tender, volunteer, vote* (≠ answer, condemn, -deny, disbelieve, discourage, -disregard, dissuade, forget, -ignore, -neglect, oppose, -refuse, -reject, repulse)

OFFER (→): *celebrate, consecrate, dedicate, devote, forfeit, give, hand, immolate, martyr, present, sacrifice, slaughter, spare, surrender, volunteer, worship, yield* (≠ -abandon, -deny, desecrate, -ignore, misapply, misuse, -neglect, profane, withhold)

OFFER (→): *act, attempt, brandish, carry, depict, display, dramatize, enact, exhibit, expose, express, extend, flaunt, give, impersonate, mount, parade, perform, play, playact, portray, present, preview, proffer, render, represent, roleplay, show, showcase, stage, tender, try, unveil* (≠ bury, camouflage, cloak, cloud, conceal, cover, deprive, disguise, ensconce, hide, mask, obscure, screen, shroud, stint, suppress, veil, withhold)

OFFSET (+): *abrogate, alleviate, annul, assuage, balance, -cancel, center, checkmate, compose, correct, counteract, counterbalance, counterpoise, countervail, ease, equalize, erase, expense, -frustrate, ground, incapacitate, invalidate, minimize, mitigate, -negate, neuter, neutralize, normalize, -nullify, outbalance, outweigh, overcome, override, overrule, pacify, realign, rectify, redeem, redress, relax, relieve, remedy, right, square, subdue, undo* (≠ accent, accentuate, aggravate, amplify, animate, assert, complicate, compound, corroborate, deepen, emphasize, exacerbate, exaggerate, expand, extend, heighten, increase, inflate, inspire, intensify, magnify, maximize, overdramatize, punctuate, raise, restore, resurrect, revive, stimulate, strengthen)

OIL (←): *anoint, bathe, beeswax, blandish, brownnose, butter, cajole, candy-coat, charm, coat, commend, compliment, con, court, douse, drench, dulcify, flannel, flatter, glad-hand, grease, humor, hustle, inveigle, jolly, lard, lube, lubricate, marinate, massage, moisturize, palaver,* *pomade, praise, salve, schmooze, sell, slick, smear, smooth, snooker, snow, soak, soften, soft-soap, souse, stroke, sucker, sugarcoat, sweeten, sweet-talk, syrup, wash, water, wax, wet, wheedle, win, woo, wow* (≠ abrade, berate, blackjack, bully, callous, chafe, coarsen, compel, condemn, criticize, dehydrate, desiccate, dry, force, harden, harshen, insult, intimidate, jeer, mock, muscle, offend, parch, railroad, repel, ridicule, rough, roughen, sear, sharpen, toughen)

-OMIT (/): *-avoid, -bypass, delete, -disregard, -ditch, drop, dump, edit, eliminate, erase, except, -exclude, expel, expunge, fail, forget, -ignore, miss, -neglect, -ostracize, -overlook, pass, -preclude, -refuse, -reject, -shirk, -shun, -sidestep, skimp, skip, stint, withhold* (≠ add, admit, assimilate, combine, contain, cover, embrace, enclose, encompass, hold, include, incorporate, insert, integrate, introduce, involve, mention, mix, span, subsume, unite)

OPEN (→): *break, broach, burst, bust, clear, crack, disclose, disengage, display, disrupt, expose, force, jimmy, lacerate, lance, penetrate, perforate, pierce, pop, prize, puncture, push, release, reveal, rupture, separate, sever, slide, slip, slit, slot, split, tap, unbar, unblock, unbolt, unbuckle, unbutton, unclasp, unclench, unclothe, uncork, uncover, undo, unfasten, unlatch, unlock, unseal, untie, unzip, ventilate* (≠ bar, barricade, bolt, button, cinch, clasp, clench, clinch, close, cordon, deadbolt, fasten, latch, lock, padlock, plug, seal, secure, shut, stopper, zip)

OPEN (→): *broaden, diffuse, dilate, enlarge, expand, extend, fan, flare, outstretch, part, scatter, separate, split, spread, stretch, unfold, unfurl, unroll, widen* (≠ close, compact, compress, concentrate, condense, contract, crease, fold, narrow, pucker, reduce, tighten, wrinkle)

OPEN (+): *access, adopt, begin, commence, convene, create, embrace, enter, establish, father, found, generate, hatch, inaugurate, initiate, innovate, institute, invent, jump, launch, meet, organize, originate, pioneer, sire, spawn, start* (≠ -abandon, abolish, -abort, cease, close, complete, conclude, -discontinue, end, extinguish, finish, -forsake, -halt, leave, pause, -quit, stop, terminate)

OPEN (+): *aerate, clean, clear, decongest, disentangle, ease, expose, extricate, facilitate, fissure, free, loosen, oxygenate, release, rid, slack, slacken, smooth, strip, unblock, unclog, unclutter, uncork, unplug, unstop, vent, ventilate, wash* (≠ barricade, block, blockade, clog, close, clutter, constipate, constrict, cork, dam, encumber, fill, hamper, hinder, impede, obstruct, occlude, plug, seal, shut, stem, stop, stopple)

OPERATE (→): *administer, align, apply, balance, channel, command, conduct, control, deploy, dial, direct, drive, employ, exert, fly, guide, handle, implement, influence, man, manage, maneuver, manipulate, marshal, pilot, realign, run, steer, synchronize, use, utilize, wield, work* (≠ -abandon, -avoid, break, damage, -desert, destroy, discard, -disdain, drop, -eschew, -halt, hinder, -ignore, lose, misapply, mismanage, misuse, -neglect, -overlook, -refuse, -reject, ruin, stop, withdraw, wreck)

OPPOSE (/): *answer, antagonize, argue, assail, assault, attack, -avert, baffle, balance, bar, barricade, battle, block, blockade, blunt, bombard, bottleneck, brake, buffer, bung, burden, catch, challenge, check, checkmate, choke, clog, combat, compare, complicate, confound, confront, confute, congest, constipate, constrain, contest, contradict, contrast, contravene, controvert, counter, counteract, counterattack, counterbalance, countercheck, counterpunch, cover, cramp, crimp, cripple, cross, curb, dam, debate, defend, defy, delay, demotivate, -deny, detain, -deter, disapprove, discourage, discredit, disfavor, disgrace, disobey, -disown, disprove, dispute, distrust, drag, encumber, entangle, entrap, expose, face, fetter, fight, foul, -frustrate, gainsay, gaslight, guard, hamper, hamstring, handicap, hassle, hinder, impair, impede, impugn, inhibit, intercept, interrupt, invalidate, jam, juxtapose, match, mire, -negate, neutralize, obstruct, offset, oppress, override, overturn, paralyze, parry, pit, plug, police, preempt, -prevent, protest, race, -rebuff, rebut, refute, -reject, repel, repress, -repudiate, repulse, resist, restrain, restrict, retort, return, reverse, safeguard, save, scotch, screen, secure, shelter, shelve, shield, short-circuit, snag, snarl, stall, stay, stop, straightjacket, subvert, support, suppress, tangle, taunt, -thwart, withstand, wrestle* (≠ abet, abide, absorb, accede, accept, accommodate, admit, aid, align, assist, back, befriend, concede, contribute, encourage, endorse, endure, favor, follow, foster, harmonize, help, join, nourish, nurture, obey, oblige, observe, promote, protect, reconcile, represent, reunite, second, support, sustain, tolerate, uncomplicate, unite, uphold)

OPPRESS (/): *abuse, afflict, agitate, ail, anguish, appall, blackjack, bother, break, bridle, browbeat, brutalize, bully, burden, bury, clog, concern, confute, constrain, control, cramp, crucify, crush, curb, dash, daunt, defeat, deluge, demoralize, depress, devastate, discipline, discomfort, discompose, discourage, disfavor, dishearten, dismay, dispirit, disquiet, distress, disturb, drown, encumber, enslave, floor, foist, -frustrate, grind, hamper, harass, harm, harry, hinder, hurt, impede, injure, intimidate, lumber, maltreat, menace, muscle, outrage, overcome, overextend, overload, overpower, overwhelm, persecute, perturb, plague, press, prostrate, quash, quell, railroad, refute, repress, restrain, ride, rock, sadden, saddle, scotch, shatter, sicken, sink, squeeze, stagger, steamroller, stress, subdue, subjugate, suppress, swamp, terrorize, threaten, throw, torment, torture, trammel, trample, trash-talk, traumatize, trouble, tyrannize, unhinge, unman, unnerve, unsettle, upset, vex, victimize, violate, weigh, worry, wound, wrong* (≠ accommodate, animate, appease, assure, boost, brighten, buoy, cheer, comfort, console, delight, elate, elevate, encourage, enliven, entertain, excite, exhilarate, favor, featherbed, gladden, gratify, hearten, humor, inspire, invigorate, lift, lighten, nourish, nurse, nurture, oblige, pacify, pamper, pity, placate, please, prioritize, protect, reassure, reward, satiate, satisfy, soothe, spoil, spoon-feed, stimulate, thrill, treat, uplift)

ORCHESTRATE (+): *adjust, align, arrange, array, assemble, balance, blend, build, calibrate, captain, cast, categorize, chair, chart, choreograph, class, classify, collate, compose, concert, contemporize, control, convene, coordinate, design, devise, direct, establish, facilitate, finalize, fix, form, formalize, frame, govern, grade, group, harmonize, integrate, lead, machinate, maintain, manage, marshal, mastermind, mediate, normalize, order, organize, pace, pigeonhole, place, plan, plot, prep, prepare, present, prioritize, program, quarterback, rank, rate, rationalize, ready, referee, regulate, reintegrate, right, schedule, schematize, scheme, score, script, separate, set, settle, shape, sift, sketch, slate, solve, sort, spearhead, stabilize, stage, stage-manage, steer, strategize, structure, subordinate, summon, support, synchronize, synthesize, systematize, time, tune, tweak, type, unify, unsnarl, untangle, weave* (≠ addle, baffle, bewilder, blow, bobble, bomb, botch, bungle, butcher, capsize, clutter, confound, confuse, damage, destroy, disorder, disorganize, disperse, disrupt, disturb, divide, doom, flub, flunk, forget, fudge, fumble, half-ass, -ignore, jumble, mangle, mar, mishandle, mismanage, miss, muddle, muff, muss, -neglect, overset, perplex, puzzle, ruffle, ruin, scotch, scramble, separate, -shirk, spoil, tousle, upset, wreck)

ORDER (→): *adjure, advise, appoint, ask, assign, authorize, beg, beseech, bid, boss, call, chair, charge, charter, coerce, command, commission, compel, conduct, constrain, control, counsel, decree, demand, dictate, direct, enjoin, entreat, force, greenlight, herd, hire, instruct, lead, license, manage, mandate, muscle, oblige, ordain, oversee, petition, railroad, request, require, requisition, solicit, superintend, supervise, tell, warn* (≠ -cancel, contradict, countermand, -decline, deprogram, follow, -ignore, keep, mind, obey, observe, oppose, -refuse, -reject, -rescind, stall, stop)

ORDER (+): *adapt, adjust, align, alphabetize, arbitrate, arrange, array, assign, assure, balance, barber, calibrate, cast, categorize, center, ceremonialize, chain, chart, choreograph, class, classify, codify, collate, command, compose, concatenate, conduct, control, coordinate, cue, design, devise, display, dispose, distribute, establish, file, fix, form, formalize, frame, furnish, govern, grade, groom, group, guide, gussy, harmonize, hierarchize, instruct, integrate, line, link, locate, maintain, manage, manicure, map, marshal, mediate, neaten, normalize, orchestrate, organize, pace, pigeonhole, place, plan, plot, police, prepare, prioritize, program, queue, range, rank, rate, rationalize, ready, rectify, referee, regiment, regulate, reintegrate, right, ritualize, schedule, schematize, scheme, score, screen, script, separate, sequence, set, settle, shape, sift, slot, sort, space, spruce, stabilize, standardize, straighten, stratify, streamline, string, structure, subordinate, support, synchronize, systematize, tabulate, thread, tidy, time, tune, type, unify, unscramble, unsnarl* (≠ agitate, bother, churn, confuse, derange, diffuse, disarrange, disarray, dishevel, disorder, disturb, jumble, mess, mismatch, mix, muddle, muss, ruffle, rumple, scatter, scramble, tousle, untidy, upset)

ORGANIZE (+): *adapt, adjust, align, alphabetize, arrange, array, assemble, balance, book, calendar, calibrate, cast, catalog, categorize, center, ceremonialize, chart, choreograph, class, classify, codify, collate, combine, compose, configure, construct, contemporize, control, coordinate, create, cue, depersonalize, design, develop, devise, display, dispose, docket, establish, fashion, file, fix, form, formulate, foster, found, frame, grade, groom, group, gussy, harmonize, herd, hierarchize, index, institute, integrate, line, machinate, maintain, manage, map, marshal, mediate, micromanage, mold, normalize, orchestrate, order, originate, overcommit, pace, pigeonhole, place, plan, plot, prepare, prioritize, program, queue, range, rank, rate, rationalize, referee, regiment, regulate, reintegrate, right, ritualize, run, schedule, schematize, scheme, score, screen, separate, sequence, set, settle, shape, shelve, sift, slot, sort, spiff, spruce, stabilize, standardize, straighten, stratify, structure, subordinate, support, synchronize, systematize, tabulate, tailor, tidy, time, type, unify, unscramble, unsnarl* (≠ botch, break, churn, confuse, customize, derange, destroy, diffuse, disarrange, disarray, discombobulate, dishevel, disorder, disorganize, disrupt, disturb, fracture, fragment, improvise, jumble, mess, mismatch, mix, muddle, muss, perplex, pulverize, ruin, rumple, scatter, scramble, shatter, tousle, untidy, upset, wing)

ORGANIZE (+): *administer, aim, arrange, blueprint, book, boss, broker, budget, calculate, chair, chart, choreograph, concert, conduct, contemplate, contrive, coordinate, design, devise, direct, draft, figure, frame, graph, guide, handle, inspect, intend, machinate, manage, manipulate, map, meditate, monitor, number, numerate, orchestrate, outline, oversee, pace, plan, plot, premeditate, prepare, project, ready, renegotiate, run, scheme, script, shape, sketch, stage-manage, strategize, superintend, supervise, target, transact* (≠ -abandon, annul, botch, bugger, bungle, -cancel, confound, demolish, destroy, disorganize, disperse, disrupt, disturb, doom, half-ass, improvise, interrupt, -nix, nuke, oppose, -prevent, -prohibit, scratch, stop, terminate, wing)

ORIENT (+): *accommodate, accustom, acquaint, adapt, adjust, advise, align, apprise, ascertain, attune, brief, calculate, calibrate, compute, contextualize, coordinate, deduce, detect, determine, direct, discern, edify, educate, enlighten, evaluate, expose, familiarize, figure, graph, grok, ground, habituate, inform, initiate, install, instruct, introduce, juxtapose, locate, map, orientate, pinpoint, place, position, present, reacquaint, scan, school, scrutinize, set, site, situate, station, subject, tell, train, turn, warn* (≠ addle, baffle, bewilder, conceal, confound, confuse, daze, deceive, disarrange, discombobulate, disorder, disorient, gaslight, guess, mask, misread, miss, muddle, mystify, nonplus, obscure, perplex, puzzle, stump, throw, trick, wonder)

ORNAMENT (+): *accessorize, adjust, adorn, appliqué, arrange, array, beautify, bedazzle, bedeck, bedizen, bejewel, beribbon, bestow, blazon, boss, braid, brighten, caparison, chase, costume, dandify, deck, decorate, diamond, drape, dress, drizzle, edge, elaborate, embellish, emblaze, emblazon, emboss, embroider, enrich, fancify, fancy, feather, festoon,* *figure, filigree, fillet, flounce, freshen, frill, fringe, garland, garnish, gem, gild, glitter, glitz, grace, hang, impearl, increase, jewel, lace, neaten, order, paint, pearl, pigment, provide, raddle, redecorate, ribbon, sculpt, set, smarten, spangle, spruce, stipple, stud, swag, tidy, tinsel, tool, trim, wreathe* (≠ bare, blemish, blot, decrease, deface, deform, denude, disfigure, disgrace, dismantle, display, disrobe, divest, dull, efface, expose, harshen, mar, mismatch, reveal, scalp, scar, simplify, smudge, spoil, spot, stain, streamline, strip, sully, tarnish, uglify, unclothe, uncomplicate, uncover)

-OSTRACIZE (→): *alienate, -avoid, ban, banish, bar, blackball, blacklist, -boycott, -cold-shoulder, cordon, -cut, debunk, demean, demonize, denounce, -deny, disallow, discomfit, disgrace, dishonor, displace, disqualify, drop, eradicate, excise, -exclude, -excommunicate, exile, exorcise, expatriate, expel, expose, -forbid, humiliate, -ignore, incriminate, isolate, malign, mock, -omit, oppose, oust, outlaw, picket, pillory, -prohibit, proscribe, protest, quarantine, -reject, relegate, -renounce, -repudiate, ridicule, scandalize, seclude, segregate, shame, -shun, -snub, stigmatize, vilify* (≠ accept, admit, allow, befriend, embrace, enlist, enroll, greet, harbor, help, high-five, house, include, invite, nurture, permit, promote, receive, recruit, reunite, shelter, shield, summon, support, wait-list, welcome)

OUST (→): *alienate, ban, banish, bar, blackball, blacklist, boot, bounce, -boycott, cloister, closet, confine, cordon, -deny, deport, depose, deprive, detach, dethrone, disallow, disbar, discard, discharge, disinherit, dislodge, dismiss, displace, dispossess, disqualify, -ditch, divest, dump, eject, eliminate, eradicate, evacuate, evict, excise, -exclude, -excommunicate, exile, exorcise, expatriate, expel, extirpate, extradite, fire, -forbid, -ignore, insulate, isolate, kick, offload, -omit, -ostracize, overthrow, -prohibit, proscribe, -reject, relegate, remove, -renounce, replace, -repudiate, sack, screen, seclude, segregate, separate, sequester, supersede, supplant, topple, toss, transport, unhorse, uninstall, unseat* (≠ access, admit, appoint, assign, attach, constitute, crown, designate, elect, elevate, enter, greet, house, include, indulge, install, invite, meet, nominate, permit, prioritize, promote, receive, retain, reunite, room, shelter, summon, welcome)

OUTCLASS (→): *amaze, astonish, beat, best, better, checkmate, clobber, conquer, crush, dazzle, defeat, dominate, drub, eclipse, enthrone, exceed, finesse, humble, humiliate, lick, master, one-up, outcompete, outdistance, outdo, outgun, outmatch, outpace, outperform, outplay, outrace, outrank, outreach, outrun, outsell, outshine, outstrip, outthink, outweigh, overcome, overshadow, overtake, pass, rout, shame, skunk, stagger, subdue, surpass, thrash, top, transcend, trim, trounce, trump, usurp, wallop, whip* (≠ -abandon, aggrandize, augment, bastardize, belittle, blow, bobble, bomb, boost, botch, brutalize, bungle, cheapen, coach, corrupt, debase, defame, defile, degrade, demean, develop, diminish, disgrace, dishonor, elevate, enhance, exalt, fail, flub, flunk, forfeit, -forsake, fumble, glorify, half-ass, humiliate, improve, lose, lower, miss, mortify, muff, pervert, promote, prostitute, ruin, sabotage, shame, spoil, sully, teach, train, undercut, uplift, wreck)

OUTLAW (/): *abolish, ban, banish, bar, blackball, blacklist, block, condemn, constrain, control, criminalize, curb, curtail, damn, delegitimize, -deny, disallow, disapprove, disqualify, embargo, enjoin, -exclude, -excommunicate, -forbid, inhibit, oppose, oppress, -ostracize, oust, -preclude, -prevent, -prohibit, proscribe, protest, -refuse, -reject, restrain, restrict, stop, suppress, taboo* (≠ accredit, authorize, certify, charter, cultivate, decriminalize, empower, enable, encourage, endorse, foster, greenlight, legalize, legitimize, nourish, nurture, order, permit, promote, qualify, rubber-stamp, sanction, tolerate)

OUTPLAY (→): *beat, best, better, cap, checkmate, clobber, conquer, crush, defeat, dominate, dwarf, eclipse, exceed, minimize, one-up, outbid, outclass, outgun, outlast, outmaneuver, outperform, outreach, outrun, outshine, outsmart, outstrip, outwit, overcome, overshadow, overtake, pass, reduce, strip, surmount, surpass, top, topple, transcend, trounce, trump, usurp, wallop, whip, win* (≠ abet, aggrandize, aid, amplify, assist, augment, back, bolster, boost, cede, cheat, coach, concede, defend, develop, elevate, enhance, expand, extend, fail, forfeit, glorify, guard, heighten, help, hold, increase, lose, maximize, nurture, please, promote, protect, -quit, relinquish, -renounce, sacrifice, straighten, support, surrender, train)

OUTRAGE (/): *abuse, aggrieve, anger, appall, assault, belittle, blame, blast, boo, -cut, defame, defile, degrade, deride, desecrate, disgust, disparage, displease, disrespect, distress, disturb, enrage, force, horrify, humiliate, hurt, incense, infuriate, injure, insult, jar, jeer, libel, madden, malign, maltreat, miff, mistreat, misuse, mock, muckrake, offend, oppress, pain, persecute, rape, ravage, ravish, revile, ridicule, scandalize, shame, shock, slander, slap, -slight, slur, smear, -snub, sorrow, spoil, taunt, torment, torture, trouble, upset, violate, wound, wrong* (≠ acclaim, applaud, approve, assist, benefit, blandish, bless, calm, commend, compliment, delight, eulogize, exalt, flatter, glad-hand, glorify, gratify, hail, heal, honor, inveigle, lull, mellow, mitigate, moderate, mollify, pacify, persuade, placate, please, praise, remedy, satisfy, soften, sweet-talk, thrill, woo)

OUTRAGE (/): *affront, aggravate, anger, annoy, antagonize, burn, cross, embitter, enrage, envenom, exasperate, get, harass, hassle, heckle, hound, incense, inflame, infuriate, irritate, madden, miff, nag, needle, nettle, nitpick, offend, peeve, pique, provoke, rankle, rile, roil, ruffle, troll, vex* (≠ allay, appease, assuage, beguile, bewitch, calm, captivate, charm, comfort, conciliate, console, delight, disarm, ease, enchant, gratify, help, humor, lull, mellow, mitigate, moderate, mollify, pacify, placate, please, quiet, relieve, sedate, settle, soothe, stabilize, steady, tranquilize)

OUTSHINE (→): *assert, beat, best, better, cap, clobber, conquer, control, crush, defeat, display, dominate, drub, dwarf, eclipse, exceed, finagle, lick, maneuver, master, minimize, one-up, outclass, outdistance, outdo,* *outgrow, outmaneuver, outpace, outperform, outrace, outrank, outrun, outsell, outstrip, outthink, outweigh, overcome, overshadow, overtake, pass, rout, shame, skunk, subdue, surmount, surpass, thrash, top, transcend, trounce, trump, upstage, wallop, whip* (≠ aggrandize, amplify, augment, bolster, boost, cede, coach, concede, defend, defer, develop, elevate, -elude, enhance, enlarge, exalt, expand, extend, extol, fail, glorify, heighten, hide, highlight, hype, improve, increase, magnify, maximize, nurture, plug, promote, protect, publicize, reduce, relinquish, showcase, shrink, spotlight, support, surrender, survive, train, uplift)

OUTSMART (←): *assert, baffle, -balk, bar, beat, best, better, bewilder, block, cap, cheat, checkmate, -circumvent, con, confound, confuse, conquer, convince, cozen, deceive, defeat, defraud, double-talk, dupe, entrap, euchre, finagle, finesse, foil, fool, fox, frustrate, gull, hinder, hoodwink, impede, lick, monkey-wrench, obstruct, outclass, outdistance, outdo, outflank, outfox, outguess, outmaneuver, outperform, outshine, outslick, outstrip, outthink, outwit, overcome, overtake, puzzle, rival, scam, second-guess, stump, sucker, surpass, swindle, -thwart, top, trick, trounce* (≠ abet, aid, assist, baby, back, bolster, boost, clarify, coach, confess, defend, edify, educate, encourage, enlighten, explain, expose, give, glorify, guard, help, illuminate, inform, instruct, lose, nurture, protect, reveal, support, teach, train, uncover)

OUTWIT (←): *baffle, bamboozle, bar, beat, bewilder, block, bluff, buffalo, cheat, checkmate, -circumvent, con, confound, confuse, convince, corner, deceive, defeat, defraud, delude, dupe, -elude, euchre, finagle, finesse, foil, fool, fox, goose, gull, hinder, hoax, hocus-pocus, hoodwink, impede, manipulate, mislead, monkey-wrench, obstruct, one-up, outdo, outfox, outguess, outmaneuver, outslick, outsmart, outthink, overreach, scam, stall, stump, stymie, sucker, swindle, -thwart, top, trap, trick, trip, trump* (≠ aid, assist, back, bolster, boost, clarify, coach, coddle, concede, confess, confront, defend, develop, divulge, drill, educate, enhance, explain, expose, give, guard, help, illuminate, inform, instruct, lose, nurture, promote, protect, support, teach, train, tutor)

OVERCHARGE (←): *bilk, cheat, clip, con, deceive, defraud, double-talk, exaggerate, extort, fleece, gazump, gouge, hornswoggle, inflate, magnify, milk, misrepresent, overstate, pad, rob, scam, short, shortchange, skin, soak, steal, stick, sting, surcharge, swindle, trick, victimize* (≠ buy, confess, divulge, expose, honor, import, outbid, outlay, overpay, overspend, remunerate, repay, restore, steal, stiff, stint, undercharge, underpay)

OVERCOME (→): *amaze, annihilate, beat, best, better, bomb, break, bury, cap, climb, clobber, conquer, convince, cream, crush, defeat, dispatch, drub, eclipse, enslave, exceed, finish, flatten, foil, hammer, lick, master, outdistance, outdo, outfight, outlast, outlive, outmaneuver, outplay, outsell, outshine, outslick, outsmart, outstrip, outthink, outwit, overpower, overtake, overthrow, overwhelm, prostrate, reduce, rout, ruin, score, shellac, shock, skin, skunk, slaughter, smoke, steamroller, stop, stun,* *subdue, subjugate, surmount, surpass, survive, sweep, take, thrash, top, topple, transcend, trounce, trump, unseat, upend, upset, vanquish, wallop, weather, whip, whup, wrack, wreck* (≠ -abandon, abdicate, assist, augment, boost, botch, bungle, elevate, endure, fail, flunk, follow, forfeit, half-ass, help, lose, mind, muff, obey, relinquish, -renounce, resign, serve, stomach, strengthen, suffer, surrender, tolerate, weather, withstand)

OVERHAUL (+): *adapt, adjust, automate, calibrate, check, computerize, copy, cure, darn, debug, doctor, examine, fix, gentrify, heal, improve, inspect, investigate, mend, modernize, optimize, patch, perfect, reassemble, rebuild, recondition, reconstitute, reconstruct, recreate, rectify, reexamine, refashion, refurbish, rehabilitate, reimagine, reinvigorate, rejuvenate, remake, remodel, renew, renovate, reorganize, repair, replace, reproduce, reprogram, reshape, reshuffle, restimulate, restore, restructure, retool, retread, revamp, revive, revolutionize, rework, service, sew, tune, tweak, update, upgrade* (≠ afflict, annihilate, blemish, blight, boobytrap, break, crack, damage, deep-six, degrade, demolish, destroy, diminish, disadvantage, doom, eradicate, erase, fracture, fragment, impede, mar, monkey-wrench, -neglect, nuke, obliterate, pulverize, raze, ruin, sabotage, scotch, scupper, scuttle, shatter, shelve, undercut, undermine, vandalize, vaporize, wreck)

OVERHEAR (←): *apprehend, attend, bug, catch, descry, devour, discern, discover, find, hear, heed, mark, mind, monitor, note, observe, perceive, read, receive, spy, surveil, tap, wire, wiretap* (≠ conceal, debate, -deny, disobey, dispute, -disregard, forget, hide, hush, -ignore, keep, lose, mishear, miss, misunderstand, -neglect, -omit, -refuse, -reject, silence) **(¿) ABSTRACTION ALERT. Concrete goals essential!**

OVERINDULGE (+): *accommodate, baby, caress, cherish, coddle, corrupt, cosset, cotton, cradle, cuddle, debauch, deluge, engulf, exceed, favor, featherbed, fondle, glut, gratify, humor, indulge, infantilize, inundate, mollycoddle, nurse, nurture, oblige, overdose, overprotect, pamper, pet, smother, spoil, spoon-feed, treat* (≠ anger, control, -deny, disappoint, discipline, disfavor, hurt, -ignore, munch, -neglect, nibble, oppress, -overlook, punish, -refuse, reserve, restrain, -slight, starve, stint, straight-jacket, torment, upset, withhold)

OVERLOAD (→): *burden, clog, constipate, encumber, hamper, handicap, hinder, impede, inconvenience, lumber, oppress, overburden, overcharge, overextend, overtax, retard, saddle, strain, tax, trammel, weigh* (≠ alleviate, drop, dust, lessen, lift, lighten, pull, relieve, remove, scant, skimp, sprinkle, stint, trim, unburden, unload, withhold)

-OVERLOOK (→): *accept, -avoid, -blank, blind, blindfold, -bypass, confuse, convince, -cut, deceive, -disdain, disguise, -disregard, drop, eliminate, -exclude, fail, forget, -ignore, leave, mask, miss, -neglect, -omit, pass, pooh-pooh, -reject, -repudiate, scant, -scorn, -shirk, skimp, skip, -slight, -snub, -spurn* (≠ acknowledge, appreciate, attend, bemoan, cherish, clock, cultivate, follow, foster, greet, heed, honor, indulge, lament, mark, mind, mourn, note, notice, nurse, nurture, observe, pamper, prize, regard, regret, remark, remember, scan, scope, scrutinize, tend, treasure, value, watch, weigh)

OVERLOOK (+): *absolve, acquit, brook, clear, condone, countenance, disbelieve, -discount, dismiss, disobey, -disregard, exculpate, excuse, exonerate, explain, forgive, gloss, handle, -ignore, justify, pardon, rationalize, remit, spare, vindicate, waive, whitewash* (≠ accuse, admonish, await, blame, condemn, -deny, discipline, fault, finger, follow, frame, heed, incriminate, mark, mind, note, penalize, punish, -refuse, resent, scapegoat, -veto, weigh)

OVERPOWER (/): *affect, amaze, astonish, astound, baffle, bewilder, blindside, boggle, break, bushwhack, confound, confuse, crush, daze, dazzle, deafen, defeat, deluge, demoralize, devastate, distress, disturb, drown, dumbfound, flabbergast, floor, gobsmack, hypnotize, move, nauseate, oppress, overcome, overrule, overwhelm, paralyze, perplex, prostrate, pulverize, razzle-dazzle, repulse, rock, shake, shatter, shock, sink, stagger, stun, stupefy, surprise, swamp, throw, torpefy, touch, unman, unnerve, upset, wow* (≠ amuse, annoy, bore, bother, buffer, bug, calm, clarify, cushion, explain, irk, lull, mitigate, moderate, nag, needle, nettle, niggle, nitpick, numb, pester, poke, tickle, weary)

OVERPOWER (/): *annihilate, beat, break, bulldoze, burke, bury, capture, checkmate, clobber, confound, conquer, cream, crush, decimate, defeat, dominate, domineer, drown, drub, enslave, immobilize, lick, master, murder, oppress, outlast, overcome, overtake, overthrow, overwhelm, pacify, prostrate, quash, quell, railroad, reduce, repress, rout, ruin, shellac, silence, skunk, slaughter, smash, smother, snuff, squash, squelch, squench, steamroller, subdue, subject, subjugate, subordinate, suppress, swamp, thrash, torpedo, total, trash, trounce, vanquish, wallop, waste, whip, wrack, wreck* (≠ cede, discharge, emancipate, enfranchise, forfeit, free, liberate, manumit, release, spring, subvert, survive, unbind, uncage, unchain, unfetter)

OVERRIDE (→): *abrogate, accent, accentuate, amplify, annul, assert, -cancel, contradict, count, counter, countercheck, defeat, displace, -disregard, dominate, emphasize, exceed, invalidate, -negate, -nullify, oppose, outreach, outweigh, overcome, overrule, quash, rectify, replace, reverse, revoke, supersede, surpass, trample, usurp, -veto, void* (≠ aid, allow, approve, assist, back, champion, concede, encourage, endorse, enforce, follow, grant, greenlight, keep, legalize, maintain, observe, permit, ratify, sanction, second, support, validate)

OVERRULE (→): *abrogate, annul, break, -cancel, command, countermand, demand, disallow, erase, invalidate, invert, lift, -negate, -nullify, override, overthrow, overturn, quash, -reject, repeal, -rescind, reverse, revoke, revolutionize, strike, subvert, tip, topple, turn, upset, vacate, vanquish, -veto, void* (≠ allow, approve, authorize, certify, endorse, enforce, establish, follow, guarantee, keep, mind, obey, permit, promise, promote, ratify, sanction, support, validate, verify)

OVERSEE (→): *administer, boss, bridle, captain, chair, command, contain, control, curb, determine, dictate, direct, discipline, dominate, front, govern, guide, handle, harness, head, inhibit, lead, manage, master, micromanage, order, organize, pace, pilot, quarterback, restrain, rule, run, shepherd, show, spearhead, steer, steward, superintend, supervise* (≠ aid, allow, assist, begrudge, botch, bungle, -deny, deregulate, follow, -frustrate, fumble, help, liberate, loose, mismanage, misrule, -neglect, obey, overrule, permit, -refuse, release, serve, subvert, unleash, vent)

OVERSEE (←): *analyze, appraise, assess, audit, categorize, check, classify, comb, con, consider, dissect, estimate, evaluate, examine, explore, gauge, grade, inspect, investigate, judge, notice, observe, parse, peruse, pigeonhole, plumb, police, prioritize, probe, research, review, scan, scope, scrutinize, slot, study, survey, view, watch, weigh* (≠ addle, -avoid, baffle, blind, blindfold, cheat, con, confuse, deceive, defraud, disguise, -disregard, euchre, fake, fudge, half-ass, -ignore, mask, miss, mistake, muddle, mystify, -neglect, outwit, -overlook, perplex, poach, puzzle, scam, skim, steal, sucker, swipe, trick, worry)

OVERSEE (+): *arbitrate, attend, baby, babysit, chaperone, conduct, guard, keep, mind, monitor, mother, nanny, operate, pace, patrol, police, proctor, protect, referee, regulate, safeguard, sentinel, shield, stage-manage, tend, umpire, watch* (≠ -abandon, -avoid, -blank, -desert, -disregard, -ditch, fail, forget, -forsake, -ignore, leave, lose, maroon, misplace, miss, -neglect, -overlook, skip, starve)

OVERSHADOW (→): *ail, assert, beat, becloud, bedim, befog, belittle, best, bite, blear, clobber, cloud, coarsen, command, contaminate, cost, damage, darken, deemphasize, dehumanize, dent, depreciate, dim, diminish, dominate, doom, downgrade, downplay, dwarf, eclipse, extinguish, finagle, govern, harm, haze, hide, impair, marginalize, minimize, -negate, neutralize, -nullify, obfuscate, obscure, offset, one-up, outclass, outdo, outgrow, outgun, outperform, outrank, outsell, outshine, outstrip, outweigh, overcloud, overtake, poison, rule, shade, shroud, skew, soft-pedal, spoil, surpass, taint, top, transcend, trivialize, underplay, understate, veil* (≠ boost, brighten, cede, commend, concede, confront, defer, disclose, discover, divulge, -elude, expose, floodlight, illuminate, light, prioritize, relinquish, reveal, spotlight, survive, uncloak, uncover, unmask, unveil)

OVERTAKE (→): *attain, beat, better, -bypass, capture, catch, clear, engulf, exceed, fulfill, gain, outdistance, outdo, outflank, outgrow, outpace, outperform, outrun, outsell, outshine, outstrip, outwit, overcome, overhaul, overrun, overshoot, overstep, overwhelm, pass, race, reach, rival, strike, subdue, surmount, surpass, target, top, transcend, transgress* (≠ -abandon, cede, chase, -desert, -disregard, dog, exhaust, fail, follow, forfeit, -ignore, leave, lose, miss, -neglect, pursue, quit, release, relinquish, shadow, surrender, tail, withdraw)

OVERTHROW (/): *abolish, beat, best, capture, checkmate, confound, conquer, crush, defeat, demolish, depose, dethrone, dominate, evict, foil,* *humble, master, oust, outdo, outplay, overcome, overpower, overturn, overwhelm, quash, quell, replace, rout, subdue, subvert, supersede, supplant, surmount, topple, trounce, trump, unhorse, unseat, upset, usurp, vanquish, whip, win* (≠ authorize, boost, build, confirm, crown, defend, elect, establish, guard, install, institute, maintain, preserve, protect, reinstate, renew, repair, restore, revive, settle, stimulate, uphold)

OVERTURN (/): *abolish, abrogate, annul, beat, -cancel, cant, capsize, capture, change, check, checkmate, conquer, contradict, contravene, counterbalance, countercheck, countermand, crush, debate, defeat, demolish, -deny, disavow, disclaim, discredit, disprove, dispute, efface, foil, invalidate, invert, monkey-wrench, -negate, -nullify, oppose, overcome, overpower, override, overset, overthrow, parry, quash, quell, rebut, recall, refute, -renounce, repeal, -repudiate, retract, reverse, revoke, revolutionize, rout, spill, subdue, subject, subvert, surmount, topple, transpose, trounce, trump, unhorse, unseat, upend, upset, vanquish, -veto, -void, whip* (≠ accept, allow, back, bless, build, coin, conceive, construct, continue, create, defend, devise, enact, erect, establish, initiate, institute, legislate, maintain, make, ordain, permit, preserve, promote, propose, protect, raise, reinforce, repair, restore, right, shield, spitball, strengthen, support)

OVERWHELM (→): *amaze, astonish, astound, beat, best, bewilder, blindside, blitzkrieg, boggle, bulldoze, bury, clobber, confuse, conquer, consume, cream, crush, daze, dazzle, deafen, defeat, deluge, destroy, devastate, drown, drub, engulf, envelop, floor, flummox, flush, gobsmack, hammer, impress, infest, inundate, lick, massacre, mob, move, oppress, outlast, outplay, outsmart, outwit, overburden, overcome, overpower, overrun, overthrow, quash, quell, railroad, razzle-dazzle, rout, seize, slaughter, smash, stagger, steamroller, stun, subdue, subjugate, submerge, surprise, swamp, thrash, touch, trounce, vanquish, wallop, wow* (≠ assist, baby, build, coddle, comfort, conceal, defend, discover, guard, handle, hide, humor, investigate, invite, placate, protect, seek, strengthen, support, suss, underwhelm, welcome)

OWE (+): *acknowledge, appreciate, bond, borrow, charge, guarantee, hazard, hock, honor, hook, incur, mortgage, obligate, offload, pawn, pledge, promise, recognize, require, risk, swear* (≠ advance, defray, deprive, deserve, lend, loan, overpay, overspend, pay, recoup, refund, reimburse, repay, resolve, settle, square, steal, stiff, stint) **(¿) ABSTRACTION ALERT. Concrete goals essential!**

OWN (←): *acquire, appropriate, boast, claim, colonize, control, corner, dominate, enjoy, get, grab, hog, hold, inhabit, inherit, keep, maintain, monopolize, obtain, occupy, possess, procure, reserve, retain, secure, seize, settle, snag, take, tenant, use, withhold* (≠ borrow, circulate, commend, consign, deliver, discard, -disown, disseminate, drop, entrust, -forsake, gainsay, give, hand, lease, lose, maroon, mislay, misplace, -refuse, -reject, remainder, -renounce, rent, require, sell, toss) **(¿) ABSTRACTION ALERT. Concrete goals essential!**

P

PACE (←): *arrest, baffle, -balk, bench, block, blockade, bottleneck, catch, check, choke, clog, conclude, dam, defer, delay, detain, -discontinue, divert, end, -evade, fence, filibuster, -halt, hamper, hinder, hold, impede, interrupt, obstruct, parry, pause, postpone, rein, repress, shelve, sideline, slow, snag, squash, squelch, stagnate, staunch, stay, stem, still, stonewall, stop, stunt, suppress, suspend, terminate, -thwart* (≠ accelerate, actuate, advance, aid, allow, assist, boost, budge, catalyze, coerce, drive, enable, encourage, facilitate, further, goad, grease, hasten, help, hurry, impel, instigate, muscle, prioritize, propel, push, quicken, railroad, rush, smooth, spur, stir, trigger)

PACE (+): *adjust, administer, arrange, assess, balance, calculate, conduct, control, determine, direct, estimate, evaluate, govern, guard, guide, handle, judge, keep, lead, manage, micromanage, mind, moderate, monitor, operate, order, organize, oversee, pilot, prioritize, protect, rule, run, safeguard, set, settle, square, stage-manage, steer, steward, superintend, supervise, synchronize, tend, tune, watch, weigh* (≠ challenge, contradict, counter, counteract, cramp, debate, defy, -deny, disobey, dispute, flout, follow, gainsay, heed, hold, keep, mind, mismanage, obey, observe, obstruct, oppose, resist, -scorn, serve)

PACIFY (←): *allay, ameliorate, appease, assist, assuage, baby, blandish, butter, cajole, calm, coax, coddle, comfort, compose, conciliate, console, content, cool, cosset, counteract, crush, defuse, delight, demilitarize, diminish, disarm, domesticate, dulcify, dull, ease, facilitate, flannel, gentle, gladden, glad-hand, gratify, grease, housebreak, housetrain, humor, hush, indulge, infantilize, ingratiate, lull, mellow, mitigate, moderate, mollify, mollycoddle, neutralize, offset, pamper, placate, please, propitiate, quell, quiet, quieten, reconcile, relax, relieve, satisfy, settle, silence, smooth, soften, soft-pedal, soothe, stabilize, steady, still, subdue, sugarcoat, sweeten, sweet-talk, tame, temper, thrill, tranquilize, wheedle* (≠ affront, aggravate, agitate, anger, annoy, antagonize, bother, brutalize, bug, chafe, cross, distress, disturb, earbash, enrage, exasperate, fret, gall, harass, harry, heckle, incense, inflame, infuriate, insult, irk, irritate, lynch, madden, militarize, nag, needle, nettle, nitpick, offend, outrage, peeve, persecute, perturb, pester, provoke, rankle, rile, roil, rouse, ruffle, -slight, terrorize, troll, unhinge, unsettle, upset, vex, worry)

PACIFY (/): *annihilate, beat, break, clobber, conquer, crush, defeat, dominate, drub, enslave, lick, overcome, overpower, quash, quell, reduce, repress, rout, silence, skunk, smash, smother, snuff, squash, squelch, squench, subdue, subject, subjugate, subordinate, suppress, tame, thrash, trounce, vanquish, wallop, whip* (≠ discharge, emancipate, enfranchise, free, liberate, manumit, release, spring, subvert, survive, unbind, uncage, unchain, unfetter, weather)

PACK (→): *bloat, bulk, charge, compact, compress, cram, crate, crowd, crush, fill, heap, honeycomb, jam, jam-pack, load, mat, mob, overcharge, overcrowd, overfill, overflow, overstuff, penetrate, press, ram, refill, refresh, reload, repack, replenish, sardine, saturate, shove, squash, squeeze, stow, stuff, wedge* (≠ bleed, clean, clear, consume, deplete, depredate, drain, draw, dump, eliminate, empty, evacuate, exhaust, flush, leech, lighten, purge, scour, sweep, unload, unpack, vacate, void)

PACK (→): *block, bung, bury, caulk, chink, choke, clog, close, clot, congest, constipate, dam, drench, fill, flood, glut, inundate, jam, obstruct, occlude, overfill, plug, seal, stem, stop, stuff, surfeit, swamp* (≠ clear, core, drain, empty, excavate, extract, hollow, leach, loosen, remove, scoop, shovel, vacate, void)

PACK (+): *bale, bind, box, bundle, cluster, cover, crate, fasten, gather, package, parcel, pickle, prep, stash, store, stow, tie, truss, wrap* (≠ bare, crack, diffuse, distribute, expose, open, reveal, scatter, share, shed, spread, strew, uncover, unwrap)

PAD (+): *accent, accentuate, accrue, amplify, assert, augment, belabor, caricature, color, elaborate, embellish, embroider, emphasize, enhance, enlarge, exaggerate, expand, fudge, hedge, heighten, heroicize, heroize, honor, hyperbolize, idealize, idolize, increase, inflate, intensify, lengthen, magnify, maximize, overdo, overdramatize, overdraw, overemphasize, overplay, oversell, overstate, poeticize, romanticize, satirize, sentimentalize, spin, stress, stretch* (≠ belittle, deemphasize, deprecate, diminish, -discount, dismiss, disparage, downplay, lessen, marginalize, minimize, shrink, soft-pedal, trivialize, underemphasize, underestimate, underplay, understate)

PAD (+): *allay, alleviate, assuage, baffle, blanket, blunt, buffer, cushion, dampen, deaden, dull, ease, fill, gentle, lighten, line, mitigate, moderate, modulate, pack, protect, relieve, soften, stuff, temper, upholster, wad, weaken, wrap* (≠ compromise, endanger, exacerbate, expose, heighten, imperil, intensify, jeopardize, risk, sharpen, strip, threaten)

PAINT (→): *characterize, conjure, define, delineate, demonstrate, depict, describe, display, draft, draw, elaborate, evoke, exhibit, hint, illustrate, image, label, limn, narrate, outline, picture, portray, profile, qualify, recite, recount, rehearse, relate, render, report, represent, show, showcase, silhouette, sketch, suggest, summarize, tell, trace* (≠ alter, color, confuse, contort, distort, embellish, embroider, falsify, garble, miscommunicate, mislabel, misrepresent, misstate, pervert, twist, warp) **(¿) ABSTRACTION ALERT. Concrete goals essential!**

PAINT (+): *apply, brighten, coat, color, cover, dapple, darken, daub, decorate, dye, fleck, glaze, lacquer, lard, lighten, marble, mottle, pigment, plaster, redecorate, slather, smear, spackle, speck, speckle, spray, stain,* *streak, striate, stripe, syrup, tincture, tinge, tint, variegate, varnish, wash, whitewash* (≠ blanch, bleach, clean, cleanse, decolorize, rinse, scour, scrub, smear, strip, wash, whiten, wipe)

PAMPER (+): *accommodate, amuse, appease, assuage, baby, blandish, butter, cajole, calm, caress, charm, cherish, coddle, comfort, conciliate, console, content, cosset, cotton, court, cradle, cuddle, delight, divert, dulcify, ease, endow, entertain, favor, featherbed, flannel, fondle, foster, furnish, gladden, glad-hand, gratify, guard, help, humor, indulge, infantilize, ingratiate, lull, mellow, mitigate, moderate, mollify, mollycoddle, mother, nourish, nurse, nurture, oblige, offer, overindulge, overprotect, pacify, pet, pity, placate, please, pleasure, propitiate, protect, provide, regale, relax, relieve, reward, romance, satiate, satisfy, schmooze, shelter, smooth, smother, soft-pedal, soothe, spoil, spoon-feed, subdue, sugarcoat, supply, sweeten, sweet-talk, tame, tickle, tolerate, treat, woo* (≠ abuse, affront, aggravate, anger, anguish, annoy, antagonize, bother, bridle, brutalize, bug, -bypass, chafe, check, constrain, control, cross, curb, -deny, deprive, discipline, disfavor, distress, disturb, enrage, exasperate, forget, fret, gall, gaslight, harass, harm, hassle, hector, incense, infuriate, injure, irk, lynch, malnourish, maltreat, manhandle, menace, mistreat, nag, needle, -neglect, oppress, outrage, persecute, pester, rankle, restrain, rile, sadden, sicken, skimp, starve, stint, terrorize, threaten, torment, torture, traumatize, troll, unsettle, upset, vex, victimize, violate, worry, wound, wrong)

PANIC (/): *affright, agitate, alarm, amaze, appall, astound, awe, brutalize, chill, clutch, confound, daunt, demoralize, discomfort, discompose, disconcert, discourage, dishearten, dismay, dispirit, disquiet, distract, distress, disturb, emasculate, floor, fluster, frighten, horrify, intimidate, jolt, perturb, psych, rattle, scare, scarify, shake, shock, spook, startle, terrify, terrorize, unman, unnerve, unsettle, unstring, upset, worry* (≠ amuse, anchor, appease, assuage, bolster, buoy, calm, comfort, console, content, encourage, humor, hush, inspire, lull, mellow, mitigate, moderate, mollify, placate, reassure, relax, sedate, soothe, stabilize, steady, steel, tranquilize)

PARALYZE (/): *anesthetize, arrest, attenuate, cripple, daze, deactivate, deaden, debilitate, devitalize, disable, disqualify, drug, dull, dumbfound, enervate, enfeeble, fix, freeze, -halt, hamstring, hobble, hypnotize, immobilize, inactivate, incapacitate, kneecap, lame, maim, mesmerize, mutilate, numb, palsy, petrify, pinion, prostrate, sap, shock, stagnate, stale, stall, stiffen, stop, stun, stupefy, suspend, terrify, tire, torpefy, transfix, undercut, undermine, unnerve, weaken* (≠ activate, animate, empower, energize, fortify, galvanize, goad, invigorate, melt, refresh, regenerate, reinvigorate, rejuvenate, restore, revitalize, revive, stimulate, strengthen, thaw, wake, weaponize)

PARDON (+): *absolve, accept, acquit, allow, clear, commute, condone, defray, discharge, -discount, dismiss, dispel, -disregard, except, exculpate, excuse, exempt, exonerate, explain, forget, forgive, free, gloss,*

-ignore, justify, legalize, liberate, mitigate, -omit, -overlook, palliate, permit, rationalize, redeem, release, relieve, remit, reprieve, rescue, shrive, spare, spring, tolerate, unburden, vindicate, waive, whitewash (≠ abhor, abominate, accuse, allege, attack, avenge, begrudge, blame, castigate, charge, chasten, chastise, condemn, convict, -despise, -detest, discipline, execrate, fault, fine, finger, frame, -hate, heed, impeach, implicate, impugn, incriminate, indict, -loathe, mind, note, penalize, prosecute, punish, rebuke, redress, resent, revenge, scapegoat, -scorn, sentence, shame)

PARENT (+): *baby, bear, bequeath, bestow, bottle-feed, carry, cherish, coddle, cradle, cultivate, discipline, educate, father, foster, generate, gestate, guard, harbor, hatch, host, indulge, infantilize, mother, nanny, nourish, nurse, nurture, overprotect, pamper, produce, protect, raise, rear, respect, reward, school, scold, shelter, sire, spoil, teach, tend, train, welcome* (≠ -abandon, abuse, betray, -deny, -desert, disavow, discard, disclaim, -disown, exterminate, -forsake, murder, -neglect, orphan, -reject, -repudiate, uproot, wrong)

PARRY (→): *anticipate, -avert, -avoid, bend, block, -bypass, challenge, -circumvent, counter, counterpunch, deflect, divert, -dodge, -duck, -elude, -evade, fence, field, foil, forestall, miss, monkey-wrench, -preclude, -prevent, protest, -rebuff, rebuke, redirect, reorient, repel, repulse, resist, retort, reverse, shift, -shirk, -shun, shunt, -sidestep, sidetrack, stop, sway, swivel, -thwart, transfer, turn, twist* (≠ accost, allow, attack, attract, brave, compel, confront, demand, face, fight, invite, lance, meet, obligate, oppose, penetrate, render, request, stab, submit, tackle, take, taunt, thrust, welcome, wrestle)

PART (/): *bisect, break, chunk, cleave, detach, disassemble, disconnect, disengage, disentangle, disintegrate, dismantle, dissect, dissolve, divide, divorce, estrange, fracture, halve, insulate, isolate, orphan, oust, partition, pull, quarter, rend, resolve, rip, rive, rupture, seclude, segment, segregate, separate, sequester, sever, split, subdivide, sunder, tear, uncouple, unlink, unravel, untie, unyoke* (≠ accumulate, assemble, associate, attach, bind, blend, cement, cinch, close, combine, connect, couple, fasten, fuse, hybridize, integrate, join, knit, link, mingle, mix, mortar, network, reintegrate, reunite, stick, stockpile, synthesize, unify, unite, weld)

PASS (→): *beat, best, better, checkmate, clobber, conquer, crush, defeat, drub, eclipse, exceed, lap, leave, lick, lose, master, one-up, outclass, outdistance, outdo, outgrow, outlast, outpace, outperform, outrank, outreach, outrun, outshine, outstrip, outweigh, overcome, overshadow, overtake, rout, shame, skunk, subdue, surmount, surpass, thrash, top, topple, transcend, trim, trounce, trump, wallop, whip* (≠ -abandon, aggrandize, amplify, augment, back, bolster, boost, cede, coach, concede, defend, defer, develop, elevate, enhance, fail, forfeit, -forsake, glorify, lose, magnify, maximize, miss, nurture, promote, protect, relinquish, -renounce, sacrifice, support, survive, train)

PASS (→): *advance, assign, bear, bequeath, bestow, buck, carry, cede, commend, commit, confer, confide, consign, contribute, delegate, deliver, deposit, dispense, disperse, distribute, divide, dole, dollop, entrust, finger, furnish, give, grant, hand, handle, leave, lend, loan, offload, paw, reach, recommend, relay, release, relinquish, render, submit, supply, surrender, transfer, transmit, trust, vest, will, yield* (≠ accept, coopt, demand, -deny, deprive, detain, hold, keep, own, poach, possess, receive, reserve, retain, steal, stint, take, withhold)

PASS (+): *accept, administer, adopt, allow, approve, authorize, confirm, constitute, decree, dictate, effect, enact, execute, legalize, legislate, legitimate, legitimize, make, ordain, permit, proclaim, ratify, sanction, validate, warrant* (≠ abolish, abrogate, annul, -cancel, delegitimize, invalidate, kill, -nullify, overturn, repeal, -rescind, reverse, revoke, void)

PASTE (+): *adhere, affix, attach, cement, connect, fasten, fix, glue, gum, hang, join, link, mend, pin, plaster, reaffix, reattach, refasten, repair, stick, tack, unite* (≠ detach, divide, loose, loosen, part, rip, separate, sever, split, sunder, tear, unbind, undo, unfasten)

PATCH (+): *aid, ameliorate, bandage, better, bind, condition, cover, cure, doctor, dress, enhance, enrich, fix, freshen, furbish, heal, help, improve, maintain, mend, overhaul, prepare, ready, rebuild, recondition, reconstruct, refresh, refurbish, regenerate, reinforce, rejuvenate, renew, renovate, repair, restimulate, restore, revamp, revitalize, revive, service, sew, splint, stitch, wrap* (≠ blemish, break, cripple, damage, deface, disable, disfigure, efface, flaw, harm, harshen, hurt, impair, injure, maim, mangle, mar, monkey-wrench, mutilate, rip, ruin, savage, spoil, tear, unsew, vandalize, wreck)

PATROL (→): *-avert, check, conserve, cover, cruise, defend, guard, inspect, keep, monitor, oppose, oversee, police, pound, preserve, -prevent, protect, resist, safeguard, screen, secure, sentinel, shield, tour, withstand* (≠ -abandon, assail, assault, attack, beset, besiege, bombard, boobytrap, burgle, forfeit, -forsake, -ignore, kill, murder, -neglect, overrun, pickpocket, poach, rob, sabotage, shelve, slay, steal, storm, swipe, vandalize)

PATRONIZE (+): *abet, adopt, advance, advocate, aid, assist, back, bankroll, befriend, bolster, boost, buttress, champion, embrace, encourage, endorse, espouse, favor, finance, forward, foster, fund, furnish, further, help, maintain, plug, preach, prioritize, promote, protect, push, reinforce, second, sponsor, supply, support, underwrite* (≠ antagonize, attack, baffle, cheat, check, checkmate, counter, defund, -desert, disappoint, discredit, disfavor, disinherit, -disown, fail, fight, foil, -frustrate, monkey-wrench, muzzle, oppose, sabotage, scotch, scupper, scuttle, shelve, stiff, stint, stymie, subvert, -thwart, undercut, undermine, withhold)

PATRONIZE (/): *affront, belittle, brandish, -cold-shoulder, -cut, -despise, -disdain, disparage, -disregard, disrespect, flaunt, flourish, high-hat, humble, humiliate, -ignore, indulge, insult, miff, mortify, offend, parade,*

-rebuff, rebuke, ridicule, -scorn, shame, -shun, -slight, -snub, -spurn, squash, wave (≠ assist, commend, compliment, elevate, encourage, glorify, gratify, honor, idolize, praise, respect, serve, support, treasure, venerate)

PAW (→): *caress, clap, claw, clutch, dig, feel, finger, fondle, grab, grate, grope, handle, manhandle, maul, mishandle, molest, palpate, pat, poke, rake, rasp, riffle, rub, scratch, search, slap, smite, stroke, strum, touch* (≠ -avoid, defend, -dodge, drop, -elude, -escape, -evade, guard, hit, -ignore, leave, miss, please, protect, stab, strike)

PAWN (→): *bond, borrow, commercialize, commodify, deposit, guarantee, hazard, hock, hook, monetize, mortgage, offload, pledge, risk, sell, stash, stow* (≠ advance, buy, lend, loan, recover, redeem, refund, reimburse, repay, steal, stiff, stint, win)

PAY (→): *adjust, bequeath, bestow, blow, clear, compensate, confer, defray, disburse, discharge, dissipate, drop, expend, extend, foot, fritter, give, grant, handle, honor, indemnify, invest, lavish, liquidate, offer, outlay, pony, prepay, present, proffer, purchase, rain, recompense, recoup, refund, reimburse, remit, remunerate, render, repay, restitute, reward, satisfy, settle, slather, spare, spend, squander, stake, stand, subsidize, underwrite, volunteer, waste* (≠ acquire, borrow, cache, cheat, defraud, disinherit, -disown, dupe, earn, filch, fool, gain, garner, hoard, make, palm, pillage, plunder, procure, realize, -repudiate, rifle, rob, save, secure, steal, stiff, stint, swindle, swipe, win)

PEDDLE (→): *advertise, auction, ballyhoo, barter, boost, bootleg, bundle, carry, cold-call, commercialize, commodify, deal, disburse, dispense, display, distribute, dump, endorse, exchange, export, flog, franchise, handle, hard-sell, hawk, hustle, hype, keep, launch, leverage, market, merchandize, monetize, offer, offload, outsell, package, pimp, plug, presell, promote, promulgate, provide, publicize, push, reissue, remainder, retail, sell, shill, stock, supply, swap, tout, trade, traffic, vend, wholesale* (≠ acquire, archive, bank, borrow, buy, collect, conceal, discard, hide, hoard, hold, import, keep, lend, loan, maintain, obtain, possess, preserve, procure, purchase, retain, secure, source, store, withhold)

PEEL (/): *bare, bark, denude, disrobe, divulge, excoriate, expose, find, flake, flay, hull, husk, pare, remove, scale, scalp, shell, shuck, skin, strip, unbuckle, unbutton, uncover, undress, unveil* (≠ apparel, clothe, conceal, costume, cover, drape, dress, envelop, garb, hide, jacket, pall, swathe, tog, wrap)

PEG (→): *bowl, buck, cant, cast, catapult, chuck, dart, dash, eject, fire, fling, flip, gun, heave, hook, hurl, hurtle, impel, launch, lob, loft, pass, pelt, pitch, precipitate, project, propel, rifle, roll, shoot, skitter, sling, throw, thrust, toss, wing* (≠ accept, acquire, block, bring, carry, catch, clutch, collect, convey, draw, gain, gather, get, give, grab, grasp, grip, hand, hold, keep, obtain, receive, retain, seize, snatch, take)

PEG (→): *alphabetize, array, ascertain, catalog, categorize, clump, cluster, control, cull, deduce, detect, determine, diagnose, discern, dispose, file, fix, freeze, hierarchize, identify, index, limit, list, order, organize, pigeonhole, pinpoint, prioritize, recategorize, reclassify, recognize, refer, scan, screen, scrutinize, set, shelve, sieve, sift, slot, stabilize, stereotype, systematize, typecast, understand, winnow* (≠ baffle, believe, confound, confuse, deceive, disarrange, disguise, -disregard, hide, -ignore, jumble, lump, mask, misclassify, misread, missort, mistype, misunderstand, mix, muddle, mystify, obscure, perplex, puzzle, scatter, scramble, wonder)

PELT (→): *bowl, cast, catapult, chuck, dart, dash, eject, fire, fling, flip, gun, heave, hook, hurl, hurtle, impel, launch, lob, loft, pass, peg, pitch, precipitate, project, propel, rifle, roll, shoot, sling, throw, thrust, toss, wing* (≠ accept, block, bring, carry, catch, clutch, collect, contain, convey, draw, gain, gather, give, grab, grasp, grip, hand, hold, keep, obtain, receive, restrain, retain, save, seize, snatch, take, welcome)

PELT (/): *assail, assault, attack, bash, baste, bat, batter, beat, belabor, belt, beset, birch, bludgeon, bombard, box, buffet, bust, charge, clobber, clout, club, crack, cudgel, cuff, drub, flog, hammer, hide, hit, knock, lace, lambaste, lash, lather, lick, maul, mortar, paddle, paste, pepper, pound, pour, pummel, punch, rain, rush, shower, slam, slap, slate, sling, slog, smack, smash, sock, spank, speed, stone, storm, strike, swat, swipe, switch, tan, tear, thrash, thresh, thump, thwack, wallop, whack, whale, wham, whip, whomp, whup* (≠ armor, -avoid, brush, caress, counterpunch, cover, defend, deflect, expose, fondle, guard, -ignore, lose, miss, nurture, parry, pat, pet, protect, repel, safeguard, screen, secure, shelter, shield, slow, stroke, support, tap, tickle)

PEN (+): *chronicle, communicate, compose, concoct, copy, create, draft, draw, email, impart, inscribe, jot, journalize, mark, message, notate, note, print, record, register, schedule, scrawl, scribble, transcribe, write* (≠ anonymize, censor, cut, delete, destroy, efface, erase, expunge, gag, hush, obliterate, purge, quash, read, redact, silence)

PEN (/): *armor, bound, box, cage, circumscribe, closet, confine, contain, coop, corral, delimit, encapsulate, encase, encircle, enclose, encompass, enfold, envelop, fence, frame, hedge, hem, herd, house, immure, include, leash, limit, mew, restrict, ring, shut, surround, wall, wrangle, wrap* (≠ bail, deliver, discharge, emancipate, free, loose, manumit, ransom, release, rescue, spring, uncage, unchain, unfetter, unleash, unshackle)

PENALIZE (/): *assess, blackball, blister, -boycott, castigate, charge, chasten, chastise, condemn, convict, correct, criticize, crucify, damn, denounce, disadvantage, discipline, dock, exile, expel, fine, ground, handicap, impose, imprison, incarcerate, intern, jail, judge, keelhaul, levy, mulct, punish, rebuke, reprimand, reprove, scold, sentence, torture, wreak* (≠ absolve, acquit, alibi, coddle, commute, compensate, condone, defend, excuse, exonerate, forfeit, forgive, honor, incriminate, indemnify, indulge, lionize, outlay, overindulge, -overlook, overpay, pamper, pardon, pay, praise, protect, ransom, release, remunerate, reward, shield, spare, vindicate)

PENETRATE (→): *access, bayonet, bore, broach, charge, core, crack, crash, crucify, cut, disembowel, drill, drive, enter, fill, force, gaff, gash, gate-crash, gimlet, gore, gut, harpoon, honeycomb, hurt, imbue, impale, impregnate, infest, infiltrate, injure, inseminate, insert, insinuate, introduce, invade, jab, kebab, knife, lance, occupy, perforate, permeate, pervade, pick, pierce, pike, pink, poke, poniard, pop, prick, probe, prong, punch, puncture, ram, ravage, ream, riddle, rupture, saturate, screw, shank, shiv, sink, skewer, slit, spear, spike, spindle, spit, split, stab, stake, stick, storm, suffuse, thrust, transfix, wound* (≠ armor, bandage, bar, barricade, block, buffer, cloak, close, clothe, cloud, cordon, cover, defend, deflect, disguise, draw, eject, expel, extract, fill, -forbid, guard, heal, help, invite, leach, leave, leech, mend, miss, open, oust, parry, patch, plaster, pluck, plug, prize, protect, pull, remove, restore, seal, secure, sheathe, shield, tug, veil, welcome, withdraw, wrench, yank)

PERFECT (+): *advance, ameliorate, amend, augment, better, boost, correct, cultivate, debug, develop, edit, elaborate, emend, enhance, enrich, fine, fine-tune, flavor, fortify, glitz, heighten, help, hone, idealize, improve, intensify, machine, magnify, marinate, maximize, mitigate, optimize, overhaul, polish, prioritize, punctuate, realign, rectify, redraft, refine, reform, refurbish, rehab, rehabilitate, reimagine, reinforce, remedy, repair, rephrase, restore, rethink, retool, retouch, revamp, revise, revolutionize, rework, right, season, shine, slick, smooth, sophisticate, spice, strengthen, upgrade, weed* (≠ -abandon, afflict, aggravate, barbarize, blemish, blight, callous, coarsen, compromise, damage, deface, degrade, -desert, destroy, diminish, -discontinue, disfigure, doom, drop, efface, eradicate, exacerbate, flaw, -forsake, harm, harshen, hurt, impair, injure, lessen, lower, mar, reduce, ruin, spoil, taint, tarnish, vitiate, vulgarize, worsen, wreck)

PERFECT (+): *accomplish, achieve, actualize, ameliorate, amend, better, cap, claim, complete, consummate, crest, crown, discharge, effect, enhance, enrich, execute, finalize, finish, fulfill, improve, mature, optimize, overhaul, perform, polish, realize, refine, round* (≠ -abandon, begin, -cancel, commence, -desert, -discontinue, drop, -forsake, initiate, instigate, launch, level, -nullify, originate, -quit, ruin, start)

PERFORATE (→): *bore, broach, burst, core, cut, drill, drive, enter, gaff, gash, gimlet, gore, gouge, groove, harpoon, hollow, honeycomb, impale, insert, invade, jab, kebab, knife, lance, notch, peck, penetrate, permeate, pierce, pike, pin, pink, pit, poke, poniard, prick, probe, punch, puncture, ream, rend, riddle, rupture, shank, shiv, shoot, skewer, slash, slit, spear, spike, spindle, spit, split, stab, stake, stick, tap, tear, thrust, transfix* (≠ armor, bandage, block, buffer, close, cover, defend, deflect, draw, eject, extract, fill, guard, heal, mend, parry, patch, plaster, plug, protect, pull, remove, repair, seal, secure, shield, withdraw)

PERFUME (→): *anoint, bathe, brush, cloud, cologne, conceal, dab, disguise, douse, drench, embellish, emit, enhance, exude, hide, intensify, mist, oil, release, scent, smear, splash, spray* (≠ breathe, detect, discern, discover, find, identify, inhale, nose, notice, perceive, recognize, retrace, sense, smell, sniff, trace, track, whiff)

PERMEATE (→): *brine, charge, diffuse, drench, fill, flood, glut, imbue, impregnate, infect, infiltrate, infuse, ingrain, instill, interpenetrate, inundate, invade, marinate, penetrate, percolate, pervade, pierce, presoak, riddle, saturate, soak, spread, stalk, steep, suffuse, surfeit, transfuse* (≠ clear, deprive, divide, drain, eliminate, empty, extract, filter, isolate, leach, leech, purge, quarantine, remove, segregate, separate, sift, siphon, tap, withdraw)

PERMIT (+): *accept, admit, allow, approve, authorize, bear, bless, commission, concede, condone, countersign, deputize, designate, empower, enable, endorse, endure, enfranchise, entitle, excuse, facilitate, give, grant, greenlight, indulge, legalize, let, license, lubricate, notarize, ordain, pardon, qualify, rubber-stamp, sanction, spare, stand, stomach, suffer, take, task, tolerate, unlock, validate, warrant, weather, withstand* (≠ -avoid, ban, bar, battle, block, check, coerce, condemn, counteract, criminalize, curb, denounce, -deny, -deter, -escape, fight, -flee, flout, force, -halt, hinder, -ignore, impede, muscle, -nix, obstruct, oppose, outlaw, protest, railroad, -refuse, -reject, repel, resist, restrain, stall, stem, straight-jacket, suppress, withhold)

PERPLEX (/): *abash, addle, agitate, amaze, baffle, bamboozle, beat, befog, befuddle, beguile, bemuse, bewilder, blindside, block, boggle, bother, buffalo, chagrin, cloud, confound, confuse, cozen, daze, deceive, delude, discombobulate, discomfit, discomfort, discompose, disconcert, dismay, disorient, disquiet, distress, disturb, double-talk, dumbfound, dupe, embarrass, faze, floor, flummox, fluster, foil, fool, fox, frustrate, gaslight, gull, harass, hoax, hobble, hocus-pocus, hoodwink, humbug, jumble, manipulate, misguide, mislead, mismatch, monkey-wrench, mortify, muddle, muddy, mystify, nonplus, obscure, outwit, perturb, puzzle, rattle, snow, stump, stun, stupefy, surprise, tangle, throw, trick, trouble, unhinge, unsettle, upset, vex* (≠ abbreviate, assure, clarify, decipher, deduce, detect, disentangle, ease, edify, educate, enlighten, explain, facilitate, floodlight, illuminate, inform, instruct, oversimplify, reassure, satisfy, school, shorten, simplify, solve, straighten, streamline, teach, train, tutor, uncomplicate, unravel, untangle)

PERSECUTE (/): *affront, aggravate, agitate, anger, annoy, antagonize, assail, badger, bait, belittle, berate, besmirch, blackguard, blacklist, blame, blast, blemish, bother, bug, bullyrag, burn, censure, chafe, chastise, decry, defame, demean, demonize, deprecate, deride, devil, diminish, discomfort, discompose, disgrace, dishonor, disparage, disquiet, distress, dog, earbash, eat, enrage, exasperate, exercise, freak, fret, frost, gall, get, hagride, harangue, harass, harry, hassle, haunt, heckle, hector, hound, humble, hunt, impugn, incense, inflame, infuriate,* *insult, irk, irritate, knock, madden, malign, miff, molest, nag, needle, nettle, nitpick, offend, outrage, peeve, perturb, pester, pillory, pique, plague, provoke, pursue, rankle, rasp, rebuke, revile, ridicule, rile, roil, rouse, ruffle, shame, slander, -slight, slur, -snub, soil, spite, taunt, tease, troll, undo, unhinge, unsettle, upset, vex, vilify, worry, zing* (≠ admire, appease, applaud, assure, back, blandish, cheer, comfort, commend, conciliate, console, content, court, defend, delight, expiate, flatter, gladden, gratify, honor, indulge, infantilize, mollify, oblige, pacify, pamper, placate, please, promote, propitiate, quiet, reassure, revere, reward, romance, salute, satisfy, solace, soothe, spoil, thrill, woo)

PERSECUTE (/): *abuse, afflict, aggravate, aggrieve, agitate, agonize, ambush, anathematize, anguish, annoy, assail, attack, badger, beat, bedevil, beset, besiege, bestialize, blackball, blackjack, blackmail, bombard, bother, -boycott, browbeat, brutalize, bug, bully, chafe, constrain, crucify, crush, curse, damage, debase, degrade, dehumanize, demote, deprave, discipline, discomfort, discompose, disquiet, distress, disturb, dog, dragoon, exasperate, excruciate, exile, expel, exploit, fluster, gall, gaslight, get, grieve, hagride, harass, harm, harrow, harry, hassle, heckle, hound, humiliate, hurt, ill-treat, impair, injure, intimidate, irk, irritate, lynch, malnourish, maltreat, manhandle, mar, martyr, menace, mistreat, misuse, molest, mortify, nag, needle, -neglect, nettle, nitpick, oppress, outrage, overpower, overwhelm, pain, peeve, perturb, pester, picket, pique, plague, prick, -prohibit, protest, pursue, restrain, ride, rile, ruin, sadden, sandbag, sicken, smite, sorrow, spoil, stab, sting, strain, stress, strike, sully, threaten, torment, torture, trample, trash-talk, traumatize, trouble, try, tyrannize, upset, use, vex, victimize, violate, worry, wound, wrack, wring, wrong* (≠ abet, accommodate, advantage, aid, appease, assist, avenge, baby, benefit, bless, cherish, coddle, comfort, console, content, cosset, cotton, cradle, defend, delight, deliver, dignify, elevate, entertain, favor, featherbed, foster, free, gratify, heal, help, humor, infantilize, mollycoddle, nourish, nurse, nurture, oblige, pacify, pamper, pity, placate, please, promote, protect, quiet, rectify, regret, release, relieve, remedy, reprieve, rescue, reward, satiate, satisfy, save, soothe, spoon-feed, succor, support, tickle, treasure, treat)

PERSUADE (+): *advise, allure, argue, assure, bed, beguile, blandish, blarney, brainwash, bring, bullshit, buttonhole, cajole, coax, coerce, convert, convince, counsel, court, encourage, enlist, entice, entreat, exhort, fast-talk, gain, get, goad, impel, impress, incite, incline, induce, influence, inveigle, lead, lobby, lubricate, lure, midwife, mollify, move, palaver, press, prod, prompt, retrain, romance, rouse, satisfy, schmooze, seduce, sell, snooker, snow, soft-sell, stroke, sway, tantalize, tease, tempt, touch, urge, wheedle, win, woo* (≠ -avoid, bulldoze, delay, demotivate, -deter, discourage, disenchant, dissuade, -forbid, force, -halt, hamper, hinder, -ignore, muscle, -neglect, postpone, -prevent, -prohibit, protest, railroad, repel, repress, restrain, shelve, short-circuit, stall, steamroller, stop, suppress, -thwart, unsell, -veto)

PERVERT (/): *abase, abuse, adulterate, bastardize, befoul, bend, bestialize, blemish, brainwash, bribe, cheapen, contaminate, contort, corrupt, damage, debase, debauch, deface, defile, deform, degrade, dehumanize, demean, dement, demoralize, deprave, derange, desecrate, destroy, deteriorate, dilute, dirty, disgrace, dishonor, distort, doctor, doom, falsify, flaw, fudge, garble, gaslight, harm, humble, humiliate, hurt, impair, lessen, mar, misapply, misconstrue, misdirect, misinterpret, mislead, misrepresent, mistreat, misuse, nobble, poison, pollute, profane, prostitute, retrain, ruin, shame, spoil, stain, suborn, subvert, taint, tarnish, thin, turn, twist, vitiate, warp, weaken, whore, wreck, wrong* (≠ assist, better, clarify, clean, cleanse, decontaminate, dignify, elevate, enhance, ennoble, enrich, exalt, help, heroicize, honor, idealize, idolize, improve, moralize, optimize, overhaul, perfect, purify, rarefy, refine, respect, restore, sanctify, straighten, uplift)

PERVERT (/): *belie, bend, bowdlerize, camouflage, censor, color, complicate, confound, confuse, cook, disguise, distort, embellish, embroider, falsify, fudge, garble, gloss, half-ass, heighten, mask, miscommunicate, misdescribe, mishear, misinterpret, misread, misrepresent, misstate, mistake, mistranslate, mix, mystify, obfuscate, obscure, rephrase, romanticize, sentimentalize, slant, spin, twist, veil, warp, whitewash* (≠ betray, clarify, clear, communicate, decipher, declare, decode, decrypt, delineate, demonstrate, depict, evince, explain, expose, illuminate, illustrate, interpret, limn, portray, render, reveal, untangle)

PESTER (→): *afflict, aggravate, agitate, anger, annoy, antagonize, badger, bait, bedevil, beleaguer, beset, besiege, bother, browbeat, bug, bully, chafe, chaff, chivy, confound, craze, devil, discommode, distress, disturb, dog, dun, earbash, enrage, exasperate, fret, frustrate, gall, gate-crash, gnaw, harangue, harass, harry, hassle, heckle, hector, henpeck, hound, importune, incense, incommode, inconvenience, inflame, infuriate, invade, irk, irritate, jeer, madden, mock, molest, nag, needle, nettle, niggle, nitpick, nudge, outrage, panhandle, peeve, persecute, perturb, pique, plague, poke, prick, prod, provoke, rankle, rasp, remind, ride, ridicule, rile, roil, ruffle, sandbag, stalk, tantalize, taunt, tease, torment, trespass, troll, trouble, vex, worry* (≠ amuse, appease, captivate, charm, comfort, console, content, court, delight, disarm, -disregard, enchant, energize, enliven, entertain, fascinate, forget, gladden, gratify, -ignore, leave, mollify, oblige, pacify, placate, please, satisfy, seduce, -slight, -snub, thrill, titillate, welcome, woo)

PET (+): *baby, caress, clasp, coddle, cosset, cradle, cuddle, dandle, embrace, enfold, fondle, gentle, hold, hug, indulge, infantilize, knead, love, massage, mollycoddle, nurse, nuzzle, pamper, pat, paw, rub, smooch, snuggle, spoil, spoon, stroke, strum, touch* (≠ abuse, assault, attack, -avoid, batter, crucify, harm, hurt, -ignore, injure, mangle, maul, murder, -neglect, punish, smash, strangle, strike, torment, torture)

PETITION (←): *adjure, beg, beseech, besiege, bid, cadge, claim, coerce, command, compel, constrain, covet, crave, demand, desire, entreat,* *force, implore, importune, induce, insist, invoke, memorialize, mooch, oblige, plead, pray, press, reclaim, recover, request, require, retrieve, scavenge, seek, solicit, sponge, sue, target, urge* (≠ allow, appease, assist, assuage, -avoid, comfort, console, content, deliver, -disregard, gratify, help, hint, -ignore, imply, intimate, mollify, oblige, -overlook, pacify, permit, placate, please, quiet, relieve, satisfy, -sidestep, suggest)

PETRIFY (←): *calcify, crystallize, fossilize, freeze, harden, immobilize, ossify, paralyze, set, solidify, toughen, transfix* (≠ crumble, disintegrate, dissolve, liquefy, melt, relax, release, soften, thaw, unstiffen, weaken)

PETRIFY (/): *alarm, amaze, appall, astonish, astound, boggle, castrate, chill, confound, damp, dampen, daunt, daze, deactivate, deaden, debilitate, dehydrate, demoralize, desiccate, devitalize, discourage, dishearten, dismay, dispirit, drain, dumbfound, emasculate, enervate, enfeeble, exhaust, fatigue, frighten, gobsmack, horrify, immobilize, lobotomize, numb, panic, paralyze, rattle, sap, scare, shake, spook, startle, stun, stupefy, terrify, transfix, undermine, unman, weaken, wear* (≠ aid, arouse, boost, bore, brace, buoy, calm, charge, cheer, comfort, convulse, ease, electrify, energize, enliven, excite, fortify, galvanize, inspire, invigorate, kindle, lift, lull, mellow, mitigate, moderate, mollify, pacify, placate, provoke, quicken, relax, rouse, soothe, spark, steady, stimulate, stir, trigger, vivify, weary)

PICK (→): *abet, activate, advance, begin, brew, cultivate, detonate, encourage, energize, enliven, excite, ferment, fire, foment, forward, foster, further, galvanize, incite, inflame, inspire, instigate, invigorate, kindle, motivate, nourish, nurture, prod, produce, promote, prompt, provoke, quicken, raise, rouse, set, sow, spur, start, stimulate, stir, trigger, vitalize* (≠ allay, bridle, calm, cease, check, conclude, constrain, curb, defuse, demotivate, discourage, end, finish, -halt, hamper, hold, inhibit, quiet, regulate, rein, restrain, settle, soothe, still, stop, subdue, tame, terminate, -thwart, tranquilize)

PICK (→): *breach, crack, crowbar, dent, dislodge, force, hack, hit, hoist, jimmy, lever, lift, nose, open, poke, pop, prize, pry, raise, shift, strike, unfasten, unlock, winkle* (≠ bolt, chain, close, connect, deadbolt, fasten, guard, join, latch, lock, protect, seal, secure, shut)

PICK (←): *accept, adopt, appoint, cherry-pick, choose, cull, designate, elect, embrace, espouse, fancy, favor, finger, fix, handpick, mark, name, nominate, prefer, preselect, prioritize, select, set, slot, tab, tag, take, tap* (≠ ban, blackball, blacklist, -decline, discard, discredit, disfavor, disgrace, dismiss, fire, jettison, -omit, -ostracize, oust, -refuse, -reject, -repudiate, -shun, -spurn)

PICK (←): *accumulate, acquire, amass, bag, capture, choose, collect, compile, crop, cull, cut, download, draw, forage, gain, garner, gather, glean, grow, harvest, hoard, hunt, net, obtain, pluck, procure, pull, raise, reap, recycle, salvage, scavenge, secure, seek, select, separate, snare, sort, source, stockpile, trap, winnow* (≠ crop, diffuse, disperse, distribute, divide, grow, lose, nurture, plant, -refuse, -reject, scatter, seed, source, sow, spend, squander, start, waste, yield)

PIERCE (→): *access, bore, break, broach, cleave, core, crack, cut, drill, enter, excavate, gaff, gash, gouge, groove, hack, hollow, impale, incise, invade, jab, knife, lance, notch, penetrate, perforate, plow, poke, prick, probe, punch, puncture, razor, rend, riddle, rupture, shank, shiv, skewer, slash, slice, slit, spear, spike, split, stab, stake, stick, tap, transfix* (≠ armor, bar, barricade, block, cloak, close, clothe, cloud, defend, deflect, disguise, eject, extract, fill, -forbid, guard, heal, invite, leach, leave, leech, open, oust, parry, plug, protect, seal, secure, shield, veil, welcome, withdraw)

PIGEONHOLE (→): *box, cage, catalog, categorize, class, classify, compartmentalize, constrain, defer, delay, dismiss, file, group, hierarchize, hinder, hold, label, limit, package, peg, pin, postpone, prioritize, rank, shelve, sideline, slot, sort, stall, tab, table, tag, trap, typecast* (≠ conflate, confuse, elevate, jumble, mislabel, miss, mistake, mix, muddle, -omit, -overlook, promote, recategorize, reclassify, scatter, scramble)

PILFER (←): *annex, appropriate, bag, borrow, burglarize, collar, cop, crib, defalcate, embezzle, filch, grab, grasp, heist, hijack, hoist, hook, liberate, lift, loot, misappropriate, mooch, nail, nick, nip, nobble, palm, pick, pillage, pinch, pluck, plunder, poach, pocket, pull, purloin, remove, requisition, rifle, rob, rustle, sack, scrounge, seize, shanghai, shoplift, snaffle, snag, snare, snatch, sneak, snitch, sponge, steal, swipe, take, thieve, whip* (≠ bestow, buy, comp, contribute, donate, entrust, furnish, give, guard, hand, leave, offer, present, preserve, purchase, receive, recoup, recover, restore, retain, return, share, shield, supply, tender, volunteer)

PILLAGE (←): *arrogate, burgle, cannibalize, confiscate, consume, damage, depredate, desecrate, desolate, despoil, destroy, devastate, devour, freeboot, gut, invade, loot, mar, maraud, misappropriate, nab, pilfer, pinch, plunder, purloin, raid, ransack, ravage, raze, rend, rifle, rob, ruin, sack, spoil, steal, strip, thieve, vandalize, waste, wreck* (≠ build, construct, create, defend, grow, guard, help, improve, maintain, offer, preserve, protect, rebuild, receive, release, rescue, safeguard, save, shield, withstand)

PILLORY (/): *attack, blackguard, blame, blast, blemish, blister, boo, brand, burn, chide, condemn, cook, criticize, critique, crucify, deflate, demean, demonize, denounce, denunciate, deride, discipline, discredit, disgrace, disparage, disrespect, expose, flout, fulminate, grill, harangue, harass, hassle, heckle, hector, hound, humiliate, incriminate, insult, jeer, knock, label, lampoon, lash, mark, mock, needle, out, poke, punish, rag, razz, -repudiate, rib, ridicule, satirize, scold, scorch, -scorn, shame, shrivel, -shun, -spurn, stain, stigmatize, taunt, tease, unmask, vilify, vilipend, wither* (≠ acclaim, admire, adore, anonymize, applaud, blandish, bless, cheer, commend, compliment, conceal, confess, congratulate, defend, -disregard, exalt, exonerate, extol, flannel, flatter, glorify, gratify, hail, hide, high-five, honor, -ignore, magnify, praise, promote, protect, reward, salute, sanctify, vindicate, worship)

PILOT (→): *administer, boss, bridle, captain, chair, command, conduct, control, direct, discipline, dominate, drive, execute, fly, govern, guide, handle, harness, head, influence, lead, manage, maneuver, manipulate, monitor, navigate, negotiate, operate, order, oversee, quarterback, rule, run, sail, shepherd, skipper, spearhead, steer, superintend, supervise* (≠ -abandon, chase, crash, cripple, -deny, -desert, foil, follow, -frustrate, hamper, hamstring, heed, hinder, -ignore, maroon, mind, mishandle, mismanage, misrule, monkey-wrench, -neglect, obey, obstruct, pursue, -refuse, relinquish, ride, sabotage, serve, sideswipe, smash, submit, subvert, target)

PIMP (→): *abuse, advertise, aggrandize, announce, auction, ballyhoo, bleed, boost, broker, cheat, commercialize, commodify, distribute, exploit, fleece, hard-sell, hawk, hustle, hype, leverage, limelight, manipulate, market, milk, mistreat, monetize, negotiate, overcharge, peddle, play, plug, presell, procure, promo, promote, promulgate, prostitute, provide, publicize, push, renegotiate, sell, shill, skin, soak, solicit, steer, stick, tout, trade, traffic, use, whore, work, wrong* (≠ borrow, buy, cherish, compliment, defend, donate, encourage, guard, lease, nurture, pamper, prize, protect, raise, -refuse, -reject, rent, respect, safeguard, shelter, shield, support, treasure, value, withhold)

PIN (→): *affix, attach, bind, cinch, clasp, clinch, clip, close, fasten, fix, immobilize, join, nail, peg, pinion, press, secure, staple, stick, tack* (≠ detach, disconnect, divide, move, pull, remove, separate, split, unfasten, unlatch, unpin, yank)

PIN (←): *arrest, bind, bridle, captivate, chain, check, collar, confine, constrain, constrict, control, curb, detain, fetter, govern, hinder, hogtie, hold, immobilize, impede, imprison, inhibit, leash, manacle, obstruct, press, -prevent, regulate, restrain, restrict, shackle, stop, straightjacket, subdue, suppress, tether, tie* (≠ deliver, emancipate, encourage, expedite, fast-forward, fast-track, forget, free, fuel, hurry, liberate, loose, -overlook, quicken, rush, unleash, unshackle, untie)

PINCH (←): *apprehend, arrest, bag, bind, book, bust, cage, capture, catch, collar, commit, condemn, confine, constrain, convict, detain, enchain, fetter, get, grab, grapple, handcuff, hold, hook, immure, impound, imprison, incarcerate, intern, jail, jug, keep, land, limit, manacle, nab, nail, nick, pen, remand, restrain, restrict, seize, sentence, shackle, shanghai, snaffle, snare, snatch, trammel, trap* (≠ acquit, alibi, bail, discharge, emancipate, enfranchise, exculpate, exonerate, free, incriminate, liberate, loose, loosen, manumit, pardon, redeem, release, spare, spring, unbind, uncage, unchain, vindicate)

PINCH (←): *appropriate, bag, burglarize, burgle, carjack, collar, cop, crib, filch, glom, grab, grasp, heist, hijack, hook, lift, loot, misappropriate, mooch, nab, nail, nick, nip, nobble, pick, pilfer, pillage, plunder, poach, pocket, purloin, rifle, rob, rustle, sack, seize, shoplift, snaffle, snag, snatch, snitch, sponge, steal, swipe, take, thieve* (≠ bestow, buy, comp, contribute, donate, give, hand, offer, present, purchase, receive, refund, reimburse, repay, restore, save, secure, tender, volunteer)

PINCH (←): *afflict, budget, conserve, cut, -deny, deprive, distress, economize, famish, hoard, husband, maintain, malnourish, manage, oppress, preserve, press, reserve, save, scant, scrape, scrimp, skimp, spare, starve, stiff, stint, underfeed, withhold* (≠ blow, dissipate, force-feed, fritter, fuel, give, grant, host, lard, lavish, misspend, offer, overfeed, shower, slather, spare, spend, squander, syrup, volunteer, waste)

PINCH (/): *chafe, check, clasp, clutch, compress, confine, cramp, crimp, crush, grasp, grip, harm, hold, hurt, injure, lace, mark, nip, pain, pincer, press, shut, squeeze, tweak, twitch, wrench, wrest, wring* (≠ aid, calm, comfort, dilate, drop, ease, enlarge, expand, free, loose, loosen, open, release, slacken, spring, uncompress)

PINPOINT (+): *ascertain, betray, calculate, check, clock, compute, deduce, define, detect, determine, diagnose, discern, disclose, discover, distinguish, establish, evaluate, examine, find, finger, identify, inspect, investigate, isolate, learn, locate, notice, observe, orient, place, position, recall, recognize, remember, reveal, scan, scope, scrutinize, situate, specify, spot, suss, uncloud, uncover* (≠ addle, -avoid, baffle, bewilder, blur, bury, camouflage, cloak, clothe, cloud, conceal, confound, confuse, counterfeit, deceive, disguise, -disregard, fake, feign, fudge, half-ass, hide, -ignore, lose, mask, misdiagnose, misread, miss, mistake, misunderstand, muddle, muddy, mystify, obscure, -overlook, perplex, puzzle, scatter, simulate, trick, veil, wonder)

PIONEER (+): *anticipate, arrange, author, bankroll, begin, brainstorm, coin, colonize, conceive, concoct, constitute, construct, contrive, create, develop, devise, discover, endow, enlarge, establish, expand, explore, fabricate, father, finance, foreshadow, foster, found, fund, generate, hatch, head, inaugurate, initiate, innovate, instigate, institute, introduce, invent, launch, lead, map, open, organize, originate, patent, plant, prepare, produce, sire, spearhead, start, subsidize, systematize, trail-blaze, underwrite* (≠ abolish, abrogate, annihilate, annul, axe, -cancel, close, copy, deep-six, defund, destroy, -discontinue, doom, dump, duplicate, eliminate, end, eradicate, finish, follow, -halt, invalidate, mind, -nullify, obey, obliterate, overthrow, overturn, quash, repeal, -rescind, revoke, scrap, shut, sink, stop, subvert, suppress, terminate, wrap) **(¿) ABSTRACTION ALERT. Concrete goals essential!**

PIRATE (←): *annex, appropriate, arrogate, assume, attach, borrow, claim, collar, commandeer, confiscate, convert, copy, crib, despoil, embezzle, freeboot, grab, grasp, hack, hijack, impound, infringe, invade, lift, loot, misapply, misappropriate, misuse, nick, occupy, pillage, pinch, plagiarize, poach, preempt, press, purloin, reap, repossess, reproduce, scavenge, seize, sequester, snatch, steal, trespass, usurp, wrench, wrest* (≠ authenticate, block, defend, disclose, expose, guard, notarize, preserve, protect, reclaim, recoup, recover, redeem, rescue, restore, retain, safeguard, salvage, shield, validate, verify)

PITCH (→): *assemble, boost, brace, buttress, crane, elevate, erect, fix, heave, heft, heighten, hike, hoist, jack, lift, locate, place, plant, prop, raise, rear, settle, station, support, upend, uphold, uplift* (≠ annihilate, compress, crush, -cut, demolish, destroy, devastate, dismantle, flatten, level, raze, ruin, squash, topple, wreck)

PITCH (→): *bowl, buck, bung, cant, cast, catapult, chuck, dash, eject, fire, fling, flip, gun, heave, hook, hurl, hurtle, impel, launch, lob, loft, pass, peg, pelt, precipitate, project, propel, roll, shoot, sling, throw, thrust, toss, wing* (≠ accept, block, bring, carry, catch, clutch, collect, convey, gain, gather, give, grab, grasp, grip, hand, hold, keep, obtain, receive, restrain, retain, save, schlep, seize, snatch, take, welcome)

PITCH (→): *acclaim, advertise, announce, ballyhoo, bark, broadcast, cold-call, commercialize, commodify, describe, endorse, hail, hard-sell, hawk, hype, laud, limelight, market, merchandize, offer, peddle, pimp, plug, praise, presell, promote, publicize, publish, push, recommend, review, sell, shill, telegraph, tout* (≠ accept, acquire, buy, contract, demand, import, procure, purchase, -reject, secure, solicit, take)

PITCH (→): *-abandon, abdicate, abolish, annihilate, boot, cant, cashier, chuck, -desert, discard, dismiss, -ditch, dump, eject, eliminate, eradicate, exorcise, expunge, exterminate, extinguish, extirpate, -forsake, jettison, junk, liquidate, lose, -reject, remove, root, scrap, shed, shuck, slough, squander, toss, unload, unseat* (≠ adopt, appropriate, arrogate, assume, back, choose, embrace, employ, endorse, espouse, follow, hold, keep, recycle, rescue, retain, salvage, save, select, support, use, utilize)

PITY (+): *accept, allow, appreciate, bemoan, bewail, comfort, comprehend, console, deplore, encourage, fathom, get, grasp, grok, lament, love, mourn, recognize, regret, rue, spare, tolerate, understand* (≠ belittle, celebrate, -despise, -disregard, -hate, -ignore, -neglect, -overlook, -rebuff, -reject, relish, -scorn, -slight, -snub, -spurn, torment, torture, undervalue) **(¿) ABSTRACTION ALERT. Concrete goals essential!**

PLACATE (←): *allay, alleviate, appease, assuage, baby, blandish, cajole, calm, coax, coddle, comfort, compose, conciliate, console, content, delight, demilitarize, disarm, dulcify, ease, featherbed, flannel, flatter, gentle, gladden, gratify, harmonize, heal, help, humor, hush, indulge, infantilize, ingratiate, lighten, lull, mellow, mitigate, mollify, mollycoddle, overindulge, overprotect, pacify, palliate, pamper, placate, please, propitiate, quell, quiet, reconcile, relax, relieve, salve, satisfy, sedate, settle, smooth, soften, soothe, spoil, spoon-feed, still, stroke, sugarcoat, sweeten, sweet-talk, temper, tranquilize, wheedle* (≠ affront, aggravate, agitate, anger, antagonize, bug, burn, chafe, cross, distress, disturb, earbash, enrage, exasperate, gall, harass, henpeck, incense, inflame, infuriate, irritate, militarize, nag, nettle, niggle, noodge, offend, outrage, persecute, pester, provoke, rankle, rile, troll, unsettle, upset, vex)

PLACE (→): *affix, align, anchor, arrange, array, assemble, berth, carry, clap, collect, contextualize, coordinate, depose, deposit, dispose, ensconce, establish, fix, garrison, install, juxtapose, lay, leave, locate, lock, lodge, move, niche, orient, park, plank, plant, plonk, plop, plump, plunk, position, queue, rank, rearrange, rejigger, reorder, rest, set, settle, shift, site, situate, slap, stand, station, stick, wedge* (≠ -abandon, banish, change, discard, dislodge, displace, drop, forget, lose, relegate, relocate, remove, replace, shed, supersede, supplant, take, uninstall, unsettle, upset)

PLACE (+): *alphabetize, array, ascertain, assort, attune, calculate, catalog, categorize, class, classify, clump, cluster, codify, compartment, compartmentalize, compute, cull, deduce, detect, determine, digest, direct, discern, dispose, distinguish, distribute, establish, evaluate, familiarize, file, grade, grok, group, hierarchize, identify, index, list, map, marshal, order, organize, orient, peg, pigeonhole, pinpoint, prioritize, range, rank, recategorize, reclassify, recognize, refer, regiment, regroup, relegate, screen, separate, set, shelve, sieve, sift, slot, sort, subcategorize, systematize, type, winnow* (≠ addle, baffle, bewilder, bury, churn, clutter, confound, confuse, disarrange, disguise, disperse, jumble, lump, mess, misclassify, mislabel, missort, mistype, mix, muddle, mystify, obscure, perplex, puzzle, scatter, scramble, shuffle)

PLAGUE (/): *afflict, aggravate, anguish, annoy, antagonize, assail, attack, badger, bedevil, beleaguer, besiege, bother, brutalize, bug, burden, chafe, crucify, curse, cuss, destroy, distress, disturb, dog, earbash, exasperate, expose, frequent, fret, gall, gnaw, hamper, harass, harry, hassle, haunt, heckle, hector, hinder, hound, impugn, infest, irk, irritate, molest, nag, needle, nettle, nitpick, oppress, overextend, pain, persecute, pester, pursue, ride, tease, terrorize, torment, torture, trouble, upset, vex, weary, worry, wound* (≠ advantage, aid, amuse, appease, assist, benefit, bless, charm, cheer, comfort, console, content, defend, delight, delouse, divert, entertain, gratify, guard, heal, medicate, mend, placate, please, protect, relieve, remedy, satisfy, shield, solace, soothe, support, thrill, tickle, titillate, treat, wow)

PLAN (+): *adumbrate, aim, arrange, blueprint, brainstorm, budget, calculate, chart, choreograph, concert, contemplate, contrive, daydream, design, develop, devise, draft, dream, figure, formulate, frame, graph, intend, intrigue, invent, machinate, map, mastermind, meditate, number, numerate, orchestrate, organize, outline, overcommit, patent, plot, premeditate, prepare, program, project, ready, regulate, rehearse, schedule, scheme, shape, sketch, strategize, synchronize, time* (≠ addle, ad-lib, adopt, baffle, blow, bobble, bomb, botch, bugger, bungle, butcher, clone, copy, copycat, disorganize, disrupt, duplicate, emulate, fake, flub, forget, fudge, fumble, gamble, gum, half-ass, hazard, imitate, improvise, jumble, louse, mangle, mess, mimic, mishandle, -neglect, reduplicate, replicate, reproduce, risk, scramble, wing)

PLAN (+): *accomplish, achieve, aim, attempt, await, calculate, consider, contemplate, debate, design, destine, effect, envisage, execute, foresee,* *hope, intend, meditate, mull, perform, plot, ponder, propose, purport, resolve, scheme, seek, spitball, target, want, wish* (≠ -abandon, -bypass, disbelieve, dismiss, -disregard, -eschew, forget, half-ass, hasten, -ignore, misuse, -neglect, rush, squander, use, waste) **(¿) ABSTRACTION ALERT. Concrete goals essential!**

PLANT (→): *broadcast, bury, cover, cultivate, culture, develop, double, drill, embed, engender, evoke, farm, fertilize, germinate, ground, grow, implant, nourish, nurture, originate, pitch, pot, produce, promote, propagate, provoke, quicken, raise, rear, replant, reseed, scatter, seed, sow, start, stock, tend, transplant, turf* (≠ afflict, blight, choose, collect, cull, defoliate, deforest, devour, dig, diminish, eat, gather, glean, harvest, hay, kill, mow, -neglect, pick, pluck, poison, pull, raze, reap, recycle, ripen, ruin, salvage, scavenge, scorch, select, shrivel, sicken, sprout, squander, stunt, uproot, waste, weed, wither, yield)

PLANT (→): *breed, cram, deposit, drive, ease, embed, entrench, establish, fix, found, hammer, imbue, implant, inculcate, infuse, ingrain, inoculate, inseminate, insert, install, instill, institute, invest, juxtapose, lodge, park, place, plank, plop, plunk, position, pound, ram, root, set, settle, situate, sow, station, steep, stuff, suffuse, thrust* (≠ delete, disorder, disorganize, erase, excise, jar, jolt, lift, move, pull, push, remove, shift, shoulder, shove, shunt, unsettle, upset)

PLANT (/): *archive, bury, cache, coffer, conceal, disguise, ensconce, hide, hoard, insert, inter, lodge, nestle, niche, place, secrete, sheathe, situate, squirrel, stash, store, stow, submerge, tuck, wedge* (≠ bare, brandish, disclose, display, exhibit, expose, extract, flaunt, parade, remove, reveal, show, showcase, uncover, unearth, unmask, unveil, unwrap, yank)

PLAY (→): *attempt, bet, bid, chance, endanger, gamble, hazard, imperil, jeopardize, lay, offer, stake, venture, wager* (≠ bank, defend, guard, hoard, keep, preserve, protect, save, secure, shield, store)

PLAY (→): *address, brave, command, control, direct, engineer, face, field, finagle, finesse, grapple, guide, hack, handle, jockey, manage, maneuver, manipulate, micromanage, negotiate, outsmart, outthink, outwit, regulate, run, steer, swing, take, treat, weather* (≠ -avoid, bobble, bomb, botch, bungle, -bypass, -circumvent, foozle, fumble, half-ass, louse, mishandle, muff, scamp, skip)

PLAY (→): *act, adopt, ape, copy, depict, dramatize, emulate, enact, hoke, imitate, impersonate, interpret, mime, mimic, mock, overplay, pantomime, parody, perform, playact, portray, render, represent, roleplay, travesty, underplay* (≠ color, conceal, costume, disguise, distort, falsify, garble, hide, mask, miscommunicate, misrepresent, misstate, obscure, pervert, twist, warp)

PLEASE (←): *amuse, animate, applaud, attract, beguile, bewitch, bolster, boost, brighten, buoy, captivate, charm, cheer, comfort, congratulate, console, content, delight, distract, divert, elate, elevate, embolden,* *enchant, encourage, energize, engage, enliven, enrapture, entertain, enthrall, entrance, excite, exhilarate, fascinate, fire, fortify, galvanize, gladden, gratify, grip, hearten, honor, humor, hypnotize, indulge, inspire, intrigue, invigorate, lighten, mesmerize, monopolize, occupy, placate, pleasure, rally, reassure, refresh, reinvigorate, relax, revive, rouse, satiate, satisfy, seduce, spellbind, stimulate, stir, strengthen, sustain, thrill, tickle, uplift, vitalize, warm, woo, wow* (≠ abuse, affront, aggravate, agitate, alarm, anger, annoy, appall, blame, blast, boo, bore, bother, bug, busy, chafe, cross, dampen, deaden, demoralize, demotivate, depress, disappoint, discourage, dismay, displease, disquiet, distract, distress, disturb, enrage, exasperate, exhaust, fatigue, fret, frustrate, gall, get, harass, harry, heckle, hound, hurt, incense, inflame, infuriate, insult, irk, irritate, knacker, madden, nag, nauseate, needle, nettle, niggle, nitpick, noodge, numb, offend, outrage, pain, peeve, perturb, pester, pique, provoke, rankle, repulse, revolt, rile, roil, rouse, ruffle, sadden, sicken, tire, troll, trouble, underwhelm, upset, vex, weary, worry, wound, wrong)

PLEDGE (+): *bond, commit, contract, covenant, dedicate, deposit, engage, ensure, guarantee, hock, mortgage, oblige, pass, pawn, promise, secure, soak, swear, undertake, vow* (≠ breach, break, buy, disavow, disobey, falsify, flout, forswear, redeem, -reject, release, resist, subvert, violate, win)

PLOT (+): *adumbrate, angle, brainstorm, brew, calculate, conceive, concoct, contrive, design, devise, draft, finagle, frame, hatch, imagine, lay, machinate, maneuver, map, operate, organize, outline, plan, project, promote, regiment, script, sketch, structure, wangle* (≠ addle, ad-lib, baffle, botch, bugger, bungle, demolish, disorganize, disrupt, forget, gamble, half-ass, improvise, jumble, -neglect, risk, scramble, wing)

PLOW (→): *break, bulldoze, cultivate, dig, fallow, farm, furrow, harrow, harvest, hoe, list, push, rake, reap, ridge, rototill, rush, shove, smash, spade, till, trench, turn, work* (≠ blight, -bypass, deaden, fill, freeze, harden, -ignore, leave, miss, -neglect, -omit, -overlook, -shirk, skip)

PLUCK (←): *acquire, capture, catch, clutch, collect, crop, cull, discover, drag, draw, extract, finger, garner, gather, glean, grab, grasp, grip, harvest, haul, hitch, hunt, jerk, locate, mine, net, obtain, pick, pincer, procure, pull, reap, remove, salvage, scavenge, scrounge, secure, seize, select, snag, snare, snatch, source, strip, strum, take, tow, tug, tweak, twitch, wrench, yank* (≠ -abandon, deprive, diffuse, discard, dissipate, donate, drop, -eschew, fill, fling, furnish, give, grow, heave, implant, insert, junk, lavish, leave, lose, offer, plant, push, ram, -reject, scatter, scrap, seed, shove, skip, sow, squander, stint, supply, thrust, toss, trash, waste, withhold)

PLUG (→): *advance, advertise, aggrandize, aid, announce, assist, auction, back, bait, ballyhoo, barter, boost, broadcast, bulletin, carry, champion, circulate, commend, commercialize, commodify, condone, declare, display, disseminate, distribute, elevate, encourage, endorse, exchange, export, favor, feature, further, handle, hawk, highlight, hustle, hype,* *inform, inspire, keep, kindle, laud, leverage, license, limelight, lobby, lure, mainstream, market, mention, merchandize, monetize, motivate, notify, offer, overestimate, overstate, peddle, pimp, pitch, popularize, praise, presell, prioritize, proclaim, promo, promote, promulgate, propagandize, provide, publicize, publish, puff, push, recommend, retail, sanction, sell, shill, spark, spotlight, spur, stimulate, stock, supply, support, telegraph, tout, trade, traffic, upgrade, wholesale* (≠ attack, ban, battle, -boycott, bury, buy, camouflage, conceal, condemn, criticize, critique, demean, demonize, denigrate, denounce, deride, discourage, discredit, disguise, dismiss, disparage, -eschew, foil, hide, insult, knock, mock, monkey-wrench, muffle, muzzle, neg, pan, picket, pillory, -prohibit, protest, purchase, recall, recant, -refuse, -reject, reserve, ridicule, -scorn, -shun, slam, -snub, -spurn, suppress, -thwart, undersell, understate, withhold)

PLUG (→): *block, bung, caulk, chink, choke, clog, close, clot, congest, constipate, cork, cover, dam, fill, jam, mute, muzzle, obstruct, occlude, pack, plaster, ram, repack, restuff, seal, secure, silence, spackle, stem, stifle, stop, stopper, stopple, stuff, wedge* (≠ clear, decongest, dig, excavate, extract, extricate, hollow, open, remove, scoop, shovel, unclog, uncork, unplug, unseal, unstopper)

PLUNDER (←): *appropriate, burglarize, burgle, comb, demolish, despoil, devastate, filch, fleece, forage, grab, harry, hijack, hunt, lift, loot, maraud, misappropriate, nab, pilfer, pillage, pinch, pluck, poach, pocket, purloin, raid, rake, ransack, ravage, ravish, remove, rifle, rob, rummage, sack, seize, shanghai, shoplift, snatch, sneak, steal, strip, swindle, take, waste, wreck* (≠ aid, bank, bankroll, bestow, buy, compensate, covet, defend, deposit, donate, earn, endow, finance, fund, furnish, gift, give, guard, help, hoard, offer, pay, preserve, protect, receive, reclaim, recoup, recover, rescue, restore, return, save, secure, shield, spare, stash, stockpile, store, supply, tender, underwrite, volunteer, yield)

POACH (←): *appropriate, bag, bogart, boost, borrow, burgle, copy, crib, embezzle, filch, heist, hijack, hoist, hunt, knap, lift, loot, misappropriate, nick, nobble, peculate, pilfer, pinch, pocket, purloin, rob, seek, shoplift, snaffle, snag, snatch, sneak, steal, swipe, take, thieve* (≠ conserve, contribute, defend, give, guard, hoard, keep, maintain, preserve, protect, purchase, receive, recoup, recover, replace, replenish, restore, save, secure, shelter, shield, stash, stock, tuck)

POCKET (←): *appropriate, burglarize, burgle, carjack, filch, gain, grab, grasp, heist, hijack, hook, lift, loot, misappropriate, mooch, nail, nick, nip, pick, pilfer, pillage, pinch, plunder, poach, purloin, rifle, rob, rustle, sack, seize, shoplift, snag, snatch, snitch, sponge, steal, swipe, take, thieve* (≠ bestow, buy, comp, confer, contribute, donate, give, grant, impart, offer, present, purchase, spare, supply, tithe, volunteer, will)

POISON (/): *adulterate, afflict, befoul, begrime, besmirch, blacken, contaminate, corrupt, defile, dilute, dirty, doctor, dose, embitter, envenom, foul, grime, infect, mire, muddy, overdose, pollute, rot, sicken, smirch, smudge, soil, sour, spike, spoil, stain, sully, taint* (≠ aid, clarify, clean, cleanse, clear, cure, decontaminate, disinfect, distill, doctor, drug, filter, heal, hospitalize, isolate, medicate, nurse, purge, purify, quarantine, rarefy, rectify, refine, sanitize, sterilize)

POISON (/): *abase, alienate, bastardize, befoul, begrime, besmear, besmirch, bestialize, blacken, blemish, blight, blur, cheapen, cloud, contaminate, corrupt, damage, darken, debase, debauch, deface, defile, degrade, demean, demoralize, deprave, depreciate, descend, destroy, deteriorate, dilute, dirty, discolor, discredit, disgrace, dishonor, doom, downgrade, flaw, foul, harm, humble, humiliate, hurt, impair, injure, lessen, lower, mar, pervert, pollute, profane, prostitute, ruin, shame, sink, smear, smirch, smudge, soil, spoil, stain, suborn, subvert, sully, taint, tar, tarnish, thin, touch, vitiate, warp, water, weaken, wreck* (≠ ameliorate, amend, better, clarify, clean, cleanse, dignify, elevate, enhance, ennoble, enrich, exalt, flavor, honor, improve, moralize, optimize, overhaul, perfect, purify, rarefy, refine, respect, restore, season, spice, uplift)

POISON (/): *allure, beguile, bias, blandish, blarney, brainwash, bribe, cajole, coax, convert, convince, dispose, entreat, exhort, fast-talk, gaslight, incline, induce, influence, lure, move, persuade, predetermine, predispose, prejudge, prejudice, prepossess, prompt, retrain, seduce, sell, snow, suggest, sway, tantalize, tease, tempt, turn, urge, wheedle* (≠ counter, demotivate, -deter, discourage, dissuade, hinder, impede, inhibit, -prevent, resist, restrain, unsell)

POKE (→): *annoy, arouse, awaken, badger, bother, bug, butt, clip, contact, crowd, dig, earbash, elbow, goose, harass, hassle, hit, irk, irritate, jab, jostle, nag, needle, nettle, niggle, nitpick, nudge, nuzzle, pester, pick, prick, prod, provoke, punch, push, ram, rouse, shoulder, shove, stab, stick, stimulate, stir, taunt, tease, thrust* (≠ -avoid, blandish, block, -bypass, calm, coddle, compliment, -disregard, envelop, -eschew, flatter, gratify, help, humor, -ignore, lull, mellow, mitigate, moderate, mollify, -neglect, outrun, outstrip, -overlook, pacify, placate, praise, pull, shield, -shun, -sidestep, skip, skirt, stabilize, steady)

POLARIZE (+): *align, assemble, blend, center, centralize, coalesce, collect, combine, compact, concentrate, consolidate, coordinate, fuse, gather, harmonize, hybridize, incorporate, integrate, join, link, merge, orchestrate, reduce, reunify, reunite, synthesize, unify, unite* (≠ decentralize, deconcentrate, scatter, segregate, separate, split, spread)

POLARIZE (/): *affront, alienate, anger, annoy, antagonize, detach, disaffect, disgruntle, distance, disunite, divide, divorce, enrage, estrange, isolate, needle, nettle, offend, outrage, part, peeve, rile, roil, segregate, separate, split, unnerve, upset* (≠ alleviate, assuage, blend, coalesce, combine, fuse, harmonize, hybridize, integrate, join, merge, pacify, placate, reunite, synthesize, unite)

POLICE (←): *check, control, cruise, defend, detect, examine, guard, inspect, investigate, monitor, note, observe, oversee, pace, patrol, pound, probe, proctor, protect, regulate, retrace, safeguard, scan, scour, scout,* *scrutinize, secure, sentinel, supervise, tour, trace, track, watch* (≠ -abandon, aggravate, ambush, attack, blackjack, blackmail, blind, bully, confound, deceive, disguise, exacerbate, -forsake, harm, injure, intimidate, menace, miss, mistake, muddle, mystify, -neglect, -overlook, puzzle, scare, stalk, terrorize, threaten, trick)

POLISH (→): *beeswax, brighten, buff, burnish, clean, coat, dress, face, file, finish, furbish, glaze, gloss, grind, lacquer, oil, pomade, pumice, rasp, rub, sand, sandblast, sandpaper, scour, scrape, scrub, shine, sleek, slick, smooth, varnish, veneer, wax* (≠ blemish, coarsen, deface, dent, ding, dirty, dull, harshen, mar, nock, notch, rough, roughen, ruffle, score, scrape, scratch, scuff, sully, tarnish)

POLISH (+): *adapt, ameliorate, amend, beautify, better, civilize, complete, correct, cultivate, enhance, enrich, file, finalize, finish, glamorize, glitter, glitz, improve, mature, mend, optimize, overhaul, perfect, rectify, refine, refurbish, remedy, revolutionize, right, shine, sophisticate, sugarcoat* (≠ -abandon, barbarize, bedraggle, bury, conceal, corrupt, damage, deface, -desert, destroy, drop, efface, erase, -forsake, harm, hide, injure, obliterate, obscure, ruffle, ruin, spoil, suborn, sully, taint, upset, worsen, wreck)

POLL (←): *assess, ballot, benchmark, canvass, consult, detect, determine, gauge, grill, interrogate, interview, question, sample, solicit, survey* (≠ -disregard, document, elect, estimate, fancy, guess, -ignore, misgauge, miss, -neglect, report, skip, wonder)

POLLUTE (/): *abase, adulterate, alloy, bastardize, befoul, begrime, besmear, besmirch, blacken, blemish, blight, blot, contaminate, corrupt, damage, debase, debauch, defile, degrade, demean, demote, deprave, desecrate, devalue, dilute, diminish, dirty, disgrace, dishonor, doctor, foul, harm, humble, humiliate, infect, injure, insult, libel, lower, malign, mar, mire, mortify, muddy, offend, outrage, poison, profane, reduce, ridicule, rot, ruin, shame, slander, -slight, smear, smirch, smudge, -snub, soil, spike, spoil, stain, suborn, sully, taint, tarnish, trample, violate, water* (≠ boost, clarify, clean, cleanse, clear, decontaminate, dignify, disinfect, distill, filter, filtrate, improve, purge, purify, quarantine, rarefy, rectify, refine, remedy, rinse, sanitize, sift, sterilize, strain, upgrade, wash)

PORTRAY (→): *caricature, delineate, depict, describe, diagram, document, doodle, draw, etch, ghostwrite, illustrate, image, limn, map, outline, paint, photograph, pictorialize, picture, render, replicate, represent, show, silhouette, simulate, sketch, trace, visualize* (≠ blur, cloak, cloud, conceal, contort, costume, disguise, distort, erase, expunge, fog, hide, mask, muddle, muddy, obfuscate, obliterate, obscure, scramble, screen, smudge, veil)

PORTRAY (→): *characterize, connote, corroborate, define, delineate, demonstrate, depict, describe, detail, display, document, draft, elaborate, elucidate, evince, evoke, exemplify, exhibit, expose, flaunt, hint, illuminate, illustrate, label, narrate, outline, picture, précis, present, profile, qualify, recite, recount, rehearse, relate, render, report, represent,* *show, showcase, silhouette, sketch, spiel, substantiate, suggest, summarize, take, tell, trace, uncover, unmask, vignette* (≠ color, confound, confuse, debunk, disprove, distort, embellish, embroider, falsify, garble, miscommunicate, misdescribe, mishear, misinterpret, mislabel, misread, misrepresent, misstate, perplex, pervert, puzzle, rebut, refute, twist, warp)

PORTRAY (→): *act, adopt, ape, characterize, conjure, depict, dramatize, duplicate, echo, emulate, enact, ghostwrite, imitate, impersonate, interpret, mime, mimic, overplay, pantomime, perform, personify, play, playact, render, represent, roleplay, underplay* (≠ coin, confuse, contradict, -deny, disguise, gainsay, invent, obscure, oppose, originate, reverse) **(¿) ABSTRACTION ALERT. Concrete goals essential!**

POSITION (→): *affix, align, anchor, arrange, array, assemble, berth, carry, clap, clinch, collect, contextualize, deploy, deposit, dispose, ensconce, establish, fix, install, lay, locate, lock, lodge, move, niche, orient, park, place, plank, plant, plonk, plop, plump, plunk, queue, rank, rearrange, rejigger, reorder, set, settle, shift, situate, slap, stand, station, stick, wedge* (≠ banish, discombobulate, dislodge, displace, invalid, relegate, relocate, remove, replace, ruffle, seclude, shove, shunt, supersede, supplant, take, transfer, vacate)

POSSESS (→): *acquire, claim, colonize, corner, download, get, grab, hog, inhabit, keep, maintain, obtain, occupy, reap, reclaim, recoup, recover, redeem, rescue, reserve, retain, retrieve, salvage, seize, settle, take, tenant, withhold* (≠ -abandon, cede, -decline, disclaim, dispossess, -forsake, leave, -reject, -renounce, -repudiate, require, -spurn) **(¿) ABSTRACTION ALERT. Concrete goals essential!**

POSSESS (→): *bewitch, control, demonize, direct, dominate, eclipse, enchant, govern, haunt, induce, infatuate, influence, inhabit, manipulate, master, mold, overwhelm, rule, sway, transform, witch* (≠ banish, -decline, defy, -deny, eject, -exclude, exorcise, free, -ostracize, -reject, release, -repudiate, resist, -spurn)

POSSESS (←): *acquire, bear, boast, brandish, carry, command, contain, employ, enjoy, gain, get, handle, hold, own, procure, retain, secure, sport, utilize, wield* (≠ -abandon, bequeath, bestow, discard, -disown, dump, give, hand, lose, miss, relinquish, remainder, request, surrender, want, yield) **(¿) ABSTRACTION ALERT. Concrete goals essential!**

POST (→): *advertise, advise, announce, apprise, bill, billboard, blare, blaze, blazon, blurb, broadcast, bulletin, call, circulate, communicate, concede, confess, confide, confirm, declare, disclose, disseminate, divulge, enunciate, externalize, feature, flash, herald, hype, impart, inform, intimate, introduce, manifest, message, notify, pitch, placard, plug, presell, proclaim, promote, promulgate, publicize, publish, puff, release, report, reveal, show, sound, spotlight, spread, telegraph, text, trumpet, verbalize* (≠ -avoid, bury, censor, conceal, -deny, expurgate, gag, hide, hush, mask, obscure, quash, recall, recant, redact, retract, revoke, shush, silence, stifle, suppress, withhold)

POST (→): *affix, attach, bulletin, display, exhibit, nail, pin, placard, plaster, publicize, show, stick, tack* (≠ bury, conceal, detach, free, hide, -ignore, loosen, -overlook, pull, remove, tear, unfasten)

POSTPONE (←): *adjourn, block, defer, delay, detain, encumber, extend, foil, freeze, -frustrate, hamper, hinder, hold, impede, lengthen, monkey-wrench, mothball, obstruct, pause, pigeonhole, prolong, refer, remit, reschedule, retard, shelve, short-circuit, slow, stall, stay, stretch, stymie, suspend, table, -thwart, waive, withhold* (≠ accelerate, advance, boost, brainstorm, catalyze, expedite, fast-forward, fast-track, forward, frogmarch, further, grease, hasten, hurry, march, overcommit, prioritize, quicken, race, rush, speed)

POUND (→): *backhand, bang, bash, bat, batter, beat, belt, biff, bludgeon, bonk, bop, box, bruise, buffet, bust, clap, clip, clobber, clock, clout, club, concuss, conk, crack, drub, drum, hammer, hit, knead, knock, nail, palpitate, paste, pelt, pummel, punch, rap, slam, slap, slog, slug, smack, smash, smite, sock, stomp, strike, swat, swipe, tag, thrash, thump, thwack, wallop, whack, whale, zap* (≠ -bypass, caress, clasp, counter-punch, defend, deflect, grip, guard, heal, help, miss, -neglect, nurse, parry, protect, shield, skip, stroke)

POUND (/): *atomize, beat, break, bust, crack, crumble, crunch, crush, dash, disintegrate, fracture, fragment, granulate, grate, grind, kibble, mash, mill, pestle, powder, pulverize, shatter, shiver, smash, splinter, stamp, trample* (≠ assemble, construct, create, doctor, fashion, fix, forge, form, fuse, glue, heal, meld, melt, mend, mold, preserve, produce, protect, rebuild, reconstruct, repair, restore, revamp, save, sculpt, seal, sew, shape)

POWER (→): *activate, animate, boost, catapult, charge, drive, electrify, empower, enable, encourage, energize, facilitate, fan, feed, ferment, fire, foment, force, force-feed, fortify, fuel, goad, hasten, impel, incite, induce, inflame, inspire, instigate, invigorate, jolt, launch, lubricate, motivate, move, nourish, poke, prime, prioritize, prod, prompt, propel, provoke, punch, punt, push, ram, reboot, recharge, reinvigorate, restimulate, revive, rouse, shoot, shove, spark, stimulate, stoke, strengthen, super-charge, sustain, thrust, trigger, urge, vitalize* (≠ -abort, cannibalize, castrate, consume, cripple, curb, dampen, deactivate, deaden, debilitate, deplete, dissuade, drain, emasculate, enervate, enfeeble, exhaust, fatigue, freeze, -halt, hamper, hamstring, hinder, impair, impede, inactivate, inhibit, leech, overextend, paralyze, quell, quench, repress, restrain, sap, sedate, shrivel, slow, stifle, still, stop, stunt, suppress, tax, tire, undermine, unman, waste, weaken, weary, wither, worsen, wound)

PRAISE (+): *acclaim, accredit, acknowledge, admire, adore, adulate, aggrandize, applaud, appreciate, approve, ballyhoo, beatify, blandish, bless, boost, celebrate, cheer, commend, compliment, congratulate, deify, dignify, elevate, emblazon, endorse, ennoble, eulogize, exalt, extol,* *favor, fête, flannel, flatter, glorify, gold-star, gratify, hail, hallow, heighten, honor, idolize, laud, lift, lionize, magnify, overpraise, promote, raise, recognize, recommend, revere, reverence, reward, salute, sanction, strengthen, support, swell, thank, toast, tout, trumpet, venerate, worship* (≠ abuse, admonish, belittle, berate, blame, blast, boo, castigate, censure, chastise, chide, criticize, critique, demean, denigrate, discredit, disfavor, disgrace, dismiss, disparage, excoriate, fault, finger, frame, -ignore, keelhaul, knock, lambaste, neg, pan, rebuke, regret, repent, reprimand, reproach, reprove, revile, rue, scold, skewer, slam, vilify, warn, wrong)

PREACH (→): *address, admonish, adopt, advise, advocate, back, brainwash, champion, countenance, defend, educate, encourage, endorse, enlighten, equip, espouse, evangelize, exhort, favor, groom, guide, harangue, inculcate, indoctrinate, influence, instill, instruct, justify, lecture, mold, patronize, plug, praise, prepare, prescribe, prime, proclaim, promote, prophesy, propose, recommend, school, sermonize, shape, support, teach, transform, tune, uphold, urge, worship* (≠ assail, attack, belittle, berate, censure, challenge, criticize, critique, debate, deprecate, discredit, disparage, disprove, dispute, disrespect, doubt, grill, impugn, interrogate, invalidate, oppose, question, resist, revile, -scorn, scruple, suspect, traduce, vilify, vituperate) **(¿) ABSTRACTION ALERT. Concrete goals essential!**

PREDICT (+): *adumbrate, alert, announce, anticipate, augur, caution, declare, divine, envision, forecast, foresee, foreshadow, foretell, forewarn, hallucinate, harbinger, herald, portend, presage, proclaim, prognosticate, promise, prophesy, reveal, scent, sense, smell, soothsay, tip, warn* (≠ assure, calculate, demonstrate, describe, establish, guess, insure, investigate, narrate, prove, recount, relate, report, settle, warrant)

PREEMPT (←): *acquire, annex, anticipate, appropriate, arrogate, assume, attach, claim, collar, commandeer, confiscate, convert, despoil, embezzle, forestall, grab, grasp, impound, infringe, invade, loot, misapply, misappropriate, misuse, occupy, pillage, pirate, press, -prevent, procure, reap, recoup, recover, repossess, retrieve, salvage, save, secure, seize, sequester, snag, snatch, steal, take, trespass, usurp, wrench, wrest* (≠ -abandon, abdicate, bequeath, bestow, doubt, drop, fail, forfeit, give, hand, keep, lose, offer, -refuse, -reject, release, relinquish, -renounce, surrender, waive)

PREOCCUPY (←): *absorb, allure, attract, beguile, bemuse, bewitch, busy, captivate, charm, distract, enchant, engage, engulf, enthrall, fascinate, fixate, grip, hog, hypnotize, immerse, interest, intrigue, involve, mesmerize, monopolize, occupy, prepossess* (≠ annoy, -balk, bore, bother, bug, dampen, deaden, depress, disappoint, dull, -exclude, frustrate, irk, irritate, jade, misinterpret, miss, mistake, misunderstand, nauseate, -neglect, numb, offend, outrage, -overlook, repulse, revolt, sicken, tire, underwhelm, weary) **(¿) ABSTRACTION ALERT. Concrete goals essential!**

PREPARE (+): *adapt, adjust, arm, arrange, assemble, author, bake, brew, build, calibrate, cast, compose, compound, concoct, configure, construct,* *contribute, contrive, cook, couch, craft, customize, devise, draft, equip, express, fabricate, fashion, fix, form, frame, ghostwrite, improvise, make, mold, organize, pave, pen, plan, prime, produce, provide, redraft, reframe, script, sculpt, sculpture, shape, state, stock, supply, tune, tweak, verbalize, warn, weave, word, write* (≠ adopt, appropriate, break, bulldoze, clone, consume, copy, copycat, demolish, destroy, disassemble, dismantle, duplicate, emulate, flatten, imitate, level, mimic, pulverize, raze, replicate, reproduce, ruin, separate, shred, smash, splinter, strip, tatter, tear, topple, usurp)

PREPARE (+): *arrange, blueprint, brainstorm, budget, calculate, chart, choreograph, conceive, consult, contemplate, contrive, design, devise, draft, figure, formulate, frame, graph, intrigue, machinate, map, orchestrate, organize, outline, plan, plot, premeditate, project, regiment, scheme, script, shape, sketch, strategize* (≠ distrust, doom, doubt, fake, forget, fudge, gamble, hazard, -ignore, improv, improvise, measure, mistrust, -neglect, -overlook, question, suspect, time, wing, worry)

PREPARE (+): *accustom, acquaint, adapt, adjust, adopt, advise, aid, apprentice, apprise, arm, arrange, assist, authorize, beautify, brace, brainwash, brief, catechize, caution, civilize, coach, cock, command, compel, condition, convince, counsel, cram, cultivate, demonstrate, develop, direct, discipline, domesticate, draft, drill, edify, educate, elevate, embattle, empower, enable, enhance, enlighten, entitle, equip, exercise, expand, extend, familiarize, fit, fix, forearm, fortify, foster, frame, furnish, gird, groom, ground, guide, gussy, habituate, help, housebreak, housetrain, impart, implant, improve, inculcate, indoctrinate, inform, initiate, inspire, instill, instruct, introduce, lay, lead, learn, lecture, manicure, mentor, monitor, moralize, mount, notify, nurture, order, outfit, parrot, perfect, perfume, practice, preach, prep, prime, proctor, provide, qualify, question, quiz, read, ready, rear, rehearse, retrain, reveal, school, scold, season, set, shape, sharpen, show, spread, steady, steel, steer, strain, stretch, study, supervise, supply, tailor, take, tame, tax, teach, test, train, tutor, update* (≠ abuse, addle, attend, baffle, ban, bar, barbarize, bewilder, block, bury, censor, cheat, conceal, confound, confuse, constrain, consult, debase, deceive, defraud, delude, demean, discombobulate, discourage, disguise, disqualify, -exclude, fabricate, fluster, follow, -forbid, forget, gaslight, hamper, heed, hide, hinder, -ignore, impede, inhibit, keep, learn, lower, mind, misinform, mislead, miss, muddle, mystify, -neglect, nonplus, obey, obscure, observe, obstruct, outlaw, perplex, pester, -preclude, -prevent, -prohibit, protest, puzzle, ruffle, sabotage, scotch, scupper, scuttle, shelve, study, stump, subvert, suppress, surprise, -veto, withhold)

PRESCRIBE (→): *advise, appoint, arrange, assign, bid, charge, choose, coerce, command, compel, conduct, constrain, control, decree, define, demand, dictate, direct, enjoin, fix, foist, force, force-feed, govern, impose, insist, instruct, lead, limit, manage, obligate, oblige, ordain, order, promulgate, require, rule, select, set, settle, specify, stipulate, tell* (≠ abolish, -avoid, ban, bar, -cancel, disallow, disorganize, enjoin, -exclude,

-forbid, -halt, hamper, hinder, invalidate, mislead, -negate, -neglect, -nullify, -prevent, -prohibit, proscribe, -refuse, -reject, -rescind, strike, unsettle, -veto)

PRESENT (→): *administer, aid, assist, award, benefit, bestow, comp, confer, contribute, dish, dispense, dole, dollop, donate, dower, endow, entrust, extend, force-feed, fork, furnish, give, grant, hand, help, impart, issue, lard, lavish, mete, offer, overfeed, proffer, provide, push, regale, render, sacrifice, slather, spitball, submit, supply, tender, tithe, unspool, volunteer* (≠ advance, beg, coopt, demand, -deny, grab, hold, keep, lend, loan, poach, pocket, preserve, request, require, retain, save, sell, snag, steal, swipe, withhold)

PRESENT (→): *act, announce, carry, compère, demonstrate, display, dramatize, emcee, enact, exhibit, expose, extend, flaunt, give, host, impersonate, mount, offer, organize, parade, perform, play, playact, portray, preview, proffer, render, represent, roleplay, show, showcase, stage, tender, unveil* (≠ bury, -cancel, close, conceal, costume, disguise, ensconce, hide, mask, niche, obscure, -omit, shutter, stash, stow, tuck, veil, withhold)

PRESENT (→): *characterize, define, delineate, depict, describe, distinguish, elaborate, identify, picture, portray, profile, propound, represent, specify, typecast* (≠ color, distort, embellish, embroider, falsify, garble, miscommunicate, misrepresent, misstate, pervert, twist, warp) **(¿) ABSTRACTION ALERT. Concrete goals essential!**

PRESENT (→): *acquaint, address, advertise, announce, communicate, connect, enlighten, greet, hail, inform, introduce, join, link, meet, notify* (≠ affront, cloak, clothe, cloud, -cut, embrace, -ignore, invite, mortify, -rebuff, receive, -shun, -slight, -snub, -spurn, welcome)

PRESERVE (+): *accommodate, accumulate, anchor, appease, archive, armor, assist, bolster, budget, bury, camouflage, cloak, clothe, cloud, cocoon, colonize, commemorate, conceal, conserve, continue, cover, cure, cushion, defend, deflect, disguise, embalm, ensconce, fence, fix, fortify, foster, guard, harbor, heal, help, hide, hoard, hog, house, husband, indemnify, insulate, insure, keep, maintain, manage, mask, mend, mind, mothball, mummify, nourish, nurse, nurture, obscure, obstruct, outlast, patch, patronize, perpetuate, placate, police, protect, rebuild, reconstruct, recycle, rehabilitate, rejuvenate, remedy, rescue, reserve, restore, retain, retrieve, return, reward, safeguard, salvage, save, screen, secure, service, shelter, shield, shroud, stockpile, stonewall, store, strengthen, support, sustain, tolerate, uphold, ward, watch, weather, withstand* (≠ -abandon, abuse, assail, assault, attack, besiege, betray, break, compromise, crack, crucify, damage, defile, demolish, -desert, destroy, -disregard, disrupt, dissipate, doom, double-cross, endanger, erase, expose, forfeit, forget, -forsake, fracture, fragment, harm, hurt, -ignore, impair, imperil, impugn, injure, jeopardize, liquidate, lose, malign, malnourish, mangle, menace, molest, monkey-wrench, -neglect, nuke, obliterate, persecute, pervert, provoke, pulverize, ravish, raze, release, relinquish, risk, ruin, sabotage, scotch, scupper, scuttle, shatter, shelve, sicken, spend, squander, storm, subvert, target, tear, threaten, torment, torture, traumatize, undermine, upset, vandalize, victimize, vilify, violate, wound, wreck, wrong)

PRESERVE (/): *bottle, brine, bronze, can, candy, chill, cure, desiccate, dry, embalm, freeze, jar, pickle, process, refrigerate, salt, season, smoke, store, stow, wrap* (≠ consume, contaminate, damage, distribute, eat, pollute, ruin, squander, thaw, use, waste, wither)

PRESS (→): *accelerate, afflict, assail, beg, beset, besiege, bribe, buttonhole, coerce, compel, constrain, convince, demand, encourage, enjoin, entreat, exhort, fast-talk, force, goad, grease, harass, hasten, impel, implore, importune, induce, muscle, nudge, panhandle, persuade, petition, plague, plead, pressure, push, railroad, rush, sell, soft-sell, soft-soap, spur, sue, sweet-talk, thrust, torment, trouble, urge, vex, worry* (≠ block, coax, convince, daunt, delay, demotivate, -deter, discourage, -disregard, dissuade, foil, -halt, hamper, hinder, impede, monkey-wrench, nobble, pause, postpone, -prevent, protest, restrain, shelve, short-circuit, stall, stem, stop, straightjacket, stymie, suppress, -thwart)

PRESS (→): *bear, bulldoze, compact, compel, compress, condense, constrict, contract, cram, crowd, crush, deflate, depress, drive, flatten, force, iron, jam, jam-pack, knead, level, mangle, mash, muscle, pack, pinch, pressure, propel, punch, push, railroad, ram, roll, scrunch, shove, smooth, squash, squeeze, squish, squoosh, steamroll, stuff, swarm, throng, thrust, trample, wedge, weigh, wring* (≠ amplify, bend, bulge, crack, crimp, crinkle, decompress, dent, distend, enlarge, expand, extend, fill, grow, increase, inflate, kink, loose, loosen, puff, release, restore, roughen, rumple, sharpen, swell, uncompress, wiggle)

PRESS (←): *caress, clasp, clench, clutch, contact, crush, cuddle, embrace, enfold, envelop, fold, grapple, grasp, greet, grip, hold, hug, keep, knead, lock, massage, retain, seize, squeeze, squish, squoosh, welcome, wrap* (≠ bequeath, bestow, deliver, discharge, disparage, drop, liberate, loose, lose, miss, open, receive, -reject, release, relinquish, -shun, unclasp, unfasten, unhand)

PRESSURE (→): *antagonize, badger, blackjack, blackmail, bludgeon, bluff, bribe, browbeat, brutalize, bug, bulldoze, bully, buttonhole, coerce, compel, constrain, convince, cow, daunt, drag, dragoon, drive, earbash, enforce, fast-talk, force, gaslight, goad, harass, hector, hound, impel, impress, insist, intimidate, lobby, make, menace, muscle, nag, obligate, oblige, overcommit, palaver, press, push, railroad, rush, sandbag, sell, shame, squeeze, steamroller, stress, sway, terrorize, threaten, trash-talk, urge, victimize* (≠ allow, argue, block, cajole, coax, convince, demotivate, -deter, discourage, dissuade, ease, free, help, hinder, impede, induce, leave, let, loosen, lubricate, midwife, mitigate, move, nobble, permit, persuade, -prevent, protest, pull, relax, release, restrain, satisfy, slow, soft-sell, soft-soap, stall, stem, stymie, suggest, sweet-talk, -thwart, win)

PRETEND (→): *act, adopt, affect, emulate, ghostwrite, imagine, imitate, impersonate, make-believe, mime, mimic, play, playact, portray, pose, purport, represent, reproduce, roleplay, simulate, suppose* (≠ admit, concede, confess, confide, confirm, confront, disclose, divulge, expose, face, humiliate, lampoon, leak, reveal, unmask, unveil)

PRETEND (←): *act, affect, allege, assume, beguile, bluff, cheat, claim, convince, counterfeit, cozen, deceive, delude, dissimulate, double-talk, dupe, fabricate, fake, feign, fish, fool, fudge, half-ass, hoodwink, imagine, jazz, jive, mislead, profess, purport, roleplay, simulate, spin, stonewall, sucker, suppose, whitewash* (≠ authenticate, confess, confide, confirm, confront, corroborate, debunk, dismantle, disprove, notarize, prove, ruin, substantiate, testify, validate, verify, wreck) **(¿) ABSTRACTION ALERT. Concrete goals essential!**

-PREVENT (→): *-abort, anticipate, arrest, -avert, -avoid, baffle, -balk, ban, banish, bar, block, bottleneck, brake, bung, burden, catch, censor, chain, check, checkmate, chill, choke, clog, complicate, condemn, congest, constipate, constrain, cordon, counter, counteract, cramp, crimp, cripple, curb, dam, damn, dampen, daunt, delay, demotivate, depress, detain, -deter, disadvantage, disallow, discourage, dishearten, disincline, disqualify, disrupt, dissuade, drag, embargo, encumber, enjoin, entangle, entrap, -exclude, -excommunicate, fetter, foil, -forbid, forestall, foul, freeze, -frustrate, -halt, hamper, hamstring, handicap, hinder, hogtie, impair, impede, inconvenience, inhibit, intercept, interrupt, invalidate, jam, -kibosh, kneecap, knot, limit, lumber, mire, monkey-wrench, muzzle, obstruct, occlude, oppose, -ostracize, outlaw, overload, paralyze, pause, plug, preempt, -prohibit, proscribe, redact, resist, restrain, restrict, retard, scotch, shackle, shelve, short-circuit, slow, snag, snarl, stagnate, stall, staunch, stay, stem, stifle, stop, straightjacket, stultify, stunt, stymie, suppress, taboo, tangle, throttle, -thwart, trammel, -veto, wing* (≠ accelerate, accommodate, advance, aid, allow, assist, boost, brainstorm, catalyze, clear, compel, cultivate, decongest, disencumber, disentangle, ease, enable, encourage, expedite, extricate, facilitate, fast-forward, fast-track, foster, free, frogmarch, fuel, further, grease, hasten, heal, help, hurry, improve, incite, instigate, legalize, liberate, loosen, lubricate, march, mend, midwife, nurture, oblige, open, permit, prioritize, promote, prompt, propel, protect, push, quicken, release, relieve, remedy, rush, smooth, spark, speed, spur, steady, stimulate, stir, stoke, strengthen, support, transact, transcend, unclog, uncomplicate, unleash, unlock, untangle, untie, urge)

PRICE (←): *adjudge, appraise, arrange, ascertain, assess, charge, collect, compare, cost, decide, define, demand, determine, discount, estimate, evaluate, exact, figure, finalize, fix, impose, levy, mark, name, rate, reduce, resolve, set, settle, specify, sticker, tax, toll, valuate, value* (≠ abate, acquire, assume, bestow, bury, conceal, diminish, -disregard, donate, hide, lessen, mistake, -neglect, obtain, outlay, pay, predetermine, purchase, secure)

PRICK (+): *bite, bore, cut, drill, enter, gash, gore, hurt, impale, jab, lance, nick, penetrate, perforate, pierce, pink, point, poke, prod, punch, puncture, scratch, slash, slit, spike, spur, stab, sting, wound* (≠ bandage, block, close, deflect, doctor, eject, extract, guard, heal, preserve, seal, sew, shield, smooth, withdraw)

PRICK (/): *afflict, aggravate, agonize, anguish, annoy, bother, bug, chafe, cramp, discomfort, distress, gall, gravel, harass, harry, hurt, inflame, irk, irritate, nag, needle, nettle, nitpick, pain, plague, sting, torment, torture, trouble, vex, worry, wrack, wrench* (≠ aid, alleviate, amuse, assuage, buffer, calm, comfort, console, defend, delight, ease, entertain, gratify, help, lighten, lull, mellow, mitigate, moderate, mollify, pacify, placate, please, protect, quiet, relieve, rescue, salve, soften, soothe)

PRIME (+): *arm, brief, coach, cock, cram, drill, energize, equip, excite, fit, galvanize, groom, inform, mentor, motivate, move, notify, prep, prepare, provoke, ready, rehearse, season, stimulate, tell, train* (≠ -abandon, block, -disregard, fool, forget, -forsake, hamper, mislead, -neglect, -overlook, -rebuff, short-circuit, -spurn, stymie)

PRIMP (+): *adorn, barber, beautify, brush, clip, costume, dandify, decorate, dress, embellish, enhance, fancify, garnish, glamorize, glitter, glitz, grace, groom, gussy, improve, manicure, optimize, ornament, overhaul, pomade, smarten, tidy, tinsel, titivate, trim, wax* (≠ bedraggle, blemish, damage, deface, deform, dirty, disfigure, draggle, efface, flaw, harshen, maim, mar, muddy, ruin, scar, soil, spoil, untidy)

PRIORITIZE (+): *adjust, align, arrange, assess, balance, benchmark, book, budget, calculate, catalog, categorize, class, classify, codify, compile, compute, coordinate, design, dispose, distribute, estimate, figure, file, filter, formulate, grade, group, handle, hierarchize, index, itemize, juxtapose, list, manage, marshal, methodize, operate, pace, poll, position, prearrange, process, range, rank, rate, register, regulate, reorganize, restructure, schedule, set, settle, sift, slate, slot, sort, structure, systematize, tidy* (≠ botch, bungle, confuse, disorder, disorganize, disperse, flub, fluff, jumble, mismanage, muddle, -neglect, overcommit, -refuse, scatter, scramble, shuffle, unsettle)

PRIORITIZE (+): *accent, accentuate, adulate, advertise, assert, belabor, blandish, bolster, boost, butter, charm, concentrate, count, court, deepen, display, elevate, emphasize, encourage, energize, escalate, exaggerate, exhibit, favor, feature, flaunt, floodlight, focus, foreground, foster, heighten, highlight, hype, identify, illuminate, increase, intensify, lift, limelight, magnify, mark, maximize, overemphasize, overplay, oversell, overstate, overstress, pinpoint, plug, power, praise, present, press, promote, publicize, punctuate, push, reinforce, sharpen, show, spotlight, stimulate, strengthen, stress, support, underline, underscore, upgrade, uplift, weight* (≠ attack, -avoid, belittle, blame, blast, blister, boo, bury, -cancel, conceal, condemn, cover, criticize, curb, decrease, deemphasize, delegate, denounce, deride, diminish, -discount, dismiss, disparage, -disregard, downgrade, downplay, erase, -eschew, forget, half-ass, hide,

-ignore, knock, lessen, malign, marginalize, mask, minimize, miss, neg, -neglect, obscure, obstruct, -omit, -overlook, pan, quiet, reduce, ridicule, rubbish, -scorn, -shun, sideline, silence, skip, slam, slate, -snub, stifle, subdue, temper, trash, trivialize, undercut, underemphasize, underestimate, undermine, underrate, understate, undervalue, weaken)

PRIORITIZE (+): *accommodate, baby, bolster, coax, coddle, compliment, cosset, favor, featherbed, flannel, flatter, follow, fondle, gratify, grease, heed, honor, humor, indulge, inveigle, mollify, mollycoddle, obey, overindulge, pamper, permit, pet, placate, please, praise, romance, satisfy, soap, soft-soap, soothe, spoil, spoon-feed, stroke, sweet-talk, tolerate, treat, woo* (≠ abase, abuse, banish, belittle, bench, bereave, challenge, debase, declass, degrade, demean, demote, -deny, deport, deprecate, deprive, disfavor, disgrace, downgrade, eject, -exclude, exile, expatriate, expel, humble, humiliate, injure insult, lower, oppose, -refuse, relegate, resist, sideline, transfer, vulgarize, withhold)

PRIZE (←): *draw, eradicate, excavate, extract, extricate, fish, harvest, haul, mine, pluck, pry, pull, remove, select, snatch, take, tear, tow, tug, uproot, weed, withdraw, wrench, wrest, wring, yank* (≠ cram, embed, implant, insert, install, instill, jam, ram, stuff, wedge)

PRIZE (+): *accumulate, admire, adore, affirm, amass, appreciate, archive, cherish, coffer, count, covet, enjoy, enshrine, esteem, fancy, fetishize, gather, guard, heap, idolize, love, preserve, rate, regard, relish, revere, save, savor, seek, squirrel, stash, stockpile, store, treasure, value, worship* (≠ blackguard, chide, -despise, dismiss, disparage, disrespect, -loathe, minimize, mock, ridicule, scold, -scorn, -spurn, squander, undervalue, waste) **(¿) ABSTRACTION ALERT. Concrete goals essential!**

PROBE (←): *analyze, browse, check, compute, consult, cross-examine, cruise, detect, dig, disclose, discover, dissect, examine, explore, eye, eyeball, fathom, feel, grill, hunt, inspect, interrogate, investigate, learn, penetrate, peruse, pierce, plumb, poke, police, prod, prospect, prowl, pump, query, question, quiz, reconnoiter, reference, research, reveal, rifle, scan, scout, scrutinize, search, seek, sift, skim, sound, study, surf, suss, test, thumb, unearth, verify* (≠ -abandon, bury, -bypass, -circumvent, cloak, clothe, cloud, conceal, detour, -discount, disguise, -disregard, drop, forget, hide, -ignore, miss, -neglect, obscure, -overlook, screen, -sidestep, skim, skip)

PROCESS (+): *absorb, acculturate, accustom, adapt, adjust, alphabetize, alter, amalgamate, array, assimilate, attend, automate, blend, catalog, categorize, change, class, classify, clump, cluster, codify, combine, commingle, compartmentalize, condition, convert, coopt, cull, digest, dispose, distinguish, distribute, embody, enculturate, file, fuse, grade, group, habituate, handle, hybridize, identify, incorporate, index, initiate, integrate, intermingle, internalize, list, marshal, mechanize, merge, metabolize, metamorphose, mingle, modify, motorize, naturalize, order, organize, peg, place, prepare, prioritize, range, rank, recast, recategorize, reclassify, recognize, redefine, redesign, redo, reengineer, refashion, refer,* *refine, regenerate, regroup, reimagine, relegate, remake, remodel, rethink, retool, revamp, revise, rework, screen, separate, set, sieve, sift, slot, sort, synthesize, systematize, transfigure, transform, transmute, treat, type, vary, winnow* (≠ -blank, -bypass, confuse, disarrange, -disregard, elaborate, -ignore, jumble, lump, misclassify, missort, mistype, mix, muddle, -neglect, -omit, -overlook, -refuse, -reject, scramble, -shun, -spurn) **(¿) ABSTRACTION ALERT. Concrete goals essential!**

PROCURE (←): *accomplish, accumulate, achieve, acquire, amass, annex, appropriate, attain, bag, beg, buy, capture, carry, catch, claim, clear, compass, cop, corral, download, draw, earn, effect, enlist, finagle, find, gain, garner, get, grab, gross, harvest, import, induce, land, lobby, lubricate, make, manage, net, nobble, notch, obtain, occupy, persuade, pick, pull, purchase, reacquire, realize, reap, recapture, recruit, regain, requisition, rescue, rustle, score, secure, select, smuggle, snag, solicit, source, steal, stockpile, wangle, win, wrangle* (≠ accord, bequeath, bestow, bootleg, commit, comp, confer, contribute, donate, forfeit, furnish, give, grant, hand, lose, market, offer, outbid, outlay, overpay, overspend, own, pay, peddle, pimp, possess, relinquish, sell, -shun, spare, -spurn, squander, starve, stiff, stint, supply, surrender, tender, tithe, volunteer, withhold, yield)

PROD (→): *bore, butt, chuck, crowd, dig, drill, drive, elbow, goad, goose, jab, jog, knock, nudge, perforate, pierce, poke, press, prick, probe, propel, punch, puncture, push, ram, remind, shove, spur, stab, stick, thrust* (≠ -avoid, bar, block, -bypass, -circumvent, -elude, -evade, guard, hamper, impede, pull, shield, -sidestep, skip, skirt, yank)

PROD (→): *adjure, animate, arouse, beseech, blandish, bribe, cajole, coax, convince, drive, egg, encourage, excite, exhort, fast-forward, foment, frogmarch, galvanize, goad, goose, hurry, hustle, impel, implore, importune, incite, inspire, instigate, kindle, march, motivate, move, nag, needle, nudge, persuade, pique, press, pressure, prompt, propel, provoke, push, rabble-rouse, remind, rouse, rush, sic, soft-soap, sound, spark, spur, stimulate, sting, stir, trigger, urge, wheedle* (≠ brake, calm, check, checkmate, constrain, curb, deactivate, delay, demotivate, depress, -deter, discourage, dissuade, foil, -frustrate, -halt, hold, hush, inactivate, inhibit, mellow, mitigate, moderate, monkey-wrench, nobble, pacify, pause, placate, postpone, -prevent, pull, quiet, repress, restrain, schmooze, shelve, short-circuit, slow, soft-sell, stall, stop, stymie, suppress, -thwart)

PRODUCE (→): *advance, assemble, bear, beget, begin, brainstorm, breed, bring, build, catalyze, compose, construct, craft, create, cultivate, decide, deliver, determine, develop, effect, effectuate, enact, encourage, engender, establish, evoke, fabricate, fashion, father, forward, foster, found, further, generate, gestate, greenlight, grow, hatch, inaugurate, induce, initiate, innovate, institute, introduce, invent, invoke, launch, make, manufacture, nourish, nurture, originate, patent, pioneer, prepare, promote, prompt, provoke, ready, render, sculpt, set, sire, spawn, start, whelp, work, yield* (≠ abolish, arrest, check, control, crush, curb, dampen, demolish, destroy, doom, eradicate, erase, exterminate, extinguish, -forbid, impede, inhibit, limit, liquidate, quash, quell, quench, rein, repress, restrain, restrict, retard, scotch, smother, squash, squelch, stifle, subdue, suppress)

PRODUCE (→): *advance, advertise, air, announce, bare, blaze, brandish, bring, broadcast, concede, confess, confide, confirm, demonstrate, discover, display, divulge, exhibit, expose, flash, flaunt, flourish, forward, furnish, give, herald, offer, parade, placard, post, present, proclaim, proffer, provide, publicize, reveal, show, showcase, sound, sport, supply, telegraph, trumpet, uncloak, uncover, unmask, unsheathe, unveil, wave* (≠ camouflage, cloak, cloud, conceal, cover, curtain, disguise, enshroud, hide, holster, mask, obscure, occlude, occult, sheathe, shroud, veil)

PRODUCE (+): *assemble, brainstorm, brew, build, coin, conceive, concoct, construct, contrive, cook, craft, create, design, devise, envisage, erect, establish, fabricate, fashion, father, forge, form, frame, generate, handcraft, hatch, hew, imagine, improvise, institute, integrate, invent, machine, make, manufacture, mint, mold, organize, originate, picture, prefabricate, raise, rear, refashion, remake, sculpt, sew, shape, sire, stitch, structure, unify, unite, visualize, weld* (≠ atomize, break, disassemble, dismantle, dismember, explode, flatten, pulverize, raze, repair, restore, ruin, shatter, shred, smash, splinter, sunder, tatter, tear, topple, unsew, wreck)

PRODUCE (+): *arrange, assemble, bankroll, capitalize, carry, contribute, depict, direct, display, dramatize, enact, exhibit, expose, extend, finance, fund, furnish, give, greenlight, impersonate, make, manage, mount, offer, organize, parade, percolate, perform, play, portray, present, preview, proffer, render, represent, roleplay, show, showcase, stage, underwrite, unveil* (≠ act, bury, close, conceal, defund, end, ensconce, finish, hide, kill, niche, obscure, -reject, shutter, terminate, withhold, write)

PROFANE (/): *abase, abuse, affront, bastardize, befoul, begrime, bestialize, blaspheme, blemish, blight, cheapen, contaminate, corrupt, curse, cuss, damage, damn, debase, debauch, deconsecrate, deface, defame, defile, degrade, demean, demoralize, deprave, depreciate, desacralize, desanctify, desecrate, despoil, destroy, deteriorate, devastate, dilute, dirty, disgrace, dishonor, disrespect, downgrade, efface, flame, flaw, foul, harm, humble, humiliate, hurt, impair, insult, lessen, mar, misapply, misemploy, misuse, mock, muddy, offend, outrage, pervert, pimp, poison, pollute, prostitute, ransack, ravage, revile, ruin, -scorn, shame, soil, spoil, stain, subvert, sully, taint, tar, tarnish, trash, twist, violate, vitiate, warp, weaken, whore, wreck, wrong* (≠ ameliorate, amend, better, bless, clean, cleanse, consecrate, decontaminate, dedicate, devote, dignify, elevate, enhance, ennoble, enrich, enshrine, exalt, fetishize, hallow, honor, improve, moralize, perfect, purify, rarefy, refine, respect, restore, revere, sanctify, treasure, uplift, venerate, worship)

PROFILE (←): *aggregate, amalgamate, analyze, anatomize, appraise, ascertain, assay, assess, assimilate, benchmark, calculate, clarify, classify, compare, compile, consider, construe, contrast, critique, decipher, decode, deduce, define, delineate, depict, determine, discern, dissect, divide, elucidate, estimate, evaluate, examine, expect, explain, explore, extract, extrapolate, gauge, generalize, glean, grok, illustrate, infer, inspect, integrate, interpret, investigate, judge, portray, postulate, predict, probe, process, project, rationalize, read, reckon, reconstruct, reduce, render, resolve, review, sample, scan, scope, scrutinize, search, separate, sift, solve, study, summarize, surmise, suss, synthesize, take, test, theorize, translate, understand, weigh* (≠ assume, -bypass, confuse, -discount, -disregard, distort, forget, guess, -ignore, misapprehend, misconceive, misconstrue, misinterpret, misjudge, mislabel, misread, miss, mistake, misunderstand, mystify, -neglect, -omit, -overlook, perplex, presume, puzzle, scatter, -sidestep)

PROFIT (→): *advantage, aid, assist, award, benefit, bestow, better, bless, content, contribute, delight, deliver, earn, endow, fulfill, fund, furnish, gain, gladden, grant, gratify, gross, help, improve, net, offer, outbid, outlay, overpay, overspend, pay, please, provide, satisfy, serve, supply, support, sustain* (≠ afflict, charge, cost, damage, defund, disadvantage, distress, harm, hinder, hurt, impair, impede, injure, lose, obstruct, ruin, squander, starve, steal, stiff, stint, upset, waste, withhold, worsen)

PROGRAM (+): *appoint, arrange, ask, assign, authorize, automate, book, budget, calculate, calendar, charge, code, coerce, command, commission, compel, compile, compute, conduct, constrain, control, design, direct, draft, edit, engage, engineer, enjoin, enter, estimate, feed, figure, force, formulate, hack, instruct, itemize, lead, list, manage, map, mechanize, oblige, order, overcommit, oversee, petition, plan, poll, prearrange, prioritize, process, regiment, register, reprogram, request, require, schedule, script, set, spearhead, superintend, supervise, synchronize, task, tell, time* (≠ break, -cancel, counteract, crash, damage, derail, destroy, disorder, disorganize, disperse, execute, follow, forget, keep, mind, muddle, -neglect, obey, observe, overturn, rattle, scatter, scramble, spoil, -thwart, unsettle, -veto)

-PROHIBIT (/): *arrest, -balk, ban, banish, bar, barricade, blackball, block, blockade, -boycott, censor, check, checkmate, choke, clog, close, condemn, confound, confront, congest, cordon, criminalize, curb, curse, dam, damn, delay, delegitimize, -deter, disallow, discourage, disqualify, embargo, enjoin, -exclude, -forbid, freeze, -frustrate, gag, -halt, hamper, handicap, hinder, impede, indict, inhibit, intercept, -negate, obstruct, occlude, -omit, oppose, -ostracize, oust, outlaw, picket, -preclude, preempt, -prevent, proscribe, protest, redact, restrain, restrict, scotch, seal, shelve, short-circuit, stall, stem, stonewall, stop, stopper, straight-jacket, stump, stymie, suppress, taboo, tackle, -thwart, -veto, zing* (≠ accept, accord, allow, approve, authorize, buy, command, direct, empower, enable, encourage, endorse, endure, facilitate, grant, grease, greenlight, help, import, include, incorporate, instigate, legalize, legitimize, nudge, order, permit, persuade, promote, push, ratify, recall, reinstate, reinvigorate, require, restore, revive, sanction, stimulate, stomach, support, sustain, tolerate, transact, unblock, uphold, urge, welcome)

PROJECT (→): *adumbrate, aim, anticipate, arrange, await, blueprint, budget, calculate, cast, chart, choreograph, conceive, concert, contemplate, contrive, delineate, design, destine, devise, diagram, draft, envisage, envision, estimate, expect, extrapolate, feature, figure, forecast, frame, gauge, graph, hallucinate, imagine, intend, intrigue, machinate, map, meditate, orchestrate, organize, outguess, outline, plan, plot, predetermine, predict, premeditate, prepare, propose, ready, reckon, scheme, script, shape, sketch, spitball, strategize, target, think, time, visualize* (≠ accept, assume, believe, bemoan, credit, destroy, disbelieve, disorder, disorganize, -disregard, forget, guess, -ignore, lament, mourn, recall, regret, remember, sabotage, scotch, scupper, shelve, trust)

PROJECT (→): *bowl, bunt, butt, cant, cast, catapult, chuck, compel, discharge, drive, fire, flick, fling, goad, heave, hurl, impel, launch, lob, pelt, pitch, precipitate, prod, propel, push, ram, shoot, shove, shunt, sling, throw, thrust, toss, transmit, wing* (≠ block, catch, clasp, clutch, fasten, field, grasp, grip, hold, hook, keep, nail, receive, seize, snatch, take)

PROJECT (→): *absolve, account, accredit, acknowledge, acquit, apply, assign, associate, assume, attach, attribute, blame, brand, cast, charge, cite, conceive, conclude, condone, conjecture, connect, credit, deduce, detect, divine, educe, excuse, explain, extrapolate, fancy, forgive, generalize, guess, imagine, infer, intuit, judge, justify, link, mark, perceive, place, rationalize, recognize, refer, scapegoat, sense, surmise, suspect, theorize, universalize* (≠ ascertain, contradict, contrast, couch, -deny, differentiate, discern, disconnect, distinguish, imply, individualize, prove, separate, sever, sunder) **(¿) ABSTRACTION ALERT. Concrete goals essential!**

PROLONG (→): *accent, accentuate, amplify, attenuate, delay, elongate, enlarge, expand, extend, hamper, hinder, increase, lengthen, maximize, obstruct, pause, postpone, protract, shelve, short-circuit, stall, stretch, sustain, thin* (≠ abbreviate, abridge, accelerate, compress, curtail, -cut, decrease, diminish, fast-forward, grease, hasten, hurry, lessen, lubricate, minimize, reduce, shorten, speed)

PROMISE (+): *affirm, assert, assure, attest, avow, betroth, certify, claim, confirm, contend, contract, convince, corroborate, countersign, declare, demonstrate, depose, engage, ensure, espouse, forswear, guarantee, indicate, insist, insure, maintain, pledge, proclaim, profess, prove, ratify, reassure, safeguard, secure, state, stipulate, swear, testify, trust, validate, verify, vow, warrant* (≠ believe, bluff, breach, break, bullshit, cheat, contradict, debate, deceive, denounce, -deny, disavow, discourage, discredit, disprove, dispute, distrust, double-talk, doubt, -ignore, invalidate, lose, mislead, mistrust, -prohibit, protest, -refuse, -reject, -repudiate, scruple, stiff, suspect, trick) **(¿) ABSTRACTION ALERT. Concrete goals essential!**

PROMOTE (→): *acclaim, advertise, announce, bait, ballyhoo, broadcast, bulletin, champion, circulate, commercialize, disseminate, hustle, hype, laud, limelight, lure, mainstream, market, merchandize, monetize, overestimate, overstate, peddle, pimp, pitch, plug, popularize, praise, presell, promo, promulgate, propagandize, publicize, publish, puff, push, recommend, schmooze, sell, shill, spotlight, telegraph, tout* (≠ attack, battle, conceal, condemn, criticize, critique, deride, discredit, disparage, hide, mock, ridicule, -scorn, slam, suppress)

PROMOTE (+): *abet, advance, advantage, advertise, advocate, aid, assist, back, befriend, benefit, bolster, boost, champion, commend, condone, contribute, develop, encourage, endorse, energize, espouse, favor, forward, foster, further, help, improve, inspire, invigorate, kindle, motivate, nourish, nurture, patronize, prioritize, push, recommend, rubber-stamp, sanction, second, serve, spark, speed, sponsor, spur, stimulate, strengthen, subsidize, succor, support, uphold, urge* (≠ belittle, bench, blackguard, checkmate, condemn, cramp, curb, demote, deride, disrespect, foil, -frustrate, hamstring, harm, hurt, impede, injure, monkey-wrench, muzzle, -prevent, protest, restrain, restrict, scotch, shame, -shun, sideline, slow, -spurn, straightjacket, stymie, -thwart)

PROMOTE (+): *advance, aggrandize, better, dignify, elevate, ennoble, exalt, favor, graduate, honor, increase, magnify, prefer, raise, skip, up, upgrade* (≠ bench, block, daunt, declass, degrade, demote, discredit, disfavor, dishonor, hamper, humble, impair, impede, inhibit, obstruct, shame, -thwart)

PROMPT (→): *activate, advise, aid, arouse, assist, beseech, blandish, bribe, buzz, cajole, coax, convince, cue, draw, drive, egg, encourage, evoke, exhort, fast-forward, foment, frogmarch, goad, hurry, hustle, ignite, impel, implore, importune, incite, induce, inspire, instigate, jog, kick-start, march, mention, midwife, motivate, nag, needle, nudge, persuade, prepossess, press, pressure, prick, prod, propel, provoke, push, refresh, remind, rush, seed, soft-soap, sow, spark, spur, stimulate, stir, suggest, trigger, urge, wheedle* (≠ bind, brake, cage, check, constrain, curb, curtail, deactivate, demotivate, -deter, discourage, dissuade, freeze, -halt, hamper, hinder, hobble, impair, impede, inhibit, leash, nobble, paralyze, pin, restrain, shackle, shelve, slow, soft-sell, stall, still, stop, straightjacket)

PROMPT (+): *advance, beget, begin, brainstorm, breed, bring, catalyze, create, cultivate, decide, determine, develop, effect, effectuate, enact, encourage, engender, establish, father, forward, foster, found, further, generate, hatch, inaugurate, induce, initiate, innovate, institute, introduce, invoke, launch, make, midwife, nourish, nurture, open, originate, pioneer, produce, promote, propose, render, set, sire, spawn, start, trigger, yield* (≠ abolish, arrest, check, clamp, control, cramp, crush, curb, dampen, demolish, destroy, doom, eradicate, erase, exterminate, extinguish, hamstring, impede, inhibit, limit, liquidate, quash, quell, quench, rein, repress, restrain, restrict, retard, scotch, smother, squash, squelch, squench, stifle, subdue, suppress)

PROP (+): *bolster, brace, buoy, buttress, carry, embattle, fortify, harden, hold, maintain, rest, secure, set, shore, stand, stay, steady, steel, strengthen, strut, support, sustain, toughen, truss, underpin, underwrite, uphold* (≠ afflict, capsize, cripple, damage, debilitate, drop, erode, harm, hobble, impair, incapacitate, injure, lame, push, sabotage, scotch, scupper, shrivel, subvert, topple, undermine, unhorse, unseat, weaken, wither, wound)

PROPAGATE (→): *advertise, announce, broadcast, circulate, communicate, convey, diffuse, dispense, disperse, disseminate, dissipate, distribute, impart, proclaim, promote, promulgate, publicize, publish, report, scatter, sow, spread, transfer, transmit* (≠ ban, bury, censor, cloak, collect, conceal, contain, enshroud, gather, -halt, hide, limit, mask, muffle, obscure, redact, restrict, secrete, shroud, silence, stifle, stop, veil)

PROPAGATE (+): *bear, beget, breed, cultivate, culture, engender, farm, father, generate, get, grow, hatch, increase, mother, multiply, parent, produce, proliferate, raise, ranch, rear, reproduce, sire, spawn, spread, whelp* (≠ afflict, collect, decrease, deplete, destroy, diminish, doom, eradicate, erase, finish, gather, glean, harvest, hold, kill, lessen, poison, reduce, slaughter, stunt, weed)

PROPEL (→): *accelerate, actuate, bowl, brainstorm, budge, bulldoze, bump, bunt, butt, cant, cast, catalyze, catapult, chuck, compel, compress, disturb, drive, fire, flick, fling, force, frogmarch, fuel, funnel, goad, grease, hasten, heave, hurl, impel, incite, jam, jolt, launch, lob, manhandle, march, mobilize, move, muscle, nudge, paddle, pelt, pitch, poke, pole, power, precipitate, press, pressure, prod, project, prompt, pump, punt, push, railroad, ram, row, sail, send, shoot, shove, shunt, sling, spur, squash, squeeze, start, steamroller, stimulate, throw, thrust, toss, trigger, wheel, wing* (≠ -avert, ban, bar, brake, cage, capture, catch, check, clasp, clutch, cripple, curb, deactivate, decelerate, -discontinue, disrupt, foil, freeze, grab, grasp, grip, hamper, hamstring, haul, hinder, hobble, hook, impede, inactivate, keep, monkey-wrench, nail, paralyze, postpone, -preclude, -prevent, -prohibit, protest, pull, receive, sabotage, scotch, scupper, seize, shackle, shelve, short-circuit, slacken, stall, stop, subvert, -thwart, tow, yank)

PROPHESY (+): *alert, announce, anticipate, augur, call, caution, declare, divine, forebode, forecast, foresee, foretell, forewarn, harbinger, herald, outguess, portend, predetermine, predict, presage, proclaim, prognosticate, promise, read, soothsay, warn* (≠ ascertain, assure, bemoan, calculate, deduce, demonstrate, describe, determine, ensure, establish, guarantee, insure, lament, mourn, narrate, prove, recite, recount, regret, relate, report, settle, tell)

PROPITIATE (←): *amuse, appease, arbitrate, assuage, baby, blandish, brownnose, butter, cajole, calm, charm, cheer, coax, coddle, comfort, conciliate, console, content, cosset, court, delight, disarm, divert, dulcify, endear, entertain, flannel, flatter, gentle, gladden, glad-hand, gratify, help, humor, hush, indulge, infantilize, ingratiate, lull, mediate, mellow, mitigate, moderate, mollify, mollycoddle, overprotect, pacify, pamper, placate, please, quiet, reconcile, referee, reunite, satisfy, schmooze, soften, soft-pedal, soothe, spoil, stroke, sugarcoat, sweeten, sweet-talk, tranquilize, wheedle, win, woo* (≠ affront, aggravate, agitate, anger, annoy, antagonize, bother, bug, burden, chafe, challenge, cross, discomfort, distress, disturb, enrage, exasperate, fret, gall, harass, harry, heckle, hound, incense, inflame, infuriate, insult, irk, irritate, lynch, madden, nag, needle, nettle, nitpick, offend, oppose, outrage, peeve, persecute, perturb, pester, provoke, rankle, rile, roil, rouse, ruffle, troll, unhinge, unsettle, upset, vex, victimize, weary, worry, wound, wrong)

PROPOSE (→): *adduce, advance, advise, advocate, affirm, assert, bounce, broach, contend, counsel, file, introduce, invite, lodge, move, name, nominate, offer, pitch, place, plan, pose, prefer, present, press, proffer, proposition, propound, recommend, request, slate, solicit, spare, spitball, state, submit, suggest, table, tender, urge, volunteer, vote* (≠ blackball, blacklist, castigate, condemn, criticize, denounce, -deny, fulminate, oppose, -refuse, -reject, slate, -snub, -veto, withhold)

PROPOSE (→): *aim, arrange, attempt, calculate, chart, consider, contemplate, contrive, cover, debate, design, destine, dream, frame, hope, intend, map, mind, mull, plan, plot, ponder, purport, scheme, shape, target, try, wish* (≠ check, consult, contradict, cross-examine, disbelieve, distrust, doubt, dread, fear, grill, interrogate, oppose, question, -refuse, -reject, repulse, scruple, -spurn, suspect)

PROPOSITION (→): *accost, address, approach, ask, bed, bother, bug, buttonhole, coax, confront, detain, flatter, hint, hustle, importune, insinuate, inveigle, molest, persuade, pester, pose, prefer, propose, pursue, schmooze, seduce, solicit, suggest, waylay* (≠ alarm, bully, caution, coerce, daunt, demand, -deny, force, insist, intimidate, menace, muscle, nauseate, obligate, railroad, -refuse, -reject, repulse, warn)

PROSECUTE (/): *accuse, allege, arraign, blame, charge, cite, compel, contest, criticize, fault, finger, frame, impeach, implicate, impugn, incriminate, indict, involve, litigate, negotiate, process, reproach, subpoena, sue, summon, try* (≠ -abandon, acquit, alibi, condone, defend, -desert, exonerate, forgive, -forsake, free, ingratiate, liberate, pardon, release, relinquish, -renounce, represent, -repudiate, retract, spare, vacate, vindicate)

PROSTITUTE (→): *abase, abuse, auction, bastardize, bedraggle, befoul, begrime, bestialize, blemish, canker, cheapen, commercialize, commodify, contaminate, corrupt, damage, debase, debauch, deface, defile, degrade, demean, demoralize, deprave, desecrate, destroy, deteriorate, dilute, dirty, disgrace, dishonor, downgrade, flaw, hard-sell, harm, hawk,* *humble, humiliate, hurt, impair, lessen, mar, market, misapply, mismanage, misuse, monetize, nobble, pervert, pimp, poison, pollute, profane, promote, ruin, sell, shame, spoil, stain, suborn, subvert, taint, tarnish, thin, twist, vitiate, vulgarize, warp, weaken, whore, wreck* (≠ ameliorate, amend, apply, better, clarify, clean, cleanse, dignify, elevate, employ, enhance, ennoble, enrich, exalt, honor, improve, moralize, perfect, purify, refine, respect, restore, uplift, use, utilize)

PROSTRATE (/): *bulldoze, capsize, castrate, checkmate, cripple, crush, damage, debilitate, defeat, deplete, depress, destroy, devitalize, disable, disarm, drain, drown, emasculate, enervate, enfeeble, exhaust, fatigue, fell, flatten, floor, frazzle, hamstring, harm, hurt, immobilize, impair, impoverish, incapacitate, injure, invalid, kneecap, lame, leech, level, mow, oppress, outlast, overcome, overextend, overpower, overset, overthrow, overtire, overturn, overwhelm, paralyze, reduce, ruin, sap, shrivel, soften, steamroller, subdue, subvert, tire, topple, unhorse, unman, unseat, waste, weaken, weary, wither, wizen, wrack, wreck* (≠ activate, aid, assist, assuage, build, construct, create, embattle, enable, encourage, energize, erect, fight, fortify, harden, help, improve, increase, inure, invigorate, mobilize, please, raise, recruit, refresh, rejuvenate, repair, right, save, season, soothe, straighten, strengthen, toughen, vitalize, weaponize)

PROTECT (+): *accommodate, advantage, aid, archive, arm, armor, assist, assure, -avert, baby, bar, barricade, battle, bear, benefit, bless, blockade, blunt, bolster, brave, budget, buffer, bulwark, bury, buttress, camouflage, champion, chaperone, chauffeur, cloak, clothe, cloud, cocoon, combat, commemorate, conceal, confront, conserve, continue, cosset, costume, cotton, counter, counterattack, cover, cradle, cushion, defend, deflect, disguise, embalm, embattle, ensconce, ensure, escort, face, favor, fence, fight, forfend, fortify, foster, galvanize, gestate, gratify, guarantee, guard, harbor, heal, hedge, help, hide, house, humor, indemnify, infantilize, inoculate, insulate, insure, keep, maintain, mask, mind, mother, nourish, nurse, nurture, oblige, obscure, oppose, outlast, pamper, parry, patrol, patronize, perpetuate, placate, please, police, preserve, -prevent, prove, rebut, rescue, reserve, resist, retain, retort, retrieve, return, reward, safeguard, salvage, sanction, save, screen, secure, shade, shelter, shield, shingle, shroud, spare, stand, stonewall, store, stow, strengthen, support, survive, sustain, tolerate, uphold, ward, watch, weather, withhold, withstand, wrap* (≠ -abandon, abuse, accost, anguish, assail, assault, atomize, attack, backstab, beset, besiege, betray, blitz, bombard, boobytrap, compromise, constrain, curb, damage, deep-six, defame, defile, demolish, -desert, destroy, discipline, disparage, dissipate, doom, double-cross, endanger, eradicate, erase, expose, forfeit, -forsake, harass, harm, hurt, imperil, impugn, injure, jeopardize, liquidate, lose, lynch, malign, maltreat, menace, molest, nuke, obliterate, oppress, outrage, overrun, persecute, pervert, plunder, profane, pulverize, ravish, raze, relinquish, -renounce, reproach, revile, risk, ruin, sabotage, scotch, scupper, scuttle, shatter, shelve, sic, sicken, slander, spend, squander, storm, submit, subvert, surrender, target, threaten, torment, traumatize, two-time, undercut, undermine, upset, vandalize, vaporize, vex, victimize, vilify, violate, weed, wound, wrong, yield)

PROTEST (/): *abhor, argue, -balk, blast, boo, -boycott, break, buck, censure, challenge, combat, criticize, critique, dare, debate, defy, denounce, disapprove, disobey, dispute, -disregard, except, fight, flout, gag, hassle, kick, mock, nag, oppose, picket, -prohibit, -reject, resist, revolt, ridicule, -scorn, -spurn, stick, subvert, violate, withstand* (≠ accede, accept, advocate, applaud, approve, champion, cheer, commend, congratulate, defend, follow, gold-star, gratify, maintain, mind, obey, observe, praise, sanction, support, sustain, uphold)

PROVE (+): *affirm, analyze, ascertain, assay, attest, authenticate, back, certify, check, confirm, contextualize, convince, corroborate, crosscheck, declare, demonstrate, detect, determine, document, double-check, establish, evidence, evince, examine, explain, externalize, find, fix, justify, manifest, notarize, settle, show, substantiate, sustain, test, testify, try, uphold, validate, verify, warrant, witness* (≠ abrogate, allege, annul, -cancel, challenge, contradict, debate, -deny, disavow, disclaim, -discount, discredit, disprove, dispute, distrust, doubt, embellish, embroider, falsify, guess, hypothesize, invalidate, presume, pulverize, rebut, refute, scruple, shake, shatter, surmise, suspect, theorize, wonder)

PROVIDE (→): *accommodate, add, administer, afford, allocate, apportion, arm, arrange, assign, bestow, bootleg, bring, budget, cater, cede, contribute, deal, deed, deliver, dish, dispense, distribute, dole, dollop, equip, favor, feather, feed, fit, force-feed, fuel, furnish, give, grant, hand, impart, implement, indulge, keep, lend, line, maintain, mete, offer, outfit, overfeed, parcel, portion, prepare, present, procure, produce, proffer, provision, ration, ready, render, repair, replenish, serve, spare, stake, stock, store, supply, support, sustain, tender, transfer, victual, volunteer, yield* (≠ block, conserve, demand, -deny, deprive, disarm, famish, hoard, hold, keep, maintain, malnourish, poach, preserve, -refuse, -reject, remove, reserve, retain, save, scant, skimp, starve, steal, stint, take, underfeed, withhold)

PROVISION (→): *accoutre, allocate, allot, apportion, arm, assign, bestow, contribute, deal, disburse, dispense, distribute, dole, donate, equip, fit, fortify, furnish, gird, give, hand, mete, outfit, parcel, portion, prepare, present, prorate, rig, stock, store, supply, tender, tithe, transfer, yield* (≠ appropriate, arrogate, confiscate, -decline, -deny, deprive, dispossess, divest, -forsake, -neglect, pinch, -refuse, -reject, retain, scant, skimp, stint, strip, withdraw, withhold)

PROVISION (→): *banquet, batten, board, cater, fatten, feast, feed, fill, force-feed, fuel, hand-feed, nourish, nurture, overfeed, regale, reprovision, satisfy, serve, spoon-feed, surfeit, sustain, victual* (≠ contaminate, -deny, deprive, famish, husband, malnourish, poison, remove, scant, skimp, spoil, starve, stint, stockpile, underfeed, waste, withhold)

PROVOKE (→): *anger, animate, annoy, arouse, attract, awaken, bait, bother, challenge, drive, egg, electrify, elicit, encourage, energize, enrage, enthuse, entice, exasperate, excite, fan, ferment, fire, foment, fuel, gall, galvanize, goad, ignite, impassion, incite, incur, induce, inflame, infuriate, inspire, instigate, invigorate, irritate, jeer, kindle, lure, madden, motivate, move, pique, prime, prod, prompt, quicken, rabble-rouse, raise, rally, rev, revitalize, rouse, spark, spur, stimulate, stir, subvert, tantalize, taunt, tease, tempt, tickle, titillate, trigger, troll, upset, vex, vitalize, wake, whet* (≠ appease, bore, calm, deaden, debilitate, demoralize, demotivate, desensitize, -deter, discourage, dispirit, dissuade, drain, enervate, exhaust, fatigue, frustrate, gratify, humor, hush, lull, mellow, mitigate, moderate, mollify, numb, pacify, paralyze, placate, relax, sedate, soothe, stall, stem, stifle, stymie, subdue, -thwart, tire, tranquilize, trouble, weary)

PROVOKE (+): *abet, activate, advance, animate, arouse, birth, breed, brew, call, create, cultivate, detonate, drive, elicit, encourage, energize, engender, enliven, evoke, excite, fan, ferment, fire, foment, form, forward, foster, further, galvanize, generate, hatch, ignite, impassion, incite, incur, induce, inflame, initiate, inspire, instigate, invigorate, kindle, liven, lubricate, make, motivate, move, nourish, nurture, originate, pick, pique, precipitate, produce, proliferate, promote, prompt, propagate, quicken, raise, rev, rouse, roust, set, sow, spark, spawn, stimulate, stir, trigger, vitalize* (≠ allay, appease, bridle, cage, calm, check, constrain, curb, deactivate, demotivate, depress, discourage, dismay, end, exterminate, -forbid, freeze, -halt, hamper, hamstring, hobble, hold, impede, inhibit, kill, lull, mellow, mitigate, moderate, mollify, neutralize, numb, pace, pacify, paralyze, placate, -prevent, -prohibit, protest, quiet, regulate, rein, restrain, sadden, settle, smother, soothe, still, straightjacket, subdue, tame, -thwart, tranquilize)

PROVOKE (/): *abrade, affront, aggravate, agitate, anger, annoy, antagonize, appall, bait, beget, bother, bug, chafe, condemn, criticize, dare, defy, denounce, deride, destabilize, detonate, discompose, disconcert, disrupt, dominate, earbash, enrage, exacerbate, exasperate, fan, fire, fret, gall, galvanize, generate, harangue, harass, harry, hassle, heckle, hector, hound, incense, incite, inflame, infuriate, instigate, insult, irk, irritate, jeer, judge, knock, madden, miff, mock, motivate, nag, needle, nettle, niggle, nitpick, offend, perturb, pester, pique, promote, quicken, rattle, -refuse, -reject, ridicule, rile, roil, rouse, ruffle, sabotage, set, slam, slate, subvert, taunt, tease, threaten, topple, torment, traumatize, trigger, troll, undercut, undermine, upset, vex, wound* (≠ alleviate, amuse, beguile, bore, cajole, calm, charm, coax, daunt, distract, divert, drain, entertain, exhaust, fascinate, flannel, gentle, glad-hand, gratify, help, humor, hush, jade, leech, lull, mellow, mitigate, moderate, mollify, pacify, placate, schmooze, sedate, soft-soap, soothe, subdue, sweet-talk, tire, tranquilize, weary)

PRUNE (/): *barber, bob, clip, crop, curtail, -cut, dock, eliminate, -exclude, groom, gut, lop, manicure, mow, neaten, nip, pare, pinch, poll, pollard, reduce, shape, shave, shear, shorten, skive, snip, stump, thin, tidy, trim,* *whittle* (≠ accept, augment, cultivate, elongate, extend, fertilize, include, lengthen, -neglect, nurture, tangle, thicken, untidy, welcome)

PUBLICIZE (→): *acclaim, advertise, advise, announce, apprise, bait, ballyhoo, bark, bellow, bill, billboard, blare, blaze, blazon, blurb, broadcast, bulletin, circulate, commercialize, commodify, communicate, confess, confirm, declare, disclose, disseminate, divulge, endorse, enunciate, feature, flash, hail, herald, hustle, hype, impart, inform, intimate, introduce, laud, limelight, lure, mainstream, manifest, market, merchandize, notify, overestimate, overstate, peddle, pimp, pitch, placard, plug, popularize, post, praise, presell, proclaim, promo, promote, promulgate, publish, puff, push, recommend, release, report, reveal, review, sell, shill, show, sound, spotlight, spread, telegraph, tout, trumpet* (≠ axe, bury, conceal, contain, cover, criticize, disparage, ensconce, hide, hush, kill, niche, quash, recall, recant, repress, restrain, retract, revoke, -scorn, silence, slam, smother, spin, stifle, suppress, withhold)

PULL (←): *attract, carry, cart, conduct, convey, convoy, dislocate, drag, draw, ferry, fetch, grab, haul, heave, hump, jerk, lug, move, relay, schlep, ship, tow, trail, transport, truck, tug, yank* (≠ -abandon, boost, discard, drive, drop, force, forfeit, impel, jam, nudge, propel, punt, push, ram, -refuse, scrap, shove, thrust)

PULL (←): *acquire, appropriate, choose, compile, confiscate, cull, debit, deduct, exact, extract, gather, glean, grab, gut, mine, obtain, pick, pluck, prize, pry, quarry, recover, remove, rip, seize, select, slurp, snag, source, suck, take, tear, uninstall, uproot, vacuum, weed, wheedle, withdraw, worm, wrench, wrest, wring, yank* (≠ -avoid, cram, -decline, dismiss, drop, -ignore, implant, insert, install, instill, jam, jettison, leave, lose, -overlook, ram, -refuse, -reject, -spurn, stuff, wedge, withhold)

PULL (←): *absorb, adduce, allure, amuse, attract, bear, bewitch, bring, captivate, carry, charm, convey, drag, draw, enchant, engage, engross, enthrall, entice, fascinate, fetch, galvanize, grip, hypnotize, induce, intrigue, invite, involve, lure, magnetize, mesmerize, obsess, obtain, pick, preoccupy, rally, secure, seduce, stimulate, tantalize, taunt, tease, tempt, transfer, transport, vamp, win* (≠ annoy, block, bore, bug, chill, deaden, demoralize, desensitize, -deter, discourage, disgust, dissuade, drain, exhaust, fatigue, frustrate, irk, irritate, knacker, numb, -omit, oppose, paralyze, -prevent, protest, -reject, release, repel, repulse, -shun, stifle, warn) **(¿) ABSTRACTION ALERT. Concrete goals essential!**

PULL (/): *bruise, cripple, damage, dislocate, harm, hurt, impair, injure, lame, rend, rip, sprain, strain, stress, stretch, tax, tear, turn, twist, weaken, wound, wrack, wrench* (≠ adjust, align, alleviate, bandage, bind, brace, doctor, dress, heal, mend, nurse, push, remedy, repair, restore, soothe, splint, strap, treat)

PULP (/): *beat, bruise, compress, contort, crush, demolish, distort, flatten, grind, liquidize, macerate, mash, pestle, pound, powder, press, pulverize, purée, shred, smash, squash, squeeze, squoosh, stamp, trample*

(≠ assemble, assist, build, craft, form, generate, heal, inflate, mold, nurture, preserve, protect, reconstruct, renovate, shape, support)

PULVERIZE (/): *annihilate, atomize, beat, best, blast, break, bust, checkmate, clobber, comminute, conquer, crack, cream, cripple, crumb, crumble, crunch, crush, damage, dash, decimate, deface, defeat, demolish, desolate, despoil, destroy, deteriorate, devastate, dilapidate, disassemble, disfigure, disintegrate, dismantle, dissolve, doom, drub, dynamite, efface, eradicate, erode, expunge, exterminate, extinguish, extirpate, flatten, fracture, fragment, grate, grind, gut, hammer, harm, impair, injure, kibble, lick, liquidate, loot, mangle, mar, master, mill, mince, mortar, mutilate, nuke, obliterate, overcome, pestle, pillage, plunder, pound, powder, pulp, ravage, raze, remove, root, rout, ruin, sack, savage, scotch, scour, shatter, skunk, smash, snuff, splinter, spoil, squash, stamp, subdue, surmount, tear, thrash, total, trample, trash, trim, trounce, unbuild, undo, unmake, vandalize, vanquish, vaporize, vitiate, wallop, waste, wax, wear, whip, wrack, wreck* (≠ armor, assemble, build, conserve, constitute, construct, craft, create, doctor, erect, establish, fabricate, fashion, father, fix, forge, form, found, frame, institute, invent, machine, maintain, make, manufacture, mend, mold, organize, patch, preserve, produce, protect, raise, rear, rebuild, recondition, reconstruct, remodel, renovate, repair, restore, revamp, revive, save, sculpt, shape, shield, survive, sustain, weather, withstand)

PUMMEL (→): *assail, assault, attack, backhand, bang, bash, bat, batter, beat, belabor, belt, beset, birch, blackjack, bludgeon, box, break, buffet, bust, cane, chop, clobber, clout, club, concuss, conk, cowhide, crack, crumble, crunch, crush, cudgel, cuff, dash, drub, flagellate, flog, fracture, fragment, gore, grate, hammer, hide, hit, horsewhip, knock, lace, lacerate, lash, lick, maim, mangle, mash, maul, mutilate, organize, paddle, paste, patch, pelt, pistol-whip, pommel, pound, pulverize, punch, raid, ram, rawhide, rush, savage, scourge, shatter, slam, slap, slate, slug, smack, smash, sock, spank, splinter, storm, strap, strike, swat, swipe, switch, tan, thrash, thresh, thump, thwack, trounce, wallop, whack, whale, wham, whip, whomp, whup, wound* (≠ -avoid, bar, block, counterpunch, cover, defend, deflect, -deter, -dodge, -duck, -escape, guard, -halt, hamper, harbor, hinder, miss, parry, protect, repel, safeguard, save, screen, shelter, shield, stonewall, stop, -thwart, withstand)

PUMP (→): *bob, dilate, distend, drive, elevate, force, gush, inflate, inject, jerk, jet, jiggle, jog, jounce, push, rock, screw, send, shake, spout, spurt, supply, sway, swell, swing, wiggle* (≠ drain, draw, extract, leach, leech, remove, sap, settle, siphon, stabilize, steady, tap)

PUMP (←): *bleed, cannibalize, clean, clear, consume, debilitate, decant, deplete, depredate, draft, drain, draw, effuse, empty, evacuate, exhaust, extract, flush, leach, leech, milk, pour, purge, remove, siphon, suck, tap, vacate, vacuum, void, withdraw* (≠ add, bathe, deluge, douse, drench, drizzle, drown, fill, flood, furnish, inundate, marinate, overflow, replenish, restore, soak, souse, stock, submerge, supply, swamp, trickle, wash, water, wet)

PUMP (←): *annoy, ask, canvas, catechize, challenge, check, coax, cross-examine, cross-question, debrief, disbelieve, dispute, doubt, examine, grill, hammer, harass, hound, interrogate, interview, investigate, nag, needle, niggle, nitpick, pester, poll, probe, query, question, quiz, research, roast, test* (≠ answer, conceal, confide, distort, -evade, fabricate, feign, hide, hoodwink, -ignore, mislead, -neglect, silence, staunch, stifle, stonewall)

PUNCH (→): *backhand, bang, bash, bat, batter, bean, beat, belt, biff, black, blast, blitz, bludgeon, bob, boff, bonk, bop, box, brain, buffet, bump, bung, bunt, bust, butt, cane, chop, clap, clip, clobber, clock, clout, club, conk, counterpunch, crack, cream, cudgel, cuff, dab, deck, ding, drub, fell, flail, flick, flog, floor, hammer, hit, hook, jab, jog, jostle, kick, knee, knock, lace, lambaste, lash, level, lick, mangle, maul, nail, nudge, paste, pelt, pepper, plug, poke, pommel, pop, pound, prod, pummel, push, rabbit-punch, ram, rap, rough, sap, scuff, shove, skull, slam, slap, slash, sledge, sledgehammer, slug, smack, smash, smite, sock, spear, stab, stamp, stone, strike, stroke, sucker-punch, swat, swipe, switch, tap, thrash, thrust, thump, thwack, trash, uppercut, wallop, whack, whale, whip, wind, zap* (≠ aid, assist, -avoid, block, brave, cajole, coddle, compliment, counter, defend, deflect, -dodge, -duck, endure, flatter, guard, help, -ignore, miss, parry, praise, preserve, protect, repel, secure, shield, soothe, steady, stroke, suffer, support, tap, weather)

PUNCTURE (→): *bayonet, bore, burst, crack, cut, deflate, drill, gaff, gimlet, gore, harpoon, impale, inject, insert, invade, jab, kebab, knife, lance, mainline, nick, peck, penetrate, perforate, pick, pierce, pike, pin, pink, poke, prick, probe, prong, punch, riddle, rupture, shank, shiv, shoot, skewer, spear, spike, spit, stab, stake, stick, thrust, transfix* (≠ absorb, armor, block, close, defend, deflect, eject, extract, fill, fuse, heal, inflate, mend, patch, plug, praise, protect, prove, rectify, repair, seal, sew, shield, smooth, stitch, withdraw, yank)

PUNISH (/): *afflict, assess, avenge, bang, batter, beat, belt, bench, blacklist, blister, cane, castigate, charge, chasten, chastise, condemn, convict, correct, criticize, critique, crucify, damn, defrock, demote, denounce, disadvantage, discipline, dismiss, dock, execute, exile, expel, fine, flagellate, flog, ground, hang, harm, hide, hurt, immure, impose, imprison, incarcerate, injure, institutionalize, intern, jail, judge, keelhaul, kneecap, lash, lather, lecture, levy, lick, maltreat, misuse, oppress, paddle, penalize, rebuke, reprimand, reprove, revenge, scold, scour, scourge, sentence, sideline, slap, slipper, slug, smack, spank, starve, stiff, stint, strafe, strap, strike, switch, tan, thrash, thwack, torture, train, trounce, wallop, whack, whip, wreak* (≠ absolve, acquit, baby, blame, coddle, commute, compensate, condone, cosset, defend, excuse, exonerate, forfeit, forgive, honor, incriminate, indemnify, lionize, -neglect, overindulge, -overlook, pamper, pardon, patronize, pay, praise, protect, ransom, release, remunerate, reward, shield, spare, vindicate)

PURCHASE (←): *accumulate, achieve, acquire, add, amass, annex, assume, attain, bag, bid, buy, capture, catch, claim, collect, cop, corner, download, earn, fetch, finance, gain, garner, get, harvest, incur, invest, land, lure, negotiate, net, obtain, offer, outbid, outlay, overpay, overspend, palm, patronize, pay, pick, pocket, procure, reap, receive, retrieve, score, secure, select, source, stockpile, take, trade, truck, underpay, win, wrangle* (≠ bandy, barter, bootleg, borrow, broker, commercialize, commodify, deal, discard, dispense, dole, exchange, forfeit, freeboot, give, hawk, -ignore, import, loan, lose, market, merchandize, miss, monetize, peddle, pilfer, pirate, poach, presell, remainder, renegotiate, retail, sell, spare, spend, steal, stiff, stint, swap, swipe, vend, volunteer, withhold)

PURGE (/): *abolish, absolve, acquit, amend, annihilate, annul, anonymize, barf, blackball, blot, -cancel, clarify, cleanse, clear, deep-six, delete, depose, destroy, disgorge, dismiss, doom, efface, eject, elevate, empty, enhance, ennoble, eradicate, erase, excrete, exonerate, exorcise, expel, expiate, expunge, exterminate, extinguish, extirpate, forgive, heal, improve, kill, liquidate, obliterate, oust, pardon, -prevent, protest, purify, raze, refine, regenerate, regurgitate, remove, restore, rid, sanctify, spew, spit, splutter, unload, unpack, uplift, vindicate, vomit, wash, weed, wipe* (≠ accumulate, bastardize, bear, bestialize, build, collect, compile, construct, corrupt, create, debase, debauch, defile, degrade, demean, deprave, dirty, gather, gestate, glean, herd, hold, incorporate, incriminate, institute, invite, keep, maintain, pervert, plant, poison, possess, profane, prostitute, recycle, rehabilitate, retain, salvage, scavenge, spike, stain, stockpile, suborn, sully, survive, sustain, tarnish, warp, weather, welcome, withstand)

PURIFY (+): *aerate, bolt, chasten, clarify, clean, cleanse, clear, decontaminate, delouse, deodorize, disinfect, distill, expurgate, extract, filter, freshen, fumigate, leach, process, purge, quarantine, rarefy, rectify, refine, sanitize, screen, scrub, sieve, sift, sterilize, wash* (≠ bedraggle, begrime, besmirch, cloud, contaminate, dirty, dull, foul, infect, muddy, poison, pollute, soil, spike, stain, sully, taint, tarnish)

PURIFY (+): *absolve, acquit, amend, cleanse, clear, consecrate, dedicate, devote, elevate, ennoble, exonerate, expiate, hallow, heal, improve, moralize, perfect, purge, rarefy, rectify, redeem, refine, regenerate, restore, sanctify, shrive, uplift, vindicate* (≠ bestialize, corrupt, debase, debauch, defile, degrade, demean, deprave, disgrace, incriminate, pervert, poison, profane, prostitute, stain, suborn, sully, taint, tarnish, violate, warp)

PURLOIN (←): *abduct, appropriate, boost, burglarize, burgle, carjack, cheat, collar, defalcate, defraud, embezzle, filch, glom, grab, grasp, heist, hijack, hook, kidnap, lift, loot, misappropriate, mooch, nab, nail, nick, nip, nobble, pick, pilfer, pillage, pinch, pluck, plunder, poach, pocket, ransack, remove, rifle, rob, rustle, sack, seize, shanghai, shoplift, snaffle, snag, snatch, sneak, snitch, spirit, sponge, steal, swindle, swipe, take, thieve* (≠ add, bestow, buy, comp, contribute, defend, donate, earn, give, guard, hand, increase, keep, offer, present, protect, purchase, receive, recover, -refuse, -reject, replace, rescue, restore, return, save, secure, shield, tender, volunteer)

PURSUE (→): *accompany, attend, backtrack, badger, bait, bird-dog, bug, chaperone, chase, chivy, court, desire, dog, entice, escort, eye, ferret, fish, follow, forage, harass, harry, haunt, hound, hunt, investigate, learn, mob, observe, oppress, persecute, plague, retrace, ride, romance, root, run, scent, search, seek, shadow, spoor, stalk, study, tag, tail, target, trace, track, trail, watch, win, woo* (≠ -abandon, aid, assist, -avoid, banish, blind, -boycott, cease, conceal, deceive, direct, -discontinue, disguise, -dodge, -duck, -eschew, expel, -flee, forget, -forsake, guide, -halt, head, help, hide, -ignore, lead, leave, lose, miss, muddle, -neglect, pilot, shake, -shun, spearhead, stop, support, -thwart, trick)

PUSH (→): *accelerate, bore, budge, bulldoze, bump, butt, compress, constrain, cram, crash, crowd, crush, depress, dig, drive, elbow, fast-forward, force, frogmarch, gore, grease, hasten, hurry, hustle, impel, jam, jolt, jostle, knock, launch, manhandle, march, move, muscle, nudge, plunge, poke, press, pressure, prod, propel, punt, railroad, ram, shift, shoulder, shove, shunt, sideswipe, squash, squeeze, squish, squoosh, steamroll, stir, strong-arm, thrust* (≠ bridle, check, constrain, contain, curb, delay, discourage, dissuade, drag, end, finish, hamper, hinder, hold, impede, inhibit, keep, pace, pause, postpone, pull, regulate, rein, repress, restrain, shelve, short-circuit, slow, stall, stop, weight)

PUSH (→): *advance, advertise, boost, commercialize, commodify, float, hawk, hype, leverage, limelight, market, monetize, offer, peddle, pimp, plug, presell, prioritize, promote, propagandize, publicize, puff, sell, shill, spitball, tout, traffic* (≠ acquire, attack, buy, camouflage, cloak, cloud, combat, conceal, disguise, hide, import, mock, procure, purchase, ridicule, scathe, -scorn, secure, seek, -shun)

PUSH (+): *bribe, browbeat, bulldoze, catalyze, champion, coerce, compel, constrain, convince, dragoon, egg, encourage, escalate, expedite, fast-track, force, frogmarch, further, goad, goose, hasten, hurry, impel, influence, inspire, march, motivate, muscle, oblige, persuade, press, pressure, prod, promote, railroad, speed, spur, squeeze, steamroll, strong-arm, urge* (≠ -cancel, cripple, daunt, demotivate, -deter, discourage, hamper, hamstring, hinder, kneecap, nobble, postpone, -prevent, protest, quell, scotch, shelve, stifle, stymie, suppress, -thwart)

PUZZLE (/): *abash, addle, agitate, amaze, baffle, bamboozle, beat, befog, befuddle, beguile, bemuse, bewilder, block, boggle, bother, buffalo, chagrin, cloud, confound, confuse, cozen, daze, deceive, delude, discombobulate, discomfit, discomfort, discompose, disconcert, dismay, disorient, disquiet, distress, disturb, double-talk, dumbfound, dupe, embarrass, encode, faze, floor, flummox, fluster, foil, fool, fox, frustrate, gaslight, gull, harass, hoax, hobble, hocus-pocus, hoodwink, humbug, impede, jumble, manipulate, misguide, mislead, mismatch, mortify, muddle, muddy, mystify, nonplus, obscure, obstruct, outwit, perplex, perturb, rattle, scatter, snow, stick, stump, stun, stupefy, surprise, tangle, throw, -thwart, trick, trouble, unhinge, unsettle, upset, vex* (≠ assure, clarify, decipher, decode, deduce, derange, detect, distract, edify, educate, -elude, enlighten, explain, floodlight, illuminate, inform, instruct, profile, reassure, satisfy, school, simplify, solve, teach, train, tutor, untangle)

Q

QUAFF (←): *belt, consume, down, drain, drink, empty, gulp, guzzle, hoist, imbibe, ingest, kill, lap, lick, mouth, nip, pledge, pound, sip, slug, slurp, suck, swallow, swig, swill, toast* (≠ barf, belch, crave, decant, -decline, disgorge, eject, expel, fill, pour, puke, -refuse, regurgitate, -reject, spew, spill, spit, vomit)

QUALIFY (←): *adapt, alleviate, alloy, alter, assuage, circumscribe, classify, color, define, delimit, diminish, distort, ease, lessen, limit, minimize, misrepresent, misstate, mitigate, moderate, modify, modulate, narrow, pace, pervert, reduce, regulate, restrain, restrict, soften, temper, twist, underemphasize, warp, weaken* (≠ accent, accentuate, affirm, align, amplify, assert, boost, broaden, emphasize, exacerbate, expand, magnify, maximize, prioritize, punctuate, raise, supplement, widen) **(¿) ABSTRACTION ALERT. Concrete goals essential!**

QUALIFY (+): *accredit, accustom, adapt, adjust, affirm, allow, approve, authorize, calibrate, certify, clear, coach, commission, compare, condition, confirm, credential, educate, empower, enable, endorse, enfranchise, entitle, equip, fit, graduate, groom, ground, habituate, inaugurate, indoctrinate, induct, initiate, install, instate, instruct, invest, legalize, legitimize, let, license, okay, pass, permit, prepare, privilege, ratify, ready, rubber-stamp, sanction, school, season, shape, tailor, teach, train, tutor, validate, vest, warrant* (≠ ban, bar, block, constrain, decertify, delegitimize, -deny, disable, disallow, disbar, discourage, disenfranchise, disqualify, enjoin, -exclude, -forbid, hinder, hold, impede, inhibit, -interdict, invalidate, -nullify, obstruct, -omit, oppose, outlaw, -prevent, -prohibit, proscribe, protest, stop, -veto)

QUANTIFY (←): *appraise, ascertain, assess, benchmark, calculate, calibrate, caliper, check, compare, compute, count, deduce, detect, determine, enumerate, evaluate, figure, gauge, measure, number, numerate, rank, rate, read, size, specify, time, value, weigh* (≠ assume, distrust, estimate, fudge, grill, guess, half-ass, -ignore, interrogate, misgauge, mistrust, -omit, -overlook, question, suspect, wonder)

QUASH (/): *abrogate, annihilate, annul, beat, -cancel, checkmate, conquer, crush, decimate, deep-six, defeat, demolish, desolate, destroy, devastate, dissolve, dominate, doom, douse, eradicate, erase, exterminate, extinguish, invalidate, -negate, nuke, obliterate, outlast, outwit, overcome, overpower, override, overrule, overthrow, overturn, overwhelm, quell, quench, repeal, repress, -rescind, reverse, revoke, ruin, scotch, silence, smash, smother, snuff, squash, squelch, squench, steamroller, stifle, strangle, subdue, subjugate, suppress, throttle, vanquish, -veto,*

-void, waste, weed, wreck (≠ abet, advance, aid, approve, assist, back, bolster, buttress, confirm, cultivate, encourage, enforce, establish, foment, forward, foster, further, help, incite, instigate, maintain, nourish, nurture, perpetuate, promote, prop, provoke, rabble-rouse, stir, support, survive, sustain, uphold, urge, validate, withstand)

QUELL (/): *allay, alleviate, appease, assuage, beat, calm, capture, checkmate, compose, conciliate, conquer, console, cool, crush, deaden, defeat, defuse, demilitarize, demolish, destroy, doom, ease, extinguish, foil, humble, hush, lull, master, mellow, minimize, mitigate, moderate, mollify, monkey-wrench, muzzle, overcome, overpower, pacify, placate, quash, quiet, reconcile, relieve, repress, reunite, rout, sedate, silence, smooth, soften, soothe, squash, stabilize, stifle, still, subdue, subject, subjugate, suppress, tranquilize, trounce, trump, vanquish* (≠ accentuate, advance, affirm, aggravate, agitate, amplify, assert, assist, back, cultivate, deepen, disturb, emphasize, encourage, exacerbate, excite, foment, foster, incite, instigate, intensify, irritate, magnify, maximize, militarize, nourish, nurture, prolong, promote, prompt, provoke, punctuate, rabble-rouse, reinvigorate, revive, start, stimulate, stir, strengthen, support, tease, unnerve, upset)

QUENCH (←): *allay, alleviate, appease, assuage, check, content, engorge, fill, glut, gorge, gratify, lighten, mitigate, relieve, sate, satiate, satisfy, saturate, slake, stuff, surfeit* (≠ arouse, entice, exacerbate, excite, frustrate, ignite, inflame, kindle, light, provoke, stimulate, tantalize, taunt, tease, tempt, trigger)

QUENCH (/): *annihilate, burke, choke, cool, crush, dampen, decimate, demolish, dismantle, douse, end, hush, kill, moisten, muffle, quash, quell, raze, repress, ruin, shatter, smother, snuff, stifle, strangle, suppress, throttle, wreck* (≠ bake, barbecue, broil, burn, fire, ignite, inflame, kindle, light, scorch, sear, survive, withstand)

QUESTION (→): *assail, attack, berate, censure, challenge, combat, contest, criticize, critique, defy, discredit, disprove, dispute, distrust, doubt, fight, impeach, impugn, malign, mistrust, oppose, protest, query, resist, revile, traduce, vilify, vituperate* (≠ abide, accept, advocate, await, back, believe, champion, defend, embrace, endure, promote, stomach, support, swallow, tolerate, withstand)

QUESTION (←): *annoy, ask, besiege, blitz, bombard, canvass, catechize, challenge, check, consult, contest, cross-examine, cross-question, debate, debrief, disbelieve, dispute, distrust, doubt, examine, explore, grill, hammer, harass, hector, hound, interrogate, interview, investigate, nag, needle, niggle, nitpick, pester, poll, probe, pump, query, quiz, research, survey, suspect, test* (≠ answer, assert, attest, -avoid, conceal, confide, -duck, -evade, hide, -ignore, mislead, -neglect, observe, remark, retort, silence, stifle, validate, verify)

QUESTION (←): *absorb, analyze, assimilate, believe, chew, conceive, conclude, consider, contemplate, debate, deliberate, digest, entertain,* *examine, explore, eye, eyeball, incorporate, integrate, learn, mull, ponder, reason, reinvestigate, review, second-guess, study, turn, weigh, wrestle* (≠ disbelieve, -discount, discredit, dismiss, -disregard, distrust, -ignore, invalidate, mistrust, -neglect, -overlook, pooh-pooh, -reject, -repudiate, -scorn, scruple, -slight, -spurn, suspect)

QUESTION (/): *challenge, debunk, -deny, disavow, disbelieve, -discount, discredit, distrust, doubt, dread, fear, invalidate, mistrust, -negate, -rebuff, rebut, refute, -reject, -repudiate, scruple, suspect, wonder* (≠ accept, adjudge, anticipate, assume, assure, await, believe, credit, debunk, detect, determine, expect, fancy, presume, prove, suppose, trust, verify)

QUICKEN (→): *accelerate, activate, advance, aid, bundle, catalyze, dispatch, drive, ease, encourage, expedite, facilitate, fast-forward, fast-track, frogmarch, goad, grease, hasten, hurry, lubricate, march, midwife, oil, precipitate, press, prod, propel, push, race, rush, speed, spur, supercharge, urge, whisk* (≠ arrest, brake, check, cripple, decelerate, delay, disqualify, dull, encumber, enervate, fetter, hamper, hinder, hobble, hold, impede, incapacitate, manacle, obstruct, pause, postpone, rein, restrain, retard, shackle, shelve, short-circuit, slow, stall, stay, still, stop, stymie, -thwart, tie, trammel)

QUICKEN (→): *abet, activate, actuate, amp, animate, arouse, awaken, boost, brace, buoy, charge, cheer, drive, electrify, embolden, energize, enkindle, enliven, excite, exhilarate, ferment, fire, foment, fortify, galvanize, ginger, hearten, impel, incite, inflame, infuse, inspire, instigate, invigorate, jazz, juice, jump-start, kindle, lift, liven, motivate, move, prioritize, provoke, raise, rally, reactivate, reanimate, reawaken, recharge, recreate, reenergize, refresh, regenerate, reinvigorate, rejuvenate, rekindle, renew, resurrect, resuscitate, revitalize, revive, rouse, spark, spike, steel, stimulate, stir, strengthen, tantalize, tease, tempt, trigger, vitalize, vivify, wake* (≠ cage, check, cripple, curb, damp, dampen, daunt, deactivate, deaden, debilitate, demoralize, discourage, dishearten, dispirit, drain, dull, enervate, enfeeble, exhaust, fatigue, freeze, hamper, handicap, harass, hinder, impair, impede, inhibit, jade, kill, overextend, paralyze, quell, quench, repress, restrain, sap, slake, slow, stagnate, stall, still, straightjacket, stunt, suppress, tucker, undermine, weaken, wear, weary)

QUIET (←): *allay, alleviate, appease, assuage, calm, comfort, compose, curb, deaden, diminish, dose, drug, dull, ease, gag, hush, hypnotize, lower, lull, mellow, mesmerize, mitigate, moderate, mollify, muffle, mute, muzzle, narcotize, pacify, placate, quell, quieten, reduce, relax, sedate, settle, shush, silence, smooth, sober, soften, soothe, squelch, squench, stifle, still, subdue, suppress, throttle, tranquilize* (≠ agitate, alarm, alert, disturb, exacerbate, excite, goad, harass, heckle, hound, incite, irk, irritate, jab, nettle, noodge, panic, pester, prod, provoke, rankle, rattle, roil, rouse, shake, spur, stimulate, stir, tease, torment, traumatize, vex, wake)

QUIZ (←): *annoy, ask, besiege, bombard, canvas, canvass, catechize, challenge, check, consult, contemplate, cross-examine, cross-question,* *debate, debrief, deride, dispute, earbash, examine, explore, gibe, grill, harass, hector, hound, interpolate, interrogate, interview, investigate, mock, nag, needle, niggle, nitpick, pester, poll, probe, prove, pump, puzzle, query, question, scrutinize, seek, survey, test* (≠ answer, -avoid, bury, cheat, conceal, deceive, disguise, -disregard, -duck, forget, hide, -ignore, -neglect, observe, -omit, retort, solve, study, trick)

RACE (→): *battle, beat, best, better, challenge, confront, defeat, double, eclipse, -elude, engage, escalate, exceed, excel, face, fight, hasten, hurry, increase, jockey, jostle, maneuver, match, multiply, oppose, outclass, outdo, outmatch, outperform, outplay, outrank, outrun, outshine, outstrip, overtake, pass, play, pound, raise, resist, rival, rush, surpass, test, train, win, work* (≠ -abandon, brake, bungle, cede, concede, cripple, delay, drop, follow, forfeit, hamper, help, hinder, hobble, impede, lose, relinquish, -renounce, ruin, sacrifice, slow, stall, waive, wreck)

RAID (→): *ambush, assail, assault, attack, battle, beleaguer, beset, besiege, blindside, blitz, blockade, bomb, bombard, breach, bum-rush, burglarize, burgle, bushwhack, bust, charge, combat, conquer, crush, despoil, devastate, dominate, envelop, fight, flank, forage, garrison, gate-crash, harass, harry, heat, infringe, invade, invest, loot, maraud, mob, mug, nuke, occupy, overcome, overpower, overrun, overwhelm, pillage, pirate, plunder, press, rake, ransack, ravage, rifle, rob, rush, sack, sandbag, seize, shell, steamroller, storm, strafe, strike, strip, subdue, subject, subjugate, surprise, swarm, sweep, torpedo, trash, trespass, vanquish, waste, waylay* (≠ aid, assist, build, cede, construct, convince, cover, defend, defy, guard, help, invite, oppose, patrol, persuade, police, protect, repel, resist, restore, safeguard, save, screen, secure, sentinel, shelter, shield, support, survive, ward, welcome, withstand)

RAILROAD (→): *badger, blackjack, bludgeon, bluff, bogart, browbeat, bulldoze, bully, bullyrag, coerce, command, compel, constrain, control, cow, decree, demand, dictate, direct, dragoon, drive, enforce, force, frogmarch, guide, hound, hustle, impel, intimidate, make, march, muscle, oblige, order, press, press-gang, pressure, push, require, sandbag, steamroll, steamroller, steer, strong-arm, threaten, trample, urge* (≠ allow, argue, bait, beg, beseech, bribe, cajole, coax, console, convince, court, entice, gauge, induce, influence, inspire, lubricate, lure, midwife, move, permit, persuade, request, romance, satisfy, schmooze, solicit, sway, tantalize, tease, tempt, trigger, win, woo)

RAISE (→): *advance, animate, ascend, boost, brace, brighten, buttress, crane, elate, elevate, encourage, erect, escalate, heave, heft, hike, hoist, jack, levitate, lift, mount, pitch, prop, rear, shore, soar, up, upend, uphold, uplift, upraise* (≠ bear, capsize, demolish, depress, dip, drop, flatten, knock, level, lower, pitch, plunge, press, push, raze, sink, submerge, topple)

RAISE (→): *accelerate, accentuate, accrue, accumulate, add, aggrandize, amass, amplify, assert, augment, beef, boost, broaden, build, bump, catalyze, collect, complement, compound, deepen, develop, dilate,* *distend, double, elongate, emphasize, enhance, enlarge, ennoble, escalate, exalt, excite, exhilarate, expand, extend, fatten, flesh, foster, grow, hearten, heighten, hype, increase, inflate, intensify, lengthen, magnify, maximize, multiply, optimize, overhaul, prioritize, prolong, promote, protract, pump, punctuate, ratchet, reinforce, revolutionize, spike, steel, stir, stoke, strengthen, stretch, supersize, supplement, support, swell, treble, triple, up, upgrade, widen* (≠ abate, abbreviate, abridge, compress, concentrate, condense, constrict, contract, curtail, decrease, de-escalate, downsize, lessen, lower, minimize, reduce, shorten, subtract, underemphasize)

RAISE (→): *acclaim, advance, affirm, aggrandize, apotheosize, applaud, bless, boost, celebrate, cite, commend, commission, compliment, congratulate, decorate, deify, deputize, elevate, empower, enfranchise, enhance, ennoble, enshrine, entitle, eulogize, exalt, extol, fetishize, forward, further, glorify, gratify, hail, heighten, honor, idolize, improve, knight, laud, lift, lionize, magnify, ordain, praise, prioritize, promote, salute, treasure, upgrade, uplift, worship* (≠ abase, bastardize, belittle, bench, bestialize, blacklist, blast, boo, censure, condemn, criticize, critique, damn, debase, declass, decry, degrade, demean, demote, denounce, depose, dethrone, diminish, disgrace, dishonor, dismiss, disparage, downgrade, expel, humble, humiliate, impeach, incriminate, lessen, lower, mortify, oust, overthrow, raze, reduce, remove, reproach, ruin, shame, sideline, topple, unhorse, unmake, unseat, weaken, wrack, wreck)

RAISE (→): *advertise, air, announce, articulate, broach, broadcast, circulate, cite, communicate, convey, debate, declare, define, describe, discuss, disseminate, expound, express, give, interject, interrupt, introduce, mention, name, offer, place, proclaim, propose, publish, sound, spitball, state, submit, suggest, telegraph, vent, ventilate, verbalize, vocalize, voice, volunteer, write* (≠ ban, blue-pencil, bowdlerize, censor, cut, delete, edit, erase, expurgate, hush, quiet, redact, rephrase, restrain, restrict, silence, stifle, strike, suppress) **(¿) ABSTRACTION ALERT. Concrete goals essential!**

RAISE (←): *accrue, accumulate, add, amass, arouse, ask, assemble, beckon, bewitch, call, charm, collect, compel, conjure, cultivate, elicit, evoke, externalize, gather, generate, glean, hoard, increase, invite, invoke, manifest, materialize, muster, obtain, prompt, provoke, pull, rally, recruit, salvage, scavenge, source, stimulate, stockpile, summon, welcome* (≠ banish, decrease, deliver, disperse, dissipate, dissuade, distribute, divide, donate, drop, expel, give, lessen, lose, oust, pay, -prevent, protest, reduce, -refuse, scatter, spend, squander, tender, tithe, waste)

RAISE (+): *adopt, advance, attend, breed, cradle, crop, cultivate, culture, develop, direct, discipline, dress, edify, educate, enlighten, father, feed, forward, foster, further, gather, generate, germinate, glean, grow, guide, harvest, hatch, indoctrinate, instruct, lead, mentor, mind, mother, nourish, nurse, nurture, parent, plant, prepare, produce, promote,* *propagate, quicken, reap, rear, ripen, root, school, shelter, shepherd, show, sire, sow, spawn, sprout, supply, teach, tend, train, tutor, watch* (≠ abuse, curb, cut, dig, discourage, extirpate, harm, harvest, hay, hinder, hobble, hurt, -ignore, ill-treat, injure, kill, maltreat, mishandle, mistreat, mow, mutate, -neglect, pick, pluck, pulverize, ruin, shatter, stifle, stunt, uproot, wreck, wrong)

RALLY (→): *animate, awaken, boost, comfort, encourage, foment, improve, incite, inspire, invigorate, prod, quicken, reactivate, reanimate, reawaken, recover, reestablish, refresh, reintroduce, reinvigorate, rekindle, renew, restore, resurrect, resuscitate, revitalize, revive, rouse, stimulate, strengthen, wake* (≠ bore, bug, burden, checkmate, curb, dampen, debilitate, depress, -deter, discourage, disenchant, dishearten, dissuade, downplay, enervate, exhaust, -frustrate, -halt, hamper, hamstring, hinder, impede, inhibit, quell, quench, restrain, sap, sicken, slow, stunt, tax, tire, undermine, weaken, weary)

RALLY (←): *assemble, collect, congregate, conjure, convene, gather, group, herd, integrate, marshal, mobilize, muster, organize, reassemble, reform, regroup, reorganize, reshape, retool, summon, unify, unite* (≠ alienate, detach, diffuse, disaffect, disconnect, dislodge, dismiss, disperse, divide, estrange, foil, isolate, leave, monkey-wrench, -ostracize, oust, part, scatter, seclude, segregate, send, separate, split, spread, -thwart)

RAM (→): *attack, bang, bash, beat, bounce, brush, bulldoze, bump, butt, charge, contact, crash, dash, drive, drum, elbow, graze, hammer, hit, horn, impact, jostle, kiss, knock, land, muscle, nudge, poke, pound, press, push, ricochet, scrape, shave, skim, skip, slam, smash, stab, stem, stick, strike, sweep, swipe, touch* (≠ -avoid, -bypass, -circumvent, deflect, -evade, miss, parry, -rebuff, -sidestep, sideswipe, skirt, stroke, strum, tap)

RAM (→): *compress, cram, crowd, crush, drive, fill, force, heap, jam, jam-pack, load, pack, sandwich, sardine, shoehorn, sink, squeeze, stuff, tamp, tap, thrust, wedge* (≠ cull, drag, draw, ease, extract, glean, pluck, prize, pull, remove, strip, tug, withdraw, wrench, wrest, yank)

RANK (+): *align, alphabetize, arrange, array, assort, catalog, categorize, class, classify, clump, cluster, codify, compare, compartment, compartmentalize, contextualize, coordinate, cull, digest, dispose, distinguish, distribute, establish, estimate, evaluate, eyeball, file, fix, gauge, grade, group, hierarchize, identify, include, index, judge, juxtapose, list, locate, marshal, order, organize, peg, pigeonhole, place, position, prioritize, range, rate, recognize, refer, regard, relegate, screen, separate, set, shelve, sieve, sift, situate, slot, sort, systematize, tab, type, typecast, valuate, value, winnow* (≠ churn, confuse, disarrange, disorder, disorganize, jumble, level, lump, misclassify, misgauge, missort, mistype, mix, scatter, scramble)

RANKLE (/): *affront, aggravate, agitate, anger, annoy, antagonize, bother, bug, burn, canker, chafe, chagrin, cross, earbash, embitter,* *enrage, exasperate, fret, gall, get, harass, heckle, hector, hound, hurt, incense, inflame, infuriate, irk, irritate, madden, miff, mortify, nag, needle, nettle, niggle, nitpick, nonplus, noodge, offend, outrage, pain, peeve, pester, pique, plague, provoke, rile, roil, ruffle, torment, troll, unnerve, upset, vex, weary, worry* (≠ allay, alleviate, appease, assuage, buoy, calm, captivate, charm, comfort, console, delight, disarm, favor, gratify, humor, hush, hypnotize, lull, mellow, mesmerize, mitigate, moderate, mollify, pacify, placate, please, quiet, relax, relieve, satisfy, sedate, settle, smooth, soothe, stabilize, steady, still, tranquilize)

RANSACK (←): *ascertain, audit, browse, check, comb, descry, detect, determine, discover, dredge, examine, explore, ferret, find, fish, frisk, hit, hunt, inspect, investigate, learn, locate, peruse, probe, prowl, rake, review, rifle, rummage, scan, scour, scrutinize, search, seek, sound, spy, study, survey* (≠ -abandon, bury, conceal, cover, disguise, ensconce, hide, -ignore, leave, lose, -neglect, niche, obscure, stash, tuck, veil, withhold)

RANSACK (/): *appropriate, burglarize, burgle, comb, depredate, despoil, devastate, filch, gut, harry, hunt, loot, maraud, overhaul, pilfer, pillage, pinch, plunder, poach, purloin, raid, rake, rape, ravage, ravish, rifle, rob, rustle, sack, seize, spoil, steal, strip, thieve, toss* (≠ clean, defend, fill, give, guard, hoard, hold, keep, maintain, neaten, offer, order, organize, patrol, preserve, protect, receive, repair, restore, right, save, secure, shield, straighten, tidy)

RANSOM (+): *bail, buy, deliver, emancipate, extricate, free, liberate, pay, recover, redeem, regain, release, repay, reprise, rescue, retrieve, salvage, save, unchain, unfetter* (≠ abduct, blackmail, coerce, demand, disappear, extort, extract, hijack, kidnap, persecute, shanghai, steal, stiff, stint, victimize)

RAPE (/): *abuse, assault, attack, debauch, defile, deflower, degrade, demean, demote, desecrate, despoil, devastate, humiliate, impregnate, inseminate, loot, maltreat, molest, mortify, penetrate, pillage, plunder, raid, ransack, ravage, ravish, rob, ruin, sack, seduce, strip, torment, violate, wreck, wrong* (≠ benefit, comfort, console, defend, dignify, guard, heal, honor, nurture, obey, preserve, protect, purify, rescue, respect, revere, save, shield, vindicate)

RATE (+): *analyze, appraise, ascertain, assay, assess, benchmark, calculate, categorize, class, classify, compare, compute, conclude, consider, contrast, correlate, count, critique, decide, deduce, determine, discover, esteem, estimate, evaluate, eyeball, figure, gauge, grade, guesstimate, hierarchize, judge, learn, measure, misjudge, misprize, price, prioritize, rank, reappraise, reassess, reckon, reevaluate, regard, sample, settle, subdivide, survey, test, time, underestimate, undervalue, value, weigh* (≠ accept, assume, dismiss, -disregard, excuse, -ignore, miss, -neglect, -overlook, pardon, pooh-pooh, predetermine, -reject, skip, -slight)

RATIFY (+): *accept, accredit, acknowledge, affirm, allow, approve, authenticate, authorize, back, bless, canonize, certify, champion, clear,* *confirm, corroborate, countersign, enable, endorse, establish, favor, finalize, formalize, initial, legalize, legitimate, legitimize, license, notarize, okay, pass, permit, reapprove, recommend, rubber-stamp, sanctify, sanction, seal, second, sign, support, uphold, validate, warrant* (≠ abolish, ban, -decline, delegitimize, -deny, disallow, disapprove, -disregard, enjoin, -forbid, -ignore, -interdict, invalidate, -negate, negative, -neglect, oppose, -overlook, -prohibit, proscribe, -rebuff, rebut, -refuse, -reject, -renounce, repeal, -repudiate, revoke, -spurn, turn down, -veto)

RATION (→): *accord, administer, afford, allocate, allot, allow, apportion, assign, award, bestow, budget, chunk, confer, conserve, contribute, deal, deliver, designate, dispense, distribute, divide, dole, dollop, donate, earmark, furnish, give, grant, impart, issue, limit, measure, mete, meter, parcel, part, portion, present, proffer, prorate, provide, reallocate, reapportion, reassign, redistribute, reserve, restrain, restrict, save, share, split, supply, tender* (≠ accept, acquire, appropriate, arrogate, begrudge, commandeer, confiscate, -deny, deprive, impound, keep, lavish, obtain, procure, -rebuff, -refuse, -reject, -rescind, retain, revoke, rob, seize, squander, stint, swipe, withhold)

RATIONALIZE (+): *absolve, acquit, attribute, clear, condone, confirm, contextualize, defend, establish, exculpate, excuse, exonerate, explain, forgive, justify, maintain, pardon, prove, spare, spin, substantiate, support, sustain, uphold, validate, verify, vindicate, warrant* (≠ berate, blame, chastise, chide, condemn, criticize, critique, curse, damn, fault, finger, -forsake, incriminate, punish, rebuke, rebut, refute, scold, -scorn)

RATTLE (/): *addle, agitate, alarm, bash, bewilder, bother, bug, confound, confuse, daunt, discombobulate, discomfit, discompose, disconcert, discountenance, disorient, disquiet, distract, distress, disturb, embarrass, faze, flummox, frighten, harrow, haunt, horrify, indispose, intimidate, menace, mismatch, muddle, nonplus, panic, perplex, perturb, petrify, puzzle, rile, roil, ruffle, scare, shake, shock, spook, terrify, threaten, throw, unman, unnerve, unsettle, upset* (≠ appease, assure, balance, buoy, calm, center, cheer, clarify, comfort, compose, console, educate, encourage, enlighten, explain, gladden, gratify, hearten, help, lull, mellow, mitigate, moderate, mollify, organize, pacify, placate, please, quiet, reassure, regiment, relieve, sedate, soothe, stabilize, steady, still, tranquilize)

RAVAGE (/): *annihilate, bulldoze, burgle, cannibalize, capture, consume, crack, cream, crush, damage, decimate, demolish, depredate, desecrate, desolate, despoil, destroy, devastate, dismantle, disorganize, disrupt, doom, eradicate, erase, exterminate, extinguish, forage, fracture, fragment, gut, harry, impair, level, loot, maraud, nuke, obliterate, overpower, overrun, overthrow, overwhelm, pillage, pirate, plunder, prostrate, pulverize, raid, rape, raze, rob, ruin, sack, scourge, seize, shatter, sink, smash, spoil, strip, total, trample, trash, vaporize, waste, wrack, wreck, wrest* (≠ advantage, aid, armor, fix, guard, help, inspire, maintain, mend, patch, patrol, protect, recondition, recover, rectify, redeem, rehabilitate, repair, restore, resuscitate, revamp, shield, spark, survive, sustain, weather, withstand)

RAVISH (←): *absorb, allure, amuse, attract, bewitch, captivate, charm, delight, draw, elate, enchant, engage, enrapture, enthrall, entice, entrance, excite, exhilarate, fascinate, galvanize, gladden, gratify, grip, hold, hypnotize, intrigue, magnetize, mesmerize, monopolize, obsess, please, possess, preoccupy, satisfy, seduce, spellbind, stimulate, stir, thrill, transport, wow* (≠ annoy, appall, -balk, bore, bother, bug, burden, dampen, deaden, demoralize, depress, desensitize, discourage, disenchant, disgust, disillusion, dispirit, drain, dull, enervate, exhaust, fatigue, frustrate, infuriate, irk, irritate, knacker, nauseate, needle, nettle, numb, offend, paralyze, repel, repulse, sadden, sicken, stifle, tire, trouble, underwhelm, vex, weary, worry)

RAVISH (/): *abduct, abuse, assault, attract, bewitch, captivate, charm, debauch, defile, deflower, delight, enchant, enrapture, enthrall, entice, entrance, fascinate, force, maltreat, molest, oppress, outrage, rape, ruin, spellbind, violate, wrong* (≠ benefit, cherish, conserve, defend, displease, guard, nurture, protect, purify, respect, sanctify, shield, sustain, tend, uphold, vindicate)

RAZE (/): *abolish, annihilate, atomize, bulldoze, -cancel, crush, -cut, decimate, demolish, desolate, destroy, devastate, disintegrate, dismantle, doom, dynamite, efface, eradicate, erase, explode, exterminate, extirpate, fell, flatten, level, obliterate, pulverize, ruin, smash, topple, vaporize, wreck* (≠ brace, build, -bypass, construct, defend, develop, embattle, erect, fabricate, fortify, foster, guard, keep, maintain, manufacture, protect, raise, rear, shield, steady, strengthen, survive, sustain, weather, withstand)

REACH (→): *access, accomplish, achieve, acquire, actualize, approach, attain, bag, beat, capture, carry, claim, complete, consummate, contact, crest, draw, earn, effect, equal, execute, find, finish, fulfill, gain, garner, get, grasp, hit, land, log, make, manage, match, meet, net, notch, obtain, outdo, perform, procure, produce, realize, rival, score, secure, surpass, tie, top, touch, win* (≠ -abandon, accord, attempt, begin, consider, cordon, fail, forfeit, -forsake, give, grant, lose, miss, part, pay, ponder, relinquish, start, surrender, try, undershoot, yield) **(¿) ABSTRACTION ALERT. Concrete goals essential!**

REACH (→): *accrue, amplify, augment, broaden, continue, deepen, develop, elongate, enlarge, expand, extend, increase, intensify, lengthen, maximize, project, prolong, protract, spread, stretch, unwind, widen* (≠ compress, condense, contract, curtail, decrease, diminish, draw, lessen, minimize, reduce, shorten, shrink, shrivel, tense)

REACH (→): *brush, caress, contact, feel, finger, fondle, grasp, graze, handle, hit, hold, pat, pet, skim, strike, stroke, strum, tap, tickle, touch* (≠ -avoid, -bypass, -circumvent, -disregard, -dodge, -duck, -elude, -evade, miss, outwit, -overlook, -refuse, -shun, -sidestep, -thwart)

REACH (→): *access, acquaint, address, advise, apprise, approach, brief, buzz, call, clue, contact, email, enlighten, familiarize, get, inform, instruct, message, notify, phone, ring, telephone, tell, text, write* (≠ belie, conceal, distort, garble, hide, hush, -ignore, miscommunicate, misinform, mislead, misrepresent, -neglect, obscure, suppress, withhold)

REACH (→): *affect, afflict, agitate, allure, attract, bewitch, bias, bother, captivate, charm, color, concern, dazzle, discomfort, discompose, disquiet, distress, disturb, enchant, energize, engage, enrapture, enthrall, entrance, excite, fascinate, fluster, harass, harry, impact, impress, influence, inspire, interest, intrigue, involve, move, penetrate, perturb, pester, pierce, plague, ravish, smite, stimulate, stir, strain, stress, strike, sway, touch, transport, trouble, try, upset, worry, wring* (≠ annoy, bore, bother, bug, -circumvent, dampen, deaden, desensitize, dispirit, drain, exhaust, fatigue, frustrate, irk, jade, knacker, miss, nag, needle, nettle, numb, paralyze, stagnate, tire, trouble, underwhelm, vex, weary, worry) **(¿) ABSTRACTION ALERT. Concrete goals essential!**

READ (→): *articulate, communicate, declaim, deliver, depict, describe, detail, enumerate, impart, lecture, narrate, perform, portray, pronounce, recite, recount, rehearse, relate, repeat, report, speak, spiel, spout, tell, unfold, utter, verbalize, vocalize* (≠ attend, baffle, bewilder, bury, conceal, -disregard, heed, hush, miss, muddle, muddy, mystify, -neglect, observe, perplex, puzzle, quiet, silence, watch)

READ (←): *analyze, assess, benchmark, browse, categorize, classify, clock, consume, devour, examine, explore, eye, eyeball, inspect, investigate, peruse, prioritize, probe, proofread, rank, rate, review, riffle, scan, scope, scrutinize, search, sift, skim, speed-read, study* (≠ chronicle, communicate, compose, correct, create, draft, edit, -ignore, jumble, misinterpret, misread, miss, notate, -overlook, pen, punctuate, record, rephrase, scramble, scribble, tweak, write)

READ (←): *appreciate, apprehend, browse, catch, comprehend, construe, consult, decipher, decode, deduce, detect, devour, diagnose, discern, examine, fathom, gobble, grasp, grok, interpret, learn, make, penetrate, perceive, peruse, profile, proofread, pry, question, regard, review, scan, scrutinize, skim, speed-read, study, survey, suss, translate, understand, view* (≠ -blank, confuse, -disregard, distort, forget, garble, -ignore, jumble, miscommunicate, misconstrue, misdiagnose, mishear, misinterpret, misread, misrepresent, miss, mistake, misunderstand, -overlook, scramble, skim, twist)

READ (←): *anticipate, augur, call, comprehend, construe, decipher, decode, divine, forecast, foretell, harbinger, interpret, outguess, predetermine, predict, presage, prognosticate, prophesy, understand* (≠ describe, narrate, recite, recount, regret, relate, report, spiel, tell)

READY (→): *arm, arrange, assemble, barber, batten, bestow, boot, brace, compose, construct, cook, curry, develop, devise, draft, dress, educate, embattle, endow, equip, fabricate, fashion, fit, fix, forearm, formulate,* *fortify, foster, frame, furnish, gather, get, gird, groom, gussy, incline, indoctrinate, instruct, lay, make, manicure, marshal, mobilize, mount, order, organize, outfit, predispose, prep, prepare, prime, provide, regiment, school, sculpt, seize, set, spread, steel, strengthen, supply, train, tutor, uncomplicate, warm, weaponize* (≠ arrogate, baffle, botch, bungle, confiscate, confuse, -deny, deprive, disorganize, divest, forget, fumble, half-ass, mangle, mismanage, preempt, -refuse, remove, rob, ruin, sabotage, scant, scotch, scupper, scuttle, sequester, shelve, skimp, starve, stint, strip, undermine, usurp, withdraw, withhold, wreck)

READY (+): *accustom, adapt, adjust, alert, arrange, authorize, cock, condition, customize, educate, empower, enable, entitle, equip, fit, groom, habituate, indoctrinate, instruct, license, order, organize, prepare, prime, qualify, school, season, set, shape, tailor, teach, train, tutor* (≠ conceal, deceive, delude, discombobulate, disorganize, gaslight, hide, mislead, mismatch, -neglect, -omit, -overlook, traumatize, wound)

READY (+): *animate, arm, bolster, boost, brace, buoy, buttress, case-harden, cheer, comfort, embolden, encourage, energize, enforce, enliven, excite, exhilarate, fire, forearm, fortify, freshen, harden, hearten, inspire, inure, invigorate, liven, motivate, nerve, poise, prioritize, prop, psych, quicken, rally, reassure, refresh, reinforce, rejuvenate, renew, revitalize, rouse, season, steel, stimulate, stir, strengthen, support, sustain, tone, toughen, uncomplicate, vitalize, weaponize* (≠ abuse, alarm, baffle, bewilder, chagrin, confuse, daunt, debilitate, demoralize, demotivate, -deter, discomfit, discourage, dishearten, dismay, dispirit, disturb, embarrass, enervate, enfeeble, fluster, nonplus, overextend, perplex, prostrate, psych, rattle, ruffle, sap, shake, soften, startle, surprise, terrorize, tire, undercut, undermine, unnerve, unsettle, upset, weaken)

REAP (←): *accumulate, bag, capture, crop, cut, fish, forage, garner, gather, glean, grow, harvest, hay, hunt, mow, net, pick, raise, select, snare, stockpile, trap* (≠ bury, diffuse, grow, hand, implant, lose, miss, plant, -reject, relinquish, scatter, seed, sow, squander, starve, transplant, waste)

REAP (←): *accomplish, accumulate, achieve, acquire, actualize, amass, annex, attain, bag, capture, carry, catch, claim, clear, collect, compile, derive, download, draw, earn, gain, garner, get, gross, land, make, net, notch, obtain, occupy, procure, reacquire, realize, reattain, recapture, receive, recycle, regain, remake, salvage, scavenge, score, secure, source, stockpile, take, win* (≠ accord, bequeath, bestow, forfeit, give, grant, hand, lose, misunderstand, offer, part, pay, relinquish, spare, steal, stiff, stint, surrender, tender, volunteer, yield)

REAR (+): *advance, attend, bottle-feed, breed, cradle, cultivate, develop, direct, discipline, edify, educate, enlighten, father, feed, forward, foster, further, guide, hatch, indoctrinate, instruct, lead, mentor, mind, mother, nourish, nurse, nurture, parent, prepare, promote, provide, raise, school, shelter, shepherd, show, sire, supply, teach, train, tutor, watch* (≠ abuse, damage, destroy, doom, eradicate, erase, harm, hurt, -ignore, ill-treat, impair, injure, maltreat, mishandle, mistreat, mutate, -neglect, pervert, stifle, stymie, subvert)

REASSURE (+): *allay, alleviate, amuse, assuage, assure, bolster, boost, brace, buoy, buttress, calm, cheer, comfort, console, convince, cross-check, elevate, embolden, encourage, ensure, fortify, gratify, guarantee, hearten, humor, inspire, invigorate, lift, lull, mellow, mitigate, moderate, mollify, nerve, pacify, placate, prove, quiet, rally, relax, relieve, settle, solace, soothe, stabilize, steady, stimulate, strengthen, sustain, tranquilize, uplift* (≠ aggravate, agitate, alarm, anguish, annoy, bother, bug, crucify, demoralize, demotivate, discourage, dishearten, distress, exacerbate, exasperate, fret, harass, heckle, hound, intensify, irk, irritate, nag, needle, nettle, niggle, nitpick, panic, pester, terrify, torment, torture, troll, trouble, unnerve, upset, vex, worry, worsen)

REBUILD (+): *adapt, adjust, better, craft, doctor, enhance, fix, gentrify, improve, mend, modernize, optimize, overhaul, patch, perfect, reassemble, recondition, reconstitute, reconstruct, rectify, refashion, refurbish, rehabilitate, rejuvenate, remake, remodel, renew, renovate, repair, reproduce, reshuffle, restore, restructure, retool, revamp, revolutionize, service, tune, tweak, update, upgrade* (≠ annihilate, blemish, boobytrap, break, crack, cripple, damage, deep-six, deface, demolish, destroy, disable, disfigure, dismantle, doom, efface, eradicate, erase, flaw, fracture, harm, harshen, hurt, impair, injure, maim, mangle, mar, mutilate, -neglect, nuke, obliterate, pulverize, raze, ruin, sabotage, savage, scotch, scupper, shatter, spoil, topple, vandalize, wreck)

REBUKE (/): *abuse, admonish, assail, attack, badmouth, belittle, berate, blackguard, blame, blast, blister, boo, castigate, censure, chastise, chide, condemn, countercheck, criticize, critique, crucify, demean, demonize, denounce, denunciate, deprecate, deride, disparage, disrespect, diss, excoriate, fault, finger, flay, fry, fulminate, gibbet, hammer, harangue, impugn, incriminate, jaw, jeer, keelhaul, knock, lambaste, lash, lecture, lesson, mock, oppose, pan, pillory, punish, rag, rate, ream, reprimand, reproach, reprove, resent, revile, ridicule, rip, scapegoat, scold, score, -scorn, scourge, slam, slap, -snub, tongue-lash, trim, trounce, upbraid, vituperate, zap, zing* (≠ acclaim, applaud, approve, blandish, bless, cite, commend, compliment, congratulate, endorse, eulogize, extol, flannel, flatter, gratify, hail, honor, ingratiate, laud, lionize, okay, praise, rubber-stamp, salute, sanction, tout)

REBUT (/): *abnegate, abrogate, belie, break, challenge, confound, confute, contest, contradict, contravene, controvert, counter, cross, cross-examine, debate, debunk, defeat, defend, deflect, -deny, disavow, discredit, discuss, disprove, dispute, doubt, explode, falsify, grill, interrogate, invalidate, justify, mistrust, -negate, oppose, overthrow, overturn, parry, quash, query, question, -rebuff, refute, rejoin, repeal, repel, -repudiate, repulse, retort, scruple, subvert, top* (≠ adduce, approve, attest, authenticate, buttress, certify, chronicle, concede, confirm, corroborate, cosign, demonstrate, display, document, establish, evidence, evince, illustrate, manifest, notarize, prove, record, show, substantiate, support, validate, verify, witness)

RECEIVE (←): *accept, accumulate, acquire, add, admit, amass, annex, apprehend, appropriate, arrogate, assume, bag, buy, capture, catch, claim, collect, compile, cop, corner, corral, derive, download, draw, earn, fetch, gain, garner, gather, get, glean, grab, harvest, heap, hear, hold, import, incur, inherit, land, lure, make, net, obtain, palm, perceive, pocket, procure, pull, purchase, reap, reclaim, recoup, recover, recycle, redeem, rescue, retrieve, salvage, scavenge, score, secure, seize, snag, source, take, win, wrangle* (≠ -abandon, bestow, comp, contribute, -decline, deliver, -deny, disburse, discourage, dispatch, dispense, distribute, -ditch, donate, drop, dump, forfeit, furnish, give, hand, junk, leave, lose, miss, offer, outbid, pass, pay, pitch, present, provide, push, -refuse, -reject, release, -renounce, select, send, spend, steal, stop, supply, swipe, tender, throw, tithe, toss, volunteer)

RECEIVE (+): *accept, accommodate, accost, acknowledge, admit, approach, contain, embrace, entertain, greet, hail, hold, host, hug, induct, initiate, install, introduce, invite, meet, notice, permit, salaam, salute, signal, take, welcome* (≠ -avoid, ban, banish, bar, blackball, blacklist, block, -deny, disallow, dissuade, eject, -evade, evict, -exclude, exile, expel, -forsake, -halt, -omit, -ostracize, oust, -prohibit, -rebuff, rebuke, -reject, repel, -shun, -snub, -spurn) **(¿) ABSTRACTION ALERT. Concrete goals essential!**

RECLAIM (←): *appropriate, arrogate, commandeer, confiscate, impound, reacquire, recapture, recoup, recover, recruit, recycle, redeem, regain, regenerate, reinstate, replenish, repossess, repurchase, rescue, restore, retake, retrieve, salvage, seize* (≠ -abandon, claim, discard, drop, forfeit, forget, -forsake, -ignore, jettison, lose, mislay, misplace, -overlook, -reject, relinquish, -renounce, skip, surrender)

RECOGNIZE (+): *absorb, accept, acknowledge, adjudge, admit, allow, appreciate, apprehend, ascertain, assimilate, calculate, catch, clock, compass, comprehend, compute, concede, conceive, confess, decipher, decode, deduce, descry, detect, determine, diagnose, dig, digest, discern, distinguish, endorse, espy, evaluate, eye, eyeball, fathom, finger, get, grant, grasp, identify, incorporate, integrate, internalize, intuit, know, make, nail, note, notice, observe, own, peg, penetrate, perceive, pierce, pinpoint, place, plumb, profile, realize, recall, recollect, register, remark, remember, savvy, scan, scope, scrutinize, see, seize, sense, spot, suss, tag, tell, track, twig, understand, verify* (≠ baffle, bewilder, blind, cloak, clothe, cloud, conceal, confound, confuse, costume, cover, debate, deceive, -deny, -discount, disguise, -disown, disprove, dispute, -disregard, distrust, doubt, erase, forget, gainsay, hide, -ignore, invalidate, mask, misapprehend, misconceive, misconstrue, misdiagnose, mishear, misinterpret, misperceive, misread, miss, mistake, misunderstand, muddle, mystify, -negate, obscure, -overlook, perplex, puzzle, rebut, -renounce, scruple, trick, -veto, wonder) **(¿) ABSTRACTION ALERT. Concrete goals essential!**

RECOGNIZE (+): *accept, acclaim, acknowledge, admit, allow, applaud, appreciate, apprehend, approve, avow, celebrate, ceremonialize, cheer, cite, commemorate, commend, compliment, comprehend, concede, confess, congratulate, credit, decorate, elevate, endorse, extol, fête, glorify, gold-star, grant, gratify, greet, hail, high-five, honor, laud, make, memorialize, observe, own, perceive, praise, realize, respect, reward, ritualize, salute, sanction, thank, tout, understand, validate* (≠ badmouth, blackguard, blast, boo, censure, condemn, damn, defame, demean, denounce, disapprove, discredit, -disdain, disgrace, dishonor, -disregard, exploit, humble, humiliate, -ignore, incriminate, jeer, libel, malign, misunderstand, mock, -neglect, oppose, -refuse, regret, repent, ridicule, rue, shame, slander, -slight, -snub, -spurn)

RECOMMEND (→): *acclaim, admire, admonish, advance, advise, advocate, affirm, applaud, approve, assign, back, bequeath, blandish, brief, caution, celebrate, commend, commit, compliment, confer, confide, confirm, consign, consult, counsel, cue, deal, delegate, deliver, dignify, direct, dispense, disperse, distribute, divide, encourage, endorse, enjoin, entrust, esteem, eulogize, exalt, exhort, extol, favor, flatter, furnish, give, glorify, grant, guide, hand, hype, inform, ingratiate, instruct, justify, laud, leave, lend, loan, magnify, move, notify, pass, plug, praise, preach, prescribe, presell, prize, prompt, propose, ratify, release, relinquish, sanction, second, shill, steer, submit, suggest, supply, support, surrender, task, tout, transfer, transmit, trust, uphold, urge, value, vest, will, yield* (≠ accept, assail, blame, castigate, caution, censure, condemn, criticize, critique, debase, denounce, detain, disapprove, discourage, discredit, disfavor, disgrace, -disregard, dissuade, fault, finger, frame, fulminate, -hate, hold, humiliate, impugn, incriminate, insult, keep, knock, mock, neg, occupy, oppose, own, pan, possess, protest, receive, -refuse, regret, -reject, repent, reserve, retain, rue, -scorn, slam, take, trash, -veto, warn, withhold)

RECONCILE (+): *accommodate, accord, adapt, adjust, align, approximate, arrange, array, attune, balance, blend, calibrate, center, combine, compose, conciliate, connect, coordinate, correlate, defray, dovetail, equalize, even, fit, fuse, harmonize, hybridize, integrate, join, key, match, mend, merge, orchestrate, order, pair, proportion, rebate, rectify, regularize, remedy, resolve, settle, square, standardize, suit, synchronize, synthesize, tune, tweak, unskew* (≠ bother, bug, confuse, customize, disarray, disorder, disorganize, disrupt, disturb, jumble, mismatch, muddle, rattle, scramble, skew, upset)

RECONCILE (+): *accept, accommodate, appease, connect, content, coordinate, expiate, forgive, heal, integrate, invite, merge, mollify, pacify, placate, propitiate, redeem, reintegrate, reunite, unify, unite, welcome* (≠ alienate, banish, blackball, blame, boot, bounce, deport, disaffect, disconcert, distance, eject, -eschew, estrange, evict, -exclude, exile, fault, finger, fire, frame, isolate, oppose, orphan, oust, -reject, repel, repulse, sack)

RECONSTRUCT (←): *analyze, anticipate, assess, benchmark, calculate, conceive, conclude, contemplate, deduce, deduct, derive, detect,* *determine, elaborate, envisage, envision, estimate, expect, extrapolate, eye, eyeball, gather, gauge, imagine, infer, model, picture, plan, profile, project, read, reckon, recreate, revisit, sample, scrutinize, solve, understand, visualize* (≠ alter, baffle, blind, blur, confuse, -disregard, doubt, embellish, embroider, fabricate, fake, falsify, guess, -ignore, mistake, mystify, overwhelm, perplex, puzzle, stump, witness, wonder)

RECONSTRUCT (+): *automate, computerize, craft, doctor, fix, gentrify, mechanize, mend, modernize, overhaul, patch, reassemble, rebuild, recapture, recast, reconceive, reconceptualize, recondition, reconstitute, recreate, rectify, recycle, reestablish, refashion, refine, reform, regain, regenerate, rehabilitate, reimagine, reinvent, rejuvenate, remake, remodel, remold, renew, renovate, reorganize, reorient, repair, replace, reproduce, reshape, reshuffle, restore, restructure, retool, revamp, revolutionize, rework, salvage, survive, sustain, update, upgrade, weather, withstand* (≠ -abandon, annihilate, antique, blast, bulldoze, deep-six, demolish, destroy, devastate, dismantle, doom, downgrade, eradicate, flatten, fracture, fragment, level, obliterate, raze, remove, ruin, sabotage, scotch, scrap, scupper, shatter, shelve, wreck, zap)

RECORD (←): *bug, burn, capture, chronicle, cut, document, edit, film, photo, photograph, picture, produce, retake, shoot, take, tape, tape-record, video, videotape, witness* (≠ block, bury, -cancel, censor, classify, conceal, delete, ensconce, erase, expunge, hide, -ignore, loose, misrepresent, miss, -neglect, obfuscate, obscure, screen, shroud)

RECORD (+): *book, calendar, card, catalog, chalk, chronicle, classify, clock, collect, compile, docket, document, draft, enroll, enter, enumerate, file, index, inscribe, itemize, jot, journalize, list, log, mark, minute, notch, note, pencil, register, report, reschedule, schedule, score, slate, summarize, tabulate, tally, transcribe, wait-list* (≠ access, -cancel, conceal, consult, cover, -decline, delete, eradicate, erase, forget, hide, -nix, pass, reconsider, reference, secrete, shelve, withhold)

RECOUP (←): *clear, compensate, earn, gross, indemnify, inherit, make, net, profit, reacquire, recapture, reclaim, recompense, recover, recruit, redeem, refund, regain, reimburse, repay, replenish, repossess, repurchase, rescue, retake, retrieve* (≠ borrow, cadge, cheat, compromise, defalcate, drop, embezzle, endanger, forfeit, gamble, lend, loan, lose, mislay, misplace, miss, pilfer, poach, risk, scrounge, squander, steal, stiff, stint, swipe, threaten, waste)

RECOVER (←): *catch, collect, conserve, correct, cull, detect, discover, earn, extract, find, fix, gain, grab, gross, grow, harvest, improve, locate, mend, mine, monetize, net, obtain, patch, pinpoint, pocket, preserve, process, pull, rally, reacquire, reap, recapture, receive, reclaim, recollect, reconcile, recoup, recruit, rectify, recycle, redeem, regain, repair, replenish, repossess, reprocess, repurchase, rescue, restore, resume, retain, retake, retrieve, reunite, reuse, right, salvage, save, seize, settle, snag, source, take, unearth, win* (≠ -abandon, boobytrap, -desert, -ditch, dump, forfeit,

-forsake, lose, mislay, misplace, offload, -refuse, -reject, sabotage, scotch, scupper, scuttle, shelve, starve, steal, stiff, stint, withhold)

RECOVER (+): *appease, assuage, better, comfort, cure, decontaminate, divert, enhance, enliven, exhilarate, foster, freshen, gratify, heal, improve, invigorate, mend, nourish, nurse, nurture, palliate, quarantine, quicken, rally, reanimate, recharge, recoup, recuperate, refresh, reinvigorate, rejuvenate, remedy, renew, rescue, restimulate, restore, resurrect, resuscitate, revitalize, revive, salve, satiate, satisfy, save, soothe, spoon-feed, stimulate, treat* (≠ afflict, ail, anguish, assault, attack, brutalize, burden, contaminate, curse, -deny, deprive, distress, grieve, harass, harm, hurt, impair, incapacitate, infect, injure, malnourish, -neglect, oppress, overextend, pain, persecute, plague, poison, sicken, starve, strain, stress, strike, terrorize, threaten, torment, torture, traumatize, trouble, upset, victimize, wound, wrong)

RECRUIT (←): *acquire, advance, apprentice, assemble, assume, augment, better, conscript, contract, deliver, draft, employ, engage, enlist, enroll, gain, gather, headhunt, hire, impress, improve, induct, levy, mobilize, muster, obtain, partner, pay, place, procure, promote, proselytize, raise, reanimate, recoup, recover, recuperate, refresh, regain, reinforce, reinvigorate, renew, repair, replenish, repossess, restore, retain, retrieve, revive, scout, secure, select, sign, subcontract, upgrade* (≠ axe, ban, banish, bar, blackball, blacklist, boot, can, cashier, discard, discharge, -discount, dismiss, exorcise, expel, fire, furlough, -reject, release, sack, -shun, -spurn, wait-list)

RECTIFY (+): *adapt, adjust, align, alter, ameliorate, amend, better, blue-pencil, calibrate, change, coordinate, correct, cure, cut, debug, develop, doctor, edit, emend, enhance, fix, improve, mend, modify, modulate, moralize, pace, patch, perfect, polish, punctuate, rarefy, realign, red-pen, red-pencil, redraft, redraw, redress, refine, reform, regulate, remedy, repair, rephrase, restore, restyle, retool, revamp, revise, rework, rewrite, right, shine, shorten, tune, tweak* (≠ aggravate, botch, bungle, callous, coarsen, compromise, contaminate, corrupt, damage, destroy, eradicate, erase, flub, harm, hurt, impair, injure, jumble, mar, muddle, pervert, poison, pollute, ruin, scramble, spoil, taint, tarnish, warp, worsen)

RECYCLE (+): *conserve, convert, preserve, process, reclaim, reconceive, reconceptualize, recover, redeem, redefine, refine, reimagine, reinvent, repair, reprocess, rescue, restore, retain, rethink, retool, retrieve, reuse, salvage, save* (≠ -abandon, discard, -ditch, dump, endanger, harm, hurt, junk, lose, ruin, scrap, squander, toss, trash, waste)

REDEEM (←): *bail, buy, cash, change, claim, collect, convert, deliver, emancipate, exchange, expense, glean, liberate, nab, offset, outweigh, preserve, ransom, recapture, reclaim, recoup, recover, recuperate, regain, release, repossess, repurchase, rescue, restore, retrieve, salvage, save, swap, switch, trade* (≠ -abandon, chuck, -desert, discard, -disown, -ditch, drop, dump, endanger, -eschew, forfeit, -forsake, imperil, jeopardize, junk, lose, offload, -reject, risk, scrap, squander, stiff, stint, surrender, waste, yield)

REDEEM (+): *absolve, acquit, amend, balance, bless, buy, cleanse, compensate, consecrate, correct, counterbalance, counterpoise, countervail, defray, deliver, discharge, emancipate, expiate, forgive, free, fulfill, hallow, improve, indemnify, keep, liberate, meet, mend, moralize, offset, outweigh, pardon, perfect, propitiate, purify, ransom, realign, reclaim, recompense, rectify, redress, reeducate, refine, reform, refund, regenerate, rehabilitate, reimburse, reinstate, release, remit, remunerate, repay, reprieve, rescue, restore, right, sanctify, sanitize, satisfy, save, shrive, spare* (≠ abase, accuse, allege, attaint, bestialize, blame, blemish, blotch, bribe, canker, cheat, contaminate, corrupt, debauch, deceive, defraud, degrade, demean, demoralize, deprave, -disregard, double-talk, fault, foul, -ignore, implicate, incriminate, indict, lower, nobble, pervert, poison, profane, prosecute, prostitute, steal, suborn, subvert, sully, taint, tarnish, trick, trouble, warp, wound)

REDIRECT (→): *-avert, bend, bounce, channel, concentrate, curve, deflect, distract, divert, dribble, focus, funnel, jog, move, nudge, rechannel, refract, reroute, reverse, rotate, shift, shove, shunt, sidetrack, sway, swerve, swing, switch, swivel, transfer, turn, twist, wheel, whip, whirl, withdraw, wriggle, zigzag* (≠ advance, conserve, continue, defend, demand, develop, finish, grow, hold, initiate, keep, lose, maintain, perpetuate, preserve, retain, shield, start, stay, stop, straighten, sustain, terminate, upset)

REDUCE (/): *abate, abbreviate, abridge, attenuate, bob, cheapen, chop, clip, compact, compress, concentrate, condense, contract, crop, cull, curtail, -cut, decrease, deduct, deflate, deplete, depress, digest, dilute, diminish, -discontinue, -discount, dock, downgrade, downsize, drain, elide, erode, fragment, impair, lessen, lighten, lose, lowball, lower, melt, miniaturize, minimize, moderate, nip, pare, prune, pucker, quash, rarefy, refine, repress, restrict, retrench, shave, shear, shorten, shrink, simplify, slash, slim, strip, subdue, subjugate, subtract, taper, thin, tighten, trim, truncate, underbid, underemphasize, weaken, weed* (≠ accent, accentuate, accrue, amplify, assert, boost, broaden, compound, develop, elaborate, emphasize, encourage, enhance, enlarge, exaggerate, expand, expound, extend, flavor, foster, increase, inflate, intensify, invigorate, lengthen, magnify, marinate, maximize, overdramatize, oversell, prioritize, promote, punctuate, raise, reinforce, season, spice, strengthen, stretch, supplement)

REDUCE (/): *bankrupt, bastardize, beggar, bench, break, cannibalize, cheapen, consume, cripple, deaden, debase, debilitate, degrade, demote, deplete, depress, deprive, devalue, diminish, disable, drain, enervate, exhaust, humble, impair, impoverish, leach, lower, overextend, pauperize, ruin, salvage, sap, scant, sideline, starve, straiten, subjugate, subordinate, vanquish, weaken* (≠ augment, boost, cultivate, elevate, energize, enhance, enrich, expand, extend, feed, fuel, galvanize, improve, increase, magnify, motivate, nourish, nurture, prioritize, refill, replenish, restore, revitalize, stimulate, sustain, unspool, upgrade, value)

REFEREE (+): *adjudge, adjudicate, arbitrate, ascertain, broker, chair, command, conclude, consider, control, decide, determine, direct, equalize, examine, handle, inspect, judge, manage, mediate, moderate, mull, negotiate, pacify, ponder, propitiate, prosecute, reconcile, renegotiate, resolve, reunite, rule, scrutinize, settle, size, solve, transact, umpire, unskew, weigh* (≠ baffle, bias, challenge, cheat, confound, confront, confuse, debate, defy, demand, dismiss, -disregard, exacerbate, favor, fight, -ignore, inflame, instigate, manipulate, misrepresent, miss, mistake, muddle, oppose, -overlook, predetermine, prejudge, prejudice, provoke, skew, skirt, slant, twist)

REFINE (+): *clarify, cleanse, clear, decontaminate, delouse, disinfect, distill, filter, freshen, polish, process, purge, purify, rarefy, rectify, sanitize, shine, sift, sterilize, strain, sublimate, treat* (≠ bedraggle, besmirch, blend, callous, coarsen, contaminate, corrupt, dirty, foul, infect, infiltrate, mix, muddy, poison, pollute, soil, spoil, spot, stain, sully, taint, tarnish)

REFINE (+): *advance, ameliorate, amend, better, boost, civilize, clarify, correct, cultivate, deepen, develop, edit, educate, elaborate, elevate, embellish, emend, enhance, enrich, exalt, explain, fine-tune, flavor, fortify, further, garnish, help, hone, improve, intensify, magnify, marinate, maximize, mend, minimize, moralize, optimize, overhaul, perfect, polish, prioritize, punctuate, realign, rectify, redraft, reform, refurbish, rehab, rehabilitate, reinforce, remedy, renovate, rephrase, retouch, revamp, revise, revolutionize, rework, right, round, season, sleek, slick, smooth, spice, strengthen, temper, treat, upgrade* (≠ barbarize, bestialize, blemish, blight, callous, canker, coarsen, compromise, damage, deface, diminish, disfigure, efface, flaw, hamper, harm, harshen, hurt, impair, injure, lessen, lower, mar, reduce, ruin, spoil, stain, taint, tarnish, vitiate, worsen)

REFLECT (→): *allow, articulate, communicate, conjecture, demonstrate, depict, display, evince, exhibit, express, externalize, guess, manifest, note, observe, portray, remark, reveal, show, showcase, speak, state, suppose, surmise, talk, tell, verbalize, vocalize, voice* (≠ camouflage, censor, choke, cloak, clothe, cloud, conceal, costume, disguise, gag, hide, hush, mask, muffle, mute, muzzle, quiet, redact, screen, silence, stifle, strangle, suppress, veil) **(¿) ABSTRACTION ALERT. Concrete goals essential!**

REFLECT (→): *adopt, approximate, cast, catch, clone, copy, duplicate, echo, emulate, equalize, follow, ghostwrite, image, imitate, match, mimic, mirror, reduplicate, repeat, replicate, reproduce, reverse, scatter* (≠ absorb, conceal, cover, discard, dismiss, -disregard, forget, generate, hide, -ignore, mismatch, miss, -neglect, originate, request, take, withhold)

REFORM (+): *align, ameliorate, amend, better, clean, cleanse, convert, correct, cure, depersonalize, improve, mend, purify, realign, rearrange, rebuild, reclaim, reconceive, reconceptualize, reconstitute, reconstruct, rectify, redeem, redefine, reeducate, refashion, refine, regenerate,* *rehabilitate, reimagine, reinvent, rejigger, remake, remedy, remodel, renew, renovate, reorganize, repair, reshape, reshuffle, resolve, restore, rethink, retool, revamp, revise, revolutionize, rework, right, standardize, transform* (≠ blemish, bribe, bungle, canker, coddle, corrupt, damage, degrade, demean, hamper, harm, impair, injure, lower, mangle, mar, mutate, nobble, pervert, poison, pollute, prostitute, -refuse, spoil, suborn, subvert, undermine, warp, worsen)

REFRESH (+): *assist, brace, cheer, cool, encourage, energize, enliven, exhilarate, fortify, freshen, galvanize, gentrify, heal, invigorate, liven, modernize, prod, prompt, quicken, rally, reanimate, recharge, recondition, recoup, recover, recreate, recuperate, refurbish, reinvigorate, rejuvenate, renew, renovate, repair, replenish, restimulate, restore, restructure, resuscitate, revamp, revitalize, revive, revolutionize, rouse, steady, stimulate, strengthen, update, upgrade* (≠ age, antique, blemish, break, canker, castrate, corrode, cripple, damage, dampen, deaden, depress, desiccate, destroy, disable, discourage, dissuade, drain, dull, energize, enervate, eradicate, erase, erode, fatigue, fray, gnaw, -halt, hamstring, harass, harm, hurt, incapacitate, injure, jade, kill, leech, mangle, mar, outwear, paralyze, ruin, scar, scuff, stagnate, stale, tire, wear, weary, wreck)

REFURBISH (+): *automate, clean, computerize, enhance, fix, gentrify, improve, mend, modernize, overhaul, recondition, redecorate, redo, reequip, refit, refresh, rehab, rehabilitate, rejuvenate, remodel, renew, renovate, repair, reshuffle, restore, retread, revamp, revolutionize, service, spiff, spruce, tool, update, upgrade, wallpaper* (≠ break, damage, demolish, dent, destroy, -disregard, eradicate, erase, harm, hurt, kill, level, mar, -neglect, nock, ruin, scar, scrape, scratch, wreck)

-REFUSE (-): *-balk, ban, check, constrain, curb, -decline, -deny, disallow, disapprove, -dodge, enjoin, -evade, -forbid, hinder, hold, impede, keep, -negate, -nix, obstruct, -prohibit, proscribe, -rebuff, -reject, repel, repress, restrain, restrict, -spurn, -veto, withhold* (≠ accede, accept, accord, afford, allow, authorize, commission, concede, disburse, dispense, furnish, give, grant, invite, let, license, offer, okay, permit, provide, sanction, solicit, spare, spitball, supply, tender, volunteer, vouchsafe, warrant, welcome)

-REFUSE (/): *abjure, -avoid, -balk, -bypass, challenge, contradict, controvert, countermand, debate, -decline, -deny, deselect, detour, disallow, disapprove, disavow, disclaim, -disdain, dismiss, -disown, disprove, dispute, disrespect, -exclude, -forbid, forswear, gainsay, -ignore, -negate, negative, -nix, -omit, oppose, -ostracize, oust, overrule, pass, -prohibit, proscribe, protest, -rebuff, rebut, recall, recant, refute, regret, -reject, -renounce, -repudiate, retract, revoke, -scorn, scout, -shun, -spurn, stick, -veto, withdraw* (≠ accede, accept, admit, adopt, approve, assert, brook, choose, condone, countenance, defend, embrace, espouse, face, handpick, incur, maintain, permit, receive, select, support, swallow, take, tolerate, uphold, welcome)

REFUTE (/): *abnegate, argue, break, burn, -cancel, challenge, contradict, contravene, convict, counter, crush, debate, deflect, demolish, -deny, disallow, disavow, disclaim, discredit, -disown, disprove, dispute, doubt, expose, gainsay, invalidate, -negate, oppose, overthrow, parry, quash, rebut, -reject, -repudiate, retort, silence, squelch* (≠ accept, acknowledge, admit, adopt, affirm, authenticate, avow, concede, confess, confirm, corroborate, declare, embrace, endorse, maintain, notarize, own, prove, ratify, sanction, substantiate, support, validate, verify)

REGAIN (←): *discover, find, locate, reacquire, recapture, reclaim, recollect, recoup, recover, recruit, redeem, rediscover, replenish, repossess, repurchase, rescue, retake, retrieve, salvage, save, win* (≠ -abandon, deep-six, destroy, fail, forfeit, forget, -forsake, lose, mislay, misplace, obliterate, ruin)

REGENERATE (+): *change, charge, cure, energize, exhilarate, heal, invigorate, mend, produce, reanimate, reawaken, reconstitute, reconstruct, recreate, reestablish, reform, refresh, reinvigorate, rejuvenate, rekindle, remedy, renew, renovate, reproduce, restimulate, restore, resuscitate, revitalize, revive, stimulate, uplift* (≠ damage, degrade, demoralize, destroy, eradicate, erase, extinguish, hamstring, injure, kill, lower, pervert, poison, ruin, stagnate, stale, stifle, stultify, subvert, suppress, warp)

REGISTER (→): *chronicle, clock, engrave, enter, inscribe, jot, journalize, list, log, mark, minute, notch, note, record, report, scan, score, scrutinize, trademark, transcribe* (≠ annihilate, anonymize, censor, conceal, -cut, edit, eradicate, erase, expunge, expurgate, hide, -ignore, -nullify, obliterate, -omit, redact, rephrase, strike)

REGISTER (→): *arrange, book, calendar, card, catalog, classify, compile, docket, enroll, enter, file, index, inscribe, list, notate, note, organize, record, reschedule, schedule, slate, tabulate, tally* (≠ -cancel, delete, -exclude, expunge, -omit, -overlook, -reject, scratch, terminate, wait-list, withdraw)

REGISTER (←): *book, cast, conscript, draft, enlist, enroll, induct, inscribe, list, muster, overcommit, schedule* (≠ banish, blackball, -exclude, expel, expunge, -omit, oust, -overlook, -refuse, -reject, wait-list)

REGISTER (+): *absorb, appreciate, apprehend, assimilate, catch, compass, comprehend, conceive, decipher, decode, deduce, detect, diagnose, dig, digest, discern, eye, eyeball, fathom, get, grasp, incorporate, integrate, internalize, intuit, know, make, penetrate, perceive, pierce, realize, recognize, savvy, see, seize, sense, suss, understand* (≠ -blank, -bypass, -disregard, forget, -ignore, lose, misapprehend, misconceive, misconstrue, misdiagnose, mishear, misinterpret, misperceive, misread, miss, mistake, misunderstand, -omit, -overlook) **(¿) ABSTRACTION ALERT. Concrete goals essential!**

REGRET (←): *bemoan, berate, bewail, blame, castigate, censure, condemn, confess, criticize, denounce, deplore, deprecate, disparage, grieve, lament, miss, mourn, recant, repent, reproach, reprove, resent, revile, rue, slam, slate, sorrow, upbraid* (≠ absolve, accept, adore, applaud, appreciate, blame, celebrate, commend, desire, embrace, enjoy, excuse, forget, hope, invite, justify, love, -overlook, pardon, relish, sanction, savor, welcome) **(¿) ABSTRACTION ALERT. Concrete goals essential!**

REGULATE (→): *administer, chair, conduct, control, direct, govern, guard, guide, handle, keep, lead, manage, mastermind, micromanage, mind, operate, oversee, patrol, pilot, police, protect, run, safeguard, stage-manage, steer, steward, superintend, supervise, tend, watch* (≠ challenge, contradict, counter, counteract, debate, defy, -deny, disobey, dispute, flout, follow, gainsay, heed, hold, mind, mismanage, misrule, obey, observe, oppose, resist, -scorn, serve)

REGULATE (→): *adapt, adjust, administer, align, allocate, arbitrate, arrange, array, balance, calibrate, cast, categorize, center, chair, chart, choreograph, class, classify, collate, compose, conduct, control, coordinate, correct, customize, defray, depersonalize, design, determine, devise, direct, dispose, establish, fit, fix, form, frame, govern, grade, ground, group, guide, handle, harmonize, harness, improve, integrate, legislate, machinate, maintain, manage, marshal, measure, mediate, methodize, moderate, modulate, monitor, normalize, orchestrate, order, organize, oversee, pace, pigeonhole, place, plan, plot, police, prepare, prioritize, program, rank, rate, rationalize, readjust, ready, realign, reconcile, rectify, referee, regiment, regularize, reintegrate, reunite, right, rule, run, schedule, schematize, scheme, score, screen, script, separate, set, settle, shape, sift, slot, sort, square, stabilize, standardize, stratify, structure, subordinate, superintend, supervise, support, synchronize, systematize, tame, temper, time, tune, type, unify, unsnarl, weaponize* (≠ break, brew, bungle, clutter, confuse, damage, deprogram, deregulate, diffuse, dishevel, disorder, disorganize, disperse, disrupt, disturb, divide, express, flout, -ignore, jumble, liberate, loosen, mismatch, muddle, -neglect, overcommit, ruin, scatter, scramble, separate, spoil, tousle, trouble, unleash, upset)

REGULATE (/): *arrest, block, bottle, bridle, check, choke, constrain, contain, control, curb, gag, govern, hamper, handcuff, hinder, hold, housebreak, housetrain, impede, inhibit, interrupt, keep, measure, mince, muffle, muzzle, obstruct, pace, pocket, rein, repress, restrain, rule, silence, sink, smother, squelch, stifle, stop, straightjacket, strangle, suppress, swallow, tame* (≠ air, evince, express, foment, incite, instigate, liberate, loose, loosen, lose, propel, provoke, rabble-rouse, slacken, uncork, unleash, vent, verbalize, vocalize)

REHABILITATE (+): *adjust, align, amend, calibrate, cleanse, clear, convert, darn, elevate, enhance, furbish, gentrify, improve, mend, normalize, nourish, nurse, nurture, overhaul, purify, rebuild, reclaim, recondition, reconstitute, reconstruct, recover, rectify, redeem, reeducate, reestablish,* *refine, reform, refurbish, regenerate, rehab, reinstate, reintegrate, reinvent, remodel, renew, renovate, restore, tune, tweak* (≠ -abandon, abase, anguish, bestialize, bribe, canker, corrupt, damage, debauch, degrade, demean, demoralize, deprave, destroy, doom, eradicate, erase, harm, hurt, injure, lower, mutate, nobble, pervert, poison, profane, prostitute, ruin, scathe, suborn, subvert, threaten, torment, torture, traumatize, victimize, warp, wound, wrong)

REHABILITATE (+): *alleviate, attend, bandage, cure, develop, doctor, exercise, fix, fortify, heal, hospitalize, medicate, mend, nurse, patch, physic, reinvigorate, rejuvenate, relieve, remedy, renew, repair, restimulate, resuscitate, revitalize, revive, save, splint, train, treat* (≠ afflict, ail, cripple, damage, debilitate, disable, drain, enervate, enfeeble, harm, hurt, impair, infect, injure, kneecap, lacerate, lame, leech, maim, mangle, mutilate, overextend, palsy, sap, savage, shrivel, sicken, waste, weaken, wither, wound)

REIN (←): *arrest, bind, brake, bridle, check, collect, compose, contain, control, cool, curb, govern, -halt, halter, hamper, hinder, hold, impede, inhibit, lash, leash, limit, master, moderate, repress, restrain, restrict, retard, slow, smother, snaffle, stall, stop, straightjacket, stymie, subdue, suppress, tether* (≠ abet, boost, encourage, foster, free, incite, instigate, liberate, loose, prod, spur, unleash, untether)

REINFORCE (+): *accent, accentuate, affirm, amplify, assert, augment, back, beef, belabor, bolster, boost, brace, buttress, case-harden, confirm, consolidate, corroborate, echo, embattle, emphasize, establish, fortify, fuel, harden, improve, increase, inure, overemphasize, parrot, prioritize, prop, prove, punctuate, raise, replenish, secure, shore, stabilize, stay, steady, steel, stiffen, strengthen, stress, strut, substantiate, supplement, support, toughen, underline, validate, verify* (≠ attack, boobytrap, damage, disrupt, harm, incapacitate, sabotage, scotch, scupper, scuttle, subvert, undercut, underemphasize, undermine, weaken)

REINVIGORATE (+): *aid, assist, bolster, boost, enliven, exhilarate, feed, force-feed, fuel, liven, modernize, nourish, prioritize, reanimate, recondition, refresh, refurbish, regenerate, rehabilitate, rejuvenate, renew, renovate, restimulate, restore, retread, revitalize, revive, revolutionize, rouse, stimulate, strengthen, update, upgrade* (≠ blight, castrate, daunt, debilitate, demotivate, depress, destroy, discourage, dissuade, doom, drain, emasculate, encumber, enervate, eradicate, erase, hamper, harm, incapacitate, kill, leech, paralyze, ruin, sedate, unman, weaken, wither, wizen)

-REJECT (/): *-abandon, banish, betray, blackball, blacklist, -boycott, chuck, condemn, -decline, deflect, defy, -deny, deselect, -desert, -despise, disallow, disbelieve, discard, disclaim, -discount, discredit, -disdain, disgorge, dismiss, -disown, -disregard, -ditch, divorce, drop, dump, eject, eliminate, enjoin, -exclude, exorcise, expel, -forsake, -ignore, jettison, jilt, kill, -nix, offload, -omit, oppose, -ostracize, oust, picket, pooh-pooh, -rebuff, -refuse, -renounce, repel, -repudiate, repulse, -scorn, scrap, shed,*

-shun, -sidestep, -snub, -spurn, -veto (≠ accept, adopt, allow, assimilate, await, choose, colonize, concede, crave, demand, desire, embrace, expect, fancy, grant, hunt, incorporate, integrate, invite, permit, possess, pursue, request, sanction, seek, select, solicit, welcome)

REJUVENATE (+): *activate, animate, electrify, encourage, energize, exhilarate, galvanize, invigorate, modernize, motivate, provoke, quicken, reanimate, recharge, reclaim, recondition, reconstruct, recover, refresh, refurbish, regenerate, rehab, reinvigorate, rekindle, renew, renovate, restimulate, restore, retread, revitalize, revive, revolutionize, rouse, spruce, spur, stimulate, stir, strengthen, update, upgrade, uplift* (≠ abuse, afflict, damage, destroy, doom, drain, eradicate, erase, harm, injure, kill, leech, ruin, shrivel, weaken, weary, wither, wizen)

RELAX (+): *abate, allay, alleviate, anesthetize, appease, assuage, calm, comfort, diminish, ease, gratify, hush, lessen, lighten, loose, loosen, lower, lull, massage, mellow, mitigate, moderate, modify, modulate, mollify, pacify, placate, quiet, reduce, release, relieve, remit, sedate, settle, slack, slacken, slow, soften, soothe, tranquilize, weaken* (≠ bond, constrain, exacerbate, exercise, flex, grow, hump, hustle, increase, intensify, man, panic, pucker, restrain, stiffen, strain, stretch, sweat, tense, tighten, work, worry)

RELEASE (→): *air, belch, cast, discharge, disgorge, drizzle, effuse, ejaculate, eject, eliminate, emit, erupt, evacuate, evolve, excrete, exhale, expel, express, exude, gush, irradiate, issue, jet, ooze, pour, radiate, regurgitate, secrete, send, shoot, spew, splutter, spout, spray, spurt, squirt, throw, trickle, uncork, upchuck, vent, vomit* (≠ absorb, contain, fill, gather, glean, holster, inhale, marinate, slurp, smell, smother, sniff, soak, sponge, suck, swallow, take, throttle)

RELEASE (→): *advertise, advise, announce, apprise, bark, bellow, blare, blaze, blazon, blurb, broadcast, bulletin, circulate, communicate, concede, confess, confirm, confront, declare, disclose, disseminate, divulge, enunciate, feature, flash, herald, hype, impart, inform, intimate, introduce, launch, manifest, notify, pitch, placard, plug, post, presell, proclaim, produce, promote, promulgate, publicize, publish, puff, report, reveal, show, sound, spotlight, spread, telegraph, trumpet* (≠ bury, censor, collect, conceal, contain, ensconce, erase, hide, hoard, hush, keep, kill, mask, obscure, quiet, recall, recant, redact, restrict, retract, revoke, silence, suppress, withhold)

RELEASE (+): *clear, deliver, disencumber, disengage, disentangle, extricate, free, liberate, redeem, rescue, save, unburden, unravel, unsnarl, untangle, untie, untwine* (≠ block, burden, embroil, encumber, entangle, hamper, hinder, impede, load, lumber, obstruct, overextend, weigh)

RELEASE (+): *absolve, acquit, bail, deliver, discharge, disengage, disentangle, emancipate, enfranchise, excuse, exempt, exonerate, extricate, loose, loosen, manumit, parole, ransom, redeem, relieve, slack, slacken, spring, unbind, unbridle, unburden, uncage, unchain, unclasp,* *undo, unfasten, unfetter, unhook, unlace, unleash, unlock, unmoor, unshackle, untie* (≠ bind, bridle, burden, capture, catch, check, cinch, commit, conceal, confine, conquer, constrain, control, convict, curb, detain, enslave, fetter, govern, halter, hamper, handcuff, harness, hoard, hogtie, hold, immure, implicate, imprison, incarcerate, incriminate, inhibit, institutionalize, intern, jail, keep, lock, manacle, niche, pace, regulate, rein, restrain, shackle, straightjacket, subdue, subjugate, tame, trammel)

RELEASE (/): *axe, bench, boot, bounce, can, cashier, chuck, close, degrade, demote, discharge, -discontinue, dismiss, downsize, end, fire, furlough, -halt, interrupt, pink-slip, reduce, remit, remove, retire, sack, separate, sideline, suspend, terminate, trim, unseat* (≠ contract, employ, engage, hire, induct, keep, recruit, reemploy, rehire, retain, sign, subcontract)

RELEGATE (→): *array, assign, assort, banish, bench, blackball, boot, -boycott, categorize, charge, class, classify, codify, commit, compartment, compartmentalize, consign, cull, declass, degrade, delegate, demote, deport, digest, dispatch, dispose, distinguish, distribute, downgrade, eject, entrust, exile, expatriate, expel, file, grade, group, index, list, marshal, order, organize, peg, pigeonhole, place, prioritize, range, rank, reduce, refer, screen, separate, set, shelve, sideline, sieve, sift, slot, sort, stereotype, systematize, transfer, type, typecast, winnow* (≠ accept, admit, advance, allow, assume, benefit, better, confuse, -deny, disarrange, elevate, entertain, harbor, hold, honor, house, jumble, keep, lump, naturalize, permit, promote, receive, repatriate, scramble, upgrade, welcome)

RELIEVE (+): *abate, aid, allay, alleviate, ameliorate, amend, appease, assist, assuage, better, clear, comfort, console, correct, cure, cushion, defang, ease, emend, enhance, enrich, fix, free, heal, help, improve, lessen, lighten, lull, mend, mitigate, moderate, mollify, pacify, palliate, perfect, reassure, rectify, reduce, refine, reform, relax, release, remedy, repair, rescue, save, settle, slacken, soften, soothe, spare, support, sustain, temper, unburden* (≠ aggravate, damage, deepen, exacerbate, exasperate, harm, heighten, hurt, impair, injure, intensify, panic, sharpen, terrify, troll, worry, worsen)

RELIEVE (+): *clear, deliver, discharge, disencumber, disengage, disentangle, divest, emancipate, enfranchise, extricate, free, liberate, loose, loosen, manumit, redeem, release, rescue, rid, slack, slacken, spring, unbind, unburden, uncage, unchain, unfetter* (≠ bog, burden, encumber, fetter, hamper, lumber, overextend, restrain, saddle, shackle, subject, tire, weary, weight)

RELINQUISH (→): *-abandon, abdicate, abjure, abnegate, cede, commit, consign, deliver, -deny, -desert, disavow, discard, disclaim, -discontinue, -disown, drop, entrust, forfeit, forgo, -forsake, give, hand, jilt, leave, -quit, release, render, -renounce, -repudiate, resign, shed, surrender, transfer, vacate, waive, yield* (≠ adopt, appropriate, arrogate, assume, claim, colonize, confiscate, defend, guard, inhabit, keep, maintain, obtain, protect, recover, rescue, retain, safeguard, secure, seek, seize, source, take, tenant, usurp, withhold, wrest)

RELISH (←): *admire, adore, applaud, appreciate, celebrate, cherish, clock, congratulate, consume, detect, devour, dig, drink, eat, enjoy, esteem, experience, extol, eye, fancy, favor, gobble, heed, idolize, indulge, inhale, love, mull, note, observe, ponder, prefer, prize, recognize, respect, revere, savor, scrutinize, sense, smell, sniff, taste, touch, treasure, value, venerate, whiff, wolf, worship* (≠ abhor, abominate, boo, chide, condemn, criticize, -despise, -detest, -disdain, disfavor, disrespect, -dodge, -hate, -loathe, protest, -refuse, regret, -reject, -renounce, repent, -repudiate, resent, ridicule, rue, scold, -scorn, -shun, -sidestep, -spurn) **(¿) ABSTRACTION ALERT. Concrete goals essential!**

REMEDY (+): *aid, allay, alleviate, assuage, attend, bandage, clean, control, correct, counteract, cure, diagnose, doctor, dose, drug, ease, fix, heal, help, hospitalize, improve, lighten, medicate, mend, mitigate, moderate, nurse, palliate, quarantine, realign, recalibrate, rectify, redress, reform, relieve, renew, repair, restore, right, salve, scrub, solve, soothe, sort, splint, temper, treat* (≠ afflict, aggravate, blemish, break, contaminate, damage, harm, hurt, impair, indispose, infect, injure, misdiagnose, nauseate, overdose, palsy, poison, pollute, ruin, sicken, spike, spoil, sprain, traumatize, trouble, worsen, wound, wreck)

REMEDY (+): *adjust, alter, ameliorate, amend, better, blue-pencil, calibrate, change, control, correct, cut, debug, defray, edit, emend, fix, improve, launder, mend, mitigate, modify, modulate, override, pace, perfect, polish, punctuate, realign, rebate, rectify, red-pen, red-pencil, redraft, redraw, redress, reform, regulate, repair, rephrase, restore, restyle, rethink, retool, retouch, revamp, revise, rework, rewrite, right, shine, shorten, square, tune, tweak, upgrade* (≠ aggravate, callous, coarsen, compromise, damage, harm, hurt, impair, injure, mar, spoil, vulgarize, worsen)

REMIND (→): *bare, confess, confide, confirm, disclose, discover, divulge, evince, evoke, expose, hint, impel, nudge, prod, prompt, reveal, spur, uncover, unmask, unveil* (≠ bury, conceal, -disregard, erase, forget, hide, -ignore, miss, -negate, -neglect, -nullify, -overlook, secrete, shroud) **(¿) ABSTRACTION ALERT. Concrete goals essential!**

REMODEL (+): *adapt, adjust, align, alter, amend, change, commute, convert, customize, deform, exchange, fashion, fit, harmonize, match, metamorphose, modernize, modify, mutate, prepare, qualify, ready, recast, reconceive, reconceptualize, redo, refashion, regenerate, reimagine, reinvent, rejigger, remake, reshape, restructure, rethink, retool, revamp, revise, revolutionize, rework, sculpt, shape, suit, tailor, transfigure, transform, transmute, vary, weaponize* (≠ boobytrap, damage, destroy, eradicate, fix, freeze, harm, hurt, monkey-wrench, paralyze, ruin, sabotage, scotch, scupper, scuttle, set, shelve, stabilize, topple, undermine, vandalize, wreck)

REMOVE (→): *abolish, anonymize, blue-pencil, boot, delete, delouse, discard, discharge, dislodge, dismiss, efface, eject, eliminate, evacuate, evict, excise, -exclude, expel, expunge, exterminate, extract, extricate, junk, -omit, purge, relegate, sack, scratch, shed, strip, take, throw, uninstall, uproot* (≠ affix, commission, conceive, concoct, connect, create, draft, fix, install, invent, mount, preserve, retain, submit)

REMOVE (→): *axe, ban, banish, boot, bounce, bump, bust, can, cashier, chuck, deselect, discard, discharge, dismiss, displace, dispossess, downsize, drum, eject, excuse, exempt, exorcise, expel, fire, furlough, -nix, -ostracize, oust, pink-slip, release, relieve, replace, retire, rout, sack, separate, sideline, spare, supersede, supplant, suspend, terminate, toss, trim, turf, unload, unseat* (≠ appoint, assign, contract, delegate, employ, engage, hire, invite, keep, promote, protect, recruit, reemploy, rehire, retain, sign, subcontract, task, welcome)

REMOVE (←): *abstract, alter, bear, budge, carry, cart, clear, convey, -cut, detach, dislocate, dislodge, displace, disturb, -ditch, drag, draw, drive, drop, extract, extricate, haul, lose, lug, manhandle, modify, move, pull, redo, refashion, relegate, relocate, remake, remodel, replace, reposition, revamp, revise, rework, schlep, separate, shift, ship, shuttle, skim, smuggle, supersede, supplant, take, tote, transfer, transmit, transplant, transport, transpose, unload, vary, withdraw* (≠ affix, anchor, clamp, clinch, control, embed, entrench, fix, freeze, hitch, implant, ingrain, juxtapose, lodge, moor, mount, pin, place, position, -prevent, reclaim, recoup, recover, rescue, retrieve, root, salvage, secure, set, site, situate, stabilize, stay, stick)

REMOVE (/): *change, disrobe, doff, douse, excoriate, expose, husk, peel, reveal, shed, strip, unbuckle, unbutton, undress, unwrap* (≠ apparel, array, attire, bedeck, clothe, costume, don, dress, garb, hide, holster, jacket, mask, rig, robe, sheathe, sport, suit, wear)

REMOVE (/): *annihilate, asphyxiate, assassinate, behead, bump, butcher, chill, claim, croak, deep-six, delouse, depopulate, destroy, dispatch, doff, doom, drown, eliminate, eradicate, erase, execute, exterminate, fell, get, guillotine, hang, ice, kill, liquidate, massacre, murder, obliterate, orphan, purge, sacrifice, shoot, slaughter, slay, smite, smother, snuff, sterilize, strangle, suffocate, terminate, uproot, waste, weed, zap* (≠ animate, bear, benefit, birth, defend, embalm, guard, help, nourish, pickle, raise, reinvigorate, rescue, restore, resurrect, resuscitate, revive, save, survive, sustain)

REMOVE (/): *alter, amputate, anatomize, behead, butcher, carve, castrate, chop, circumcise, cut, deball, decapitate, desex, dismember, eliminate, emasculate, eviscerate, excavate, excise, extract, extricate, geld, gore, harvest, lop, maim, mangle, mutilate, razor, rip, savage, select, separate, sever, slice, split, sunder, truncate, unsex, vivisect, withdraw* (≠ attach, create, doctor, generate, graft, heal, implant, insert, introduce, mend, nurse, nurture, plant, repair, restore, revive, sew, stitch, suture, transplant, unite, weld)

RENEW (+): *automate, beautify, boost, brace, enhance, exhilarate, extend, freshen, gentrify, groom, improve, innovate, jump-start, kick-start, manicure, mend, modernize, optimize, overhaul, prioritize, prolong, reactivate, reaffirm, reanimate, reawaken, recharge, reclaim, recondition, reconstitute, recreate, redesign, redevelop, reengineer, reestablish, refill, refit, reform, refresh, refurbish, regenerate, rehabilitate, reinvent, reinvigorate, rejuvenate, remodel, renovate, reopen, repair, repeat, replace, replenish, reshuffle, restart, restimulate, restock, restore, resume, resupply, resuscitate, retread, revitalize, revive, revolutionize, spiff, spruce, steady, stimulate, survive, transform, update, upgrade* (≠ -abandon, annihilate, break, can, -cancel, cease, check, complete, conclude, consummate, cut, damage, deep-six, drop, dump, exhaust, extinguish, finalize, finish, -halt, kill, obliterate, offload, quench, ruin, sabotage, scotch, scupper, scuttle, shelve, snuff, subvert, suppress, terminate, undermine, wreck)

-RENOUNCE (→): *-abandon, abdicate, abjure, -boycott, cede, -deny, -desert, disavow, discard, disclaim, -disown, -eschew, -forsake, jettison, leave, -nullify, picket, -quit, -refuse, -reject, relinquish, -repudiate, resign, revoke, sacrifice, -shun, -spurn, surrender, vacate, waive, yield* (≠ accept, advocate, appropriate, arrogate, assume, claim, confiscate, defend, embrace, espouse, guard, permit, protect, reap, reclaim, recover, redeem, safeguard, secure, seize, support, take, usurp, wrest)

-RENOUNCE (/): *-abandon, abjure, bolt, contradict, controvert, -deny, disallow, disavow, disclaim, discredit, -disown, disprove, dispute, doubt, drop, -forsake, forswear, gainsay, -negate, rebut, recall, recant, refute, relinquish, repeal, -repudiate, retract, revoke, -spurn, surrender, withdraw* (≠ accept, acknowledge, adhere, admit, adopt, affirm, assert, avow, back, claim, confess, confirm, contend, declare, defend, embrace, endorse, espouse, maintain, proclaim, profess, state, support, uphold, vow)

RENOVATE (+): *aid, ameliorate, automate, better, clean, cleanse, computerize, condition, cure, doctor, enhance, enrich, face-lift, fix, freshen, furbish, gentrify, heal, help, improve, mend, modernize, optimize, overhaul, patch, prepare, reactivate, ready, rebuild, recondition, reconstruct, recreate, redecorate, refit, reform, refresh, refurbish, regenerate, rehabilitate, reinvigorate, rejuvenate, rekindle, remake, remedy, remodel, renew, repair, reprogram, reshuffle, restore, resurrect, resuscitate, retread, revamp, revitalize, revive, revolutionize, service, spiff, spruce, stimulate, update, upgrade, wallpaper* (≠ annihilate, blemish, boobytrap, break, bulldoze, condemn, cripple, damage, deface, demolish, disable, disfigure, efface, flaw, harm, harshen, hurt, impair, injure, level, maim, mangle, mar, mutilate, ruin, sabotage, savage, scotch, scupper, scuttle, shelve, spoil, vandalize, wreck)

RENT (←): *acquire, arrange, bespeak, book, charter, contract, engage, hire, lease, let, lodge, obtain, order, procure, reserve, secure, sublease, sublet* (≠ borrow, buy, close, commandeer, lend, loan, outbid, own, possess, purchase, steal)

REPAIR (+): *adjust, aid, align, ameliorate, amend, automate, balance, better, calibrate, center, compose, condition, connect, coordinate, correct, cure, darn, debug, defray, doctor, edit, enhance, enrich, fine-tune, fit, fix, focus, freshen, furbish, grind, heal, help, improve, maintain, mechanize, mend, modernize, motorize, optimize, overhaul, patch, polish, prepare, readjust, ready, realign, reassemble, rebuild, recalibrate, reclaim, recondition, reconstitute, reconstruct, recover, rectify, redesign, redevelop, redo, redress, reengineer, refit, reform, refresh, refurbish, regenerate, regulate, rehab, rehabilitate, reinvigorate, rejuvenate, remake, remedy, remodel, renew, renovate, repaint rephrase, reshuffle, restore, retool, retread, retrieve, retrofit, revamp, revise, revitalize, revive, revolutionize, right, service, set, settle, sew, sharpen, shine, square, tighten, troubleshoot, tune, tweak, update, upgrade* (≠ blemish, botch, break, bungle, callous, coarsen, compromise, cripple, damage, deface, destroy, disable, disfigure, doom, efface, eradicate, erase, flaw, harm, harshen, hurt, impair, incapacitate, injure, kneecap, maim, mangle, mar, monkey-wrench, mutilate, ruin, savage, spoil, unsew, vandalize, wreck)

REPAY (→): *avenge, bankroll, compensate, counter, counteract, defray, disburse, discharge, dole, exchange, indemnify, liquidate, outlay, overpay, pay, rebate, recompense, redress, refund, reimburse, remit, remunerate, render, reprise, retort, revenge, reward, satisfy, settle, square, substitute, swap, switch* (≠ absolve, acquit, beggar, damage, deprive, disinherit, excuse, extort, forget, forgive, lend, loan, mortgage, -neglect, -overlook, owe, pardon, penalize, poach, -refuse, seize, -slight, spare, steal, stiff, stint, take, withhold)

REPEL (/): *affront, aggrieve, anger, annoy, antagonize, appall, boot, bother, bounce, buck, bug, check, cut, disappoint, disgust, -disown, displease, disquiet, distress, disturb, horrify, insult, irritate, jar, nag, nauseate, needle, nettle, nitpick, offend, outrage, provoke, repulse, revolt, rile, scandalize, shock, sicken, -spurn, ward* (≠ allure, attract, bed, beguile, bewitch, captivate, charm, delight, disarm, draw, enchant, enrapture, enthrall, entice, entrance, fascinate, gratify, interest, intrigue, lure, please, pull, rejoice, seduce, tantalize, tease, tempt, thrill, tickle) **(¿) ABSTRACTION ALERT. Concrete goals essential!**

REPEL (/): *baffle, -balk, battle, buck, challenge, check, combat, confront, contest, contradict, counter, counterpunch, debate, -decline, deflect, defy, dismiss, dispute, duel, fight, foil, -frustrate, hinder, kick, obstruct, oppose, parry, -rebuff, rebut, -refuse, -reject, repulse, resent, resist, -snub, -spurn, stem, -thwart, ward, withstand* (≠ accept, accost, approve, chase, clasp, clutch, demand, desire, embrace, encourage, follow, grab, hail, hunt, invite, pursue, request, seek, shadow, tail, track, welcome)

REPLACE (→): *adjust, appoint, deliver, fix, foist, heal, mend, overhaul, reappoint, recall, reestablish, reimpose, reinforce, reinstate, reintroduce, release, relinquish, reload, render, replenish, restock, restore, return, service, substitute, surrender, tend, yield* (≠ appropriate, commandeer, confiscate, destroy, drop, end, eradicate, exterminate, lose, maintain, -nullify, obliterate, remove, repeal, reverse, revoke, seize, sustain, weed)

REPLACE (+): *change, depose, deputize, disinherit, dislodge, dismiss, displace, dispossess, eject, evict, exchange, expel, follow, oust, overthrow, preempt, refund, relieve, replace, replant, substitute, succeed, supersede, supplant, swap, switch, topple, unseat, usurp* (≠ bogart, borrow, catch, filch, grab, hold, nab, pinch, place, poach, purloin, settle, situate, snag, steal, swipe, take)

REPLENISH (→): *accoutre, allocate, allot, apportion, arm, assign, bestow, contribute, disburse, dispense, distribute, dole, dollop, donate, equip, feed, fill, fit, fortify, furnish, gird, give, mete, outfit, parcel, portion, prepare, present, prorate, provide, provision, recharge, refill, refresh, reload, renew, replace, reprovision restock, restore, rig, stock, store, supply, tender, tithe, top, victual* (≠ cannibalize, consume, cripple, debilitate, deplete, depredate, deprive, dispossess, dissipate, divest, drain, eat, empty, exhaust, malnourish, overextend, require, sap, squander, strip, tap, tax, waste)

REPRESENT (→): *agent, assign, broker, constitute, contract, depict, display, embody, engineer, epitomize, evoke, exteriorize, externalize, finesse, invoke, jockey, lobby, manage, manifest, negotiate, obligate, oblige, portray, renegotiate, wangle* (≠ -abandon, botch, bungle, cheat, -desert, foozle, -forsake, fumble, half-ass, manipulate, mishandle, mislead, muff, swindle) **(¿) ABSTRACTION ALERT. Concrete goals essential!**

REPRESS (←): *bottle, bridle, bury, chasten, check, cloak, clothe, cloud, collect, compose, constrain, contain, control, cool, cork, cover, crush, curb, -deny, disguise, efface, exorcise, fetter, forget, govern, hide, hinder, hold, hush, inhibit, lock, manage, mask, master, muffle, muzzle, overcome, overpower, pocket, quash, quell, rein, restrain, shush, silence, sink, smother, squelch, staunch, stifle, subdue, subjugate, sublimate, submerge, suppress, swallow, withdraw* (≠ advance, aid, allow, arouse, assist, confess, cultivate, disclose, disperse, emancipate, encourage, evince, excite, expose, express, foment, forward, foster, free, help, impel, incite, instigate, liberate, loose, out, permit, provoke, release, reveal, scatter, share, stir, support, unleash, unlock, vent, verbalize, vocalize)

REPRESS (/): *annihilate, choke, clamp, conquer, decimate, demolish, desolate, destroy, devastate, dominate, douse, exterminate, extinguish, kill, nuke, obliterate, overcome, overpower, overwhelm, quench, ruin, smash, smother, snuff, squash, squelch, staunch, stifle, strangle, subdue, subjugate, suppress, throttle, vanquish, waste, wreck* (≠ advance, aid, assist, back, boost, cultivate, encourage, foment, forward, foster, further, help, incite, instigate, nourish, nurture, prioritize, promote, prop, provoke, rabble-rouse, stir, subvert, support, tantalize, tease, tempt, trigger, whip)

REPRIMAND (/): *admonish, advise, berate, blame, boo, castigate, caution, censure, chastise, check, chide, correct, counsel, criticize, critique,* *denigrate, denounce, discipline, disparage, exhort, fault, finger, frame, fulminate, judge, lambaste, lecture, lesson, punish, rap, -rebuff, rebuke, reproach, reprove, school, scold, -shun, slate, upbraid, warn, zap* (≠ admire, applaud, approve, blandish, bless, commend, compliment, congratulate, endorse, eulogize, excuse, exonerate, extol, flatter, forgive, glorify, gratify, honor, lionize, pardon, praise, reward, salute, sanction, spare, tout)

-REPUDIATE (/): *-abandon, abjure, -balk, -boycott, -bypass, controvert, -decline, -deny, detour, disapprove, discard, -disdain, dismiss, -disown, -disregard, -eschew, -forbid, -forsake, forswear, gainsay, -ignore, jettison, -negate, -nix, overrule, pass, -prohibit, proscribe, -rebuff, -refuse, -reject, relinquish, -renounce, repeal, revoke, -scorn, scout, -shun, -spurn, surrender, -veto, waive, withdraw* (≠ accept, acknowledge, adopt, advocate, aid, allow, approve, assert, back, brook, choose, condone, confirm, countenance, covet, crave, defend, embrace, endorse, endure, face, fancy, fetishize, handpick, invite, maintain, permit, receive, seek, select, stomach, support, swallow, take, tolerate, uphold, welcome)

-REPUDIATE (/): *abdicate, abjure, challenge, confute, contradict, criticize, critique, cross-examine, debate, -deny, disallow, disavow, disclaim, discredit, -disown, disprove, dispute, distrust, doubt, gainsay, grill, interrogate, -negate, -nullify, oppose, override, question, rebut, recant, refute, -reject, -renounce, retort, retract, traverse* (≠ accept, acknowledge, admit, adopt, affirm, allow, announce, assert, authenticate, avow, claim, concede, confess, confirm, consult, corroborate, declare, embrace, espouse, grant, maintain, notarize, own, profess, reclaim, recognize, submit, substantiate, validate, verify)

REPULSE (/): *affront, appall, brutalize, disgust, displease, disquiet, distress, horrify, insult, nauseate, offend, outrage, rattle, repel, revolt, scandalize, shake, shock, sicken, terrorize, traumatize, unnerve, upset* (≠ attract, bed, beguile, bewitch, captivate, charm, delight, disarm, draw, entice, fascinate, gratify, intrigue, lure, please, pull, seduce, tantalize, taunt, tease, tempt, thrill, tickle) **(¿) ABSTRACTION ALERT. Concrete goals essential!**

REPULSE (→): *check, curb, defeat, deflect, defy, -disdain, -disregard, fight, -nix, oppose, overthrow, -rebuff, rebuke, rebut, -refuse, -reject, repel, resist, -snub, -spurn, ward, withstand* (≠ accept, beckon, call, chase, coax, draw, embrace, hail, include, invite, pull, pursue, seek, solicit, summon, welcome)

REQUISITION (←): *appropriate, arrogate, charter, commandeer, commission, confiscate, demand, hijack, hire, impound, license, occupy, request, seize, sequester, solicit, summon, take, use, usurp* (≠ bestow, give, keep, offer, provide, receive, -refuse, -reject, relinquish, spare, stop, submit, surrender, tender, volunteer, yield)

RESCUE (←): *absolve, acquit, aid, assist, -avert, champion, conserve, counterattack, counterpunch, defend, deliver, discharge, disengage,* *disentangle, emancipate, enfranchise, escort, exonerate, extricate, free, insulate, keep, liberate, manumit, nourish, pardon, patronize, pluck, preserve, protect, ransom, recapture, reclaim, recover, recycle, redeem, regain, release, relieve, reprieve, retain, retrieve, safeguard, salvage, save, secure, shelter, shield, spring, support, unburden, unchain, unfetter, unleash, unshackle, untie, uphold, ward, watch* (≠ abduct, abuse, assault, attack, bash, betray, bind, brutalize, capture, compromise, demolish, destroy, devastate, disappear, dismantle, endanger, enslave, -forsake, gamble, harm, hazard, hurt, impair, imperil, imprison, injure, institutionalize, jail, jeopardize, kidnap, menace, persecute, punish, risk, ruin, savage, seize, target, terrorize, threaten, torment, torture, traumatize, venture, victimize, violate, wreck)

RESEARCH (←): *analyze, ascertain, assay, assess, benchmark, browse, calculate, categorize, check, compile, compute, consult, cram, cross-examine, cruise, deduce, detect, determine, diagnose, discern, evaluate, examine, explore, eye, eyeball, ferret, gather, grill, grok, hunt, inspect, interrogate, interview, investigate, learn, monitor, notice, observe, peruse, prioritize, probe, prove, prowl, pump, question, rank, read, reconstruct, reinvestigate, review, scan, scope, scrutinize, search, seek, sift, skim, spot, study, surf, suss, test, try, verify* (≠ accept, addle, assume, baffle, bewilder, blind, bury, -bypass, conceal, confound, confuse, conjecture, deceive, defraud, -disregard, fake, fancy, forget, fudge, guess, half-ass, hide, -ignore, mask, miscalculate, mislead, misread, miss, misunderstand, muddle, mystify, -neglect, obscure, -omit, -overlook, perplex, predetermine, puzzle, -reject, -shirk, skirt, surmise, trick, wonder)

RESENT (/): *alienate, begrudge, blame, chide, covet, crave, denounce, desire, disaffect, disappoint, disenchant, disillusion, disrespect, dissatisfy, embitter, endure, envy, estrange, face, fault, grudge, isolate, poison, scant, scold, skimp, sour, stint, stomach, suffer, tolerate, want, weather* (≠ accept, admire, appreciate, approve, cherish, esteem, fetishize, forgive, give, invite, love, offer, relish, respect, satisfy, savor, spare, tender, treasure, understand, volunteer, welcome, wish) **(¿) ABSTRACTION ALERT. Concrete goals essential!**

RESERVE (←): *accumulate, archive, bear, boast, budget, cherish, coffer, command, conserve, control, defer, delay, detain, direct, -duck, earmark, enjoy, guard, harbor, hoard, hold, hug, keep, maintain, manage, own, pause, pickle, plant, possess, postpone, preserve, protect, retain, rule, save, shelve, squirrel, stash, stockpile, store, stow, treasure, tuck, withhold* (≠ -abandon, bequeath, bestow, blow, cede, circulate, comp, consume, contribute, -decline, diffuse, discard, disseminate, dissipate, distribute, donate, drop, dump, gamble, give, lard, lavish, lose, offer, overfeed, -reject, release, relinquish, -repudiate, risk, scatter, slather, spare, -spurn, squander, surrender, tender, tithe, volunteer, waste, yield)

RESERVE (←): *arrange, bespeak, book, calendar, charter, claim, commit, contract, earmark, engage, hire, lease, note, order, plan, prearrange, promise, register, rent, retain, schedule, secure, select, utilize* (≠ -abort, break, -cancel, -decline, -deny, discard, -dodge, forfeit, lose, -nix, pass, postpone, reconsider, -rescind, revoke, scrap, shelve, spend, -spurn, squander, use, waste, withdraw)

RESERVE (←): *allocate, apply, arrange, bespeak, bestow, bless, book, commit, confide, consecrate, consign, contract, dedicate, devote, earmark, employ, engage, entrust, hallow, hire, order, prearrange, retain, sanctify, save, schedule, secure, use* (≠ break, discard, -ignore, lose, misapply, misuse, -neglect, spend, use, waste)

RESIST (/): *antagonize, assail, assault, -avert, -avoid, baffle, -balk, bar, barricade, battle, block, -boycott, brave, brazen, buck, challenge, check, combat, confront, contest, contradict, contrast, counter, counteract, countermand, counterpunch, cross, curb, dare, debate, deflect, defy, disobey, dispute, disturb, duel, embattle, face, fight, flout, foil, forgo, -frustrate, -halt, hassle, hinder, impede, impugn, inhibit, intercept, obstruct, oppose, override, parry, picket, -prevent, protest, race, -rebuff, -refuse, -reject, repel, repress, restrain, -scorn, stay, stem, stonewall, stop, tackle, -thwart, traverse, wrangle, wrestle* (≠ -abandon, abide, accept, advance, aid, allow, assist, bear, brook, concede, condone, contribute, defend, -desert, -discontinue, encourage, enjoy, forfeit, guard, help, indulge, ingratiate, invite, maintain, okay, permit, promote, protect, provide, safeguard, sanction, save, screen, secure, shelter, shield, stand, stomach, suffer, sustain, tolerate, uphold, weather, welcome, withstand)

RESPECT (+): *accept, acclaim, accredit, admire, adore, adulate, applaud, appreciate, approve, canonize, cherish, cleanse, commend, compliment, congratulate, consecrate, consider, credit, deify, devote, dig, dignify, elevate, enjoy, ennoble, esteem, exalt, fancy, favor, follow, hallow, heed, honor, idolize, improve, lionize, love, mind, note, obey, observe, praise, pray, prize, purify, recognize, regard, relish, restore, revere, reverence, salute, sanctify, tend, treasure, uphold, uplift, value, venerate, worship* (≠ abhor, abominate, abuse, advise, bastardize, bestialize, blacken, blackguard, boo, command, condemn, contaminate, counsel, debase, decry, defame, defile, demand, demean, demonize, -deny, deplore, desecrate, -despise, -detest, direct, disapprove, -discount, discredit, -disdain, disfavor, disgrace, dismiss, -disregard, disrespect, educate, enlighten, execrate, guide, -hate, humble, humiliate, -ignore, instruct, insult, -loathe, mandate, mock, -neglect, order, -overlook, pervert, pillory, pollute, profane, require, restrain, ridicule, -scorn, slander, taunt, teach, vilify, violate, warn, wrong) **(¿) ABSTRACTION ALERT. Concrete goals essential!**

RESTORE (→): *allot, allow, assign, assist, attribute, award, bequeath, bestow, consign, contribute, deliver, devote, disburse, dispense, dole, donate, endow, expend, extend, fund, furnish, give, grant, help, impart, indemnify, lavish, lend, offer, outlay, overpay, pay, pledge, present, provide, ration, rebate, recharge, recoup, refill, refund, reimburse, reinstate, reintroduce, reload, render, renew, repay, replace, replant, replenish, reprovision, restock, return, send, serve, share, shower, submit, supply, tender, tithe, underwrite, volunteer* (≠ bleed, cannibalize, consume, defund, deplete, depredate, disinherit, drain, drink, dry, empty, exhaust, keep, leach, leech, nobble, overextend, poach, purloin, remove, sap, slurp, steal, stiff, stint, strain, suck, swallow, take, tax, weaken, withhold)

RESTORE (+): *aid, alleviate, assist, cure, enliven, fix, freshen, gentrify, heal, help, improve, mend, modernize, overhaul, rebuild, reclaim, recondition, reconstruct, recover, recycle, redecorate, redeem, reform, refresh, refurbish, regenerate, rehabilitate, reinvigorate, rejuvenate, renew, renovate, repair, replace, rescue, reshuffle, retouch, revamp, revitalize, revive, salvage, strengthen, update, upgrade* (≠ -abandon, abolish, abrogate, break, castrate, cripple, damage, debilitate, demolish, destroy, doom, emasculate, eradicate, erase, harm, hurt, indispose, injure, kill, leech, level, malnourish, -neglect, repeal, -rescind, ruin, sabotage, scotch, scrap, scupper, shelve, sicken, sink, starve, subvert, undermine, unman, weaken, wear, weed, wither, wizen, wound, wreck, wrong)

RESTRAIN (←): *arrest, bind, block, book, bridle, capture, categorize, censor, chain, chasten, check, confine, constrain, constrict, control, convict, cramp, curb, curtail, delay, detain, encumber, fetter, frogmarch, gag, govern, -halt, hamper, handcuff, hinder, hogtie, impede, impound, imprison, incarcerate, inhibit, institutionalize, intern, jail, leash, manacle, march, muzzle, obstruct, pace, pin, pinion, police, -prevent, -prohibit, ration, redact, regulate, repress, restrict, secure, shackle, shelve, short-circuit, stall, stifle, stop, straightjacket, subdue, suppress, tackle, tether, tie, tighten* (≠ aid, air, allow, animate, arouse, assist, -avoid, compel, emancipate, enable, encourage, evince, excite, express, force, free, help, -ignore, impel, incite, indulge, liberate, loosen, lose, -neglect, permit, promote, provoke, release, rescue, save, slack, slacken, spring, start, tolerate, unbind, unchain, unleash, untie, vent)

RESTRICT (/): *ban, bar, bind, block, bottle, bound, cage, categorize, chain, condition, confine, constrain, constrict, contain, control, convict, cramp, curb, curtail, debilitate, demarcate, detain, disable, disqualify, encumber, enervate, enfeeble, fetter, -forbid, gate, hamper, handcuff, handicap, hinder, hogtie, hold, impede, impound, incapacitate, incarcerate, inhibit, -interdict, intern, limit, localize, pinch, -prohibit, ration, regulate, restrain, straiten, strangle, suppress, taboo, temper, tether, tie, tighten, trammel, weaken* (≠ allow, assist, broaden, develop, encourage, enlarge, exceed, expand, extend, foster, free, help, increase, legalize, lengthen, liberate, loose, loosen, open, outreach, permit, promote, raise, release, slacken, stretch, unbind, unleash, untie, widen)

RESURRECT (+): *awaken, energize, enkindle, ensoul, gentrify, jump-start, kick-start, reactivate, reanimate, reawaken, reboot, recharge, reconceive, reconceptualize, redefine, reestablish, refresh, regenerate, reinstall, reintroduce, reinvent, reinvigorate, rejuvenate, rekindle, renew, rescue, restart, restimulate, restore, resuscitate, revitalize, revive, save* (≠ assassinate, crush, destroy, doom, end, eradicate, erase, execute, extinguish, kill, lobotomize, murder, neutralize, orphan, quench, slay, snuff, stifle, suppress, terminate, wizen)

RESUSCITATE (+): *arouse, awaken, energize, enliven, ensoul, exhilarate, heal, invigorate, jolt, oxygenate, quicken, rally, reanimate, recharge, recoup, recover, recuperate, refresh, reinvigorate, rejuvenate, rekindle, renew, renovate, rescue, restimulate, restore, resurrect, revitalize, revive, save, spark, stimulate, stir, wake* (≠ anesthetize, bludgeon, chloroform, concuss, conk, destroy, doom, dope, dose, drug, eradicate, execute, injure, kill, lynch, maim, murder, overdose, poison, sedate, sicken, smother, strangle, suffocate, terminate, throttle, tranquilize)

RETAIN (←): *absorb, accumulate, amass, assemble, bear, boast, budget, cherish, clasp, clutch, collect, colonize, command, concentrate, conglomerate, conserve, contain, continue, control, corner, detain, direct, embrace, enjoy, enshrine, gather, grasp, grip, guard, harbor, hoard, hog, hold, hug, husband, keep, maintain, manage, memorize, mind, monopolize, own, possess, preserve, protect, recall, recognize, recollect, remember, reserve, restrain, rule, save, scant, seize, shelter, skimp, sport, stash, stint, store, stow, treasure, withhold* (≠ -abandon, abolish, anonymize, bequeath, bestow, -cancel, cede, circulate, comp, contribute, -decline, destroy, discard, -disown, disseminate, donate, doom, drop, dump, entrust, eradicate, erase, expunge, forfeit, forget, -forsake, give, grant, impart, lavish, lose, -nullify, offload, -reject, release, relinquish, -repudiate, scrap, sell, share, spend, -spurn, squander, surrender, tender, tithe, waste, weed, yield)

RETAIN (←): *advance, assume, commission, contract, employ, engage, enlist, headhunt, hire, keep, maintain, occupy, overpay, partner, pay, place, promote, recruit, reserve, scout, sign, subcontract, upgrade* (≠ axe, can, -deny, discharge, dismiss, fire, furlough, -rebuff, -refuse, -reject, sack, scrap, -spurn, stiff, stint, terminate, transfer)

RETARD (←): *arrest, baffle, boobytrap, bottleneck, brake, check, constrain, curb, decelerate, delay, detain, disqualify, encumber, foil, -frustrate, -halt, hamper, hamstring, handicap, hinder, hobble, impede, incapacitate, inhibit, monkey-wrench, obstruct, pause, postpone, rein, restrain, restrict, sabotage, scotch, shelve, short-circuit, slacken, slow, stall, stop, subvert, -thwart, undercut, undermine* (≠ accelerate, advance, aid, augment, boost, brainstorm, catalyze, dispatch, drive, ease, encourage, enhance, expedite, facilitate, fast-forward, feed, forward, fuel, further, goad, grease, hasten, help, hurry, nurture, optimize, prioritize, propel, punt, push, quicken, revolutionize, rush, speed, spur, stimulate, stir, urge)

RETRACT (←): *-abandon, abjure, abnegate, back, bolt, -cancel, contradict, controvert, countermand, debate, deep-six, -deny, disallow, disavow, disclaim, -disown, disprove, dispute, eliminate, -exclude, -forsake, forswear, gainsay, invalidate, -negate, -nix, rebut, recall, recant, refute, relinquish, -renounce, repeal, -repudiate, -rescind, reverse, revoke, sheathe, -spurn, surrender, suspend, withdraw* (≠ accent, accentuate, accept, admit, adopt, advance, advocate, affirm, amplify, approve, assert, avow, back, belabor, boost, cherish, claim, confess, corroborate, court, embrace, emphasize, endorse, enforce, espouse, extend, favor, forge, keep, maintain, profess, protect, prove, reaffirm, repeat, sanction, seek, support, unspool, uphold, verify, vindicate, vow, welcome, woo)

RETRIEVE (←): *acquire, download, fetch, gain, mend, obtain, procure, reacquire, recall, recapture, reclaim, recollect, recoup, recover, recruit, redeem, regain, remedy, repair, replenish, repossess, repurchase, rescue, restore, retake, return, salvage, save, secure, seize, source* (≠ -abandon, -desert, -disown, -ditch, dump, -forsake, give, lose, mislay, misplace, offer, relinquish, resign, surrender, tender, volunteer)

REVEAL (+): *acknowledge, admit, advertise, air, announce, avow, bare, betray, blab, blaze, blurt, broadcast, bulletin, circulate, clue, communicate, concede, confess, confide, confirm, confront, debunk, decipher, declare, disclose, discover, disinter, display, disseminate, divulge, elaborate, evince, exhibit, expose, express, exteriorize, externalize, impart, inform, leak, manifest, own, placard, post, proclaim, promulgate, publicize, publish, relate, share, show, showcase, spill, spud, squeal, talk, telegraph, tell, tender, uncloak, unclothe, uncloud, uncover, undeceive, undrape, unearth, unfold, unmask, unveil, verbalize, vocalize, volunteer, vouchsafe* (≠ alter, bleep, bluff, blur, box, bullshit, bury, camouflage, cheat, cloak, clothe, cloud, conceal, costume, cover, curtain, darken, deceive, -deny, disguise, distort, double-cross, double-talk, embellish, embroider, enshroud, entomb, erase, eyeball, falsify, fence, fool, fudge, garble, hide, hood, impersonate, mask, miscommunicate, mislead, misrepresent, muddy, notice, obscure, occlude, pretend, -refuse, scramble, screen, shadow, shroud, spackle, spin, trick, varnish, veil, watch, whitewash, wrap)

REVENGE (/): *avenge, castigate, chasten, chastise, compensate, correct, counter, defend, discipline, even, exact, exonerate, fix, get, incriminate, justify, lynch, match, penalize, persecute, punish, recompense, rectify, redress, repay, retort, return, right, scourge, sentence, square, torment, torture, vindicate, wreak* (≠ absolve, allow, approve, brook, comfort, condone, defend, -disregard, encourage, endure, excuse, exonerate, forgive, pardon, permit, remit, spare, stomach, tolerate)

REVERE (+): *acknowledge, admire, adore, advance, aggrandize, apotheosize, applaud, appreciate, award, canonize, cheer, cherish, congratulate, consecrate, defend, deify, delight, dignify, elevate, enjoy, ennoble, enshrine, esteem, exalt, extol, fetishize, glorify, gratify, guard, honor, idolize, laud, lionize, love, magnify, please, praise, prize, promote, protect, regard, respect, reverence, reward, sanctify, satisfy, support, toast, treasure, value, venerate, worship* (≠ abhor, abominate, affront, blackguard, blaspheme, castigate, condemn, criticize, critique, decry, defame, demean, demonize, denounce, denunciate, deride, desecrate, -despise, -detest, dishonor, disparage, displease, -disregard, disrespect, execrate, insult, libel, malign, mock, offend, outrage, pillory, pique, profane, ridicule, -scorn, slander, -slight, slur, smear, violate) **(¿) ABSTRACTION ALERT. Concrete goals essential!**

REVIEW (←): *amend, analyze, bemoan, categorize, check, correct, debrief, detect, determine, emend, eyeball, prioritize, readdress, reanalyze, reappraise, reassess, recall, recap, recapitulate, recollect, reconceive, reconceptualize, reconsider, rectify, redefine, reenvision, reevaluate, reexamine, reexplore, reform, regret, rehash, reimagine, reinvestigate, remedy, remember, rethink, revamp, revise, revisit, reweigh, sample, slot, sort* (≠ aid, assert, assist, assume, condone, defend, discover, excuse, forgive, give, guess, help, -ignore, lessen, maintain, -neglect, pardon, preview, uphold) **(¿) ABSTRACTION ALERT. Concrete goals essential!**

REVIEW (←): *analyze, appraise, assess, audit, badmouth, benchmark, check, comb, commend, compare, con, correct, criticize, critique, discuss, dissect, evaluate, examine, explore, eye, eyeball, inspect, investigate, judge, knock, learn, mark, neg, notice, observe, oversee, pan, parse, peruse, plumb, praise, probe, prowl, rank, read, recapitulate, reference, research, rip, sample, scan, scope, scrutinize, slam, study, survey, trash, view, watch, weigh, zap* (≠ approve, baffle, blind, -bypass, confound, confuse, deceive, disguise, -disregard, forget, fudge, half-ass, -ignore, leave, mask, miss, mistake, -neglect, -omit, -overlook, perplex, peruse, praise, puzzle, quiet, -shirk, -shun, silence, skim, skip)

REVILE (/): *abuse, admonish, assail, berate, blackguard, blame, boo, calumniate, castigate, censure, chide, criticize, defame, denigrate, denounce, deride, -despise, discredit, disfavor, disgrace, disparage, disrespect, execrate, fault, finger, frame, fulminate, -hate, lambaste, lecture, libel, malign, maltreat, persecute, ream, reprimand, reproach, reprove, resent, scapegoat, scold, -scorn, shame, slander, smear, tongue-lash, traduce, upbraid, vilify, vituperate, wrong* (≠ acclaim, admire, applaud, blandish, cheer, cherish, commend, compliment, congratulate, consider, eulogize, exalt, extol, favor, flatter, glorify, hail, honor, laud, praise, promote, protect, regard, respect, shield, sustain, vindicate, worship)

REVISE (+): *accommodate, adapt, adjust, align, alter, amend, blue-pencil, calibrate, change, clean, commute, compare, convert, coordinate, correct, cut, debug, deform, develop, edit, emend, exchange, expurgate, fine-tune, improve, launder, mend, metamorphose, modify, mutate, overhaul, perfect, peruse, polish, punctuate, realign, recalibrate, recast, reconceive, reconceptualize, reconsider, rectify, redefine, redo, red-pen, redraft, redraw, reexamine, refashion, refine, regenerate, rehash, reimagine, reinvent, rejigger, remake, remodel, reorganize, repair, rephrase, reshape, reshuffle, restyle, retool, revamp, review, revolutionize, reword, rework, rewrite, right, scan, scrub, scrutinize, shuffle, square, study, substitute, supersede, supplant, swap, switch, tighten, transfigure, transform, transmute, tune, tweak, update, upgrade, vary* (≠ -abandon, blemish, blight, -cancel, chuck, coarsen, compromise, corrupt, damage, diminish, disarrange, discard, disorganize, -ditch, draft, dump, fix, freeze,

-halt, harm, hurt, -ignore, impair, jettison, keep, lock, maintain, mangle, mar, preserve, repeal, replace, ruin, salvage, save, scrap, set, sketch, spoil, stabilize, suspend, tarnish, toss, trash, upset, vitiate, vulgarize, weaken, worsen)

REVITALIZE (+): *animate, assure, automate, cheer, comfort, console, embolden, encourage, fire, fortify, freshen, gentrify, hearten, incite, inflame, inspire, invigorate, jump-start, kick-start, modernize, nerve, overhaul, rally, reactivate, reanimate, reassure, recharge, reclaim, reconceive, reconceptualize, recondition, reconstitute, recreate, redesign, redevelop, redo, reengineer, refill, refresh, refurbish, regenerate, rehab, rehabilitate, reinvent, reinvigorate, rejuvenate, rekindle, remake, remodel, renew, renovate, repair, replenish, reshuffle, restart, restimulate, restore, resupply, resurrect, resuscitate, revive, revolutionize, rouse, stiffen, stimulate, stir, strengthen, sustain, trigger, update, upgrade, vitalize* (≠ attenuate, burden, cannibalize, checkmate, conquer, consume, cripple, crush, damage, debilitate, defeat, deplete, destroy, drain, enervate, erode, exhaust, extinguish, hamstring, handicap, harm, hurt, impair, incapacitate, infect, injure, kill, leech, murder, overpower, overwhelm, quench, sap, sicken, subjugate, suppress, tire, weaken, weary, wither, wizen)

REVIVE (+): *aid, animate, arouse, assist, awaken, brighten, charge, cheer, comfort, console, encourage, energize, exhilarate, freshen, gladden, invigorate, lift, overcome, please, quicken, rally, reactivate, reanimate, recondition, recover, refresh, regenerate, reinvigorate, rejuvenate, rekindle, relieve, renew, renovate, repair, restimulate, restore, resurrect, resuscitate, revitalize, rouse, strengthen, supercharge, wake* (≠ -abandon, anesthetize, cannibalize, chloroform, consume, cripple, dampen, deaden, debilitate, deplete, dose, drain, drug, dull, exhaust, exterminate, hypnotize, infect, injure, leech, murder, -negate, neutralize, numb, offset, overdose, ruin, sedate, stupefy, subdue, suppress, tire, torpefy, tranquilize, weary, wither, wizen)

REVOKE (←): *-abandon, abjure, abolish, -abort, abrogate, annul, call, -cancel, countermand, -deny, disclaim, -discontinue, dismantle, dismiss, -disown, drop, end, erase, expunge, forswear, -halt, interrupt, invalidate, lift, -negate, -nix, -nullify, obliterate, overrule, quash, recall, recant, relinquish, remove, -renounce, repeal, -repudiate, -rescind, retract, reverse, scrap, scrub, stop, surrender, suspend, terminate, vacate, -void, withdraw* (≠ affirm, allow, approve, authorize, begin, bequeath, certify, commence, confirm, continue, enact, enforce, engage, establish, initiate, keep, launch, legalize, permit, pledge, promise, ratify, regulate, sanction, start, stipulate, support, undertake, validate)

REVOLT (/): *afflict, affront, agitate, appall, discomfit, disgust, dismay, displease, disquiet, distress, harm, horrify, indispose, infect, inflict, insult, nauseate, offend, outrage, pain, rattle, repel, repulse, scandalize, shake, shock, sicken, terrorize, traumatize, unhinge, unnerve, unsettle, upset, weary, wound* (≠ allure, attract, bed, beguile, bewitch, captivate, charm, comfort, console, delight, disarm, draw, entertain, entice, entrance, fascinate, gratify, heal, intrigue, lure, please, pull, restore, seduce, steady, tantalize, taunt, tease, tempt, thrill, tickle, woo, wow) **(¿) ABSTRACTION ALERT. Concrete goals essential!**

REVOLUTIONIZE (+): *adapt, adjust, automate, calibrate, change, computerize, convert, electrify, gentrify, improve, inspire, jolt, metamorphose, modernize, outdo, outgrow, outperform, outsell, outshine, outstrip, overhaul, overtake, overthrow, overturn, patch, perfect, pioneer, rebuild, recast, reconceive, reconceptualize, reconstruct, recreate, rectify, refashion, reform, refurbish, reimagine, reinvent, reinvigorate, rejuvenate, remake, remodel, renew, renovate, reorganize, reprogram, reshape, reshuffle, restructure, retool, retread, revamp, rework, surpass, top, transfigure, transform, transmogrify, tune, tweak, update, upgrade* (≠ annihilate, blemish, blight, boobytrap, conserve, continue, deep-six, demolish, destroy, diminish, doom, duplicate, echo, eradicate, erase, fracture, impede, maintain, mar, monkey-wrench, -neglect, nuke, obliterate, paralyze, perpetuate, preserve, pulverize, raze, ruin, sabotage, scotch, shatter, shelve, sustain, undercut, undermine, vandalize, vaporize, wreck)

REWARD (→): *acclaim, applaud, appreciate, award, boost, celebrate, cherish, cite, commemorate, commend, compensate, compliment, congratulate, crown, decorate, enrich, enshrine, favor, glorify, gold-star, gratify, hail, honor, indulge, laud, memorialize, observe, outlay, overpay, pay, praise, prioritize, recognize, recompense, refund, reimburse, remember, remunerate, repay, return, revere, salute, stroke, thank, treasure* (≠ belittle, blame, boo, castigate, chasten, chastise, correct, criticize, denounce, deprive, disavow, discipline, discount, discredit, disfavor, disgrace, dishonor, dispute, -disregard, disrespect, excuse, fault, fine, forget, forgive, frame, -neglect, -omit, -overlook, pardon, penalize, pooh-pooh, punish, resent, scold, -scorn, shame, -slight, starve, steal, stiff, stint, take, withhold)

RIDE (→): *board, carry, control, cruise, direct, drive, float, guide, handle, manage, move, pedal, post, progress, restrain, roll, straddle, tour, travel* (≠ -avoid, brake, debark, dismount, -flee, leave, stop)

RIDE (+): *badger, cajole, chaff, deride, earbash, fool, harass, harry, hassle, haunt, heckle, hound, irk, jive, josh, kid, nag, needle, noodge, palaver, pester, rag, rally, razz, rib, roast, tease, vex* (≠ abuse, attack, -avoid, berate, chastise, injure, punish, -shun, -snub, terrorize, wrong)

RIDE (/): *abuse, aggravate, assail, castigate, chasten, chastise, compensate, correct, counter, defend, discipline, even, exact, exonerate, fix, impugn, justify, match, penalize, persecute, punish, recompense, rectify, redress, repay, return, right, scourge, sentence, square, torment, torture, vindicate, wreak, wrong* (≠ allay, assist, assuage, benefit, comfort, free, help, ingratiate, lull, mitigate, mollify, placate, please, release, right)

RIDICULE (/): *ape, badmouth, bait, belittle, boo, bug, burlesque, caricature, cartoon, catcall, chaff, crucify, decry, deflate, demean, deride, disparage, disrespect, diss, expose, flout, harass, harry, hassle, haze, heckle, humiliate, imitate, insult, jeer, josh, kid, knock, lampoon, mimic, mock, needle, neg, pan, parody, parrot, patronize, pester, pillory, poke, pooh-pooh, rag, razz, rib, ride, roast, satirize, -scorn, shame, skewer, -slight, target, taunt, tease, torment, travesty, tweak, twit, unmask* (≠ applaud, approve, blandish, commend, congratulate, endorse, exalt, flannel, flatter, glorify, gold-star, gratify, honor, idolize, lionize, praise, respect, sanction, support)

RIFLE (←): *ascertain, audit, browse, burgle, capture, check, comb, descry, despoil, detect, determine, dig, discover, dredge, examine, explore, ferret, filch, find, frisk, get, grab, grub, hijack, hit, hunt, inspect, investigate, learn, lift, locate, loot, misappropriate, nab, peruse, pilfer, pillage, pinch, pluck, plunder, poach, pocket, poke, probe, purloin, rake, ransack, remove, review, rob, rummage, scan, scour, scrutinize, search, seek, seize, shanghai, shoplift, snatch, sneak, sort, steal, study, survey, swindle, swipe, take, track* (≠ -abandon, bury, conceal, defend, donate, earn, ensconce, fix, give, hide, -ignore, lose, -neglect, offer, protect, recover, rescue, restore, return, secure, shield, stash, stow, tuck, wedge, withhold)

RIG (→): *allocate, allot, appoint, apportion, arm, array, assign, attire, bestow, clothe, contribute, costume, dispense, distribute, dole, donate, dress, endow, equip, fortify, furnish, gear, gird, give, mete, outfit, portion, prepare, present, prorate, provide, provision, ready, reequip, refit, refurnish, stock, store, supply, uniform* (≠ appropriate, bogart, boobytrap, burgle, cheat, confiscate, -deny, deprive, dispossess, divest, embezzle, expose, hinder, -ignore, impair, impede, pilfer, -refuse, remove, rob, sabotage, skim, skimp, steal, stint, strip, swipe, undermine, withdraw, withhold)

RIG (/): *arrange, cheat, con, cook, deceive, defraud, distort, doctor, double-talk, embellish, embroider, engineer, fake, falsify, fiddle, fix, forge, gerrymander, jerry-build, jerry-rig, juggle, manipulate, massage, misrepresent, outsmart, outwit, pervert, pretend, scam, stiff, sucker, swindle, trick, twist* (≠ audit, authenticate, confirm, corroborate, document, establish, evince, prove, substantiate, validate, verify, witness)

RILE (/): *affront, aggravate, agitate, anger, annoy, antagonize, badger, bait, bother, bug, bullyrag, burn, chafe, cross, devil, discomfort, discompose, disquiet, distress, disturb, eat, embitter, enrage, envenom, exasperate, exercise, freak, fret, frost, gall, get, gravel, hagride, harass, harry, hassle, heckle, incense, inflame, infuriate, insult, irk, irritate, itch, madden, miff, nag, needle, nettle, niggle, nitpick, offend, outrage, peeve, persecute, perturb, pester, pique, plague, provoke, rankle, rasp, roil, rouse, ruffle, spite, spur, taunt, tease, troll, undo, unhinge, unsettle, upset, vex, worry* (≠ allay, appease, assuage, calm, captivate, charm, cheer, comfort, console, court, delight, disarm, enchant, gratify, help, humor, hush, lull, mellow, mitigate, moderate, mollify, pacify, placate, please, propitiate, quiet, reassure, relieve, romance, satisfy, settle, soothe, thrill, woo)

RINSE (+): *bathe, clean, cleanse, decontaminate, deluge, dip, douche, douse, drench, engulf, flood, flush, hose, inundate, irrigate, marinate, presoak, saturate, slosh, sluice, soak, spatter, splash, splatter, swamp, wash, water, wet* (≠ bake, barbecue, bedraggle, besmirch, broil, contaminate, desiccate, dirty, dry, foul, infect, muddy, parch, pollute, scorch, soil, sully, tarnish)

RIP (/): *amputate, anatomize, break, burst, butcher, carve, chop, claw, cleave, crosscut, cut, dice, dismember, dissect, fray, frazzle, gash, hack, hacksaw, incise, lacerate, maim, mangle, maul, mince, notch, pierce, razor, rend, ribbon, rive, rupture, saw, scissor, score, section, separate, sever, shank, shear, shiv, shred, slash, slice, slit, split, stab, tatter, tear, unsew, vivisect* (≠ attach, close, connect, fuse, heal, join, mend, nurse, overhaul, repair, restore, reunite, seal, secure, sew, solder, stitch, suture, unite, weld)

RISK (→): *ante, back, beard, bet, bid, brave, chance, compromise, confront, dare, defy, endanger, face, gamble, hazard, imperil, invest, jeopardize, lay, menace, play, spitball, stake, tackle, target, threaten, venture, wager, wrestle* (≠ block, certify, crosscheck, defend, design, ensure, guarantee, harbor, indemnify, insure, plan, preserve, protect, prove, script, secure, shelter, shield, sustain)

RIVAL (/): *adopt, approach, battle, challenge, contest, copy, displace, duplicate, echo, emulate, engage, equal, fight, imitate, impersonate, jockey, jostle, maneuver, match, meet, mimic, mirror, oppose, parallel, parrot, play, race, reflect, replicate, roleplay, simulate, tie, touch, train, work* (≠ aid, alleviate, assist, boost, champion, defend, follow, help, mind, obey, prioritize, promote, protect, support, uphold)

RIVET (←): *absorb, amaze, arrest, bewitch, captivate, compel, concern, consume, employ, enchant, engage, engross, entertain, enthrall, entice, excite, fascinate, fasten, fill, freeze, grab, grip, hold, hypnotize, immerse, interest, intrigue, involve, mesmerize, monopolize, nail, obsess, occupy, paralyze, petrify, pin, preoccupy, seduce, spellbind, spike, stimulate, stun, transfix* (≠ annoy, appall, baffle, bewilder, bore, bother, bug, confuse, dampen, deaden, demotivate, depress, detach, disappoint, disconnect, discourage, disgust, distract, drain, dull, enrage, exhaust, fatigue, frustrate, infuriate, irk, irritate, knacker, mystify, nauseate, numb, offend, outrage, paralyze, perplex, repel, ruin, stagnate, stale, tire, underwhelm, weary) **(¿) ABSTRACTION ALERT. Concrete goals essential!**

ROAST (+): *bake, barbecue, braise, broil, burn, caricature, chide, cook, crucify, deflate, demean, deride, disparage, flout, griddle, grill, heat, heckle, hound, humble, humiliate, insult, jeer, knock, lampoon, mock, needle, neg, pillory, poke, rag, razz, rib, ridicule, satirize, sauté, scold, scorch, sear, shrivel, taunt, tease, wither* (≠ applaud, approve, blandish, butter, commend, congratulate, douse, drench, flannel, flatter, glorify, gold-star, gratify, heroicize, honor, idealize, idolize, praise, respect, support, wet)

ROB (←): *appropriate, blackmail, burglarize, burgle, capture, cheat, confiscate, cop, defraud, deprive, despoil, embezzle, extort, filch, fleece, freeboot, grab, haul, heist, hijack, hotwire, lift, loot, misappropriate, mug, nab, nip, palm, pilfer, pillage, pinch, pirate, plagiarize, pluck, plunder, poach, pocket, purloin, ransack, remove, rustle, seize, shanghai, shoplift, snag, snatch, sneak, steal, swindle, swipe, take* (≠ bank, bestow, defend, donate, give, guard, hoard, keep, leave, offer, patrol, police, protect, recover, rescue, restore, return, secure, shield, stash, tender, tithe, undercharge)

ROCK (+): *alleviate, appease, assuage, calm, cant, comfort, console, cradle, ease, hush, jiggle, lull, mellow, mollify, oscillate, pacify, pitch, placate, quiet, reassure, relieve, roll, sedate, shake, soothe, stagger, subdue, sway, swing, tilt, tip, toss, wag, wiggle, wobble* (≠ attack, bang, bash, bump, crash, dash, disturb, hit, jar, jolt, knock, nail, pin, pinion, pound, rap, rattle, slap, smack, stamp, strap, strike, tap, thump, tie, upset)

ROCK (/): *agitate, alarm, amaze, astonish, astound, bewilder, blindside, boggle, bother, daze, deafen, discombobulate, disconcert, disquiet, disturb, dumbfound, frighten, gobsmack, harrow, haunt, horrify, intimidate, jog, jolt, jounce, panic, petrify, roil, ruffle, scare, shake, shock, stagger, startle, stun, surprise, terrify, threaten, undermine, unnerve, unsettle* (≠ alleviate, anchor, baby, bore, calm, clarify, coddle, contextualize, explain, gratify, help, hold, humor, indulge, lull, mellow, mitigate, moderate, mollify, pacify, pamper, placate, relax, sedate, stabilize, steady)

ROMANCE (←): *blandish, charm, chase, court, date, desire, embellish, encourage, escort, exaggerate, fancy, fantasize, flatter, overdramatize, overstate, poeticize, pursue, push, romanticize, serenade, target, urge, win, woo, wow* (≠ abuse, assault, attack, -avoid, -cut, -deter, -disregard, -elude, foil, -ignore, -neglect, -rebuff, -refuse, -reject, repel, -shun, -snub, -spurn, terrorize)

ROMANTICIZE (+): *adulate, aggrandize, amplify, apotheosize, canonize, celebrate, deify, dignify, dramatize, elevate, embellish, encourage, ennoble, enshrine, enthrone, eulogize, euphemize, exaggerate, fantasize, fetishize, flatter, glamorize, glorify, hail, heighten, heroicize, heroize, idealize, idolize, immortalize, intensify, lionize, magnify, overdramatize, overemphasize, oversell, overstate, panegyrize, poeticize, praise, sensationalize, sentimentalize, soften, sweeten, treasure, varnish, venerate, worship* (≠ bare, belittle, chide, condemn, criticize, decry, deemphasize, defile, deglamorize, demean, denigrate, deprecate, deride, diminish, disparage, downplay, humble, humiliate, judge, knock, marginalize, minimize, mock, pan, regret, repent, ridicule, rue, scold, shame, -shun, slam, slate, -spurn, trash, trivialize, underemphasize, vilify)

ROOK (←): *bamboozle, beat, beguile, bemuse, betray, bilk, bluff, buffalo, bullshit, cajole, cheat, con, convince, counterfeit, deceive, defraud, delude, diddle, dupe, embellish, embroider, euchre, exploit, falsify, fiddle, finagle, fleece, flimflam, fool, forge, fox, fudge, gouge, gull, hoax, hocus-pocus, hoodwink, hornswoggle, hustle, manipulate, mislead, outwit, overcharge, palaver, persuade, scam, schmooze, screw, shaft, snooker, snow, stiff, sting, sucker, swindle, trick, underpay, upset, victimize, wrong* (≠ accuse, assume, assure, believe, compensate, confess, confide, confirm, confront, disabuse, disclose, discredit, disillusion, divulge, exonerate, expose, indemnify, pillory, protect, prove, punish, reassure, -repudiate, restore, reveal, reward, substantiate, support, trust, unmask, verify, vindicate)

ROOT (→): *affix, anchor, arrest, attach, balance, base, bed, brace, cage, catch, check, clamp, clinch, compose, control, curb, deactivate, dock, embed, empower, entrench, equalize, establish, fasten, fix, freeze, ground, -halt, hamstring, hitch, hobble, hold, immobilize, impact, implant, inactivate, incapacitate, infuse, ingrain, instill, juxtapose, leash, lodge, moor, nourish, nurture, paralyze, pinion, place, plant, position, postpone, restrain, secure, set, settle, soothe, stabilize, stay, steady, stick, still, stop, subdue, support, transfix, wedge* (≠ accelerate, animate, blackball, boost, destroy, detach, discombobulate, disconnect, disengage, dislodge, displace, doom, drive, eject, eliminate, eradicate, erode, expel, extract, force, grease, hasten, launch, loose, loosen, mobilize, move, prioritize, prize, propel, pry, pull, punt, quicken, release, remove, roil, root, rush, send, shake, shift, shunt, speed, tear, terminate, thrust, unfasten, unleash, untie, uproot, weed, wiggle, wobble, wrench, wrest, yank)

ROOT (←): *deep-six, displace, eliminate, eradicate, erase, exorcise, expunge, exterminate, extinguish, extract, haul, heave, jerk, mine, obliterate, pluck, prize, pry, pull, remove, snatch, spud, tear, tug, uninstall, uproot, weed, withdraw, wrench, wrest, wring, yank* (≠ cram, embed, fix, implant, insert, install, instill, jam, place, plant, ram, root, seed, sow, stabilize, steady, stuff, wedge)

ROPE (←): *bind, capture, catch, chain, engage, enlist, fasten, fetter, -halt, harness, hitch, hogtie, immobilize, involve, lash, lasso, leash, moor, persuade, rein, seize, snag, stop, tether, tie, trap, truss, yoke* (≠ deliver, disengage, disentangle, drop, free, liberate, loose, release, slip, unbind, unhitch, unknot, unwrap)

ROUGHEN (/): *abrade, adapt, adjust, blunt, brutalize, callous, chafe, chap, coarsen, deaden, debase, dehumanize, demoralize, deprave, desensitize, develop, dull, embitter, granulate, graze, habituate, harden, harshen, indurate, inure, numb, paralyze, rasp, scuff, season, steel, stiffen, strengthen, thicken, toughen, vitiate, vulgarize, warp* (≠ baby, buff, burnish, civilize, clean, cultivate, file, fix, groom, gussy, help, improve, indulge, manicure, neaten, oil, pamper, perfect, polish, primp, protect, pumice, rectify, refine, sensitize, shine, smarten, smooth, soften, spoil, tenderize, tidy, titivate, wax)

ROUSE (+): *activate, agitate, anger, animate, arouse, awaken, bestir, boost, brighten, call, charge, conjure, disturb, drive, egg, elate, electrify, elevate, encourage, energize, enliven, enthuse, evoke, excite, exhilarate, fan, foment, force, freshen, galvanize, generate, hearten, incite, incur, induce, inflame, infuriate, inspire, instigate, invigorate, jolt, kindle, move, needle, nerve, persuade, power, prioritize, provoke, quicken, raise, rally, razzle-dazzle, recharge, reinvigorate, restimulate, resuscitate, revive, rout, shock, spark, start, stimulate, stir, strengthen, summon, thrill, trigger, uplift, vitalize, wake, waken* (≠ appease, block, bore, cage, calm, check, curb, dampen, deactivate, deaden, demotivate, -deter, disappoint, discourage, dissuade, dull, fail, freeze, -frustrate, -halt, hamper, hamstring, hinder, hobble, hush, hypnotize, immobilize, impede, inactivate, intoxicate, knacker, lull, mellow, mesmerize, mollify, numb, pacify, paralyze, placate, please, -prevent, -prohibit, quash, quiet, retard, sedate, slow, soothe, stall, stifle, tranquilize)

ROUT (→): *axe, banish, boot, bounce, can, cashier, chase, defenestrate, deport, discharge, dismiss, dispel, displace, dispossess, eject, evict, exile, exorcise, expatriate, expel, extrude, fire, -ostracize, oust, out, pink-slip, release, remove, repulse, retire, sack, scatter, scuttle, terminate* (≠ accept, admit, entertain, harbor, house, lodge, nurture, protect, receive, shelter, take, treasure, welcome)

ROUT (/): *annihilate, bash, beat, best, better, blitzkrieg, bomb, break, bulldoze, bury, chase, checkmate, clobber, conquer, cream, cripple, crush, decimate, defeat, demolish, desolate, despoil, destroy, devastate, discomfit, dispatch, doom, drub, dust, eclipse, eradicate, erase, exceed, exterminate, extinguish, finish, flatten, gut, hammer, hunt, hurdle, kill, kneecap, lambaste, larrup, lick, maraud, master, murder, nuke, obliterate, orphan, outdistance, outdo, outfight, outmaneuver, outperform, outsell, outshine, outstrip, overcome, overpower, overrun, overtake, overthrow, overwhelm, paste, pillage, plunder, pulverize, ravage, raze, ruin, sack, savage, scourge, shatter, shellac, shred, sink, skin, skunk, slaughter, smash, snuff, splinter, subdue, subjugate, surmount, surpass, swamp, sweep, take, target, thrash, throw, top, topple, torpedo, total, trample, transcend, trash, trounce, undercut, undermine, unhorse, unseat, upend, upset, vanquish, vaporize, wallop, waste, wax, whip, whomp, whup, wrack, wreck, zap* (≠ aid, appease, arm, assemble, assist, bear, build, cede, coddle, concede, conserve, construct, craft, create, defend, develop, encourage, endure, erect, establish, fabricate, face, fashion, forfeit, forge, form, foster, found, generate, hatch, help, improve, initiate, lose, mend, mold, nurture, obey, pacify, placate, preserve, produce, protect, raise, rear, rebuild, reconstruct, recover, renovate, repair, repel, rescue, resign, resist, restore, revamp, save, secure, shape, shield, sire, soothe, spawn, strengthen, support, surrender, survive, sustain, -thwart, tolerate, weather, withstand, yield)

RUB (→): *apply, brush, buff, caress, fondle, grip, knead, manipulate, massage, pat, pummel, roll, scratch, shampoo, stroke* (≠ aggravate, beat, cut, displease, harm, hit, injure, irritate, wound)

RUB (→): *anoint, beeswax, brush, buff, burnish, clean, coat, daub, dress, dust, furbish, glaze, gloss, grind, lap, moisturize, polish, pomade, scour, scrape, scrub, shine, sleek, slick, smooth, sponge, wax, wipe* (≠ abrade, blemish, callous, chafe, coarsen, dehydrate, dent, desiccate, dim, dirty, dry, harden, harm, harshen, mar, mark, nick, nock, roughen, score, scrape, scratch, scuff, sully, tarnish)

RUB (/): *abrade, bite, canker, chafe, chew, corrode, decompose, disintegrate, dissolve, eat, erase, erode, excoriate, file, fray, frazzle, fret, gall, gnash, gnaw, grate, graze, grind, hone, nibble, obliterate, pinch, rasp, reduce, sandblast, sandpaper, scour, scrape, scratch, scuff, sharpen, shave, wear, whet, wipe* (≠ buff, buffer, burnish, cushion, guard, polish, preserve, protect, repair, restore, seal, shield, shine, smooth, soften, wax)

RUFFLE (/): *aggravate, agitate, anger, annoy, bother, bug, confuse, crease, crumple, daze, discomfit, discomfort, discompose, disconcert, dishevel, disturb, dizzy, earbash, exasperate, fluster, fret, hassle, heckle, irk, irritate, nag, needle, nettle, niggle, nitpick, perturb, pucker, rankle, rattle, rile, rumple, shake, tangle, tousle, troll, trouble, unsettle, upset, vex, wrinkle* (≠ appease, assuage, calm, comfort, compose, gratify, help, humor, lull, mellow, mitigate, moderate, mollify, order, organize, pacify, placate, please, propitiate, quiet, regiment, regulate, satisfy, settle, smooth, soothe, straighten, tranquilize, uncrumple)

RUIN (/): *annihilate, atomize, bankrupt, beat, beggar, best, betray, blast, bleed, boobytrap, botch, break, bulldoze, bust, canker, cannibalize, clobber, conquer, consume, corrode, corrupt, crack, cream, cripple, crumple, crush, damage, debauch, debilitate, decimate, deface, defeat, defile, deform, demolish, deplete, deplore, depredate, desecrate, desolate, despoil, destroy, deteriorate, detonate, devastate, devour, dilapidate, disassemble, disfigure, disintegrate, dismantle, dissolve, doom, drain, drub, dynamite, efface, eradicate, erase, erode, exhaust, expunge, exterminate, extinguish, extirpate, finish, fracture, fragment, gut, half-ass, harm, harry, impair, injure, kneecap, leech, lick, liquidate, loot, maim, mangle, mar, maraud, master, monkey-wrench, mortar, mow, mutilate, nuke, obliterate, overcome, overpower, overrun, overthrow, overturn, overwhelm, pillage, plunder, pulverize, rape, ravage, ravish, raze, remove, rout, sabotage, sack, savage, scotch, scour, scourge, scupper, shatter, shiver, shred, skunk, smash, snuff, splinter, spoil, strip, subdue, subvert, surmount, tatter, tear, thrash, topple, total, trample, trash, trounce, unbuild, undercut, undermine, unmake, vandalize, vaporize, vitiate, wallop, waste, whip, wrack, wreak, wreck* (≠ aid, appease, arm, assemble, bronze, build, coddle, conserve, constitute, construct, craft, create, defend, develop, doctor, embalm, encourage, endure, erect, establish, fabricate, fashion, father, fix, forfeit, forge, form, foster, found, frame, generate, hatch, heal, help, improve, institute, invent, machine, make, manufacture, mend, mold, nurture, obey, organize, pacify, patch, patent, pickle, placate, preserve, produce, protect, raise, rear, rebuild, recondition, reconstruct, recover, redeem, rehabilitate, remodel, renovate, repair, repel, rescue, resist, restore, revamp, save, sculpt, secure, shape, shield, sire, soothe, spawn, strengthen, support, survive, sustain, uncrumple, weather, withstand)

RUIN (/): *bankrupt, beggar, break, bust, cripple, defund, deplete, deprive, devastate, diminish, disinherit, drain, exhaust, fleece, impoverish, pauperize, reduce, straiten, waste, wreck* (≠ augment, bankroll, budget, capitalize, develop, dower, endow, enrich, fund, furnish, indulge, keep, leech, maintain, subsidize, supplement, supply, underwrite)

RULE (→): *administer, boss, bridle, browbeat, captain, chair, choreograph, coach, coerce, command, conduct, conquer, control, coordinate, crush, curb, decree, defeat, demand, dictate, direct, discipline, dominate, domineer, eclipse, enslave, govern, grasp, grip, guide, handle, harness, head, influence, inform, instruct, intimidate, lead, manage, manipulate, master, micromanage, monopolize, muscle, nobble, officiate, oppress, orchestrate, order, outmaneuver, outrank, outshine, outthink, overcome, overpower, override, overrule, oversee, overshadow, pace, pacify, pilot, police, railroad, regulate, restrain, rout, run, sandbag, spearhead, steamroller, steer, subdue, subject, subjugate, subordinate, superintend, supervise, sway, thrash, threaten, train, trounce, trump, tyrannize, vanquish* (≠ -abandon, accept, attack, baby, back, battle, bobble, bolster, botch, bungle, challenge, collapse, combat, concede, constrain, contest, contradict, counteract, defer, defy, -disdain, -disregard, disrespect, emancipate, enfranchise, fluff, follow, forfeit, forget, free, fumble, hamper, heed, humor, -ignore, indulge, invalidate, liberate, lull, mellow, mind, mishandle, mismanage, misrule, miss, muff, -neglect, obey, observe, obstruct, oppose, override, pacify, pamper, placate, release, relinquish, resist, serve, short-circuit, soften, spring, submit, subvert, support, topple, unbind, uncage, unchain, unfetter, weaken)

RULE (←): *arrest, block, bottle, bridle, cage, check, choke, constrain, contain, control, cuff, curb, curtail, foil, gag, govern, hamper, hamstring, handcuff, hinder, hold, impair, impede, inhibit, interrupt, keep, leash, limit, measure, mince, muffle, muzzle, obstruct, pace, pocket, pull, quash, quell, regulate, rein, repress, restrain, restrict, scotch, shackle, shrink, silence, sink, skunk, smother, snuff, squash, squelch, stifle, stop, strangle, subdue, suppress, swallow, tame* (≠ air, blab, blaze, blurt, boost, brandish, broadcast, develop, discharge, disclose, elevate, emit, enlarge, exalt, exhibit, expand, express, extend, extol, flaunt, glorify, heighten, highlight, hype, increase, liberate, loose, loosen, lose, magnify, maximize, nurture, parade, plug, promote, publicize, reveal, spill, sport, spotlight, trumpet, unleash, vent, voice, wreak)

RUMOR (→): *advertise, air, allege, announce, appall, bandy, bare, beam, bear, broadcast, bulletin, buzz, carry, circulate, clue, communicate, conduct, confess, confide, confirm, contradict, convey, corroborate, couch, defame, -deny, diffuse, disclose, dish, dispatch, disseminate, distribute, divulge, expose, forward, hint, impart, imply, insinuate, intimate, libel, mediate, muckrake, -negate, out, pass, proclaim,* *promulgate, propagate, publicize, publish, relay, remit, report, reveal, scandalize, scatter, send, shame, shock, slander, spill, spread, suggest, telegraph, televise, tell, transfer, transmit, transport, verbalize, vocalize, voice, whisper* (≠ bury, censor, conceal, contain, cover, defuse, disclaim, disguise, ensconce, gag, hide, hush, mute, muzzle, prove, quash, quell, recall, recant, retract, revoke, secrete, silence, smother, stifle, suppress, verify, withhold)

RUMPLE (/): *contract, corrugate, crease, crimp, crinkle, crumple, crush, derange, dishevel, disorder, fold, furrow, knit, mess, muss, pleat, pucker, ripple, ruck, ruffle, scrunch, tousle, untidy, wrinkle* (≠ barber, beautify, even, flatten, groom, iron, launder, neaten, order, organize, press, primp, shine, smooth, straighten, tidy, uncrumple, unfold, unwrinkle)

RUN (→): *administer, boss, bridle, captain, chair, command, conduct, control, coordinate, decree, dictate, direct, discipline, dominate, drive, execute, govern, guide, handle, harness, head, helm, lead, manage, master, micromanage, officiate, operate, oppress, orchestrate, order, organize, override, overrule, oversee, own, pace, pilot, police, regiment, regulate, restrain, rule, spearhead, steer, subdue, subjugate, superintend, supervise, sway, tyrannize* (≠ -abandon, bobble, bomb, botch, bungle, challenge, collapse, contest, contradict, defer, destabilize, -disdain, -disregard, disrespect, disrupt, fluff, follow, forget, fumble, half-ass, heed, -ignore, mind, mishandle, mismanage, misrule, miss, muff, -neglect, obey, observe, oppose, relinquish, sabotage, serve, subvert, undercut, undermine)

RUPTURE (/): *anatomize, breach, break, burst, cleave, crack, crumble, cut, decay, decompose, disintegrate, disrupt, dissect, dissolve, divide, divorce, erupt, explode, fracture, fragment, obliterate, open, part, penetrate, pierce, pulverize, puncture, rend, rive, rot, separate, sever, shatter, split, spoil, sunder, tear, vivisect* (≠ attach, barricade, bind, bolster, brace, buttress, cinch, close, fasten, fortify, fuse, harden, hybridize, join, marry, mend, patch, repair, seal, secure, shield, solder, strengthen, synthesize, unite, weld)

RUSH (→): *accelerate, aid, bundle, catalyze, charge, chase, dash, dispatch, drive, ease, encourage, expedite, facilitate, fast-forward, fast-track, frogmarch, goad, grease, hasten, hurry, hustle, lubricate, march, nudge, press, prod, prompt, propel, push, quicken, race, run, speed, spur, stampede, stir, urge, whisk* (≠ -abort, arrest, brake, check, decelerate, delay, encumber, fetter, hamper, hinder, hobble, hold, impede, manacle, obstruct, pause, postpone, rein, restrain, retard, shackle, shelve, short-circuit, slow, stall, stay, still, stop, -thwart, trammel, weight)

SABOTAGE (/): *attenuate, block, blunt, boobytrap, break, bugger, canker, castrate, checkmate, compromise, contaminate, corrode, corrupt, counteract, cripple, damage, debilitate, deep-six, demoralize, deplete, destroy, devitalize, diminish, disable, disarm, disqualify, disrupt, disturb, doom, emasculate, enfeeble, erode, foil, -frustrate, half-ass, -halt, hamper, hamstring, harm, hinder, hobble, hollow, honeycomb, hurt, impair, impede, inactivate, incapacitate, inhibit, injure, interrupt, invalidate, kneecap, mar, monkey-wrench, muzzle, obstruct, overextend, paralyze, pervert, pickle, poison, queer, rock, ruin, sandbag, sap, scotch, scupper, scuttle, shelve, shrivel, sideline, soften, spoil, subvert, taint, threaten, -thwart, torpedo, undercut, undermine, unhinge, unman, unnerve, unsettle, upset, vandalize, warp, weaken, wear, whittle, wither, wizen, wobble, wreck* (≠ animate, assist, augment, bolster, boost, brace, build, buoy, buttress, calibrate, catalyze, choreograph, compose, defend, develop, devise, embolden, enable, encourage, energize, enhance, enshrine, expedite, facilitate, fix, fortify, galvanize, guard, help, heroicize, heroize, idolize, improve, inspire, maintain, mend, midwife, motivate, optimize, orchestrate, organize, overhaul, patrol, perfect, preserve, prioritize, protect, rebuild, rectify, relieve, remedy, repair, rescue, restructure, revolutionize, safeguard, save, stabilize, steady, strengthen, support, sustain, tidy, tweak, vitalize, worship)

SACK (→): *axe, banish, boot, bounce, can, chuck, discharge, dislodge, dismiss, eject, fire, furlough, oust, pink-slip, release, remove, retire, terminate, unseat* (≠ contract, employ, engage, hire, invite, keep, praise, promote, recruit, rehire, retain, solicit, subcontract)

SACK (/): *besiege, burglarize, comb, despoil, devastate, flatten, harry, hunt, level, loot, maraud, pillage, plunder, raid, rake, ransack, ravish, rifle, rob, rummage, strip, vandalize* (≠ barricade, blockade, build, construct, defend, earn, erect, guard, hold, keep, maintain, outlast, preserve, protect, rebuild, replace, restore, sustain)

SACRIFICE (→): *-abandon, bequeath, bestow, cede, consecrate, contribute, dedicate, devote, donate, forfeit, give, immolate, kill, molochize, offer, propitiate, relinquish, -renounce, slaughter, spare, submit, surrender, tender, tithe, volunteer, yield* (≠ begrudge, cheat, -deny, deprive, grip, hoard, indulge, keep, protect, reserve, retain, save, scant, skimp, squander, stockpile, survive, waste, withhold)

SADDEN (/): *afflict, ail, alarm, bother, burden, concern, dampen, dash, daunt, demoralize, demotivate, deplore, depress, desolate, discomfort, discompose, discourage, dishearten, dismay, dispirit, disquiet, distress,* *disturb, down, exercise, grieve, oppress, perturb, press, torment, torture, trouble, unhinge, unnerve, unsettle, upset, worry* (≠ amuse, animate, boost, brighten, buoy, cheer, comfort, console, delight, elate, elevate, encourage, entertain, excite, exhilarate, gladden, gratify, heal, hearten, inspire, lift, nurture, please, quiet, reassure, soothe, stabilize, steady, stimulate, thrill, uplift, wow)

SALUTE (+): *acclaim, accost, accredit, acknowledge, address, adulate, applaud, approach, approve, ballyhoo, blandish, buttonhole, call, cap, celebrate, cheer, clap, commend, congratulate, deify, emblazon, endorse, eulogize, exalt, extol, favor, flag, flatter, glad-hand, glorify, greet, hail, high-five, honor, idolize, knight, laud, magnify, mark, meet, praise, receive, recognize, recommend, signal, support, tout, trumpet, wave, waylay, welcome* (≠ admonish, affront, -avoid, belittle, blame, boo, castigate, censure, chastise, chide, -cold-shoulder, criticize, critique, -cut, denigrate, discredit, disfavor, disgrace, disparage, -elude, excoriate, fault, finger, -ignore, knock, -overlook, pan, pass, rebuke, regret, reprimand, reproach, reprove, resent, rue, scapegoat, scold, -shun, skewer, slam, -spurn, threaten, vilify, zap)

SALVAGE (←): *accumulate, amass, assemble, budget, build, capture, cherish, claim, collect, conserve, convert, cull, defend, deliver, emancipate, embrace, extract, extricate, find, gather, glean, grab, harvest, hoard, keep, liberate, locate, maintain, manage, mend, nab, overcome, overhaul, patch, preserve, protect, ransom, reap, rebuild, recapture, reclaim, reconstruct, recoup, recover, rectify, recuperate, recycle, redeem, refurbish, regain, reimagine, reinvent, relieve, renew, renovate, repair, repossess, rescue, restore, retain, retrieve, retrofit, reuse, revamp, safeguard, salve, save, scavenge, snatch, stockpile, unify, unite, uphold* (≠ -abandon, -cancel, chuck, consume, demolish, -desert, destroy, discard, -disown, -ditch, doom, drop, dump, endanger, eradicate, -eschew, finish, forfeit, -forsake, fritter, harm, hurt, imperil, injure, jeopardize, jettison, junk, lose, miss, misuse, -nix, -nullify, offload, -omit, -overlook, -refuse, -reject, risk, ruin, -scorn, scrap, scupper, scuttle, -sidestep, -spurn, squander, terminate, trash, waste, wreck)

SALVE (+): *allay, alleviate, appease, assuage, butter, calm, comfort, compose, ease, grease, hush, lay, lighten, lotion, lull, medicate, mellow, mitigate, mollify, narcotize, oil, pacify, palliate, placate, quell, quiet, relax, relieve, sedate, settle, soften, solace, soothe, still, stupefy, temper, tranquilize* (≠ aggravate, agitate, arouse, chafe, discompose, disquiet, disturb, exacerbate, exasperate, excite, foment, harm, heighten, hurt, incite, inflame, injure, intensify, irritate, perturb, rouse, stir, troll, trouble, upset, vex, worry)

SAMPLE (←): *appraise, assess, audit, benchmark, beta, browse, check, chew, clock, consider, determine, examine, experience, explore, eye, eyeball, identify, inspect, investigate, learn, locate, notice, peruse, pick, probe, read, reference, resample, research, review, riffle, savor, scan, scope, screen, scrutinize, sip, size, skim, study, surf, survey, suss, taste, test,* *try, vet, view, weigh* (≠ assimilate, -avoid, -blank, -bypass, confound, -decline, digest, -disregard, -dodge, -evade, forget, grok, -ignore, integrate, leave, misconstrue, miss, mistake, -neglect, -omit, -overlook, -shun, -sidestep, sidetrack, skip, skirt)

SANCTIFY (+): *absolve, anoint, apotheosize, baptize, beatify, bless, canonize, chasten, cleanse, consecrate, dedicate, deify, devote, dignify, enshrine, exalt, exorcise, glorify, hallow, idolize, purify, rarefy, wash, worship* (≠ condemn, curse, damn, deconsecrate, defile, desecrate, execrate, maledict, pollute, profane, punish, soil, taint, violate)

SANCTION (+): *accept, accredit, acknowledge, affirm, allow, approve, authorize, back, bless, canonize, certify, clear, condone, confirm, delegate, empower, enable, endorse, entitle, favor, finalize, formalize, greenlight, initial, legalize, legitimize, license, okay, pass, permit, ratify, recommend, rubber-stamp, safeguard, sanctify, sign, support, sustain, underwrite, validate, warrant* (≠ ban, -decline, delegitimize, -deny, disallow, disapprove, -disregard, enjoin, -forbid, -ignore, -neglect, -nullify, -prohibit, proscribe, -rebuff, rebut, -refuse, -reject, -spurn, -veto)

SANITIZE (+): *bathe, cauterize, censor, clarify, clean, cleanse, clear, decontaminate, delouse, deodorize, disinfect, distill, filter, freshen, fumigate, launder, purge, purify, quarantine, rectify, redact, refine, scour, scrub, sieve, sift, sterilize, wash* (≠ bedraggle, besmirch, contaminate, defile, dirty, foul, infect, muddy, poison, pollute, soil, spike, sully, taint, tarnish)

SAP (-): *attenuate, bleed, blunt, burgle, cannibalize, castrate, consume, cripple, dampen, deaden, debilitate, deflate, demoralize, deplete, depredate, depress, devitalize, dilute, diminish, disable, discourage, disqualify, dissuade, drain, dull, emasculate, enervate, enfeeble, erode, exhaust, extract, fatigue, filter, impair, impoverish, incapacitate, jade, leach, leech, paralyze, prostrate, rarefy, reduce, remove, rob, ruin, shrivel, steal, strain, subvert, tire, undermine, unman, vitiate, weaken, wither, wizen, wreck* (≠ advantage, amp, benefit, bless, boost, build, buoy, charge, dose, energize, excite, flavor, fortify, ginger, heal, help, increase, infuse, invigorate, jazz, juice, maintain, motivate, reinvigorate, replenish, restimulate, restore, revive, stimulate, strengthen)

SATE (-): *alleviate, assuage, cater, cloy, fill, glut, gorge, gratify, humor, indulge, lighten, overfill, quench, relieve, replenish, satiate, satisfy, saturate, sicken, slake, stuff, surfeit* (≠ arouse, deplete, deprive, dissatisfy, excite, famish, malnourish, pique, -prevent, sap, starve, stimulate, tantalize, taunt, tease, tempt, trigger, underfeed, underwhelm)

SATIRIZE (/): *ape, burlesque, caricature, cartoon, criticize, critique, demean, deride, distort, exaggerate, fake, haze, humiliate, impersonate, jeer, jive, josh, kid, lampoon, mimic, misrepresent, mock, needle, parody, pasquinade, pillory, playact, razz, rib, ride, ridicule, roast, roleplay, spoof* (≠ acclaim, applaud, cherish, commend, compliment, congratulate, defend, enshrine, exalt, extol, glorify, gratify, hallow, honor, idolize, lionize, panegyrize, praise, protect, respect, revere, venerate)

SATISFY (+): *amuse, appease, assuage, captivate, capture, cheer, cloy, comfort, content, delight, enliven, entertain, fascinate, fill, flatter, fulfill, gladden, glut, gorge, gratify, humor, indulge, mollify, overfill, pacify, placate, please, propitiate, quench, sate, satiate, saturate, score, sell, sicken, slake, suffuse, suit, surfeit, thrill, uplift* (≠ anger, appall, bore, bother, burden, depress, deprive, disgruntle, dismay, dissatisfy, famish, frighten, frustrate, malnourish, sadden, scare, skimp, starve, stint, tantalize, taunt, tease, tempt, terrify, trigger, underfeed, underwhelm, weary, worry)

SATISFY (+): *accomplish, allay, alleviate, appease, assuage, assure, bolster, brace, bribe, buoy, cheer, comfort, convince, encourage, equip, fill, fulfill, furnish, hearten, induce, inspire, inveigle, meet, observe, perform, persuade, placate, provide, qualify, quiet, rally, reassure, restore, score, sell, serve* (≠ alarm, anger, block, bully, checkmate, -deter, discourage, dissuade, enrage, fail, frighten, frustrate, hamper, harm, hinder, hobble, impede, incense, irritate, menace, panic, scare, terrorize, threaten, unnerve, upset, vex)

SATURATE (→): *bathe, brine, douche, douse, drench, drown, engulf, flood, immerse, inundate, lubricate, marinate, moisturize, overfill, percolate, permeate, presoak, soak, sop, souse, steep, swamp, syrup, wash, waterlog, wet* (≠ air, bake, barbecue, broil, dehumidify, dehydrate, desiccate, drain, dry, harden, leech, mummify, parch, scorch, sear, staunch, toughen, withhold)

SATURATE (→): *burden, charge, cram, fill, flood, glut, imbue, impregnate, infuse, interpenetrate, invade, jam, jam-pack, occupy, overfill, pack, penetrate, permeate, pervade, sardine, sate, satiate, stuff, suffuse, surfeit, transfuse* (≠ cull, deduct, -deny, deprive, dissatisfy, drain, draw, empty, extract, leach, leech, remove, siphon, slurp, starve, suck, unpack, waterproof, wilt, withdraw, wither, withhold, wring)

SAVAGE (/): *abuse, anguish, attack, berate, blame, browbeat, bulldoze, bully, censure, chastise, condemn, criticize, deaden, dehumanize, denigrate, denounce, denunciate, depersonalize, desensitize, discredit, -disdain, disfavor, disgrace, fault, frame, fulminate, harden, intimidate, inure, knock, mistreat, neg, objectify, rebuke, reprimand, rubbish, scapegoat, scold, slam, slate, torment, trash, trash-talk, violate, wrong* (≠ acclaim, appease, applaud, boost, celebrate, champion, commend, defend, endorse, enshrine, favor, fetishize, gratify, honor, idolize, laud, lionize, praise, promote, protect, rescue, revere, save, support, treasure, venerate, worship)

SAVAGE (/): *anguish, assault, attack, bestialize, bite, brutalize, claw, crucify, crush, deface, dehumanize, disfigure, eviscerate, gash, gore, harm, hurt, injure, lacerate, maim, mangle, maul, mutilate, rend, rip, scalp, shred, slash, smash, splinter, tatter, tear, terrorize, torment, torture, traumatize, victimize, welt, wound, wrong* (≠ defend, delight, dignify, elevate, exalt, foster, gratify, guard, heal, honor, humanize, humor, nourish, nurse, nurture, pamper, pity, placate, please, protect, regret, repair, respect, restore, reward, soothe, spoil, thrill, treat, uplift)

SAVE (←): *absolve, acquit, aid, assist, -avert, champion, conserve, counterattack, counterpunch, defend, deliver, discharge, disengage, disentangle, emancipate, enfranchise, escort, exonerate, extricate, free, insulate, keep, liberate, manumit, nourish, pardon, patronize, pluck, preserve, protect, ransom, recapture, reclaim, recover, recycle, redeem, regain, release, relieve, reprieve, rescue, retain, retrieve, safeguard, salvage, secure, shelter, shield, spring, support, unburden, unchain, unfetter, unleash, unshackle, untie, uphold, ward, watch* (≠ abduct, abuse, assault, attack, bash, betray, bind, brutalize, capture, compromise, demolish, destroy, devastate, disappear, dismantle, endanger, enslave, -forsake, gamble, harm, hazard, hurt, impair, imperil, imprison, injure, institutionalize, jail, jeopardize, kidnap, menace, persecute, punish, risk, ruin, savage, seize, target, terrorize, threaten, torment, torture, traumatize, venture, victimize, violate, wreck)

SAVE (←): *accrue, accumulate, amass, archive, bank, budget, cache, coffer, collect, compile, conserve, deposit, gather, glean, harvest, heap, hoard, hog, hold, keep, maintain, manage, monopolize, pack, pile, preserve, reap, recycle, reserve, retain, salvage, scant, scavenge, scrimp, skimp, spare, squirrel, stash, stockpile, store, stow, treasure, tuck, wedge* (≠ chuck, consume, contribute, diffuse, discard, dispense, dole, dollop, donate, dump, eliminate, forfeit, give, lose, provide, scatter, scrap, share, spend, squander, use, waste)

SAVE (+): *brine, bronze, conserve, defend, embalm, guard, hinder, keep, maintain, -obviate, pickle, preserve, -prevent, protect, safeguard, screen, shield, spare, sustain* (≠ bruise, compromise, contaminate, damage, destroy, endanger, expose, harm, imperil, jeopardize, risk, target, threaten, wither, wreck)

SAVOR (←): *admire, adore, applaud, appreciate, celebrate, cherish, clock, congratulate, consume, detect, devour, dig, drink, eat, enjoy, esteem, experience, extol, eye, fancy, favor, gobble, heed, idolize, indulge, inhale, love, mull, note, observe, ponder, prefer, prize, recognize, relish, respect, revere, scrutinize, sense, smell, sniff, taste, touch, treasure, value, venerate, whiff, wolf, worship* (≠ -abandon, abhor, abominate, -avoid, boo, chide, condemn, criticize, -despise, -disdain, disfavor, -dodge, -eschew, forfeit, -hate, -loathe, protest, -refuse, regret, -reject, -renounce, repent, -repudiate, resent, ridicule, rue, -scorn, -shun, -sidestep, -spurn) **(¿) ABSTRACTION ALERT. Concrete goals essential!**

SCALE (→): *ascend, beat, best, clamber, climb, conquer, crest, exceed, mount, outreach, overcome, overtake, surmount, surpass, tackle, top, vanquish* (≠ -bypass, circumnavigate, compress, descend, dip, dismount, -disregard, -dodge, drop, -flee, miss, mistake, -overlook, plumb, plunge, sink, submerge)

SCAM (←): *bamboozle, beat, beguile, bilk, blackmail, bleed, bluff, bribe, buffalo, bullshit, burn, cajole, cheat, chisel, con, convince, cozen, crib, deceive, defraud, delude, diddle, double-cross, double-deal, double-talk, dupe, embezzle, euchre, exploit, fake, fiddle, finagle, fleece, flimflam, fool, fox, fudge, goldbrick, gouge, gull, hoax, hocus-pocus, hoodwink, hornswoggle, hose, lull, manipulate, milk, mislead, nobble, outslick, outsmart, outwit, palaver, persuade, pretend, rob, rook, sandbag, screw, shaft, short, shortchange, skin, snooker, snow, stiff, sting, sucker, swindle, thimblerig, trick, two-time, underpay, victimize, wrong* (≠ accuse, afford, assess, assume, assure, audit, authenticate, believe, confess, confirm, confront, corroborate, debunk, deflate, discredit, disgrace, dispute, divulge, document, doubt, evince, expose, fund, give, humiliate, malign, mock, offer, -ostracize, pillory, pity, protect, prove, provide, regret, -repudiate, respect, restore, reveal, scruple, shame, stigmatize, substantiate, supply, support, trust, underwrite, verify, vilify)

SCAN (←): *browse, check, compute, consider, contemplate, examine, flash, inspect, investigate, learn, liken, police, prowl, read, regard, riffle, scour, scrutinize, search, skim, spell, study, survey, suss, sweep, x-ray* (≠ -blank, blind, blindfold, confuse, discard, -disregard, forget, -ignore, miss, mystify, -neglect, perplex, puzzle, skim, skip)

SCANDALIZE (/): *affront, aggrieve, anger, annoy, antagonize, appall, disgruntle, disgust, dish, dismay, disoblige, distress, disturb, exasperate, fret, gall, horrify, hurt, insult, irritate, jar, miff, muckrake, nauseate, nettle, offend, outrage, pain, pique, provoke, repel, repulse, revolt, rile, shock, sicken, slur, -snub, sting, troll, upset, vex, wound, zing* (≠ aggrandize, aid, assist, bolster, compliment, conceal, dignify, elevate, enhance, ennoble, exalt, glorify, guard, help, honor, impress, inspire, please, praise, promote, protect, raise, secure, support, uplift)

SCAPEGOAT (/): *abuse, accuse, admonish, assail, attack, attaint, badmouth, belittle, berate, blame, blast, blister, castigate, censure, charge, chastise, chide, clobber, condemn, criticize, crucify, decry, demonize, denigrate, denounce, deride, discipline, disparage, drub, excoriate, fault, finger, flay, frame, fulminate, gibbet, hammer, impugn, incriminate, keelhaul, knock, lambaste, lash, pan, penalize, pillory, punish, rebuke, reprimand, reproach, reprove, resent, scalp, scold, skewer, slam, slash, upbraid, zap* (≠ absolve, acquit, adore, advantage, alibi, approve, benefit, bless, boost, cherish, clear, commend, condone, defend, elevate, encourage, endorse, excuse, exonerate, favor, forgive, guard, ingratiate, pardon, praise, promote, protect, reassure, recommend, release, remedy, rescue, respect, revere, sanction, save, shield, spare, sponsor, treasure, venerate, worship)

SCAR (/): *beat, blemish, blight, blot, brand, burn, cauterize, cut, damage, deface, deform, discolor, disfigure, efface, flaw, injure, maim, mar, mark, pinch, scald, scalp, scorch, score, scratch, sear, shock, slash, spoil, spot, stab, stigmatize, traumatize, welt, wound* (≠ adorn, beautify, clear, conceal, correct, decorate, doctor, enhance, erase, heal, hide, mend, ornament, perfect, rectify, refine, smooth)

SCARE (/): *affright, agitate, alarm, amaze, appall, astound, awe, blackjack, blackmail, bludgeon, boggle, browbeat, brutalize, bulldoze, bully, chill, cow, daunt, deafen, demoralize, demotivate, -deter, discomfort, discompose, disconcert, discourage, dishearten, dismay, dispirit, disquiet, distract, distress, disturb, emasculate, faze, floor, freeze, frighten, funk, haunt, horrify, intimidate, jolt, menace, numb, panic, paralyze, perturb, petrify, railroad, rattle, repel, sandbag, savage, shake, shock, spook, startle, strong-arm, stun, stupefy, terrify, terrorize, threaten, trash-talk, traumatize, unhinge, unman, unnerve, unsettle, unstring, upset, victimize, warn, worry* (≠ allay, amuse, assuage, assure, baby, boost, buoy, calm, charm, cheer, coddle, comfort, compose, console, delight, embolden, enchant, encourage, entertain, exhilarate, fortify, gladden, guard, hearten, help, humor, inspire, invigorate, lull, mellow, mitigate, moderate, mollify, nurture, pacify, placate, please, protect, quiet, reassure, release, relieve, save, secure, seduce, soothe, stabilize, steady, steel, stimulate, strengthen, thrill, uplift, vamp, woo, wow)

SCATTER (/): *break, broadcast, cast, circulate, diffuse, disassemble, disband, disintegrate, dispel, disperse, disseminate, dissipate, dissolve, disunite, divide, dot, fling, fracture, fragment, intersperse, isolate, litter, melt, orphan, part, pepper, segregate, separate, shake, shatter, shower, sow, spatter, spill, split, splutter, spray, spread, sprinkle, squander, strew, telegraph* (≠ agglomerate, assemble, cluster, collect, compile, concentrate, conglomerate, congregate, gather, glean, herd, integrate, maintain, preserve, reclaim, recoup, recover, reintegrate, reunite, salvage, scavenge, sustain, unify, unite, withhold)

SCAVENGE (←): *accumulate, acquire, arrogate, bogart, claim, collect, comb, confiscate, convert, forage, gather, glean, grab, hunt, loot, nab, obtain, pick, pilfer, pillage, plunder, poach, preserve, probe, procure, rake, ransack, reap, reclaim, recover, recycle, rescue, retrieve, rifle, rummage, salvage, save, scour, scrounge, search, secure, seek, seize, snaffle, snag, snatch, source, stockpile, strip* (≠ -abandon, -avoid, bestow, bury, buy, cache, conceal, contribute, deposit, discard, dissipate, donate, dump, fritter, furnish, hide, hoard, -ignore, jettison, keep, leave, lose, -neglect, offer, -omit, -overlook, present, purchase, recoup, -refuse, -reject, replace, replenish, restore, scatter, spare, squander, stock, tender, volunteer, waste, withhold)

SCENT (→): *anoint, bathe, brush, cloud, cologne, conceal, dab, disguise, douse, drench, embellish, emit, enhance, exude, hide, intensify, mist, oil, perfume, release, smear, splash, spray* (≠ breathe, detect, discern, discover, find, identify, inhale, nose, notice, perceive, recognize, retrace, sense, smell, sniff, trace, track, whiff)

SCENT (←): *breathe, detect, discern, discover, find, identify, inhale, nose, notice, perceive, recognize, retrace, sense, smell, sniff, snuff, trace, track, trail, whiff* (≠ choke, cloak, clothe, cloud, conceal, dab, disguise, exude, hide, perfume, plug, release, spray) **(¿) ABSTRACTION ALERT. Concrete goals essential!**

SCHEDULE (+): *appoint, arrange, assign, book, calendar, card, catalog, classify, compile, contract, docket, enroll, enter, file, index, inscribe, list, manage, mark, micromanage, note, order, organize, overcommit, plan, program, record, regiment, register, reschedule, slate, table, tabulate, tally, task, time, timetable, wait-list* (≠ -abort, axe, -cancel, -decline, delete, disarrange, disorder, disorganize, drop, -dump, end, erase, expunge, finish, forget, -halt, kill, -neglect, -nix, -omit, -overlook, purge, reconsider, -rescind, revoke, scrap, scratch, shelve, terminate)

SCHLEP (+): *bear, bring, carry, cart, chauffeur, convey, convoy, deliver, drag, draw, ferry, fetch, haul, heave, hump, lift, lug, move, pack, pull, push, shift, ship, shuttle, smuggle, take, tote, tow, trail, transfer, transport, tug* (≠ -abandon, discard, dispatch, drop, dump, eliminate, -forsake, fumble, jettison, leave, lose, miss, -omit, -refuse, -reject, repel, send, thrust)

SCHMOOZE (+): *bamboozle, beguile, bluff, butter, buttonhole, cajole, charm, coax, convince, cozen, dazzle, encourage, extort, fast-talk, finagle, finesse, flimflam, glad-hand, grease, honey, hustle, induce, influence, inveigle, leverage, lobby, lubricate, manipulate, nudge, oil, palaver, persuade, pressure, seduce, sell, snow, soft-sell, soft-soap, sway, tempt, urge, wheedle* (≠ abuse, affront, anger, assume, attack, believe, confess, defend, disturb, doubt, expose, harm, incense, injure, insult, irk, irritate, offend, outrage, shield, -slight, -snub, suspect, trust, verify, vex, wrong)

SCHOOL (+): *advance, brief, catechize, civilize, coach, control, cultivate, develop, direct, discipline, drill, edify, educate, elevate, enlighten, familiarize, fit, foster, ground, guide, impart, implant, improve, inculcate, indoctrinate, inform, initiate, instill, instruct, introduce, lead, lecture, manage, mentor, nurture, prepare, prime, qualify, rear, reeducate, reschool, reteach, retrain, teach, train, tutor* (≠ -abandon, barbarize, cloud, conceal, confuse, darken, -desert, forget, hide, -ignore, learn, misguide, mislead, mismanage, -neglect, obscure, perplex, puzzle, -reject, resist, study)

SCOLD (/): *abuse, accuse, admonish, attaint, berate, blame, blast, browbeat, castigate, caution, censure, chasten, chastise, chide, condemn, correct, criticize, critique, demean, denigrate, denounce, disparage, earbash, exasperate, fault, flog, hector, henpeck, lambaste, lecture, lesson, mock, nag, pillory, punish, rate, ream, rebuke, reprimand, reproach, reprove, revile, ridicule, scapegoat, taunt, trash-talk, upbraid, vilify, vituperate, wrong* (≠ approve, blandish, commend, compliment, congratulate, endorse, flannel, flatter, glorify, gratify, heroicize, idolize, praise, respect, reward, sanction, venerate)

SCOPE (+): *analyze, appraise, assay, assess, audit, benchmark, case, categorize, check, classify, clock, compare, consider, consult, critique, diagnose, discover, dissect, evaluate, examine, explore, eye, eyeball, gauge, inspect, investigate, learn, mull, observe, peruse, police, ponder,* *prioritize, probe, process, prowl, rank, read, reckon, reference, research, review, sample, scan, scrutinize, search, sift, slot, sort, study, survey, tabulate, test, value, vet, weigh* (≠ addle, -avoid, baffle, blind, blindfold, -bypass, -circumvent, cloak, clothe, cloud, conceal, confound, confuse, deceive, detour, -discount, disguise, -disregard, -evade, forget, -ignore, mask, misdiagnose, mislead, miss, mistake, muddle, mystify, -neglect, -overlook, perplex, puzzle, skirt, trick)

SCORCH (/): *bake, blacken, blast, blister, broil, burn, cauterize, char, cook, deep-fry, discolor, dry, frizzle, fry, griddle, grill, melt, panfry, parch, roast, sauté, scald, scathe, sear, shrivel, simmer, singe, sizzle, stale, stew, wither, zap* (≠ butter, chill, cool, douse, drench, freeze, grease, heal, oil, rinse, salve, spatter, wet)

SCORE (→): *blemish, cleave, crosshatch, cut, damage, deface, dent, ding, efface, engrave, furrow, gash, gouge, graze, groove, incise, indent, line, mark, mill, nick, nock, notch, scrape, scratch, serrate, slash, slit* (≠ beautify, blend, buff, fill, fix, mend, patch, perfect, plaster, polish, repair, shine, smooth, spackle)

SCORE (←): *accomplish, achieve, actualize, add, amass, attain, calculate, chalk, claim, count, crest, earn, enumerate, gain, get, impress, make, notch, number, procure, reach, realize, reckon, record, register, secure, tally, total, win* (≠ dismiss, -disregard, estimate, exaggerate, fake, falsify, forget, -ignore, lose, miss, -overlook, pretend, undershoot)

-SCORN (/): *blackball, blackguard, blacklist, condemn, crucify, defy, demean, demonize, deride, -despise, -disdain, dismiss, disparage, -disregard, flout, -hate, -ignore, jeer, mock, pillory, -rebuff, -refuse, refute, -reject, -renounce, -repudiate, ridicule, scorch, shame, -shun, -slight, -spurn, taunt, trash, zing* (≠ accept, admire, allow, approve, champion, cherish, compliment, covet, crave, desire, embrace, enjoy, esteem, fancy, fetishize, flannel, flatter, gratify, include, invite, involve, lionize, love, note, praise, prioritize, regard, relish, respect, sanction, tolerate, treasure, welcome)

SCOTCH (/): *abnegate, abrogate, annihilate, annul, atomize, -blank, bulldoze, -cancel, decimate, deep-six, delete, demolish, -deny, desolate, destroy, devastate, disavow, disintegrate, dismantle, dismiss, dissolve, divorce, efface, eliminate, end, eradicate, erase, expunge, exterminate, extinguish, extirpate, flatten, -halt, invalidate, level, -negate, neutralize, -nullify, obliterate, overturn, pulverize, quash, raze, refute, -repudiate, retract, revoke, ruin, scrap, scupper, scuttle, smash, snuff, stop, suppress, terminate, topple, undo, uproot, vaporize, -veto, vitiate, -void, wreck* (≠ authorize, begin, brainstorm, bring, build, catalyze, commence, create, enact, establish, fashion, forge, form, found, generate, greenlight, hatch, inaugurate, induce, initiate, institute, introduce, launch, legislate, make, notarize, ordain, retain, shape, spawn, survive, weather)

SCOUR (→): *brush, buff, burnish, clean, cleanse, flush, furbish, lather, mop, oil, polish, pumice, purge, rub, sand, scrape, scrub, shine, sweep, wash,* *wax, whiten, wipe* (≠ bedraggle, blemish, callous, canker, coarsen, corrode, dirty, exfoliate, pollute, spot, stain, sully, tarnish)

SCOUR (←): *ascertain, audit, beat, browse, check, comb, descry, detect, determine, discover, drag, dredge, examine, explore, expose, ferret, find, forage, frisk, get, grub, hit, hunt, inspect, investigate, learn, locate, peruse, poke, police, probe, prowl, rake, ransack, reinvestigate, review, rifle, rout, rummage, scan, scope, scrutinize, search, seek, study, survey, track* (≠ -abandon, bury, conceal, cover, ensconce, forget, hide, -ignore, lose, -neglect, niche, -overlook, presume)

SCOURGE (/): *afflict, beat, belt, birch, brutalize, burden, cane, castigate, chastise, crucify, curse, devastate, discipline, excoriate, flail, flog, harass, hit, horsewhip, lambaste, lash, penalize, persecute, plague, punish, scathe, scorch, strap, tan, terrorize, thrash, torment, torture, trounce, wallop, whip* (≠ advantage, armor, baby, benefit, coddle, comfort, console, defend, delight, gratify, guard, help, humor, indulge, maintain, protect, shield, spoil, support, thrill, uplift)

SCOUT (→): *case, check, clock, examine, explore, eye, ferret, hunt, inspect, investigate, observe, patrol, police, probe, prowl, reconnoiter, scan, scope, scrutinize, search, seek, spot, spy, survey, suss, watch* (≠ -avoid, blind, blindfold, -bypass, -circumvent, cloud, conceal, deceive, detour, disguise, -dodge, -duck, -evade, fake, forget, guard, hide, -ignore, mask, mislead, miss, mystify, -omit, -overlook, perplex, puzzle, screen, shield, -shun, -sidestep, skip, skirt)

SCRAMBLE (/): *adulterate, agitate, alloy, amalgamate, blend, clutter, commingle, compound, cross, disorder, disorganize, disturb, fuse, garble, incorporate, infuse, jumble, lump, merge, mess, mingle, miscommunicate, mislabel, misrepresent, mix, stir, synthesize, tangle, unite, untidy* (≠ align, arrange, catalog, classify, colander, compose, consolidate, filter, hierarchize, index, neaten, order, organize, regiment, regulate, sift, slot, sort, strain, tidy, unscramble)

SCRAP (→): *-abandon, abdicate, annihilate, axe, cashier, chuck, deep-six, demolish, -desert, discard, dismiss, -ditch, drop, dump, eliminate, eradicate, exorcise, expunge, exterminate, extinguish, extirpate, forfeit, -forsake, jettison, junk, liquidate, lose, offload, pitch, -reject, remove, shed, shuck, slough, toss, unload* (≠ adopt, amass, collect, compile, conserve, embrace, employ, gather, hoard, hold, keep, preserve, recover, restore, retain, spare, stockpile, store, use, utilize)

SCRAP (/): *-abandon, abolish, -abort, abrogate, annul, call, -cancel, countermand, -discontinue, drop, end, -halt, interrupt, invalidate, -nullify, recall, recant, relinquish, repeal, -rescind, retract, reverse, revoke, scrub, stop, surrender, suspend, terminate, -void, withdraw* (≠ begin, brainstorm, bronze, commence, continue, embalm, engage, found, initiate, keep, maintain, pledge, preserve, promise, start, sustain, undertake)

SCRAPE (→): *bang, clash, crunch, dent, ding, drag, gnash, grate, grind, grit, jangle, jar, mark, rasp, rub, score, scratch, scrunch* (≠ buffer, cushion, hush, muffle, mute, pad, quiet, shush, silence, upholster)

SCRAPE (←): *abrade, bark, bruise, chafe, claw, clean, contuse, curette, cut, de-ice, descale, erase, file, flesh, fret, gall, grate, graze, grind, hoe, lacerate, maul, paw, rake, rasp, raze, remove, rub, scalp, scour, scratch, scuff, shave, shred, skin* (≠ assist, butter, ease, grease, lard, lubricate, oil, polish, shine, smooth, soften, wax)

SCRATCH (/): *abrade, bark, bruise, chafe, claw, contuse, cut, damage, fret, gall, grate, graze, grind, lacerate, maim, maul, nick, pick, prick, rasp, rub, score, scrape, scuff, skin, slice, tear, wound* (≠ bandage, bind, buff, butter, cover, dress, glide, grease, heal, mend, nurse, oil, polish, rectify, remedy, repair, seal, sew, shield, shine, slide, smooth, soften, stitch, wax)

SCREEN (←): *analyze, appraise, ascertain, assay, assess, benchmark, beta, calculate, check, colander, compare, compute, critique, decide, deduce, determine, diagnose, discern, discover, estimate, evaluate, examine, figure, filter, gauge, grade, guesstimate, investigate, judge, leach, learn, notice, number, percolate, price, process, rank, rate, read, reassess, reevaluate, reinvestigate, riddle, sample, scan, scrutinize, set, sieve, sift, slot, sort, strain, survey, test, total, valuate, value, vet* (≠ addle, assume, baffle, believe, bewilder, bury, conceal, confound, confuse, conjecture, deceive, defraud, disguise, -disregard, guess, hide, -ignore, mask, misgauge, misjudge, misprize, misread, mistake, misunderstand, muddle, mystify, -neglect, obscure, overestimate, -overlook, overvalue, perplex, predetermine, puzzle, snooker, snow, trick, trust, underestimate, undervalue)

SCREEN (/): *becloud, bedim, befog, belie, blanket, bleep, block, blot, bury, camouflage, canopy, cap, cloak, clothe, cloud, conceal, costume, cover, curtain, darken, defend, disguise, drape, eclipse, enshroud, gild, gloss, guard, hide, mask, obscure, obstruct, occlude, occult, overlap, overshadow, pall, paper, protect, safeguard, shade, shelter, shield, shroud, smother, spackle, suppress, varnish, veil, whitewash* (≠ accost, advertise, air, bare, broadcast, circulate, clarify, concede, confess, confide, confirm, confront, disclose, display, disseminate, divulge, expose, floodlight, illuminate, present, proclaim, publicize, publish, reveal, show, spread, telegraph, uncloak, uncover, unmask, unveil)

SCREW (+): *ball, bang, bed, boff, boink, bone, bonk, debauch, deflower, devour, diddle, drill, enter, fuck, hump, impale, jump, nail, penetrate, pillage, pleasure, plow, plunder, poke, pork, pound, rail, ravish, ride, seduce, shag, shtup, skewer, tap, tumble* (≠ -avoid, block, -deny, -disdain, dismiss, -disregard, -ditch, drop, -dump, -ignore, jilt, -neglect, -rebuff, -refuse, -reject, -shun, -snub, -spurn)

SCROUNGE (←): *abuse, appropriate, beg, bilk, bleed, bogart, borrow, bum, cadge, cheat, crib, defalcate, drain, embezzle, employ, exploit, fleece, gouge, hunt, leech, lift, manipulate, milk, mooch, panhandle, pilfer, scam,* *schnorr, seek, sponge, stint, swindle, tap, use, weasel, wheedle* (≠ bestow, deserve, disburse, dispense, donate, earn, endow, furnish, give, help, lend, merit, offer, outbid, outlay, overpay, overspend, pay, provide, recoup, replace, restore, serve, supply, support, tender, tithe, volunteer)

SCRUB (→): *abrade, brush, buff, burnish, clean, cleanse, dress, dust, file, flush, furbish, gloss, grind, polish, pumice, purge, rasp, rub, sand, sandblast, sandpaper, scour, scrape, shine, smooth, wash, wipe* (≠ bedraggle, begrime, blacken, dirty, muddy, pollute, smear, smirch, smudge, soil, spoil, sully, taint, tarnish)

SCRUB (/): *-abandon, abolish, -abort, abrogate, annul, axe, brush, call, -cancel, clean, cleanse, countermand, delete, -discontinue, drop, end, forget, -halt, interrupt, invalidate, -nullify, recall, recant, relinquish, repeal, -rescind, retract, reverse, revoke, rub, scour, scrap, stop, surrender, suspend, terminate, -void, wash, wipe, withdraw* (≠ begin, brainstorm, commence, continue, endure, engage, extend, hold, initiate, keep, maintain, pledge, promise, start, sustain, undertake)

SCRUTINIZE (←): *analyze, assess, audit, benchmark, canvass, case, categorize, check, classify, clock, comb, con, consider, consult, contemplate, dig, dissect, examine, explore, eye, eyeball, filter, grade, inspect, investigate, learn, mark, notice, observe, oversee, parse, peg, penetrate, peruse, pierce, plumb, police, prioritize, probe, prowl, rank, ransack, read, reference, reinvestigate, research, review, rifle, scan, scope, scour, search, sift, smoke, study, survey, suss, vet, view, vivisect, watch, weigh, winnow, x-ray* (≠ baffle, -blank, blind, blindfold, bury, -bypass, cheat, cloak, conceal, confound, confuse, deceive, disguise, -disregard, ensconce, erase, fake, forget, fudge, gaslight, half-ass, hide, -ignore, mask, mislead, misplace, miss, misunderstand, mystify, -neglect, niche, -overlook, perplex, puzzle, scam, skim, skip, sucker, trick, veil)

SCULPT (+): *adapt, adjust, alter, calibrate, carve, cast, chisel, contour, convert, correct, customize, cut, doctor, edit, engrave, etch, fake, fashion, fine-tune, fit, form, hew, incise, inscribe, model, modify, mold, prepare, prime, ready, recast, recycle, redesign, redevelop, reengineer, refashion, reinvent, rejigger, remake, remodel, represent, restore, retool, revamp, revise, rework, rig, salvage, sculpture, shape, square, tailor, transform, tune, tweak* (≠ batter, borrow, break, canker, copy, corrode, crack, damage, deface, destroy, disfigure, dissolve, disturb, duplicate, efface, eradicate, erase, hurt, mangle, melt, obliterate, pulverize, ruin, sabotage, scar, scatter, scotch, scramble, shatter, shelve, smash, spoil, topple, vandalize, worsen, wreck)

SCUPPER (/): *axe, compromise, defeat, demolish, destroy, disable, doom, endanger, foil, imperil, invalidate, kill, monkey-wrench, overthrow, overwhelm, ruin, scuttle, sink, submerge, torpedo, wreck* (≠ advance, advantage, assist, benefit, defend, foster, guard, preserve, promote, protect, support, survive, weather)

SEAL (+): *block, bung, caulk, chink, choke, cinch, clog, close, clot, congest, cork, dam, fasten, fill, jam, obstruct, occlude, pack, plug, plumb, pucker, secure, shut, stem, stop, stopper, stopple, stuff, tighten, waterproof* (≠ aerate, broach, clear, core, crack, excavate, force, hollow, open, oxygenate, prize, scoop, shovel, steam, unblock, uncork, unseal, ventilate)

SEAL (+): *accept, affirm, approve, authorize, certify, clear, clinch, conclude, confirm, consign, counterseal, endorse, finalize, formalize, initial, legalize, okay, ratify, rubber-stamp, settle, sign, stamp, validate* (≠ botch, -cancel, -decline, -deny, disallow, disapprove, jettison, -negate, -prohibit, -rebuff, -refuse, -reject, -spurn, -veto)

SEAR (/): *bake, barbecue, brand, broil, burn, cauterize, char, cremate, fire, ignite, immolate, incinerate, inflame, kindle, light, scald, scar, scathe, scorch, singe, steam* (≠ chill, cool, douse, extinguish, freeze, heal, marinate, rinse, smother, soak, wash, water, wet)

SEARCH (→): *check, dig, disclose, discover, dredge, evaluate, examine, excavate, explore, expose, fathom, fish, forage, frisk, hunt, inspect, investigate, mine, patrol, perambulate, pilfer, plumb, probe, prospect, prowl, pry, raid, rake, ransack, ravage, reconnoiter, research, reveal, rummage, scoop, scour, scout, scrutinize, seek, shovel, sift, sound, spade, survey, suss, tour, transit, travel, traverse, trowel, unearth, visit, wander* (≠ -abandon, -avoid, block, -bypass, circumnavigate, -circumvent, conceal, cover, defend, donate, -evade, guard, hide, -ignore, impede, keep, mask, mislead, miss, mistake, neaten, -neglect, orbit, -overlook, -prevent, -prohibit, protect, receive, -refuse, -reject, return, shield, skip, skirt, stash, stow, supply, tidy, volunteer, yield)

SEARCH (←): *ascertain, assess, audit, benchmark, browse, check, comb, deduce, descry, detect, determine, dig, discern, discover, dredge, evaluate, examine, explore, ferret, find, frisk, get, grok, hit, hunt, inspect, investigate, learn, locate, mark, notice, peruse, plumb, probe, rake, ransack, read, review, riffle, rifle, rummage, scan, scope, scour, scrounge, scrutinize, seek, sift, slot, sort, study, survey, suss, track* (≠ -abandon, baffle, bewilder, blanket, bury, cloak, conceal, confound, confuse, cover, deceive, defraud, -discount, disguise, disprove, -disregard, forget, -forsake, hide, -ignore, lose, mask, misjudge, mislay, misread, miss, mistake, misunderstand, muddle, mystify, -neglect, obscure, -omit, -overlook, perplex, puzzle, screen, shroud, trick, unlearn, veil)

SEASON (+): *acclimate, acclimatize, accommodate, accustom, adapt, adjust, age, authorize, bolster, boost, brace, buttress, calibrate, case-harden, condition, discipline, educate, empower, enable, enforce, entitle, equip, familiarize, fit, fortify, groom, habituate, harden, immunize, indoctrinate, instruct, inure, invigorate, limber, mature, mellow, moderate, naturalize, orient, prep, prepare, prime, qualify, ready, rehabilitate, reinforce, ripen, school, shape, steady, steel, strengthen, support, tailor, teach, temper, tone, toughen, train, treat, tutor, tweak, vitalize* (≠ castrate, cripple, debilitate, disqualify, emasculate, enervate, enfeeble, exhaust, hamstring, impair, incapacitate, overextend, sap, scotch, sensitize, soften, unman, weaken, wither)

SEASON (+): *appetize, brighten, color, dress, drizzle, dulcify, enhance, enliven, enrich, entice, flavor, garnish, ginger, imbue, improve, infuse, lace, leaven, liven, magnify, marinate, maximize, optimize, overhaul, pepper, perfume, prepare, revolutionize, richen, salt, saturate, sauce, savor, sour, spice, sugar, sweeten, syrup, zest* (≠ blemish, blunt, blur, bore, cloud, contaminate, damage, dampen, deaden, dilute, diminish, dull, foul, harm, hurt, impair, maintain, muddle, nauseate, repel, repulse, simplify, sully, taint, water)

SECLUDE (/): *alienate, cage, cloister, closet, confine, detach, detain, disengage, hold, immure, incarcerate, institutionalize, insulate, isolate, jail, keep, -omit, -ostracize, oust, quarantine, remove, restrain, restrict, segregate, separate, sequester, withdraw* (≠ annex, assemble, assimilate, associate, combine, connect, desegregate, discharge, free, include, incorporate, integrate, join, liberate, link, loose, merge, network, reintegrate, release, unite)

SECOND (+): *abet, advance, advocate, aid, approve, assist, back, champion, defend, encourage, endorse, espouse, forward, foster, further, help, praise, promote, rubber-stamp, sanction, support* (≠ attack, censure, condemn, denounce, incriminate, kill, monkey-wrench, revile, ruin, sabotage, scupper, subvert, undercut, vilify)

SECRETE (/): *appropriate, bury, cache, cloak, clothe, cloud, conceal, cover, disguise, ensconce, entomb, hide, hoard, holster, inter, screen, sequester, sheathe, shroud, squirrel, stash, take, tuck, veil* (≠ bare, brandish, disclose, disinter, display, exhibit, exhume, expose, flaunt, niche, parade, reveal, show, showcase, uncover, unearth, unmask, unveil, unwrap)

SECURE (←): *access, accomplish, accumulate, achieve, acquire, actualize, amass, annex, assure, attain, bag, bring, buy, capture, carry, catch, cinch, claim, clear, crest, crosscheck, download, draw, earn, ensure, gain, garner, get, grasp, gross, guarantee, hook, import, insure, knock, land, lock, make, net, notch, obtain, occupy, pick, procure, pull, rack, reacquire, realize, reap, reattain, recapture, regain, score, source, stockpile, take, win* (≠ -abandon, accord, bequeath, bestow, drop, forfeit, give, grant, lose, miss, pay, -refuse, release, relinquish, starve, steal, stiff, stint, surrender, undershoot, withhold, yield)

SECURE (+): *adjust, affix, anchor, attach, attain, batten, bind, bolt, button, catch, cement, chain, chock, cinch, clamp, clinch, close, deadbolt, embed, entrench, fasten, fix, hitch, hogtie, implant, ingrain, jam, lash, leash, lock, lodge, moor, mortar, nail, padlock, peg, pin, pinion, reinforce, rivet, seal, set, settle, shut, steady, strap, stuff, tack, tether, tie, tighten, wedge* (≠ detach, extract, loose, loosen, prize, pry, pull, secure, slack, slacken, tear, unfasten, untie, uproot, wrest, yank)

SECURE (+): *armor, assure, attach, -avert, ban, bar, barricade, battle, blockade, bulwark, colonize, conserve, cordon, cover, defend, embattle, ensure, fence, fight, fix, forfend, fortify, guarantee, guard, indemnify, insure, keep, lock, oppose, outlast, patrol, preserve, -prevent, protect, prove, reinforce, resist, safeguard, save, screen, shield, strengthen, support, wall, ward, withstand* (≠ ambush, assail, assault, attack, beset, besiege, blindside, blitz, bombard, boobytrap, bushwhack, compromise, damage, endanger, harm, hurt, injure, overrun, penetrate, protest, sabotage, sandbag, scupper, storm, submit, target, threaten, undermine, yield)

SECURE (+): *assure, attest, certify, choreograph, cinch, confirm, endorse, ensure, establish, guarantee, ice, insure, orchestrate, pledge, promise, sponsor, stipulate, swear, underwrite, warrant, witness* (≠ annul, -cancel, damage, destabilize, discourage, enfeeble, impugn, overthrow, rock, sabotage, scotch, shake, shelve, subvert, topple, undercut, undermine, unhorse, unman, unseat, weaken)

SEDATE (←): *allay, alleviate, anesthetize, appease, assuage, balance, calm, chloroform, compose, daze, deaden, defuse, dope, dose, drug, ease, etherize, hush, hypnotize, intoxicate, lighten, lull, medicate, mellow, mesmerize, mitigate, moderate, mollify, narcotize, numb, pacify, placate, quell, quiet, quieten, relax, relieve, restrain, settle, shanghai, silence, smooth, soften, soothe, stabilize, steady, still, stupefy, subdue, torpefy, tranquilize, unruffle* (≠ aggravate, agitate, anger, arouse, bait, bother, chafe, charge, convulse, discompose, disturb, dizzy, energize, enrage, excite, fluster, foment, goad, incite, inflame, infuriate, irk, irritate, jolt, madden, needle, nettle, perturb, provoke, rankle, rattle, rile, roil, rouse, shake, spur, stimulate, stir, terrorize, trouble, unnerve, upset, vex, wake, worry)

SEDUCE (←): *absorb, allure, amuse, arouse, arrest, attract, bait, bamboozle, beckon, bedevil, beguile, bewitch, bribe, cajole, candy-coat, captivate, capture, catch, charm, coax, conquer, convince, court, dare, dazzle, deceive, decoy, delight, delude, disarm, draw, enamor, enchant, engage, engross, enlist, enmesh, enrapture, ensnare, entangle, entertain, enthrall, entice, entrance, entrap, excite, fascinate, galvanize, grab, grant, gratify, grip, honey, hoodwink, hook, hypnotize, incite, indoctrinate, induce, influence, inspire, instigate, interest, intrigue, inveigle, invite, lead, lure, magnetize, manipulate, mesmerize, mislead, monopolize, motivate, move, obsess, occupy, oil, palaver, paralyze, persuade, please, preoccupy, provoke, pull, ravish, razzle-dazzle, romance, rope, rouse, schmooze, seize, sell, snare, snooker, snow, solicit, spellbind, steer, stimulate, stir, strike, suborn, sugarcoat, suggest, sway, sweeten, tangle, tantalize, taunt, tease, tempt, thrill, titillate, train, transfix, transport, trap, treat, trigger, turn, urge, vamp, welcome, wheedle, whet, win, woo, wow* (≠ affront, alarm, alert, anger, annoy, appall, badger, -balk, beleaguer, blackjack, blackmail, block, bore, bother, browbeat, bug, bully, burden, caution, command, content, covet, crave, dampen, daunt, deaden, demoralize, demotivate, depress, desensitize, -deter, disappoint, discourage, disenchant, disgust, dismay, dissuade, drain, dull, enervate, enrage, exhaust, fatigue, force, frustrate, fulfill, glut, gratify, harass, hassle, horrify, hunt, -ignore, infuriate, intimidate, irk, irritate, knacker, lose, menace, nag, nauseate, needle, nettle, niggle, nitpick, nobble, numb, offend, outrage, paralyze, pester, plague, pursue, quench, -reject, repel, repulse, revolt, sadden, sate, satiate, satisfy, scare, seek, shake, sicken, slake, -spurn, stifle, stymie, surfeit, terrify, threaten, -thwart, tire, torment, trouble, underwhelm, upset, vex, ward, warn, weary, worry)

SEDUCE (/): *abuse, assault, bed, beguile, betray, corner, corrupt, debauch, deceive, defile, deflower, deprave, desecrate, despoil, dishonor, disturb, dominate, force, harm, lure, mar, mislead, mistreat, molest, rape, ravish, ruin, spoil, submit, suborn, tantalize, tempt, trap, violate, wreck, wrong* (≠ benefit, bless, cherish, defend, guard, honor, preserve, protect, -refuse, respect, -scorn, shield, -shun, -spurn, sustain, tend)

SEEK (→): *aim, ask, attempt, beg, bird-dog, chase, comb, consult, desire, dog, explore, fan, ferret, fish, follow, forage, hunt, intend, investigate, invite, petition, probe, pursue, ransack, request, rifle, root, rummage, scour, scout, scratch, search, sift, spoor, stalk, tail, target, track, trail, try, undertake, want, winnow* (≠ achieve, acquire, bury, -bypass, conceal, crest, discard, -discount, discover, -disregard, -ditch, drop, dump, ensconce, entreat, find, forfeit, forget, grasp, hide, -ignore, junk, lose, misread, miss, mistake, -neglect, niche, offload, -omit, -overlook, pass, procure, -quit, secure, seize, -shun, -sidestep, skip, skirt, solicit, toss)

SEEK (←): *ask, beg, bid, call, claim, conjure, covet, crave, demand, desire, enjoin, entreat, exact, fancy, favor, fetishize, importune, insist, interrogate, interview, invite, invoke, petition, plead, press, probe, query, question, reclaim, recoup, recover, request, require, requisition, rescue, resent, retrieve, salvage, scavenge, solicit, summon, target, tempt, urge, want, wish* (≠ abhor, -avoid, blame, -boycott, criticize, -decline, decry, denounce, -deny, -detest, disclaim, disfavor, -dodge, -duck, -eschew, fault, finger, -forsake, -loathe, -negate, -rebuff, -refuse, -reject, repel, -repudiate, reserve, resist, -scorn, scrap, -shun, -spurn, withhold)

SEGREGATE (/): *alienate, confine, detain, disengage, divide, -exclude, hold, immure, incarcerate, institutionalize, insulate, isolate, jail, keep, -omit, -ostracize, oust, polarize, quarantine, remove, restrain, restrict, seclude, separate, sequester, split* (≠ annex, assimilate, associate, combine, connect, desegregate, discharge, free, incorporate, integrate, join, liberate, link, loose, mingle, mix, network, reintegrate, release, reunite, unite)

SEIZE (←): *abduct, bag, capture, catch, clasp, claw, clench, clinch, clutch, compass, cop, corner, corral, detain, disappear, embrace, enclose, enfold, enmesh, ensnare, entangle, entrap, envelop, fasten, fence, gain, get, glom, glove, grab, grapple, grasp, grip, halter, herd, hold, hook, incorporate, keep, kidnap, land, lasso, lift, nab, nail, net, pinch, pluck, rap, rend, rope, rustle, secure, snag, snap, snare, snatch, squeeze, take, trap, wrangle, wrap, wrest* (≠ -abandon, bestow, deliver, discharge, drop, furnish, give, liberate, loosen, lose, mislay, misplace, miss, offer, ransom, redeem, release, remove, save, slacken, supply, tender, unhand, volunteer)

SEIZE (←): *ambush, annex, appropriate, arrogate, assume, attach, blindside, bogart, captivate, claim, collar, commandeer, confiscate, convert, corner, despoil, embezzle, embrace, exact, force, freeboot, glom, grab, grasp, hijack, impound, infringe, invade, loot, misapply, misappropriate, misuse, nobble, occupy, overcome, overpower, overrun, overwhelm, pillage, pirate, pluck, poach, possess, preempt, press, raid, repossess, secure, sequester, snatch, steal, subdue, swipe, take, throttle, trap, trespass, usurp, wrench, wrest* (≠ bestow, confer, deed, dismiss, donate, drop, earn, endow, enthrone, exchange, free, give, honor, impart, liberate, offer, release, replace, respect, restore, return, spring, square, trade, unbind, volunteer)

SEIZE (←): *apprehend, arrest, bag, bind, bust, cage, capture, catch, chain, collar, commit, condemn, confine, conquer, contain, convict, coop, cuff, detain, enchain, fetter, get, grab, grapple, handcuff, hogtie, hold, hook, immure, imprison, incarcerate, institutionalize, intern, jail, jug, land, manacle, nab, nail, pinch, remand, restrain, shackle, snaffle, snare, snatch, straightjacket, trammel, trap* (≠ acquit, bail, discharge, emancipate, free, liberate, loose, loosen, manumit, pardon, release, rescue, slack, slacken, spring, unbind, unchain, uncuff)

SELECT (←): *accumulate, acquire, adopt, amass, appoint, approve, assemble, bag, cache, capture, cherry-pick, choose, claim, collect, compile, covet, cull, decide, designate, desire, download, elect, embrace, espouse, fancy, favor, fix, gain, garner, gather, glean, grasp, handpick, harvest, hoard, hunt, invite, mark, name, nominate, obtain, peg, pick, pluck, predetermine, prefer, preselect, prioritize, procure, pull, reap, salvage, scavenge, secure, seize, set, slot, snag, snare, source, strip, tab, tag, take, tap, winnow* (≠ -abandon, -avoid, bandy, -decline, deep-six, deselect, discard, discredit, disfavor, dismiss, dissipate, -ditch, donate, drop, dump, eliminate, -eschew, -exclude, -forsake, furnish, give, -ignore, jettison, junk, lavish, lose, -neglect, -nix, offer, -omit, predetermine, -refuse, -reject, remove, -repudiate, retain, scatter, -scorn, scrap, skip, -spurn, squander, supply, toss, trash, -veto, waste, withhold)

SELL (→): *auction, barter, bootleg, bundle, carry, commodify, deal, dispense, dispose, distribute, dump, exchange, export, flog, franchise, handle, import, keep, launch, market, merchandize, monetize, offload, outsell, package, peddle, pimp, presell, prostitute, provide, reissue, remainder, retail, stock, supply, swap, trade, traffic, vend, wholesale, whore* (≠ acquire, borrow, buy, hoard, hold, import, keep, lend, loan, obtain, outbid, possess, preserve, procure, purchase, retain, secure, source)

SELL (→): *acclaim, advertise, announce, ballyhoo, bark, boost, broadcast, commercialize, convince, endorse, flog, hail, hawk, hype, laud, market, merchandize, peddle, persuade, pitch, plug, praise, presell, promote, publicize, publish, push, recommend, review, shill, telegraph, tout* (≠ bury, conceal, cover, hide, hush, recall, recant, retract, revoke, secrete, silence, suppress, veil, withhold)

SEND (→): *accelerate, address, advance, assign, beam, bestow, commission, comp, consign, contribute, convey, courier, delegate, deliver, dispatch, donate, drop, expedite, export, express, forward, freight, give, grant, hand, hasten, import, mail, pack, pass, post, present, redirect, relay, remit, render, resend, return, route, rush, schlep, ship, tender, tithe, transfer, transmit, transport* (≠ accept, acquire, collect, download, draw, earn, find, gain, garner, get, keep, obtain, procure, receive, save, secure, source, take)

SEND (→): *cast, catapult, chuck, direct, discharge, drive, emit, fire, fling, flip, heave, hurl, launch, lob, move, pitch, project, propel, shoot, sling, throw, toss, wing* (≠ catch, clasp, clutch, detain, grab, grip, -halt, hinder, hold, impede, keep, receive, rescue, salvage, slow)

SEND (→): *address, beam, broadcast, channel, circulate, communicate, concentrate, convey, detail, dispatch, email, emit, focus, forward, funnel, impart, issue, mail, message, post, radio, relay, telegraph, televise, text, transfer, transmit, wire* (≠ cloak, conceal, contain, hide, hush, obscure, recant, retract, shroud, silence, suppress, veil, withhold)

SEND (←): *amaze, amuse, animate, astonish, astound, bewitch, charm, delight, dizzy, elate, electrify, enrapture, entertain, enthrall, enthuse, excite, exhilarate, inspire, intoxicate, move, ravish, stimulate, stir, thrill, titillate, transfix, transport, wow* (≠ appall, bore, bother, bug, burden, demoralize, depress, discourage, dismay, displease, distress, fatigue, frustrate, irk, irritate, knacker, nauseate, numb, oppress, repel, repulse, sadden, sicken, weary, worry)

SENSE (←): *anticipate, ascertain, assume, await, believe, conjecture, consider, credit, descry, detect, determine, discover, distinguish, divine, espy, expect, experience, eye, feel, foresee, guess, hear, hold, note, notice, observe, read, regard, remark, scent, see, sight, smell, spoor, spy, taste, view, whiff, witness* (≠ -avoid, blind, blindfold, -bypass, -circumvent, cloak, clothe, cloud, conceal, confuse, deafen, disguise, dull, -evade, hide, -ignore, mask, muffle, -neglect, -overlook, screen, shield, -sidestep, skirt, stifle) **(¿) ABSTRACTION ALERT. Concrete goals essential!**

SENSE (←): *absorb, adjudge, appreciate, apprehend, assimilate, catch, clock, compass, comprehend, conceive, decipher, decode, deduce, detect, determine, diagnose, dig, digest, discern, fathom, get, grasp, incorporate, internalize, intuit, know, learn, make, penetrate, perceive, pierce, plumb, presume, realize, recognize, register, savvy, scan, scope, scrutinize, seize, suppose, surmise, suspect, suss, think, twig, understand, wonder* (≠ cloak, cloud, conceal, confound, confuse, -discount, disguise, -disregard, distort, encode, encrypt, garble, hide, -ignore, jumble, lump, misapprehend, misconceive, misconstrue, misdiagnose, mishear, misinterpret, misperceive, misread, miss, mistake, misunderstand, muddle, -neglect, -overlook, perplex, puzzle, scramble, screen, shield, -sidestep, skip, skirt, veil) **(¿) ABSTRACTION ALERT. Concrete goals essential!**

SEPARATE (+): *alphabetize, array, assign, assort, catalog, categorize, class, classify, cluster, codify, colander, comb, compartment, compartmentalize, cull, digest, dispose, distinguish, distribute, file, grade, group, hierarchize, identify, index, insulate, list, marshal, order, organize, partition, peg, pigeonhole, place, prioritize, range, rank, recategorize, reclassify, regroup, relegate, screen, shelve, sieve, sift, slot, sort, space, stereotype, systematize, type, winnow* (≠ churn, confuse, desegregate, disarrange, disorder, disorganize, gather, integrate, join, jumble, level, lump, misclassify, missort, mistype, mix, scatter, scramble, strew, unify, unite)

SEPARATE (/): *bisect, break, chunk, cleave, comminute, decompose, decouple, detach, dichotomize, disassemble, disassociate, disconnect, disengage, disentangle, disintegrate, disjoin, disjoint, dismantle, dissect, dissolve, distribute, disunite, divide, divorce, estrange, fracture, halve, insulate, intersect, isolate, orphan, part, partition, pull, quarter, remove, rend, resolve, rip, rive, rupture, seclude, segment, segregate, sequester, sever, split, subdivide, sunder, tear, uncouple, unlink, unravel, untie, unyoke, vivisect, withdraw* (≠ accumulate, assemble, associate, attach, bind, blend, cement, close, collect, combine, compile, connect, couple, fasten, fuse, hybridize, integrate, join, knit, link, mingle, mix, mortar, recover, reintegrate, reunite, stick, synthesize, unify, unite, unmarry, weld)

SEPARATE (/): *abstract, alienate, bifurcate, confine, cordon, depart, detach, detain, disaffect, -discontinue, disengage, disunite, divorce, drop, -eschew, estrange, hold, immure, imprison, incarcerate, institutionalize, insulate, isolate, jail, keep, leave, part, quarantine, remove, restrain, restrict, seclude, segregate, sequester, sideline, split, uncouple* (≠ assimilate, associate, connect, desegregate, incorporate, integrate, join, link, marry, network, reclaim, recoup, reintegrate, release, unite, wed)

SEQUESTER (←): *appropriate, arrogate, attach, bogart, commandeer, confiscate, dragoon, garnish, impound, preempt, seize, take, usurp* (≠ bestow, cede, deliver, forfeit, give, hand, release, relinquish, render, surrender, yield)

SEQUESTER (/): *abstract, alienate, confine, detach, detain, disengage, hold, immure, incarcerate, institutionalize, insulate, isolate, jail, keep, quarantine, remove, restrain, restrict, seclude, segregate, separate* (≠ assimilate, associate, connect, desegregate, discharge, free, incorporate, integrate, join, liberate, link, loose, reintegrate, release, reunite, unite)

SERVE (→): *administer, allocate, apportion, assign, chunk, contribute, deliver, dish, dispense, distribute, dole, dollop, feed, force-feed, fuel, furnish, give, hand, ladle, offer, portion, present, prorate, provide, scoop, spoon, supply, transfer* (≠ budget, conserve, -deny, deprive, hold, keep, maintain, preserve, remove, reserve, retain, save, seize, starve, withdraw, withhold)

SERVE (+): *advantage, aid, assist, attend, benefit, better, bless, content, delight, favor, follow, further, gladden, gratify, help, improve, obey, oblige, please, profit, satisfy, service, succor, support* (≠ afflict, blemish, blight, damage, distress, harm, hinder, hurt, impair, impede, inhibit, injure, irk, maltreat, mar, plague, upset, weary, worry)

SERVE (+): *accomplish, achieve, answer, assuage, complete, content, discharge, finish, fulfill, justify, perform, quench, realize, sate, satiate, satisfy, slake, suit* (≠ affront, aggravate, anger, annoy, bother, bug, disappoint, distress, gall, infuriate, insult, irk, nag, needle, nettle, niggle, offend, rankle, rile, upset, vex)

SERVICE (+): *adjust, aid, ameliorate, attend, better, bolster, brace, chauffeur, check, condition, conserve, correct, cure, defend, doctor, enhance, enrich, fix, freshen, furbish, furnish, guard, heal, help, husband, improve, maintain, manage, mend, modify, nourish, nurture, optimize, overhaul, patch, patrol, prepare, preserve, protect, ready, rebuild, recondition, reconstruct, rectify, redress, reform, refresh, refurbish, regenerate, rehabilitate, reinvigorate, rejuvenate, remedy, renew, renovate, repair, restore, revamp, revitalize, revive, right, safeguard, save, strengthen, supply, support, sustain, tune, tweak* (≠ blemish, break, cripple, damage, deface, destroy, disable, disfigure, -disregard, efface, flaw, harm, harshen, hurt, -ignore, impair, incapacitate, injure, maim, mangle, mar, monkey-wrench, mutilate, -neglect, ruin, sabotage, scotch, scupper, shelve, spoil, undermine, vandalize, wreck)

SETTLE (+): *accept, affirm, appoint, approve, arrange, authorize, blueprint, broker, calculate, chart, choose, clear, clinch, close, complete, compromise, concert, conclude, confirm, contract, decide, defray, design, determine, draft, end, establish, figure, finalize, finish, fix, frame, graph, intrigue, machinate, maneuver, manipulate, map, negotiate, numerate, okay, plan, pledge, program, promise, reconcile, resolve, sanction, schematize, scheme, script, set, shape, solve, square, transact, warrant, wrap* (≠ -abort, contest, counter, counteract, debate, defy, discredit, -disown, disprove, dispute, distrust, doubt, drop, invalidate, oppose, predetermine, -prohibit, protest, recall, -refuse, renegotiate, repeal, -rescind, resist, revoke, scruple)

SETTLE (+): *adjust, align, allay, alleviate, appease, arrange, assuage, assure, balance, calibrate, calm, center, complete, compose, conciliate, ease, ground, harmonize, heal, help, hush, lull, mellow, mitigate, moderate, mollify, order, organize, pace, pacify, placate, quell, quiet, reassure, regiment, regulate, relax, relieve, reunite, salve, sedate, smooth, solace, soothe, still, stupefy, tranquilize, tweak* (≠ aggravate, agitate, arouse, bother, confuse, convulse, derange, disconcert, distress, disturb, exacerbate, exasperate, excite, fluster, foment, heighten, incite, intensify, irritate, muddle, panic, rabble-rouse, rattle, shake, startle, stir, trouble, unnerve, unsettle, upset, vex, worry)

SEVER (/): *alienate, amputate, axe, behead, bisect, break, chop, chunk, circumcise, cleave, cut, decapitate, detach, disarticulate, disassemble, disassociate, disconnect, disengage, disintegrate, disjoin, dismantle, dissect, disunite, divide, divorce, estrange, excise, fragment, guillotine, hack, halve, hew, incise, insulate, isolate, joint, pare, part, partition, razor, remove, rend, rip, rupture, scissor, segregate, separate, slash, slice, slit, split, sunder, tear, truncate, uncouple, vivisect* (≠ associate, attach, begin, bind, blend, cement, close, combine, connect, continue, couple, establish, fetter, fuse, heal, join, knit, link, maintain, marry, mend, mix, mortar, repair, reunite, secure, sew, solder, start, stick, unite, uphold, weld)

SHACKLE (/): *attach, bind, chain, confine, constrain, curb, encumber, enslave, entangle, fasten, fetter, hamper, hamstring, handcuff, handicap, hinder, hobble, hogtie, hold, impede, inhibit, iron, join, lash, limit, link, manacle, obstruct, pinion, restrain, restrict, secure, tangle, tether, -thwart, tie, trammel, truss* (≠ detach, disengage, emancipate, free, liberate, loose, loosen, manumit, release, rescue, save, slacken, unbind, undo, unfasten, unfetter, unlock, unshackle, untie)

SHADOW (→): *accompany, attend, bird-dog, chaperone, chase, darken, dog, escort, eye, follow, guard, guide, hide, hound, hunt, obscure, observe, pursue, retrace, run, scent, screen, seek, shade, shield, spoor, stalk, tag, tail, target, trace, track, trail, usher, watch* (≠ beacon, brighten, -escape, floodlight, guide, head, illuminate, lead, lose, pilot)

SHAKE (→): *agitate, beat, blend, bounce, bump, churn, convulse, disturb, faze, flutter, froth, heave, jerk, jiggle, joggle, jolt, jounce, jumble, mix, oscillate, palpitate, quiver, rattle, razzle-dazzle, ripple, rock, roll, ruffle, scramble, seesaw, shiver, stagger, stir, sway, swing, thrill, twitch, undermine, unnerve, vibrate, wag, wave, wiggle, wobble* (≠ affix, anchor, attach, balance, calm, center, compose, fasten, fix, mitigate, moderate, nail, pin, pinion, root, settle, stabilize, steady)

SHAKE (/): *-avert, -avoid, ban, bar, -bypass, -circumvent, debar, deflect, -ditch, divert, -dodge, -duck, eliminate, -elude, -escape, -evade, except, -exclude, finesse, foil, fox, frustrate, miss, -obviate, -ostracize, oust, outfox, outmaneuver, outsmart, outwit, overreach, parry, -preclude, -prevent, -shirk, -shun, skirt, -thwart, ward* (≠ accept, capture, catch, contract, court, detect, embrace, find, follow, incur, invite, join, pursue, seek, spot, welcome, woo)

SHAME (/): *abase, abash, abuse, affront, badmouth, bait, bastardize, belittle, bench, besmear, besmirch, bestialize, blackguard, blister, boo, castigate, censure, chasten, chastise, cheapen, condemn, confound, confuse, criticize, critique, damn, debase, decry, defame, defile, degrade, demean, demonize, demote, denounce, denunciate, depreciate, detract, devalue, diminish, discomfit, disconcert, -discount, discredit, disgrace, dishonor, disparage, disrespect, diss, embarrass, execrate, expose, faze, fluster, foul, fulminate, humble, humiliate, hurt, incriminate, injure, insult, jeer, libel, lower, malign, minimize, mock, mortify, nonplus, offend, out,* *outrage, pillory, profane, rattle, -rebuff, rebuke, reduce, reveal, ridicule, -scorn, sideline, sink, slander, -slight, slur, smirch, -snub, soil, spoil, stain, sully, taint, taunt, trample, violate, wound, wrong* (≠ acknowledge, admire, affirm, aggrandize, applaud, blandish, bless, boost, buoy, canonize, celebrate, cheer, cite, commend, compliment, congratulate, decorate, deify, dignify, elevate, encourage, ennoble, enshrine, exalt, extol, flannel, flatter, glorify, gratify, heroicize, heroize, highlight, honor, hype, idealize, idolize, limelight, lionize, magnify, plug, praise, presell, prioritize, promote, raise, recognize, revere, romanticize, salute, shill, spotlight, support, tout, upgrade, uplift, venerate, worship)

SHANGHAI (←): *abduct, appropriate, attack, bag, bundle, capture, coopt, ensnare, entangle, entrap, freeboot, grab, hijack, hook, hotwire, implicate, kidnap, lure, nab, nobble, pirate, pluck, poach, ransom, remove, seize, snag, snatch, steal, swipe, take, waylay* (≠ -bypass, chauffeur, defend, deliver, -escape, -evade, foil, preserve, -prevent, protect, ransom, redeem, rescue, restore, safeguard, save, secure, shelter, shield, skip, stymie, -thwart)

SHAPE (→): *acclimate, acclimatize, accommodate, accustom, acquaint, adapt, adjust, align, alter, attune, automate, bend, block, calibrate, carve, case-harden, cast, coin, concoct, condition, constitute, construct, contour, convert, correct, create, curl, customize, cut, define, design, determine, develop, devise, doctor, edit, educate, equalize, equip, establish, familiarize, fashion, fiddle, fine-tune, fit, fold, forge, form, foster, frame, gear, guide, habituate, harden, harmonize, improve, influence, inure, knead, make, match, mechanize, model, modify, mold, naturalize, organize, orient, pace, pattern, plan, prepare, prime, produce, punctuate, readjust, ready, realign, rebuild, recast, reclaim, reconceive, reconceptualize, recycle, redesign, redevelop, redo, reengineer, refashion, refit, refocus, register, regulate, rehearse, reinvent, rejigger, remake, remodel, reorient, rephrase, reshuffle, rethink, revamp, revise, rework, rig, right, root, rotate, script, sculpt, sculpture, season, settle, shuffle, square, suit, tailor, tone, toughen, transform, tune, tweak, twist, weaponize, whittle* (≠ atomize, break, crack, damage, deface, deform, demolish, disfigure, dissolve, distort, fracture, fragment, liquefy, mangle, melt, misadjust, mismatch, mutate, obliterate, pulverize, ruin, shatter, skew, unbalance, unsettle, warp, wreck, wrinkle)

SHAPE (+): *adjust, aim, arrange, blueprint, budget, calculate, calibrate, chart, choreograph, concert, contemplate, contrive, design, destine, devise, draft, figure, frame, graph, improvise, intend, intrigue, machinate, map, meditate, orchestrate, organize, outline, phase, plan, plot, premeditate, prepare, project, scheme, script, settle, sketch, strategize* (≠ blow, botch, bungle, butcher, derange, disarrange, disarray, disorder, disorganize, duplicate, flub, fumble, gum, half-ass, louse, mangle, mess, mishandle, muss, replicate, rumple, unsettle, upset, wing)

SHARE (→): *accord, administer, allocate, allot, allow, apportion, assign, award, bestow, chunk, circulate, contribute, deal, disburse, dispense,* *disseminate, distribute, divide, divvy, dole, dollop, donate, earmark, furnish, give, grant, halve, hand, issue, measure, mete, parcel, part, partition, pledge, portion, prorate, provide, ration, reallocate, receive, redistribute, reserve, scatter, shift, slice, split, spread, supply, yield* (≠ aggregate, appropriate, arrogate, begrudge, collect, combine, composite, compound, confiscate, consolidate, -decline, -deny, deprive, gather, hold, keep, maintain, misallocate, oppose, pool, receive, recycle, -refuse, -reject, retain, salvage, skimp, starve, stint, unite, withhold)

SHARPEN (+): *amplify, better, boost, correct, emend, enhance, fine-tune, flavor, fortify, grasp, hone, improve, intensify, learn, magnify, manage, marinate, master, maximize, perfect, polish, realign, rectify, refine, reform, rehabilitate, remedy, revamp, richen, season, shine, spice, strengthen, study, uncloud, upgrade, vitalize* (≠ agitate, blunt, compromise, corrupt, damage, debilitate, disable, dull, harm, hurt, impair, incapacitate, injure, mar, pollute, ruin, scramble, spoil, tarnish, undermine, vitiate, weaken, worsen)

SHARPEN (/): *dress, edge, file, grind, hone, polish, refine, shine, stroke, strop, taper, whet* (≠ blunt, blur, buff, buffer, burnish, cushion, dull, muffle, polish, round, smooth, soften, weaken)

SHATTER (/): *annihilate, atomize, batter, beat, best, burst, bust, clobber, conquer, cream, cripple, damage, dash, decimate, deface, defeat, demolish, desolate, despoil, destroy, deteriorate, devastate, dilapidate, disable, disassemble, disfigure, disintegrate, dismantle, dissolve, disunite, divide, doom, drub, efface, eradicate, erode, exhaust, expunge, exterminate, extinguish, extirpate, gut, harm, impair, implode, injure, kneecap, lick, liquidate, loot, mangle, mar, master, mutilate, nuke, obliterate, overcome, pillage, plunder, ravage, raze, remove, rout, ruin, sack, scotch, scour, skunk, snuff, spoil, subdue, surmount, thrash, torpedo, total, trample, trash, trim, trounce, unbuild, unmake, vandalize, vaporize, vitiate, wallop, waste, whip, wrack, wreck* (≠ build, conserve, constitute, construct, create, doctor, erect, establish, fabricate, fashion, fix, form, found, frame, institute, invent, machine, make, manufacture, mold, organize, patch, preserve, produce, protect, raise, rear, rebuild, recondition, reconstruct, remodel, renovate, revamp, save, sculpt, shape, survive, weather, withstand)

SHATTER (/): *atomize, bash, batter, blast, blow, break, burst, bust, chip, crack, crash, crumble, crunch, crush, detonate, discharge, disintegrate, dismantle, dynamite, efface, explode, fracture, fragment, grind, mangle, mortar, nuke, pop, pound, powder, pulverize, pummel, rupture, shiver, smash, snap, splinter, split, spoil, total, trash, vaporize, waste, zap* (≠ assemble, bind, build, combine, construct, create, erect, fabricate, fashion, fasten, fix, forge, form, fuse, glue, invent, join, make, manufacture, melt, mend, mold, organize, patch, preserve, produce, protect, raise, rear, rebuild, reconstruct, repair, restore, revamp, save, secure, shape, solder, unite, weld)

SHAVE (/): *barber, bob, brush, clip, crop, curtail, cut, dock, fleece, graze, groom, lop, manicure, mow, nip, pare, peel, plane, poll, pomade, prune, razor, reduce, scrape, shear, shingle, shorten, shred, skim, skin, slash, slice, snip, strip, thin, touch, trim, whittle* (≠ cultivate, develop, -disregard, elongate, extend, foster, grow, increase, lengthen, -neglect, nurture, stretch)

SHELTER (+): *accommodate, barrack, bestow, billet, board, chamber, conceal, cover, defend, domicile, enclose, ensconce, fortify, garrison, guard, harbor, hide, house, invite, lodge, place, preserve, protect, quarter, roof, room, safeguard, screen, secure, shade, shadow, shield, shingle, shroud, stable, surround, ward, welcome* (≠ -abandon, abuse, assault, ban, banish, bar, betray, compromise, damage, eject, endanger, evict, exile, exorcise, expel, expose, harm, hurt, imperil, injure, -rebuff, -refuse, -reject, repel, reveal, risk, -shun, target, threaten, uncover)

SHELVE (+): *-abort, abrogate, adjourn, annul, banish, bank, bench, -blank, bury, cache, call, cellar, close, coffer, conceal, conclude, deactivate, defer, degrade, delay, demote, deposit, detain, disband, disbar, -discontinue, dismiss, disperse, dissolve, downgrade, drop, eject, end, ensconce, -exclude, exile, expel, extend, ground, -halt, hold, inactivate, interrupt, invalidate, jettison, kill, lengthen, mothball, -negate, -nullify, offload, -ostracize, oust, pause, postpone, prolong, protract, quash, recall, recess, relegate, remove, repeal, -rescind, reserve, retard, revoke, sack, sideline, slow, squirrel, stash, stay, stop, store, stow, stretch, suspend, table, terminate, transfer, tuck, unload, -void, warehouse, withdraw, wrap* (≠ activate, assemble, begin, brainstorm, call, circulate, continue, convene, convoke, elicit, encourage, establish, expedite, expend, extend, found, inaugurate, incite, induce, initiate, inspire, instigate, institute, introduce, launch, lavish, motivate, muster, nominate, open, organize, prod, prolong, promote, prompt, provoke, rally, renew, reopen, resume, scatter, spend, spur, start, stimulate, summon, trigger, urge)

SHEPHERD (+): *accompany, advise, assess, attend, brief, chair, chaperone, chauffeur, check, coach, conduct, control, convoy, counsel, cultivate, detect, direct, drill, engineer, enlighten, escort, follow, foster, gauge, godfather, govern, guard, guide, handle, herd, inculcate, indoctrinate, inform, inspect, instruct, judge, lead, maintain, manage, marshal, mentor, mind, monitor, nanny, nurture, observe, organize, oversee, pastor, pilot, proctor, protect, regiment, safeguard, scan, school, show, squire, steer, supervise, support, survey, sway, teach, track, train, tutor, usher, watch* (≠ -abandon, abuse, addle, baffle, blind, blindfold, compromise, confound, confuse, damage, deceive, -desert, -disregard, -ditch, -exclude, forget, forgo, -forsake, harm, hurt, -ignore, imperil, injure, maroon, misdirect, misguide, mishandle, mislead, mismanage, miss, -neglect, oppose, -ostracize, oust, -overlook, perplex, puzzle, -reject, risk, shake, -shun, -snub, -spurn, strand, trick)

SHIELD (+): *armor, -avert, bar, barricade, buffer, bulwark, conceal, conserve, cordon, counter, counterattack, cover, cushion, defend, fence,* *forfend, guard, harbor, house, insulate, keep, maintain, oppose, outlast, police, preserve, -prevent, protect, rebut, resist, safeguard, save, screen, secure, sentinel, shade, shadow, shelter, stonewall, support, sustain, uphold, wall, ward, withstand* (≠ -abandon, assail, assault, attack, beset, besiege, blitz, bombard, compromise, -desert, endanger, imperil, impugn, jeopardize, mortar, offend, overrun, risk, storm, target, threaten)

SHIELD (/): *block, canopy, cap, cloak, clothe, cloud, conceal, costume, cover, crown, curtain, darken, dim, disguise, drape, hide, mask, obscure, overlap, overshadow, pall, protect, screen, shade, shadow, shroud, veil* (≠ accost, bare, betray, compromise, concede, confess, confide, confirm, confront, denounce, detect, display, divulge, expose, incriminate, out, present, strip, uncover, unmask, unveil)

SHIFT (→): *adapt, adjust, alter, beam, bear, budge, calibrate, carry, cart, change, convert, convey, dislocate, displace, disturb, drive, haul, improve, lug, modify, move, recline, redo, refashion, relegate, relocate, remake, remodel, remove, replace, reposition, rethink, revamp, revise, rework, schlep, shove, shunt, shuttle, sideline, situate, supersede, supplant, tote, transfer, transform, transmit, transplant, transport, transpose, tune, tweak, vary* (≠ -abort, anchor, embed, endure, entrench, fix, freeze, -ignore, immobilize, implant, ingrain, lodge, maintain, moor, paralyze, perpetuate, preserve, root, secure, set, stabilize, stop, sustain, transfix)

-SHIRK (/): *-avert, -avoid, ban, bar, -bypass, -circumvent, debar, deflect, detour, divert, -dodge, -duck, eliminate, -elude, -escape, -eschew, -evade, except, -exclude, fake, finesse, foil, forget, fox, -frustrate, fudge, half-ass, miss, -neglect, -obviate, -omit, oppose, outfox, outsmart, outwit, parry, -preclude, -prevent, shake, -shun, skirt, -thwart, ward* (≠ accept, accomplish, accost, achieve, catch, confront, contract, court, embrace, enjoy, exceed, execute, incur, invite, locate, maintain, perform, pursue, relish, seek, welcome)

SHOCK (→): *agitate, alarm, amaze, appall, astonish, astound, awe, baffle, bewilder, blindside, boggle, bushwhack, confound, confuse, consternate, daze, dazzle, deafen, discombobulate, discomfit, disconcert, disgust, dismay, distress, disturb, dumbfound, electrify, excite, flabbergast, floor, flummox, fluster, frighten, galvanize, gaslight, gobsmack, horrify, invigorate, jar, jolt, muckrake, muddle, nauseate, nonplus, numb, offend, outrage, overwhelm, panic, paralyze, perplex, petrify, rattle, razzle-dazzle, repel, revolt, rile, rock, roil, rouse, scandalize, scare, shake, sicken, stagger, startle, stir, stump, stun, stupefy, surprise, terrify, thrill, throw, traumatize, trigger, unnerve, unsettle, upset, wow* (≠ anchor, annoy, anticipate, appease, assure, balance, blunt, bore, calm, caution, center, charm, cheer, clarify, comfort, compose, console, cushion, dampen, deaden, delight, -disregard, dull, elucidate, embolden, encourage, entice, expect, explain, follow, forecast, foretell, gratify, hearten, help, hypnotize, -ignore, jade, lull, mellow, mesmerize, mind, miss, mitigate, moderate, mollify, orchestrate, organize, outguess, -overlook, pacify, placate, please, predetermine, predict, quiet, reassure, regiment, regret, relax, remind, sedate, signal, soothe, stabilize, steady, steel, stultify, tease, tempt, threaten, tranquilize, warn, weary) **(¿) ABSTRACTION ALERT. Concrete goals essential!**

SHOOT (→): *aim, bandy, barrage, blast, blaze, bombard, burn, cast, catapult, destroy, direct, discharge, dispatch, drill, empty, execute, expel, explode, finish, fire, fling, fry, fusillade, gun, heave, hit, hurl, hurtle, ignite, injure, kick, kill, launch, lob, loose, mortar, murder, pelt, pepper, pitch, plug, pop, project, propel, pump, skitter, sling, snipe, strafe, target, throw, torpedo, toss, trigger, wing, wound, zap* (≠ absorb, accept, acquire, armor, cover, deactivate, defend, disarm, drag, draw, gain, garner, hold, holster, load, poke, procure, receive, reload, secure, shield, slow, suck, suppress, unload, withhold)

SHORTCHANGE (←): *bamboozle, beat, betray, bilk, bleed, bluff, cheat, chisel, clip, con, cozen, deceive, defraud, diddle, double-cross, dupe, exploit, extort, fast-talk, fiddle, fleece, flimflam, fool, gouge, gull, hoodwink, hustle, manipulate, milk, mislead, nick, overcharge, pluck, ream, rook, rope, screw, short, skin, soak, squeeze, stick, stiff, sting, stint, swindle, trick, underpay, victimize, withhold, wrench, wrest, wring, wrong* (≠ believe, comp, confess, confront, disclose, divulge, donate, expose, give, help, honor, indemnify, offer, refund, reimburse, repay, restore, reveal, reward, tender, trust, uncover, undeceive, unmask)

SHOULDER (→): *bash, bludgeon, bump, butt, coerce, crowd, drive, elbow, force, hit, hustle, jam, jar, jolt, jostle, knock, move, muscle, nudge, oblige, pack, poke, press, pressure, prod, prompt, propel, push, railroad, ram, shove, shunt, slam, smash, steamroller, stuff, thrust* (≠ -avoid, -balk, bar, barricade, block, curb, daunt, -deter, -ditch, -dodge, draw, -duck, -elude, -evade, extract, -flee, fling, -halt, hamper, hinder, impede, miss, -prevent, pull, push, remove, repel, restrain, stall, stymie, -thwart, tug, withstand, yank)

SHOULDER (+): *abide, accept, allow, assume, bear, brave, brook, buck, carry, concede, condone, confront, countenance, endure, experience, face, hack, harden, incur, indulge, know, lug, outlast, overcome, permit, receive, sanction, season, stand, stomach, suffer, support, surmount, survive, sustain, swallow, sweat, take, tolerate, weather, withstand* (≠ -avoid, battle, combat, contest, -decline, denounce, -deny, -deter, disallow, disappoint, drop, embrace, enjoy, fight, flout, -forbid, forgo, oppose, -prevent, pull, -quit, -refuse, -reject, -repudiate, surrender, -veto, withdraw)

SHOVE (→): *bash, bulldoze, bully, bump, compel, cram, crowd, dash, drive, elbow, force, frogmarch, hammer, hustle, impel, jam, jam-pack, jolt, jostle, knock, march, move, muscle, nudge, pack, poke, pound, press, pressure, prod, propel, punt, push, ram, sardine, shoulder, shunt, slam, smash, squash, squeeze, strike, stuff, thrust, urge, wedge* (≠ -avoid, barricade, block, brake, check, clutch, cradle, curb, defend, deflect, delay, -deter, discourage, dissuade, -dodge, draw, embrace, extract, fling, grasp, grip, guard, -halt, hinder, pull, push, remove, repel, restrain, tug, wall, yank)

SHOW (→): *advertise, air, announce, bare, bellow, betray, blaze, brandish, broadcast, communicate, concede, confess, confide, confirm, confront, declare, demonstrate, disclose, discover, display, divulge, elaborate, embody, evince, exhibit, expose, externalize, flash, flaunt, flourish, herald, hype, manifest, offer, outshine, parade, placard, plug, post, present, proclaim, produce, project, publicize, reveal, showcase, sound, spitball, sport, telegraph, televise, tender, trumpet, uncloak, uncover, unmask, unsheathe, unveil, volunteer, wave* (≠ camouflage, cloak, clothe, cloud, conceal, costume, counterfeit, cover, curtain, disguise, distort, embellish, embroider, enshroud, falsify, garble, gild, gloss, hide, holster, mask, miscommunicate, misrepresent, obscure, occlude, occult, rotate, sheathe, shroud, spackle, twist, varnish, veil, whitewash)

SHOW (→): *accompany, attend, chaperone, conduct, control, convoy, direct, escort, guide, lead, manage, marshal, pilot, route, steer, take, usher* (≠ -abandon, -desert, -ditch, dog, dump, follow, forget, -forsake, hound, -ignore, -neglect, shadow, tail, tailgate, trail)

SHOW (+): *admit, affirm, ascertain, assert, attest, authenticate, certify, claim, confess, confirm, contend, corroborate, declare, demonstrate, document, double-check, endorse, establish, evidence, express, justify, maintain, pledge, proclaim, profess, promise, pronounce, prove, ratify, state, substantiate, support, sustain, testify, uphold, validate, verify, warrant* (≠ challenge, confute, contest, contradict, cross-examine, debate, -deny, discredit, disprove, dispute, distrust, doubt, gainsay, grill, interrogate, interview, invalidate, oppose, question, rebut, refute, -repudiate, scruple)

SHOW (+): *accompany, attend, brief, chaperone, clarify, coach, contextualize, convoy, counsel, cultivate, demonstrate, direct, drill, elucidate, engineer, enlighten, escort, explain, foster, godfather, guide, illustrate, inculcate, indoctrinate, inform, instruct, lead, mentor, nurture, oversee, pilot, school, see, shepherd, squire, steer, superintend, supervise, sway, teach, train, tutor* (≠ baffle, checkmate, confound, confuse, faze, fox, frustrate, gaslight, muddle, mystify, nonplus, pall, perplex, puzzle, throw, -thwart, upset)

SHRED (/): *break, butcher, chop, cleave, cut, destroy, dismember, dissect, doom, eradicate, fray, frazzle, gash, hack, incise, lacerate, mangle, reduce, rend, ribbon, rip, rive, rupture, shave, slash, slice, sliver, split, strip, tatter, tear, trash, unsew, vivisect* (≠ aggregate, amend, braid, correct, darn, fix, fuse, glue, heal, improve, mend, patch, rectify, remedy, renew, renovate, repair, restore, sew, stitch, weave)

SHRINK (/): *abate, abridge, collapse, compress, concentrate, condense, constrict, contract, decrease, deflate, digest, diminish, excise, flatten, fritter, lessen, lighten, lower, miniaturize, minimize, mitigate, moderate, narrow, prune, reduce, shorten, shrivel, sink, squander, truncate, waste, weaken, wilt, wither* (≠ accent, accentuate, accrue, accumulate, amplify, assert, augment, balloon, broaden, elongate, emphasize, expand, expound, extend, grow, increase, inflate, punctuate, stretch, swell, unspool)

SHROUD (←): *blanket, bower, circle, cloak, cocoon, curtain, drape, embed, embrace, encase, encircle, enclose, encompass, enfold, enlace, enshroud, envelop, involve, lap, mantle, mask, muffle, overlay, pall, screen, swaddle, swathe, veil, wind, wrap* (≠ bare, denude, disclose, divest, expose, shred, shuck, strip, tatter, tear, uncloak, uncover, unveil, unwrap)

SHROUD (/): *belie, blear, blot, burke, bury, camouflage, censor, cloak, clothe, cloud, conceal, cover, curtain, disguise, ensconce, gild, gloss, haze, hide, mask, mist, obliterate, obscure, occult, overcloud, paper, quash, redact, repress, screen, secrete, silence, smother, spackle, spike, squash, squelch, stash, stifle, store, stow, strangle, suppress, throttle, varnish, veil, whitewash* (≠ advertise, affirm, air, blab, blaze, blurt, broadcast, circulate, concede, confess, confront, debunk, declare, disclose, divulge, expose, present, proclaim, publicize, publish, push, recount, report, reveal, show, shrive, spill, spread, telegraph, uncloak, uncover, unmask, unveil)

SHROUD (/): *becloud, bedim, befog, blanket, block, blur, cloud, conceal, cover, darken, eclipse, fog, obstruct, occlude, overshadow, shade, shadow, smother, varnish, veil, withhold* (≠ brighten, broadcast, clarify, confide, confirm, disclose, display, divulge, expose, flash, floodlight, illuminate, illumine, light, lighten, uncloud, uncover)

SHUFFLE (/): *agitate, change, clutter, confuse, derange, disarrange, disarray, discompose, dishevel, disjoint, dislocate, disorder, disorganize, disrupt, disturb, entangle, hash, infuse, intermix, jumble, mix, muddle, muss, perturb, rearrange, rejigger, reorganize, reshuffle, retool, rumple, scramble, shift, snarl, stir, swap, switch, tangle, tousle, tumble, unsettle, untidy, upset* (≠ adjust, align, arrange, array, calibrate, classify, codify, compose, fix, groom, marshal, methodize, neaten, order, organize, queue, regiment, regulate, spruce, straighten, systematize, systemize, tidy, tune, unscramble)

-SHUN (→): *-abandon, -avert, -avoid, ban, bar, bilk, -blank, -boycott, -bypass, -circumvent, -cold-shoulder, -cut, debar, -decline, deflect, -desert, -despise, detour, -disdain, disrespect, -ditch, divert, -dodge, -duck, eliminate, -elude, -escape, -eschew, -evade, except, -exclude, finesse, -flee, foil, fox, -frustrate, -ignore, isolate, maroon, miss, -neglect, -obviate, -omit, oppose, -ostracize, oust, outfox, outsmart, outwit, overreach, parry, -preclude, -prevent, -refuse, regret, -reject, rue, -scorn, seclude, shake, -shirk, shortcut, skirt, -snub, stall, -thwart, ward, weasel* (≠ accept, accost, acknowledge, admire, catch, celebrate, chauffeur, colonize, confront, contract, court, covet, crave, desire, embrace, enjoy, esteem, face, fetishize, incur, meet, pursue, relish, reunite, sanction, seek, target, welcome, win, woo)

SHUNT (→): *alter, -avert, bend, bring, budge, bump, butt, carry, deflect, dislodge, displace, divert, elbow, fetch, focus, force, funnel, hustle, impel, jam, jig, jostle, knock, move, muscle, nudge, press, pressure, prod, propel,* *pull, punt, push, ram, rechannel, redirect, rejigger, relegate, relocate, reorient, reposition, reverse, shift, shoulder, shove, shuttle, sidetrack, slam, smash, strike, sway, swerve, swing, switch, swivel, take, thrust, transfer, transport, transpose, tug, turn, twist, urge, whirl, wiggle, wrench, yank* (≠ affix, aid, allow, assist, -avoid, barricade, block, bolt, brake, check, clamp, clasp, clutch, concentrate, curb, defend, deflect, delay, dement, -deter, discourage, dissuade, draw, extract, fasten, fix, fling, freeze, fuse, grasp, grip, guard, -halt, hamper, hinder, hold, impede, keep, lose, maintain, paralyze, pin, restrain, retain, stabilize, steady, straighten, support, trace, trap, weld)

SHUT (/): *bar, bolt, cage, choke, cinch, close, confine, cork, draw, enclose, -exclude, fasten, fold, imprison, latch, lock, -omit, pen, plug, push, seal, secure, slam, squeeze, stop, stopple, strangle, throttle, wall* (≠ accept, broach, clear, crack, expose, include, loose, loosen, open, release, take, unbar, unbolt, unchain, uncover, unfasten, unfold, unlock, unseal)

SICKEN (/): *affect, afflict, affront, aggrieve, ail, alarm, anguish, appall, blackjack, bother, browbeat, brutalize, bully, burden, coerce, contaminate, curse, daunt, dement, derange, disconcert, disgust, dismay, disorder, -disown, displease, disquiet, distress, frighten, grieve, harass, harm, horrify, hurt, indispose, infect, inflict, insult, intimidate, menace, nauseate, offend, oppress, outrage, overextend, pain, plague, poison, press, pressure, repel, repulse, revolt, scare, shock, strain, stress, strike, terrify, terrorize, threaten, torment, trouble, try, unhinge, unnerve, unsettle, upset, weary, wound* (≠ allure, attract, beguile, bewitch, captivate, charm, cure, delight, diagnose, disarm, draw, drug, enchant, encourage, enrapture, enthrall, entice, entrance, fascinate, gratify, heal, help, interest, intrigue, isolate, lure, medicate, mend, nurse, order, please, pull, quarantine, reassure, recover, rectify, rejoice, remedy, restore, seduce, soothe, tantalize, taunt, tease, tempt, thrill, tickle, uplift, vaccinate, wow)

SIDELINE (/): *banish, bench, blackball, degrade, delegate, demote, denigrate, deport, discard, discharge, discourage, dismiss, disparage, dispatch, downgrade, eject, -exclude, -excommunicate, exile, expatriate, expel, hinder, humble, -ostracize, oust, reassign, relegate, remove, sack, transfer* (≠ advance, aggrandize, boost, elevate, encourage, favor, feature, forward, foster, further, honor, hype, praise, prefer, prioritize, promote, reward, select, shelve, target, task, upgrade)

-SIDESTEP (→): *-avert, -avoid, beat, -blank, -boycott, -bypass, -circumvent, deflect, detour, disobey, -disregard, -ditch, divert, -dodge, -duck, -elude, -end-run, -escape, -eschew, -evade, -flee, flout, fudge, half-ass, -ignore, -obviate, -omit, outflank, outrun, -overlook, parry, -prevent, shake, -shirk, -shun, skip, skirt, slip, subvert, trick, ward, weasel* (≠ accept, accost, address, brave, catch, confront, contact, contract, court, embrace, face, follow, incur, keep, mind, note, obey, observe, oppose, pursue, seek, tackle, welcome, woo, wrestle)

SIDETRACK (←): *agitate, alter, -avert, bother, bug, change, concern, confound, daunt, deflect, derail, discomfit, discompose, disconcert, displace, disquiet, disrupt, distract, distress, disturb, divert, dizzy, exasperate, faze, fluster, frazzle, freak, fret, funnel, gall, hamper, harass, harry, haunt, heckle, impede, indispose, irk, irritate, jar, misguide, mislead, mortify, needle, nettle, niggle, nonplus, obstruct, overturn, peeve, perturb, pester, plague, -prevent, rankle, rattle, redirect, refocus, reorient, rile, roil, shake, short-circuit, sideline, startle, swerve, switch, unhinge, unnerve, unsettle, unsteady, upset, vex, worry, wreck* (≠ advance, aid, aim, assist, balance, boost, brace, calibrate, calm, center, chair, compose, concentrate, continue, dedicate, direct, enable, encourage, equalize, expedite, facilitate, focus, forward, further, guide, help, keep, maintain, prioritize, quiet, settle, smooth, soothe, stabilize, steady, steer, support, sustain, target, tranquilize, tune, tweak)

SIFT (←): *analyze, appraise, ascertain, assess, audit, benchmark, categorize, check, clock, compare, consider, contemplate, critique, decide, deduce, detect, determine, discover, evaluate, examine, explore, eye, eyeball, fathom, gauge, grade, inspect, investigate, judge, learn, measure, observe, peruse, prioritize, probe, prowl, rank, rate, read, reappraise, reassess, reevaluate, regard, reinvestigate, review, sample, scan, scope, scrutinize, search, settle, slot, sort, study, survey, suss, test, weigh* (≠ accept, assume, blind, -bypass, cheat, cloak, cloud, conceal, confuse, deceive, -discount, disguise, -disregard, dump, forget, half-ass, -ignore, jumble, mimic, misjudge, mislead, miss, mistake, muddle, -neglect, -omit, overestimate, -overlook, predetermine, puzzle, scramble, skim, skip, swallow, trick, underestimate)

SIFT (/): *clarify, clean, colander, comb, decontaminate, drain, filter, grade, leach, pan, part, percolate, prospect, purify, rarefy, refine, riddle, screen, separate, sieve, size, sort, strain, winnow* (≠ adulterate, besmirch, blemish, blend, churn, combine, compile, contaminate, damage, defile, dirty, disgrace, dishonor, join, jumble, mar, mix, pollute, scramble, soil, spoil, spot, stain, sully, taint, tarnish)

SIGNAL (→): *acquaint, advise, alert, beam, beckon, broadcast, buzz, caution, circulate, communicate, convey, diffuse, dispatch, disseminate, express, flag, flash, impart, inform, mark, mime, pantomime, propagate, relate, relay, remit, report, salute, show, sign, spread, telegraph, tell, transfer, transmit, warn, wave* (≠ bury, camouflage, cloak, clothe, cloud, conceal, confuse, disguise, -disregard, ensconce, hide, -ignore, misconstrue, misread, perplex, puzzle, translate) **(¿) ABSTRACTION ALERT. Concrete goals essential!**

SILENCE (→): *asphyxiate, calm, choke, comfort, curb, curtail, deaden, diminish, dispel, douse, dull, dumbfound, ease, extinguish, gag, hush, lower, lull, mellow, minimize, mitigate, moderate, mollify, muffle, mute, muzzle, pacify, placate, quell, quench, quiet, quieten, reduce, relax, repress, settle, shush, smother, snuff, soften, soothe, squash, squench, startle, stifle, still, stop, strangle, subdue, suffocate, suppress, throttle,* *tranquilize, weaken* (≠ accent, accentuate, affirm, aggravate, agitate, alert, amplify, arouse, assert, broadcast, champion, circulate, communicate, deafen, disseminate, disturb, emphasize, encourage, exacerbate, excite, foment, foster, incite, instigate, intensify, maximize, nourish, nurture, permit, promote, provoke, publicize, release, rouse, spread, stir, support, telegraph, trigger, vex, wake)

SILENCE (/): *annihilate, conquer, crush, decimate, defeat, demolish, desolate, destroy, devastate, dominate, exterminate, master, nuke, obliterate, overcome, overpower, overwhelm, quash, quell, rout, ruin, smash, squelch, subdue, subjugate, suppress, vanquish, waste, wreck* (≠ abet, advance, aid, assist, back, bolster, boost, cultivate, develop, encourage, foment, forward, foster, further, help, incite, instigate, nourish, nurture, promote, prompt, provoke, raise, stir, support, urge)

SIMPLIFY (+): *abridge, chasten, clarify, clean, ease, edit, expedite, facilitate, generalize, mitigate, order, oversimplify, paraphrase, popularize, précis, prune, punctuate, purify, rarefy, reduce, refine, rephrase, shorten, smooth, streamline, strip, summarize, trim, unclog, unriddle* (≠ aggrandize, baffle, bewilder, complicate, confuse, decorate, dumbfound, elaborate, embellish, exaggerate, glitz, impede, magnify, muddy, obfuscate, perplex, sophisticate, stud, stump)

SIMPLIFY (+): *analyze, annotate, clarify, clear, construe, decipher, decode, define, demonstrate, demystify, disentangle, elucidate, explain, explicate, expound, gloss, illuminate, illustrate, interpret, resolve, solve, specify, spell, uncomplicate, undo, unravel, unriddle, unscramble, untangle* (≠ befog, cloud, complicate, confound, confuse, disorder, encode, encrypt, entangle, jumble, knot, muddle, muddy, mystify, obfuscate, obscure, perplex, puzzle, scramble, tangle)

SIMULATE (←): *act, adopt, affect, ape, assume, bluff, bootleg, borrow, camouflage, cheat, clone, conceal, concoct, copy, costume, counterfeit, crib, deceive, disguise, dissimulate, double, duplicate, echo, emulate, exaggerate, fabricate, fake, feature, feign, fence, forge, ghostwrite, imitate, impersonate, invent, lift, mask, mimic, mirror, misrepresent, mock, overdramatize, parallel, parrot, phony, pirate, play, playact, pose, pretend, profess, reflect, render, replicate, reproduce, roleplay, steal* (≠ bare, coin, conceive, create, destroy, disclose, -disregard, distinguish, expose, face, finger, formulate, generate, identify, -ignore, invent, originate, patent, pioneer, produce, propose, -reject, reveal, start, unmask) **(¿) ABSTRACTION ALERT. Concrete goals essential!**

SINGE (/): *bake, barbecue, blacken, blaze, brand, broil, brown, burn, cauterize, char, cook, cremate, crisp, fire, flame, griddle, grill, heat, ignite, incinerate, inflame, kindle, light, parch, scald, scathe, scorch, sear, toast, torch* (≠ bleach, chill, cool, douse, extinguish, freeze, heal, ice, mend, oil, protect, remedy, repair, shield, smooth, smother, soothe, stifle, subdue)

SINK (→): *bore, bury, conceal, depress, dig, dip, down, drill, drive, drop, drown, embed, ensconce, excavate, force, immerse, implant, insert, lay,* *lower, penetrate, plumb, plunge, ram, scuttle, set, shank, shiv, stab, stick, submerge, swamp, thrust* (≠ buoy, extract, float, lift, pluck, prize, pull, quarry, raise, recover, remove, soar, suck, support, sustain, uproot, withdraw)

SINK (/): *abridge, attenuate, bastardize, break, cheapen, compress, contract, debase, deepen, deflate, demonetize, depreciate, depress, devaluate, devalue, downgrade, downsize, lessen, lowball, lower, moderate, reduce, shrink, underbid, underestimate, underprice, underrate, undervalue* (≠ amplify, augment, bloat, boost, bump, escalate, extend, fetishize, hike, increase, inflate, intensify, monetize, overestimate, overprice, overrate, overvalue, prioritize, raise)

SINK (/): *abate, corrupt, crumble, debilitate, decay, -decline, decompose, de-escalate, degrade, demolish, descend, destroy, deteriorate, devastate, dilapidate, diminish, disintegrate, doom, downsize, foil, lessen, lower, minimize, monkey-wrench, reduce, rot, ruin, scupper, scuttle, sour, spoil, undermine, waste, weaken, wilt, worsen, wreck* (≠ accentuate, advance, ameliorate, amplify, better, develop, embattle, enhance, enrich, fortify, foster, heighten, improve, intensify, march, maximize, optimize, overhaul, progress, revolutionize, strengthen, sugarcoat, upgrade)

SINK (/): *abase, abash, affront, badmouth, belittle, blackguard, castigate, censure, chasten, cheapen, condemn, confound, confuse, criticize, damn, debase, decry, defame, defile, degrade, demean, denounce, depreciate, detract, diminish, discomfit, disconcert, -discount, discredit, disgrace, dishonor, disparage, embarrass, execrate, faze, fluster, foul, fulminate, humble, humiliate, incriminate, insult, libel, lower, malign, minimize, mortify, nonplus, pillory, rattle, ridicule, shame, slander, smirch* (≠ acclaim, affirm, aggrandize, applaud, boost, canonize, celebrate, commend, compliment, congratulate, deify, dignify, elevate, ennoble, enshrine, enthrone, exalt, fetishize, float, glorify, hail, heighten, heroicize, honor, idealize, idolize, laud, magnify, praise, prioritize, romanticize, salute, spitball, tout, upgrade)

SIPHON (←): *bankrupt, beggar, bleed, catheterize, clean, clear, consume, debilitate, debit, decant, decrease, deplete, divert, draft, drain, draw, drink, effuse, empty, evacuate, exhaust, expend, exploit, express, extract, flush, leech, milk, press, pump, purge, remove, sap, slurp, squeeze, suck, swallow, tap, tax, use, vacate, vacuum, void, waste, withdraw, wring* (≠ bank, bathe, clog, constipate, deluge, deposit, douse, drench, drown, fill, flood, furnish, increase, inundate, invest, marinate, replenish, soak, souse, stash, staunch, stock, store, submerge, swamp, wash, water, wet)

SKEWER (→): *bayonet, cut, disembowel, gaff, gimlet, gore, gut, harpoon, impale, jab, kebab, knife, lance, peck, penetrate, perforate, pick, pierce, pike, pin, pink, poke, poniard, prick, probe, prod, prong, punch, puncture, ram, riddle, shank, shiv, slice, spear, spike, spit, stab, stick, thrust, transfix* (≠ block, close, deflect, extract, extricate, fill, guard, heal, parry, pull, -rebuff, remove, repel, seal, sew, withdraw)

SKEWER (/): *ape, badmouth, bait, belittle, blackguard, boo, bug, burlesque, caricature, castigate, catcall, chaff, chide, decry, demean, demonize, deride, disparage, disrespect, diss, harangue, harass, harry, hassle, heckle, hound, imitate, jeer, jive, josh, kid, lampoon, mimic, mock, needle, parody, parrot, pester, pillory, pooh-pooh, quiz, rag, razz, -repudiate, rib, ride, ridicule, satirize, scold, -scorn, shame, target, taunt, tease, torment, travesty, tweak* (≠ applaud, approve, commend, congratulate, defend, endorse, glorify, gratify, heroize, honor, idealize, idolize, praise, promote, protect, respect, revere, reward, sanction, treasure, worship)

SKIM (→): *bounce, brush, bump, caress, contact, cuddle, float, fly, fondle, glide, graze, kiss, love, miss, nudge, osculate, pat, pet, plane, ricochet, sail, scrape, shave, sideswipe, skip, skirt, skitter, strike, stroke, strum, sweep, swipe, touch* (≠ bang, bash, bump, clash, clench, crash, grasp, grip, hit, hold, impact, knock, press, punch, ram, slam, slap, smack, smash, swipe, thwack, whack)

SKIM (←): *browse, check, con, consult, dip, flip, glimpse, graze, observe, peruse, preview, read, riffle, scan, skip, spot, spy, surf, thumb, view* (≠ blind, blindfold, examine, explore, grill, heed, inspect, interrogate, investigate, learn, memorize, ogle, oversee, prowl, question, scrutinize, study, survey, suss)

SKIN (/): *abrade, bare, bark, denude, excoriate, expose, flay, fleece, gall, grate, graze, hull, husk, pare, peel, pull, remove, rind, scale, scalp, scrape, shave, shed, shell, shuck, slough, strip, trim, uncover* (≠ adorn, bandage, clothe, cover, decorate, drape, enfold, garnish, hide, regenerate, robe, shroud, trim, veil, wrap)

SLAKE (←): *abate, allay, alleviate, assuage, cater, cloy, extinguish, gratify, humor, indulge, lighten, mitigate, moderate, moisten, oblige, quench, reduce, relieve, sate, satiate, satisfy, saturate, surfeit* (≠ amplify, arouse, entice, exacerbate, excite, frustrate, intensify, lure, pique, provoke, stimulate, tantalize, taunt, tease, tempt, trigger)

SLAM (→): *backhand, bang, bash, bat, batter, bean, beat, belt, bludgeon, bonk, bop, box, brain, buffet, bulldoze, bump, bung, bunt, bust, butt, cane, chop, clap, clip, clobber, clock, clout, club, concuss, conk, crack, crash, cream, cudgel, cuff, dash, deck, drub, fell, fling, flog, floor, hammer, hit, hurl, impact, jab, jostle, kick, knee, knock, lambaste, level, lick, maul, muscle, nail, paste, pelt, poke, pommel, pound, prod, propel, pummel, punch, push, rabbit-punch, ram, rap, rough, sap, shove, skull, slap, sledge, sledgehammer, slog, slug, smack, smash, smite, sock, stamp, strike, sucker-punch, swat, swipe, thrash, thump, thwack, wallop, whack, whale, wing, zap* (≠ aid, armor, -avoid, block, caress, defend, guard, heal, help, miss, protect, riffle, save, secure, shield, sideswipe, skim, skirt, stroke)

SLAM (→): *bang, bar, batten, bolt, chain, close, deadbolt, fasten, latch, lock, seal, secure, shut, stop* (≠ clear, crack, open, unbar, unbolt, unfasten, unlatch, unlock, unseal)

SLAM (/): *abuse, affront, assail, attack, badmouth, bash, belabor, belittle, berate, blackguard, blast, castigate, chastise, chide, criticize, critique, curse, damn, decry, defame, denounce, denunciate, deride, disparage, excoriate, execrate, fault, flay, fulminate, harangue, harass, harry, impugn, incriminate, insult, lambaste, libel, neg, pan, profane, rebuke, reprimand, revile, rubbish, savage, scathe, scold, scourge, shred, slander, slap, slash, slate, slur, traduce, vilify, vituperate, whip, wrong, zap* (≠ acclaim, blandish, cajole, commend, compliment, elevate, flannel, flatter, gratify, hail, ingratiate, laud, lionize, praise, promote, recommend, revere, schmooze, venerate)

SLANDER (/): *assail, attack, backbite, badmouth, belittle, besmirch, blacken, blister, calumniate, curse, damage, decry, defame, denigrate, discredit, disfavor, disgrace, dishonor, disparage, impugn, insult, knock, libel, malign, muckrake, revile, roast, scorch, slam, -slight, slur, smear, sully, tarnish, taunt, traduce, vilify* (≠ applaud, blandish, cherish, commend, compliment, congratulate, defend, esteem, eulogize, extol, favor, flatter, glorify, gratify, honor, idealize, idolize, ingratiate, laud, praise, protect, respect, revere, shield, uphold, venerate, vindicate, worship)

SLAP (→): *bang, bash, bat, bump, burst, bust, clap, clip, clock, clout, crash, cuff, drub, flap, hit, knock, lash, lick, punch, rap, slam, smack, snap, strike, swat, swipe, tap, thump, thwack, wallop, whack* (≠ block, brush, coddle, deflect, -dodge, -duck, miss, nudge, parry, repel, save, shave, shield, skim)

SLASH (/): *amputate, anatomize, bruise, butcher, carve, chip, chisel, chop, cleave, cut, dice, dissect, gash, gouge, hack, incise, injure, knife, lacerate, mangle, mince, notch, pierce, razor, rend, rip, rive, saw, score, section, sever, shank, shear, shiv, slice, slit, split, stab, strike, tear, vivisect, wound* (≠ aid, block, close, combine, create, cure, defend, enlarge, expand, extend, fix, heal, help, increase, lengthen, mend, raise, sew, unite)

SLATHER (+): *anoint, apply, bedaub, befoul, begrime, besmear, besmirch, blacken, burnish, butter, coat, cover, daub, dirty, foul, glaze, gloss, grease, grime, gum, lard, mire, moisturize, mop, muck, muddy, oil, paint, perfume, pigment, pitch, plaster, polish, pomade, shine, smear, smirch, smooth, smudge, soil, spray, spread, stain, sully, swab, syrup, tar, wax, wet* (≠ abrade, bathe, bedraggle, chafe, clean, cleanse, clear, dehydrate, desiccate, dry, erase, harden, mop, purify, remove, rinse, scour, sterilize, swab, wash, wipe)

SLAUGHTER (/): *annihilate, assassinate, behead, blitzkrieg, butcher, decimate, defeat, demolish, depopulate, destroy, devastate, dispatch, doom, eliminate, eradicate, erase, execute, expunge, exterminate, extinguish, fell, finish, guillotine, kill, liquidate, mangle, massacre, molochize, murder, mutilate, obliterate, orphan, overwhelm, purge, remove, rout, slay, smite, snuff, terminate, trounce, vanquish, waste*

(≠ absorb, armor, bear, birth, build, conserve, construct, create, cultivate, defend, develop, doctor, embalm, endure, foster, gestate, guard, hatch, heal, help, lose, maintain, nourish, nurture, outlast, preserve, produce, protect, repair, repel, resuscitate, revive, save, shield, spawn, support, surrender, survive, sustain, weather, withstand)

SLAY (/): *annihilate, assassinate, butcher, claim, croak, decimate, destroy, dispatch, doom, eliminate, eradicate, execute, exterminate, fell, finish, get, kill, martyr, massacre, mow, murder, off, orphan, retire, slaughter, smite, snuff, take, terminate, waste* (≠ animate, assist, create, defend, doctor, heal, mend, nurse, nurture, protect, raise, rescue, restore, resurrect, resuscitate, revive, save, support, survive)

SLICE (/): *amputate, anatomize, bite, butcher, carve, chip, chisel, chop, circumcise, cleave, clip, crop, dice, dismember, dissect, divide, dock, excise, gash, gouge, hack, hash, hew, hurt, incise, knife, lacerate, lop, mangle, mince, nick, notch, part, perforate, pierce, prick, prune, raze, razor, rend, rip, rive, saw, scissor, score, scratch, scythe, section, segment, separate, sever, shred, slash, slit, sliver, snip, splinter, split, stab, sting, strike, tatter, tear, unsew, vivisect, wound* (≠ aid, bandage, block, combine, create, cure, expand, extend, fix, fuse, grow, heal, increase, join, leave, lengthen, meld, mend, nurse, repair, restore, seal, sew, shield, smooth, stitch, stretch, suture, unite, unspool)

-SLIGHT (/): *abhor, abominate, affront, belittle, boo, contemn, defame, deplore, deprecate, -despise, -detest, -disdain, disfavor, disgrace, disparage, displease, disrespect, distress, disturb, execrate, -hate, high-hat, hurt, insult, jeer, libel, -loathe, malign, miff, mock, offend, oppress, outrage, pain, persecute, revile, ridicule, -scorn, scout, slander, slap, slur, smear, -snub, taunt, torment, torture, trouble, upset, victimize, wound, wrong* (≠ admire, applaud, appreciate, blandish, buoy, cherish, commend, compliment, delight, esteem, eulogize, exalt, favor, flatter, glad-hand, glorify, gratify, hail, hallow, honor, lionize, persuade, please, praise, prize, respect, revere, satisfy, sweet-talk, thrill, treasure, uplift, value, venerate, worship)

-SLIGHT (/): *alienate, -blank, -bypass, -cold-shoulder, -cut, -disdain, disparage, -disregard, fail, forget, high-hat, -ignore, isolate, miss, -neglect, -omit, -ostracize, -overlook, pass, pooh-pooh, -rebuff, -reject, repel, repulse, scant, -scorn, skimp, slur, -snub, -spurn, wrong* (≠ advance, appreciate, attend, boost, cherish, cultivate, follow, foster, heed, indulge, mark, mind, note, notice, nurse, nurture, observe, pamper, prize, regard, remark, remember, serve, spoil, spoon-feed, tend, treasure, value, watch)

SLOT (→): *allocate, allot, appoint, arrange, array, assign, banish, cage, choose, commend, commission, consign, convey, delegate, deliver, deploy, designate, detail, determine, devote, dispense, dispose, distribute, ensconce, entrench, establish, fit, fix, give, grant, insert, install, juxtapose, locate, lodge, name, nestle, niche, nominate, pigeonhole, place, position, prioritize, range, rank, regiment, relegate, select, send, set, settle, shackle, site, situate, specify, stand, station, stereotype, stipulate, straightjacket,* *task, transfer, transmit, trap* (≠ confuse, disarrange, disorder, disorganize, displace, extract, extricate, free, invalidate, liberate, loose, move, remove, uninstall, unleash, unsettle, upset)

SLOW (←): *arrest, baffle, brake, check, constrain, curb, decelerate, delay, detain, ease, encumber, foil, -frustrate, -halt, hamper, handicap, hinder, hobble, hold, impair, impede, inhibit, leash, monkey-wrench, obstruct, pause, postpone, reduce, rein, restrain, restrict, retard, shelve, short-circuit, slacken, stall, stop, stymie, -thwart, weight* (≠ accelerate, advance, aid, dispatch, drive, ease, encourage, expedite, facilitate, fast-forward, fast-track, forward, frogmarch, further, goad, grease, hasten, help, hurry, lubricate, march, propel, punt, push, quicken, rush, speed, spur, stampede, stir, urge)

SMACK (→): *backhand, bang, bash, bat, batter, bean, beat, belt, biff, blow, bludgeon, bob, bonk, bop, box, brain, buffet, bump, bung, bunt, bust, butt, cane, chop, clap, clip, clobber, clock, clout, club, concuss, conk, crack, crash, cream, cudgel, cuff, deck, drub, fell, flail, flick, flog, floor, hammer, hit, jab, jostle, kick, knee, knock, lace, lambaste, lash, level, lick, mangle, maul, nail, paste, pat, pelt, pepper, poke, pommel, pound, prod, pummel, punch, push, rabbit-punch, rap, rough, sap, scuff, shove, sideswipe, skull, slam, slap, slash, sledge, sledgehammer, slug, smite, snap, sock, spank, spear, stab, stamp, strike, sucker-punch, swat, swipe, switch, tag, tap, thrash, thump, thwack, wallop, whack* (≠ armor, block, caress, -circumvent, defend, deflect, -deter, -dodge, -duck, -escape, -evade, grasp, grip, guard, massage, miss, -prevent, protect, repel, riffle, shield, squeeze, stroke, strum)

SMASH (→): *bang, bash, bump, crash, disrupt, drive, hit, knock, overthrow, overturn, plow, run, strike, thump, topple, trash, trounce, tumble, unhorse, unman, unseat, wrack, wreck* (≠ -avoid, block, -bypass, -circumvent, defend, -evade, guard, miss, parry, preserve, protect, secure, shelter, shield, skip)

SMASH (/): *annihilate, atomize, bang, belt, blast, break, burst, clobber, crack, crash, crush, dash, decimate, defeat, deform, demolish, destroy, disintegrate, doom, efface, eradicate, fracture, fragment, hit, kibble, mangle, pound, powder, pulverize, ram, raze, rive, ruin, scrunch, shatter, shiver, slam, slog, slug, splinter, squash, squish, topple, trash, wallop, wreck* (≠ assemble, build, cherish, construct, erect, fashion, fix, forge, form, fortify, gather, guard, mend, mold, organize, patch, preserve, produce, promote, protect, raise, rebuild, reconstruct, recover, renew, renovate, repair, restore, sculpt, shape, support, sustain, weather, withstand)

SMEAR (→): *anoint, apply, bedaub, bedraggle, befoul, begrime, besmear, besmirch, blacken, blur, butter, coat, cover, dab, daub, defile, dirty, discolor, foul, grease, grime, gum, lard, mire, moisturize, muck, muddy, oil, overlay, paint, patch, pigment, pitch, plaster, pomade, rub, slap, slop, smirch, smudge, soil, spatter, spray, spread, sprinkle, stain, streak, sully, taint, tar* (≠ bathe, chafe, clean, cleanse, clear, dehydrate, desiccate, dry, erase, mop, purify, remove, rinse, scour, sterilize, swab, towel, uncloud, wash, wipe)

SMEAR (/): *abase, abuse, badmouth, bait, befoul, belittle, besmirch, bestialize, blacken, blackguard, blister, boo, calumniate, debase, defame, defile, degrade, denigrate, detract, dirty, discolor, discredit, -disdain, disgrace, dishonor, disparage, disrespect, diss, hit, humble, humiliate, incriminate, injure, insult, knock, libel, malign, neg, pan, rubbish, scorch, -scorn, shame, slam, slander, slur, soil, stain, sully, taint, tar, tarnish, traduce, trash, vilify, wrong* (≠ acclaim, admire, adore, alibi, applaud, augment, benefit, boost, commend, congratulate, defend, esteem, exalt, exonerate, flatter, glorify, gratify, help, honor, idealize, idolize, praise, promote, protect, regard, respect, revere, upgrade, venerate, worship)

SMELL (←): *anticipate, ascertain, assume, breathe, conjecture, detect, discern, discover, distinguish, divine, expect, feel, find, guess, identify, inhale, learn, nose, note, notice, observe, perceive, presume, realize, recognize, regard, savor, scent, sense, sniff, snuff, spoor, suppose, surmise, suspect, taste, whiff* (≠ -avoid, block, -bypass, choke, cloak, clog, clothe, cloud, cologne, conceal, -discount, disguise, -disregard, hide, -ignore, launder, miss, -overlook, perfume, plug, rinse, scour, smother, wash) **(¿) ABSTRACTION ALERT. Concrete goals essential!**

SMITE (→): *afflict, assault, bang, bash, bat, batter, bean, beat, behead, belt, biff, blitzkrieg, bludgeon, bob, bonk, bop, box, brain, buffet, bung, bunt, bust, butt, cane, chop, clap, clip, clobber, clock, clout, club, conk, crack, cream, crush, cudgel, cuff, curse, deck, destroy, doom, down, drub, eliminate, eradicate, execute, fell, flail, flog, floor, hammer, harm, hit, hurt, inflict, jab, jostle, kick, kill, knee, knock, lace, lambaste, lash, level, lick, mangle, massacre, maul, nail, overthrow, pain, paste, pelt, pepper, plague, poke, pommel, pound, prod, pummel, punch, punish, push, rabbit-punch, rap, raze, rough, sap, scuff, shove, skull, slam, slap, slash, slaughter, sledge, sledgehammer, slog, slug, smack, sock, spear, stab, stamp, strike, sucker-punch, swat, swipe, switch, tag, thrash, thump, thwack, torment, torture, trouble, wallop, whack, whale, whip, wound, wreck, zap* (≠ aid, armor, assist, -avoid, boost, cheer, comfort, compliment, console, defend, encourage, fail, flatter, guard, harbor, heal, help, inspirit, lose, miss, nurse, praise, protect, repair, revive, shelter, shield, succor, support, tap)

SMOOTH (→): *bob, bone, brighten, buff, burnish, card, clear, clip, coat, comb, crop, dress, even, face, file, finish, flatten, flush, furbish, glaze, gloss, grade, grind, iron, japan, lacquer, lay, level, pare, perfect, plane, plaster, polish, pomade, press, prune, pumice, rake, rasp, refine, resurface, roll, round, rub, sand, sandblast, sandpaper, scour, scrape, scrub, shave, shine, sleek, slick, spackle, spread, surface, trim, varnish, veneer* (≠ bend, blemish, break, callous, coarsen, crack, crosshatch, dent, ding, harshen, kink, nick, nock, notch, pit, plow, rough, roughen, ruffle, rumple, scratch, scuff, serrate, wrinkle)

SMOOTH (+): *abet, accelerate, advance, aid, allay, alleviate, appease, assist, assuage, bribe, calm, comfort, cool, disentangle, ease, encourage, expedite, facilitate, fast-track, forward, further, gratify, grease, hasten, help, humor, hurry, improve, loosen, mellow, mend, mitigate, moderate, mollify, oil, pacify, palliate, pat, patch, placate, promote, quicken, right, rush, simplify, soften, soothe, speed, straighten, streamline, stroke, unclog, uncomplicate, untangle* (≠ aggravate, agitate, complicate, confound, exacerbate, hinder, impede, incite, intensify, irk, muddy, nobble, obscure, perplex, postpone, provoke, retard, shelve, sophisticate, upset, worsen)

SMOTHER (/): *asphyxiate, burke, check, choke, coddle, cosset, cover, deaden, devoice, douse, envelop, extinguish, gag, garrote, heap, inhibit, kill, muffle, overpower, overwhelm, quash, quell, quench, rein, repress, restrain, shroud, shush, silence, snuff, squeeze, squelch, squench, squoosh, stifle, strangle, subdue, suffocate, suppress, surround, swathe, throttle* (≠ aerate, brighten, encourage, energize, free, loose, oxygenate, refresh, release, resuscitate, revitalize, strengthen, uncover, ventilate)

SMUGGLE (←): *bootleg, cache, commodify, conceal, consign, convey, cover, deal, deliver, dispense, distribute, dump, exchange, export, fence, filch, freight, furnish, hide, monopolize, obscure, peddle, pirate, push, resell, run, schlep, secrete, sell, ship, snake, sneak, stash, stow, supply, swap, trade, traffic, transfer, transport, tuck* (≠ arrest, ban, bar, blackball, block, -boycott, bust, criminalize, donate, -exclude, exhibit, expose, -forbid, nab, nick, offer, outlaw, -prevent, -prohibit, reveal, show, withhold)

SNAG (←): *abduct, apprehend, arrest, bag, capture, catch, clasp, clutch, collar, cop, corner, corral, detain, disappear, enmesh, ensnare, entangle, entrap, get, glom, glove, grab, grapple, grasp, grip, halter, hold, hook, kidnap, land, lasso, nab, nail, net, nobble, pinch, poach, rap, rend, rope, rustle, secure, seize, snaffle, snare, snatch, steal, swipe, take, trap, wrest* (≠ bestow, contribute, discharge, drop, free, furnish, give, grant, guard, liberate, loosen, miss, offer, protect, release, repay, replace, replenish, reserve, restore, spare, starve, steal, stiff, stint, supply, tender, unhand, volunteer, withhold)

SNAP (←): *capture, chronicle, document, film, photo, photograph, picture, record, retake, shoot, take, videotape, witness* (≠ bury, conceal, ensconce, hide, -ignore, loose, misrepresent, -neglect, screen, shroud)

SNAP (/): *break, burst, chop, collapse, crack, explode, fissure, fracture, fragment, mangle, pop, pulverize, rend, rive, separate, shatter, splinter, split* (≠ affix, attach, brace, dissolve, fuse, glue, join, melt, mend, patch, repair, splint, steady, strengthen)

SNARE (←): *arrest, bag, birdlime, capture, catch, collar, corral, decoy, embroil, enmesh, ensnare, entangle, entrap, hook, implicate, involve, land, lasso, lure, mire, net, rope, seduce, seize, snaffle, tangle, tantalize, taunt, tease, tempt, trap* (≠ clear, detach, disengage, disentangle, extricate, free, liberate, loose, miss, untangle)

SNATCH (←): *abduct, bogart, bundle, burgle, capture, disappear, entrap, filch, glom, grab, hijack, kidnap, lift, lure, nab, nobble, pilfer, pluck, poach, pocket, purloin, ransom, remove, rob, seize, shanghai, snag, sneak, steal, swipe, take, waylay* (≠ bestow, comp, defend, discharge, donate, drop, free, give, liberate, loosen, lose, miss, offer, protect, push, receive, recover, release, rescue, return, secure, shield, target, tender, unhand, volunteer)

SNOOKER (←): *baffle, bait, -balk, bamboozle, beguile, bilk, bleed, bluff, buffalo, burn, candy-coat, cheat, chisel, con, confound, convince, cozen, deceive, defeat, defraud, delude, diddle, doctor, double-cross, double-talk, dupe, enmesh, ensnare, entangle, entice, entrap, euchre, fake, fleece, flimflam, flummox, foil, fool, frame, gouge, gull, hamper, hinder, hoax, hocus-pocus, hoodwink, hornswoggle, humbug, hustle, impede, inveigle, juggle, lure, maneuver, manipulate, misdirect, misguide, misinform, mislead, nonplus, outfox, outwit, puzzle, rook, rope, sandbag, scam, schmooze, shortchange, skin, snow, spin, spoof, squeeze, stick, stiff, stonewall, stump, sucker, swindle, tantalize, tempt, -thwart, trap, trick, two-time, underpay, vamp, victimize, whitewash, wrong* (≠ assume, assure, believe, blab, blurt, confess, confide, confirm, confront, debunk, disabuse, disclose, disenchant, disillusion, divulge, expose, face, honor, protect, regret, restore, reveal, show, tell, trust, uncloak, uncover, undeceive, unmask, unveil)

SNOW (←): *act, allure, attract, bamboozle, beguile, bewitch, bleed, bluff, buffalo, burn, cajole, captivate, catch, charm, cheat, con, convince, counterfeit, deceive, defraud, delight, delude, diddle, draw, dupe, enamor, enchant, enrapture, exaggerate, fabricate, fake, falsify, fascinate, feign, fleece, fool, forge, hoax, hocus-pocus, hoodwink, hornswoggle, hustle, imitate, intrigue, manipulate, mesmerize, misinform, mislead, please, pretend, rook, seduce, shortchange, simulate, sucker, swindle, take, tease, trick, win* (≠ believe, compel, confess, confront, disclose, disenchant, disgust, disillusion, divulge, enlighten, expose, repel, repulse, reveal, trust, uncloak, uncover, undeceive, unmask, unveil)

-SNUB (→): *-abandon, abhor, abominate, affront, alienate, belittle, -blank, -boycott, censure, chill, -cold-shoulder, contemn, cool, -cut, deplore, deprecate, -desert, -despise, -detest, -disdain, disfavor, disparage, -disregard, disrespect, -ditch, -duck, execrate, forget, -hate, high-hat, humble, humiliate, ice, -ignore, insult, isolate, -loathe, mortify, -neglect, offend, -ostracize, -overlook, -rebuff, rebuke, -reject, repel, repulse, scold, -scorn, scout, scratch, seclude, shame, -shun, -slight, slur, -spurn, squash, squelch, upstage* (≠ accept, admire, appreciate, approve, brook, cherish, commend, contact, countenance, embrace, endure, entertain, esteem, face, favor, greet, hail, hallow, high-five, honor, host, include, invite, lionize, okay, praise, prize, respect, revere, salute, stomach, tolerate, treasure, value, venerate, welcome, worship)

SOAK (→): *absorb, bathe, bloody, braise, brine, dampen, dip, douse, drench, drown, humidify, hydrate, imbrue, immerse, impregnate,* *infiltrate, infuse, inundate, macerate, marinate, moisten, mop, penetrate, permeate, saturate, slather, sop, souse, spatter, splatter, sponge, steep, submerge, swamp, swill, syrup, wash, water, wet* (≠ bake, barbecue, broil, burn, dehumidify, dehydrate, desiccate, drain, dry, empty, leach, leech, parch, scorch, sear, staunch)

SOAP (+): *adulate, applaud, blandish, blarney, bribe, butter, cajole, coax, commend, compliment, congratulate, court, eulogize, extol, flannel, flatter, glad-hand, glorify, gratify, grease, hero-worship, honey, honor, humor, idealize, idolize, laud, massage, oil, overpraise, palaver, praise, puff, romance, schmooze, soft-sell, soft-soap, stroke, sweet-talk, wheedle, woo, worship, wow* (≠ badmouth, belittle, boo, chaff, criticize, decry, demean, deprecate, deride, disparage, disrespect, diss, insult, knock, mock, neg, pan, ridicule, -scorn, slam, slate, vilify)

SOBER (+): *adjust, align, allay, assuage, awaken, balance, calm, center, civilize, compose, control, cool, depress, energize, fix, govern, harmonize, leash, mellow, mitigate, moderate, pace, palliate, regulate, relieve, restrain, right, sedate, settle, stabilize, steady, support, tame, temper, wake* (≠ agitate, amaze, befuddle, confuse, daze, derange, dizzy, dose, drug, enrage, hallucinate, indulge, inebriate, infuriate, intoxicate, numb, pickle, rattle, shake, stimulate, stun, stupefy, unhinge)

SOFTEN (+): *abate, allay, alleviate, appease, assuage, baffle, blunt, buffer, calm, castrate, compose, conciliate, cool, cushion, dampen, deaden, defuse, desensitize, diminish, disintegrate, dull, ease, enfeeble, gentle, hush, knead, lessen, lighten, lower, lull, mash, mellow, mitigate, moderate, modify, modulate, mollify, muffle, pacify, pad, palliate, placate, qualify, quell, quicken, quiet, reconcile, relax, relieve, restrain, sedate, smooth, soothe, stabilize, stifle, still, subdue, temper, tranquilize, weaken* (≠ aggravate, agitate, chafe, deepen, disrupt, disturb, embattle, embitter, exacerbate, exasperate, fortify, heighten, incite, increase, intensify, invigorate, irritate, militarize, provoke, roil, ruffle, serrate, sharpen, strengthen, trouble, upset, vex, worry, worsen)

SOFTEN (/): *bend, dissolve, liquefy, loosen, marinate, melt, moisten, presoak, reduce, slack, slacken, soak, steep, tenderize, thaw, weaken* (≠ calcify, coagulate, congeal, freeze, harden, reinforce, set, solidify, starch, stiffen, toughen)

SOIL (/): *bastardize, bedraggle, befoul, begrime, besmirch, bespatter, blacken, callous, coarsen, compromise, confuse, contaminate, crumb, damage, daub, debase, defile, degrade, dirty, disarrange, disarray, discolor, disgrace, dishevel, disorder, draggle, foul, grime, jumble, mess, muddle, muddy, muss, pollute, puddle, shame, smear, smirch, smudge, spatter, spoil, spot, stain, sully, taint, tar, tarnish, untidy* (≠ brighten, brush, clean, cleanse, decontaminate, delouse, disinfect, dust, freshen, launder, polish, purge, purify, rinse, sanitize, scour, scrub, shine, sponge, sterilize, swab, sweep, tidy, wash, wet, wipe)

SOLICIT (+): *ask, beg, beseech, cadge, canvass, claim, coerce, command, compel, conjure, court, covet, crave, demand, desire, drum, enjoin, entreat, exact, fetishize, force, implore, importune, insist, invite, invoke, mooch, petition, plead, pray, press, reclaim, recoup, recover, request, require, requisition, retrieve, scavenge, scrounge, seek, sponge, sue, target, tout, urge, wish, woo* (≠ appease, comfort, compel, conciliate, console, constrain, content, deliver, force, furnish, gratify, hand, hint, imply, intimate, mollify, oblige, offer, pacify, placate, please, quiet, require, satisfy, suggest, supply, tender, volunteer)

SOLICIT (+): *accost, allure, bait, bash, beguile, betray, bewitch, bribe, captivate, catch, charm, decoy, enchant, enmesh, ensnare, entice, entrap, fascinate, hustle, importune, inveigle, lure, magnetize, mesh, persuade, proposition, rope, schmooze, seduce, snare, snooker, snow, tangle, tantalize, taunt, tease, tempt, trap* (≠ alert, -avert, block, caution, disallow, drive, -forbid, forewarn, hamper, hamstring, hobble, nobble, outlaw, -prevent, -prohibit, repulse, turn, ward, warn)

SOLVE (+): *answer, assume, break, clarify, clear, conclude, conjecture, crack, decide, decipher, decode, deduce, detect, determine, diagnose, disentangle, divine, educe, explain, expound, fathom, gather, glean, guess, infer, interpret, judge, presume, profile, read, reason, rectify, remedy, resolve, riddle, settle, suss, translate, uncomplicate, undo, unfold, unravel, unriddle, unscramble, untangle, untie, work* (≠ baffle, befuddle, bewilder, bug, complicate, confound, confuse, defer, destroy, dumbfound, encode, encrypt, fail, frustrate, gaslight, hide, lose, mend, misconstrue, misdiagnose, misrepresent, miss, misunderstand, -neglect, obscure, perplex, pose, predetermine, puzzle, question, search, stump, tangle, twist, unsettle, wonder)

SOOTHE (+): *aid, align, allay, alleviate, appease, assuage, assure, balance, beguile, boost, buoy, calm, center, charm, cheer, coddle, comfort, compose, conciliate, console, cradle, cuddle, defang, dulcify, ease, elevate, harmonize, heal, help, hush, inspire, lift, lighten, lull, massage, mellow, mitigate, mollify, pacify, palliate, pet, placate, propitiate, quell, quiet, reassure, relax, relieve, salve, sedate, settle, smooth, soften, stabilize, steady, still, stroke, sugarcoat, sweeten, temper, tranquilize, uplift* (≠ aggravate, agitate, anger, anguish, annoy, antagonize, arouse, bother, crucify, demoralize, depress, distress, disturb, dizzy, earbash, enrage, exacerbate, exasperate, excite, fluster, gall, harass, harm, hassle, haunt, heckle, hound, hurt, incense, incite, inflame, infuriate, injure, intensify, irk, irritate, kindle, nag, needle, nettle, niggle, nitpick, noodge, outrage, pester, provoke, ruffle, sadden, stimulate, stir, torment, torture, troll, trouble, upset, vex, worry)

SOPHISTICATE (+): *adorn, better, burnish, civilize, coach, complexify, complicate, confound, confuse, correct, cultivate, develop, edify, educate, elaborate, embarrass, embroider, emend, enlighten, entangle, expand, fancify, glitz, groom, housebreak, housetrain, humanize, improve, instruct, intensify, magnify, manicure, mature, mentor, muddle,* *ornament, perfect, perplex, polish, rarefy, realign, refine, school, shine, snarl, socialize, tame, tangle, teach, train* (≠ abbreviate, barbarize, callous, coarsen, compromise, cut, degrade, dehumanize, disentangle, ease, facilitate, oversimplify, roughen, ruin, shorten, simplify, spoil, straighten, streamline, uncomplicate, unravel, untangle, vulgarize)

SORT (+): *align, alphabetize, arrange, array, assort, catalog, categorize, class, classify, clump, cluster, codify, compartment, compartmentalize, cull, digest, dispose, distinguish, distribute, divide, docket, file, grade, group, hierarchize, identify, index, list, marshal, order, organize, peg, pigeonhole, place, prioritize, range, rank, recategorize, reclassify, recognize, refer, regiment, regroup, relegate, screen, segregate, separate, set, shelve, sieve, sift, slot, stereotype, systematize, type, typecast, winnow* (≠ churn, clutter, confuse, disarrange, dishevel, garble, intermix, jumble, lump, misclassify, missort, mistype, mix, randomize, rearrange, rummage, scramble, shuffle)

SOUR (/): *acidify, canker, contaminate, curdle, embitter, ferment, poison, pollute, spike, spoil, taint, turn* (≠ candy, dulcify, ease, flavor, honey, marinate, mellow, season, soothe, spice, sugar, sugarcoat, sweeten, syrup, temper)

SOUR (/): *aggravate, alienate, anger, antagonize, disaffect, disappoint, disenchant, disgruntle, disillusion, disunite, divide, embitter, enrage, envenom, estrange, exacerbate, exasperate, incense, inflame, infuriate, irritate, madden, outrage, rankle, rile, roil, separate, sever, split, sunder, uncouple, unlink, unyoke* (≠ alleviate, appease, comfort, conciliate, disarm, endear, impress, ingratiate, inspire, mollify, pacify, placate, propitiate, reconcile, sweeten)

SOURCE (←): *accumulate, acquire, amass, annex, attain, bag, capture, carry, catch, download, draw, fish, gain, garner, get, harvest, land, locate, mine, notch, obtain, occupy, pick, procure, pull, reacquire, realize, reap, recapture, score, secure, seize, select, stockpile, win* (≠ accord, ban, bequeath, bestow, forfeit, fritter, give, grant, hand, lose, pay, -prohibit, relinquish, squander, starve, steal, stiff, stint, surrender, take, waste, withhold, yield)

SPACKLE (+): *amend, beautify, close, coat, cobble, conceal, correct, cover, daub, disguise, enhance, fill, fix, hide, improve, mask, mend, mortar, patch, plaster, rectify, reform, remedy, renew, renovate, repair, restore, resurface, revise, roughcast, seal, smear, spread, surface* (≠ blemish, break, chip, crack, damage, disfigure, expose, harm, harshen, injure, mar, mark, peel, scar, scrape, scuff, spoil, strip)

SPANK (→): *bang, beat, belt, cane, chastise, discipline, flagellate, flog, hide, hurt, lash, lather, lick, paddle, pain, penalize, punish, slap, slipper, slug, smack, strap, strike, tan, thrash, thwack, torment, wallop, whack, whip* (≠ absolve, acquit, baby, blame, coddle, defend, dismiss, excuse, exonerate, humor, indulge, mollify, -neglect, pamper, pardon, praise, protect, reward, shield, spare, spoil, vindicate)

SPARE (→): *afford, allow, assist, award, bankroll, bequeath, bestow, comp, consign, contribute, deliver, devote, disburse, dispense, dole, donate, dower, endow, expend, extend, forego, fund, furnish, give, grant, help, impart, lend, offer, outbid, outlay, overpay, overspend, pay, pledge, present, provide, relinquish, render, salt, send, serve, submit, supply, surrender, tender, tithe, underwrite, volunteer, yield* (≠ beg, check, conceal, control, crave, curb, debit, deduct, defund, disinherit, entreat, hide, implore, importune, panhandle, petition, plead, -refuse, request, require, reserve, retain, seek, starve, steal, stiff, stint, sue, take, target, withhold)

SPARE (→): *allocate, allot, assign, budget, conserve, cut, deal, divide, earmark, economize, famish, hoard, husband, maintain, malnourish, manage, measure, mete, nurse, parcel, partition, pinch, portion, preserve, ration, reserve, retrench, save, scant, scrape, scrimp, segment, short, shortchange, skimp, slice, split, starve, stash, stint, tuck, withhold* (≠ blow, circulate, disseminate, dissipate, dole, fritter, heap, lavish, misspend, pour, rain, share, shower, spend, squander, take, waste)

SPARE (+): *absolve, acquit, condone, discharge, dispense, exculpate, excuse, exempt, exonerate, forgive, free, leave, liberate, -overlook, pardon, pity, release, relieve, remit, reprieve, rescue, save, spring, vindicate, withhold* (≠ abuse, accuse, anguish, arrest, bully, confine, damage, discipline, fault, finger, frame, harass, harm, imprison, incriminate, indict, injure, intimidate, lynch, maltreat, muscle, oppress, persecute, punish, railroad, sandbag, torment, traumatize, victimize, wrong)

SPARE (+): *aid, assist, conserve, cover, defend, deliver, guard, harbor, keep, maintain, preserve, protect, recover, recycle, redeem, safeguard, salvage, save, screen, secure, shelter, shield, support, sustain, uphold, ward* (≠ attack, betray, bully, compromise, decry, demean, demonize, endanger, hazard, imperil, intimidate, jeopardize, mock, molest, pillory, ridicule, risk, target, threaten, torment)

SPARK (→): *accelerate, activate, actuate, animate, arouse, brainstorm, catalyze, charge, crank, discharge, drive, electrify, energize, excite, facilitate, fire, fuel, generate, ignite, incite, initiate, instigate, jump-start, kick-start, kindle, launch, midwife, move, power, precipitate, prod, prompt, provoke, push, quicken, reactivate, recharge, release, run, speed, spur, start, stimulate, supercharge, switch, trigger, trip, vitalize* (≠ -abort, arrest, brake, cease, check, cripple, -cut, deactivate, decelerate, douse, end, finish, freeze, -halt, hamper, hinder, hobble, impair, impede, inactivate, incapacitate, inhibit, jam, kill, paralyze, repress, slow, stagnate, stall, stick, stop, stunt, suffocate, suppress, terminate, throttle)

SPARK (→): *abet, activate, anger, animate, annoy, arouse, bother, drive, encourage, energize, enrage, exasperate, excite, fan, ferment, fire, foment, gall, galvanize, ignite, impassion, incite, incur, induce, inflame, inspire, instigate, irritate, jeer, kindle, madden, motivate, move, needle, pique, provoke, quicken, rabble-rouse, raise, revitalize, rouse, stimulate, stir, taunt, tease, trigger, troll, upset, vex, vitalize* (≠ appease, buffer, calm, coddle, douse, dull, hush, lull, mellow, mitigate, moderate, mollify, pacify, placate, sedate, smother, soothe, stifle, strangle, subdue, tranquilize)

SPATTER (→): *band, bar, bedaub, bedraggle, bespatter, besprinkle, blemish, blot, blotch, dapple, daub, diffuse, dirty, dot, dye, fleck, freckle, intersperse, marble, mark, mottle, pepper, scatter, shower, soil, speck, speckle, splash, splatter, splotch, spot, spray, sprinkle, stain, stipple, streak, stripe, stud, taint* (≠ blanch, bleach, clean, cleanse, erase, fade, launder, miss, mop, purify, remove, rinse, sponge, wash, wet, whiten, wipe)

SPAWN (+): *advance, beget, begin, brainstorm, breed, brew, bring, catalyze, coin, conceive, concoct, contrive, create, cultivate, decide, design, determine, develop, devise, effect, effectuate, enact, encourage, engender, envision, establish, father, formulate, forward, foster, found, further, generate, hatch, improvise, inaugurate, incubate, induce, initiate, innovate, institute, introduce, invent, invoke, issue, launch, machinate, make, mother, nourish, nurture, originate, parent, patent, pioneer, plan, plot, produce, project, promote, prompt, render, reproduce, scheme, script, set, sire, start, yield* (≠ abolish, -abort, arrest, attack, check, control, crush, curb, dampen, demolish, destroy, doom, eradicate, exterminate, extinguish, -forbid, impede, inhibit, kill, limit, liquidate, mutate, predetermine, -prevent, quash, quell, quench, repress, restrain, restrict, slaughter, smother, snuff, squash, squelch, stifle, stop, subdue, suppress, weed)

SPECIFY (+): *adjure, advertise, announce, arrange, articulate, ascertain, assign, bid, blueprint, broach, broadcast, charge, choose, cite, clarify, coerce, command, compel, conduct, constrain, control, declare, decree, define, delineate, describe, designate, destine, detail, determine, dictate, differentiate, direct, distinguish, elucidate, enjoin, enumerate, establish, explain, explicate, finger, fix, flag, force, govern, individualize, instruct, intend, interject, interpolate, interpose, introduce, itemize, label, lead, list, manage, mark, mention, name, nominate, note, notice, obligate, oblige, ordain, order, package, particularize, peg, pinpoint, prescribe, prioritize, proclaim, profile, pronounce, publicize, publish, quote, require, select, set, settle, signal, signify, sound, specialize, state, stipulate, tab, tag, telegraph, tell, touch* (≠ anonymize, confuse, contradict, debate, -deny, destroy, discourage, disprove, dispute, -disregard, dissuade, forget, gainsay, generalize, -halt, -ignore, mislabel, -neglect, oppose, -overlook, refute, -repudiate, retract, suggest, unsettle, waive)

SPELLBIND (←): *absorb, allure, amaze, amuse, arouse, arrest, attract, bait, bedazzle, beguile, bemuse, bespell, bewilder, bewitch, bind, captivate, capture, charm, conjure, curse, delight, enamor, enchant, energize, engage, engross, enrapture, ensnare, ensorcel, entangle, entertain, enthrall, entrance, excite, fascinate, galvanize, glamour, grip, hex, hoodoo, hook, hypnotize, ignite, inspire, intrigue, involve, kindle, lure, mesmerize, monopolize, obsess, occupy, paralyze, petrify, possess, preoccupy, razzle-dazzle, seduce, spark, stimulate, stir, strike, tangle, tantalize, thrill, transfix, transport, trap, voodoo, weave, whammy, witch,* *woo, wow* (≠ anger, annoy, appall, -balk, bore, bother, bug, demoralize, demotivate, deplete, depress, desensitize, disappoint, discourage, disenchant, disgust, dispirit, drain, enrage, exhaust, fatigue, frustrate, infuriate, irk, irritate, knacker, madden, nag, nauseate, needle, nettle, nitpick, numb, paralyze, rankle, repel, rile, roil, sadden, sicken, stifle, tire, trouble, underwhelm, vex, weary, worry) **(¿) ABSTRACTION ALERT. Concrete goals essential!**

SPEND (→): *allocate, apply, award, bankroll, bestow, blow, cannibalize, compensate, concentrate, confer, consume, contribute, cripple, debilitate, defray, deplete, devour, disburse, dispense, dissipate, dole, donate, drain, drop, employ, empty, exhaust, expend, finance, finish, fritter, fund, give, invest, lard, lavish, liquidate, lose, maintain, meet, misspend, outbid, outlay, overpay, overspend, pay, redeem, refund, reimburse, remunerate, repay, scatter, settle, slather, sponsor, squander, support, tender, treat, underwrite, use, waste* (≠ accept, accumulate, aggregate, amass, bank, beggar, budget, collect, conserve, defund, deposit, earn, gather, get, glean, heap, hoard, inherit, keep, maintain, preserve, receive, recycle, -refuse, reserve, salvage, save, scavenge, scrimp, squirrel, starve, stash, steal, stiff, stint, stockpile, stow, sustain, take, tuck, withhold)

SPICE (+): *animate, appetize, brighten, dress, drizzle, dulcify, energize, enhance, enliven, entice, flavor, garnish, ginger, honey, imbue, improve, infuse, invigorate, lace, liven, magnify, marinate, maximize, pepper, prepare, richen, rouse, salt, saturate, sauce, season, sour, stimulate, stir, sugar, sweeten, syrup, vitalize, zest* (≠ blunt, bore, contaminate, dilute, dull, muddle, muddy, nauseate, poison, pollute, repel, repulse, ruin, simplify, spoil, sully, taint, water)

SPIKE (→): *bayonet, broach, core, cut, disembowel, drill, drive, enter, fill, gaff, gash, gimlet, gore, gut, harpoon, hurt, impale, injure, insert, invade, jab, kebab, knife, lance, peck, penetrate, perforate, pick, pierce, pike, pink, poke, poniard, prick, probe, prong, punch, puncture, ram, ream, riddle, rupture, shank, shiv, skewer, slice, spear, spindle, spit, split, stab, stake, stick, thrust, transfix, wound* (≠ armor, bandage, block, buffer, close, cover, defend, deflect, draw, eject, expel, extract, guard, heal, help, mend, miss, parry, patch, plaster, pluck, plug, prize, pull, remove, restore, seal, secure, sheathe, shield, tug, withdraw, wrench, yank)

SPIKE (+): *add, amp, blend, boost, brace, contaminate, dose, drizzle, drug, flavor, fortify, ginger, imbue, infuse, jazz, juice, lace, marinate, mix, overdose, poison, strengthen* (≠ deaden, decontaminate, distill, drain, dull, enfeeble, extract, filter, leach, leech, purge, purify, rarefy, remove, strain, weaken)

SPIN (←): *circle, circulate, coil, crank, dial, orbit, pivot, reel, revolve, roll, rotate, screw, swing, swirl, swivel, turn, twiddle, twirl, twist, unscrew, wheel, whirl, wind* (≠ block, constrain, fix, freeze, grip, hold, immobilize, lock, nail, pin, restrain, stop, straighten)

SPLICE (+): *ally, assemble, associate, bind, braid, chain, cluster, compound, congregate, conjoin, connect, constellate, convene, couple, entwine, fasten, fuse, gather, graft, hitch, hook, hybridize, integrate, interlace, intertwine, interweave, join, knit, link, marry, mate, meet, mesh, plait, raddle, recombine, reconnect, rejoin, reunify, reunite, stitch, synthesize, tie, unify, unite, weave, wed, yoke* (≠ break, cut, detach, disband, disconnect, disjoin, disjoint, disperse, disunite, divide, divorce, isolate, part, resolve, scatter, seclude, section, separate, sever, split, sunder, unbraid, uncouple, unfasten, unlink, unsplice, unyoke)

SPLINTER (/): *atomize, break, burst, chip, cleave, crack, crumble, dice, disintegrate, explode, fracture, fragment, hash, mince, pulverize, rive, shatter, shiver, smash, split* (≠ affix, blend, combine, fuse, glue, lump, melt, merge, repair, restore, unite)

SPLIT (+): *allocate, allot, apportion, carve, chunk, comminute, dispense, distribute, divide, divvy, dole, dollop, halve, mete, parcel, partition, separate, share, slice* (≠ collect, confiscate, consolidate, -deny, deprive, hoard, keep, receive, -refuse, retain, seize, stint, withhold)

SPLIT (/): *atomize, bifurcate, bisect, break, burst, chop, cleave, crack, crumb, crumble, cut, decompose, decouple, detach, dichotomize, disassemble, disassociate, disband, disconnect, disengage, disentangle, disintegrate, disjoin, disjoint, dissect, dissolve, disunite, divide, divorce, fissure, fracture, fragment, gouge, hack, halve, incise, insulate, isolate, open, orphan, part, partition, polarize, pull, pulverize, quarter, rend, resolve, rip, rive, rupture, seclude, segment, segregate, separate, sequester, sever, shatter, shiver, slash, slit, snap, splinter, subdivide, sunder, tear, uncouple, unlink, unravel, untie, unyoke, vivisect* (≠ accumulate, affix, assemble, associate, attach, bind, blend, cement, churn, cinch, close, combine, connect, couple, fasten, fuse, glue, hybridize, integrate, join, knit, link, mend, mingle, mix, mortar, network, reintegrate, reunite, scramble, splice, stick, stockpile, synthesize, unify, unite, unmarry, weld)

SPOIL (+): *accommodate, baby, caress, cherish, coddle, corrupt, cosset, cotton, cradle, cuddle, debauch, favor, featherbed, fondle, gratify, humor, indulge, infantilize, mollycoddle, nurse, nurture, oblige, overindulge, overprotect, pamper, pet, pity, protect, smother, spoon-feed, treat* (≠ abuse, control, crucify, deprive, discipline, disfavor, harass, harm, hurt, -ignore, injure, mistreat, molest, -neglect, oppress, outrage, -overlook, persecute, punish, respect, restrain, spank, torment, torture, victimize, violate, wrong)

SPOIL (/): *bastardize, blemish, blight, botch, break, bugger, bungle, butcher, contaminate, contort, cook, corrupt, crack, damage, debase, deface, defile, deform, demolish, desecrate, desolate, despoil, destroy, devastate, disfigure, disgrace, distort, efface, flaw, foul, half-ass, harm, harshen, hurt, impair, infect, infest, injure, louse, maim, mangle, mar, maul, misdiagnose, murder, mutilate, obliterate, pillage, plunder, poison, pollute, predetermine, prejudice, queer, ravage, raze, ruin, sack, scotch,* *shatter, shiver, smash, spike, squash, stale, suborn, taint, tarnish, topple, trash, upset, vitiate, waste, wreck* (≠ adorn, advantage, assemble, beautify, benefit, better, bless, build, clean, cleanse, create, cure, decontaminate, decorate, defend, develop, doctor, elevate, embellish, enhance, ennoble, enrich, fix, flavor, grace, guard, heal, help, improve, injure, marinate, mend, optimize, ornament, overhaul, patch, perfect, pickle, preserve, prize, protect, purify, rarefy, rectify, refine, reform, refresh, rehabilitate, remedy, renovate, repair, restore, rethink, revamp, revise, revolutionize, richen, season, spice, tinsel, tool, trim)

SPONGE (←): *appropriate, beg, beggar, bilk, borrow, bum, cadge, cheat, chisel, claim, exploit, fleece, grub, hustle, importune, inherit, inveigle, leech, mooch, obtain, panhandle, reap, reclaim, recoup, recover, request, salvage, scavenge, schnorr, score, scrounge, solicit, steal, take, tap, touch, use, weasel, wheedle* (≠ bankroll, bestow, capitalize, contribute, deliver, dower, endow, finance, float, fund, furnish, garner, offer, provide, refund, reimburse, repay, save, spare, sponsor, subsidize, supply, tender, underwrite, volunteer, withhold)

SPONSOR (→): *advance, advocate, approve, authorize, back, bankroll, capitalize, certify, champion, commend, countersign, endorse, ensure, finance, fund, guarantee, invest, patronize, promise, promote, ratify, recommend, rubber-stamp, subsidize, support, underwrite, validate* (≠ beggar, blackball, blacklist, -boycott, -cold-shoulder, defund, -deny, disinherit, -exclude, oppose, -ostracize, picket, protest, -refuse, -reject, -shun, -snub, withhold)

SPOOK (/): *affright, agitate, alarm, appall, awe, blackjack, blackmail, brutalize, bully, chill, daunt, demoralize, discomfort, discompose, disconcert, disgust, dismay, dispirit, disquiet, distract, distress, disturb, floor, frighten, funk, haunt, horrify, intimidate, jolt, menace, offend, outrage, panic, perturb, petrify, rattle, repel, revolt, scandalize, scare, shake, shock, sicken, startle, terrify, terrorize, threaten, undo, unhinge, unman, unnerve, unsettle, unstring, upset, worry* (≠ amuse, assuage, assure, bolster, brace, buoy, buttress, calm, comfort, console, delight, embolden, encourage, gratify, hearten, inspire, lull, mellow, mitigate, moderate, mollify, pacify, placate, please, reassure, soothe, steady, steel, strengthen, support, thrill, toughen, uplift, woo, wow)

SPOT (→): *band, bar, bespatter, blemish, blot, blotch, dapple, dot, dye, fleck, freckle, intersperse, marble, mark, mottle, pepper, set, soil, spatter, speck, speckle, splotch, sprinkle, stain, stipple, streak, stripe, stud, taint* (≠ blanch, bleach, clean, cleanse, erase, fade, launder, miss, remove, rinse, wash, whiten)

SPOT (←): *catch, clock, consider, descry, detect, discern, distinguish, espy, examine, eye, heed, identify, inspect, mark, mind, note, notice, observe, perceive, recognize, regard, remark, scan, scope, scrutinize, see, sight, spy, study, survey, view, watch, witness* (≠ -blank, blind, blindfold, bury, -bypass, camouflage, conceal, cover, disguise, -disregard, hide, -ignore, lose, mask, mislay, misplace, miss, mystify, -neglect, -overlook, pass, perplex, -sidestep)

SPOTLIGHT (→): *accent, accentuate, advertise, affirm, amplify, assert, belabor, boost, concentrate, emphasize, feature, floodlight, focus, highlight, hype, identify, illuminate, limelight, overemphasize, overplay, pimp, pinpoint, plug, presell, press, prioritize, promote, publicize, punctuate, shill, stress, underline* (≠ belittle, bury, conceal, cover, curtain, deemphasize, -discount, disparage, -disregard, forget, hide, lessen, lose, minimize, obscure, screen, underemphasize, understate)

SPREAD (→): *accelerate, accumulate, advance, appreciate, arrange, broaden, bulk, cover, deepen, develop, dilate, distend, double, enlarge, escalate, exacerbate, expand, extend, fan, foster, gain, grow, heighten, increase, inflate, intensify, lay, multiply, open, order, proliferate, puff, redouble, set, stretch, swell, treble, triple, unfold, unfurl, unroll, widen* (≠ close, contract, crease, decrease, diminish, fold, lessen, remove, retract, shrink, withdraw, wrinkle)

SPREAD (→): *anoint, apply, bedaub, besmear, blanket, butter, carpet, coat, cover, dab, daub, douse, grease, lard, lavish, lay, layer, mantle, moisturize, muddy, oil, overlay, paint, pigment, plaster, pomade, roughcast, slather, smear, smudge, soil, spackle, stain, sully, surface, syrup, tar, wax* (≠ abrade, bare, blot, dehydrate, desiccate, dry, excoriate, expose, lather, peel, rinse, scour, scrape, strip, towel, uncover, wash, wet)

SPREAD (→): *advertise, broadcast, bulletin, circulate, communicate, conduct, contaminate, convey, deliver, diffuse, dish, dispense, disperse, disseminate, dissipate, distribute, give, impart, infect, pass, poison, promulgate, propagate, publicize, publish, radiate, rumor, scatter, sow, strew, surrender, telegraph, transfer, transfuse, transmit* (≠ catch, cleanse, cloak, conceal, contain, contract, decontaminate, enshroud, hide, isolate, limit, mask, obscure, purify, quarantine, restrict, seclude, secrete, sequester, shroud, sterilize, suppress, veil)

SPRING (+): *aid, allow, assist, bail, benefit, clear, defend, deliver, detach, discharge, disengage, disentangle, disenthrall, distrust, doubt, drop, emancipate, enfranchise, extract, extricate, free, help, liberate, loose, loosen, lose, manumit, open, outmaneuver, outsmart, outwit, parole, preserve, protect, ransom, recapture, reclaim, recoup, recover, redeem, regain, release, repossess, rescue, retrieve, safeguard, salvage, save, slack, slacken, solve, unbind, uncage, unchain, unfetter, unhand, unleash, unshackle, untangle* (≠ abduct, apprehend, arrest, bind, blindside, box, cage, capture, catch, chain, collar, commit, confine, corral, detain, disappear, endanger, enmesh, enslave, ensnare, ensnarl, entangle, entrap, fasten, fetter, grab, handcuff, hold, hook, immure, imperil, imprison, incarcerate, intern, jail, jeopardize, kidnap, lasso, latch, lock, lure, manacle, nab, restrain, risk, secure, seize, shackle, snag, snatch, subdue, subjugate, trammel, trap)

SPUR (→): *accelerate, animate, annoy, arouse, assist, awaken, badger, boost, brainstorm, bribe, bustle, buttonhole, catalyze, coerce, compel, convince, countenance, drive, egg, encourage, energize, excite, exhort, expedite, fast-forward, fast-track, forward, frogmarch, further, galvanize, generate, goad, goose, harass, hasten, hound, hurry, hustle, impel, incite, incur, induce, influence, inspire, instigate, irritate, jolt, lobby, lubricate, march, midwife, mobilize, motivate, muscle, nag, needle, nudge, persuade, poke, prick, prioritize, prod, promote, prompt, propel, provoke, push, quicken, railroad, rouse, rush, sic, spark, speed, stampede, stimulate, sting, stir, strengthen, support, trigger, uphold, urge, vex, vitalize* (≠ -abort, axe, block, cage, calm, check, curb, daunt, deactivate, deaden, delay, demotivate, -deter, discourage, dissuade, freeze, -halt, hamper, hamstring, hinder, hobble, hush, impair, impede, inactivate, incapacitate, inhibit, interrupt, kill, mellow, mitigate, moderate, mollify, nobble, paralyze, pause, postpone, -prevent, repress, scotch, shelve, short-circuit, stall, stem, stifle, stop, stymie, throttle, -thwart)

-SPURN (→): *abjure, -avoid, banish, blackball, blacklist, -boycott, -bypass, condemn, contradict, controvert, -cut, -decline, -deny, -desert, -despise, detour, disallow, disavow, discard, disclaim, -disdain, dismiss, -disown, disprove, dispute, -disregard, drop, dump, eject, -exclude, exorcise, expel, flush, -forbid, forswear, gainsay, -ignore, -negate, -nix, -omit, oppose, -ostracize, oust, overrule, pass, picket, -prohibit, proscribe, protest, -rebuff, rebut, recall, recant, -refuse, refute, -reject, -renounce, -repudiate, repulse, retract, revoke, -scorn, scout, -slight, -snub, stick, -veto, withdraw* (≠ accede, accept, adopt, approve, brook, choose, condone, countenance, embrace, endure, espouse, face, handpick, receive, select, stomach, support, swallow, take, tolerate, want, welcome, withstand)

SPY (←): *attend, bug, case, clock, consider, cover, detect, discern, discover, espy, examine, eye, eyeball, glimpse, heed, identify, inspect, mark, mind, monitor, note, notice, observe, overhear, perceive, recon, reconnoiter, regard, retrace, scan, scope, scout, scrutinize, search, see, shadow, sight, spot, study, surveil, survey, tail, tap, trace, trail, view, watch, wire, wiretap, witness* (≠ baffle, blind, blindfold, bury, -bypass, camouflage, cloak, clothe, cloud, conceal, confound, confuse, costume, deceive, disguise, -disregard, expose, hide, -ignore, mask, miss, mistake, -neglect, -omit, -overlook, puzzle, screen, -sidestep, skim, skip, trick)

SQUANDER (/): *abuse, bankrupt, blow, botch, bungle, bust, cannibalize, compromise, consume, deplete, devastate, devour, diffuse, disburse, disperse, dissipate, down, drain, endanger, erode, exceed, exhaust, expend, flub, fritter, gamble, gorge, half-ass, imperil, impoverish, indulge, jeopardize, lard, lavish, lose, louse, mishandle, misspend, misuse, muck, muddle, neutralize, overdo, overfeed, overindulge, overspend, overuse, pay, plunge, ravage, risk, scatter, shoot, shrink, shrivel, slather, spend, spoil, surpass, threaten, waste, wither* (≠ accumulate, assemble, bank, bankroll, budget, collect, concentrate, conserve, deposit, earn, economize, finance, fund, furnish, gather, glean, hoard, invest, manage, preserve, protect, recoup, recover, recycle, retain, salvage, save, scant, scavenge, scrimp, skimp, starve, stash, steal, stiff, stint, stockpile, store, stow, sustain, take, tuck, underwrite, unify, unite, withhold)

SQUARE (+): *accord, adapt, adjust, align, answer, balance, calibrate, center, check, compose, coordinate, customize, dovetail, equal, equalize, even, expiate, fit, harmonize, level, match, parallel, reconcile, register, regulate, remedy, resolve, right, settle, sort, straighten, suit, tailor, tally, tune, tweak* (≠ challenge, cheat, contest, contradict, debate, debunk, -deny, deprive, dispute, gainsay, jar, misdiagnose, mismatch, -negate, -nullify, oppose, refute, -repudiate, steal, stiff, stint, withhold)

SQUASH (/): *annihilate, attack, bear, bruise, bulldoze, compress, contort, crowd, crush, defeat, distort, extinguish, flatten, grind, jam, kill, macerate, mash, -negate, obliterate, pack, pound, press, -prevent, pulp, pulverize, push, quash, quell, repress, scrunch, smash, squeeze, squoosh, stamp, subdue, suppress, terminate, trample* (≠ advance, assist, brainstorm, build, encourage, establish, expand, extend, fill, foment, further, help, increase, inflate, instigate, nurture, permit, praise, promote, provoke, rouse, stimulate, stir, stretch, support, survive, sustain, uphold, withstand)

SQUEEZE (→): *cram, crowd, crush, fill, heap, jam, jam-pack, jostle, load, overcrowd, pack, ram, ream, sandwich, sardine, saturate, shoehorn, stock, stuff, thrust, wedge* (≠ allow, clean, clear, deplete, drain, eliminate, empty, evacuate, exhaust, flush, lighten, open, pull, purge, release, remove, unpack, vacate, void)

SQUEEZE (→): *abbreviate, abridge, capsule, capsulize, collapse, compact, compress, concentrate, condense, consolidate, constrict, contract, cram, crowd, curtail, decrease, diminish, downsize, jam, jam-pack, lessen, narrow, pack, scrunch, shorten, shrink, simplify, streamline, stuff, telescope* (≠ broaden, bulge, decompress, diffuse, dilate, disperse, dissipate, distend, expand, free, increase, inflate, lengthen, open, release, scatter, stretch, swell)

SQUEEZE (←): *bear, choke, clasp, clinch, clip, clutch, crush, cuddle, embrace, enfold, express, extract, extrude, force, grip, hug, juice, mash, milk, nip, pack, pincer, pinch, press, pucker, pulp, quash, squash, squish, strain, strangle, suck, throttle, tighten, twist, wedge, wring* (≠ cram, fill, implant, inflate, insert, loose, open, replace, replenish, restore, unclench, uncompress, wedge)

SQUEEZE (←): *acquire, attain, bamboozle, betray, bilk, blackmail, bleed, bluff, buffalo, cheat, chisel, clip, con, deceive, defraud, double-cross, draw, dupe, earn, euchre, exploit, extort, extract, fast-talk, fiddle, fleece, flimflam, fool, force, gain, gazump, gouge, gull, hoax, hustle, land, mangle, manipulate, milk, mulct, nick, obtain, oppress, overcharge, pinch, pluck, pressure, procure, ream, rook, rope, scam, screw, scrounge, secure, short, shortchange, skin, skunk, soak, stick, stiff, sting, sucker, sweat, swindle, take, trick, underpay, victimize, wrench, wrest, wring* (≠ accuse, afford, audit, bankroll, confess, contribute, debunk, discredit, disperse, donate, expose, fund, furnish, give, grant, offer, -ostracize, permit, provide, respect, restore, reveal, scatter, shame, spare, stuff, substantiate, supply, support, tender, tithe, trust, underwrite, volunteer, withhold, yield)

SQUELCH (/): *annihilate, burke, check, conquer, crush, curb, curtail, decimate, demolish, desolate, destroy, devastate, dominate, doom, douse, exterminate, extinguish, nuke, obliterate, outlast, overcome, overpower, overwhelm, police, quash, quell, quench, reduce, repress, restrain, restrict, ruin, silence, smash, smother, snuff, squash, squeeze, squench, stifle, strangle, subdue, subjugate, suppress, throttle, trample, vanquish, waste, wreck* (≠ abet, advance, aid, assist, back, bolster, buttress, cultivate, encourage, foment, forward, foster, further, help, incite, instigate, nourish, nurture, promote, prop, provoke, rabble-rouse, stir, subvert, support, survive, weather)

SQUIRE (+): *accompany, associate, attend, bring, chaperone, chauffeur, conduct, convoy, defend, escort, follow, guard, guide, join, lead, partner, pilot, protect, see, shadow, steer, tag, tail, usher, walk* (≠ -abandon, alienate, -desert, -ditch, drop, dump, -forsake, isolate, leave, maroon, -ostracize, seclude, -shun, -snub, -spurn)

SQUIRREL (←): *accumulate, acquire, amass, archive, assemble, bank, budget, bury, cache, coffer, collect, conceal, concentrate, conserve, deposit, ensconce, garner, gather, heap, hide, hoard, hold, husband, keep, niche, pile, preserve, procure, reserve, retain, salt, save, secrete, secure, stack, stash, stock, stockpile, store, stow, treasure, tuck, wedge, withhold* (≠ blow, circulate, consume, deplete, discard, disperse, dissipate, -ditch, divest, dump, exhaust, expend, fritter, impoverish, jettison, lavish, offload, overfeed, relinquish, scatter, spend, squander, surrender, unload, waste)

STAB (→): *bayonet, bore, broach, burst, chop, cleave, clip, core, crack, cut, disembowel, drill, drive, enter, fill, gaff, gash, gimlet, gore, gouge, groove, gut, harpoon, hollow, honeycomb, hook, hurt, impale, injure, insert, invade, jab, kebab, knife, lance, nick, peck, penetrate, perforate, pick, pierce, pike, pin, pink, plow, plunge, poke, poniard, prick, probe, prong, punch, puncture, ram, razor, ream, rend, riddle, rupture, screw, shank, shiv, skewer, slice, spear, spike, spindle, spit, split, stake, stick, tap, tear, thrust, transfix, wound* (≠ aid, armor, assist, bandage, bind, block, buffer, close, cover, cure, defend, deflect, draw, eject, expel, extract, fill, guard, heal, help, mend, miss, nurse, nurture, parry, patch, plaster, plug, protect, pull, remove, repair, restore, seal, secure, sheathe, shield, tug, unite, withdraw, yank)

STABILIZE (+): *adjust, align, anchor, arrange, array, assure, balance, ballast, bolster, bolt, brace, buttress, calibrate, center, compose, control, coordinate, counterbalance, ensure, equalize, establish, fasten, firm, fix, fortify, freeze, harmonize, integrate, maintain, marshal, mediate, normalize, orchestrate, order, organize, pace, place, plan, plot, poise, prepare, preserve, prop, rationalize, referee, regiment, regulate, right, root, schematize, secure, set, settle, shape, sort, splint, square, steady,* *steel, stiffen, structure, strut, support, sustain, systematize, time, tone, toughen, tune, tweak, untangle, uphold* (≠ agitate, attack, boobytrap, change, convulse, damage, disturb, inflame, jumble, monkey-wrench, sabotage, scotch, scupper, scuttle, shake, subvert, topple, undermine, unhorse, unman, unnerve, unseat, unsettle, weaken)

STACK (←): *accumulate, amass, assemble, bank, bunch, clump, collect, compile, concentrate, garner, gather, group, heap, hoard, layer, load, lump, mass, mound, pile, pyramid, save, stash, stockpile, store, tuck, wedge* (≠ chunk, cut, diffuse, disperse, dissipate, distribute, divide, parcel, portion, scatter, separate, split, unload, waste)

STAGE (+): *act, arrange, carry, choreograph, depict, direct, display, dramatize, enact, engineer, exhibit, expose, extend, give, impersonate, mount, offer, orchestrate, organize, parade, perform, play, playact, portray, present, preview, produce, proffer, render, represent, roleplay, show, showcase, stage-manage, tender, unveil* (≠ attend, -cancel, close, conclude, criticize, critique, end, enjoy, finish, shutter, terminate, watch, wrap)

STAGGER (/): *amaze, astonish, astound, boggle, confound, daze, dazzle, deafen, devastate, dumbfound, faze, flabbergast, floor, flummox, gobsmack, nonplus, numb, overpower, overwhelm, paralyze, perplex, puzzle, razzle-dazzle, shake, shatter, shock, startle, stump, stun, stupefy, surprise, wow* (≠ balance, bore, calm, center, comfort, compose, enlighten, explain, hush, lull, mellow, mitigate, moderate, mollify, pacify, placate, reassure, settle, soothe, stabilize, steady)

STAIN (+): *brighten, brown, color, dapple, darken, daub, discolor, dye, fleck, lighten, marble, mottle, paint, pattern, pigment, speck, speckle, stipple, streak, striate, stripe, tincture, tinge, tint, variegate, varnish* (≠ blanch, bleach, clear, decolorize, strip, whiten, whitewash, wipe)

STAIN (/): *abase, bastardize, bedraggle, befoul, begrime, besmear, besmirch, bestialize, blacken, blemish, blot, blotch, blur, brutalize, cheapen, cloud, confuse, contaminate, corrupt, damage, darken, daub, debase, debauch, defile, degrade, demean, demoralize, deprave, dirty, disarrange, disarray, discolor, discredit, disgrace, dishevel, dishonor, disorder, draggle, foul, grime, injure, jumble, lower, mar, mark, mess, mire, muck, muddle, muddy, pervert, poison, pollute, shame, sink, smear, smirch, smudge, soil, spoil, spot, suborn, subvert, sully, taint, tar, tarnish, tinge, tint, touch, victimize, vitiate, worsen, wrong* (≠ brighten, brush, clean, cleanse, decontaminate, deodorize, dignify, disinfect, dry-clean, dust, elevate, ennoble, enshrine, expiate, freshen, glorify, hallow, launder, magnify, mop, purge, purify, rinse, sanitize, scour, scrub, sweep, uncloud, uplift, wash, wipe)

STAKE (→): *bear, bind, bolster, brace, buttress, carry, fasten, fortify, hold, pierce, prop, reinforce, secure, steady, strengthen, support, sustain, tether, tie, underpin* (≠ break, damage, destroy, disrupt, endanger, erode, sabotage, scotch, scupper, subvert, weaken, wreck)

STAKE (→): *assert, base, declare, demand, ensure, establish, institute, lodge, plant, requisition, secure, settle, state* (≠ -abandon, betray, challenge, cross-examine, -deny, -desert, distrust, doubt, grill, hinder, interrogate, question, scruple, undermine)

STAKE (→): *ante, bet, bid, chance, compromise, endanger, gamble, hazard, imperil, jeopardize, lay, offer, parlay, play, spare, venture, volunteer, wager* (≠ assure, ensure, guarantee, indemnify, insure, pledge, promise, protect, recoup, secure, warrant)

STAKE (→): *advocate, aid, back, bankroll, capitalize, champion, clear, cofinance, defray, discharge, dower, endorse, endow, finance, foot, fund, grubstake, liquidate, maintain, nourish, offer, outbid, outlay, overpay, patronize, pay, provide, -quit, recompense, refinance, settle, sponsor, stand, subsidize, support, underwrite* (≠ bankrupt, beggar, -cancel, defund, -deny, disinherit, forfeit, hoard, indemnify, keep, lose, owe, refund, -refuse, reimburse, repay, sacrifice starve, steal, stiff, stint, take, withhold)

STALK (→): *ambush, approach, chase, dog, drive, ferret, flush, follow, harass, harry, hassle, haunt, hector, hound, hunt, nag, persecute, pester, pursue, scout, seek, shadow, spoor, surveil, tail, target, track, trail, wheedle* (≠ attract, -avoid, bait, charm, -dodge, -elude, -evade, -ignore, invite, -sidestep, skirt, welcome)

STALL (←): *arrest, baffle, -balk, bench, block, blockade, bottleneck, catch, check, choke, clog, conclude, dam, defer, delay, detain, -discontinue, divert, end, -evade, fence, filibuster, -halt, hamper, hamstring, handicap, hinder, hobble, hold, impede, interrupt, obstruct, occlude, parry, pause, postpone, rein, repress, root, shelve, short-circuit, sideline, slow, snag, squash, squelch, stagnate, stale, staunch, stay, stem, still, stonewall, stop, stunt, suppress, suspend, terminate, -thwart* (≠ accelerate, actuate, advance, aid, allow, assist, boost, brainstorm, budge, catalyze, coerce, compel, drive, ease, enable, encourage, facilitate, frogmarch, fuel, further, goad, grease, hasten, help, impel, instigate, kindle, march, muscle, nurture, prioritize, propel, push, race, railroad, rush, smooth, spark, speed, spur, stir, trigger)

STAMP (→): *brand, categorize, characterize, claim, designate, dub, emboss, engrave, establish, etch, fix, identify, imbue, implant, impress, imprint, inculcate, infuse, ingrain, inscribe, instill, label, mark, monogram, package, print, seal, set, tool* (≠ anonymize, blot, bury, conceal, erase, expunge, garble, hide, mislabel, muddy, -negate, -nullify, obliterate, scramble, smooth, veil)

STAMP (/): *beat, boot, crush, kick, mash, override, overrun, pound, pulp, smash, squash, squelch, stomp, trample, tread* (≠ aid, assist, -bypass, -circumvent, cure, -elude, -escape, heal, help, inflate, observe, restore, uncompress)

STAND (→): *build, erect, install, juxtapose, locate, place, position, post, raise, rear, set, station, upend* (≠ cant, capsize, collapse, overbalance, overset, overturn, pitch, topple, tumble, upset)

STAND (+): *abide, absorb, accept, allow, bear, brook, countenance, endure, experience, face, hack, handle, meet, permit, pocket, reconcile, respect, stick, stomach, suffer, support, sustain, swallow, sweat, take, tolerate, weather, withstand* (≠ -avoid, -bypass, -circumvent, combat, contest, -decline, dismiss, -dodge, -elude, -escape, -evade, fight, miss, oppose, -refuse, -reject, -repudiate, resist, -spurn)

STANDARDIZE (+): *accredit, align, average, certify, codify, control, coordinate, depersonalize, equalize, even, formalize, govern, harmonize, homogenize, integrate, marshal, mass-produce, methodize, normalize, order, organize, pace, reconcile, regiment, regularize, regulate, rule, square, stereotype, synthesize, systematize* (≠ accommodate, adapt, alter, change, convert, customize, differentiate, disorder, disorganize, individualize, mix, modify, personalize, -prevent, tailor, vary, weaponize)

STARTLE (/): *agitate, amaze, astonish, astound, awe, baffle, befuddle, bewilder, blindside, boggle, bushwhack, confound, confuse, daze, dazzle, deafen, discombobulate, discomfit, disconcert, dismay, dumbfound, electrify, excite, flabbergast, floor, flummox, fluster, galvanize, gobsmack, invigorate, jar, jolt, jump, muddle, nonplus, overwhelm, perplex, rattle, razzle-dazzle, rock, rouse, shake, shock, stagger, start, stimulate, stir, stump, stun, stupefy, surprise, thrill, throw, unsettle, wow* (≠ anchor, annoy, anticipate, balance, blunt, bore, buffer, calm, center, clarify, compose, dampen, deaden, demystify, -disregard, dull, elucidate, expect, explain, follow, forecast, foretell, hypnotize, -ignore, jade, lull, mellow, mesmerize, mind, miss, numb, orchestrate, organize, outguess, -overlook, predetermine, predict, regiment, relax, remind, sedate, settle, signal, soothe, stabilize, steady, stultify, tire, weary) **(¿) ABSTRACTION ALERT. Concrete goals essential!**

STARTLE (/): *affright, alarm, alert, amaze, appall, astound, awe, browbeat, bully, chill, consternate, cow, daunt, demoralize, discomfort, discompose, disconcert, disgust, dismay, dispirit, disquiet, distract, distress, disturb, emasculate, floor, freak, frighten, gaslight, horrify, intimidate, jolt, nauseate, numb, offend, outrage, panic, paralyze, perturb, petrify, repel, revolt, rile, rock, roil, sandbag, scandalize, scare, shake, shock, sicken, signal, spook, stupefy, terrify, terrorize, traumatize, trigger, undo, unman, unnerve, unsettle, unstring, upset, worry* (≠ anticipate, appease, assure, blunt, buffer, calm, caution, charm, cheer, comfort, compose, console, cushion, dampen, deaden, delight, dull, embolden, encourage, entice, gratify, hearten, help, inspire, mitigate, moderate, mollify, pacify, placate, please, quiet, reassure, relax, sedate, soothe, stabilize, steady, steel, tease, tempt, threaten, tranquilize, warn) **(¿) ABSTRACTION ALERT. Concrete goals essential!**

STARVE (/): *-deny, deprive, disadvantage, dismiss, -forbid, -ignore, -neglect, -prohibit, reduce, -reject, remove, scant, scrimp, skimp, stint,* *weaken, withdraw, withhold* (≠ beef, bolster, bottle-feed, cook, feed, fill, force-feed, fuel, furnish, gratify, nourish, nurture, offer, overfeed, satisfy, supply, support, tender, victual, volunteer)

STASH (←): *accumulate, acquire, amass, archive, assemble, bank, budget, bury, cache, closet, coffer, collect, conceal, concentrate, conserve, deposit, ensconce, garner, gather, heap, hide, hoard, hold, husband, keep, mothball, niche, pickle, pile, preserve, procure, reserve, retain, salt, save, secrete, secure, squirrel, stack, stock, stockpile, store, stow, treasure, warehouse, withhold* (≠ blow, cast, circulate, consume, deplete, diffuse, discard, dispel, disperse, dissipate, -ditch, divest, dump, exhaust, expend, fritter, impoverish, jettison, lavish, misspend, offload, overfeed, relinquish, scatter, spend, squander, surrender, throw, toss, unload, waste)

STEADY (←): *allay, appease, assuage, calm, check, compose, conciliate, control, cool, curb, defuse, discipline, domesticate, ease, gentle, hush, lull, mellow, mitigate, moderate, mollify, pacify, placate, quell, quiet, reconcile, relax, relieve, restrain, reunite, sedate, smooth, soften, soothe, squelch, still, subdue, suppress, tame, temper, tranquilize* (≠ agitate, anger, arouse, bait, enrage, excite, incense, infuriate, irritate, militarize, outrage, provoke, rouse, ruffle, unleash)

STEADY (+): *adjust, align, arrange, array, balance, brace, buttress, calibrate, center, compose, constrain, control, coordinate, counterbalance, equalize, fix, harmonize, integrate, maintain, marshal, mediate, normalize, orchestrate, order, organize, pace, place, plan, plot, prepare, preserve, prop, rationalize, referee, regularize, regulate, right, schematize, secure, set, settle, shape, sort, splint, stabilize, structure, strut, support, sustain, systematize, tune, tweak, unsnarl, untangle, uphold* (≠ alarm, alter, ambush, attack, blindside, boobytrap, bushwhack, confuse, convulse, disconcert, exacerbate, exasperate, intensify, monkey-wrench, perplex, puzzle, rattle, rile, roil, sabotage, sandbag, scupper, shake, shift, shunt, subvert, troll, undermine, unnerve, weaken)

STEAL (←): *abduct, appropriate, bogart, burglarize, burgle, capture, carjack, cheat, collar, defraud, despoil, embezzle, filch, freeboot, glom, grab, grasp, heist, hijack, hook, hotwire, kidnap, lift, loot, maraud, misappropriate, mooch, nab, nail, nip, nobble, pick, pilfer, pillage, pinch, pirate, pluck, plunder, poach, pocket, purloin, ransack, remove, rifle, rob, rustle, sack, seize, shanghai, shoplift, snag, snatch, sneak, snitch, sponge, stiff, sucker, swindle, swipe, take, thieve* (≠ afford, bestow, buy, comp, contribute, defend, donate, furnish, give, hand, offer, present, protect, provide, purchase, recover, restore, return, secure, shield, spare, supply, tender, transfer, volunteer, yield)

STEAMROLLER (→): *abuse, beat, bluff, browbeat, bulldoze, bully, bullyrag, clear, clobber, coerce, command, compel, constrain, control, cow, cream, crush, daunt, defeat, demand, demolish, dominate, domineer, drub, fell, flatten, force, frighten, haze, hector, intimidate, level, menace, muscle, oppress, overcome, overpower, overthrow, overwhelm, persecute, pulverize, railroad, raze, sandbag, scare, shellac, smash, smear,* *steamroll, subdue, subjugate, terrorize, thrash, threaten, topple, torment, traumatize, trounce, tyrannize, upset, usurp, vanquish, victimize, violate, wallop, wrong* (≠ accommodate, aid, amuse, appease, assemble, assist, authorize, baby, bribe, build, cajole, clarify, coax, coddle, comfort, convince, court, delight, discourage, dissuade, ease, empower, enable, encourage, enlighten, entertain, erect, favor, featherbed, foster, gauge, grant, gratify, help, humor, inspire, mollycoddle, nobble, nudge, nurture, oblige, organize, pacify, pamper, permit, persuade, pull, raise, reassure, reward, romance, satisfy, schmooze, soothe, steel, subvert, suggest, underwhelm, woo)

STEEL (+): *acclimate, accustom, adapt, adjust, animate, anneal, assure, beef, bolster, boost, brace, buoy, buttress, calibrate, case-harden, cheer, condition, consolidate, embattle, embolden, empower, encourage, energize, enforce, enliven, excite, forearm, fortify, galvanize, gird, habituate, harden, hearten, immunize, indurate, inspire, inure, invigorate, naturalize, nerve, prepare, prioritize, prop, provoke, psych, quicken, rally, ready, reassure, reinforce, season, stabilize, steady, stiffen, stimulate, stir, strengthen, support, temper, tone, toughen, train, tweak, vaccinate, vitalize* (≠ castrate, cripple, daunt, debilitate, demoralize, demotivate, deplete, depress, -deter, diminish, discourage, dissuade, emasculate, enervate, enfeeble, exhaust, fatigue, hamstring, harm, impair, incapacitate, intimidate, kneecap, melt, overextend, sadden, sap, scotch, sensitize, shake, shrivel, soften, undercut, undermine, unman, unnerve, weaken, wither, wizen, worsen)

STEEP (+): *animate, bathe, brine, charge, damp, deluge, dip, drench, drown, embalm, enliven, fill, flood, imbrue, imbue, immerse, implant, impregnate, inculcate, infuse, ingrain, inoculate, instill, inundate, invest, invigorate, leaven, macerate, marinate, moisten, overwhelm, penetrate, permeate, pervade, pickle, plant, presoak, saturate, soak, sop, souse, submerge, suffuse, syrup* (≠ clear, dehydrate, delete, deplete, deprive, desiccate, divest, drain, dry, eliminate, empty, eradicate, erase, flush, leach, leech, parch, purge, remove, strip, wring)

STEER (→): *accompany, attend, captain, chair, chaperone, chauffeur, commandeer, conduct, control, convoy, direct, dominate, escort, govern, guide, helm, hijack, influence, lead, manage, maneuver, manipulate, marshal, navigate, negotiate, operate, outsmart, outthink, pilot, route, see, shepherd, show, skipper, turn, usher* (≠ crash, dog, follow, hound, mishandle, shadow, sideswipe, smash, subvert, tail, tailgate, trail)

STERILIZE (+): *bleach, boil, bolt, clarify, clean, cleanse, clear, decontaminate, disinfect, distill, eliminate, expurgate, exterminate, extract, filter, filtrate, fine, freshen, fumigate, launder, leach, process, purge, purify, quarantine, rectify, refine, sanitize, scour, screen, scrub, sieve, sift, wash* (≠ befoul, begrime, besmirch, blacken, cloud, contaminate, corrupt, defile, dirty, dull, foul, grime, infect, infest, mire, muddy, poison, pollute, rot, smirch, smudge, soil, spoil, stain, sully, taint)

STERILIZE (/): *alter, blight, caponize, castrate, deball, desex, doctor, dress, emasculate, excise, extract, fix, geld, mutilate, neuter, remove, spay, unman, unsex* (≠ arouse, boost, buoy, charge, fertilize, heal, invigorate, keep, renew, replace, restore, retain, stimulate)

STICK (→): *bayonet, cut, gimlet, gore, harpoon, impale, insert, jab, knife, lance, peck, penetrate, perforate, pick, pierce, pike, pink, poke, prick, prong, punch, puncture, push, ram, razor, riddle, shank, shiv, skewer, slice, spear, spike, spit, stab, thrust, transfix* (≠ aid, armor, assist, close, cure, defend, extract, guard, heal, help, parry, -rebuff, remove, sew, shield)

STICK (→): *affix, anchor, array, assemble, berth, carry, clap, collect, depose, deposit, dispose, drop, ensconce, establish, fix, install, juxtapose, lay, line, locate, lock, lodge, move, nestle, niche, orient, park, place, plank, plant, plonk, plop, plump, plunk, position, queue, rank, rearrange, rejigger, reorder, set, settle, shift, site, situate, slap, wedge* (≠ banish, dislodge, displace, eject, extricate, find, force, lose, oust, relegate, relocate, remove, replace, shift, shove, shunt, supersede, supplant, take)

STICK (+): *adhere, affix, attach, bind, bond, cement, cleave, fasten, fix, fuse, glue, grip, gum, hew, hold, join, mortar, paste, pin, secure, solder, tack, tape, unite, weld* (≠ cut, detach, disconnect, drop, loosen, pull, remove, rip, slacken, snatch, tear, unfasten, wrench, yank)

STIFFEN (+): *anneal, bake, brace, buttress, cake, calcify, cement, clot, coagulate, congeal, consolidate, contract, crystallize, curdle, dry, firm, fix, flex, fortify, fossilize, freeze, gird, harden, ossify, petrify, precipitate, press, pucker, reinforce, set, settle, solidify, starch, steel, strengthen, temper, tense, thicken, tighten, toughen* (≠ corrode, dilute, dissolve, liquefy, loosen, marinate, melt, moisten, presoak, rarefy, slacken, soak, soften, tenderize, thaw, weaken)

STIFFEN (+): *acclimate, acclimatize, accustom, adapt, adjust, augment, bolster, boost, brace, buttress, condition, embolden, enforce, forearm, fortify, habituate, harden, harshen, immunize, indurate, inure, invigorate, naturalize, prop, reinforce, season, steel, strengthen, support, sustain, temper, toughen, vitalize* (≠ bend, cripple, crumple, debilitate, ease, emasculate, enervate, enfeeble, erode, exhaust, fatigue, fold, hamstring, harm, heat, impair, incapacitate, lessen, moderate, quiver, sabotage, sap, sensitize, soften, thin, undermine, unman, weaken, wiggle)

STIFLE (/): *asphyxiate, ban, burke, censor, choke, cork, cripple, curb, cushion, dampen, daunt, deaden, depress, -deter, devoice, discourage, dishearten, disincline, dissuade, extinguish, -forbid, -frustrate, gag, garrote, hamper, hamstring, hinder, hurt, hush, impair, impede, inhibit, kill, muffle, mute, muzzle, paralyze, pinch, pound, -prevent, quell, quench, quiet, repress, restrain, scorch, silence, smother, snuff, spike, squash, squelch, squench, stagnate, stale, stall, still, stop, strangle, stultify, subdue, suffocate, suppress, throttle, trouble* (≠ aerate, aid, amplify, assist, boost, create, deepen, encourage, enhance, enliven, escalate, exaggerate, express, free, heighten, help, increase, inspire, intensify, loose, magnify, maximize, oxygenate, persuade, prioritize, reinvigorate, release, resuscitate, revive, start, strengthen, support, vent, ventilate)

STIGMATIZE (/): *badmouth, besmirch, blacken, blackguard, blacklist, blame, blemish, brand, characterize, class, classify, condemn, criticize, critique, debunk, defame, demonize, denigrate, denounce, deride, designate, discredit, disgrace, dishonor, disparage, disrespect, diss, expose, fault, finger, frame, harm, humiliate, incriminate, injure, insult, label, libel, malign, mark, mock, muckrake, -ostracize, pillory, pollute, rebuke, reprimand, reproach, resent, revile, ridicule, scandalize, scapegoat, scorch, -scorn, shame, slam, slander, smear, stain, stamp, sully, tag, taint, tarnish, vilify, villainize* (≠ alibi, anonymize, approve, assist, blandish, boost, commend, compliment, defend, elevate, exalt, exonerate, extol, flatter, gratify, honor, idolize, lionize, mislabel, pardon, praise, prioritize, protect, revere, reward, spare, treasure, venerate, vindicate, worship)

STILL (←): *arrest, baffle, -balk, block, blockade, bottleneck, cage, catch, check, choke, clog, conclude, confine, cripple, curb, curtail, dam, deactivate, detain, disable, -discontinue, end, extinguish, freeze, -halt, hinder, hold, immobilize, impede, incapacitate, obstruct, paralyze, pin, rein, repress, restrain, snag, squash, squelch, stall, staunch, stay, stem, stifle, stop, stunt, suppress, suspend, terminate, transfix* (≠ accelerate, actuate, advance, budge, continue, drive, encourage, foment, fuel, goad, hasten, impel, kindle, mobilize, move, prompt, propel, provoke, punt, push, quicken, rouse, shove, shunt, spur, stir)

STILL (+): *abate, allay, alleviate, appease, assuage, calm, comfort, compose, conciliate, dampen, deaden, dull, ease, hush, hypnotize, lighten, lull, mesmerize, mitigate, moderate, mollify, narcotize, numb, pacify, placate, quell, quiet, relax, relieve, salve, sedate, settle, silence, smooth, solace, soothe, stifle, stupefy, subdue, tranquilize, unruffle* (≠ aggravate, agitate, alarm, arouse, discompose, disquiet, distress, disturb, energize, exacerbate, excite, foment, heighten, incite, intensify, irritate, jar, jostle, perturb, rattle, rouse, shake, spur, stimulate, stir, trouble, unsettle, upset, vex)

STIMULATE (→): *actuate, agitate, amp, animate, applaud, arouse, awaken, boost, brace, buoy, charge, cheer, compel, dazzle, disquiet, disturb, drive, elate, electrify, embolden, energize, enkindle, enliven, excite, exhilarate, ferment, fire, foment, fortify, freshen, galvanize, gentrify, ginger, grab, hearten, impassion, impel, incite, inflame, infuse, inspire, instigate, invigorate, jazz, juice, jump-start, kindle, lift, liven, motivate, move, pique, prioritize, propel, provoke, quicken, raise, rally, razzle-dazzle, reactivate, reanimate, reassure, reawaken, recharge, recreate, reenergize, refresh, regenerate, reinvigorate, rejuvenate, rekindle, renew, restimulate, resurrect, resuscitate, revitalize, revive, rouse, shock, spark, spike, startle, steel, stir, strengthen, tantalize, taunt, tease, tempt, thrill, tickle, titillate, trigger, vitalize, vivify, wake, zap*

(≠ bridle, castrate, check, consume, cripple, curb, damp, dampen, daunt, deactivate, deaden, debilitate, demoralize, demotivate, depress, -deter, discourage, dishearten, dispirit, drain, dull, enervate, enfeeble, exhaust, fatigue, freeze, hamper, harass, hinder, hobble, immobilize, incapacitate, inhibit, jade, kill, leech, numb, overextend, pacify, paralyze, quell, quench, repress, restrain, sap, sedate, slake, slow, still, stunt, suppress, tranquilize, tucker, undermine, weaken, wear, weary, wither)

STIMULATE (→): *abet, activate, amaze, anger, animate, annoy, arouse, astound, bother, bug, drive, encourage, energize, enrage, exasperate, excite, fan, ferment, fire, foment, gall, galvanize, goad, hasten, hook, ignite, impassion, incite, incur, induce, inflame, infuriate, inspire, instigate, irritate, jeer, jolt, kindle, lubricate, madden, midwife, motivate, move, nag, needle, nettle, pique, prod, prompt, provoke, quicken, rabble-rouse, raise, rev, send, shake, spark, spawn, spur, stir, stoke, stretch, taunt, tease, trigger, upset, urge, vex, vitalize* (≠ anesthetize, appease, bore, burden, calm, cripple, dampen, deactivate, deaden, depress, dope, dose, drug, dull, hamper, hamstring, hinder, hobble, hush, hypnotize, impair, impede, lull, mellow, mesmerize, mitigate, moderate, mollify, narcotize, numb, pacify, placate, poison, postpone, -prevent, sadden, sedate, sicken, soothe, stagnate, stale, stifle, stunt, stupefy, subdue, suppress, throttle, torpefy, tranquilize)

STING (←): *bamboozle, beat, betray, bilk, bleed, buffalo, cheat, chisel, clip, con, cozen, deceive, defraud, double-cross, dupe, embezzle, exploit, extort, fast-talk, fiddle, fleece, flimflam, fool, gazump, gouge, gull, hocus-pocus, hustle, lull, manipulate, milk, nick, outwit, overcharge, pluck, ream, rook, rope, scam, screw, short, shortchange, skin, soak, squeeze, stick, stiff, sucker, swindle, trick, underpay, victimize, wrench, wrest, wring, wrong* (≠ accuse, aid, assist, assume, assure, believe, catch, confess, credit, defend, discredit, encourage, expose, fund, give, help, lose, -prevent, protect, shield, trust, undercharge, watch)

STING (/): *annoy, bite, cut, distress, exasperate, goad, grieve, harm, heckle, hurt, incense, injure, nag, needle, nettle, nitpick, offend, pierce, prick, prod, provoke, stab, torment, upset, wound* (≠ aid, benefit, better, cure, doctor, fix, guard, heal, help, mend, patch, protect, rehabilitate, remedy, shield)

STIPULATE (+): *ask, badger, bind, claim, command, compel, constrain, contract, demand, dun, enjoin, exact, foist, harass, hound, impose, insist, mandate, obligate, overcommit, plead, press, request, require, requisition, specify, take, want, warrant* (≠ -abandon, cede, concede, forfeit, -forsake, lose, relinquish, -renounce, resign, surrender, waive, yield)

STIR (→): *abet, activate, agitate, anger, animate, annoy, arouse, astound, bother, challenge, charge, churn, disorder, disorganize, disrupt, disturb, drive, encourage, energize, enrage, exasperate, excite, fan, ferment, foment, gall, galvanize, generate, gladden, heat, ignite, impassion, incite, incur, induce, inflame, infuriate, inspire, instigate, invigorate, irritate, jolt, kindle, madden, motivate, move, muddle, nag, needle, nerve, nettle,* *niggle, nitpick, pique, poke, prod, provoke, quicken, rabble-rouse, raise, rattle, razzle-dazzle, rev, roil, rouse, rout, rustle, shake, shift, shock, spark, startle, stimulate, stoke, surprise, taunt, tease, thrill, touch, trigger, unsettle, upset, vex, vitalize, wake* (≠ appease, calm, cripple, deactivate, demotivate, -deter, discourage, dissuade, finish, freeze, -halt, hamper, hinder, hush, hypnotize, impede, incapacitate, lull, mellow, mitigate, moderate, mollify, pacify, paralyze, placate, -prevent, quiet, restrain, satisfy, sedate, soothe, stabilize, stall, steady, stupefy, subdue, tranquilize)

STIR (+): *agitate, bandy, beat, blend, churn, convulse, fold, froth, jumble, mingle, mix, muddy, paddle, reel, roil, scramble, shake, shuffle, slosh, splash, swirl, toss, wash, wheel, whip, whirl, whisk* (≠ bottle, colander, contain, distill, divide, extract, filter, insulate, isolate, order, purify, rarefy, rend, separate, sift, slot, sort, split, strain)

STITCH (+): *alter, baste, bind, connect, couple, crochet, darn, embroider, fasten, finish, hem, knit, lash, line, mend, patch, plait, pleat, repair, seam, sew, suture, tack, tether, tuck, weave, zip* (≠ cleave, comfort, cut, ease, lacerate, mangle, release, rend, rip, shred, slice, slit, split, tatter, tear, unpick, unsew)

STOCKPILE (←): *accumulate, acquire, amass, archive, assemble, bank, budget, bury, cache, coffer, collect, conceal, concentrate, conserve, deposit, ensconce, ensure, garner, gather, heap, hoard, hold, husband, keep, maintain, pickle, pile, preserve, procure, recycle, reserve, retain, salt, salvage, save, scavenge, secrete, secure, squirrel, stack, stash, stock, store, stow, treasure, tuck, wedge, withhold* (≠ blow, cannibalize, cast, consume, deplete, depredate, diffuse, discard, dispel, disperse, dissipate, distribute, -ditch, dump, exhaust, expend, fritter, impoverish, jettison, lard, lavish, misspend, offload, overfeed, relinquish, scatter, slather, spend, squander, surrender, unload, waste)

STOKE (→): *accelerate, accent, accentuate, accrue, accumulate, activate, add, affirm, aggrandize, amass, amplify, assert, augment, beef, boost, brainstorm, build, catalyze, collect, complement, compound, deepen, develop, dilate, distend, double, egg, elongate, emphasize, encourage, enhance, enlarge, escalate, exacerbate, expand, extend, feed, foment, foster, fuel, goad, heighten, hype, ignite, incite, increase, inflate, instigate, intensify, kindle, lengthen, magnify, maximize, multiply, poke, prioritize, prod, prolong, prompt, protract, pump, rabble-rouse, raise, reinforce, rouse, spur, stimulate, stir, strengthen, stretch, supersize, supplement, swell, treble, triple, up* (≠ abate, abbreviate, abridge, compress, condense, constrict, contract, curtail, decrease, de-escalate, delay, -deter, diminish, downsize, foil, -frustrate, hamper, hinder, lessen, lower, minimize, monkey-wrench, muzzle, pause, postpone, -prevent, reduce, shelve, short-circuit, shorten, stall, stem, stymie, subtract, -thwart, underemphasize)

STOMACH (+): *abide, absorb, accept, allow, bear, brave, brook, buck, concede, condone, confront, countenance, endure, experience, face, hack, handle, incur, indulge, know, meet, outlast, overcome, permit,* *pocket, receive, respect, sanction, season, stand, suffer, support, surmount, survive, sustain, swallow, sweat, take, tolerate, weather, withstand* (≠ -avoid, battle, -bypass, -circumvent, combat, contest, -decline, denounce, disallow, dismiss, -dodge, -elude, -escape, -evade, fight, -flee, flout, -hate, miss, misunderstand, oppose, -prevent, -refuse, -reject, -repudiate, resist, -shun, -spurn, stop)

STONE (/): *annihilate, attack, cream, crucify, crumble, crush, decimate, demolish, demonize, desolate, destroy, devastate, discipline, doom, excoriate, execute, extinguish, grind, lynch, martyr, mill, nuke, pelt, penalize, persecute, pillory, pound, powder, pulp, pulverize, pummel, punish, raze, ruin, scourge, shame, shatter, smash, squash, stigmatize, strike, target, torture, total, vaporize, waste, wrack, wreck* (≠ absolve, acquit, aid, benefit, boost, clear, conceal, defend, exonerate, forgive, pardon, praise, promote, rescue, spare, survive, sustain, vindicate, weather, withstand)

STONEWALL (←): *baffle, -balk, bamboozle, beguile, block, bullshit, check, checkmate, conceal, confound, confuse, cross, deceive, defeat, delay, -dodge, double-talk, -evade, fence, flummox, foil, forestall, -frustrate, hamper, hamstring, hide, hinder, hogtie, hornswoggle, impede, inhibit, misdirect, mislead, monkey-wrench, mystify, nobble, nonplus, obscure, obstruct, occlude, oppose, perplex, postpone, preempt, -prevent, protest, puzzle, ruin, scotch, shelve, shift, short-circuit, shuffle, snooker, spite, spoil, stall, stem, stop, stump, stymie, -thwart* (≠ accelerate, advance, assist, assuage, boost, brainstorm, catalyze, clarify, define, ease, elucidate, enable, encourage, expedite, explain, explicate, expound, facilitate, floodlight, gloss, grease, hasten, help, illuminate, instigate, interpret, lubricate, nurture, promote, prompt, resolve, simplify, spark, speed, spur, translate, trigger, trust)

STOP (→): *block, bung, caulk, chink, choke, clog, close, clot, congest, constipate, cork, cover, dam, fill, jam, mute, muzzle, obstruct, occlude, pack, plaster, plug, repack, restuff, seal, secure, silence, spackle, stem, stifle, stopper, stopple, stuff, wedge* (≠ clear, decongest, dig, excavate, extract, extricate, hollow, open, remove, scoop, shovel, unclog, uncork, unplug, unseal, unstopper)

STOP (←): *apprehend, arrest, baffle, -balk, block, blockade, bottleneck, cage, catch, check, choke, clog, confine, constrain, contain, control, cripple, curb, dam, deflect, delay, detain, freeze, -frustrate, hamper, hinder, hobble, hold, immobilize, impede, inactivate, inhibit, intercept, interrupt, limit, obstruct, paralyze, pause, -prevent, rein, repress, restrain, restrict, shelve, short-circuit, snag, squash, squelch, stall, staunch, stay, stem, still, stunt, suppress, -thwart* (≠ accelerate, actuate, advance, aid, assist, benefit, boost, budge, continue, drive, encourage, expedite, facilitate, fast-forward, fast-track, frogmarch, goad, grease, hasten, help, hurry, impel, march, move, prioritize, progress, promote, propel, punt, push, spur, stimulate, stir)

STOP (/): *-abandon, abolish, -abort, annul, anticipate, arrest, ban, bar, block, blockade, brake, break, call, can, cease, check, checkmate, close, complete, conclude, -cut, dam, deactivate, demolish, destroy, detain, -discontinue, dissolve, doom, drop, end, eradicate, erase, finish, forestall, -halt, hamstring, hold, inactivate, -interdict, -kibosh, kick, kill, obstruct, -prevent, -prohibit, -quit, rein, rest, ruin, scuttle, snuff, squash, squelch, stamp, staunch, stay, stem, suppress, suspend, terminate* (≠ activate, actuate, advance, animate, begin, brainstorm, catalyze, commence, continue, drive, extend, impel, initiate, institute, introduce, keep, launch, legalize, permit, progress, prolong, propel, reboot, restart, resume, spur, start, stir, unspool)

STORE (←): *accumulate, acquire, amass, assemble, bank, budget, bury, cache, cellar, coffer, collect, conceal, concentrate, conserve, cram, deposit, ensconce, ensure, file, garage, garner, gather, hangar, heap, hoard, hold, house, husband, jam, keep, mothball, niche, pack, pickle, pile, preserve, procure, reserve, retain, salt, save, secrete, secure, shelve, squirrel, stack, stash, stock, stockpile, stow, treasure, tuck, warehouse, wedge, withhold* (≠ bandy, blow, cast, circulate, consume, deplete, diffuse, discard, dispel, disperse, dissipate, -ditch, download, dump, exhaust, expend, fritter, jettison, lavish, misspend, offload, overfeed, relinquish, scatter, scavenge, spend, squander, surrender, toss, unload, waste)

STORM (→): *ambush, assail, assault, attack, barrage, batter, beleaguer, beset, besiege, blindside, blitz, bomb, bombard, buffet, bum-rush, bushwhack, cannon, charge, claim, envelop, flank, gate-crash, harry, infest, invade, loot, mob, mortar, nuke, occupy, overrun, pillage, plunder, press, raid, ransack, ravage, reclaim, rush, sack, sandbag, seize, stomp, strike, surprise, swarm, trash, trespass, violate, waylay* (≠ assist, -avoid, bar, barricade, befriend, block, blockade, calm, cover, defend, guard, mitigate, moderate, outlast, placate, preserve, protect, repel, rescue, resist, restore, save, secure, shelter, shield, support, sustain, uphold, warn, withdraw, withstand)

STOW (←): *accumulate, acquire, amass, archive, assemble, bank, budget, bundle, bury, cache, cellar, coffer, collect, conceal, concentrate, conserve, cram, deposit, ensconce, file, garage, garner, gather, hangar, heap, hoard, hold, house, husband, jam, jam-pack, keep, load, mothball, niche, overstuff, pack, pile, place, preserve, procure, reserve, retain, salt, save, secrete, secure, shelve, squirrel, stack, stash, stock, stockpile, store, stuff, treasure, tuck, warehouse, wedge, withhold* (≠ -abandon, blow, cast, consume, deplete, diffuse, discard, dispel, disperse, dissipate, -ditch, drop, dump, exhaust, expend, expose, forfeit, fritter, impoverish, jettison, lavish, lose, misspend, offload, overfeed, relinquish, scatter, spend, squander, surrender, toss, unload, waste)

STRAIGHTEN (+): *adjust, align, arrange, bend, calibrate, compose, coordinate, correct, disentangle, equalize, even, expand, extend, flatten, hook, iron, level, neaten, order, plumb, realign, rectify, right, simplify, smooth, streamline, tidy, tune, tweak, unbend, uncoil, uncrumple, uncurl,* *unfold, unkink, unravel, unroll, unskew, unsnarl, untangle, untwine, untwist, unwind* (≠ alter, bend, bow, coil, contort, corrugate, crease, crimp, crook, curl, curve, distort, entwine, fold, kink, loop, mangle, quiver, ripple, rotate, round, shift, skew, slant, spiral, swirl, turn, twine, twist, untidy, warp, wiggle, wind, wriggle, wrinkle)

STRAIN (/): *aggravate, agitate, annoy, bother, compel, compromise, demand, drive, exact, exasperate, exert, extract, fatigue, force, gall, grate, harass, harry, hassle, importune, irk, irritate, nettle, overtax, overwork, pain, peeve, pester, plague, press, pressure, push, rile, spite, stretch, tax, test, tire, try, vex, weaken* (≠ alleviate, assuage, calm, cheer, comfort, console, ease, encourage, enliven, gladden, gratify, hearten, help, humor, invigorate, lull, mellow, mitigate, moderate, mollify, pacify, placate, reassure, refresh, relax, release, relieve, soothe, strengthen, support)

STRAIN (/): *batter, bruise, cinch, constrict, crack, cripple, damage, dislocate, displace, elongate, extend, fray, harm, hurt, impair, injure, lame, lengthen, mangle, mutilate, pull, rack, rick, rupture, sever, shred, split, sprain, stretch, tauten, tax, tear, tense, tighten, turn, twist, weaken, wound, wrench* (≠ adjust, alleviate, bandage, brace, doctor, ease, fix, heal, help, loosen, medicate, mend, nurse, relax, remedy, repair, restore, slack, slacken, soothe, treat)

STRAIN (/): *bolt, clarify, clean, cleanse, clear, colander, compress, decontaminate, disinfect, distill, divide, drain, express, expunge, extract, filter, fine, garble, leach, percolate, process, purge, purify, quarantine, rarefy, rectify, refine, remove, riddle, sanitize, screen, separate, sieve, sift, squeeze, wash, winnow, wring* (≠ agitate, amalgamate, besmirch, blend, churn, cloud, combine, contaminate, defile, dirty, dull, foul, fuse, infest, integrate, jumble, meld, mix, muddy, poison, pollute, scramble, soil, spoil, stain, stir, sully, taint, unify, unite)

STRANGLE (/): *asphyxiate, burke, check, choke, confine, constrict, control, curb, dampen, daunt, demotivate, depress, -deter, discourage, dishearten, disincline, dissuade, endanger, extinguish, -frustrate, gag, garrote, hamper, hinder, hush, impede, imperil, inhibit, kill, limit, lynch, muffle, murder, mute, muzzle, paralyze, quiet, repress, restrain, shush, silence, smother, squeeze, squelch, stifle, stop, stymie, subdue, suffocate, suppress, throttle, wring* (≠ aerate, air, clear, free, heal, help, inhale, inspire, loose, nurture, open, oxygenate, reinvigorate, release, relieve, restore, resuscitate, revive, unclog, unseal, vent, ventilate, verbalize, vocalize, voice)

STRAP (+): *attach, bandage, bind, chain, cinch, confine, connect, constrain, couple, curb, entangle, fasten, fetter, fix, hamper, handcuff, hinder, hobble, hogtie, impede, iron, join, knot, lace, lash, limit, link, manacle, moor, pinion, restrict, rope, secure, shackle, tangle, tether, tie, trammel, truss, unite* (≠ -abandon, detach, disengage, divide, drop, eject, emancipate, free, jettison, liberate, loose, loosen, release, repel, rescue, separate, sever, slack, slacken, split, unbind, undo, unfasten, unfetter, unhitch, unshackle, untangle, untie)

STRAP (/): *beat, belt, birch, blackjack, cane, chastise, clobber, clout, club, cudgel, cuff, drub, flagellate, flail, flog, hide, hit, horsewhip, lace, lambaste, lash, lick, maul, paddle, pelt, pummel, punish, scourge, slap, slate, smack, smite, spank, swat, swipe, switch, tan, thrash, thwack, wallop, whack, whip, whup* (≠ aid, assist, block, caress, coddle, defend, deflect, guard, heal, help, indulge, mollycoddle, nurse, parry, protect, reward, shield, spoil, stroke, support, tend)

STREAMLINE (+): *abridge, automate, clarify, compact, computerize, concentrate, condense, consolidate, correct, decipher, enhance, focus, improve, incorporate, modernize, modify, optimize, overhaul, oversimplify, paraphrase, perfect, prune, purify, realign, reconceive, reconceptualize, reduce, refine, refurbish, reimagine, reinvent, remodel, renovate, reorganize, reshape, reshuffle, rethink, retool, revamp, revise, revolutionize, simplify, strip, trim, uncomplicate, unify, unravel, untangle, update, upgrade* (≠ adorn, complicate, compound, decorate, elaborate, embellish, fancify, garnish, glitz, grace, jumble, muddle, ornament, pad, sophisticate, stud, tangle, tinsel, tool, trim)

STRENGTHEN (+): *acclimate, acclimatize, accustom, adapt, adjust, aid, anneal, arm, assist, assuage, bolster, boost, brace, buttress, case-harden, condition, cure, doctor, edify, empower, enable, enforce, fix, forearm, fortify, freshen, galvanize, habituate, harden, heal, heighten, help, immunize, indurate, inure, invigorate, kindle, limber, mend, mobilize, motivate, naturalize, nurture, patch, patronize, prop, protect, reassure, refresh, regenerate, rehabilitate, reinforce, rejuvenate, remedy, renew, repair, restimulate, restore, revitalize, revive, season, steady, steel, stiffen, support, sustain, temper, toughen, train, vaccinate, vitalize* (≠ canker, castrate, checkmate, corrode, cripple, damage, daunt, debilitate, demoralize, destroy, discourage, dishearten, dissolve, dissuade, emasculate, enervate, enfeeble, eradicate, erase, exhaust, fracture, fragment, -halt, hamstring, harm, imperil, incapacitate, -neglect, overthrow, prostrate, ruin, sabotage, sap, scotch, scupper, scuttle, sensitize, shake, shatter, short-circuit, soften, undermine, unman, unsettle, upset, weaken)

STRENGTHEN (+): *anneal, beef, develop, drill, embattle, energize, enhance, exercise, facilitate, firm, fortify, fuel, harden, invigorate, nourish, perfect, practice, prepare, refine, rehearse, repeat, review, study, temper, tone, toughen, train, vitalize, work* (≠ cripple, damage, debilitate, doom, enervate, enfeeble, hamstring, harm, hurt, impair, incapacitate, injure, paralyze, rupture, sap, scar, scupper, shelve, strain, tear, undercut, undermine, weaken)

STRENGTHEN (+): *abet, accelerate, accentuate, aggravate, amp, amplify, augment, back, beef, boost, broaden, comfort, concentrate, condone, consolidate, deepen, develop, elevate, emphasize, encourage, endorse, enforce, enhance, enlarge, enliven, exacerbate, excite, expand, extend, favor, feed, force-feed, foster, fuel, further, hasten, heighten, help, improve, increase, inspire, intensify, jazz, lengthen, magnify, maximize, nourish, nurture, prioritize, promote, protect, provoke, quicken, raise, rally,* *redouble, refresh, reinforce, reinvigorate, restore, revitalize, rouse, sanction, second, secure, sharpen, spur, stress, supplement* (≠ abate, -abort, abridge, alleviate, ameliorate, annul, block, -cancel, checkmate, contradict, counter, cramp, curb, curtail, decrease, dent, diminish, drop, ease, foil, -frustrate, -halt, hamper, hinder, hobble, impede, inhibit, lessen, lighten, lose, lower, moderate, monkey-wrench, muzzle, obstruct, -prevent, reduce, -reject, restrain, restrict, sabotage, scotch, shrink, shrivel, slow, stop, subdue, subtract, taper, -thwart, tone, undermine, weaken)

STRESS (+): *accent, accentuate, advertise, amplify, assert, augment, beef, belabor, bolster, boost, coerce, compel, concentrate, deepen, dictate, dragoon, drive, emphasize, enhance, enlarge, enliven, escalate, exaggerate, feature, focus, foment, foreground, galvanize, heighten, highlight, hijack, identify, illuminate, impel, incite, increase, intensify, jazz, magnify, mandate, maximize, overdramatize, overemphasize, overplay, oversell, pinpoint, plug, press, prioritize, promote, propel, publicize, punctuate, push, reinforce, sharpen, spark, spotlight, stimulate, strengthen, supplement, underline, underscore, urge* (≠ belittle, blunt, buffer, bury, conceal, cover, cut, decrease, deemphasize, diminish, -discount, disparage, downplay, hide, lessen, mediate, minimize, mitigate, obscure, obstruct, reduce, shrink, slacken, soften, subdue, tune, underemphasize, understate, weaken)

STRESS (/): *afflict, agitate, alarm, anger, annoy, appall, blackjack, bother, browbeat, bug, bulldoze, bully, burden, concern, crunch, daunt, demotivate, depress, disappoint, disconcert, discourage, dishearten, disillusion, dismay, dispirit, distend, distress, disturb, dread, earbash, force, fret, frighten, goad, gravel, harass, hassle, horrify, intimidate, irk, irritate, motivate, nag, needle, nettle, niggle, nitpick, oblige, overdo, overextend, panic, pressure, pull, rattle, ruffle, scare, shake, shock, strain, stretch, tense, traumatize, trouble, unnerve, unsettle, upset, worry* (≠ allay, alleviate, amuse, appease, assist, assuage, calm, cure, cushion, delight, drug, ease, entertain, fix, gratify, help, humor, hypnotize, lull, mellow, mitigate, moderate, mollify, pacify, placate, please, referee, relax, relieve, remedy, satisfy, sedate, stupefy, sugarcoat, thrill, tranquilize, uplift, woo, wow)

STRETCH (→): *accentuate, amplify, attenuate, broaden, challenge, demand, drag, elongate, emphasize, enlarge, expand, extend, increase, lengthen, maximize, project, prolong, protract, push, reach, spread, stimulate, strain, tauten, tax, test, thin, tighten, try, unfold, unspool, widen* (≠ abbreviate, abridge, break, concentrate, condense, contract, crumble, curtail, cut, decrease, diminish, lessen, minimize, reduce, shorten, shrink, thicken)

STRIKE (→): *amaze, assault, astound, attack, backhand, bang, bat, batter, beat, belt, biff, box, break, bruise, buffet, bump, cane, castigate, charge, chastise, clobber, clock, clout, club, crash, crown, cudgel, cuff, cut, dash, hammer, hit, knock, know, lash, pelt, pound, punch, ram, rap, shake, sideswipe, slam, slap, slash, slog, slug, smack, sock, spank, stone, strap,* *stun, swat, swipe, tan, tap, thrash, thump, thwack, wallop, whack, wound* (≠ aid, assist, block, counter, counterpunch, cover, deflect, guard, help, miss, nurse, parry, protect, shield)

STRIKE (/): *abuse, ambush, assail, assault, attack, besiege, blindside, brutalize, bushwhack, charge, harm, hurt, injure, launch, push, ravage, rush, sandbag, smash, storm, strangle, thrash, victimize, wound, wrong* (≠ armor, assemble, barricade, blockade, build, -bypass, defend, -disregard, guard, help, -overlook, please, preserve, protect, secure, shelter, shield, skirt, support)

STRIP (←): *bare, bark, denude, disrobe, divest, expose, flay, peel, remove, shuck, skin, tear, unbuckle, unbutton, unclothe, uncover, undrape, undress, unmask, unveil* (≠ accoutre, apparel, arm, blanket, buckle, button, caparison, cloak, clothe, costume, cover, deck, drape, dress, equip, furnish, garb, gown, mantle, outfit, rig, robe, swaddle, swathe, tog, veil)

STRIP (←): *abate, bankrupt, beggar, bereave, burgle, cheat, clean, clear, defraud, deprive, despoil, disinherit, displace, dispossess, divest, empty, expose, gut, impoverish, lift, loot, pillage, plunder, ransack, ravage, remove, rob, shave, shortchange, spoil, unpack, withdraw* (≠ bankroll, capitalize, compensate, cover, defend, earn, endow, envelop, fill, finance, fund, recoup, replace, replenish, restore, stock, supply, underwrite)

STRIP (/): *clear, excoriate, flay, hull, husk, pare, peel, remove, rind, rip, scale, scalp, scour, scrape, shed, shuck, skin, tear, zest* (≠ bale, buffer, cocoon, cover, cushion, encase, envelop, package, sheathe, shield, shroud, wrap)

STRIP (/): *annihilate, bankrupt, beggar, decimate, deconstruct, demolish, deprive, destroy, detach, disarticulate, disassemble, disconnect, disjoin, disjoint, dismantle, dismember, disunite, divest, divide, fell, gut, level, raze, remove, ruin, separate, split, strike, subvert, topple, unsew, wrack, wreck* (≠ affix, assemble, build, combine, construct, craft, erect, fabricate, fashion, fasten, glue, machine, make, manufacture, pin, pitch, raise, sew, stitch, survive, sustain, unite, weather, weld, withstand)

STROKE (→): *baby, bounce, brush, caress, chuck, coddle, comfort, cradle, cuddle, dandle, embrace, enfold, fondle, gentle, hug, indulge, infantilize, knead, love, massage, mollycoddle, nestle, nuzzle, pamper, pat, paw, pet, rub, smooth, snuggle, soothe, spoil, spoon, tickle, touch* (≠ abuse, backhand, batter, beat, club, harm, hit, injure, maim, pain, punch, punish, shank, shiv, spank, stab, terrify, torment, whip, wrong)

STROKE (←): *adulate, applaud, blandish, blarney, butter, cajole, coax, commend, compliment, congratulate, court, endear, eulogize, extol, flannel, flatter, glad-hand, gratify, grease, hero-worship, honey, hustle, idolize, ingratiate, massage, oil, overpraise, palaver, persuade, praise, puff, romance, schmooze, soft-sell, soft-soap, sweet-talk, wheedle, woo, worship* (≠ afflict, anger, annoy, -avoid, badmouth, belittle, boo, decry, depreciate, disconnect, disparage, divide, enrage, humiliate, infuriate, insult, irritate, nag, needle, nettle, niggle, nitpick, separate, shame, torment, vex, worry)

STRONG-ARM (→): *abuse, affright, alarm, appall, assault, awe, badger, blackjack, blackmail, bleed, bludgeon, bluff, bogart, browbeat, brutalize, bulldoze, bully, bullyrag, coerce, compel, constrain, cow, daunt, demoralize, discompose, disconcert, dismay, disquiet, distress, disturb, dragoon, entreat, force, frighten, harass, hector, hijack, horrify, hound, implore, importune, intimidate, make, manhandle, mau-mau, menace, molest, muscle, nobble, oblige, oppress, perturb, petrify, press, pressure, push, railroad, ram, sandbag, scare, shock, spook, startle, terrify, terrorize, threaten, trash-talk, unman, unnerve, upset, violate, wrong* (≠ allow, amuse, assuage, bamboozle, bribe, cajole, calm, cheer, coax, comfort, con, console, convince, court, deceive, delight, embolden, encourage, entice, gratify, hearten, help, hint, humor, induce, influence, lubricate, lull, manipulate, mellow, mitigate, moderate, mollify, outmaneuver, outslick, outsmart, outwit, pacify, permit, persuade, placate, please, reassure, romance, scam, schmooze, soothe, steel, suggest, sway, swindle, tantalize, taunt, tease, tempt, trick, wheedle, woo)

STUDY (←): *analyze, appraise, ascertain, audition, brainstorm, calculate, caliper, canvass, case, categorize, check, clock, compare, compute, consult, contextualize, critique, decide, determine, discover, dissect, estimate, evaluate, examine, explore, eyeball, figure, gauge, inspect, investigate, judge, measure, numerate, observe, peg, peruse, prioritize, probe, prowl, pursue, research, review, sample, scan, scope, scrutinize, search, sift, solve, suss, test, time, vivisect* (≠ accept, assume, -blank, blind, blindfold, bury, -bypass, cloak, clothe, cloud, conceal, confound, confuse, deceive, demonstrate, disguise, dismiss, -disregard, explain, expose, fake, fudge, half-ass, hide, -ignore, illuminate, improvise, mask, miscalculate, misgauge, misplace, misread, mistake, mystify, -overlook, perplex, pooh-pooh, predetermine, pretend, puzzle, -reject, reveal, wing)

STUDY (←): *absorb, accept, apprehend, comprehend, con, digest, grasp, grok, know, learn, memorize, recall, recollect, relive, remember, retain, understand* (≠ -avoid, -disregard, forget, grade, -ignore, jumble, misremember, muddle, -neglect, -omit, -overlook, -slight, slur, unlearn)

STUDY (+): *absorb, analyze, apply, apprehend, ascertain, assimilate, believe, chew, coach, comprehend, con, conceive, conclude, consider, consult, contemplate, cram, debate, deduce, detect, determine, dig, digest, entertain, examine, explore, eye, find, grasp, grind, incorporate, integrate, internalize, interview, investigate, know, learn, memorize, mind, mull, plumb, ponder, profile, question, read, reason, reference, reinvestigate, research, rethink, review, revise, scan, scope, scrutinize, second-guess, survey, suss, train, turn, tutor, understand, weigh, wrestle* (≠ bomb, cheat, clarify, deceive, -discount, -disregard, edify, educate, flub, flunk, forget, -ignore, illuminate, instill, lose, mislead, miss, misunderstand, muff, -neglect, -overlook, school, -shirk, teach, trick, unlearn, wonder)

STUFF (→): *block, clog, compress, congest, constipate, cram, crowd, fill, force, jam, jam-pack, load, obstruct, occlude, overcrowd, overfill, overstuff, pack, pad, press, push, ram, sardine, shove, squeeze, stow, tamp, thrust, wad, wedge* (≠ clear, declutter, drain, empty, leach, loosen, offer, remove, unload, unpack, unstuff, vacate, void)

STUFF (←): *bolt, cram, devour, eat, glut, gobble, gorge, guzzle, ingest, inhale, nosh, overindulge, sate, satiate, scarf, swallow, wolf* (≠ belch, -decline, disgorge, expel, munch, nibble, -refuse, regurgitate, sample, sip, spew, spill, spit, taste, vomit)

STUMP (/): *baffle, bamboozle, befuddle, bemuse, bewilder, block, bother, cloud, confound, confuse, daze, defeat, disconcert, disturb, dumbfound, -elude, embarrass, faze, floor, flummox, foil, forestall, gaslight, -halt, harass, hobble, jumble, muddle, mystify, nonplus, obscure, outwit, perplex, puzzle, stir, stoke, stymie, tangle, throw, -thwart, trouble* (≠ aid, assist, clarify, describe, edify, educate, elucidate, encourage, enlighten, explain, help, illuminate, illustrate, reveal, school, show, simplify, solve, streamline, teach, train, tutor, uncomplicate, untangle)

STUN (→): *ambush, backhand, bang, bash, batter, beat, belt, blindside, bludgeon, buffet, bung, bushwhack, chop, clobber, clout, club, concuss, conk, cuff, daze, deaden, drub, hammer, hit, numb, paralyze, paste, pelt, pound, pummel, punch, rap, rock, slam, slap, slug, smack, smite, sock, strike, stupefy, swat, thump, thwack, torpefy, trap, wallop, waylay, whack, whale* (≠ armor, awaken, cover, defend, deflect, guard, parry, protect, resuscitate, revive, rouse, secure, shield, stir, wake)

STUN (/): *alarm, amaze, appall, arrest, astonish, astound, befuddle, bemuse, bewilder, blindside, boggle, bushwhack, confound, confuse, daze, dazzle, deafen, discomfit, disconcert, dismay, disturb, dumbfound, electrify, excite, flabbergast, floor, flummox, fluster, freeze, frighten, galvanize, gobsmack, immobilize, jar, jolt, muddle, nonplus, numb, overcome, overpower, overwhelm, paralyze, perplex, petrify, razzle-dazzle, rile, rock, sandbag, scare, shake, shock, spook, stagger, startle, strike, stupefy, surprise, thrill, torpefy, unnerve, unsettle, upset, wind, wow* (≠ anchor, anesthetize, anticipate, assuage, bore, calm, clarify, comfort, compose, deaden, distract, drain, encourage, enlighten, enliven, exhaust, expect, explain, hush, hypnotize, inspire, lull, mellow, mitigate, moderate, mollify, organize, pacify, placate, quell, quiet, relax, relieve, root, sedate, soothe, stabilize, steady, survive, tire, underwhelm, unruffle, vex, weary, withstand)

STUNT (/): *arrest, baffle, -balk, barricade, bind, block, blockade, bottleneck, brake, catch, chain, check, choke, clog, conclude, confine, constrain, cramp, cripple, curb, dam, defeat, delay, derail, detain, diminish, -discontinue, disrupt, dominate, domineer, downsize, dwarf, embarrass, encumber, end, fetter, foil, -frustrate, -halt, halter, hamper, hamstring, handcuff, handicap, hinder, hobble, hogtie, hold, impede, inhibit, leash, manacle, mire, muzzle, obstruct, oppress, overpower, rein, repress, restrain, restrict, retain, retard, roadblock, sabotage, scotch,* *shackle, short-circuit, shrink, slow, smother, squash, squelch, stagnate, stale, stall, staunch, stay, stem, stifle, still, stop, strangle, stump, stymie, suffocate, suppress, suspend, terminate, tether, -thwart, tie, trammel* (≠ accelerate, actuate, advance, aid, assist, augment, boost, brainstorm, budge, catalyze, clear, drive, encourage, enhance, enrich, expand, expedite, facilitate, forward, foster, free, further, goad, help, impel, improve, liberate, loosen, midwife, move, nourish, nurture, open, optimize, overhaul, prioritize, promote, propel, push, quicken, release, rush, smooth, spur, stir, unclog, unplug, unstop, untie)

STYMIE (←): *-abort, anticipate, arrest, -avert, -avoid, baffle, -balk, bamboozle, ban, banish, bar, barricade, bind, block, blockade, bog, boobytrap, bottleneck, brake, bung, burden, cage, catch, censor, chain, check, checkmate, chill, choke, -circumvent, clog, complicate, condemn, confine, confound, confuse, congest, constipate, constrain, cordon, counter, counteract, cramp, crimp, cripple, cross, curb, dam, damn, dampen, dash, daunt, deactivate, defeat, defy, delay, demotivate, depress, derail, detain, -deter, disadvantage, disallow, disappoint, discommode, discourage, dishearten, disincline, disqualify, disrupt, dissuade, -ditch, double-cross, drag, -elude, embargo, embarrass, encumber, enjoin, entangle, entrap, -exclude, -excommunicate, fetter, flummox, foil, -forbid, forestall, foul, freeze, -frustrate, -halt, halter, hamper, hamstring, handcuff, handicap, hem, hinder, hobble, hogtie, hold, impair, impede, inactivate, incapacitate, incommode, inconvenience, inhibit, intercept, interrupt, invalidate, jam, -kibosh, kneecap, knot, leash, limit, lumber, manacle, minimize, mire, monkey-wrench, muzzle, mystify, nonplus, obstruct, occlude, oppose, -ostracize, outlaw, outwit, overload, paralyze, parry, pause, plug, postpone, preempt, -prevent, -prohibit, proscribe, puzzle, redact, rein, repress, resist, restrain, restrict, retain, retard, roadblock, ruin, sabotage, scotch, scupper, shackle, shelve, short-circuit, skin, slow, smother, snag, snarl, snooker, spite, stagnate, stall, staunch, stay, stem, stifle, stop, straightjacket, strangle, stultify, stump, stunt, stymie, subvert, suffocate, suppress, taboo, tangle, tether, throttle, -thwart, tie, trammel, undercut, undermine, -veto, wing* (≠ accelerate, accent, accentuate, accommodate, accrue, advance, affirm, aid, allow, amplify, assert, assist, boost, brainstorm, catalyze, clear, compel, cultivate, decongest, disencumber, disentangle, ease, enable, encourage, expedite, extricate, facilitate, fast-forward, fast-track, foster, free, frog-march, fuel, further, grease, hasten, heal, help, hurry, improve, incite, instigate, legalize, liberate, loosen, lubricate, march, maximize, mend, midwife, nurture, oblige, open, optimize, overhaul, permit, prioritize, promote, prompt, propel, protect, push, quicken, release, relieve, remedy, rush, slack, slacken, smooth, spark, speed, spur, steady, stimulate, stir, stoke, strengthen, support, transact, transcend, trigger, unclog, uncomplicate, unleash, unlock, unstop, untangle, untie, urge)

SUBDUE (←): *break, bridle, cage, charm, chasten, chastise, check, contain, control, cow, curb, damp, daunt, deactivate, defeat, discipline, harness, humble, hush, leash, master, mellow, moderate, mortify, oppress,* *overcome, pacify, quash, quell, quiet, quieten, reduce, repress, restrain, silence, soften, soft-pedal, squelch, squench, starve, stifle, suppress, tame* (≠ advance, aggravate, boost, bug, encourage, exacerbate, exasperate, fast-forward, fast-track, foment, hasten, help, hurry, incite, instigate, intensify, prioritize, provoke, rabble-rouse, release, stir, trigger, trouble, unleash)

SUBDUE (/): *annihilate, beat, best, blitzkrieg, bomb, break, bury, cap, checkmate, clobber, conquer, cream, crush, decimate, defeat, demolish, desolate, destroy, devastate, dispatch, dominate, douse, drub, eclipse, enslave, exceed, exterminate, extinguish, finish, flatten, get, lick, lynch, master, nuke, obliterate, outdistance, outdo, outfight, outlast, outperform, outshine, outstrip, overcome, overpower, overrun, overthrow, overwhelm, pacify, quash, quell, quench, reduce, repress, rout, ruin, shellac, skin, skunk, slake, slaughter, smash, smoke, smother, snuff, squash, squelch, stifle, strangle, subject, subjugate, subordinate, suppress, surmount, surpass, sweep, take, thrash, throttle, top, transcend, trounce, unseat, upend, upset, vanquish, wallop, waste, whip, whup, wreck* (≠ advance, aid, assist, back, cultivate, discharge, emancipate, encourage, enfranchise, foment, forward, foster, free, further, help, incite, instigate, liberate, manumit, nourish, nurture, promote, prop, provoke, release, spring, stir, subvert, support, unbind, uncage, unchain, unfetter)

SUBJUGATE (/): *annihilate, beat, bind, break, bulldoze, bully, capture, checkmate, clobber, coerce, compel, conquer, crush, defeat, discipline, domesticate, dominate, drub, enslave, enthrall, force, gain, hogtie, housebreak, housetrain, indenture, lick, master, muscle, oppress, overcome, overpower, overthrow, pacify, quash, quell, railroad, reduce, repress, rout, rule, silence, skunk, smash, smother, snuff, squash, squelch, subdue, subject, subordinate, suppress, tame, thrash, trounce, vanquish, wallop, whip, wrack, wreck* (≠ -abandon, discharge, emancipate, enfranchise, follow, forfeit, free, liberate, manumit, mind, obey, rabble-rouse, release, resign, resist, spring, subvert, surrender, survive, tolerate, unbind, uncage, unchain, unfetter, weather, withstand, yield)

SUBMERGE (→): *bury, deluge, dip, douse, drench, drown, -duck, dunk, engulf, ensconce, flood, immerse, impregnate, inundate, overflow, overwhelm, plunge, sink, sound, souse, swamp* (≠ dehydrate, drain, dry, elevate, expose, express, float, grow, increase, lift, loose, parch, raise, release, reveal, soar, underwhelm, unleash, vent)

SUBMIT (→): *advance, advise, affirm, argue, assert, claim, commit, contend, float, introduce, move, offer, posit, prefer, present, propose, proposition, propound, refer, render, serve, spitball, state, suggest, table, tender, theorize, urge, volunteer* (≠ blackball, conceal, counter, -deny, discourage, dissuade, hide, -refuse, -reject, withdraw, withhold) **(¿) ABSTRACTION ALERT. Concrete goals essential!**

SUBORDINATE (/): *annihilate, beat, blackjack, bludgeon, boss, break, clobber, conquer, control, crush, decrease, defeat, deflate, denigrate, devalue, diminish, dismiss, disparage, dominate, drub, eclipse, enslave, hamper, intimidate, knock, lessen, lick, lower, master, minimize, outrank,* *overcome, overpower, override, overrule, overshadow, pacify, quash, quell, reduce, reevaluate, repress, rout, rule, silence, skunk, slam, slate, smash, smother, snuff, squash, squelch, subdue, subject, subjugate, suppress, thrash, trounce, trump, underemphasize, underrate, undervalue, vanquish, wallop, whip* (≠ accent, accentuate, accrue, affirm, aggrandize, amplify, assert, augment, boost, discharge, emancipate, emphasize, enfranchise, fetishize, free, heighten, increase, inflate, liberate, manumit, overestimate, overrate, overvalue, prioritize, promote, punctuate, raise, release, spring, subvert, swell, unbind, uncage, unchain, unfetter, upgrade)

SUBSTANTIATE (+): *actualize, affirm, approve, argue, assert, attest, authenticate, avow, certify, concretize, confirm, consult, contextualize, corroborate, crosscheck, cross-examine, debunk, declare, demonstrate, document, ensure, establish, evidence, grill, guarantee, incarnate, interrogate, interview, justify, manifest, materialize, notarize, objectify, personify, profess, prove, ratify, realize, reify, reinforce, show, support, suss, sustain, test, testify, uphold, validate, verify, vindicate, warrant, witness* (≠ break, challenge, cheat, con, confute, contest, contradict, debate, debunk, defraud, -deny, disavow, disclaim, discredit, disprove, dispute, distrust, doubt, fake, gainsay, invalidate, mislead, pretend, question, rebut, refute, scam, scruple, sucker, swindle)

SUBTRACT (/): *abate, abbreviate, abridge, clip, crop, curtail, cut, debit, decrease, deduct, deep-six, detract, diminish, discount, divide, dock, downsize, eliminate, lessen, lower, minimize, pare, prune, reduce, remove, retrench, shorten, shrink, slash, take, trim, truncate, whittle, withdraw, withhold* (≠ accrue, add, aggrandize, amplify, annex, append, augment, boost, broaden, complement, compound, double, enhance, enlarge, escalate, expand, extend, heighten, increase, intensify, magnify, maximize, multiply, supplement, tack, treble, triple)

SUBVERT (/): *belie, capsize, checkmate, confound, confute, contradict, contravene, counter, counteract, counterpunch, defeat, demolish, demoralize, -deny, depress, destroy, dismantle, disobey, disprove, -disregard, disrupt, dominate, doom, extinguish, gaslight, invalidate, invert, level, monkey-wrench, -negate, oppose, overthrow, overturn, parry, raze, rebut, refute, retrain, reverse, ruin, sabotage, scotch, scupper, shelve, supersede, supplant, suppress, topple, tumble, undermine, unhorse, unman, unseat, upset, usurp, vitiate, wreck* (≠ back, boost, brainwash, choreograph, consecrate, convince, crown, defend, dignify, enthrone, establish, feature, follow, found, guard, highlight, inaugurate, insist, institute, maintain, mind, obey, optimize, orchestrate, ordain, overhaul, preserve, prioritize, protect, repair, respect, second, select, sustain, uphold)

SUBVERT (/): *abase, bastardize, befoul, begrime, bestialize, blemish, cheapen, contaminate, corrupt, damage, debase, debauch, deface,* *defile, degrade, demean, demoralize, deprave, depreciate, destroy, deteriorate, dilute, dirty, disgrace, dishonor, downgrade, flaw, harm, humble, humiliate, hurt, impair, lessen, mar, mutate, nobble, pervert, poison, pollute, profane, prostitute, ruin, shame, spoil, stain, taint, tarnish, vitiate, warp, weaken, wreck* (≠ align, amend, better, clarify, clean, cleanse, decontaminate, dignify, elevate, enhance, ennoble, enrich, exalt, expiate, honor, improve, moralize, optimize, overhaul, perfect, purify, refine, respect, restore, uplift)

SUCK (←): *absorb, bleed, drain, draw, drink, empty, exhaust, exploit, express, extract, gulp, guzzle, hoover, imbibe, leach, leech, milk, press, pull, pump, quaff, remove, sap, sip, siphon, slurp, sponge, squeeze, suckle, swallow, swig, swill, tap, use, vacuum, withdraw, wring* (≠ bottle-feed, feed, fill, fuel, furnish, inject, load, plug, replace, replenish, restore, satisfy, soak, supply)

SUCKLE (+): *bottle-feed, breastfeed, coddle, cradle, feed, fill, fuel, nourish, nurse, nurture, victual, wet-nurse* (≠ -deny, deprive, -halt, malnourish, -neglect, scant, skimp, starve, stint, wean, withhold)

SUE (←): *accuse, appeal, beg, beseech, charge, claim, contest, demand, enjoin, entreat, exact, file, indict, invite, invoke, litigate, petition, plead, prosecute, request, require, requisition, seek, solicit, summon, urge* (≠ acquit, alibi, condone, defend, discharge, excuse, exonerate, forgive, judge, -overlook, pardon, prove, release, represent, spare, vindicate)

SUFFER (+): *abide, accept, accord, admit, allow, assimilate, authorize, bear, brave, brook, commission, concede, condone, countenance, digest, endure, experience, face, grant, greenlight, harden, incur, indulge, know, license, outlast, overcome, permit, receive, sanction, season, stand, stomach, support, surmount, survive, sustain, swallow, sweat, take, taste, tolerate, vouchsafe, warrant, weather, withstand, witness* (≠ ban, bar, begrudge, block, censure, check, curb, -deny, deplore, -deter, disallow, disapprove, disfavor, -dodge, embrace, enjoin, enjoy, -exclude, fight, -forbid, hinder, impede, -interdict, keep, obstruct, oppose, oust, -prevent, -prohibit, proscribe, protest, -refuse, -reject, repel, repress, resist, restrain, revoke, stem, stop, suppress, -veto, withhold)

SUFFOCATE (/): *asphyxiate, bar, block, burke, check, choke, clog, close, confine, constrict, control, curb, dampen, daunt, demotivate, depress, -deter, discourage, dissuade, endanger, extinguish, -frustrate, gag, garrote, hamper, hinder, hush, impede, imperil, inhibit, kill, limit, lynch, muffle, murder, mute, muzzle, obstruct, overpower, overwhelm, paralyze, plug, quash, quiet, repress, restrain, shush, silence, smoke, smother, squeeze, squelch, stifle, stop, strangle, stymie, subdue, suppress, throttle, wring* (≠ aerate, clear, encourage, evince, express, free, heal, help, inspire, loose, nurture, open, oxygenate, reinvigorate, release, restimulate, restore, resuscitate, revive, unclog, unseal, vent, ventilate)

SUFFUSE (→): *bathe, charge, color, cover, douse, drench, drown, fill, flood, imbue, immerse, implant, infiltrate, infuse, interpenetrate, inundate,* *macerate, mantle, marinate, moisten, penetrate, perfume, permeate, pervade, pigment, presoak, satisfy, saturate, scent, soak, sop, souse, spread, steep, submerge, swamp, swill, transfuse, wash, water* (≠ clear, close, dehydrate, deplete, deprive, desiccate, divest, drain, dry, eliminate, empty, extract, leach, parch, remove, strip, void, withdraw, wring) **(¿) ABSTRACTION ALERT. Concrete goals essential!**

SUGAR (→): *alleviate, appease, assuage, blandish, cajole, candy, candy-coat, cushion, dulcify, ease, flannel, flatter, gratify, grease, harmonize, honey, ingratiate, mellow, mitigate, mollify, oil, pacify, palaver, placate, propitiate, relieve, schmooze, soften, soothe, spin, sugarcoat, sweeten, syrup, temper* (≠ alienate, annoy, bother, bug, disaffect, displease, disrupt, embitter, irk, malign, salt, sour, traumatize, trouble, worry, wrong)

SUGGEST (→): *admonish, advance, advise, advocate, affirm, brief, broach, caution, commend, condone, conjecture, counsel, countenance, direct, encourage, endorse, envisage, exhort, float, forward, goad, greenlight, guide, inform, insist, instruct, move, nominate, notify, offer, plug, pose, prefer, present, press, prompt, propose, proposition, push, recommend, spitball, spur, steer, submit, table, tender, theorize, tip, tout, urge, validate, volunteer, vote, warn* (≠ block, bury, command, conceal, condemn, cover, criticize, demand, denounce, -deny, discourage, -halt, hide, hush, oppose, order, pooh-pooh, -refuse, -reject, stifle, suppress, withdraw, withhold) **(¿) ABSTRACTION ALERT. Concrete goals essential!**

SUGGEST (→): *allege, allude, conjure, connote, couch, evoke, hint, imply, infer, insinuate, intimate, promise, prompt, represent, savor, shadow, signify* (≠ announce, declare, delineate, demand, describe, dictate, explain, proclaim, profile, specify) **(¿) ABSTRACTION ALERT. Concrete goals essential!**

SULLY (/): *abase, adulterate, bastardize, bedraggle, besmear, besmirch, bestialize, blacken, blackguard, blemish, blight, blot, callous, coarsen, compromise, contaminate, corrupt, damage, debase, debauch, defame, defile, degrade, demean, demote, deprave, desecrate, devalue, diminish, dirty, disgrace, dishonor, foul, harm, humble, humiliate, infect, injure, insult, libel, lower, malign, mortify, muddy, offend, outrage, poison, pollute, reduce, ridicule, ruin, shame, slander, -slight, smear, -snub, soil, spike, spoil, stain, suborn, taint, tarnish, trample, violate, vulgarize* (≠ acclaim, admire, brush, cherish, clean, cleanse, decontaminate, delouse, dignify, disinfect, filter, honor, launder, polish, praise, purge, purify, rarefy, refine, rinse, sanitize, scour, scrub, shine, upgrade, wash)

SUMMON (←): *amass, arouse, ask, assemble, beckon, bid, buzz, call, challenge, charge, cite, collect, command, conjure, convene, convoke, demand, direct, draft, educe, elicit, enjoin, evoke, gather, group, hail, herd, invite, invoke, mobilize, muster, order, page, petition, provoke, raise, rally, recall, recollect, request, requisition, ring, rouse, sign, signal, subpoena* (≠ ban, banish, bar, blackball, block, boot, discharge, dismiss, dissolve, eject, exorcise, expel, free, -ostracize, oust, release, remove, repel, repulse, rout, send)

SUNDER (/): *bisect, break, chop, chunk, cleave, cut, detach, disassociate, disconnect, disengage, disentangle, disintegrate, disjoin, disjoint, dissect, dissolve, disunite, divide, divorce, estrange, fracture, halve, insulate, isolate, orphan, oust, part, partition, pull, quarter, razor, rend, resolve, rip, rive, rupture, seclude, segment, segregate, separate, sequester, sever, slice, split, subdivide, tear, uncouple, unlink, unravel, untie, unyoke, vivisect* (≠ accumulate, annex, assemble, associate, attach, bind, blend, cement, churn, cinch, close, combine, connect, couple, fasten, fuse, integrate, join, jumble, knit, link, meld, mingle, mix, mortar, reintegrate, return, reunite, scramble, stick, unify, unite, weld)

SUPERVISE (→): *administer, arbitrate, boss, captain, chair, chaperone, command, conduct, control, determine, direct, edit, govern, guard, guide, handle, inspect, keep, lead, manage, micromanage, mind, monitor, nanny, observe, operate, order, organize, oversee, patrol, pilot, proctor, protect, quarterback, referee, regiment, regulate, rule, run, safeguard, settle, shepherd, show, stage-manage, steer, steward, superintend, survey, tend, umpire, watch* (≠ -abandon, challenge, contradict, debate, -deny, -disregard, follow, forget, heed, -ignore, mind, mismanage, misrule, miss, -neglect, note, obey, oppose, -overlook, -refuse, respect, serve)

SUPPLANT (→): *bounce, crowd, displace, eject, expel, force, oust, overthrow, preempt, relieve, remove, replace, ring, substitute, succeed, supersede, topple, transfer, undermine, unman, unseat, usurp* (≠ authorize, cherish, defend, establish, gentrify, preserve, promote, reinstate, renew, restore, support, survive, sustain)

SUPPLY (→): *accoutre, afford, allocate, allot, apportion, arm, assign, bestow, bootleg, budget, cater, commodify, comp, contribute, deal, deliver, dispense, distribute, dole, dollop, donate, dower, drop, earmark, endow, equip, feed, fill, find, fit, fortify, fuel, fulfill, furnish, gird, give, grant, gratify, hand, mete, outfit, parcel, portion, prepare, present, produce, prorate, provide, provision, remainder, replenish, rig, satisfy, sell, source, stake, stock, store, tender, tithe, transfer, victual, yield* (≠ cannibalize, commandeer, confiscate, consume, cripple, demand, -deny, deplete, depredate, deprive, disarm, dispossess, divest, drain, empty, exhaust, grab, hold, impound, keep, leach, poach, pocket, -refuse, remove, reserve, rob, scant, scrimp, seize, skimp, snag, steal, stint, strip, suppress, swipe, take, tap, unload, unpack, withhold)

SUPPORT (→): *back, bankroll, bequeath, capitalize, deliver, donate, endow, equip, finance, fund, furnish, grant, greenlight, hand, keep, kindle, maintain, patronize, promote, prop, provide, secure, sponsor, stake, subsidize, succor, supply, sustain, underwrite, upgrade* (≠ bankrupt, beggar, defalcate, defund, disinherit, -disown, embezzle, impoverish, -neglect, obstruct, ruin, swindle)

SUPPORT (←): *anchor, back, base, bear, beef, bolster, brace, buffer, build, bulwark, buoy, buttress, carry, cover, cradle, defend, embattle, embed, entrench, fence, fix, fortify, found, garrison, gird, ground, guard, harden, hold, patch, pillow, poise, prepare, prop, rampart, ready, reinforce, safeguard, secure, shore, shoulder, stabilize, stand, stay, steady, steel, stiffen, strengthen, strut, sustain, temper, toughen, truss, undergird, underpin, uphold, wall* (≠ agitate, attack, boobytrap, breach, break, burden, canker, compromise, convulse, corrode, corrupt, crack, damage, destabilize, destroy, doom, drop, endanger, erode, fail, forget, harm, hurt, -ignore, imperil, injure, loosen, lumber, mar, melt, monkey-wrench, -neglect, rattle, release, roil, sabotage, scuttle, shake, short-circuit, soften, subvert, threaten, undercut, undermine, weaken)

SUPPORT (+): *abet, accept, advance, advocate, affirm, aid, approve, assert, assist, assure, attest, authenticate, authorize, back, bolster, boost, brook, carry, certify, champion, cheer, claim, comfort, condone, confirm, contend, corroborate, countenance, crosscheck, declare, defend, document, endorse, energize, espouse, establish, express, forward, foster, further, greenlight, help, hold, justify, legalize, maintain, optimize, overhaul, pledge, prioritize, proclaim, profess, promise, promote, propound, prove, ratify, recommend, rubber-stamp, sanction, second, sponsor, state, submit, substantiate, sustain, testify, tolerate, uphold, validate, verify, vindicate, warrant* (≠ annul, block, challenge, contest, contradict, counteract, cross-examine, debate, -deny, disapprove, disavow, disclaim, discredit, -disown, disprove, dispute, doubt, gainsay, grill, hamper, interrogate, invalidate, oppose, -prevent, question, rebut, -refuse, refute, -reject, -repudiate)

SUPPORT (+): *abet, aid, assist, attend, befriend, benefit, boost, buoy, chaperone, cherish, comfort, commend, defend, empower, encourage, energize, enliven, facilitate, favor, feed, fortify, foster, fuel, further, guard, help, inspire, invigorate, kindle, lift, maintain, mother, motivate, nourish, nurse, nurture, optimize, overhaul, preserve, prioritize, promote, prop, protect, provoke, raise, reinforce, relieve, restimulate, revive, save, secure, serve, shield, spur, stiffen, strengthen, stroke, succor, sustain, tend, upgrade, uphold* (≠ block, checkmate, counteract, damage, discourage, discredit, disfavor, disgrace, dissuade, foil, -frustrate, hamper, hamstring, harm, hinder, hurt, -ignore, injure, monkey-wrench, muzzle, -neglect, obstruct, oppose, override, -refuse, -reject, resist, sabotage, scotch, scupper, scuttle, shelve, -shun, -snub, subvert, -thwart, undermine, withstand)

SUPPRESS (/): *abolish, abuse, arrest, ban, block, bottle, burke, -cancel, censor, check, choke, clamp, conceal, contain, control, crush, curb, cushion, deaden, demotivate, -deter, devoice, discourage, extinguish, gag, hamper, hamstring, hinder, hush, impair, incapacitate, inhibit, interrupt, -kibosh, mince, muffle, muzzle, obstruct, oppress, overcome, overpower, overthrow, -prevent, quash, quell, quench, quiet, redact, repress, restrain, restrict, shush, silence, sink, smother, squash, squelch, stifle, still, stop, strangle, stultify, stymie, subdue, subjugate, submerge,* *subvert, taboo, throttle, -thwart, trample, tyrannize, vanquish, withhold, wrong* (≠ activate, add, advance, aid, authorize, back, boost, dish, encourage, endorse, enhance, foment, greenlight, help, incite, inspire, instigate, legalize, liberate, optimize, overhaul, praise, prioritize, promote, provoke, rabble-rouse, reinvigorate, release, renew, repair, restore, revive, revolutionize, rouse, rumor, sanction, spread, spur, stimulate, stir, support, tantalize, tease, tempt, trigger, uphold, urge)

SURF (→): *ascend, brave, conquer, dominate, endure, face, handle, manage, maneuver, manipulate, master, mount, navigate, negotiate, outlast, overcome, ride, rule, subdue, survive, tackle, tame, tolerate, use, weather, withstand, wrestle* (≠ attack, battle, block, -bypass, -circumvent, combat, debate, defy, -dodge, -duck, fight, -ignore, leave, oppose, resist, stop)

SURFACE (+): *armor, asphalt, blanket, bronze, cake, canopy, carpet, caulk, cement, cloak, coat, concrete, cover, curtain, daub, deck, decorate, drape, dust, electroplate, enamel, encase, enfold, enshroud, envelop, face, flag, floor, gild, glaze, ice, japan, lacquer, layer, mantle, overlay, paint, palliate, panel, paper, pave, plaster, plate, render, resurface, roughcast, seal, shellac, shield, shroud, size, spackle, spread, stucco, sugarcoat, swathe, tar, thatch, tile, turf, upholster, veil, wallpaper, wax, whitewash, wrap* (≠ bare, burnish, callous, coarsen, crack, denude, excoriate, expose, flay, fleece, graze, husk, peel, pierce, polish, remove, reveal, scalp, scorch, scour, scrape, scrub, shine, shred, shuck, skin, strip, tatter, uncover)

SURPASS (→): *beat, best, better, checkmate, clobber, conquer, crush, defeat, drub, eclipse, exceed, lap, leave, lick, lose, master, one-up, outclass, outdistance, outdo, outgun, outlast, outpace, outrank, outreach, outrun, outsell, outshine, outstrip, outthink, outweigh, overcome, overshadow, overtake, pass, rout, shame, skunk, subdue, surmount, thrash, top, topple, transcend, trim, trounce, trump, wallop, whip* (≠ -abandon, cede, concede, defer, fail, forfeit, -forsake, lose, miss, -neglect, -omit, -overlook, relinquish, -renounce, sacrifice, skip, support)

SURPRISE (→): *agitate, alarm, amaze, appall, astonish, astound, awe, baffle, befuddle, bewilder, blindside, boggle, bushwhack, confound, confuse, consternate, daze, dazzle, deafen, discombobulate, discomfit, disconcert, disgust, dismay, distress, disturb, dumbfound, electrify, excite, flabbergast, floor, flummox, fluster, frighten, galvanize, gaslight, gobsmack, horrify, invigorate, jar, jolt, muckrake, muddle, nauseate, nonplus, numb, offend, outrage, overwhelm, panic, paralyze, perplex, petrify, rattle, razzle-dazzle, repel, revolt, rile, rock, roil, rouse, scandalize, scare, shake, shock, sicken, stagger, startle, stir, stump, stun, stupefy, terrify, thrill, throw, traumatize, trigger, unnerve, unsettle, upset, wow* (≠ anchor, annoy, anticipate, appease, assure, balance, blunt, bore, buffer, calm, caution, center, charm, cheer, clarify, comfort, compose, console, cushion, dampen, deaden, delight, -disregard, dull, elucidate, embolden, encourage, entice, expect, explain, follow, forecast, foretell, gratify, hearten, help, hypnotize, -ignore, jade, lull, mellow, mesmerize, mind, miss, mitigate, moderate, mollify, numb, obey, orchestrate, organize, outguess, -overlook, pacify, placate, please, predetermine, predict, quiet, reassure, regiment, regret, relax, remind, sedate, signal, soothe, stabilize, steady, steel, stultify, tantalize, tease, tempt, threaten, tranquilize, warn, weary) **(¿) ABSTRACTION ALERT. Concrete goals essential!**

SURPRISE (→): *accost, ambush, arrest, assail, assault, attack, blindside, bushwhack, buttonhole, capture, catch, charge, checkmate, corner, ensnare, entrap, hunt, intercept, jump, mousetrap, mug, net, sabotage, sandbag, seize, snare, spring, stalk, storm, strike, tackle, trap, waylay* (≠ announce, anticipate, await, -circumvent, -elude, -evade, expect, foresee, intercept, outguess, -preclude, predict, preempt, -prevent, second-guess, -sidestep)

SURRENDER (→): *-abandon, abnegate, bequeath, bestow, cede, chuck, commit, concede, consign, deliver, -desert, discard, -ditch, drop, dump, entrust, forfeit, -forsake, give, hand, offload, release, relinquish, render, -renounce, -repudiate, resign, sacrifice, shed, submit, transfer, waive, yield* (≠ adopt, archive, cache, claim, conserve, defend, hoard, hold, keep, maintain, pickle, preserve, protect, reserve, resist, retain, seek, stash, store, stow, tuck, withhold)

SURRENDER (/): *-abandon, abdicate, abjure, cede, concede, -deny, -desert, disavow, disclaim, -disown, -forsake, hand, -quit, relinquish, -renounce, resign, survive, vacate, waive, yield* (≠ appropriate, arrogate, assume, claim, confiscate, defend, guard, protect, safeguard, secure, seize, usurp, wrest)

SURROUND (←): *abut, belt, beset, besiege, blockade, border, bound, box, cage, circle, circumscribe, -circumvent, compass, confine, contain, cordon, corner, corral, cover, delimit, edge, embrace, encase, encircle, enclose, encompass, enfold, engulf, entrench, envelop, fence, flank, fringe, gird, girdle, hem, herd, hold, hug, impound, imprison, inundate, invest, limit, loop, margin, orbit, outline, package, rim, ring, round, skirt, swarm, trap, wall, wrangle, wrap, wreathe* (≠ -abandon, allow, -avoid, center, expel, expose, -forsake, free, -ignore, invade, lose, occupy, -omit, open, outlast, peel, penetrate, permit, pierce, release, shuck, -shun, -sidestep, strip, uncover)

SURVEY (←): *analyze, appraise, audit, benchmark, calculate, calibrate, case, check, climb, clock, comb, compare, compute, con, consider, contemplate, critique, detect, determine, dissect, estimate, evaluate, examine, explore, inspect, investigate, judge, learn, measure, notice, observe, oversee, parse, peruse, plan, plumb, poll, probe, prospect, prowl, quantify, quantize, rank, rate, read, reconnoiter, reference, research, review, sample, scale, scan, scope, score, scrutinize, size, spy, study, summarize, supervise, suss, test, time, triangulate, valuate, verify, view, watch* (≠ assume, blind, blindfold, browse, bury, -bypass, cloak, clothe, cloud, conceal, disguise, -disregard, doctor, embellish, embroider, falsify, fiddle, fudge, garble, guess, guesstimate, hide, -ignore, manipulate, mask, massage, misrepresent, miss, mistake, muddy, mystify, -neglect, -overlook, pass, perplex, puzzle, riffle, skim, skip)

SURVEY (←): *ask, canvass, catechize, challenge, consult, contemplate, cross-examine, debate, dispute, examine, explore, grill, interpolate, interrogate, interview, investigate, poll, probe, query, question, quiz, seek, solicit* (≠ analyze, answer, debrief, declare, -disregard, forget, -ignore, learn, miss, -neglect, -overlook, present, report, study)

SURVIVE (+): *abide, accept, allow, bear, brave, brook, confront, continue, countenance, endure, face, indulge, know, outlast, outlive, overcome, permit, receive, ride, sanction, shoulder, stand, stomach, suffer, support, surmount, swallow, sweat, take, tolerate, weather, withstand* (≠ -avoid, -bypass, cease, depart, -deter, -ditch, -dodge, -duck, end, -escape, -eschew, fail, -flee, foil, -ignore, miss, -preclude, -prevent, -reject, -sidestep, spoil, stop, -thwart)

SUSPECT (+): *anticipate, assume, await, believe, conceive, conclude, conjecture, deduce, dread, expect, fancy, fear, feel, gather, guess, hypothesize, imagine, infer, judge, presume, profile, reckon, suppose, surmise, suss, take, theorize, think, understand, wonder* (≠ adjudge, ascertain, deduce, demonstrate, determine, discover, document, establish, learn, observe, prove, substantiate, validate, verify) **(¿) ABSTRACTION ALERT. Concrete goals essential!**

SUSPECT (/): *accuse, attaint, believe, blame, challenge, charge, cite, cross-examine, debate, disbelieve, -discount, discredit, dispute, distrust, doubt, fault, finger, gainsay, grill, impeach, implicate, interrogate, interview, involve, mistrust, -negate, question, refute, scruple* (≠ accept, attest, clear, consult, credit, crosscheck, discover, disprove, ensure, frame, guarantee, know, prove, trust, verify, warrant, witness)

SUSPEND (+): *append, attach, balance, dangle, drape, extend, festoon, garland, hang, hook, mount, pin, poise, project, sling, stick, string, swing, tack, unspool, wave* (≠ cut, drop, elevate, jerk, lift, lose, pull, raise, remove, retract, strip, tear, tug, wrench, yank)

SUSPEND (/): *-abort, abrogate, adjourn, annul, -blank, call, close, conclude, defer, depose, dethrone, disband, disbar, -discontinue, dismiss, disperse, dissolve, drop, end, -exclude, exile, expel, ground, -halt, interrupt, invalidate, -negate, -nullify, -ostracize, oust, postpone, quash, recall, recess, remove, repeal, -rescind, reserve, revoke, sack, shelve, stop, table, terminate, unfrock, -void, wrap* (≠ assemble, brainstorm, call, continue, convene, convoke, extend, inaugurate, launch, muster, nominate, open, prolong, rally, renew, reopen, resume, summon)

SUSTAIN (→): *board, cater, cloy, feed, fill, fortify, fuel, furnish, nourish, nurse, nurture, provide, provision, ration, replenish, sate, satiate, satisfy, strengthen, suckle, supply, surfeit, victual* (≠ appropriate, burgle, confiscate, -deny, deprive, dispossess, divest, famish, malnourish, -refuse, rob, starve, steal, strip, underfeed, withhold)

SUSTAIN (←): *abide, absorb, accept, allow, assimilate, bear, brave, brook, countenance, digest, endure, experience, face, feel, hack, handle, know, meet, pass, permit, pocket, receive, respect, see, stand, stomach, suffer, support, swallow, sweat, take, taste, tolerate, weather, witness* (≠ -avoid, -bypass, -circumvent, combat, contest, -decline, dismiss, -dodge, -elude, -escape, -evade, fight, miss, oppose, -refuse, -reject, -repudiate, resist, -spurn)

SUSTAIN (+): *aid, assist, augment, back, bear, bolster, brace, buoy, buttress, carry, comfort, delay, elongate, embolden, encourage, endorse, extend, foster, gestate, help, hold, increase, invigorate, lengthen, maintain, maximize, prolong, prop, protract, provide, reassure, recommend, relieve, stand, stay, steady, stretch, support, truss, undergird, underpin, uphold* (≠ abbreviate, -abort, abridge, accelerate, circumvent, combat, compress, contradict, curtail, -cut, decrease, diminish, drop, lessen, minimize, -negate, oppose, reduce, -refuse, resist, shorten, -spurn)

SWALLOW (←): *absorb, accept, assimilate, await, believe, consume, devour, dispatch, down, drink, eat, enfold, engulf, envelop, expect, gobble, gorge, gulp, guzzle, imbibe, incorporate, ingest, inhale, quaff, sip, slurp, swig, swill, take, trust, wolf* (≠ assemble, belch, brew, concoct, cook, create, -decline, disgorge, eject, excrete, expel, hunt, make, offer, prepare, -refuse, regurgitate, -reject, spew, spit, splutter, -spurn, steep, vomit)

SWAMP (→): *avalanche, besiege, consume, deluge, douse, drench, drown, engulf, envelop, flood, flush, gush, inundate, marinate, mire, overcome, overflow, overload, overrun, overwhelm, pour, saturate, sink, sluice, smother, soak, splatter, spout, submerge, syrup, wet* (≠ -abandon, dehydrate, desiccate, diffuse, drain, drizzle, dry, empty, leach, liberate, outlast, parch, rescue, scatter, scorch, sear, staunch, towel, trickle)

SWAT (→): *backhand, bash, bat, beat, belt, biff, blow, bop, box, buffet, bump, clip, clobber, clock, clout, conk, cuff, ding, hit, knock, lash, lick, paste, punch, rap, slap, slog, slug, smack, smash, smite, sock, spank, strike, swipe, thwack, wallop, whack* (≠ -avert, block, coddle, counter-punch, defend, deflect, -dodge, -duck, guard, miss, parry, protect, repel, shield, soothe, tap)

SWAY (←): *affect, afflict, agitate, allure, attract, bewitch, bias, bother, bribe, cajole, captivate, charm, coax, coerce, color, con, concern, convert, convince, dazzle, deceive, direct, discomfort, discompose, disquiet, distress, disturb, dominate, enchant, engage, enrapture, enthrall, entrance, fascinate, fluster, govern, harass, harry, impact, impress, induce, influence, inspire, interest, inveigle, involve, move, nudge, override, overrule, palaver, penetrate, persuade, perturb, pester, pierce, plague, predetermine, prejudge, prejudice, prompt, ravish, reach, rule, scam, schmooze, smite, stir, strain, stress, strike, sucker, taint, tantalize, tarnish, taunt, tease, tempt, touch, transport, trick, trouble, try, upset, wheedle, worry, wring* (≠ -avoid, bore, bully, coerce, command, compel, daunt, demand, demotivate, -deter, discourage, dissuade, dragoon, force, frighten, hamper, hinder, hobble, jade, muscle, nobble, oppress, overpower, overwhelm, railroad, restrain, stall, stymie, subvert, terrorize, -thwart, tire, underwhelm, weary)

SWEAR (+): *accede, affirm, assert, attest, avow, betroth, contract, convince, covenant, declare, depose, engage, ensure, forswear, guarantee, insist, maintain, pledge, promise, prove, testify, trust, undertake, verify, vow, warrant, witness* (≠ break, condemn, contradict, contravene, debate, deceive, -deny, discredit, disprove, dispute, distrust, double-talk, doubt, gainsay, invalidate, mistrust, oppose, refute, -renounce, -repudiate, retract, scruple, suspect, waive) **(¿) ABSTRACTION ALERT. Concrete goals essential!**

SWEETEN (→): *alleviate, ameliorate, appease, assuage, candy, cushion, ease, embellish, enhance, enrich, flavor, honey, improve, magnify, marinate, maximize, mellow, mitigate, mollify, optimize, overhaul, pacify, placate, propitiate, relieve, season, soften, soothe, spice, temper, thaw* (≠ acidify, alienate, bug, canker, disaffect, displease, embitter, envenom, exacerbate, exasperate, isolate, offend, poison, repel, sour, spike, spoil, taint, tarnish, trouble)

SWEET-TALK (←): *beg, beguile, beseech, blandish, blarney, bribe, bullshit, butter, cajole, charm, coax, con, convince, court, cozen, diddle, dupe, enchant, entice, euchre, finagle, flannel, flatter, glad-hand, gratify, grease, honey, humbug, humor, importune, inveigle, jolly, juggle, leverage, lure, manipulate, massage, mislead, nudge, oil, outsmart, outwit, palaver, persuade, salve, schmooze, seduce, sell, serenade, snooker, snow, soften, soft-sell, soft-soap, soothe, stroke, sucker, sway, tantalize, tease, tempt, urge, wangle, wheedle, woo* (≠ accuse, blackjack, blackmail, bludgeon, browbeat, bug, bulldoze, bully, chide, coerce, command, compel, condemn, constrain, cow, criticize, daunt, demand, force, harass, hassle, intimidate, irritate, knock, make, menace, muscle, nag, nobble, noodge, oblige, offend, outrage, pester, -prevent, railroad, repel, require, sandbag, scold, slam, slate, tease, trash-talk, traumatize, victimize, wound, wrong)

SWINDLE (←): *bamboozle, beguile, betray, bilk, blackmail, bleed, bluff, burn, cajole, cheat, chisel, clip, con, convince, cozen, deceive, defraud, delude, diddle, double-cross, double-deal, dupe, embezzle, euchre, exploit, extort, fake, fast-talk, fiddle, finagle, finesse, fleece, flimflam, fool, fox, fudge, gazump, goldbrick, gouge, gull, hoax, hoodwink, hornswoggle, hustle, manipulate, milk, mislead, mulct, nick, outwit, overcharge, peculate, pretend, rob, rook, rope, sandbag, scam, screw, shaft, short, shortchange, shuck, skin, snooker, snow, soak, squeeze, stick, stiff, sting, sucker, trick, underpay, victimize, wrench, wrest, wring, wrong* (≠ accuse, afford, assume, audit, authenticate, bankroll, believe, confess, corroborate, disabuse, discredit, disgrace, dispute, document, donate, doubt, earn, evince, expose, fund, give, indemnify, malign, offer, pillory, protect, provide, refund, regret, reimburse, repay, respect, restore, reveal, shame, stigmatize, substantiate, supply, support, trust, verify)

SWING (→): *bend, circle, circulate, coil, corner, crank, curve, dial, incline, loop, manipulate, negotiate, orbit, oscillate, pass, pivot, reel, revolve, roll, rotate, round, screw, shunt, spin, sway, swirl, swivel, turn, twiddle, twirl, twist, unscrew, weave, wheel, whip, whirl, wind* (≠ bind, correct, direct, fasten, freeze, hobble, hold, level, lock, nail, paralyze, pin, smooth, stabilize, steady, stop, straighten, tie, unbend)

SWING (→): *acquire, afford, back, bankroll, bid, capitalize, contribute, cover, defray, endow, expend, facilitate, finance, float, foot, fuel, furnish, grant, guarantee, lend, loan, obtain, offer, outlay, patronize, pay, pony, procure, proffer, provide, purchase, secure, sponsor, stake, stand, subsidize, supply, support, sustain, take, underwrite* (≠ bankrupt, borrow, cadge, consume, cost, defund, demand, -deny, deplete, deprive, disappoint, drain, earn, exhaust, exploit, foil, -frustrate, hinder, leech, -neglect, pauperize, -refuse, request, ruin, sabotage, sap, scant, scotch, scupper, shelve, skimp, squander, stiff, stint, straiten, -thwart, waste, withhold)

SWING (+): *accept, accomplish, achieve, address, assume, brave, broker, command, complete, control, direct, endure, engineer, execute, face, field, finagle, finesse, finish, fix, grapple, guide, hack, handle, jockey, manage, maneuver, manipulate, micromanage, negotiate, pace, play, pull, realize, regulate, rig, run, steer, stomach, tackle, take, treat, undertake, wangle, weather, work, wrangle* (≠ -abandon, abdicate, bobble, bomb, botch, bugger, bungle, fail, fake, flub, flunk, foozle, forfeit, -forsake, fudge, fumble, goof, half-ass, lose, louse, mess, mishandle, miss, muff, -neglect, -omit, overestimate, -overlook, -refuse, scamp, -shirk, skimp, skip)

SWING (/): *-avert, bend, curve, deflect, divert, move, rechannel, redirect, reverse, shift, shunt, sidetrack, sway, swerve, switch, swivel, transfer, turn, twist, wheel, whip, whirl, zigzag* (≠ anchor, balance, correct, direct, level, root, simplify, smooth, stabilize, steady, steel, straighten)

SWIPE (→): *backhand, bang, bash, bat, batter, bean, beat, belt, bludgeon, bob, bonk, bop, box, brain, buffet, bump, bung, bunt, bust, butt, cane, chop, clap, clip, clobber, clock, clout, club, concuss, conk, crack, cream, cudgel, cuff, deck, drub, fell, flail, flick, flog, floor, hammer, hit, jab, jostle, kick, knee, knock, lace, lambaste, lash, level, lick, mangle, maul, nail, paste, pelt, pepper, poke, pommel, pound, prod, pummel, punch, push, rap, sap, scuff, shove, skull, slam, slap, slash, sledge, sledgehammer, slug, smack, smite, sock, spear, stab, strike, stroke, sucker-punch, swat, switch, tap, thrash, thump, thwack, wallop, whack, whale, whip, wipe, zap* (≠ armor, defend, deflect, -dodge, -duck, guard, harbor, heal, help, nurse, parry, preserve, protect, repel, safeguard, save, shelter, shield, uphold)

SWIPE (←): *appropriate, bogart, burglarize, burgle, collar, filch, grab, hijack, hook, hotwire, lift, loot, misappropriate, mooch, nab, nobble, pick, pilfer, pillage, pinch, pluck, plunder, poach, pocket, purloin, remove, rifle, rob, rustle, seize, shanghai, shoplift, snag, snatch, sneak, steal, swindle, take* (≠ bestow, buy, comp, contribute, defend, donate, earn, furnish, give, grant, guard, offer, present, protect, purchase, recover, rescue, restore, return, secure, shield, stash, store, supply, tender, tuck, volunteer)

SWITCH (/): *adjust, alter, bandy, barter, cede, change, commute, convert, deflect, displace, divert, exchange, interchange, invert, move, rearrange, rejigger, reorder, replace, reverse, shift, shunt, sidetrack, substitute, supersede, supplant, surrender, swap, trade, transfer, transpose, turn, yield* (≠ affix, cement, clasp, clutch, demand, freeze, grip, guard, hold, keep, leave, paralyze, pinion, preserve, reserve, retain, trap, withhold)

SYNTHESIZE (+): *align, alloy, amalgamate, arrange, articulate, blend, brainstorm, brew, cast, choreograph, coalesce, coin, combine, compose, compound, conceive, concoct, conflate, coordinate, create, define, design, detail, develop, devise, express, fashion, form, formulate, fuse, harmonize, hybridize, incorporate, integrate, invent, itemize, meld, merge, mingle, mix, orchestrate, organize, originate, patent, plan, prepare, propose, reintegrate, script, sculpt, specify, state, unify, unite, weld* (≠ analyze, -avoid, crush, demolish, destroy, detach, disconnect, dismantle, disperse, dissect, dissolve, distill, divide, doom, eradicate, erase, estrange, filter, forget, mangle, -omit, oust, -overlook, part, resolve, ruin, sabotage, scotch, scupper, separate, shelve, sift, split, vivisect, wreck)

T

TACKLE (→): *accept, accost, address, approach, attack, attempt, begin, brave, broach, confront, consider, defy, engage, face, grasp, handle, intercept, introduce, launch, learn, manage, meet, oppose, pursue, resist, seize, study, treat, undertake, withstand* (≠ -avoid, -bypass, complete, conclude, continue, delay, detour, -dodge, end, -evade, finish, forget, miss, mistake, misunderstand, -neglect, pause, postpone, propose, raise, -reject, shelve, -shun, stall, -thwart)

TACKLE (→): *ambush, assault, attack, bash, batter, blindside, block, bushwhack, catch, challenge, charge, check, checkmate, clip, clutch, combat, confront, counter, crush, down, flip, -frustrate, grab, grapple, grasp, -halt, intercept, jump, nail, obstruct, ram, rush, sack, sandbag, seize, shove, slam, smash, smear, smite, stop, take, throw, topple, unhorse, unseat, upend, upset, waylay, wrestle* (≠ armor, assist, -avoid, block, brave, -circumvent, defend, deflect, -dodge, -duck, -elude, embrace, endure, -evade, face, free, guard, help, invite, liberate, loose, protect, receive, release, rescue, shelter, shield, -shirk, -sidestep, skip, skirt, weather, welcome, withstand)

TAIL (→): *accompany, bird-dog, chaperone, chase, dog, escort, eye, follow, hound, hunt, mark, observe, pursue, retrace, run, search, seek, shadow, stalk, tag, target, trace, track, trail, watch* (≠ -abandon, -avoid, -desert, direct, -disregard, -ditch, drop, -duck, -elude, -evade, guide, head, -ignore, lead, leave, lose, maroon, -neglect, pilot, shake)

TAILOR (+): *accommodate, adapt, adjust, alter, calibrate, camouflage, convert, coordinate, customize, cut, dovetail, fashion, fit, modify, mold, personalize, reconcile, sculpt, shape, square, style, trim, tune, tweak, uncomplicate, weaponize* (≠ botch, bungle, depersonalize, force, freeze, half-ass, hamper, hinder, maintain, mar, misadjust, preserve, retain, ruin, spoil, standardize)

TAINT (/): *abase, adulterate, bastardize, bedraggle, befoul, begrime, besmear, besmirch, bestialize, blacken, blackguard, blemish, blight, blot, cheapen, cloud, color, contaminate, corrupt, damage, darken, debase, debauch, defame, defile, degrade, demean, demoralize, demote, deprave, desecrate, devalue, dilute, diminish, dirty, discolor, discredit, disgrace, dishonor, distort, doctor, foul, grime, harm, humble, humiliate, infect, injure, insult, libel, lower, malign, mar, mire, mortify, muddy, offend, outrage, pervert, poison, pollute, profane, reduce, ridicule, rot, ruin, shame, sink, slander, smear, smirch, smudge, smut, soil, spike, spoil, stagnate, stain, stale, suborn, subvert, sully, tar, tarnish, trample, twist, violate, vitiate* (≠ admire, benefit, bless, boost, cherish, clarify, clean, cleanse, clear, congratulate, decontaminate, dignify, disinfect, distill, elevate, ennoble, enshrine, expiate, filter, flatter, glorify, gratify, hallow, honor, idealize, idolize, inoculate, isolate, launder, magnify, praise, purge, purify, quarantine, rarefy, rectify, refine, respect, revere, sanctify, sanitize, sterilize, treasure, upgrade, uplift, wash, worship)

TAKE (→): *accompany, attend, bear, bootleg, bring, buck, carry, cart, chauffeur, conduct, convey, convoy, courier, deliver, dispatch, distribute, drive, drop, escort, ferry, fetch, give, guide, hand, hand-carry, haul, heel, help, lead, lug, move, pack, pass, piggyback, pilot, remit, ride, schlep, send, shepherd, shoulder, show, shuttle, smuggle, steer, supply, tote, tour, transport, trek, truck, usher, waft, whisk* (≠ -abandon, covet, -desert, -ditch, drop, dump, -forsake, guard, hoard, hold, -ignore, keep, leave, lose, maroon, meet, -neglect, -refuse, retain, -shirk, -shun, skip, stash, stint, tuck, withhold)

TAKE (←): *accept, acquire, adopt, arrest, assume, attain, capture, catch, choose, clasp, clutch, collar, collect, compile, decide, derive, download, earn, ensnare, entrap, gain, gather, get, glean, grab, grasp, grip, handle, hold, inherit, obtain, overtake, pick, procure, reach, reap, receive, recycle, salvage, scavenge, scrounge, secure, seize, select, snag, snatch, source, strike, win* (≠ -abandon, bequeath, bestow, cast, -desert, discard, disperse, distribute, -ditch, divide, drop, dump, entrust, fling, forfeit, forgo, furnish, give, grant, hand, jettison, junk, lose, miss, pass, pay, present, -refuse, -reject, release, relinquish, -renounce, resell, sacrifice, scatter, scrap, sell, shuck, slough, spend, steal, stiff, stint, surrender, throw, unload, waive, withhold, yield)

TAKE (←): *absorb, accept, bolt, chew, consume, devour, digest, dispatch, down, drink, eat, engulf, gnaw, gobble, gorge, gulp, gum, guzzle, imbibe, ingest, inhale, lap, lick, metabolize, mouth, munch, nibble, nosh, nurse, pop, quaff, relish, ruminate, savor, scarf, sip, slurp, snarf, sniff, suck, swallow, swig, swill, taste, wolf* (≠ belch, brew, collect, concoct, cook, covet, crave, -deny, desire, disgorge, expel, famish, fancy, feed, force-feed, fuel, furnish, gratify, hoard, malnourish, preserve, -refuse, regurgitate, -reject, save, serve, spew, spit, starve, supply, underfeed, victual, vomit, withhold)

TAKE (←): *abduct, annex, appropriate, arrogate, bogart, borrow, carry, colonize, commandeer, confiscate, debit, deduct, draw, eliminate, extract, filch, hotwire, kidnap, lift, misappropriate, nab, nick, nobble, pinch, pluck, poach, pocket, preempt, purloin, remove, rustle, salvage, seize, sequester, snaffle, snag, snare, snatch, snitch, steal, subtract, swipe* (≠ -abandon, add, bequeath, bestow, comp, disperse, distribute, donate, earn, forfeit, forgo, furnish, give, grant, hand, lose, miss, offer, pay, plant, provide, recoup, release, relinquish, -renounce, replace, restore, sacrifice, scatter, sell, spare, spend, spitball, squander, substitute, supply, surrender, tender, tithe, volunteer, waste, withhold, yield)

TAKE (←): *bamboozle, beat, bilk, bluff, burgle, cheat, con, cozen, deceive, defraud, dupe, embezzle, exploit, fleece, flimflam, gull, hoodwink, manipulate, milk, outwit, rob, rook, sandbag, scam, screw, shortchange,* *steal, stiff, sucker, swindle, trick* (≠ assume, assure, believe, blab, confess, expose, give, indemnify, provide, refund, reimburse, repay, respect, restore, trust, validate, verify)

TAKE (+): *abide, accept, accommodate, bear, brave, brook, contain, control, endure, experience, face, hack, handle, harbor, hold, house, lodge, manage, receive, room, shelter, stand, stomach, suffer, supervise, swallow, tackle, tolerate, weather, welcome, withstand* (≠ abuse, alienate, anger, -avoid, battle, block, bother, bug, denounce, -deny, -desert, -dodge, eject, estrange, evict, fight, -flee, flout, hinder, impede, irk, isolate, molest, obstruct, oppose, orphan, -prevent, -refuse, -reject, resist, retort, seclude, stop)

TALLY (←): *add, calculate, chalk, chronicle, compute, count, figure, notch, note, number, reckon, record, score, total* (≠ confuse, estimate, exaggerate, miscount, mistake, -overlook, oversell, overstate, undersell, understate)

TAME (+): *arrest, bind, block, bottle, break, bridle, bust, cage, calm, check, choke, collar, colonize, confine, conquer, constrain, contain, control, curb, deactivate, discipline, domesticate, dominate, enslave, fetter, freeze, gag, gentle, govern, -halt, halter, hamper, handcuff, harness, hinder, hold, housebreak, housetrain, humble, hush, impede, incapacitate, inhibit, interrupt, keep, leash, manacle, master, measure, mellow, mince, mitigate, mollify, muffle, mute, muzzle, obstruct, overcome, pace, pacify, paralyze, placate, pocket, quell, quiet, regulate, rein, repress, restrain, rule, shackle, silence, sink, smother, soften, squelch, stifle, stop, straightjacket, strangle, stymie, subdue, subjugate, suppress, swallow, temper, -thwart, train, trammel, truss, vanquish, whip, whup* (≠ -abandon, agitate, air, catalyze, craze, drive, egg, encourage, express, foment, force, free, galvanize, goad, hasten, hurry, hustle, induce, inflame, instigate, jolt, liberate, loose, loosen, lose, motivate, -neglect, nudge, poke, prod, propel, provoke, push, quicken, rabble-rouse, release, rush, stimulate, subvert, trigger, unbridle, uncage, unhinge, unleash, upset, urge, vent)

TANGLE (←): *bag, bind, birdlime, block, brake, burden, capture, catch, check, choke, clog, collar, complicate, confuse, congest, constipate, constrain, counter, cramp, crimp, cripple, curb, dam, delay, detain, -deter, drag, embroil, encumber, enmesh, ensnare, ensnarl, entangle, entrap, entwine, fetter, foul, -frustrate, hamper, hamstring, handicap, hinder, impair, impede, implicate, inhibit, interweave, involve, mesh, mire, net, obstruct, oppose, paralyze, pause, postpone, resist, restrain, restrict, snag, snare, snarl, stay, stop, -thwart, trap* (≠ clarify, clear, cut, detach, disengage, disentangle, emancipate, explain, extricate, free, liberate, right, separate, straighten, streamline, uncomplicate, unravel, untangle)

TANGLE (/): *bedraggle, braid, coil, confound, confuse, disarrange, disarray, dishevel, disorganize, embroil, enlace, entangle, entwine, interlace, intertwine, interweave, involve, jumble, knot, mat, muddle, muss, obstruct, perplex, plait, raddle, rat, ravel, rumple, scramble, snarl, tease, trash, twine, twist, untidy, upset, weave, wind, wreathe, wreck*

(≠ arrange, barber, brush, comb, cut, disentangle, groom, manicure, neaten, organize, pomade, primp, ravel, razor, sleek, slice, slick, smooth, spiff, spruce, straighten, tidy, unbind, unbraid, undo, unfasten, unknot, unravel, unscramble, unsnarl, untangle, untwine, untwist, unweave)

TANTALIZE (←): *allure, arouse, arrest, attract, award, bait, bamboozle, beckon, bedevil, beguile, bewitch, bribe, cajole, candy-coat, captivate, capture, catch, charm, coax, conquer, convince, court, dare, dazzle, decoy, delight, disarm, draw, dulcify, educe, enamor, enchant, engage, engross, enlist, enrapture, ensnare, entangle, enthrall, entice, entrance, entrap, fascinate, grab, grant, gratify, grip, honey, hoodwink, hook, hypnotize, incite, indoctrinate, induce, influence, instigate, interest, intrigue, inveigle, invite, lead, lure, magnetize, manipulate, mesmerize, motivate, move, oil, outbid, overpay, paralyze, persuade, please, provoke, pull, ravish, razzle-dazzle, reward, rouse, schmooze, seduce, seize, sell, solicit, spellbind, stimulate, strike, suborn, sugarcoat, suggest, sway, sweeten, tangle, taunt, tease, tempt, test, thrill, tip, titillate, train, transfix, transport, trap, treat, trigger, urge, vamp, welcome, wheedle, whet, win, woo, wow* (≠ affront, alarm, annoy, appall, assuage, badger, baffle, -balk, beleaguer, bore, browbeat, bug, bully, burden, caution, cloy, command, content, covet, crave, daunt, demand, demotivate, -deter, disappoint, discourage, disgust, dismay, displease, dissuade, exhaust, fill, force, frustrate, fulfill, glut, gratify, hassle, horrify, hunt, irk, irritate, lose, menace, nag, nauseate, needle, niggle, nitpick, offend, pester, plague, pursue, quench, -reject, repel, repulse, revolt, sadden, sate, satiate, satisfy, scare, seek, shake, shock, sicken, slake, surfeit, terrify, threaten, -thwart, tire, torment, upset, vex, warn, weary, worry, wound)

TAP (→): *bang, bash, bat, beat, bob, bonk, bop, chuck, clap, click, clink, dab, drum, flick, hammer, hit, knock, nudge, palpate, paste, pat, ping, poke, pound, rap, slam, smack, sock, strike, swat, tag, thud, thump, thwack, tip, touch, wallop, whack* (≠ bash, batter, beat, -bypass, choke, deflect, grasp, grip, -ignore, miss, penetrate, pierce, pummel, punch, shank, shiv, slap, smash, stab, whack)

TAP (←): *bleed, bore, broach, clean, clear, decant, deplete, draft, drain, draw, drill, effuse, empty, evacuate, exhaust, exploit, flush, lance, leech, milk, mine, open, penetrate, perforate, pump, purge, quarry, riddle, scrounge, siphon, spear, spike, stab, suck, unplug, unstopper, use, utilize, vacate, -void* (≠ bathe, close, contribute, deluge, douse, drench, drown, fill, flood, inundate, marinate, plug, replace, replenish, restore, seal, soak, staunch, stock, submerge, supply, swamp, wash, water, wet)

TARGET (→): *aim, attend, backtrack, badger, bait, bird-dog, bug, chase, chivy, court, desire, direct, dog, entice, eye, ferret, fish, flag, focus, follow, harass, harry, haunt, hound, hunt, identify, investigate, learn, mark, note, observe, oppress, persecute, place, plague, point, pursue, retrace, ride, romance, root, run, scan, scope, search, seek, shadow, snipe, specify, spoor, stalk, study, tag, tail, trace, track, trail, watch, win, woo* (≠ -abandon, -avoid, baffle, blind, blindfold, blur, -boycott, cloud, conceal, diffuse, disperse, disrupt, divide, -dodge, -duck, -eschew, -flee, forget, -forsake, help, hide, -ignore, leave, lose, miss, -neglect, -overlook, scatter, shake, -shun, skim, skip, -spurn)

TARNISH (/): *abase, bastardize, befoul, begrime, besmear, besmirch, bestialize, blacken, blemish, blot, blur, canker, cheapen, cloud, color, contaminate, corrode, corrupt, damage, darken, debase, debauch, defame, defile, degrade, demean, demoralize, deprave, dim, dirty, discolor, discredit, disgrace, dishonor, distort, dull, embarrass, foul, grime, harm, hurt, impair, injure, libel, lower, mar, muddy, pervert, poison, pollute, rust, shame, sink, slander, smear, smirch, smudge, smut, soil, spoil, spot, stain, stigmatize, suborn, subvert, sully, taint, tar, touch, twist, vitiate* (≠ advantage, aid, assist, beautify, benefit, brighten, burnish, clean, cleanse, cure, decontaminate, dignify, elevate, ennoble, enshrine, expiate, fetishize, fix, glorify, hallow, heal, help, honor, improve, lighten, magnify, mend, please, polish, praise, purify, rectify, refine, scour, shine, uncloud, uplift, wash, whiten)

TASK (→): *allocate, allot, assign, authorize, burden, charge, commission, commit, confer, confide, consign, delegate, empower, encumber, entrust, exhaust, foist, impose, invest, oppress, overload, push, recommend, relegate, saddle, test, trust, weary, weigh* (≠ accept, aid, assist, confuse, disarrange, entertain, exonerate, follow, heed, help, jumble, mind, note, obey, relieve, scramble, shelter, unburden)

TASTE (←): *anticipate, ascertain, assay, bite, chew, consume, discern, discover, distinguish, divine, eat, enjoy, espy, eye, feel, hear, imbibe, learn, lick, nibble, nosh, note, notice, observe, perceive, realize, regard, relish, remark, sample, savor, scent, see, sense, sight, sip, smack, smell, spy, suspect, test, touch, try, view, whiff, witness* (≠ abjure, -avoid, -boycott, -bypass, -decline, deride, -disdain, -eschew, protest, -refuse, -reject, resist, -scorn, -shun) **(¿) ABSTRACTION ALERT. Concrete goals essential!**

TASTE (+): *accept, anticipate, appreciate, ascertain, assimilate, assume, conjecture, detect, determine, differentiate, digest, discern, discover, distinguish, divine, endure, expect, experience, eye, feel, foresee, guess, hear, judge, know, learn, meet, note, notice, observe, pass, perceive, presume, realize, receive, regard, remark, savor, scent, see, sense, sight, smell, spy, suffer, surmise, suspect, sustain, view, whiff, witness* (≠ -avoid, block, -bypass, -disregard, -eschew, -ignore, miss, -neglect, -overlook, -refuse, -reject, skip)

TAUNT (/): *aggravate, aggrieve, agitate, annoy, attack, badger, bait, bedevil, beleaguer, blast, bother, browbeat, bug, bully, caricature, chafe, chaff, chastise, condemn, criticize, defame, denigrate, denounce, deprecate, deride, discomfort, disparage, diss, disturb, dog, earbash, exasperate, fault, fret, frost, gall, goad, grate, hagride, harass, harry, hassle, haze, heckle, hector, hound, humiliate, importune, insult, irk, irritate, itch, jeer, josh, kid, knock, lambaste, mimic, mock, nag, needle, nettle, niggle, nitpick, nudge, peeve, perplex, persecute, perturb, pester,* *pillory, pique, plague, poke, prod, provoke, rag, rally, razz, rebuke, reprimand, rib, ride, ridicule, rile, roast, ruffle, -scorn, shame, slam, slander, spite, tantalize, tease, terrorize, test, torment, torture, trash-talk, troll, trouble, try, vex, worry* (≠ acclaim, admire, applaud, blandish, buoy, cajole, celebrate, comfort, commend, compliment, congratulate, ease, encourage, esteem, eulogize, exalt, extol, fête, flannel, flatter, glorify, gratify, hail, heroicize, honor, idealize, idolize, -ignore, inspire, lionize, please, praise, protect, respect, revere, safeguard, salute, save, schmooze, soap, soft-soap, soothe, sweet-talk, toast, venerate, welcome)

TAX (→): *aggravate, agitate, annoy, bother, burden, consume, deplete, drain, encumber, enervate, exact, exasperate, exhaust, foist, gall, gnaw, harass, harry, hassle, impose, irk, irritate, knacker, load, lumber, needle, nettle, niggle, nitpick, oppress, overburden, overextend, overload, overtax, overuse, overwork, pain, peeve, pester, pressure, push, rile, saddle, sap, spite, strain, stress, stretch, task, test, tire, vex, weaken, weary, weigh, weight* (≠ -abandon, chuck, discard, -ditch, dump, jettison, lighten, lose, miss, offload, remove, unburden, unload)

TAX (←): *assess, bill, charge, claim, debit, demand, dictate, enact, enforce, exact, extract, figure, fine, importune, impose, invoice, involve, leech, levy, order, penalize, press, pressure, price, push, rate, require, stipulate, take, tithe, toll* (≠ bankroll, cheat, contribute, donate, excuse, forgive, fund, offer, outlay, overpay, pay, rebate, recoup, refund, reimburse, repay, replace, reserve, restore, scant, scrimp, skimp, spare, steal, stiff, stint, supply, tender, tithe, volunteer, withhold, yield)

TEACH (+): *acquaint, advise, aid, apprentice, apprise, assist, brainwash, brief, catechize, civilize, coach, command, compel, condition, convince, counsel, cram, cultivate, demonstrate, develop, direct, discipline, domesticate, drill, edify, educate, elevate, enlighten, expand, extend, familiarize, fit, foster, groom, ground, guide, help, housebreak, house-train, impart, implant, improve, inculcate, indoctrinate, inform, initiate, inspire, instill, instruct, introduce, lead, lecture, mentor, monitor, moralize, notify, nurture, order, parrot, perfect, preach, prepare, prime, proctor, qualify, question, quiz, read, ready, rear, rehearse, retrain, reveal, school, scold, season, shape, sharpen, show, steer, strain, stretch, supervise, take, tame, tax, test, train, tutor, update* (≠ abuse, addle, attend, baffle, barbarize, bewilder, bury, censor, cheat, conceal, confound, confuse, consult, debase, deceive, defraud, delude, demean, discombobulate, disguise, fabricate, fluster, follow, gaslight, hamper, heed, hide, hinder, -ignore, impede, keep, learn, lower, mind, misinform, mislead, muddle, mystify, -neglect, nonplus, obey, obscure, observe, -omit, -overlook, perplex, pester, puzzle, ruffle, study, stump, suppress, surprise, withhold)

TEAR (←): *drag, draw, extract, force, grab, haul, jerk, nab, pluck, prize, pry, pull, rip, seize, snag, snatch, strain, tow, tug, twist, unsew, uproot, withdraw, wrench, wrest, wring, yank* (≠ affix, attach, bury, clamp, cram, drop, embed, ensconce, fasten, glue, implant, insert, install, jam, leave, push, release, sew, shove, stitch, stroke, wedge)

TEAR (/): *bite, break, butcher, claw, cleave, crack, cut, damage, dismember, dissect, divide, fray, frazzle, gash, gouge, hack, impair, incise, injure, lacerate, maim, mangle, maul, mutilate, rend, ribbon, rip, rive, run, rupture, savage, scalp, scratch, separate, sever, shred, slash, slit, split, sunder, tatter, vivisect, wound* (≠ fix, fuse, guard, heal, join, mend, protect, repair, restore, sew, stitch, suture, unite, weave)

TEASE (/): *aggravate, aggrieve, agitate, annoy, badger, bait, bedevil, beleaguer, bother, browbeat, bug, bully, burn, chafe, chaff, deride, discomfort, disturb, dog, exasperate, fool, fret, frost, gall, get, goad, harass, harry, hassle, haze, heckle, hector, hound, importune, irk, irritate, jeer, jive, josh, kid, mock, needle, nettle, nitpick, nudge, peeve, perplex, persecute, perturb, pester, pique, plague, poke, prod, provoke, rag, rally, razz, rib, ride, ridicule, rile, roast, ruffle, slam, spite, tantalize, target, taunt, terrorize, test, tickle, torment, torture, trash-talk, trouble, try, vex, worry, zing* (≠ appease, assuage, blandish, blunt, buffer, butter, cajole, calm, charm, coax, comfort, console, content, cushion, defend, gratify, guard, honor, mellow, mitigate, moderate, mollify, mollycoddle, oblige, pacify, placate, please, protect, quell, relieve, rescue, respect, salve, satisfy, save, settle, soften, soft-soap, soothe, still, sweet-talk)

TEMPER (→): *armor, bake, braze, case-harden, cement, chill, fortify, harden, harshen, inure, mold, petrify, prepare, roughen, set, shield, solidify, starch, steel, stiffen, strengthen, toughen* (≠ bend, corrode, crack, crumble, damage, debilitate, destroy, dissolve, flex, fracture, fragment, harm, mar, melt, pulverize, shatter, soften, undermine, weaken)

TEMPER (+): *abate, adjust, allay, alleviate, assuage, calibrate, calm, cool, coordinate, curb, cushion, dilute, diminish, domesticate, dull, ease, except, fine-tune, help, housebreak, housetrain, hush, lessen, limit, lull, mellow, minimize, mitigate, moderate, modify, modulate, mollify, pacify, pad, palliate, placate, qualify, reduce, relieve, reserve, restrain, season, soften, soft-pedal, soothe, stipulate, tame, tune, tweak, underemphasize, weaken* (≠ accent, accentuate, accrue, affront, aggravate, agitate, amplify, anger, appall, arouse, assert, augment, chafe, deepen, emphasize, enrage, exacerbate, exasperate, excite, gall, harass, heighten, incense, incite, increase, infuriate, intensify, irk, irritate, magnify, nettle, offend, outrage, peeve, pester, provoke, punctuate, rouse, ruffle, sharpen, stimulate, upset, vex, worry, worsen)

TEMPT (←): *allure, arouse, arrest, attract, award, bait, bamboozle, beckon, beguile, bewitch, bribe, cajole, candy-coat, captivate, catch, charm, coax, compensate, conquer, convince, court, dare, dazzle, decoy, delight, disarm, draw, dulcify, educe, enamor, enchant, engage, engross, enlist, enrapture, ensnare, entangle, enthrall, entice, entrance, entrap, fascinate, give, grab, grant, gratify, grip, honey, honor, hoodwink, hook, hypnotize, incite, indoctrinate, induce, influence, instigate, interest, intrigue, inveigle, invite, lead, lure, magnetize, manipulate, mesmerize, motivate, move, oil, outbid, outlay, overpay, overspend, paralyze, pay, persuade, please, promote, provoke, pull, ravish, razzle-dazzle, remuner-*

ate, reward, risk, rouse, schmooze, seduce, seize, sell, solicit, spellbind, stimulate, strike, suborn, sugarcoat, suggest, sway, sweeten, tangle, tantalize, test, thrill, tip, train, transfix, transport, trap, treat, urge, vamp, wheedle, whet, win, woo, wow (≠ affront, alarm, annoy, appall, assuage, badger, baffle, -balk, beleaguer, bore, browbeat, bug, bully, burden, caution, cloy, command, content, covet, crave, daunt, demand, demotivate, -deter, disappoint, discourage, disgust, dismay, displease, dissuade, exhaust, force, frustrate, glut, gnaw, gratify, hassle, horrify, hunt, irk, irritate, lose, menace, nag, nauseate, needle, nettle, niggle, nitpick, offend, pester, plague, pursue, quench, -reject, repel, repulse, revolt, sadden, sate, satiate, satisfy, scare, seek, shake, shock, sicken, slake, surfeit, terrify, threaten, -thwart, tire, torment, upset, vex, warn, weary, worry, wound)

TEND (→): *administer, attend, baby, babysit, carry, chaperone, codirect, conduct, control, cradle, direct, govern, guard, guide, handle, keep, lead, manage, micromanage, mind, mother, operate, oversee, pace, patrol, pilot, protect, regulate, run, safeguard, shepherd, shield, stage-manage, steer, steward, superintend, supervise, watch* (≠ -abandon, abuse, attack, damage, destroy, -disregard, eradicate, erase, forget, -forsake, harm, hurt, -ignore, indispose, kill, murder, -neglect, orphan, -overlook, sabotage, scupper, -shirk, -shun, -sidestep, torment, torture, undermine)

TEND (+): *breed, crop, cultivate, culture, cut, develop, dig, domesticate, dress, extirpate, fallow, farm, feed, fertilize, garden, gather, germinate, gestate, glean, grow, harrow, harvest, hay, hoe, husband, kill, manage, manure, mow, nourish, nurture, pick, plant, plow, pluck, pot, prepare, produce, promote, propagate, pull, quicken, raise, ranch, reap, rear, replant, reseed, ripen, root, rototill, seed, sharecrop, sow, sprout, suckle, till, transplant, uproot, work* (≠ -abandon, afflict, blight, butcher, consume, contaminate, cull, damage, destroy, devastate, devour, diminish, disease, eat, exterminate, gather, glean, harvest, -ignore, impair, infect, infest, injure, jettison, junk, kill, malnourish, mow, -neglect, pick, pickle, pluck, poison, pollute, pull, raze, reap, recycle, ruin, scavenge, scorch, select, shrivel, sicken, slaughter, squander, stunt, uproot, waste, weed, wither, yield)

TENDER (→): *accord, adduce, advance, bestow, bid, cite, confer, contribute, deliver, disburse, dispense, entrust, extend, forward, furnish, give, grant, impart, introduce, offer, pose, posit, present, proffer, propose, propound, provide, recommend, render, sell, spitball, submit, suggest, supply, volunteer* (≠ accept, accredit, approve, authorize, clear, confirm, -decline, -deny, disallow, disapprove, -disregard, finalize, formalize, -ignore, negative, -neglect, okay, -overlook, ratify, -rebuff, rebut, receive, -refuse, -reject, retract, sanction, -spurn, take, -veto, warrant, withdraw)

TERMINATE (/): *abolish, -abort, adjourn, annihilate, annul, bounce, -cancel, cease, close, complete, conclude, confine, consummate, crown, deep-six, determine, discharge, -discontinue, dismiss, dissolve, drop, eliminate, end, euthanize, execute, extinguish, finish, fire, -halt, kill, limit, murder, perfect, restrict, sack, scratch, scrub, slay, stop, suspend, wrap*

(≠ allow, back, begin, brainstorm, commence, concoct, create, defend, engender, generate, guard, hatch, inaugurate, initiate, keep, launch, maintain, open, originate, preserve, promote, rescue, save, spawn, spitball, start, survive, sustain, trigger)

TERRIFY (/): *affright, agitate, alarm, amaze, appall, astound, awe, blackjack, blackmail, bludgeon, boggle, browbeat, brutalize, bulldoze, bully, chill, cow, daunt, deafen, demoralize, demotivate, -deter, discomfort, discompose, disconcert, discourage, dishearten, dismay, dispirit, disquiet, distract, distress, disturb, emasculate, faze, floor, freeze, frighten, funk, haunt, horrify, intimidate, jolt, menace, numb, panic, paralyze, perturb, petrify, railroad, rattle, repel, sandbag, savage, scare, shake, shock, spook, startle, strong-arm, stun, stupefy, terrorize, threaten, trash-talk, traumatize, unhinge, unman, unnerve, unsettle, unstring, upset, victimize, warn, worry* (≠ allay, amuse, assuage, assure, baby, boost, buoy, calm, charm, cheer, coddle, comfort, compose, console, delight, embolden, enchant, encourage, entertain, exhilarate, fortify, gladden, guard, hearten, help, humor, inspire, invigorate, lull, mellow, mitigate, moderate, mollify, nurture, pacify, placate, please, protect, quiet, reassure, release, relieve, save, secure, seduce, soothe, stabilize, steady, steel, stimulate, strengthen, thrill, uplift, vamp, woo, wow)

TERRORIZE (/): *abuse, agitate, alarm, blackjack, blackmail, blindside, bludgeon, browbeat, brutalize, bulldoze, bully, chill, coerce, daunt, dehumanize, demoralize, dismay, endanger, frighten, hijack, horrify, intimidate, jeopardize, jump, lynch, maltreat, menace, mistreat, molest, muscle, oppress, outrage, panic, persecute, perturb, petrify, plague, railroad, rattle, sandbag, scare, shock, startle, steamroll, strong-arm, surprise, target, terrify, threaten, traumatize, unnerve, upset, warn, wrong* (≠ aid, allay, alleviate, amuse, assist, assuage, assure, baby, boost, buoy, calm, coddle, comfort, defend, delight, elevate, embattle, encourage, entertain, fortify, gladden, gratify, guard, help, humor, hush, -ignore, inspire, lift, lull, mellow, mitigate, moderate, mollify, nurture, pacify, patrol, placate, please, protect, reassure, relieve, rescue, save, secure, sedate, shelter, shield, soothe, thrill, uplift, woo)

TEST (←): *analyze, appraise, ascertain, assay, assess, audition, benchmark, beta, burden, calculate, calibrate, categorize, check, compare, compute, confirm, consult, critique, cross-examine, decide, demonstrate, determine, discover, evaluate, examine, eyeball, gauge, grill, impose, inspect, interrogate, interview, investigate, judge, measure, peg, probe, prove, quantify, question, quiz, rank, rate, read, reappraise, reassess, reevaluate, reinvestigate, sample, scale, scan, score, screen, scrutinize, settle, substantiate, survey, suss, time, try, validate, verify, weigh* (≠ accept, assume, await, believe, blow, bomb, botch, bungle, cheat, conclude, deceive, discredit, disprove, estimate, excuse, fake, flub, flunk, fudge, half-ass, invalidate, learn, misgauge, misjudge, mistake, muff, -neglect, overestimate, -overlook, pass, predetermine, pretend, ruin, -shirk, skip, study, trick, trust, underestimate, wreck)

TEST (/): *aggravate, agitate, annoy, bother, bug, burden, demand, drain, earbash, encumber, enervate, exact, exasperate, exhaust, gall, harass, harry, hassle, importune, impose, irk, irritate, load, lumber, nag, needle, nettle, niggle, nitpick, overextend, overload, pain, peeve, pester, press, pressure, push, rile, sap, spite, strain, stretch, tax, tire, try, vex, weaken, wear, weary* (≠ animate, boost, brace, energize, enhance, fortify, hearten, help, inspire, invigorate, motivate, prioritize, protect, redeem, rejuvenate, restore, save, strengthen, toughen)

TESTIFY (→): *affirm, assert, assure, attest, avow, certify, confirm, convince, corroborate, declare, demonstrate, depose, endorse, establish, forswear, guarantee, maintain, pledge, promise, prove, show, state, substantiate, support, swear, verify, vow, warrant, witness* (≠ contradict, deceive, -deny, disavow, disclaim, -disown, double-talk, -ignore, recant, refute, -repudiate, retract, silence) **(¿) ABSTRACTION ALERT. Concrete goals essential!**

THANK (+): *accredit, acknowledge, admire, appreciate, bless, cherish, credit, enjoy, esteem, owe, praise, prize, recognize, regard, relish, repay, respect, reward, savor, treasure, value, welcome* (≠ beg, beseech, conceal, desire, entreat, -ignore, implore, -negate, -neglect, -omit, -overlook, plead, press, request, resent, solicit)

THAW (+): *crack, defrost, de-ice, disarm, dissolve, flux, fuse, heat, liquefy, mellow, melt, relax, render, soften, sweeten, thin, warm* (≠ clot, coagulate, congeal, fortify, freeze, harden, set, solidify, stiffen, thicken, toughen)

THREATEN (/): *abuse, admonish, alarm, blackjack, blackmail, browbeat, brutalize, bully, caution, challenge, command, compromise, cow, curse, daunt, demand, endanger, enforce, extort, hector, hijack, imperil, insist, intimidate, jeopardize, menace, muscle, pressure, railroad, sandbag, scare, target, terrorize, trash-talk, traumatize, undermine, victimize, warn, worry* (≠ alleviate, amuse, approve, assist, calm, commend, compliment, defend, entertain, flatter, gratify, guard, help, humor, lull, mellow, mitigate, moderate, mollify, nurture, pacify, patrol, placate, please, praise, preserve, protect, reassure, relax, relieve, safeguard, satisfy, save, shelter, shield)

THRILL (→): *amaze, amuse, animate, arouse, astonish, astound, bewitch, captivate, charge, charm, dazzle, delight, distract, dizzy, electrify, enchant, energize, enrapture, entertain, enthrall, enthuse, excite, exhilarate, galvanize, gobsmack, grab, hypnotize, incite, inspire, interest, intoxicate, intrigue, jolt, juice, mesmerize, move, provoke, quicken, rally, razzle-dazzle, rivet, rouse, send, shock, spellbind, startle, stimulate, stir, surprise, tantalize, tickle, titillate, transport, wow* (≠ anger, bore, bother, bug, burden, dampen, daunt, deaden, demoralize, demotivate, depress, discourage, dishearten, dispirit, drain, exhaust, hallucinate, jade, nag, nauseate, needle, repel, repulse, revolt, sadden, sicken, tire, traumatize, vex, weary, worry, wrack)

THROTTLE (/): *asphyxiate, burke, check, choke, confine, constrict, control, curb, dampen, daunt, demotivate, depress, -deter, discourage,* *dishearten, disincline, dissuade, endanger, extinguish, -frustrate, gag, garrote, hamper, hinder, hush, impede, imperil, inhibit, kill, limit, lynch, muffle, murder, mute, muzzle, paralyze, quiet, repress, restrain, shush, silence, smother, squeeze, squelch, stifle, stop, strangle, stymie, subdue, suffocate, suppress, wring* (≠ air, clear, encourage, evince, express, flood, free, heal, help, inhale, inspire, loose, nurture, open, oxygenate, reinvigorate, release, restimulate, restore, resuscitate, revive, unclog, unseal, vent, ventilate, verbalize, vocalize, voice)

THROW (→): *bowl, bunt, butt, cant, cast, catapult, chuck, compel, direct, distract, drive, fire, flick, fling, flip, floor, goad, heave, hurl, impel, launch, lob, pelt, pitch, precipitate, prod, project, propel, push, ram, send, shed, shove, shunt, shy, skitter, sling, thrust, toss, wing* (≠ accept, acquire, bring, carry, catch, clasp, clutch, convey, drag, give, grab, grasp, grip, hand, hold, keep, obtain, procure, pull, receive, retain, schlep, secure, snag, tow, tug, yank)

THRUST (→): *bulldoze, burden, butt, compel, compress, depress, drive, foist, force, force-feed, frogmarch, further, hustle, impel, impose, inflict, jab, jam, lunge, march, move, muscle, pierce, plunge, poke, press, pressure, prod, propel, punt, push, ram, saddle, shove, squash, squeeze, stab, stick, urge, wedge* (≠ accept, attract, bore, discourage, dissuade, draw, drop, extract, guard, -halt, pull, -rebuff, receive, repress, slide, stop, yank)

THWACK (→): *backhand, bang, bash, bat, batter, beat, buffet, clout, club, cuff, flick, flog, hit, knock, rap, slap, smack, sock, spank, strike, swat, thrash, thump, wallop, whack* (≠ block, brush, caress, deflect, -dodge, -duck, miss, nudge, pet, repel, shave, shield, skim)

-THWART (←): *-abort, anticipate, arrest, -avert, baffle, -balk, bar, beat, block, bottleneck, brake, bung, burden, cage, catch, check, checkmate, choke, -circumvent, clog, complicate, confuse, congest, conquer, constipate, constrain, counter, counteract, cramp, crimp, cripple, cross, curb, dam, dampen, dash, daunt, defeat, defy, delay, demotivate, depress, detain, -deter, disadvantage, disappoint, discomfit, discourage, dishearten, disincline, dissuade, -ditch, double-cross, drag, -duck, -elude, encumber, entangle, entrap, fetter, flummox, foil, forestall, foul, -frustrate, -halt, hamper, hamstring, handicap, hinder, hobble, hogtie, hold, impair, impede, inhibit, interrupt, jam, -kibosh, kneecap, lumber, manacle, mire, monkey-wrench, muzzle, -negate, neutralize, -nullify, obstruct, -obviate, offset, oppose, outlast, outwit, overcome, override, paralyze, parry, pause, plug, postpone, -preclude, preempt, -prevent, -prohibit, resist, restrain, restrict, retard, ruin, scotch, shackle, shelve, short-circuit, skin, snag, snarl, snooker, spite, stagnate, stall, stay, stem, stifle, stop, straightjacket, stultify, stump, stunt, stymie, tangle, throttle, -thwart, trammel, wing* (≠ abet, accelerate, accommodate, advance, aid, assist, await, boost, brainstorm, catalyze, clear, compel, cultivate, disencumber, disentangle, ease, encourage, expedite, extricate, facilitate, fast-forward, fast-track, forward, foster, free, frogmarch, fuel, further, grease, hasten, heal, help, hurry, improve, inspire, instigate, legalize, liberate, loosen, lubricate, march, mend, midwife, nurture, oblige, open, optimize, overhaul, prioritize, prod, promote, prompt, propel, quicken, release, relieve, remedy, rush, slacken, smooth, speed, steady, stimulate, stir, stoke, strengthen, support, transcend, unclog, uncomplicate, unleash, unlock, untangle, untie, urge)

TICKLE (→): *amaze, amuse, astonish, brush, caress, cheer, contact, convulse, delight, distract, divert, enchant, entertain, excite, gratify, hearten, interest, itch, lift, pat, pet, please, provoke, rub, stimulate, stroke, strum, tease, thrill, titillate, touch, uplift, wow* (≠ anger, annoy, bore, bother, compose, depress, disappoint, discipline, disenchant, disturb, irritate, nag, needle, nettle, pain, pester, placate, repulse, sicken, trouble, upset, vex, weary)

TIDY (+): *arrange, barber, brush, clean, clear, dandify, declutter, groom, gussy, manicure, neaten, order, organize, police, pomade, preen, primp, rectify, regiment, right, sleek, slick, smarten, sort, spiff, spruce, straighten, tauten, titivate, trim* (≠ bedraggle, clutter, diffuse, dirty, dishevel, disorder, disorganize, jumble, litter, muss, rumple, scatter, scramble, shuffle, smudge, trash, untidy, wreck)

TIE (→): *approach, approximate, beat, better, compare, eclipse, equal, excel, match, meet, oppose, outdistance, outdo, outperform, outrank, outshine, outstrip, parallel, reach, rival, suggest, surpass, top, touch, transcend* (≠ abide, advance, back, bear, cede, concede, endure, fail, flunk, foster, further, nurture, promote, suffer, support, survive)

TIE (←): *band, bind, chain, cinch, coil, confine, constrain, constrict, cord, curb, encumber, enslave, entangle, entwine, fetter, fix, gird, hamper, handcuff, hinder, hogtie, hold, interlace, intertwine, interweave, knot, lace, lash, leash, lock, manacle, pinion, restrain, restrict, rope, secure, shackle, snarl, straightjacket, strap, subjugate, tangle, tether, thread, truss, twist, wind, wire* (≠ cut, detach, disentangle, divide, divorce, emancipate, free, loose, loosen, release, separate, unbind, uncoil, unfasten, unlace, unlash, unleash, unlock, unloose, unravel, unsnarl, unspool, unstrap, unstring, untangle, untether, unthread, untie, untwine, untwist, unwind)

TIGHTEN (←): *brace, check, choke, cinch, close, constrict, control, cramp, crush, curb, -deter, discourage, dissuade, extinguish, fasten, fix, flex, -frustrate, gag, garrote, hamper, hinder, impede, inhibit, limit, lynch, narrow, pucker, restrain, screw, secure, squeeze, squelch, stiffen, stop, strangle, stretch, stymie, subdue, suppress, tauten, tense, wring* (≠ allow, clear, ease, encourage, enlarge, evince, expand, extend, flood, free, help, increase, lengthen, loose, loosen, open, reinvigorate, relax, release, restore, revive, slack, slacken, stretch, unclog, unfasten, unseal, unspool)

TILT (→): *angle, bank, bend, cant, careen, cock, -decline, descend, dip, heel, incline, lean, list, pitch, rake, recline, rock, seesaw, shift, slant, slope, swag, sway, swerve, tip, toss, trip, turn, wiggle, wriggle* (≠ align, anchor, balance, calm, center, equalize, even, flatten, level, position, right, root, settle, stabilize, steady, straighten)

TIME (→): *adjust, arrange, calendar, calibrate, choreograph, coordinate, direct, fix, govern, integrate, manage, mastermind, orchestrate, organize, prepare, present, program, schedule, set, stage-manage, steer, timetable* (≠ addle, -cancel, confuse, disarrange, discompose, disorder, disorganize, disrupt, disturb, end, forget, jumble, mess, miss, mix, muddle, unsettle, unstring, upset)

TIME (←): *appraise, ascertain, assess, benchmark, calculate, clock, compare, compute, control, count, determine, estimate, evaluate, fathom, gauge, judge, measure, meter, order, quantify, rank, read, record, regulate, survey, weigh* (≠ allege, conceal, conjecture, contradict, -deny, -discount, dispute, -disregard, estimate, guess, guesstimate, hide, -ignore, invalidate, miss, mistake, -neglect, skim, skip)

TIRE (/): *bore, burden, debilitate, depress, drain, enervate, enfeeble, exasperate, exhaust, fatigue, harass, incapacitate, irk, irritate, jade, leech, nauseate, overextend, overload, pain, prostrate, sap, sicken, sink, strain, tax, vex, weaken, wear, weary* (≠ activate, agitate, animate, charge, electrify, enliven, excite, inspire, jolt, kindle, motivate, quicken, reinvigorate, restimulate, revitalize, revive, spark, stimulate, stir)

TITILLATE (←): *amuse, arouse, attract, beguile, bewitch, captivate, charge, charm, delight, dizzy, electrify, enchant, entertain, enthrall, excite, exhilarate, fascinate, galvanize, grab, grapple, heat, hook, hypnotize, ignite, incite, inspire, interest, intoxicate, intrigue, mesmerize, palpate, provoke, razzle-dazzle, rivet, seduce, spark, spellbind, stimulate, tantalize, tease, thrill, tickle, trigger, warm* (≠ aggravate, blunt, bore, bother, buffer, bug, confound, deaden, demoralize, demotivate, depress, discourage, dishearten, dispirit, dull, exasperate, frustrate, irk, irritate, jade, lull, nauseate, sadden, tire, vex, weary)

TOAST (→): *bake, barbecue, braise, broil, brown, burn, char, cook, crisp, desiccate, dry, fire, griddle, grill, heat, overheat, parch, roast, sauté, scald, scorch, sear, singe, warm* (≠ chill, cool, dampen, douse, drench, extinguish, freeze, frost, ice, marinate, refrigerate, soak, water, wet)

TOAST (+): *applaud, approve, celebrate, commend, congratulate, esteem, exalt, extol, flatter, glorify, gratify, hail, honor, idealize, idolize, pledge, praise, salute, trumpet, venerate, welcome* (≠ attack, blame, blast, boo, censure, chastise, condemn, criticize, critique, defame, denigrate, denounce, disparage, diss, fault, finger, frame, fulminate, insult, knock, lambaste, rebuke, regret, repent, reprimand, rue, shame, -shun, slam)

TOLERATE (+): *abide, accept, allow, bear, brave, brook, concede, condone, confront, countenance, endure, experience, face, hack, harden, incur, indulge, know, outlast, overcome, permit, receive, sanction, season, shoulder, stand, stomach, suffer, support, surmount, survive, sustain, swallow, sweat, take, weather, withstand* (≠ bar, battle, block, -bypass,

-circumvent, combat, contest, -deter, discourage, dismiss, -dodge, -elude, enjoy, -escape, -evade, fight, -forbid, oppose, -prevent, -prohibit, -reject, -repudiate, resist, seek, -shun, -spurn)

TOP (→): *ace, beat, best, better, checkmate, clobber, conquer, crush, defeat, drub, eclipse, exceed, finagle, fox, goose, lick, master, one-up, outclass, outdistance, outdo, outfox, outgrow, outgun, outlast, outpace, outperform, outrank, outreach, outrun, outsell, outshine, outsmart, outstrip, outthink, outweigh, outwit, overcome, overrun, overshadow, overtake, rout, rule, shame, skunk, subdue, surmount, surpass, thrash, total, transcend, trounce, trump, wallop, whip* (≠ blow, botch, buck, bungle, concede, counter, defer, -dodge, fail, flub, flunk, follow, forfeit, -forsake, fumble, incapacitate, lose, mind, muff, obey, oppose, quit, relinquish, stop, surrender, topple)

TOPPLE (/): *capsize, collapse, crash, crumple, depose, dethrone, displace, drop, knock, oust, overbalance, overset, overthrow, overturn, pitch, plunge, precipitate, raze, sabotage, scotch, scupper, scuttle, skittle, stagger, tip, trip, tumble, unbalance, undermine, unhorse, unseat, upend, upset, usurp, wreck* (≠ ascend, boost, build, carry, construct, elect, elevate, enthrone, erect, hoist, lift, mount, pile, raise, right, stack, stand, straighten, uplift)

TORCH (/): *ash, bake, bank, barbecue, blacken, blaze, brand, brighten, broil, burn, cauterize, char, consume, cook, cremate, damage, destroy, enkindle, fire, flame, frizzle, griddle, grill, heat, ignite, illuminate, illumine, immolate, incinerate, inflame, inspire, irradiate, kindle, light, lighten, melt, parch, radiate, reignite, rekindle, relight, roast, sauté, scald, scathe, scorch, sear, singe, spark, stoke, trigger* (≠ blacken, bolster, chill, choke, cool, darken, defend, dim, douse, drench, dull, extinguish, freeze, obscure, preserve, quench, rebuild, save, smother, snuff, stifle, suffocate, wet)

TORMENT (/): *afflict, aggravate, agitate, agonize, anguish, annoy, assail, attack, badger, bait, bedevil, beset, besiege, bother, bug, burden, chafe, crucify, crush, curse, demean, demonize, discomfort, discompose, disquiet, distress, disturb, dog, earbash, exasperate, excruciate, fluster, gall, get, grieve, hagride, harass, harrow, harry, heckle, hound, hurt, impugn, irk, irritate, martyr, mistreat, molest, nag, needle, nettle, nitpick, oppress, overpower, overwhelm, pain, peeve, persecute, perturb, pester, pillory, pique, plague, prick, provoke, punish, pursue, rack, rag, rasp, ride, ridicule, rile, smite, stab, sting, strain, stress, strike, tantalize, tease, torture, troll, trouble, try, tyrannize, upset, vex, victimize, welt, worry, wrack, wrench, wring, wrong* (≠ abet, aid, amuse, assist, befriend, buoy, comfort, console, content, deliver, help, -ignore, inspire, pity, please, protect, quiet, regret, relax, release, relieve, reprieve, satisfy, settle, solace, soothe, steady, succor, thrill, uplift)

TORTURE (/): *abuse, afflict, aggravate, agitate, agonize, anguish, assail, attack, avenge, badger, beat, bedevil, beset, besiege, bestialize, blister, break, brutalize, castigate, chafe, chasten, chastise, confine, correct, crucify, crush, curse, dehumanize, discipline, excruciate, execute, exploit,* *fine, grieve, grill, harm, harrow, hurt, ill-treat, impale, imprison, incarcerate, inflame, injure, interrogate, judge, lacerate, lambaste, maim, malnourish, mangle, martyr, menace, mistreat, molest, mutilate, nettle, oppress, outrage, overpower, overwhelm, pain, penalize, persecute, pillory, plague, punish, rack, reprise, ride, rile, scalp, scourge, sentence, sicken, smite, stab, sting, strain, stress, strike, terrorize, threaten, torment, traumatize, trouble, tyrannize, upset, victimize, whip, worry, wound, wrack, wring, wrong* (≠ abet, accommodate, aid, alleviate, amuse, assist, assuage, baby, buoy, cherish, coddle, comfort, console, content, cuddle, delight, deliver, elevate, entertain, favor, foster, gratify, help, humor, lift, mollify, nourish, nurse, nurture, oblige, pamper, pity, placate, pleasure, protect, quiet, regret, release, relieve, reprieve, reward, satisfy, soothe, spoil, stabilize, succor, thrill, tolerate, treat, uplift, wow)

TORTURE (/): *ball, bend, buckle, bunch, coil, contort, crimp, crook, crumple, curl, damage, deface, deform, disfigure, distort, gnarl, loop, mangle, mar, metamorphose, misshape, mold, mutilate, reshape, ruin, scalp, screw, spiral, squinch, twine, twist, vandalize, warp, wind, wreathe, wreck, wrench, wrest, wring, wrinkle* (≠ align, craft, fabricate, flatten, form, level, mold, shape, smooth, straighten, unbend, uncurl, weave)

TOSS (→): *bowl, buck, bung, cast, catapult, chuck, dart, dash, eject, fire, flick, fling, flip, gun, heave, hook, hurl, hurtle, impel, launch, lob, loft, pass, peg, pelt, pitch, precipitate, project, propel, rifle, roll, shoot, skitter, sling, throw, thrust, twirl, wing* (≠ accept, adopt, catch, clasp, clutch, drop, grasp, grip, hold, keep, receive, seize, stabilize, steady, take)

TOSS (/): *-abandon, abdicate, abolish, annihilate, boot, cashier, chuck, deep-six, -desert, discard, dismiss, -ditch, dump, eighty-six, eliminate, eradicate, exorcise, expunge, exterminate, extinguish, extirpate, fire, -forsake, jettison, junk, liquidate, lose, pitch, -reject, remove, scotch, scrap, shed, shuck, slough, terminate, unload, weed, wipe* (≠ adopt, embrace, employ, hire, hold, include, invite, keep, maintain, retain, take, use, utilize)

TOUCH (→): *brush, caress, clap, clasp, clench, clutch, contact, dab, embrace, examine, feel, finger, flick, fondle, frisk, grasp, graze, grip, grope, handle, hit, hold, hug, inspect, jab, join, kiss, knock, lick, lip, manipulate, massage, meet, nose, nudge, nuzzle, palm, palpate, pat, paw, peck, pet, pound, probe, push, rap, reach, riffle, rub, scrutinize, shave, sip, skim, smooth, stir, strike, stroke, strum, suck, sweep, tag, tap, taste, tickle, whack* (≠ aggravate, annoy, -avoid, -bypass, deflect, disbelieve, displease, -dodge, -eschew, -ignore, insult, miss, observe, offend, -ostracize, -overlook, provoke, release, -shun, -sidestep, tease, vex, watch, wound)

TOUCH (←): *affect, afflict, agitate, arouse, attract, bewitch, bother, captivate, charm, concern, dazzle, discomfort, discompose, disquiet, distress, disturb, embroil, enchant, engage, enrapture, entangle, enthrall, entrance, excite, fascinate, fluster, grab, harass, harry, impact, implicate, impress, influence, inspire, interest, involve, mark, melt, move, penetrate, perturb, pester, pierce, plague, quicken, ravish, reach, regard, sadden, soften, stimulate, stir, strain, stress, strike, stroke, sway, transport, trouble,* *try, upset, worry* (≠ alienate, anger, annoy, bore, deaden, desensitize, disgust, drain, exasperate, exhaust, forget, harden, infuriate, inure, irk, irritate, isolate, numb, repel, repulse, revolt, sap, seclude, sicken, tax, test, tire, toughen, underwhelm, vex, weary) **(¿) ABSTRACTION ALERT. Concrete goals essential!**

TOUGHEN (+): *acclimate, acclimatize, accustom, adapt, adjust, anneal, bolster, boost, brace, brutalize, buttress, callous, case-harden, condition, deaden, dehumanize, desensitize, develop, discipline, embattle, energize, enforce, familiarize, firm, forearm, fortify, habituate, harden, immunize, indurate, inure, invigorate, numb, protect, reinforce, school, season, steel, stiffen, strengthen, substantiate, support, teach, temper, tone, train, vitalize* (≠ castrate, consume, cripple, damage, debilitate, emasculate, enervate, enfeeble, exhaust, hamstring, harm, hurt, impair, incapacitate, injure, liquefy, melt, monkey-wrench, overextend, paralyze, sabotage, sap, scotch, scupper, sensitize, soften, stretch, subvert, tenderize, thaw, undercut, undermine, unman, victimize, weaken, wither)

TOUT (→): *accentuate, acclaim, advance, advertise, affirm, amplify, announce, applaud, assert, ballyhoo, blandish, blare, blaze, blazon, boost, broadcast, celebrate, claim, commend, communicate, compliment, congratulate, declare, emphasize, endorse, eulogize, extol, flatter, glorify, gratify, hail, hard-sell, herald, honor, hype, idealize, idolize, laud, limelight, magnify, market, offer, peddle, petition, pimp, pitch, plug, praise, presell, prioritize, proclaim, promote, pronounce, publicize, push, recommend, salute, seek, shill, solicit, support, telegraph, trumpet, volunteer* (≠ belittle, blacken, blackguard, boo, bury, chide, conceal, criticize, critique, deride, disrespect, hide, insult, knock, minimize, mock, neg, pan, regret, repent, ridicule, rue, scold, -scorn, skewer, slam, underemphasize, vilify)

TOW (←): *attract, carry, convey, drag, draw, ferry, haul, heave, jerk, lug, move, propel, pull, push, schlep, shuttle, trail, transport, trawl, tug, yank* (≠ alienate, bobble, drive, drop, fumble, lose, propel, punt, push, ram, -rebuff, -reject, repel, repulse, shove, thrust)

TRACE (→): *accompany, analyze, ascertain, backtrack, bird-dog, chaperone, chase, derive, detect, determine, discern, discover, dog, escort, eye, ferret, find, follow, hound, hunt, observe, perceive, pursue, run, search, seek, shadow, spoor, spot, stalk, tag, tail, target, track, trail, uncover, unearth, watch* (≠ -avoid, blind, blindfold, -bypass, captain, confound, confuse, -discount, -disregard, -ditch, -duck, dump, -elude, -evade, guide, head, -ignore, lead, lose, mislead, -neglect, -omit, -overlook, perplex, pilot, -sidestep, skip, skirt, steer)

TRACK (→): *accompany, apprehend, bird-dog, capture, catch, chaperone, chase, cover, discover, dog, escort, expose, eye, eyeball, ferret, find, follow, harry, haunt, hound, hunt, monitor, observe, pursue, retrace, scout, search, seek, shadow, spoor, stalk, tag, tail, target, trace, trail, uncover, watch* (≠ arrest, cage, catch, confine, confound, cripple, detain, -disregard, forget, guide, hamper, head, hobble, -ignore, impede, incarcerate, jail, lead, lose, mislay, misplace, miss, mistake, -neglect, -overlook, perplex, pilot, restrain, skip, trap)

TRADE (→): *auction, barter, bootleg, broker, buy, commercialize, commodify, corner, deal, distribute, exchange, export, fence, horse-trade, market, merchandize, monetize, monopolize, negotiate, peddle, presell, purchase, remainder, renegotiate, resell, retail, run, sell, smuggle, supply, swap, take, traffic, transact, transfer, vend, wholesale* (≠ ban, bar, blackball, -boycott, budget, buy, close, -deny, deplete, embargo, hoard, impede, import, outbid, -prohibit, purchase, -refuse, restrict, suppress, swindle, withhold)

TRADE (+): *alternate, bandy, cede, change, commute, displace, divert, exchange, imitate, interchange, rearrange, rejigger, replace, represent, second, shift, substitute, supersede, supplant, surrender, swap, switch, transfer, transpose, turn, yield* (≠ block, cement, conserve, hold, keep, leave, maintain, pin, preserve, -prevent, resist, retain, sustain)

TRAIL (→): *dangle, drag, draw, extend, flutter, hang, haul, pull, sweep, tow, track, unspool* (≠ coil, contract, cut, drop, loop, pull, retract, retrieve, withdraw)

TRAIL (→): *accompany, bird-dog, chaperone, chase, dog, escort, eye, follow, hound, hunt, observe, pursue, retrace, run, seek, shadow, spoor, stalk, tag, tail, target, trace, track, watch* (≠ -bypass, -circumvent, detour, direct, -elude, -escape, -evade, guide, head, -ignore, lead, pilot, -shun, steer)

TRAIN (+): *acclimate, accustom, acquaint, adapt, adjust, aim, apprentice, brainwash, brief, catechize, challenge, civilize, coach, condition, convince, cultivate, develop, direct, discipline, domesticate, drill, edify, educate, enlighten, equip, exercise, familiarize, focus, fortify, groom, ground, guide, habituate, harden, hone, housebreak, housetrain, impart, implant, improve, inculcate, indoctrinate, inform, initiate, instill, instruct, introduce, inure, lead, learn, lecture, mentor, mold, naturalize, nurture, orient, prepare, prime, qualify, question, ready, rear, rehearse, retrain, school, scold, season, shape, sharpen, show, steel, strain, strengthen, stretch, study, tame, tax, teach, test, tone, toughen, tutor, update* (≠ -abandon, abuse, confound, consult, decondition, decrease, dement, derange, destroy, forget, gaslight, harm, hinder, -ignore, impede, injure, learn, madden, mislead, -neglect, obstruct, stall, stymie unhinge, unnerve, upset, worry)

TRAMPLE (/): *-abandon, abuse, attack, bash, batter, betray, boot, breach, break, bruise, brutalize, bulldoze, bully, crush, damage, dehumanize, destroy, devalue, discredit, -disregard, flatten, foil, gate-crash, grind, harm, hoof, hurt, -ignore, injure, invade, kick, maltreat, mash, menace, miss, mistreat, -neglect, objectify, offend, oppress, outrage, -overlook, override, overwhelm, penalize, persecute, poach, pound, pulp, ravage, -reject, sandbag, shortchange, smash, squash, squelch, stamp, steamroller, stomp, taunt, threaten, torment, trash, traumatize, trespass,* *tyrannize, victimize, violate, wound, wrong* (≠ advantage, aid, assist, -avoid, baby, benefit, cherish, coddle, cosset, cure, cushion, favor, fluff, follow, foster, gratify, guard, heal, heed, help, honor, humor, indulge, keep, mind, mollycoddle, note, nourish, nurture, obey, observe, overindulge, overprotect, pamper, pet, pity, placate, please, protect, recognize, respect, satisfy, shield, -sidestep, skip, skirt, soothe, spoil, treat, uncompress)

TRANQUILIZE (←): *allay, alleviate, anesthetize, appease, assuage, balance, calm, center, chloroform, compose, conciliate, console, daze, deaden, defuse, dope, dose, drug, ease, etherize, hush, hypnotize, intoxicate, lighten, lull, medicate, mellow, mesmerize, mitigate, moderate, mollify, narcotize, numb, pacify, placate, quell, quiet, quieten, relax, relieve, restrain, sedate, settle, silence, smooth, soften, soothe, stabilize, steady, still, stupefy, subdue, torpefy* (≠ aggravate, agitate, anger, arouse, bait, bother, brace, brutalize, charge, convulse, discompose, disturb, energize, enrage, excite, fluster, foment, goad, incite, inflame, infuriate, irk, irritate, jolt, madden, needle, nettle, perturb, provoke, rattle, rile, roil, rouse, shake, spur, stimulate, stir, terrorize, trouble, unnerve, upset, vex, wake, worry)

TRANSCEND (→): *beat, best, better, clobber, conquer, crush, defeat, drub, eclipse, exceed, lick, master, outclass, outdistance, outdo, outgrow, outpace, outperform, outrank, outreach, outrun, outsell, outshine, outstrip, outthink, outweigh, overcome, overshadow, overtake, pass, rival, rout, shame, skunk, subdue, supersede, supplant, surmount, surpass, thrash, top, transform, trounce, trump, usurp, wallop, whip* (≠ adopt, ape, approximate, copy, counterfeit, disappoint, duplicate, emulate, equal, equalize, follow, forfeit, ghostwrite, lose, maintain, match, mimic, obey, originate, preserve, reproduce, shrink, stall, sustain, trail, waste)

TRANSFER (→): *beam, bear, broadcast, carry, cede, communicate, conduct, contaminate, convey, deliver, diffuse, disburse, dispense, disseminate, give, hand, handle, impart, infect, pass, poison, pollute, propagate, reach, relay, release, relinquish, render, spread, supply, surrender, transfuse, transmit, yield* (≠ accept, acquire, brave, brook, catch, claim, collect, conceal, contract, discern, discover, -dodge, drop, endure, experience, face, gather, -halt, hide, hold, isolate, keep, maintain, obtain, partition, quarantine, receive, -refuse, reserve, retain, seclude, source, stop, suffer, take, weather, withhold)

TRANSFER (→): *address, advance, beam, bestow, consign, contribute, convey, deliver, dispatch, donate, drop, export, forward, furnish, give, hand, import, launch, pack, pass, present, provide, render, resend, return, schlep, send, ship, shoot, shuttle, smuggle, spirit, supply, taxi, transmit, transport* (≠ accept, acquire, choose, draw, earn, gain, garner, get, lose, obtain, order, procure, receive, -refuse, secure, select, source)

TRANSFER (→): *alter, bear, budge, carry, cart, change, convey, dislocate, displace, disturb, drive, exchange, haul, lug, modify, move, redo, refashion, relegate, relocate, remake, remodel, remove, replace,* *reposition, revamp, revise, rework, schlep, shift, shove, shunt, sideline, supersede, supplant, swap, switch, take, tote, transmit, transplant, transport, transpose, vary* (≠ affix, anchor, detain, embed, entrench, fight, fix, freeze, glue, implant, ingrain, lodge, maintain, moor, oppose, preserve, retain, root, secure, set, stabilize, stay)

TRANSFER (→): *accord, advance, alienate, allow, assign, bequeath, bestow, cede, commend, commit, comp, confer, confide, consign, contribute, convey, deal, deed, delegate, deliver, dispense, disperse, distribute, divide, donate, endow, entrust, furnish, give, grant, hand, lease, leave, lend, loan, move, pass, present, recommend, release, relinquish, rent, submit, supply, surrender, tender, transmit, trust, vest, will, yield* (≠ accept, assume, claim, collect, demand, deserve, detain, exact, hoard, hold, inherit, keep, occupy, own, possess, receive, remove, request, require, requisition, reserve, retain, take, withhold)

TRANSFIX (→): *bayonet, cut, fix, freeze, gaff, gimlet, gore, -halt, harpoon, hold, hypnotize, impale, jab, knife, lance, mesmerize, nail, paralyze, peck, penetrate, perforate, petrify, pick, pierce, pike, pin, pink, poke, poniard, prick, prong, punch, puncture, riddle, skewer, slice, spear, spellbind, spike, spindle, spit, stab, stick, stop, thrust, torpefy* (≠ accelerate, charge, empower, energize, extract, extricate, invigorate, move, pull, push, reinvigorate, release, remove, restore, revive, shunt, spur, start, stir, yank)

TRANSFIX (←): *amaze, arouse, arrest, astonish, astound, attract, beguile, bewitch, captivate, capture, charm, dazzle, delight, enchant, engross, enrapture, enslave, ensnare, entertain, enthrall, enthuse, entrance, excite, fascinate, fixate, floor, grab, grip, hold, hook, hypnotize, inspire, interest, intrigue, mesmerize, motivate, paralyze, petrify, ravish, razzle-dazzle, rivet, root, seize, spellbind, stagger, stimulate, stun, thrill, uplift, win, wow* (≠ annoy, appall, bore, bother, bug, burden, caution, chill, disenchant, disgust, disillusion, dissuade, irk, irritate, nag, needle, nitpick, offend, repel, repulse, revolt, rouse, sicken, startle, tire, wake, weary)

TRANSFORM (+): *adapt, adjust, alter, automate, calibrate, change, commute, contort, convert, cook, coordinate, customize, deform, disfigure, displace, distort, doctor, gentrify, harshen, improve, mechanize, metamorphose, modify, mold, motorize, mutate, pervert, rebuild, recast, reconceive, reconceptualize, reconstruct, redefine, redesign, redo, reengineer, refashion, reform, regenerate, reimagine, reinvent, remake, remodel, renew, replace, resolve, rethink, retool, revamp, revise, revolutionize, rework, shift, substitute, supersede, supplant, switch, transfer, transfigure, translate, transmogrify, transmute, transpose, tune, turn, tweak, uncomplicate, vary, weaponize* (≠ abide, -abort, annihilate, conserve, continue, destroy, endure, freeze, hold, immobilize, keep, maintain, obliterate, outlive, paralyze, perpetuate, preserve, prolong, protect, retain, ruin, stagnate, stale, stall, stomach, stop, sustain, terminate, transfix, uphold, weather, wreck)

TRANSLATE (+): *clarify, construe, contextualize, decipher, decode, deduce, detect, elucidate, encode, explain, generalize, illuminate, interpret,* *paraphrase, recapitulate, reduce, reiterate, render, rephrase, restate, reword, simplify, solve, summarize, transcribe, transform, turn* (≠ confuse, copy, echo, encode, garble, jumble, miscommunicate, misconstrue, misrepresent, mistranslate, muddle, puzzle, quote, repeat, reproduce, transcribe)

TRANSMIT (→): *air, beam, bear, broadcast, buzz, carry, channel, communicate, conduct, contaminate, convey, deliver, diffuse, dispatch, disseminate, email, forward, funnel, give, hand, impart, infect, mediate, message, network, pipe, poison, propagate, publicize, radiate, relay, report, send, spread, surrender, telegraph, televise, text, transfer, transfuse, transport* (≠ accept, block, catch, collect, conceal, contract, -dodge, drop, earn, gather, glean, -halt, hide, hold, isolate, keep, obscure, obtain, partition, procure, quarantine, receive, -refuse, retain, seclude, secure, source, stop, withhold)

TRANSMIT (→): *address, advance, bear, bestow, carry, cart, consign, contribute, convey, deliver, dispatch, donate, drop, export, express, forward, give, haul, import, launch, move, pack, pass, present, remove, render, resend, return, schlep, send, shift, ship, shoot, transfer, transport* (≠ accept, acquire, draw, drop, earn, forget, gain, garner, get, lose, obtain, order, -overlook, procure, receive, request, secure)

TRANSMUTE (+): *adjust, alter, change, contort, convert, deform, disfigure, displace, distort, metamorphose, modify, mutate, recast, reconceive, redefine, redesign, redo, reengineer, refashion, regenerate, reimagine, reinvent, remake, remodel, replace, rethink, retool, revamp, revise, rework, shift, substitute, supersede, supplant, transfigure, transform, translate, transmogrify, transpose, vary* (≠ abide, annihilate, continue, destroy, endure, hold, increase, keep, maintain, obliterate, perpetuate, preserve, protect, -refuse, retain, ruin, stagnate, stale, stay, sustain, terminate, uphold, wreck)

TRANSPORT (→): *address, advance, beam, bear, bestow, bring, carry, chauffeur, conduct, consign, contribute, convey, courier, deliver, deport, dispatch, donate, drive, drop, exile, export, ferry, fetch, fly, forward, give, hand, haul, hump, import, launch, lug, move, pack, pass, piggyback, present, remove, render, resend, return, run, sail, schlep, send, shift, ship, shoot, shoulder, smuggle, spirit, take, taxi, tote, transfer, transmit, truck* (≠ accept, acquire, block, draw, earn, freeze, gain, garner, get, grip, keep, obtain, procure, receive, retain, secure, source, stop, -thwart)

TRANSPORT (←): *agitate, bewitch, captivate, charm, content, delight, dizzy, elate, electrify, elevate, enchant, enrapture, enthrall, entrance, excite, exhilarate, fascinate, gladden, gratify, hypnotize, inflame, inspire, intoxicate, mesmerize, move, please, provoke, quicken, ravish, razzle-dazzle, rejoice, satisfy, send, slay, spellbind, stimulate, stir, thrill, uplift, warm, wow* (≠ anguish, annoy, appall, bore, crucify, demoralize, demotivate, depress, discourage, dishearten, dismay, dispirit, distress, fatigue, hallucinate, irritate, nag, needle, nettle, oppress, repulse, sadden, tire, torment, torture, vex, weary)

TRAP (←): *abduct, ambush, apprehend, arrest, bag, beguile, bind, birdlime, blindside, boobytrap, box, bushwhack, cage, capture, catch, chain, clasp, clutch, collar, confine, convince, cop, corner, corral, deceive, decoy, detain, disappear, double-cross, double-talk, dupe, embroil, endanger, enmesh, ensnare, ensnarl, entangle, entrap, fasten, fetter, fool, frame, get, glom, grab, grapple, grasp, grip, halter, handcuff, herd, hoax, hold, hook, immure, imperil, implicate, imprison, incarcerate, institutionalize, intern, inveigle, involve, jail, kidnap, land, lasso, latch, lock, lure, manacle, mine, mire, nab, nail, net, outmaneuver, outsmart, outwit, overtake, package, pigeonhole, pin, restrain, rope, secure, seduce, seize, shackle, snaffle, snag, snare, snatch, spirit, subdue, surprise, take, tangle, trammel, trick, wrangle, wrest* (≠ aid, allow, assist, benefit, clear, deliver, detach, discharge, disengage, disentangle, -disregard, distrust, doubt, dread, drop, emancipate, enfranchise, -exclude, extricate, fear, forget, free, help, -ignore, liberate, loose, loosen, lose, manumit, miss, mistake, -neglect, open, -overlook, ransom, redeem, release, rescue, save, solve, spring, unbind, uncage, unchain, unhand, unshackle, untangle, warn)

TRASH (/): *abrade, assail, attack, badmouth, batter, blackguard, blame, boo, break, censure, chastise, condemn, criticize, critique, decry, defame, demolish, denigrate, denounce, denunciate, depreciate, destroy, detract, devastate, diminish, -discount, disparage, doom, eradicate, erase, excoriate, fault, finger, frame, fulminate, impugn, knock, lessen, malign, mar, mock, neg, pulverize, ravage, rebuke, reduce, reprimand, resent, ridicule, ruin, scapegoat, shatter, sink, slam, slate, smash, spoil, violate, vituperate, weed, wreck, zap* (≠ accept, acclaim, aggrandize, applaud, canonize, cherish, compliment, congratulate, dignify, elevate, enshrine, exalt, fetishize, flatter, glamorize, glitz, glorify, gratify, heroicize, heroize, honor, idealize, idolize, ingratiate, overrate, praise, protect, respect, revere, romanticize, sentimentalize, shield, treasure, uphold, venerate, vindicate)

TRAUMATIZE (/): *abuse, amaze, anguish, appall, assault, astound, attack, batter, beat, bestialize, break, castrate, confuse, constrain, cripple, crucify, damage, daze, deaden, deafen, debase, debilitate, deduct, degrade, demote, deplete, depredate, deprive, devalue, diminish, disable, discipline, dismay, distress, drain, emasculate, enervate, exhaust, exploit, famish, fracture, grieve, harass, harm, hit, horrify, humble, hurt, impair, impoverish, imprison, injure, lower, maim, malnourish, menace, molest, mutilate, numb, offend, oppress, outrage, overextend, paralyze, persecute, rape, sadden, sap, scalp, scant, shock, shrivel, sicken, stagger, startle, starve, stun, stupefy, subjugate, subordinate, terrify, threaten, torment, torture, trouble, underfeed, unman, unnerve, upset, vanquish, vex, victimize, violate, weaken, welt, wither, wound, wrong* (≠ aid, amuse, appease, assist, baby, bandage, calm, coddle, cosset, defend, delight, doctor, entertain, favor, fix, foster, gratify, heal, help, humor, infantilize, inspire, lull, mellow, mend, misdiagnose, mitigate, moderate, mollify, mollycoddle, nourish, nurse, nurture, oblige, pacify, pamper, pity, placate, please, pleasure, protect, regret, rehabilitate, rejuvenate, remedy, repair, rescue, restore, reward, satiate, satisfy, save, sedate, soothe, splint, spoil, spoon-feed, stabilize, steady, sustain, thrill, tickle, tolerate, treat, uplift, wow)

TREASURE (+): *admire, adore, appreciate, bronze, caress, ceremonialize, cherish, consecrate, conserve, defend, dig, embalm, enjoy, enshrine, esteem, fancy, fetishize, guard, honor, idolize, immortalize, love, memorialize, pet, preserve, prize, protect, regard, relish, respect, revere, reverence, ritualize, save, secure, value, venerate, worship* (≠ abhor, abominate, badmouth, belittle, denigrate, -despise, -detest, -discount, -disdain, disparage, disrespect, execrate, fritter, -hate, -loathe, minimize, mock, ridicule, -scorn, -slight, -snub, squander, trash, undervalue, waste) **(¿) ABSTRACTION ALERT. Concrete goals essential!**

TREAT (→): *afford, amuse, appoint, bankroll, bestow, blow, buy, decorate, delight, dispense, divert, endow, entertain, equip, escort, feast, flaunt, fund, furnish, give, grant, host, indulge, offer, outlay, overpay, patronize, pay, present, provide, regale, rig, satisfy, stake, stand, stock, supply, tender, underwrite, volunteer* (≠ bill, charge, commodify, curb, demand, -deny, deprive, disappoint, discipline, disinherit, -disown, -eschew, expense, forgo, frustrate, -ignore, loan, -neglect, -overlook, persecute, sell, -slight, starve, steal, stiff, stint, take, torment, upset, victimize, withhold, worry, wound, wrong)

TREAT (+): *administer, apply, attend, bandage, cure, decontaminate, delouse, diagnose, doctor, dose, dress, drug, heal, help, hospitalize, medicate, mend, nurse, prescribe, purify, quarantine, rectify, rehabilitate, remedy, splint, sterilize, tend* (≠ afflict, contaminate, damage, harm, hurt, impair, indispose, infect, infest, injure, maltreat, misdiagnose, mistreat, -neglect, overdose, pain, palsy, plague, poison, sicken, spike, wound)

TRICK (←): *bait, bamboozle, beard, beat, bed, beguile, betray, bilk, bleed, bluff, bootleg, bottom-deal, buffalo, bullshit, bunk, burn, candy-coat, catch, cheat, chisel, clip, con, convince, cook, cozen, deacon, deceive, defraud, delude, diddle, disinform, doctor, double-cross, double-talk, dupe, enmesh, ensnare, entangle, entice, entrap, euchre, fake, fleece, flimflam, fool, fox, frame, fudge, gammon, gas, gouge, gull, gyp, hoax, hocus-pocus, hoodwink, hook, hornswoggle, hose, humbug, hustle, hype, ice, inveigle, juggle, lure, maneuver, manipulate, misdirect, misguide, misinform, mislead, misrepresent, mousetrap, outfox, outslick, outsmart, outwit, overreach, pervert, plant, pluck, pretend, rephrase, rook, rope, salt, sandbag, scam, screw, seduce, shaft, shortchange, skin, snooker, snow, soak, spin, spoof, squeeze, stick, stiff, sting, stonewall, sucker, swindle, take, tease, tempt, trap, two-time, underpay, vamp, victimize, whitewash, wrong* (≠ assume, assure, believe, blab, blurt, confess, confide, confirm, confront, debunk, disabuse, disclose, disenchant, disillusion, divulge, expose, face, honor, protect, regret, restore, reveal, show, tell, trust, uncloak, uncover, undeceive, unmask, unveil)

TRIGGER (→): *accelerate, activate, actuate, arouse, brainstorm, buzz, catalyze, charge, crank, cue, detonate, discharge, drive, electrify, elicit,* *energize, excite, fire, flip, fuel, generate, goose, ignite, incite, initiate, instigate, jolt, jump-start, kick-start, launch, light, move, power, prod, produce, prompt, provoke, push, quicken, reactivate, reboot, recharge, release, run, spark, start, stimulate, switch, trip, vitalize, zap* (≠ -abort, arrest, brake, check, cripple, cut, dampen, deactivate, deaden, decelerate, freeze, -halt, hamper, hinder, hobble, incapacitate, jam, kill, numb, paralyze, repress, reset, sedate, slow, stall, stick, stop, stunt, stymie, suppress, -thwart)

TRIM (+): *adjust, adorn, arrange, array, beautify, bedeck, beribbon, costume, deck, decorate, dress, edge, elaborate, embellish, emblazon, embroider, fancify, festoon, fringe, garnish, glitter, grace, neaten, order, ornament, paint, provide, sculpt, set, spangle, stipple, stud, tidy, tinsel, tool* (≠ blemish, damage, deform, disfigure, dismantle, expose, harshen, hurt, mar, reduce, scar, spoil, stain, streamline, strip, uglify)

TRIM (/): *abbreviate, abridge, abstract, barber, bob, chop, clip, compact, compress, concentrate, condense, constrict, contract, crop, cull, curtail, cut, decrease, deflate, deplete, diminish, dock, drain, edit, erode, lessen, lighten, lop, minimize, mow, nip, pare, pollard, précis, prune, razor, reduce, rephrase, shave, shear, shorten, shrink, slice, snip, summarize, taper, truncate, weed, whittle* (≠ accentuate, accrue, add, amplify, augment, boost, broaden, double, elaborate, elongate, emphasize, enhance, enlarge, expand, extend, grow, heighten, increase, inflate, intensify, lengthen, magnify, maximize, multiply, raise, reinforce, strengthen, stretch, swell, treble, triple)

TRIVIALIZE (/): *abuse, badmouth, belittle, criticize, critique, decry, deemphasize, defame, denigrate, denounce, deprecate, depreciate, devalue, diminish, -discount, discredit, disgrace, dismiss, disparage, disrespect, downplay, lessen, malign, minimize, rip, -scorn, shrink, slander, -slight, slur, soft-pedal, traduce, underemphasize, underestimate, underplay, understate, undervalue, vilify* (≠ accent, accentuate, acclaim, affirm, amplify, applaud, belabor, boost, broadcast, commend, compliment, congratulate, credit, elevate, emphasize, exaggerate, exalt, flatter, glorify, gratify, honor, idealize, idolize, inflate, laud, lionize, magnify, overdramatize, oversell, overstate, praise, prioritize, punctuate, raise, revere, telegraph, worship)

TROUBLE (/): *afflict, aggravate, aggrieve, agitate, anger, annoy, badger, bedevil, bother, bug, burden, chafe, chagrin, concern, confound, confuse, crucify, discomfort, discommode, disconcert, discredit, disfavor, disgrace, disoblige, disquiet, distract, distress, disturb, encumber, exasperate, fetter, fret, gall, get, gravel, grieve, hamper, hamstring, handicap, harass, harm, harry, hassle, haunt, hinder, hobble, impede, incommode, inconvenience, inflame, inhibit, irk, irritate, manacle, muddle, nag, needle, nettle, niggle, nitpick, noodge, obstruct, pain, peeve, perplex, perturb, pester, pique, plague, provoke, psych, rile, sadden, saddle, shackle, short-circuit, sorrow, spook, strain, stress, torment, torture, trammel, traumatize, troll, try, unnerve, unsettle, upset, vex, weaken,* *weary, weigh, worry* (≠ abet, accommodate, aid, alleviate, amuse, appease, assist, comfort, console, content, delight, disarm, ease, entertain, facilitate, favor, gladden, gratify, help, mollify, oblige, pacify, placate, please, reassure, satisfy, smooth, steady, sugarcoat, support, thrill)

TROUBLESHOOT (+): *accommodate, adjust, align, alleviate, amend, balance, break, calibrate, connect, correct, crack, debug, decipher, decode, decrypt, deduce, defray, diagnose, edit, expose, fine-tune, fit, fix, focus, grind, improve, isolate, mend, overhaul, patch, polish, punctuate, quarantine, readjust, realign, reassemble, rectify, regulate, remedy, renovate, repair, rephrase, reshuffle, restore, rethink, retool, retrofit, revise, right, service, set, sharpen, simplify, solve, square, tighten, tune, tweak* (≠ afflict, blunt, breach, break, confuse, contaminate, damage, derange, destroy, disorder, disorganize, dull, hamstring, hurt, infect, misdiagnose, monkey-wrench, poison, ruin, sabotage, scotch, scupper, scuttle, shelve, spoil, stymie, undermine, upset)

TRUMPET (→): *advertise, announce, bellow, blare, blast, blazon, blurb, broadcast, bulletin, call, circulate, communicate, concede, confess, confide, confirm, confront, declare, disclose, disseminate, divulge, emblazon, extol, feature, flash, herald, impart, intimate, laud, notify, pitch, plug, praise, proclaim, promote, promulgate, publicize, publish, puff, report, reveal, roar, salute, shout, show, sound, spotlight, spread, telegraph, toast* (≠ bury, cloak, conceal, confound, denounce, devoice, erase, expunge, hide, hush, -ignore, mislead, misrepresent, muffle, mute, -omit, quiet, redact, retract, revoke, silence, smother, stifle, suppress, swallow, throttle, whisper)

TRUNCATE (/): *abate, abbreviate, abridge, abstract, compress, concentrate, condense, constrict, contract, curtail, cut, decrease, de-escalate, deflate, digest, diminish, dock, downsize, elide, encapsulate, epitomize, generalize, lessen, lower, minimize, moderate, modify, pare, précis, prune, recapitulate, reduce, retrench, shorten, shrink, slash, subtract, summarize, syncopate, taper, trim* (≠ accentuate, accrue, add, amplify, augment, broaden, build, elaborate, elongate, emphasize, enlarge, expand, extend, increase, inflate, lengthen, magnify, maximize, ornament, stretch, supplement, unspool)

TRUST (+): *accept, account, accredit, anticipate, assume, await, believe, buy, conclude, conjecture, consider, consult, credit, decide, deduce, expect, fancy, gather, guess, imagine, infer, judge, predetermine, presume, reason, reckon, suppose, surmise, suspect, swallow, take, understand* (≠ challenge, cross-examine, debate, debunk, disbelieve, discredit, dispute, distrust, double-deal, doubt, dread, fear, grill, interrogate, interview, mistrust, question, -reject, scruple, suspect) **(¿) ABSTRACTION ALERT. Concrete goals essential!**

TUG (←): *attract, carry, coax, convey, dislodge, drag, draw, ferry, fish, force, grab, haul, heave, hitch, jerk, lug, move, pluck, pull, shuttle, snag, snatch, strain, tear, tow, transport, wrench, wrest, yank* (≠ bash, bump, cast, drive, heave, nudge, pitch, propel, punt, push, ram, release, repel, repulse, shove, shunt, stab, throw, thrust, toss)

TUNE (+): *adapt, adjust, align, attune, balance, blend, calibrate, center, compose, coordinate, correct, equalize, harmonize, integrate, measure, modulate, pace, pitch, realign, rectify, regulate, right, set, streamline, synchronize, temper, tweak* (≠ agitate, crack, discombobulate, disrupt, disturb, interrupt, jangle, jar, jolt, mismatch, muddle, rattle, silence)

TURN (→): *bend, circle, circulate, coil, corner, crank, curve, dial, incline, loop, manipulate, negotiate, orbit, oscillate, pass, pivot, reel, revolve, roll, rotate, round, screw, shunt, spin, sway, swing, swirl, swivel, twiddle, twirl, twist, unscrew, weave, wheel, whip, whirl, wind* (≠ bind, correct, direct, fasten, freeze, hobble, hold, level, lock, nail, paralyze, pin, smooth, stabilize, steady, stop, straighten, tie, unbend)

TURN (→): *aim, alter, alternate, -avert, bend, capsize, change, channel, convert, curve, deflect, depart, detour, detract, direct, divert, double, face, focus, funnel, incline, invert, loop, move, pivot, rechannel, redirect, refract, reorient, reposition, retrace, return, reverse, rotate, shift, shunt, sidetrack, subvert, sway, swerve, swing, swirl, switch, swivel, tack, transfer, transform, twist, upset, vary, wheel, whip, whirl, zigzag* (≠ abide, bide, continue, defy, endure, fix, freeze, hold, keep, resist, retain, set, stabilize, stay, straighten, target)

TURN (+): *adapt, adjust, alter, calibrate, cast, change, convert, coordinate, customize, deflect, develop, divert, fashion, fit, form, get, grow, invert, make, metamorphose, modify, mold, move, mutate, refashion, remake, remodel, render, rephrase, retort, reverse, run, sculpt, shape, shift, switch, transfer, transfigure, transform, translate, transmute, transpose, tune, tweak, vary, wax* (≠ abide, bide, broaden, continue, endure, expand, fix, freeze, hold, keep, paralyze, retain, set, stabilize, stay, steady, still)

TURN (/): *bias, bribe, condition, convince, corrupt, curdle, -desert, dispose, distort, incline, influence, nobble, persuade, poison, predetermine, predispose, prejudge, prejudice, prepossess, -renounce, -repudiate, retract, slant, spike, suborn, subvert, suggest, sway, taint* (≠ -deter, discourage, dissuade, hamper, hinder, hold, inhibit, maintain, -prevent, repel, restrain, sustain, sweeten)

TUTOR (+): *advise, aid, apprentice, apprise, assist, brief, civilize, coach, compel, condition, convince, counsel, cultivate, demonstrate, develop, direct, discipline, drill, edify, educate, elevate, enlighten, familiarize, foster, groom, ground, guide, help, housebreak, housetrain, impart, implant, improve, inculcate, indoctrinate, inform, initiate, inspire, instill, instruct, introduce, lead, lecture, mentor, monitor, nurture, order, parrot, perfect, prepare, prime, qualify, question, quiz, read, ready, rear, rehearse, retrain, reveal, school, scold, season, shape, sharpen, show, steer, stretch, supervise, tame, tax, teach, test, train, update* (≠ abuse, addle, baffle, bewilder, censor, cheat, conceal, confound, confuse, consult, debase, deceive, defraud, delude, demean, discombobulate, disguise, -disregard, fabricate, fluster, follow, gaslight, hamper, heed, hide, hinder, -ignore, impair, impede, learn, lower, mind, misinform, mislead, muddle, mystify, -neglect, nonplus, obey, obscure, observe, -omit, -overlook, perplex, puzzle, ruffle, stall, study, stump, stymie, suppress, surprise, withhold)

TWEAK (+): *accommodate, adapt, adjust, align, alter, amend, arrange, balance, calibrate, change, compose, convert, coordinate, correct, customize, doctor, edit, enhance, fine-tune, fit, fix, flavor, improve, jerk, magnify, marinate, maximize, modify, modulate, nip, patch, perfect, pinch, pull, punctuate, realign, reconceive, reconceptualize, rectify, refashion, reform, regulate, reimagine, reinvent, remodel, repair, rephrase, reshape, restore, rethink, retool, revise, richen, right, season, set, shape, shift, spice, square, squeeze, strengthen, suit, temper, tug, tune, twist, uncomplicate, upgrade, weaponize* (≠ blemish, blight, break, confuse, damage, defy, destroy, diminish, disorganize, disturb, dull, freeze, harm, hurt, -ignore, impair, maintain, mar, -neglect, paralyze, preserve, -prevent, resist, retain, ruin, save, scatter, spoil, stabilize, stay, stymie, tarnish, -thwart, undermine, unsettle, vitiate, weaken, worsen)

TWIST (/): *alter, bend, braid, break, change, coil, color, contort, corkscrew, curl, deform, derange, dial, distort, embellish, embroider, entangle, entwine, falsify, flip, fold, garble, gnarl, impair, miscommunicate, misquote, misreport, misrepresent, misshape, misstate, modify, mutate, pervert, plait, raddle, rotate, screw, skew, spin, turn, twine, twirl, warp, weave, wiggle, wind, wrap, wrench, wrest, wriggle, wring, wrinkle* (≠ align, clarify, clear, expand, explain, explicate, flatten, rephrase, right, simplify, smooth, still, straighten, unbend, unbraid, uncoil, uncurl, unfold, unravel, unskew, unspool, untangle, untwist, unwind)

TYRANNIZE (/): *abase, abuse, anguish, badger, blackjack, browbeat, brutalize, bulldoze, bully, butcher, coerce, cow, crush, daunt, degrade, dehumanize, demean, depersonalize, desensitize, dictate, dominate, domineer, dragoon, enforce, enslave, frighten, grind, harass, hassle, hector, hound, humble, humiliate, intimidate, lynch, maltreat, manhandle, menace, mistreat, muscle, objectify, oppress, outrage, overpower, overwhelm, persecute, pervert, poison, pollute, pressure, profane, quash, quell, railroad, repress, ride, rule, savage, scare, subdue, subjugate, suppress, taint, terrorize, threaten, torment, torture, trample, traumatize, victimize, violate, warp, wrong* (≠ allay, alleviate, assist, baby, cherish, coddle, cosset, defend, defy, dignify, elevate, endure, ennoble, exalt, favor, foster, gratify, guard, help, honor, humanize, humor, indulge, mollycoddle, nurture, pamper, pity, preserve, protect, regret, relax, repent, resist, respect, restore, sabotage, save, secure, shield, spoil, subvert, support, topple, undermine, uplift, usurp, weather, withstand)

ULCERATE (/): *anger, annoy, bleed, blister, brew, chafe, damage, erode, gall, harm, hurt, infect, irk, nag, needle, nettle, perforate, rankle, wound* (≠ aid, calm, coat, cool, delight, doctor, grow, heal, improve, lessen, medicate, mellow, nurse, palliate, please, sedate, soothe, tranquilize, treat)

UMPIRE (+): *adjudge, adjudicate, arbitrate, ascertain, broker, chair, command, conclude, consider, control, decide, determine, direct, equalize, examine, handle, inspect, judge, manage, mediate, moderate, mull, negotiate, pacify, ponder, propitiate, prosecute, reconcile, referee, renegotiate, resolve, reunite, rule, scrutinize, settle, size, skirt, solve, unskew, weigh* (≠ baffle, bias, challenge, cheat, confound, confront, confuse, debate, defy, demand, dismiss, -disregard, exacerbate, favor, fight, -ignore, inflame, instigate, manipulate, misrepresent, miss, mistake, muddle, oppose, -overlook, predetermine, prejudge, prejudice, provoke, skew, skirt, slant, twist)

UNBALANCE (/): *agitate, anger, annoy, bother, bug, confuse, convulse, crack, craze, dement, derange, destabilize, discomfit, discompose, disconcert, disquiet, distract, disturb, dizzy, enrage, exasperate, faze, fluster, frenzy, incense, inebriate, inflame, infuriate, intoxicate, irk, irritate, madden, needle, nettle, nitpick, perturb, provoke, rattle, ruffle, shake, shock, spook, threaten, throw, trigger, trouble, unhinge, unnerve, unsettle, unsteady, unstring, upset, vex, worry* (≠ balance, calm, center, coddle, comfort, compose, defend, gratify, help, humor, lull, maintain, mellow, mitigate, moderate, mollify, nurture, pacify, placate, preserve, protect, quiet, relax, settle, shelter, soothe, steady, tranquilize)

UNBURDEN (→): *clear, discharge, disclose, disencumber, disengage, disentangle, divest, emancipate, enfranchise, extricate, free, grant, liberate, loose, loosen, manumit, redeem, release, relieve, rescue, rid, soothe, spring, unbind, uncage, unchain, uncover, unfetter* (≠ burden, bury, cloak, conceal, disavow, disguise, encumber, fetter, hamper, restrain, saddle, shackle, short-circuit, subject, withhold)

UNBURDEN (+): *alleviate, cast, clear, deliver, disburden, discharge, disencumber, disengage, disentangle, -ditch, drop, dump, ease, empty, evacuate, free, lessen, liberate, lighten, offload, reduce, release, relieve, remove, rescue, unchain, unfetter, unleash, unload, unpack, vacate, void* (≠ acquire, burden, charge, cram, encumber, fill, handicap, heap, jam, jam-pack, load, lumber, obtain, overload, overstuff, pack, saddle, sardine, stuff, weight)

UNBUTTON (/): *access, disconnect, disengage, disentangle, expose, free, locate, loose, loosen, open, relax, release, relieve, retrieve, reveal, separate, split, thaw, unbuckle, unclasp, undo, unfasten, unfetter, unfreeze, unhook, unlock, untie, unwind, unwrap, unzip* (≠ affix, attach, belt, bind, buckle, button, cinch, clasp, close, clothe, cover, dress, fasten, join, lace, seal, secure, stress, tie, worry, wrap, zip)

UNCOVER (→): *accentuate, accost, acknowledge, admit, advertise, announce, avow, bare, betray, blab, blurt, brandish, break, broadcast, circulate, communicate, concede, confess, confide, confirm, confront, convince, debunk, declare, disclose, discover, disinter, display, disseminate, divulge, exhibit, expose, feature, flaunt, flourish, highlight, illustrate, impart, inform, investigate, leak, manifest, open, own, parade, placard, post, probe, proclaim, promulgate, publicize, publish, relate, reveal, share, show, showcase, sound, spill, spotlight, squeal, suss, talk, telegraph, tell, unbosom* (≠ attest, authenticate, bury, camouflage, certify, cloak, conceal, confirm, corroborate, counterfeit, cover, deceive, disguise, document, evidence, fake, feign, fool, hide, mask, obfuscate, obscure, prove, quash, ratify, seal, secrete, spin, substantiate, support, trick, uphold, validate, veil, verify, whitewash)

UNCOVER (←): *crack, debunk, decipher, decode, deflate, demolish, demystify, deride, disclose, discredit, disparage, disprove, divulge, exhume, explode, expose, flay, invalidate, lampoon, mock, nail, out, penetrate, pierce, puncture, reveal, ridicule, showcase, skin, strip, tell, trust, uncloak, unclothe, undrape, undress, unearth, unmask, untangle, unveil, unwrap, unzip* (≠ becloud, bedim, befog, blanket, camouflage, cloak, clothe, cloud, conceal, costume, cover, darken, disguise, dress, eclipse, enshroud, eye, gild, gloss, hide, impersonate, mask, obscure, overshadow, shade, shroud, spackle, suppress, varnish, veil, wrap)

UNDERESTIMATE (/): *anticipate, belittle, bench, criticize, decry, deemphasize, denigrate, depersonalize, deprecate, depreciate, -despise, diminish, -discount, -disdain, dismiss, disparage, -disregard, disrespect, divine, downplay, gauge, insult, judge, marginalize, minimize, miscalculate, miscarry, misgauge, misjudge, miss, mock, modulate, -overlook, ridicule, -scorn, second-guess, sideline, -slight, soften, soft-pedal, trivialize, underemphasize, underrate, undersell, undervalue, vilify* (≠ accentuate, admire, adore, affirm, appreciate, assert, belabor, cherish, emphasize, esteem, exaggerate, fetishize, heighten, heroicize, heroize, honor, idealize, idolize, inflate, maximize, overestimate, overrate, oversell, overstate, overvalue, prize, regard, respect, revere, reverence, romanticize, sentimentalize, treasure, value, venerate, worship)

UNDERMINE (/): *attenuate, block, blunt, boobytrap, break, bugger, canker, castrate, checkmate, compromise, contaminate, corrode, corrupt, counteract, cripple, damage, debilitate, deep-six, demoralize, deplete, destroy, devitalize, diminish, disable, disarm, disqualify, disrupt, disturb, doom, emasculate, enfeeble, erode, foil, -frustrate, half-ass, -halt, hamper, hamstring, harm, hinder, hobble, hollow, honeycomb, hurt,* *impair, impede, inactivate, incapacitate, inhibit, injure, interrupt, invalidate, kneecap, mar, monkey-wrench, muzzle, obstruct, overextend, paralyze, pervert, pickle, poison, queer, rock, ruin, sabotage, sandbag, sap, scotch, scupper, scuttle, shelve, shrivel, sideline, soften, spoil, subvert, taint, threaten, -thwart, torpedo, undercut, unhinge, unman, unnerve, unsettle, upset, vandalize, warp, weaken, wear, whittle, wither, wizen, wobble, wreck* (≠ animate, assist, augment, bolster, boost, brace, build, buoy, buttress, calibrate, catalyze, choreograph, compose, defend, develop, devise, embolden, enable, encourage, energize, enhance, enshrine, expedite, facilitate, fix, fortify, galvanize, guard, help, heroicize, heroize, idolize, improve, inspire, maintain, mend, midwife, motivate, optimize, orchestrate, organize, overhaul, patrol, perfect, preserve, prioritize, protect, rebuild, rectify, relieve, remedy, repair, rescue, restructure, revolutionize, safeguard, save, stabilize, steady, strengthen, support, sustain, tidy, tweak, vitalize, worship)

UNDERPIN (/): *back, bear, beef, bolster, brace, build, buttress, carry, construct, defend, derive, establish, fortify, found, ground, locate, plant, predicate, prop, reinforce, rest, root, settle, stay, steady, strengthen, support, sustain, truss, uphold* (≠ assail, attack, demolish, destroy, dismantle, erode, impugn, leave, move, raze, ruin, sabotage, scotch, scupper, scuttle, undermine, unsettle)

UNDRESS (←): *bare, bark, denude, dismantle, disrobe, divest, doff, expose, flay, husk, peel, remove, rend, rip, shed, shred, shuck, skin, strip, tatter, tear, unbuckle, unbutton, uncloak, unclothe, uncover, undrape, unfasten, unhook, unlace, unmask, unveil, unzip* (≠ accoutre, apparel, array, attire, buckle, button, caparison, cloak, clothe, costume, cover, deck, drape, dress, garb, gown, mantle, outfit, robe, swaddle, swathe, zip)

UNEARTH (←): *ascertain, detect, discover, disinter, dredge, excavate, exhume, explore, expose, ferret, find, investigate, probe, rake, reveal, sleuth, spotlight, suss, uncover, uproot* (≠ bury, conceal, cover, disguise, ensconce, entomb, hide, inter, mask, obscure, seal, shroud, stash, store, stow, suppress, vault)

UNFASTEN (/): *access, disconnect, disengage, disentangle, expose, free, locate, loose, loosen, open, ravel, release, relieve, retrieve, reveal, separate, split, unbind, unbraid, unbuckle, unbutton, unclasp, undo, unfetter, unhook, unlace, unlash, unlock, unravel, unsnarl, untangle, untie, unwind, unzip* (≠ bind, braid, buckle, button, cage, cinch, clasp, close, connect, corset, entangle, fasten, fix, hook, interlace, interweave, knot, lace, lash, leash, lock, seal, secure, snarl, tangle, tie, tighten, wind, zip)

UNFOLD (→): *clarify, describe, disclose, display, elaborate, expand, explain, expound, extend, fan, flatten, illustrate, interpret, iron, narrate, present, press, relate, resolve, reveal, show, smooth, straighten, tell, tidy, uncrumple, unfurl, unspool, unwind, unwrap* (≠ bend, crease, crimp, crinkle, crumple, curl, fold, gather, package, pleat, rumple, tuck, wrap, wriggle, wrinkle)

UNHINGE (/): *aggravate, agitate, alarm, anger, annoy, bedevil, bother, confound, confuse, crack, craze, dement, derange, destabilize, disable, discombobulate, discompose, disorder, disquiet, distract, disturb, enrage, faze, fluster, freak, frenzy, haunt, incite, inebriate, infuriate, irritate, madden, needle, nettle, nitpick, panic, perturb, plague, rattle, rile, terrify, unbalance, undermine, unnerve, unsettle, unstring, upset, vex* (≠ anchor, appease, assuage, balance, buoy, calm, compose, conciliate, gratify, hush, hypnotize, lull, mellow, mesmerize, mitigate, mollify, pacify, placate, propitiate, quiet, relax, sedate, settle, soothe, stabilize, steady, still, tranquilize)

UNHOOK (/): *breach, detach, disengage, dismantle, display, expose, extricate, free, loose, loosen, open, release, replace, retrieve, reveal, separate, strip, unbind, unblock, unbuckle, unbutton, unclasp, unclothe, uncover, unfasten, unlatch, unlock, untie, unzip* (≠ affix, bar, barricade, bolt, buckle, button, cinch, clasp, clench, clinch, clip, close, cordon, deadbolt, fasten, fix, hook, join, latch, lock, padlock, peg, seal, secure, shut, tie, zip)

UNITE (+): *alloy, ally, amalgamate, associate, band, blend, cement, close, coalesce, combine, conjoin, connect, consolidate, couple, embody, fuse, graft, herd, hybridize, incorporate, integrate, join, knit, knot, lap, link, lock, marry, meld, merge, mingle, mortar, network, pool, rally, reintegrate, reunite, splice, synthesize, team, tie, twist, unify, wed, weld* (≠ alienate, atomize, break, cleave, diffuse, disaffect, disconnect, disengage, disperse, divide, divorce, estrange, -exclude, fracture, halve, isolate, -omit, oppose, orphan, -ostracize, oust, part, pulverize, scatter, seclude, section, separate, sever, share, shatter, split, spread)

UNLEASH (→): *advertise, air, announce, bellow, blab, blare, blurt, brandish, broadcast, circulate, communicate, convey, declare, describe, disseminate, enunciate, evince, exhibit, expound, express, flaunt, loose, offer, parade, proclaim, publish, raise, release, showcase, sound, spitball, state, submit, telegraph, tender, trumpet, vent, ventilate, voice, volunteer, write* (≠ allay, bottle, bridle, check, choke, constrain, contain, control, curb, govern, handle, hold, holster, inhibit, lull, manage, muffle, pocket, quell, quiet, rein, repress, restrain, sheathe, smother, soothe, squelch, squench, stifle, still, strangle, suppress, swallow, tame)

UNLEASH (+): *accelerate, brainstorm, bustle, catalyze, catapult, deliver, discharge, disengage, disentangle, drive, egg, emancipate, encourage, energize, enfranchise, expedite, fast-forward, fast-track, fire, foment, force, free, galvanize, goad, hasten, heave, hurl, hurry, hustle, induce, inflict, inspire, instigate, jolt, launch, liberate, lob, loose, loosen, lubricate, manumit, mobilize, motivate, nudge, poke, prod, propel, provoke, push, quicken, rabble-rouse, relax, release, rush, shoot, shove, speed, spring, stimulate, throw, thrust, trigger, unbind, unbridle, unburden, uncage, unchain, uncork, unfetter, unlace, unlock, unmoor, unshackle, untether, untie, urge* (≠ bind, bottle, bridle, cage, check, confine, constrain, contain, control, curb, deactivate, domesticate, enchain, fetter, freeze, govern, -halt, halter, hamper, handcuff, hold, holster, housebreak, housetrain, impair, impede, inactivate, incapacitate, inhibit, manacle, pace, paralyze, regulate, rein, repress, reset, restrain, shackle, smother, stop, straightjacket, stymie, suppress, tame, -thwart, trammel, truss)

UNLOCK (+): *air, break, crack, decipher, decode, decrypt, deduce, detect, discharge, emancipate, enfranchise, express, free, jimmy, liberate, loose, loosen, manumit, open, pop, release, solve, spring, unbar, unbind, unbolt, unbuckle, unbutton, uncage, unchain, uncork, unfasten, unfetter, unhook, unlatch, unleash, unmoor, unravel, unseal, unshackle, vent* (≠ bind, bridle, cage, check, confine, constrain, contain, control, curb, enchain, encode, fasten, fetter, govern, halter, hamper, handcuff, hold, inhibit, lock, manacle, regulate, restrain, seal, shackle, shut, straightjacket, tame, trammel)

UNMASK (+): *advertise, announce, bare, betray, blab, blaze, blurt, broadcast, communicate, confess, confide, confirm, confront, debunk, declare, demolish, detect, disclose, discover, discredit, disinter, display, disprove, divulge, exhibit, expose, impart, inform, invalidate, leak, manifest, nail, out, placard, post, proclaim, promulgate, publicize, publish, rake, relate, reveal, share, shatter, show, sound, spill, squeal, strip, talk, telegraph, tell, uncloak, unclothe, uncover, undrape, undress, unearth, unveil* (≠ becloud, bedim, befog, camouflage, cloak, clothe, cloud, conceal, costume, cover, darken, disguise, eclipse, enshroud, gild, gloss, hide, mask, obscure, overshadow, secrete, shade, shroud, spackle, varnish, veil, whitewash)

UNNERVE (/): *afflict, agitate, alarm, appall, blackjack, bother, browbeat, brutalize, buffalo, bug, bully, castrate, chill, confound, confuse, cow, craze, damp, dampen, daunt, deaden, debilitate, dement, demoralize, depress, derange, disarm, discombobulate, discompose, disconcert, discourage, dishearten, dismay, dispirit, disquiet, distract, distress, disturb, emasculate, enervate, enfeeble, faze, floor, fluster, frighten, frustrate, harrow, haunt, hocus-pocus, horrify, incapacitate, intimidate, irk, madden, mismatch, needle, neuter, panic, paralyze, perturb, petrify, prostrate, provoke, rattle, sadden, sap, scare, shake, shock, soften, spook, startle, terrify, terrorize, threaten, tire, trash-talk, trouble, try, unbalance, undermine, undo, unhinge, unman, unsettle, unsteady, unstring, upset, vex, waste, weaken, weigh, worry* (≠ agitate, alarm, alleviate, animate, assure, boost, buoy, calm, cheer, embattle, embolden, encourage, energize, enliven, excite, fortify, galvanize, gladden, gratify, hearten, help, humor, inspire, invigorate, lift, lull, mellow, mitigate, moderate, mollify, nerve, order, organize, pacify, placate, quicken, quiet, rally, reassure, regulate, reinforce, settle, soothe, stabilize, steady, steel, stimulate, stir, strengthen)

UNRAVEL (/): *clarify, comprehend, contextualize, decipher, deduce, detect, disentangle, explain, extricate, fathom, fray, free, fret, grasp, grok, interpret, investigate, penetrate, profile, read, resolve, scrutinize, separate, smooth, solve, sort, straighten, suss, unbraid, uncoil, under-*

stand, undo, unknot, unlace, unroll, unsnarl, unspool, unstring, untangle, unthread, untie, untwine, untwist, unweave, unwind (≠ braid, cipher, code, complicate, conceal, cypher, -disregard, encipher, encode, encrypt, entangle, fuse, garble, hide, -ignore, knit, knot, lace, mend, misconstrue, misinterpret, misread, miss, mistake, misunderstand, obscure, -overlook, plait, ply, raddle, ravel, scramble, snarl, splice, stitch, tangle, tie, wind)

UNSCRAMBLE (+): *adjust, crack, debug, decipher, decode, decrypt, deduce, detect, fix, interpret, jack, order, organize, read, remedy, solve, sort, translate, troubleshoot, uncomplicate, understand, unravel, untangle* (≠ complicate, confuse, destroy, disarrange, disorganize, encode, entangle, entwine, garble, jumble, knot, misdiagnose, mystify, obscure, scramble, tangle, twist)

UNSEAL (+): *aerate, assail, breach, break, broach, clear, crack, disclose, discover, expose, force, oxygenate, pry, unblock, unbolt, uncap, uncork, uncover, undo, unfasten, unlatch, unlock, unstop, untie, ventilate* (≠ bolt, bury, close, conceal, cork, deadbolt, fasten, hide, lock, plug, screw, seal, secure, shut, stopper, stopple, tighten)

UNSETTLE (/): *abash, aggravate, agitate, ail, alarm, anger, annoy, bedevil, bother, bug, chafe, concern, confound, confuse, daunt, demoralize, derail, derange, destabilize, disarrange, disarray, discomfit, discomfort, discompose, disconcert, discountenance, discourage, dishearten, dishevel, dismay, disorder, disorganize, dispirit, displace, disquiet, disrupt, distemper, distract, distress, disturb, dizzy, embarrass, exasperate, exercise, faze, fluster, frazzle, freak, fret, fuss, gall, get, grate, harass, harry, haunt, irk, irritate, jar, jumble, mortify, nag, needle, nettle, niggle, nitpick, nonplus, peeve, perturb, pester, pique, plague, rattle, rile, ruffle, shake, shock, sicken, spook, throw, trigger, trouble, unbalance, undo, unhinge, unnerve, unsteady, upset, vex, worry* (≠ adjust, allay, alleviate, anchor, appease, assuage, balance, buoy, calibrate, calm, center, compose, conciliate, coordinate, dispose, govern, gratify, group, help, humor, lull, maintain, mellow, mitigate, moderate, mollify, order, pacify, placate, propitiate, protect, quiet, regiment, regulate, settle, soothe, sort, stabilize, steady, sugarcoat, sustain, tranquilize, tune)

UNSHACKLE (+): *absolve, acquit, bail, clear, deliver, detach, discharge, disencumber, disengage, disentangle, dismiss, drop, emancipate, enfranchise, exculpate, excuse, exonerate, extricate, free, liberate, loose, loosen, manumit, open, oust, pardon, ransom, recover, redeem, release, rescue, salvage, save, spring, unbind, unburden, unchain, unfasten, unfetter, unhook, unleash, unlock, untie, unyoke* (≠ bind, burden, capture, compel, condemn, confine, convict, cuff, detain, enslave, fasten, handcuff, hogtie, hold, imprison, incarcerate, incriminate, intern, jail, keep, leash, limit, lock, maintain, pinion, -prevent, restrain, restrict, retain, sentence, shackle, suppress, tame, tie, trap, withhold)

UNTANGLE (+): *catalog, classify, clear, deliver, discharge, disencumber, disengage, disentangle, emancipate, explain, extricate, fray, free, fret,* *liberate, order, organize, redeem, release, relieve, rescue, resolve, save, smooth, solve, sort, straighten, unbraid, unburden, unchain, uncoil, undo, unfetter, unhook, unknot, unlace, unleash, unravel, unroll, unscramble, unshackle, unsnarl, unstring, unthread, untie, untwine, untwist, unweave, unwind* (≠ block, braid, burden, embroil, encumber, entangle, hamper, hinder, impede, interweave, knot, lace, link, load, mat, mix, muddle, obstruct, occlude, plait, ply, raddle, ravel, snare, snarl, spin, splice, tangle, tie, tousle, twist, weave, weigh, wind)

UNTIE (+): *disengage, disentangle, emancipate, free, liberate, loose, loosen, release, unbind, unchain, undo, unfasten, unfetter, unhitch, unknot, unleash, unravel, unshackle, unwrap* (≠ bind, braid, connect, entangle, fasten, hogtie, knot, lace, lash, restrain, snarl, tangle, tie, twist, wind)

UNVEIL (→): *advertise, air, announce, bare, bellow, betray, blab, blaze, blurt, brandish, broadcast, circulate, communicate, confess, confide, confront, debunk, declare, demonstrate, disclose, discover, disinter, display, disseminate, divulge, evince, exhibit, exhume, expose, flash, flaunt, flourish, herald, illustrate, impart, inform, leak, light, manifest, parade, post, present, proclaim, produce, promulgate, publicize, publish, rake, relate, reveal, share, show, showcase, spill, sport, squeal, telegraph, trumpet, uncloak, unclothe, uncover, undrape, unearth, unmask, unsheathe, unwrap, wave* (≠ bury, camouflage, cloak, clothe, cloud, conceal, costume, cover, curtain, darken, disguise, drape, eclipse, ensconce, enshroud, hide, holster, mask, obscure, occlude, occult, overshadow, screen, shadow, sheathe, shroud, spackle, varnish, veil, whitewash)

UNZIP (←): *bare, detach, expose, free, loosen, open, pull, release, separate, tug, unfasten, unhook, unlace, unwind, yank* (≠ button, cinch, close, clothe, confine, cover, dress, obscure, seal, veil, zip)

UPBRAID (/): *abuse, admonish, advise, assail, attack, badmouth, belittle, berate, blackguard, blame, blast, browbeat, castigate, caution, censure, chastise, chide, condemn, correct, counsel, criticize, critique, crucify, decry, demean, denigrate, denounce, discipline, disparage, disrespect, diss, excoriate, exhort, fault, flay, fulminate, hammer, harangue, hector, henpeck, impugn, jaw, jeer, judge, keelhaul, knock, lambaste, lash, lecture, lesson, mock, nag, pan, pillory, punish, rag, rate, ream, rebuke, reprimand, reproach, reprove, revile, ridicule, roast, savage, scold, scorch, score, -scorn, scourge, slam, slate, tongue-lash, trash, trash-talk, vituperate, zap, zing* (≠ admire, allow, applaud, approve, bless, boost, buoy, celebrate, cheer, commend, compliment, congratulate, countenance, defend, delight, encourage, endorse, esteem, eulogize, exalt, expiate, extol, favor, flannel, flatter, glorify, gratify, honor, idealize, idolize, ingratiate, laud, lionize, praise, protect, rescue, respect, revere, sanction, venerate, vindicate, worship)

UPDATE (+): *amend, automate, computerize, correct, improve, mechanize, modernize, modify, motorize, realign, rebuild, recast, reconceive,* *reconceptualize, redesign, redevelop, redo, reengineer, refashion, reform, refresh, refurbish, regenerate, reimagine, reinvent, rejuvenate, remake, remodel, renew, renovate, reprogram, restore, rethink, retool, revamp, revise, revolutionize, rework, right, streamline, transform, upgrade* (≠ break, confound, damage, date, diminish, disable, freeze, hamper, harm, hurt, impair, injure, keep, lose, maintain, monkey-wrench, -neglect, outmode, paralyze, ruin, stabilize, vandalize, weaken, wear, worsen, wreck)

UPGRADE (+): *accentuate, accrue, add, advance, advocate, ameliorate, amend, amplify, augment, back, beef, better, boost, broaden, champion, confirm, correct, decontaminate, deepen, defend, edit, elaborate, elevate, embellish, emend, emphasize, endorse, enhance, enlarge, enrich, expand, extend, fatten, fine-tune, fortify, further, garnish, gentrify, grow, heighten, help, hike, hone, improve, increase, inflate, intensify, justify, keep, lengthen, magnify, maximize, multiply, optimize, overhaul, perfect, polish, prioritize, progress, raise, realign, reconceive, reconceptualize, rectify, redraft, refine, reform, refurbish, rehab, rehabilitate, reimagine, reinforce, reinvent, rejigger, remedy, renovate, reshuffle, restore, rethink, retool, retouch, revamp, revise, revolutionize, rework, shine, strengthen, sustain, tweak, update, widen* (≠ abase, afflict, bench, blemish, blight, callous, coarsen, compromise, contaminate, damage, declass, deface, degrade, demote, diminish, disfigure, downgrade, efface, flaw, harm, harshen, hurt, impair, injure, lessen, lower, maintain, mar, minimize, misdiagnose, monkey-wrench, poison, pollute, preserve, reduce, relegate, retain, ruin, sideline, spike, spoil, sustain, tarnish, vitiate, vulgarize, worsen, wreck)

UPGRADE (+): *acclaim, advance, aggrandize, applaud, boost, celebrate, cite, commend, commission, compliment, congratulate, decorate, elevate, endorse, ennoble, eulogize, exalt, extol, forward, further, glorify, hail, heighten, honor, improve, knight, laud, lift, lionize, praise, prioritize, promote, raise, salute, support, uplift, vindicate* (≠ abase, bench, censure, chastise, condemn, degrade, demean, demote, denounce, depose, dethrone, disgrace, dishonor, dismiss, downgrade, expel, humble, humiliate, impeach, lower, mortify, oust, overthrow, reduce, remove, ruin, shame, sideline, unmake, unseat)

UPLIFT (+): *advance, animate, better, boost, brighten, cheer, civilize, cultivate, edify, elate, elevate, enlighten, exalt, excite, exhilarate, freshen, heave, hoist, improve, inspire, invigorate, lift, nurture, raise, refine, regenerate, rejuvenate, rouse, upgrade, vitalize* (≠ appall, burden, demoralize, demotivate, depress, descend, discourage, dismay, drop, lower, pitch, plunge, press, push, sink, submerge)

UPROOT (←): *abolish, annihilate, deep-six, destroy, eliminate, eradicate, erase, expunge, exterminate, extract, isolate, mine, obliterate, orphan, pluck, prize, pry, pull, purge, remove, root, take, tear, uninstall, weed, withdraw, wrest, wring, yank* (≠ add, cram, graft, implant, insert, install, instill, jam, place, plant, position, ram, reunite, seed, set, settle, sow, stabilize, stuff, survive, wedge)

UPSET (/): *abash, aggravate, agitate, ail, alarm, anger, annoy, appall, bedevil, bother, bug, chafe, chivy, concern, confound, confuse, craze, daunt, demoralize, demotivate, derail, derange, discombobulate, discomfit, discomfort, discompose, disconcert, discountenance, discourage, dishearten, dismay, disorganize, dispirit, disquiet, disrupt, dissatisfy, distemper, distract, distress, disturb, embarrass, exasperate, exercise, faze, fluster, frazzle, freak, fret, fuss, gall, get, grieve, harass, harry, haunt, irk, irritate, jangle, jar, madden, mismatch, mortify, nag, needle, nettle, nitpick, nonplus, offend, peeve, perturb, pester, pique, plague, rattle, rile, ruffle, sadden, shake, troll, trouble, undo, unhinge, unnerve, unsettle, vex, worry* (≠ allay, alleviate, appease, assuage, calm, comfort, compose, encourage, gratify, hearten, help, humor, hush, lull, mellow, mitigate, moderate, mollify, pacify, placate, propitiate, quiet, relax, settle, smooth, soothe, stabilize, steady, sugarcoat, tranquilize)

UPSET (/): *cant, capsize, careen, collapse, convulse, destabilize, heel, invert, jog, knock, lean, list, overset, overthrow, overturn, shove, shunt, spill, tilt, tip, topple, unhorse, unman, unseat, unsteady, upend* (≠ bolster, brace, build, buttress, erect, fortify, raise, reinforce, right, stabilize, steady, steel, straighten, strengthen)

UPSET (/): *agitate, churn, clutter, confuse, derange, disarrange, disarray, discompose, dishevel, disjoint, dislocate, disorder, disorganize, disrupt, disturb, embroil, entangle, garble, hash, jumble, mess, mingle, mix, muddle, muss, overset, perturb, rumple, scramble, shuffle, snarl, stir, tangle, tousle, tumble, unsettle, untidy* (≠ adjust, align, arrange, array, attune, calibrate, classify, codify, coordinate, dispose, fix, groom, line, marshal, methodize, order, organize, pace, queue, range, regiment, regulate, straighten, systematize, systemize, tidy, tune, tweak, unscramble)

UPSTAGE (→): *beat, best, better, cap, clobber, conquer, control, crush, defeat, display, dominate, drub, dwarf, eclipse, exceed, finagle, lick, maneuver, master, one-up, outclass, outdistance, outdo, outgrow, outgun, outpace, outperform, outrace, outrank, outreach, outsell, outshine, outstrip, outthink, outweigh, overshadow, pass, rout, shame, skunk, subdue, supersede, supplant, surmount, surpass, thrash, top, transcend, trounce, trump, undercut, undermine, whip* (≠ accent, accentuate, cede, conceal, concede, defend, defer, disguise, -elude, emphasize, feature, hide, highlight, honor, illuminate, mask, obscure, relinquish, respect, spotlight, stress, subvert, support, underline)

URGE (→): *adjure, animate, beseech, blandish, boost, bribe, cajole, coax, coerce, compel, constrain, convince, dragoon, drive, encourage, enforce, entreat, exhort, fast-forward, fast-track, foment, force, forward, frogmarch, fuel, goad, grease, hasten, hurry, hustle, impel, implore, importune, incite, incur, induce, influence, instigate, march, midwife, motivate, muscle, nag, needle, nudge, palaver, persuade, press, pressure, prioritize, prod, prompt, propel, provoke, push, quicken, rabble-rouse, railroad, rush, schmooze, soft-soap, spur, stimulate, strengthen, strong-*

arm, wheedle (≠ brake, check, constrain, curb, daunt, demotivate, -deter, discourage, dissuade, -halt, hamper, hamstring, hinder, impair, impede, inhibit, nobble, postpone, -prohibit, restrain, slow, soft-sell, stall, stem, stop, suppress, -thwart)

URGE (+): *advise, advocate, back, buttonhole, champion, counsel, defend, egg, encourage, endorse, espouse, exhort, favor, justify, lobby, patronize, plug, preach, prescribe, promote, propose, recommend, rubber-stamp, second, support, uphold* (≠ -avoid, block, check, curb, daunt, demotivate, -deter, discourage, dissuade, frighten, hamper, hamstring, hinder, impede, inhibit, intimidate, -nix, -nullify, -prevent, -prohibit, restrain, threaten, -thwart, -veto)

USE (→): *adapt, apply, cannibalize, deploy, direct, employ, exercise, exert, exploit, handle, harness, manipulate, operate, recycle, reuse, run, tap, utilize, weaponize, wield, work* (≠ conceal, conclude, discharge, displace, disturb, end, finish, fire, hide, -ignore, misapply, misuse, -neglect, retire, withhold)

USE (/): *abuse, appropriate, beguile, bleed, cheat, coerce, commercialize, commodify, con, defraud, embezzle, exploit, fleece, leverage, manipulate, milk, misappropriate, mistreat, misuse, outsmart, outthink, outwit, overcharge, rob, scam, skim, skin, soak, stick, stiff, sucker, swindle, trick, work* (≠ aid, bankroll, bestow, comp, defend, donate, elevate, endow, esteem, fund, furnish, give, grant, help, honor, offer, promote, protect, provide, respect, supply, support, underwrite, value, volunteer)

USHER (+): *accompany, attend, chaperone, conduct, control, direct, escort, guide, herald, initiate, institute, introduce, launch, lead, manage, marshal, navigate, originate, pilot, receive, route, see, show, steer* (≠ -abandon, -desert, discard, -ditch, dog, drop, finish, follow, -forsake, hound, leave, retrace, shadow, -spurn, tail, trail)

USURP (←): *annex, appropriate, arrogate, assume, attach, bogart, claim, collar, colonize, commandeer, confiscate, convert, despoil, displace, embezzle, grab, grasp, hijack, impound, invade, loot, misapply, misappropriate, misuse, nobble, occupy, overthrow, pillage, pirate, poach, preempt, press, repossess, requisition, seize, sequester, snag, snatch, steal, supersede, supplant, swipe, take, vanquish, wrench, wrest* (≠ -abandon, abdicate, abnegate, bequeath, bestow, cede, forfeit, -forsake, give, grant, keep, leave, offer, -refuse, -reject, release, relinquish, -renounce, resign, surrender, survive, tender, volunteer)

UTILIZE (→): *account, adapt, apply, appropriate, bestow, cannibalize, deploy, direct, employ, engage, exercise, exert, exploit, handle, harness, manipulate, operate, promote, recycle, reuse, run, unsheathe, use, weaponize, wield, work* (≠ -abandon, cease, drop, -eschew, -halt, hinder, -ignore, impede, invalid, misapply, misuse, -neglect, -overlook, -renounce, skip, -spurn, stop)

VACCINATE (+): *cure, doctor, dose, immunize, infuse, inject, inoculate, jab, mainline, medicate, mitigate, -prevent, protect, quarantine, remedy, shield, treat, worm* (≠ afflict, blight, contaminate, corrupt, indispose, infect, pass, pollute, sicken, sully, taint, transmit, weaken)

VALIDATE (+): *accredit, affirm, argue, assert, attest, authenticate, authorize, avow, certify, champion, confirm, consult, corroborate, crosscheck, declare, demonstrate, detect, determine, document, endorse, ensure, establish, eye, eyeball, formalize, guarantee, interview, justify, legalize, legitimize, notarize, okay, permit, profess, prove, ratify, reinforce, rubber-stamp, sanction, scrutinize, sponsor, substantiate, support, testify, underwrite, verify, vindicate, warrant, witness* (≠ annul, challenge, condemn, contest, contradict, debate, debunk, decry, delegitimize, -deny, disavow, disclaim, discredit, disprove, dispute, distrust, doubt, gainsay, invalidate, -nix, -nullify, -omit, oppose, question, rebut, refute, suspect, void)

VALUE (←): *account, add, appraise, ascertain, assess, audit, benchmark, calculate, categorize, classify, compute, conclude, consider, count, critique, deduce, detect, determine, divide, educe, enumerate, estimate, evaluate, examine, figure, gauge, grade, infer, inspect, judge, learn, measure, multiply, price, prioritize, quantify, quantize, rank, rate, rationalize, reckon, review, schedule, scheme, score, slot, study, sum, suppose, surmise, survey, systematize, tally, think, total, valuate, weigh* (≠ assume, -disregard, distrust, doubt, forget, guess, -ignore, miss, mistrust, -neglect, -overlook, question, suspect)

VALUE (+): *acclaim, admire, adore, applaud, appreciate, approve, blandish, cherish, commend, compliment, congratulate, covet, dignify, endorse, enjoy, enshrine, esteem, estimate, eulogize, exalt, extol, fetishize, flatter, glorify, gratify, honor, idealize, idolize, love, praise, prefer, prize, recommend, relish, respect, revere, sanction, treasure* (≠ abhor, bastardize, belittle, boo, cheapen, condemn, criticize, debase, defame, deflate, degrade, demean, -despise, -detest, devalue, diminish, discount, disrespect, execrate, -hate, -loathe, lowball, mock, pillory, -reject, ridicule, -scorn, shame, smear, underbid, underestimate, underrate, undervalue, vilify) **(¿) ABSTRACTION ALERT. Concrete goals essential!**

VAMP (←): *absorb, allure, arouse, attract, bait, beguile, bewitch, captivate, charm, coax, convince, court, dazzle, delight, draw, enchant, engross, enrapture, ensnare, enthrall, entice, entrance, entrap, fascinate, hook, hypnotize, interest, intrigue, inveigle, invite, lure, mesmerize, persuade, razzle-dazzle, rivet, snare, snooker, snow, solicit, spellbind, sway, tangle,* *tempt, thrill, titillate, transfix, trap, woo, wow* (≠ alarm, anger, annoy, bore, bother, bug, disgust, distract, enrage, exasperate, henpeck, -ignore, infuriate, irk, irritate, nag, nauseate, needle, nettle, nitpick, plague, repel, repulse, revolt, sicken, unnerve, upset, vex, weary, worry)

VANDALIZE (/): *annihilate, bash, boobytrap, break, burn, crack, damage, deface, demolish, depredate, desecrate, despoil, destroy, devastate, disfigure, efface, fracture, graffiti, harm, hurt, impair, loot, mar, maraud, monkey-wrench, pillage, plunder, pulverize, ransack, ravage, raven, ravish, raze, rend, ruin, sabotage, sack, scorch, scourge, shatter, shred, sink, slash, smash, splinter, spoil, tatter, tear, torpedo, total, trash, undermine, violate, waste, wrack, wreck* (≠ bronze, build, clean, cleanse, conserve, construct, defend, embalm, erect, guard, maintain, mend, patrol, preserve, protect, rebuild, rectify, recycle, renovate, repair, rescue, restore, salvage, save, shield, sustain, wall, wash)

VANQUISH (→): *annihilate, beat, break, checkmate, clobber, confound, conquer, crush, defeat, demolish, destroy, devastate, dominate, doom, drub, enslave, eradicate, hammer, humble, lick, master, outlast, outmaneuver, outthink, overcome, overpower, overwhelm, pacify, quash, quell, reduce, repress, rout, silence, skunk, slaughter, smash, smother, snuff, squash, squelch, subdue, subject, subjugate, subordinate, suppress, thrash, thump, trounce, trump, wallop, whip, whup* (≠ assist, bolster, defend, discharge, emancipate, encourage, enfranchise, free, guard, liberate, manumit, offer, promote, protect, rebuild, release, rescue, restore, revive, save, shield, spring, subvert, support, survive, sustain, tender, unbind, uncage, unchain, unfetter, volunteer, withstand)

VAPORIZE (/): *annihilate, atomize, beat, best, blast, blow, break, clobber, condense, conquer, cream, cripple, crush, damage, decimate, deface, defeat, demolish, derive, desolate, despoil, destroy, deteriorate, devastate, dilapidate, disassemble, disfigure, disintegrate, dismantle, dissolve, drub, dynamite, efface, eradicate, erode, evaporate, express, expunge, exterminate, extinguish, extirpate, extract, gut, harm, impair, injure, leak, level, lick, liquidate, loot, mangle, mar, master, mortar, mutilate, nuke, obliterate, overcome, pillage, plunder, pulverize, purify, ravage, raze, refine, remove, root, rout, ruin, sack, scotch, scour, shatter, skunk, smash, snuff, splinter, spoil, subdue, sublimate, surmount, thrash, topple, total, trample, trash, trim, trounce, unbuild, undo, unmake, vandalize, vitiate, wallop, waste, whip, wrack, wreck, zap* (≠ assemble, bronze, build, conserve, constitute, construct, craft, create, doctor, embalm, erect, establish, fabricate, fashion, father, fix, forge, form, found, frame, institute, invent, make, manufacture, mend, mold, organize, patch, preserve, produce, protect, raise, rear, rebuild, recondition, reconstruct, remodel, renovate, repair, restore, revamp, save, sculpt, shape, survive, sustain, withstand)

VARNISH (+): *adorn, caulk, coat, cover, decorate, enamel, finish, gild, glaze, gloss, japan, lacquer, paint, pave, plaster, polish, shellac, shine, spackle, sugarcoat, surface, veneer, wax, whitewash* (≠ air, bare, blast, coarsen, dull, excoriate, expose, open, peel, reveal, roughen, sand, scour, shuck, strip, uncover, unmask)

VEIL (/): *becloud, bedim, befog, belie, blanket, block, blot, bury, camouflage, circle, cloak, clothe, cloud, conceal, costume, cover, curtain, darken, dim, disguise, drape, eclipse, encircle, enshroud, envelop, gild, gloss, hide, launder, mask, obscure, obstruct, occlude, occult, overshadow, pall, screen, secrete, shade, shadow, shield, shroud, smother, spackle, stonewall, suppress, varnish, whitewash, wrap* (≠ accost, advertise, air, bare, blast, brandish, broadcast, circulate, clarify, concede, confess, confirm, confront, denude, disclose, display, disseminate, divulge, excoriate, expose, flaunt, hype, illuminate, light, parade, peel, plug, present, proclaim, publicize, publish, reveal, show, showcase, spread, strip, telegraph, uncloak, uncover, unmask, unveil)

VENERATE (+): *acclaim, admire, adore, adulate, aggrandize, apotheosize, applaud, appreciate, approve, beatify, blandish, bless, boost, cajole, canonize, celebrate, cheer, cherish, commemorate, commend, compliment, congratulate, consecrate, deify, delight, dignify, endorse, enjoy, enshrine, esteem, eulogize, exalt, extol, fête, fetishize, flannel, flatter, glorify, gold-star, gratify, hail, hallow, hero-worship, high-five, honor, hype, idealize, idolize, immortalize, laud, limelight, lionize, love, magnify, memorialize, observe, panegyrize, please, plug, praise, presell, prioritize, prize, promote, protect, publicize, push, recommend, regard, respect, revere, reverence, romanticize, salute, sanction, satisfy, sentimentalize, solemnize, stroke, treasure, trumpet, value, worship* (≠ abominate, accuse, admonish, affront, anathematize, attaint, badmouth, belittle, berate, bestialize, blame, blaspheme, blast, boo, castigate, censure, chastise, chide, condemn, criticize, critique, debase, defame, demean, demonize, denigrate, denounce, deride, desecrate, -detest, -disdain, disgrace, dishonor, disparage, displease, disrespect, execrate, fault, frame, fulminate, humiliate, incriminate, insult, lambaste, libel, malign, offend, oppose, -ostracize, oust, outrage, pillory, pique, profane, rebuke, regret, repent, reprimand, reproach, ridicule, rue, scathe, scold, -scorn, shame, slander, -slight, slur, smear, trash, vilify, violate) **(¿) ABSTRACTION ALERT. Concrete goals essential!**

VENTURE (→): *act, advance, aim, approach, assay, attempt, bet, brave, challenge, commit, compromise, contract, dare, defy, endanger, engage, exploit, gamble, grant, hazard, imperil, initiate, jeopardize, maneuver, perform, presume, pretend, pursue, risk, scheme, spitball, suggest, undertake, volunteer* (≠ block, -decline, -deny, hamper, hamstring, hinder, hoard, hobble, impede, -prevent, -refuse, scotch, short-circuit, -sidestep, skirt, withhold)

VERBALIZE (→): *advertise, affirm, air, allege, announce, articulate, assert, attest, broadcast, clarify, communicate, convey, couch, declare, depict, describe, disclose, discuss, divulge, draft, enunciate, expand, explain, expound, express, formulate, intimate, post, proclaim, promulgate, publicize, publish, report, reveal, share, sound, speak, state, testify, utter,* *vent, ventilate, vocalize, voice, whisper, word, write* (≠ -avoid, bowdlerize, bury, censor, conceal, confuse, corrupt, disguise, distort, expurgate, gag, garble, hide, hush, -ignore, misrepresent, muddle, muffle, mute, muzzle, quell, quiet, silence, stifle, still, subdue, suppress, twist, withhold) **(¿) ABSTRACTION ALERT. Concrete goals essential!**

VERIFY (+): *accredit, affirm, argue, ascertain, assert, attest, audit, authenticate, avow, certify, check, compute, confirm, consult, corroborate, crosscheck, debunk, declare, demonstrate, detect, determine, document, double-check, endorse, ensure, establish, eye, eyeball, guarantee, interview, notarize, profess, prove, reinforce, scrutinize, settle, substantiate, support, test, testify, validate, vindicate, warrant, witness* (≠ challenge, contest, contradict, debate, debunk, -deny, disavow, disclaim, discredit, disprove, dispute, distrust, doubt, gainsay, invalidate, oppose, question, rebut, refute, -reject, scruple, suspect, warn, wonder)

VET (+): *analyze, anatomize, appraise, audit, case, catechize, certify, check, consider, critique, dissect, evaluate, examine, explore, eye, eyeball, frisk, gauge, inspect, interrogate, investigate, judge, monitor, observe, parse, peruse, probe, prove, prowl, query, quiz, read, reconnoiter, reference, research, review, sample, scan, scope, screen, scrutinize, sift, sound, study, survey, test, validate, verify, weigh, winnow* (≠ accept, allow, baffle, believe, blind, blindfold, -bypass, confound, confuse, -disregard, forget, -ignore, misgauge, misread, miss, mistake, misunderstand, -neglect, -overlook, perplex, puzzle, -reject, skim, skip, trust)

-VETO (/): *ban, blackball, blacklist, block, -cut, -decline, defeat, -deny, disallow, disapprove, dismiss, -forbid, kill, -negate, negative, -nix, -nullify, oppose, override, overrule, -prohibit, -refuse, -reject, subvert* (≠ admit, allow, approve, champion, confirm, elect, legalize, okay, pass, promote, propose, ratify, sanction, spitball, submit, support)

VEX (/): *afflict, aggravate, agitate, anger, annoy, antagonize, arouse, badger, bait, bedevil, bother, bug, burden, chafe, chagrin, depress, discompose, discountenance, discourage, distress, disturb, earbash, embarrass, enrage, envenom, exacerbate, exasperate, fluster, fret, gall, harass, harry, hassle, hound, incense, inflame, infuriate, irk, irritate, molest, nag, needle, nettle, niggle, nitpick, noodge, offend, oppose, -ostracize, peeve, perplex, persecute, perturb, pester, plague, provoke, rankle, ride, rile, ruffle, tease, torment, traumatize, troll, trouble, unnerve, upset, victimize, weary, worry* (≠ aid, amuse, appease, assist, assuage, baby, calm, coddle, comfort, console, defend, delight, entertain, gratify, guard, help, humor, indulge, inspire, lull, mellow, mitigate, moderate, mollify, pacify, pamper, placate, please, protect, reassure, relieve, restore, salve, satisfy, settle, shield, soothe, spoil, stabilize, steady, sugarcoat, support, thrill, tranquilize, treat, uplift, wow)

VICTIMIZE (/): *bamboozle, beat, betray, bilk, blackjack, blackmail, bleed, bludgeon, bluff, browbeat, brutalize, bully, burn, cheat, chisel, clip, coerce, con, convince, cozen, daunt, deceive, defraud, discredit, disfavor,* *disgrace, double-cross, double-deal, double-talk, dupe, excruciate, exploit, extort, fast-talk, fiddle, fleece, flimflam, fool, frame, frighten, frogmarch, gazump, gouge, gull, hoodwink, hustle, intimidate, lynch, manipulate, martyr, menace, milk, mulct, muscle, nick, oppose, oppress, -ostracize, oust, overcharge, persecute, pluck, ream, rook, rope, sandbag, scare, screw, shake, short, shortchange, skin, slam, snooker, snow, soak, squeeze, stick, stiff, sting, sucker, swindle, terrorize, threaten, trash-talk, trick, underpay, use, wrench, wrest, wring* (≠ advantage, aid, assist, benefit, bless, boost, cherish, defend, favor, heal, help, nourish, nurture, optimize, pity, praise, prioritize, profit, protect, regard, regret, rescue, respect, save, shield, strengthen, trust, value)

VILIFY (/): *abase, abuse, accuse, assail, attack, attaint, backbite, badmouth, belittle, berate, besmirch, bestialize, blacken, blackguard, blame, blast, blister, boo, castigate, chastise, condemn, criticize, crucify, curse, debase, decry, defame, defile, degrade, dehumanize, demean, denigrate, denounce, denunciate, detract, dirty, discredit, -disdain, disfavor, disgrace, dishonor, disparage, disrespect, diss, embarrass, excoriate, fault, flay, fulminate, hammer, harangue, harm, hector, humble, humiliate, impugn, incriminate, injure, insult, jinx, judge, knock, lambaste, libel, malign, misrepresent, mock, mortify, neg, -ostracize, pan, pillory, pollute, rag, ream, rebuke, regret, reprimand, reproach, revile, roast, rue, scorch, -scorn, scourge, shame, slam, slander, slate, slur, smear, soil, stain, stigmatize, sully, taint, tarnish, traduce, trash, trash-talk, traumatize, victimize, villainize, vituperate, wrong, zap* (≠ acclaim, admire, adore, applaud, benefit, blandish, bless, boost, buoy, celebrate, cheer, cherish, commend, compliment, congratulate, defend, deify, elevate, emulate, encourage, endorse, esteem, eulogize, exalt, expiate, favor, flannel, flatter, glorify, gratify, honor, hype, idealize, idolize, imitate, ingratiate, inspire, lionize, mimic, plug, praise, promote, protect, publicize, purify, regard, rescue, respect, revere, sanctify, save, showcase, uphold, uplift, venerate, vindicate, worship)

VINDICATE (+): *absolve, acquit, affirm, alibi, avenge, champion, cleanse, clear, condone, consult, corroborate, defend, defray, deliver, discharge, dismiss, disprove, endorse, exculpate, excuse, exempt, exonerate, expiate, forgive, free, justify, liberate, mitigate, pardon, prove, purge, purify, redeem, redress, refute, rehabilitate, release, relieve, remit, reprieve, revenge, second, shield, spare, substantiate, support, unburden, uphold, warrant, whitewash* (≠ accuse, allege, arraign, attack, blame, castigate, charge, condemn, contradict, convict, damn, denounce, -desert, destroy, discipline, discredit, -disown, disprove, dispute, distrust, doom, doubt, fault, finger, forget, frame, gainsay, impeach, implicate, imprison, impugn, incriminate, indict, interview, jail, oppose, prosecute, prove, punish, question, rebut, refute, -reject, resent, revile, ruin, scapegoat, sentence, spin, subvert)

VIOLATE (/): *abase, abuse, affront, anguish, assail, assault, attack, bait, bastardize, bed, befoul, belittle, besmear, besmirch, bestialize, betray, blaspheme, boink, contaminate, curse, debase, debauch, deconsecrate,* *defame, defile, deflower, degrade, demean, demonize, desacralize, desanctify, desecrate, despoil, disgrace, dishonor, disrupt, disturb, foul, fuck, gate-crash, humiliate, hurt, impugn, injure, insult, invade, libel, lower, malign, molest, mortify, offend, outrage, pillory, poison, pollute, profane, rape, ravish, -rebuff, reduce, ridicule, screw, shame, slander, slur, soil, spoil, stain, sully, taint, taunt, torment, wound, wreck, wrong* (≠ bless, cleanse, compliment, consecrate, dedicate, defend, dignify, exalt, expiate, guard, hallow, heal, heed, honor, mind, nourish, nurse, nurture, patrol, pity, protect, purge, purify, regret, respect, revere, sanctify, shield, withstand, worship)

VIOLATE (/): *abuse, assail, assault, attack, breach, break, contradict, contravene, defy, -deny, dismiss, disobey, -disregard, disrespect, flout, fracture, -ignore, infringe, -neglect, offend, oppose, -ostracize, -overlook, pooh-pooh, resist, -scorn, -slight, -snub, subvert, traduce, trample, transgress, trespass, withstand* (≠ attend, follow, fulfill, hear, heed, honor, mark, mind, note, notice, obey, observe, regard, respect, serve, watch)

VITIATE (/): *adulterate, afflict, anesthetize, bastardize, blemish, blight, botch, contaminate, corrupt, cramp, cripple, deaden, debase, debauch, defile, deform, degrade, demoralize, deprave, deteriorate, devalue, disable, disarm, dull, enfeeble, hamper, hamstring, handicap, harm, hinder, hobble, impair, incapacitate, infect, injure, invalidate, lame, mar, neutralize, -nullify, overextend, paralyze, pervert, poison, pollute, prostrate, ruin, sap, scotch, spike, spoil, stagnate, stale, stun, stupefy, sully, taint, torpefy, twist, undermine, warp, weaken* (≠ assist, better, cure, doctor, elevate, enhance, ennoble, fix, glorify, hallow, heal, help, mend, nurture, optimize, overhaul, patch, perfect, purify, rehabilitate, remedy, repair, revamp, revolutionize, strengthen, validate)

VIVISECT (/): *anatomize, carve, cleave, cut, disarticulate, dismember, dissect, divide, examine, inspect, joint, probe, quarter, razor, scrutinize, section, sever, slice, sunder* (≠ amalgamate, assimilate, combine, connect, consolidate, fix, fuse, heal, -ignore, integrate, join, meld, mend, repair, restore, revive, sew, stitch, suture, unify, unite)

-VOID (/): *abate, abnegate, abolish, -abort, abrogate, annihilate, annul, -avoid, ban, call, -cancel, countermand, -cut, delegitimize, -deny, deprive, disallow, discharge, -discontinue, dismiss, dissolve, drop, eliminate, enjoin, eradicate, erase, -forbid, gut, invalidate, launder, liquidate, -negate, null, -nullify, -omit, -ostracize, oust, outlaw, override, overrule, overturn, -prohibit, quash, recall, -reject, remove, repeal, -rescind, retract, reverse, revoke, sanitize, sterilize, strike, suspend, trim, vacate, -veto, withdraw* (≠ allow, approve, authorize, clear, command, decree, enact, endorse, establish, formalize, found, institute, legalize, legislate, legitimate, legitimize, mandate, order, pass, permit, prescribe, ratify, sanction, validate, warrant, weather, withstand)

VOLUNTEER (+): *administer, advance, afford, aid, allocate, allot, apportion, assist, authorize, award, benefit, bequeath, bestow, commend, commit, comp, concede, confer, consign, contribute, deliver,* *disburse, dish, dispense, distribute, dole, donate, endow, entrust, extend, forward, furnish, gift, give, grant, hand, help, impart, issue, lavish, mete, offer, outlay, overpay, pay, permit, pledge, present, proffer, promise, propose, propound, provide, regale, relegate, render, replenish, restore, sacrifice, suggest, supply, tender, tithe, trust, vouchsafe, will, yield* (≠ accept, advance, appropriate, beg, begrudge, bully, claim, coerce, commandeer, compel, debit, demand, -deny, deprive, force, hoard, hog, hold, keep, lend, loan, monopolize, obligate, obtain, order, overcommit, pinch, pocket, preserve, -prevent, purchase, receive, refund, -refuse, reimburse, -reject, remove, request, require, resent, reserve, retain, save, sell, snatch, solicit, source, steal, stiff, swipe, take, wean, withdraw, withhold)

VOLUNTEER (→): *advise, announce, articulate, bare, bellow, betray, blab, blurt, breathe, broadcast, communicate, confess, confirm, counsel, declare, deliver, direct, disclose, display, divulge, enunciate, exhibit, expose, express, frame, impart, leak, manifest, offer, present, proclaim, pronounce, propose, proposition, publicize, publish, recommend, reveal, show, speak, spitball, state, suggest, supply, trumpet, uncover, undeceive, unearth, unfold, unmask, unveil, utter, verbalize, vocalize, voice, warn* (≠ annul, -avoid, blind, bury, camouflage, censor, cloak, compel, conceal, delete, disguise, enshroud, expunge, expurgate, -forbid, force, hide, hush, -ignore, mask, obscure, -omit, redact, sanitize, screen, silence, stifle) **(¿) ABSTRACTION ALERT. Concrete goals essential!**

VOW (+): *affirm, assert, assure, attest, avow, betroth, consecrate, contract, convince, covenant, declare, dedicate, depose, devote, ensure, forswear, guarantee, maintain, pledge, promise, prove, stipulate, swear, testify, trust, warrant* (≠ abjure, abnegate, betray, cheat, contradict, counter, debate, deceive, -deny, discredit, disprove, dispute, distrust, double-talk, doubt, fool, forswear, invalidate, recant, -renounce, -repudiate, retract, scruple, stiff, suspect, withdraw) **(¿) ABSTRACTION ALERT. Concrete goals essential!**

VULGARIZE (/): *abase, adulterate, bastardize, cheapen, coarsen, contaminate, corrupt, damage, debase, defile, degrade, demean, democratize, devalue, dirty, disgrace, dishonor, disseminate, familiarize, generalize, hype, lessen, lower, plug, pollute, popularize, propagate, roughen, simplify, spread, sully, taint, tarnish, universalize* (≠ burnish, civilize, clarify, cultivate, edify, educate, elevate, enhance, enlighten, hone, humanize, improve, indulge, instruct, perfect, polish, purify, refine, shine, smooth, socialize, soften, sophisticate, spoil, tame, upgrade, withhold)

WAGE (+): *accomplish, achieve, administer, begin, commence, complete, conduct, consummate, deliver, discharge, dispatch, effect, enact, enforce, engineer, execute, expedite, finish, fulfill, implement, levy, make, perform, practice, prosecute, pursue, realize, render, serve, stage, undertake, validate* (≠ -avert, cease, destroy, doom, end, -eschew, fail, foil, -forbid, forget, -halt, lose, miss, monkey-wrench, -neglect, -prevent, -prohibit, -quit, -refuse, stop)

WAGER (→): *bet, bid, chance, endanger, expose, gamble, game, hazard, hustle, imperil, jeopardize, lay, offer, parlay, play, pledge, propose, risk, stake, tender, venture, volunteer* (≠ bank, deposit, ensure, guarantee, guard, hoard, hold, invest, keep, lose, preserve, protect, prove, safeguard, secure, stash, stockpile, win, withhold)

WAIVE (/): *-abandon, abdicate, -cancel, cede, deep-six, defer, disclaim, dismiss, -disown, eliminate, forfeit, forgo, grant, leave, -nullify, -omit, pardon, postpone, -reject, release, relinquish, remit, remove, -renounce, -rescind, resign, shelve, spare, surrender, suspend, table, undercharge, vacate, -void, yield* (≠ affirm, assert, claim, command, compel, decree, demand, employ, enact, enforce, expect, maintain, mandate, necessitate, obtain, owe, propose, request, require, sustain)

WAKE (→): *activate, agitate, alert, animate, arouse, awaken, buzz, disturb, enliven, excite, fire, galvanize, generate, goad, ignite, incite, inspire, jab, jostle, kindle, notify, nudge, poke, prod, provoke, raise, reawaken, reinvigorate, restimulate, revive, rouse, roust, rout, signal, sober, spur, stimulate, stir, vitalize, vivify, warn, whet* (≠ anesthetize, bewitch, bore, calm, deaden, drug, dull, entrance, hypnotize, impair, incapacitate, lull, mellow, mesmerize, numb, quiet, relax, sedate, tire, trank, tranquilize, weary)

WANGLE (+): *accomplish, achieve, arrange, attain, brew, broker, captain, chart, command, compass, conclude, concoct, conduct, contrive, cook, direct, engineer, exploit, fiddle, finagle, finesse, finish, fix, frame, gerrymander, handle, hatch, improv, improvise, lobby, machinate, manage, maneuver, manipulate, mastermind, negotiate, obtain, plot, quarterback, reach, renegotiate, run, scheme, shuffle, source, steer, transact, weaponize, wing, work* (≠ block, blow, bobble, bomb, botch, bugger, bungle, butcher, challenge, combat, contest, drop, fight, flub, flunk, fumble, half-ass, lose, mangle, mishandle, misjudge, misread, miss, mistake, muff, oppose, -prevent, ruin, spoil, stop, stymie, -thwart, wreck)

WARD (+): *anticipate, -avert, -avoid, battle, block, bulwark, check, conserve, cover, defend, deflect, -deter, divert, -dodge, -evade, fence, fight, foil, forestall, forfend, -frustrate, guard, keep, -omit, oppose, outlast, parry, -preclude, preserve, -prevent, protect, -rebuff, rebut, repel, resist, safeguard, save, screen, secure, shield, stymie, -thwart, withstand* (≠ accept, allow, assail, assault, attack, beset, besiege, betray, blitz, bombard, encourage, expel, expose, gather, invite, meet, offend, open, overrun, -refuse, -reject, storm, welcome)

WARM (→): *bake, barbecue, boil, braise, brighten, broil, burn, char, cook, fire, frizzle, fry, griddle, grill, heat, ignite, irradiate, kindle, light, melt, overheat, panfry, parboil, parch, poach, reheat, reignite, roast, sauté, scald, scorch, sear, simmer, singe, steam, stew, stoke, superheat, thaw, toast* (≠ chill, cool, darken, dim, douse, drench, extinguish, freeze, frost, ice, quench, refrigerate, smother, snuff, stifle, suffocate, supercool, wet)

WARM (+): *amuse, animate, appease, arouse, assuage, calm, captivate, charm, cheer, coddle, comfort, content, delight, divert, entertain, enthuse, excite, feast, galvanize, gladden, gratify, humor, indulge, interest, lull, mellow, melt, mollify, mollycoddle, pacify, pamper, placate, please, prepare, quench, rejoice, rouse, sate, satiate, satisfy, soothe, spoil, stimulate, stir, suit, thrill, tickle, titillate, treat* (≠ aggravate, agitate, anger, annoy, bother, chafe, cross, depress, displease, distress, disturb, enrage, exasperate, fret, gall, harass, harry, incense, infuriate, irk, irritate, madden, nettle, nitpick, outrage, peeve, perturb, pester, pique, provoke, rankle, rile, roil, rouse, ruffle, upset, vex)

WARN (→): *admonish, adumbrate, advise, alarm, alert, apprise, augur, buzz, caution, counsel, direct, discourage, dissuade, exhort, -forbid, forebode, forecast, foreshadow, foretell, forewarn, harbinger, hint, inform, motion, notify, outguess, portend, predetermine, predict, prepare, presage, prognosticate, prompt, prophesy, rebuke, recommend, remind, reprimand, reprove, signal, suggest, tell, threaten, tip, urge, wake* (≠ abet, allow, applaud, approve, brook, cheer, commend, compliment, compromise, conceal, congratulate, countenance, encourage, endanger, hide, -ignore, impel, imperil, incite, instigate, mislead, -neglect, -omit, permit, pity, praise, -prevent, regret, risk, seek, tolerate, withhold)

WARP (/): *abase, bastardize, bedraggle, befoul, begrime, bestialize, blemish, brutalize, castrate, cheapen, contaminate, corrupt, damage, debase, debauch, deface, defile, degrade, dehumanize, demean, dement, demoralize, deprave, depreciate, derange, destroy, deteriorate, dilute, dirty, disgrace, dishonor, doom, downgrade, emasculate, flaw, harm, humble, humiliate, hurt, impair, lessen, mar, pervert, poison, pollute, profane, prostitute, ruin, sabotage, shame, spike, spoil, stain, suborn, subvert, sway, taint, tarnish, thin, vitiate, water, weaken, wreck* (≠ ameliorate, amend, better, clean, cleanse, dignify, elevate, enhance, ennoble, enrich, exalt, honor, improve, moralize, optimize, overhaul, perfect, purify, redeem, refine, reform, rehabilitate, respect, restore, upgrade, uplift)

WARP (/): *alter, bend, break, buckle, coil, compress, contort, corrugate, crease, crinkle, crook, crumple, curl, deface, deform, disfigure, distort, fold, gnarl, kink, loop, mar, misshape, modify, rotate, screw, shift, spiral, squinch, stretch, torture, turn, twine, twist, weight, wind, wreathe, wrench, wrest, wriggle, wring, wrinkle* (≠ align, beautify, equalize, even, extend, flatten, hold, iron, keep, press, render, right, smooth, straighten, unbend, uncrumple, uncurl, unfold, untwist, unwrinkle)

WARP (/): *alter, belie, bend, bowdlerize, camouflage, censor, change, cloud, color, complicate, confound, confuse, cook, disguise, distort, embellish, embroider, falsify, fudge, garble, gloss, half-ass, mask, miscommunicate, misdescribe, mishear, misinterpret, misread, misrepresent, misstate, mistake, mistranslate, modify, mystify, obscure, pervert, redact, skew, slant, spin, sway, twist, veil, whitewash* (≠ clarify, clear, decipher, deduce, detect, display, educate, elucidate, explain, expose, illuminate, illustrate, interpret, read, rephrase, reveal, school, simplify, streamline, teach, translate, unskew)

WARRANT (→): *affirm, allege, announce, argue, assert, attest, avow, back, broadcast, certify, claim, confirm, contend, declare, defend, insist, justify, maintain, proclaim, profess, promise, protest, purport, rationalize, reaffirm, reason, reassert, second, substantiate, support, swear, uphold, validate, verify, vindicate* (≠ -abandon, betray, challenge, confute, contradict, counter, debate, denounce, -deny, disavow, disbelieve, disclaim, -disown, disprove, dispute, distrust, doubt, -forsake, gainsay, -negate, negative, oppose, question, rebut, refute, -reject, -repudiate, -scorn, scruple) **(¿) ABSTRACTION ALERT. Concrete goals essential!**

WARRANT (→): *adhere, affirm, answer, assert, assure, attest, authenticate, avow, back, bond, certify, contract, corroborate, covenant, crosscheck, declare, deserve, earn, endorse, ensure, guarantee, indemnify, insist, insure, notarize, pledge, promise, prove, stipulate, support, swear, testify, undertake, underwrite, uphold, vouchsafe, vow, witness* (≠ allege, breach, break, contradict, debate, debunk, -deny, disavow, -disown, disprove, invalidate, -neglect, oppose, refute, -reject, -repudiate, -rescind, sabotage, scotch, scupper, shelve, -thwart, undermine)

WARRANT (←): *ask, bear, beg, challenge, claim, command, compel, demand, enjoin, entail, exact, insist, involve, merit, oblige, press, request, require, stipulate, take, want* (≠ -decline, eliminate, hold, -obviate, own, possess, -prevent, -refuse, -reject, stop, -thwart)

WARRANT (+): *accept, accredit, acknowledge, affirm, allow, approve, authorize, bless, canonize, certificate, certify, clear, commission, confirm, credential, empower, enable, endorse, enfranchise, entitle, excuse, finalize, formalize, inaugurate, induct, initial, initiate, install, instate, invest, justify, legalize, let, license, okay, pass, permit, privilege, qualify, ratify, require, rubber-stamp, sanctify, sanction, sign, support, validate, vest* (≠ abolish, annul, ban, bar, block, -cancel, constrain, -decline, -deny, disallow, disapprove, disbar, discourage, disenfranchise, disqualify, enjoin, -exclude, -forbid, hinder, impede, inhibit, -interdict, invalidate, -nullify, obstruct, oppose, oust, outlaw, -prevent, -prohibit, proscribe, -rebuff, rebut, -refuse, -reject, -spurn, stop, -veto)

WASH (+): *bathe, clean, cleanse, decontaminate, dip, disinfect, douse, drench, flush, freshen, immerse, inundate, lather, launder, moisten, mop, rinse, scour, scrub, shampoo, shower, soak, soap, spatter, splatter, sponge, steam, swab, wet, wipe* (≠ bedraggle, befoul, begrime, besmirch, contaminate, corrupt, defile, dehydrate, dirty, dry, foul, muddy, parch, pollute, pour, roll, scorch, sear, soil, spoil, stagnate, stain, stream, sully, taint, tarnish)

WASTE (/): *blow, consume, decrease, deplete, depredate, destroy, devastate, disburse, dissipate, divert, doom, drain, empty, enfeeble, erode, exhaust, expend, fritter, impoverish, indulge, lard, lavish, leech, lose, misapply, misspend, misuse, overextend, overfeed, overindulge, overspend, sap, shoot, sink, slather, spend, spoil, squander, straiten, thin, undermine, wither* (≠ bankroll, budget, conserve, contribute, economize, endow, famish, fill, fund, furnish, grant, hoard, increase, keep, malnourish, offer, preserve, protect, retain, save, scant, scrimp, skimp, supply, underfeed, underwrite, withhold)

WASTE (/): *annihilate, atomize, beat, best, blast, blot, break, clobber, conquer, cream, cripple, crush, damage, decimate, deface, defeat, demolish, desolate, despoil, destroy, deteriorate, devastate, dilapidate, disassemble, disfigure, disintegrate, dismantle, dissolve, doom, drub, dynamite, efface, eradicate, erode, expunge, exterminate, extinguish, extirpate, gut, harm, impair, injure, lick, liquidate, loot, mangle, mar, master, mortar, mutilate, nuke, obliterate, outlast, overcome, pillage, plunder, pulverize, ravage, raze, remove, root, rout, ruin, sack, scotch, scour, shatter, skunk, smash, snuff, spoil, subdue, surmount, sweep, thrash, topple, total, trample, trash, trim, trounce, unbuild, undo, unmake, vandalize, vaporize, vitiate, wallop, whip, wrack, wreck* (≠ assemble, brine, build, conserve, constitute, construct, craft, create, doctor, erect, establish, fabricate, fashion, father, fix, forge, form, found, frame, generate, hatch, initiate, institute, invent, make, manufacture, mend, mold, organize, patch, pickle, preserve, produce, protect, raise, rear, rebuild, recondition, reconstruct, remodel, renovate, repair, restore, revamp, save, sculpt, shape, sire, start, survive, sustain, weather, withstand)

WASTE (/): *cannibalize, consume, cripple, damage, debilitate, deplete, depress, devitalize, disable, enervate, enfeeble, exhaust, grind, hamstring, harm, hurt, impair, impoverish, incapacitate, injure, invalid, overextend, paralyze, prostrate, sap, soften, tire, unman, weaken, wither* (≠ brace, cure, energize, fortify, harden, heal, help, invigorate, preserve, protect, recruit, rejuvenate, remedy, season, strengthen, sustain, tone, toughen, vitalize)

WAYLAY (→): *accost, ambush, assail, assault, attack, blindside, bother, box, bushwhack, buttonhole, capture, catch, charge, corner, detain, ensnare, entrap, hound, hunt, intercept, jump, mousetrap, mug, net, prowl, sandbag, seize, snare, stalk, storm, strike, surprise, tackle, trap,* *trouble, wrestle* (≠ alert, allow, caution, defend, forward, give, guard, -ignore, inform, miss, notify, patrol, permit, -prevent, protect, secure, tolerate, waive, warn)

WEAKEN (/): *afflict, attenuate, blight, boobytrap, break, cannibalize, castrate, consume, cripple, damage, dampen, deaden, debilitate, decrease, demilitarize, demoralize, demotivate, deplete, depress, deprive, destabilize, destroy, -deter, deteriorate, devitalize, diminish, disable, disarm, disconcert, discourage, disorganize, disperse, dissuade, divide, doom, drain, dull, emasculate, enervate, enfeeble, etiolate, exhaust, fade, fatigue, -halt, hamper, hamstring, harm, hobble, hurt, impair, impoverish, inactivate, incapacitate, injure, kneecap, leech, lessen, lose, lower, malnourish, mar, monkey-wrench, overextend, overthrow, palsy, paralyze, prostrate, restrict, ruin, sabotage, sap, scatter, scotch, scupper, scuttle, separate, short-circuit, shrivel, sink, soften, starve, subvert, tire, trouble, undercut, undermine, unman, vitiate, waste, wither, wizen, worsen, wound* (≠ activate, agitate, aid, animate, assist, beef, better, bolster, boost, buttress, develop, emphasize, encourage, energize, enhance, enlarge, exacerbate, excite, expand, extend, fix, fortify, foster, grow, harden, help, improve, incite, invigorate, magnify, maximize, militarize, nurture, optimize, overhaul, praise, prioritize, prolong, raise, rally, recruit, refresh, reinforce, rejuvenate, revitalize, revolutionize, season, stabilize, steel, strengthen, toughen, vitalize)

WEAKEN (/): *adulterate, attenuate, befoul, cheapen, contaminate, corrupt, counterfeit, cut, debase, decrease, defile, degrade, diffuse, dilute, diminish, dirty, doctor, dose, envenom, extend, fake, falsify, foul, fudge, half-ass, infect, invalidate, lace, lessen, load, lose, lower, manipulate, mar, minimize, misrepresent, mitigate, moderate, modify, poison, pollute, qualify, reduce, soil, sophisticate, spike, spoil, sully, taint, temper, thin, water* (≠ accentuate, accrue, augment, better, boost, clarify, clean, cleanse, compact, compliment, concentrate, condense, decontaminate, deepen, distill, embattle, enhance, enrich, fertilize, filter, flavor, flush, fortify, gain, improve, increase, lard, leach, magnify, marinate, maximize, pasteurize, punctuate, purge, purify, refine, reinforce, richen, season, spice, strengthen, supplement)

WEAN (/): *alienate, -deny, deprive, detach, divest, divide, isolate, orphan, remove, scant, scrimp, separate, sequester, skimp, starve, stint, withdraw, withhold* (≠ bottle-feed, breastfeed, feed, force-feed, indulge, nourish, nurse, offer, overfeed, suckle, supply, tender, volunteer)

WEAPONIZE (+): *accelerate, accentuate, activate, adapt, adjust, aggravate, alter, ambush, amplify, arm, bomb, boobytrap, change, charge, convert, corroborate, customize, deepen, equip, exacerbate, exaggerate, exploit, fashion, harness, hone, increase, intensify, load, match, maximize, mechanize, militarize, mine, modify, plant, plug, poison, prepare, prime, qualify, raise, rearm, reconceive, reimagine, reinvent, remodel, restore, shape, sharpen, snare, strengthen, suit, tailor, transform, trap, trigger, tweak, wire* (≠ armor, buffer, counteract, cushion, deactivate, decelerate, defeat, defuse, demilitarize, disable, disarm, erase, -frustrate, ground, immobilize, incapacitate, invalidate, minimize, -negate, neutralize, -nullify, offset, overcome, override, personalize, relieve, remedy, shield, soften, standardize, subdue, unload, weaken)

WEARY (/): *annoy, bore, bug, burden, cloy, debilitate, demoralize, depress, disable, discourage, disgust, dishearten, dispirit, drain, earbash, enervate, enfeeble, exasperate, exhaust, fail, fatigue, frustrate, glut, harass, irk, irritate, jade, nag, needle, nettle, niggle, nitpick, numb, oppress, plague, sap, sicken, strain, stultify, tax, tire, trouble, tucker, vex, wear* (≠ absorb, allure, amuse, animate, arouse, attract, beguile, bewitch, busy, captivate, charm, enchant, energize, engage, engross, entertain, enthrall, excite, fascinate, galvanize, grip, immerse, inspire, interest, intrigue, invigorate, mesmerize, monopolize, obsess, occupy, please, preoccupy, stimulate, stir) **(¿) ABSTRACTION ALERT. Concrete goals essential!**

WEARY (/): *break, bust, cripple, debilitate, drain, enervate, enfeeble, exhaust, fatigue, finish, frazzle, harass, kill, leech, overextend, overwhelm, ruin, sap, sicken, strain, stress, tax, tire, tucker, waste, weaken, wear* (≠ activate, boost, energize, feed, fuel, heal, help, invigorate, nourish, rally, rejuvenate, relax, resuscitate, revive, rouse, stimulate, strengthen, vitalize, wake)

WEASEL (←): *bilk, borrow, -bypass, cadge, cheat, -circumvent, con, disguise, -dodge, -duck, -elude, -eschew, euchre, -evade, fudge, scam, schnorr, scrounge, shake, -shirk, shuck, -shun, -sidestep, skirt, slip, sneak, stiff, straddle, wheedle* (≠ afford, bestow, comp, confront, contribute, deliver, donate, face, furnish, give, grant, honor, meet, offer, provide, subsidize, supply)

WEATHER (+): *abide, accept, allow, bear, brave, brook, concede, condone, countenance, endure, experience, face, harden, incur, indulge, know, outlast, outlive, overcome, permit, receive, sanction, season, shoulder, stand, stomach, suffer, support, surmount, survive, sustain, swallow, sweat, take, tolerate, withstand* (≠ -abandon, -avoid, battle, cease, challenge, combat, croak, denounce, depart, -elude, end, -escape, -eschew, -evade, fight, -flee, flout, oppose, pass, -prevent, -prohibit, -refuse, -reject, resist, skip, stop, -thwart)

WEAVE (+): *blend, braid, build, complicate, compose, concoct, construct, contrive, create, enlace, entwine, fabricate, fashion, fuse, hybridize, improvise, incorporate, interlace, intermingle, intertwine, interweave, join, knit, knot, lace, link, loop, make, manufacture, merge, mix, plait, ply, raddle, sculpt, sew, shape, snake, spin, splice, synthesize, twine, twist, unite, wind, wreathe* (≠ cut, disentangle, divide, razor, rip, separate, shred, slice, split, synthesize, tatter, tear, unbraid, uncoil, unknot, unravel, unsew, unspool, untangle, untwine, unwind)

WED (+): *affiance, betroth, commit, dedicate, engage, espouse, marry, match, mate, pledge, promise, splice, vow* (≠ -abandon, alienate, distance, divorce, estrange, mismatch, -ostracize, oust, -reject, separate, split, sunder)

WEDGE (→): *affix, block, chock, cram, crowd, crush, fill, fit, fix, force, heap, jam, jam-pack, load, lodge, overcrowd, overstuff, pack, push, ram, sandwich, sardine, shoehorn, splice, squeeze, stuff, tamp, thrust* (≠ detach, dislodge, dissolve, ease, expand, extend, free, loosen, open, release, remove, stretch, unblock, unclog, unlock, wrest, wring, yank)

WEED (/): *abolish, annihilate, cull, deep-six, delouse, destroy, eliminate, eradicate, erase, expunge, exterminate, gather, groom, isolate, kill, manicure, pick, pluck, pull, purge, remove, uproot, yank* (≠ add, cultivate, encourage, farm, fertilize, grow, -ignore, -neglect, nurture, plant, produce, propagate, protect, raise, seed, sow, sprout, survive, tend)

WEIGH (←): *absorb, analyze, anatomize, appraise, assimilate, balance, brainstorm, calculate, chew, compare, compute, conclude, consider, consult, contemplate, critique, debate, deliberate, digest, dissect, entertain, estimate, evaluate, examine, explore, eye, eyeball, gauge, measure, mind, mull, ogle, ponder, question, read, rehash, review, sample, scrutinize, second-guess, study, sweat, time* (≠ abdicate, -avoid, -blank, -bypass, -discount, dismiss, -disregard, -ditch, -dodge, drop, -duck, forget, -forsake, guesstimate, -ignore, invalidate, lose, misgauge, misjudge, -neglect, -nullify, -omit, -overlook, pooh-pooh, -reject, -shirk, -slight) **(¿) ABSTRACTION ALERT. Concrete goals essential!**

WEIGHT (←): *afflict, angle, ballast, bias, burden, clog, clutter, encumber, fill, freight, hamper, handicap, heap, load, lumber, mound, oppress, overburden, overload, overtax, pack, pile, predetermine, prejudge, prejudice, press, pull, rephrase, sadden, saddle, skew, slant, stack, strain, surcharge, sway, task, tax, tip, trouble, twist, unbalance, weigh, worry* (≠ alleviate, calibrate, cheer, detach, discharge, discredit, disencumber, disgrace, dishonor, -disregard, divest, dump, ease, lighten, offload, part, relieve, remove, unburden, unload, unskew)

WELCOME (+): *accept, acclaim, accost, admit, adopt, applaud, befriend, cherry-pick, choose, compère, cull, drink, eat, elect, embrace, emcee, enjoy, entertain, espouse, flag, glad-hand, greet, hail, handpick, high-five, host, hug, invite, meet, name, pick, please, prefer, receive, reunite, salute, select, take* (≠ alienate, ban, banish, bar, blackball, boo, -boycott, -decline, disaffect, -disregard, disrespect, diss, -eschew, estrange, exorcise, expel, -ignore, insult, isolate, -neglect, oppose, -ostracize, oust, pass, picket, protest, -refuse, -reject, resent, -scorn, seclude, -shun, -spurn)

WELD (+): *affix, attach, bind, bond, cement, combine, connect, fix, fuse, heat, hybridize, join, link, melt, mortar, seal, solder, synthesize, unite* (≠ break, cleave, crack, cut, disconnect, dissolve, divide, fracture, mangle, rupture, scatter, separate, shatter, split, sunder)

WET (→): *bathe, damp, dampen, deluge, dip, douse, drench, drown, flood, hose, imbrue, imbue, irrigate, marinate, moisten, presoak, puddle, rinse,* *saturate, sluice, soak, sop, spatter, splash, splatter, spray, sprinkle, steep, swamp, wash, water* (≠ bake, burn, dehydrate, desiccate, dry, harden, mop, parch, scorch, staunch, towel, waterproof, wipe, wring)

WHACK (→): *backhand, bang, bash, bat, batter, bean, beat, belt, biff, bludgeon, bob, bonk, bop, box, brain, buffet, bump, bust, butt, cane, chop, clap, clip, clobber, clock, clout, club, conk, crack, cudgel, cuff, deck, drub, fell, flail, flog, floor, hammer, hit, jab, jostle, kick, knee, knock, lace, lambaste, lash, level, lick, nail, paste, poke, pound, prod, pummel, punch, push, rabbit-punch, rap, sap, shove, skull, slam, slap, sledgehammer, slog, slug, smack, smite, sock, spank, stamp, strike, sucker punch, swat, swipe, tag, thrash, thump, thwack, wallop, whale* (≠ aid, baby, block, coddle, deflect, -dodge, -duck, guard, massage, miss, mollify, parry, pet, placate, please, protect, repel, shelter, shield, -sidestep, skim, stroke, tap)

WHACK (/): *ambush, annihilate, assassinate, bury, butcher, claim, croak, decimate, defeat, destroy, dispatch, doom, eliminate, eradicate, erase, execute, exterminate, fell, hit, ice, kill, liquidate, massacre, murder, neutralize, off, shoot, slaughter, slay, smite, snuff, terminate, waste, weed, zap* (≠ animate, assist, defend, guard, heal, help, preserve, protect, raise, rescue, restore, resurrect, resuscitate, revive, safeguard, save, secure, shield)

WHEEDLE (←): *adulate, beg, beguile, beseech, blandish, blarney, bribe, butter, cadge, cajole, charm, coax, cozen, entice, finagle, flannel, flatter, gratify, importune, induce, inveigle, juggle, lure, massage, overpraise, palaver, panhandle, praise, schmooze, scrounge, seduce, soft-sell, soft-soap, sweet-talk, tempt, urge, wangle, woo* (≠ blackjack, blackmail, bludgeon, browbeat, bug, bulldoze, bully, coerce, command, compel, constrain, cow, daunt, demand, force, harass, intimidate, make, muscle, nag, nobble, oblige, pester, require, sandbag, tease)

WHET (→): *activate, actuate, animate, appetize, arouse, awaken, boost, buoy, catalyze, challenge, charge, drive, electrify, enhance, enkindle, excite, ferment, foment, fortify, galvanize, hearten, impel, incite, increase, inflame, infuse, inspire, instigate, kindle, motivate, move, pique, propel, provoke, quicken, raise, rally, reanimate, reawaken, recharge, reenergize, refresh, reinvigorate, rejuvenate, rekindle, renew, restimulate, resurrect, resuscitate, revitalize, revive, rouse, spark, spur, steel, stimulate, stir, stoke, strengthen, tantalize, tease, tempt, titillate, trigger, wake, waken* (≠ blunt, calm, check, choke, crush, curb, dampen, daunt, deaden, debilitate, decrease, demotivate, depress, -deter, discourage, dishearten, drain, dull, enfeeble, exhaust, hamper, hinder, hush, inhibit, kill, lose, mitigate, numb, quell, quench, repress, restrain, sap, satisfy, slake, slow, smother, spoil, stifle, still, stunt, stymie, subdue, suppress, throttle, undermine, weaken)

WHET (/): *burnish, edge, file, finish, grind, hone, polish, refine, serrate, sharpen, stone, stroke, strop* (≠ blunt, blur, buff, buffer, burnish, cushion, dull, gloss, polish, round, shine, smooth, soften)

WHIP (→): *bash, beat, belt, birch, blackjack, blister, bludgeon, cane, castigate, chastise, clobber, clout, club, cowhide, cudgel, cuff, discipline, drub, flagellate, flail, flog, hide, hit, horsewhip, lace, lambaste, lash, lather, lick, maul, paddle, pelt, pound, pulverize, pummel, punish, scourge, slap, slate, smack, smite, spank, strap, strike, swat, swipe, switch, tan, thrash, thwack, trash, wallop, whack, whup* (≠ aid, assist, block, caress, coddle, compliment, defend, deflect, guard, heal, help, indulge, mollycoddle, nurse, parry, praise, protect, reward, shield, spoil, stroke, support, tend)

WHIP (/): *ace, annihilate, assault, attack, beat, best, better, bomb, break, bury, cap, checkmate, clobber, conquer, cow, cream, crush, decimate, defeat, demolish, destroy, devastate, discomfit, dispatch, doom, drub, dust, eclipse, edge, engulf, enslave, exceed, excel, finish, flatten, hammer, lick, master, obliterate, outdistance, outdo, outfight, outsell, outshine, outstrip, overcome, overpower, overthrow, overwhelm, paste, quash, quell, reduce, rout, ruin, shellac, sink, skin, skunk, slaughter, smash, smoke, smother, subdue, subjugate, surmount, surpass, sweep, take, tame, thrash, throw, top, topple, transcend, trim, trounce, upend, upset, vanquish, wallop, wax, whomp, whup* (≠ admit, aid, assist, build, cherish, conserve, construct, defend, elevate, encourage, fix, follow, forfeit, free, guard, help, institute, invite, liberate, maintain, mend, nourish, nurture, obey, preserve, promote, protect, release, relinquish, renew, repair, rescue, restore, revamp, revive, save, serve, shield, support, survive, sustain, upgrade, welcome)

WHITEWASH (←): *absolve, acquit, alibi, alleviate, bleach, bleep, blur, camouflage, candy-coat, clear, cloak, clothe, cloud, conceal, costume, cover, decorate, deemphasize, disguise, downplay, ease, exculpate, excuse, exonerate, explain, gloss, hide, justify, launder, lessen, liberate, lighten, mask, minimize, mitigate, moderate, obscure, -omit, paint, palliate, rationalize, screen, soften, soft-pedal, spackle, spin, sugarcoat, suppress, temper, underemphasize, varnish, veil, veneer, vindicate, whiten* (≠ accent, accentuate, accost, address, admit, affirm, amplify, assert, betray, blab, blacken, blame, condemn, confess, confide, confirm, confront, criticize, darken, debunk, defame, denounce, discredit, disprove, dispute, divulge, doubt, emphasize, exaggerate, expose, eyeball, fault, finger, frame, fulminate, incriminate, judge, libel, out, punctuate, reveal, shame, slander, unmask)

WHITTLE (→): *carve, chip, contour, cut, fashion, form, hew, model, mold, pare, scrape, sculpt, shape, shave, trim* (≠ augment, buff, build, construct, create, develop, enlarge, expand, fill, increase, inflate, keep, pad, polish, shine, smooth, swell)

WHITTLE (/): *bleed, cannibalize, consume, cripple, damage, debilitate, decrease, deplete, destroy, devour, diminish, drain, eat, erode, exhaust, impair, injure, kneecap, leach, lessen, mar, sabotage, sap, subvert, undercut, undermine, use, weaken* (≠ broaden, earn, expand, feed, fuel, grow, heal, increase, nourish, nurture, remedy, repair, replenish, restore, stock)

WIELD (→): *apply, brandish, command, conduct, control, employ, exercise, exert, flourish, handle, hold, maintain, manage, maneuver, manipulate, operate, ply, possess, shake, swing, throw, unsheathe, use, utilize, wave, work* (≠ abuse, conceal, discard, drag, drop, forget, forgo, hide, holster, lose, misapply, misplace, misuse, -neglect, -reject, sheathe, stay, store, suppress)

WIN (→): *accomplish, achieve, actualize, beat, best, carry, colonize, conquer, crest, outlast, overcome, overwhelm, sweep, trump, whip, whup* (≠ -abandon, bomb, concede, fail, flunk, forfeit, -forsake, leave, lose, miss, -neglect, -nullify, skimp, start, stop, waste)

WIN (←): *achieve, acquire, allure, annex, approach, attain, attract, bag, captivate, capture, carry, catch, charm, collect, convince, derive, disarm, draw, earn, enamor, enchant, equal, gain, garner, get, harvest, hit, land, log, make, match, meet, net, notch, obtain, outdo, outperform, persuade, procure, reach, realize, receive, rival, score, secure, select, source, surpass, top* (≠ -abandon, accord, bequeath, bestow, bore, demand, -deny, disappoint, give, grant, lose, miss, pay, relinquish, repel, steal, stiff, stint, surrender, tithe, undershoot, waste, withhold, yield)

WIND (→): *bend, coil, contort, corkscrew, curl, dial, distort, encircle, entwine, fold, loop, reel, roll, rotate, screw, skew, snake, spin, turn, twine, twirl, twist, weave, wrap, wreathe, wring* (≠ bind, free, grind, loose, loosen, release, smooth, stick, straighten, uncoil, unravel, unspool, untwist, unwind, unwrap)

WING (→): *bowl, buck, bung, bunt, butt, cant, cast, catapult, chuck, compel, dart, dash, direct, dispatch, distract, drive, eject, fire, flick, fling, flip, floor, goad, gun, heave, hook, hurl, hurtle, impel, launch, lob, loft, loose, pass, peg, pelt, pitch, precipitate, prod, project, propel, push, rifle, roll, send, shoot, shy, skitter, sling, throw, thrust, toss* (≠ absorb, accept, acquire, bring, carry, catch, clasp, clutch, convey, cover, drag, gain, garner, give, grab, grasp, grip, hand, hold, keep, obtain, procure, pull, receive, request, retain, secure, snag, tow, tug, welcome, yank)

WING (+): *ad-lib, bluff, brainstorm, coin, con, concoct, contrive, counterfeit, deceive, devise, double-talk, extemporize, fake, falsify, feign, forge, form, fudge, half-ass, hatch, imitate, improve, improvise, invent, jive, misrepresent, pretend, scam, spin, vamp* (≠ choreograph, compose, crosscheck, orchestrate, order, organize, plan, prepare, prove, rehearse, study, substantiate, test, validate, verify)

WING (/): *barrage, bash, batter, beat, bench, blast, bludgeon, bombard, break, bruise, buffet, burn, clip, club, crack, cripple, damage, deactivate, debilitate, disable, disfigure, dispatch, disqualify, drill, drub, fracture, fry, fusillade, hammer, hamper, hamstring, handicap, harm, hinder, hit, hobble, hurt, immobilize, impair, impede, incapacitate, injure, kneecap, lacerate, lame, maim, mangle, maul, mutilate, paralyze, paste, pelt,* *pepper, plug, pop, prostrate, sabotage, scar, scotch, shatter, shoot, short-circuit, shrivel, sideline, smash, snipe, spoil, strafe, target, thump, torpedo, trigger, undercut, undermine, wallop, weaken, whip, wither, wizen, wound, zap* (≠ absorb, aid, armor, assist, bolster, brace, brave, cover, cure, defend, disarm, doctor, draw, enable, face, fix, guard, heal, help, mend, militarize, nurse, outlast, overcome, patch, rehabilitate, reintegrate, rejuvenate, remedy, renew, repair, restore, secure, shield, splint, steady, strengthen, support, suture, tolerate, unify, unite, weaponize, weather, weld, withstand)

WINNOW (/): *categorize, choose, classify, clean, clear, comb, compartmentalize, cull, distinguish, divide, examine, filter, glean, grade, hierarchize, identify, organize, part, pigeonhole, prioritize, rank, refine, screen, select, separate, sieve, sift, slot, sort, systematize, type* (≠ addle, baffle, blend, churn, combine, confuse, disarrange, dishevel, disorganize, fuse, garble, jumble, knot, lump, meld, mingle, misclassify, missort, mistype, mix, muddle, muddy, perplex, scramble, shuffle, stir, tangle)

WIPE (/): *abolish, annihilate, anonymize, -blank, blot, brush, -cancel, clean, cleanse, clear, -cut, dab, decimate, delete, demolish, destroy, devastate, discard, dismantle, -ditch, doom, dry, dust, efface, eject, eradicate, erase, excise, expel, expunge, exterminate, extirpate, flatten, jettison, liquidate, mop, mow, -nullify, obliterate, oust, purge, ravage, raze, remove, rub, ruin, smear, snuff, sponge, swab, sweep, total* (≠ bedraggle, begrime, besmirch, build, conserve, construct, contaminate, create, dirty, fabricate, fashion, fix, forge, form, foul, frame, make, manufacture, mend, muddy, patch, pollute, preserve, protect, rebuild, recondition, reconstruct, renew, renovate, repair, replace, restore, revamp, save, sculpt, shape, soil, spoil, spot, stain, sully, taint, tarnish)

WIRE (+): *angle, bend, bow, coil, contract, crimp, crook, curve, double, establish, fit, fix, fold, insert, insinuate, install, introduce, lay, locate, lodge, loop, network, place, plant, ply, position, settle, situate, station, stretch, thread, tighten, twist* (≠ cut, detach, disconnect, eradicate, extract, fish, isolate, pull, relocate, remove, separate, sever, strip, unplug, unwire, yank)

WISH (+): *accept, allow, anticipate, ask, assume, await, beg, believe, bid, choose, command, conjure, contemplate, covet, crave, desire, direct, envy, expect, fancy, fetishize, instruct, invite, order, plead, prefer, presume, request, require, seek, solicit, summon, target, trust, want, welcome, will* (≠ -avoid, begrudge, bestow, -decline, -despise, discard, dump, envy, furnish, give, -hate, -loathe, offer, -refuse, -reject, remove, repel, -repudiate, resent, stint, withdraw, withhold) **(¿) ABSTRACTION ALERT. Concrete goals essential!**

WITHDRAW (+): *abstract, budge, clear, -cut, debit, derive, dislocate, dislodge, displace, disturb, draw, elicit, exact, excavate, extract, extricate, gather, glean, move, obtain, place, pluck, position, pull, quarry, recover, remove, shift, slurp, suck, take, transfer, transpose, vacuum, worm, wrench, wrest, wring* (≠ anchor, clamp, deposit, earn, embed, entrench, fix, hitch, implant, ingrain, lodge, moor, mount, plonk, recoup, replace, restore, return, root, secure, set, situate, spitball, stick)

WITHER (/): *afflict, bake, barbecue, blight, broil, canker, castrate, corrode, corrupt, cripple, crumble, debilitate, decay, -decline, decrease, degrade, demolish, destroy, deteriorate, devastate, dilapidate, diminish, disfigure, disintegrate, doom, dry, emasculate, fade, foil, hamstring, harm, harshen, hurt, impair, incapacitate, injure, lessen, lower, mummify, reduce, rot, ruin, scorch, scupper, scuttle, shrink, shrivel, taint, undermine, unman, waste, weaken, wilt, wizen, worsen, wound, wreck* (≠ advance, ameliorate, augment, better, boost, develop, enhance, enrich, fortify, foster, freshen, grow, heighten, improve, increase, nourish, nurture, optimize, overhaul, prioritize, reinvigorate, restimulate, revive, strengthen, upgrade, wax)

WITHHOLD (←): *amass, bear, boast, cherish, command, conceal, conserve, control, -deny, detain, direct, enjoy, guard, harbor, hide, hoard, hog, hold, hug, keep, maintain, manage, mass, own, possess, preserve, protect, reserve, retain, rule, safeguard, save, shelter, shield, squirrel, stockpile, treasure* (≠ -abandon, accord, bequeath, bestow, cede, circulate, comp, contribute, -decline, discard, disseminate, -ditch, donate, drop, dump, eject, forfeit, -forsake, give, grant, hand, jettison, lose, -reject, release, relinquish, -repudiate, scrap, scuttle, spend, -spurn, squander, surrender, tender, tithe, yield)

WITHHOLD (/): *-balk, ban, bridle, budget, check, conceal, constrain, control, curb, -decline, deduct, -deny, deprive, disadvantage, disallow, disapprove, drizzle, enjoin, -forbid, hamper, hide, hinder, hoard, hold, impede, inhibit, keep, malnourish, -nix, obstruct, -omit, -prohibit, proscribe, -rebuff, recall, -refuse, -reject, remove, repel, repress, reserve, resist, restrain, restrict, retain, retract, revoke, skimp, spike, -spurn, stall, starve, steal, stiff, stint, stymie, suppress, trickle, -veto, withdraw* (≠ accord, afford, allow, authorize, bestow, commission, comp, concede, contribute, cosset, deliver, disburse, dispense, donate, furnish, give, grant, greenlight, humor, indulge, let, license, offer, okay, outbid, outlay, overpay, overspend, pamper, patronize, pay, permit, provide, release, sanction, spare, spitball, spoil, supply, tender, tithe, treat, volunteer, vouchsafe, warrant)

WITHSTAND (+): *abide, accept, allow, battle, bear, brace, brave, brook, buck, combat, concede, condone, confront, contest, countenance, debate, defend, defy, dispute, duel, endure, experience, face, fight, -forbid, handle, harden, incur, indulge, know, oppose, outlast, overcome, permit, preserve, -rebuff, receive, regularize, repel, repulse, resist, sanction, season, -snub, stabilize, stand, stick, stomach, suffer, support, surmount, survive, sustain, swallow, sweat, take, -thwart, tolerate, traverse, violate, weather* (≠ accept, accost, aid, allow, assist, -avoid, battle, budge, combat, concede, -dodge, -duck, enjoy, forfeit, -forsake, grant, gratify, help, hound, humor, indulge, mind, obey, oblige, permit, -prevent, -refuse, -reject, resist, spoil, suffer, support, surrender)

WITNESS (←): *advise, affirm, analyze, anatomize, ascertain, assess, attest, audit, authenticate, avow, backtrack, benchmark, certify, chaperone, chart, check, chronicle, clock, comb, con, conclude, confirm, connect, consider, consult, contemplate, contextualize, contrast, correlate, corroborate, criticize, critique, crosscheck, debunk, deconstruct, deduce, detect, determine, differentiate, discern, dissect, distill, document, double-check, endorse, ensure, establish, examine, explore, eye, eyeball, follow, gauge, glimpse, graph, guarantee, guesstimate, heed, inspect, investigate, judge, learn, mind, monitor, nanny, notarize, note, notice, number, numerate, observe, oversee, parse, patrol, perceive, plumb, police, prioritize, probe, proctor, profess, prove, read, reconnoiter, record, referee, reference, regard, reinforce, research, retrace, review, rifle, sample, scan, scope, scout, scrutinize, search, settle, spy, study, substantiate, supervise, support, surveil, survey, suss, test, testify, trace, track, validate, verify, vet, view, vindicate, visit, vivisect, warrant, watch* (≠ -abandon, baffle, believe, bewilder, -blank, blind, blindfold, bury, challenge, conceal, confound, confuse, contest, contradict, cross-examine, debate, deceive, defraud, -deny, disavow, disbelieve, disclaim, -discount, discredit, disguise, disprove, dispute, -disregard, distrust, doubt, erase, expunge, fake, fancy, forget, fudge, gainsay, grill, half-ass, hide, -ignore, imagine, invalidate, lose, mask, mislead, miss, mistake, muddle, mystify, -neglect, obfuscate, obliterate, obscure, -omit, oppose, -overlook, perplex, pretend, puzzle, question, rebut, refute, -reject, scam, scruple, skim, skip, suspect, trick, warn, wonder) **(¿) ABSTRACTION ALERT. Concrete goals essential!**

WOLF (←): *bolt, consume, cram, demolish, devour, eat, finish, gobble, gorge, gulp, guzzle, ingest, inhale, overeat, pack, ravage, raven, scarf, slop, slosh, stuff, swallow, swill* (≠ -avoid, concoct, cook, -decline, hunt, nibble, peck, pick, prepare, -refuse, -reject, skip, spew, spit, splutter, vomit)

WONDER (+): *admire, anticipate, assume, attribute, await, believe, conceive, conclude, conjecture, consider, deduce, disbelieve, distrust, doubt, dread, dream, estimate, evaluate, examine, guess, infer, judge, mistrust, mull, ponder, presume, project, puzzle, query, question, rationalize, reckon, scruple, suppose, surmise, survey, suspect, theorize, think, weigh* (≠ adjudge, affirm, anticipate, ascertain, assert, assume, assure, await, believe, corroborate, demonstrate, detect, determine, discern, discover, document, establish, expect, explain, guarantee, insist, insure, know, learn, orient, presume, prove, substantiate, validate, verify, warrant) **(¿) ABSTRACTION ALERT. Concrete goals essential!**

WOO (←): *attract, beg, beguile, bewitch, cajole, captivate, charm, chase, coax, court, cuddle, cultivate, date, encourage, entice, entreat, escort, flannel, flatter, gratify, hunt, importune, ingratiate, invite, magnetize, please, praise, propose, provoke, pursue, romance, schmooze, search, seduce, seek, serenade, solicit, sway, sweet-talk, tantalize, target, tempt, welcome, win, wow* (≠ abuse, alienate, annoy, assault, attack, -avoid, bore, brutalize, chastise, chide, -cut, daunt, -despise, discourage, disgust, disrespect, dissuade, -elude, -ignore, insult, irk, irritate, lesson, menace, nauseate, -neglect, offend, -omit, oppose, -ostracize, -overlook, pass, punish, rebuke, -refuse, -reject, repel, repulse, -scorn, -shun, sicken, -snub, -spurn, terrorize, threaten, troll)

WORK (→): *arrange, command, control, cultivate, dial, direct, drive, engineer, execute, farm, fashion, form, guide, handle, influence, man, manage, maneuver, manipulate, model, mold, operate, perform, pilot, ply, process, run, sculpt, shape, shift, steer, use, wield* (≠ -abandon, botch, bungle, -disregard, flub, flunk, fumble, half-ass, -neglect, -omit, -overlook, -shirk, spoil)

WORK (+): *advance, beget, begin, breed, bring, catalyze, concoct, create, cultivate, decide, determine, develop, effect, effectuate, enact, encourage, engender, establish, father, forward, foster, found, further, generate, hatch, inaugurate, induce, initiate, innovate, institute, introduce, invoke, launch, make, nourish, nurture, pioneer, produce, promote, prompt, render, set, sire, spawn, start, yield* (≠ abolish, arrest, check, control, crush, curb, dampen, demolish, destroy, exterminate, extinguish, hamper, impede, inhibit, limit, liquidate, -prevent, quash, quell, quench, repress, restrain, restrict, retard, smother, squash, squelch, stifle, subdue, suppress)

WORK (/): *abuse, arrange, beguile, bilk, bleed, bluff, buffalo, bullshit, cadge, cheat, chisel, commercialize, commodify, con, contrive, convince, cozen, deceive, defraud, delude, devise, dupe, engineer, exploit, finagle, finesse, fleece, fool, gazump, gull, gyp, hoax, hocus-pocus, hoodwink, hustle, impose, inveigle, jockey, kid, leverage, maneuver, manipulate, mastermind, milk, mistreat, misuse, outsmart, outthink, outwit, overcharge, play, prostitute, schnorr, shanghai, skin, snooker, snow, soak, stick, stiff, sucker, swindle, trick, use* (≠ accuse, confess, defend, discredit, expose, guard, honor, maintain, protect, provide, repay, respect, restore, save, secure, shame, support)

WORM (→): *edge, infiltrate, inject, insert, insinuate, interpolate, interpose, introduce, replace, restore, slip, snake, sneak, wiggle, wind, wriggle* (≠ cull, derive, distill, draw, elicit, extract, get, glean, obtain, prize, pull, take, withdraw, wrest, wring)

WORRY (←): *abash, aggravate, agitate, ail, alarm, anger, annoy, badger, bedevil, bother, bug, chafe, concern, confound, confuse, convulse, daunt, demoralize, demotivate, depress, derail, -deter, discomfit, discomfort, discompose, disconcert, discourage, dishearten, dismay, dispirit, disquiet, distemper, distract, distress, disturb, dog, embarrass, exasperate, exercise, faze, fluster, frazzle, freak, fret, fuss, gall, get, gravel, harass, harry, hassle, haunt, hector, irk, irritate, jar, mortify, nag, needle, nettle, niggle, nitpick, nonplus, peeve, persecute, perturb, pester, pique, plague, rattle, rile, shake, sweat, tease, torment, traumatize, trouble, undo, unhinge, unnerve, unsettle, upset, vex* (≠ allay, alleviate, amuse, appease, assuage, bolster, brace, buoy, calm, candy-coat, comfort, compose, conciliate, content, ease, entertain, gratify, help, humor, hush, lull, mellow, mitigate, moderate, mollify, pacify, placate, propitiate, quiet, reassure, relax, settle, soothe, steady, sugarcoat, tranquilize)

WORSHIP (+): *admire, adore, affirm, apotheosize, beatify, bless, bronze, canonize, celebrate, ceremonialize, cherish, consecrate, dedicate, deify, delight, devote, dignify, enshrine, esteem, eternalize, exalt, extol, fetishize, glorify, gratify, guard, hallow, honor, idealize, idolize, immortalize, laud, lionize, love, magnify, memorialize, please, praise, preserve, protect, purify, regard, respect, revere, reverence, ritualize, romanticize, sanctify, satisfy, sentimentalize, treasure, value, venerate* (≠ -abandon, affront, bastardize, belittle, bestialize, blaspheme, condemn, contaminate, debase, decry, defame, defile, demean, demonize, desecrate, dishonor, disparage, disrespect, humble, -ignore, insult, libel, -loathe, malign, minimize, offend, outrage, pillory, pollute, profane, ridicule, -scorn, shame, slander, -slight, slur, smear, tarnish, vandalize, violate)

WOUND (/): *abuse, afflict, aggrieve, bash, batter, beat, belt, bench, bite, blemish, blight, bloody, bludgeon, break, bruise, buffet, castrate, club, contort, crack, crease, cripple, crucify, cut, damage, debilitate, deface, defeat, deform, deprive, destroy, disable, disfigure, dismember, drub, emasculate, enervate, enfeeble, flog, fracture, fragment, gash, gore, gouge, graze, hack, hammer, hamstring, handicap, harm, hit, hobble, hurt, immobilize, impair, incapacitate, injure, kill, kneecap, knife, lacerate, lambaste, lame, lash, maim, maltreat, mangle, mar, maul, murder, mutilate, nick, palsy, paralyze, paste, pelt, pierce, pound, prostrate, pummel, puncture, ruin, sabotage, scald, scalp, scar, scathe, scotch, scrape, scratch, shank, shatter, shiv, short-circuit, shrivel, singe, slash, slit, smash, sorrow, spoil, stab, stifle, strain, strike, tear, thrash, thump, torment, torture, undermine, unman, wallop, weaken, welt, whip, wing, wither, wizen, wrong* (≠ aid, assist, bolster, brace, brave, correct, cure, defend, doctor, dose, drug, ease, face, fix, guard, heal, help, hospitalize, medicate, mend, misdiagnose, nurse, patch, rectify, rehabilitate, reintegrate, rejuvenate, remedy, renew, repair, restore, sedate, splint, steady, strengthen, suture, tolerate, unify, unite, weld, withstand)

WOUND (/): *abuse, affront, blame, boo, canker, crucify, cut, defame, demean, demoralize, disparage, displease, disqualify, disrespect, diss, distress, disturb, -frustrate, grieve, hamper, hurt, impede, injure, insult, jeer, libel, malign, maltreat, miff, mistreat, mock, mortify, offend, oppress, -ostracize, oust, outrage, pain, persecute, pillory, prejudice, revile, ridicule, ruin, shock, sideline, slander, slap, -slight, slur, smear, -snub, spoil, stigmatize, sting, swipe, tarnish, taunt, torment, torture, traumatize, trouble, undercut, undermine, upset, weaken, wrong* (≠ acclaim, applaud, blandish, boost, buoy, commend, compliment, congratulate, delight, elevate, enable, enhance, eulogize, flatter, glorify, gratify, hail, honor, idealize, idolize, inspire, outlast, overcome, please, praise, satisfy, support, sweet-talk, thrill, uplift, weaponize, weather, woo, wow)

WOW (→): *amaze, animate, astonish, astound, attract, bewilder, bewitch, blindside, boggle, charm, cheer, confound, daze, dazzle, disconcert, dumbfound, energize, entertain, enthuse, excite, fascinate, flabbergast, floor, flummox, gobsmack, grab, impress, inspire, interest, intrigue, kill, motivate, move, overwhelm, razzle-dazzle, rouse, shock, slay, stagger,* *startle, stimulate, stir, stun, stupefy, surprise, sway, tickle* (≠ anesthetize, annoy, -balk, blunt, bore, bother, bug, clarify, comfort, confound, cushion, dampen, deaden, depress, disappoint, disenchant, dismay, displease, dull, exhaust, explain, irk, muffle, nag, needle, nettle, niggle, nitpick, numb, sedate, stifle, tire, underwhelm, vex, weary, worry)

WRACK (/): *abuse, afflict, agonize, annihilate, beat, best, blast, bother, break, clobber, conquer, cream, cripple, crucify, crush, damage, decimate, deface, defeat, demolish, desolate, despoil, destroy, deteriorate, devastate, dilapidate, disassemble, disfigure, disintegrate, dismantle, dissolve, distress, doom, drub, dynamite, efface, eradicate, erode, expunge, exterminate, extinguish, extirpate, fracture, grill, gut, harm, harrow, impair, injure, lick, liquidate, loot, mangle, mar, master, monkey-wrench, mutilate, nuke, obliterate, overcome, pain, persecute, pillage, plague, plunder, pulverize, punish, ravage, raze, remove, rout, ruin, sack, scalp, scotch, scour, shatter, skunk, smash, snuff, spoil, subdue, surmount, thrash, torture, total, trample, trash, trim, trouble, trounce, unbuild, vandalize, vaporize, vitiate, wallop, waste, whip, worry, wreck* (≠ assemble, build, calm, comfort, conserve, constitute, construct, create, doctor, ease, erect, establish, fabricate, fashion, father, fix, forge, form, found, frame, gratify, heal, help, humor, institute, invent, lull, make, manufacture, mellow, mend, mitigate, moderate, mold, mollify, nurse, organize, pacify, patch, placate, preserve, produce, protect, rebuild, recondition, reconstruct, remodel, renovate, repair, restore, revamp, save, shape, survive, sustain, tend, weather, withstand)

WRANGLE (←): *argue, bandy, butt, challenge, consider, contest, controvert, dare, debate, defy, discuss, dispute, fence, fight, hassle, jar, kick, litigate, nitpick, protest, wrestle* (≠ accept, allow, calm, concede, deflect, endure, grant, gratify, lull, mellow, mitigate, pacify, permit, placate, sedate, stomach, surrender, tolerate)

WRAP (←): *bale, band, bandage, belt, bind, blanket, bower, bundle, camouflage, chain, circle, circumscribe, clasp, cloak, clothe, cocoon, cord, costume, cover, curtain, disguise, drape, embed, embrace, encase, enchain, encircle, enclose, encompass, enfold, enshroud, envelop, fold, gird, girdle, invest, involve, lap, lash, loop, mantle, mask, muffle, overlay, pack, package, protect, rope, shackle, shroud, straightjacket, surround, swaddle, swathe, tape, tie, truss, veil, wind, wire, wreathe* (≠ bare, denude, disclose, disrobe, divulge, exhibit, expose, open, peel, reveal, shuck, strip, tear, trumpet, unbind, uncover, unroll, untie, unveil, unwind, unwrap, wrinkle)

WREAK (→): *accomplish, ace, achieve, actualize, attain, bestow, bring, commit, compass, complete, create, effect, effectuate, end, execute, exercise, express, finish, force, force-feed, fulfill, implement, impose, inflict, make, manipulate, nail, negotiate, perform, perpetrate, practice, prosecute, realize, reduplicate, reenact, repeat, unleash, vent, visit, work* (≠ baffle, bar, block, destroy, fail, forget, -frustrate, -halt, hamper, hinder, hobble, -ignore, impair, impede, inhibit, miss, -neglect, obstruct, -overlook,

-prevent, -prohibit, -slight, stop, stymie, -thwart, withhold) **(¿) ABSTRACTION ALERT. Concrete goals essential!**

WRECK (/): *annihilate, atomize, bash, beat, best, blast, boobytrap, break, capsize, checkmate, clobber, conquer, crash, cream, cripple, crush, damage, dash, debauch, decimate, deface, defeat, demolish, desolate, despoil, destroy, deteriorate, detonate, devastate, dilapidate, disable, disassemble, disfigure, disintegrate, dismantle, dissolve, doom, drub, dynamite, efface, eradicate, erode, expunge, exterminate, extinguish, extirpate, fracture, gut, harm, impair, injure, kneecap, lick, liquidate, loot, mangle, mar, master, monkey-wrench, mortar, mutilate, nuke, obliterate, overcome, pillage, plunder, pulverize, ravage, ravish, raze, remove, rout, ruin, sabotage, sack, scotch, scour, scupper, scuttle, shatter, sink, skunk, smash, snuff, split, spoil, subdue, surmount, thrash, torpedo, total, trample, trash, trim, trounce, unbuild, undermine, undo, unmake, vandalize, vaporize, vitiate, wallop, waste, whip, wrack* (≠ assemble, bronze, budget, build, concoct, configure, conserve, construct, craft, create, doctor, embalm, erect, establish, fabricate, fashion, father, fix, forge, form, found, frame, institute, invent, machine, make, manufacture, mend, mold, organize, patch, preserve, produce, protect, raise, rear, rebuild, recondition, reconstruct, recycle, remodel, renovate, repair, restore, revamp, salvage, save, sculpt, shape, sideswipe, sire, survive, sustain, weather, withstand)

WRENCH (←): *amputate, budge, compel, contort, detach, dislocate, dislodge, displace, distort, disturb, drag, draw, dredge, extract, force, grab, jerk, jimmy, lever, lug, nab, pluck, prize, pry, pull, remove, rip, root, rotate, ruin, seize, sever, shift, snag, snatch, strain, take, tear, transfer, transpose, tug, tweak, twist, uproot, win, wrest, wring, yank* (≠ attach, coax, -deter, give, heave, leave, push, ram, reattach, release, shove, straighten, thrust, untwist)

WRESTLE (←): *bash, batter, battle, beat, box, buffet, challenge, clutch, combat, confront, contest, duel, engage, face, fight, grapple, grasp, grip, handle, hit, punch, race, slug, strike, tackle, wrangle* (≠ -avoid, -bypass, coddle, -disregard, -dodge, drop, -duck, -elude, -escape, -evade, loose, -omit, pacify, placate, release, -sidestep, skip)

WRING (←): *acquire, attain, blackmail, bleed, cheat, coerce, compel, debit, draw, earn, exact, extort, extract, fleece, force, gain, gouge, inherit, land, milk, mine, obtain, pluck, prize, procure, pry, pull, remove, root, scrounge, secure, skin, source, squeeze, swindle, take, tear, uproot, withdraw, wrest, yank* (≠ bank, bankroll, bestow, comp, deposit, distribute, donate, earn, finance, fund, furnish, give, grant, hoard, hog, insert, keep, offer, -omit, owe, pack, provide, replenish, restore, spare, supply, tender, underwrite, volunteer, withhold)

WRING (/): *budge, choke, coerce, compress, dislocate, displace, disturb, draw, dredge, exact, extort, extract, force, hurt, jerk, jimmy, lever, lug, mangle, pinch, pluck, pry, pull, remove, screw, shift, squeeze, strain, strangle, throttle, transfer, transpose, tug, turn, tweak, twist, wrench,* *wrest, yank* (≠ cram, implant, infuse, insert, install, protect, ram, replenish, restore, straighten, suffuse, unbend, untwist)

WRINKLE (/): *adapt, adjust, angle, arch, bend, bow, break, buckle, bulge, collapse, contort, corrugate, crease, crimp, crinkle, crook, crumple, curl, deform, distort, double, flex, fold, furrow, gather, hook, incline, line, mutate, pervert, pleat, plow, pucker, ridge, ripple, ruck, ruffle, rumple, shrivel, tilt, turn, twist, unsmooth, warp, wiggle, wilt, wriggle, zigzag* (≠ align, bolster, brace, comb, correct, flatten, groom, iron, level, plane, press, rectify, right, roll, smooth, steady, steam, straighten, tidy, unbend, uncrumple, uncurl, unfold, untwist, withstand)

WRONG (/): *abuse, afflict, anguish, antagonize, assault, attack, batter, blackjack, blackmail, bludgeon, browbeat, brutalize, bully, burn, cheat, crucify, deceive, defraud, dehumanize, discredit, disfavor, disgrace, dishonor, distress, double-cross, gaslight, harass, harm, hurt, ill-treat, impair, injure, intimidate, lynch, malign, malnourish, maltreat, manhandle, martyr, maul, menace, mishandle, misrepresent, mistreat, misuse, molest, -neglect, oppose, oppress, -ostracize, oust, outrage, persecute, plague, ravish, restrain, sadden, sandbag, savage, scam, sicken, stiff, sucker, swindle, terrorize, threaten, torment, torture, trash-talk, traumatize, trick, tyrannize, upset, victimize, violate, wound* (≠ accommodate, advance, aid, amuse, appease, assist, baby, cherish, coddle, compensate, defend, delight, elevate, enhance, entertain, favor, featherbed, foster, gratify, guard, heal, help, humor, improve, indulge, inspire, mend, mollycoddle, nourish, nurse, nurture, oblige, overindulge, overprotect, pacify, pamper, pet, pity, placate, please, pleasure, profit, promote, protect, raise, rectify, refine, regale, regret, repair, repay, rescue, reward, right, satiate, satisfy, save, serve, soothe, spoil, spoon-feed, tend, thrill, tickle, tolerate, treat, uplift, wow)

YANK (←): *acquire, corkscrew, drag, draw, extract, force, gain, grab, haul, heave, hitch, jerk, mine, nab, obtain, pluck, prize, pry, pull, remove, rip, root, seize, snag, snap, snatch, source, take, tear, tow, tug, uninstall, uproot, withdraw, wrench, wrest, wring* (≠ cram, drop, hammer, heave, implant, insert, install, instill, jam, knock, nudge, push, ram, retain, shove, shunt, stuff, thrust, wedge)

YIELD (→): *accord, admit, afford, allow, bear, bring, contribute, deliver, disburse, discharge, dispense, earn, fetch, furnish, gain, generate, give, grant, gross, net, offer, outbid, outlay, overpay, pay, produce, proffer, provide, realize, restore, return, supply, tender, tithe, volunteer* (≠ accrue, acquire, charge, consume, cost, debit, deduct, demand, -deny, forfeit, lose, offer, steal, stiff, stint, take, withhold)

YIELD (+): *advance, beget, begin, breed, bring, catalyze, create, cultivate, decide, determine, develop, effect, effectuate, enact, encourage, engender, establish, father, forward, foster, found, further, generate, hatch, inaugurate, induce, initiate, innovate, institute, introduce, invoke, launch, make, midwife, nourish, nurture, pioneer, produce, promote, prompt, render, set, sire, spawn, start* (≠ abolish, arrest, check, control, crush, curb, dampen, defy, demolish, destroy, erase, exterminate, extinguish, impede, inhibit, limit, liquidate, predetermine, quash, quell, quench, retard, smother, squash, stall, stifle, stymie, subdue, suppress)

YIELD (/): *-abandon, abdicate, abnegate, accept, acknowledge, admit, bequeath, bestow, cede, commit, concede, consign, deliver, -desert, discard, entrust, forfeit, forgo, -forsake, give, grant, hand, permit, release, relinquish, render, -renounce, resign, sacrifice, shed, surrender, transfer, waive* (≠ challenge, clutch, colonize, counter, defy, -deny, disallow, -forbid, keep, protect, -refuse, -reject, resist, retain, safeguard, -veto, withhold)

YOKE (+): *align, bind, bond, bracket, cement, chain, coalesce, combine, compound, concatenate, conjugate, connect, couple, dovetail, fuse, harness, hitch, hogtie, hook, integrate, interconnect, interlink, join, link, span, strap, string, team, tie, unite, weld, wire* (≠ cleave, cut, detach, disconnect, disengage, divide, loose, part, rupture, separate, sever, split, sunder, unchain, uncouple, unhitch, unlink, unshackle, unyoke)

Z

ZAP (/): *bake, bang, barbecue, bash, bat, batter, bean, beat, belt, blast, blitz, bludgeon, bob, bombard, bonk, bop, box, brain, broil, buffet, bump, bung, bunt, burn, bust, butt, cane, chop, clap, clip, clobber, clock, clout, club, concuss, conk, crack, cream, cudgel, cuff, deck, destroy, drub, fell, finish, flail, flick, flog, floor, fry, fusillade, hammer, hit, jab, jostle, kick, kill, knee, knock, lace, lambaste, lash, level, lick, mangle, maul, mortar, nail, paste, pelt, pepper, poke, pommel, pound, prod, pummel, punch, push, rabbit-punch, rap, rough, sap, sauté, scorch, scuff, shoot, shove, skull, slam, slap, slash, sledge, sledgehammer, slug, smack, smite, snipe, sock, spear, stab, stamp, strafe, strike, stroke, sucker-punch, swat, swipe, switch, tag, tap, thrash, thump, thwack, wallop, whack, whip* (≠ absorb, accept, armor, augment, bandage, bear, bolster, boost, buffer, cover, defend, deflect, disarm, draw, gain, garner, guard, heal, hold, holster, mend, overhaul, protect, receive, recharge, refurbish, repair, rescue, restore, secure, shelter, shield, suppress, withhold)

ZING (/): *abuse, attack, badmouth, blackguard, blister, boo, castigate, chide, condemn, criticize, critique, demean, denigrate, disparage, excoriate, fault, flay, fry, impugn, injure, insult, judge, knock, nag, needle, neg, -ostracize, oust, pan, pillory, poke, rebuke, ridicule, rip, roast, scorch, sear, slam, slate, sting, trash, wound* (≠ applaud, commend, compliment, congratulate, defend, flatter, forget, glorify, gratify, honor, idealize, idolize, -ignore, ingratiate, lionize, praise, protect, retort, shield, -shun, skip, -slight, -snub)

ZONE (/): *allocate, allot, apportion, bisect, chunk, compartmentalize, define, delimit, delineate, demarcate, divide, fence, halve, outline, parcel, partition, portion, screen, section, segment, segregate, share, split, subdivide, wall* (≠ absorb, annex, attach, combine, connect, couple, gather, incorporate, integrate, join, link, meld, network, reintegrate, unify, unite)

Part II: Genres

"We expect literary revolutions to come from above, from the literary end of the spectrum—the difficult, the avant-garde, the high-end, the densely written....Instead we're getting a revolution from below, coming up from the supermarket aisles. Genre fiction is the technology that will disrupt the literary novel as we know it."

Lev Grossman[7]

Fans of a given genre show up with expectations you must meet and exceed. It's a sword that cuts both ways. As an author, conventional solutions will help you survive, but to stand out and thrive, you'll need to keep your writing fresh and fascinating with every new project or your audience will get bored and head off in search of better, bolder books.

Every genre stakes out an imaginal terrain that its readers enjoy and defend. Most of that comes down to WHAT HAPPENS. In a sense, all conventional story patterns common to a genre (aka *tropes*) are nothing more than *actions and tactics* common to a genre.

Verb shapes vibe.

Remember: when I say "verb," I'm referring to character actions *and* tactics, both. The verbs that comprise a characterization simply express the character's energy flowing through the narrative.

Always factor in the type of story you're writing and the connotations of those verbs for genre and subgenre. Subtle variations in meaning really will recast an entire scene or character. Turning a boat even one degree can land you somewhere miles from the original destination.

What verbs serve your story and your characters best?

What actions and tactics get overused in your (sub)genre?

What are the actions and tactics used by protagonists of current bestsellers in this stretch of the bookshelf? How about genre classics?

Which actions and tactics would move this book into a different genre/subgenre? How would that transform your story for better and worse?

For my part, I suspect that audience tastes actually come down specifically to the kinds of verbs and vibes readers find entertaining. When a reader is bored by one type of book or drawn to another, it's because the actions (and tactics) resonate and evoke appealing emotions. Genre audiences show up expecting certain obligatory scenes, beloved archetypes, and timeless tropes...new wine in old bottles. How can you stretch your readers' imaginations and expand the landscape of your genre?

Remember: **the best way to predict the future is to invent it.**

Different actions and tactics can change a cozy into a noir into a romantic suspense into a paranormal. Obsessive fan devotion *flourishes* in the subtle distinctions between these subgenres, and canny verbalization will help you navigate the emotional landscape and determine the kind of audience you attract. And of course, actions and tactics will always be transitive and specific to the characters and their context.

Use language to put your story on the right genre shelf for its audience. Readers gravitate to their favorite kinds of emotional rides; your job is to engineer the most satisfying emotional ride possible within the framework of their expectations.

Genre language operates as a kind of promise to the reader and a fulfillment of that promise. Lazy authors recycle the half-assery of other lazy recyclers, and overuse eventually turns the perfect word into a feeble cliché—know the difference!

Genres evolve via their language, which means you'll need to keep abreast of developments and mutations in your neck of the fictional woods. To do your job and grow as an artist, you'll need to meet and exceed reader expectations with every new project.

> "If you have a story that seems worth telling, and you think you can tell it worthily, then the thing for you to do is to tell it, regardless of whether it has to do with sex, sailors, or mounted policemen."
>
> Dashiell Hammett[8]

Action-Adventure

Representative Authors and Titles

- **Steve Berry,** *The Templar Legacy*
- **Michael Crichton,** *Jurassic Park*
- **Clive Cussler,** *Raise The Titanic!*
- **Anthony Hope,** *The Prisoner of Zenda*
- **George MacDonald Fraser,** *The Pyrates*
- **Katherine Neville,** *The Eight*
- **Rafael Sabatini,** *Captain Blood*

-abort, access, accrue, accumulate, acknowledge, acquire, adjudge, advise, afflict, aggravate, alarm, alert, ally, amass, amaze, ambush, analyze, anchor, anger, arbitrate, arrange, arrest, assault, assemble, assess, auction, audition, authenticate, avenge, -avert, award

bait, ballyhoo, barricade, batter, beam, beat, beckon, bedraggle, beguile, belittle, benchmark, benefit, best, bestow, betray, bias, bid, bilk, blackball, blackjack, blacklist, blind, blindside, blitz, block, bluff, blunt, blurt, bogart, boggle, bolster, bombard, boobytrap, boost, bootleg, borrow, botch, box, -boycott, brace, brandish, breach, bribe, bridge, broadcast, bulldoze, bump, burden, burglarize, burst, bury, bushwhack, bust, butter, -bypass

calculate, calibrate, camouflage, capsize, captain, capture, carry, carve, catalog, catalyze, categorize, caution, certify, chafe, challenge, champion, chart, charter, chase, cheat, chisel, choreograph, churn, circle, circumnavigate, -circumvent, claim, clarify, clasp, classify, clean, climb, cloak, clobber, close, cloud, clout, clutch, coerce, coffer, collect, combat, commandeer, commend, compact, compare, compel, complicate, compute, concatenate, conceal, concede, concoct, condemn, condense, conduct, confide, confiscate, conflate, confound, confront, conk, conquer, conserve, consign, consolidate, construct, consult, consume, contain, contest, convey, convict, convince, convulse, coordinate, cop, corner, corrode, cost, counsel, countermand, counterpunch, cover, covet, cow, cram, cramp, crank, crash, crate, credential, crest, cripple, criticize, cross, crosscheck, cross-examine, crowd, crush, cue, cuff, cull, customize

damage, dangle, dare, dazzle, deactivate, decipher, decode, decrease, decrypt, deep-six, defame, defang, defeat, defend, deflate, defraud, defray, defuse, defy, delay, delegate, deliver, delouse, demand, demilitarize, demolish, demonstrate, denigrate, deplete, deploy, deposit, desire, destabilize, destroy, detach, detain, detect, -deter, detonate, detour, devalue, devise, diagnose, dictate, diddle, dig, direct, disable, disappear, disarm, discharge, discipline, -discount, discourage, discover, discredit, disillusion, dislodge, dismantle, dispatch, dispirit, display, disqualify, -disregard, disrupt, dissuade, distill, distract, distrust, divide, doctor, -dodge, dog, donate, double-cross, double-deal, down, draw, drive, drown, dump

earmark, earn, edify, efface, eighty-six, electrify, elevate, elicit, eliminate, -elude, embalm, embroider, embroil, emphasize, empty, encrypt, endorse, engross, enrich, ensconce, enslave, entomb, entrap, entrust, erode, escalate, -escape, -eschew, escort, estimate, evacuate, -evade, evoke, exact, examine, excavate, excuse, exhort, exhume, expedite, expel, expense, explain, exploit, explore, expose, extort, extract, extricate

face, fake, familiarize, fast-forward, fast-track, fathom, fatigue, faze, feed, feign, fetch, fetishize, fight, finance, fine-tune, fix, flag, flaunt, -flee, fleece, fling, flummox, foist, follow, forage, -forbid, force, forfeit, forgive, fortify, frogmarch, -frustrate, fry, fuel, fumble, furnish

garble, garner, gather, gauge, gild, glamorize, glean, glorify, goad, gobsmack, gouge, grab, grasp, grease, greenlight, grill, gross, guard, guide

half-ass, haul, hawk, hazard, heal, heap, hide, highlight, hijack, hoard, hoax, hog, hoist, hollow, holster, hoodwink, hook, hose, hospitalize, hotwire, hound, hunt, hurl, hurry, hustle, hype

identify, immortalize, impair, impersonate, implicate, import, impound, impress, improvise, incapacitate, incarcerate, indemnify, indulge, inflate, injure, instigate, instruct, insure, intercept, interpret, interrogate, interrupt, intrigue, inventory, invest, investigate, invite, invoice, itemize

jack, jam, jeopardize, jerk, jog, juggle, junk, justify

-kibosh, kick, kick-start, kidnap, kneecap, knife

lasso, launch, launder, lead, leash, lecture, legitimize, level, leverage, libel, license, limelight, link, liquidate, load, loan, lobby, locate, lock, loot, lowball, lubricate, lug, lure

machinate, maim, maltreat, mandate, maneuver, map, mar, maroon, mask, master, mastermind, maximize, mechanize, menace, micromanage, misappropriate, mismanage, misplace, misread, mistake, mobilize, moderate, modify, mold, monkey-wrench, monopolize, mortar, mothball, motivate, mug, mummify, mystify

nab, nail, navigate, negotiate, net, neutralize, niche, nitpick, nominate, numerate, nurse

obey, obfuscate, obscure, obstruct, obtain, offload, open, optimize, orchestrate, order, organize, orient, oust, outbid, outclass, outdistance, outdo, outgun, outlay, outmaneuver, outperform, outplay, outrace, outrank, outshine, outsmart, outstrip, outwit, overcome, overemphasize, overhaul, overload, overpower, override, overrule, oversell, overtake

pace, pack, palaver, pass, patent, patrol, paw, penetrate, perplex, petition, pick, pierce, pile, pilfer, pillage, pilot, pimp, pinion, pinpoint, pirate, placate, plot, pluck, plumb, plunder, poke, police, polish, position, praise, predetermine, preempt, presell, preserve, pressure, -prevent, price, prime, prioritize, probe, process, procure, profile, profit, program, -prohibit, prolong, promote, prop, propel, propose, publicize, pulp, pummel, pump, punch, punctuate, purloin, pursue, push, puzzle

quantify, quash, quell, question, quiz

race, raid, ransack, ransom, ration, ravage, reach, ream, reclaim, reconnoiter, recoup, recover, recruit, recycle, redact, redeem, -refuse, regret, rehabilitate, rejigger, release, remove, renegotiate, rent, reorient, repair, represent, reprimand, repurpose, rescue, research, resist, restore, resuscitate, retain, retool, retrieve, review, revoke, revolutionize, reward, rifle, rig, rile, rob, rope, rotate, rue, rupture, rush

sabotage, sack, safeguard, salvage, sample, sap, save, scald, scale, scam, scan, scavenge, schedule, schmooze, scoop, scope, scorch, -scorn, scour, scout, scrap, scruple, scrutinize, scuttle, search, seize, select, sell, sensationalize, shadow, shanghai, shine, shock, shoot, short-circuit, shove, showcase, shroud, -shun, -sidestep, sideswipe, signal, siphon, skewer, skim, skunk, slug, smash, smuggle, snap, snare, snatch, sneak, snipe, snooker, soft-sell, solicit, solve, sour, source, spark, spearhead, specify, spitball, sponge, sponsor, sport, spot, spotlight, spring, spur, square, squeeze, squirrel, stage-manage, stagger, startle, stash, staunch, steal, steamroller, steel, steer, stiff, stipulate, stockpile, stonewall, store, stow, straighten, stress, strew, strip, strong-arm, stump, stupefy, stymie, suborn, subvert, sucker-punch, sugarcoat, supercharge, supersize, supply, suppress, surf, surprise, surrender, survey, suspend, swamp, swear, sweet-talk, swindle, swipe, synchronize, synthesize

taboo, tabulate, tackle, tail, tally, tangle, tantalize, target, tarnish, taste, taunt, tax, telegraph, test, tether, throw, -thwart, toast, tolerate, top, topple, torch, torpedo, tote, toughen, tour, tout, tow, track, trail, tranquilize, transcend, translate, transmit, transport, trap, trash, trash-talk, travel, traverse, trick, trigger, trivialize, troubleshoot, trump, truncate, turn

uncover, undercut, underpay, undervalue, underwrite, unearth, unfasten, unleash, unload, unlock, unman, unpack, unravel, unscramble, unshackle, untangle, update, upgrade

valuate, vanquish, verify, vet, -veto, vindicate, -void, volunteer, vouchsafe

waive, wangle, want, ward, warehouse, warn, waste, weaken, weaponize, wedge, weigh, weld, wheedle, whet, whitewash, whittle, win, withdraw, worm, wound, wow, wreck, wrest, wrestle, wring, wrinkle

yank

zap, zone

Fantasy

Representative Authors and Titles

- **Peter Beagle,** *The Last Unicorn*
- **S.A. Chakraborty,** *The City of Brass*
- **Robin Hobb,** *Assassin's Apprentice*
- **Barry Hughart,** *The Bridge of Birds*
- **Ursula K. LeGuin,** *A Wizard of Earthsea*
- **Patricia McKillip,** *The Riddle-Master of Hed*
- **Naomi Novik,** *His Majesty's Dragon*

-abandon, abase, abdicate, abduct, abolish, absorb, accept, access, acclimate, accompany, accost, accumulate, accuse, achieve, acquire, adopt, adumbrate, advantage, affirm, afflict, affront, aggrandize, aggrieve, aid, aim, align, allay, allot, allure, amass, anguish, animate, annihilate, annoy, anoint, apotheosize, appease, appoint, appraise, apprise, archive, arm, armor, arrange, arrogate, assail, assassinate, assemble, assert, assimilate, astonish, attain, attire, attract, augment, augur, avenge, await, awe, axe

badger, bait, balance, -balk, bandage, banish, barbarize, barricade, barter, battle, bear, beg, begrudge, behead, bejewel, believe, bemoan, beseech, bet, betray, betroth, bewitch, bid, bind, bite, blackguard, blame, blazon, blend, bless, blockade, borrow, botch, bother, bottle, brainstorm, brave, break, breathe, brew, bring, broach, bronze, bully, bungle, buoy, burgle, bury

cadge, cage, cajole, camouflage, captivate, cart, center, chain, champion, charm, check, checkmate, cheer, cherish, choke, choose, chronicle, circulate, civilize, claim, clash, claw, cleanse, clear, cloak, clothe, club, cocoon, codify, coerce, collect, combat, comfort, command, commit, compile, complete, compose, concretize, confine, confirm, congratulate, conjecture, conjure, conquer, consecrate, consign, contribute, contrive, control, convene, counsel, counter, counteract, covenant, covet, craft, crest, crown, crush, crystallize, cudgel, cull, curse, curtail

dare, daunt, dazzle, decant, deceive, decipher, declare, decode, decrypt, dedicate, deface, defeat, defile, defy, degrade, deify, delay, delegate, delegitimize, delight, demonize, demoralize, depredate, desecrate, desire, desolate, destine, detain, -deter, determine, dethrone, devastate, devise, devote, dictate, diffuse, dilute, diminish, direct, disband, discard, disclose, discourage, discover, disembowel, disenchant, disfavor, disgrace, disguise, disobey, disorient, dispense, disrespect, disrupt, dissatisfy, disseminate, distill, distinguish, divine, dominate, doom, douse, dragoon, drain, draw, drink, drop, drug, dub, -duck, dulcify, dull, dumbfound

earn, echo, educe, elaborate, elucidate, embarrass, embattle, emblazon, embody, empower, enchant, encircle, encode, encompass, encourage, encumber, endure, enforce, engender, enrapture, enroll, enshrine, ensoul, ensure, entertain, enthrall, enthrone, entitle, entrance, entreat, entrust, entwine, equip, eradicate, escort, eulogize, evacuate, -evade, even, evoke, exact, exalt, excavate, exchange, -exclude, excoriate, excruciate, exert, exhilarate, exhort, exile, exorcise, explore, externalize, extol, extort

face, fascinate, fashion, father, fathom, fell, ferry, fight, fire, flout, foil, force, foresee, foretell, forewarn, forfeit, forge, formulate, -forsake, foster, fragment, fête, fulfill, fuse

galvanize, gammon, garnish, gate, gather, gauge, gird, girdle, glamour, glean, goad, govern, grace, grant, grapple, grasp, greet, ground, group, guard, guide, guzzle

-halt, hamstring, handicap, handle, handpick, harangue, harbinger, harbor, harmonize, harness, harshen, harvest, hatch, heal, heat, helm, hex, hoard, hocus-pocus, holster, honor, hornswoggle, host, humiliate

idealize, imbue, immortalize, impart, imperil, implicate, implore, impose, impregnate, impress, imprison, improv, incite, include, inconvenience, incubate, infatuate, infect, infiltrate, inflame, influence, inform, infuse, inherit, initiate, integrate, interrogate, intertwine, intimate, intimidate, intrigue, intuit, invade, invent, investigate, invigorate, invite, invoke, isolate

jab, jail, jar, jilt, join, jolly, judge, jumble, juxtapose

keep, kidnap, kindle, knight, knit

lard, lash, launch, lavish, lead, legitimize, levy, liberate, light, limit, lionize, loose, loosen, loot, lull, lumber

magnify, maintain, malign, manacle, manage, maneuver, maraud, march, marinate, mark, marshal, mask, master, mature, maul, mediate, meld, mellow, mesmerize, mimic, mine, minimize, mirror, misdirect, mislead, misrepresent, misrule, mistreat, mitigate, mock, moisten, mollify, mooch, mother, mourn, muddle, muscle, muster, mystify

-negate, -neglect, nourish, -nullify, nurse, nurture

obey, obligate, obliterate, obscure, occult, occupy, offend, offer, one-up, open, oppose, oppress, order, orient, originate, orphan, -ostracize, outfox, outgrow, outrage, overcharge, overcome, overindulge, overpower, overrule, oversee, overshadow, overthrow, overwhelm, owe, own pamper, pardon, parent, patch, permeate, permit, perplex, personalize, personify, persuade, petition, pierce, pilfer, pillage, plan, pledge, plot, plunder, plunge, pocket, ponder, possess, praise, précis, preach, predict, pretend, prioritize, proclaim, procure, prod, profane, profit, project, prompt, prophesy, propitiate, prostrate, protect, prove, provide, provoke, pummel, puncture, punish, purge, purify, purloin, puzzle

quaff, quash, quell, quench, question

raid, rally, ransack, ransom, ravage, raze, reach, reactivate, ready, realign, reanimate, reap, rear, reassemble, rebuke, recapture, reclaim, recruit, rectify, redeem, reduce, reference, refine, reflect, regale, regard, regenerate, regiment, rein, reinforce, reintegrate, reinvigorate, -reject, rejoin, rejuvenate, release, relish, remedy, remind, rend, renew, repay, replace, replenish, reproach, reprovision, repulse, request, rescue, resent, reserve, resist, respect, restore, restrict, resurrect, retrace, retrain, retrieve, reveal, revenge, reverence, revive, reward, right, risk, ritualize, rob, roleplay, rook, rouse, rout, rule, run

sacrifice, salt, salve, sanctify, sanction, sandbag, satisfy, save, savor, scapegoat, scatter, scavenge, scent, school, scorch, scotch, scourge, scrape, scrimp, scrounge, scrutinize, sculpt, seal, sear, search, secrete, secure, sedate, seek, seize, select, sentinel, serve, set, sever, shackle, shadow, shape, share, sharpen, shatter, sheathe, shed, shelter, shelve, shepherd, shield, shift, shill, -shirk, shortchange, shoulder, show, shrink, shroud, shut, sidetrack, signify, singe, skew, skull, slake, slaughter, slay, slow, smite, smother, snag, snitch, soak, soften, soil, solicit, solidify, solve, spare, spawn, spellbind, spend, spirit, spite, split, spook, spur, -spurn, squire, stable, stalk, starve, steal, stimulate, stipulate, stir, stockpile, stoke, storm, strategize, strong-arm, study, stultify, subdue, subjugate, submerge, subordinate, substantiate, subvert, suckle, suffocate, suffuse, suggest, summon, sunder, supplant, support, suppress, surpass, surprise, surrender, survive, swathe, sway, swipe

taboo, tame, tantalize, target, taunt, teach, temper, tempt, tend, tender, test, thank, threaten, thrust, -thwart, tickle, tidy, tilt, tire, titillate, tone, tool, topple, torment, trace, track, trade, train, trammel, transcend, transform, transmute, transplant, trash-talk, traverse, treasure, treat, treble, trespass, trigger, troll, trumpet, truss, tuck, tune, tutor, typecast, tyrannize

unbind, unbuckle, unburden, unchain, undermine, undo, unearth, unfasten, unfold, unify, unite, unleash, unlock, unmask, unseal, unseat, unshackle, unspool, untangle, untidy, untie, upset, upstage, urge, usher, usurp

vamp, vanquish, venerate, venture, verbalize, -veto, vex, villainize, violate, vocalize, vow

wag, wager, wangle, warm, warn, warp, warrant, waylay, weave, weigh, welcome, whip, whisk, wield, win, wind, wish, witch, wither, withhold, wonder, woo, worm, worship, wreak, wrest, wring, wrinkle

Historical

Representative Authors and Titles

- **Dorothy Dunne,** *Niccolò Rising*
- **Umberto Eco,** *The Name of the Rose*
- **Robert Graves,** *I Claudius,*
- **Toni Morrison,** *Beloved*
- **Patrick Suskind,** *Perfume*
- **Gore Vidal,** *Creation*
- **Sarah Waters,** *Fingersmith*

-abandon, abdicate, abduct, abet, abjure, abolish, abrogate, absolve, abuse, accentuate, acclaim, accommodate, accuse, ace, acquaint, actualize, address, adjust, administer, admonish, adopt, adorn, adulate, afford, aid, alienate, alleviate, allocate, allow, alter, amaze, amend, amuse, anchor, annex, annul, antagonize, appease, appraise, appropriate, arouse, arrange, arrogate, assail, assassinate, assign, assist, attend, attest, attract, avenge, axe

baby, backhand, bait, bandy, banish, bankroll, bankrupt, bathe, battle, beat, beatify, beautify, bed, bedeck, beggar, beguile, behead, bellow, bend, bequeath, beseech, besmirch, bestow, betray, betroth, better, bid, bind, blackguard, blackmail, blandish, block, blockade, bolster, bootleg, borrow, bowdlerize, brave, bridge, broaden, broker, browbeat, brush, budget, buffalo, build, bulletin, bungle, burden, burke, burnish, bury, butcher, buttonhole, buttress, buy

cadge, call, canonize, capture, castigate, caution, celebrate, cement, censure, chafe, chair, challenge, champion, chance, chaperone, charm, chart, chase, chasten, chastise, chauffeur, cheat, cherish, chide, civilize, claim, cleanse, cloak, cloister, coarsen, coax, coddle, coerce, coin, collect, colonize, combat, command, commandeer, commission, commodify, compel, compensate, complicate, compose, compromise, conceal, concentrate, condemn, confer, configure, confine, confiscate, confront, congest, conserve, console, consolidate, constrain, construct, construe, consummate, contact, contemn, content, contest, contract, convert, correct, corrode, corrupt, cosset, costume, counsel, countenance, court, cozen, crab, credit, crib, critique, cross, crown, crush, cuddle, cudgel, cure, curse dam, damage, dampen, dandify, deacon, debase, debauch, deceive, decipher, decorate, decry, deep-six, defeat, defend, defer, defile, deflower, defray, defy, delegitimize, deliver, demand, demean, denunciate, -deny, depict, depopulate, deport, depose, deprave, desecrate, destroy, dethrone, devise, devour, dignify, disadvantage, disaffect, disallow, discern, discipline, disclaim, discomfit, discomfort, discountenance, discover, disenfranchise, disgrace, disguise, dish, dishevel, dishonor, dislodge, disobey, -disown, disparage, dispatch, dispel, displease, dispute, dissipate, distort, divert, divide, divine, divorce, document, dog, dole, domesticate, domineer, donate, dower, draft, drizzle, duel, dupe

earmark, earn, eclipse, educate, emancipate, embellish, embezzle, embroider, emulate, endanger, endow, endure, enervate, enforce, enhance, enlarge, ennoble, enrage, enrich, enshrine, enslave, ensnare, entertain, enthrall, enthrone, entice, entitle, envelop, eradicate, erect, escort, establish, esteem, estrange, etherize, euchre, -evade, evaluate, evangelize, evict, exacerbate, exalt, exasperate, exceed, excite, -exclude, excuse, execute, exhaust, exile, exonerate, expel, expiate, exploit, explore, expose, expound, extinguish, extirpate, extort, exude

fabricate, falsify, famish, fashion, fault, favor, feature, feign, fence, festoon, fetter, fight, filch, filter, finance, finesse, flannel, flatter, flaunt, flavor, flimflam, flounce, flout, foil, foist, follow, foment, fool, -forbid, forecast, forfeit, forge, fortify, foster, found, frame, fuel, fulminate, furnish, further

gamble, garner, garrison, gate-crash, gauge, gentrify, gird, gladden, glad-hand, glamorize, glean, glitz, govern, grant, grasp, grieve, groom, gross, guard, guillotine, gussy

habituate, hamper, hang, harbor, harm, harness, hazard, heal, heave, help, hide, hijack, hitch, hoard, honor, hoodwink, host, humble, humbug, husband, hustle

ignite, imitate, impart, impersonate, impoverish, impress, imprison, impugn, inaugurate, incommode, increase, incriminate, indenture, index, indispose, indulge, infect, inflict, inherit, inspect, inspire, install, institute, instruct, insulate, insult, intern, interrupt, intimidate, intoxicate, introduce, invade, invalidate, inveigle, investigate

jade, jeopardize, jilt, judge

keelhaul, kidnap, knight

label, lambaste, lavish, learn, leech, legalize, legislate, legitimate, lend, lessen, level, leverage, levy, libel, liberate, limn, lionize, litigate, loan, lobby, locate, loose, lynch

machine, malnourish, manage, manhandle, manicure, manipulate, manufacture, manumit, map, maraud, marginalize, maroon, marry, martyr, mask, master, measure, melt, memorialize, menace, mentor, midwife, misdiagnose, mishandle, misjudge, mismanage, misrule, moderate, modernize, modulate, monetize, monopolize, moralize, mortify, motorize, muckrake name, navigate, needle, -negate, negotiate, nettle, nobble, nominate, notarize, notch, notify, nourish, number, nurse, nurture

obey, obfuscate, offset, oil, operate, oppose, orchestrate, ordain, ornament, orphan, -ostracize, oust, outbid, outlast, outlaw, overextend, overpay, oversee, overspend, overtake, overthrow, overwhelm

pacify, paint, pall, palliate, pamper, panhandle, parade, pardon, parry, patent, patrol, pause, pave, peddle, penalize, penetrate, persecute, persuade, pervert, petition, pilfer, pillage, pillory, pimp, pioneer, pirate, place, plague, plan, plant, plaster, plead, pledge, plot, plow, plunder, poison, polish, pomade, pooh-pooh, portray, postpone, praise, preach, predict, prejudice, prepossess, present, preserve, pressure, pretend, primp, prize, procure, profit, -prohibit, promise, propel, propose, prosecute, prostitute, protect, protest, provoke, prune, punish, purge, purloin, puzzle

quaff, quarantine, quash, quell, quench, quiet, -quit

raid, railroad, rally, rank, rankle, rate, ratify, ravage, ravish, raze, rebuke, recommend, recompense, reconcile, record, recoup, recover, rectify, redeem, refine, reform, refurbish, refute, regain, regulate, reimburse, -reject, relaunch relegate, relinquish, relocate, -renounce, renovate, repair, repay, repel, repent, reprimand, reproach, reproduce, -rescind, rescue, research, reshape, resist, restimulate, restore, restrain, restrict, restructure, retard, retort, retract, retrench, reunite, revenge, revere, reverse, revile, revitalize, revoke, revolutionize, reward, ridicule, risk, roast, roleplay, romance, romanticize, rope, roust, rout, rue, ruffle, ruin, rule, rumple, rush

sack, safeguard, salute, sanitize, satirize, scalp, scandalize, scapegoat, scar, scathe, scavenge, scold, -scorn, scour, scourge, scout, scrounge, scupper, scuttle, seal, second, secure, seduce, seek, segregate, seize, sentence, sentimentalize, separate, serve, service, shackle, shame, shave, shine, shortchange, simplify, situate, skimp, slam, slander, slap, slate, slaughter, slay, -slight, smash, smear, smite, smooth, snatch, snow, -snub, solve, sophisticate, source, spoil, sponge, sponsor, -spurn, squander, stabilize, stain, stale, stalk, steal, steam, steward, stigmatize, stipulate, stitch, stock, stoke, storm, straiten, strike, strong-arm, structure, study, subdue, subjugate, submit, sucker, suckle, sully, sunder, supplant, surrender, surround, sustain, sweeten

tailor, taint, tarnish, task, tatter, tax, tempt, tender, test, testify, -thwart, topple, torture, touch, trade, train, translate, treasure, trick, trim, trounce, trumpet, twist, tyrannize

uncover, undercut, underestimate, underpin, unfetter, unhorse, unlock, unseal, untangle, unveil, upbraid, upgrade, uplift, uproot, usurp

validate, value, vanquish, varnish, veil, venerate, vex, vilify, vindicate, violate, vitiate, vomit, vouchsafe, vow, vulgarize

wager, wallop, ward, waste, waylay, weaponize, weather, wed, welcome, whore, winnow, withdraw, withhold, woo, worship, wound, wreak, wrestle, wrong

yield, yoke

Horror

Representative Authors and Titles

- **Clive Barker**, *The Hellbound Heart*
- **Poppy Z. Brite**, *Drawing Blood*
- **William Hjortsberg**, *Falling Angel*
- **Steven King**, *Misery*
- **Ira Levin**, *Rosemary's Baby*
- **Shirley Jackson**, *The Haunting of Hill House*
- **Bram Stoker**, *Dracula*

-abandon, abase, abridge, abuse, accrue, adulterate, advance, agitate, agonize, aid, allege, alleviate, amalgamate, amplify, amputate, anesthetize, anguish, annihilate, anticipate, ape, appall, approach, archive, arouse, articulate, ascertain, asphyxiate, assault, assemble, assimilate, assist, assure, astound, atomize, attaint, attenuate, -avert, await, awaken, awe

bag, ban, banish, baptize, bar, bathe, bear, bedevil, befoul, beget, beguile, behead, belch, beleaguer, bemoan, bereave, besmear, bestialize, betray, better, bind, bite, blast, bleed, blemish, blight, bludgeon, blunt, blur, botch, bother, brainwash, brandish, brave, break, brew, bring, broach, bruise, brutalize, bug, bully, burden, burn, burst, bury, butcher, buttress

cage, camouflage, canker, cannibalize, capture, caress, carve, castrate, catalyze, catch, cauterize, caution, chagrin, chaperone, charm, chill, chip, chronicle, clamp, clarify, claw, cleanse, cleave, climb, cloak, clone, clothe, cloud, club, coagulate, coat, codify, coerce, commingle, compel, compress, conceive, concern, concuss, condemn, condone, confound, confuse, conjecture, conjure, conquer, consecrate, consternate, constrict, consult, consume, contain, contaminate, contort, contrive, control, convince, corner, corroborate, corrode, corrupt, couch, cover, covet, cozen, crack, create, cripple, crisp, cross, crossbreed, crucify, crumple, crush, cultivate, culture, cure, curse

damage, damn, dangle, darken, dash, daunt, deadbolt, deaden, debase, debauch, debilitate, decant, decay, deceive, decimate, deconstruct, decontaminate, deduce, deepen, deface, defeat, defend, defile, deform, degrade, dehumanize, deify, delouse, delude, dement, demolish, demonstrate, demystify, denounce, -deny, depersonalize, deplete, deprave, depredate, depress, deprive, deprogram, desecrate, -desert, design, desolate, destabilize, destroy, detain, detect, -deter, deteriorate, devastate, develop, devise, devour, dig, digest, dirty, disable, disappoint, disarticulate, disbelieve, discard, discompose, disconcert, disconnect, -discount, discourage, disembowel, disentangle, disfigure, disgorge, disgrace, disgust, disintegrate, disjoint, dismantle, dismember, dismiss, disorient, display, disprove, disqualify, -disregard, dissect, disseminate, dissolve, dissuade, distress, disturb, doctor, dominate, doom, dose, double-talk, downplay, drag, draggle, drain, dread, drink, drown, drug, dumbfound

ease, eclipse, educe, efface, elevate, eliminate, emasculate, embalm, embrace, empty, encase, enclose, encompass, encourage, encrypt, endure, enfeeble, enfold, engross, engulf, enlighten, enmesh, ensconce, enslave, ensnare, ensoul, entangle, entice, entomb, entrap, envelop, erode, -escape, evince, eviscerate, evoke, examine, excavate, excise, excoriate, excruciate, execrate, execute, exert, exhibit, exhume, exorcise, expect, expiate, exploit, explore, express, expunge, exterminate, externalize, extinguish, eye

facilitate, falsify, farm, father, fertilize, fetishize, film, finish, fissure, fixate, flay, flood, fluster, fondle, force, forward, fossilize, foster, foul, fracture, fragment, freeze, frighten, fumigate, fuse

gag, gain, garland, gash, gaslight, generate, gestate, glamour, glorify, gnaw, goad, gobble, gore, gouge, graft, grant, grapple, grasp, gravel, grind, grip, groom, grope, gut

hallow, hamper, hamstring, handicap, harass, harbinger, harm, harness, harpoon, harvest, hasten, haunt, heal, hector, help, hew, hobble, hollow, hone, honey, horrify, hospitalize, host, hound, humiliate, humor, hunt, hurt, hush, hypnotize

idealize, -ignore, illuminate, imagine, immerse, immobilize, immolate, impair, impale, impersonate, implant, implore, impose, impregnate, imprison, inactivate, incapacitate, incense, incinerate, incorporate, incubate, incur, indict, indoctrinate, infantilize, infect, infest, infiltrate, inflict, ingest, ingratiate, inhale, inject, injure, innovate, insert, institutionalize, integrate, intensify, interbreed, internalize, interrogate, intimate, intimidate, inundate, inure, invade, invalidate, invent, investigate, involve, irk, irritate, isolate

jam, jar, jeopardize, jilt, jinx, jolt, juice

kill, knife, knit, knot

lace, lacerate, lame, lament, lance, leach, lead, leech, lick, limit, liquefy, lobotomize, lock, lure

maim, maledict, manacle, mangle, mar, mash, mask, massacre, maul, mechanize, medicate, melt, menace, mend, metabolize, midwife, mine, mirror, misinform, misrepresent, mistreat, mitigate, mock, modify, moisten, mold, molest, mollify, monitor, mortify, mother, mount, mourn, multiply, mummify, murder, mutate, mutilate

nauseate, -negate, -neglect, nonplus, normalize, numb

obey, obliterate, obscure, obsess, obstruct, occlude, open, oppose, oppress, originate, orphan, outrage, outthink, -overlook, overpower, overturn, overwhelm

palsy, panic, paralyze, pass, paw, peel, peg, pen, penetrate, perfect, perforate, permeate, pervert, petrify, pierce, pin, pinch, pinion, pity, plague, plot, plug, plumb, poison, poke, pollute, possess, pound, power, preoccupy, prepare, presell, preserve, press, probe, process, prod, profane, -prohibit, proliferate, prolong, prophesy, propitiate, proselytize, prostrate, prove, prowl, pull, pulp, pulverize, puncture, punish, purify, pursue, quell

quicken

ram, rape, rarefy, ration, rationalize, rattle, ravage, razor, reactivate, read, ready, reanimate, reap, rear, -rebuff, rebuild, rebut, recreate, rectify, recycle, reference, -refuse, refute, regenerate, regret, reinvestigate, -reject, rejuvenate, relax, relish, remedy, remove, rend, repair, repel, replace, replicate, represent, repress, -repudiate, repulse, rescue, resolve, resurrect, resuscitate, retrace, reveal, revolt, rile, rinse, rip, risk, ritualize, rivet, ruffle, ruin, rule, rupture

sacrifice, sadden, sanctify, sanction, sandbag, sanitize, sap, satisfy, saturate, savage, scald, scalp, scar, scare, scatter, scent, scour, scratch, screen, screw, script, scrub, sculpt, seal, sear, seclude, secrete, sedate, seduce, seize, sensationalize, sermonize, sever, shackle, shadow, shake, shame, sharpen, shatter, shed, shelter, shield, shock, shred, shrivel, shroud, -shun, shunt, sicken, sift, signify, simulate, singe, skin, slash, slaughter, slay, slice, slit, smash, smell, smother, snare, soil, soothe, sorrow, sound, span, spare, spawn, spice, spike, splatter, splinter, split, spoof, spook, squander, squash, squelch, stab, stagger, stagnate, stain, stake, stale, stalk, stamp, starve, stash, steel, steep, sterilize, stiffen, stigmatize, stimulate, sting, stint, stomach, store, stow, straightjacket, strangle, study, stun, stunt, subdue, subjugate, submerge, subtract, subvert, suck, suffer, suffocate, suffuse, sully, summon, suppress, surface, surrender, survive, suss, suture, swallow, swamp, synthesize

taboo, taint, tangle, tantalize, taste, teach, tend, terrify, terrorize, thrash, threaten, throttle, throw, thump, tie, tighten, torch, torment, torpefy, torture, trample, transfix, trap, traumatize, trouble, twist, tyrannize

ulcerate, unbalance, unbury, undercut, underwrite, unearth, unfold, unhinge, unmask, unnerve, unravel, unseal, unsex, untangle, untidy, untie, unveil, uplift, upset, utilize

vaccinate, vamp, vandalize, vanquish, vaporize, veil, venture, verify, vet, victimize, violate, vitiate, vivisect, -void, vomit wake, ward, warn, warp, wash, weaken, wean, weave, weed, weight, welcome, wet, whammy, wither, withstand, witness, wizen, worry, worship, wound, wrack, wrangle, wrap, wreak, wreck, wrench, wrinkle, wrong

zone

Humor

Representative Authors and Titles

- **Douglas Adams,** *The Hitchhiker's Guide to the Galaxy*
- **Carl Hiaasen,** *Native Tongue*
- **Kevin Kwan,** *Crazy Rich Asians*
- **Anita Loos,** *Gentlemen Prefer Blonds*
- **Christopher Moore,** *Island of the Sequined Love Nun*
- **Terry Pratchett,** *The Color of Magic*
- **P.G. Wodehouse,** *The Code of the Woosters*

abase, abash, abdicate, accelerate, accent, accommodate, accost, accrue, achieve, adapt, add, addle, address, adopt, adulate, advance, advertise, advise, affront, aggravate, alarm, alibi, allay, allege, allow, ambush, amplify, amuse, anger, animate, antagonize, ape, appall, appease, applaud, apply, appraise, arouse, assuage, assume, astonish, attach, attain, audition, automate, axe

baby, badger, badmouth, baffle, bait, bake, ballyhoo, bamboozle, bankroll, bankrupt, barbecue, barter, bastardize, bat, bed, befriend, befuddle, beggar, believe, belittle, bemuse, benefit, bestow, bet, betray, bewilder, bilk, blackmail, blame, blandish, blast, blindside, blister, block, bluff, boast, bogart, boggle, boink, bombard, book, bore, borrow, botch, brainstorm, breach, brew, broker, browbeat, brownnose, bruise, budget, buffalo, buffer, bug, bully, bungle, buzz

cadge, cajole, call, -cancel, candy-coat, caricature, castigate, catch, censor, censure, chafe, chaff, chagrin, challenge, chance, channel, chasten, cheapen, cheat, check, cherish, chide, choreograph, churn, circulate, claim, clear, clinch, clock, clog, cloud, clutch, clutter, coach, coax, collect, combine, commercialize, comp, compact, compartmentalize, compensate, complicate, compliment, con, conceal, concoct, condemn, condense, confess, confide, conflate, confound, confuse, conquer, consign, console, constipate, consume, contradict, contrast, contribute, contrive, convulse, coopt, copy, correct, corrupt, cost, costume, couple, court, cow, cram, cramp, crash, crave, critique, cross-examine, crumble, crumple, crush, cue, curb, cushion

dampen, debase, debate, deceive, declare, decorate, defame, defeat, defer, deflate, deflect, defraud, defy, degrade, deliver, delude, demand, demean, demonize, demote, denigrate, dent, -deny, derail, deride, -desert, -despise, despoil, devise, dichotomize, dictate, diddle, discombobulate, discomfort, discredit, -disdain, disenchant, disgrace, disguise, dishevel, dismay, disobey, disparage, dispirit, displease, disqualify, -disregard, disrespect, diss, dissatisfy, dissipate, distort, distress, disturb, -ditch, divine, divorce, divulge, dizzy, -dodge, douse, downplay, dramatize, draw, drench, dress, drill, drizzle, dull, dump, dupe, duplicate

earn, edit, eject, elaborate, elbow, elevate, emasculate, embarrass, embellish, embrace, embroider, emphasize, encourage, endear, energize, engulf, enjoy, enlarge, ensnare, entertain, enthrall, entice, entrap, espouse, -evade, exacerbate, exaggerate, exasperate, exceed, exchange, exhaust, exhilarate, expand, expense, exploit, expose, extend, extol, eyeball

fabricate, falsify, familiarize, fancify, fancy, fascinate, feature, feign, fetch, fiddle, finagle, fine-tune, fire, fix, flabbergast, flag, flaunt, fleece, flimflam, fling, flip, flog, flout, flub, flummox, fluster, fondle, fool, forestall, forfeit, -forsake, frazzle, -frustrate, fry, fudge, fumble, funnel, further

gain, galvanize, game, generalize, glitz, glue, goad, gobble, gobsmack, grab, grace, grade, grant, gratify, grease, ground, gull, guzzle

half-ass, -halt, hammer, hamper, harangue, hard-sell, harry, hassle, hatch, hawk, heckle, hector, heighten, henpeck, hide, hinder, hoax, hock, hog, honor, hoodwink, hornswoggle, housetrain, humble, humiliate, hurt, hustle, hype

idolize, ignite, imbue, imitate, impede, impel, impersonate, implicate, impoverish, impress, improve, improvise, impugn, inconvenience, indulge, infantilize, infatuate, inflame, inflate, influence, inform, infringe, infuriate, infuse, inherit, inhibit, inject, injure, instigate, insult, intercept, interrupt, intoxicate, introduce, inveigle, invent, invert, irritate

jab, jeer, jerk, jettison, jilt, jimmy, jolly, jostle, juggle, juice, jumble, junk, justify, juxtapose

-kibosh, kick, kick-start, kid, kindle, knead, knock

label, lambaste, lampoon, lance, land, lard, leech, lend, lengthen, lessen, level, libel, lionize, litigate, loan, loosen, lose, louse, lowball, lube, lubricate

madden, magnify, malign, manipulate, marinate, market, mask, massage, master, maximize, mellow, milk, mimic, mince, minimize, misappropriate, miscalculate, miscommunicate, mishear, misinterpret, mislabel, mislay, mislead, mismatch, misplace, misread, mistake, mistreat, mix, mock, moderate, molest, mollycoddle, monetize, monkey-wrench, monopolize, mooch, mortify, motivate, muckrake, muddle, muffle

nag, neaten, needle, neg, net, neuter, nibble, niggle, nitpick, nudge, -nullify obscure, observe, offend, offload, oil, one-up, orbit, orientate, outdistance, outgrow, outplay, outrage, outsell, outsmart, outwit, overcharge, overdramatize, overemphasize, overindulge, overload, -overlook, overprotect, oversell, oversimplify, overspend, overstuff, overwork

package, palaver, panic, parade, parody, parrot, parry, paste, patronize, pawn, peddle, perfect, permit, perplex, persecute, persuade, peruse, pester, pickle, pigeonhole, pimp, plan, pleasure, pledge, plonk, plot, plow, poach, pocket, poll, pollute, popularize, pork, position, postpone, praise, prejudge, prepare, pretend, -prevent, price, prick, primp, prize, proclaim, prod, profane, profess, -prohibit, promise, promote, prompt, proposition, provoke, publicize, punctuate, punish, purchase, purge, pursue

quantify, quell, quench

rate, ravish, razzle-dazzle, reap, reassure, -rebuff, rebuke, recreate, redirect, referee, refine, refund, regulate, reimburse, rein, reinvigorate, -reject, rejigger, remodel, rent, repel, rephrase, repossess, repress, reprimand, reproach, repulse, repurpose, restrain, retort, retrench, reverence, reverse, revile, reward, ridicule, roast, rock, roleplay, romance, rook, roughen, rouse, ruffle, ruin, rumple

sabotage, sample, sap, sardine, satirize, sauté, savage, scam, scandalize, scathe, schedule, schlep, schmooze, schnorr, school, scold, score, -scorn, scotch, scourge, scrape, screw, scruple, season, second, sell, sentimentalize, separate, service, shake, shame, shanghai, shape, share, shift, shill, -shirk, shock, shortchange, shove, showcase, shred, shrink, shuffle, sicken, sideline, -sidestep, sidetrack, sink, siphon, skew, skewer, skimp, skin, skirt, skunk, slake, slam, slander, slant, slate, slather, -slight, sling, slot, slur, slurp, smack, smother, smudge, snag, snap, snooker, snow, -snub, soap, sober, soften, soft-soap, solicit, sophisticate, sort, spackle, spank, spark, spend, spiff, spin, splatter, splice, spoil, spoon-feed, spring, spur, -spurn, squander, squeeze, stall, startle, steam, steamroll, stereotype, stiff, stifle, stimulate, sting, stipulate, stir, stoke, straddle, stretch, stroke, stump, stupefy, submit, sucker, sue, sugar, sugarcoat, support, surfeit, surpass, surprise, swallow, swat, swear, sweet-talk, swill, swindle, switch, syrup

tailor, tally, taunt, tease, tempt, thimblerig, thrill, throw, thrust, thwack, tickle, tilt, titillate, tolerate, toss, tout, trade, trample, trash, trick, trigger, trivialize, troll, trump, trust, tug, turn, tutor, tweak, twist, two-time, typecast

unbalance, unbutton, unchain, uncomplicate, underestimate, undermine, underpay, underrate, undervalue, underwhelm, undress, unleash, unload, unnerve, unseat, unsettle, unskew, untie, unzip, upbraid, upchuck, upset, upstage, urge, use

varnish, venture, verbalize, verify, vex, vow, vulgarize

wag, wager, wangle, warrant, waste, waylay, wean, weasel, wed, wedge, wet, wheedle, whitewash, win, wind, winnow, wish, wither, withhold, wolf, worry, worship, wound, wow, wreck, wrong

yank

zing

Military

Representative Authors and Titles

- **Bernard Cornwell,** *The Archer's Tale*
- **Joe Haldeman,** *The Forever War*
- **Jack Higgins,** *The Eagle Has Landed*
- **Alistair MacLean,** *The Guns of Navarone*
- **Patrick O'Brian,** *Master and Commander*
- **Michael Shaara,** *The Killer Angels*
- **Herman Wouk,** *The Caine Mutiny*

-abandon, abduct, -abort, abuse, accelerate, accent, acclaim, accompany, accomplish, accost, ace, acknowledge, acquire, actualize, adorn, affect, affirm, aggrandize, aim, alert, align, allocate, ally, amplify, analyze, anesthetize, annihilate, annoy, apply, apportion, approach, appropriate, approve, arm, armor, arrange, arrogate, assault, assemble, assign, assimilate, assuage, atomize, attack, audit, augment, automate, avenge, -avert, avow, award

bait, -balk, bandage, batter, battle, bear, beat, begrudge, bellow, belt, benchmark, bend, berate, besiege, best, bewilder, bind, blackjack, blazon, blemish, bless, blight, blitz, blitzkrieg, blockade, bludgeon, bolster, boobytrap, boost, boot, bother, bounce, box, brace, brand, brandish, brave, breach, break, bridle, brigade, bronze, browbeat, buff, buffer, build, bulldoze, bump, buoy, bushwhack, buttress, -bypass

calibrate, call, cant, capsize, captain, capture, case-harden, cede, certify, chafe, chair, champion, chaperone, chart, charter, chasten, check, checkmate, cheer, choke, chunk, circle, -circumvent, civilize, clarify, classify, clobber, clog, clout, coach, coarsen, colonize, combat, comfort, command, commandeer, commemorate, commend, commission, commit, compare, compromise, concede, condition, conduct, confiscate, confront, congest, congratulate, conquer, conscript, conserve, constrain, constrict, construct, contain, control, convert, convict, cordon, corral, correct, counterfeit, countermand, counterpunch, court, cover, crate, crease, credit, cripple, criticize, crop, crosscheck, crush, curb, cure

damage, dare, deactivate, deaden, debilitate, debrief, debug, deck, declass, decorate, decoy, decrease, decree, deface, defeat, defend, deflect, defraud, defund, defuse, defy, dehumanize, deliver, delude, demilitarize, demolish, demonstrate, demoralize, demote, denigrate, denounce, deploy, depopulate, depose, deputize, derange, -desert, designate, destabilize, detonate, devastate, dictate, dignify, direct, disable, disappear, disarm, disband, discard, discharge, discipline, discover, discredit, disencumber, disengage, disfigure, disgrace, disguise, dishearten, dishonor, disillusion, dismantle, dismiss, disparage, dispatch, dispense, disperse, disrespect, disrupt, distinguish, distort, distribute, disturb, divert, -dodge, dog, dole, domesticate, dominate, double-deal, down, downgrade, downsize, draft, dragoon, drill, dull, dupe

ease, echo, educate, eighty-six, eliminate, emancipate, embattle, employ, emulate, encircle, encompass, endorse, endure, engineer, enhance, enlarge, enlist, ennoble, enrage, enroll, ensure, entreat, entrench, entrust, equal, equalize, equip, eradicate, escalate, escort, establish, esteem, estimate, eulogize, -evade, evaluate, even, -exclude, excoriate, execute, exercise, exhibit, exhort, exonerate, expect, expel, expend, explode, explore, exterminate, extinguish, extort, extract, extricate

face, fast-forward, fast-track, fatigue, fell, fence, ferry, festoon, fight, finish, flabbergast, flank, flannel, flatten, flog, flub, flunk, focus, follow, foment, forage, forewarn, forge, forgive, -forsake, fortify, foster, found, frame, free, frogmarch, fête, fulminate, furnish, further, fusillade

gain, gamble, garland, garnish, garrison, gather, gauge, generate, gouge, govern, grieve, groom, ground, group, guarantee, guard, guide, gull, gut

hail, -halt, halve, handicap, harangue, harbor, harden, harm, harshen, head, heave, hedge, helm, hijack, hog, hoist, hold, honor, hose, hotwire, hump, hurl

illustrate, immobilize, impose, improve, inactivate, inaugurate, incapacitate, incarcerate, incorporate, incriminate, incur, indoctrinate, influence, injure, inspect, install, institute, instruct, intersect, intimidate, intoxicate, inure, invade, invalid, inventory, investigate, invigorate, invoice, issue

jail, jam, jeopardize, jerry-build, jerry-rig, jettison, jilt, jog, jump, junk

keep, kidnap, kneecap, knight

lacerate, lament, lather, launch, lead, leak, learn, leash, legitimate, level, levy, liberate, license, lobby, lodge, lose, lug, lumber, lynch

machinate, malnourish, manage, mandate, map, march, marginalize, mark, maroon, marshal, mash, massage, master, mature, mechanize, mediate, medicate, melt, memorialize, mend, meter, micromanage, minute, miscalculate, misgauge, mismanage, misrepresent, mitigate, mobilize, modernize, moralize, mortar, mothball, motivate, motorize, mount, mourn, muster, mute

nail, -negate, negotiate, neutralize, nominate, notch, numb, numerate

obliterate, obtain, occupy, offset, operate, oppose, oppress, optimize, orchestrate, order, organize, orient, orientate, orphan, -ostracize, oust, outclass, outguess, outgun, outmaneuver, outperform, outrank, outreach, outshine, outthink, overcommit, overextend, overhaul, overpay, override, oversee, overset, overshadow, overthrow

pace, pacify, paralyze, pardon, partition, patch, patrol, penalize, perforate, perplex, pigeonhole, pile, pilfer, pillage, pilot, pioneer, placate, place, plan, plot, plumb, point, police, post, pound, precipitate, preempt, prepare, prescribe, preserve, -prevent, prime, primp, promote, propose, prostitute, prostrate, protect, provision, provoke, pulverize, pummel, pump, punch, punish, purchase, purge, pursue, push

quarantine, quell, quench, query, quicken, -quit

raid, rally, rampart, rank, ransack, ransom, rate, ratify, ration, rationalize, ravage, ready, ream, recapture, reclaim, recognize, recommend, recon, reconcile, reconnoiter, record, recover, recruit, redact, redeem, reform, regale, regard, regiment, regulate, rehabilitate, reinforce, rejoin, relax, release, relegate, relieve, remedy, remove, renegotiate, -renounce, renovate, repair, replenish, repress, reprieve, requisition, -rescind, rescue, resent, resign, respect, restock, restore, restructure, retard, retool, retrieve, reunite, revere, revise, revive, revolutionize, reward, rig, risk, rival, roil, rotate, rubber-stamp, run, rupture

sabotage, sack, sacrifice, safeguard, salute, salvage, salve, sandbag, save, scale, scan, scandalize, scant, scar, scavenge, schedule, school, scope, scotch, scout, screen, scrimp, scrounge, scupper, scuttle, season, secure, sentinel, settle, shave, sheathe, shelter, shelve, shepherd, shine, -shirk, shock, shoot, short, shoulder, show, -shun, shuttle, sideline, sidetrack, signal, situate, skipper, skull, slam, slash, slaughter, slot, smash, smooth, snaffle, snarl, snipe, soak, sober, solidify, source, spare, specify, spin, spotlight, spy, squash, stabilize, stage, stagger, stand, standardize, station, steady, steamroller, steel, steer, steward, stigmatize, stitch, stockpile, store, storm, strafe, strategize, streamline, strengthen, stress, strike, stultify, subdue, subjugate, submit, subordinate, suborn, suffer, supercharge, supervise, supply, support, suppress, surrender, surround, sustain, swat, synchronize

tabulate, tackle, taint, tally, tap, target, tarnish, task, taunt, teach, tear, telegraph, temper, tend, terrify, terrorize, thaw, thrash, thrust, thump, -thwart, time, tire, toast, top, topple, torpedo, toughen, tow, trace, train, transfix, transmit, transport, trash-talk, traumatize, treat, trim, troubleshoot, trounce, trump, trumpet, tug, turf, tutor, tweak, twist, tyrannize

unburden, undershoot, unearth, unhorse, uniform, unman, unmask, unnerve, upbraid, update, upgrade, uphold, usurp, utilize

validate, value, venerate, vet, -veto, victual, vilify, volunteer

wage, waive, warehouse, warn, warp, waste, weaken, weaponize, weather, welt, whip, whup, wield, wire, withdraw, withstand, wound, wrack, wreak, wreck

yank, yield

zone

Mystery & Suspense

Representative Authors and Titles

- **James Anderson**, *The Affair of the Bloodstained Egg Cosy*
- **Agatha Christie**, *And Then There Were None*
- **Elmore Leonard**, *Get Shorty*
- **Peter Lovesey**, *The False Inspector Dew*
- **Walter Mosley**, *Devil in a Blue Dress*
- **Arturo Perez-Reverte**, *The Club Dumas*
- **Barbara Vine (aka Ruth Rendell)**, *The Brimstone Wedding*

abduct, absolve, access, accuse, acquaint, acquit, addle, adjudge, adjudicate, admit, afflict, affront, aggravate, agitate, agonize, alert, alibi, allay, allege, amend, analyze, antagonize, anticipate, appease, applaud, appraise, apprehend, arbitrate, archive, arraign, arrest, articulate, ascertain, asphyxiate, assemble, assert, assess, assist, attack, attaint, attest, authenticate, avenge

badger, baffle, bag, bamboozle, bar, barricade, barter, bastardize, batter, befuddle, behead, belittle, bend, bequeath, beseech, betray, bias, bilk, blab, blackball, blacklist, blackmail, blame, blast, bleed, blind, blindfold, blindside, block, bludgeon, bluff, blunt, blur, blurt, bogart, boggle, bootleg, botch, -boycott, brainstorm, brew, bribe, brief, broadcast, broker, brutalize, bug, bulldoze, bully, bungle, burden, burglarize, burgle, burke, bury, bust, buttonhole, buy

calculate, camouflage, canonize, case, castrate, catalog, catalyze, catch, categorize, center, challenge, charge, chase, chastise, cheat, check, checkmate, chill, chronicle, churn, cinch, cipher, circle, circulate, -circumvent, claim, clarify, cloak, clock, clue, clutter, codify, coerce, coin, collar, collate, comb, commodify, compel, compile, complicate, compress, compromise, compute, con, conceal, concentrate, conclude, concoct, concuss, condemn, condense, confess, confide, confine, confirm, confound, confuse, confute, conjecture, conk, connect, consider, construe, consult, contemplate, contend, contest, contextualize, contradict, contrive, convict, convince, cook, coordinate, cop, copy, corner, correlate, corroborate, corrupt, couch, counter, counterfeit, cover, cozen, crack, crib, criminalize, cross-examine, crowbar, crucify, cuff, curb

dangle, dare, daunt, deadbolt, deal, debase, debate, debit, debunk, deceive, decipher, declare, decode, deconstruct, decontaminate, decry, decrypt, deduce, deepen, deface, defend, defer, deform, defraud, delay, delegitimize, delete, delude, demonstrate, denounce, dent, -deny, depersonalize, depict, deport, deposit, destroy, detach, detain, detect, -deter, determine, devalue, devise, devote, dictate, disabuse, disclaim, disclose, discombobulate, -discount, discover, discredit, disgrace, disintegrate, dismay, -disown, disparage, dispel, dispute, -disregard, dissect, disseminate, dissipate, distinguish, distract, distress, distrust, divide, divulge, doctor, document, -dodge, dog, double-check, double-cross, double-talk, downgrade, drag, dredge, dupe, duplicate

educe, efface, elaborate, elicit, eliminate, elucidate, -elude, embezzle, emphasize, encode, endanger, endow, enfold, enforce, enlighten, enmesh, enrage, enshrine, ensure, entangle, entrap, erase, escalate, -escape, -eschew, escort, espouse, estimate, estrange, euchre, euthanize, -evade, exacerbate, exact, examine, exceed, excise, excruciate, exhume, exonerate, expense, expiate, exploit, expose, expunge, extinguish, extort, extrapolate

fabricate, fake, falsify, fast-track, fathom, fault, faze, feign, ferret, fiddle, filch, film, filter, finger, finish, flood, floodlight, flub, flummox, flush, foil, follow, force, forge, forgive, fortify, frame, frisk, fudge, fuel

gag, gamble, game, gammon, garble, gaslight, gate-crash, gauge, glad-hand, glamorize, grab, grasp, gratify, grease, grill, grope, guard

hack, -halt, hammer, hamper, hamstring, handcuff, handle, hang, harass, harbor, haunt, hide, highlight, hijack, hinder, hoard, hock, hocus-pocus, hogtie, honey, honor, hook, hound, humiliate, humor, hunt, hush, hustle

identify, idolize, ignite, -ignore, illuminate, imitate, impart, impede, imperil, impersonate, implicate, imply, impound, incarcerate, incriminate, indemnify, index, indict, indispose, induce, inflame, inform, infuse, inherit, inhibit, insinuate, inspect, instruct, insulate, insure, intercept, interest, intern, interpret, interrogate, interrupt, intertwine, interview, intimate, intimidate, intrigue, intuit, invade, invalidate, inveigle, invent, inventory, invest, investigate, itemize

jab, jack, jade, jail, jimmy, jolly, judge, justify

keep, kidnap, knife, knit

label, lampoon, lance, launder, leak, learn, legislate, legitimate, legitimize, level, leverage, libel, light, limn, link, liquidate, lock, lodge, loot, lull, lure, lynch

maim, malign, manhandle, manicure, manipulate, marinate, mark, mask, master, mastermind, measure, mediate, mind, mirror, miscommunicate, misconstrue, misdiagnose, misdirect, misguide, mishandle, mishear, misinform, misjudge, mislabel, mislay, mislead, misplace, misread, misrepresent, mistake, misuse, modulate, molest, monetize, monkey-wrench, monopolize, muckrake, muddle, muddy, muffle, mug, murder, muscle, muzzle, mystify

nab, nag, nail, narrow, navigate, -negate, neutralize, nobble, notify, -nullify, number

obfuscate, obscure, observe, obstruct, occlude, -omit, outbid, outfox, outsmart, outwit, overdose, -overlook, overpower, owe

paint, pardon, parrot, pawn, peg, penetrate, permit, perplex, persecute, persuade, pester, pierce, pilfer, pimp, pinch, pinpoint, pirate, pity, plagiarize, plague, plan, plant, plead, pledge, plot, pluck, poach, pocket, poke, police, pollute, ponder, predetermine, prejudice, preoccupy, prepare, prescribe, press, pressure, -prevent, prick, prioritize, probe, process, prod, profess, profile, profit, promise, prosecute, protect, prove, provoke, prowl, pulp, pump, punctuate, puncture, punish, purchase, purloin, pursue, puzzle

quash, query, question, quiet, quiz

railroad, rake, rankle, ransack, ransom, rape, rattle, razor, read, reassure, -rebuff, rebuke, rebut, reconstruct, redact, redirect, reference, refute, regret, regulate, reinvestigate, remind, repay, repent, -repudiate, request, research, resent, restrict, retain, retrace, retract, retrain, reveal, revenge, reverse, review, rig, rile, rip, risk, rivet, rob, romanticize, rook, root, rout

sabotage, sadden, sanction, savage, scam, scandalize, scapegoat, scare, schmooze, school, scoop, score, scour, scramble, scrap, scratch, screen, screw, scrub, scruple, scrutinize, search, secrete, secure, seize, sell, sentence, sequester, sever, shadow, shake, shame, shanghai, shank, shield, shiv, shred, shroud, shuffle, -sidestep, sidetrack, sift, silence, simplify, simulate, siphon, skew, skim, slander, slash, slice, slow, slur, smear, smother, smuggle, snag, snare, snatch, sneak, sniff, snooker, soap, soil, solicit, solve, sour, spearhead, spend, spike, spitball, split, sponge, sponsor, spoon-feed, spotlight, spy, squander, square, squeeze, squirrel, stain, stalk, stall, startle, stash, steal, steep, stifle, stigmatize, sting, stipulate, stir, stoke, stonewall, strong-arm, study, stump, stun, stunt, stymie, submerge, suborn, subpoena, substantiate, subtract, sucker, sue, suffer, sugar, surf, surface, surpass, suspect, suss, swamp, sway, sweep, sweet-talk, swindle, swipe, switch

tabulate, tail, tame, tangle, target, tatter, tease, terminate, test, testify, threaten, throttle, throw, thump, tidy, tie, torment, trace, track, trade, trail, translate, trap, trash, trawl, trick, trigger, trouble, trounce, tuck, twist

uncomplicate, uncover, uncrumple, uncuff, undercut, undo, undress, unearth, unmask, unnerve, unpack, unravel, unscramble, unskew, unspool, untangle, uphold, urge validate, vamp, vandalize, ventilate, verify, victimize, vilify, villainize, vindicate, violate, -void, vow

waive, wangle, waste, weasel, wedge, weed, weigh, weight, whack, wheedle, whitewash, whore, wind, wiretap, withhold, witness, wonder, worm, worry, wrap, wring, wrinkle, wrong

x-ray

Paranormal & Urban Fantasy

Representative Authors and Titles

- **Jim Butcher**, *Storm Front*
- **Mike Carey**, *The Devil You Know*
- **Mercedes Lackey**, *The Serpent's Shadow*
- **China Miéville**, *Perdido Street Station*
- **Anne Rice**, *Interview with the Vampire*
- **Nalini Singh**, *Slave to Sensation*
- **Chris Wooding**, *The Haunting of Alaizabel Cray*

-abandon, abdicate, abduct, abolish, absorb, accelerate, access, acclimate, accrue, acquire, activate, adapt, admonish, adopt, adulterate, adumbrate, advance, advise, advocate, affirm, aggrandize, alarm, alert, alienate, alleviate, ally, alter, amaze, anguish, animate, annex, anoint, apotheosize, arouse, ascertain, assail, assault, assert, assess, assimilate, assure, astonish, astound, attach, attract, attune, augment, authorize, avenge, -avert, await, awaken, awe

balance, ban, banish, baptize, bar, bash, bathe, beat, beatify, beckon, bedevil, bedraggle, beg, beguile, bemuse, bequeath, bestialize, bestow, betray, bewilder, bewitch, bite, blacken, blast, blemish, bless, blight, blind, blot, blur, boast, bolster, boost, borrow, bowdlerize, box, brainwash, break, brighten, brush, buoy, burden, burst, bury, bushwhack, bust, butcher, buttress

cache, cage, call, camouflage, cannibalize, captivate, capture, carve, cast, catalyze, categorize, cauterize, caution, cement, censure, chain, champion, change, charge, charm, chase, check, cherish, chisel, choose, chronicle, circumscribe, claim, claw, cleanse, climb, clothe, cloud, coach, color, comfort, command, commingle, complete, conceal, concretize, condense, confess, confide, confirm, confiscate, conflate, conjecture, conjure, consolidate, consume, consummate, contaminate, contort, contract, contravene, contribute, control, convert, convince, correct, couch, counter, counterfeit, court, cow, crack, craft, crave, craze, crisp, crossbreed, crown, crucify, crush, crystallize, cull, curse, curtail damage, damn, darken, dash, daunt, daze, dazzle, debilitate, decant, deepen, deep-six, deface, defang, defeat, defend, defile, deflate, deflower, deform, defy, deify, delegate, delight, delouse, demand, demean, demonize, demystify, denigrate, deplete, deprave, depredate, deprive, deride, desecrate, designate, destine, destroy, detect, dethrone, develop, devour, diagnose, dictate, diffuse, digest, dirty, disabuse, disaffect, disappoint, disbelieve, discern, discipline, disclose, disconcert, -discount, discredit, -disdain, disenchant, disfavor, disgorge, disguise, disjoint, dislodge, dismantle, disobey, dispel, display, disprove, -disregard, dissolve, dissuade, distill, distrust, divine, divulge, domesticate, dominate, domineer, donate, doom, doubt, douse, downplay, drag, drain, draw, dread, dredge, drench, dress, drill, drink, drown, drug

educate, efface, elicit, emancipate, embalm, embed, embody, embrace, embroider, empty, enchant, encircle, encrypt, endanger, enervate, enfold, engender, engross, engulf, enlighten, enrapture, enslave, ensorcel, ensoul, enthrall, enthrone, entrance, entrust, entwine, envelop, erase, escort, establish, eternalize, evacuate, -evade, evaluate, evoke, exact, exalt, excite, excuse, exempt, exert, exhume, exile, exorcise, expedite, expel, expiate, expose, expound, express, externalize, extirpate, extort, extract, extricate, eyeball

familiarize, fascinate, father, fathom, faze, fear, feed, feign, fell, festoon, fetch, fetishize, fetter, fixate, flay, flout, flush, follow, forage, -forbid, forfeit, formulate, fossilize, foster, foul, fracture, frighten, frogmarch, fuel, fulfill, further, fuse

gainsay, garner, gash, gather, glamour, glean, glorify, goad, gobble, gobsmack, gore, graft, greenlight, greet, groom, group, guarantee, guard, guide, guzzle

hallow, hammer, handpick, harbinger, harbor, harden, harm, harpoon, harvest, haunt, heal, heat, hex, hide, hobble, hornswoggle, hospitalize, host, humble, hunt, husband, hustle, hybridize, hypnotize

ignite, illustrate, imbibe, imitate, immerse, immortalize, impair, impale, imperil, impersonate, implant, implore, impregnate, imprison, incapacitate, include, incubate, indoctrinate, induct, infect, infest, infiltrate, influence, inherit, inhibit, initiate, injure, innovate, inoculate, inspire, instruct, insulate, insult, integrate, interbreed, internalize, interrogate, intrigue, introduce, intuit, invoke, involve, isolate

jangle, jar, jeopardize, jinx, join, juxtapose

keep, kidnap, kindle, knot

lacerate, lambaste, lament, leach, lead, leash, leech, legalize, levy, liberate, limit, locate, lock, loose, lull

magnetize, magnify, maintain, maledict, manacle, mangle, manifest, manumit, mar, maraud, martyr, materialize, maul, medicate, meld, mellow, menace, mentor, mesmerize, metabolize, midwife, mimic, minimize, mishandle, misinterpret, misread, mistake, mistreat, mix, mobilize, mock, mold, mollify, monitor, muddy, muster, mutate, muzzle, mystify

name, navigate, -neglect, neutralize, nonplus, normalize, nourish, numb, nurse, nurture, nuzzle

obey, obligate, obliterate, obscure, occult, offend, orbit, order, originate, -ostracize, oust, outgrow, outlast, outlaw, overrule, overtake, overthrow, overturn, overwhelm

parent, pave, paw, penalize, perfect, permeate, perplex, personify, pervert, petition, petrify, pigeonhole, pillory, placate, plaster, plead, plunder, plunge, poison, possess, post, power, preach, predict, preserve, probe, procure, produce, profane, profile, proliferate, promote, prompt, prop, propel, prophesy, propitiate, proselytize, protect, prove, provide, provoke, prowl, pulverize, pummel, puncture, purify, pursue

quantify, question, quieten

raid, raise, rarefy, rationalize, ravish, reactivate, read, realign, reanimate, reap, rear, reassemble, reassure, -rebuff, recruit, referee, reflect, refract, refresh, refurbish, -refuse, regain, regenerate, rein, reinforce, -reject, rejigger, rejuvenate, release, relegate, relinquish, relocate, rend, renew, -renounce, reorient, repel, reproduce, repulse, rescue, reserve, reshape, restimulate, resurrect, reunite, reveal, reverence, revitalize, revive, revoke, rip, risk, ritualize, rive, roughen, rouse, rue, rule

sacrifice, safeguard, salt, salvage, sample, sanctify, sap, savage, scald, scapegoat, scare, scatter, scavenge, scent, scorch, scourge, scratch, sculpt, seclude, second, sedate, seduce, seek, segregate, seize, select, sensationalize, sense, sequester, serve, set, shackle, shadow, shatter, shed, shelter, shepherd, shift, shock, show, shrivel, -shun, shut, sicken, sift, signify, singe, sizzle, slather, slaughter, slug, smash, smear, smell, smite, smother, smuggle, snare, snatch, sniff, snow, sober, soil, solicit, solidify, sort, sour, span, spank, spark, spawn, specify, spellbind, splice, splinter, split, spoil, spook, spoor, spot, spread, spring, spruce, spur, -spurn, squander, squelch, stagger, stain, stake, stalk, startle, steer, stipulate, stir, stoke, stomach, stonewall, strangle, strengthen, strike, study, stump, stun, stymie, subdue, subjugate, submit, subordinate, suborn, substantiate, suck, suckle, suffuse, sugarcoat, sully, summon, sunder, supplant, support, surfeit, surpass, survive, suspect, suspend, sustain, swallow, swamp, swear, synthesize

taint, tame, tantalize, tap, target, tarnish, taste, teach, tear, tender, tether, thrash, threaten, tighten, tilt, tone, torch, torment, torpefy, torture, touch, toughen, track, train, transcend, transfigure, transfix, transform, transgress, transmit, transmute, transplant, trap, traumatize, treasure, trespass, trigger, trivialize, tug, tune, tutor, tweak

unbind, uncover, undermine, underpin, unearth, unfasten, unfetter, unfold, unify, unleash, unlock, unmask, unravel, unseal, unseat, unshackle, uphold, uplift, uproot, upstage, usurp vaccinate, validate, vamp, venerate, verify, violate, vitiate, vivisect, vocalize, vouchsafe

wag, ward, warn, warrant, wean, weave, weigh, welcome, weld, whammy, wield, wind, witch, witness, wizen, wolf, wonder, worm, worship, wound, wow, wrap, wreck, wrest, wring

yoke

zap

Romance

Representative Authors and Titles

- **Loretta Chase**, *Lord of Scoundrels*
- **Georgette Heyer**, *The Grand Sophy*
- **Beverly Jenkins**, *Indigo*
- **Susan Elizabeth Phillips**, *It Had to be You*
- **Nora Roberts**, *Montana Sky*
- **LaVyrle Spencer**, *Morning Glory*
- **Mary Stewart**, *Nine Coaches Waiting*

With romance in particular, the antonymic relationship between the actions of the main characters becomes essential. Because of the need for constant, fascinating tension between the lovers, actions need to be primal and oppositional to map out a satisfying emotional landscape. Some classic pairings from the genre's canonic titles include: *protect/risk, chase/escape, puzzle/solve, preserve/provoke, corrupt/redeem, explore/ignore, sweeten/sour, disguise/expose, demand/defy, heal/harm, muscle/mind, pierce/block, build/demolish, gamble/plan, tame/unleash, avenge/forgive, bind/free, corrupt/purify, freeze/melt, catch/release, wreck/repair, believe/deceive, feed/starve, blame/forgive, rush/slow, rule/ruin, judge/pardon, amplify/simplify, guard/attack, dull/sharpen, rock/steady, torture/nurture.*

Giving your duo a pair of dazzling antonyms can practically write the book for you, because a great action (and the attendant tactics) supplies your story with a range of interesting contrasts and potential confrontations. Consider the sheer *range* of antonyms for

- **Secure ≠** lose, attack, expose, unleash, endanger, drop, oppose, traumatize
- **Entice ≠** repulse, terrorize, upset, bore, offend, insult, discourage, expel
- **Defile ≠** cleanse, worship, scour, sanitize, bless, scold, sterilize, purify
- **Confess ≠** withhold, dispute, betray, mask, conceal, mislead, accuse, swindle

Each of those actions encompasses a swath of behavior, leaving all kinds of dramatic potential on hand for those hot opposites that need attracting. When verbalizing your couple, don't forget the complexity of verbs that allow for a broad spectrum of antonyms with different connotations. The spectrum of oppositions will result in variegated, flexible relationships with room to develop on the page.

-abandon, abide, abolish, accentuate, accept, accommodate, accost, acknowledge, actualize, addle, adjust, adore, advance, advantage, advocate, affront, aggravate, agitate, aid, alienate, allege, allure, amplify, amuse, anchor, anger, annoy, anticipate, appraise, appreciate, approach, arbitrate, arouse, arrogate, assess, assist, assuage, assure, attack, attract, attune, audition, avenge, -avert, awaken, award

back, backbite, bait, bandy, bankroll, battle, bear, beautify, bed, beg, beguile, bejewel, believe, bend, benefit, besiege, besmirch, bestow, betray, better, bewitch, bias, bind, blame, blandish, blast, blend, blind, block, blurt, bolster, book, borrow, bother, bounce, brace, brave, breathe, brew, bribe, broach, broaden, buck, budget, buffer, build, bulldoze, burn, burnish, bury, butter, buttress

cadge, cajole, -cancel, captivate, capture, carry, castigate, catch, celebrate, center, chaff, chagrin, chair, challenge, champion, chaperone, charge, charm, chase, chastise, check, cherish, chide, chill, choose, choreograph, civilize, claim, clasp, clean, clear, clobber, clutch, coax, coddle, combat, comfort, command, commit, comp, compact, compartmentalize, compel, complement, compose, compound, compromise, conceal, condone, confide, confine, confound, confront, congratulate, consecrate, conserve, consign, console, consume, contact, contrive, control, convert, convince, cook, copy, correct, corrode, corrupt, cosset, cost, costume, counsel, counter, counteract, court, covet, cramp, crave, credit, crest, criticize, critique, cross, crown, crush, cuddle, cultivate, curb

damn, dandify, dare, deaden, debate, debauch, deceive, declare, dedicate, defame, defend, defer, deflate, deflower, defray, defrost, defy, delight, deliver, demand, demolish, demonize, -deny, deprave, deprive, -desert, desire, -despise, destabilize, destroy, devise, dictate, direct, disadvantage, disappoint, disarm, discombobulate, discomfit, discomfort, -discount, discountenance, discourage, disfavor, disguise, dish, dishevel, dishonor, disillusion, disobey, disorient, disparage, dispirit, displease, disqualify, diss, distress, distrust, -ditch, divorce, dizzy, dog, domesticate, dominate, dull, dump, dupe

ease, eclipse, edit, elaborate, elevate, elicit, -elude, embarrass, embellish, embrace, emulate, enable, enchant, encourage, encumber, endear, endure, energize, enhance, ennoble, enrage, enrapture, enrich, enshrine, ensnare, enthrall, entice, entitle, entrance, envelop, equalize, erode, -escape, esteem, estrange, -evade, evaluate, even, evince, exacerbate, exact, exaggerate, exalt, exasperate, excavate, exceed, exchange, -exclude, excuse, exempt, exhibit, exhilarate, expedite, expend, explore, expose, express

fabricate, face, facilitate, falsify, fancy, fascinate, fault, feature, feed, fence, fight, filter, finance, finesse, fire, flatter, flaunt, flavor, flip, follow, fool, -forbid, forfeit, forgive, fortify, foster, frazzle, free, freeze, fuel, furnish

galvanize, gamble, garnish, gate-crash, gild, glamorize, glitter, glitz, glue, goad, govern, grab, grace, grant, grasp, gratify, grill, groom, ground, guarantee, guard, guide, gussy

-halt, handle, harbor, harm, harmonize, harness, hassle, heal, heighten, hide, highlight, hinder, hold, honor, hook, host, hound, housetrain, humble, hurl, hurt

idealize, idolize, ignite, immortalize, impede, impel, impersonate, implore, improve, improvise, impugn, incense, incite, include, incommode, increase, induce, indulge, inflame, influence, infuriate, ingratiate, injure, insert, inspire, instigate, insult, insure, intensify, interrupt, intimate, intoxicate, intrigue, invalidate, inveigle, invent, invert, invigorate, invite, irk, irritate

jab, jilt, jinx, jolly, judge, juggle, jumble, justify

kick-start, kindle, knead, knock

land, lavish, lead, learn, leave, lend, level, light, litigate, loan, loosen, loot, lose, lubricate, lure

madden, magnify, malign, manage, mangle, manicure, market, marry, mask, massage, master, mediate, melt, menace, mend, mesmerize, mince, mine, mirror, misconstrue, misinform, misjudge, mislabel, mislead, mismatch, misplace, misrepresent, mistake, mistreat, misuse, mock, moderate, mold, monopolize, mooch, mother, motivate, mourn, move

nag, neaten, needle, -negate, negotiate, nettle, nitpick, nourish, nurse, nurture

obey, obscure, obsess, obstruct, offend, offer, oil, one-up, oppose, oppress, orchestrate, ornament, outfox, outshine, outsmart, outwit, overcommit, overdramatize, overemphasize, overindulge, overspend, owe

package, pamper, parade, pardon, parry, partition, patronize, pause, paw, penetrate, perfect, permit, personalize, persuade, pester, pierce, pillage, plague, plan, play, plead, please, pleasure, pledge, plot, pluck, poeticize, polish, popularize, portray, possess, postpone, praise, predetermine, prejudge, preoccupy, prepare, prepossess, preserve, press, pressure, -prevent, prime, primp, prioritize, prize, proclaim, prod, -prohibit, project, prolong, promise, promote, prop, propose, protect, protest, prove, provide, provoke, prune, publicize, pull, punish, purify, pursue, push, puzzle

quash, quench, quicken, -quit, quiz

race, ram, rate, ravish, razzle-dazzle, reactivate, ream, rebuild, recapture, reclaim, reconcile, recover, rectify, redeem, reform, -refuse, regard, regret, rehabilitate, reinforce, reintegrate, reinvigorate, -reject, rekindle, relax, release, relieve, relinquish, relish, remind, renew, renovate, repair, repel, rephrase, replenish, represent, reproach, reprove, -repudiate, rescue, reserve, resist, resolve, respect, restore, restrain, retain, retort, retract, retrieve, reunite, revile, ridicule, rile, risk, rivet, roast, rock, roleplay, romanticize, rope, rouse, ruffle, ruin, rule, rumor, rumple, rush

sabotage, sacrifice, salvage, save, savor, scale, scandalize, schmooze, school, scold, -scorn, scotch, scramble, scrimp, script, sear, season, second, secure, seduce, seek, seize, sentimentalize, separate, serve, settle, shadow, shake, share, sharpen, shelter, shield, shift, -shirk, shoulder, showcase, shred, shuffle, sideline, simplify, skewer, skimp, slake, slam, slander, slap, slice, -slight, slow, smack, smooth, snag, -snub, soak, soap, soften, soft-sell, solicit, solve, soothe, sophisticate, sour, spackle, spank, spare, spark, spellbind, spend, spice, spiff, split, spoil, sponge, spoof, spotlight, spruce, spur, -spurn, squander, squire, stage-manage, stain, stale, starve, steady, steal, steam, steer, stereotype, stimulate, stint, stipulate, stir, stitch, stoke, straighten, streamline, strengthen, stroke, subdue, subvert, sucker, suffocate, supervise, support, surprise, surrender, sustain, sway, sweeten, switch

taboo, tailor, tame, tantalize, tarnish, taste, taunt, teach, tease, tempt, tend, thank, thaw, threaten, thrill, thrust, -thwart, tickle, tie, titillate, tolerate, torment, torture, toss, track, trammel, transform, trash, treasure, treble, trick, troll, trumpet, trust, tune, two-time, typecast

unbalance, unbind, unburden, unbutton, unchain, undercharge, undercut, underestimate, underpin, undervalue, underwhelm, underwrite, undo, undress, unite, unleash, unload, unlock, unman, unpack, unscramble, untangle, unveil, unzip, update, upgrade, urge, use

validate, value, vamp, varnish, veil, violate, vulgarize

wake, warm, warn, warrant, waste, wean, weather, weave, wed, wedge, weed, welcome, whet, whisk, wind, winnow, wish, wither, withhold, withstand, woo, worship, wound, wow, wrack, wrangle, wreck, wrench, wrestle, wrong

yield

Science Fiction

Representative Authors and Titles

- **Lois McMasters Bujold**, *The Warrior's Apprentice*
- **Philip José Farmer**, *To Your Scattered Bodies Go*
- **William Gibson**, *Neuromancer*
- **Frank Herbert**, *Dune*
- **Anne McCaffrey**, *Dragonflight*
- **Larry Niven & Steven Barnes**, *Dream Park*
- **Neal Stephenson**, *The Diamond Age*

-abort, abrogate, absorb, abuse, acclimate, accommodate, accost, accustom, achieve, activate, adapt, administer, adorn, advise, advocate, agonize, alarm, alienate, allay, allot, amalgamate, amaze, amplify, analyze, anesthetize, annex, annihilate, ape, appall, appraise, apprentice, appropriate, armor, ascertain, assassinate, assemble, assign, astound, atomize, attune, auction, augment, authorize, automate, await, awaken, awe

badmouth, bag, bait, ballyhoo, bamboozle, bankrupt, barbarize, barricade, barter, bastardize, beam, beat, bedeck, benchmark, best, bet, bid, blacklist, blaze, blitz, block, blockade, boggle, bolt, bombard, boost, botch, -boycott, braid, brainstorm, brand, brave, breach, bridge, bring, broadcast, broker, browbeat, brownnose, buffalo, bug, bully, buzz

cadge, cajole, calculate, calibrate, capsize, captain, captivate, categorize, caution, celebrate, cement, censor, chafe, charge, chart, chauffeur, cheat, chip, chisel, choke, circumnavigate, clamp, classify, cloak, clog, clone, clothe, clout, clutter, coalesce, coat, coax, cocoon, code, codify, coin, collect, colonize, combat, command, commend, commercialize, commission, compact, compensate, compile, complicate, compute, con, conceive, condemn, condense, conduct, confine, confirm, confiscate, confront, congest, connect, conquer, consolidate, constrain, construct, consult, contact, contain, contaminate, contour, contract, control, convene, convince, coopt, correct, corrode, crack, craft, crank, crash, crave, criminalize, cross, crosscheck, crumple, crush, culture, curb, cure, customize

dare, daze, deactivate, debrief, deceive, decode, decontaminate, decouple, decrypt, dedicate, deduce, defuse, defy, dehumanize, delegate, deliver, delouse, dent, depersonalize, deplete, depopulate, deport, depredate, deprive, deprogram, design, desolate, detain, -deter, deteriorate, devastate, develop, devise, dictate, dilute, disabuse, disarticulate, disconnect, disenfranchise, disengage, disgrace, disintegrate, dislodge, -disown, dispatch, dispense, disprove, dispute, disqualify, disrupt, dissect, disseminate, distill, distinguish, divide, -dodge, dose, double-talk, doubt, download, downsize, drag, draw, drive, duel, dumbfound, dupe, duplicate

earmark, earn, eat, echo, eclipse, edify, educate, educe, eject, elbow, electrify, elevate, emancipate, embattle, empower, encase, encrypt, endanger, endow, endure, energize, enforce, engender, engineer, engulf, enhance, enmesh, enslave, ensoul, entertain, enthrone, eradicate, erect, -eschew, escort, evacuate, evaluate, evict, exacerbate, exaggerate, excavate, exceed, -exclude, execute, exert, exhaust, exonerate, expel, expense, exploit, explore, expunge, extend, exterminate, extinguish, extort, extricate

fabricate, face, fake, fast-forward, fault, feed, fell, ferry, fertilize, fight, filch, find, fix, flank, flatter, flimflam, flood, flout, flub, flummox, flunk, foist, foment, force, forecast, forego, forewarn, forfeit, forge, formulate, fortify, fragment, frame, freeboot, fry, fête, fuel, fumigate, fuse

gain, galvanize, gamble, gather, gestate, gird, glean, govern, graft, graph, grease, grind, grip, grok, guard, guide, gull

habituate, hack, half-ass, halve, hammer, handle, harbor, hard-sell, harshen, harvest, hatch, haul, hazard, head, hector, heighten, helm, hide, hijack, hire, hocus-pocus, hose, host, house, humor, hunt, hustle, hybridize, hype, hypnotize

idolize, illuminate, imagine, impair, imperil, impersonate, implant, import, impound, impress, imprison, inactivate, incite, incorporate, incriminate, incubate, indemnify, index, induce, indulge, infatuate, infect, infest, infiltrate, inflict, infuriate, infuse, inject, innovate, inoculate, inspect, install, instigate, institute, insulate, insult, integrate, interbreed, intercept, intermingle, interpret, interrogate, interrupt, intimidate, inundate, invade, inventory, investigate, invoice, involve, issue

jack, jam, jerry-build, jerry-rig, jettison, jolt, jostle, juice, junk

keelhaul, kill

lame, lard, launch, lead, leech, level, leverage, liberate, license, liquefy, lobby, lobotomize

machine, maintain, mandate, maneuver, manhandle, manufacture, map, mar, march, marginalize, mark, market, maroon, massacre, master, mastermind, maul, maximize, measure, mechanize, medicate, menace, merge, metabolize, mimic, mine, misappropriate, miscalculate, misdiagnose, misgauge, mislabel, misrule, mobilize, modernize, modify, monetize, monitor, monkey-wrench, monopolize, mortar, motorize, multiply, mutate

nab, name, navigate, negotiate, net, network, neuter, neutralize, nudge, -nullify, numb, numerate occlude, offload, open, operate, optimize, orbit, order, organize, orient, originate, orphan, -ostracize, oust, outclass, outdistance, outlay, outmaneuver, outperform, outrank, outsell, outthink, overcharge, overcome, overhaul, -overlook, overpower, override, oversell, overthrow

pacify, pack, partition, pass, patch, patent, patrol, pawn, peddle, peruse, pet, pierce, pilot, pinpoint, pioneer, pirate, plague, plan, plot, plug, plumb, plunder, poke, poll, pollute, position, power, prescribe, presell, pressure, pressurize, pretend, price, prime, prize, process, procure, profit, program, proliferate, propel, propitiate, prostitute, prostrate, protect, provoke, punch, puncture, punish, purchase, purge, pursue, puzzle

quaff, qualify, quantify, quarantine, quench, query, quicken

race, rank, rankle, ransom, ravage, raze, reach, reap, reboot, recoup, recreate, recruit, recycle, redeem, reference, refine, reflect, refract, refurbish, regenerate, regiment, regulate, rehabilitate, rejigger, rejuvenate, relaunch, remedy, render, renew, renovate, repair, repay, replace, replenish, replicate, repurpose, requisition, rescue, research, reserve, reshape, resist, restock, restore, restrict, restructure, resuscitate, retain, retool, retrain, retrieve, revenge, revere, review, revitalize, revoke, revolutionize, reward, rifle, rig, right, rinse, rip, risk, rivet, rob, rook, rubber-stamp, rupture

safeguard, salvage, salve, sample, sandbag, sanitize, saturate, scale, scam, scan, scathe, scavenge, schlep, scoop, scope, scorch, scour, scout, scrap, screen, scrounge, scrub, scrutinize, sculpt, scuttle, seal, search, sedate, segregate, send, serve, service, shade, shanghai, shed, shield, shill, shortchange, short-circuit, shorten, shrink, shunt, shuttle, sicken, sift, signal, simplify, simulate, siphon, slam, sling, slit, slough, slow, smash, snarl, snatch, snooker, -snub, solder, solve, sort, sour, source, spark, spawn, spitball, splatter, splice, splinter, sponge, sponsor, square, squash, squelch, stabilize, stake, standardize, stash, steal, steamroller, steep, steer, sterilize, steward, stiff, stiffen, stigmatize, stimulate, stipulate, stock, stoke, store, stow, stretch, strong-arm, structure, study, stupefy, subdue, subordinate, substantiate, suck, supercharge, supervise, supplant, supply, surf, survey, suss, sway, swear, sweeten, swipe, switch, synthesize, syrup

tackle, tail, tame, tap, tax, tempt, tender, terminate, test, tether, thrash, threaten, thump, tone, tool, top, topple, torpedo, tote, toughen, tout, tow, trace, trade, traffic, train, transcend, transform, translate, transmit, transmute, transport, trash-talk, trick, trigger, trouble, troubleshoot, turn, tweak, twist, tyrannize

ulcerate, uncork, underrate, underwrite, unite, unlock, unseal, unskew, untidy, unwind, update, upgrade, uproot, urge, usurp, utilize

value, vaporize, ventilate, verify, vex, vindicate, vivisect, -void, volunteer

waive, wake, wangle, want, warehouse, warn, warp, wash, waylay, weaken, weaponize, weasel, weld, wet, wield, wing, wire, worm, worry, wow, wrack, wreak, wrench

yoke

zap, zone

Thriller

Representative Authors and Titles

- **Lee Child**, *Killing Floor*
- **Frederick Forsyth**, *Day of the Jackal*
- **Thomas Harris**, *Silence of the Lambs*
- **Patricia Highsmith**, *The Talented Mr. Ripley*
- **Stieg Larsson**, *The Girl with the Dragon Tattoo*
- **Helen MacInnes**, *Above Suspicion*
- **John Le Carré**, *Tinker Tailor Soldier Spy*

abase, abduct, abet, abolish, abridge, absolve, absorb, accelerate, accentuate, accomplish, accumulate, accuse, ace, acquit, activate, adulterate, advise, affect, afford, agitate, alibi, align, allege, amass, ambush, anchor, anguish, annihilate, anonymize, antagonize, appease, apprehend, approve, arm, arrange, arrest, asphyxiate, assassinate, assemble, assess, assign, attack, attaint, attest, audit, augment, award, axe

backhand, badger, bait, battle, beam, beguile, behead, beleaguer, believe, belt, beseech, besmirch, bestialize, bestow, bet, betray, bewilder, bilk, blackmail, blame, bleed, blind, blindside, block, bludgeon, bluff, blunt, bolster, bombard, bond, boobytrap, boost, brainwash, brief, broach, brutalize, buck, bug, bulldoze, bungle, burglarize, burn, burnish, butcher, butter, -bypass

cage, cajole, calculate, calibrate, camouflage, -cancel, candy-coat, canonize, capture, carve, case, case-harden, castrate, catch, chagrin, challenge, chance, charge, charm, chase, chastise, check, checkmate, chide, chill, churn, cinch, circulate, -circumvent, clarify, clinch, cloak, clobber, clone, cloud, club, clue, coach, coerce, collar, collate, combat, commandeer, commit, compare, compel, compensate, compile, compromise, compute, concatenate, conceal, concentrate, concern, conclude, concoct, concuss, condense, condition, condone, confess, confound, confront, congratulate, conk, constipate, constrain, constrict, consume, contaminate, contest, contextualize, contract, contradict, convert, convict, convulse, coordinate, copy, corner, corrupt, counter, counteract, counterfeit, cover, covet, crab, craze, create, credential, cross-examine, crush, cudgel, cuff, cultivate, curb, curtail damage, dare, dazzle, deactivate, deadbolt, debase, debrief, debug, debunk, deceive, decide, decipher, decode, deconstruct, decoy, decrease, decrypt, deduce, deepen, deep-six, defend, deflect, defraud, defuse, defy, dehumanize, delay, delegate, delete, delude, demolish, demonstrate, demoralize, denounce, depose, -desert, desire, destabilize, destroy, detect, determine, detonate, devise, devour, diagnose, dignify, diminish, direct, disable, disappear, disappoint, disarm, disbelieve, discern, discharge, discipline, disconcert, -discount, discredit, -disdain, disembowel, disguise, disgust, dismantle, dismember, disobey, disorient, -disown, disperse, dispute, -disregard, disrespect, disrupt, dissatisfy, dissipate, distort, distract, divulge, dizzy, doctor, dog, domineer, doom, double-check, doubt, down, dragoon, dread, drill, drive, drug, dumbfound, dupe

earn, eighty-six, eject, elect, eliminate, -elude, embed, embellish, embezzle, emphasize, employ, empty, encircle, enclose, encode, encrypt, endorse, engineer, engross, enrage, ensconce, ensnare, ensure, entangle, entice, entomb, entrap, equal, equip, eradicate, erase, erode, escalate, -escape, escort, evacuate, -evade, even, eviscerate, exact, examine, excavate, excise, excuse, exempt, exhibit, exhort, exhume, exonerate, expedite, expel, expend, expiate, expose, expunge, exterminate, extinguish, extract, extrapolate, extricate, eyeball

face, facilitate, fake, falsify, fashion, fast-track, fathom, faze, fight, filch, film, finagle, finesse, fine-tune, finger, finish, flatter, flaunt, flay, fleece, flip, flout, flummox, flush, foil, foist, follow, force, forestall, forfeit, forge, formulate, -forsake, foul, fracture, freeze, frighten, -frustrate, fuel, fumble, fumigate, funnel, fuse

gainsay, gamble, game, gash, gaslight, generalize, generate, goad, grade, grapple, grasp, greenlight, grieve, grill, ground, guard, guesstimate, guillotine

hack, handpick, harangue, harness, hassle, hasten, hatch, hazard, hide, hijack, hinder, hobble, holster, hoodwink, hook, hospitalize, hotwire, humiliate, humor, hush, hustle, hype, hypnotize

identify, -ignore, immobilize, immolate, impair, impart, impede, imperil, impersonate, implant, implicate, improvise, incapacitate, incense, incinerate, incriminate, indict, indoctrinate, induct, infect, infiltrate, inflame, inoculate, institutionalize, instruct, intensify, intercept, interest, internalize, interpret, interrogate, interrupt, intersect, interview, intrigue, intuit, inure, investigate, isolate, itemize

jack, jade, jar, jeopardize, jettison, jinx, juggle, juxtapose

kidnap, kill

label, land, launch, launder, lavish, lead, leak, lecture, legislate, legitimize, level, lick, lift, lionize, liquidate, lock, loot, lubricate, lull, lure

machinate, magnetize, magnify, malign, maneuver, manipulate, manufacture, mar, marinate, mask, massacre, mastermind, maximize, medicate, menace, minimize, miscalculate, mishandle, mishear, misinform, misinterpret, misjudge, mismanage, misread, mitigate, modulate, molest, monitor, motivate, muscle, muster, mutilate, mystify

narrow, nauseate, needle, -negate, neutralize, normalize

obligate, oblige, obliterate, obscure, obsess, offset, oil, -omit, oppose, orchestrate, orient, outguess, outlast, outplay, outrace, outrun, outsmart, outwit, overdose, -overlook, overpay, oversee, overtake, overturn, overwhelm

pace, pacify, palm, panic, paralyze, parry, pause, penalize, perfect, perforate, perplex, persecute, petrify, pinion, placate, plan, plant, plot, poach, pocket, poison, police, portray, posit, position, postpone, pound, precipitate, predetermine, preempt, prejudice, prepare, present, press, pressure, -prevent, prioritize, probe, profess, profile, program, prolong, promise, prosecute, protect, prove, provoke, prowl, publicize, pulverize, pummel, pump, punctuate, puncture, purloin, pursue, puzzle

quash, question, quicken

race, railroad, rally, ransack, ransom, rape, ratify, ration, rationalize, reap, reassure, recapture, recommend, recon, reconnoiter, recover, recreate, redact, redeem, redirect, referee, refine, -refuse, reinvestigate, -reject, release, relegate, relinquish, relish, repel, represent, reprimand, reproduce, rescue, resist, restrain, restructure, resuscitate, reverence, reverse, revise, revive, ridicule, rile, risk, ritualize, rob, romance, rue, rush

sabotage, sacrifice, safeguard, sanitize, savage, save, savor, scan, scapegoat, scar, schedule, scout, scramble, screen, script, scruple, scrutinize, scupper, search, secure, sedate, seduce, seize, sell, sense, sentence, sentinel, sequester, sever, shadow, sharpen, shatter, shelve, shield, shiv, shock, short, shoulder, show, shroud, -shun, shunt, sicken, sideline, -sidestep, sideswipe, signal, silence, simulate, singe, sink, skew, skin, skyjack, slake, slander, slash, slate, slaughter, slay, slice, slot, smash, smuggle, snap, snatch, sneak, snipe, sober, solidify, solve, sophisticate, spare, spearhead, specify, spend, spike, spin, split, spoof, spook, -spurn, spy, squeeze, stab, stage-manage, stagger, stalk, stand, stash, sterilize, stiff, stockpile, stomach, straightjacket, strangle, strategize, streamline, stress, strong-arm, stun, stymie, submerge, subpoena, supersize, suppress, surprise, surrender, survey, survive, suspect, suspend, swat, swindle, swipe, synchronize

tail, tap, target, telegraph, terminate, terrify, terrorize, testify, threaten, thrill, throttle, time, titillate, tolerate, torch, torment, torture, trace, track, trail, train, tranquilize, transfix, translate, trap, trash, traumatize, trawl, trigger, troubleshoot, truck, truncate, turf, tweak

uncuff, undermine, unfold, unhinge, unlock, unpack, unravel, unscramble, unseat, unsettle, unshackle, unveil, upbraid, upset, upstage, usurp, utilize vaccinate, value, vandalize, vaporize, varnish, veil, venture, vet, -veto, victimize, villainize, vindicate, violate

wager, warn, weaken, weaponize, weather, weigh, weight, weld, welt, whack, wheedle, whitewash, wipe, wire, wiretap, withdraw, withhold, withstand, witness, wreck, wrestle

x-ray

yank

Western

Representative Authors and Titles

- **Willa Cather,** *Death Comes for the Archbishop*
- **Zane Grey,** *Riders of the Purple Sage*
- **Louis L'Amour,** *Hondo*
- **Cormac McCarthy,** *All the Pretty Horses*
- **Larry McMurtry,** *Lonesome Dove*
- **Charles Portis,** *True Grit*
- **Glendon Swarthout,** *The Shootist*

abduct, abrade, abuse, accept, accompany, accost, accrue, accuse, acknowledge, acquaint, acquire, actualize, adjudge, adjudicate, adjust, admire, adopt, adore, advantage, afflict, affright, aggrandize, aggravate, agitate, aim, alert, alienate, alleviate, allocate, allow, alter, amaze, ambush, annex, annoy, antagonize, anticipate, appall, appease, applaud, apply, appropriate, arbitrate, arrest, arrogate, assault, assemble, assert, assimilate, assuage, auction, authorize, await

backbite, bait, bake, balance, bale, -balk, bandage, bankrupt, baptize, barbecue, barricade, bat, battle, beat, beautify, bedraggle, befriend, beggar, begrudge, belittle, bemoan, bequeath, berate, better, bewilder, bind, blackguard, blackjack, blame, blast, bless, blight, bluff, boot, bootleg, borrow, brand, brandish, break, breathe, bribe, bridle, bring, broach, browbeat, buck, budget, buff, build, bulletin, burden, burgle, burke, bury, bushwhack

cage, calm, castigate, catch, cauterize, cede, challenge, champion, chance, chaperone, chasten, cheapen, cheat, check, cheer, chew, circle, civilize, claim, classify, clean, climb, close, clothe, clout, coarsen, coerce, collect, colonize, comfort, command, commingle, complete, compliment, concede, conciliate, condemn, conduct, confine, confirm, confound, confront, congest, conquer, conserve, consider, construct, contain, content, contest, control, convince, corner, corral, correct, corroborate, counterpunch, court, cover, cowhide, cradle, crease, crib, cripple, criticize, crucify, crush, cull, cultivate, culture, curse, cushion

dam, damage, damn, dampen, dare, daunt, debate, deceive, declare, decry, deface, defeat, defend, defray, defy, delegitimize, deliver, demand, demarcate, demote, denounce, depopulate, deprive, deputize, -desert, designate, -despise, despoil, detain, -deter, devalue, develop, devote, dichotomize, diffuse, dig, dirty, disband, discard, disconcert, discover, discredit, disenfranchise, disfavor, disfigure, dishearten, disjoint, dismantle, dismay, dismiss, dispatch, disrupt, dissolve, distract, distress, distrust, disturb, dole, domesticate, donate, double-deal, downgrade, downplay, draft, drag, draw, drill, drown, dub, dull

ease, eliminate, elucidate, emasculate, embroil, emulate, enclose, encompass, encumber, end, endear, endure, enforce, enfranchise, enlarge, enlist, enrage, entertain, entitle, entrust, equalize, erect, escalate, -escape, -eschew, escort, establish, esteem, estimate, eulogize, even, exact, exalt, examine, exasperate, -exclude, excoriate, excuse, execute, exhaust, expand, expect, expel, expiate, explore, extend, extinguish, extol, extort, extract

fake, fallow, famish, fancify, fancy, farm, fashion, fatigue, favor, faze, fence, finance, fix, flag, flannel, flatten, -flee, fleece, fluster, focus, foil, forge, forgive, -forsake, fortify, found, fracture, frame, free, -frustrate, fulminate, furnish

gag, garble, garner, gauge, gladden, glorify, gore, gouge, govern, grade, grapple, gravel, griddle, grill, grip, guarantee, guide, gussy, gut

habituate, hamper, handle, hang, harass, harbor, harden, harm, harness, harshen, harvest, hassle, haul, head, heat, heave, heckle, help, hire, hitch, hoard, hogtie, hoist, hold, holster, honey, honor, host, hound, humbug, hump, hunt, hurl

ignite, implicate, impoverish, imprison, improve, impugn, inaugurate, incarcerate, inconvenience, increase, incriminate, incur, indict, inform, ingratiate, inhibit, initiate, injure, inspect, institute, instruct, insult, insure, interrupt, intimidate, intoxicate, inundate, invade, invest, investigate, invite, involve, irritate, isolate

jail, jerk, jilt, join, jostle, judge, jumble, jump

keep, kick, kidnap, kill, knife, knock, knot

lame, lament, lasso, launch, leave, lecture, legalize, legislate, lessen, license, lift, limit, link, liquidate, litigate, load, loan, locate, loosen, loot, lowball, lug, lumber, lynch

maim, maintain, manage, manhandle, mark, mask, master, mature, mediate, mellow, memorialize, meter, milk, mind, mine, misconstrue, misdirect, misjudge, mismanage, misplace, mock, modernize, mollify, mooch, moralize, mortgage, mortify, motivate, mount, mourn, muffle, muster, muzzle

nab, nag, nail, -neglect, negotiate, nettle, niggle, nitpick, nock, nominate, notarize, notch, notify, nourish, number, nurse, nurture

obligate, observe, obstruct, occupy, offend, officiate, operate, ordain, order, organize, orientate, orphan, -ostracize, oust, outbid, outgun, outlaw, outrage, outrun, overextend, overload, oversee, overshadow, overthrow, overturn, overwork, owe

palaver, pamper, panic, pardon, parent, patrol, peddle, peel, pelt, permeate, perplex, perturb, pester, petition, pigeonhole, pile, pilfer, pillory, pilot, pinion, pioneer, pity, place, plan, plaster, pledge, plow, poach, poison, polish, pooh-pooh, post, praise, preach, prepossess, preserve, prime, profane, promise, promote, prop, propitiate, propose, prosecute, protect, provide, provoke, prune, pulp, punch, punish, purchase, purge, pursue, puzzle

quarantine, quell, quench, quiet, -quit

raid, raise, rally, ram, rankle, ransom, rattle, ravage, rawhide, raze, ready, ream, rear, -rebuff, rebuild, reclaim, recover, recruit, rectify, redeem, reduce, refine, reform, refresh, refund, regain, regard, regret, regulate, reimburse, rein, reintegrate, -reject, release, relieve, remodel, remove, renegotiate, renovate, rent, repair, repay, repent, replace, replenish, repress, reprovision, -repudiate, requisition, rescue, resent, reserve, reshape, resign, resolve, restimulate, restore, restrict, restructure, retire, retrench, retrieve, reunite, revenge, revere, revile, revitalize, reward, ride, rifle, rinse, roast, rob, rock, romanticize, root, rope, rototill, roughen, rout, rule, rumple, rustle

sack, sacrifice, sadden, saddle, safeguard, salt, salvage, sanctify, sanction, save, scam, scant, scare, scatter, scavenge, scent, school, scold, -scorn, scourge, scout, scrape, screen, scrounge, scrub, sear, search, season, seclude, secrete, separate, sermonize, settle, shackle, shame, shape, share, shave, shelter, shepherd, -shirk, shock, shoot, shortchange, shoulder, shrivel, shuffle, -shun, shut, signify, silence, simplify, skimp, skin, skunk, slice, slur, smooth, snaffle, snare, sneak, snitch, snow, soak, soap, sober, socialize, soften, soft-sell, soothe, sorrow, sour, source, span, spark, splinter, spread, spring, spur, squire, stable, stake, stalk, stampede, startle, starve, staunch, steady, steal, steel, steer, stifle, stigmatize, stint, stockpile, stomach, stonewall, store, stow, straddle, strip, stultify, subdue, subtract, sucker-punch, sue, sully, supervise, supply, support, surrender, surround, survey, swallow, sway, swear, sweeten, sweet-talk, swipe

tabulate, taint, tally, tame, tangle, tarnish, task, taunt, tax, tear, tease, telegraph, temper, terrify, thank, throw, -thwart, tidy, tie, tire, tolerate, tool, tote, tout, train, trample, treat, trouble, truss, trust, tuck, tug, tutor

unbuckle, unburden, uncover, undercut, underestimate, underwrite, unearth, unhorse, unite, unnerve, unsettle, untie, upgrade, uplift, uproot, upset, usher

validate, vandalize, venerate, venture, vet, vex, victual, vilify, vindicate, vow, vulgarize

warm, warn, warrant, waste, weary, weather, weed, welcome, whittle, win, winnow, withdraw, wither, withstand, woo, worsen, worship, wrangle, wreck, wrong

yank, yield, yoke

Part III: Directions

"A story's energy comes from the degree to which its characters are warring elements, complementary aspects that illuminate each other by contrast and conflict. The only practical reason for a particular character's existence, in fact, is to interact with other characters."

Alexander MacKendrick[9]

A character who sticks with a single tactical mode gets old fast, and so writers instinctively change the tune to keep readers paying attention. Verbs *move*, so we can add texture and drama to any character arc by considering *direction*.

Character transformation requires a tactical cocktail that mixes it up. Yes, your characters will pursue their singular actions, but their tactics need to cover a range of possibilities in order to be fully realized. Contrast creates opposition and friction.

Transformation and escalation don't happen in straight lines.

If we treat any character as a distinct point of view, then energy moves along one axis in relation to a character and another in relation to the external world. Because energy moves, the *direction* of that movement will shift and evolve in response to context.

From the character's POV, their energy can either move away from or toward them, either *Push* or *Pull*. This division includes actions and tactics that *give/take*, *repel/attract*, *command/request*, and *threaten/persuade*. You can think of Push/Pull as the forces of will and desire, (or brawn and brains, *viz* Achilles vs. Odysseus, for any Homer fans). With these verbs, ask yourself: Is this character's action moving to or from? Does Muhammad go to the mountain or the mountain come to Muhammad?

Of course, not all verbs involve the character personally. Often a character does stuff to or with the world that changes external things and people.

With verbs affecting the world outside the character, their energy unites or divides people, things, ideas, relationships: either *Join* or *Split*. These modes also include actions and tactics that *heal/harm*, *create/destroy*, *protect/attack*, and *teach/confuse*. You can think of Join/Split as the forces of love and war (or Eros and Eris, for the mythologically minded). Ask yourself: Is this character's action moving things together or apart? Is their energy a spoon that gathers the food or a knife that cuts it?

At core, what I'm describing is essential direction, and many verbs hybridize them. It may help to visualize them like so:

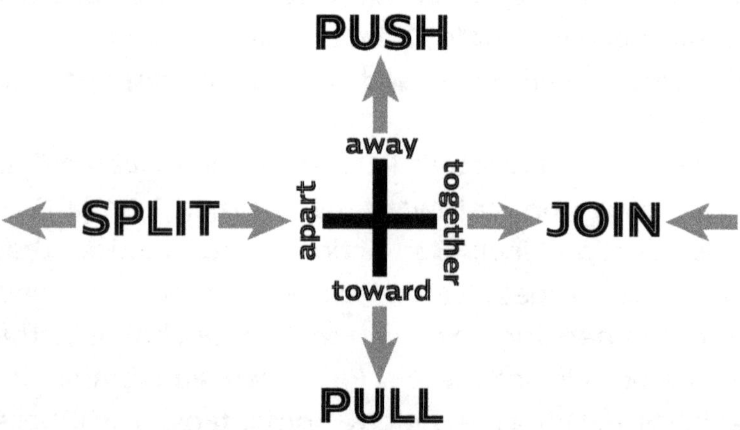

Most verbs fall somewhere between both axes. When it comes to directions, being "right" is less important than changing the tune meaningfully. The goal is *contrast*. By revealing and contrasting the different directions, you provide a dimensional portrait of a character.

All writers get into ruts. Deadlines, bad days, and intense pressure can leave us regurgitating the same stale stories or scenes over and over, but once you focus on shifting the trajectory of a character's action and tactics, you stave off redundancy and monotony.

The purpose of this section is not to split hairs, but to offer easy options for variation on the fly so that you don't get yourself into ruts and trouble. Please don't feel you need to agree with the directions I've assigned to these verbs. As with anything in genre fiction, voice is choice and your mileage may vary.

Keep things escalating, important, and entertaining. The critical element is *meaningful variation*: keep changing the tune to build a satisfying emotional ride for your audience. Let the energy of the characters flow through the story and spill off the page into your readers' imaginations.

Move them!

Push (→)

"Push" verbs extend out, up, and away from the subject, moving objects farther or emitting energy into the surrounding environment. Because they direct a character's efforts outward, they tend to include behaviors that appear authoritative, assertive, energetic, public, decisive, and instructive.

"Push" verbs move away from the subject toward the object and the environment beyond, e.g. *donate, attack, flaunt, manhandle*. These are verbs of authority and order that impose a POV upon the world by asserting internals and extending energy. Vibe-wise, these verbs especially center on the kind of will and brawn that makes Achilles such a formidable force in the Trojan War.

Along the POV character's **internal** axis, "push" verbs *give, extend, repel, threaten*, and *lead*. In these instances, Muhammad goes to the mountain, the stick threatens the donkey from behind.

accelerate, accent, accentuate, accost, accuse, ace, achieve, address, administer, advance, advertise, advise, advocate, afford, aggrandize, agitate, aim, alarm, alert, allege, allocate, allot, amaze, ambush, amplify, apply, appoint, apportion, apprise, approach, arm, arraign, assail, assert, astonish, astound, auction, -avert, -avoid, award

backhand, badger, -balk, ballyhoo, ban, bandy, banish, bankroll, bat, beam, beat, belch, beleaguer, bellow, belt, bequeath, besiege, best, bestow, bet, better, bias, blab, blitz, bludgeon, bluff, blurt, boast, bombard, boost, boot, bother, bounce, box, -boycott, brand, brandish, breathe, bribe, brief, broach, broadcast, broaden, brush, buck, buff, bug, bulldoze, bulletin, bump, buoy, burden, butt, buttonhole, buzz, -bypass cant, captain, caress, caricature, case, cast, catalyze, caution, chair, challenge, champion, chance, charge, chase, choreograph, churn, circulate, clear, climb, clobber, clock, clout, club, clue, coat, coerce, cold-call, colonize, command, commercialize, commodify, communicate, comp, compel, compensate, concuss, condense, confer, confide, confront, congest, conk, conquer, contact, contest, contour, contribute, contrive, control, convince, convulse, cork, corner, counsel, counter, counterpunch, cover, cram, crest, crisp, cross, cross-examine, crowd, cudgel, cue

dare, daunt, dazzle, decant, declare, decree, deepen, defray, delegate, deliver, demonstrate, dent, depict, deposit, deputize, describe, -deter, devote, dictate, diddle, direct, disallow, discard, discharge, discipline, disclose, disgorge, dish, dislodge, dismiss, dispatch, dispense, display, dispose, disseminate, disturb, divulge, doctor, dog, dole, dominate, domineer, donate, dose, douse, dower, dragoon, dramatize, drench, drill, drive, drizzle, drop, drown, duel

edify, eject, elaborate, elbow, elect, electrify, elevate, -elude, embed, emphasize, empower, encourage, encumber, endow, enforce, enrich, enthrone, entrust, equal, equip, escalate, -escape, evacuate, -evade, evangelize, evict, evince, exacerbate, exaggerate, exasperate, exceed, excite, execute, exert, exhibit, exhort, exile, expand, expel, expend, explore, expound, express, extend, externalize, exude

fan, fast-forward, fast-track, father, feature, feed, fill, finance, finger, fire, flabbergast, flatten, flaunt, -flee, fling, flip, flog, floodlight, floor, flout, flush, flutter, foist, follow, foment, force, force-feed, forecast, foresee, foretell, forewarn, forfeit, frogmarch, froth, fudge, fuel, fund, furnish, further, fusillade

gamble, gate-crash, give, goad, gobsmack, govern, grace, grant, grope

hammer, hard-sell, harpoon, hasten, haunt, hawk, hazard, head, heat, hedge, heighten, helm, hex, highlight, hock, hoke, hound, hunt, hurl, hurry, hype

illustrate, immerse, impale, impart, impel, implant, implicate, imply, impose, impregnate, incense, incite, infest, infiltrate, inflame, inflate, infringe, inject, insert, insinuate, instigate, intensify, interpenetrate, intersect, intimate, introduce, inundate, invade, invest, iron

jab, jam, jar, jettison, jimmy, jog, jolt, jostle, jump

kick, kick-start, knead, knife, knock

label, lance, lather, launch, lavish, leak, lecture, lend, leverage, lick, limn, load, loan, loose, lower, lumber

magnify, mainline, manage, mandate, maneuver, manhandle, manifest, march, marinate, market, massage, master, mastermind, maximize, mentor, micromanage, mislay, misplace, mobilize, moisten, molest, monetize, motivate, mount, mug, muscle

nag, nail, navigate, needle, nock, nominate, notify, nudge

obligate, occupy, offer, offload, one-up, operate, -ostracize, oust, outbid, outclass, outdistance, outdo, outgun, outlay, outmaneuver, outplay, outrace, outrank, outreach, outrun, outsell, outshine, outstrip, overcome, overcrowd, overdramatize, overemphasize, overfeed, overhaul, overindulge, overload, overpay, overpower, override, overrule, oversee, oversell, overshadow, overspend, overstuff, overtake, overwhelm, overwork

pack, package, paint, parade, parry, pass, patrol, patronize, paw, pawn, pay, peddle, peg, pelt, penetrate, perforate, permeate, pester, pierce, pigeonhole, pilot, pimp, pinpoint, pioneer, plan, plane, plant, plow, plug, plunge, poeticize, poke, polish, pomade, pooh-pooh, portray, posit, position, post, pound, power, preach, predetermine, prejudge, prejudice, prepossess, prescribe, presell, present, press, pressure, -prevent, prick, print, probe, proclaim, prod, profess, profit, project, prolong, promote, prompt, propel, propose, proposition, proselytize, prostitute, prostrate, provide, provision, prowl, publicize, pummel, punch, punctuate, puncture, pursue, push

quicken, -quit

race, raid, railroad, ram, ravish, reach, -rebuff, rebut, recommend, recompense, redirect, refill, refund, regale, reimburse, release, relegate, relinquish, relocate, remind, remunerate, -renounce, renovate, repay, repel, replenish, represent, retort, retrace, revolt, reward, ride, riffle, risk, rock, roll, ruffle, rule, run, rush

sacrifice, saddle, salt, sandbag, saturate, scale, scope, scour, scout, scramble, scrap, scratch, scrub, sculpt, sell, send, sensationalize, sentimentalize, sermonize, shadow, shake, shape, share, shed, shift, shill, shine, shock, shoot, shove, show, showcase, shuffle, -shun, shunt, sideline, -sidestep, sideswipe, signal, signify, silence, sink, situate, skewer, skipper, skull, slam, slap, slather, sling, slot, slough, slug, smack, smite, smooth, snipe, -snub, soak, soil, spank, spark, spearhead, spend, spike, spoil, spotlight, spread, spur, -spurn, squash, stake, stalk, stamp, stampede, startle, station, steam, steamroll, steamroller, steer, steward, stiffen, stimulate, stock, stoke, storm, strafe, strangle, stress, stretch, strew, strike, stroke, strong-arm, stuff, submerge, submit, suborn, subpoena, sucker-punch, suffuse, sugar, supercharge, supervise, supplant, supply, surf, surfeit, surpass, surprise, swamp, swat, sweep

tack, tackle, tail, target, task, telegraph, tender, testify, text, throw, thrust, thump, thwack, tickle, tilt, tithe, tool, top, topple, toss, touch, tout, trace, track, trail, transcend, transfigure, transmit, trespass, trigger, trump, trumpet, turf

unbalance, underwrite, unload, unspool, upstage, urge, utilize

vanquish, venture, verbalize, victual, vocalize, volunteer, vomit, vouchsafe

wag, wage, wager, wallop, warm, warn, warp, wedge, wet, whet, whup, wield, wind, wipe, witch, wow

Pull (←)

"Pull" verbs contract in, down, and toward the subject, moving objects closer or absorbing energy from the surrounding environment. Because they direct efforts inward, they tend to include behaviors that appear submissive, receptive, persuasive, private, flexible, and attentive.

"Pull" verbs move the object out of the environment toward the subject, e.g., *borrow, lure, hamper, hog*. These are verbs of influence and appetite that handle the outside world by attracting externals and assimilating energy. Vibe-wise, these verbs gravitate to the kind of skill and brains that bring Odysseus home safe a decade after the Trojan War.

Along the POV character's **internal** axis, "pull" verbs *take, retract, attract, persuade*, and *hinder*. In these instances, the mountain comes to Muhammad, the carrot coaxes the donkey to advance.

abduct, absorb, accept, accrue, accumulate, acquire, admit, adopt, affect, aggregate, allure, alter, amuse, analyze, anesthetize, ape, apprehend, apprentice, appropriate, archive, arouse, arrest, arrogate, ascertain, assess, assimilate, assume, attain, attend, attract, audit, audition, authenticate, awe

baby, bag, bait, bamboozle, bare, beckon, befriend, beg, begrudge, beguile, bemoan, benchmark, bereave, beseech, bewitch, bid, bilk, blandish, bleed, blindfold, blindside, bogart, book, bootleg, borrow, bottle, bowdlerize, bridle, bring, brownnose, budget, bum, burglarize, burgle, butter, buy

cadge, cajole, calculate, call, candy-coat, captivate, capture, carry, cart, catch, channel, charm, charter, chauffeur, cheat, check, chill, choose, cinch, circumnavigate, claim, clasp, clip, clone, clutch, coax, cocoon, coddle, coil, collar, collect, comb, commandeer, commission, compare, con, conduct, confiscate, conjure, conscript, conserve, consider, constrain, constrict, construe, consult, consume, contain, contemplate, contract, convey, cool, coopt, cop, copy, cosset, cost, counterfeit, countermand, courier, court, covet, cozen, crab, crave, crib, crop, cuddle, cull, curb

dam, dangle, deacon, debit, debrief, deceive, decoy, deduce, defang, defer, defraud, delay, delight, demand, demilitarize, demotivate, deplete, deprive, derive, desire, despoil, detain, detect, determine, devour, diagnose, dig, disappear, disarm, discern, discover, disencumber, disentangle, disguise, disrobe, distill, distract, divest, double-check, double-deal, double-talk, down, download, draft, drag, drain, draw, dredge, drink, drug, dupe, duplicate

earmark, earn, eat, echo, economize, educe, elicit, embezzle, embrace, embroil, employ, emulate, enamor, enchant, enclose, encompass, endear, enfold, engage, engross, engulf, enlist, enmesh, enrapture, enroll, enshrine, ensnare, ensorcel, entangle, entertain, enthrall, entice, entrance, entrap, entreat, entwine, envelop, envy, estimate, euchre, evaluate, evoke, exact, examine, excavate, exhaust, exhume, expense, exploit, extort, extract, extricate, eye, eyeball

fake, fancy, fascinate, fathom, feign, ferret, ferry, fetch, fiddle, filch, film, filter, finagle, finesse, fixate, flag, flannel, flatter, fleece, flimflam, focus, foil, fondle, fool, forage, forestall, fox, freeboot, freeze, frisk, frost, -frustrate, funnel

gain, game, gammon, garner, gather, gauge, gazump, get, ghostwrite, glamour, glean, glom, gobble, goldbrick, gorge, grab, grapple, grasp, gratify, grill, grip, grok, gross, gull, guzzle, gyp

-halt, hamper, hamstring, hand-carry, handpick, hang, harbor, harvest, haul, heap, heave, hijack, hinder, hire, hoard, hoax, hocus-pocus, hog, hoist, hold, holster, honey, hoodwink, hook, hornswoggle, hose, hotwire, house, hug, humbug, hump, husband, hustle, hypnotize

ice, imbibe, imitate, impede, impersonate, implore, import, impound, impress, incline, include, inconvenience, incur, induce, infantilize, infatuate, influence, ingest, ingratiate, inhale, inherit, inhibit, inspect, intercept, interest, internalize, interpret, interrogate, intertwine, interview, intrigue, intuit, inveigle, investigate, invite, invoice, invoke, involve

jerk, jolly, juice, juggle

keep, kid, kidnap

lament, land, lasso, leach, lead, learn, lease, leech, levy, lobby, loot, lowball, lug, lull, lure

magnetize, manipulate, maraud, materialize, measure, mesmerize, metabolize, meter, midwife, milk, mimic, mine, minimize, minute, mirror, misappropriate, misdirect, misguide, mislead, misrepresent, mollycoddle, monitor, monopolize, mooch, mother, mourn, mousetrap, move, muckrake, muster nab, name, net, niche, nick, nobble, nosh

observe, obsess, obtain, oil, orbit, outfox, outguess, outslick, outsmart, outthink, outwit, overcharge, overhear, overprotect, own

pacify, page, palaver, palm, pamper, panhandle, parrot, pause, personify, persuade, peruse, petition, pick, pickle, piggyback, pilfer, pillage, pincer, pinch, pirate, placate, plagiarize, plead, please, pleasure, pluck, plumb, plunder, poach, pocket, police, poll, ponder, possess, postpone, preempt, preoccupy, pretend, price, procure, profile, propitiate, provoke, pucker, pull, pump, purchase, purloin

quaff, quantify, quarry, quench, query, question, quiet, quiz

raise, rake, ransack, razzle-dazzle, read, reap, recall, recapture, receive, reclaim, recollect, recon, reconnoiter, record, recoup, recover, recruit, reference, reflect, refrigerate, regain, regret, rein, reinvestigate, relish, remember, remove, rent, replicate, repossess, repress, reprieve, reproduce, request, require, requisition, rescue, research, reserve, restrain, retain, retard, retract, retrieve, review, revoke, rifle, rob, roleplay, romance, rook, root, rope, rustle

sack, salvage, sample, sap, sate, satiate, satisfy, save, savor, scam, scan, scant, scavenge, schlep, schmooze, schnorr, scoop, score, scrimp, scrounge, scrutinize, search, secure, sedate, seduce, seek, seize, select, sense, shanghai, sheathe, shelter, shelve, short, shortchange, shuttle, sidetrack, sift, simulate, siphon, skim, skimp, slake, slow, slurp, smell, smuggle, snaffle, snag, snare, snarl, snatch, sneak, sniff, snitch, snooker, snow, soap, soft-sell, soft-soap, solicit, solve, source, spellbind, spin, spirit, sponge, spoof, spoon-feed, spot, spud, spy, squeeze, squelch, squirrel, stack, stall, stash, staunch, steal, stiff, stint, stockpile, stonewall, stop, store, stow, strip, strum, study, stultify, suck, sucker, sue, sugarcoat, summon, surround, survey, suspect, suspend, suss, swallow, sway, sweet-talk, swig, swill, swindle, swipe

tabulate, take, tally, tangle, tantalize, tap, taste, taunt, tax, tease, temper, tempt, test, thrill, -thwart, tighten, titillate, tote, tow, trademark, transfer, transfix, transport, trap, trawl, trick, truck, truss, tug, turn

unburden, unbury, unclothe, uncork, uncover, undercharge, underemphasize, underpay, undress, unearth, uninstall, unpack, unzip, uproot, use, usurp

vacuum, vamp, ventilate, vet

waft, want, warehouse, watch, waylay, weasel, weed, weigh, weight, whammy, wheedle, whisk, whitewash, win, wiretap, wish, withdraw, withhold, witness, wolf, wonder, woo, worm, wrangle, wrap, wrench, wrest, wrestle, wring

x-ray

yank

Join (+)

"Join" verbs connect objects in the environment outside the subject, linking items together or creating a sense of cohesion and community out of constituent components. Because they assemble pieces into a coherent whole, they tend to include behaviors that appear logical, sociable, pleasurable, supportive, cooperative, and creative.

"Join" verbs create common ground between people, things, groups, and concepts, e.g., *teach, exonerate, kindle, transform*. These are verbs of inclusion and cooperation, often seen as benevolent because of their unifying force and the emphasis on constructive, social coherence...like a spoon gathering things together. Vibe-wise, these verbs reflect the magnetic attraction of Eros, god of love, and the cooperative benevolence of any community.

Along the POV character's **external** axis, "join" verbs *heal, build, protect, organize*, and *improve*. In these instances, the characters opt to encourage community and show hospitality.

abet, absolve, access, acclaim, acclimate, accommodate, accompany, accomplish, accustom, acknowledge, acquaint, acquit, activate, actualize, adapt, add, adjudge, adjudicate, adjust, admire, adore, adorn, adulate, advantage, affirm, affix, agglomerate, aid, alibi, align, allay, alleviate, allow, ally, amalgamate, amass, ameliorate, amend, anchor, animate, annex, anticipate, apotheosize, appease, applaud, appraise, appreciate, approve, approximate, arbitrate, armor, arrange, articulate, assemble, assign, assist, associate, assuage, assure, attach, attest, attire, attune, augment, augur, authorize, automate, avow, await, awaken back, balance, bandage, baptize, barber, barter, bathe, bear, beatify, beautify, bed, bedeck, beget, bejewel, believe, benefit, betroth, bind, blazon, blend, bless, bolster, bolt, bond, brace, braid, brainstorm, brainwash, brave, brew, bridge, brigade, brighten, broker, bronze, buckle, build, button, buttress

calibrate, canonize, case-harden, catalog, categorize, celebrate, cement, center, certify, change, chaperone, characterize, cheer, cherish, chronicle, circle, civilize, clamp, clarify, classify, clean, cleanse, clinch, clip, clothe, coach, coagulate, code, codify, coin, collage, collate, combine, comfort, commemorate, commend, commingle, commit, compile, complement, complete, complexify, complicate, compliment, compose, compound, compute, computerize, concatenate, concede, concentrate, concoct, concretize, condition, condone, confess, confirm, conflate, congratulate, conjecture, conjugate, connect, consecrate, consign, console, consolidate, construct, consummate, content, convene, convert, cook, coordinate, corral, correct, corroborate, costume, couple, cradle, craft, create, credential, credit, crossbreed, crosscheck, cross-fertilize, cross-pollinate, crown, crystallize, cultivate, culture, cure, cushion, customize

dandify, debug, debunk, decide, decipher, deck, decode, decontaminate, decorate, decrypt, dedicate, defend, defrost, defuse, deify, delouse, demystify, design, designate, destine, develop, devise, dignify, divine, document, domesticate, double, dress, dulcify

ease, edit, educate, elucidate, emancipate, embattle, embellish, emblazon, embroider, enable, encircle, endorse, endure, energize, enfranchise, engender, engineer, enhance, enjoy, enlarge, enlighten, enliven, ennoble, ensoul, ensure, entitle, equalize, erect, escort, espouse, establish, esteem, eternalize, eulogize, even, exalt, exchange, excite, excuse, exercise, exhilarate, exonerate, expect, expedite, expiate, explain, expose, extol, extrapolate

fabricate, face, facilitate, fallow, familiarize, fancify, farm, fashion, fasten, favor, feast, fertilize, festoon, fetishize, fine-tune, fix, flavor, flood, flounce, forge, forgive, form, formulate, fortify, foster, free, fry, fête, fulfill, fuse

galvanize, garland, garnish, generalize, generate, gentrify, gestate, gild, gird, girdle, gladden, glad-hand, glamorize, glitter, glitz, glorify, glue, gold-star, grade, graft, graph, grease, greenlight, greet, griddle, groom, ground, group, grow, guarantee, guard, guide, gussy

habituate, hallow, handle, harbinger, harmonize, harness, hatch, heal, help, hierarchize, hitch, honor, hospitalize, host, housetrain, humor, hybridize

idealize, identify, idolize, ignite, illuminate, imagine, imbue, immortalize, improv, improve, improvise, inaugurate, incorporate, increase, incubate, indemnify, index, indoctrinate, induct, indulge, inform, infuse, initiate, innovate, inoculate, inspire, install, institute, instruct, insulate, insure, integrate, interbreed, intermingle, intermix, intoxicate, inure, invent, inventory, invigorate, itemize

jack, jerry-build, jerry-rig, join, judge, justify

kindle, knight, knit, knot

lace, lard, latch, launder, legalize, legislate, legitimate, legitimize, lengthen, liberate, license, lift, light, link, lionize, locate, loosen, love, lube, machinate, lubricate

machine, maintain, make, manicure, manufacture, manumit, map, marry, marshal, mass, match, mature, mechanize, mediate, medicate, meet, meld, mellow, memorialize, mend, merge, mingle, mitigate, mix, moderate, modernize, modify, modulate, moisturize, mold, mollify, mongrelize, moralize, motorize, multiply

narrow, neaten, negotiate, network, normalize, notarize, nourish, number, numerate, nurse, nurture, nuzzle

obey, oblige, officiate, offset, open, optimize, orchestrate, ordain, order, organize, orient, orientate, ornament, outlast, overcommit, overestimate, overvalue, owe

pace, palliate, pardon, parent, partner, paste, patch, patent, pave, perfect, permit, personalize, pile, pin, pity, place, plaster, pledge, plot, popularize, pork, praise, predict, prepare, preserve, prime, primp, prioritize, prize, process, produce, program, proliferate, promise, prop, prophesy, protect, prove, purify

qualify

rally, rank, ransom, rarefy, rate, ratify, rationalize, reactivate, ready, realign, reanimate, rear, reassemble, reassure, reboot, rebuild, reconcile, reconstruct, recreate, rectify, recycle, redeem, referee, refine, reform, refresh, refurbish, regard, regenerate, regiment, regulate, rehabilitate, reinforce, reintegrate, reinvigorate, rejigger, rejoin, rejuvenate, rekindle, relax, relieve, remedy, remodel, renegotiate, renew, reorient, repair, rephrase, replace, repurpose, reshape, resolve, respect, restore, restructure, resurrect, resuscitate, retool, retrain, reunite, reveal, revere, reverence, revise, revitalize, revive, revolutionize, richen, rig, ritualize, rivet, romanticize, rouse, roust, rubber-stamp

safeguard, salute, salve, sanctify, sanction, sanitize, sauté, schedule, school, screw, script, seal, season, second, sentinel, serve, service, set, settle, shepherd, shield, shoulder, simplify, sleek, slick, sober, soften, solder, solidify, soothe, sophisticate, sort, sound, spackle, span, spare, spawn, specify, spice, splice, sponsor, spruce, square, squire, stabilize, stable, stage-manage, stand, standardize, steady, steel, steep, stereotype, sterilize, stick, stipulate, stir, stitch, stomach, straddle, straighten, strap, strategize, streamline, strengthen, stud, subdue, substantiate, suckle, suffer, suit, supersize, support, surface, surrender, survive, sustain, suture, swear, sweeten, synchronize, synthesize tailor, tame, teach, tether, thank, thaw, tidy, tie, time, titivate, toast, tolerate, tone, toughen, trade, traffic, train, transfigure, transform, translate, transmute, transplant, treasure, treat, triangulate, triple, troubleshoot, trust, tune, tutor, tweak

umpire, unbuckle, unchain, uncomplicate, uncrumple, uncuff, underpin, unfetter, unfold, uniform, unify, unite, unleash, unlock, unmask, unscramble, unseal, unshackle, unskew, untangle, unveil, update, upgrade, uphold, uplift, usher

vaccinate, validate, valuate, value, varnish, venerate, verify, vindicate, vitalize, vow

wake, wangle, warrant, wash, weaponize, weather, weave, wed, welcome, weld, wire, withstand, worship

yield, yoke

zip

Split (/)

"Split" verbs divide objects in the environment outside the subject, separating items into detached fragments or abusing, rejecting, and dissolving anything whole. Because they tear a totality into shreds and threads, they tend to include behaviors that appear confusing, hostile, painful, alienating, dominant, and destructive.

"Split" verbs isolate or damage people, things, communities, and concepts, e.g., *corrupt, demolish, insult, lacerate*. These are verbs of separation and disturbance, often seen as aggression because of the potential for retaliation or ill will in a winners/losers dynamic. Vibe-wise, these verbs reflect the disruptive antagonism of Eris, goddess of strife, and the combative force that drives all competitors.

Along the POV character's **external** axis, "split" verbs *harm, destroy, segregate, distort,* and *confuse*. In these instances, the characters opt to inflict harm and show selfishness.

-abandon, abase, abash, abdicate, abjure, abolish, -abort, abrade, abridge, abrogate, abuse, addle, admonish, adulterate, afflict, affright, affront, aggravate, aggrieve, agonize, alienate, amputate, anger, anguish, annihilate, annoy, annul, antagonize, appall, asphyxiate, assassinate, assault, atomize, attack, attaint, attenuate, avenge, axe

badmouth, baffle, bankrupt, bar, barbarize, barricade, bash, bastardize, batter, battle, bedevil, befoul, befuddle, beggar, behead, belittle, bemuse, bend, berate, besmear, besmirch, bestialize, betray, bewilder, bisect, bite, blackball, blacken, blackguard, blackjack, blacklist, blackmail, blame, -blank, blanket, blast, bleep, blemish, blight, blind, block, blockade, blot, blunt, blur, boggle, boobytrap, bore, botch, breach, break, browbeat, bruise, brutalize, buffalo, buffer, bully, bungle, burke, burn, burst, bury, bushwhack, bust, butcher

cache, cage, camouflage, -cancel, canker, capsize, carve, castigate, castrate, cauterize, cede, censor, censure, chafe, chagrin, chain, chasten, chastise, cheapen, chew, chide, chip, chisel, choke, chop, chunk, circumcise, circumscribe, -circumvent, claw, cleave, cloak, clog, cloister, close, cloud, clutter, coarsen, coffer, combat, comminute, compartmentalize, compress, compromise, conceal, concern, conclude, condemn, confine, confound, confuse, consternate, constipate, contaminate, contemn, contort, contradict, contrast, convict, corrode, corrupt, counteract, cow, crack, cramp, crash, crate, craze, crease, cripple, criticize, critique, crucify, crumble, crumple, crush, cuff, curse, curtail, cut

damage, damn, dampen, darken, dash, daze, deactivate, deaden, debase, debate, debauch, debilitate, decapitate, decimate, -decline, deconstruct, decrease, decry, deduct, deep-six, deface, defame, defeat, defile, deflate, deflect, deflower, deform, defy, degrade, dehumanize, delegitimize, delete, delude, demarcate, demean, demolish, demonize, demoralize, demote, denigrate, denounce, -deny, depersonalize, deport, depose, deprave, depredate, depress, derail, deride, desecrate, -desert, -despise, destabilize, destroy, detach, deteriorate, dethrone, detonate, devalue, devastate, diffuse, digest, dilute, diminish, dirty, disable, disabuse, disadvantage, disaffect, disappoint, disapprove, disarticulate, disassemble, disband, disbelieve, disclaim, discombobulate, discomfit, discomfort, discompose, disconcert, disconnect, -discount, discourage, discredit, -disdain, disembowel, disenfranchise, disfavor, disfigure, disgrace, disgust, dishearten, dishevel, dishonor, disillusion, disintegrate, disjoint, dismantle, dismay, dismember, disobey, disorient, -disown, disparage, dispel, disperse, dispirit, displease, disprove, dispute, disqualify, -disregard, disrupt, diss, dissatisfy, dissect, dissipate, dissolve, dissuade, distinguish, distort, distress, distrust, disunite, -ditch, divert, divide, divorce, dizzy, -dodge, doom, double-cross, doubt, downgrade, downplay, downsize, dread, dull, dumbfound, dump

eclipse, efface, eighty-six, eliminate, emasculate, embalm, embarrass, empty, encase, encode, encrypt, end, endanger, enervate, enfeeble, enrage, ensconce, enslave, entomb, eradicate, erase, erode, -eschew, estrange, eviscerate, excise, -exclude, excoriate, excruciate, execrate, exempt, exorcise, expunge, exterminate, extinguish, extirpate

falsify, fatigue, fault, faze, fell, fence, fetter, fight, finish, fissure, flay, flub, flummox, flunk, fluster, -forbid, forget, -forsake, fossilize, foul, fracture, fragment, frame, frazzle, frighten, fulminate, fumble, fumigate

gag, gainsay, garble, gash, gnaw, gore, gouge, grieve, grind, guillotine, gut

hack, half-ass, halve, handcuff, handicap, harangue, harass, harden, harm, harry, hassle, heckle, hector, henpeck, hew, hide, hobble, hollow, horrify, humble, humiliate, hurt, hush

-ignore, immobilize, immolate, impair, imperil, impoverish, imprison, impugn, inactivate, incapacitate, incarcerate, incinerate, incommode, incriminate, indenture, indict, infect, inflict, infuriate, injure, insult, inter, interrupt, intimidate, invalidate, irk, irritate, isolate

jade, jail, jangle, jeopardize, jilt, jinx, joint, jumble, junk

keelhaul, -kibosh, kill, kneecap

lacerate, lambaste, lame, lampoon, lash, leash, leave, lessen, level, libel, limit, liquefy, liquidate, litigate, lobotomize, lock, lop, lose, lynch

maim, malign, maltreat, manacle, mangle, mar, marginalize, mark, maroon, mash, mask, massacre, maul, melt, menace, mince, miscalculate, misconstrue, misdiagnose, mishandle, mishear, misinform, misinterpret, misjudge, mislabel, mismanage, mistake, mistreat, misuse, mock, monkey-wrench, mortgage, mortify, mothball, muddle, muddy, muffle, mummify, murder, mutate, mute, mutilate, muzzle, mystify

nauseate, -negate, -neglect, nettle, neuter, neutralize, nibble, nick, nonplus, notch, -nullify, numb

obfuscate, obliterate, obscure, obstruct, occlude, occult, offend, -omit, oppose, oppress, orphan, outlaw, outrage, -overlook, overthrow, overturn

pall, panic, paralyze, parody, part, partition, peel, pen, penalize, perplex, persecute, pervert, petrify, pillory, pinion, plague, poison, pollute, profane, -prohibit, prosecute, protest, prune, pulp, pulverize, punish, purge, puzzle

quarantine, quash, quell

rankle, rape, ration, rattle, ravage, raze, razor, ream, rebuke, redact, reduce, -refuse, refute, -reject, rend, reprimand, reproach, reprove, -repudiate, repulse, -rescind, resent, resist, restrict, retrench, revenge, reverse, revile, ridicule, rile, rip, roast, roughen, rout, ruin, rumple, rupture

sabotage, sadden, satirize, savage, saw, scald, scalp, scandalize, scapegoat, scar, scare, scathe, scatter, scold, scorch, -scorn, scotch, scourge, screen, scruple, scupper, scuttle, sear, seclude, secrete, segregate, separate, sequester, sever, shackle, shame, sharpen, shatter, -shirk, short-circuit, shred, shrink, shrivel, shroud, shut, sicken, singe, sizzle, skew, skin, skip, skunk, slander, slash, slate, slaughter, slay, slice, -slight, slit, slur, smash, smear, smother, smudge, snap, sorrow, sour, splinter, split, spook, squander, stab, stagger, stain, starve, stifle, stigmatize, sting, straightjacket, straiten, stump, stun, stunt, stupefy, stymie, subjugate, subordinate, subtract, subvert, suffocate, sully, sunder, suppress, switch

taboo, taint, tarnish, tear, terminate, terrify, terrorize, thrash, threaten, throttle, tire, torment, torpedo, torpefy, torture, trammel, trample, trash, trash-talk, traumatize, trim, trivialize, trouble, trounce, truncate, tuck, twist, two-time, tyrannize ulcerate, unbutton, undercut, underestimate, undermine, undo, unfasten, unhinge, unhorse, unnerve, unravel, unseat, unsettle, untidy, untie, upbraid, upset

vandalize, vaporize, veil, -veto, vex, victimize, vilify, villainize, violate, vitiate, vivisect, -void, vulgarize

waive, waste, weaken, wean, welt, whack, whip, whittle, winnow, wither, wizen, worry, wound, wrack, wreak, wreck, wrinkle, wrong

zap, zing, zone

BONUS EXERCISE: Reverberations

Characters are what characters do.

Every member of your story's cast will affect and be affected by the action and tactics of your protagonist as they pursue their version of happiness. One of the easiest ways to start brainstorming, untangle story, and guarantee razzle-dazzle is to look at the way that central action reverberates throughout the narrative. Secondary characters *reflect* or *reject* the primary action and tactics, altering the emotional flow of the story in satisfying and transformative ways.

As an example, here's a cast breakdown for *Pride & Prejudice*...starting from Lizzie (*Provoke*) and countered by Darcy (*Preserve*):

EXAMPLE: *Pride & Prejudice*

LIZZIE (Provoke)		(supporting cast)		DARCY (Preserve)
charm	≠	*tease* (Mr. Bennet)	≠	*dismiss*
judge	≠	*pester* (Mrs. Bennet)	≠	*thwart*
encourage	≠	*believe* (Jane Bennet)	≠	*offend*
criticize	≠	*fancy* (Lydia Bennet)	≠	*disdain*
outshine	≠	*exhibit* (Mary Bennet)	≠	*admonish*
baffle	≠	*scorn* (Caroline Bingley)	≠	*endure*
challenge	≠	*please* (Charles Bingley)	≠	*protect*
defy	≠	*demand* (Catherine de Bourgh)	≠	*withstand*
mock	≠	*flatter* (Mr. Collins)	≠	*overlook*
dare	≠	*respect* (Georgianna Darcy)	≠	*defend*
doubt	≠	*settle* (Charlotte Lucas)	≠	*support*
bait	≠	*include* (Sir William Lucas)	≠	*intimidate*
goad	≠	*squander* (George Wickham)	≠	*banish*

Notice that each secondary character in the cast is an antonym of one of Lizzie's tactics, denoting her actions in a main scene involving them. Notice also that Darcy's tactics are antonyms in turn, both of the other characters, creating friction with them, and with Lizzie's individual tactics as well, maximizing his friction with her in particular.

Herein lies the inestimable power of artistic alignment. Once you establish your protagonist's action, every other cast member and action in the story plugs directly into it, drawing power from it. Your own cast list can be built in the same way.

Based upon what you know about your protagonist, identify oppositional actions (reflection/rejection) for the rest of main cast. Seek fascinating collisions and friction between them.

- Identify your **protagonist's action** and **four to six synonymous tactics** they might use in different pivotal moments.
- Identify a list of **antonyms** for the action. Choose the most interesting and emotionally resonant verb to serve as the **action for your antagonist, love interest, or pivotal second role**.
- Identify a list of **antonyms** for each of the protagonist's tactics. Identify the most emotionally resonant antonym for each. These antonyms become the primary **actions for the significant secondary characters** with a transformative role to play.

EXERCISE: *Reverberations*

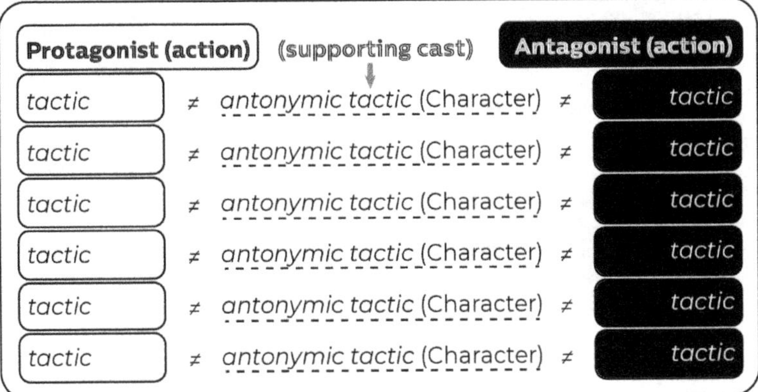

Perhaps you don't know your protagonist but you have a keen sense of the love interest. Maybe you can visualize a couple of minor characters but none of your leading roles—no prob! Every member of the cast connects to every other via their actions. Start with what you know; you just have to trace the dramatic friction to the various connected actions.

Any character's action can (and does) lead you back to the other significant actions that drive the story. Because every characterization aligns with every other, you can start a project from ANY point; even a secondary character can lead you to your protagonist and antagonist. The energy of the story flows through those verbs.

Yay, alignment!

If you'd like to download a **Reverberations** worksheet, you can find it on my website (www.damonsuede.com/a-reverb).

"Theatre is conflict, struggle, movement, transformation, not simply the exhibition of states of mind. It is a verb, not an adjective. To act is to produce an action, and every action produces a reaction—conflict."

Augusto Boal, director & teacher[10]

About the Author

Thank you so much for purchasing and using ***Activate***. I hope you've found it practical and useful to your writing process.

As a working author, you know how important reviews and word of mouth can be to a book's success. When you have a moment, please leave a good word for this book online mentioning whatever specifics you found helpful, so writers who'd benefit from verbalizing their stories can find what you dug and why.

BIO:

Damon Suede grew up out-n-proud deep in the anus of right-wing America, and escaped as soon as it was legal. He has lived all over and along the way, he's earned his crust as a model, a messenger, a promoter, a programmer, a sculptor, a singer, a stripper, a bookkeeper, a bartender, a techie, a teacher, a director...but writing has ever been his bread and butter. He has been happily partnered for over a decade with the most loving, handsome, shrewd, hilarious, noble man to walk this planet.

Damon is a proud member of the Romance Writers of America and currently serves on its national Board of Directors. He has been a full-time writer for print, stage, and screen for over two decades, which is both more and less glamorous than you might imagine. He's won some awards, but counts his blessings more often: his amazing friends, his demented family, his beautiful husband, his loyal fans, and his silly, stern, seductive Muse who keeps whispering in his ear, year after year.

Damon also loves teaching workshops and seminars. If you'd like him to present to your group or conference hit him up via:

- **DamonSuede.com**
- **Twitter** (@DamonSuede)
- **Facebook** (facebook.com/damon.suede.author)
- **Newsletter** (eepurl.com/blmkir)

Additionally, the @LiveWireGuides twitter account features a *#DailyVerb* hashtag as well as article links, updates, and more.

Notes

1. Constance Hale's *Vex, Hex, Smash, Smooch*, p. 276.
2. Scott McCloud, *Making Comics*, pp. 5-6.
3. Joseph Conrad, Preface to *The Children of the Sea*, p. 4.
4. cf. Michael Hauge, *Writing Screenplays That Sell.*
5. Judith Weston, *Directing Actors*, p. 36.
6. Dean Koontz, *How to Write Best Selling Fiction.*
7. Lev Grossman, "Literary Revolution in the Supermarket Aisle: Genre Fiction Is Disruptive Technology" in *Time* (23 May 2012).
8. From a 1924 interview Hammett did, quoted in *Legends of Literature: The Best Articles, Interviews, and Essays from the Archives of Writer's Digest Magazine* by Phillip Sexton, p. 34.
9. Alexander Mackendrick, *On Film-Making*, p. 18.
10. Augusto Boal, *Games for Actors and Non-Actors*, p. 39.

Bibliography

Oxford American Writer's Thesaurus by David Auburn and Rae Armantrout

Actions: The Actors' Thesaurus by Marina Caldarone and Maggie Lloyd-Williams

Chamber's Thesaurus, 12th Edition (2012)

The Slang of Sin by Tom Dalzell

Vex, Hex, Smash, Smooch: Let Verbs Power Your Writing by Constance Hale

The Well-Spoken Thesaurus: The Most Powerful Ways to Say Everyday Words and Phrases by Tom Heehler

The Random House Thesaurus of Slang by Esther and Albert E. Lewin

Roget's Super Thesaurus, 4th Edition by Marc McCutcheon (2010)

The Merriam-Webster Dictionary of Synonyms and Antonyms

The Merriam-Webster Thesaurus (2006)

Roget's Cloud: The Ultimate Thesaurus by Lucas Nicolato

Roget's Thesaurus of Words for Writers: Over 2,300 Emotive, Evocative, Descriptive Synonyms, Antonyms, and Related Terms Every Writer Should Know by David Olsen, Michelle Bevilacqua, Justin Cord Hayes, and Robert W Bly

The Synonym Finder by JJ Rodale

The Word Finder by JJ Rodale

Roget's 21st Century Thesaurus, Third Edition (2005)

Shorter Oxford English Dictionary (2007)

Verbalize: bring life to stories and stories to life by Damon Suede